Governing States and Localities

7th Edition

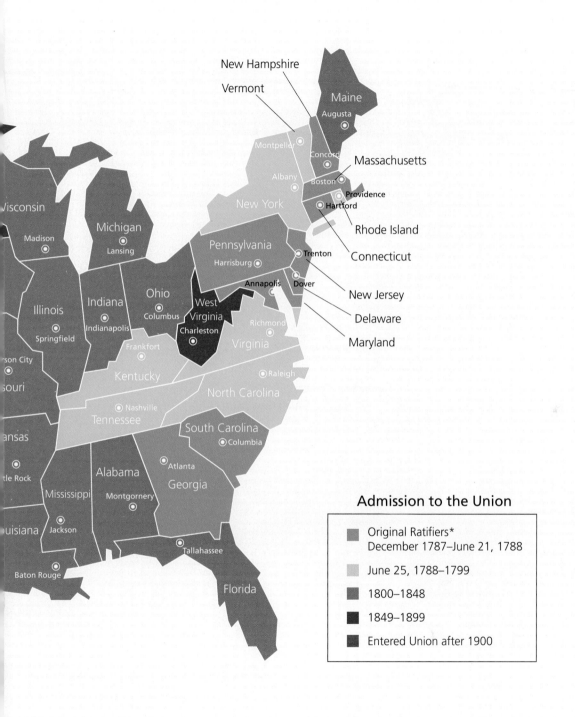

New Hampshire
Vermont
Maine
Augusta
Montpelier
Concord
Massachusetts
Albany
Boston
New York
Providence
Hartford
Rhode Island
Pennsylvania
Harrisburg
Trenton
Connecticut
Wisconsin
Michigan
Lansing
Madison
Annapolis
Dover
New Jersey
Ohio
West
Virginia
Columbus
Illinois
Indiana
Indianapolis
Charleston
Richmond
Delaware
Springfield
Frankfort
Virginia
Maryland
son City
Kentucky
Raleigh
souri
North Carolina
ansas
Nashville
Tennessee
South Carolina
Columbia
tle Rock
Atlanta
Mississippi
Alabama
Georgia
Montgornery
uisiana
Jackson
Tallahassee
Baton Rouge
Florida

Admission to the Union

- Original Ratifiers*
  December 1787–June 21, 1788
- June 25, 1788–1799
- 1800–1848
- 1849–1899
- Entered Union after 1900

For my students.

     —Kevin B. Smith

For my son, Simon.

     —Alan Greenblatt

Governing States and Localities

7th Edition

Kevin B. Smith
University of Nebraska–Lincoln

Alan Greenblatt
Governing magazine

FOR INFORMATION:

CQ Press

An imprint of SAGE Publications, Inc.

2455 Teller Road

Thousand Oaks, California 91320

E-mail: order@sagepub.com

SAGE Publications Ltd.

1 Oliver's Yard

55 City Road

London EC1Y 1SP

United Kingdom

SAGE Publications India Pvt. Ltd.

B 1/I 1 Mohan Cooperative Industrial Area

Mathura Road, New Delhi 110 044

India

SAGE Publications Asia-Pacific Pte. Ltd.

18 Cross Street #10-10/11/12

China Square Central

Singapore 048423

Executive Publisher: Monica Eckman

Editorial Assistant: Sam Rosenberg

Content Development Editor: Scott Harris

Production Editor: Laureen Gleason

Copy Editor: Melinda Masson

Typesetter: C&M Digitals (P) Ltd.

Proofreader: Susan Schon

Indexer: Maria Sosnowski

Cover Designer: Candice Harman

Marketing Manager: Erica DeLuca

Printed in Canada

Library of Congress Cataloging-in-Publication Data

Names: Smith, Kevin B., author. | Greenblatt, Alan, author.

Title: Governing states and localities / Kevin B. Smith, University of Nebraska-Lincoln, Alan Greenblatt, Governing magazine.

Description: Seventh Edition. | Thousand Oaks, California : SAGE | CQ PRESS, [2019] | Includes bibliographical references and index.

Identifiers: LCCN 2018042302 | ISBN 9781544325422 (Paperback : acid-free paper)

Subjects: LCSH: State governments—United States—Textbooks. | Local government—United States—Textbooks. | Comparative government—Textbooks.

Classification: LCC JK2408 .S57 2019 | DDC 320.473—dc23
LC record available at https://lccn.loc.gov/2018042302

This book is printed on acid-free paper.

19 20 21 22 23 10 9 8 7 6 5 4 3 2

• Brief Contents •

• Detailed Contents •

• Tables, Figures, and Maps •

Tables

Figures

Maps

• Preface •

The mission of the seventh edition of *Governing States and Localities* is the same as its predecessors: to provide a comprehensive introduction to state and local governments and to do it with a difference. This book is a unique collaboration between academic and professional writers that rests on a foundation of academic scholarship, more than two decades of experience teaching undergraduates about state and local governments, and the insight and experience of a journalist with decades of experience covering state and local politics.

This book provides fresh and contemporary perspective on state and local politics, not just in terms of coverage and content, but also in its look and feel. The text deliberately follows a newsmagazine's crisp journalistic style, and the book employs magazine-quality, full-color layout and design. Our intent is to deliver a text that meets the highest academic and pedagogical standards while remaining engaging and easily accessible to undergraduates. *Governing* magazine remains an important partner for this edition, and many of the feature boxes draw directly from the work of its award-winning reporters, bloggers, and correspondents.

All chapters have been revised substantially, with the content updated throughout to reflect the latest issues, trends, and political changes, including the following:

- Analysis of the results of the most recent legislative and gubernatorial elections

- Discussion of the most important state supreme court decisions and constitutional debates

- The growing impact of political polarization at the state and even local levels, and the implications of the nationalization of party politics for subnational governance

- The impact of the Donald Trump presidency on intergovernmental relations and issues of central interest to states and localities

- In-depth examination of recent events and issues that have had impacts on (and in some cases transformed) states and localities, such as the federal–state tugs of war over immigration reform, school shootings and gun control, and the impact of tax cuts on public services and economic performance

- Updates to "The Latest Research" sections at the ends of all chapters, where recent scholarship is put into the context of what students have just read

Although these represent significant revisions, the current edition retains the pedagogical philosophy of the comparative method. This approach compares similar units of analysis to explain *why* differences exist. As scholars know well, state and local governments make excellent units of analysis for comparison because they operate within a single political system. The similarities and differences that mark their institutional structures, laws and regulations, political cultures, histories, demographics, economies, and geographies make them exciting laboratories for asking and answering important questions about politics and government. Put simply, their differences make a difference.

The appeal of exploring state and local government through comparison is not just that it makes for good political science. It is also a great way to engage students because it gives undergraduates an accessible, practical, and systematic way to understand politics and policy in the real world. Students learn that even such seemingly personal concerns as why their tuition is so darned high are not just relevant to their particular situation and educational institution but also fundamental to the interaction of that institution with its state's political culture, economy, history, and tax structure, and even to the school's geographic and demographic position within the state and region. Using the comparative method, this book gives students the resources they need to ask and answer such questions themselves.

Key Features

This book includes several elements designed to show-case and promote its main themes. Each chapter begins with a list of chapter objectives. Based on Bloom's taxonomy, these present straightforward, big-picture statements of key information students should take away from each chapter. Instructors may easily turn these into class discussion topics or homework assignments.

Following the objectives, each chapter presents an opening vignette modeled after a lead in a newsmagazine article—a compelling story that segues naturally into the broader themes of the chapter. Many of these vignettes (as well as many of the feature boxes) represent original reporting.

Each vignette concludes with a set of chapter-specific questions intended to engage student interest and prompt students to look systematically for answers using the comparative method. The idea is not simply to spoon-feed the answers to students but, rather, to demonstrate how the comparative method can be used to explore and explain questions about politics and policy.

The feature boxes in each chapter emphasize and reinforce the comparative theme:

- "A Difference That Makes a Difference" boxes provide clear examples of how variations among states and localities can be used to explain a wide range of political and policy phenomena. These pieces detail the ways the institutions, regulations, political culture, demographics, and other factors of a particular state shape its constitution, the way its political parties function, how its citizens tend to vote, how it allocates its financial resources, and why its courts are structured the way they are, to name a few.

- "Local Focus" boxes spotlight the ways localities function independently of the states and show how they are both constrained and empowered by intergovernmental ties. From battles to wrest control of their budgets from the state to constitutional restrictions on how they can tax and spend, the topics addressed in these boxes showcase the rich variety represented in these nearly 87,000 substate entities.

- "Policy in Practice" boxes demonstrate how different states and localities have interpreted and implemented the legislation handed down from higher levels of government, and the consequences of these decisions. The impact of declining agency fees on public unions, the difficulties and implications of city–county mergers, and the policy implications of the power imbalance between states and localities are just some of the issues addressed.

- "States under Stress" boxes demonstrate how states deal with challenges such as the long-lingering effects of the Great Recession and the impact of natural disasters.

Another key feature that serves the comparative theme is the design and use of graphics and tables. Nearly 30 full-color, 50-state maps, including three unique cartograms, provide a visual representation of and intuitively easy way to grasp the differences among states and localities—whether the sizes of the state economies, the party affiliation requirements for voting in direct primaries, the methods of judicial selection, or state incarceration rates. Similarly, more than 40 tables and figures emphasize how states and localities differ and what these differences mean to politics and policy. State rankings of voter turnout rates, recent regional murder rates, and many other features support comparisons made in the text.

To help students assimilate content and review for tests, each chapter concludes with a list of "Top Ten Takeaways" that reinforces key themes and ideas. Each chapter also includes a set of highlighted key concepts. These terms are defined near the places where they are introduced in the text and are compiled into a list at the end of each chapter, with corresponding page numbers. A comprehensive glossary of key terms precedes the book's index.

Organization of the Book

The book is organized so that each chapter logically builds on previous chapters. The first chapter (subtitled "They Tax Dogs in West Virginia, Don't They?") is essentially a persuasive essay that lays the conceptual groundwork for the book. Its aim is to convince students that state and local politics are important to their day-to-day lives and to their futures as professionals and citizens. That is, it makes the case for why students should care about state and local politics. Along the way, it introduces the advantages of the comparative method as a systematic way to explore this subject. In introducing the book's approach, the chapter provides the basic context for studying state and local governments, especially the differences in economics, culture, demographics, and geography that drive policy and politics at the regional level.

The next two chapters cover federalism and state constitutions. These chapters provide a basic understanding of what state and local governments are and what powers, responsibilities, and roles they have within the political system of the United States, as well as a sense of how they legally can make different political and policy choices.

Chapter 4 examines the finances of state and local governments. This highlights the fact that, a full decade after the Great Recession's official end date, recovery from the biggest economic downturn in five generations continues to have an impact on state budgets. Compounding the uneven financial picture across subnational governments are a range of differing decisions that influence not only the key revenue streams for states and localities—income, sales, and property taxes—but also the sorts of policy and program choices that governments can and cannot make. This chapter gives students a fundamental sense of the revenues and expenditures of state and local governments and their central importance to virtually everything government does.

Chapter 5 examines political participation with an eye to helping students understand how citizens connect to the core policymaking institutions of government. Chapters 6 through 10 are separate treatments of those core institutions: parties and interest groups, legislatures, governors and executives, courts, and the bureaucracy. There is special emphasis in each chapter on how variations in the structure, powers, and responsibilities of these institutions have real-life implications for citizens of states and localities.

Chapters 11 and 12 focus on local government. Chapter 11 concentrates on laying out the basic structure, authority, and responsibilities of local government. Chapter 12 examines the relations among local governments from a regional perspective. The final four chapters are devoted to specific policy areas—education, crime and punishment, health and welfare, and the environment—that represent a selection of the most critical policy functions of state and local governments.

Digital Resources

$ SAGE coursepacks

SAGE coursepacks makes it easy to import our quality instructor and student resource content into your school's learning management system (LMS). Intuitive and simple to use, **SAGE coursepacks** gives you the control to focus on what really matters: customizing course content to meet your students' needs.

Customized and curated for use in:

Blackboard

Canvas

Desire2Learn (D2L)

Moodle

Created specifically for *Governing States and Localities*, Seventh Edition, by Kevin B. Smith and Alan Greenblatt, **SAGE coursepacks** is included FREE! *Instructors*, contact your sales representative to request a brief demonstration or additional information. Learning and teaching has never been easier!

SAGE coursepacks for INSTRUCTORS supports teaching with quality content and easy-to-integrate course management tools, featuring:

✓ Our content delivered **directly into your LMS**

✓ **Intuitive and easy-to-use format** that makes it easy to integrate **SAGE coursepacks** into your course with minimal effort

✓ **Pedagogically robust assessment tools** that foster review, practice, and critical thinking, and offer a better, more complete way to measure student engagement, including:

  ○ **Instructions** on how to use and integrate the comprehensive assessments and resources provided

  ○ **Diagnostic chapter pretests and posttests** that identify opportunities for student improvement, track student progress, and ensure mastery of key learning objectives

- ○ **Test banks** built on Bloom's taxonomy that provide a diverse range of test items

- ○ **Activity and quiz options** that allow you to choose only the assignments and tests you want

- ○ **Exercises based on State Stats,** a password-protected, interactive database that is part of the SAGE Stats product, which delivers a dynamic and engaging user experience that is unmatched in other resources; features data from more than 80 different government and nongovernment sources; and is backed by a rich collection of more than 2,000 current and historical data series on popular topics of research interest

- ✓ **Chapter-specific discussion questions** to help launch classroom interaction by prompting students to engage with the material and by reinforcing important content

- ✓ **Video resources tied to learning objectives and accompanied by quiz tools** that automatically feed to your gradebook

- ✓ **Comprehensive, downloadable, easy-to-use guides for every video resource** that list the chapter to which the video content is tied, associated learning objective(s), a helpful description of the video content, and assessment questions

- ✓ Editable, chapter-specific **PowerPoint® slides** that offer flexibility when creating multimedia lectures, so you don't have to start from scratch but can customize to your exact needs

- ✓ **Sample course syllabi** with suggested models for structuring your course that give you options to customize your course in a way that is perfect for you

- ✓ **Lecture notes** that summarize key concepts on a chapter-by-chapter basis to help you with preparation for lectures and class discussions

- ✓ **All tables and figures** from the textbook

SAGE coursepacks for STUDENTS enhances learning in an easy-to-use environment that offers:

- ✓ **Chapter-specific discussion questions** to help launch classroom interaction by prompting students to engage with the material and by reinforcing important content

- ✓ Mobile-friendly **practice quizzes** that allow students to practice and assess how much they've learned and where they need to focus their attention

- ✓ Mobile-friendly **flashcards** to strengthen understanding of key concepts

- ✓ **Multimedia resources tied to learning objectives** covered in each chapter

In addition, students and instructors alike will find *Governing* magazine's website especially useful for further research and in-class discussion. To help them bring the latest word from the states and localities into their classrooms, adopters may receive a free semester-long subscription to *Governing* magazine.

Acknowledgments

A lot of effort and dedication go into the making of a textbook such as this, only a fraction of which is contributed by those whose names end up on the cover. Emily Johnson deserves special recognition for her crucial contributions as a research assistant. We'd also like to acknowledge the contributions made by John Buntin, Melissa Feinberg, and Michele Mariani Vaughn to prior editions of this work.

A huge thanks also goes out to the team at SAGE/CQ Press who did so much to make the book possible: Monica Eckman, Erica DeLuca, Scott Harris, Sam Rosenberg, Charisse Kiino, the project's original champion and advocate, and particularly Melinda Masson, our copy editor extraordinaire. We especially want to thank our many reviewers, past and present, for their careful and detailed assistance with reading and commenting on the manuscript:

Sharon Alter, William Rainey Harper Community College

Jeff Ashley, Eastern Illinois University

Alex Badas, Indiana University Bloomington

Jenna Bednar, University of Michigan

Neil Berch, West Virginia University

John J. Bertalan, University of South Florida

Nathaniel Birkhead, Kansas State University

Michael Bobic, Alderson Broaddus University

John Bohte, University of Wisconsin–Milwaukee

Shannon Bow O'Brien, University of Texas–Austin

Jane Bryant, John A. Logan College

Jaclyn Bunch, University of South Alabama

Adam Butz, Marshall University

William Cassie, Appalachian State University

Jennifer Clark, University of Houston

Douglas Clouatre, Mid-Plains Community College

Chris Cooper, Western Carolina University

Margery Coulson-Clark, Elizabeth City State University

Gary Crawley, Ball State University

Warren Dixon, Texas A&M University

Nelson Dometrius, Texas Tech University

Jaime Dominguez, DePaul University

Deborah Dougherty, Illinois Central College–Peoria

Regina Durante, Eastern University

Nicholas Easton, Clark University

Craig Emmert, University of Texas–Permian Basin

David Floreen, Northeastern University

David H. Folz, University of Tennessee–Chattanooga

Patricia Freeland, University of Tennessee–Knoxville

Keneshia Grant, Howard University

Michael E. Greenberg, Shippensburg University

Simon F. Haeder, West Virginia University

Donald Haider-Markel, University of Kansas

George Hale, Kutztown University

William Hall, Bradley University

Susan Hansen, University of Pittsburgh

Dana Michael Harsell, University of North Dakota

Aubrey Jewett, University of Central Florida

Avra Johnson, Minnesota State University–Mankato

Wendy L. Johnston, SUNY Adirondack

Nicole Kalaf-Hughes, Bowling Green State University

John Kennedy, West Chester University

Douglas Kuberski, Florida State College–Jacksonville

Lisa Langenbach, Middle Tennessee State University

William Lester, Jacksonville State University

Angela Lewis, University of Birmingham

Malene Little, University of South Dakota

Daniel J. Mallinson, Pennsylvania State University

Andrea McAtee, University of South Carolina

Madhavi McCall, San Diego State University

Bryan McQuide, University of Idaho

Gary Moncrief, Boise State University

Scott Moore, Colorado State University

Angela Narasimhan, Keuka College

Lawrence Overlan, Bentley College

Kevin Parsneau, Minnesota State University

David Peterson, Iowa State University

Elizabeth Prough, Madonna University

Lori Riverstone-Newe, Illinois State University

Pamela M. Schaal, Ball State University

James Sheffield, University of Oklahoma–Norman

Kelly Sills, Washington State University–Vancouver

Lee Silvi, Lakeland Community College

Zachary Smith, Northern Arizona University

Kendra Stewart, Eastern Kentucky University

Sharece Thrower, University of Pittsburgh

Lee Trepanier, Saginaw Valley State University

Charles Turner, California State University–Chico

Kenn Vance, John Jay College of Criminal Justice–CUNY

Lyle Wind, Suffolk County Community College

John Woodcock, Central Connecticut State University

Heather Yates, Illinois College

Stephen Yoder, Towson University

We hope and expect that each of them will be able to find traces of their numerous helpful suggestions throughout this final product.

Finally, in general, we express our appreciation to those political scientists and journalists who pay attention not only to Washington, D.C., but also to what is happening throughout the rest of the country.

• About the Authors •

Kevin B. Smith is the Leland J. and Dorothy H. Olson Chair of Political Science at the University of Nebraska–Lincoln. He is the author or coauthor of 10 books on politics and policy, as well as numerous scholarly articles on state politics and policy. He is also the longtime editor of CQ Press's annual *State and Local Government* reader as well as the former associate editor of *State Politics & Policy Quarterly*. Prior to becoming an academic, he covered state and local politics as a newspaper reporter.

Alan Greenblatt, a reporter at *Governing* magazine, has been writing about politics and government in Washington, D.C., and the states for more than two decades. As a reporter for *Congressional Quarterly*, he won the National Press Club's Sandy Hume Award for political journalism. At *Governing*, he has covered many issues of concern to state and local governments, such as budgets, taxes, and higher education. Along the way, he has written about politics and culture for numerous other outlets, including NPR, the *New York Times*, and the *Washington Post*.

Milton Brown/Caiaimage/Getty Photos

Introduction to State and Local Government

They Tax Dogs in West Virginia, Don't They?

Is government going to the dogs? Well, some do, some don't. State and local governments can tax virtually anything, including dogs. In some places, man's best friend is not only a family pet, but also a source of money for government.

Chapter Objectives

After reading this chapter, you will be able to

- Identify the ways state and local governments can affect daily life,

- Discuss how the comparative method can help explain differences between states,

- Describe the importance of state and local government within the wider context of American government,

- Identify the factors that influence how states and localities exercise their independent decision-making authority, and

- Summarize how this book will foster your knowledge of the roles and importance of state and local governments.

Saira Blair is an unusual college student in that she's very interested in state politics. How interested? So much so that she ran for her first election before she was old enough to vote. And won. In 2014, at the age of 17, she defeated an incumbent two decades her senior in the Republican primary election for the 59th District of the West Virginia House of Delegates. In the November 2014 general election, Blair—by then 18 years old and eligible to cast a ballot—cruised to a comfortable victory. The next day, the West Virginia University freshman was up early to make it to geology class. In early 2015, she officially became the youngest sitting state legislator in the nation. In 2016—at the ripe old age of 20—she was elected to a second two-year term (you can check out her policy and political activities on her web page: sairablair.com).

Blair, needless to say, is not a typical state legislator. Most state legislators are middle-aged men (see Chapter 7) who haven't worried about term papers or final exams in a long time. Blair, though, is also an unusual college student. Clearly she is very interested in politics and in state politics in particular—so much so that during her legislative career she has deferred her spring semesters because that's when the House of Delegates holds its annual 60-day session.[1] Most college students are not interested enough in politics to delay their studies so they can help run a government. Heck, most college students are not that into politics, period. At the same time Blair was campaigning for her second term, the United States was facing one of the most controversial presidential elections in a generation, yet voter turnout among the college-aged voting cohort barely scraped

50 percent (in comparison, turnout as a whole that year topped 60 percent). According to one study conducted during the same fall of that high-profile and contentious presidential campaign, less than half of the nation's college freshmen thought that keeping up with political affairs was important, and only about a quarter thought it was important to exert influence on the political system.[2] Even though the report showed only a small fraction of college students actively engaged and interested in politics, these numbers were higher compared to previous years and election cycles. The fact that college students today are fractionally less apathetic about politics than were their counterparts a few years ago was greeted as good news.

Regardless, if only half of college students are going to bother to vote and less than half think politics is important, then any way you cut it, a textbook like this has a big problem. We can expect, at most, that roughly half of our potential readers have some sort of minimal interest and curiosity about state and local politics. To this group, the Saira Blairs among you, we say welcome and enjoy the ride—given your interest in state politics, there is a lot to enjoy and soak up in what follows.

What about the rest of you, though—why should you care? Why should you have an interest in politics? More specifically, why should you give a hoot about politics and government at the state and local level? Fair question. The first goal of this textbook is to answer it. Everyone, and we mean *everyone*, should be interested in state and local politics. Here we explain why.

As you read through this chapter, keep in mind the following questions:

- **What are the advantages and disadvantages of federalism?**

- **What is the comparative method, and why is it a useful way to talk about state and local governments?**

- **What role do state and local politics play in determining how much certain services—such as a college education—cost?**

The Impact of State and Local Politics on Daily Life

Regardless of who you are, what you do, or what you want to do, if you reside in the United States, state and local governments play a large role in your life. Regardless of what you are interested in—graduating, starting a career, beginning a family, or just good old-fashioned sex, drugs, and rock 'n' roll—state and local governments shape how, whether, and to what extent you are able to pursue those interests. To make things immediately relevant, let's consider your college education. The vast majority of college students in the United

States—more than 70 percent—attend public institutions of higher education.[3] Public colleges and universities are created and supported by state governments. For many readers of this book, the opportunity to get a college education is possible only because each state government created a system of higher education. For example, California has three major higher education systems: the University of California, the California State University, and the California Community Colleges system. State governments require that taxpayers subsidize the operation of these education systems; in other words, the systems were designed not just to provide educational opportunities but also to make those opportunities broadly accessible, with tuition covering only a portion of the actual costs of a student's education.

Much of the rest comes from the taxpayers' pockets via the state government. When that state subsidy falls, college students inevitably end up paying more in tuition. If you wonder why your tuition bill keeps going up, wonder no more. State support for higher education was battered hard by the Great Recession of 2008–2009 and more than a decade later has yet to fully recover. Adjusted for inflation, state governments spent less on higher education in 2017 than they did in 2008.[4] In 2000, state government appropriations in 47 states covered a bigger portion of higher education costs than student tuition and fees. In other words, if you went to a public university or college in 2000, there was a very good chance that your state government paid more for your college education than you did. That's no longer true. In many states, students now cover more of the cost than state government does.[5]

If you take a longer view, an even more dramatic drop in state support for higher education is evident. In the mid-1980s, state governments routinely accounted for 50 percent or more of the revenues of state universities. These days, state support for some public universities has fallen so low that the institutions have effectively been privatized. For example, the proportion of revenues coming from state appropriations at places like the University of Colorado Boulder and the University of Michigan at Ann

Saira Blair is an unusual college student. Not just passionately interested in state politics, she successfully ran for the West Virginia House of Delegates while an 18-year-old freshman.

AP Photo/The Journal Newspaper, Ron Agnir

Arbor has fallen into the single digits. Yet while state appropriations are footing a smaller and smaller fraction of higher education's costs, demand for a college education has skyrocketed. Something has to give in such a situation, and it has: Tuition has gone up, often way up. In inflation-adjusted terms, the cost of going to college at the type of institution most students attend—a four-year public university—has increased by roughly 50 percent in a decade.[6]

The budgetary decisions being made by your state government don't affect only your tuition bill; they might be shaping the entire context of your educational experience. For example, in recent years, the University of Wisconsin–Superior cut a swath of educational programs (including nine majors, 15 minors, and a graduate field), Eastern Illinois University cut a quarter of its employees, and the Kansas Board of Regents cut nearly a million dollars in student scholarships.[7] What you can study, and whether you can afford it, is driven in no small part by the decisions of state government. True, the situation is slightly different if you go to a private university, but don't for a minute think you are not affected by state politics. For example, most students at private universities receive some sort of financial aid, and a goodly chunk of this comes from state and local taxpayers. In fact, undergraduates at private colleges receive on average more than $2,500 in state grants or other financial aid from state or local government. Not including tuition, that amount of financial aid is several hundred dollars more than what the average undergraduate at a public college receives from the state.[8]

State governments do not just play an outsize role in what you pay to go to college; they may also determine what classes you pay for, whether you want to take those classes or not. Some states have curriculum mandates. You may be taking a course on state and local politics—and buying and reading this book—because your state government decided it was a worthy investment of your time and money. In Texas, for example, a state politics course is not just a good idea; it's the law. According to Section 51.301 of the Texas Education Code, to receive a bachelor's degree from any publicly funded college in the state, a student must successfully complete a course on state politics.

And, dear college student, if you think all of this adds up to government having a big impact on your life, dream on. The government's role in shaping your college education is actually pretty small. Compared with the heavy involvement of state and local governments in shaping K–12 education, colleges have pretty much free rein. For 2018, it was estimated that more than 90 percent of students in Grades 9–12 were attending public high schools.[9] Local units of government operate most of these schools. Private grade schools also are subject to a wide variety of state and local government regulations, from teacher certification and minimum curriculum requirements to basic health and safety standards. Whether you attended public or private school—or were homeschooled—at the end of the day, you had no choice in the decision to get a basic grade school education. Although the minimum requirements vary, every state in the union requires that children receive at least a grade school education.

Believe it or not, state and local governments do not exist simply to regulate large areas of your life, even if it sometimes seems that way. Their primary purpose is to provide services to their respective populations. In providing these services, state and local governments shape the social and economic lives of their citizens. Education is a good example of a public service that extends deep into the daily lives of Americans, but it is far from the only one. The roads you use to get to school are there because state and local authorities built them and maintain them. The electricity that runs your computer comes from a utility grid regulated by state government, local government, or both. State and local governments are responsible for the sewer and water systems that make the bathroom down the hall functional. They make sure that the water you drink is safe and that the burger, sushi, or salad you bought in your student union does not make you sick.[10] State governments determine the violations and punishments that constitute criminal law. Local governments are responsible primarily for law enforcement and fire protection. The services that state and local governments supply are such a part of our lives that in many cases we notice only their absence—when the water does not run, when the road is closed, or when the educational subsidy either declines or disappears.

The Comparative Method in Practice: Yes, They Really Do Tax Dogs in West Virginia

Recognizing the impacts of state and local government may be a reasonable way to spark an interest in the topic, but interest alone does not convey knowledge. To gain a coherent understanding of the many activities, responsibilities, and levels of state and local governments, you need a systematic approach to learning. In this book, that systematic approach is the **comparative method**, which uses similarities and differences as the basis for explaining why the world is the way it is. Think of it this way: Any two states or localities that you can think of will differ in a number of ways. For example, they really do tax dogs in West Virginia—a dollar per head for male and spayed female dogs and two dollars a head for unspayed females. This is not the case in, say, Nebraska, where dogs have to be licensed but are not taxed.[11] Another example: Texas has executed hundreds of criminals since the national moratorium, or ban, on the death penalty was lifted in the 1970s; other states have executed none.

Or consider the electoral differences among states. Kansans and Nebraskans reliably send Republicans to the U.S. House of Representatives, while the people of Massachusetts send Democrats. Differences among states and localities are not limited to oddities like the tax status of the family pet or such big political questions as the balance of power in the House of Representatives. Those of you who do something as ordinary as buying a soda after class may pay more than your peers in other states or cities. Some readers of this book are certainly paying more in tuition and fees than those attending other colleges. Why is that? Why do those differences exist?

The comparative method seeks answers to these kinds of questions by looking for systematic **variance**, or differences, between comparable units of analysis. For our purposes, states are comparable units of analysis. Local governments—governments below the state level, such as county boards of commissioners and city councils—are another. Governments at each of these levels, state or local, have basic similarities that make comparisons of their differences meaningful. One way to think of this is that the comparative method is based on the idea that you can learn more about apples by comparing them with other apples than you can by comparing them with oranges or bananas.

> Governments at each of these levels, state or local, have basic similarities that make meaningful comparisons possible. One way to think of this is that the comparative method is based on the idea that you can learn more about apples by comparing them with other apples than you can by comparing them with oranges or bananas.

For example, governmentally speaking, all 50 states have a lot in common. Their governmental structures are roughly the same. All have a basic division of powers among the executive, legislative, and judicial branches of government. All have to operate within the broad confines of the single set of rules that is the U.S. Constitution. There's a bit more variety below the state level, with many different kinds and levels of local government (counties, municipalities, townships, and so forth), but broadly speaking, all these governments share a basic set of responsibilities, and all have to operate within the rules set down within their respective state constitutions. These similarities among states and among local governments make meaningful comparisons possible. Paradoxically, what makes such comparisons meaningful are not the similarities but the differences. This is because even though states share similar political structures and follow the same overall set of rules, they make very different choices. These differences have consequences—as in the example of college tuition and fees. Figure 1-1 shows how differences in the size of a state government's contribution to higher education relate to differences in the tuition and fees paid. See the trend? As the per-student state appropriation—the amount the state kicks in per student— goes up, the average tuition bill goes down. In short, the state-level differences plotted on the horizontal axis systematically map onto the state-level differences on the vertical axis. That's an example of the comparative method in action. Similar sorts of systematic differences among the states explain why some of you will pay more for a soda after class than others will. The sales tax on a can of soda ranges from 0 to 8 percent, depending on the city and state, hence the different prices in different locales.[12] These examples demonstrate the essence of

---

Comparative method A learning approach based on studying the differences and similarities among similar units of analysis (such as states).

Variance The difference between units of analysis on a particular measure.

FIGURE 1-1 ● State Appropriations and Tuition, 2017

Sources: Data from State Higher Education Executive Officers Association, *State Higher Education Finance: FY 2016* (Boulder, CO: SHEEO, 2016), http://www.sheeo.org/sites/default/files/project-files/SHEEO_SHEF_2016_Report.pdf, and College Board, "2017–18 Tuition and Fees at Public Four-Year Institutions by State," https://trends.collegeboard.org/college-pricing/figures-tables/2017-18-state-tuition-and-fees-public-four-year-institutions-state-and-five-year-percentage.

the comparative method—from your tuition bills to the price of soda, differences among political jurisdictions make a difference in the daily lives of citizens.

Such differences can lend themselves to sophisticated and useful statistical analyses. For example, just exactly how much is a tuition bill influenced by state support of public higher education? Using the data in Figure 1-1, we can calculate a precise relationship between contributions from state government and college costs. On average, for every appropriation of $1,000 per student by state government, tuition and fees at public four-year universities fall by about $615.[13] Of course, the reverse is also true: For every reduction of $1,000 per student in state aid, tuition and fees go up by an average of $615.

This basic approach of looking for differences that make a difference can be used to answer a broad range of "why" questions. For example, we know that how much a state gives to higher education helps determine how much you pay in tuition. So why do some states provide more support to higher education than others do? This is a question about one difference (variation in how much state governments spend on higher education) that can be answered by looking at other differences. What might these differences be? Well, they could stem from partisan politics in a state's legislature, a state's traditions and history, or a state's relative wealth, among many other possibilities. As a starting point for using the comparative approach to analyze such questions, consider the following basic differences among states and among localities.

Sociodemographics

The populations of states and localities vary enormously in size, age, and ethnicity. The particular mix of these characteristics, or **sociodemographics**, in a specific state or community has a profound impact on the state or community's politics. California is the most populous state in the nation, with nearly 39 million residents. This is a racially and ethnically diverse population, with Hispanics and Latinos constituting about 39 percent, whites about 38 percent, Asians nearly 15 percent, and blacks around 7 percent. Roughly 14

As of 2015, **CALIFORNIA, HAWAII, NEW MEXICO,** and **TEXAS** were the only states where minorities, or those not identifying themselves as non-Hispanic whites, already made up the majority of the population.

·······································

Sociodemographics The characteristics of a population, including size, age, and ethnicity.

percent of Californians live in poverty. Compare this with New Hampshire, which has about 1.3 million residents, more than 90 percent of whom are non-Hispanic whites and only about 7 percent of whom live below the poverty line.[14] These population characteristics present different challenges to the governments in these two states. Differences in populations are likely to promote different attitudes about and policies on welfare, affirmative action, bilingual education programs, and even the roles and responsibilities of government in general.

All these sorts of population characteristics are dynamic—that is, they change. Between the two most recent census periods (2000 and 2010), the population of McKinney, Texas, grew by more than 200 percent.[15] During roughly the same period, the population of Parkersburg, West Virginia, shrank by more than 21 percent. Such population expansions and contractions create very different problems and policy priorities for local governments—the struggle to accommodate new growth in a fast-developing area versus the challenge of maintaining even basic services in a rural county in which there are ever fewer taxpayers to tax. The same is true at the state level. Population-wise, some states are actually shrinking. Illinois, for example, had roughly 30,000 fewer residents in 2017 than in 2010. In the same period, Texas grew by more than 3 million. Such population shifts have potentially huge impacts, influencing everything from housing starts to job creation to demand for public services to state and local tax collections.[16]

The population of ILLINOIS shrank by roughly 30,000 between 2010 and 2017.

The population of TEXAS grew by more than 3 million between 2010 and 2017.

Sociodemographics might even be related to your tuition bill. Consider the age distribution of a state's population, from young to old. There is less demand for college education among those older than 65 than there is among those in the traditional undergraduate demographic of 18 to 24. Given this, states with higher percentages of their populations in older age groups face a different set of education policy pressures than those with higher concentrations in younger groups. States with large aging populations are likely to face less demand for spending on higher education and more demand for public programs that address the needs of the elderly, such as access to health care. Why do some states provide more support to higher education than others? At least a partial answer to this question is that different sociodemographics create different demands for higher education.

Study Map 1-1 for a moment. Believe it or not, you are actually looking at the United States. The reason the states look so strange is that this is a special kind of map called a cartogram. Instead of using actual geographical space to determine the size of a particular area represented in the map—the number of square miles in each state, for instance—cartograms use other variables to determine how size is represented. This cartogram depicts the size of each state's population, another useful way to compare states. Notice that some states that are geographically pretty big, such as New Mexico at 122,000 square miles, are very small on this map because they have small populations. Other states that are geographically quite small, such as Connecticut (with only 5,000 square miles), look much bigger on this map because they have large populations. Some states, such as Virginia, don't look that different in size at all from their appearance on a traditional map.

Culture and History

States and localities have distinct "personalities" that are apparent in everything from the "bloody bucket" shoulder patch worn by the Pennsylvania National Guard to the drawl that distinguishes the speech of West Texas natives. Some states have been part of the union for more than 200 years and still project an Old World connection to Europe. Hawaii and Alaska became states within living memory and are more associated with the exoticism of the Pacific and the Old West. New York City prides itself on being a cosmopolitan center of Western civilization. The visitors' bureau of Lincoln, Nebraska, touts the city's small-town ambience and Middle American values. These differences are more than interesting variations in accent and local points of pride; they are visible symbols that represent distinct values and attitudes. Political scientists generally accept that these differences extend to government and that

MAP 1-1 ● Population by State, 2017

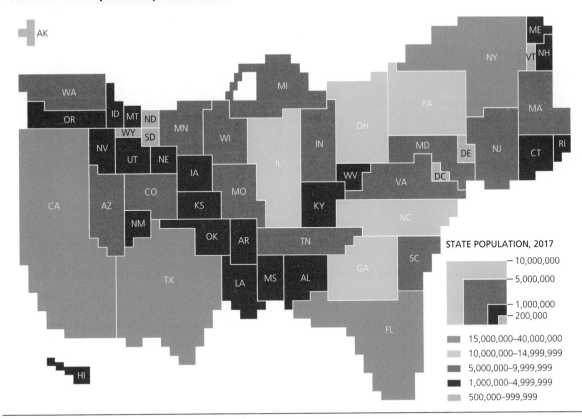

STATE POPULATION, 2017

— 10,000,000
— 5,000,000
— 1,000,000
— 200,000

15,000,000–40,000,000
10,000,000–14,999,999
5,000,000–9,999,999
1,000,000–4,999,999
500,000–999,999

Source: U.S. Census Bureau, "Estimates of Resident Population Change for the United States, Regions, States, and Puerto Rico: July 1, 2016 to July 1, 2017," https://www.census.gov/data/tables/2017/demo/popest/state-total.html.

each state has a distinct **political culture**, identifiable general attitudes and beliefs about the role and responsibility of government.

Daniel Elazar's *American Federalism: A View from the States* is the classic study of political culture. In this book, first published more than 50 years ago, Elazar not only describes different state cultures and creates a classification of those still in use today but also explains why states have distinctly different political cultures. Elazar argues that political culture is a product of how the United States was settled. He says that people's religious and ethnic backgrounds played the dominant role in establishing political cultures. On this basis, there were three distinct types of settlers who fanned out across the United States in more or less straight lines from the East Coast to the West Coast. These distinct migration patterns created three different types of state political cultures: moralistic, individualistic, and traditionalistic.[17]

States with **moralistic cultures** are those in which politics is the means used to achieve a good and just society. Such states tend to be clustered in the northern parts of the country (New England, the upper Midwest, and the Pacific Northwest). Elazar argues that the Puritans who originally settled the Northeast came to the New World seeking religious freedom. Their political culture reflected a desire to use politics to construct the best possible society. This notion, that government and politics represent the means to the greater good, creates a society that values involvement in politics and views government as a positive force for addressing social problems. This general orientation toward government and politics spread across the

....

Political culture The attitudes and beliefs broadly shared in a polity about the role and responsibility of government.

Moralistic culture A political culture that views politics and government as the means to achieve the collective good.

▲

Demographics and culture give each state a unique "personality." So does geography. The wide-open spaces of the Midwest and the dense urban concentration of New York City, for example, create different expectations about and demands on government.

northern and middle parts of the country in successive waves of migration. Wisconsin, for example, is a classic moralistic state. First settled by Yankees and later by Scandinavians, Germans, and Eastern Europeans, the state has long had a reputation for high levels of participation in politics (e.g., high levels of voter turnout), policy innovation, and scandal-free government.

States with **individualistic cultures** have a different view of government and politics. In individualistic cultures, people view government as an extension of the marketplace, something in which people participate for individual reasons and to achieve individual goals. Government should provide the services people want, but it is not viewed as a vehicle to create a "good society" or intervene in private activities. In individualistic states, politics is viewed the same as any other business. Officeholders expect to be paid like professionals, and political parties are, in essence, corporations that compete to provide goods and services to people. Unlike those in moralistic states, as long as the roads are paved and the trains run on time, folks in individualistic states tend to tolerate a certain level of corruption in government. Illinois is an individualistic culture state—and four of its last nine governors have served jail terms for corruption, bribery, and fraud.

In a **traditionalistic culture**, politics is the province of elites, something that average citizens should

Individualistic culture A political culture that views politics and government as just another way to achieve individual goals.

Traditionalistic culture A political culture that views politics and government as the means of maintaining the existing social order.

not concern themselves with. Traditionalistic states are, as their name suggests, fundamentally conservative, in the sense that they are concerned with preserving a well-established society. Like moralistic states, traditionalistic states believe that government serves a positive role. But there is one big difference—traditionalistic states believe the larger purpose of government is to maintain the existing social order. Those at the top of the social structure are expected to play a dominant role in politics, and power is concentrated in the hands of these elites. Traditionalistic states tend to be rural (at least historically); in many of these states, agriculture, rather than a broader mix of competing commercial activities, is the main economic driver.

Traditionalistic cultures tend to be concentrated in the Deep South, in states such as Georgia, Mississippi, and South Carolina. In these states, politics is significantly shaped by tradition and history. Like the settlers of individualistic states, those who settled the South sought personal opportunity. The preindustrial, agrarian economy of the South, however, led to a culture that was little more than a variation of the feudal order of the European Middle Ages. As far back as the 1830s, French aristocrat and writer Alexis de Tocqueville, writing about the United States, noted that "as one goes farther south . . . the population does not exercise such a direct influence on affairs. . . . The power of the elected officials is comparatively greater and that of the voter less."[18]

States have changed considerably since Elazar's pioneering research. Some traditionalistic states (e.g., Florida) have seen huge influxes of people from northern states, people who often are not from

A DIFFERENCE THAT MAKES A DIFFERENCE
IS IT BETTER TO BE A WOMAN IN MINNESOTA OR A GAL IN ALABAMA?

According to the Institute for Women's Policy Research (IWPR), it is better to be a woman in Minnesota than a gal in Alabama.

Why? Well, in an analysis of the status of women in the states, the IWPR had several reasons for ranking Minnesota as the best state for women and Alabama as the worst. For each state, the IWPR created composite indexes (combinations of different indicators collapsed onto a single measure) to rank women's status in six areas: political participation, employment and earnings, work and family, poverty and opportunity, reproductive rights, and health and well-being. Minnesota got its top billing by scoring in the top 10 in five of these six indices. Alabama never got into the top half on anything. That tells us why the IWPR ranked Minnesota higher than Alabama, but it is really only a partial answer to our question. To learn the rest of the answer, we must ask: *Why* would women have greater economic autonomy and more reproductive rights in Minnesota than in Alabama?

The comparative approach to answering this question involves looking for other differences between Minnesota and Alabama—differences that might explain the variance in the status of women. One candidate for an explanatory difference is presented in Table 1-1, which shows the top five and the bottom five states in the 2015 IWPR rankings along with the dominant political culture in each state. Notice any patterns?

You may have caught that all the top five states have either moralistic or individualistic cultures, and all the bottom five states have traditionalistic cultures. Political culture thus might explain some of the differences in women's status. States in which the dominant political values stress the importance of everyone getting involved might offer more opportunities for women. So might states that emphasize the value of hard work as the predominant basis for getting ahead in life. States in which the dominant political values stress leaving the important decisions to established elites might offer fewer opportunities for women because, traditionally, elites have been male.

Political culture, though, is not the be-all and end-all of the comparative method. Other differences may help explain why the status of women can vary so much across states. Consider Figure 1-2. The vertical axis in this graph

TABLE 1-1 ● Political Culture and the Status of Women in the States, 2015

Five Best States for Women	Dominant Political Culture
1. Minnesota	Moralistic
2. Connecticut	Individualistic
3. Massachusetts	Moralistic
4. Vermont	Moralistic
5. California	Moralistic

Five Worst States for Women	Dominant Political Culture
46. Florida	Traditionalistic
47. Tennessee	Traditionalistic
48. Kentucky	Traditionalistic
49. Mississippi	Traditionalistic
50. Alabama	Traditionalistic

Sources: Cynthia Hess, Jessica Milli, Jeff Hayes, and Ariane Hegewisch, with Yana Mayayeva, Stephanie Román, Julie Anderson, and Justine Augeri, *The Status of Women in the States: 2015* (Washington, DC: Institute for Women's Policy Research, 2015), http://statusofwomendata.org/publications/2015-national-report; Daniel J. Elazar, *American Federalism: A View from the States* (New York: Crowell, 1966); National Conference of State Legislatures, "Women in State Legislatures for 2014," April 1, 2014, http://www.ncsl.org/legislators-staff/legislators/womens-legislative-network/women-in-state-legislatures-for-2014.aspx.

charts women's earnings ratio—the amount women earn relative to men—by state. The horizontal axis is the IWPR political participation index, which combines several indicators, such as the percentage of women registered to vote and the number of women holding elective office, into a single measure. Again, there appears to be a pretty clear

(Continued)

(Continued)

FIGURE 1-2 ● Political Participation and Women's Earnings, 2015

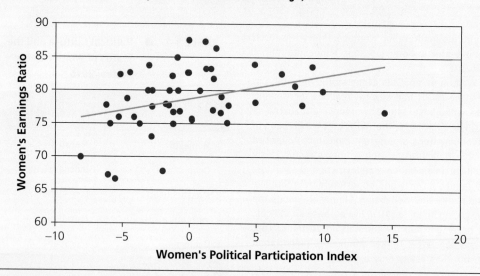

Source: Data from Cynthia Hess, Jessica Milli, Jeff Hayes, and Ariane Hegewisch, with Yana Mayayeva, Stephanie Román, Julie Anderson, and Justine Augeri, *The Status of Women in the States: 2015* (Washington, DC: Institute for Women's Policy Research, 2015), http://statu-sofwomendata.org/publications/2015-national-report.

trend here: The greater the political participation, the higher the earnings ratio. In other words, in states where women are more involved in politics and wield more political influence, women's earnings get closer to parity with male earnings. Why do women earn less than men? Figure 1-2 suggests that at least a partial answer is that in some places they wield less political power than men. Once you get the hang of using the comparative method at the state level to frame an analysis like this, you will likely see potential applications of the comparative method to a wide variety of questions with political, social, and economic importance.

traditionalistic cultures. The Deep South is also considerably more urban than it used to be, thus the agricultural foundation of many traditionalistic states has changed. The upshot of these sorts of shifts is that many states these days tend to encompass a mix of two or even all three cultures.

Even with such changes, however, political culture is remarkably resilient. In most states, one of Elazar's three political cultures is likely to be dominant, as shown in Map 1-2. In a recent examination of state differences, one journalist deduced that those cultural classifications still hold explanatory power and concluded, "It is unlikely that we'll see the erosion of these different state cultures in the near future."[19] A 2014 academic study undertaken by non–political scientists (who were apparently unaware of Elazar's work) engaged in a highly sophisticated statistical analysis of state differences based on a wide range of variables, from disease rates to the threat of natural disasters. The resulting state rankings are highly correlated with the moralistic/traditionalistic/individualistic typology—indeed, so highly correlated that it is reasonable to argue that these researchers effectively rediscovered Elazar's cultural classification more than 50 years later.[20] This new cultural ranking scheme joins a long list of studies that have found that political culture (however measured) shapes politics and policy in important ways. Policy change and innovation, for example, are more likely in moralistic states. Individualistic states are more likely to offer businesses tax breaks. Traditionalistic states tend to commit less public money to areas such

MAP 1-2 ● Dominant Political Culture by State

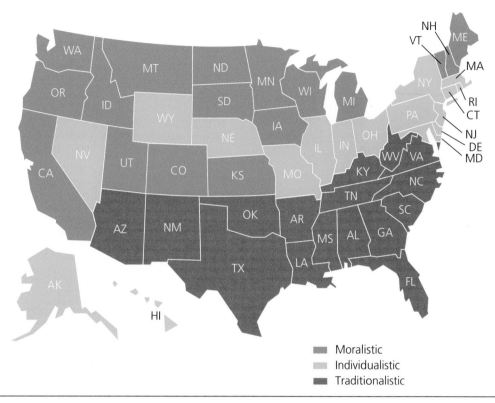

Moralistic
Individualistic
Traditionalistic

Source: Virginia Gray, "The Socioeconomic and Political Contexts of States," in *Politics in the American States: A Comparative Analysis*, 10th ed., ed. Virginia Gray and Russell Hanson (Washington, DC: CQ Press, 2013), 22.

as education.[21] Faced with similar problems, therefore, the Texas and Wisconsin state legislatures may propose radically different policy responses. These differences are at least partially products of the political cultures that still distinguish each state. In other words, culture and history matter.

These cultural differences certainly are apparent when it comes to states' support for higher education. Moralistic states commit considerably more resources to higher education than do individualistic and traditionalistic states. They spend about 13 percent more per capita on colleges and universities than do states with the other two cultures. Because moralistic states are those in which attitudes support higher levels of commitment to the public sector, these spending differences make sense in cultural terms. Why do some states provide more support to higher education than others do? Apparently, another part of the answer is that some political cultures see higher education in more communal than individual terms. See Table 1-2 for a summary of the three political cultures as classified by Elazar.

Economy

The relative size and health of a state's economy has a huge impact on its capacity to govern and provide public services. Among the states, the per capita gross domestic product—the state equivalent of the gross national product—varies from about $31,607 in Mississippi to $66,910 in North Dakota.[22] (See Map 1-3.) This means government in North Dakota has the ability to tap a greater amount of resources than can government in Mississippi. The difference in wealth, in effect, means that if North Dakota and Mississippi were to implement identical and equivalent public services, Mississippi would have a considerably higher tax rate. This is because Mississippi would have to use a greater proportion of its smaller amount of resources, compared with North Dakota. These sorts of differences also are visible at the local level. Wealthy suburbs can enjoy lower tax rates and still spend more on public services than can economically struggling urban or rural communities.

TABLE 1-2 ● Political Cultures at a Glance

	Elazar Classification		
	Moralistic	**Individualistic**	**Traditionalistic**
Role of Government	Government should act to promote the public interest and policy innovation.	Government should be utilitarian, a service provider.	Government should help preserve the status quo.
Attitude of Public Representatives	Politicians can effect change; public service is worthwhile and an honor.	Businesslike—politics is a career like any other, and individual politicians are oriented toward personal power. High levels of corruption are more common.	Politicians can effect change, but politics is the province of the elites.
Role of Citizens	Citizens actively participate in voting and other political activities; individuals seek public office.	The state exists to advance the economic and personal self-interest of citizens; citizens leave politics to the professionals.	Ordinary citizens are not expected to be politically involved.
Degree of Party Competition	Highly competitive	Moderate	Weak
Government Spending on Services	High	Moderate—money goes to basic services but not to perceived "extras."	Low
Political Culture	Strong	Fragmented	Strong
Most Common in . . .	Northeast, northern Midwest, Northwest	Middle parts of the country, such as the Mid-Atlantic; parts of the Midwest, such as Missouri and Illinois; parts of the West, such as Nevada	Southern states, rural areas

Source: Adapted from Daniel J. Elazar, *American Federalism: A View from the States*, 2nd ed. (New York: Crowell, 1972).

Regional economic differences do not determine only tax burdens and the level of public services; they also determine the relative priorities of particular policy and regulatory issues. Fishing, for example, is a sizable industry in coastal states in the Northeast and Northwest. States such as Maine and Washington have numerous laws, regulations, and enforcement responsibilities tied to the catching, processing, and transporting of fish. Regulating the economic exploitation of marine life occupies very little government attention and resources in places such as Kansas and Nevada, although agriculture in the former and gambling in the latter create just as many policy challenges and demands for government action.

Regardless of the basis of a state's economy, greater wealth does not always translate into more support for public programs. States with above-average incomes actually tend to spend *less* per capita on higher education. Why would less wealthy states concentrate more of their resources on higher education? There are a number of possible explanations. Education is a critical component of a postindustrial economy, so states that are less well-off may direct more of their resources into education in hopes of building a better economic future. Citizens in wealthy states simply may be better able to afford higher tuition costs. Whatever the explanation, this example suggests another advantage of employing the comparative

MAP 1-3 ● Economy by State, 2016

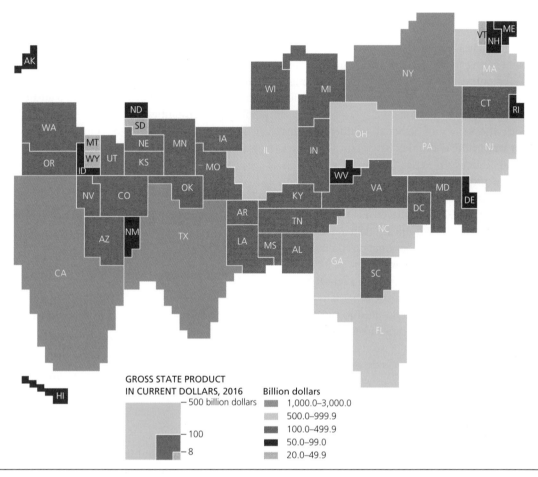

GROSS STATE PRODUCT
IN CURRENT DOLLARS, 2016

— 500 billion dollars

— 100

— 8

Billion dollars

▥	1,000.0–3,000.0
▢	500.0–999.9
▥	100.0–499.9
■	50.0–99.0
▥	20.0–49.9

The relative size of state economies is measured in terms of gross state product. Notice how geographically big states with small economies (Montana and Alaska) compare with geographically small states with big economies (New Jersey and Massachusetts).

Source: Bureau of Economic Analysis, "Gross Domestic Product by State: Second Quarter 2017," press release, November 21, 2017, Table 3, "Current-Dollar GDP by State, 2016:Q1–2017:Q2," https://www.bea.gov/system/files/2018-02/qgsp1117.pdf.

method—it shows that the obvious assumptions are not always the correct ones.

Geography and Topography

There is wild variation in the physical environments in which state and local governments operate. Hawaii is a lush tropical island chain in the middle of the Pacific Ocean, Nevada encompasses a large desert, Michigan is mostly heavily forested, and Colorado is split by the Rocky Mountains. Such geographical and topographical variation presents different challenges to governments. State and local authorities in California devote

considerable time and resources to preparing for earthquakes. Their counterparts in Texas spend comparatively little time thinking about earthquakes, but they do concern themselves with tornadoes, grass fires, and hurricanes.

Combine geography with population characteristics, and the challenges become even more complex. Montana is a large rural state in which the transportation logistics—simply getting students to school—can present something of a conundrum. Is it better to bus students long distances to large, centrally located schools, or should there be many smaller schools within easy commuting distance for relatively few students?

The first is cheaper. Larger schools can offer academic and extracurricular activities that smaller schools cannot afford. But the busing exacts a considerable cost on students and families. The second alternative eases transportation burdens, but it requires building more schools and hiring more teachers, which means more taxes. Geographical and population differences often not only shape the answers to such difficult policy issues but also pose the questions.

Consider the variety of seasonal weather patterns that occur within the enormous geographical confines of the United States. In Wisconsin, snow removal is a key service provided by local governments. Road-clearing crews are often at work around the clock during bad weather. The plows, the crews, and the road salt cost money. They all require a considerable investment in administration and coordination to do the job effectively. In Florida, snow removal is low on local governments' lists of priorities, for good reason—it rarely snows in the Sunshine State. On the other hand, state and local authorities in Florida do need to prepare for the occasional hurricane. Hurricanes are less predictable and less common than snow in Wisconsin, and it takes only one to create serious demands on the resources of local authorities.

And, yes, even basic geography affects your tuition bill, especially when combined with some of the other characteristics discussed here. Many large public colleges and universities are located in urban centers because central geographical locations serve more people more efficiently. Delivering higher education in rural areas is a more expensive proposition simply because there are fewer people in the service area. States with below-average population densities tend to be larger and more sparsely populated. They also tend to spend more on higher education. Larger government subsidies are necessary to make tuition affordable.

Recognizing the Stakes

The variation across states and localities offers more than a way to help make sense of your tuition bill or to explain why some public school systems are better funded or to understand why taxes are lower in some states. These differences also serve to underline the central role of states and localities in the American political system. Compared with the federal government, state and local governments employ more people and buy more goods and services from the private sector. They

have the primary responsibility for addressing many of the issues that people care about the most, including education, crime prevention, transportation, health care, and the environment. Public opinion polls often show that citizens place more trust in their state and local governments than in the federal government. These polls frequently express citizens' preference for having the former relieve the latter of a greater range of policy responsibilities.[23] With these responsibilities and expectations, it should be obvious that state and local politics are played for high stakes.

> Compared with the federal government, state and local governments employ more people and buy more goods and services from the private sector. They have the primary responsibility for addressing many of the issues that people care about the most, including education, crime prevention, transportation, health care, and the environment.

High stakes, yes, but it is somewhat ironic that state and local governments tend to get less attention in the media, in private conversation, and in curricula and classrooms than does their federal counterpart.[24] Ask most people to think about American government, and chances are they will think first about the president, Congress, Social Security, or some other feature of the national government. Yet most American governments are state or local. Only 535 elected legislators serve in the U.S. Congress. Thousands of legislators are elected at the state level, and tens of thousands more serve in the legislative branches of local government.

In terms of people, state and local governments dwarf the federal government. There are more teachers working for public schools—about 3 million—than the entire combined civilian workforce of the federal government (about 2.7 million).[25] Roughly 5 million state employees and more than 14 million local government employees punch the time clock every day. (See Map 1-4.) In terms of dollars, state and local governments combined represent about the same spending force as the

MAP 1-4 ● Number of State Government Employees by State, 2016

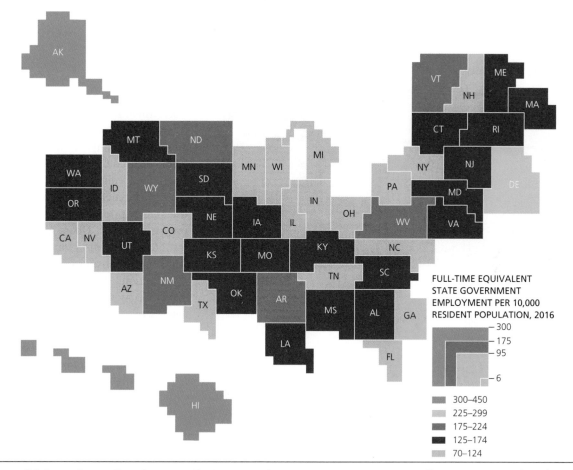

FULL-TIME EQUIVALENT STATE GOVERNMENT EMPLOYMENT PER 10,000 RESIDENT POPULATION, 2016
— 300
— 175
— 95
— 6

300–450
225–299
175–224
125–174
70–124

Source: U.S. Census Bureau, "State Government Employment and Payroll Data: March 2016," 2017, https://factfinder.census.gov/faces/tableser vices/jsf/pages/productview.xhtml?src=bkmk.

federal government. In 2015, state and local government expenditures totaled about $3.4 trillion.[26]

The size of state and local government operations is commensurate with these governments' 21st-century role in the political system. After spending much of the 20th century being drawn closer into the orbit and influence of the federal government, states and localities have spent the last few decades aggressively asserting their independence. This maturing of nonfederal, or subnational, government made its leaders and policies—not to mention its differences—among the most important characteristics of our political system.

The context of the federal system of government, and the role of state and local governments within that system, is given more in-depth coverage in Chapter 2.

For now, it is important to recognize that governance in the United States is more of a network than a hierarchy. The policies and politics of any single level of government are connected and intertwined with the policies and politics of the other levels of government in a complex web of interdependent relationships. The role of states and localities in these governance partnerships has changed considerably in the past few decades.

What states and localities do, and how they go about doing it, turns out to shape national life overall, as well as the lives of individual citizens. Given what is at stake at the state and local levels, no citizen can fully comprehend the role and importance of government without understanding subnational politics.

▲

It has a local government much like any other major municipality and electoral votes like a state, but it is ultimately ruled by Congress even though it has no representatives with full voting rights in the national legislature. Technically, Washington, D.C., is a federal city, the only political jurisdiction of its kind in the United States.

Laboratories of Democracy: Devolution and the Limits of Government

U.S. Supreme Court justice Louis Brandeis famously described the states as **laboratories of democracy**. This metaphor refers to the ability of states—and, to a lesser extent, localities—to experiment with policy. Successful experiments can be replicated by other states or adopted by the national government. For much of the past 30 years, state–federal relations have been characterized by **devolution**, or the process of taking power and responsibility away from the federal government and giving it to state and local governments. As a result, the states for a time aggressively promoted new ways to solve old problems in such high-profile policy areas as welfare, gun control, and education. That trend of increasing state policy autonomy was temporarily halted by the severe economic contraction of 2008–2009, the so-called Great Recession. For several years after the Great Recession,

states became critically dependent on federal money to stay solvent, and that meant they had to pay attention to federal policy priorities. As the economy recovered and states became less reliant on federal grant dollars, however, states in the past decade have once again begun to assert their independence from the federal government. This independence is increasingly characterized by ideological and partisan differences. States with conservative Republican governors frequently sought to resist the policy priorities of Democratic president Barack Obama's administration, pushing back on everything from the expansion of Medicaid to immigration. More recently, blue state Democratic governors have aggressively opposed Republican president Donald Trump's attempts to back away from climate change policies and to tighten immigration.

We'll take a closer look at the details of intergovernmental relations in the next chapter, but it is important here to recognize that how state and local governments exercise their independent decision-making authority is dependent on a number of factors. Some of these factors are external. The U.S. Constitution, federal laws and regulations, nationwide recessions, and the like constrain what states and localities can and cannot do. Internal factors, such as the characteristics of a particular state, also play a critical role in setting limits on what the state decides to do.

The big three of these internal factors are wealth, the characteristics of the state's political system, and the relative presence of organized interest groups, those individuals who organize to support policy issues that concern them. Public programs cost money. Wealth sets the limits of possible government action. Simply speaking, wealthier states can afford to do more than poorer states can. For most states, lack of funds is currently the biggest factor limiting independent policy action at the state and local levels. Simply put, many subnational governments do not have the money to launch expensive new policy initiatives. Indeed, in recent years, many of these governments have not had the money to keep funding their existing programs

----

Laboratories of democracy A metaphor that emphasizes the states' ability to engage in different policy experiments without interference from the federal government.

Devolution The process of taking power and responsibility away from the federal government and giving it to state and local governments.

and services (higher education, for example) at previous levels. While it is important, however, money is not the only factor that influences policy directions at the subnational level. Political system characteristics are the elements of the political environment that are specific to a state. States in which public opinion is relatively conservative are likely to pursue different policy avenues than are states in which public opinion is more liberal. States in which Republicans dominate the government are likely to opt for different policy choices than are states in which Democrats dominate. States with professional full-time legislatures are more likely to formulate and pursue sustained policy agendas than are states in which legislators are part-timers who meet only periodically. States in which the government perceives an electoral mandate to reform government are more likely to be innovative than are states in which the government perceives an electoral mandate to retain the status quo.[27] Organized interest group activity helps determine what sorts of policy demands government responds to. Governments in states with powerful teachers' unions, for example, experience different education policy pressures than do governments in states where teachers' unions are politically weak. These three factors constitute the basic ingredients for policymaking in the states. Specifics vary enormously from state to state, and the potential combinations in this democratic laboratory are virtually infinite.

Localities face more policymaking constraints than states do because they typically are not sovereign governments. This means that, unlike states, local governments get their power from the level of government above them rather than directly from citizens. The states have much greater control over local governments than the federal government has over the states. Yet, even though local governments are much more subordinate to state government than state government is to the federal government, they do not simply take orders from the state capital. Many have independent taxing authority and broad discretion to act within their designated policy jurisdictions.

These policy jurisdictions, nevertheless, are frequently subject to formal limits. The authority of school districts, for example, extends only to funding and operating public schools. State government may place limits on districts' tax rates and set everything from minimal employment qualifications to maximum teacher-to-pupil ratios. Even within this range of tighter restrictions, however, local governments retain considerable leeway to act independently. School districts often decide to contract out cafeteria and janitorial services, cities and counties actively seek to foster economic development with tax abatements and loan guarantees, and police commissions experiment with community-based law enforcement. During the past two decades, many of the reforms enthusiastically pursued at all levels of government—reforms from innovative management practices to the outright privatization of public services—have had their origins in local government.[28]

> **States and localities are not just safe places to engage in limited experimentation; they are the primary mechanisms connecting citizens to the actions of government.**

What all this activity shows is that states and localities are not only the laboratories of democracy but also the engines of the American republic. States and localities are not just safe places to engage in limited experimentation; they are the primary mechanisms connecting citizens to the actions of government.

Conclusion

There are good reasons for developing a curiosity about state and local governments. State politics determines everything from how much you pay for college to whether your course in state and local governments is required or elective. Above and beyond understanding the impact of state and local governments on your own life and interests, studying such governments is important because of their critical role in the governance and life of the nation. Subnational, or nonfederal, governments employ more people than the federal government and spend as much money. Their responsibilities include everything from repairing potholes to regulating pot. It is difficult, if not impossible, to understand government in the United States and the rights, obligations, and benefits of citizenship without first understanding state and local governments.

This book fosters such an understanding through the comparative method. This approach involves looking for patterns in the differences among states

LOCAL FOCUS

THE FEDERAL CITY

Riddle me this: It is a city. It is sort of a state. It is ruled by Congress. What is it? It is the District of Columbia, otherwise known as Washington, D.C. It is also the nation's capital—and surely the most unusual local government in the country.

Technically, Washington, D.C., is a federal city. Article I, Section 8, Paragraph 17 of the U.S. Constitution gives Congress the power to rule over an area not to exceed 10 square miles that constitutes the seat of national government; yet it has never been quite clear what that means in terms of governance. Should Congress rule the city directly? Should the citizens of the city be given the right to elect a representative government? If they do this, should the government be subordinate to Congress, or should it be counted as equivalent to a state and thus free to make any laws that do not violate the U.S. Constitution?

Throughout the city's history, these questions have been answered very differently. In the early 1800s, the district was a strange collection of cities and counties, each governed by different means. Washington City and Georgetown were municipalities run by a chief executive (a mayor) and a legislature (a council). Depending on the time period, however, the mayors were sometimes appointed by the federal government and sometimes elected. In addition to the two cities, there were two counties. Maryland laws governed Washington County; Virginia laws governed Alexandria County.

In the 1870s, Washington City, Georgetown, and Washington County were combined into a single governmental unit, a federal territory with a governor appointed by the president and a legislature elected by the territorial residents. This eventually became the District of Columbia, or Washington, D.C. For most of its history, commissioners appointed by the federal government governed the district. It was not until 1974 that the residents of Washington, D.C., gained home rule and the right to elect their own mayor and council.

This mayor–council arrangement, however, is unlike any other municipal government in the United States. The laws passed by the council have to be reviewed and approved by Congress. The laws that govern federal–state relationships treat the district as a state, even though it is not a state and cannot operate like one. The mayor is not considered the head of a federal agency, but he or she is expected to act like one when seeking appropriations from Congress.

This odd hybrid of local, state, and federal governments is reflected in the unique electoral status of Washington, D.C., voters. Voters in the district have a local vote but only half of a federal vote. They can vote for the president but not for a member of Congress. They can vote for a mayor and council, but they have no voting representative in Congress; yet Congress has the power to overturn laws passed by the council. The district now has three electoral votes. Prior to 1963, it had none, and D.C. voters could not cast a ballot for president.

All this makes Washington, D.C., the nation's most unusual local government. It is the only municipality that is a creature of the United States rather than of a state constitution, and, as such, it is the only really national city in the country.

Source: Mark David Richard, "History of Local Government in Washington, D.C.," 2002, https://www.dcvote.org/inside-dc/history-local-government-washington-dc.

and localities. Rather than advocating a particular perspective on state and local politics, the comparative method is predicated, or based, on a systematic way of asking and answering questions. Why is my tuition bill so high? Why does Massachusetts send mostly Democrats to the U.S. House of Representatives? Why are those convicted of capital crimes in Texas more likely to be executed than those convicted of comparable crimes in Connecticut? Why are sales taxes high in Alabama? Why is there no state income tax in South Dakota? We can answer each of these questions by comparing states and looking for systematic patterns in their differences. The essence of the comparative method is to use one difference to explain another.

This book's examination of state and local politics is organized into three distinct sections. The first section consists of five chapters designed to set the basic framework, or context, for studying state and local politics. Included here are chapters on federalism, state constitutions, budgets, political participation, and political

THE LATEST RESEARCH

As discussed extensively in this chapter, the comparative method is an important tool used by scholars to understand how state-level differences translate into meaningful political and policy differences. A lot of these differences that make a difference are not static—indeed, some may be changing even as you read this textbook.

The "granddaddy" of all differences—though far from the only one—is political culture, a concept originated by Daniel Elazar that continues to be widely respected for its explanatory power. While scholars in the past few decades have conducted a number of more fine-grained analyses of political culture that take advantage of new data sources and more sophisticated statistical techniques, Elazar's original classification system remains a disciplinary standard. Below we summarize some of the newest research that uses the comparative method and investigates state political cultures and their impact on politics and policy.

- **Dincer, Oguzhan, and Michael Johnston,** "Political Culture and Corruption Issues in State Politics: A New Measure of Corruption Issues and a Test of Relationships to Political Culture," *Publius: The Journal of Federalism* 47, no. 1 (2016): 131–148.

- **Fisher, Patrick I.,** "Definitely Not Moralistic: State Political Culture and Support for Donald Trump in the Race for the 2016 Republican Presidential Nomination," *PS: Political Science and Politics* 49, no. 49 (2016): 743–747.

The two studies listed here use Elazar's classification to examine the impact of political culture in two very different areas of politics. Fisher is examining whether political culture can help explain state-level voting patterns in the 2016 Republican presidential primary. He finds this is indeed the case. For example, Donald Trump's share of the primary vote was significantly lower in states with a moralistic political culture. Dincer and Johnston are interested in what explains patterns of corruption in state government, and hypothesize that political culture may play an important role in predicting these trends. Their analysis concludes that culture is a "sticky" determinant of corruption patterns, where states with moralistic cultures have fewer corruption issues than states with traditionalistic or individualistic cultures. What these two studies show is that more than 50 years after Elazar first developed his theory of political culture, contemporary scholars continue to find his cultural classifications have a lot of explanatory power across various dimensions of politics and policy.

- **Harrington, Jesse R., and Michele J. Gelfand,** "Tightness-Looseness across the 50 United States," *Proceedings of the National Academy of Sciences* 111, no. 22 (2014): 7990–7995.

Harrington and Gelfand's study is different from the two papers discussed above. These researchers are not analyzing an existing concept of state-level culture, but trying to create a new one. Specifically, they are taking a theory used to explain differences in political culture between nations and seeing if it works for the states. This theory makes a distinction between "tight" and "loose" cultures. Tight cultures are characterized by strongly enforced rules and norms, with less tolerance for deviance. Loose cultures have fewer strongly enforced rules and high levels of tolerance. The basic idea is that nations that face a lot of stress—wars, environmental or economic threats, internal strife—gravitate toward a tighter culture to maintain social cohesion (or even survival). Nations that face fewer threats tend to gravitate toward a looser culture. Harrington and Gelfand find that the basic idea also works at the state level. They create a state-level index of cultural "tightness" that successfully predicts various state characteristics in exactly the way you would expect culture to affect laws and policy choices.

parties and interest groups. The second section covers the institutions of state and local government: legislatures, executives, courts, and bureaucracy. Although elements of local government are discussed in all these, there are also two chapters in this section devoted solely to local politics and government. The final section covers a series of distinct policy areas: education, crime, health care, and the environment. These chapters not only cover areas of substantive policy interests but also offer concrete examples of how a broad understanding of the context and institutions of state and local governments can be combined with the comparative method to promote a deeper understanding of the politics of states and localities.

CHAPTER 1

for CQ Press

Want a better grade?

Get the tools you need to sharpen your study skills. SAGE edge offers a robust online environment featuring an impressive array of free tools and resources.

Access practice quizzes, eFlashcards, video, and multimedia at **edge.sagepub.com/smithgreenblatt7e**

Top Ten Takeaways

1. Most citizens know comparatively little about state and local politics, even though these governments have a significant impact on their daily lives.

2. State and local governments have the primary policy responsibility in areas such as education and law enforcement, and decisions made by these governments affect everything from the size of a tuition bill to the size of an elementary school class, from the licensing requirements to become a barber to the licensing requirements to become a doctor.

3. States are different in many ways, from topography and weather to population size and sociodemographics.

4. Despite their differences, all states have a core set of political similarities—they all must operate within the guidelines of the U.S. Constitution, and they have similarly structured governments, with an elected legislature, an independently elected executive, and an independent judiciary.

5. States are sovereign governments. In other words, as long as they are not in violation of the U.S. Constitution, they are free to do as they please. They draw their power not from the federal government, but from the U.S. Constitution, their own state constitutions, and their own citizens.

6. These differences and similarities make the states unique laboratories for investigating a wide range of important political and policy questions. The states constitute 50 truly comparable and sovereign governments.

7. The comparative method uses the similarities and differences of the states as a basis for looking at systematic variance. In other words, this method seeks to see whether one set of differences among the states can help explain other differences.

8. There are three basic types of political culture in the states. Moralistic cultures tend to view government as a means to make society better. Individualistic cultures view government as an extension of the marketplace. Traditionalistic cultures tend to view government and politics as the concern of elites, not average citizens.

9. Political culture provides a good example of how "a difference makes a difference." Variation in political culture helps explain a wide variety of political and policy differences among the states—everything from differences in voter turnout to differences in the political status of women.

10. It is virtually impossible to understand politics, policy, and governance in the United States without understanding state and local government.

Key Concepts

comparative method (p. 4)
devolution (p. 16)
individualistic
    culture (p. 8)

laboratories of democracy
    (p. 16)
moralistic culture (p. 7)
political culture (p. 7)

sociodemographics (p. 5)
traditionalistic
    culture (p. 8)
variance (p. 4)

Suggested Websites

- **www.csg.org.** The website of the Council of State Governments, an organization that represents elected and appointed officials in all three branches of state government. Publishes on a wide variety of topics and issues relevant to state politics and policy.

- **libguides.princeton.edu/politics/american/states.** A site containing links to a wide variety of state-level data sources that have been collected and made available to the public by scholars and government agencies.

- **www.census.gov/quickfacts.** A U.S. Census Bureau website that lists state rankings on population, per capita income, employment, poverty, and other social and economic indexes.

- **us.sagepub.com/en-us/nam/state-stats.** A comprehensive and searchable database of state-level information (requires subscription).

Scott Olson/Getty Images

Federalism

The Power Plan

Like it or not, states and the federal government need each other. Big economic development projects, for example, sometimes require the efforts of both levels of government. President Donald Trump and former Wisconsin governor Scott Walker are seen here attending the groundbreaking of a massive factory in Walker's state.

Chapter Objectives

After reading this chapter, you will be able to

- Identify the three systems of government and how they divide power,
- Explain what federalism is and why it was chosen as a system for the United States,
- Discuss the advantages and disadvantages of federalism,
- Describe the ways elements in the U.S. Constitution provide a basis for federalism,
- Summarize the different types of federalism that developed over time, and
- Discuss the Supreme Court's role in U.S. federalism.

In 2017, roughly $1.5 billion worth of marijuana was legally sold in the state of Colorado.[1] Well, sort of. Technically, it was all illegal, even though the people doing the selling were running aboveboard, legitimate businesses. Huh? How can selling marijuana be legal and illegal at the same time? Simple: federalism.

Federalism is a political system in which national and regional governments share powers and are considered independent equals. The upshot of federalism in the United States is that the national government and state governments can have pretty different ideas about what should or should not be done. And you don't have to get too far into the legal weeds to figure this out. You just have to get into weed. See, the reason selling pot is both legal and illegal in Colorado boils down to a difference between state and federal law. In 2012, voters in Colorado approved Amendment 64, a ballot initiative that among other things permitted the commercial cultivation and retail sale of marijuana. Since this new law took effect in 2014, legal sales of marijuana have skyrocketed, and at last count, taxes on those sales were bringing about $250 million a year into the state treasury. Nothing that's happened in Colorado or the other eight states and the District of Columbia (and counting) that have legalized marijuana, however, changes anything about federal law.

At least in theory, federal law in this instance is supposed to take precedence over state law, and federal law takes a dim view of selling spliffs or herb-enhanced candy. It classifies marijuana as a Schedule I drug, which basically means it's treated more like heroin than booze. As far as federal law is concerned, possessing and/or selling marijuana is a serious no-no that can

be punished with stiff fines and jail time. Except it isn't. Or at least, not until it is. If this sounds confusing, it's because, well, it *is* confusing. When states started to adopt full-on legalization of marijuana a half-decade or so ago, the federal government basically said, "No worries, we've got bigger fish to fry." The administration of President Barack Obama adopted an official policy of telling federal prosecutors not to expend their limited time and resources going after people selling pot where the practice had been legalized. In January 2018, the administration of Donald Trump formally ended that policy. So where did that leave pot sellers in Colorado? Well, running a legal business by state law that was illegal by federal law.

This confusing state of affairs is actually a good metaphor for federalism as it is practiced in the United States. State governments want to do one thing and go their own way, while the federal government wants the nation as a whole to go in a different direction. Clearly, both of these things cannot happen. So, who ultimately has the power and the authority to get their way? The states or the federal government? In a nutshell, finding the answer to this question drives a good deal of political conflict in the United States. The only way any of that makes sense is if you understand federalism. Indeed, the bottom line is that you cannot understand politics in the United States—and that means national as well as state and local politics—without understanding federalism. Certainly, a thorough understanding of this system of shared powers is critical to understanding

....

Federalism A political system in which national and regional governments share powers and are considered independent equals.

the politics of states and localities and the important role they play in the political life of the nation. Figuring out who—the federal or state governments—has the power to do what is not just the only way to resolve the legal status of pot; it is one of the most central questions of the entire American political system. This chapter provides a basic understanding of federalism, its history and evolution in the United States, and its implications for politics and governance in states and localities. As you read through the chapter, keep in mind the following questions:

- **What are the advantages and disadvantages of federalism?**

- **Why has policy activity increasingly moved from the federal government to the states?**

- **Why would some businesses prefer to be regulated by the federal government rather than by state governments?**

Systems of Power

We typically think of a nation as being ruled by a single sovereign government—that is, a government that depends on no other government for its political authority or power. This does not mean, however, that every nation has one government. Power and policy responsibility are distributed throughout any given political system in one of three ways, and all typically involve multiple levels of government. (See Figure 2-1.) The first option is to concentrate power in a single central government. Nations in which legal authority is held exclusively by a central government are known as **unitary systems**. Unitary systems typically do have regional and/or local governments, but these can exercise only the powers and responsibilities granted them by the central government. In other words, these governments are not sovereign; how much or how little power they are allowed to wield is up to the central government, not the citizens of the particular localities. The United Kingdom is a good example of a unitary system. Historically, the United Kingdom

has a strong tradition of local and regional government; power is concentrated in the nation's Parliament. If it so chooses, Parliament can expand or contract the powers and responsibilities of these lower governments or even shut them down entirely.

In contrast to unitary systems, confederal systems concentrate power in regional governments. A **confederacy** is defined as a voluntary association of independent, sovereign states or governments. This association stands the power hierarchy of a unitary system on its head. In a confederacy, the central government depends on the regional governments for its legal authority. The United States has experimented with confederal systems twice during its history. The Articles of Confederation was the first constitution of the United States. It organized the U.S. political system as an agreement of union among sovereign states. The national government consisted of a legislature in which all states had equal representation. There was no national executive branch, such as the presidency, and no national judiciary, such as the Supreme Court.

This confederal system was adopted during the Revolutionary War and remained in effect for more than a decade. Many of the nation's founders saw its flaws, however, and wrote its replacement at the Constitutional Convention of 1787 in Philadelphia. The product of that gathering—the U.S. Constitution—was ratified in 1788 and replaced the Articles of Confederation as the basis of the U.S. political system.[2] The second experiment with confederacy began in 1861 at the onset of the Civil War. Southern states seeking to secede from the Union organized their political system as a confederacy. All this ended with the South's surrender in 1865 and the return of the seceded states to the Union.

Federal systems operate in a middle range between unitary systems and confederacies. Responsibilities in a federal system are divided between the two levels of government, and each is given the appropriate power and legal authority to fulfill those responsibilities. The system's defining feature is that neither level of government is dependent on the other for its power. Within its defined areas of responsibility, each is considered independent and autonomous. In the United States, the two levels of government considered sovereign are the federal government and state governments. States are legally equal partners with the national government and occupy a central role in the political system. Although required to operate within the rules laid

---

Unitary systems Nations in which legal authority is held exclusively by a central government.

Confederacy A voluntary association of independent, sovereign states or governments.

FIGURE 2-1 ● How It Works

Systems of Government

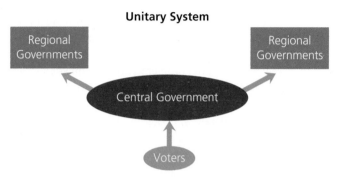

Unitary System

Central government grants powers to the regional governments.

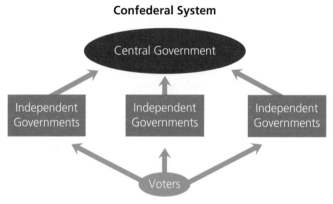

Confederal System

Independent states or governments grant legal authority to central government.

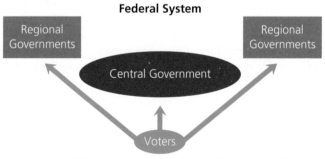

Federal System

Responsibilities and powers are divided between central government and regional governments or states; neither level is dependent upon the other for its power.

down by the U.S. Constitution, states are considered sovereign because their power and legal authority are drawn not just from the U.S. Constitution but also from their own citizens as codified in their own state constitutions. Local governments are treated very differently than are states. Within their own borders, states are very much like unitary systems; substate governments such as cities and counties get their power from the state, and they exercise only the policymaking authority the state is willing to grant. The specifics of local governments' powers and policy responsibilities are discussed in more depth in Chapter 11.

Why Federalism? The Origins of the Federal System in the United States

The United States is a federal system for a number of reasons. Largely because of their experiences with the Articles of Confederation, the framers of the Constitution rejected the possibility of a confederacy. The national government was so weak under the Articles that prominent figures such as James Madison and George Washington feared it doomed the newly independent republic to failure.

These fears were not unfounded. Following the successful conclusion of the Revolutionary War in 1783, the new United States found itself in the grip of an economic recession, and the central government had little power to address the crisis. Indeed, it actually contributed to the problem by constantly threatening to default on its debts. Independence had brought political freedom, but it also meant that American-made products were now in head-to-head competition with cheap, high-quality goods from Great Britain. This made consumers happy but threatened to cripple American businesses. The economic difficulties pitted state against state, farmer against manufacturer, and debtor against banker. The weak central government really did not have the power to attempt a coordinated, nationwide response to the problem. It could do little but stand by and hope for the best.

As internal tensions mounted within the United States, European powers still active in the Americas threatened the nation's very sovereignty. Spain shut down shipping on the Mississippi River. The British refused to withdraw from some military posts until the U.S. government paid off its debts to British creditors. George Washington believed the United States, having won the war, was in real danger of losing the peace. He said that something had to change "to avert the humiliating and contemptible figure we are about to make on the annals of mankind."[3]

For a loose coalition of the professional classes who called themselves Federalists, that "something" that needed to change was obviously the central government. This group of lawyers, businessmen, and other individuals, drawn mostly from the upper social strata, sought to create a stronger and more powerful national government. Americans, however, were not particularly enthusiastic about handing more power to the central government, an attitude not so different from that held by many today. Most recognized that the Articles had numerous flaws, but few were ready to copy the example of the British and adopt a unitary system.

Two events in fall 1786 allowed the Federalists to overcome this resistance and achieve their goal of creating a more powerful national government. The first was the Annapolis Convention. This meeting in Maryland's capital was convened for the purpose of hammering out an interstate trade agreement. Few states sent delegates, and those who did show up had strong Federalist sympathies. They took advantage of the meeting and petitioned Congress to call for a commission to rewrite the Articles of Confederation.

The second event was Shays's Rebellion, named for its leader, Daniel Shays, a hero of the recently won Revolutionary War. The rebellion was an uprising of Massachusetts farmers who took up arms in protest of state efforts to take their property as payment for taxes and other debts. It was quickly crushed, but with further civil unrest threatening to boil over into civil war and with mounting pressure from powerful elites within the Federalist ranks, the Continental Congress was pushed to call for states to send delegates to Philadelphia in summer 1787. The purpose of the meeting, which came to be known as the Constitutional Convention, was the rewriting of the Articles of Confederation.

Once convened, the group quickly abandoned its mandate to modify the Articles and decided to write an entirely new constitution. In doing so, the Federalists who dominated the convention rejected confederacy as an adequate basis for the American political system. Their experience under the Articles had taught them that a central government subordinate to the states was not much of a government at all. What they wanted was a government capable of dealing effectively with national problems, and this meant a strong central government whose power was independent of the states.

Some Federalists, notably Alexander Hamilton, were attracted to the idea of a unitary government, but such a system was never seriously considered at the Constitutional Convention. Popular sentiment did not favor a unitary system, which was understandable given that the Revolutionary War had been fought in no small part because of the perceived arrogance of and abuse by a central government toward its regional subordinates (the states were originally colonies of the British Crown). Political realities also argued against pushing for a unitary system. To have any legal force, the new constitution would have to be ratified by the states, and it was highly unlikely the states would voluntarily agree to give up all their powers to a national government. Federalism was thus the only practical option.

Yet a federal system meant more than the political price that had to be paid to achieve a stronger national government. The founders were attempting to construct a new form of **representative government**, in which citizens would exercise power indirectly, on the basis of a paradox. Convention delegates wanted a more powerful national government, but at the same time, they did not want to concentrate power for fear that would lead to tyranny. Their solution to this problem was to create a system of separated powers and checks and balances. They divided their new and stronger national government into three branches—legislative, executive, and judicial—and made each branch partially reliant on the others to carry out its own responsibilities. This made it difficult for any single group to gain the upper hand in all three divisions of government and gave each branch the power to check the excesses of the other branches.

The delegates achieved a similar set of goals by making state and national governments coequal partners. By letting states remain independent decision makers in a wide range of policy arenas, they divided power between the national and subnational levels of

---

Representative government A form of government in which citizens exercise power indirectly by choosing representatives to legislate on their behalf.

government. The national government was made more powerful by the new constitution, but the independence of the states helped set clear limits on this power.

The Advantages and Disadvantages of Federalism

Federalism solved a political conundrum for the founders and helped achieve their philosophical aims of dispersing and separating power. Yet federalism is not necessarily better than a confederal or a unitary system—it's just different. In the United States, the pros and cons of federalism have benefited and bedeviled the American political system for more than two centuries.

There are four key advantages to the federal system. (See Table 2-1.) First, it keeps government closer to the people. Rather than the federal government's imposing one-size-fits-all policies, states have the freedom and authority to match government decisions to local preferences. This freedom also results in the local variance in laws, institutions, and traditions that characterizes the U.S. political system and provides the comparative method with its explanatory strength.

Second, federalism allows local differences to be reflected in state and local government policy and thereby reduces conflict. Massachusetts, for example, tends to be more liberal than, say, Alabama. California has a much more ethnically and culturally diverse population than does Nebraska. Rather than having the various interests and preferences that spring from state-to-state differences engage in a winner-take-all policy struggle at the federal level, they can be accommodated at the state level. This reduces the friction among interests and lessens conflict.

Third, independent subnational governments allow for flexibility and experimentation. The states, as Supreme Court justice Louis Brandeis famously put it, are "the laboratories of democracy." Successful policy innovations in one state can be adopted by other states and copied by the federal government. Fourth, the achievement of at least some national goals is made easier by the participation of independent subnational governments. For example, the Patient Protection and Affordable Care Act (popularly known as Obamacare) is the most sweeping reform of health care regulation in half a century. The primary goal of Obamacare was to reduce the number of people without health insurance, and one of the law's key provisions is the establishment of health insurance exchanges, basically centralized places where people can buy federally subsidized health insurance packages. As state governments constitute ready-made centralized regulatory bodies geographically distributed across the nation, it made sense to have them set up and run these exchanges rather than have the federal government do it from scratch, and that was the original intent when Obamacare was initiated.

Along with its benefits, however, federalism confers a set of disadvantages. First, while allowing local differences does keep government closer to the people, it also creates complexity and confusion. For example, if you own a nationwide business, you have to deal with state *and* federal regulations—51 sets of regulations in all. That means, among other things, 51 tax codes and 51 sets of licensing requirements. And many communities have their own restrictions and requirements for businesses as well.

Second, federalism can increase conflict as easily as reduce it. The Constitution is very vague on the exact division of powers between state and federal governments, and doesn't mention local governments at all (see the box "Local Focus: States and Cities Are Not Equal Partners"). This results in a constant struggle—and a lot of litigation—to resolve which level of government has the responsibility and legal authority to take the lead role in a given policy area. For example, while some states followed through on the Obamacare intent of setting up exchanges, other states—especially states characterized by conservative

TABLE 2-1 ● Advantages and Disadvantages of Federalism

Advantages	Disadvantages
Allows for flexibility among state laws and institutions.	Increases complexity and confusion.
Reduces conflict because states can accommodate citizens' interests.	Sometimes increases conflict when jurisdictional lines are unclear.
Allows for experimentation at the state level.	Duplicates efforts and reduces accountability.
Enables the achievement of national goals.	Makes coordination difficult.
	Creates inequality in services and policies.

LOCAL FOCUS

STATES AND CITIES ARE NOT EQUAL PARTNERS

Texas governor Greg Abbott famously doesn't like taking orders from Washington, D.C. He made his reputation as a crusading attorney general fighting federal government overreach—he sued the Obama administration 31 times—and championing the cause of states' rights.

Abbott's commitment to decentralization of government power within the federal system, though, pretty much stops at the state border. While Abbott supports states having the freedom to chart their own political and policy course, he's not a big fan of extending that philosophy outside the state capitol. Quite the reverse. He might favor hands-off regulation by the federal government, but he is considerably less keen on the states giving local governments the same sort of freedom.

The reason state governments want a free rein from the feds while keeping a whip hand over local governments is not hard to fathom. Cities in big states tend to lean liberal, and though local elections are often nonpartisan, they tend to be dominated by Democratic officials. In recent years, cities controlled by Democratic-leaning politicians have passed ordinances on everything from banning plastic grocery bags; to extending civil rights protections to LGBT residents; to discouraging cooperation with federal immigration efforts.

Yet, while big cities lean liberal and Democratic, state governments have increasingly leaned right and Republican. Indeed, in the past five or so years, the Grand Old Party (GOP) has had historically high levels of control over state governments. The people controlling state government, in other words, are often not happy with the policy directions being pursued at the local level. That not only creates political tension; it creates a certain paradox: the same politicians fighting to keep state governments out from under the

thumb of the federal government are often the same politicians actively seeking to put local governments under the thumb of the state.

Certainly, critics of Abbott's support for limiting local authority argue it is inconsistent with his staunch defense of states' rights. If he's so against the federal government intruding in states, it only seems logical to assume he would defend local governments from regulatory overreach at the state level.

Yet that seeming contradiction—favoring policy freedom for state but not for local governments—is not necessarily inconsistent with how federalism works in the United States. It is important to remember that although the Constitution divides sovereign power between federal and state governments, it says nothing at all about local governments. The upshot is that local governments have no constitutional claim to exercise independent sovereign power; they have to make do with whatever power states allow them to exercise.

We have whole chapters devoted to local government later in the book, but it is important to recognize now that local governments do not occupy the same place in the federal system as state governments. The bottom line is that if cities are doing things the state government doesn't want them to, legally speaking the chances are that states can order them to stop.

While the legal position of local governments with the federal system might make that true, it does not mean people have to like state governments pushing around their local government. As Bennett Sandlin, executive director of the Texas Municipal League, put it, "Texans don't want to be told they have to conform to one way of thinking or one way of living—whether it comes from Washington or from the governor's office in Austin."

Source: Adapted from Daniel C. Vock, "The End of Local Laws? War on Cities Intensifies in Texas," *Governing*, April 5, 2017, http://www.governing.com/topics/politics/gov-texas-abbott-preemption.html.

Republican leadership—balked and left the job up to the federal government. Governments in many such states saw Obamacare as federal government overreach into state sovereignty and not only refused to set up exchanges but also avoided participating in other key

provisions of Obamacare—most notably by refusing to take advantage of federal subsidies to expand Medicaid, a program that helps provide health care coverage to poorer citizens. When Republicans gained control of the White House and both houses of Congress following

2016, political support for Obamacare at the federal level plummeted, even though an effort to end it outright was unsuccessful. This left states that had embraced Obamacare and/or expanded Medicaid still expecting the federal government to follow through on its Obamacare obligations, even though the leaders of the federal government were openly hostile to the program. In other words, throughout this program's history, state and federal governments have clashed as much as cooperated, with both sides arguing that the other was ignoring the appropriate roles and limitations of the federal division of powers.

Third, although federalism promotes flexibility and experimentation, it also promotes duplication and reduces accountability. For example, local, state, and national governments have all taken on law enforcement responsibilities. In some areas, this means there may be municipal police departments, a county sheriff's department, and the state patrol, plus local offices of the Federal Bureau of Investigation and the U.S. Drug Enforcement Administration. The responsibilities and jurisdictions of these organizations overlap, which means taxpayers end up paying twice for some law enforcement activities. Also, when these agencies are unsuccessful or ineffective, it can be very difficult to figure out which is responsible and what needs to change.

Fourth, the federal system can make it hard to coordinate policy efforts nationwide. For example, police and fire departments on opposite sides of a state border, or even within adjacent jurisdictions in the same state, may have different communication systems. It is hard to coordinate a response to a large-scale emergency if the relevant organizations cannot talk to each other, but the federal government cannot force state and local governments to standardize their radio equipment.

Finally, a federal system creates inequality in services and policies. The uneven implementation of Obamacare is an obvious example: Health care options can differ fairly dramatically from state to state. The quality of

AP Photo/Mike Wintroath

▲
Emergency management provides a classic example of how different levels of government work together. The Federal Emergency Management Agency (FEMA) is critical to any effective response to disaster, but that effectiveness is also dependent upon FEMA's ability to coordinate with state and local agencies.

public schools and welfare services more generally also depends heavily on the choices state and local governments make. This inevitably means that some states offer better educational opportunities and do more for the needy than others do.

The Constitutional Basis of Federalism

The relationship between national and state governments is like a sibling rivalry. It is hard to imagine either level of government getting along without the other, yet because each is independent and focused on its own interests, conflict is common. The ink was barely dry on the newly ratified Constitution before the federal government and the states were squabbling over who had the power and authority in this or that policy area. In writing the Constitution, the founders recognized that the differences between states and the federal government were likely to be a central and lasting feature of the political system. Accordingly, they attempted to head off the worst of the disputes—or at least to provide a basis for resolving them—by making a basic division of powers between the national and state governments.

The Constitution grants the federal government both enumerated and implied powers. **Enumerated powers** are grants of authority explicitly given by the Constitution. Among the most important of these is the **national supremacy clause** contained in Article VI. This states that the Constitution "shall be the supreme law of the land; and the judges in every state shall be bound thereby." In other words, federal law takes precedence over all other laws. This allows the federal government to preempt, or override, areas regulated by state law. In recent decades, the federal government has aggressively used this power to extend its authority over states in a wide range of policy issues, so much so that **preemption** has been called "the gorilla that swallows state laws."[4]

Other enumerated powers are laid out in Article I, Section 8. This part of the Constitution details a set of **exclusive powers**—grants of authority that belong solely to the national government. These include the powers to regulate commerce, to declare war, and to raise and maintain an army and navy. Article I, Section 8, also confers a set of **concurrent powers** on the national government. Concurrent powers are those granted to the national government but not denied to the states. Both levels of government are free to exercise these prerogatives. Concurrent powers include the power to tax, borrow, and spend.

....

Enumerated powers Grants of authority explicitly given by the Constitution.

National supremacy clause A constitutional clause that states that federal law takes precedence over all other.

Preemption The process of the federal government's overriding areas regulated by state law.

Exclusive powers Powers given by the Constitution solely to the federal government.

Concurrent powers Powers that both federal and state governments can exercise.

Implied powers Broad, but undefined, powers given to the federal government by the Constitution.

General welfare clause A constitutional clause that gives Congress an implied power through the authority to provide for the "general welfare."

Necessary and proper clause A constitutional clause that gives Congress an implied power through the right to pass all laws considered "necessary and proper" to carry out the federal government's responsibilities as defined by the Constitution.

Full faith and credit clause Constitutional clause that requires states to recognize each other's public records and acts as valid.

Privileges and immunities clause Constitutional clause that prohibits states from discriminating against citizens of other states.

Finally, this same section of the Constitution gives the national government **implied powers**. The basic idea behind implied powers is that the authors of the Constitution realized they could not possibly list every specific power that the national government would require to meet the needs of a developing nation. Accordingly, they gave Congress the flexibility to meet unforeseen challenges by granting the federal government a set of broad and largely undefined powers. These include the **general welfare clause**, which gives the federal government the authority to provide for "the general welfare of the United States," and the **necessary and proper clause**, which authorizes Congress "to make all laws which shall be necessary and proper" to carry out its responsibilities as defined by the Constitution. (See Table 2-2 for explanations of these and other provisions.)

The Constitution says a good deal about the powers of the federal government but very little about the powers of the states. The original, unamended Constitution spent much more time specifying the obligations of the states than it did defining their power and authority. The list of obligations includes Article IV, Section 2, better known as the **full faith and credit clause**. The clause requires all states to grant "full faith and credit" to each other's public acts and records. This means that wills, contracts, and marriages that are valid under one state's laws are valid under all. Under the **privileges and immunities clause**, states are prohibited from discriminating against citizens from other states. The idea here was to protect people traveling across state boundaries or temporarily residing in a state because of business or personal reasons from becoming the targets of discriminatory regulation or taxation.

The Constitution also sets out an often criticized system for electing the nation's president and vice president. The presidency goes not to the candidate who wins the most votes but, rather, to the one who wins the most states. Article II, Section 1, charges the states with appointing electors—one for each of a state's U.S. senators and representatives—who actually choose the president based on the winner of the state's popular vote. (If the Republican candidate gets the most votes in a state, the state's delegation to the Electoral College is made up of Republican Party loyalists who vote for the Republican nominee.) A presidential candidate needs a majority in the Electoral College, which requires the votes of at least 270 of the 538 state electors, to be named the winner.

Other than these responsibilities and explicitly granting the states the right to enter into compacts,

TABLE 2-2 ● The U.S. Constitution's Provisions for Federalism

What It Is	What It Says	What It Means
Article I, Section 8 (commerce clause)	The Congress shall have Power . . . To regulate Commerce with foreign Nations, and among the several States, and with the Indian Tribes.	Gives Congress the right to regulate interstate commerce. This clause has been broadly interpreted to give Congress a number of implied powers.
Article I, Section 8 (necessary and proper clause)	The Congress shall have Power . . . To make all Laws which shall be necessary and proper for carrying into Execution the foregoing Powers, and all other Powers vested by this Constitution in the Government of the United States, or in any Department or Officer thereof.	An implied power giving Congress the right to pass all laws considered "necessary and proper" to carry out the federal government's responsibilities as defined by the Constitution.
Article IV, Section 3 (admission of new states)	New States may be admitted by the Congress into this Union; but no new State shall be formed or erected within the Jurisdiction of any other State; nor any State be formed by the Junction of two or more States, or Parts of States, without the Consent of the Legislatures of the States concerned as well as of the Congress.	Allows the U.S. Congress to admit new states to the union and guarantees each state sovereignty and jurisdiction over its territory.
Article IV, Section 4 (enforcement of republican form of government)	The United States shall guarantee to every State in this Union a Republican Form of Government, and shall protect each of them against Invasion; and on Application of the Legislature, or of the Executive (when the Legislature cannot be convened) against domestic Violence.	Ensures that a democratic government exists in each state and protects states against foreign invasion or insurrection.
Article VI (supremacy clause)	This Constitution, and the Laws of the United States which shall be made in Pursuance thereof; and all Treaties made, or which shall be made, under the Authority of the United States, shall be the supreme Law of the Land; and the Judges in every State shall be bound thereby, any Thing in the Constitution or Laws of any State to the Contrary notwithstanding.	States that federal law takes precedence over all other laws.
Tenth Amendment	The powers not delegated to the United States by the Constitution, nor prohibited by it to the States, are reserved to the States respectively, or to the people.	Guarantees that a broad, but undefined, set of powers be reserved for the states and the people, as opposed to the federal government.
Fourteenth Amendment	All persons born or naturalized in the United States, and subject to the jurisdiction thereof, are citizens of the United States and of the state wherein they reside. No state shall make or enforce any law which shall abridge the privileges or immunities of citizens of the United States; nor shall any state deprive any person of life, liberty, or property, without due process of law; nor deny to any person within its jurisdiction the equal protection of the laws.	Prohibits any state from depriving individuals of the rights and privileges of citizenship, and requires states to provide due process and equal protection guarantees to all citizens.
Sixteenth Amendment	The Congress shall have the power to lay and collect taxes on incomes, from whatever source derived, without apportionment among the several States, and without regard to any census or enumeration.	Enables the federal government to levy a national income tax, which has helped further national policies and programs.
Seventeenth Amendment	The Senate of the United States shall be composed of two Senators from each State, elected by the people thereof, for six years; and each Senator shall have one vote. . . . When vacancies happen in the representation of any State in the Senate, the executive authority of each State shall issue writs of election to fill such vacancies: Provided that the legislature of any State may empower the executive thereof to make temporary appointments until the people fill the vacancies by election as the legislature may direct.	Provides for direct election of U.S. senators, rather than election by each state's legislature.

or binding agreements, with each other on matters of regional concern, the Constitution is virtually silent on the powers of the states. This lopsided attention to the powers of the federal government was a contentious issue in the battle to ratify the Constitution. Opponents of the document, collectively known as Anti-Federalists, feared that states would become little more than puppets of the new central government. Supporters of the Constitution sought to calm these fears by arguing that states would remain sovereign and independent and that the powers not specifically granted to the federal government were reserved for the states. As James Madison put it, in writing the Constitution the Federalists were seeking "a middle ground which may at once support due supremacy of the national authority" and also preserve a strong independent role for the states.[5]

Madison and his fellow Federalists offered to put these assurances in writing. In effect, they promised that if the Constitution was ratified, the first order of business for the new Congress would be to draft a set of amendments that would spell out the limits of central government power and specify the independence of the states. Although Anti-Federalist skepticism remained, the Federalists kept their promise. The First Congress formulated a series of changes that eventually became the first 10 amendments to the Constitution, which are collectively known as the **Bill of Rights**.

Most of these amendments set specific limits on government power. The aim was to guarantee certain individual rights and freedoms, and, at least initially, they were directed at the federal government rather than at state governments. The **Tenth Amendment**, however, finally addressed the power of the states. In full, the Tenth Amendment specifies: "The powers not delegated to the United States by the Constitution, nor prohibited by it to the states, are reserved to the states respectively, or to the people." This provided no enumerated, or specific, powers to the states, but those implied by the language of the amendment are considerable. The so-called reserved powers encompass all the concurrent powers that allow the states to tax, borrow, and

spend; to make laws and enforce them; to regulate trade within their borders; and to practice eminent domain, which is the power to take private property for public use. The reserved powers also have been traditionally understood to mean that states have the primary power to make laws that involve the health, safety, and morals of their citizens. Yet the powers reserved for the states are more implied than explicit, and they all rest in an uneasy tension with the national supremacy clause of Article VI.

After the Tenth Amendment, the **Fourteenth Amendment** is the most important in terms of specifying state powers. Ratified in 1868, the Fourteenth Amendment is one of the so-called Civil War Amendments that came in the immediate wake of the bloody conflict between the North, or the Union, and the South, or the Confederacy. The Fourteenth Amendment prohibits any state from depriving individuals of the rights and privileges of citizenship and requires states to provide due process and equal protection guarantees to all citizens. The Supreme Court has used these guarantees to apply the Bill of Rights to state governments as well as to the federal government and to assert national power over state power in issues ranging from the desegregation of public education to the reapportioning of state legislatures.

The implied powers of the federal government, the limitations set on states by the Fourteenth Amendment, and the undefined "leftovers" given to the states by the Tenth Amendment mean that the scope and authority of both levels of government are, in many cases, dependent on how the Constitution is interpreted. The Constitution, in other words, provides a basic framework for solving the sibling-rivalry squabbles between the states and the federal government. (See Figure 2-2.) It does not, however, provide an unambiguous guide to which level of government has the primary power, responsibility, and authority on a broad range of policy issues. This, as we will see, means that the U.S. Supreme Court is repeatedly thrust into the role of referee in power disputes between national and state governments.

Bill of Rights The first 10 amendments to the U.S. Constitution, which set limits on the power of the federal government and set out the rights of individuals and the states.

Tenth Amendment Constitutional amendment guaranteeing that a broad, but undefined, set of powers be reserved for the states and the people.

Fourteenth Amendment Constitutional amendment that prohibits states from depriving individuals of the rights and privileges of citizenship and requires states to provide due process and equal protection guarantees.

The Development of Federalism

Although clearly establishing a federal political system, the provisions of the U.S. Constitution leave considerable room for disagreement about which level of government—federal or state—has the power to do what.

FIGURE 2-2 ● Powers of National and State Governments

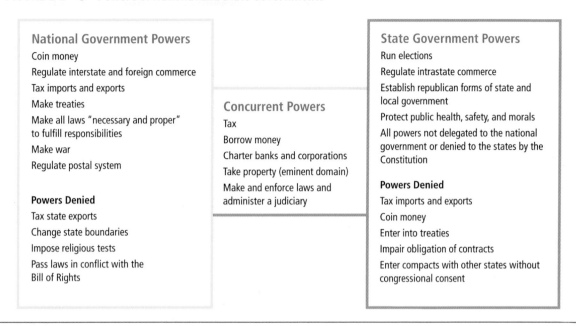

National Government Powers

Coin money

Regulate interstate and foreign commerce

Tax imports and exports

Make treaties

Make all laws "necessary and proper" to fulfill responsibilities

Make war

Regulate postal system

Powers Denied

Tax state exports

Change state boundaries

Impose religious tests

Pass laws in conflict with the Bill of Rights

Concurrent Powers

Tax

Borrow money

Charter banks and corporations

Take property (eminent domain)

Make and enforce laws and administer a judiciary

State Government Powers

Run elections

Regulate intrastate commerce

Establish republican forms of state and local government

Protect public health, safety, and morals

All powers not delegated to the national government or denied to the states by the Constitution

Powers Denied

Tax imports and exports

Coin money

Enter into treaties

Impair obligation of contracts

Enter compacts with other states without congressional consent

Source: Adapted from Samuel Kernell, Gary C. Jacobson, and Thad Kousser, *The Logic of American Politics*, 6th ed. (Washington, DC: CQ Press, 2013), Figure 3-2.

Disagreements about the scope and authority of the national government arose almost immediately when the First Congress convened in 1789. The issue of a national bank was one of the most controversial of these early conflicts and the one with the most lasting implications. Alexander Hamilton, secretary of the treasury under President George Washington, believed a central bank was critical to stabilizing the national economy, but there was nothing in the Constitution that specifically granted the federal government the authority to create and regulate such an institution.

Lacking a clear enumerated power, Hamilton justified his proposal for a national bank by using an implied power. He argued that the necessary and proper clause implied the federal government's power to create a national bank because the bank would help the government manage its finances as it went about its expressly conferred authority to tax and spend. Essentially, Hamilton was interpreting *necessary* as "convenient" or "appropriate." Secretary of State Thomas Jefferson objected, arguing that if the Constitution was going to establish a government of truly limited powers, the federal government needed to

stick to its enumerated powers and interpret its implied powers very narrowly. He thus argued that the *necessary* in the necessary and proper clause should properly be interpreted as "essential" or "indispensable." Hamilton eventually won the argument, and Congress approved the national bank. Still, the issue simmered as a controversial—and potentially unconstitutional—expansion of the national government's powers.

The issue was not fully resolved until 1819, when the Supreme Court decided the case of *McCulloch v. Maryland*. This case stemmed from the state of Maryland's attempts to shut down the national bank, which was taking business from state-chartered banks, by taxing its operations. The chief cashier of the national bank's Baltimore branch refused to pay the tax, and the parties went to court. The Supreme Court, in essence, backed Hamilton's interpretation of the Constitution over Jefferson's. This was important above and beyond the issue of a national bank. It suggested that the Constitution gave the national government a broad set of powers relative to the states. Key to this early affirmation of the federal government's power was

U.S. Chief Justice John Marshall, whose backing of a broad interpretation of implied powers laid the foundation for later expansions in the scope and authority of the federal government.

The full impact of *McCulloch v. Maryland*, however, would not be felt for some time. For the most part, the federal government began to feel its way into the gray areas of its constitutional powers pretty cautiously. Federalism went on to develop in four distinct stages— dual federalism, cooperative federalism, centralized federalism, and New Federalism—and the first of these stages leaned toward the more limited role of the federal government favored by Jefferson.

Dual Federalism (1789–1933)

Dual federalism is the idea that state and federal governments have separate jurisdictions and responsibilities. Within these separate spheres of authority, each level of government is sovereign and free to operate without interference from the other. Dual federalism represents something of a middle ground in the initial interpretations of how the Constitution divided power. On one side of the debate were Federalists such as Hamilton, who championed a nation-centered view of federalism. They wanted to interpret the Constitution as broadly as possible to give the national government supremacy over the states. On the other side were fierce **states' rights** advocates such as John Calhoun of South Carolina, who served as vice president in the administrations of John Quincy Adams and Andrew Jackson. Supporters of states' rights wanted the federal government's power limited to the greatest possible extent and

saw any expansion of that power as an encroachment on the sovereignty of the states.

In the 1820s and 1830s, Calhoun formulated what became known as the **compact theory** of federalism. The idea was that the Constitution represented an agreement among sovereign states to form a common government. It interpreted the Constitution as essentially an extension of the Articles of Confederation, a perspective that viewed the U.S. political system as more confederal than federal. The compact theory argued that if sovereignty ultimately rested with the states, then the states rather than the Supreme Court had the final say in how the Constitution should be interpreted. The states also had the right to reject federal laws and make them invalid within their own borders. This process was known as **nullification**, and the compact theory took it to an extreme. Calhoun argued that states could reject the entire Constitution and choose to withdraw, or secede, from the Union. In the 1820s, national policies— especially a trade tariff—triggered an economic downturn in the southern states, which created wide support for nullification and **secession** arguments. These extreme states' rights views were not completely resolved until the Union victory in the Civil War ended them for good.

Dual federalism walked the line of moderation between the extremes of **nation-centered federalism** and **state-centered federalism**. Basically, dual federalism looks at the U.S. political system as a layered cake. The state and federal governments represent distinct and separate layers of this cake. To keep them separate, advocates of dual federalism sought to limit the federal government to exercising only a narrow interpretation of its enumerated powers. If the Constitution was to be interpreted broadly, that interpretation should favor the states rather than Congress. This became the central operating philosophy of the U.S. Supreme Court for much of the 19th century and is most closely associated with the tenure of Chief Justice Roger B. Taney, who served from 1836 to 1864. Compared with his immediate predecessor, John Marshall, Taney was much less sympathetic to arguments that interpreted the federal government's powers broadly.

Dual federalism The idea that state and federal governments have separate and distinct jurisdictions and responsibilities.

States' rights The belief that states should be free to make their own decisions with little interference from the federal government.

Compact theory The idea that the Constitution represents an agreement among sovereign states to form a common government.

Nullification The process of a state's rejecting a federal law and making it invalid within state borders.

Secession The process of a government's or political jurisdiction's withdrawal from a political system or alliance.

Nation-centered federalism The belief that the nation is the basis of the federal system and that the federal government should take precedence over state governments.

State-centered federalism The belief that states are the basis of the federal system and that state governments should take precedence over the federal government.

Even at the height of the dual federalism era, state and federal governments were collaborating as much as they were fighting.

The dual federalism doctrine gave rise to some infamous Supreme Court decisions on the powers and limitations of the federal government. Perhaps the best known is *Scott v. Sandford* (1857). This case dealt with Dred Scott, a slave taken by his master from Missouri, a slave state, to Illinois, a free state, and on into what was then called the Wisconsin Territory, where slavery had been outlawed by the Missouri Compromise of 1820. This federal law stipulated which new states and territories could and could not make slavery legal. After his master's death, Scott sued for his freedom, arguing that his residence in a free territory had legally ended his bondage. Scott's case was tied to the Missouri Compromise, which the Supreme Court subsequently ruled unconstitutional. The justices' justification was that Congress did not have the enumerated, or the implied, power to prohibit slavery in the territories. Thus, Scott remained a slave, although his owners voluntarily gave him his freedom shortly after the Supreme Court decision. He died of tuberculosis in 1858, having spent only 1 of his nearly 60 years as a free man.

Cooperative Federalism (1933–1964)

In theory, dual federalism defines and maintains a clear division between state and national governments and sets a clear standard for doing so. If the federal government has the enumerated power to take a disputed action or make a disputed law, it has supremacy over the states in the particular case; if it does not have the enumerated power, then the Tenth Amendment reserves that power for the states, and state preferences take precedence.

The problem was that dual federalism's clarity in theory rarely matched the complex realities of governance in practice. State and national governments share interests in a wide range of issues, from education to transportation. To divide these interests cleanly into separate spheres of influence was not only difficult; in many cases, it was impractical and not desirable. Even at the height of the dual federalism era, state and

federal governments were collaborating as much as they were fighting. The federal government, for example, owned vast tracts of land in the Midwest and West, and it made extensive grants of these lands to the states to help develop transportation and education systems. Many of the nation's best-known state universities got their start this way, as land-grant colleges.

In the 19th century, the federal government also gave out cash grants to support Civil War veterans housed in state institutions, gave money to the states to support agricultural research, and lent federal manpower—primarily U.S. Army engineers—to help state and local development projects.[6] Rather than a layered cake, some experts believe a more appropriate metaphor for federalism is a marble cake, with the different levels of government so thoroughly mixed with one another that they are impossible to separate. (See Figure 2-3.)

Certainly as the nation became increasingly industrialized and more urban, state and federal interests became increasingly intertwined. As the 19th century

FIGURE 2-3 ● The Varieties of Federalism

Dual or "Layer Cake" Federalism

Cooperative or "Marble Cake" Federalism

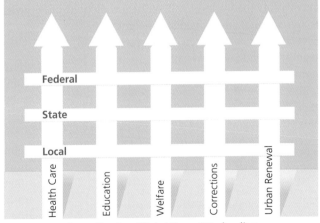
Centralized or "Picket Fence" Federalism

The Sixteenth Amendment gave the federal government the power to levy an income tax. Some of the money collected by the federal government in income taxes is returned to the states in the form of grants to support a wide range of domestic policies and programs.

During World War II (1939–1945), that power was centralized even further. The need to fight global conflicts pushed the federal government to assert its authority on a wide range of economic and social issues. Even more important to the long-term relationship between state and national governments was the Great Depression of the 1930s, a social and economic catastrophe that swept aside any remaining vestiges of dual federalism.

The central catalyst for a fundamental change in the nature of state–federal relations was the election of Franklin Delano Roosevelt to the presidency in 1932. In an effort to combat economic and social malaise, Roosevelt aggressively pushed the federal government into taking a lead role in areas traditionally left to the states, and in the 1930s, the federal government became deeply involved in regulating the labor market, creating and managing welfare programs, and providing significant amounts of direct aid to cities. The general approach of Roosevelt's so-called New Deal agenda defined the central characteristics of **cooperative federalism**— using the federal government to identify a problem, set up the basic outline of a program to address the problem, and make money available to fund that program and then turning over much of the responsibility for implementing and running the program to the states and localities. This arrangement dominated state and federal relations for the next three decades.

Centralized Federalism (1964–1980)

Having all levels of government addressing problems simultaneously and cooperatively paid dividends. It combined the need to attack national problems with the flexibility of the decentralized federal system. Cooperative federalism, however, also signaled a significant shift in power away from the states and toward the federal government. The key to this power shift was money, specifically federal **grants-in-aid**, which are cash appropriations given by the federal government to the states. An ever-increasing proportion of state and local budgets came from federal coffers. At the beginning of the 19th century, federal grants constituted less

drew to a close and the 20th century began, the federal government undertook a significant expansion of its policy responsibilities. In 1887, it began to regulate the railroads, a policy area with enormous significance for the economic development of states and localities. In economic and social terms, this was roughly equivalent to the federal government of today announcing its comprehensive regulation of the Internet and software manufacturers. By fits and starts, dual federalism gradually fell out of favor with the Supreme Court. The Court instead began to interpret the powers of the federal government very broadly and to allow the jurisdictions of state and national governments to merge gradually.

Several events accelerated this trend. In 1913, the Sixteenth Amendment was ratified, giving the federal government the ability to levy a nationwide income tax. The new taxing and spending authority helped further national policies designed during the next decades.[7] World War I (1914–1918) resulted in a significant centralization of power in the federal government.

....

Cooperative federalism The notion that it is impossible for state and national governments to have separate and distinct jurisdictions and that both levels of government must work together.

Grants-in-aid Cash appropriations given by the federal government to the states.

FIGURE 2-4 ● Key Dates in the History of American Federalism

Left column	Year		Year	Right column
Revolutionary War starts	1775		1776	Declaration of Independence adopted
Articles of Confederation ratified	1781		1783	Revolutionary War ends
Annapolis Convention	1786		1786	Shays's Rebellion
Constitutional Convention drafts new constitution	1787		1788	U.S. Constitution ratified
First Congress adopts Bill of Rights	1791			
McCulloch v. Maryland establishes that the federal government has a broad set of powers over the states	1819			
Roger Taney sworn in as chief justice; adopts dual federalism as model for federal–state relations	1836		1832	South Carolina attempts to nullify federal law
			1857	*Scott v. Sandford* demonstrates the limits of the federal government
Southern states experiment with confederacy as Civil War starts	1861		1860	South Carolina secedes from the Union in December; hostilities between North and South begin a month later
			1865	Civil War ends with Union victory; Thirteenth Amendment abolishes slavery
Fourteenth Amendment passes	1868			
			1887	Federal government regulates the railroads
Sixteenth Amendment passes	1913			
Great Depression begins	1930			
			1933	Franklin Delano Roosevelt takes office; era of cooperative federalism begins
Era of centralized federalism begins	1964			
			1972	Richard Nixon begins revenue sharing
Ronald Reagan is elected; New Federalism emerges	1980			
Supreme Court decides *Bush v. Gore;* George W. Bush receives Florida's contested electoral votes and becomes president	2000		1986	William Rehnquist becomes chief justice; Supreme Court begins to look more favorably on states' rights arguments
			2008	Great Recession
			2012	*National Federation of Independent Business v. Sebelius* expands federal government power by upholding the government's right to mandate that individuals purchase health care coverage; the Court upholds state sovereignty in the case by ruling that the federal government cannot force states to expand Medicaid.
			2013	Supreme Court decides *Shelby v. Holder;* states with histories of disenfranchising minority voters no longer have to get voting laws and regulations approved by federal government

than 1 percent of state and local government revenues. By the middle of the 1930s, federal grants accounted for close to 20 percent of state and local revenues.[8]

For the next 30 years, the federal government continued to rely on grants to administer programs, including the 1950s construction of the federal highway system that Americans drive on today. The 1960s marked a shift, however. **Centralized federalism**, ushered in with Lyndon Baines Johnson's presidency, further increased the federal government's involvement in policy areas previously left to state and local governments. It is commonly associated with Johnson's Great Society program, which used state and local governments to help implement such national initiatives as the Civil Rights Act and the War on Poverty. This is sometimes called "picket-fence federalism" because in practice the relationships among local, state, and national governments were centered on particular programs and the agencies that managed them. These policy-specific agencies (bureaucracies dealing with education, transportation, welfare, and the like) were laid across the levels of government like pickets on a three-rail fence.

Those initiatives meant more money—and more regulations—for states and localities. The federal government began aggressively attaching strings to this money through **categorical grants**. Federal–state relations evolved into a rough embodiment of the Golden Rule of politics—he who has the gold gets to make the rules.

Richard Nixon's presidential administration took a slightly different tack. It cut some strings but continued to increase the number of grants doled out by the federal government.[9] In the late 1960s, the administration pioneered the idea of **general revenue sharing grants**, federal funds turned over to the states and localities with essentially no strings attached. Although popular with states and localities—from their perspective it was "free" money—this type of grant-in-aid had a short life span; it was killed by the Ronald Reagan administration in the early 1980s.

Federal grants, strings or no strings, do not sound so bad on the surface. Money is money, and a government can never have too much. The problem was that the grants were not distributed equitably to states and localities, and a central feature of cooperative federalism was the often fierce competition to control and access these revenues. The politics became complex. One form of conflict arose between the states and the federal government over what types of grants should be used for particular policies or programs. States and localities favored federal grants with fewer strings. Congress and the president often favored putting tight guidelines on federal money because this allowed them to take a greater share of the credit for the benefits of federal spending.

Perhaps the most important dimension of the politics of grants-in-aid, however, was the federal government's increasing desire to use its purse strings to pressure states and localities into adopting particular policies and laws. Beginning in the 1960s and 1970s, cooperative federalism began a new, more coercive era with the rise of ever more stringent grant conditions. These included **crosscutting requirements**, or strings that applied to all federal grants. For example, one requirement a state or locality must meet to receive virtually any federal government grant is an assessment of the environmental impact of the proposed program or policy. Accordingly, most state and local governments began writing—and defending—environmental impact statements for any construction project that involved federal funds.

The federal government also began applying **crossover sanctions**. Crossover sanctions are strings that require grant recipients to pass and enforce certain laws or policies as a condition of receiving funds. One example is the drinking age. As a condition of receiving federal highway funds, the federal government requires states to set 21 as the minimum legal age for drinking alcohol.

Increasingly, the strings came even if there were no grants. State and local governments were issued direct orders, essentially were commanded, to adopt certain laws or rules, such as clean-water standards and minimum-wage laws.[10] These **unfunded mandates** became a particular irritant to state and local governments. Even when there was broad agreement on the substance of a mandate, subnational governments

---

Centralized federalism The notion that the federal government should take the leading role in setting national policy, with state and local governments helping implement the policies.

Categorical grants Federal grants-in-aid given for specific programs that leave states and localities with little discretion over how to spend the money.

General revenue sharing grants Federal grants-in-aid given with few constraints, leaving states and localities almost complete discretion over how to spend the money.

Crosscutting requirements Constraints that apply to all federal grants.

Crossover sanctions Federal requirements mandating that grant recipients pass and enforce certain laws or regulations as a condition of receiving funds.

Unfunded mandates Federal laws that direct state action but provide no financial support for that action.

resented the federal government's taking all the credit while leaving the dirty work of finding funds and actually running the programs to the states and localities.

Congress eventually passed a law banning unfunded mandates in the mid-1990s, but it is full of loopholes. For example, the law does not apply to appropriations bills—the laws that actually authorize the government to spend money. The National Conference of State Legislatures has estimated that in the period from 2004 to 2008, the federal government shifted $131 billion in costs to the states in unfunded mandates.[11] Congress, in other words, continues to pass laws that subnational governments must obey, and Congress also passes on the costs of implementing these laws to the states.

New Federalism (1980–2002)

Centralized federalism's shift of power toward the national government always faced opposition from states' rights advocates, who viewed the growing influence of the national government with alarm. By the end of the 1970s, centralized federalism also was starting to face a practical crisis—the federal government's revenues could not keep up with the demand for grants. With the election of Ronald Reagan in 1980, the

practical and ideological combined to create pressure for a fundamental shift in state and federal relations.

Reagan was not the first president to raise concerns about the centralization of power in the national government. A primary reason for Nixon's support of general revenue sharing, for example, was the attraction of giving states more flexibility by cutting the strings attached to federal grants. It was not until Reagan, however, that a sustained attempt was made to reverse the course of centralized federalism. Reagan believed the federal government had overreached its boundaries, and he wanted to return power and flexibility to the states. At the core of his vision of state-centered **New Federalism** was the desire to reduce federal grants-in-aid. In return, states would be given more policymaking leeway with the money they did get through **block grants**.

Reagan's drive to make this vision a reality had mixed success. The massive budget deficits of the 1980s made cutting grants-in-aid a practical necessity. We can see this in Figure 2-5, which shows federal government

New Federalism The belief that states should receive more power and authority and less money from the federal government.

Block grants Federal grants-in-aid given for general policy areas that leave states and localities with wide discretion over how to spend the money within the designated policy area.

FIGURE 2-5   ●   Federal Grants to States, 1940–2022 (in billions of constant 2009 dollars)

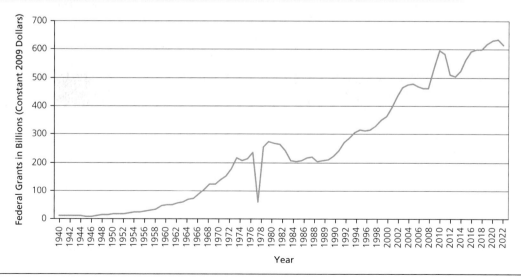

Source: U.S. Office of Management and Budget, *Budget of the United States*, Historical Tables, Table 12.1, "Summary Comparison of Total Outlays for Grants to State and Local Governments: 1940–2012 (in Current Dollars, as Percentages of Total Outlays, as Percentages of GDP, and in Constant [FY 2009] Dollars)," https://www.whitehouse.gov/sites/whitehouse.gov/files/omb/budget/fy2018/hist12z1.xls.

grants to state and local governments in billions of constant dollars from 1940 through 2014. There was a clear upward trend beginning in the 1960s that peaked in about 1978. After that, federal grants to states stayed relatively constant for about a decade—while the federal government was not really drastically cutting grants in the 1980s, in real terms it did not increase them either. At least for a while, the federal government managed to rein in the grant dollars flowing to states and localities. Reducing the federal government's influence over states and localities turned out to be another matter.

Reagan, like many conservatives, was a modern heir to a states' rights perspective that dated back to the Anti-Federalist movement. This means he believed that government should be as close to the voters as possible—in the city hall or the state capitol—rather than far away in Washington, D.C. Yet believing that government should be closer to the people in the abstract is far different from putting that belief into practice. Taking power from the federal government did advance a core philosophical belief of the Reagan administration, but it also created problems for Reagan supporters, who were not shy about voicing their displeasure.

Such core conservative constituencies as business and industry quickly realized that dealing with a single government was much less of a headache than dealing with 50 governments. They almost immediately began to put counter pressure on the movement toward expanded state policymaking authority. The result was something of a push and pull, with the Reagan administration trying to shove power onto the states with one set of legislative priorities and yank it back to the federal government with another. Ultimately, Reagan did succeed in cutting grants-in-aid. He consolidated 57 categorical grants into 9 new block grants. General revenue sharing and another 60 categorical grants were eliminated entirely. This reduced the amount of money sent to the states while increasing the states' ability to act independently.[12] Yet Reagan also engaged in a number of fairly aggressive preemption movements and backed a number of unfunded mandates. This reduced the independence of states and forced them to fund programs they did not necessarily support.

The seeds of New Federalism had a hard time taking root at the national level, but the roots sank fast and sank deep at the state and local levels. States were caught between the proverbial rock of a cash-strapped federal government and the hard place of the demand for the programs traditionally supported by federal

funds. They slowly and often painfully worked themselves out of this dilemma by becoming less reliant on the federal government. States began aggressively pursuing innovative policy approaches to a wide range of social and economic problems. By the 1990s, as one author puts it, there was "a developing agreement among state and national political elites that states should have greater authority and flexibility in operating public programs."[13]

The effort to take power away from the federal government and give it to the states was broadly supported by public opinion, as polls consistently showed that Americans placed more trust in state and local governments than they did in the federal government.[14] In the 1990s, the Bill Clinton administration championed the idea of devolution, an extension of New Federalism that sought a systematic transition of power from the federal to the state level in certain policy areas.

Probably the best-known example of devolution is the Personal Responsibility and Work Opportunity Reconciliation Act of 1996, popularly known as the law that "ended welfare as we know it." The law, which Clinton signed under Republican pressure during the 1996 presidential campaign after vetoing it twice, ended Aid to Families with Dependent Children and replaced it with a block grant. In essence, the law embodied the deal between state and federal governments that embodied devolution—the federal government would provide less money, and the states would get more policymaking authority.

Like its parent, New Federalism, the devolution revolution faced strong resistance, often from an old enemy. Conservatives, at least rhetorically, still were the strongest states' rights advocates. Yet when states' rights conflicted with key portions of the conservative political agenda, conservative groups fought tenaciously for federal supremacy over the states, just as they had during the 1980s. An example of this contradictory behavior is the 1996 Defense of Marriage Act. This federal law was proposed in the wake of movements in Hawaii and Vermont to legalize same-sex civil unions. Now, remember, the full faith and credit clause means that a contract made under the laws of one state is legally recognized and binding in all states. So if one state made same-sex unions legal, it raised the possibility that the other 49 would have to recognize such civil unions as the legal equivalent of marriages. There was a strong push from many traditional states' rights advocates for the federal government to, in essence, grant states exceptions from their full faith and credit obligations. The Defense of Marriage Act did this. It also put the federal government into the business of defining what constitutes a marriage, an area traditionally left to the states.[15]

Ad Hoc Federalism (2002–Present)

For a variety of reasons, the commitment to New Federalism, at least at the federal level, more or less dissolved entirely by the end of the administration of President George W. Bush. Bush came to the White House from the Texas governor's mansion and, at least initially, was a champion of pushing power away from Washington, D.C. Circumstances and policy priorities, however, led Bush to advocate for greater federal authority in a number of policy areas. For example, Bush's signature domestic policy was the No Child Left Behind Act, which asserted federal control over important aspects of public education, a policy area traditionally under the jurisdiction of state and local governments. Peter Harkness, editor of *Governing* magazine, summed up the Bush administration's record on federalism thus: "The administration has mandated more, preempted more and run roughshod over state initiatives that didn't conform to its own ideology."[16]

This did not mean that federal–state relations in the Bush era shifted from a commitment to devolution to a commitment to centralizing power in Washington, D.C. What it meant was that a principled guiding philosophy of state–federal relations—such as dual federalism, cooperative federalism, or New Federalism—was abandoned. Instead a new, more partisan or ideologically based approach to state–federal relations came to the fore, an approach described as **ad hoc federalism**.[17] Ad hoc federalism is the process of choosing a state-centered or nation-centered view of federalism on the basis of political or partisan convenience. In other words, the issue at hand, not a core philosophical commitment to a particular vision of federalism, determines a policymaker's commitment to state or federal supremacy.

The rise of ad hoc federalism, which continues to this day, is explained at least in part by the nationalization of party politics. Historically, national political parties were little more than confederations of state party organizations that were strongly focused on their own issues and priorities. The result of that sort of decentralized party structure was that Democrats in Texas might have more in common with Republicans in New

York than Democrats in California. These days, that's hard to imagine. In the past couple of decades, party polarization has gone national, with Republicans and Democrats at all levels of government aligning themselves with consistent and opposing ideological agendas. As a number of scholars have noted, one result is that it is now not uncommon for members of Congress to vote the interests of their party over the interests of their constituents, and for candidates competing for state and local offices to run on issues aligned with national party positions.[18] A big implication of this political environment is that who favors federal or state supremacy on any given issue depends on its partisan implications. And even that support can be temporary. When Barack Obama was president, conservative Republican governors resisted a range of federal policy initiatives in areas like health care, immigration, and the environment, arguing federal overreach was unconstitutionally limiting the prerogatives of states. More liberal Democratic governors tended to cheer on and support these same initiatives. After Donald Trump was elected in 2016 and Republicans took control of the federal government, however, those positions flipped. Now it was Republican state lawmakers cheering on the federal initiatives while Democrats pushed back, filing lawsuits and arguing the federal government should not limit state discretion on everything from marijuana legalization to LGBT rights to establishing sanctuary cities.[19]

This new, more confrontational face of ad hoc federalism has raised real questions about the future of state–federal relations and the ability of different levels of government to work cooperatively with each other (see the box "States under Stress: Two-Speed Federalism"). What we are currently witnessing is ad hoc federalism with a vengeance. State as well as national leaders are increasingly varying their views of the appropriate role of state and federal governments according to ideological or partisan preferences on a policy-by-policy basis.

MICHIGAN was the first state to plow its roads and to use the yellow dividing line on its highways.

....

Ad hoc federalism The process of choosing a state-centered or nation-centered view of federalism on the basis of political or partisan convenience.

The Supreme Court: The Umpire of Federalism

Article VI of the Constitution contains the national supremacy clause, which declares that the Constitution, laws passed by Congress, and national treaties are the "supreme law of the land." This does not mean that the states are always subordinate to the national government. Don't forget—the Tenth Amendment also counts as part of that supreme law. However, it does mean that federal courts often have to referee national–state conflicts. Because it has the final say in interpreting the Constitution, the Supreme Court is, in effect, the umpire of federalism. Its rulings ultimately decide the powers and limitations of the different levels of government.

The Rise of Nation-Centered Federalism on the Court

Throughout U.S. history, the Supreme Court has cycled through trends of state-centered and nation-centered philosophies of federalism. As we have already seen, the early Supreme Court under Chief Justice John Marshall pursued a fairly broad interpretation of the federal government's powers in such cases as *McCulloch v. Maryland*. Marshall's successor, Roger Taney, took the Court in a more state-centered direction by establishing dual federalism as the Court's central operating philosophy. The shift from dual federalism to cooperative federalism required a return to a more nation-centered judicial philosophy. Although the Court initially took a more nation-centered direction in its rulings following the Civil War, it was not until the Great Depression and Roosevelt's New Deal that a decisive tilt in the Court's rulings cleared the way for the rise of cooperative federalism and the centralization of power in the national government.

The shift toward a liberal interpretation of the federal government's powers dominated the Supreme Court's operating philosophy for much of the next 60 years and is exemplified by its decision in *United States v. Darby Lumber Co.* (1941). The substantive issue at stake in this case was whether the federal government had the power to regulate wages. The Supreme Court said yes, but the decision is of more lasting interest because of the majority opinion's dismissive comment on the

Tenth Amendment. Once considered the constitutional lockbox of state power, the amendment, according to the Court's ruling, now did little more than state "a truism that all is retained which has not been surrendered." In other words, the Tenth Amendment was simply a basket for the "leftover" powers the federal government had not sought or did not want.

During and after the New Deal era, the Supreme Court also accelerated a trend of broadly interpreting Congress's powers to regulate interstate commerce. It did this through its interpretation of the **interstate commerce clause**. In *Wickard v. Filburn* (1942), the Court ruled that the clause gave Congress the power to regulate what a farmer could feed his chickens. The case involved an Ohio farmer, Roscoe Filburn, who was growing more wheat than allowed under federal production limits. He wasn't selling the excess wheat; he was feeding it to his chickens. The Court reasoned that this reduced the amount of chicken feed Filburn needed to buy on the open market, and because that market was an interstate market, which meant interstate commerce, Congress could regulate what Filburn was doing. In *Heart of Atlanta Motel v. United States* (1964) and *Katzenbach v. McClung* (1964), the justices ruled that this clause gave Congress the power to regulate private acts of racial discrimination. These cases involved the owners of a motel and a restaurant, respectively, who wanted to refuse service to blacks. The Court ruled that these businesses served interstate travelers, and that was interstate commerce, so Congress had the power to force them to obey federal antidiscrimination laws.

A series of such decisions over the course of more than 50 years led some judicial scholars to conclude that the Supreme Court had essentially turned the concept of enumerated and reserved powers on its head. In effect, the assumption now seemed to be that the federal government had the power to do anything the Constitution did not specifically prohibit.[20] The states and localities were drawn ever closer into roles as subordinate satellites in orbit around the federal government. This situation continued until just before the end of the 20th century. At that point, the Court once again began siding with the states over the federal government.

A Tenth Amendment Renaissance or Ad Hoc Federalism?

By the mid-1990s, the Supreme Court was dominated by justices appointed by New Federalists. Reagan,

---

Interstate commerce clause Constitutional clause that gives Congress the right to regulate interstate commerce. This clause has been broadly interpreted to give Congress a number of implied powers.

STATES UNDER STRESS
TWO-SPEED FEDERALISM

At first glance, the policy topics of immigration, LGBT rights, health care, homeland security, education, and abortion seem to have little in common. Substantively, that is true enough. Structurally, though, they all share something important: Congress and/or the Supreme Court has taken actions intended to guarantee equal and uniform application of laws and policy regulation nationwide. Yet that uniformity is breaking down, as there are now large policy differences among the states in all these areas.

Widening differences in politics and policy priorities, many of them rooted in differences in political culture, are contributing to increasing policy—and ideological—polarization among the states. These differences are readily apparent in the public policies originating in the states, whether they be legalization of marijuana use, "stand your ground" gun laws, or climate change policies. The yawning ideological gulfs between states are also affecting the implementation of federal programs.

Recent elections brought a good deal of polarization to state governments. In 2018, state government was controlled by a single party in roughly two-thirds of the states: Half the states had a Republican governor and Republican legislative majorities, and seven states had a Democratic governor and Democratic legislative majorities. One-party dominance at the state level emphasized and, in many cases, exacerbated the growing ideological distance between the two parties that also underlies partisan conflict in Congress. Republican Donald Trump became president after losing the popular vote and, at least through the early part of his administration, suffered historically low approval ratings. That provided Democratic lawmakers with plenty of incentive to mount serious challenges to federal mandates and policy prescriptions.

At a minimum, growing ideological differences across states clearly help to explain the widely varying levels of participation by states in major federal policy programs. For example, the Affordable Care Act intended for states to expand Medicaid (a health care program for the poor) and to set up their own online health insurance exchanges. Roughly a dozen states have refused to do either. State participation in federal programs is increasingly reflective of the ideological and partisan composition of state government. What can the federal government do when state governments flat-out refuse to work with it, even to the extent of turning down big federal monetary incentives to participate? The answer seems to be, work with the states you have rather than the states you want. Out of necessity, national officials have taken ad hoc federalism to a new extreme by adopting flexible strategies that largely enable states to participate in new federal initiatives as much or as little as their politics permit. These initiatives include the following:

- *Partial preemptions* These establish a floor but not a ceiling for new regulations, allowing some states to go beyond a federally required level of regulation. California, for example, has long taken advantage of this with the Clean Air Act, which allows states to impose stricter limits on automobile emissions than what is federally mandated.

- *Waivers* These tools have been used for several decades, first in welfare reform and later in Medicaid. States have been able to tailor federal entitlement and grant programs to achieve cost savings, shifts in service-delivery approaches, and other innovations.

- *Opt-outs* These have allowed conservative states to avoid participating in some federal programs altogether. In the case of regulatory opt-outs, the federal government typically stands by to enforce federal rules in nonparticipating states, thereby ensuring some level of national uniformity. This has been most notable with the Affordable Care Act, which allows states to opt out of operating their own insurance exchanges. When states opt out of grants, however, there is typically no federal fallback.

Where is all this leading? No one is quite sure. People increasingly talk of a two-speed European Union, where, for example, some member states adopt the euro while others do not. It seems as though something similar is happening in the political system of the United States; a sort of "two-speed federalism" is emerging where states opt in or out of federal policy initiatives based on their ideological and partisan leanings. Whether this is good or bad remains to be seen. On one hand, states could emerge as newly empowered actors in charge of federal programs. On the other, the polarization that gave rise to wide variations among the states could become institutionalized, further segmenting the nation into radically different policy worlds.

Two-speed federalism could also be temporary. If the goals of national programs become more deeply rooted, this may prompt a push for stronger forms of nationalization of policy programs. In other words, if state governments will not implement policy programs that state citizens decide they want, they might ask the federal government not to take away state options to opt out.

Source: Adapted from Paul Posner and Timothy Conlan, "The Future of Federalism in a Polarized Country," *Governing*, February 2014.

who had campaigned on his intention to nominate federal judges who shared his conservative philosophy, appointed four. He also elevated a fifth, William Rehnquist—originally appointed as an associate justice by Nixon—to the position of chief justice. Reagan's vice president and presidential successor, George H. W. Bush, appointed two more justices. The end result was a mid-1990s Supreme Court chosen largely by conservative Republican presidents who wanted limits set on the federal government's powers and responsibilities. The justices obliged.

In a series of narrow (mostly 5–4) decisions in the 1990s, the Court began to back away from the nation-centered interpretation of the Constitution that had dominated its rulings during the era of cooperative federalism (see Table 2-3). *United States v. Lopez* (1995) was a significant victory for states' rights and a clear break from a half-century of precedent. This case involved the Gun-Free School Zones Act of 1990, which made it a federal crime to possess a firearm within 1,000 feet of a school. Following a good deal of precedent, Congress justified its authority to regulate local law enforcement by using a very liberal interpretation of the interstate commerce clause, the basic argument being that the operation of public schools affected interstate commerce, so the federal government had the constitutional authority to ban guns near schools. The Supreme Court disagreed and argued that the commerce clause granted no such authority.

The justices used similar reasoning in *United States v. Morrison* (2000) to strike down the Violence Against Women Act. Congress had passed this law in 1994 out of concern that the states, although having primary responsibility for criminal law, were not adequately dealing with the problem of violence against women. The key provision of the act gave assault victims the right to sue their assailants in federal court. Congress argued that it was authorized to pass such a law because fear of violence prevented women from using public transportation or going out unescorted at night. Such fears, the reasoning went, placed limits on economic opportunities for women. This argument made the connection to commerce and Congress's constitutional authority, but the Supreme Court rejected this broad interpretation of the commerce clause.

At the same time it was narrowly interpreting the Constitution to limit federal power, the Supreme Court after 1990 began to interpret the Constitution broadly to expand state power. Notably, the Court made a series of rulings that broadly interpreted the Eleventh Amendment's guarantee of **sovereign immunity** to the states. Sovereign immunity is essentially "the right of a government to be free from suits brought without its consent."[21] In cases such as *Seminole Tribe of Florida v. Florida* (1996) and *Alden v. Maine* (1999), the Supreme Court adopted an interpretation of the Eleventh Amendment that limited the right of citizens to sue states for violations of federal law. These rulings not only lessened the power of the federal government over the states but also arguably gave the states more power over their own citizens.

Although these and other rulings resurrected the Tenth Amendment and underlined the independent power of the states, there has been an element of inconsistency to Supreme Court decisions since 1990. In *Bush v. Gore* (2000), the Court abandoned its commitment to states' rights by overruling the Florida Supreme Court and ordering a halt to the contested recount of presidential ballots. Democratic presidential nominee Al Gore indisputably won the popular vote in 2000, but the outcome of the presidential election was decided by Florida's electoral votes. Gore and Bush ran neck and neck in this state, the decision so close that a series of controversial and hotly contested recounts were undertaken with the approval of the Florida courts. In effect, the U.S. Supreme Court overturned the state court's interpretation of state law—which allowed the recounts—and decided the presidency in favor of George W. Bush. Another decision that favored federal power over state power came in *Lorillard Tobacco Co. v. Reilly* (2001). Here, the Court overturned a Massachusetts law that regulated the advertising of tobacco products. The Court argued that federal law—specifically, the Federal Cigarette Labeling and Advertising Act—legitimately preempts state law on this issue.

The Court also trumped 10 states that had legalized the use of marijuana for medical purposes. In *Gonzales v. Raich* (2005), the Court, led by its more liberal justices, ruled that federal law enforcement officers, prosecutors, and judges can prosecute and punish anyone possessing marijuana. This ruling is interesting because, while it upheld federal laws, it did not overturn state laws and left state and local officials free not to participate in any federal efforts to seize medical marijuana.[22]

Sovereign immunity The right of a government not to be sued without its consent.

TABLE 2-3 ● Key U.S. Supreme Court Rulings Regarding Federalism, 1995–2018

Case	Decision
United States v. Lopez (1995)	Court strikes down a federal law prohibiting possession of firearms near public schools. First time since World War II that Court placed limits on Congress's powers under the interstate commerce clause.
Seminole Tribe of Florida v. Florida (1996)	Court rules Congress cannot allow citizens to sue states in a federal court except for civil rights violations. State claim upheld.
Printz v. United States (1997)	Court strikes down a federal law requiring mandatory background checks for firearms purchases. State claim upheld.
Alden v. Maine (1999)	Court rules that Congress does not have the power to authorize citizens to sue in state court on the basis of federal claims. State claim upheld.
United States v. Morrison (2000)	Court strikes down the federal Violence Against Women Act. State claim upheld.
Reno v. Condon (2000)	Court upholds a federal law preventing states from selling driver's license information. State claim overturned.
Bush v. Gore (2000)	Court overrules a Florida Supreme Court action allowing hand recounts of contested election ballots. State claim overturned.
Alabama v. Garrett (2001)	Court rules that state employees cannot sue their employers in federal court to recover monetary damages under the provisions of the Americans with Disabilities Act. State claim upheld.
Lorillard Tobacco Co. v. Reilly (2001)	Court strikes down Massachusetts laws regulating the advertising of tobacco products. State claim overturned.
Kelo v. City of New London (2005)	Court rules that government can seize private property for public purposes, including economic development. State claim upheld.
Gonzales v. Raich (2005)	Court rules that federal laws outlawing marijuana can be upheld by federal law enforcement officers in states where medical marijuana has been legalized. State law enforcement groups, however, do not have to participate in federal efforts to seize marijuana.
Gonzales v. Oregon (2006)	Court rules that the U.S. attorney general overstepped his authority by threatening to eliminate prescription-writing privileges for doctors who follow state law allowing physician-assisted suicide. State claim upheld.
Arizona v. United States (2012)	Court rules that states do not have the authority to enact and enforce immigration laws; however, it allows states to implement "show me your papers" regulations that require law enforcement officers to determine the immigration status of anyone they stop or detain.
National Federation of Independent Business v. Sebelius (2012)	Court rules that the federal government can require individuals to purchase health insurance and that doing so does not violate powers reserved to the states under the Tenth Amendment.
Environmental Protection Agency v. EME Homer City Generation (2014)	Court rules that the Environmental Protection Agency can regulate greenhouse gas emissions over the opposition of state governments.

Just 6 months later, however, the Court upheld a state law related to serious illnesses when it ruled in *Gonzales v. Oregon* (2006) against the federal government's challenge of Oregon's law that allows physician-assisted suicide. In recent years, the Court has reviewed a number of preemptions of state law on everything from banking regulation to labor arbitration, and, for the most part, it has sided with federal authority.[23]

This was certainly the case in the Court's 2012 landmark ruling in *National Federation of Independent Business v. Sebelius*, which bitterly disappointed many conservatives. This case decided the federal government's power to enact the Patient Protection and Affordable Care Act, in particular the federal government's authority to require individuals to purchase health insurance. Chief Justice John Roberts, appointed by President George W. Bush and typically seen as a member of the Court's conservative bloc, surprised many by voting with the more liberal justices to affirm that power. Yet in another landmark case decided the same year, the Court put caveats on federal supremacy. In *Arizona v. United States* (2012), the Supreme Court essentially ruled that only the federal government has the power to set immigration policy but affirmed that states have the right to check the immigration status of people within their borders. In other words, the Court sort of split the difference between state and federal claims to power. Similarly, the Court in 2014 ruled in *Environmental Protection Agency v. EME Homer City Generation* that the federal Environmental Protection Agency could regulate major producers of greenhouse gas emissions—something opposed by coal-producing states—but then in 2016 issued an order that blocked the Obama administration's attempts to implement such regulations.

So over the past quarter-century or so, the Supreme Court has sometimes zigged and sometimes zagged on state–federal relations. In the 1990s, its rulings seemed to herald a resurrection of states' rights by conservative justices, but this commitment was never consistent, and something of that inconsistency is seen in the landmark cases affecting state–federal relations in the past few years. Some scholars argue that these sorts of inconsistencies have always been characteristic of the Supreme Court's federalism rulings. Ideology—not a firm commitment to a particular vision of state–national relations—is what ultimately decides how a justice rules in a particular case.[24] Therefore, a Court dominated by conservative appointees will occasionally depart from the state-centered notion of federalism if

a nation-centered view is more ideologically pleasing, whereas a Court dominated by liberal appointees will do the opposite. The Supreme Court, like the president, finds it hard to resist the temptations of ad hoc federalism.

Ideology—not a firm commitment to a particular vision of state–national relations—is what ultimately decides how a justice rules in a particular case.

Conclusion

The Constitution organizes the United States into a federal political system. This means that the states are powerful independent political actors that dominate important policy areas. Many of these policy areas are those with the most obvious and far-reaching roles in the day-to-day lives of citizens. Education, law enforcement, utility regulation, and road construction are but a handful of examples. The independence states are granted under the federal system allows them broad leeway to go their own way in these and many other policy areas.

The resulting variation has a number of advantages, such as making it easier to match local preferences with government action and allowing states and localities to experiment with innovative programs and policies. There are also a number of disadvantages. These include the complexity and difficulty in coordinating policy at the national level. The interests of state and national governments overlap in many areas. Because of this and because the Constitution does not clearly resolve the question of who has the power to do what in these arenas of shared interest, conflict is inevitable.

What is the future of federalism? That is a hard question to answer because across the partisan and ideological spectrum it has become increasingly difficult to see any sort of consistent commitment to an overarching philosophy of federalism. The eras of dual, cooperative, and centralized federalism are history. The federal government's commitment to New Federalism essentially collapsed during the George W. Bush administration. What has emerged since then is ad hoc federalism, with views on which level of government has primacy shifting from policy to policy on the basis of partisan and ideological preferences. Under the Obama administration, the federal government increasingly worked with the states that were willing; other states sought opt-outs or even effectively sought to nullify federal programs and laws. The administration of Donald Trump sought to impose a new set of federal policy priorities in areas such as immigration and environmental regulation only to encounter fierce resistance, often from the same states that had worked enthusiastically with the Obama administration. The era of ad hoc federalism is one of fractured state–federal relations, with conflicts breaking out along openly partisan and ideological lines. This creates a situation ripe for continued conflicts between state and federal governments, conflicts that in many cases will have to be resolved by the Supreme Court. The Court recently has exhibited some inconsistency in its own commitment to favoring states' rights in resolving state–federal conflicts. Yet, regardless of how these conflicts are ultimately resolved, the future undoubtedly will find states and localities continuing to play a central role in the U.S. political system, both as independent policymakers and as cooperative partners with the federal government.

THE LATEST RESEARCH

Federalism in the United States is dynamic. The roles and responsibilities of federal and state governments are constantly evolving based on political and economic context, policy demands and innovation, Supreme Court rulings, and the political philosophies, ideological preferences, and partisan fortunes of lawmakers at both levels of government. Current scholars of federalism find themselves in a particularly interesting period in the development of intergovernmental relations. The growing ideological and partisan divisions within and between states, and between states and the federal government, are leading to a resurgence of independent state policy activity. Federal, state, and local governments are resetting their relationships to deal with a political system that is increasingly politically polarized.

Below are summaries of some of the most recent research on federalism. Two constant themes emerge from this stream of scholarship: First, intergovernmental relations are increasingly defined by partisan and ideological differences, and second, states are aggressively seeking to assert their independence as policy actors.

- **Goelzhauser, Greg, and Shanna Rose,** "The State of American Federalism 2016–17: Policy Reversals and Partisan Perspectives on Intergovernmental Relations," *Publius: The Journal of Federalism* 47, no. 3 (2017): 285–313.

In this article Goelzhauser and Rose report on the contemporary state of American federalism. What they find is that state–federal relations are increasingly characterized by ideological and partisan division. Notably, they find a sharp reversal of partisan perspectives of state-federal relations in the wake of the 2016 elections. With the GOP controlling the White House and Congress, Republicans suddenly become much more supportive of federal primacy, especially in areas such as immigration, LGBT rights, and the environment. In contrast, Democrats and progressives—traditionally more supportive of nation-centered governance—became much more aggressive in defending state prerogatives.

- **Conlan, Timothy J.,** "The Changing Politics of American Federalism," *State and Local Government Review* 49, no. 3 (2018): 1–14.

This is an interesting companion study to the Goelzhauser and Rose article. Here, Conlan looks at three political trends that have affected intergovernmental relations and policy: nationalization, polarization, and delegitimation. Conlan argues that politics, especially party politics, have increasingly become nationalized, to the point where even state and local races are fought on national issues such as immigration. Concurrent with that nationalization is an ever-growing ideological gap, with the two now largely national political parties planting their flags on opposing sides of an ideological canyon that is increasingly difficult to bridge. At the same time, the national government itself is suffering from delegitimation, a steady erosion of trust and confidence in its ability to represent the public interest and effectively respond to social and economic problems. This creates a volatile situation where the level of government

(Continued)

(Continued)

least favored by the public is increasingly setting the terms of policy debates.

- **Nicholson-Crotty, Sean,** *Governors, Grants, and Elections: Fiscal Federalism in the American States* (Baltimore: Johns Hopkins University Press, 2015).

In this book, Nicholson-Crotty examines how governors strategically pursue and use federal grant dollars for their own political ends. At the heart of the book is a massive comparative study that looks at federal grant revenue and expenditure in all 50 states across several decades. Based on these revenue and expenditure patterns, Nicholson-Crotty concludes that governors use federal grants to serve their own political purposes—to fund programs favored by key constituencies in their states and to attract funds that support the governors' own policy agendas. This puts a somewhat different spin on the traditional story of fiscal federalism, of the federal government setting policy priorities and providing money to the states, which use the money to implement those policy targets. Nicholson-Crotty's findings suggest that governors are strategically using federal grants to improve their own political fortunes.

- **McCann, Pamela J. Clouser, Charles R. Shipan, and Craig Volden,** "Top-Down Federalism: State Policy Responses to National Government Discussions," *Publius: The Journal of Federalism* 45, no. 4 (2015): 495–525.

While many scholars are investigating how states are increasingly acting as independent policy actors and frequently disagreeing with the federal government on a range of policy issues, it is worth pointing out that the two levels of government are far from going their separate ways. Regardless of whether either side is happy about it, the state–federal relationship is symbiotic, with the actions and decisions of one level of government affecting the other. This study is an example of that. McCann and her colleagues examine how the federal government influences state policies in ways other than through direction action, such as providing grant incentives or imposing legal mandates. They find that when the federal government pays particular attention to a policy issue—the example they use is antismoking initiatives—states also pay attention, often taking independent action even when they are not explicitly encouraged or directed to by the federal government.

CHAPTER 2

for CQ Press

Want a better grade?

Get the tools you need to sharpen your study skills. SAGE edge offers a robust online environment featuring an impressive array of free tools and resources.

Access practice quizzes, eFlashcards, video, and multimedia at **edge.sagepub.com/ smithgreenblatt7e**

Top Ten Takeaways

1. A unitary political system concentrates power in a single central government. Confederal systems concentrate power in regional governments. In federal systems, power and policy responsibilities are divided between central and regional governments.

2. The framers of the U.S. Constitution chose a federal system for several reasons. Their experience with the confederal system under the Articles of Confederation convinced them of the need for a more powerful central government. Their experience under a unitary system—as colonies of the United Kingdom—made that option unpalatable to many.

3. A federal system also fit with the framers' preferences for division of powers and allowed states to retain sovereign powers.

4. Federalism has advantages and disadvantages. For example, it allows policy experimentation by the states, but it also creates legal and political complexity and confusion.

5. Federal–state division of powers is governed by the U.S. Constitution. While the Constitution provides a number of explicit grants of power to the federal government, powers of the states are more vague and are derived in large part from the Tenth Amendment.

6. Disagreements about which level of government has the power and authority to do what inevitably lead to conflicts between state and local governments. These conflicts ultimately have to be resolved by the Supreme Court.

7. Relationships between state and federal governments have evolved considerably, being characterized by dual federalism initially and by cooperative and centralized federalism for much of the last century. This evolution generally shifted power toward the federal government.

8. The New Federalism movement of the late 20th century sought to push power away from the federal government and back to the states.

9. Current state–federal government relations are characterized by ad hoc federalism, where political actors favor state power or federal power based on the issue and their own political preferences.

10. After signaling a return to supporting states' rights in the 1990s, Supreme Court rulings have been inconsistent in the 21st century, favoring state authority in some cases and federal authority in others.

Key Concepts

ad hoc federalism (p. 41)

Bill of Rights (p. 32)

block grants (p. 39)

categorical grants (p. 38)

centralized federalism (p. 38)

compact theory (p. 34)

concurrent powers (p. 30)

confederacy (p. 24)

cooperative federalism (p. 36)

(Continued)

(Continued)

crosscutting requirements
   (p. 38)
crossover sanctions (p. 38)
dual federalism (p. 34)
enumerated powers (p. 30)
exclusive powers (p. 30)
federalism (p. 23)
Fourteenth Amendment
   (p. 32)
full faith and credit clause
   (p. 30)
general revenue sharing
   grants (p. 38)

general welfare clause (p. 30)
grants-in-aid (p. 36)
implied powers (p. 30)
interstate commerce clause
   (p. 42)
nation-centered federalism
   (p. 34)
national supremacy clause
   (p. 30)
necessary and proper clause
   (p. 30)
New Federalism (p. 39)
nullification (p. 34)

preemption (p. 30)
privileges and immunities
   clause (p. 30)
representative government
   (p. 26)
secession (p. 34)
sovereign immunity (p. 44)
state-centered federalism
   (p. 34)
states' rights (p. 34)
Tenth Amendment (p. 32)
unfunded mandates (p. 38)
unitary systems (p. 24)

Suggested Websites

- **www.nga.org**. Website of the National Governors Association; includes a section devoted to state–federal relations.

- **www.publius.oxfordjournals.org**. Website of *Publius*, a scholarly journal dedicated to the study of federalism.

- **www.supremecourt.gov**. Website of the U.S. Supreme Court; includes text of the Court's opinions.

3

State of *Massachusetts-Bay.*

In the House of REPRESENTATIVES, February 19, 1779.

WHEREAS the Constitution or Form of Civil Government, which was proposed by the late Convention of this State to the People thereof, hath been disapproved by a Majority of the Inhabitants of said State :

And whereas it is doubtful, from the Representations made to this Court, what are the Sentiments of the major Part of the good People of this state as to the Expediency of now proceeding to form a new Constitution of Government :

Therefore, *Resolved,* That the Selectmen of the several Towns within this State cause the Freeholders, and other Inhabitants in their respective Towns duly qualified to vote for Representatives, to be lawfully warned to meet together in some convenient Place therein, on or before the last Wednesday of *May* next, to consider of and determine upon the following Questions.

First, Whether they chuse at this Time to have a new Constitution or Form of Government made.

Secondly, Whether they will impower their Representatives for the next Year to vote for the calling a State Convention, for the sole Purpose of forming a new Constitution.

Constitutions

Operating Instructions

State constitutions differ from the U.S. Constitution in many ways. Some are older—the Massachusetts Constitution, shown here, was written about a decade before the U.S. Constitution was adopted. Most state constitutions are longer, more detailed, and much easier to change than their federal counterpart.

Chapter Objectives

After reading this chapter, you will be able to

- Describe the role of state constitutions,

- Explain how state constitutions evolved in early American history,

- Discuss the role of bicameral legislatures in the first generation of state constitutions,

- Identify the ways state constitutions can be formally changed,

- Identify informal means of changing constitutions,

- Discuss why constitutions vary from state to state,

- Explain how state constitutions differ, and

- Relate the ways local governments may be subject to governing documents such as constitutions.

It's pretty clear that, at least in theory, the president of the United States could be an atheist. It's equally clear that, at least technically, the same nonbeliever could not become governor of Texas. How the heck can that be? How can someone who qualifies to hold the top job in the federal government be barred on religious grounds from being eligible to be the chief executive of the Lone Star State? The answer is pretty simple. It's what the constitution says. Both of them.

Article VI of the U.S. Constitution states pretty plainly that "no religious test shall ever be required as a qualification to any office or public trust under the United States." Believe what you want, or believe nothing at all, but as a federal official, your faith or lack thereof is a nonissue. At least, that is, in a legal sense. Politically speaking, good luck getting elected after publicly professing your agnosticism or longtime membership in the Church of the Flying Spaghetti Monster (that's a real thing, by the way—it has its own Wikipedia page and everything). Still, while religious skepticism might cost a candidate votes, nonbelief in an office-seeker is constitutionally kosher. You cannot be barred from running, and you cannot be removed from federal office, simply because you have an unpopular set of ideas about religion.

Article I, Section 4, of the Texas Constitution says something pretty similar to Article VI of the U.S. Constitution. Specifically: "No religious test shall ever be required as a qualification to any office, or public trust, in this state; nor shall anyone be excluded from

holding office on account of his religious sentiments." Well, that sounds pretty clear-cut, too. Ah, but there's a catch. Section 4 concludes, "provided he acknowledges the existence of a Supreme Being." That would seem to limit Texas officials to people who believe in God, or at least a god. That, admittedly, is a pretty big set of people in Texas, especially as *he* still technically qualifies as a gender-neutral pronoun, even if to modern eyes it smacks of being a bit on the male-centric side. While the rules of grammar make gender a nonissue, though, there's no getting around that bit about belief in a supreme being. The bottom line: if you are a nonbeliever, then you are constitutionally unqualified to hold office in the state of Texas.

In reality, the U.S. Constitution almost certainly prevents Texas from requiring its officials to have some form of religious belief. And Texas knows it. This clause of the state constitution has never been enforced, and any attempt to do so would likely result in a fast legal challenge with a very high probability of success. The U.S. Supreme Court ruled decades ago that a state could not require any candidate for public office to profess a belief in God (*Torcaso v. Watkins*, 1961), and the legal bottom line is that if a state constitution is in conflict with the U.S. Constitution, the latter wins.

Outside of that limitation, though, state constitutions can say pretty much whatever citizens and their lawmakers want them to. They can expand or grant rights, protections, and freedoms not found in the U.S. Constitution. They can also restrict those rights to the bare minimum required. For example, there has been a long-running debate over whether and to what extent the Second Amendment to the Constitution of the United States grants individuals an unrestricted right to possess firearms. There's no debate in Alabama, though, where the state's constitution plainly states, "Every citizen has a fundamental right to bear arms in defense of himself or herself and the state."[1] Do the citizens of Alabama have a right to keep and bear arms? You bet. Indeed, it is a "fundamental right," and Alabama's constitution specifies that any attempt to restrict that right "shall be subject to strict scrutiny." In other words, state and local officials are going to have a very high legal hurdle to jump if they want to regulate firearms ownership. In contrast, the California Constitution has no provision at all on the right (or lack thereof) to bear arms, and California has some of the most restrictive gun control laws in the nation. Do you have an unrestricted constitutional right to keep and bear arms in California? Heck, no. You get whatever the minimum guarantee is from the U.S. Constitution and not a bit more.

Many people are surprised to find out that their constitutional rights vary from state to state. True, your rights under the U.S. Constitution are (mostly) the same in every state. But that does not mean rights are uniform. It's not just your right to own a gun; it's everything from your free speech rights to your right to run for office. Even your right to participate in the political process can vary pretty drastically from state to state. Among other things, that's because some states have some form of **direct democracy**, which allows citizens to make laws themselves rather than outsourcing the job to elected representatives. Citizens of Alabama do not have the ability to propose and vote on amendments to their state's constitution, but in other states, including Nebraska, California, and Missouri, members of the **electorate**—those individuals who can vote—are free to take policy matters into their own hands. Ballot initiatives and referendums allow voters to amend the constitution or override the decisions of the state's elected officials, or even remove the officials entirely, with ease.

Whether or not states allow for direct democracy is among the reasons that constitutions, and the rights and regulations they mandate, differ so much from state to state. What else explains the tremendous variation among state constitutions? A state constitution reflects that state's particular historical experiences, its political culture, its geography, and its notions of what makes good government. We'll look at these sorts of differences and their implications in this chapter.

Before getting to that, though, it is critical to understand the importance of state constitutions, which serve an underappreciated role not just in organizing state and local governance but also in determining individual rights and the operation of the entire federal system. Since the 1990s, the U.S. Supreme Court has made a number of decisions strengthening the role of states in the federal system, decisions that elevate the importance of state constitutions. The Court's insistence on determining the boundaries of federalism and evaluating state laws and regulations—a form of activism sometimes referred to as **judicial federalism**—even gained former chief justice William Rehnquist the nickname "Governor Rehnquist."[2]

State supreme courts also are becoming more assertive. In 1977, Supreme Court justice William Brennan, a former justice of the New Jersey Supreme Court, wrote a now-famous article for the *Harvard Law Review* noting that state constitutions afford their citizens a layer of rights above and beyond those protected in the U.S. Constitution. He urged state courts to pay more attention to these rights and to assert themselves more forcefully. They have. State courts, for example, ruled same-sex couples had the same marriage rights as heterosexuals long before the U.S. Supreme Court's landmark ruling in *Obergefell v. Hodges* (2015). This is just one example of assertive state supreme courts finding rights in state constitutions that are not under the protection of the U.S. Constitution. This means that the documents that reflect and determine what state and local governments can and cannot do have become even more important to an understanding of politics in the United States.

As you read through this chapter, keep in mind the following questions:

- **What impact do state constitutions have on our lives?**

- **Why do state constitutions differ?**

- **How do constitutions determine what state and local governments can and cannot do?**

Direct democracy A system in which citizens make laws themselves rather than relying on elected representatives.

Electorate The population of individuals who can vote.

Judicial federalism The idea that the courts determine the boundaries of state–federal relations.

What State Constitutions Do: It's Probably Different from What You Think

Mention "the constitution" and chances are good that your listener will think instantly of the U.S. Constitution. The founders have gotten more than two centuries of good press for their work in 1787. Schoolchildren memorize "We the People of the United States, in order to form a more perfect Union . . . " and venerate the document's wisdom. Yet the U.S. Constitution is only half the story. As residents of the United States, we live under a system of **dual constitutionalism**, in which the federal government and state governments are cosovereign powers. Both levels of government run in accordance with the rules laid out in their respective constitutions. Despite the important role state constitutions play in establishing our rights and organizing our local and state governments, most people know very little about them.

The U.S. Constitution and all state constitutions have some basic things in common. Constitutions at both state and federal levels lay down the roles, responsibilities, and institutional structure of government and establish the basic procedures for operating key government institutions. For example, like the U.S. Constitution, all state constitutions create three primary branches of government (legislative, executive, and judicial) and provide a general governmental framework for what each branch is supposed to do (or not do) and how it should go about doing it. Similar to the U.S. Constitution, all state constitutions contain something roughly equivalent to a bill of rights, with those rights firmly placed in the context of **natural law**, also known as **higher law**. Natural (or higher) law is a philosophy that certain rights are divine endowments rather than political creations. Natural law thus holds that basic rights and values, such as those guaranteed by the Bill of Rights, are not created by governments through law. If these rights were created by governments, after all, then governments could take them away. Instead, governments merely "discover" the rights that nature bestows on all people and restrain any interference with those rights. Constitutions and any subsequent **constitutional amendments**, or changes, thus do not create rights; they are there to make sure those natural rights are not taken from anyone.

Yet while federal and state constitutions share a good deal in terms of their functions and underlying legal philosophy, in many ways it is misleading to compare state constitutions with their better-known federal counterpart. Consider the important differences discussed below.

Powers Granted to Government

Perhaps the most important and surprising difference between the U.S. Constitution and state constitutions is the scope of the documents. The U.S. Constitution's original purpose was to organize a federal government with sharply limited powers. In contrast, state governments have what is called **plenary power**, which means their powers are not limited to those laid down in the U.S. Constitution or their own state constitutions. As the Tenth Amendment to the U.S. Constitution makes clear, *all* powers not expressly delegated or forbidden to the federal government are reserved for the states. In other words, this is not a limited grant of power in the sense of laying out the specifics of what states have the authority to do or not do. It basically says that states can do whatever they want—they have complete or plenary power—as long as they do not contravene the U.S. Constitution.

That plenary power is vested in the lawmaking bodies of state government—that is, state legislatures. This does not mean that these legislatures can go around arbitrarily breaking the rules laid down by their own constitutions, which can be quite restrictive. What it means is they can act without express permission of the constitution; as long as their actions are not prohibited, they are good to go. Think of it like this: When passing a law, Congress must address the key question, "Is this allowed (by the U.S. Constitution)?" For state legislatures, the key question is, "Is this prohibited (by the state constitution)?" That's the difference between limited and plenary powers in the federal system. State legislatures, through the U.S. Constitution and their own state constitutions, have these powers. Congress does not. State constitutions, in short, do not establish limited governments in the same way the U.S. Constitution establishes a limited federal government.[3]

....

Dual constitutionalism A system of government in which people live under two sovereign powers. In the United States, these are the government of their state of residence and the federal government.

Natural law or higher law A set of moral and political rules based on divine law and binding on all people.

Constitutional amendments Proposals to change a constitution, typically enacted by a supermajority of the legislature or through a statewide referendum.

Plenary power Power that is not limited or constrained.

Permanence

The U.S. Constitution is widely seen as the document that created the United States—the embodiment of the founders' wisdom. As such, it is held in the highest regard by politicians and the public alike. It has lasted more than two centuries and has been formally changed only 27 times. In contrast, state constitutions are amended and even replaced much more frequently. Most states have replaced their original constitutions at least once. California is currently on its second constitution. New York is on its fourth. Louisiana is on its eleventh. In fact, one political scientist has estimated that the average state constitution lasts for only about 70 years.[4]

Length

The federal constitution is a relatively short document. At about 7,400 words, it is shorter than most chapters in this book. In contrast, state constitutions tend to be much longer—about 26,000 words on average. Some are much, much longer. New York's constitution and California's ruling document are each roughly 50,000 words long. The longest state constitution, Alabama's, clocks in at 310,296 words, more than 40 times the length of the U.S. Constitution.[5] This entire textbook is only about two-thirds as long as Alabama's 300,000-plus-word constitution.

Specificity

Why are state constitutions so much longer than the federal constitution and so much more likely to change? Part of the answer has to do with how the functions of the federal constitution differ from those of state constitutions. The U.S. Constitution is primarily concerned with setting up the basic structures and procedures of government. State constitutions do these things too, but they often set forth procedures and address policies in much greater detail than the federal constitution does. Whereas the federal constitution creates a framework for government, state constitutions often get into policy details. South Dakota, for instance, is one of several states whose constitution once sanctioned the state prison to produce twine and cordage. Oklahoma's constitution mandates that home economics be taught in school; Maryland's regulates off-street parking in Baltimore. Political scientist Christopher Hammons has estimated that 39 percent of the total provisions in state constitutions are devoted to specific

policy matters of this sort. In contrast, only 6 percent of the U.S. Constitution deals with such specific issues.[6] Some political scientists think this narrow policy focus may help explain why states are more likely to replace their constitutions: if influential political constituencies start to part ways with the policy preferences embedded in a state constitution, they have an obvious incentive to tear up that constitution and write a new one more agreeable to their views.[7]

Whereas the federal constitution creates a framework for government, state constitutions often get into policy details. South Dakota, for instance, is one of several states whose constitution once sanctioned the state prison to produce twine and cordage.

Embrace of Democracy

The U.S. Constitution creates a system of representative democracy; it purposefully rejects direct democracy as a basis for governance. The founders went to great pains to check "the whimsies of the majority" by designing a system of checks and balances that deliberately keeps policymaking at arm's length from the shifting winds of popular opinion. During the Progressive Era in the early 1900s, many states revamped their constitutions to do just the opposite. This was particularly true of the newer western and midwestern states, in which old-school politics was less entrenched and political cultures tended toward the moralistic or individualistic.

Progressive reformers believed that old constitutional arrangements were outmoded and that citizens should have the opportunity to participate directly in making laws. Moreover, they worried that state legislatures had been captured by wealthy special interests. In other words, they thought that representative democracy was working for the benefit of a few rather than for the benefit of all. Their solution was to give the people the ability to amend their constitutions and pass laws directly through the use of referendums and ballot initiatives. Thus, in about half the states, state constitutions champion direct democracy in a way that the U.S. Constitution purposefully does not.

Finances

Congress and the White House can run up as much national debt as they can persuade bond buyers to swallow. In contrast, 32 state constitutions require the legislative and executive branches to balance their budgets. Another 17 states have statutes that mandate balanced budgets. Only Vermont can choose to run up debt as the feds do. Even state constitutions that do not require a balanced budget take a much more proscriptive, or restrictive, view of budget matters than does the U.S. Constitution. California's constitution, for instance, mandates that almost 40 percent of the state budget go toward education, a requirement that has constrained legislators' options when the state has been faced with budget shortfalls.

Other state constitutions mandate a specific style and format for laws that allow the transfer of money to the executive branch. These are known as **appropriations bills**. Some state constitutions require supermajorities—two-thirds or three-fifths of the electorate—instead of simple majorities of the legislature to increase revenues or taxes.[8] Sometimes constitutions get more specific still, prohibiting legislators from attaching riders (amendments or additions unrelated to the main bill) to appropriations bills and requiring a single subject for each bill. State constitutions can also shape state finances by explicitly requiring legislatures to make certain expenditures. For example, Article VI, Section 6(b), of the Kansas Constitution requires the legislature to "make suitable provision for finance of the educational interests of the state." In 2016, the Kansas Supreme Court ruled that the state legislature's school funding formula violated that provision, creating a political firestorm in a state that was already dealing with widening budget deficits.

The Evolution of State Constitutions

The first state constitutions were not technically constitutions at all. Rather, they were **colonial charters**

Mike Hutmacher/The Wichita Eagle via AP

State constitutions contain provisions on everything from free speech to parking fees. The Kansas Constitution requires the legislature to adequately fund public schools, a provision that has direct implications for this second-grade class in Wichita.

awarded by the king of England. These charters typically were brief documents giving individuals or corporations the right to establish "plantations" over certain areas and govern the inhabitants therein. King James I of England granted the first charter in 1606. It created the Virginia Company of London, which in 1607 established the first English settlement in North America at Jamestown in what is now the state of Virginia.

As the colonies expanded, many of these charters were amended to give the colonists "the rights of Englishmen." Just what those rights were was never entirely clear. Britain's constitution was not (and is not) a written document. It is a tradition based on the Magna Carta of 1215 and on a shared understanding of what government should and should not do. From the start, some colonies took an expansive view of their rights and privileges. The Massachusetts Bay Colony, like other English settlements in North America, was organized as a corporation and was controlled by a

....

Appropriations bills Laws passed by legislatures authorizing the transfer of money to the executive branch.

Colonial charters Legal documents drawn up by the British Crown that spelled out how the colonies were to be governed.

small group of stockholders. But whereas the charters of the other companies remained in England, within easy reach of the British courts, Puritan leader John Winthrop took his colony's charter with him when he sailed for the New World in 1630. This made it difficult for the English government to seize and revoke the charter if the company misbehaved or operated illegally, which it soon did. The Puritans excluded non-churchgoers from local governments, punished people who violated their sense of morals, and generally behaved as an independent polity. This misbehavior eventually incurred the displeasure of King Charles II, who revoked the charter in 1691. Massachusetts then received a new royal charter that provided for a royal governor and a general assembly—a form of governance that lasted until the Revolutionary War, nearly a century later.[9]

When the colonies won their independence, it was clear that the colonial charters had to be replaced or at least modified. It was less clear what should replace them. Some colonial leaders believed that the Continental Congress should draft a model constitution that every state should adopt. Richard Henry Lee, a Virginia politician, explained the idea in a letter to John Adams in May 1776: "Would not a uniform plan of government, prepared for America by the Congress, and approved by the colonies, be a surer foundation of unceasing harmony to the whole?"[10]

Adams thought not. Although he liked the idea of uniform state constitutions in principle, he worried about what would happen in practice. He believed that effective government required a strong executive. The colonists' experience dealing with royal governors, however, had created an aversion to executive power. Adams feared that the Continental Congress would create governments dominated by powerful **unicameral legislatures** or even do away with governors altogether and create a special committee of legislators to handle the everyday business of governing. This would violate what he saw as the wise precautionary principle of the **separation of powers**.

....

Unicameral legislatures Legislatures that have only one chamber. Nebraska is currently the only U.S. state with a unicameral legislature.

Separation of powers The principle that government should be divided into separate legislative, executive, and judicial branches, each with its own powers and responsibilities.

Bicameral legislatures Legislatures made up of two chambers, typically a house of representatives, or assembly, and a senate.

Franchise The right to vote.

Ultimately, despite being a unicameral body itself, the Continental Congress rejected that particular idea. Instead, it passed a resolution that urged the 13 colonies to reorganize their authority solely "on the basis of the authority of the people."[11] This set the stage for the states to create their own varied blueprints for government.

After independence was declared and secured, the states convened special assemblies to draft new constitutions. Most adopted lightly modified versions of their old colonial charters. References to the king of England were deleted and bills of rights added. In most of the new states, power was concentrated in the legislative branch to diminish the possibility that tyrannical governors would appear in the political arena.

The First Generation of State Constitutions

This first generation of state constitutions created powerful **bicameral legislatures**—with a few exceptions. Georgia, Pennsylvania, and Vermont opted for unicameral legislatures. Governors and state judiciaries were clearly subordinate in most cases. In fact, legislatures often appointed both the governor and judges. No one envisioned that one day a state supreme court would have the power to overrule the acts of a legislature on the grounds that its laws were unconstitutional. Indeed, the states that did provide for constitutional review entrusted that function to special "councils of revision" or to "councils of censor."

Nor did the early state constitutions embrace the now commonplace idea of "one person, one vote." Every early state constitution except Vermont's restricted voting access to white males who met certain minimum property requirements. Vermont gave the vote to every adult male. Supporters of a limited **franchise** defended these limitations as essential to the new republic. Without property qualifications, John Adams warned,

> there will be no end to it. New claims will arise; women will demand a vote; lads from 12 to 21 will think their rights are not enough attended to; and every man who has not a farthing will demand an equal voice with any other, in all acts of the state. It tends to confound and destroy all distinctions, and prostrate all ranks to one common level.[12]

Indeed, Adams wanted to restrict the franchise even further by setting still higher property requirements.

In practice, the actual requirements necessary to achieve the right to vote varied widely. Some states, such as New Hampshire, let all white male taxpayers vote. This reflected the fact that New Hampshire was a state of small landowners with a fairly egalitarian political culture. However, even this fair state specified a higher threshold of property ownership that must be met should a man wish to hold office. In Virginia, a state with a more hierarchical political culture dominated by a small group of wealthy landowners and planters, the property qualifications were stiff. Only white males who owned at least 25 acres and a 12-foot-by-12-foot house, 50 acres unsettled, or a town lot with a 12-foot-by-12-foot house could vote. It is not entirely clear how many people met these qualifications. Most scholars believe that in the more democratic northern states 60 to 80 percent of white males could vote. Needless to say, women and nonwhites could not.

Over the course of the 19th century, the franchise was expanded gradually, although in a very uneven and often unjust fashion. A number of southern states, for example, rewrote their constitutions to allow minorities to vote only when such changes were forced on them as part of the price for their readmission to the Union after the Civil War. African American rights also were enshrined in the Fourteenth Amendment of the U.S. Constitution. Yet, despite these protections, gains for African Americans proved short-lived. In the last decade of the 1800s, African Americans' ability to vote and to participate in all aspects of society were harshly limited by the passage of **Jim Crow laws**. These laws provided for the systematic separation of races, sharply restricted access to the franchise, and permitted the outright intimidation of African Americans.

Women fared only slightly better. Wyoming began to allow women to vote in 1869. By 1912, only 13 states had followed suit. It took the Nineteenth Amendment, ratified in 1920, to secure the right to vote, or suffrage, for all women nationwide.

The limitations on the franchise imposed by many early state constitutions did little to promote good governance. State legislatures quickly developed an impressive record of corruption and fiscal extravagance because some of the men who had the legal right to vote also had money to influence politicians, an easy task in many states. But the era of unlimited legislative power did not last very long. New territories entering the Union, such as Indiana and Mississippi, opted for elected governors, as did older states that began to revise or replace their constitutions in the 1820s. The intention was to create more balance among the branches of government and allow all voters (not just the rich ones) more of a voice in deciding who would run a state. By 1860, South Carolina was the only state with a governor selected by the legislature.[13] In hindsight, the 19th century is recognized as a period of tumultuous constitutional change.

Formal Constitutional Changes

Every state constitution provides a method for making changes. Fourteen states actually require citizens to vote periodically on whether or not they want to convene a **constitutional convention**. Voters can decide if they want to amend or replace their state's constitution.[14]

In the early 19th century, suggesting such change could be an exciting—and dangerous—business. In 1841, a patrician attorney and renegade lawmaker by the name of Thomas Wilson Dorr convened an illegal constitutional convention with the intention of replacing Rhode Island's colonial charter with a more modern and progressive constitution. The state's aged document still limited the franchise to voters owning land valued at $134 or more at a time when other states had long since abandoned such requirements. Dorr's supporters elected him "governor" the following year on a platform that proposed allowing all white males—even Catholic immigrants, a group viewed by the Protestant majority with great suspicion—to vote, which caused the sitting governor to order Dorr arrested and tried for treason. Thus began the Dorr War, or Dorr's Rebellion. Dorr's supporters then attempted to seize the arsenal in Providence but were repelled when their cannons failed to discharge. A month later, Dorr and his followers tried again. This time, a force of militiamen and free blacks from Providence repelled them.[15] Still, Rhode Island's establishment got the hint. A new, more liberal constitution was quickly enacted.

The amendment process has since become a bit more routinized in most states. Amending or replacing a state constitution is typically a two-step process. First, a constitutional amendment or a new constitution must be

Jim Crow laws Legislative measures passed in the last decade of the 19th century that sought to systematically separate blacks and whites.

Constitutional convention An assembly convened for the express purpose of amending or replacing a constitution.

A DIFFERENCE THAT MAKES A DIFFERENCE
THE PECULIAR CONSTITUTION OF EARLY PENNSYLVANIA

The original American colonies were established for a wide variety of purposes. The Massachusetts Bay Colony, for example, started off as a haven for a persecuted religious sect. The Puritans were determined to create, in the words of Massachusetts's first governor, John Winthrop, "a city upon a hill" to serve as an example of a holy community for all people. Other colonies, such as Virginia, began as business ventures. Still others, including Pennsylvania, were both.

Pennsylvania's first colonial charter reflected the colony's dual purposes as a religious settlement and an investment. It illustrates how state charters were created to serve very particular goals—and how "rights" that Americans now take for granted, such as the right to self-governance, were by no means obvious to this country's founders.

The colony started out as a business venture. In 1681, William Penn received a proprietary interest—the controlling share—in what is now the state of Pennsylvania as repayment for a debt that England's King Charles II owed Penn's father. Penn was already deeply involved in land speculation in North America. He and 11 other investors already owned East Jersey (present-day New Jersey). Soon after buying into Pennsylvania, they acquired a lease on Delaware.

Penn, however, wasn't just a businessman. He was also a devout Quaker, a member of a peace-loving religious group that was often at odds with the official Church of England. Pennsylvania was to Penn "a holy experiment"—a unique chance to found a province dedicated to Quakerism's vision of equality and religious freedom.

William Markham, Penn's deputy, was sent in 1681 to establish a seat of government for Penn's new colony. Penn also instructed his representative to construct a "City of Brotherly Love"—Philadelphia. One year later,

Penn himself arrived in his fledgling colony. His first major action was to draw up a constitution, or charter, for the new colony, which he called the "Frame of Government." His second major act was to establish friendly relations with the American Indians in the area—an unusual action that reflected his pacific religious beliefs.

In many ways, the Frame of Government echoed Quakerism's progressive dogmas. Penn's constitution guaranteed religious freedom to everyone who believed in God. It also set forth a humane penal code and encouraged the emancipation of slaves. In contrast, the early settlers of Massachusetts were interested not in individual religious freedom but in establishing a just Puritan society. As a result, the functions of local churches and town governments were intertwined in early Massachusetts. Indeed, the colony was governed as a virtual theocracy for its first 200 years.

However, the Pennsylvania model was not a uniform triumph of humane liberalism. Penn did use his charter to protect his business interests. The Frame of Government provided for an elected general assembly, but it also concentrated almost all power in the executive branch of government, which was controlled by Penn and the other proprietors.

It was not long before colonists began to chafe at some of the less progressive features of Penn's early constitution. Penn was forced to return to Pennsylvania in 1701 and issue a new constitution, the Charter of Privileges, which granted more power to the provincial assembly. However, the conflict between proprietary and antiproprietary forces did not diminish until 1776. That year, noted revolutionary Benjamin Franklin led a convention to assemble and approve a new constitution for the state as it struggled for independence from Great Britain.

proposed and meet a certain threshold of support. Then it must be ratified.

Changes to state constitutions are generally proposed in four primary ways: through legislative proposals, ballot initiatives or referendums, constitutional conventions, and constitutional commissions.

Legislative Proposals

Most attempts to change state constitutions begin with legislative proposals. Forty-nine state constitutions

allow the state legislature to propose constitutional amendments to the electorate as a whole.[16] This is how Alabama ended up enshrining strong gun rights in its constitution. The Alabama Right to Bear Arms was a legislatively referred constitutional amendment; in other words, the legislature put it on the ballot for an up-or-down vote by the electorate, who approved it with a walloping 72 percent in favor. While virtually all state legislatures can propose constitutional amendments to submit to voters for approval or disapproval,

MAP 3-1 ● **Number of Constitutions per State**

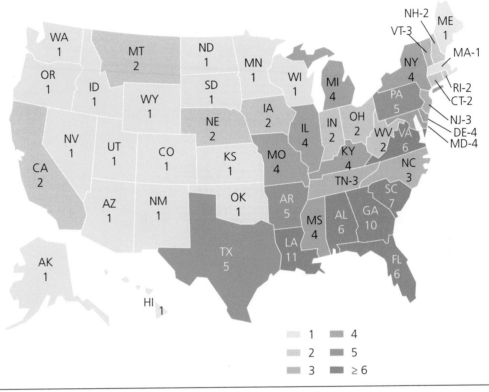

Source: Data from Heather Perkins, "State Constitutions," in *The Book of the States 2017*, ed. Council of State Governments (Lexington, KY: Council of State Governments, 2017), Table 1.1, http://knowledgecenter.csg.org/kc/content/book-states-2017-chapter-1-state-constitutions.

what state legislatures actually have to do to make that happen varies quite a bit. In 17 states, a simple majority vote in both houses of the legislature is enough to send a constitutional amendment on to the voters for **ratification**. Most other states require a supermajority for legislative approval of a constitutional amendment. Some states set the bar even higher. The constitutions of 11 states—Delaware, Indiana, Iowa, Massachusetts, Nevada, New York, Pennsylvania, South Carolina, Tennessee, Virginia, and Wisconsin—require the legislature to vote for a constitutional amendment in two consecutive sessions before it can be ratified.[17] In principle, some state legislatures also can propose completely new constitutions to voters. However, no state legislature has successfully proposed a wholesale constitutional change since Georgia did so in 1982.

Ballot Initiatives and Referendums

Twenty-four states give voters another way to propose constitutional amendments—through **ballot** **initiatives** or popular **referendums**. These ballot measures offer citizens a way to amend the constitution or enact new legislation without working through the legislature. South Dakota was the first state to provide voters with the option of ballot initiatives, in 1898, but it was only after Oregon embraced the initiative process in 1902 that the push for direct democracy really got under way. In the 16 years that followed, nearly two dozen states followed Oregon's lead. The last of these states to approve ballot initiatives was Mississippi in 1992, some 70 years after that state's supreme court tossed out its first ruling allowing initiatives.[18]

Ratification A vote of the entire electorate to approve a constitutional change, referendum, or ballot initiative.

Ballot initiatives Processes through which voters directly convey instructions to the legislature, approve a law, or amend the constitution.

Referendums Procedures that allow the electorate to accept or reject a law passed by the legislature.

MAP 3-2 ● Number of Amendments Adopted per State

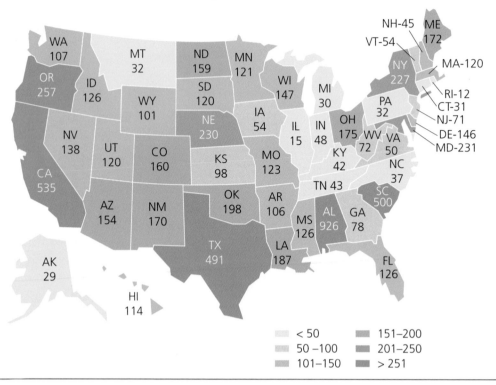

Legend:
- < 50
- 50–100
- 101–150
- 151–200
- 201–250
- > 251

WA 107, OR 257, ID 126, MT 32, ND 159, MN 121, WI 147, MI 30, NH-45, VT-54, ME 172, NY 227, MA-120, RI-12, CT-31, NJ-71, DE-146, MD-231, PA 32, NV 138, UT 120, WY 101, SD 120, NE 230, IA 54, IL 15, IN 48, OH 175, WV 72, VA 50, CA 535, CO 160, KS 98, MO 123, KY 42, NC 37, TN 43, SC 500, AZ 154, NM 170, OK 198, AR 106, MS 126, AL 926, GA 78, TX 491, LA 187, FL 126, AK 29, HI 114

Source: Data from Heather Perkins, "State Constitutions," in *The Book of the States 2017*, ed. Council of State Governments (Lexington, KY: Council of State Governments, 2017), Table 1.1, http://knowledgecenter.csg.org/kc/content/book-states-2017-chapter-1-state-constitutions.

SOUTH DAKOTA became the first state to adopt the initiative in 1898. Since then, more than 2,000 initiatives have appeared on state ballots across the nation.

How ballot measures work in practice varies widely from state to state, although there are some common elements to the process. In most states, citizens must first provide the text of their proposal to an oversight body, usually the secretary of state's office or a legislative review committee. Then they need to gather enough signatures to place the proposal on the ballot. This threshold varies widely among states. Wyoming sets the bar high, requiring a number of signatures equal to 15 percent of the votes cast for governor in the most recent election. The bar is lower in Colorado, where proponents need only gather signatures equal to 5 percent of the votes tallied for secretary of state in the previous election. The signatures are then verified, again by the secretary of state or the attorney general. Proposals that pass each test make it onto the ballot at the next election.

Ballot measures typically combine the proposal and ratification stages of the amendment process. Once a proposed amendment is on the ballot, it usually requires a simple majority to pass and become part of the constitution, although some state constitutions require a supermajority. The practical result is laws without lawmakers; the initiative process is commonly employed by people who seek policy changes that, for whatever reason, are not being considered or undertaken by the legislature.

Constitutional Conventions

The most freewheeling approach to changing or replacing a state constitution is to convene a constitutional convention. Massachusetts, whose constitution was drafted in 1780 and is the nation's oldest, was the first state to adopt a constitution via a convention. Most other states quickly followed. Currently, the only states that make no provisions for changing their constitutions through the use of constitutional conventions are Arkansas, Indiana, Mississippi, New Jersey, Pennsylvania, and Texas.

A constitutional convention typically begins when a state legislature passes a resolution that calls for a state-wide referendum on whether a convention should be held. If a majority of the electorate votes in favor of the proposal, then the next step is to hold elections for convention delegates. In most states, a law is passed that provides for the election of convention members from local election districts. Of course, there are exceptions. The legislatures of Georgia, Louisiana, Maine, South Dakota, and Virginia can call a constitutional convention without the approval of the electorate. Iowa holds an automatic constitutional assembly every 10 years, and Alaska's lieutenant governor can propose a constitutional convention through a ballot question if one has not occurred within the past decade.

Once delegates are selected, the constitutional convention can convene. The delegates are free to amend, revise, or even replace their state's constitution; they can change the existing document in any way they see fit or write an entirely new constitution. Ultimately, the handiwork of the constitutional convention goes before the electorate as a whole to be voted in or cast out.

Or a constitutional convention can do nothing at all. In 1974, Texas convened a convention to rewrite the state's creaky 1876 constitution. The delegates spent several months drafting a new constitution, but when it came time to put it to a vote, a majority of the delegates unexpectedly came out against it. The next year, the state legislature voted to put the newly drafted constitution to the public anyway as a referendum. The voters turned it down.[19]

> **State legislators tend to be wary of constitutional conventions and rarely convene them. The reason for this caution is that, once convened, a constitutional convention theoretically can examine any and all aspects of state and local government.**

State legislators tend to be wary of constitutional conventions and rarely convene them. The reason for this caution is that, once convened, a constitutional convention theoretically can examine any and all aspects of state and local government. Lawmakers who approve a convention might end up initiating a "runaway convention," or a process that leads to more far-reaching changes than they had expected. Voters seem to share this skepticism and have regularly rejected referendums that would have provided for constitutional conventions. Under the New York Constitution, for example, voters are asked once every 20 years if they would like to call a constitutional convention. This last happened in 2017, and the voters overwhelmingly said thanks, but no thanks. More than 80 percent voted against the proposal.[20] This helps explain why last U.S. state constitutional convention was held in 1986 in Rhode Island.[21]

Constitutional Revision Commissions

If constitutional conventions are for the bold and trusting, then **constitutional revision commissions** are often the cautious technocrat's preferred route to constitutional change. A constitutional revision commission typically consists of a panel of citizens appointed by the governor, the state legislature, or both. The commission suggests, but cannot mandate, changes to the state constitution. Because their powers are largely advisory, the impact of revisions commissions is often pretty minimal. For example, Alabama's legislature created a constitutional revision commission in 2011 and charged it with a multiyear effort to recommend piecemeal changes to that state's bloated constitution. (See Figure 3-1.) Only a handful of recommendations originating from the commission were submitted to voters for approval, and even some of those were rejected.[22] Yet, even today, supporters of the reforms championed by the revision commission continue pushing to streamline and modernize Alabama's mammoth constitution.

Two states go even further in their enthusiasm for constitutional commissions. Florida's constitution requires that a constitutional revision commission convene every 20 years. It also gives this commission a unique power—the right to present proposed changes directly to voters for their approval or rejection. Florida's latest constitutional revision commission met in 2018 and considered proposals ranging from establishing

....

Constitutional revision commissions Expert committees formed to assess constitutions and suggest changes.

FIGURE 3-1 ● How It Works

Alabama's State Constitution: The More Things Change, the More They Stay the Same

Since 1819, Alabama has adopted six different constitutions. The most recent was ratified in 1901 and consists of more than 310,000 words (that's over 40 times longer than the U.S. Constitution). The bulk of this comes from the 926 (and counting) amendments that make it the world's longest operating constitution. It was the product of a constitutional delegation comprising 155 white males who, like convention president John Knox, were mostly large planters. They wished to hold back the industrialization that had left Alabama in great debt. Knox, however, described the constitution's primary purpose as "secur[ing] white supremacy." African American voters were stripped of voting rights, and interracial marriage was forbidden (as recently as 2012, the state's legislature was still working to strip racist language from the constitution). Civil rights advocate Booker T. Washington, among others, condemned the document.

Many of its original provisions are now defunct or have been retracted, but that doesn't mean there are not still big problems with the constitution. Some provisions allow the continuing disfranchisement of many citizens, delay of economic development, and denial of governing powers to localities. Critics have accused the constitution of encouraging unproductive government action; the state legislature spends more than half of its time debating issues that have only local relevance, and two-thirds of the constitutional amendments address issues specific to one town or county.

There have been numerous efforts to change Alabama's constitution—six different governors have tried to change the existing 1901 document. In each case, they were met with resistance from the legislature, the state supreme court, or powerful planters and industrialists. The latest attempt at reform involves a constitutional revision commission created in 2011 by the legislature. The job of this 16-member commission is to comb through the constitution and recommend changes. These are recommendations, though, not mandates. Recommendations by the commission can be rejected by the legislature and must be approved by voters before taking effect. So while Alabama's constitution is likely not set in stone forever, the prospects of a start-from-scratch do-over still seem slim.

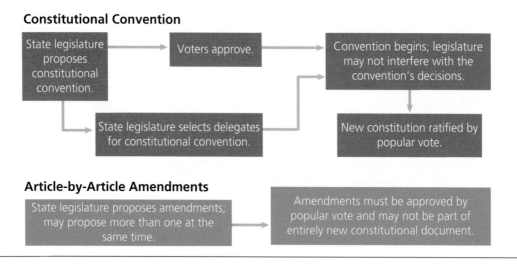

Constitutional Convention

State legislature proposes constitutional convention. → Voters approve. → Convention begins; legislature may not interfere with the convention's decisions.

State legislature selects delegates for constitutional convention.

New constitution ratified by popular vote.

Article-by-Article Amendments

State legislature proposes amendments; may propose more than one at the same time. → Amendments must be approved by popular vote and may not be part of entirely new constitutional document.

Source: Alabama Citizens for Constitutional Reform, http://www.constitutionalreform.org.

term limits on school board members to eliminating greyhound racing. Most controversially, the commission also weighed a constitutional ban on assault weapons that took on particular significance in the wake of the February 2018 school shooting in Parkland, Florida, that left 17 high school students and teachers dead. The commission actually has a history of putting gun control measures to a statewide ballot. In 1998, for example, it sent to the voters a provision to allow local governments to expand their requirements for background

checks and waiting periods for firearms purchases. More than 70 percent of voters supported the measure.

The other state with an unusual constitutional revision commission is Utah, the only state whose commission is permanent. Members of the Utah Constitutional Revision Commission are appointed by the governor, by the leaders of both houses of the legislature, and by sitting commission members. Unlike Florida's commission, Utah's commission issues its recommendations only in the form of a public report to the governor.

Although a permanent body, the Utah commission has not met much lately. After the legislature passed a law mandating that the commission can meet only if it is specifically requested to do so by the governor or legislature, few such requests have been issued.

Ratification

Once a constitutional amendment has been proposed and found acceptable, it must be ratified before it can go into effect. In most states, this is a straightforward process: the proposed amendment or new constitution is put before the voting public in the next statewide election, and the electorate either approves or rejects it. Two states add a twist to this process. In South Carolina, a majority of both houses of the state legislature must vote to approve a constitutional amendment—after a successful popular referendum—before the amendment can go into effect. In Delaware, approval by a two-thirds vote in two successive general assemblies gets a constitutional amendment ratified. As already discussed, the ballot initiative essentially combines the proposal and ratification stages. Once a proposed amendment is qualified for the ballot, it usually requires only a simple majority vote to become part of the constitution.

Informal Methods for Changing Constitutions

Constitutions can change even if the actual words in them do not. Indeed, such informal changes can be pretty dramatic and have far-reaching policy implications. The most common route of informal constitutional change is via the state supreme courts. For instance, this is the case when a court interprets an existing constitution in a way that creates a new right, such as the right to an adequate or equitable education (discussed in Chapter 13, on education).

Sometimes constitutional changes also come about from **judicial review**, which is the power of courts to review the actions of the legislative and executive branches of government and invalidate them if they are not in compliance with the constitution. When state supreme courts in places like Vermont, Iowa, and Massachusetts began ruling that their state constitutions gave same-sex couples the same (or at least similar) marriage rights as heterosexual couples, they helped set off two decades of political conflict. Many states responded to the securing of gay marriage rights through judicial review by seeking to change the constitutions being

reviewed. Many states—more than half—amended their constitutions to specify, in language that no one could misinterpret, that gay marriage was not allowed. All those amendments, however, were effectively nullified by another exercise of judicial review, this time by the U.S. Supreme Court in *Obergefell v. Hodges* (2015), which held that same-sex couples are guaranteed equal marriage rights under the due process and equal protection clauses of the Fourteenth Amendment of the U.S. Constitution. When the U.S. Constitution is found to be in conflict with a state constitution, the U.S. Constitution wins, so all those state constitutional amendments banning gay marriage no longer had a legal basis and could not be enforced.

State constitutions also can change when other branches of government successfully lay claim to broader powers. For example, Rhode Island's legislature has used its strong constitutional position—a clause in the state constitution says that the General Assembly "can exercise any power" unless the constitution explicitly forbids it—to take control of functions that most states delegate to governors. This means that in Rhode Island legislators not only sit on the boards and commissions that oversee a range of state agencies, but they also dominate the board that sets the salaries for high-ranking executive branch officials. Not surprisingly, this has given the legislature a great deal of power over executive branch decisions. In short, Rhode Island has just the type of government that John Adams feared.

Southern states such as Florida, Mississippi, and Texas also tend to have constitutions that provide for weak governors. In these cases, this arrangement is a legacy of the post–Civil War **Reconstruction** period. During Reconstruction, the victorious Union army forced most of the former Confederate states to replace their constitutions. Reconstruction ended in 1876, and the Union troops withdrew. With the exception of Arkansas, North Carolina, and Tennessee, the southern states soon abandoned their revised constitutions in favor of new ones that greatly weakened gubernatorial powers.[23] Part of the reasoning for this was that weak governors could be kept from enacting policies that the federal government encouraged but that were contrary to the norms of these traditionalistic states. This had happened during Reconstruction, when the governors of the states that had seceded from the Union

Judicial review The power of courts to assess whether a law is in compliance with the constitution.

Reconstruction The period following the Civil War when the southern states were governed under the direction of the Union army.

Procedures for Constitutional Amendment

MAP 3-3 ● **Legislative Vote Required for Approval**

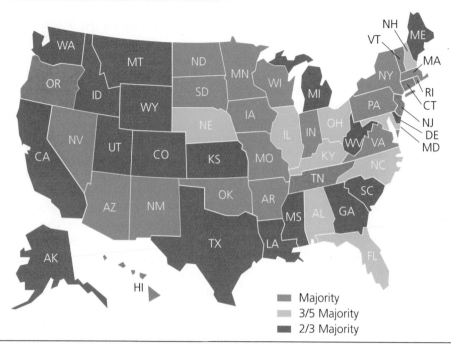

Majority

3/5 Majority

2/3 Majority

Source: Data from Heather Perkins, "State Constitutions," in *The Book of the States 2017*, ed. Council of State Governments (Lexington, KY: Council of State Governments, 2017), http://knowledgecenter.csg.org/kc/content/book-states-2017-chapter-1-state-constitutions.

MAP 3-4 ● **Vote Required for Ratification**

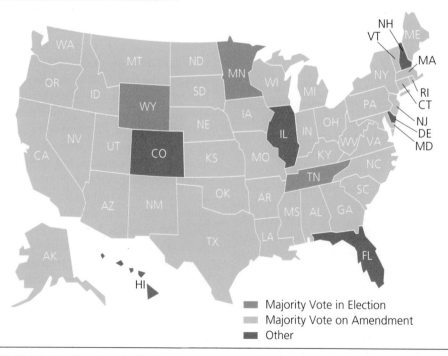

Majority Vote in Election

Majority Vote on Amendment

Other

Source: Data from Heather Perkins, "State Constitutions," in *The Book of the States 2017*, ed. Council of State Governments (Lexington, KY: Council of State Governments, 2017), Table 1.2, http://knowledgecenter.csg.org/kc/content/book-states-2017-chapter-1-state-constitutions.

were replaced by individuals sympathetic to the federal government in Washington or were forced to cooperate with federal policy in regard to such issues as African American rights. For example, in 1885, Florida passed a constitution that took away the governor's right to appoint his own cabinet; members were elected instead. Although it has been amended many times since, that constitution is still in effect today. As a result, Florida has one of the weakest governorships in the country.[24]

Of course, state legislatures do not always gain the upper hand. In states whose constitutions give governors the edge, some chief executives have been very aggressive in expanding their powers. Although their techniques do not involve written amendments to the state constitutions themselves, they do affect the distribution of powers within state government—a function that is a primary concern of state constitutions.

State constitutions may also be changed in another way—through simple neglect. Sometimes state governments just stop enforcing obscure or repugnant sections of their state constitutions, effectively changing the constitutions in the process. No politician today would dare to argue for denying the vote to individuals simply because they are poor or do not own land or belong to a minority group, yet until 1999 Texas's constitution contained a provision that limited the right to vote to citizens who owned land and paid a poll tax. The state government had stopped enforcing these objectionable requirements long before but had neglected to actually repeal them. Likewise, Alabama's constitution outlawed interracial marriages until an amendment overturned the ban in 2000; the state had informally dropped enforcement of the provision years earlier.

Why State Constitutions Vary

Without a doubt, constitutions vary widely from state to state. What explains these differences? Four factors seem particularly important: historical circumstances, political culture, geography, and changing notions of good government.

To understand how historical circumstances and culture can create a constitution—and then be shaped by that constitution—consider the case of Texas. The Lone Star State's current constitution was written in 1876, soon after federal troops had withdrawn and Reconstruction had ended. During Reconstruction, a strong Unionist governor backed by federal troops had governed the state, centralized police and education functions in state hands

in Austin, and generally defied the white Democrats who had been in power before the Civil War. So Texas followed in the footsteps of other southern states and drew up a constitution designed to ensure that the state would never again have an activist state government. Toward that end, the new constitution allowed the legislature to meet only infrequently, limited the governor's power over the executive branch, and provided for an elected judiciary. The document's sole progressive feature was a provision that for the first time allowed women to continue to own property after they were married.[25]

White Democrats' antipathy toward Reconstruction explains much of the content of Texas's 1876 constitution. The state's political culture explains why its constitution has endured to the present. Political scientist Daniel Elazar classifies Texas as a traditionalistic/individualistic state that, in his words, "places a premium on limiting community intervention" and "accepts a natural hierarchical society as part of the ordered nature of things."[26] Although Elazar's categories have blurred in recent years, state constitutions continue to bear them out. In short, Texas's constitution is well suited to the state's political culture—a culture that views strong activist government with suspicion.

In contrast, a constitution that allowed the legislature to meet only every other year would suit a moralistic state poorly. Not surprisingly, moralistic states such as Michigan, Minnesota, and Wisconsin allow their legislatures to meet far more frequently than does Texas. Because they envision fairly robust styles of governance, the constitutions in these states allow the legislatures to meet throughout the year, creating what are, for all intents and purposes, full-time professional legislatures.

New England's propensity for short, framework-oriented constitutions is a variation based noticeably on geography. One political scientist has hypothesized that such a variation may reflect the fact that New England states are small and relatively homogeneous and their citizens are thus less inclined to fight to include in their states' constitutions policies they support.[27]

Of course, history, political culture, and geography aren't the only factors that determine the kind of constitution a state will have. Another important factor is the changing sense of what works best.

Of course, history, political culture, and geography aren't the only factors that determine the kind of constitution a state will have. Another important factor is the changing sense of what works best. In the early 19th century, many states concluded that a system in which the legislature operates with unbridled power simply did not work well, so they changed their constitutions in ways that strengthened the chief executive. Eighty years ago, groups such as the National Municipal League argued that state constitutions should be more like the federal constitution; that is, they should be much shorter documents that provide a framework for governance rather than long documents that get into the details of policies. That argument gave rise to the **model constitution**, a kind of ideal notion of a constitution that states interested in "improving" could adopt. During the 1960s and 1970s, many states did revise their constitutions in ways designed to make their governments more effective, although the latest edition of the model constitution was written in 1968.

Since the mid-20th century, however, some political scientists have questioned the assumptions behind the model constitution movement. To these revisionists, the fact that most state constitutions outside New England are long and policy rich is actually a good thing—a healthy sign of an engaged electorate. Revisionists argue that, although Americans have essentially left it to the U.S. Supreme Court to interpret and on occasion to change the federal constitution, citizens have defended their right to participate by shaping their state constitutions.[28]

How State Constitutions Differ

The most obvious ways state constitutions differ involve their length and ease of amendment. These differences are not simply cosmetic; they almost always reflect the different functions that state constitutions serve. Vermont has the shortest state constitution. Like the U.S. Constitution, its goal is primarily to establish a framework for effective government, not to regulate the details of specific policy matters. This is true to a lesser extent of other states in New England as well.

In contrast, constitutions in other regions of the country tend to be longer and more specific in their policy prescriptions. In most states, voters and interest

groups that want to accomplish particular goals, such as increased state spending on education, will lobby the governor or the legislature. In California, a state with a long, policy-specific constitution that provides for a high degree of direct democracy, people often attempt to amend the constitution instead. Although the majority of political scientists wring their hands about this tendency, it is undeniable that Californians play a role in shaping their constitution that voters in New England cannot. Also note that these two aspects—length and ease of amendment—not only reflect differences in goals and purposes but also directly influence each other. If a constitution is easier to amend, it makes sense that it is more likely to get amended—and that usually means it gets longer. Again, a difference makes a difference.

Operating Rules and Selection for Office

State constitutions create varying organizational structures and operating rules for the constituent elements of state government. They establish different methods and requirements for serving in state politics. Some of these differences reflect the historical differences among states as well as variations in political culture and geography. Other differences reflect differing notions of what makes good government. Sometimes these notions can be quite quirky. Consider the following, for example. To serve as the governor of Oklahoma, a state of 3.8 million people, you must be at least 31 years old. In contrast, to be the chief executive of California's population of 38 million, you need only be 18. You might be eligible to lead one of the nation's largest states, but don't plan on buying beer or wine, even at your own fundraising events!

In addition, state constitutions differ widely in how many statewide elected positions they create and how those positions are filled. One of the most important of these differences has to do with the judiciary. At the federal level, judges are selected by the president and approved by the U.S. Senate. Things work very differently in the states. Some states elect their judges, some states appoint their judges, many states use a combination of appointment and election, and some states use different selection methods for different types of courts. The details of these various systems and their particular pros and cons are discussed in depth in Chapter 9. What's important for our purposes here is that there are big differences from state to state in how judges end up on the bench, and those differences are products

....

Model constitution An expert-approved generic or "ideal" constitution that states sometimes use as a yardstick against which to measure their existing constitutions.

A DIFFERENCE THAT MAKES A DIFFERENCE
KNOW YOUR RIGHTS

Citizens in Missouri have a constitutional right to farm. Californians have a constitutional right to fish, but not to hunt. Hoosiers have a constitutional right to fish and to hunt. Residents in Arkansas have no constitutional right to sue the state government, even if the legislature explicitly gives them permission to do so. Citizens in every state have a constitutional right to a free K–12 education, though how much the state is constitutionally obligated to spend on that education varies wildly.

As discussed in the text, your rights under the U.S. Constitution are uniform; they do not change when you cross state lines. What does change are your rights under state law. Indeed, the fact that state constitutions are not the same is arguably the mother of all differences that make a difference. This is because those constitutional differences make a difference in the liberties and freedoms you are (or are not) guaranteed as a citizen. For example, in California, you have a constitutional right to get copies of pretty much any local government documents you want, and the local government has to foot the bill for providing them. In Ohio, crime victims have a constitutional right to be treated with fairness and respect. Neither of these rights is guaranteed by the U.S. Constitution or by all state constitutions.

There are a number of reasons for all these state constitutional differences. Some are simply idiosyncratic, a product of the politics, issues, personalities, and power dynamics of a particular state's unique history. Some are due to institutional factors, notably the presence or absence of the ballot initiative. This provides a mechanism to bypass the legislature and take proposed constitutional amendments directly to the people. Some are due to informal changes, such as constitutional interpretation in rulings by state supreme courts.

As examples of how these mechanisms translate into meaningful differences, consider hunting and fishing rights in Indiana, and the lack of a right to sue the state government in Arkansas. Prior to 1996, only one state (Vermont) had a guaranteed right to hunt and fish. Currently, more than 20 states do. Indiana offers a fairly typical case study in how and why states have expanded these rights. A freedom to hunt and fish amendment was debated in the state legislature, where it was supported by the National Rifle Association (NRA) and

opposed by environmental groups. The latter saw the proposed amendment as unneeded because no one was proposing to prevent or limit existing hunting and fishing rights. The NRA argued hunting and fishing rights were under increasing attack from environmental groups and constitutional protections were necessary. The legislature passed the proposed amendment and submitted it to the voters, where it was approved by a huge majority in November 2016. The result is that in Indiana, the state constitution now plainly declares that "people have a right . . . to hunt, fish, and harvest wildlife."

While hunting and fishing rights were secured in Indiana through a formal constitutional change, people in Arkansas lost their right to sue their government through an informal change. Specifically, the right to sue the state government was lost because of a 2018 ruling by the Arkansas Supreme Court. The ruling was not arbitrary; it was a product of how the court interpreted the "sovereign immunity" clause of the Arkansas constitution. Sovereign immunity is legal doctrine that basically assumes the government cannot commit a legal wrong and therefore should not be subject to criminal prosecution or a civil lawsuit. Yet, for decades, the legislature had been passing laws allowing a variety of exceptions to the sovereign immunity provision. For example, it gave citizens the right to take the state to court over pay disputes.

The court ruling basically said the legislature did not have the legal authority to do that; in other words, legislators could not pass laws that waived provisions of the state constitution. The court's reasoning was that if a law passed by the legislature conflicts with the state constitution, the constitution trumps the statute. The result of that line of reasoning? No suing the state. The bottom line is that the right to sue state government given by the legislature was nullified by the court's interpretation of the state constitution.

Multiply the Indiana and Arkansas examples by a thousand; substitute hunting, fishing, and the right to sue with scattered political issues that include everything from gun rights to marriage rights to special education needs; and you have a lot of differences—differences that make a difference to your rights.

Sources: J. B. Wogan, "Indiana and Kansas Make Fishing and Hunting a Constitutional Right," *Governing*, November 9, 2016, http://www.governing.com/topics/elections/gov-indiana-kansas-hunting-2016-state-ballot-measure.html; "Want to Sue Your State? In Arkansas, You Can't," *Governing*, January 22, 2018, http://www.governing.com/topics/public-justice-safety/Want-to-Sue-Your-State-You-Cant-in-Arkansas.html.

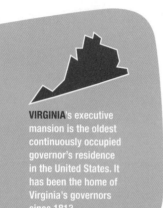

VIRGINIA's executive mansion is the oldest continuously occupied governor's residence in the United States. It has been the home of Virginia's governors since 1813.

of different constitutional approaches to structuring and staffing the judicial branch of government.

Even seemingly small institutional differences created by different constitutional approaches can have big impacts on how state governments work. For example, if a state's constitution gives the executive strong veto powers, the governor may have an easier time getting a recalcitrant legislature to consider his or her point of view on a particular piece of legislation than would a governor with weak veto powers. Similarly, some studies have shown that elected judges are more likely than those more insulated from the ballot box to uphold the death penalty in cases involving capital crimes.[29] In short, the different operating rules embedded in state constitutions lead to very different types of governance.

Distribution of Power

State constitutions make widely differing decisions about where power should reside. Although all state constitutions make at least a bow toward the principle of the separation of powers, in actuality many give one branch of government a preponderance of power. Under some state constitutions, the reins of government are clearly in the hands of the legislature or general assembly. Other states have amended their constitutions to give executives the upper hand.

Traditionally, state constitutions tended to create stronger legislatures and weaker executives. In recent decades, however, even though strong state legislatures are still the norm, constitutional changes in many states have bolstered governors' powers. More than 40 state constitutions now give governors the important power of the **line-item veto**, the ability to veto certain portions of appropriations bills while approving the rest. Exactly what counts as an item, and thus what is fair game for a governor's veto pen, is often unclear. As a result, line-item veto court cases have become a common part of the legal landscape.

....

Line-item veto The power to reject a portion of a bill while leaving the rest intact.

Some states go even further. In Wisconsin, for example, the state constitution allows the governor the power to strike out an appropriation entirely and write in a lower figure.[30] During his term in office, Wisconsin governor Tommy Thompson pushed the power of the partial veto to strike passages and even individual words from bills that came to his desk. In some cases, Thompson would strike individual letters from words within bills, creating new words to change the entire meaning of the legislation. Critics came to call Thompson's creative writing "the Vanna White veto." In one case, Thompson used the Vanna White veto and his Scrabble skills to transform a piece of legislation from a bill that set the maximum detention period for juvenile offenders at 48 hours into one that allowed for a 10-day detention period, a move that enraged the Democratic legislature.[31] Voters later amended the constitution to prohibit that particular veto maneuver. Yet, despite the controversies that surrounded such actions, during his record 14-year reign, Thompson never saw any of his more than 1,900 budget vetoes overturned by the legislature.[32]

The power structures set up by the constitutional systems of some states resist easy classification. Take Texas, for example. The fact that the legislature meets for only five or six months every other year might lead you to think that power in Texas resides primarily with the governor. Not so. In fact, the Texas Constitution arguably makes the office of lieutenant governor the most powerful in the state. In Texas, the lieutenant governor presides over the Senate, appoints Senate committees and assigns bills, and chairs the powerful Texas Legislative Council, which is responsible for researching and drafting bills. Indeed, many observers attribute George W. Bush's two successful terms as governor to his close relationship with his lieutenant governor, Bob Bullock, a Democrat.

Rights Granted

State constitutions differ not only in the mechanisms of governance they create and the sets of constraints and powers they give to government but also in the rights they confer on citizens (see "A Difference That Makes a Difference: Know Your Rights"). For example, the U.S. Constitution does not explicitly mention a right to privacy, although the U.S. Supreme Court did define a limited right to privacy in *Griswold v. Connecticut* (1965). In contrast, Montana's constitution states that "the right to individual privacy is essential to the

Meeting the budget bottom line sometimes means a choice between raising taxes and cutting spending. Illinois governor Bruce Rauner, pictured here, has been a staunch champion of spending cuts.

Daniel Acker/Bloomberg via Getty Images

Representative Government versus Direct Democracy

One of the most striking differences among state constitutions is the degree to which they have (or have not) embraced direct democracy. Most Americans celebrate the United States as a democracy, but the founders believed that they were establishing something somewhat different—a representative democracy. This is a form of government in which qualified representatives of the public make the decisions. Most of the founders viewed direct, or pure, democracy with suspicion. A "pure democracy, by which I mean a society consisting of a small number of citizens, who assemble and administer the government in person, can admit of no cure for the mischiefs of faction," warned James Madison, one of the primary authors of the U.S. Constitution, in his famous argument for the document in *Federalist* No. 10:

> A common passion or interest will, in almost every case, be felt by a majority of the whole . . . and there is nothing to check the inducements to sacrifice the weaker party or an obnoxious individual. Hence it is that such democracies have ever been spectacles of turbulence and contention; have ever been found incompatible with personal security or the rights of property; and have in general been as short in their lives as they have been violent in their deaths.[35]

In other words, Madison believed that entrusting a simple majority with the power to carry out its will would lead to fickle and tyrannical behavior and to a government that would teeter between anarchy and autocracy.

The U.S. Constitution's solution to the problem of pure democracy was to create a representative government, or, as Madison saw it, government by a small group of elected officials "whose wisdom may best discern the true interest of their country."[36] In accordance with this belief, the U.S. Constitution created an upper chamber—the Senate—whose members would be selected by state legislatures from among their eminent men. The document also created an electoral college to elect the president. Both of these decisions were made to insulate the federal government from the whims of the majority. The Constitution makes no provision for direct democratic processes. There is not a single federal officeholder *directly* elected by the entire nation. Indeed,

well-being of a free society and shall not be infringed without the showing of a compelling state interest."[33] As a result, courts in Montana—and in Kentucky and Tennessee—have interpreted the state constitution to protect adults' freedom to engage in consensual oral or anal sex, which until quite recently was illegal in many other states.[34]

Even rights that are directly addressed by the U.S. Constitution are often expanded, clarified, or given more specifics in state constitutions. The gun rights discussion in the introduction to this chapter provides a good example of this. It is not just Alabama, though, that has enshrined a clear right to bear arms in its constitution. The Nebraska Constitution, for example, spells out "the right to keep and bear arms for security or defense of self, family, home, and others, and for lawful common defense, hunting, recreational use, and all other lawful purposes," noting that "such rights shall not be denied or infringed." That leaves a lot less room for argument about gun rights than does the Second Amendment.

as we saw in 2016 with the election of Donald Trump, the Electoral College system can result in a candidate's winning the presidency after losing the popular vote.

Whereas the creators of the federal government took great care to ensure it was insulated from direct democratic processes, many states decided to do just the opposite during the Progressive Era. By giving their citizens the chance to make laws and change their constitutions directly, the Progressives sought to circumvent legislatures and executives they viewed as being beholden to wealthy special interests. As Robert M. La Follette, a leader of the Progressive Party in Wisconsin and later a governor and senator from the state, put it:

> The forces of the special privileges are deeply entrenched. Their resources are inexhaustible. Their efforts are never lax. Their political methods are insidious. It is impossible for the people to maintain perfect organization in mass. They are often taken unaware and are liable to lose at one stroke the achievements of years of effort. In such a crisis, nothing but the united power of the people expressed directly through the ballot can overthrow the enemy.[37]

For politicians such as La Follette, direct democratic mechanisms, such as the ballot initiative and the referendum, represented the general populace's best hope for breaking the power of political bosses and moneyed interests. From 1902 through 1918, direct democracy enjoyed a great vogue in the states. Sixteen states adopted the ballot initiative in that period. After World War I, ballot initiatives lost some of their luster as popular enthusiasm for Progressive ideas waned. Only five states—Alaska (1959), Florida (1968), Wyoming (1968), Illinois (1970), and Mississippi (1992)—have amended their constitutions to allow for ballot initiatives since the end of the Progressive Era.[38] What's more, note where these states are located. The majority of the states that allow direct democracy lie west of the Mississippi River, where the practice fits with much of the West's populist history.[39]

For much of their existence, initiatives and referendums were used sparingly. Then came Proposition 13 in California. In the 1970s, taxpayer activist Howard Jarvis and retired real estate salesman Paul Gann launched what at first seemed a foolishly impractical campaign to roll back California property taxes and cap the rate

at which they could grow. Their campaign struck a chord with many Californians. The state's booming economy had sent property values skyrocketing. Higher property assessments led to higher real estate taxes, which created a huge revenue boom for the state and local governments. Indeed, at the time, the state government had a $5 billion annual surplus. Yet despite the public outcry for relief from rising property costs, Governor Jerry Brown and the rest of the politicians in Sacramento could not agree on a tax reduction plan.

In 1978, California voters passed Proposition 13 and took the decision out of politicians' hands. The proposition directed the state to roll back real estate taxes to 1975 levels and decreed that property assessments could not increase by more than 2 percent a year, regardless of inflation. Most localities previously had reassessed real estate taxes every two years. Proposition 13 decreed that property could be reassessed only when it was sold. The legislation also cut property tax receipts in half and marked the beginning of a nationwide "taxpayer revolt." The revolt culminated in the election of former California governor Ronald Reagan to the presidency two years later.

California's political establishment viewed the passage of Proposition 13 with great trepidation. Politicians worried that the legislation would cripple their ability to pay for the schools and infrastructure that had contributed so much to California's post–World War II successes. These fears proved well founded. In the wake of Proposition 13, California went from having one of the nation's best-funded public school systems (in the top third in terms of per-pupil spending) to having one of the worst (in the bottom third). The proposition put such draconian limits on the ability of local governments to raise revenues that municipalities and counties became increasingly dependent on the state for their funding—so much so that 10 years later, in 1988, California teachers' unions pushed through Proposition 98, which mandated that upwards of 40 percent of California's general revenue go to education.[40]

In addition to complicating government finances and drastically reducing the flexibility of lawmakers in California, the successful passage of Proposition 13 revived interest in ballot initiatives in the 24 other states in which they were permitted. In the three decades from 1940 through 1970, an average of 19 initiatives appeared on ballots per two-year election cycle in the United States. In the 1980s, that number shot up to 50 initiatives in the average election cycle. In the 1990s, it hit 76 per election cycle.[41] In 2016, there were 71 initiatives on state ballots, plus an additional 69 proposed constitutional amendments submitted to a popular vote after passing state legislatures.[42] These numbers suggest that states allowing ballot initiatives are now engaged in an almost continuous cycle of changing their constitutions. These changes are increasingly less about broad questions of good governance and more about pushing narrow agendas.

In the past two decades, the initiative process has been used to push through legislation on some of the most controversial political issues in the entire country. Oregon voters used a ballot initiative to narrowly (51–49 percent) approve physician-assisted suicide in 1994. In California, voters have used initiatives to impose some of the nation's strictest term limits on elected officials (Proposition 140), to end affirmative action (Propositions 209 and 96), to deny education and health benefits to families of illegal immigrants (Proposition 87), to spend $3 billion on stem-cell research (Proposition 71), and to recall a sitting governor and replace him with an action-movie star. In 2016, Colorado voted to give its citizens a constitutionally guaranteed minimum wage (Amendment 70). You can check out the latest ballot initiatives and their electoral fates at Ballotpedia.org, which keeps a running tally of these proposals and how they fare at the ballot box.

The initiative process has become big business. Hundreds of millions can be spent in a single election cycle on battles waged over ballot measures.[43] Several companies are devoted to gathering the signatures needed to get issues placed on ballots for anyone who can afford their services, and signature gathering can be a pretty lucrative business. For example, in the 2016 election cycle, roughly $45 million was spent on gathering signatures for proposed ballot initiatives in California. On average, backers of California's 2016 crop of proposed initiatives shelled out roughly $4 for every signature gathered.[44] Those who have used them successfully see ballot initiatives as tools for circumventing hostile legislatures and acting on the will of the majority. But most political scientists

and close observers of state politics have a different viewpoint. They argue that the results of the use of ballot initiatives only reinforce the wisdom of the founders in their decision to keep direct democratic processes out of the U.S. Constitution. A number of those who have examined initiatives have concluded that the process has been

In the November 1914 election in **CALIFORNIA**, 48 propositions appeared on the statewide ballot.

Lyn Alweis/The Denver Post via Getty Images

▲ An example of a controversial state ballot initiative with far-reaching implications is Colorado's Amendment 70. Passed in 2016, this amendment constitutionally mandates a minimum wage of $12 per hour by 2020.

hijacked by organizations with deep pockets and by individuals who use the initiatives to further their own self-interests. Veteran *Washington Post* political reporter David Broder describes ballot initiatives in scathing terms, calling them "the favored tool of millionaires and interest groups that use their wealth to achieve their own policy goals—a lucrative business for a new set of political entrepreneurs."[45]

Exploiting the public's disdain for politics and distrust of politicians, interest groups with deep pockets now have a mechanism through which they can literally rewrite state constitutions to advance their own agendas. For example, in 1997, Microsoft cofounder and Seattle Seahawks owner Paul Allen made an end run around a balky state legislature and spent $6 million on a ballot initiative that required the state of Washington to foot much of the cost for a new stadium for his team. It proved to be a good investment; the initiative passed with 51 percent of the vote. Although this was welcome news for many football fans, most political scientists probably see it as an illustration of the very problem that Madison identified in *Federalist* No. 10. In some ways, the initiative has created a very odd form of governance in which citizens live under laws that are often resisted by their elected legislators. With its ability to make sweeping changes in state constitutions, the initiative process could radically change the American system of government in the next few decades.

Constitutions for Local Government?

For the most part, substate governments, such as school districts, counties, and many municipalities, are considered subordinate arms of the state. They may seem like autonomous political units, but they in fact operate under state constitutions and at the discretion of state governments. The courts generally have viewed only the federal government and the states as sovereign entities with the right to determine how their authority should be exercised. The authority and power of local governments is largely confined, if not outright dictated, by the states (these issues are discussed in more depth in Chapter 11).

There are some exceptions to this rule. The **municipal charter** is a key example. In a rough sense, municipal charters are similar to the charters that served as the governing documents for the original colonies. Legally, most municipalities are corporations, and their charters describe the purposes of the municipalities and the processes for achieving these objectives. A charter is not a constitution; rather, it is a grant of authority derived from a constitution or from state law. Some states have home rule, which allows municipalities the right to draft and amend their own charters and to regulate local matters within their jurisdictions without interference from the state (see Chapter 11). Some states have

Municipal charter A document that establishes operating procedures for a local government.

municipal home rule provisions in their constitutions; others grant home rule to municipalities through legislation. Municipal home rule means that some local governments are operated by charters that "can take on many characteristics of a constitution."[46] Even in the most liberal home rule states, however, state constitutions and state law generally take precedence over municipal charters.

Conclusion

Even though they tend to fly under the radar, especially compared with the U.S. Constitution, state constitutions play *the* critical role in defining the possibilities of politics in most states. All state constitutions set the basic structure of government, apportion power and responsibilities to particular institutions and political actors, and determine the rights and privileges of citizenship. State constitutions reflect states' distinctive political cultures and, over time, reinforce or alter those traditions.

Beyond this common core of shared functions, however, state constitutions vary greatly. Some protect and extend the rights of the individual beyond the guarantees of the U.S. Constitution; others do not. Perhaps the single biggest difference among state constitutions is the degree to which they serve as a venue for policymaking. In western states, whose constitutions provide for a high degree of direct democracy, advocates and interest groups often attempt to enshrine their policy positions in the state constitutions. As a result, these states have long, detailed constitutions. In contrast, the constitutions of the eastern states, particularly in New England, more closely resemble the U.S. Constitution.

State constitutions tend to have a bad reputation with political scientists, for understandable reasons. Although many function well, in more than a few instances they play an outright disruptive role. In states such as Alabama and Texas, antiquated constitutions have made it difficult for state governments to promote economic development—a function that most people believe the state government should serve. In California and other states, interest groups have used state constitutions to ensure that the states' general revenues flow toward the programs they support. In the process, they have reduced—in some areas drastically—the flexibility of legislatures to make independent decisions, a set of constraints that amounts to putting limits on representative democracy.

But, as political scientist Christopher Hammons has argued from another perspective, the fact that constitutions continue to be a contentious venue for politics in many states is not necessarily all bad. Although it is still theoretically possible to change the U.S. Constitution, for all practical purposes we as a society have given that right over to the U.S. Supreme Court. It takes an extraordinarily contentious issue, such as reproductive rights, to provoke talk about changing the federal constitution. In contrast, citizens continue to exercise their right to tamper with and tweak their state constitutions. Is that all bad?

THE LATEST RESEARCH

State constitutions are one of the most important and understudied aspects of subnational government. While it is not hard to find constitutional scholars in political science, the vast majority of these study the U.S. Constitution, not its state counterparts. More attention is paid to state constitutions in the field of law, but even there scholars focusing on state constitutions regularly lament the relative lack of research available on these centrally important legal documents.

This lack of attention is surprising because, as the studies listed below amply demonstrate, state constitutions are important—not just as the bases for much of the criminal and civil law in the United States but also as documents that reflect deeper philosophical notions of what a government is, what it should do, and what rights citizens should or should not have. Below we summarize some of the more recent and prominent research on state constitutions. All these studies reflect a constant theme: not just the central importance of state constitutions to the American political system but also how those constitutions are constantly changing and creating differences in state-level legal structure that have big, real-world impacts on the lives of state residents.

- **Versteeg, Mila, and Emily Zackin,** "Constitutions Unentrenched: Toward an Alternative Theory of Constitutional Design," *American Political Science Review* 110 (2016): 657–674.

It's conventional wisdom among constitutional theorists that constitutions seek to entrench political principles. In other words, whatever political arrangements are laid down in a constitution tend, as a rule, to be resistant to change and stable over the long term. That conventional wisdom, however, is strongly influenced by thinking about the U.S. Constitution. Versteeg and Zackin's study mounts a persuasive case to the contrary by looking at constitutional change in other democratic countries and, especially important for our purposes, in the states. What they find is that far from preserving a broad set of principles in political amber, constitutions are dynamic and constantly being revised. A key part of their analysis is a comparative study of state constitutions on the basis of an "entrenchment score." The latter simply is the number of years the state has existed divided by the total number of years in which it has experienced a constitutional change, through either amendment or replacement. Higher numbers indicate more "entrenchment," in other words, less change. Over the past two centuries, entrenchment scores have steadily decreased—today, they are roughly 75 percent lower than their historical highs. In other words, state constitutions are so frequently revised they almost certainly cannot support conventional wisdom on constitutional entrenchment.

- **Zackin, Emily,** *Looking for Rights in All the Wrong Places: Why State Constitutions Contain America's Positive Rights* (Princeton, NJ: Princeton University Press, 2013).

The U.S. Constitution is different from the constitutions of other nations in that it almost exclusively emphasizes negative rather than positive rights. A negative right is a right that you are free to exercise without government interference; Congress, for example, is constitutionally prohibited from interfering with your right to speak your mind or practice your religious beliefs. A positive right, in contrast, requires government to take positive action, to provide you with a good or service. The U.S. Constitution is pretty quiet on what services government owes its people, and this has led a lot of legal scholars to conclude that the United States really has no established tradition of positive rights. In this book, Zackin disagrees, arguing that there is a strong tradition of positive rights in the United States; legal scholars haven't found these rights because they have been looking in the wrong

(Continued)

(Continued)

place. She suggests that Americans actually have quite a lot of positive rights—for example, they have a right to a free public education. These positive rights, however, are found not in the U.S. Constitution but in state constitutions.

- **Tarr, G. Alan**, "Explaining State Constitutional Change," *The Wayne Law Review* 60 (2014): 9–30.

This is an in-depth examination of the "constitutional space" of the states and how they use it. Tarr, one of the best-known contemporary scholars of state constitutions, begins by explaining how, constitutionally speaking, the states are relatively unconstrained in what they can do with their constitutions. The federal constitution takes precedence over state constitution and laws, but outside of that, states are pretty much free to fashion their constitutions as they see fit. What

have they done with that "space"? Tarr provides an in-depth analysis that shows states have done quite a lot. States have used their constitutional space to aggressively experiment and innovate, frequently revising their constitutions and moving them in directions that have no real analogue at the federal level. They have provided for mechanisms of direct democracy, created (local) governments not mentioned in the U.S. Constitution, and guaranteed gender equality, privacy, and other rights and freedoms that go far beyond the federal constitution. All this activity in the constitutional space made available to states raises a lot of questions. Is change constant, or are there periods of heavy reform activity and periods of stability? Where do states get their ideas for constitutional change? Why do states pursue different avenues of constitutional change? In examining potential answers to those questions, Tarr details patterns in the dynamics of state-level constitutional change.

CHAPTER 3

for CQ Press

Want a better grade?

Get the tools you need to sharpen your study skills. SAGE edge offers a robust online environment featuring an impressive array of free tools and resources.

Access practice quizzes, eFlashcards, video, and multimedia at **edge.sagepub.com/ smithgreenblatt7e**

Top Ten Takeaways

1. The United States operates under a system of dual constitutionalism, which means state and federal governments are cosovereign powers and run in accordance with the rules laid down in their respective constitutions.

2. State constitutions fulfill many of the same functions as the U.S. Constitution. For example, all create three primary branches of government (executive, legislative, judicial), provide a general governmental framework, and guarantee certain rights to citizens.

3. While similar in general terms, state constitutions vary enormously, so the powers and responsibilities of different government actors and institutions, as well as the rights of citizens, vary from state to state.

4. State constitutions are different from the U.S. Constitution in important ways. For example, they tend to be longer, more specific, and easier to change, and they grant plenary rather than limited powers to government.

5. State constitutions originated in colonial charters, documents issued by the British monarchy granting individuals or corporations the right to govern areas within the American colonies. State constitutions as we know them were developed after independence and have changed considerably—much more so than the U.S. Constitution—in the past 250 years.

6. State constitutions can be formally changed in several ways, including through legislative proposals, ballot initiatives, and constitutional conventions. Typically, all proposed changes to a state constitution must be ratified by popular vote.

7. State constitutions can also be changed informally, notably through the process of judicial review.

8. State constitutions differ from one another because they are reflections of the different histories, political cultures, and politics of individual states.

9. One of the most important differences between state constitutions, and between state constitutions and the U.S. Constitution, lies in whether or not they permit direct democracy. Roughly half of the states allow some form of direct democracy. Other states, and the U.S. Constitution, allow only representative democracy.

10. Unlike states, local governments are not sovereign governments and therefore do not have constitutions. However, in some states, at least some municipalities operate under municipal charters, which have some of the basic elements of a constitution, although they are all clearly subordinate to the state constitution.

Key Concepts

appropriations bills (p. 57)
ballot initiatives (p. 61)
bicameral legislatures (p. 58)
colonial charters (p. 57)

constitutional amendments (p. 55)
constitutional convention (p. 59)

constitutional revision commissions (p. 63)
direct democracy (p. 54)
dual constitutionalism (p. 55)
electorate (p. 54)

(Continued)

(Continued)

franchise (p. 58)	model constitution (p. 68)	ratification (p. 61)
Jim Crow laws (p. 59)	municipal charter (p. 74)	Reconstruction (p. 65)
judicial federalism (p. 54)	natural law or higher law	referendums (p. 61)
judicial review (p. 65)	(p. 55)	separation of powers (p. 58)
line-item veto (p. 70)	plenary power (p. 55)	unicameral legislatures (p. 58)

Suggested Websites

- **www.iandrinstitute.org**. Website for the Initiative and Referendum Institute at the University of Southern California, a clearinghouse for information about the initiative and referendum processes of the states.

- **statecon.camden.rutgers.edu**. Website for the Center for State Constitutional Studies at Rutgers University–Camden, an interdisciplinary institute focused on studying state constitutions.

State of *Massachusetts-Bay.*

In the House of REPRESENTATIVES, February 19, 1779.

WHEREAS the Constitution or Form of Civil Government, which was proposed by the late Convention of this State to the People thereof, hath been disapproved by a Majority of the Inhabitants of said State:

And whereas it is doubtful, from the Representations made to this Court, what are the Sentiments of the major Part of the good People of this State as to the Expediency of now proceeding to form a new Constitution of Government:

Therefore, *Resolved,* That the Selectmen of the several Towns within this State cause the Freeholders, and other Inhabitants in their respective Towns duly qualified to vote for Representatives, to be lawfully warned to meet together in some convenient Place therein, on or before the last Wednesday of *May* next, to consider of and determine upon the following Questions.

First, Whether they chuse at this Time to have a new Constitution or Form of Government made.

Secondly, Whether they will impower their Representatives for the next Year to vote for the calling a State Convention, for the sole Purpose of forming a new Constitution.

Scott Heins/Bloomberg via Getty Images

Finance

Filling the Till and Paying the Bills

For a decade or so, many states helped keep budgets in check by underinvesting in public education. In 2018, teachers in a number of these states responded to low wages and poor working conditions by engaging in wildcat strikes to pressure lawmakers into spending more.

Chapter Objectives

After reading this chapter, you will be able to

- Explain what taxes generate revenue to the states,
- Identify other state revenue sources,
- Discuss why taxing varies between state and local governments, and
- Describe the budget process and restraints on budgeting.

State governments spend a lot of money on public education. Roughly 20 cents out of every dollar going out the state treasury door is headed toward K–12 schools, a total of roughly $385 billion in fiscal 2017 (the latest data available).[1] And that, quite literally, is only the half of it. Local governments spend a similar amount, and the federal government also kicks in billions. While a precise figure is hard to nail down, a reasonable guess is that something north of $700 billion is spent every year on public schools. That sounds like a lot of money. And it is.

What is not a lot of money is the average teacher's paycheck. On average, public school teachers earn between $50,000 and $60,000, which may not sound that bad. Keep in mind, though, that the average teacher has been working for a decade or two and, more often than not, has a master's degree.[2] Right out of college, some teachers still start their careers earning under $30,000 a year, and hourly wages in some districts can skate pretty close to the flipping-burgers pay scale—as low as 15 bucks an hour.[3] In 2018, teacher frustration with low wages, increasingly expensive benefits, and often nonexistent annual salary increases boiled over into political action. Teachers in West Virginia, Oklahoma, Kentucky, and Arizona threatened strikes and, in some cases, made good on their threats. To take a specific example, by 2018 teachers in Oklahoma hadn't had a state-funded pay increase in 10 years. Wages were so low emergency teaching certificates had to be issued just to get someone—anyone—to step in and take up one of the nearly 2,000 unfilled teaching jobs in the state. Many schools were so financially strapped they couldn't afford new textbooks and were operating on a four-day week.[4] In spring 2018, Oklahoma teachers had had enough. They staged a walkout demanding not just a pay hike but that the state legislature reverse years of underinvestment in public education.

What the heck is going on here? How can we spend all those hundreds of billions of dollars, and yet teachers are paid so little in some districts they literally qualify for food stamps?[5] How can all that money still leave some districts so starved for cash they operate on four-day weeks and use out-of-date textbooks over and over? Well, like most government services, public education is a people-intensive business. And people—even if you just pay them subsistence wages—are expensive. A whole swath of states—Kansas, Oklahoma, Arizona, Louisiana, Texas, and many more—have spent the better part of a decade focusing on cutting taxes, which left them with less revenue to spend on things like keeping teacher salaries up with inflation. State officials can justifiably say they spend a lot on education. And teachers can justifiably say it's not nearly enough. Welcome to the basic problem of government budgeting: everyone wants something from government, but they mostly want someone else to pay for it. Most people agree that public education is an important priority, and most would allow that the full-time, college-educated professionals in the classroom should be paid at least enough to keep them out of the welfare line. But how much, exactly, should we spend on education? And where is that money coming from? Good luck finding a consensus on answers to those questions. Disagreement leads to fierce political fights, not to mention a situation where we collectively spend $700 billion on a public service and expect the people who provide it to consign themselves to a life of tight budgets and eroding purchasing power.

Education is a good example of the central conflict at the heart of public budgeting: what do we want from government, and how much are we willing to pay for it? The problem, of course, is that we want a lot—good schools, good roads, safe streets, affordable health care—and, all else equal, we'd prefer that somebody else pay for it. Squaring that financial circle is harder for state governments than for the federal government because states operate within tighter financial constraints. Virtually all states (Vermont is the only exception) are required by law to balance their operating budgets every year, and most local governments are in the same boat. At the federal level, when the bills add up to more than what's coming in, Congress is free to borrow to cover the gap. It can also, quite literally, print more money. In other words, the federal government can run **budget deficits**, or **shortfalls**, as much as it likes. Not so for state and local governments. They can delay the inevitable by cooking the books with fancy accounting tricks and hoping for the best, but even the sharpest of bean counters cannot shield them from the hard fact that the law requires their ledgers to be balanced. Sooner or later, when income minus expenditure consistently results in a negative number, there is no avoiding the painful choices to be made, whether that involves increasing revenue (higher taxes) or cutting spending (reducing programs or services). That's exactly what happened in some states with public education. For years, many states have managed to balance the books and cut taxes, in part, by underfunding education. To raise teacher pay and reinvest in schools, lawmakers have little choice but to increase expenditures, and that means higher taxes. And that creates a big stink: most people want good public schools, but no one wants a higher tax bill.

There is a tendency among some students to think of taxes and budgets as a bit of a yawn—isn't this topic dry, technical, and boring? In reality, budgets and taxes are among the most important and consequential topics in this book. Budgets are the subject of some of the most intense political struggles in state and local politics. As the 2018 teacher strikes demonstrated, budgetary conflicts are not just about dollars and cents—they are fundamentally about policy and conflicting political

visions. Indeed, in many ways, budgets are *the* central policy documents of government. If you want to know what is important to government and the people who run it, the budget will tell you. Even if the choices are all painful—raising taxes and/or figuring out what gets cut and by how much—the decisions will still tell you what your state or local government's priorities are.

In 2015 (the latest figures available), state and local governments pulled in around $3.4 trillion in **revenues**—mostly from income, sales, and property taxes; intergovernmental transfers; and assorted **user fees**.[6] They spent a roughly equal amount. By anyone's standards, that is a lot of money. Are these governments taxing and spending too much? Too little? Attempts to answer these questions are at the heart of some of the most heated conflicts in state and local (not to mention national) politics. In this chapter, we are going to take a look at how state and local governments raise all this money and what they spend it on. We will examine why state and local governments make such different taxing and spending choices, and explore the consequences of these varying choices. As you read through this chapter, keep in mind the following questions:

- **What are the differences between progressive and regressive tax systems?**
- **Why are property taxes so important to communities?**
- **How does the federal government support state and local budgets?**
- **Are states' revenue and spending programs sustainable?**

Budgets are extremely important because they are fundamentally about policy. Indeed, in many ways, they are the central policy documents of government. They determine and reflect the policy orientations of elected leaders. If you want to know what your state or local government's priorities are, the budget will tell you.

Budget deficits or shortfalls Cash shortages that result when the amount of money coming into the government falls below the amount being spent.

Revenues The money governments bring in, mainly from taxes.

User fees Charges levied by governments in exchange for services. Such fees constitute a type of hidden tax.

Show Me the Money: Where State Tax Revenues Come From

Six types of taxes constitute the major funding sources of state and local governments, accounting for roughly half of all revenues. These are sales taxes, including **excise taxes**, often referred to as **sin taxes**, on tobacco and alcohol; property taxes; income taxes; motor vehicle taxes; **estate taxes**, also called death taxes; and **gift taxes**.

Sales Taxes

In 2015, state and local governments took in about $544 billion in **sales taxes**—about 15 percent of total state and local government tax revenues.[7] Sales taxes are especially important to state governments; roughly 80 percent of all sales taxes go into state coffers. Most states also allow at least some counties and cities to levy additional sales taxes. Currently, about 7,500 localities do so. Some states, such as California, return a small percentage of sales taxes to the areas in which the purchases were made. State governments and, to a much lesser extent, local governments also take in significant sums from gasoline taxes and sin taxes on tobacco and alcohol. States differ widely in how they apply sin taxes, and various factors often influence what gets taxed and how much. For example, North Carolina, which has a large tobacco-growing industry, levied a tax of only $0.45 on each pack of cigarettes sold in 2018. In New York, which has no large-scale tobacco industry, the tax on a pack of cigarettes was $4.35.[8]

Politicians like sales taxes because they tend to be less visible to constituents than taxes on income are. As such, sales taxes are less likely to cause voters to retaliate against the politicians at the polls. Economists like sales taxes because they are **focused consumption taxes** that do not distort consumer behavior. That is, sales taxes, even relatively high ones, often do not cause consumers to buy less.

This does not mean that sales taxes do not receive their share of criticism. Many liberals and advocates for low-income people complain that these are **regressive taxes**. If Bill Gates buys a grande latte, he pays about $0.28 in sales tax; a freshman at the University of Washington pays exactly the same. While the amount of the tax is the same, the student is paying a much higher percentage of his or her income to the government than Gates is. Put another way, if Gates's income

were even a mere $5 million a year and a typical student's income is $2,500 a year, guess how much Gates would have to pay in sales tax on that latte to face the same **tax burden** as a typical student. Give up? His grande latte would cost him a whopping but tax-proportionate $560. Of course, as already noted, it doesn't really work that way. If and when Gates goes to a coffee shop, he pays the same price and the same sales tax as anyone else.

States often do attempt to make their sales taxes less of a burden on low-income residents by exempting necessities such as food, clothing, and electric and gas utilities from taxation. In general, however, states that rely heavily on sales taxes tend to have more regressive tax systems than do other states. Take, for example, Tennessee, a state that relies heavily on sales taxes rather than assessing personal income taxes. Rich and poor alike pay a 7 percent state sales tax at the cash register. That's bad enough, but local governments can add an extra sales tax on top of that. For instance, residents in Memphis have to pay an additional 2.25 percent sales tax; effectively, the sales tax in Memphis is 9.25 percent. The upshot of such a heavy reliance on sales taxes is that low-income residents pay a higher percentage of their incomes in taxes than they might if they lived in a state that relies more on income taxes. That makes Tennessee's tax system highly regressive.

Sales taxes have another problem: they still have not been fully adjusted for a 21st-century economy. Modern sales taxes basically date to the 1930s, when states began introducing them as a Depression-era revenue raiser.[9] At the time, sales were largely conceived of as transactions in which customers went into real brick-and-mortar stores and bought products. In other words, the levy was conceived as percentage of the monetary value of a

Excise or sin taxes Taxes on alcohol, tobacco, and other similar products that are designed to raise revenues and reduce use.

Estate taxes Taxes levied on a person's estate or total holdings after that person's death.

Gift taxes Taxes imposed on money transfers made during an individual's lifetime.

Sales taxes Taxes levied by state and local governments on purchases.

Focused consumption taxes Taxes that do not alter spending habits or behavior patterns and therefore do not distort the distribution of resources.

Regressive taxes Taxes levied on all taxpayers regardless of income or ability to pay, placing proportionately more of a burden on those with lower incomes.

Tax burden A measurement of taxes paid as a proportion of income.

tangible thing—a car, a can of beans, a shovel—bought in a store geographically located within state borders. These days, though, a lot of what we buy are not tangible things, but services. And we are increasingly purchasing the things we buy online, not down at the local general store. Think of it like this: Given that 45 states impose a general sales tax, if you buy a massage chair at a local store, you will very likely pay a percentage of the price to the government. If you just go get a massage instead—in other words, you purchase a service rather than a thing—there's a decent chance you will pay no sales tax. If you buy a massage chair online, depending on which state you live in and which state the chair is actually shipped from, there's also a reasonable chance you could escape paying sales tax.

This sort of thing creates a fiscal double whammy for the state. The government loses sales tax revenues from the online purchase, and the brick-and-mortar stores selling massage chairs the old-fashioned way are put at a competitive disadvantage because the products they sell are subject to sales tax. If those businesses start to suffer and jobs are lost, the state might lose not only sales tax revenue but also income tax revenue.

Because sales taxes are such an important revenue source, states have begun to adapt to these new economic realities. Many states now levy sales taxes on services. For example, many states have started levying what is sometimes called a "yoga tax"—that is, a sales tax on services related to physical fitness.[10] There is no general agreement, however, on what services (if any) are appropriate to subject to a sales tax. And even extending the reach of sales taxes to a broad set of services does little to prevent the loss of sales taxes to e-commerce. Large e-retailers can choose to locate their businesses physically in places with tax advantages and other economic benefits and do business online with residents in other states.[11] If a retailer has no physical presence in a state, how is that state supposed to collect taxes from the company's online transactions? States have been urging Congress to impose a national set of regulations for taxing online sales. The basic idea is to establish a national tax on Internet sales, the money from which would be distributed to the states, allowing them to recoup the tax revenue lost to online purchases. Congress, though, has yet to pass a law imposing a uniform online sales tax framework nationwide.

Frustrated with federal inaction, states have taken matters into their own hands—a number of them have passed so-called Amazon laws, regulations that allow them to tax online and/or out-of-state sellers. These laws are tough to enforce, but the plan in passing them was not just to try and collect sales taxes, but also a legal maneuver. States wanted to provoke litigation with online retailers with the goal of working that lawsuit through the legal system and ultimately getting the U.S. Supreme Court to reconsider its ruling in *Quill Corp. v. North Dakota* (1992).[12] In that case, the Court held that a state could not impose sales taxes on a business that did not have a physical location in the state. This ruling, though, was made at the dawn of the Internet age, before e-commerce was part of the mainstream economy and its potential to erode state sales tax collection was fully understood. Online commerce these days, of course, is a mature business model, and the states were banking on the hope that the Court would give them more leeway to tax online transactions now that buying stuff online is just what people do.

In 2018, states got their wish when the U.S Supreme Court agreed to hear arguments in *South Dakota v. Wayfair, Inc.*, which pitted an online retailer against South Dakota, which had passed a law requiring Internet businesses to collect and submit state sales taxes. The Court's ruling in this case effectively overturned the *Quill* decision and allows states to collect sales taxes from online retailers whether they have a physical presence in the state or not. What matters now is whether the sale is made to a state resident and whether the state in question has a law requiring online retailers to collect a sales tax. As such laws are now constitutional, online retailers have to charge applicable sales taxes as the price of doing virtual business in that state. The stakes in this ruling could hardly be higher—by some estimates as much as $26 billion in additional sales tax revenue.[13]

Property Taxes

While sales taxes are the biggest single source of revenue for states, property taxes are the primary funder of local governments. In 2015, state and local governments combined raised about $488 billion in property taxes, with the vast majority of that going to local governments.[14] Just about every local government relies on property tax revenues, although property tax rates vary widely not only from state to state but also from community to community. On average, homeowners in the United States pay an effective tax rate of about 1.20 percent.[15] The word *effective* simply acknowledges that some places have exemptions and adjustments that make the effective tax rate lower than the nominal tax rate.

Effective tax rates vary enormously, from an average of 2.31 percent in New Jersey to 0.32 percent in Hawaii. Why would states have such different rates? Partially, it's dependent on political decisions about how public services get paid for. So, for example, states with lower property taxes tend to have higher sales and/or income taxes—the basic rule of thumb is that if you rely less on one tax revenue stream, you have to do more to maximize another. And keep in mind that how property tax rates translate into the dollars and cents of a property tax bill also varies wildly because it's not just the rate that counts, but the value of the property. For example, New Mexico (0.97 percent) and Virginia (0.99 percent) have virtually identical average property tax rates. The average homeowner in Virginia, though, pays considerably more in property taxes—$3,181 versus $2,214—simply because homes tend to be worth more in Virginia compared to New Mexico.

Joanne Rathe/The Boston Globe via Getty Images

How much you pay in taxes depends on where you live. Property taxes are the least popular tax for homeowners.

The Education Connection

Property taxes are important for another reason: they pretty much finance public elementary and high school education, and account for roughly a third of all local government expenditures.[16] In most states, where you live determines how many education dollars your children will receive. Wealthy communities with high housing values raise the most money from property taxes. School districts in these areas tend to have the most educational resources. Conversely, school districts in the poorest areas have the fewest resources. While state and federal governments make some effort to narrow these funding gaps, the fact that school funding is so heavily reliant on local property values means these gaps are stubbornly persistent. For example, one study estimates that in Pennsylvania, per-pupil spending is about a third lower in the poorest school districts than it is in well-off school districts.[17] The bottom line is that when schools are heavily dependent on property taxes,

it is all but impossible to equalize resources. If states do nothing, schools in areas with high property values will have bigger budgets; if states try to equalize resources, they have to find the money (read: raise taxes), which is never popular and is especially resented if viewed as a tactic to divert money from local schools to nonlocal schools.

The Pros and Cons of Property Taxes

Property owners generally pay their property taxes twice a year in large lump sums. As such, these taxes tend to be highly visible and extremely unpopular with the public. However, local officials like them because property tax receipts are historically less volatile and more predictable than other types of tax revenues. Local revenue departments assess the values of houses and businesses and then send the owners their tax bills, so the local government knows exactly how much revenue a property tax will yield.

In most instances, taxes seem worse when the economy is bad. Property taxes are the exception. They tend to rise most sharply when a town or city is experiencing an economic boom and housing prices are soaring. In these circumstances, an upsurge in property values can lead to a backlash.

The most famous of such backlashes occurred in California in 1978. In response to years of rising property values and related taxes, Californians passed Proposition 13. This piece of legislation capped the property tax rate at 1 percent of a property's purchase price and froze property assessments at their 1978 levels until the property is resold. Newcomers to a neighborhood have to pay property taxes based on the actual value of their houses.

To this day, Proposition 13 is hotly debated. Conservatives have long praised the movement that gave rise to it. They say that it was the harbinger of the conservative politics that former California governor Ronald Reagan would bring to Washington three years later. Most experts, however, believe that its effects have been devastating, especially to education. Prior to Proposition 13, California was one of the most generous contributors to public education among the U.S. states; in the years since, it has become one of the least generous.

Even the most liberal electorates can be goaded into atypical action by rising property tax rates. In 1980, Massachusetts voters passed Proposition 2½, which capped property tax increases at, you guessed it, 2½ percent. As a result, towns that want to increase spending by more than that, for such needs as increased funding for education, have to hold special override sessions. Towns also have come to rely on user fees (a phenomenon examined later in this chapter).

Many state and local governments have attempted to ease the burden of property taxes on senior citizens and, in some cases, on other low-income individuals. In about 50 Massachusetts towns, senior citizens can reduce their property taxes by performing volunteer work. Cook County, Illinois, limits property tax rate increases by tying them to the national rate of inflation.[18] Despite these efforts, tensions between retirees living on fixed incomes and parents eager to spend more on local schools are commonplace. These pressures can be particularly acute in areas with large numbers of retirees. Indeed, some "active-adult retirement communities" ban families with children altogether.

Another hidden cost of property taxes is worth noting. You might think that commercial and residential property owners are the only ones who pay, right? You're off the hook if you rent, right? Wrong! Most economists believe that landlords pass the cost

of property tax increases on to renters in the form of rent increases.

Income Taxes

Personal **income taxes** account for roughly 10 percent of total state and local tax revenues, about $367 billion in 2015.[19] That makes income tax revenue the third most significant source of state and local government income. In some ways, however, this figure conceals more than it reveals. Almost all nonfederal income tax revenues go to state governments.[20] In many states, personal income taxes are assessed on a graduated scale, so those who earn more pay a greater percentage of their income in taxes. In states that rely more heavily on the income tax than on the sales tax, this structure creates a more **progressive tax system**.

As with property taxes, states have different approaches to income taxes, with some using such taxes as a primary revenue source and others shunning them altogether. Alaska, Florida, Nevada, New Hampshire, South Dakota, Tennessee, Texas, Washington, and Wyoming impose no income taxes at all. Your state's reliance (or lack of reliance) on income taxes influences not just how much you take home in your paycheck but also how much stuff costs. This is because states that do not collect income taxes usually rely heavily on sales tax revenues. States that have no sales tax tend to make up the loss by taking a bigger bite out of income. Oregon, for example, has no sales tax and is thus heavily reliant on income taxes (individual and corporate) as a primary revenue source. Voters in Oregon endorsed, and even increased, the state's reliance on its income tax in January 2010 by approving an increase in the tax rate on the highest-wage earners—the first time they had approved such an increase since 1930.

Two states, Alaska and New Hampshire, have neither income taxes nor sales taxes. How do they manage to function without two of the primary sources of revenue for most state governments? Alaska relies on geology: The Prudhoe Bay oil fields bring in so much money that the state has little need for other revenue streams. Or at least it did until the collapse of oil prices hit state revenues hard, creating a cautionary tale about relying too heavily on a single revenue source. Alaska's latest state oil revenue forecasts suggest income from oil money is going to be flat, or even decline, well into the next decade.[21] The difference for New Hampshire is mostly the residents' hardheaded resistance to taxation. Unlike

....

Income taxes Taxes on wages and interest earned.

Progressive tax system A system of taxation in which the rate paid reflects ability to pay.

Alaska, New Hampshire has no big alternate revenue source—it just makes do. According to Donald Boyd, a fellow at the Lincoln Institute of Land Policy, New Hampshire's state government simply does less than most state governments. The state relies almost exclusively on local governments to finance elementary and secondary education rather than raising state revenue for this purpose. Unlike many other states, it also has managed to avoid court orders to spend dramatically more on secondary school education. It is able to do all this, in part, because the average New Hampshire resident has one of the highest levels of income in the country. The people of New Hampshire are able to pay for a lot of goods and services for themselves.

These states are the exceptions. On average, Americans pay about $1,068 a year in state income taxes.[22] However, residents of states with high tax rates, such as Maryland, Massachusetts, New York, and Oregon, pay significantly more in income taxes. (See Table 4-1.)

Other Tax Revenue Sources: Cars, Oil, and Death

Car registrations, deaths, and oil and other natural resources also are major sources of state revenues. For example, in 2015, car licensing and registration fees brought in about $26.4 billion to state and local governments. Thirty-two states also levy **severance taxes** on natural resources that are removed, or severed, from the state. Some states are quite creative about devising severance taxes. Washington, for example, taxes oysters and salmon and other game fish caught in the state. But despite some creative taxing, the only states that raise real money from severance taxes are those with significant coal, oil, and natural gas reserves, such as Wyoming, North Dakota, and Alaska. Alaska, for example, pulled in more than a billion in oil and gas taxes in 2018.[23]

Show Me the Money: Income from Fees, Charges, and Uncle Sam

The total tax revenues discussed so far add up to a lot of money, but not to the $3.4 trillion that actually flowed into state and local government coffers in 2015. Where does the rest of the money come from? Some of it comes from a variety of miscellaneous taxes we have not specifically discussed, such as fuel taxes and corporate (as opposed to individual) income taxes. Other sources of revenue include fees and user charges, insurance trust money, and intergovernmental transfers.

These sources of revenue can be significant. In 2015, state and local governments raised $216 billion from "miscellaneous general revenue." This includes everything from highway tolls to hunting licenses to utility fees. Although they are less visible than sales, income, or property taxes, government levies in the form of university tuitions, public hospital charges, airport use fees, school lunch sales, and park permits make a big difference to the bottom line. It would take a separate book to examine all of these other sources of revenue, but two are worth mentioning here because of their big impact on the bottom lines of state and local governments: insurance trust funds and intergovernmental transfers.

Insurance Trust Funds

The amount of money shown on a pay stub before any deductions are taken out can be pretty impressive; the actual amount of the paycheck can be a bit disappointing. What many wage earners may not realize is that they are not the only ones paying the taxes and fees they see deducted from their paychecks. Their employers often have to match these payroll taxes and deductions. These **insurance trust funds** go to their state governments and to the federal government. Ultimately, the contributions are invested to support Social Security and retirement programs, workers' compensation and disability programs, and other related insurance programs that benefit employees. In 2015, insurance trust funds accounted for roughly $323 billion in state and local government revenues.[24]

Severance taxes Taxes on natural resources that are removed from a state.

Insurance trust funds Money collected from contributions, assessments, insurance premiums, and payroll taxes.

TABLE 4-1 ● State Individual Income Tax Collections per Capita, Fiscal Year 2016

State	Individual Income Tax Collections per Capita	Rank	State	Individual Income Tax Collections per Capita	Rank
Alabama	$ 719	35	Nebraska	$ 1,177	13
Alaska[a]	$ –	—	Nevada[a]	$ –	—
Arizona	$ 574	40	New Hampshire[b]	$ 66	42
Arkansas	$ 931	29	New Jersey	$ 1,488	7
California	$ 2,055	4	New Mexico	$ 676	37
Colorado	$ 1,173	14	New York	$ 2,345	1
Connecticut	$ 2,106	3	North Carolina	$ 1,186	12
Delaware	$ 1,168	17	North Dakota	$ 465	41
Florida[a]	$ –	—	Ohio	$ 703	36
Georgia	$ 1,012	23	Oklahoma	$ 764	34
Hawaii	$ 1,481	8	Oregon	$ 1,882	6
Idaho	$ 905	30	Pennsylvania	$ 933	28
Illinois	$ 1,076	22	Rhode Island	$ 1,169	16
Indiana	$ 787	31	South Carolina	$ 780	32
Iowa	$ 1,135	20	South Dakota[a]	$ –	—
Kansas	$ 768	33	Tennessee[b]	$ 49	43
Kentucky	$ 965	26	Texas[a]	$ –	—
Louisiana	$ 612	38	Utah	$ 1,108	21
Maine	$ 1,166	18	Vermont	$ 1,171	15
Maryland	$ 1,414	10	Virginia	$ 1,454	9
Massachusetts	$ 2,115	2	Washington[a]	$ –	—
Michigan	$ 937	27	West Virginia	$ 1,009	24
Minnesota	$ 1,943	5	Wisconsin	$ 1,297	11
Mississippi	$ 603	39	Wyoming[a]	$ –	—
Missouri	$ 989	25	United States (average)	$ 1,068	—
Montana	$ 1,137	19			

Source: Tax Foundation, *Facts and Figures 2016: How Does Your State Compare?* (Washington, DC: Tax Foundation, 2018), Table 13, https://taxfoundation.org/facts-figures-2018/.

[a]State does not tax wage income.

[b]State does not tax wage income but does tax interest and dividend income.

Intergovernmental Transfers

State and local governments also get significant revenues from **intergovernmental transfers**. In the case of state governments, that means transfers from the federal government. In the case of local governments, it means transfers from both state and federal governments. These can add up to significant sums. In 2015, for example, the federal government provided some $657 billion to state and local governments, and the biggest expenditure item for most state governments—K–12 education—is money that is actually spent by a local authority.[25] The vast majority of federal funds go to specific state programs. Medicaid, the joint state–federal health insurance program for low-income people and people with disabilities, is by far the largest recipient. In 2016, Medicaid costs totaled about $550 billion, 60 percent of which came from the federal government.[26] Medicaid is far from the only program wholly or partially run by state and local governments that receives federal funding: Education (both K–12 and postsecondary), transportation projects, and public welfare also receive significant dollars from the federal government. Local governments receive funding for various programs—most notably, K–12 education—from state governments as well. Many states have funding formulas that provide significant state aid to local school districts.

Local governments generally welcome money from state sources, but relationships between state governments and county and city governments have not always been easy. Over the course of the past decade, many city and county governments have found themselves stuck with unfunded mandates. These requirements have been imposed on them by federal or state legislation that forces them to perform certain tasks but fails to provide them with the money to carry out those tasks. Transfers of money and responsibilities, however, continue to be commonplace.[27]

Taxing Variations among State and Local Governments

Generalizations about state and local finances should not obscure the fact that different states and localities tax themselves in very different ways and at very different rates. As we have been hinting throughout our discussion thus far, differences make a difference. The first and most obvious difference concerns the very different tax burdens that states choose to impose on themselves.

New York residents pay more per capita in state and local taxes than do the residents of any other state in the country, forking over roughly 13 percent of their incomes in state and local taxes. In contrast, residents of states like Alaska, Texas, and Wyoming pay only about half as much in per capita taxes as New Yorkers.[28]

State and local governments do not just choose to tax themselves at different rates; they also choose to tax themselves in different ways. Residents of many Tennessee counties pay sales taxes of almost 10 percent. New Hampshire relies on property taxes to generate 18 percent of its total state tax revenue. In contrast, property taxes do not contribute anything to state coffers in 14 states, although localities rely heavily on them.[29]

In thinking about a state's tax burden, it is helpful to distinguish between its **tax capacity** and its **tax effort**. For example, according to the online real estate service Zillow, the median value of a home in Newport Beach, California, is about $1.7 million. With such high property values, even low property tax rates are going to bring in serious money. Conversely, Zillow estimates that in Odessa, Texas, the median value of a home is $141,800. That is not going to generate a lot of property tax revenue no matter how high its rates are. In other words, Newport Beach's tax capacity is high; Odessa's tax capacity is low.

Rather than tax capacity, many political scientists prefer to look at a different measurement—tax effort, which is the aggregate-level equivalent of individual-level tax burden. Basically, measurements of tax effort seek to determine the proportion of its income that a given community chooses to pay out in taxes. A community's tax effort is also a good proxy for its appetite for public services. Some communities are willing to pay for street cleaning; some are not. Some communities, such as Cambridge, Massachusetts, even are willing to pay a government employee to drive around and announce that street cleaning is about to commence.

Tax capacities and tax efforts often diverge markedly. Consider Massachusetts and New Hampshire. Both are comparatively affluent states. Personal income per capita in 2012 was $57,179 in Massachusetts and $50,287 in New Hampshire.[30] In other words, the two states have similar tax capacities. However, they make very different tax efforts. Per capita, New Hampshire

Intergovernmental transfers Funds provided by the federal government to state governments and by state governments to local governments.

Tax capacity A measure of the ability to pay taxes.

Tax effort A measure of taxes paid relative to the ability to pay taxes.

LOCAL FOCUS

AMAZON COLLECTS FOR SOME, BUT NOT FOR OTHERS

As more and more states passed laws requiring online retailers to levy sales taxes on goods bought online by their citizens, Internet retailing juggernaut Amazon evolved into an increasingly important source of public revenues. Though it spent years fighting to keep online commerce tax free, by 2017 Amazon had ditched that opposition and was collecting sales taxes for 45 states—in other words, for every state that actually had a sales tax.

There are a number of reasons for Amazon's new-found willingness to act as a tax collector. The possibility of litigation for noncompliance with a raft of new state laws requiring online sellers to collect these taxes probably played a role. So did the fact that Amazon now has distribution centers in more than half the states, and those warehouses give the retailer a physical, nonvirtual, brick-and-mortar presence that makes it much harder to escape a state government's regulatory reach. Regardless of the reasons, the bottom line is that by 2018 Amazon had reached deals with the big majority of states to collect at least some sales taxes for online purchases.

That was good news for states annually losing billions in lost sales tax collections. It did not make much of a difference, though, to local governments that collect sales taxes. For example, consider Albuquerque, New Mexico. New Mexico levies a sales tax of just over 5 percent, and Amazon will charge the state's residents for that when they click and purchase. Yet Albuquerque has its own 2.375 percent sales tax on top of the base state rate, which is an important source of revenue for the city. Amazon doesn't collect a cent of that.

In short, while Amazon was helping states get sales tax revenues, cities were not getting the same treatment. That left traditional retailers in these cities at a big disadvantage. Because Amazon does not charge city sales taxes on purchases, Amazon automatically can sell goods cheaper. The difference created pretty big price advantages for Amazon, as much as 4 percent on pretax sales prices in some cities.

That had some local officials steamed. Amazon certainly uses city services—if nothing else, it sure uses the roads to deliver all those tax-free packages to city residents. Unlike local businesses, though, Amazon wasn't kicking in to pay the bills to maintain those city streets. This state of affairs worries local lawmakers because even though the Supreme Court ruled in 2018 that states can require online retailers to collect sales taxes like Amazon, it's not clear local governments have the same leverage, and they may still be left out even if state governments enjoy a sudden sales tax boon.

A report by the Institute on Taxation and Economic Policy on the online sales tax issue concluded that this gap in state versus local online sales tax collections is "harming local governments' ability to fund vital programs, and it is contributing to an unlevel playing field for local businesses because millions of shoppers are able to pay less tax if they choose to buy products from out-of-state companies over the Internet."

Source: Institute on Taxation and Economic Policy, "Many Localities Are Unprepared to Collect Taxes on Online Purchases," March 2018, https://itep.org/wp-content/uploads/amazonlocaltax_0318.pdf.

residents pay about $3,961 in state and local taxes, while Massachusetts residents pay $5,872.[31]

Explaining Tax Variations

What accounts for differences in tax capacity and effort such as those found between Massachusetts and New Hampshire? Political culture is one difference that helps explain the difference. New Hampshire prides itself on its rugged individualism. Its motto is "Live Free or Die." Residents tend to want the government to stay out of their way. In contrast, Massachusetts was founded as a commonwealth. The founding document of the Massachusetts Bay Colony describes a single "Body Politic" dedicated to the "general good" of the colony.[32] In this tradition, state and local governments are seen as effective ways of advancing that general good; thus, higher taxes and larger governments are more acceptable.

Political culture, however, is not the only important variable that explains the very different tax efforts among states. Factors such as geography, geology, demographics, and history also influence the choices that state and local governments make.

Geography

One obvious, but easily overlooked, factor that influences state tax policies is geography. Some states use sales tax policy as a competitive edge. Delaware proudly recruits shoppers from nearby Mid-Atlantic states to its outlet malls with "no sales tax" advertisements. In contrast, Hawaii charges a 4.0 to 4.7 percent tax on nearly everything sold, including many services. How can it get away with the practice? Well, unless residents are willing to fly to the mainland for their sundries, they don't have much choice but to pay up.

Geology

As we have already seen, geology plays an important role in some state economies. This is most notably true in oil-rich and natural gas–rich states such as Alaska, Wyoming, and North Dakota. Taxes on natural resources have long meant that state and local governments in places like Alaska are able to maintain high levels of spending with very low tax burdens. Alaska used its mineral riches to help establish the Alaska Permanent Fund, which is a sovereign wealth fund—basically a state-owned investment corporation. The fund's profits are partially redistributed to state citizens; so, rather than the state taxing residents, the fund pays Alaskans for being Alaskans. The fund sends each eligible citizen a yearly **dividend** check; in 2017, the amount per person was about $1,100. While getting free money from the government sounds good, heavy reliance on oil as a revenue source can have a big downside. When oil prices plummeted in 2016, revenues in states like Alaska, North Dakota, and Wyoming were hit hard, prompting spending cuts and increased pressure to shift tax burdens from energy producers to citizens in the form of income, property, or sales taxes.

Demographics

Demographics also play an important role in determining the attitudes of state and local governments toward taxes. This is particularly true at the local level. Consider a city with a strong local economy and rising house prices. Such a city attracts a large number of young workers with children. These are people who might very well want to spend more money on local schools and are willing to deal with rising property tax revenues. However, as mentioned previously, for seniors living on fixed incomes, rising house prices and rising property taxes might spell disaster. During economic booms, conflicts between parents of school-age children and retirees are a common feature of local politics.

The Economic Cycle

Even when states make similar tax efforts and have similar cultures, their state and local finances can still vary widely because states (and even cities) can have very different economies. The national economic numbers that most people are familiar with—unemployment, productivity gains, income, and the like—are not necessarily accurate reflections of state economic conditions. Depending on the makeup of their economies, states can find themselves at very different places on an economic cycle at the same point in time. For example, industrial states such as Michigan and Indiana tend to experience economic downturns first. Texas historically has had a countercyclical economy. When rising oil prices threaten to push industrial states into recession, Texas tends to do well. The same is true of Wyoming, Alaska, and, most recently, North Dakota.

Demographics, geography, history, political culture, and the swings of the economic cycle are all important, but these variables do not explain all the financial choices that state and local governments make. Take Mississippi, for example. One of the most religious and politically conservative states in the country, Mississippi is the buckle of the Bible Belt. In 1990, however, Mississippi passed riverboat gambling legislation that allowed casino operators to build full-size casinos on barges moored permanently to the shoreline on the Mississippi River and the Gulf Coast. The goal was to turn the northwestern town of Tunica, which had gained a measure of renown after the television news-magazine *60 Minutes* profiled it as the poorest city in America, into Las Vegas East.

What's important to keep in mind here is that Nevada and Mississippi have completely different political cultures. Political scientist Daniel Elazar describes Mississippi as a traditionalistic state and Nevada as an individualistic state. In short, Nevada has the kind of political culture that might be expected to produce, well, Las Vegas. Mississippi does not. Today, however, the hamlet of Tunica has more casino square footage

Dividend A payment made to stockholders (or, in Alaska's case, residents) from the interest generated by an investment.

NORTH DAKOTA's number of oil and natural gas rigs fell from 179 to 26 from April 2014 to April 2016 as oil production across the country slowed and prices fell.

than does the East Coast gambling hot spot Atlantic City, in the individual-istic state of New Jersey. Clearly, political culture isn't everything.

Debt

The final source of money for state and local gov-ernments is debt, gener-ally issued in the form of **bonds**. These are finan-cial instruments with which state and local governments promise to pay back bor-rowed money at a fixed rate of interest on a specified date. The interest rates paid by a government depend largely on the government's bond rating. Bond rat-ings are issued by three private companies—Moody's, Standard & Poor's, and Fitch—and are based on the gov-ernment's fiscal health; many states' bond ratings fell during the Great Recession and in the years following. A rating of AAA is the best, and anything lower than BBB is considered "junk bond status" and would send a government's interest rates skyrocketing. In 2017, after years of budget stalemate between the governor and legislature, Illinois's bond rating was cut to one step above junk status, putting it at risk of becoming the first state ever to lose its status as "investment grade."[33]

State and local governments, as well as quasi-govern-mental entities such as utility and water authorities, use bonds to finance **capital investments**, typically infra-structure upgrades such as new roads, new schools, and new airports. There are two types of bonds: **general**

obligation bonds, which are secured by the taxing power of the jurisdiction that issues them, and **revenue bonds**, which are secured by the revenue from a given project, such as a new toll road. For state governments, capital investments are projects such as highway construc-tion, power plant construction and pollution control, and even land conservation. Because the issuance of general obligation bonds must be approved by voters, state and local governments turn to revenue bonds more often.

Local governments use bonds to finance projects such as construction or improvement of schools, sew-age and water lines, airports, and affordable housing. Investors like them, too, in part because the earnings from most state bonds are exempt from state income taxes. **Municipal bonds**, called munis, are gener-ally safe and attractive investments, particularly for the rich. Municipal bondholders usually are exempted from paying federal or state taxes on income they receive from bonds. Sometimes, however, munici-pal finances go disastrously awry. In 2009, Jefferson County, Alabama, the largest county in the state, announced it would file for bankruptcy after defaulting on $3 billion in bonds to finance improvements to its sewer system. In 2015, Puerto Rico began defaulting on its debt, failing to make full payments to bondholders for the simple reason that it did not have the cash to pay. Though technically not allowed to declare bank-ruptcy, Puerto Rico sought protection from its creditors in federal court in 2017, which effectively amounted to the same thing (see "States under Stress: Bankruptcy and Natural Disasters").

The Budget Process

Once state and local governments have raised money from taxes, user fees, and bonds, and have received money from intergovernmental transfers, they must decide how to spend it. These decisions are made dur-ing the **budget process**.

Most state and local governments budget for one **fiscal year**. Unfortunately for fans of simplicity in government, the fiscal year is not the same as the cal-endar year. The federal government's fiscal year runs from October 1 to September 30. Most state and local governments begin their fiscal year on July 1; Alabama, Michigan, New York, and Texas are exceptions. Thus, when legislatures debate the budget, they are almost always debating the budget for the coming fiscal year.[34] Nineteen states pass two-year budgets.[35]

Bonds Certificates that are evidence of debts on which the issuer prom-ises to pay the holders a specified amount of interest for a specified length of time and to repay the loans on their maturity.

Capital investments Investments in infrastructure, such as roads.

General obligation bonds Investments secured by the taxing power of the jurisdiction that issues them.

Revenue bonds Investments secured by the revenue generated by a state or municipal project.

Municipal bonds Bonds issued by states, counties, cities, and towns to fund large projects as well as operating budgets. Income from such bonds is exempt from federal taxes and from state and local taxes for the inves-tors who live in the state where they are issued.

Budget process The procedure by which state and local governments assess revenues and set budgets.

Fiscal year The annual accounting period used by a government.

STATES UNDER STRESS
BANKRUPTCY AND NATURAL DISASTERS

In 2017, Puerto Rico was in dire financial straits, crushed under $120 billion in debts it couldn't pay back. In March of that year, it turned to the federal courts for protection, in effect becoming the first American state or territory to declare bankruptcy. That seemed to be the absolute low point for Puerto Rico's budget woes. Then the hurricanes hit.

Irma hit the island in September that year and Maria a couple of weeks later. The second hurricane was the worst natural disaster recorded in the island's history. The power grid, already damaged by Irma, collapsed, roads became impassable, businesses closed, and tourism—the island's big economic driver—tanked. No one really knows how much the rebuilding costs and economic losses of that awful month add up to, but reasonable estimates put it at something like $100 billion. If it was cash-strapped before the hurricanes, afterwards it was in desperate need of financial help. Not just to balance the books, but just to get the lights turned on.

The obvious financial backstop that many in the islands were counting on was the federal government. Puerto Ricans, after all, are U.S. citizens, and in many ways, Puerto Rico looks and acts like a state. It has its own constitution, a governor, and a bicameral legislature. Geographically, it's bigger than Delaware, and population-wise, it's roughly comparable to Oklahoma. Legally, though, Puerto Rico is not a state; it is not a sovereign government within the federal system, but a territory of the United States. That lack of sovereignty is a big deal with big consequences. Notably, it means that even though Puerto Ricans are U.S. citizens and pay taxes to the U.S. government, they have no voting representative in Congress and no representation in the Electoral College. In short, Puerto Rico has no voting constituency to which Congress or the president answers.

Having that leverage might have helped Puerto Rico get more help from the federal government. In the weeks after the hurricanes hit Puerto Rico and the mainland United States, the Federal Emergency Management Agency (FEMA) approved $691 million in grants to victims of Hurricane Irma in Florida, and $323 million to victims of Hurricane Harvey in Texas. Puerto Rico, in contrast, got $35 million, and when President Donald Trump visited the island to check on recovery efforts, he scolded Puerto Rico for being a drain on the federal treasury, saying, "You've thrown our budget out of whack," and "We've spent a lot of money on Puerto Rico."

It is certainly true that Puerto Rico bears a good deal of responsibility for its dire financial straits. It takes years of bad financial decisions to pile up $120 billion of unpayable debt. Still, many Puerto Ricans saw their treatment as decidedly unfair. The federal government not only refused to cover their debt, but it seemed noticeably more reluctant to help out in the wake of devastating natural disasters.

Before the hurricanes hit, Congress arguably had good reason to be reluctant to do too much to dig the territory out of its financial woes because of the precedent it might set. If Congress helps out Puerto Rico, the argument goes, then other states that get into financial trouble might ask for similar consideration. After the hurricanes, though, it seemed piling on insult to injury to be less willing to help out a community with much less financial capability to deal with a natural disaster compared to states like Texas and Florida. Of course, unlike Texas and Florida, Puerto Rico did not have a powerful congressional delegation with full voting rights, which might explain why those states got dollars and sympathy while Puerto Rico got pennies and a scolding. Absent that influence, it has been left to deal with bankruptcy and natural disasters as best it can with whatever help the federal government is willing to provide.

Sources: Mary Williams Walsh, "Puerto Rico Declares a Form of Bankruptcy," *The New York Times*, May 3, 2017, https://www.nytimes.com/2017/05/03/business/dealbook/puerto-rico-debt.html; Alexia Fernández Campbell, "Puerto Rico Pays Taxes. The US Is Obligated to Help It Just as Much as Texas and Florida," *Vox*, October 4, 2017, https://www.vox.com/policy-and-politics/2017/10/4/16385658/puerto-rico-taxes-hurricane; Liz Farmer, "With Little Cash, How Will Puerto Rico and the Virgin Islands Rebuild?," *Governing*, October 4, 2017, http://www.governing.com/topics/finance/gov-puerto-rico-virgin-islands-hurricane-debt-finances.html.

Budget timelines do vary from state to state, but the budget process itself is quite similar across states. It begins with instructions from the governor's budget office. The executive branch agencies are told to draw up funding requests for the upcoming year. During the fall (assuming the typical fiscal year beginning on July 1), the budget office reviews the spending requests and helps the chief executive develop a unified budget for the executive branch.

Most chief executives unveil their budgets in their state of the state addresses in January. In 45 states,

governors and mayors are required by law to submit a **balanced budget** to the legislature or city council. The legislative body reviews the budget, authorizes spending on certain programs, appropriates the necessary money, and presents its budget to the chief executive to sign into law.

As a guard against fiscal excess and abuse, 49 states have statutory or constitutional requirements that the state legislature enact a balanced budget. Only Vermont is free to run up debt as it pleases. Most states also have laws that require lawmakers to save a certain portion of state revenues in so-called rainy-day, or budget stabilization, funds. States can draw on these funds during times of recession, when revenues fall. Although rainy-day funds rarely offset the revenue drops that

....

Balanced budget A budget in which current expenditures are equal to or less than income.

MAP 4-1 ● Municipal Bankruptcies as of September 2017

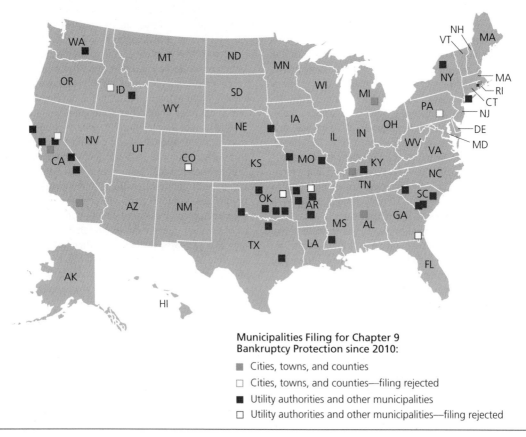

Municipalities Filing for Chapter 9
Bankruptcy Protection since 2010:

■ Cities, towns, and counties
□ Cities, towns, and counties—filing rejected
■ Utility authorities and other municipalities
□ Utility authorities and other municipalities—filing rejected

Source: "Bankrupt Cities, Municipalities List and Map," *Governing*, September 14, 2017, http://www.governing.com/gov-data/municipal-cities-counties-bankrupticies-and-defaults.html.

Note: Only about half of U.S. states allow municipalities to file for Chapter 9 bankruptcy; laws in other states prohibit such filings. Not all bankruptcy filings were approved.

occur during a recession, they do provide some cushion for the lawmakers who have to balance state budgets. For example, Georgia had $1.7 billion in its rainy-day fund in 2007, and drew heavily on that reserve over the next three years to weather a revenue crunch caused by the Great Recession (by 2010 the reserve was down to $268 million). As the economy recovered, Georgia started to replenish its rainy-day fund, topping it up to $1.6 billion by 2015.[36] That's an example of exactly how these funds are supposed to work—you build a reserve to deal with bad economic times by putting money aside during good economic times. Though that makes good financial sense, rainy-day funds sometimes face political pressure during the good times from those who do not like the idea of government sitting on a healthy bank account.

Kevin Fleming/Corbis/VCG

▲

Despite some groups' moral objections to gambling, states have turned to casinos such as this one floating on the Mississippi River in Natchez, Mississippi, to help raise much-needed revenues.

Why not use that money to lower taxes? The problem, of course, is that economic good times inevitably give way to bad times and what looks like a frivolous piggy bank in the former turns into the prudent life saver in the latter.

Expenditures, or Where the Money Goes

As you can imagine, state and local governments spend a lot of money to provide all the services and programs they are responsible for. In fiscal year 2016, state governments alone spent more than $2 trillion. (See Table 4-2.) That's about $6,560 for every resident of the United States, and that number climbs to more than $10,000 per head if local government spending is included. What do these subnational governments spend all this money on?

Wages

Salaries are the single largest source of **expenditures** for state and local governments—roughly $899 billion in 2015.[37] State and local governments are the biggest employers in the United States. In 2014, state governments employed 5 million people nationwide, and local governments employed another 14.1 million.[38]

Education

Education has long been the single largest functional spending category for state and local governments. In 2016, state governments alone spent $937 billion on education, the majority of it (about $610 billion) in the form of transfers to schools and school districts.[39]

Despite the big financial commitment by states—they provide about half the funding—primary and secondary education traditionally has been the preserve of local governments. In most states, elected local school boards hire superintendents and principals, select curricula that align with state standards, and develop school budgets. Local governments typically devote more than a third of their budgets to education.[40]

State governments also devote a portion of their expenditures to higher education; in 2018, state general fund expenditures on higher education totaled about $88 billion.[41] The fact that states spend so much on education out of general revenue funds is important because it means those expenditures fall into what's known as **discretionary spending**. In tight economic times,

. . . .

Expenditures Money spent by government.

Discretionary spending Spending controlled in annual appropriations acts.

TABLE 4-2 ● State Revenue, Expenditures, and Debt, 2016 (in thousands of dollars)

	Total Revenue	Total Expenditure	Debt at End of Fiscal Year		Total Revenue	Total Expenditure	Debt at End of Fiscal Year
United States	2,136,805,664	2,240,220,155	1,160,488,556	Montana	6,878,900	7,316,671	3,052,423
Alabama	30,502,706	30,434,595	8,667,105	Nebraska	10,881,575	11,026,935	1,950,506
Alaska	8,071,737	12,452,033	5,953,933	Nevada	16,808,682	15,315,276	3,222,367
Arizona	38,338,699	42,204,155	14,400,191	New Hampshire	8,343,685	7,687,843	7,869,122
Arkansas	21,439,227	22,910,901	4,828,756	New Jersey	65,689,159	72,617,584	66,721,791
California	322,332,341	326,837,836	151,307,658	New Mexico	18,602,071	20,158,082	6,951,535
Colorado	31,399,864	34,596,327	16,686,588	New York	185,619,993	195,571,229	137,479,990
Connecticut	28,139,072	32,202,351	37,024,731	North Carolina	55,216,582	53,857,036	16,919,235
Delaware	8,083,659	9,378,888	5,045,161	North Dakota	7,330,392	8,287,006	2,355,700
Florida	85,575,636	88,220,438	33,469,117	Ohio	78,331,623	87,016,871	33,164,507
Georgia	45,859,181	47,867,768	13,130,551	Oklahoma	22,862,875	24,950,729	8,702,914
Hawaii	13,417,610	12,425,875	9,216,583	Oregon	32,781,473	34,331,929	13,355,878
Idaho	9,405,581	9,377,948	3,542,856	Pennsylvania	90,792,145	96,439,652	47,099,314
Illinois	75,492,133	78,334,318	65,791,900	Rhode Island	8,201,456	8,625,101	9,052,017
Indiana	38,687,720	39,557,565	22,470,543	South Carolina	28,937,828	31,630,447	16,228,097
Iowa	23,715,865	23,731,772	5,956,424	South Dakota	4,537,220	5,059,935	3,366,459
Kansas	17,609,012	18,748,723	9,537,833	Tennessee	31,427,933	32,459,124	6,075,745
Kentucky	29,941,369	35,347,118	14,453,423	Texas	144,218,813	148,449,673	49,357,183
Louisiana	26,842,105	31,444,186	17,913,229	Utah	18,164,518	19,630,299	7,013,698
Maine	9,003,011	9,403,020	4,845,408	Vermont	6,488,122	6,763,948	2,492,083
Maryland	42,037,052	44,089,713	27,871,287	Virginia	51,655,912	53,747,025	28,628,254
Massachusetts	60,312,959	63,562,063	76,861,071	Washington	50,774,856	53,463,325	33,059,765
Michigan	71,188,554	70,811,041	33,744,508	West Virginia	13,928,479	14,562,503	7,223,531
Minnesota	44,247,753	46,694,801	16,213,046	Wisconsin	36,854,453	39,241,416	23,052,389
Mississippi	20,880,790	22,247,200	7,283,371	Wyoming	5,914,028	6,351,534	775,568
Missouri	33,039,255	32,778,347	19,103,212				

Source: U.S. Census Bureau, "2016 Annual Survey of State Government Finances Tables," https://www.census.gov/data/tables/2016/econ/state/historical-tables.html.

discretionary spending is one of the first parts of a government budget to come under stress—when revenues shrink, legislatures have to reduce annual appropriations, and that means cutting discretionary spending. As publicly supported colleges and universities have ways to deal with spending cuts from state government (read: jacking up your tuition and increasing your class sizes), funds for higher education have been particularly hard-hit by budget retrenchment.

Health Care

Since the late 1990s, health care spending has surged dramatically. For state governments, spending on health care is now greater than spending for any other single item—this single program accounts for approximately 29 cents out of every dollar spent by state governments.[42] Medicaid is the largest and most expensive state-run health program. When it was established in 1965, it was viewed as a limited safety net for the very poor and disabled. However, the numbers of low-income, uninsured Americans have increased, and medical care has become more expensive. The program has grown at an enormous rate as a result. In 1970, state governments spent $2 billion on Medicaid, and the federal government kicked in another $3 billion. In 2017, the states and the federal government spent $574 billion on the program.[43] The number of people served by Medicaid continues to rise dramatically, with current estimates suggesting as many as 70 million may be enrolled in this program. A big reason for the jump in Medicaid enrollments—and thus in Medicaid expenditures—is the Patient Protection and Affordable Care Act, commonly known as Obamacare. Enacted in 2010, Obamacare has the explicit aim of extending health insurance coverage to millions of uninsured people. The law is of particular interest to the states because one of its central goals is to expand Medicaid eligibility, and Medicaid is a program cooperatively run—and paid for—by state and federal governments. As such, it is an example of **fiscal federalism**, a system of delivering public services in which the federal government picks up most of the costs while states take responsibility for administering the services.

Obamacare was (and remains) a contentious and controversial law. When it was enacted, the expansion of Medicaid included in the law was opposed by some state officials, who viewed it not just as federal encroachment on state sovereignty but also as a potential budget buster. Although the federal government pledged to pick up the vast majority of the costs of adding millions to the Medicaid rolls, at least in the short term, some state governments worried that the federal fiscal commitment would not last forever. The federal government pledged to pay 100 percent of expansion costs for three years, and 90 percent of the costs after that until 2022. But what about after 2022? Some states were concerned that they could end up being saddled with huge costs at some point in the future.

The sovereignty and budget concerns raised by Obamacare were addressed in *National Federation of Independent Business v. Sebelius*, a case decided in 2012 by the Supreme Court. The Court ruled that the major provisions of Obamacare were constitutional but that the federal government could not force state governments to join in the planned expansion of Medicaid; this decision effectively gave states the right to opt out. As of 2018, 18 states—mostly conservative and Republican—had decided not to participate in the Medicaid expansion.[44]

Obamacare has added millions to the numbers covered by Medicaid, which is an **entitlement** program. This means states and the federal government are obligated by law to provide health insurance to low-income individuals who qualify for the program, regardless of the cost. While there is an ongoing debate about the pros and cons of Obamacare, there is no debate that Medicaid and other health care programs are expensive and likely to stay that way for the foreseeable future.

States do have some leeway in determining how generous they want to be with programs such as Medicaid. Eligibility for these sorts of programs is typically determined by family or wage-earner income relative to federally established poverty levels. While the federal government sets basic guidelines on those eligibility requirements, states can use more generous guidelines if they choose. For example, in Mississippi, children ages 1–5 are eligible for Medicaid benefits in families earning up to 148 percent of the federal poverty level. In Minnesota, they are eligible if their families earn up to 280 percent of the federal poverty level.[45] In other words, whether someone is eligible for Medicaid benefits is dependent not just on how much his or her family earns but also on what state the family lives in.

Welfare

Welfare has been one of the most contentious issues in U.S. politics for a long time. Like Medicaid, welfare is an entitlement program; states have some leeway to determine eligibility, but they cannot deny or restrict benefits to qualified individuals. From 1965 to 1996, women with young children were eligible to receive monetary assistance through a welfare program known as Aid to Families with Dependent Children (AFDC).

In 1996, Congress replaced AFDC with the Temporary Assistance for Needy Families (TANF) program. TANF disbursed federal money to states in block grants and gave them considerable freedom in determining how they wanted to spend those funds. Many liberals predicted that such welfare "reform" would result in disaster. Instead, the number of people on welfare rolls declined dramatically. Between 1997 and 2011, the welfare caseload declined by nearly 50 percent, from about 4 million people to 2 million people.[46]

....

Fiscal federalism The system by which federal grants are used to fund programs and services provided by state and local governments.

Entitlement A service that government must provide, regardless of the cost.

Welfare continues to be a politically contentious issue even though, from a financial viewpoint, it is actually a pretty minor program. In 2014, states and the federal government each spent about $15 billion on TANF, a tiny fraction of total spending by both levels of government.[47]

Fire, Police, and Prisons

In 2015, state and local governments spent about $105 billion on police protection and another $45 billion on fire protection. Corrections—jails and prisons—account for another $76 billion.[48] State and local government spending on police protection and prisons varies widely. New York City, with a population of 8 million, employs roughly 35,000 police officers, or about 42 cops for every 10,000 residents. In contrast, Los Angeles, a city of 3.8 million, employs fewer than 10,000 police officers, roughly 26 for every 10,000 people.[49]

States also have very different levels of enthusiasm for funding prisons. In fiscal year 2017, the average state spent roughly 3 percent of its budget on corrections. Mississippi, though, spent half of that, while California spent nearly double.[50]

Highways

In 2015, state and local governments spent about $168 billion on transportation, much of it devoted to highways and roads.[51] Most of this money came from dedicated revenue sources, such as gasoline taxes, but the federal government accounted for nearly a third of these funds.[52]

Not surprisingly, states with wide-open spaces spend more money on highway construction and transportation. In 2017, Alaska devoted 17.5 percent of total state expenditures to transportation. This was the highest percentage of any state in the country, followed by South Dakota at 14.1 percent and Florida at 13 percent. Nationwide, state governments spent 8.1 percent of total revenues on transportation in 2015.[53]

Restraints on State and Local Budgeteers

Politicians and journalists usually talk about "the budget" in the singular, as if elected officials meet every year or two to divvy up a single pot of money. That's misleading. State and local officials cannot actually lay their hands on all the revenues flowing into state and local coffers. Most of the money that comes from the federal government is earmarked for specific programs,

such as Medicaid. Revenue streams from many state sources, such as the car registration tax, are likewise dedicated to specific purposes, such as highway construction. State and local officials develop their budgets under several additional restraints as well.

Governmental Accounting Standards Board

States conduct their accounting and financial reporting according to standards set by the Governmental Accounting Standards Board (GASB). In 2004, the organization issued GASB 45, a rule that mandated that states tally and disclose the cost of health care benefits pledged to current and retired state employees. As if that were not daunting enough, the states also had to find a way to begin saving enough to cover their pension liabilities, or they risked damaging their credit ratings. GASB 45 helped expose a massive gap between what states promised public-sector retirees and what they could actually pay for, a gap that was pushed wider by the revenue crunch of the Great Recession. The basic problem is that while state pension schemes have the funds to pay for promised retiree pensions and health care benefits in the short term, they do not have the money set aside to pay for the expected long-term increases in those costs. As of 2015, the gap between the assets of state pension funds and their financial obligation to cover promised pension and health care benefits was $1.1 trillion.[54] States have taken some steps to try to close the gap by reducing benefits and increasing employee contributions to those benefits, but even with those adjustments, it is not clear that states will be able to cover their promises without resorting to getting more from taxpayers.

Unfunded Mandates

For years, state officials complained bitterly about the federal government's habit of mandating that states achieve a goal, such as an environmental cleanup, but then failing to provide any money to pay for it. State officials viewed such unfunded mandates as an affront to the notion of federalism itself. In 1995, Congress did something surprising: It passed legislation, the Unfunded Mandates Reform Act (UMRA), that dramatically curtailed the practice of imposing unfunded mandates on state governments. This measure alleviated some of the pressures on states, but it did not end the problem. In 2016, Curt Bramble, then president of

FIGURE 4-1 ● How It Works

A Year in the Life of a State Budget: Idaho's Budgetary Process

Most folks first hear about state budget priorities through their governor's state of the state address, the forum in which most state budgetary news is presented. In reality, budget planning begins well in advance of this address and involves many actors. In Idaho, for example, planning begins approximately 18 months in advance when government agencies first submit budget requests. The planning for fiscal year 2018, for example, actually began in July/August 2016. Figure 4-1 shows how the budget process works in Idaho.

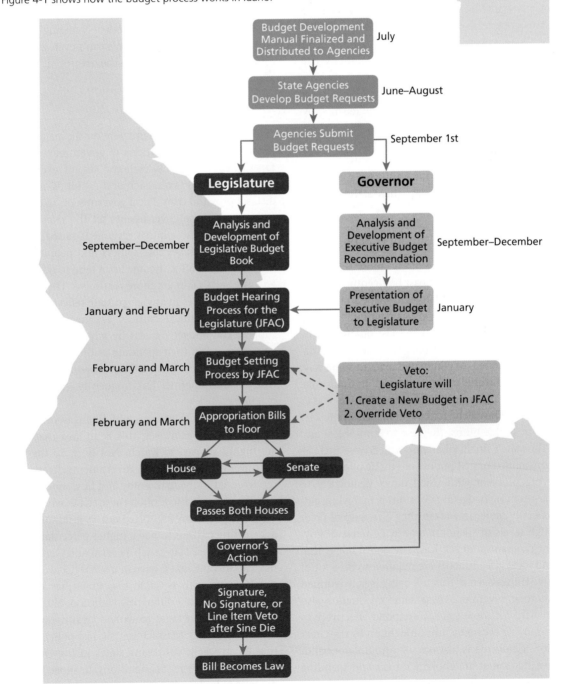

Source: Adapted from Idaho Legislative Services Office, "Budget Process and Schedules," https://legislature.idaho.gov/lso/bpa/process/.

the National Conference of State Legislatures, told a subcommittee of the U.S. Senate that the UMRA was in desperate need of updating, that it was too narrowly defined and/or too frequently ignored by Congress, which continued to pass laws that very literally passed the buck to the states. He succinctly summed up what state governments wanted Congress to do about unfunded mandates: "Knock it off."[55]

Ironically, many local government lawmakers might want state governments to listen to the exact same message. State governments have increasingly been imposing unfunded mandates on county and city governments. Evidently, many state governments were no more able to resist the temptation to set goals and make someone else pay for them than the federal government long had been. California cities, for example, control less than half of their discretionary spending. The state tells them what they must do with the rest. The situation is even worse for California's counties. They have the final say over less than a third of the money they spend.[56]

Ballot Initiatives and the Budget Process

California also illustrates one of the most significant trends in state finances in the past half-century or so—the growing use of ballot initiatives to shape and restrain state tax systems. Nationwide, voters put more than 100 tax initiatives on the ballot in the last quarter of the 20th century; roughly two-thirds were antitax initiatives that cut, limited, or eliminated taxes in some way; and roughly two-thirds of those passed.[57] In California, the net effect of all those 20th-century initiatives was to create a massive headache for budget makers in the 21st century—in simple terms, they got to control less and less of the state's financial affairs, which were increasingly constrained or just put on automatic pilot.

The big problem with using direct democracy to make far-reaching budgetary decisions is that while citizens generally prefer low taxes, they also tend to favor fairly high levels of spending on a wide range of government programs and services. The end result is that state and local governments are required to do a lot of expensive things even as they are being legally required to limit their revenues. These same constraints also made it hard for some states to respond effectively to the fast-moving economic hits brought on by the Great Recession. California is just one of a number of ballot initiative states that are choking on tax and spending policies put in place by voters.

At their worst, antitax budget initiatives can paralyze state legislatures and local governments. At least 15 states have passed initiatives or referendums that require tax decisions to gain supermajorities in a legislature to be approved. Assembling those supermajorities—typically two-thirds or three-quarters of the legislature—is an enormous challenge. In Montana, for example, the required supermajority is three-quarters of the legislature. Former state senator Roy Brown once commented on the slim chances of changing tax policy with that obstacle in place: "We can't even get a three-fourths majority vote to go to the bathroom."[58]

Conclusion

State and local governments rely on six major types of taxes to fund the operations of government: property taxes; income taxes; sales taxes; sin, or excise, taxes; user fees; and gift taxes. Each of these kinds of taxes has distinct pros and cons. Local governments like property taxes because the governments set the rates and thus control exactly how much revenue is raised. However, when property taxes rise, seniors and people on fixed incomes often suffer. Income taxes tend to be more progressive; sales taxes are more regressive. The exact configuration of taxes in any given state reflects that state's history and political culture. Tax revenues, in turn, support the budget process by which state and local governments set their spending priorities. Increasingly, governments are relying on user fees—collected in relatively small amounts but frequently—to supply key revenues.

State and local government finances can be difficult to unravel. However, this is an area that citizens are highly advised to watch. Not only do the budget decisions of state and local governments determine the services that individuals enjoy and how much they pay in taxes, but this also is often the arena in which the priorities of public life are sorted out. Is it fair or unfair to ask wealthy citizens to pay a higher percentage of their income in taxes? States such as Texas and Florida, which have no income taxes, have in a sense decided that it is unfair. States such as California, which has an income tax, have reached a different conclusion. Should everyone pay more in taxes to extend health care to low-income citizens? Massachusetts's tax policies suggest that its answer is yes. Many states in the Deep South have reached different conclusions. In short, the consequences of budget decisions are very real.

There is another reason to pay close attention to state and local finances. Over the past few years, the recovery from the most severe recession since World War II has been sluggish, and states' revenue systems are not set up to make the most of today's evolving economy. To get back in the black consistently, states will almost certainly need to change their financial structures. States such as Tennessee that rely heavily on sales tax revenues face particularly serious long-term challenges. As Internet sales and dollars spent on untaxed services continue to grow, ensuring those transactions are captured in some form by sales taxes will continue to be a priority for state and, increasingly, local government. Pressures such as the widespread teachers' revolt over years of underinvestment in public education are also likely to create a need for new revenue-raising measures. Yet states with ballot initiatives may well find new approaches blocked by antitax sentiments at the voting booth.

THE LATEST RESEARCH

It is a general article of faith among lawmakers that public policy choices can influence the economy. An especially cherished idea is the notion that tax rates influence economic performance, a perspective that has been described as "virtually universal among state politicians."[59] It's no surprise then, that over the past decade or so many states have vigorously pursued tax-cutting strategies. The hoped-for economic boost, however, does not always appear. In states like Kansas and Louisiana, aggressive tax cuts were followed by a plunge in revenues that pushed governments into fiscal crises.

This may not be surprising. Received political wisdom about the impact of tax cuts has, at best, mixed support in empirical studies. It is not that tax cuts never have positive economic effects—they sometimes do; it's more that the relationship between tax rates and economic performance is more complicated than often portrayed. A robust economy needs a well-prepared labor force, a good transportation infrastructure, and a regulatory regime that ensures fair business practices without being overly intrusive. That all requires significant investments in public goods and services—in schools and roads; in inspections and code enforcement. That requires taxes. Academics have increasingly been investigating the relationship between taxes and economic performance using comparative studies. A sampling of those studies is described below, and the results converge on two general findings: (1) cutting taxes lowers government revenues, and (2) the economic impact of a tax cut is heavily dependent on context.

- **Prillaman, Soledad Artiz, and Kenneth J. Meier,** "Assessing the Impact of Pro-business Taxes on U.S. State Economies," *The Journal of Politics* 76 (2014): 364–379.

This study looks at all 50 states for the 28-year span between 1977 and 2005 with the aim of assessing whether cuts in business taxes correlate with upticks in economic performance. The authors use a number of measures to try and capture economic performance including gross state product, job creation, personal income, and business creation. They then try to predict changes in each of these measures using state government revenue collected from business taxes. The basic hypothesis tested is that as state governments lean less on business taxes as a revenue source, economic performance will increase. They find little evidence to support this hypothesis. There is, at best, a very slight impact of business taxation on economic performance, and in a number of cases, that impact is *positive*—in other words, greater levels of business taxation lead to a better-performing economy. The authors conclude it is less the business tax regime than innate state factors such as land prices and education levels that underpin state-level economic performance.

- **Adkisson, Richard V., and Mikidadu Mohammed,** "Tax Structure and State Economic Growth During the Great Recession," *The Social Science Journal* 51 (2014): 79–89.

This study looks at economic growth and development during a particularly turbulent time for the United States: the years between 2004 and 2010. That span includes the Great Recession of 2008–2009, the economic boom years that preceded it, and the tentative recovery that occurred in the years following. What the authors are interested in is the differential tax burdens imposed by state and local governments—are these differences that make a difference in terms of predicting economic growth, especially in terms of recovering from a recession? The short answer is, well, sort of. The

(Continued)

(Continued)

authors do find a statistical relationship between short-term economic growth and tax structure, but it is very modest. While states' tax structures vary, that variation doesn't seem to play a huge role in determining economic growth. The authors conclude that "the evidence in this work suggests that minor state-by-state differences in tax structure are relatively benign in terms of short run economic growth and/or recovery from a recessionary period."

- **Gale, William G., Aaron Krupkin, and Kim Reuben,** "The Relationship between Taxes and Growth at the State Level: New Evidence," *National Tax Journal* 68, no. 4 (2015): 919–942.

A particular focus of tax cut proponents is reducing income tax burdens, especially for those in the top tax brackets. The idea here is that this will be good for the economy because, if those in the upper brackets pay less in taxes, they will be free to use their money in ways that stimulate the economy. Most states levy income taxes, and they all operate within the same national economy at the same time, so they offer a great platform to comparatively test this hypothesis. If cutting tax rates produces an economic boost, states that decide to lower their top rates compared to others should, all else equal, see a positive economic effect. This is not what the authors find. They find income tax rates (and the effect of other taxes) are pretty unstable across time and, at least in some time periods, can even have a positive effect on economic growth. The

authors' bottom-line conclusion, though, is that marginal changes in tax rates have little effect at all on economic measures such as employment and the rate of business formation.

- **Anderson, John E., and Jennifer Bernad,** "Temporal and Spatial Effects of State Taxes on Economic Growth," paper presented at the 110th Annual Conference on Taxation, National Tax Association, Philadelphia, November 9–11, 2017.

Do taxes affect economic growth? This study concludes that, well, it depends. The authors conduct a series of state-level analyses on economic performance during the years 1999–2013. Importantly, they divide those years up into different periods, and they use different sets of variables to predict economic performance. What they find is that those choices matter—what time window you pick, and what set of variables within that window you use to model economic performance, turns out to have a significant influence on whether you find an impact of taxes on economic growth. They also find that the relationship between taxes and economic growth can be significantly influenced not just by an individual state's tax policies, but by the tax and economic policies of its neighbors. For example, a state that lowers taxes with the specific aim of trying to attract new businesses may have a tough time if neighboring states have poor labor mobility. In short, the authors find that the political choices in one state inevitably affect the economic performances of others.

CHAPTER 4

for CQ Press

Want a better grade?

Get the tools you need to sharpen your study skills. SAGE edge offers a robust online environment featuring an impressive array of free tools and resources.

Access practice quizzes, eFlashcards, video, and multimedia at **edge.sagepub.com/ smithgreenblatt7e**

Top Ten Takeaways

1. Budgets are not just ledgers recording revenues and expenditures; they are central policy documents. They reveal government policy and program priorities, and there is often intense political conflict over taxing and spending.

2. State and local governments raise and spend enormous amounts of money— roughly $3.5 trillion a year according to the latest available estimates.

3. The primary sources of revenue for state and local governments are sales taxes, property taxes, income taxes, motor vehicle taxes, estate taxes, and gift taxes. Other important sources of funding include intergovernmental transfers and a wide range of fees and other taxes.

4. Generally speaking, states raise more from income and sales taxes, and local governments raise more from property taxes.

5. There is considerable variation from state to state in tax capacity and tax effort. These differences are driven by other differences in variables such as demographics, geology, and the economic cycle.

6. Education is the biggest functional expenditure category for state and local governments. Other big areas of expenditure include health care, transportation, and public safety.

7. Unlike the federal government, the vast majority of states are legally required to have balanced budgets. State and local governments can borrow money, mostly in the form of bonds, but as a general rule they cannot engage in deficit spending.

8. Local governments facing tough financial times can declare bankruptcy as a final resort to gain relief from their financial obligations. States do not have this option.

9. There is considerable variation in the financial health of states and localities. Some are doing fine, while others are dealing with budget crises brought on by economic conditions, lingering effects of the Great Recession, long-term fiscal mismanagement, or political and ideological disagreement.

10. Over the past decade or two, subnational governments have lost some budget flexibility because of new accounting standards, unfunded mandates, and ballot initiatives that have limited government budgetary discretion.

Key Concepts

balanced budget (p. 94)
bonds (p. 92)
budget deficits or shortfalls (p. 82)
budget process (p. 92)
capital investments (p. 92)
discretionary spending (p. 95)
dividend (p. 91)
entitlement (p. 97)
estate taxes (p. 83)
excise or sin taxes (p. 83)
expenditures (p. 95)
fiscal federalism (p. 97)
fiscal year (p. 92)
focused consumption taxes (p. 83)
general obligation bonds (p. 92)
gift taxes (p. 83)

income taxes (p. 86)

insurance trust funds
(p. 87)

intergovernmental transfers
(p. 89)

municipal bonds (p. 92)

progressive tax system
(p. 86)

regressive taxes (p. 83)

revenue bonds (p. 92)

revenues (p. 82)

sales taxes (p. 83)

severance taxes (p. 87)

tax burden (p. 83)

tax capacity (p. 89)

tax effort (p. 89)

user fees (p. 82)

Suggested Websites

- **www.cbpp.org.** Website of the Center on Budget and Policy Priorities. Founded in 1981, the center studies fiscal policy and public programs at the federal and state levels that affect low-income and moderate-income families and individuals. An excellent source of information on state budget issues.

- **www.census.gov.** U.S. Census Bureau site provides a wealth of state and local data; allows anyone to download detailed revenue and expenditure information from an annual survey of state government finances.

- **www.nasbo.org.** Website of the National Association of State Budget Officers.

- **www.ncsl.org.** Website of the National Conference of State Legislatures. NCSL's fiscal program produces periodic state budget and tax updates and tracks state actions to close budget gaps.

Political Attitudes and Participation

Venting and Voting

The 1965 Voting Rights Act has been a key pillar of the franchise in numerous states that had discriminated against African Americans. The Supreme Court ruled a key section of the law unconstitutional in 2013, however, and protections for voters have been weakened in many states.

Chapter Objectives

After reading this chapter, you will be able to

- Describe the role of elections within the U.S. political system,

- Identify the different positions for which elections are used, and

- Discuss the role of public opinion in elections and representation.

Voting itself has become one of the most partisan issues in American politics. That is, there is now a sharp distinction between how the two major parties view questions regarding voting. For Republicans, the security and sanctity of the ballot has become paramount. The Republican Party has succeeded in a majority of the states in enacting over the past decade or so voter identification rules to require citizens to show certain types of government-issued photo IDs. President Donald Trump, without evidence, has frequently complained that votes from up to 5 million undocumented immigrants cost him the popular vote majority in the 2016 presidential election. Other Republicans maintain that instances of voter fraud need to be protected against. In some states, they are cutting back on the number of early voting days, which allow people to vote ahead of Election Day for convenience's sake. "All three branches of government have pulled back on protecting voting rights," according to Richard L. Hasen, a professor of law and political science at the University of California, Irvine.[1]

There's been no evidence of wide-scale voter fraud; Democrats contend that the Republican Party—also known as the Grand Old Party, or GOP—is trying to rig the game in its own favor by making it harder for certain groups to vote, such as college students and members of racial and ethnic minorities, under the theory they are more likely to support Democrats. In states where Democrats are in power, they are passing laws to make registration and voting easier, such as automatic voter registration (AVR). Since Oregon became the first state to create an AVR system in 2015, there are now more than a dozen states that register people to vote when they interact with the department of motor vehicles, or in some cases other agencies. Democrats in many places are also seeking to expand same-day registration, which would allow people to register on Election Day itself. There's also been a big push in recent years to restore voting rights to former felons—or even allow individuals currently serving in prison to vote (something currently allowed only in Maine and Vermont).

It's not yet clear what effect these separate sets of laws are having—whether requiring photo IDs discourages many voters, or whether making registration easy or even automatic prompts many more people actually to vote. The upshot of all this, however, is that the two parties currently take fundamentally different positions when it comes to the ease of allowing people to register and vote. For a half-century following passage of the Voting Rights Act in 1965, the federal government and states consistently tried to find ways to make voting easier. Whether allowing people to vote by mail, or creating early voting days to offer people additional chances to exercise their franchise, all the momentum was in the direction of making voting easier. That is no longer the case. A key section of the Voting Rights Act itself was tossed out by the Supreme Court in 2013.

States are now diverging in their approaches to the most fundamental aspect of a democracy—allowing the right to vote. Nearly every state enacted laws changing some aspect of its voting procedures in the two years following the 2016 election. Many were minor, but in general, Republican-controlled states toughened registration procedures and identification requirements, while states run by Democrats moved in the opposite direction.

Before we wade into the arguments on both sides, it's worth pointing out that who shows up to vote matters—a lot. There seem to be separate electorates now. Increasingly, the two major parties rely on particular groups for support, with GOP voters typically being more rural and suburban, and Democratic voters more likely to be members of minority groups and to live in denser metropolitan areas. Support for the Democratic Party is nearly a given among African Americans, while a majority of white voters no longer support Democratic candidates for president, or often other offices. Minority voters made up nearly one-third of the electorate in 2016—an enormous shift since the days when whites accounted for more than 90 percent of voters (95 percent in 1952).[2] "The overwhelming fact about American general elections right now is that the white male voter just isn't as powerful as he used to be," journalist David S. Bernstein wrote in 2016.[3] One of the lessons of Trump's victory in 2016, however, is that while white males and females have decreasing clout, they still form a large trove of votes that can decide elections.

Voters are split not only by race but increasingly also by place. A generation ago, it was unusual for presidential candidates to carry counties by 20 percentage points or more; now, such outcomes are more common than not. Localities more and more tend to vote for one party over the other—that's one reason there are so few competitive U.S. House or state legislative seats. Progressives and conservatives not only congregate in separate communities—both in the real world and on social media—but they also tend to think that people who do not share their views are not just misguided but wrong and untrustworthy. With the GOP now more conservative and Democrats growing rapidly more progressive, there are fewer moderates ready or even willing to compromise with the other side. As a result, political campaigns are becoming less concerned with persuading voters that candidates are taking the right stands on issues; instead, they devote time and resources to motivating like-minded individuals to turn out to vote. Political pros are turning to technology to target voters individually as much as possible. Political data mining has evolved far beyond the old idea, used commonly as a way of sorting out voters just 20 years ago, that you could guess a voter's partisan leanings by looking at the types of magazines he or she subscribes to. Now, campaigns access all manner of consumer databases and social media files, gleaning near-complete portraits of individuals' habits and inclinations.

In preparation for the 2016 presidential race, Republican Ted Cruz's campaign employed a team of statisticians and behavioral scientists to engage in "psychographic targeting," using data drawn from social media posts, surveys, and consumer information sources to get a sense of individual voters' personality types so that the campaign could tailor messages that might best appeal to them.[4] "The goal of these 'digital dossiers' is to profile likely voters and identify traits that predict voting habits," according to Chris Evans, managing editor of the *Minnesota Journal of Law, Science & Technology*. "Political data-mining has proven to be a winning election tactic, but the resulting erosion of voter privacy has gone unabated."[5]

Contemporary campaigns are using data for everything. Daily reports from a data consultant informed nearly every important decision made by Republican Marco Rubio's presidential campaign in 2016, including his decision to make questionable comments about Trump's male attributes: "Even the candidate's declivitous descent into dick jokes was guided by a rigorously quantitative determination of the most effective way for Rubio to reach his targeted voters," journalist Sasha Issenberg reported.[6]

Although most people will rarely, if ever, call or write to their members of Congress or state officials, some belong to groups that make the case for particular positions on given issues, such as the National Rifle Association and the Sierra Club. Interest groups, as discussed at greater length in Chapter 6, are organizations that attempt to influence policymakers. But not all voters belong to interest groups—or think of themselves as being part of one. Politicians know that their careers depend on more than financial contributions from such organized interests. Come election time, they need the support of the vast majority of people who do not belong to such groups and who do not pay close attention to politics on a regular basis.

Given all this, how do politicians figure out what the voters back home are thinking when it seems that the only people they hear from at the capitol or city hall are part of some organized group? This chapter answers that question and also looks at how voters maintain or change the political cultures and preferences of their states and districts over time. Some of the mechanisms for change discussed include elections and the avenues for direct democracy, such as ballot initiatives and referendums. Public opinion—and how and whether politicians respond to it—is another factor that influences political outcomes. As you read through this chapter, keep in mind the following questions:

- **What causes some states or localities to change party preferences?**
- **How do state regulations affect voting?**
- **How do politicians tune in to what citizens are thinking?**

Voting Rights Disputes

The notion of equal access to the ballot for all—one person, one vote—is a cornerstone of American democracy. But how do you determine whether the person seeking to vote has the right to vote? That question is at the center of one of the major debates in U.S. politics in recent years. Numerous states have put in place greater safeguards to protect against voter fraud, demanding evidence of identification such as driver's licenses at polling places and sometimes requiring that those wishing to register to vote produce documents such as birth certificates. These laws were given the green light by the Supreme Court in 2008, when it upheld a 2005 Indiana law requiring that voters produce government-issued photo identification at the polls.

Republicans say they are instituting restrictions such as voter ID requirements in order to combat fraud. "The fact is, voter fraud is rampant," Greg Abbott, the Republican governor of Texas, said in 2016. "In Texas, unlike some other states and unlike some other leaders, we are committed to cracking down on voter fraud."[7] There's not much evidence to back up such claims. In 2014, the Alabama Republican Party went so far as to offer a reward of $1,000 to anyone who could help find examples of voter fraud, but still came up empty. States such as Alabama have had to contend with criticism that they are not doing enough to make the required IDs readily accessible. In 2015, Alabama backed away from a plan to close 31 offices of the Department of Motor Vehicles in mostly high-minority-population counties after facing criticism and lawsuits arguing that this would make it too difficult for residents to obtain driver's licenses that would allow them to vote.

Separately in 2015, Ohio secretary of state Jon Husted turned over 14 cases of alleged voter fraud to state and county prosecutors. Those cases—which hadn't been proved—represented 0.0004 percent of the 3,149,876 votes cast in Ohio the previous year.[8] Justin Levitt, a law professor at Loyola Marymount University, found 31 credible incidents of voter impersonation (someone casting an improper ballot in a way that an ID law could prevent) across the country between 2000 and 2014, out of more than 1 billion primary, special, and municipal election ballots cast.[9] Critics of voter ID laws argue that such findings prove that the laws provide a fake fix for a nonexistent problem. "We might have stopped 31 impersonation cases out of 1,000,000,000 votes to the tune of tens of millions of $ to distribute IDs & litigate," tweeted Michael McDonald, an elections expert at the University of Florida.[10] A North Carolina congressional election was marred by fraud in 2018, with hundreds of absentee ballots destroyed by bad actors. But in-person voting fraud of the type addressed by voter ID laws is vanishingly rare.

If voter fraud is not a real problem, why have so many states passed voting restrictions? Democrats accuse Republicans of acting in bad faith, seeking to make voting more difficult and disenfranchising members of groups most likely to support Democratic candidates. In 2016, students from the University of Wisconsin staged a protest at the nearby state capitol against proposed changes to voter registration procedures, which followed Wisconsin's implementation of strict voter ID requirements. "It just seems like the legislature here is trying to limit the student vote," said UW senior Kenneth Cole, who was at the protest.[11]

Complaints about GOP vote suppression have become commonplace among Democrats and civil rights groups. Republican politicians and party officials have occasionally added fuel to the fire, making comments suggesting that voter ID laws help their side win. "Any time you hail the passage of a law as potentially helping your side win elections, you're basically begging to be accused of passing it for the wrong reasons," notes political reporter Aaron Blake of the *Washington Post*.[12] In 2012, GOP consultant Scott Tranter described voter ID requirements and laws that led to long lines at polling places as part of the Republican tool kit.[13] In 2016, a former chief of staff for a Wisconsin state senator took to Facebook to explain that he had left the GOP because of the party's attempt to game the system by passing voting restrictions. "I was in the closed Senate Republican Caucus when the final round of multiple Voter ID bills were being discussed," he wrote. "A handful of the GOP Senators were giddy about the ramifications and literally singled out the prospects of suppressing minority and college voters."[14]

Brad Schimel, then the Republican attorney general in Wisconsin, suggested in 2018 that the voter ID law helped Trump narrowly carry the state in 2016. Wisconsin had supported Democratic presidential candidates in the previous seven straight elections. "We battled to get voter ID on the ballot for the November '16 election," he said during a talk radio appearance. "How many of your listeners are sure that Sen. [Ron] Johnson was going to win reelection, or President Trump was going to win Wisconsin, if we didn't have voter ID to keep Wisconsin's elections clean and honest and have integrity?"[15] Wisconsin had the second-highest turnout rate in the nation in 2008 and 2012, but voter turnout dropped markedly in 2016, particularly in largely Democratic Milwaukee. A University of Wisconsin survey found that 11 percent of nonvoting citizens in Milwaukee and Dane Counties, the latter of which includes Madison and is the state's other Democratic stronghold, had been deterred by the state's voter ID law.[16] But other political scientists have questioned the methodology of surveys that found thousands or even hundreds of thousands of voters were disenfranchised, arguing that other factors—such as simply not liking the candidates on offer—may have dampened turnout more than mechanical restrictions.[17]

And, despite the accusations that the GOP is seeking a partisan edge, voters are mostly supportive of these restrictions. Polls consistently show that upwards of 70 percent of respondents support the idea of having to show a government-issued ID in order to vote. It's not yet clear, even if the GOP's intent has been to suppress voting, that the party has succeeded. Nearly all adult Americans have some form of photo identification. And most of the people who are unable or unwilling to acquire such ID might not vote anyway.

Every election year now brings with it horror stories about citizens who have been newly disenfranchised. In 2015, Mary Lou Miller, a 101-year-old woman who had been voting since 1934, was prevented from voting in the San Antonio mayoral election due to lack of a driver's license, passport, or other identification.[18] The Government Accountability Office, Congress's investigating agency, released a study in 2014 that suggested states that adopted strict voter ID laws saw turnout drop a couple of percentage points from 2008 to 2012 in comparison with states that hadn't adopted such laws.[19]

A 2016 study by political scientists at the University of California, San Diego, found that strict ID laws would be expected to depress turnout among twice as many Democrats as Republicans. "A strict ID law could be expected to depress Latino turnout by 9.3 points, black turnout by 8.6 points and Asian American turnout by 12.5 points," they wrote.[20] Several state voter ID laws—including Wisconsin's—have been successfully challenged in court. The Fourth Circuit Court of Appeals, for example, found that North Carolina's law was

discriminatory, designed to "target African Americans with almost surgical precision."[21]

Still, some scholars have found that the laws have had minimal effects. A study of voters in Tennessee and Virginia found that informing residents with a low propensity to vote about identification requirements raised turnout among them slightly.[22] And a 2016 study by University of Michigan political scientists found that voter ID laws actually had the effect of making Democrats more likely to vote, in effect mobilizing them by making them angry.[23] "There's an active pushback going on of people wanting to say, 'Like hell you'll take my vote away,'" said Bob Hall, executive director of Democracy North Carolina, an advocacy group that registers voters in the state.[24]

The U.S. Census Bureau found that about two in three eligible African Americans (66.2 percent) voted in the 2012 election, which was higher than the share of non-Hispanic whites who voted (64.1 percent).[25] African American turnout was down in 2016. Republicans argued that was due to lack of enthusiasm among African Americans for Hillary Clinton, but progressives said it was evidence of the GOP's vote suppression efforts.

Having passed voter ID laws in more than 30 states, Republicans are turning to voter rolls—the databases of registered voters maintained by states. In 2018, the Supreme Court rejected a challenge brought against Ohio's aggressive voter purging system. Once registered voters skip four years' worth of elections, Ohio mails them a confirmation notice. It then drops from the rolls individuals who don't respond and fail to vote for another four years. In 2015 and 2016, Ohio purged 426,781 voters this way. Writing for the majority, Justice Samuel Alito said that as many as one out of eight voter registrations nationwide "are either invalid or significantly inaccurate," noting that the Ohio system purges people for failing to respond to the state's notice, not solely for failing to vote. Voting rights advocates, however, warned that the decision gave a green light to other states to find new ways to purge voters. "Concerted state efforts to prevent minorities from voting and to undermine the efficacy of their votes are an unfortunate feature of our country's history," Justice Sonia Sotomayor wrote in dissent. "Today's decision forces these communities and their allies to be even more proactive and vigilant in holding their states accountable and working to dismantle the obstacles they face in exercising the fundamental right to vote."

In most states controlled by Democrats, voting is getting easier. Blue states such as Oregon, California,

STATES UNDER STRESS

ELECTION OFFICIALS FACE INCREASED CHALLENGES IN KEEPING VOTES SAFE

A few months after the 2016 election, the Department of Homeland Security (DHS) reported that Russians had attempted—but mostly failed—to hack voting databases in 21 states. According to a leaked National Security Agency (NSA) document, Russian intelligence also attempted to crack into registration software that's used in 8 states. "Over 20 states have been hampered with in some fashion, but no one seems to know what states they are, which means the Department of Homeland Security has not shared that information," said Iowa secretary of state Paul Pate. "We're still a little frustrated on that count."

In 2017, computer hackers took less than two hours to break into voting machines at a computer security conference known as DEF CON. The security of election systems remains a primary concern. The following year, Congress approved $380 million worth of grants to states to improve election administration, including technology and security improvements.

In response to the threat, some states have rediscovered the virtue of paper ballots. For 2017 state elections, Virginia election officials decided not to stop using paperless touch-screen machines, to protect against unauthorized access. DHS and FBI officials monitored that election on the ground. "States and counties were already moving toward paper ballots before 2016," Katy Owens Hubler, a consultant to the National Conference of State Legislatures, told *Stateline*. "But the Russian hacking incident has brought the spotlight to this issue."

Shortly after taking office, President Donald Trump convened a commission to look into election matters, including security, which was led by Vice President Mike Pence and Kansas secretary of state Kris Kobach. The commission asked states to supply every voter's personal data, including addresses, partial Social Security numbers, and voting histories. More than 40 states have rejected at least part of the request, sometimes in colorful, "go jump in the Gulf of Mexico"-style language. Lawsuits poured in from privacy advocates, and the commission was soon suspended. Given the heightened concern about election security, state officials found it an odd moment to attempt to construct a national database of voter information. "States are super-conscious right now, given the concerns about voter security and their databases, in handing over this information," says Tomas Lopez, counsel for the Brennan Center for Justice at New York University Law School. "States have some reason to be wary about how this information is going to be used." In 2018, the Brennan Center released a survey of 500 election officials in 41 states. It found that two-thirds of them will need to replace voting machines by 2020 but lack the funding to do so.

News of Russian attacks have undoubtedly made state and local election officials more vigilant. But Connie Lawson, Indiana's secretary of state, says that media reports and think tank studies sometimes overstate the problem. "They were not successful. Our systems held," she says. DHS has said that while hackers attacked the systems of 21 states, they only penetrated one state, Illinois, and even there failed to make discernible changes to files.

But many voters remain nervous, not knowing whether their own votes will count or whether the final tally can be trusted. Such worries can be as damaging as the hacks themselves. "What terrorists do is instill fear into the general population," Alex Padilla, secretary of state of California, told the *Washington Post*. "If they've done that they've accomplished their goals."

Source: Adapted from Alan Greenblatt, "Ill-Prepared and Underfunded, Election Officials Brace for More Cyberattacks," *Governing*, February 14, 2018, http://www.governing.com/gov-election-cyberattacks-testimony-russia.html.

and Vermont pioneered automatic voter registration systems, which put people on voter rolls unless they specifically ask not to be registered, based on their driver's license applications or other government databases. "Democracy is served when more people participate," Jay Inslee, the Democratic governor of Washington, said in 2018 when he signed a package of bills designed to make voting easier, including creation of an automatic voter registration system.

Changes in law that made voting easier in recent decades have led to small but noticeable increases in voter turnout. That doesn't mean that automatic voter registration will automatically lead to greater turnout. Individuals who were not motivated to register themselves may not make the effort to vote. "Candidates will need to convince these *potential* voters that there is a reason to turn out," political scientists Jan Leighley and Jonathan Nagler wrote after Oregon passed its AVR law. "Strong get-out-the-vote efforts are surely critical to getting newly-registered Oregonians to cast ballots."[26] Demos, a progressive think tank, found that individuals registered through AVR in Oregon were more diverse than registered voters in the state as a whole.[27] A report by the Center for American Progress, another liberal think tank, found that, thanks to AVR, the state's registered voters were more reflective of its population as a whole, because citizens registered through the department of motor vehicles were "younger, more rural, lower-income, and more ethnically diverse."[28]

Just as Republicans may be guilty of attempting to limit voting among groups unfavorable to them, so Democrats might have an ulterior motive in expanding access to the ballot box. A 2016 Stanford University study found that only 14 percent of Americans who don't appear on voter rolls or consumer marketing lists favor the Republican Party. "We find that if unregistered and unlisted people voted at comparable rates to registered people with the same level of interest in politics, both the 2000 and 2004 Presidential elections would have been won by Democrats," the authors conclude.[29]

Let us turn now to the broader question of who turns out to vote, and why.

Elections

Voters in Missouri had no fewer than four chances to vote in 2016. Presidential primaries were held in March, with local elections following in April. Congressional and state primaries were not held until August, and the general election took place in November. This was emblematic of the odd paradox we have created as a nation. Americans like elections—we hold more of them than any other country on earth—yet we consistently score one of the lowest voter turnout rates of any democracy in the world.

State political cultures are reflected and sustained through elections, when a majority or **plurality** of voters elects officials who more or less share the political

Plurality The highest number of votes garnered by any of the candidates for a particular office but short of an outright majority.

beliefs of the majority or plurality. The use of elections to select the holders of public office is the fundamental process of representative democracies. More bluntly, elections are the main way that the will of the people connects to and influences the actions of government. Election laws are set and controlled by the states, and each state must determine what constitutes a valid vote. There has long been a great deal of variation among states regarding how easy or how hard it is for citizens to vote. As noted above, such differences are once again becoming pronounced.

But differences in election laws are not the only reason one state may tend to vote differently than its neighbors, in partisan terms. For about 100 years after the Civil War, for example, Republicans were not a true national party. They had next to no presence in the South, which still resented Republican intrusions during the Civil War and Reconstruction in support of abolition, suffrage, and economic opportunity for African Americans. That is one reason Democrats held the region for decades. In fact, the Republican Party of the 19th century bore a closer resemblance in some ways to the Democratic Party of today than to its 21st-century GOP descendant.

Times and political parties change, however. These days, the South is one of the pillars of Republican strength. The region's continuing conservatism now fits well within the GOP. Southern states and the less populous, heavily rural states of the Mountain West, such as Idaho, Wyoming, and Montana, tilt toward Republican interests. For a time in the 1970s and 1980s, they formed a bloc that helped elect presidents through their disproportionate strength in the Electoral College. Each state's Electoral College votes are equal to the size of its congressional delegation. Because each state is guaranteed at least two U.S. senators and one U.S. representative, the Electoral College gives a minimum of three votes to each state, regardless of population. This means that the voting power of smaller states in the Electoral College is disproportionately larger than the states' populations, whereas the voting power of bigger states is disproportionately lower.

For example, in 2012, California had 55 electoral votes to represent a population of nearly 37.7 million. In that presidential election, then, each of California's Electoral College votes represented about 685,000 people. Contrast that with Wyoming, which had the minimum of 3 Electoral College votes but had a population of only about 568,000. Each of Wyoming's Electoral

College votes, in other words, represented nearly 190,000 people. Political analyst Steven Hill, director of the political reform program at the New America Foundation, calls this "affirmative action for low-population states."[30] This is why Republican Donald Trump was able to win the presidency in 2016 despite losing the popular vote—the second time in five elections (the other coming in 2000) when the Republican candidate won the presidency despite receiving fewer votes than his Democratic rival. The most recent example of this happening before then was way back in 1888. "It's the result of . . . the anti-urban bias in American politics and American culture," writes historian Steven Conn. "The Founders were deeply suspicious of popular rule, which for them meant 'the mobs of great cities' in Thomas Jefferson's memorable phrase, and so they created a system in which those cities and their inhabitants would be held in check by land and by land-owners."[31] This imbalance in the representation of Electoral College votes leads to periodic efforts by groups that want to make sure no one ends up in the White House with fewer popular votes than the opponent—an incredibly tough reform to pull off without amending the Constitution. In recent years, for example, states such as Maryland, Massachusetts, and California have enacted laws that will require them to award their electoral votes according to national popular vote percentages, but those measures won't take effect until a preponderance of states are on board with the idea.

In more recent elections, however, the larger, more urbanized states have—sometimes—been able to outvote the rest. With Texas being the only highly populous state that votes reliably Republican, Democrats had the upper hand in presidential voting heading into 2016. Perhaps for this reason, in states such as Pennsylvania and Virginia, where the GOP controls the legislature but voters have tended to prefer Democratic presidential candidates, legislators have talked about awarding electoral votes by congressional district rather than sticking with the traditional winner-take-all system. Those efforts have yet to meet with success.

If there's disagreement between states about the best political approach to take, there's also disagreement within states. Some voters have felt disenfranchised lately because one party dominates state politics and they don't subscribe to that party's platform. That's always the case to some extent—politics is about picking winners and losers, after all—but in this highly polarized system, people in more conservative, rural areas may feel powerless and resentful when their state is dominated by more liberal, urban-voting blocs. That's why smaller counties in states such as California and Colorado have held secession votes in recent years. In other words, residents in those counties have been so unhappy with state laws regarding issues such as gun control and environmental regulation that they want to split off and form their own states. (Don't hold your breath waiting for that to actually happen anytime soon.) Conversely, progressive politicians in big cities have been upset by the fact that the GOP-dominated legislatures in their states have preempted the progressives' ability to pass ordinances on matters such as LGBT rights and minimum-wage increases. In 2018, California voters were presented with the choice of whether to split their state into three, but a proposal for the state to secede from the union entirely never made it off the ground.

A Voice for the Public

People do not feel well connected to government; some hate it. Less than half the voting-age population cast ballots in presidential elections. In elections in which congressional or statewide offices are at the top of the ticket, the number drops to less than 40 percent. For municipal elections, turnout rates are generally less than 20 percent.

Voting does tend to pick up for competitive races, when voters feel as though they have a genuine choice and might make a real difference. The major political parties, however, have reconciled themselves to the reality that millions of people feel that their votes don't count. Sometimes the parties are even accused of suppressing turnout by using negative ads and other means to sour people who might vote for the other side.

It is true that the majority of voters remain loyal to one party over the other throughout most of their voting lives; yet they can be convinced to cast their votes—or even to change their votes—by any number of factors. The state of the economy, the health of a state's budget, corruption scandals, or the course of a military conflict may change minds and voting habits. "Each election forces one to revisit such topics as to what's effective in voter mobilization or who you aim at," says independent political analyst Rhodes Cook.[32]

But contemporary voters seem to be pretty well set in their ways. In 2017, polling by Gallup found that a near-record 42 percent of Americans identified themselves

A DIFFERENCE THAT MAKES A DIFFERENCE
THE ELECTIONS NO ONE CARES ABOUT

Seattle voters had the chance to reshape their city council in 2015. The city changed its method of electing council members that year from at-large to separate districts around Seattle. Heading into the election, it was clear that, thanks to retirements and the primary defeat of an incumbent, at least four of the nine council seats would be won by newcomers. How much did Seattle residents care about all these changes? Not much. Turnout was below 30 percent in the city, while reaching record lows in Washington State.

It's a familiar story. Most municipal elections are held during odd-numbered years and in months far from November. Only five states (Arkansas, Kentucky, Nebraska, Oregon, and Rhode Island) hold all their municipal elections in November of even-numbered years. When elections are held on stand-alone dates, with no state or federal races to boost turnout, most voters don't show up. Local elections that fail to draw more than 10 or 20 percent of voters are common.

Voter turnout for local elections has historically lagged behind turnout for state and federal races, but recent examples suggest that the problem may be getting worse. Turnout in Los Angeles has gotten so bad that the city council has explored instituting a lottery system to offer cash prizes to some voters. That's an idea that has started to catch on. In 2015, a group called the Southwest Voter Registration Education Project, which seeks to boost Latino voting, paid $25,000 to a Los Angeles man for voting. A Philadelphia foundation handed out a $10,000 prize for voting that year.

The habit of holding local elections on dates separate from state and national elections has "outlived its usefulness," says Melissa Marschall, who leads the Local Elections in America Project at Rice University. She coauthored a study in 2016 that found turnout was double for mayoral elections in California that were timed to coincide with presidential elections, compared to elections conducted off-cycle.

Some state officials agree it's time for a change. In 2015, Kansas moved its local elections from the spring to the fall of odd-numbered years. That year, California enacted a law to force localities with low turnout—less than 25 percent on average over four elections—to move

their elections so that they overlap with state or federal contests. Such moves should make a difference. In 2013, a study by two University of Wisconsin political scientists found that shifting mayoral elections to presidential years results in a jump in turnout of 18.5 percentage points, while switching to November of a midterm election year yields an average increase of 8.7 percentage points.

There's a reason municipal elections are often held separately. Local governments began the practice during the Progressive Era of the early 20th century in the hope that it would keep state and federal elections from overshadowing the mostly nonpartisan local ones. "Any serious, in-depth examination of the effects of odd-numbered year municipal elections would examine not just voter turnout, but also voter knowledge of candidates," says Scott Mooneyham of the North Carolina League of Municipalities. "In order to enjoy viable candidacies at the local level, candidates usually have to engage in traditional political base-building gained through involvement in public institutions and civic engagement."

But focusing attention on local races may not have been the sole motivation for keeping those elections separate a century ago. According to Marschall, "The original reason was really to decrease the influence of immigrant voting and break the political machines. They thought it would be more difficult for non-English speakers to turn out, and it proved to be really effective."

In contemporary times, it remains the case that only a small subset of voters—who tend to be whiter, wealthier, and older than the population as a whole—vote during stand-alone municipal elections. That allows interest groups to "capture" local elections, Marschall says. Sarah Anzia, a political scientist at the University of California, Berkeley, notes in her book *Timing and Turnout: How Off-Cycle Elections Favor Organized Groups* that teachers' unions are often able to motivate their members to vote, helping to elect friendly candidates in low-turnout school board elections. School districts that hold off-cycle elections pay experienced teachers 3 percent more than do districts that hold concurrent elections, Anzia found.

Source: Adapted from Alan Greenblatt, "The Elections No One Cares About," *Governing*, August 11, 2015, http://www.governing.com/topics/elections/gov-moving-municipal-elections-concurrent.html.

as independents, compared with 29 percent identifying as Democrats and 27 percent as Republicans.[33] That's in keeping with other surveys, as well as with surges in the numbers of independent or unaffiliated voters in states where people register by party, such as Florida. Increasingly, people vote for the same party up and down the ballot, voting either Democratic or Republican for everything from state legislative contests on up to the presidency.

State Supervision of Elections

The U.S. Constitution gives states the authority to determine "the times, places and manner of holding elections." In nearly every state, the secretary of state has the practical duty of running elections: setting dates, qualifying candidates, and printing and counting the ballots. In a few states, the lieutenant governor or a state election board oversees these chores. The states, in turn, rely on the counties or, in some cases, cities to run the polls themselves. The localities draw precinct boundaries and set up and supervise polling places. In many cases, they have the main responsibility for registering voters. Following an election, county officials count the ballots and report the results to the appropriate individual, such as the secretary of state, who then tabulates and certifies the totals.

The styles of the ballots used vary from state to state. California currently uses a random alphabet system to decide the order in which candidate names appear, rotating the starting letter of that alphabet in each state assembly district. The **office group ballot**, also known as the **Massachusetts ballot**, lists candidates' names, followed by their party designations, under the title of the office they are seeking (governor, state representative, and so on). The other major type of ballot is the **party column ballot**, or the **Indiana ballot**, which "arranges the candidates for each office in columns according to their party designation."[34] Nine states make it even easier for citizens to vote for party nominees—voters can cast a **straight ticket** vote for all of one party's candidates with one computer click or pull of the lever. This is a practice in decline, however; several states have abolished it, most recently Iowa and Texas in 2017.[35]

Each state's election code determines the specific details about ballots and, perhaps most important, the order in which offices and candidates will appear. This varies considerably among the states. By 1992, about 80 percent of the states had replaced paper ballots with punch cards, machines in which voters pull a lever next to the name of the candidate of their choice, or optical-scan voting machines.[36] Voters in most states now use electronic systems resembling automated teller machines (ATMs), but all but a handful of states require a paper trail to allow for verification of the electronic results. Nearly all states tabulate votes for write-in candidates, although victories or even significant showings by such candidates are few and far between.

A few cities, including Minneapolis and San Francisco, use ranked-choice voting (RCV) for municipal elections. In 2018, Maine became the first state to hold a ranked-choice voting primary. Rather than picking one candidate, voters rank all the choices. If one candidate receives more than 50 percent of the first-choice votes, he or she wins. If no one receives a majority of the first-choice votes, the candidate with the lowest number of votes is disqualified, and his or her supporters' second-place choices are redistributed among the remaining candidates. This process continues until someone emerges with a majority. The benefit of such a system, supporters say, is that a candidate who is acceptable to a majority of voters will win, as opposed to the outcome in a winner-take-all election in which a candidate with only, say, 30 to 40 percent of the vote comes out on top of a large split field. But RCV has its critics, who say it can result in victories for candidates who were the first choice of few. Jean Quan, for instance, was elected mayor of Oakland, California, in 2010 after being picked as the first choice of just 24 percent of voters. Burlington, Vermont, and Aspen, Colorado, abandoned the instant-runoff voting method after complaints that it left voters confused.[37]

Regulating the Parties

A state's authority to print ballots or purchase voting software gives it enormous control over which parties and candidates are presented to the voters. Until the late 19th century, parties themselves printed the ballots, a system that obviously encouraged voters to select a straight ticket of their chosen party's nominees.

....

Office group (Massachusetts) ballot A ballot in which candidates are listed by name under the title of the office they are seeking.

Party column (Indiana) ballot A ballot in which the names of candidates are divided into columns arranged according to political party.

Straight ticket Originally, a type of ballot that allowed voters to pick all of one party's candidates at once; today, voting a straight ticket refers to voting for all of one party's candidates for various offices—for instance, voting for all Democrats or all Republicans.

A DIFFERENCE THAT MAKES A DIFFERENCE
THE PLUSES AND MINUSES OF RANKED-CHOICE VOTING

Maine voters who didn't like the way elections had turned out in the past chose an entirely different voting system in 2016. A ballot measure approved by voters made Maine the first state to implement something known as ranked-choice voting.

Under the new system, voters rank candidates from most to least preferable. If no one receives a majority on the first ballot, the candidate with the fewest votes is eliminated, and voters' second choices are counted up. The process continues until a candidate earns a majority of the remaining ballots. "People like it because they really feel strongly that candidates should be supported by a majority of voters," said Kyle Bailey, the campaign manager for the initiative.

Ranked-choice voting—sometimes known as instant-runoff voting—has already been adopted in about a dozen cities, including Minneapolis; San Francisco; and Oakland, California. It turned out to have a special appeal in Maine. Because of relatively strong independent candidates, the winner in 9 out of the previous 11 gubernatorial elections in Maine had come away with less than a majority of the vote, including GOP governor Paul LePage, who won twice with pluralities. After his first victory in 2010, some Maine residents put "61 percent" stickers on their cars, identifying themselves as part of the large majority that voted against LePage.

Ranked-choice voting, some political scientists found, can lead to more civilized politics. Candidates can't run a slash-and-burn campaign against their opponents because they can't afford to alienate anyone's supporters and risk a shot at being second choice. In the 2018 mayoral race in San Francisco, candidates Jane Kim and Mark Leno appeared in a joint TV ad, both urging their supporters to support the other. "When candidates have to campaign for a second- or third-place vote, it changes the dynamic from a zero-sum game," said Caroline Tolbert, a political scientist at the University of Iowa who has conducted surveys in cities with both ranked-choice voting and traditional voting. "Respondents in RCV cities felt that the campaigns were less negative."

But other political scientists who have studied the method have identified some problems. One challenge is voter "exhaustion," according to a study by researchers Craig Burnett and Vladimir Kogan. Looking at several local elections in California, they found that 10 to 27 percent of voters eventually stopped completing their ballots and thus did not participate in the final round that picked the winner. "This idea that a large number of people are going to have their ballots not counted is a huge problem in every context where RCV is used," said Kogan, who teaches at Ohio State University.

Ranked-choice voting may also lead to an overall decline in voter participation. According to a study by Jason McDaniel at San Francisco State University, the system led to lower turnout in San Francisco mayoral elections. "When voting is made more difficult," he said, "we should expect there to be some negative consequences with respect to ballot errors and voter participation, especially among those with less education, among certain racial minority groups who are less likely to participate, and among some portions of the elderly population."

Several localities that have adopted ranked-choice voting later eliminated it. That includes Burlington, Vermont, where people were unhappy with the candidate chosen in the 2009 mayoral election. But David Kimball, a University of Missouri–St. Louis political scientist who has studied ranked-choice voting, notes that "using the regular system, there are plenty of cities that don't like the mayor they got, either."

Source: Adapted from Alan Greenblatt, "Maine Becomes First State to Adopt a Whole New Way of Voting," *Governing*, November 9, 2016, http://www.governing.com/topics/elections/gov-maine-ranked-choice-voting-2016-ballot-measure.html.

The advent of the **secret ballot**, also known as the **Australian ballot**, led the states to print their own ballots and, therefore, to determine which parties

. . . .

Secret (Australian) ballot A ballot printed by a state that allows voters to pick and choose among different candidates and party preferences in private.

should appear on ballots. "From there," writes Kay Lawson, a retired San Francisco State University political scientist, "it seemed but a short step to requiring that parties show a minimum level of support to qualify."[38]

The Republican and Democratic Parties are themselves regulated at the state level by a bewildering array of varying state laws. Some states provide detailed

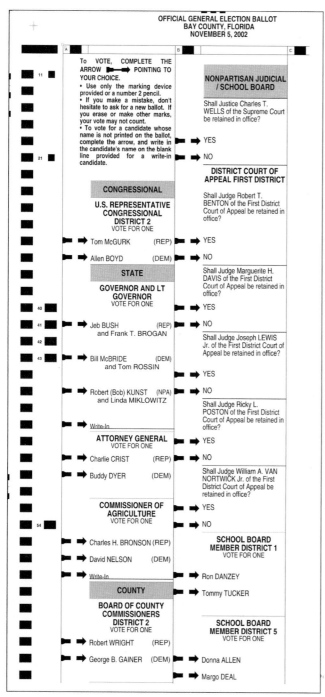

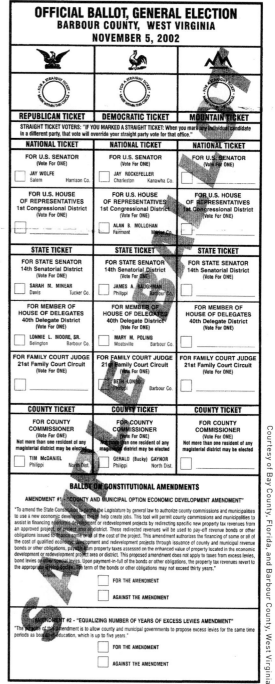

The two main types of ballots are the office group ballot and the party column ballot. These sample ballots from elections in Florida and West Virginia show the differences between the two basic approaches to ballot design. The West Virginia ballot exemplifies the party column ballot, which lists the candidates in columns that indicate their party designations. The Florida ballot, on the other hand, emphasizes office rather than party. This is the key feature of the office group ballot, which lists candidates by name and party under the title of the office they are running for.

regulations for party organization, activities, and nominating procedures. Others are silent on many specific matters. According to political scientist V. O. Key, the traditional Democratic one-party control of the South, although now a thing of the past, led to the introduction of the political primary. Voters had no real choice in the general election, so primaries gave them a say in who ultimately would hold an office.[39] For that reason, some southern states—which Democrats once entirely dominated—hold runoff elections when no candidate receives a majority of the primary vote. "They trace their lineage back to an era when there was only one party in politics," said Charles Bullock, a political scientist at the University of Georgia who wrote a book about runoff elections. "Back in the day when the South was one-party Democratic, the runoff was often the determinative election. So you often had more people participating in the runoff than in the original primary."[40] These days, nearly all states hold primary elections to pick party nominees for state offices, although some states, such as Virginia, still nominate candidates at party conventions. (A fuller discussion of political parties can be found in Chapter 6.)

The two major parties may not like all the state ballot regulations they have to comply with, but the rules in many states are designed to favor them over new or minor parties and independent candidates. Prior to a pair of Supreme Court decisions in the late 1960s, it was possible for states to have no mechanism in place to qualify new parties for their ballots. Even today, according to Richard Winger, editor of the newsletter *Ballot Access News*, in 11 states new parties cannot qualify for the ballot before they have picked their candidates, who must be listed on their ballot access petition along with voters' signatures.[41]

The Court's decisions meant that a state no longer could require that a certain percentage of signatures be collected in each county. But that did not mean states could not erect new roadblocks to keep out aspiring parties or candidates. Nine states changed their laws to require that signatures be collected in each congressional district. This kept ballot access elusive for candidates or parties that had most of their support in particular cities or regions. Fifteen states also placed time constraints on when signatures could be collected.

Some of the most restrictive ballot access laws have been repealed by various state and federal courts. For example, Ohio and California used to require new parties to qualify even before the election year began,

but these laws were struck down in 2006 and 2012, respectively. Virginia formerly blocked petitioners from gathering signatures outside their home congressional districts, but that law was also struck down in 2012. In West Virginia, the law used to require petition circulators who were trying to collect signatures to tell everyone they approached, "If you sign my petition, you can't vote in the primary." That happened not to be true—but it was the law, until a court struck it down in 2004. Why make a law requiring circulators to fib to voters? Well, such a fib benefits the major parties by keeping out the competition, and the major parties write the laws.

These sorts of laws benefiting political parties, if not the democratic process, remain on the books in various places. Texas insisted for years that voters who participated in major-party primaries were not allowed to sign petitions to get new parties on the ballot; the state also required citizens to know their voter registration numbers and to affix those numbers next to their signatures on petitions. Quick—what's your voter registration number? Those requirements were eventually tossed out following repeated court challenges. But Texas still puts up plenty of roadblocks. People looking to register voters must be deputized by individual counties after completing training courses and face misdemeanor charges if the individuals they register make mistakes on their forms, or if they turn in those forms more than five days after registering. "It is incredibly difficult and incredibly scary as an organization to be in a state . . . where you can go to jail for not trying to do anything but register another Texan to vote," said Jeremy Bird, founder of Battleground Texas, a group trying to organize the state for Democrats.[42]

In its 1971 decision in *Jenness v. Fortson*, the Supreme Court upheld a Georgia law that requires minor parties or independent candidates to collect signatures that represent 5 percent of registered voters. In 1986, the Georgia legislature lowered that threshold to 1 percent for statewide petitions, but that still means more than 50,000 signatures, a bar no one has been able to meet since 2000. Georgia continues to require signatures from 5 percent of registered voters on petitions for district and county offices, which is one big reason no minor party has appeared on the ballot for a regularly scheduled U.S. House election there since 1942. Other Republican-controlled states, such as Alabama, Oklahoma, and Tennessee, have passed laws since 2013 to discourage minor parties. "The time, money and energy spent getting on the ballot is more than the time, money and energy spent once we are on the ballot in most of these states," said Phil Huckelberry, cochair of the Green Party's ballot access committee.[43]

For third-party and independent candidates, then, it can be a real challenge to gain access to the ballot. Of course, how hard or easy it is for these political outsiders to get on the ballot varies from state to state. As with everything else, there are differences that make a difference. Given what we know about Daniel Elazar's theory regarding traditionalistic states and their hierarchical attitude toward politics, it should not surprise us that southern states such as Alabama, North Carolina, and Oklahoma have the most restrictive ballot access laws. That does not mean that hundreds of minor-party and independent candidates have not overcome all these hurdles and more to win spots on statewide ballots. A few of them have even won election as governor—for instance, in Minnesota in 1998, Maine in 1994 and 1998, and Rhode Island in 2010 (though note that all three of these examples involve moralistic or individualistic states). Their place on a ballot one year, however, is no guarantee that members of their parties will qualify the next time around. Alabama requires that a minor party poll at least 20 percent of the previous vote for state offices to win an automatic qualification for the next ballot. New Jersey and Virginia require at least 10 percent, and Pennsylvania requires 15 percent, or more than 1 million votes. Given all the restrictions, Lawson concludes, "The laws have been effective in keeping minor parties off the ballot in election after election."[44]

Minor-party candidates are concerned about ballot access in more progressive states as well. Since 2008, Washington State has used a top-two primary system, in which the top two finishers proceed to the general election, regardless of party. California voters adopted the same system in 2010. The top-two primary presents a big obstacle to minor parties and independent candidates; primary elections tend to be low-turnout affairs dominated by voters who are major-party partisans. As a result, independents and minor-party candidates rarely—if ever—have the chance to appear on general election ballots. Out of 86 instances in which minor-party candidates and at least two major-party candidates were running for federal or state office under the top-two voting system leading into 2014, the minor-party candidate qualified for the general election exactly zero times.[45] "It's the biggest threat to independent and third parties in the last 50 years," complained Christina

Tobin, a Libertarian Party candidate for California secretary of state in 2010.[46]

Why all the restrictions? Keeping minor parties off the ballot naturally helps the two major parties. Those who are in power control the rules that keep them in power. "VA's D legislature thought the rules up, knowing they would benefit themselves & friends," tweeted Larry Sabato, director of the University of Virginia's Center for Politics, in 2011. "Then Rs, once in power, liked restrictions too."[47]

Restricting Voters

The sense that the rules can rig the game is one reason restrictions on voters themselves have become controversial of late. States do not regulate only the access of parties to the ballot, after all; they also regulate the interaction of citizens with that ballot. They determine who can register to vote and how they can register. Changes in federal law over the years have removed many of the barriers that states had once imposed to restrict voting rights—those based on property ownership, literacy, race, sex, and age. But there are still differences among states in how easy or difficult it is for citizens to register to vote—a necessary step toward having the chance to vote in every state except North Dakota, which does not require voter registration.

Officials in **OHIO** removed tens of thousands of voters from registration lists because they have not cast a ballot since 2008.

As noted earlier, those differences have become more pronounced in recent years.

In the early years of the nation, most eastern states required citizens to own property to be eligible to vote. Those requirements diminished over time, in large part because the western frontier states lacked the type of class structure that reinforced them. The eastern states, however, soon came up with the idea of imposing literacy tests. Before they could vote, new immigrants had to demonstrate knowledge of the state constitution or other complex issues to the satisfaction of the local election official.[48] Native whites who were illiterate often were exempted from this requirement. Southern states took up literacy testing as a means of keeping African

Americans from voting, as African Americans generally received inadequate education in schools segregated by race. Literacy tests remained a part of the southern legal landscape until the federal Voting Rights Act of 1965 barred them. Southern states also sometimes imposed poll taxes as a means of disenfranchising African Americans and some poor whites, until the Supreme Court found such taxes unconstitutional in 1966.

Several amendments to the U.S. Constitution expanded voting rights to include minorities and women. The Fifteenth Amendment, passed following the Civil War, was meant to end discrimination against black men seeking to vote. Until the civil rights movement of the 1960s, however, southern states effectively bypassed the provisions of the amendment for a century through literacy tests, intimidation, and other means. The Voting Rights Act of 1965 gave the federal government the authority to review state requirements for registration and voting. In 1964, the Twenty-Fourth Amendment banned the use of poll taxes meant to keep African Americans and other poor people from voting. Women received the right to vote with the ratification of the Nineteenth Amendment in 1920. The voting age was lowered to 18 by the Twenty-Sixth Amendment in 1971. In 1993, Congress passed what became known as the "motor voter" law, which requires states to allow citizens to register to vote when they take tests to receive their driver's licenses.

Why all the effort to get people registered to vote? The purpose of registering voters is to prevent fraud. Registration is intended to stop people from voting more than once or outside their home jurisdictions. This makes sense, but throughout the nation's history, many states have used registration laws as a means of making voting inaccessible to some.

New York, one of the most heavily Democratic states, also has some of the most restrictive voting laws. People wishing to vote in a party primary better make their plans well in advance. The deadline for switching parties is a full year plus 25 days ahead of the general election. New York is one of only 13 states that don't allow early voting. Politicians in New York have shown no interest in allowing automatic or same-day voter registration. Not coincidentally, New York ranks among the bottom 10 states nationwide in terms of turnout. The state's election procedures might be bad for voters, but they've been good for the parties, said Susan Lerner, executive director of Common Cause in New York. "The system is meant to freeze our election administration in amber, so that nothing changes, because this way the parties are confident that they control what's going on," she said. "The fact that it's inconvenient for voters, that it discourages voters, doesn't seem to matter at all. And that is tragic."[49]

Voter Turnout

Even as some states are tightening requirements for voter registration, taking steps such as requiring individuals to provide proof of citizenship, others are seeking to make the mechanics of registering easier. The idea of coupling universal or automatic voter registration with some form of eligibility check has been around at least since a 2005 federal election commission headed by former president Jimmy Carter and former secretary of state James Baker.[50] In Oregon, which passed the nation's first automatic voter registration law in 2015, residents must provide proof of legal status in order to obtain a driver's license or identification card. The state's Elections Division will send out registration notices only to people who have provided documentation that they are U.S. citizens.

Allowing people to register online, rather than using paper forms, is one idea that has bipartisan support. In December 2016, Idaho became the 37th state to allow online voter registration—37 is more than three times the number of states allowing online registration as recently as 2012. Washington State in 2012 unveiled an app that allows citizens to register through Facebook using personal data. On a single day in March 2016, more than 13,000 people registered to vote in Washington, setting a state record. Facebook began posting a reminder that day for people to register.[51] "In this age of social media and more people going online for services, this is a natural way to introduce people to online registration and leverage the power of friends on Facebook to get more people registered," said Shane Hamlin, Washington's codirector of elections.[52]

Americans have a constitutional right to vote at age 18, but some jurisdictions are letting people vote earlier. A pair of municipalities in Maryland now let 16-year-olds vote in local elections. Other states are looking at ideas for preregistration so that people will be registered to vote as soon as they turn 18. In nearly half the states, 17-year-olds can vote in primaries, as long as they will turn 18 before the general election. In 2016, nine 17-year-olds in Ohio successfully sued Secretary of State Jon Husted over his interpretation of the law that suggested they could not vote in that year's presidential primary. Saira Blair was just 17 herself when she unseated an incumbent West Virginia legislator in a 2014 primary (see Chapter 1).[53]

An increasing number of states are allowing same-day registration (meaning voters no longer have to register weeks in advance of Election Day). But efforts to ease registration do not always lead to higher **voter turnout**. The federal motor voter law produced an initial spike in registration, but it had little or no effect on the number of people voting. A record 137 million Americans cast votes in 2016, after turnout dropped in 2012. In the midterm election of 2014, turnout was the lowest it had been since World War II, but heavy voter interest in 2018 led to the highest numbers since World War I. There are countless reasons why turnout is hit and miss, including a general disaffection with politics and government, a measurable decline in civic education and newspaper reading, a weakening of such civic-minded institutions as student government and unions, and the changing role of political parties away from engaging and educating voters and toward raising money and providing services to candidates. Turnout rates are in decline, but they are not declining uniformly across the states. The percentage of the voting-age population that turned out to vote in 2016 was more than 30 points higher in Minnesota, the best-performing state, than in Hawaii, which was the worst. There are many reasons states have such disparate turnout rates, most of which are related to political culture, demographics, and party competition.

In general, the closer you live to Canada, the more likely you are to vote. The states with turnout rates of more than 70 percent for the 2008 presidential election, including Minnesota, New Hampshire, and Iowa, were mostly in the northern tier of the country. The states with lower turnout rates, including Arkansas, Hawaii, Tennessee, and Utah, were in the South or far West. (See Table 5-1.) What explains the difference? Culture, for one thing. Elazar's theory about moralistic states appears to hold up, at least as far as voter turnout goes. "You're talking about states with fairly vigorous political parties, communications media that do cover politics and an educational system more geared toward citizen engagement than other parts of the country," said Curtis Gans, who directed the Committee for the Study of the American Electorate at American University.[54] A big state such as California has a mix of cultures—individualistic and moralistic—according to Elazar.

In 2014, lawmakers in **MASSACHUSETTS** gave residents who are at least 16 years old the ability to preregister to vote.

It is not just political culture that makes a difference. Demographics also matter, and moralistic states tend to be more likely to have demographic profiles favorable to turnout. People are more likely to vote if they are better educated, if they are elderly, and if they are white. "In states with a high percentage of minorities, you're going to have low turnout," says Steven Hill of New America. "States with higher voter turnout, such as Minnesota and Maine, tend to be fairly white states."[55] Such moralistic states historically also have bred strong two-party competition. This tends to increase turnout. Citizens in states or districts dominated by one party tend not to vote as eagerly. Their candidate of choice is certain to win—or to lose if they are "orphaned" voters whose party is weak in their home state or district. What we see here are differences that interact with other differences to produce variation in turnout.

Voter turnout rates actually have increased in the South, where many of the historical impediments to registration and voting have declined and the major parties have become more competitive than had been the case for more than 100 years. But the region has merely stabilized at a turnout rate that is slightly lower than that in the rest of the country. Its high proportion of African Americans and its historical legacy of sup-

In 2016, 13 states plus the **DISTRICT OF COLUMBIA** allowed for same-day voter registration.

pressing their votes and the votes of some whites keep the South's turnout rates sluggish, even though African Americans tend to vote in greater numbers than do other minorities, such as Hispanics.

Voter turnout The percentage of voting-eligible citizens who register to vote and do vote.

TABLE 5-1 ● Percentage of the Voting-Age Population Casting Ballots in the 2016 Presidential Election

Rank	State	Percentage of Total Voting-Age Population	Elazar Classification	Rank	State	Percentage of Total Voting-Age Population	Elazar Classification
1	Minnesota	74.2	Moralistic	27	North Dakota	60.1	Moralistic
2	New Hampshire	72.6	Moralistic	28	Georgia	60.0	Traditionalistic
3	Colorado	71.3	Moralistic	29	Wyoming	60.0	Individualistic
4	Maine	69.9	Moralistic	30	Idaho	59.7	Moralistic
5	Iowa	68.6	Moralistic	31	Kentucky	59.5	Traditionalistic
6	Wisconsin	68.3	Moralistic	32	New Jersey	59.2	Individualistic
7	Oregon	66.9	Moralistic	33	Rhode Island	58.8	Individualistic
8	Virginia	65.8	Traditionalistic	34	Alabama	58.7	Traditionalistic
9	Florida	65.6	Traditionalistic	35	South Dakota	58.7	Moralistic
10	Michigan	65.6	Moralistic	36	South Carolina	57.3	Traditionalistic
11	Massachusetts	65.3	Individualistic	37	Nevada	57.1	Individualistic
12	North Carolina	64.9	Traditionalistic	38	Arizona	56.3	Traditionalistic
13	Vermont	64.6	Moralistic	39	Indiana	56.2	Individualistic
14	Ohio	64.5	Individualistic	40	Kansas	55.7	Moralistic
15	Washington	64.4	Moralistic	41	New Mexico	54.8	Traditionalistic
16	Delaware	64.0	Individualistic	42	California	54.6	Moralistic
17	Connecticut	62.6	Individualistic	43	Mississippi	53.5	Traditionalistic
18	Montana	62.2	Moralistic	44	Arkansas	52.6	Traditionalistic
19	Missouri	61.9	Individualistic	45	New York	52.4	Individualistic
20	Nebraska	61.7	Individualistic	46	Oklahoma	52.2	Traditionalistic
21	Maryland	61.4	Individualistic	47	Texas	51.1	Traditionalistic
22	Pennsylvania	61.4	Individualistic	48	Tennessee	51.0	Traditionalistic
23	Alaska	60.6	Individualistic	49	West Virginia	51.0	Traditionalistic
24	District of Columbia	60.5		50	Utah	46.4	Moralistic
25	Louisiana	60.2	Traditionalistic	51	Hawaii	42.5	Individualistic
26	Illinois	60.1	Individualistic				

Source: United States Elections Project, "2016 November General Election Turnout Rates," September 5, 2018, http://www.electproject.org/2016g.

POLICY IN PRACTICE
SHOULD FELONS VOTE?

The idea of restoring voting rights to former felons has gained new momentum and is close to becoming a default position for Democrats. It's part of the party's pushback against Republican voting measures, such as voter ID requirements, that Democrats believe are too restrictive or even suppressive. "The policy of disenfranchising residents is unique among industrial countries. Other countries don't eliminate voting rights for citizens, even if they're incarcerated," says Nicole D. Porter, director of advocacy for The Sentencing Project, a progressive criminal justice reform group.

Voting rights restoration is also in keeping with the broader criminal justice reform effort to ease the transition of former prisoners back into society. "It's just not a credible argument to say that voting presents a threat to public safety," says Scott Novakowski, associate counsel at the New Jersey Institute for Social Justice, which advocates restoration of voting rights for felons, including those currently serving time.

The stakes are high. Nationwide, 6 million people with felony convictions are disenfranchised, including 4.7 million who have completed their prison sentences. A ban in Florida, which was challenged in courts and overturned by a ballot measure in 2018, affects 1.4 million, or 10 percent of the state's voting-age population. Florida is one of 33 states that don't automatically restore voting rights to ex-felons. (Two, Maine and Vermont, don't strip felons of voting rights, even while they're incarcerated.) Racial disparities are often highlighted by proponents of voting rights restoration. In Kentucky, 1 in 11 voting-age adults is disenfranchised by the ban on felon voting, but that number jumps to 1 in 4 among black residents.

Before leaving office in 2018, Virginia Democratic governor Terry McAuliffe restored voting rights to 170,000 felons who had served their time, which he deemed his proudest achievement. That same year, Andrew Cuomo, the Democratic governor of New York, issued an executive order restoring voting rights to felons who have been paroled. Sixteen other states allow people who are on parole or probation to vote. "It is unconscionable to deny voting rights to New Yorkers who have paid their debt and have re-entered society," Cuomo said.

The chair of the New York Republican Party, Ed Cox, condemned the move, calling it "liberal lunacy" and an "outrageous power grab." Roger Clegg, president of the Center for Equal Opportunity, a conservative think tank that studies race and ethnicity, doesn't think felons should be barred from voting forever, but argues their rights shouldn't be restored automatically because "then you lose the opportunity to incentivize people to turn over a new leaf." Nebraska GOP governor Pete Ricketts used that same argument in 2017 when he vetoed legislation that would have abolished the state's two-year waiting period for ex-felons to vote. "Requiring convicted felons to wait before allowing them to vote provides an incentive to maintain a clean record and avoid subsequent convictions," Ricketts wrote in his veto letter.

Source: Adapted from Alan Greenblatt, "Voting Rights for Felons Becoming a Key Issue for Democrats," *Governing*, April 25, 2018, http://www.governing.com/topics/politics/gov-florida-felons-voting-rights-states.html.

> **Hispanics have long been considered the "sleeping giant" of American politics because of their failure to vote in numbers commensurate with their share of the population. They cast just 6 percent of the ballots in the United States in 2004, barely half as many as African Americans, even though they constitute a larger portion of the national population.**

Hispanics have long been considered the "sleeping giant" of American politics because of their failure to vote in numbers commensurate with their share of the population. They cast just 6 percent of the ballots in the United States in 2004, barely half as many as African Americans, even though they constitute a larger portion of the national population. Their voting participation ticked upward in 2008 but still trailed well behind that of African Americans, who turned out in high numbers in support of Barack Obama. By 2012, it appeared that the sleeping giant had awakened. Hispanics made up 10 percent of voters that year, and their share of the electorate—and their influence—is considered certain

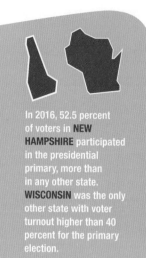

In 2016, 52.5 percent of voters in **NEW HAMPSHIRE** participated in the presidential primary, more than in any other state. **WISCONSIN** was the only other state with voter turnout higher than 40 percent for the primary election.

to grow. But the Hispanic turnout rate in the 2016 election dipped slightly from where it had been in 2012.[56]

Growth in the Latino electorate is still lagging well behind the rate of growth of the Hispanic population as a whole. In 2014, only 27 percent of eligible Latinos voted, compared with 46 percent of whites and 41 percent of African Americans.[57] The standard explanation for this lag is that Hispanics lack the well-established political organizations needed to encourage registration and turnout. But other factors are involved as well. More than 20 percent of voting-age Hispanics are noncitizens, and thus not eligible to vote. As Ruy Teixeira, a Democratic polling expert, says, "People who look at the overall size of the Hispanic population and look at the vote think, 'Oh my God, what if these people ever get mobilized?' . . . But so many of these people can't vote anyway."[58]

Then there's age. The median age of Hispanics in the United States is just 28, compared with a median age of 43 for non-Hispanic whites. A much higher percentage of Hispanics do not vote because they are simply too young. That will change. About 50,000 Hispanics will turn 18 every month for the next decade or so. This could mean that Hispanic voting rolls will swell enormously—or it could mean that young Hispanics, just like young Americans of every race, will fail to exercise their right to vote in great numbers. Hispanics, in other words, already behave pretty much like everybody else.

As previously mentioned, many other factors also determine rates of voter turnout. Elderly people tend to vote in high numbers—which is one reason Social Security and Medicare are always important political issues. Young people, by contrast, vote in lower numbers, in percentage terms. Only one out of five people under the age of 30 bothered to vote in 2014. That year, Californians over 60 voted at nearly three times the rate of those in their 20s.[59] "It's no wonder why our federal budget skews toward older folks. A whopping

24 percent is set aside for Social Security and 14 percent more for Medicare," writes *Kansas City Star* columnist Steve Kraske. "Student financial aid? Try 1 percent."[60]

People who are wealthy tend to vote more than do the poor, and people with higher levels of education vote much more regularly than do people with limited education. These are some of the reasons a high-income state with an educated population, such as Connecticut, has much higher turnout rates than a low-income state where the population is poorly educated on the whole, such as Hawaii.

What Elections Are Used For

Forty-nine states elect a governor and two sets of state legislators: state senators and members of a state house of representatives, delegates, or assemblymen. Nebraska, the only exception, elects a governor and a one-chamber legislature. Beyond that, there is quite a bit of variation among the states in what they allow people to vote for. Many states allow voters to pick a number of statewide officeholders, such as attorney general and secretary of state, whereas in a few places these are appointed positions. In most states, in addition to a governor, voters elect a lieutenant governor, treasurer, secretary of state, and attorney general. A few states elect other officers as well, such as an insurance commissioner. In Texas, the governor is only 1 of 25 different elected statewide officials.

The fact that many statewide officeholders run for office independent of the governor gives them a power base of their own. Voters pay comparatively little attention to candidates running for some state executive branch offices. Races for, say, state treasurer are just not seen as all that exciting. Most often, the party that wins the governorship takes the lion's share of the secondary executive branch offices anyway. Voters also get to select or approve judges in most states. Roughly half the states allow voters to make policy decisions directly through ballot initiatives and referendums.

Local elections also vary considerably. Most large cities, such as Chicago and Los Angeles, allow voters to elect a mayor directly. Many smaller cities have what is called a council–mayor format, in which the city council picks one of its own members to serve as mayor, while the city is administered by a city manager, who is not elected. The same holds true for counties. In some places, a county commission picks its own leader, whereas in others, voters pick a county executive on

MAP 5-1 ● States Requiring Voter Identification, 2018

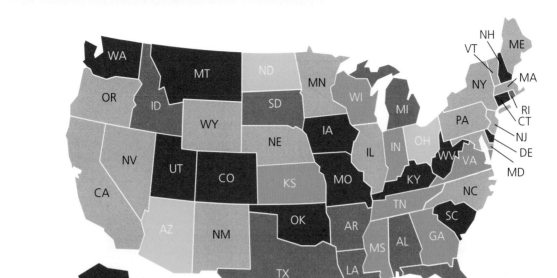

- ▨ Strict photo ID required
- ▨ Strict non-photo ID required
- ▨ Photo ID requested
- ▮ ID requested, no photo
- ▨ No document required

Source: National Conference of State Legislatures, "Voter Identification Requirements," May 15, 2018, http://www.ncsl.org/research/elections-and-campaigns/voter-id.aspx.

their own. Local elections are, for the most part, **nonpartisan elections**—that is, candidates do not run under a party label. But, again, there are exceptions, such as the highly partisan elections for mayor of New York City.

Direct Democracy

In addition to electing officials to state and local offices, voters can participate in certain forms of direct democracy. As discussed in Chapter 3, in about half the states, voters can pass legislation on their own through ballot initiatives or referendums, which also are available in hundreds of municipalities across the country. In 24 states, citizens can petition to place a piece of legislation or a constitutional amendment on the ballot

for approval or rejection by voters. Also in 24 states—mostly the same states—citizens can petition to review a law passed by the legislature and the governor, which they can then accept or reject. (See Table 5-2.)

When citizens or groups other than elected officials put a measure on the ballot to become a law, this is called a popular initiative. When citizens put a measure on the ballot to affirm or reject an action of the legislature or another political actor, this is called a popular referendum. When the legislature places a measure on the ballot to win voter approval (such as

....

Nonpartisan election An election in which the candidates do not have to declare party affiliation or receive a party's nomination; local offices and elections are often nonpartisan.

TABLE 5-2 ● Avenues for Direct Democracy

State	Popular Referendum	Ballot Initiative	Constitutional Amendment by Initiative	Recall of State Officials
Alabama	No	No	No	No
Alaska	Yes	Yes	No	Yes
Arizona	Yes	Yes	Yes	Yes
Arkansas	Yes	Yes	Yes	No
California	Yes	Yes	Yes	Yes
Colorado	Yes	Yes	Yes	Yes
Connecticut	No	No	No	No
Delaware	No	No	No	No
Florida	No	Yes	Yes	No
Georgia	No	No	No	Yes
Hawaii	No	No	No	No
Idaho	Yes	Yes	No	Yes
Illinois	Yes	Yes	No	No
Indiana	No	No	No	No
Iowa	No	No	No	No
Kansas	No	No	No	Yes
Kentucky	Yes	No	No	No
Louisiana	No	No	No	Yes
Maine	Yes	Yes	No	No
Maryland	Yes	No	No	No
Massachusetts	Yes	Yes	Yes	No
Michigan	Yes	Yes	Yes	Yes
Minnesota	No	No	No	Yes
Mississippi	No	Yes	Yes	No
Missouri	Yes	Yes	Yes	No
Montana	Yes	Yes	Yes	Yes
Nebraska	Yes	Yes	Yes	No
Nevada	Yes	Yes	Yes	Yes
New Hampshire	No	No	No	No

State	Popular Referendum	Ballot Initiative	Constitutional Amendment by Initiative	Recall of State Officials
New Jersey	No	No	No	Yes
New Mexico	Yes	No	No	No
New York	No	No	No	No
North Carolina	No	No	No	No
North Dakota	Yes	Yes	Yes	Yes
Ohio	Yes	Yes	Yes	No
Oklahoma	Yes	Yes	Yes	No
Oregon	Yes	Yes	Yes	Yes
Pennsylvania	No	No	No	No
Rhode Island	No	No	No	Yes
South Carolina	No	No	No	No
South Dakota	Yes	Yes	Yes	No
Tennessee	No	No	No	No
Texas	No	No	No	No
Utah	Yes	Yes	No	No
Vermont	No	No	No	No
Virginia	No	No	No	No
Washington	Yes	Yes	No	Yes
West Virginia	No	No	No	No
Wisconsin	No	No	No	Yes
Wyoming	Yes	Yes	No	No
Total number of states with	25	24	18	18

Source: National Conference of State Legislatures, http://www.ncsl.org/LegislaturesElections/ElectionsCampaigns/RecallofStateOfficials/tabid/16581/Default.aspx.

for a constitutional amendment or bond issue), it is called a legislative referendum. Some referendums are nonbinding—expressing the will of the people but not becoming law—but most are binding and do have the force of law once passed.

In all 50 states, the legislature or other government agencies have the power of legislative referendum. In the decades following independence, citizens in several northeastern states ratified new constitutions; Congress subsequently made legislative referendums for constitutional amendments mandatory for all new states entering the union after 1857.[61]

As discussed in Chapter 3, the notion of popular referendums and initiatives really took root because of the efforts of reformers in the Populist and Progressive movements. These individuals sought to give citizens

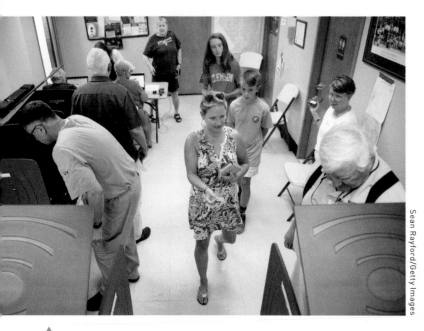

Sean Rayford/Getty Images

Voting security and ballot access have emerged as contentious issues in recent years. Here, poll workers help citizens vote in a South Carolina runoff.

teacher pay increases and school class size limitations.

Those who favor the initiative process say that it gives voters a chance to control government directly. Voters know that they are voting for an environmental safety program or a campaign finance law, as opposed to voting for candidates who say that they favor these things but may act differently once in office. Initiative states do tend to have lower state spending per capita, but that gap generally is bridged by local spending, which tends to run higher in these states.[62]

Critics of the initiative process say that it creates more problems than it solves. Because voters are presented with a straight yes-or-no choice about spending more on, say, elementary and secondary education, they do not take into account other competing state priorities, such as transportation or colleges, the way legislators must. Voters can say, as those in Washington have, that they want both lower taxes and more services but leave legislators and governors few tools for balancing the budget or responding to economic recessions.

Those opposed to initiatives also say that the idea that they express the popular will better than do elected representatives sounds good in theory but is flawed in practice. In many states—particularly California—initiatives have become big business. They are not necessarily the expressions of grassroots ideals anymore; instead, they are proposed and paid for by wealthy individuals, corporations, or interest groups, such as teachers' unions or the owners of gambling casinos. Total spending on ballot measures topped $1 billion for the first time in 2014. "Oil and gas companies in Alaska spent more than $170 for every vote they won in a successful campaign to reject higher taxes" in August 2014, the *Washington Post* reported.[63]

Still the most famous and influential modern ballot initiative is Proposition 13, approved by California voters in 1978, which limited property tax rates and made other changes to the state's tax and spending laws (see Chapter 3). The initiative was copied successfully in Michigan and Massachusetts, and most states

more influence over state political systems that they saw as dominated by moneyed interests such as banks, railroads, and mining companies. A majority of the states that have adopted the popular initiative process (under which citizens can collect a certain number of signatures to place issues directly on the ballot) did so in the late 1800s and early 1900s. Most of these states are in the West and the upper Midwest, which had political cultures that welcomed the idea of populist control. Much of the opposition in the southern and eastern states grew out of racist concerns that giving people direct authority to make laws would give too much power to African Americans or to new immigrants such as the Irish.

Recent ballot initiatives and referendums have covered a wide range of topics, from legalizing marijuana to banning the use of bait, dogs, or traps in bear hunting (a question before Maine voters in 2014). In the decade or so leading up to the 2015 Supreme Court decision recognizing the right of same-sex couples to marry, voters in more than three dozen states voted either to ban or to legalize same-sex marriage. Many initiatives, though, have to do with tax and spending issues. Sometimes voters send contradictory signals. For instance, in Washington State, voters in recent years have approved limitations on property and other taxes while at the same time approving such expensive programs as soon placed limitations on their own property tax rates. The success of Proposition 13 fueled the modern initiative movement. Only 87 statewide initiatives were proposed during the entire decade of the 1960s. Since 1978, however, about 300 initiatives have been proposed per decade. In 1996 alone, 93 statewide initiatives were placed on ballots. Initiatives have become a big-money business for consultants and a way for interest groups to promote causes when they can't succeed through the legislative process. In recent years, they've been used more routinely by progressives who, shut out of power in red states, found they could win voter approval for minimum wage increases and changes in voting procedures. In response, in 2015 the Republican State Leadership Committee established a Center for Conservative Initiatives.

Beyond initiatives and referendums is perhaps the ultimate expression of popular dissatisfaction—the **recall**. Recalls of local officials are allowed in about 30 states and 61 percent of U.S. municipalities—more local governments than allow initiatives or referendums. Like ballot initiatives, recall laws are mainly by-products of the intention of early 20th-century reformers to make state governments more responsive to average citizens. Recalls of state officials are allowed in 19 states.[64] No governor had faced a recall since the 1920s when, in 2003, California Democrat Gray Davis was recalled and replaced by Republican Arnold Schwarzenegger. In 2012, Wisconsin governor Scott Walker, a Republican, survived a recall attempt over labor issues in what became one of the most expensive state elections in U.S. history.

These high-profile recall votes helped promote growth in recalls at the local level, with everyone from county commissioners to school board members being shown the door. In 2011, at least 57 mayors faced recall attempts—up from 23 in 2009. Not all these recall attempts succeeded, but in recent years, serious recall attempts have been launched against mayors in cities such as Omaha, Kansas City, and Portland, Oregon. Once voters discovered the recall as an option, they seemed to like it. Of the 39 state legislative recall elections since states first allowed them in 1908, 18 occurred between 2010 and 2014.[65] Colorado voters unhappy with new restrictions on weapons successfully recalled two state senators—including the state Senate president—in 2013, while a third resigned rather than face a recall.[66] A total of 65 local officials faced recalls in 2017, with most either being booted out of office or resigning.[67]

Public Opinion

Randall Gnant, a former president of the Arizona Senate, says that there is quite a contrast between the politics of today and those of the 1800s. Back then, he says, "it seemed that everybody took part in the political process—there were torchlight parades, party-run newspapers for and against candidates." Today, "we're into sort of a reverse kind of period. Now, almost nobody participates in the electoral process—voter turnout rates are abysmally low." But that does not mean that citizens are not paying any attention to the political process. Given the importance of online sites and social media, which quickly spread public opinion—or at least a share of it—the old idea that voters agree to a sort of contract with politicians whom they elect to two- or four-year terms is rapidly becoming dated. Voters are more than willing to express their displeasure about a given policy well before the next scheduled Election Day. "Try to get somebody interested in electing a candidate and they just don't want to get involved," Gnant points out. "But they are perfectly willing to get involved if somebody does something they don't want them to do."[68]

Citizen opinion usually does not register loudly enough to result in a recall or other formal protest. On most issues that come before policymakers at the state level, citizen opinion hardly seems to exist or be formulated at all. After all, how many citizens are going to take the time to follow—let alone express an opinion about—an obscure regulatory issue concerning overnight transactions between banks and insurance companies? In his memoir, former state legislator and longtime Democratic congressman Barney Frank notes that people will show up for rallies and applaud speakers, but they won't follow up by writing or calling legislators and organizing others to do so. That's more important work than protest, he suggests. "I formulated a rule: If you care deeply about an issue and are engaged in group activity that is fun and inspiring and heightens your sense of solidarity with others, you are almost certainly not doing your cause any good," Frank writes.[69]

If citizens do not or cannot make their feelings known on every issue addressed in the hundreds of bills that wend through the average state legislature each year, how can legislators know that their votes

---

Recall A way for voters to oust an incumbent politician prior to the next regularly scheduled election; they collect signatures to qualify the recall proposal for the ballot and then vote on the ouster of the politician.

will reflect the will of their constituents? After all, as V. O. Key writes, "Unless mass views have some place in the shaping of policy, all the talk about democracy is nonsense."[70]

Responding to Opinion

Doug Duncan served for a dozen years as county executive of Montgomery County, Maryland. Like many veteran officeholders, he found that one of the biggest changes in his job came in the area of communications. "Doing it is half the job," he says, "and the other half is telling people about it so they know how you're spending their money."[71] The old outlets for government officials making announcements or responding to criticism—local daily newspapers and evening TV news broadcasts—have declined in audience or even gone away completely in some cases. Nevertheless, in the Internet age, more information sources are available than ever before. "The information's there," Duncan says. "It's just a question of how you make it available."

E-mail, Twitter, and Facebook groups devoted to neighborhood concerns and services such as libraries have made it easier for public officials to know what their constituents are thinking—at least those constituents who are motivated enough to make their opinions known on a given issue. And elected officials have become fairly quick to adopt social media platforms such as Facebook and Twitter. When he was a member of the Pittsburgh City Council, Dan Gilman said he didn't bother putting out old-school newsletters to his constituents, because they could follow him on Twitter.

But what about figuring out what his constituents are thinking? Let's be realistic—state officials, in particular, cannot know what the majority opinions are in their districts on every issue they confront. Mike Haridopolos, a former GOP president of the Florida Senate, cautions officials against reading too much into what they hear through social media. "I tell my members, just because you get a tweet or an e-mail doesn't mean your whole district is concerned about something," he says.[72] And even multiple e-mails might be the work of just one or two individuals using multiple aliases. Devin Nunes, a Republican congressman from California, says that 90 percent of his constituent response time used to be spent answering e-mails, calls, and letters from people who commented on specific pieces of legislation. Even before he became a leading defender of President Trump

in Congress, he was mostly hearing about conspiracy theories. "It's dramatically changed politics and politicians, and what they're doing," Nunes said.[73]

At the local level, some cities are starting to move away from the old model of holding public hearings, where members of the public show up at a certain time and place to offer their opinions about projects and policies. Surveying citizens by mail or online can yield greater feedback than soliciting comments at sparsely attended hearings. "As a career public servant who has painfully endured hundreds of government-inspired—and often legally required—public hearings over the past four decades, I can attest that sometimes the ultimate result of all that standing and testifying was that someone in a government office checked a box on a page of a bureaucratic government document," writes Ron Littlefield, former mayor of Chattanooga, Tennessee.[74]

Opening up data has become a way to make sure projects are better coordinated between departments and allow the public to know what's going on in real time. Los Angeles has set up an online site called GeoHub that hosts hundreds of types of geographic data, showing the overlap between zoning and everything from medical clinics to movie studios. City employees can see whether the road they want to repave is already scheduled to be torn up soon for some other reason, such as for replacement of a sewer pipe. If it is, they can hold off on the repaving. Residents can see the same information, so they know how long their street will be under construction. Transit planners are now using all-in-one software that allows bus routes and other services to be planned in much the same way they would be designed in a video game such as *SimCity*, instead of the old method of toggling among different programs that handled scheduling, mapping, and costs. This makes it easier for members of the public to understand why routes are laid out the way they are. Cities have found that hackathons—intensive marathon coding sessions—haven't been a silver bullet for transforming the ways in which they do business, but a few have paid off. In Boston, for instance, a 36-hour hackathon ended up revamping the way the city handles permits. Previously, residents had no clue as to where their permits stood in the approval process, and the city had no staff dedicated to helping them out. Now, they can easily download an app that allows them to check.[75]

Of course, not everyone is technologically savvy, so it's fortunate that new tools are also making traditional

STATES UNDER STRESS
PROTEST MOVEMENTS TAKE OFF DURING TRUMP'S TIME IN OFFICE

President Donald Trump's time in office has seen countless protests, from large rallies on college campuses and in big cities to NFL players kneeling during the national anthem out of anger about police brutality. Many of the most committed activists in this era, however, are suburban women who are middle-aged or older.

Anne Taussig is a 66-year-old product designer from St. Louis who opposes Trump's policies on issues such as taxes, health care, and abortion and is concerned about his campaign's possible collusion with Russia. She became an activist in 2017, even though she had not participated in a street protest since college. "We follow that strategy, to go after Trump the way the tea party went after President Obama," she says, referring to the conservative, antitax, populist movement that arose after the election of Barack Obama in 2008.

Taussig cofounded a St. Louis chapter of Indivisible, a left-leaning nationwide advocacy group that sprang up after Trump's election. Her chapter claims 3,000 members, many of whom routinely protest outside congressional offices or when administration officials come to town.

Political protests are hardly new—citizens have demonstrated against government officials and policies they oppose since before the country was born. In recent years, conservatives held protests and disrupted town halls during Obama's presidency, complaining about deficit spending and health care policy. Anti–Iraq War protests became routine during the George W. Bush administration. But Trump's election in 2016 ushered in an era of heightened protest, with large-scale street protests becoming more common than they'd been in decades.

Of course, it's not just liberals who embrace protests, and activism is not just about national politics. Angry protests have erupted on college campuses in response to both liberal and conservative speakers. Native Americans and their allies have staged long-running protests against oil pipelines built on sacred Indian lands. And some white supremacists have taken to the streets to oppose the removal of Confederate monuments, among other causes.

On campuses, some students have tried to block provocative speakers, leading to criticism they are squelching free speech. Racist speakers in particular, such as white nationalist Richard Spencer, have drawn large oppositional and disruptive crowds, some of which have turned violent. "Unfortunately, what all of us are seeing across the country, more and more, is a threat to that marketplace of ideas, with people trying to shut down others with different perspectives," says John Hardin, director of university relations at the Charles Koch Foundation, a conservative group that promotes open debate on campus.

Social media has made it easier to organize protests, regardless of the cause. "Social media is a remarkable tool not only for mobilizing people but also for spreading information about logistics, medicine, transportation and other issues," says Joshua Tucker, codirector of the Social Media and Political Participation lab at New York University.

Some street protests are organized primarily to draw media and public attention to an issue rather than to change policy, says Greg Magarian, a law professor at Washington University. "Street protest is the classic, inexpensive way of getting your message out," he says.

In politics, such protests are part of an "outside game"—a strategy of agitating for or against policies from outside formal political institutions. The strategy can be part of an activist's tool kit for changing government or corporate practices, but to effect change, it generally must be followed up by long-term commitment to an "inside game"—lobbying and participation in political campaigns. The Tea Party movement during the Obama years did just that. It started off holding large rallies, but eventually, attending such protests largely gave way to organizing local groups that aimed to influence and bolster GOP political campaigns. "Movements don't write legislation," said Nina Eliasoph, a sociologist at the University of Southern California. "They force open a line of questions that makes it possible for people to imagine new policies. That's always the first step."

Source: Adapted from Alan Greenblatt, "Citizen Protests," *CQ Researcher*, January 5, 2018.

types of communication more effective. Austin, Texas, has developed "meetings in a box," a method that allows groups in the community to use their own meetings to discuss questions that planners want answers to. The city worked with African American pastors and the Asian Chamber of Commerce and took out ads on Spanish-language television network Univision to attract participants who weren't likely to show up at official city gatherings. The city also used social media to reach younger residents and developed an online site, SpeakUp Austin, to solicit ideas and encourage public feedback on them. More than 18,000 people wound up getting involved in the development of the city's latest comprehensive plan.

A survey of local officials in California in 2013 found something of a participation paradox. Fully 88 percent of respondents said that the public has "ample opportunity" to participate in local decision making—but a vast majority also believed the public to be too busy to participate, too disengaged or ignorant to understand the issues facing their communities, and too angry and distrustful of local officials to be reliable partners.[76] This disconnect is the result of the fact that public officials typically end up hearing—a lot—from a relatively small number of people, often those with narrow agendas or those accustomed to complaining. On most issues, state legislators and city officials do not hear from any constituents at all. A few high-profile concerns, such as tax increases or the legalization of casino gambling, may lead a newspaper or an interested party to conduct a statewide poll, but even on the rare occasions when polls on state issues are conducted, the resulting data are not broken down by legislative district. Given their lack of specific information about how constituents view particular areas, public officials have to rely on a series of clues.

Some political scientists have taken data from various nationwide polls, broken them down by state, and analyzed how well elected officials have reflected the general ideologies and desires of the public in their states.[77] What they have found is that average state opinion does seem to be reflected in the policy decisions made in individual states. What does *average state opinion* mean? It encompasses the types of things we discussed earlier in regard to Elazar's classifications of the states. Some states tend to be more liberal overall, whereas others are more conservative. The average citizen's desires—whether in a conservative state such as Texas or a more progressive one such as Vermont—tend

to be pretty well reflected by state laws on issues from restrictions on abortion services to welfare spending, the death penalty, environmental protections, and gay rights.[78]

> **Elected officials devote an enormous amount of time to trying to gauge how opinion is running in their districts. They may not hear from constituents on every issue, but they pay close attention to those concerns that are registered through letters and phone calls.**

How does this happen? For one thing, elected officials devote an enormous amount of time to trying to gauge how opinion is running in their districts. They may not hear from constituents on every issue, but they pay close attention to those concerns that are registered through letters and phone calls. They go out and seek opinions by attending religious services and civic events where they can hear the concerns of constituents directly.

They use surrogates—such as newspaper articles and interest groups—as ways of determining what is on their constituents' minds. Susan Herbst, executive vice chancellor and chief academic officer for the University System of Georgia, spent some time earlier in her career hanging out with legislators in Springfield, Illinois. She found that the media were important in shaping public opinion by giving a voice to average people in their stories. The media also shaped the terms of debate. Herbst noted that people in the capital thought that lobbyists often provided good indicators of how people felt about an issue: "Staffers seem to think that the nuances and intensity of public opinion are best captured in the communications of interest groups."[79] More recently, political scientists at the University of Minnesota have found that media coverage of debates among political elites—those most directly engaged in actual legislative debates, such as trade associations—does help shape mass public opinion on issues.[80]

This is not to say that using interest groups as surrogates can't be misleading sometimes. The National Rifle Association, for example, may call on its state members to send letters to legislators in numbers that dwarf those mustered by gun control advocates—even in places where a majority of constituents favor gun control. "Intense minorities can come off potentially sounding like majorities when in fact they're not," says Illinois Wesleyan University political scientist Greg Shaw.[81] Legislators like to think that they have a pretty good sense of whether a mail-writing campaign has sprung up spontaneously or shows signs of having been organized—multiple participants signing their names to the same form letter, for example—but sometimes this is easier said than done. Nowadays, someone actually taking the time to write and mail in a letter—as opposed to tweeting or leaving an angry comment on a Facebook page—will have a disproportionate impact just because old-fashioned letters have become unusual.

Formal interest groups do not represent every constituent. Some people may favor environmental protection but not give money to the Sierra Club or the World Wildlife Fund. Still, legislators do gain some sense of how active such groups are in their states and whether they seem to have favorable support at home. A lot of this is inexact, but legislators learn from talking to people whether their constituents are most upset about crime or transportation problems. They are convinced that if they vote for things that voters broadly support, such as mandatory sentencing guidelines for drug offenders or limits on welfare benefits, they will be rewarded politically.

Conversely, a legislator's major fear is of being punished politically. Failure to get reelected can be the death knell of a political career. It is important to note, however, that if legislators or governors did not broadly reflect the wishes of the populace that elected them, they would never have won their positions in the first place. In this age of computer-assisted **redistricting**, legislative districts in particular are shaped according to the local political culture, which tends to lean in one ideological direction. Ninety-five or so times out of a hundred, a liberal is not going to get elected to a conservative district. "Legislators aren't worried about what their constituents know—they are worried about what an opponent might do with their record in the next election," says Paul Brace, a Rice University political

AP Photo/Ross D. Franklin

Arizona was one of several states in 2018 that saw large protests from teachers seeking raises. State representative Ken Clark rolled up a protest poster to use as a makeshift megaphone as he gave teachers an update on budget negotiations.

scientist. They act, therefore, as if there is someone or some group out there who has a chance of using a potentially unpopular record against them. "Legislation is written in minutiae, but you know if you vote for it, you'll get an opponent who can dumb it down and use it against you in the next election, and you won't do it."[82]

Some states offer less opportunity for using a politician's record against him or her. In a moralistic state such as Minnesota, there are more daily newspapers paying close attention to state policy matters than in, say, individualistic Wyoming. There are more public interest groups and state-level think tanks closely monitoring St. Paul than there are monitoring Cheyenne. Citizens in states with higher levels of civic engagement are more likely to keep their politicians "honest"—reflecting voters' overall policy desires—than are citizens in less engaged states. In a state such as Idaho or Maryland, one party so completely dominates state politics that only rarely are politicians voted out of office because their records do not reflect public opinion. But even Idaho Republicans or Maryland Democrats can lose—if only in the party primary—if voters sour on their records. Every state capital has engendered enough of an echo chamber that examines and

----

Redistricting The drawing of new boundaries for congressional and state legislative districts, usually following a decennial census.

discusses the work of legislators and other elected officials that an overall sense of their records—conservative or liberal, sellout or crusading—can be known to people who care enough about politics to vote.

Conclusion

This is a highly partisan era, with little civility or cooperation, it seems, between Republicans and Democrats. That extends even to how states regulate the act of voting itself. But the war between red and blue states will never be as heated as the war between the blue and the gray—the North and the South during the Civil War. Although voters today are divided, they are not as deeply divided as they have been at other moments in the country's past, such as during the Civil War or at the time of the Watergate scandal.

The outcomes of recent elections reflect the divided public mood. State and local officials still maintain a lot of control over whom citizens can vote for through their regulation of political parties and their ability to decide who deserves to get their names on the ballot.

Which state officials citizens get to vote for differs depending on where the citizens live. In most states, citizens vote for several statewide officials, such as governor, attorney general, and secretary of state. In others, they might vote for few or none aside from the governor. Similarly, in some localities citizens elect the mayor directly, whereas in others the mayor is chosen by the city council from among its own membership. Some states allow people to vote directly for judges, while in other states judges are appointed to office. Some localities allow residents to vote for school board members; in a few places, the mayor runs the schools.

In general, citizens vote for enough officeholders with the authority to control policies that the majority's will becomes law. However, because polling is done far more often at the national level than at the local or even the state level, officeholders sometimes have only an anecdotal sense of what their constituents are thinking. They do pay close attention to the clues they are given and monitor opinion as closely as they can. They are well aware that if they do not create the types of policies that most people want, they are not going to stay in office for long.

THE LATEST RESEARCH

This chapter has explained in some depth the role of state and local governments in structuring elections. As discussed above, what citizens need to do to register to vote, where they vote, when they vote, and the mechanics of how they vote are largely decisions made by state and local governments. There are differences among states on all these matters. Tougher registration requirements, for example, tend to result in lower voter turnout.

The studies discussed below represent some of the latest research on polarization and participation, as well as evidence that how states decide to regulate elections is one of the most important influences on participation in local, state, and federal elections in a highly partisan age.

- **Achen, Christopher, and Larry Bartels,** *Democracy for Realists: Why Elections Do Not Produce Responsive Government* (Princeton, NJ: Princeton University Press, 2016).

For decades, political scientists have written about the rational voters and "rational choice theory," arguing that citizens take in information about candidates, parties, and platforms and support the ones that promise

to do the most material good in their own lives. Lately, a series of studies have suggested that voters either don't have enough information to make informed choices, or vote not according to optimal policy choices but rather, as Achen and Bartels write, according to "group attachments" or "social identities." People make political decisions based on momentary feelings, they posit, not on grounded understandings of how policies will affect their lives. "For most people, partisanship is not a carrier of ideology but a reflection of judgments about where 'people like me' belong," they write. "They do not always get that right, but they have much more success than they would constructing their political loyalties on the basis of ideology and policy convictions."

- **Highton, Benjamin,** "Voter Identification Laws and Turnout in the United States," *Annual Review of Political Science* 20 (2017): 149–167.

Voter ID laws by their nature are meant to be restrictive. Some studies have found that the individuals most likely to be affected by them are members of minority groups. But reviewing the political science literature on such laws—which in some cases date back decades—Highton finds that the most careful studies have shown "modest, if any, turnout effects of voter identification laws." But the University of California, Davis, political scientist cautions that the most onerous or strictest laws are relatively recent and so their full effects may not yet be known.

- **Kalla, Joshua, and David E. Broockman,** "The Minimal Persuasive Effects of Campaign Contact in General Elections: Evidence from 49 Field Experiments," *American Political Science Review,* forthcoming.

Campaigns collectively spend millions of dollars on advertising and devote the bulk of candidate and volunteer time to what seems to be primary tasks: making contact with voters by knocking on their doors, calling them up, e-mailing them, or otherwise engaging with them. What is the payoff for all these efforts? None. At least according to this paper. The authors analyzed 40 field experiments and conducted nine of their own, finding that the net effect on voter behavior was zero. Only when candidates take unusually extreme positions, or devote unusual amounts of resources to identifying persuadable voters, do campaign pitches have a noticeable effect. "When campaigns contact voters long before election day and measure effects immediately, campaigns often appear to persuade voters," they write. "However, this early persuasion

decays before election day and the very same treatments usually cease working close to election day."

- **Mason, Liliana,** *Uncivil Agreement: How Politics Became Our Identity* (Chicago: University of Chicago Press, 2018).

Identity and ideology are becoming inextricably linked. There have been countless studies looking at the effects of a single social identity. Less well studied are the ways that various social identities work in concert. The two parties are increasingly aligned along overlapping types of identity, with Democrats likely to be not just progressive but secular and urban and members of racial and ethnic minorities. College-educated whites are increasingly Democratic, while whites without college degrees are becoming more Republican. Republicans are almost entirely white and also likely to be solidly conservative, churchgoing, and rural. In the current media environment, Democrats and Republicans "have a lot more information about who their social and partisan enemies are" (although they often stereotype subgroups in the other party) "and have little reason to find common ground." All this has helped foster a politics that is oppositional, with partisans having a sense that politics is a battle between "us" and "them," defined by anger and fear about the other side "winning."

CHAPTER 5

Want a better grade?

Get the tools you need to sharpen your study skills. SAGE edge offers a robust online environment featuring an impressive array of free tools and resources.

Access practice quizzes, eFlashcards, video, and multimedia at **edge.sagepub.com/ smithgreenblatt7e**

Top Ten Takeaways

1. From the 1960s into the 21st century, the federal government and states sought ways to expand the franchise to new groups of voters and to make voting easier. That

(Continued)

(Continued)

trend has reversed in recent years, at least in GOP-controlled states, with many new restrictions enacted on voting, such as photo identification requirements.

2. Some states are making it easier to register to vote, through either automatic voter registration systems or online registration.

3. The partisan nature of voting laws reflects the political polarization of the age. Most people vote strictly for one party or the other, with supporters sorted by factors such as race and geography.

4. Sophisticated campaigns are tapping into ever more powerful databases to target their supporters and tailor messages meant to appeal to them.

5. Americans hold many elections, but most voters aren't turning out for most of the ones that don't involve the presidential race. Turnout for stand-alone municipal elections is particularly poor.

6. Voter turnout rates vary considerably by state. In general, voters along the border with Canada are the likeliest to vote, with southerners among the least likely.

7. States regulate elections, which means that the rules for primaries and other election-related matters, such as voter registration, can vary a great deal by states. The rules regarding ballot access largely favor the two major parties.

8. Americans can vote starting at age 18, but some states allow people to vote in primaries at 17 if they will turn 18 in time for the general election. A few localities are experimenting with allowing 16-year-olds to vote in municipal elections.

9. Voters can make policy directly through ballot measures. Some measures are put on the ballot by legislatures, but in nearly half the states, citizens can put initiatives on the ballot by collecting enough signatures.

10. There's no perfect way for politicians to keep abreast of public opinion, but they do all they can to know where voters stand on issues by making constant public appearances and monitoring social media.

Key Concepts

nonpartisan election (p. 125)
office group (Massachusetts) ballot (p. 115)
party column (Indiana) ballot (p. 115)
plurality (p. 112)
recall (p. 129)
redistricting (p. 133)
secret (Australian) ballot (p. 116)
straight ticket (p. 115)
voter turnout (p. 121)

Suggested Websites

- **ballotpedia.org**. Website sponsored by the nonpartisan Lucy Burns Institute; provides thorough information about elections at all levels of government.

- **www.fairvote.org**. Website of FairVote, which promotes voting and advocates ranked-choice voting and the abolition of the Electoral College.

- **lwv.org**. Website of the League of Women Voters; provides a wealth of voter education information.

- **www.nass.org**. Website of the National Association of Secretaries of State. Secretaries of state typically serve as chief election officials, and their offices have primary responsibility for recording official election outcomes.

- **www.pewresearch.org**. Website of the Pew Research Center, which conducts surveys and publishes studies that look at the demographic trends affecting politics.

Parties and Interest Groups

Elephants, Donkeys, and Cash Cows

Georgia secretary of state Brian Kemp rode support from President Trump to victory in the GOP's gubernatorial primary in 2018. That year, GOP candidates embraced Trump while Democrats reviled him, even while running for offices that have little to do with Washington.

Chapter Objectives

After reading this chapter, you will be able to

- Describe the role of political parties in the U.S. political process and government,

- Compare why some states are more politically competitive than others,

- Identify the ways political parties are subject to regulation,

- Explain the role of third parties and independents in the political process, and

- Discuss the ways interest groups and lobbies influence politics.

ack in May 2015, a month before Donald Trump announced his bid for the presidency, the Pew Research Center conducted a survey measuring attitudes about trade. At that time, a majority of Republicans, or 51 percent, agreed that free trade agreements had been good for the country, compared with 39 percent who thought they had been bad. By the time Trump had officially been nominated the next year, views on the issue within his party had reversed. Half as many Republicans saw free trade as a good thing as had been the case a year earlier (26 percent), while two-thirds of all Republicans saw it as a net negative (68 percent).[1]

Republicans had traditionally been more supportive of free trade than Democrats, but it was one of the issues on which Trump broke with party orthodoxy as a candidate. As president, Trump has sought to renegotiate long-standing trade agreements, called the European Union a "foe" on trade, and imposed tariffs on goods from European countries, Canada, and China. Back in the first decade of the 20th century, roughly the same percentage of Democrats and Republicans thought that the North American Free Trade Agreement (NAFTA) had been good for the United States; by 2017, only 22 percent of Republicans held a positive view of NAFTA, compared with 67 percent of Democrats.[2] One poll about tariffs in 2018 found not only that Republicans and Democrats had starkly different views about them, but their feelings intensified, either negatively or positively, when Trump's name was associated with the policy of imposing them.[3]

Political scientists have found that, in many cases, the way people view a particular issue depends to a large extent on the positions their parties hold. Views of the economy among partisans are much more divided than they were 20 years ago based solely on whether their party controls the White House.[4] The Trump presidency provides a striking example of this. A month before he took office in 2017, just 14 percent of Republicans believed that the economy was in good or excellent shape. By the time he'd been in office a year, 74 percent of Republicans believed the economy was doing well.[5] By contrast, fewer Democrats believed that the economy was healthy.

The parties—and their supporters—hold differing, often conflicting views on such issues as abortion, gun control, and climate change. At times, it seems like they insist that adherents hold particular viewpoints on issues such as these, at least until a disruptive figure such as Trump manages to change where a party stands. American politics now is often described as "tribal," with people belonging to two entirely separate camps that not only fail to see eye to eye on various issues, but belong almost to separate worlds. Democrats dominate major metropolitan population centers, while rural areas have become almost exclusively Republican. Trump's candidacy and presidency has led to splits along not only racial lines but education lines as well. Whites with a college education are now more likely to vote Democratic than those without.

Adherents to the two parties tend to support separate restaurants and shops and have different habits when it comes to church attendance, the types of cars they drive, what they prefer to drink, and, importantly, where they get their news and information. Democrats largely live in cities and suburbs tied to the information economy, while Republicans are strongest in areas that rely on manufacturing, farming, and mining or other resource extraction. Democrats receive overwhelming support from members of racial and ethnic minorities, while Republicans command majority support among whites. Partisans may have different lifestyles or backgrounds, but they have developed an exaggerated sense of just how different members of the other team actually are. A study by Douglas J. Ahler and Gaurav Sood found that "people tend to considerably overestimate the extent to which party supporters belong to party-stereotypical groups."[6] For example, Republicans believe that 32 percent of Democrats are lesbian, gay, or bisexual when the correct figure is 6 percent, while Democrats believe that 44 percent of Republicans earn more than $250,000 a year when only 2 percent of Republicans make that much in reality.[7]

In her 2018 book *Uncivil Agreement: How Politics Became Our Identity*, University of Maryland political scientist Lilliana Mason argues that partisanship has become a form of "mega-identity," weaving within it factors including a person's race, religion, ethnicity, gender, and neighborhood. Each vote sends a strong signal about who a person is, or how people see themselves and others. "Identity politics is a far more powerful concept if we consider how a collection of identities is working in concert," she writes.[8] So powerful, she argues, that partisans may care more about whether their side is winning—and the other side losing—than they care about actual policy outcomes. To a large extent, American politics is now ruled by negative partisanship—the belief that the other side is not just wrong but bad and must be stopped. "We tend to define our politicians these days not by what they do, but by their attitude and their enemies," Scott Jennings, a Republican consultant, wrote in 2018.[9]

Partisan affiliation may be harder to spot from a distance than physical traits such as race and gender, but it's easy enough to find out where a person stands politically through social media posting and other cues. Political scientists Shanto Iyengar and Sean J. Westwood administered an implicit bias test to 2,000 respondents and found that underlying animosity toward the other party approaches, and in some cases surpasses, animosity based in racial bias, suggesting it is greater than previously thought. Half the participants were asked to read résumés of high school students, and about 80 percent of them managed to pick those belonging to members of their own party, showing that discrimination based on party affiliation exceeded that based on race. "Americans increasingly dislike people and groups on the other side of the political divide and face no

social repercussions for the open expression of these attitudes," the researchers write, making it clear that there is more incentive for politicians to bash the other side than to appear to be appeasers by compromising.[10]

But even as partisan loyalty, or disdain, continues to grow, the parties themselves, as entities, are weaker than they used to be. The brand of Republican or Democrat might matter a lot, but the actual party apparatus has weakened. Parties once held tight control, at least in some places, over choosing candidates. Now, candidates decide to run on their own or may be as likely to be recruited by an outside group as by party leaders. Trump himself—the nation's first president elected with no prior experience in government or the military—is a prime example of a self-selecting candidate who was able to defeat opponents with standard-issue résumés as governors or senators. In an extreme example, Arthur Jones, a former member of the American Nazi Party, in 2018 won the Republican nomination for a congressional seat in Illinois. Since the district is predominantly Democratic, the Grand Old Party—better known as the GOP—hadn't bothered to recruit a more mainstream candidate to run either in the primary or, after Jones secured the nomination, as a third-party challenger. The Illinois Republican Party denounced Jones, but he bragged about having "snookered" the party. "The Republican Party screwed up big time," he said.[11]

On the Democratic side, the party worried that it could blow winnable congressional races in California simply because it had too many candidates running. California has a top-two primary system, meaning all candidates appear on the same primary ballot, regardless of party, with the top two vote getters proceeding to the general election. In a handful of seats, Democrats had multiple candidates who threatened to split the vote, allowing two Republicans to sneak in ahead of them. Despite entreaties from party leaders, the weaker candidates didn't want to drop out, even if this boosted the chances another Democrat could win a seat. "Anybody who thinks the Democratic Party is an all-powerful primary-rigging Death Star should look at the $6 million they've spent desperately trying to clear the logjam of approx. 8 billion candidates in CA—most of whom have refused to quit under pressure," tweeted NBC reporter Alex Seitz-Wald.[12]

Other groups that may or may not be closely aligned with a party are also out there recruiting and supporting candidates. In the wake of Trump's presidential victory, a wealth of groups sprang up on the left either to push ideas, promote Democratic candidates, or both, including Indivisible, Future Now, Forward Majority, Run for Something, Sister District Project, and Flippable, joining older groups on the left such as Daily Kos, EMILY's List, and Emerge America. The parties themselves remain important conduits of candidate recruitment, voter data, and cash, but there is no Oz-like figure in control of conservatives or progressives or their messages. **Political parties** have become less hierarchical and more like networks. "There's this fallacy that some small group can get together and decide the outcome of this," said Mike Leavitt, a former Republican governor of Utah. "That does not exist. This is a marketplace of political ideas. The party is responsible for its structure, but cannot dictate the outcome."[13]

A changing media environment and the rise of fundraising vehicles such as **super PACs** have made it easier for factions within a party to organize and spread their messages. A single rich donor can be enough to help an insurgent candidate overcome resistance from party insiders, especially given the recent erosion of campaign finance regulations. As a result, the parties are less able to impose discipline when it comes to stances on issues. Candidates don't have to fear being cut off from party funds and regular donors if they know some billionaire might be willing to underwrite their efforts.

Bernie Sanders made complaints about the influence of Wall Street and billionaires the centerpiece of his 2016 campaign, a message that clearly struck a nerve with millions of people. But the evolving fundraising situation has also prompted complaints from old party regulars that politics has become an undisciplined free-for-all. "The overriding theme was that the state and local parties are just not the important players that they used to be in federal elections," said Daniel Tokaji, coauthor of *The New Soft Money*, referring to his interviews with political consultants. "On some occasions, we got laughs or chuckles when we even mentioned state or local parties."[14]

Super PACs are not allowed to coordinate their messages directly with candidates, but sometimes these organizations are run by close allies of candidates, such as former aides. Other times, they have no connection to candidates at all—which leads some observers to worry that such groups can push their own issues and end up dominating the political conversation. Candidates can end up feeling like bystanders to their own campaigns, their efforts at shaping and spreading

messages minimized as outside groups spend far more money. Some have complained even about super PAC spending that offers support, saying that they get the blame for negative advertising over which they have no control. In addition to super PACs, so-called dark money groups—organizations that ostensibly serve educational purposes and are able to spend freely in political campaigns without disclosing their donors—play an increasingly large role in American politics.

"It's one of the major problems with the current campaign finance system," said Democratic consultant Jeff Link. "A candidate is no longer the loudest speaker in his or her own campaign."[15]

The combination of all these factors—stark polarization between the parties and their supporters but weak and often undisciplined parties and coalitions—is part of the reason people generally express dissatisfaction with politics and government. Simply put, it's not a recipe for getting things done, particularly in a system that generally demands compromise. Demonization of the other side makes it harder to make deals, because politicians are punished if they're viewed as having consorted with the enemy. And, either despite or because of stark differences between the parties, rank-and-file voters are in a sense deprived of real choices, since switching allegiance isn't generally seen as a real option even if they're unhappy with the performance or views of their own party. "The defining characteristic of our moment is that parties are weak while partisanship is strong," Marquette University political scientist Julia Azari wrote in 2016. "Voters do not have to listen to elite signals. Elites do not have to listen to each other's signals. Parties have been stripped (in part by their own actions) of their ability to coordinate and bargain [and] bargaining breaks down when no one has anything that anyone else wants."[16]

The combination of weak parties and strong partisanship is dangerous, Azari argues. Parties can't control whom they nominate, but most voters will support whomever gets the nomination of the party they like best (or hate least). For that reason, parties and the party labels continue to matter a great deal. "The two-party system is about as strong as it's ever been," University

....

Political party An organization that nominates and supports candidates for elected offices.

Super PACs Political action committees that can spend unlimited funds on behalf of political candidates but cannot directly coordinate their plans with those candidates.

of Denver political scientist Seth Masket wrote in 2014. "Any candidate who wants to have even a chance at achieving office has to pick one of the two major parties to run with, and any policy idea needs an affiliation with at least one major party in order to become a law."[17]

To help better understand this paradox, we'll look at the evolving roles that parties have played and continue to play. This chapter explores the roles political parties play and how those vary by state, as well as the influence of interest groups, not only on elections but also on governance. As you read through the chapter, keep in mind the following questions:

- **Why are political parties weaker than they used to be?**

- **Why are political parties stronger in some states than in others?**

- **How do interest groups influence policymakers?**

A Primer on Political Parties

Political parties are not as dominant in American life as they once were. From roughly the 1820s until the 1940s, political parties constituted a leading organizing force in this country. They not only provided citizens with political identities but also were major sources of social activity and entertainment—and, in many cases, jobs. Today, parties are not as effective as they used to be at getting people out to vote or even at organizing them around an issue. However, they do remain important to candidates, giving them a kind of brand identification and acting as fundraisers.

Although there are two major national parties, the party organizations play larger roles at the state level than they do as national forces. Their respective strength varies widely from state to state and is affected by such factors as the different ways states regulate parties, the differences in the historical roles parties have played within each state, and the amount of competition between the major parties within a given state. In general, the more closely balanced the two main parties are in a state, the more likely that they will

....

Factional splits or factions Groups that struggle to control the message within a party; for example, a party may be split into competing regional factions.

have well-funded and well-organized state-level party organizations.

Political parties recruit candidates for offices and provide them with support for their campaigns. They give candidates money or help them raise it and offer logistical and strategic assistance. Just as important, they help coordinate the candidates' messages with those of other candidates running for other offices under the party's banner.

Since the 1850s, the vast majority of candidates for political office in the United States have run as members of either the Democratic or the Republican Party. The Democratic Party as we know it today evolved from **factional splits** in the earliest days of the American republic. The country started without a two-party system, but **factions** soon developed. The Federalists, led by Alexander Hamilton, favored a strong central government with power rooted in the industrial North. The Democratic-Republicans, led by Thomas Jefferson, emerged as the party opposing the Federalists. They argued for states' rights against a "monarchical" rule by the aristocracy and declared that farmers, craftspeople, and shopkeepers should control their own interests without interference from the capitol.

Jefferson's party, which eventually morphed into the Democratic Party that we know today, dominated politics throughout the first half of the 19th century. That same period saw the creation of numerous parties: Whigs, Know-Nothings, Barnburners, Softshells, Hunkers, and Free Soilers. They all had some success, but the Democratic Party of Jefferson and Andrew Jackson dominated so completely that, as the main source of political power, the party split into factions, with northern and southern Democrats arguing over the expansion of slavery. That argument created an opening for a new major party.

The Republican Party was formed in 1854 in opposition to slavery. It soon supplanted the Whig Party, which had been formed in 1834 to protest the spoils-system politics of Jackson. The Republican Party, also known as the Grand Old Party (GOP), quickly enjoyed congressional success. Following the election of Abraham Lincoln in 1860, Republicans dominated the presidency for decades to come. Their antislavery stance, however, guaranteed that the party remained practically nonexistent in the South until the civil rights era of the 1950s and 1960s. Democrats reemerged as the nation's dominant party in the 1930s, when Republicans took the blame for the Great Depression. The Democrats' New

Deal coalition of southerners, union workers, African Americans, the poor, and the elderly drove American politics well into the 1960s but fragmented after that, resulting in a loss of political control for the party.

Long-standing Democratic majorities at the congressional and state levels eroded. Republicans dominated presidential elections from 1968 through 1988, winning five out of the six contests. Since then, however, Democrats have met with more success, carrying the popular vote six of the last seven times. But national elections are still highly competitive. In 2004, Republican George W. Bush became the first presidential candidate since 1988 to win a majority—51 percent—of the popular vote. (He had prevailed in the Electoral College four years earlier, despite trailing in the national popular vote count by 500,000 votes.) In 2016, Trump received fewer votes nationwide than Hillary Clinton, but won the election anyway thanks to narrow victories in Electoral College battleground states such as Pennsylvania, Florida, and Wisconsin—all states Barack Obama had carried twice. The narrow margins of presidential victories suggest that, at least at the national level, the two major political parties are competitive. At the state level, Republicans control more legislatures and governorships than Democrats, as we will discuss in Chapters 7 and 8.

Overall support for the parties is split along regional lines. Democrats enjoy more support along the West Coast and in the Northeast, whereas Republicans are dominant in the South and the Plains states. The upper Midwest and parts of the Mountain West such as Colorado and Nevada have become the most competitive regions. But partisan splits within states have emerged as a striking fault line. Democrats dominate big cities and the most populated suburbs. As of 2018, no fewer than 20 out of 25 of the nation's largest cities had Democratic mayors. But Republicans rule rural areas and are competitive in suburbs. The advantage of representing people who are less densely packed is that it gives them more geographical running room, a demographic reality often exacerbated during the redistricting process. Republicans have to worry that their support is largely among groups and in places that are losing population share relative to the nation as a whole, political journalist Ronald Brownstein noted in 2018, but Democrats fear that "dominance of the largest metropolitan areas will still leave them operating with too narrow a geographic base of support to consistently control majorities not only in the House, but also in the Senate and the Electoral College."[18] This is true not only at the federal level but in states, helping to explain why Republicans have held the whip hand over most legislatures over the course of the past decade. Although most Americans are familiar with the Republican and Democratic Parties, many may not realize that political parties technically take many different shapes. When people refer to the Democratic and Republican Parties, they are really referring to officials belonging to two umbrella groups that cover a wide variety of parties. Each of the national parties is in reality a consortium of state parties. Party chairs and other representatives from the state parties dominate the national party committees. State parties, in turn, are consortia of local parties. In some states local parties are defined by counties, whereas in others they are defined by congressional districts. Although both the Democratic and Republican Parties are active in every state, some state and local parties are more active than others. Parties in densely populated states such as Florida and California are well-funded, professionally run organizations. In less populated states such as Montana and Idaho, the parties have very small full-time staffs and take on more personnel just during the few months leading up to an election.

A given state may have a particularly dominant political party, but overall, the political parties in most of the world's other Western-style democracies are much stronger than those in the United States. For example, in the United States, party leaders are not able to nominate candidates of their own choosing. Most candidates are now chosen directly by the voting public through primaries. In fact, even a party's top nominee—its presidential candidate—may not have been the first choice of party leaders. This is different from the way party politics operates in, say, Great Britain. There, political parties are much more centralized. Leadership within a party translates more cleanly into leadership in government. The parties, not voters, select the parties' nominees for the office of prime minister.

In the United States, the national Republican and Democratic Parties essentially are made up of state parties. The Republican and Democratic National Committees are made up almost exclusively of state party chairs and one male and one female representative from each state. Representatives from the territories—Puerto Rico, Guam, and the U.S. Virgin Islands, among others—form the rest of the body for each party. U.S. political parties tend to be regulated at the state level. The ways they raise and spend money,

STATES UNDER STRESS
WANING POWER OF STATE PARTIES CONTRIBUTES TO POLARIZED POLITICS

State parties matter less than they used to. They enjoy no monopoly on recruiting or training candidates. They face more federal restrictions when it comes to raising funds than do super PACs and other outside groups. A lot of their basic work—registering, educating, and turning out voters—ends up being highly regulated under federal campaign finance restrictions that don't apply to other players in the political process. "The idea that we can't coordinate with a state Senate candidate because there's also a U.S. Senate candidate on the ballot seems absurd," says Jason Perkey, executive director of the South Carolina Democratic Party.

Sometimes outside groups not only face fewer restrictions but also can have more foot soldiers in place during a campaign than the parties themselves. And, at least in off years, many state parties barely even have anyone around to answer the phone. "State parties have become really a shadow of what they used to be," says Republican consultant David Carney. "It's kind of tragic."

Still, they're far from irrelevant. Advertising can be outsourced to super PACs, but some efforts can't. State parties do the often unglamorous work of building and maintaining a base of support, year in and year out, whether there's an election or not. They mobilize loyal supporters and have a standing knowledge of voter behavior and concerns, maintaining what are generally robust databases. Parties also play a unique role in coordinating activity and messaging between candidates at all levels, from legislators to the presidency.

A super PAC can fill the airwaves and the Internet with effective, targeted messaging, but it cannot necessarily activate loyal party supporters, who rely on local elected officials for guidance and patronage. "You still build organizations with hard money," says Mo Elleithee, a former Democratic National Committee official, referring to donations that are regulated and limited in size under federal campaign finance law. "Super PAC money can do a lot, but it can't build an organization."

Still, state parties can't really compete with super PACs when it comes to raising funds. Thanks to the federal Bipartisan Campaign Reform Act of 2002, which abolished soft money—unlimited funds donated to parties by wealthy individuals, corporations, and unions—the parties have lost out in the contemporary money race. The ban on soft money was upheld by the Supreme Court in 2017, rejecting a case brought by the Louisiana Republican Party and two local party committees. Funds are instead being poured into super PACs or so-called dark money groups that don't have to disclose the identities of their donors.

Some politicians and commentators now argue that restricting the parties themselves backfired and that it would be better to lift restrictions on party fundraising. Parties are more accountable than super PACs and other outside groups due to both federal reporting requirements and the fact that they have to worry about their reputations in future election years—something not always true of super PACs, many of which support one particular candidate or are active for a single election cycle. No one seems to like the amount of money sloshing into politics, but, as the Brennan Center for Justice concluded in a 2015 report, "Organized parties plainly are more transparent than the shadow parties and other outside groups competing with them for resources."[a]

The U.S. Supreme Court's 2014 decision in *McCutcheon v. Federal Election Commission* is making it easier for parties to raise money. Individual donors who previously could give no more than $74,600 to all parties in a given cycle can now offer well over $1 million. Parties will be able to argue that giving money to them will help favored candidates to whom big donors have already maxed out their contributions. Hillary Clinton entered into joint fundraising agreements with most state Democratic parties in 2016. Increased funds coming to state parties will boost turnout and advertising efforts that assist down-ballot candidates even more than the standard-bearers.

It may also help reduce polarization, according to a 2016 study by the Brookings Institution.[b] Because the parties are concerned with winning elections and have their eye on their own long-term reputation and image, they work to balance and restrain the influence of ideologically purist groups. "Historically, and still today, state parties act as a counterforce against highly motivated, ideologically extreme minorities of the sort that are polarizing and fragmenting American politics," note the study's authors, Raymond J. La Raja and Jonathan Rauch.

As things stand, parties mostly stay neutral during primary seasons. Only 6 percent of the 56 state party leaders surveyed by La Raja and Rauch said they often take sides in competitive primaries, compared to 83 percent who rarely or never do.

It seems to make perfect sense for the party itself to act as an honest broker. But by staying neutral, parties are failing at their traditional role of vetting candidates. Instead, they have to wait on the sidelines to work with nominees who have been either supported or pummeled by highly motivated, often ideologically extreme outside groups.

Like the Brennan Center study's authors, the Brookings authors call for limits on contributions to state parties to be relaxed. It would be better for democracy, they contend, if campaign money were to flow through parties rather than through groups that are mostly unregulated. "It's simple math: If you restrict the party, you get more independent expenditures by non-party groups," La Raja says. "We think that dark money groups and super PACs are here to stay, so why handcuff state parties?"

Source: Adapted from Alan Greenblatt, "The Waning Power of State Parties," *Governing*, December 2015, http://www.governing.com/topics/politics/gov-waning-power-state-parties.html.

[a]Daniel I. Weiner and Ian Vandewalker, "Stronger Parties, Stronger Democracy: Rethinking Reform," Brennan Center for Justice, September 16, 2015, https://www.brennancenter.org/publication/stronger-parties-stronger-democracy-rethinking-reforming.

[b]Raymond J. La Raja and Jonathan Rauch, "The State of State Parties—and How Strengthening Them Can Improve Our Politics," Center for Effective Public Management, Brookings Institution, March 2016, http://www.brookings.edu/~/media/research/files/papers/2016/03/08-state-parties-la-raja-rauch/states.pdf.

their organizational structures, and the rules they follow to nominate candidates and place them on ballots are all subject to differing state regulations. How much power the national parties have in relation to the state parties shifts over time, as we will see.

In the current era of polarization, in which party loyalties are strongly divided, it's not too strong to say that many Americans not only disagree with but hate the viewpoints of the "other" party.

That is not to say that parties are not collections of interests. Parties are conglomerations of people who share some overlapping ideology, or set of political, economic, and social beliefs. These days, Democrats are supported by groups that support abortion and gay rights, as well as gun control advocates. Environmentalists, college-educated professionals, unmarried women, Hispanics, Asian Americans, and African Americans also tend to be Democrats. Republicans gain support from corporate and small businesses and from social conservatives. The 2016 election scrambled traditional alliances, with more college-educated white voters supporting Clinton than previous Democrats, while

Trump's victory was attributed to his gains among white working-class voters, while also carrying higher-income whites. Republicans are also more likely than Democrats to attend church regularly. In the current era of **polarization**, in which party loyalties are strongly divided, it's not too strong to say that many Americans not only disagree with but hate the viewpoints of the "other" party. In recent years, political reporters have delighted in playing at being pop sociologists and pointing out the differences between adherents of the two parties in everything from favorite baby names to beer preferences. Over the past 50 years, the percentage of people who say they would be upset if their children married someone from the other party has jumped from 5 percent to 40 percent.[19] One recent University of California study found that people find individuals less attractive physically if they don't share their partisan leanings.[20] In 2018, a Virginia restaurant's decision to ask White House press secretary Sarah Huckabee Sanders to leave, along with in-person confrontations with other administration officials and members of Congress, led to a spate of finger-pointing and recriminations, with partisans on both sides insisting that the other was to blame for incivility and increasing threats of violence associated with contemporary politics.

If the partisan divisions have become more entrenched, it's not necessarily the case that parties are

Polarization A split among elected officials or an electorate along strictly partisan lines.

able to stifle internal divisions within their own ranks. After Ronald Reagan and other Republicans chipped into Democratic support among certain groups in the New Deal coalition, the Democrats became a famously argumentative group, with various factions within the party struggling to find common cause with one another. As recently as 2006, a Democratic strategist wrote about "the Democratic Party's well-deserved reputation for being a fractious coalition of infighting special interests."[21] But following their poor showing in that year's elections, Republicans began to argue more loudly among themselves about which ideas should prevail within the party—a fractious debate that continued through the party's recent losing streak in presidential campaigns. Conservative, populist, so-called Tea Party groups began holding large rallies in 2009 to decry big government, President Obama's administration, and their more moderate counterparts within the Republican Party. "There is clearly a war going on in the Republican Party," Bob Smith, a Republican and former U.S. senator from New Hampshire, said. "The sooner the party's leadership recognizes that, the better off they'll be."[22] Tea Party–backed insurgents and establishment candidates have continued to square off in search of GOP support. In 2014, the establishment candidates mostly won, but they did so by co-opting the issue stances of the Tea Party.

Following the party's loss of the presidential election, the Republican National Committee commissioned a well-publicized "autopsy," which concluded that the party needed to do a better job of reaching out to younger voters and rising minority groups, notably Hispanics. "Young voters are increasingly rolling their eyes at what the party represents, and many minorities wrongly think that Republicans do not like them or want them in the country," the report concluded.[23] Nevertheless, opposition to immigration fueled the party's base and became a defining issue for Trump and other candidates in 2016. The party is also split between its donor class, which favors tax cuts for the wealthy, limits on entitlements, and reductions in environmental regulation, and many "angry conservative citizens" who "care most about stopping immigration, outlawing abortions, and cutting back on what they view as government largesse for the poor," according to Theda Skocpol, a professor of government and sociology at

Harvard University. "Today's Republican Party is being revamped and torn asunder from contradictory directions," she wrote in 2016.[24]

Having lost the White House in 2016, Democrats found themselves facing internal divisions, with plenty of commentators speculating that a "liberal Tea Party" was in the office. Believing that voters demanded a stark choice and "resistance" to the Trump administration, progressives challenged incumbent Democrats in primaries around the country, including Minneapolis mayor Betsy Hodges, New York governor Andrew Cuomo, and U.S. senator Dianne Feinstein of California. The most celebrated example in 2018 came in New York, where Alexandria Ocasio-Cortez, a young activist who was working as a bartender when she kicked off her campaign, was able to unseat Joseph Crowley, a veteran member of Congress touted as a likely future speaker of the U.S. House. Ocasio-Cortez ran on a highly progressive platform, including support for single-payer health care, free college, and the abolishment of the federal Immigration and Customs Enforcement agency. Most of the incumbent Democrats survived, but many did so by moving their positions closer to the progressive point of view on issues such as universal health care, gun control, and support for immigration and higher education.

Candidates still may rely on parties to serve as conduits to interest groups and voters, but the importance of parties to individual candidates has not been as great recently as in the past. Academics have noted a shift to **candidate-centered politics** over the past 30 years or so. What this means is that parties play less of a role in determining who is going to run for which office. Instead, candidates, in effect, select themselves. Ambitious people interested in politics and government run for the offices of their choice rather than working their way up the party ranks in roles their parties might have chosen for them. Arnold Schwarzenegger decided in 2003 to suspend his acting career to run for governor of California and won the support of the state's Republican Party. More recently, a number of businessmen have made running for governor their first political move, including Republicans Doug Burgum of North Dakota and Pete Ricketts of Nebraska. In the old days, a party's gubernatorial candidate first would have had to put in years in lower offices. He or she would have had to earn the support of party leaders throughout the state before running for the state's highest office. Today, upstarts may well decide to run against

....

Candidate-centered politics Politics in which candidates promote themselves and their own campaigns rather than relying on party organizations.

initially better-known candidates with party support. For example, Ted Cruz came seemingly out of nowhere to defeat Lieutenant Governor David Dewhurst in the 2012 Texas GOP Senate primary. Then Republican Dan Patrick prevailed over Dewhurst as the latter sought reelection in 2014.

Ocasio-Cortez, Cruz, and plenty of other insurgent candidates have given party elders lots of headaches in recent years, but they still identify themselves as Democrats or Republicans. Political candidates run under a single party label, such as Republican, Democratic, or Green. The candidate campaigns for office and is nominated as a member of that party. Bernie Sanders has served for decades in Congress as an independent and identifies himself as a democratic socialist, but he knew in order to make an impact on the 2016 race he had to run for the nomination of the Democratic Party.

For potential officeholders, there's little choice but to maintain allegiance to one party or the other. Throughout American history, the major parties have proved to be adept at embracing popular ideas presented by outsiders or third-party candidates. Democratic and Republican candidates in the 1990s took the idea of a balanced federal budget more seriously because third-party challenger Ross Perot had raised the issue. During the 1930s, Franklin D. Roosevelt lifted many of the ideas of Socialist candidate Norman Thomas. When faced with the rare strong minor-party challenge, a major-party candidate can argue that he or she offers the best vehicle for presenting any shared ideals—and stands a better chance of beating the other major-party candidate. Perot's 1992 showing was the best by a third-party candidate since Theodore Roosevelt's in 1912—and neither one of them came close to winning.

In addition to providing an important way for candidates to identify themselves, the parties are central to governance. However important interest group spending is during an election, parties remain the primary mechanisms for the organization of government. Except for Nebraska, which is nonpartisan, all state legislatures are organized by party. If Democrats have a majority of the seats in the Maine House of Representatives, for example, the Speaker and other top leaders will be Democrats, and the party will control each committee as well. As a theoretical ideal, political scientists use the **responsible party model** as a way to measure and assess political parties. The responsible party model holds that political parties should present clear policy options to voters, that voters will cast ballots based on the options they favor the most, that while in office parties try to create and implement the programs they promise, and that in the next election the parties will be judged by their performance in delivering those programs. In short, this model views political parties as connecting the wishes of citizens to government programs and policies, organizing the government to deliver on those wishes, and acting as agents to hold government accountable for delivering on what it promises.

Today, with different factions fighting one another for prominence and power, this concept remains important. During a fight between more moderate Republicans and more conservative Republicans for control of the Kansas Senate in 2012 primary contests, the balance was tipped toward conservatives thanks to more than $8 million spent by groups such as Americans for Prosperity, the Club for Growth, the Kansas Chamber of Commerce, and Kansas Right to Life.[25] The moderates sought their revenge in 2016, succeeding in defeating a dozen conservative legislators in the GOP primaries. Such an open factional split within a party is unusual, but it demonstrates the importance of the party label. Many of the super PACs that are most active in one election cycle might not even be around a few years later.

What Parties Were Like

Parties remain important organizers, and party identification offers voters a handy shortcut when it comes to figuring out where candidates are likely to stand on various issues. In their early years, political parties in the United States were a lot more than just brand identifiers and fundraisers. Many of the social services now provided by local governments, such as food assistance and job placement, were the province of political parties throughout much of the 19th century. For all the contemporary complaints about the "liberal media," one-sided social media feeds, and the domination of talk radio by conservative hosts, today's nonpartisan "mainstream" media are a far cry from the newspapers of the late 19th century, which were often openly affiliated with particular parties. The pro-Republican

....

Responsible party model The theory that political parties offer clear policy choices to voters, try to deliver on those policies when they take office, and are held accountable by voters for the success or failure of those policies.

FIGURE 6-1   ●   How It Works

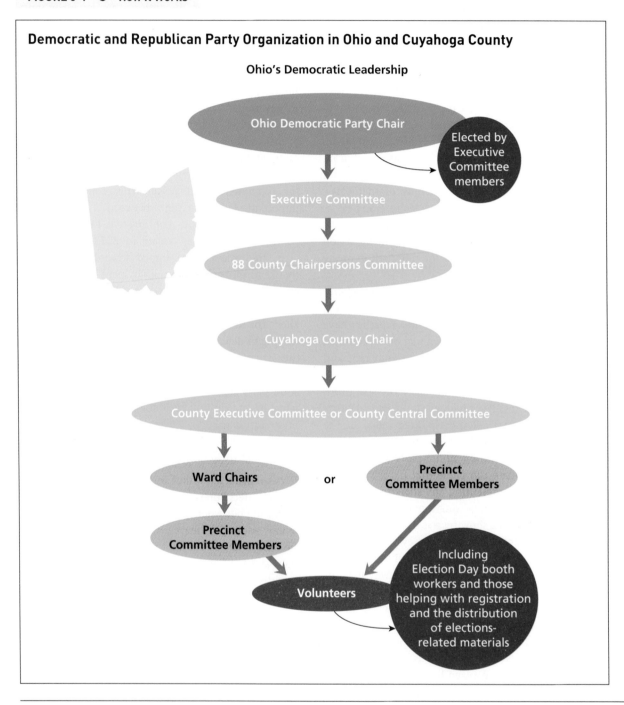

Democratic and Republican Party Organization in Ohio and Cuyahoga County

Ohio's Democratic Leadership

Ohio Democratic Party Chair

Elected by Executive Committee members

Executive Committee

88 County Chairpersons Committee

Cuyahoga County Chair

County Executive Committee or County Central Committee

Ward Chairs   or   Precinct Committee Members

Precinct Committee Members

Volunteers

Including Election Day booth workers and those helping with registration and the distribution of elections-related materials

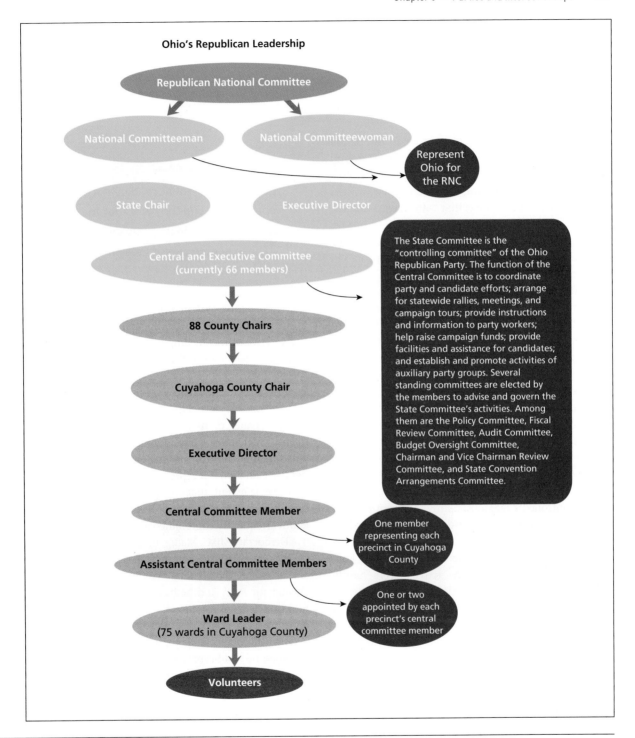

Ohio's Republican Leadership

Republican National Committee

National Committeeman

National Committeewoman

Represent Ohio for the RNC

State Chair

Executive Director

Central and Executive Committee (currently 66 members)

The State Committee is the "controlling committee" of the Ohio Republican Party. The function of the Central Committee is to coordinate party and candidate efforts; arrange for statewide rallies, meetings, and campaign tours; provide instructions and information to party workers; help raise campaign funds; provide facilities and assistance for candidates; and establish and promote activities of auxiliary party groups. Several standing committees are elected by the members to advise and govern the State Committee's activities. Among them are the Policy Committee, Fiscal Review Committee, Audit Committee, Budget Oversight Committee, Chairman and Vice Chairman Review Committee, and State Convention Arrangements Committee.

88 County Chairs

Cuyahoga County Chair

Executive Director

Central Committee Member

One member representing each precinct in Cuyahoga County

Assistant Central Committee Members

One or two appointed by each precinct's central committee member

Ward Leader (75 wards in Cuyahoga County)

Volunteers

Chicago Tribune, on learning that a Democrat had won the 1876 presidential election, ran a headline that read, "Lost. The Country Given Over to Democratic Greed and Plunder."[26] Such an openly partisan statement is unimaginable in the mainstream media of today (although not nearly as unlikely in a blog post or on Twitter).

People's party loyalties were so strong in this period because many of their livelihoods revolved around party interests. Party machines doled out jobs, government contracts, and other benefits to their workers and supporters. The idea was that "offices exist not as a necessary means of administering government but for the support of party leaders at public expense," as one political scientist wrote of 19th-century party cliques in New York State.[27]

Politics in many cities and some states was totally dominated by these usually indigenous party machines. In Rhode Island, the Democratic Party was dominant through much of the 20th century, and party leaders brooked little dissent. Only a handful of free-agent candidates were able to pry nominations away from those who had been endorsed by the party. In Providence, the state capital and largest city, only three individuals held the office of mayor from 1941 until 1974. Two of those men were state Democratic Party leaders. Over the same 30-year period, only two people served as chairs of the Providence Democratic Party. Both of them doubled as head of the city's Department of Public Works. Party leaders controlled 2,800 jobs, doling them out roughly equally among the various wards, or political districts, within the city.[28]

The close links connecting control of jobs, government spending, and party activity were hardly unique to Rhode Island. Chicago, Nassau County on Long Island, New York, and Pennsylvania were all home to legendary **political or party machines**. A long-standing joke about Chicago politics held that as many dead people voted as living ones (because the names of those who died were not removed from the election rolls and were used to cast extra votes for favored candidates). In Oklahoma, the state gave control of most government jobs—the decision-making power over hiring and firing workers—to individual

officeholders. These individuals were not afraid to exploit such control for their own benefit. "I have 85 employees—garage men, road workers, janitors, elevator operators—and they work for me when I need them," said a county commissioner. "These people care if I stay in office."[29]

> **"I have 85 employees—garage men, road workers, janitors, elevator operators—and they work for me when I need them," said a county commissioner. "These people care if I stay in office."**

The machine system used patronage to maintain firm control of power, with the ability to dole out jobs and elective offices feeding off each other (see Chapter 10). Party machines and rival factions ran "slates," or specific lists, of endorsed candidates for offices and lent their backing to the favored candidates. "Each succeeding election was viewed not as a separate contest involving new issues or new personalities," writes political scientist Joel Sibley, "but as yet another opportunity to vote for, and reaffirm, an individual's support for his or her party and what it represented."[30]

To some extent, machine politics is still practiced in certain places. As governor of Illinois, Republican Bruce Rauner frequently complained about the power wielded by Democrat Mike Madigan, the longtime speaker of the state House, through machine-style politics. "He manages the General Assembly, he controls the Democratic Party and he has a property tax appeal law firm that he owns on the side," Rauner said in 2018. "So he can set tax policy for the state, and force property taxes in Illinois to be as high as any state in America, and then he can become wealthy by charging business owners in Chicago to use his law firm to reduce their property taxes. That's corrupt. It's like a mafia protection racket."[31]

Connecticut's budget for 2016 changed 32 top-level state jobs from civil service positions to political appointments to be filled at the pleasure of the governor. For candidates, endorsements from governors and mayors often mean more than support from members of Congress, because governors and mayors have so many loyal workers at their disposal who can go out and

---

Political or party machines Political organizations controlled by small numbers of people and run for partisan ends. In the 19th and 20th centuries, these organizations controlled party nominations for public office and rewarded supporters with government jobs and contracts.

knock on doors or offer other tangible support. "The history of politics has been patronage," said Boston mayor Marty Walsh in 2016. "Helping people get jobs has always been part of the business."[32]

As Walsh noted, such practices have been curbed to a large extent. A century ago, the exposure of clear cases of corruption, such as evidence that a party was extorting union funds, running gambling operations, and taking kickbacks on government contracts, often led to the election of reform candidates for mayor and other city and state offices. Disgust over corruption in politics led to anti-machine statutes, such as the imposition of civil service requirements for many government jobs and tougher anticorruption laws. The widespread use of **nonpartisan ballots** for municipal offices was the direct result of reforms imposed in reaction to political machines. These ballots, which do not list candidates by political party, are designed to separate city government from party voting.

California may be the best example of a state that had such a progressive reaction against the machines. The state was hostile toward parties, lacked any type of patronage system, and held nonpartisan elections. Precinct and ward organizations were weak, whereas individual candidates were assertive.[33] Party organizations were once banned from endorsing candidates in primary contests. The law also limited state party chairs to two-year terms and required the rotation of chairs on a geographical basis every two years. In 1989, the U.S. Supreme Court declared the statute unconstitutional.[34]

But California was the exception to the rule. Throughout the 1800s, most states essentially treated parties as private associations and chose not to regulate them. This remains the position of many other countries today. But that all changed early in the 20th century, when the progressive backlash against machine abuse led states to intervene. Political scientists now refer to parties as equivalent to public utilities, such as

Fotosearch/Getty Images

CIVIL SERVICE REFORM.
Office-Seeker. "St. Jackson, can't you save us? Can't *you* give us something?"

"To the victor belong the spoils." President Andrew Jackson popularized a system of patronage, insisting that public offices should be filled by supporters of the party in power.

water and electricity—that is, as entities in which the public has a sufficient interest to justify state regulation.[35] Political parties, after all, are the main conduits through which elections are contested and government is organized. The legal justifications that states have used to regulate parties revolve around registration requirements—31 states and Washington, D.C., register voters by party—because party names are printed alongside the names of candidates on ballots.

Thirty-eight states regulate aspects of the structure of their state and local parties, often in explicit detail, to prevent antidemocratic, machine-boss control.[36] Some states determine, for instance, how the members of state

Nonpartisan ballots Ballots that do not list candidates by political party; still often used in local elections.

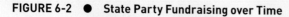

FIGURE 6-2 ● State Party Fundraising over Time

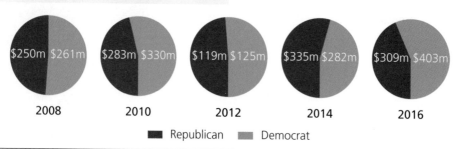

| $250m $261m | $283m $330m | $119m $125m | $335m $282m | $309m $403m |
| 2008 | 2010 | 2012 | 2014 | 2016 |

■ Republican ■ Democrat

Source: Data compiled from the National Institute for Money in State Politics.

parties' central committees should be selected and how often those committees will meet. A state might specify which party organization can name a substitute candidate if a nominee dies or withdraws prior to an election. Such regulation is practiced whether in regard to a state party in Minnesota or a local party in Pennsylvania.

A relatively limited number of state parties have challenged the laws regulating parties in the wake of the 1989 Supreme Court decision in which the Court ruled that the state of California did not have the authority to dictate how political parties are organized. The major parties in New Jersey did adopt a number of changes in party structure, but for the most part, the parties seem satisfied with the way things are being run under the systems imposed on them by the states.

The decision in 1989 was neither the first nor the last time the U.S. Supreme Court weighed in on concerns related to political parties. The nation's highest court has issued a number of other decisions in recent years to clarify the legal rights of parties. In a series of cases emanating from Illinois during the 1970s and 1980s, the Court made it clear that "party affiliations and support" are unconstitutional bases for the granting of a majority of government or public jobs, except at the highest levels.[37] In 1986, it ruled that the state of Connecticut could not prevent independents from voting in Republican Party primaries if the GOP welcomed them.[38] This precedent, which allowed the parties rather than the state to determine who could

participate in the parties' primaries, was later followed in several other states. The parties have not always gotten their way, however. In 1999, the Court determined that states have the constitutional right to regulate elections and prevent manipulation. The ruling blocked a new party in Minnesota from "fusing" with the state's Democratic Party by nominating candidates for election that the Democrats already had nominated.[39]

Parties in the 20th Century

At the dawn of the 20th century, political machines were generally locally based, and local parties were much more important political actors than were state parties in states where there were powerful big-city machines. Elsewhere, state parties often were funded and controlled by corporate interests—in many cases by just one interest, such as DuPont in Delaware or Anaconda Copper Mining Company in Montana. Following the Progressive Era move toward regulation, state parties became little more than empty shells. As late as the 1970s, many state parties lacked permanent headquarters and were run out of their chairs' homes.[40]

State parties lost much of their influence because of the rise of primary elections. In primary elections, voters select the candidates who will represent the parties in **general elections**, the contests between party nominees that decide which candidates will actually win political office. Before primary elections became common, parties picked their nominees through **party conventions**, meetings of a few hundred party officials or supporters. At conventions, party leaders closely controlled most votes and thus had enormous influence over who would or would not become the party's official nominee in the general election. This influence

....

General elections Decisive elections in which all registered voters cast ballots for their preferred candidates for a political office.

Party conventions Meetings of party delegates called to nominate candidates for office and establish party agendas.

is lost in a primary election; in a primary, members of the general public have the chance to cast secret ballots. This gives party officials less direct control over the nominating process. Some states, such as Virginia, still allow for the option of nominating candidates by party conventions, but every state now has a system in place to nominate candidates through primaries. Every party holds statewide conventions, and many hold conventions at the local or district level as well.

Direct primaries allow rank-and-file voters to choose nominees for public office through means of a direct ballot. This contrasts with the convention system, in which the role of voters is indirect—voters choose delegates to a convention, and the delegates choose the nominee. At the state level, there are three basic types of direct primaries. In a **closed primary**, only registered members of the party holding the primary are allowed to vote, meaning that an individual must be a registered Democrat to vote for the Democratic nominee for office or a registered Republican to vote for the Republican nominee. This type of primary prevents **crossover voting**, in which a member of one party votes in another party's primary (a Democrat voting in a Republican primary, for instance). This practice is not allowed in all states. In an **open primary**, independents—and in some cases members of both parties—can vote in the primary of any party they choose. In a blanket primary—a type of primary invalidated in 2000 in the U.S. Supreme Court case *California Democratic Party v. Jones*—all candidates from all parties are listed on a single ballot, and voters are allowed, in effect, to mix and match the primaries they participate in. That is, a voter could vote in one party's primary for a particular office, then switch to another party's primary for another office. Louisiana holds what is essentially a nonpartisan blanket primary—sometimes called a jungle primary—in which all candidates run in the same primary regardless of party. If no candidate wins an outright majority in the primary, the top two vote-getters—regardless of party—go on to a general election face-off. A **runoff primary** sometimes occurs in some states if no candidate receives a majority of the vote in an initial primary. In that case, the top two candidates face off. Washington State and California voters in recent years have established similar "top two" primary systems, in which candidates from all parties appear together on a single primary ballot, and the top two finishers, regardless of party, proceed to the general election. Map 6-1 shows a state-by-state breakdown of the main types of primaries.

The opposite of the relative openness of primaries is the "smoke-filled room"—a historic term referring to an area at a convention in which party barons, some puffing on big cigars, would choose a candidate of their liking. It is one of the classic images in American politics. At the 1912 Republican National Convention, President William Howard Taft had to stave off a challenge from his predecessor, Theodore Roosevelt. Roosevelt had been able to demonstrate his popularity among the party's rank and file by winning every primary that year, save the Massachusetts primary. At the time, however, only a dozen states even held primaries. Taft retained the support of the national party machinery and dominated delegate selection in the nonprimary states. Ultimately, he controlled the convention. Taft was renominated, but he was not reelected. Roosevelt bolted the party, angrily maintaining that Taft's nomination thwarted the will of the "honestly elected majority" of GOP delegates, and ran on a third-party ticket. The split within Republican ranks was enough to allow the election of Woodrow Wilson, only the second Democrat to win the White House since the Civil War.[41]

As late as 1968, party officials selected about 600 of the 2,600 delegates to the Democratic Party's national convention—almost 25 percent—two to four years ahead of the convention. Senator Eugene McCarthy, D-Minn., had made such a surprisingly strong showing in the New Hampshire primary that he drove President Lyndon Johnson from the race. But Johnson's backing was still significant enough to help his vice president, Hubert H. Humphrey, win the support of delegates controlled by party officials. McCarthy believed he had been cheated by the party rules, so he proposed that all delegates to the nominating convention be chosen through "procedures open to public participation" in the same year in which the convention was to take place.[42]

Humphrey recognized that McCarthy and Senator Robert F. Kennedy, D-N.Y., both of whom had

Closed primary A nominating election in which only voters belonging to that party may participate. Only registered Democrats can vote in a closed Democratic primary, for example.

Crossover voting Voting by a member of one party in another party's primary. This practice is not allowed in all states.

Open primary A nominating election that is open to all registered voters regardless of their party affiliations.

Runoff primary An election held if no candidate receives a majority of the vote during the regular primary. The top two finishers face off again in a runoff to determine the nominee for the general election. Such elections are held only in some states, primarily in the South.

MAP 6-1 ● Party Affiliation Requirements for Voting in Direct Primaries, 2018

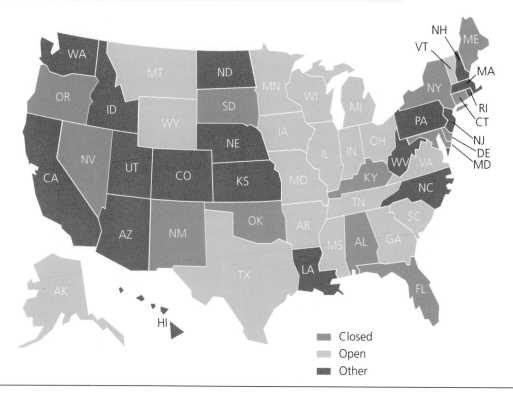

Closed
Open
Other

Sources: "Closed Primary," Ballotpedia, https://ballotpedia.org/Closed_primary; "Open Primary," Ballotpedia, https://ballotpedia.org/Open_primary.

Note: This map shows states where primaries are closed for at least one party for congressional and state races.

campaigned on anti-Vietnam platforms, had taken 69 percent of the primary vote. Respectful of what that number meant, he wanted to reward their followers with a consolation prize. So Humphrey coupled McCarthy's changes with one proposed by Senator George McGovern, D-S.D. McGovern wanted to see delegations demographically match—or at least reflect—the compositions of the states they represented. More and more states threw up their figurative hands as they tried to meet each of these new requirements. Taking the path of least resistance, they decided that the easiest thing to do was to hold popular-vote primaries. Democratic primaries were held in only 15 states in 1968, but by 1980, the number had risen to 35.[43]

But as 2016 showed, the accrual of delegates still matters. Democrats gave elected officials, such as governors and members of Congress, and party officials, such as members of the Democratic National Committee,

automatic voting privileges at nomination conventions as "superdelegates." The backing of most superdelegates was a crucial aspect of Hillary Clinton's success. In 2018, the party changed its rules, stripping superdelegates of the ability to vote at conventions on the first ballot. They'll only get to vote at contested conventions that require multiple ballots to pick a nominee—which no longer happens.

How State Parties Recovered: Campaign Reform in the Late 20th Century

Candidates no longer need hierarchical machines to reach voters. The decline of party machines was followed in time by the advent of televised campaign commercials as the dominant mode for trying to persuade citizens to vote. "Television, that's the big political party," John Coyne said as he stepped down in 1993 after serving 12 years as chair of the Cuyahoga County Democratic Party.[44]

The increasing reliance on campaign ads, ironically, led to restored strength for state and national political parties and spelled the decline of local party strength in federal elections. The move from greeting potential voters in person at party dinners and county fairs to airing TV ads meant that politicians had to run more professional campaigns. They had to hire pollsters to figure out which issues would resonate best in their ads. Consultants helped shape their messages on these issues, and media gurus produced the ads and placed them in favorable time slots. Once more changing with the times, state parties became important clearinghouses, connecting candidates with consultants. Eventually, they evolved into important consulting organizations themselves. During the 2006 campaign, when Democrats believed they had a shot at taking control of the Michigan Senate (they failed), their chief strategist sent legislative aides to run campaigns in several close races. Ken Brock, chief of staff to the Michigan Democratic Senate Campaign Committee, paid homage to the idea that candidates with a good feel for local issues were crucial. But he was equally interested in "educating our candidates" about the resources, messages, and tactics he believed would work for them. Lansing strategists provided the lists of voters that candidates should try to contact. Brock summed up his reasoning: "The way I see it is that they're all highly competent people, but they haven't had the experience of running in an expensive, marginal contest."[45]

Every Democratic and Republican state party now has a full-time chair or executive director. Most have other professional staffers as well, who handle fundraising, communications, field operations, and campaigns.[46] In general, Republican state parties tend to be better funded and often better run than their Democratic counterparts. Democratic state parties, however, often gain support from their allied groups, such as labor unions.

With their massive computer databases, maintained and updated from year to year, political parties help candidates target and reach voters who are sympathetic to their messages. It's common now for candidates to carry iPads and smartphones loaded with the latest voter registration data, instead of the old-fashioned paper printouts they used to carry on clipboards to scribble notes on. There's a race between the parties now in terms of how most effectively to harness data to make predictions about what messages will appeal most to individual voters and motivate them to vote. They might study, for example, how successful e-mail fundraising pitches are depending on response rates to different subject lines. But despite the parties' spending millions on research and sophisticated analytic tools, often "the best guide is the basic demographic information taken from public records, such as gender, age, voting history and party affiliation," the *Economist* reported in 2016.[47]

Party Competition: Why Some States Are More Competitive Than Others

Historically, most state political cultures have heavily favored one party or the other, as shown in Map 6-2. A well-known example of this is the old Democratic "Solid South." For more than a century, most southern voters were "yellow-dog Democrats," meaning they would sooner vote for a yellow dog than for a Republican. From 1880 to 1944, all 11 states of the old Confederacy voted for Democrats in every presidential election—with a couple of exceptions in 1920 and 1928. These states elected only Democrats and a few independents as governor, and they elected only Democrats to the U.S. Senate after popular voting for senators began in 1916.[48] The Democratic hegemony in the South began to break up with the civil rights era that began, roughly, with the elections of 1948.

Party control of individual states is not static. One reason is the increased mobility of the American population. In the past, people put down roots and perpetuated the political cultures of their families, but today, the country's population is constantly shifting. Immigrants to California have made the state more Democratic—Republicans politically misplayed their hand with California Hispanics by pushing an anti-immigrant ballot initiative during the 1990s. But people leaving California have made other states more Democratic as well. Californians made up half of all newcomers to Nevada during that state's recent boom years. In fact, according to the Brookings Institution, people originally from California make up more than 20 percent of Nevada's electorate, compared with 14 percent who are native-born.[49] "In the case of Nevada, the spillover effect is pretty clear," says demographer John Pitkin. "Nevada is almost a satellite of California."[50]

MAP 6-2 ● Interparty Competition, 2012–2017

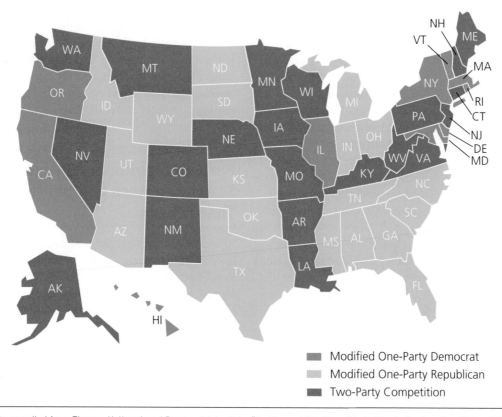

■ Modified One-Party Democrat
■ Modified One-Party Republican
■ Two-Party Competition

Source: Data compiled from Thomas Holbrook and Raymond J. La Raja, "Parties and Elections," in *Politics in the American States: A Comparative Analysis*, 11th ed., ed. Virginia Gray, Russell L. Hanson, and Thad Kousser (Washington, DC: CQ Press, 2018).

But while states don't remain static, more and more they are voting in monolithic fashion, favoring candidates of one party or the other for most elected offices. It's long been tough for a Republican to win in Connecticut or Hawaii, or for Democrats to prevail in Idaho or Utah, but single-party control has become common in many states in recent years. Fewer counties vote one way for president and another for U.S. House or state Senate. And the partisan vote has gotten more lopsided in more places. The result has been supermajority control in numerous legislative chambers. And once a party loses power in a state, it is at a disadvantage in recovering power. Its traditional allies also have a harder time pushing their agendas. We'll discuss the effects of this further in Chapter 7.

Party Factions and Activists

With party leaders prevented from dispensing prizes such as jobs, party activism and various party tasks are now carried out largely by volunteers. And because people seldom work for free unless they believe in something very strongly, political volunteers have become more ideological. People work for candidates and parties because they believe in specific causes, such as handgun control legislation or protections for small-business owners.

Just because jobs are no longer the parties' golden eggs does not mean that politicians and parties do not seek to pluck favors from their constituents through policies or promises. Both major parties court the elderly with assurances of health care benefits, such as Medicare, because senior citizens vote and thus are worth courting. The young voter turnout increased in the 2008 presidential elections from abysmally low levels—51 percent of the population between the ages of 18 and 29 cast ballots that year—but the group's participation continued to trail behind that of older voters by almost 15 percentage points.[51] Turnout among voters was roughly 50 percent in both 2012 and 2016.[52]

Remember, however, that each party is a kaleidoscope of interest groups and can appeal only so much to any one group before it risks alienating support among other groups.

It is obvious that one person cannot simultaneously support higher pay for teachers and cutting educational budgets. That is why politicians must perform the neat trick of motivating the true believers within party ranks to support their candidacies during primary elections without pinning themselves down so much that they do not appeal to members of the other party and independents during the general election. Since losing the White House in 2016, Democrats have argued amongst themselves whether their best hopes lie in motivating more of their core supporters, such as minorities, or in trying to win back former supporters such as members of the white working class. As with the Republican's earlier Tea Party experience, in 2018 Democrats nominated some ardently progressive candidates who went on to lose winnable races.

The Rise of Super PACs

What issues get talked about depends not only on what candidates believe and what they think voters want to hear but also on who is paying for the ads. In recent years, that has become something of a free-for-all. The U.S. Supreme Court's 2010 decision in *Citizens United v. Federal Election Commission* and rulings in other cases have broadened the playing field, making it possible for lightly regulated independent groups to spend unlimited sums on political campaigns. Such a group may have a broad political agenda that closely mirrors that of a party—helping support and elect more Republicans, for instance—or it may be more concerned with a single issue, such as protecting the environment or keeping taxes low.

Wealthy individuals such as the Koch brothers and Tom Steyer, a hedge-fund billionaire concerned with environmental causes, are pursuing their own agendas, spending millions to support causes and candidates near and dear to their hearts. Michael Bloomberg, the media mogul and former New York mayor, has funded a group to promote gun control. Facebook founder Mark Zuckerberg and other tech titans have launched an advocacy group pushing changes to immigration law. The list goes on and on. "Everywhere you look these days," a *National Journal* correspondent noted in 2014, "wealthy donors are . . . taking a DIY approach to their political activism."[53]

In any event, political parties—and candidates themselves—have less control over the political agenda than they did even a few years ago, simply because campaign finance is now structured in such a way as to make interest groups more influential. Three super PACs spent more than $10 million in the 2015 mayoral election in Philadelphia, which was twice the amount spent by candidates themselves, who were constrained by contribution limits imposed by the city. As such, the candidates felt themselves at a disadvantage. Lynne Abraham entered the race as the best-known candidate in the field, having served as district attorney for two decades, but she had no super PAC on her side and ended up finishing third in the Democratic primary. "I couldn't get my message out, that's it," she said. "It puts you at a tremendous competitive disadvantage."[54]

That fact—as well as the way a small number of individuals have come to dominate campaign spending—has led some to worry that American democracy is at risk of being hijacked. "Fewer than four hundred families are responsible for almost half the money raised in the 2016 presidential campaign, a concentration of political donors that is unprecedented in the modern era," the *New York Times* reported.[55] For a study published in 2014, Martin Gilens and Benjamin I. Page analyzed nearly 1,800 policy issues and found that "when the preferences of economic elites and the stands of organized interest groups are controlled for, the preferences of the average American appear to have only a minuscule, near-zero, statistically non-significant impact upon public policy."[56]

Some think that when it comes to campaign finance, the rules should be changed to allow parties to spend more. Parties are subject to campaign restrictions that don't apply to outside interest groups such as Americans for Prosperity, and that distorts the playing field, giving the "least accountable organizations . . . the most leverage over our campaigns," veteran political journalist Thomas B. Edsall concluded in 2014.[57]

Congress has attempted to regulate the flow of money into politics at various times in recent decades, notably following the Watergate scandal of the early 1970s (which involved, among other things, the funneling of illegal corporate contributions into a presidential campaign slush fund) and in 2002 when concerns were raised over the large amounts of money being spent by parties. The recent history of campaign finance laws, however, has shown that courts are skeptical about attempts to limit political spending, which is viewed as protected speech.

In 1974 and 1976, Congress enacted laws that limited the amount of money candidates could collect from individuals and political action committees. Congress revised the laws in 1979 after complaints from party leaders that the legislation almost completely eliminated participation in presidential campaigns by state and local party organizations. The laws, party leaders contended, put too many restrictions on how parties could spend money during a presidential election year. The revised law lifted all limits on what state and local parties could raise or spend for "party-building" activities. These included purchasing campaign materials (such as buttons, bumper stickers, and yard signs) and conducting voter registration and get-out-the-vote drives.[58]

In 1996, the U.S. Supreme Court lifted federal limits on how much parties could spend. Under the new rules, a party could spend as much as it liked to support a candidate, as long as the candidate did not approve the party's strategy or ads or have any say over what the party was doing. The Court decided that no one had the right to restrict **independent expenditures**—that is, funds spent on activities or advertising without the candidate's knowledge or approval. "We do not see how a Constitution that grants to individuals, candidates, and ordinary political committees the right to make unlimited independent expenditures could deny the same right to political parties," wrote Justice Stephen G. Breyer.[59] A decade later, the Court tossed out a Vermont law that sought to limit fundraising and the amounts that candidates could spend on state campaigns.

It quickly became clear that the more lax restrictions were broad enough to allow for the purchase of TV ads and the funding of other campaign-related activities with so-called **soft money** donations, which were nominally meant to support party building. Restrictions on how parties spent soft money, which was raised in increments of $100,000 and more from corporations, unions, and wealthy individuals, were nearly meaningless—as long as the parties did not coordinate directly with

candidates in spending the money. Parties violated the spirit, although not the letter, of the law, with state parties acting as virtual soft money–laundering machines for the national parties and for each other. In 2002, Congress revisited the issue and enacted the McCain–Feingold campaign finance law, which blocked the national parties from collecting soft money donations.[60]

But no matter what limitations are placed on campaign finance, money finds its way into the system because the U.S. Supreme Court held in its 1976 decision in *Buckley v. Valeo* that political expenditures are equivalent to free speech. In January 2010, in *Citizens United*, the Court ruled that political spending by corporations in candidate elections cannot be restricted. That finding was at odds with long precedent and the campaign finance laws of at least two dozen states, but in a 2012 ruling, the Court made clear that states cannot ban direct political spending by corporations. Two years later, the Court abolished the aggregate limits on how much individual donors can give to federal candidates and parties during any given election cycle. "What followed has been the most unbridled spending in elections since before Watergate," wrote *New York Times* reporter Jim Rutenberg. "In 2000, outside groups spent $52 million on campaigns, according to the Center for Responsive Politics. By 2016, that number topped $1.5 billion."[61] Says University of Virginia government professor Larry J. Sabato:

> There is no way to stop the flow of interested money and there will always be constitutional ways around the restrictions enacted into law. What is so fundamental is that politics and government determine the allocation of goods and values in society. Those goods and values are critical to the success or failure of hundreds of interest groups and millions of individuals. Those groups and individuals are going to spend the money to defend their interests, period.[62]

Third Parties and Independents

More Americans now identify themselves as politically independent than at any time since the 1930s. In 2018 polling by Gallup, as many as 45 percent of Americans described themselves as independent.[63] That was an increase from 32 percent in 2008 and 30 percent in 2004.[64] Now, political scientists will tell you that many

Independent expenditures Funds spent on ad campaigns or other political activities that are run by a party or an outside group without the direct knowledge or approval of a particular candidate for office.

Soft money Money not subject to federal regulation that can be raised and spent by state political parties. A 2002 law banned the use of soft money in federal elections.

if not most self-described independents actually tend to support one party or the other, but that raises the question: if millions of people are disenchanted with the Republican and Democratic Parties, for a variety of reasons, why isn't there more of a movement toward establishing a viable third, or minor, party as an alternative? Every election cycle seems to find more people dissatisfied with the major parties and more willing to identify themselves as independent.

In most other democracies, numerous parties exist, each with strong support. In countries such as Israel and Italy, the leading party typically does not have enough seats in parliament to construct a government on its own and has to enter into a coalition with other parties. That has never been the case in the United States, for a number of reasons. Democrats and Republicans, as we have been exploring, have established wide networks of contacts and supporters—individuals and groups that have long loyalties to one party or the other. They have officeholders at all levels who can help with strategy and fundraising.

The major parties also have many other institutional advantages. For one thing, the United States favors a winner-take-all system in which the person who receives the most votes in a district wins. In some countries, seats in the legislature are distributed on a percentage basis, so that if a party gets 5 percent of the vote it receives about 5 percent of the total seats available. But if a party took only 5 percent of the vote across the United States, it probably would not win a seat anywhere. In 1992, Texas computer billionaire Ross Perot, the most successful third-party presidential candidate in decades, took 19 percent of the vote but did not carry a single state. Senator Bernie Sanders fared unexpectedly well in the 2016 presidential contest, but he did so by running for the Democratic nomination, rather than as an independent, despite having served in Congress as an independent for decades.

Even Perot had a hard time getting on the ballot in some states—rules regarding ballot access differ across states and are often complicated. In the state of New York, for instance, a candidate must collect a certain number of signatures from each of the congressional districts to get on the ballot. Many candidates with more modest financial means than Perot's have had difficulty gaining access to ballots. After the 2012 elections, Republican-controlled legislatures in states such as Arizona, Alabama, and Tennessee enacted laws that made it harder for third parties to reach the ballot,

such as by requiring additional signatures from registered voters on petitions. In 2014, the Supreme Court denied an appeal by the Libertarian Party of Ohio to have its candidates for governor and lieutenant governor listed on the ballot. They had been kept off the ballot because of faulty candidacy petitions. "The deck is stacked by the parties against anyone but a Republican or Democrat," wrote James K. Glassman, the founding director of the George W. Bush Institute, in 2016. "An independent has to run an expensive gauntlet to gather enough signatures to get on the ballot in all the states, suffers a severe disadvantage in fund-raising, and is effectively barred from the fall presidential debates by a commission loaded with party stalwarts."[65]

Difficulties of Building Support

Following the presidential elections of 2000 and 2016, many Democrats blamed minor-party candidates for the defeat of the party's nominees, Al Gore and Hillary Clinton, each of whom won the most popular votes but was defeated in the Electoral College. In both elections, the GOP's winning margin in key states was smaller than the third-party total. Others believe that third parties help present real and needed alternatives to the Democrats and Republicans. Unless the major parties are challenged, the thinking goes, they will never change. A number of independent and third-party candidates had strong showings in statewide races in 2014, including Bill Walker, an independent candidate who won the gubernatorial election in Alaska, alongside a Democrat who gave up his own nomination to run on a unity ticket as Walker's running mate. (Walker suspended his campaign in 2018, after the Democrats decided to run their own candidate.)

Some people believe that a third-party candidate will never be anything more than a "spoiler" who deprives major-party candidates of needed votes. Others believe that third parties help present real and needed alternatives to the Democrats and Republicans.

Minor-party candidates have enjoyed some success running for lower offices. Within a state or legislative

A DIFFERENCE THAT MAKES A DIFFERENCE
PARTY ORTHODOXY ON ISSUES CAN COMPLICATE OUTREACH TO VOTERS

Annie Rice, an alderwoman in St. Louis, tried to convince the Missouri Democratic Party to adopt a resolution in 2018 to enshrine support for abortion rights. "What is the difference between supporting the rights of labor unions and supporting my rights as a woman to my own body?" Rice told the *Kansas City Star*. "One is sacrosanct to our state party, and the other is not."

Support for abortion among Democratic politicians is almost as universal as opposition among Republicans. In 1978, 175 Democrats in the U.S. House opposed abortion. By 2018, there were only three such members left.

There are still some outliers in both parties, however. And average voters are not as fixed in their views as elected officials. Not all of them, anyway. Polling consistently shows that most voters favor a compromise course, with abortion kept legal but with some limits placed on the procedure. If a party insists on one point of view on any issue, it risks losing support from people who find it doctrinaire, even if they might agree with much of the rest of its platform. As many as 20 percent of Democratic voters remain opposed to abortion rights.

Both parties have struggled with this issue over the years, which does not allow for easy compromise. In 1998, the Republican National Committee (RNC) considered a resolution barring party funds from supporting candidates who supported a procedure known as partial-birth abortion, in response to the election the previous year of Republican Christine Todd Whitman, who supported access to the procedure, as governor of New Jersey. The resolution failed. In a letter to RNC members, Jim Nicholson, then the party chair, called the procedure "indefensible," yet argued that the party could not afford to "establish a litmus test" on any particular issue.

In 2017, a Democrat named Heath Mello challenged incumbent Republican Jean Stothert as mayor of Omaha. As a state legislator, Mello supported legislation that curbed abortion rights, including a ban on the procedure after 20 weeks of pregnancy and a move to block Affordable Care Act funding from paying for abortions. He has subsequently since softened his position, saying that while his faith leads him to oppose abortion personally, he also opposes the idea of defunding Planned Parenthood and pledged to do nothing to restrict access to reproductive health care as mayor.

Mayors generally have nothing to do with abortion policy, but candidates for all kinds of offices get asked about national issues all the time. In Mello's case, a rally featuring Bernie Sanders and Minnesota representative Keith Ellison, the vice chair of the Democratic National Committee (DNC), drew attention to his history on abortion issues. Their support for his candidacy drew condemnation from national abortion rights groups. "The actions today by the DNC to embrace and support a candidate for office who will strip women—one of the most critical constituencies for the party—of our basic rights and freedom is not only disappointing, it is politically stupid," said Ilyse Hogue, the president of NARAL Pro-Choice America.

Tom Perez, the DNC chair, had said that the party should not "demand fealty" on every issue, including abortion. In response to Hogue's statement, however, he said, "Every Democrat, like every American, should support a woman's right to make her own choices about her body and her health," the chair said. "That is not negotiable."

But not everyone in the party agreed with him. In order to achieve power and be in a position to protect abortion rights, the party would have to embrace voters and some candidates who reject them, suggested Nancy Pelosi, the Democratic leader in the U.S. House. Echoing Nicholson's logic from two decades earlier, Pelosi said the party must not impose a litmus test.

In Missouri, the Democratic Party rejected Rice's resolution. Instead, it adopted language that stated, "We respect the conscience of each Missourian and recognize that members of our party have deeply held and sometimes differing positions on issues of personal conscience, such as abortion. We recognize the diversity of views as a source of strength, and welcome into our ranks all Missourians who may hold differing positions on this issue."

Source: Adapted from Alan Greenblatt, "No Politics Is Local: How America's Culture War Consumed Omaha's Race for Mayor," *Governing*, May 5, 2017, http://www.governing.com/topics/elections/gov-omaha-mayoral-race-election.html.

district, there is a better chance that an individual will enjoy enough personal popularity to equalize the playing field against Democrats and Republicans, who typically are better funded and connected. Still, only seven governors elected during the past 50 years have been neither Democrats nor Republicans. Three of the six before Walker—Walter Hickel of Alaska, Lowell Weicker of Connecticut, and Lincoln Chafee of Rhode Island—had earlier won statewide office as Republicans. Another two were elected in Maine, a state noted for the independent-mindedness of its electorate. The sixth, Jesse Ventura of Minnesota, served only one term, and the would-be successor from his Independence Party finished a distant third in 2002. Certainly, the two major parties make the argument all the time that a vote for a third-party candidate will just be wasted and make it more likely that a worse alternative will win.

A few minor parties have enjoyed periods of success in certain states, such as the Progressive Party during the 1920s in Wisconsin and the Farmer–Labor Party during the 1930s in Minnesota. Over time, however, these parties have been unable to survive the loss of early popular leaders or have been absorbed by one of the major parties. For example, the official name of Minnesota's Democratic Party is still the Democratic Farmer–Labor Party, in reference to its merger with the defunct minor party. The Liberal Party of New York boasted a New York City mayor in the 1960s named John Lindsay. New York is one of the few states that allow candidates to be listed multiple times on a ballot, as the nominee of, for instance, both the Liberal and the Republican Parties. In 1980, U.S. senator Jacob Javits was denied the nomination of the state's Republican Party and ran as the Liberal candidate. He succeeded only in splitting the votes of liberals, moderates, and Democrats, and helped elect a more conservative Republican. The Liberal Party disbanded in 2003 after failing to garner enough votes in the previous year's gubernatorial contest to maintain its guaranteed spot on state ballots. "Parties, I suppose, have a life span," said Dan Cantor, executive director of the Working Families Party. "They had their heyday in the [19]50s and [19]60s. It looks like they have come to a full stop."[66]

Ultimately, it is the states that publish the ballots and have the authority to decide which parties' nominees are going to be listed on them. It is the states that grant ballot access to parties based on their having won

a minimum percentage of the vote in a previous state-wide general election. The threshold varies from 1 percent in Wisconsin to as much as 20 percent in Georgia. Such high institutional barriers make minor parties' complaints about two-party dominance of American politics about as fruitless as trying to hold back the tide.

Despite voter dissatisfaction and the rise of outside interest groups as major financial and organizational forces, the Republicans and Democrats have dominated American politics for 150 years. They have met every challenge—both ideological and structural—and found a way to preserve their near-total control. As political scientist Jeff Fishel puts it:

> If there's any lesson of history about the two major parties in American politics, it is that they're incredible adaptive survivors. They lost the monopoly they had, particularly on candidate recruitment and finance. That certainly does not mean that they're going out of business, just that they have to compete with other groups.[67]

Interest Groups and Lobbies

On Valentine's Day 2018, a former student walked into Marjory Stoneman Douglas High School in Parkland, Florida, with an assault-style rifle, killing 17 students and staff members and injuring 17 others. Following the shooting, a number of students at the school—some of whom had been studying gun issues as part of their debate class preparations—emerged as passionate advocates for gun control. They spoke on national media outlets, urged their peers to register to vote, and vowed to make gun control a central campaign issue. A few weeks after the shooting, a set of rallies they helped prompt called March for Our Lives drew 2 million participants around the nation.[68]

It was a dramatic example of a group of people coming together to promote a cause. Public protests have a long history in this country but have grown in size and frequency during the Trump administration. There's considerable debate among academic scholars around the question of their effectiveness in changing public policy, however. Rallies are a good way to fire up supporters and garner media attention, but they have to be coupled with other techniques such as direct lobbying of lawmakers.

"Protest is effective when it takes place in concert with a range of other political activities, when it inspires people to do other things," says David Meyer, a sociologist at the University of California, Irvine. "It's not just the event, it's the context in which it takes place."

Pushing for policy change takes a persistence that protest movements can't always muster. In the immediate wake of the shooting, some 5,000 people, including students from Parkland, turned up at the Florida capitol in Tallahassee to rally for their cause. A week later, when the state Senate held a rare Saturday session to consider a gun control measure, fewer than 100 people showed up.[69] The legislature rejected a ban on assault-style weapons, but passed a law, named for the high school, raising the minimum purchasing age for rifles to 21, requiring waiting periods and background checks, and banning bump stocks, which turn rifles almost into automatic weapons. The National Rifle Association (NRA) quickly filed suit to block the law.

The NRA, the nation's leading gun rights group, became a primary target of the students and other gun control advocates. They accused politicians who had received campaign contributions from the group of having taken "blood money." David Hogg, a Stoneman Douglas student, helped launch a boycott campaign against Publix, a grocery chain that had donated $670,000 to Adam Putnam, the state's agriculture commissioner and a candidate for governor. In 2017, Putnam had called himself a "proud NRA sellout." The chain stopped making further donations.

Although a great deal of political attention was devoted to the NRA's campaign contributions, the group actually gives less and certainly spends less on lobbying than many other interest groups. What has allowed the group to block most gun control measures, while expanding gun rights provisions such as open carry permits, is not money but the ardent interest and continuing efforts of its members. Polling and some studies have shown that more people may favor certain gun control measures, but NRA members and other gun rights adherents are more likely to devote time and effort to pushing their position. "NRA members are politically engaged and politically active," said Adam Winkler, a law professor at the University of California, Los Angeles. "They call and write elected officials, they show up to vote, and they vote based on the gun issue."[70]

Lobbying is how citizens and private companies make their views known to policymakers between election seasons. When people don't like a law or regulation, they can ask their legislators to change it. That's what lobbying is all about—the right to petition for redress of grievances. Given gridlock in Congress, interest groups have vastly increased their spending on lobbying in the states in recent years. According to the *Washington Post*, interest groups spent $2.2 billion seeking to influence legislators in the 28 states where data were publicly available for the 2013–2014 legislative sessions. Such spending had gone way up in most states, with California seeing an increase of 36 percent over the previous decade and New York up by a whopping 65 percent. In 2015, lobbyists spent nearly twice as much money seeking to influence the legislature in Pennsylvania as the state paid to operate the legislature itself.[71] Spending on federal lobbying, meanwhile, had ticked down. "When nothing's happening in Washington, D.C., it's happening in the states," said Frank McNulty, a former Republican speaker of the Colorado House of Representatives. "You tend to see all these public policy issues work their way down to the state level because, whether it's an environmental organization or a Fortune 500 company, they're still going to try to move their agenda."[72]

The number of interest groups represented by professional lobbyists in the states is growing.[73] It's true that lobbyists representing big companies, unions, and other organizations often push for legislation to promote or protect their own narrow interests. That's why, if many citizens are cynical about political parties, they're even more put off by interest groups. But sometimes people lobby for altruistic reasons, rather than self-interest; for example, college students may seek to influence their university's investment decisions, or citizens may advocate for government policies to put pressure on foreign dictatorships.

But such cause campaigns—including students pushing for stricter gun control—are different in kind from the average work done by interest groups, which tend to have long-standing interests in issues or regulations that affect the groups or their members directly. Often they use the legislative or regulatory process as a means to seek advantage over their professional competitors. As should be apparent by now, interest groups have always been important resources for candidates, providing volunteers and other services as well as money. They are the organizations that take a direct interest in political activity—both in terms of supporting candidates during an election season and in terms of lobbying elected and appointed government officials regarding policy and spending matters. Still, they differ from parties in that politics and elections are not their whole reason for being. As political scientist Frank J. Sorauf notes, "The American Medical Association devotes only part of its energies to protecting its interests through political action. Not so the political party. It arises and exists solely as a response to the problems of organizing the political process."[74] In other words, the American Medical Association may spend millions of dollars annually trying to affect legislation, but it devotes more of its energy and resources to educating its members, promoting good health care techniques, and engaging in other private activities. This difference in focus illustrates a fundamental and obvious trait that separates political parties from special interest groups—political parties run candidates for office under their own labels, whereas special interest groups do not.

Interest groups basically come in five flavors. One is the membership group, such as the American Medical Association or the Sierra Club, made up of individual members with a common interest. A second type is the trade association, which represents individuals or organizations in a particular industry or field, such as the National Restaurant Association or the Alliance of Automobile Manufacturers. The third type of interest group is that consisting of an individual institution; many large companies, such as Google and Exxon, have lobbyists on staff or devote a significant portion of their executives' time to lobbying. The fourth type consists of government lobbyists (sometimes called legislative liaisons), those who represent the interests of one branch of government to another. Executive branch officials have aides designated to lobby Congress or a legislature on their behalf, and cities, counties, and states hire lobbyists to make their cases in Washington. The fifth, and smallest, category is the interest group made up of private individuals who lobby on their own behalf for a pet project or against a policy that they find reprehensible.[75]

It is worth noting that the government runs some of the most active lobbies. The White House maintains a lobbying shop to try to persuade Congress of the wisdom of its policies. Municipal governments hire lobbyists and associations to protect their interests in their state capitals. Currently about 40,000 lobbyists are working in state capitals, and the number of associations and related groups has quintupled over the past 50 years. Lobbying in the states is now a billion-dollar business every year.[76] In California alone, annual lobbying expenditures can exceed $275 million.[77] "Since

2010, the number of entities with either in-house lobbyists or part-time hired guns working in the states has grown more than 10 percent," the Center for Public Integrity reported in 2016. "That means, on average, every state lawmaker was outnumbered by six companies, trade associations, unions or other groups angling for their attention."[78]

The number of organizations with lobbyists in **WASHINGTON, D.C.**, declined 25 percent from 2010 to 2014.

It is often difficult to find out which group has influenced the outcome of a specific piece of legislation. Some interest groups play a very public game, but others are more secretive, playing an insider game in which influence is a matter of quiet access to legislators. "A third of the homes in one neighborhood adjacent to the capitol are owned by lobbyists, corporations or unions," the *Seattle Times* reported in 2018, referring to Olympia, Washington. "Seven of the top 10 earning lobbying firms in the state own homes there, which are used for fundraising and social events."[79]

Many interest groups hire **contract lobbyists**, usually lawyers or former government staffers or elected officials who are valued for possessing insider knowledge and contacts within particular state capitals. Contract lobbyists generally have a number of clients, as lawyers do. About 20 percent of lobbyists registered to ply their trade in a given capital are contract.[80] They use their relationships and contacts to convince legislators that they should or should not pass particular bills. And although lobbyists ignore the executive branch at their peril, given that spending decisions and regulatory action are carried out there, more lobbying activity happens in the legislative arena. "You don't change their minds," said a California lobbyist. "You find ways of making them think they agreed with you all along."[81]

Legislators often rely on lobbyists to provide them with information, whether simply data about an industry's economic outlook or their opinions about whether a bill would cost jobs in the legislators' districts. Dr. Brundha Balaraman, a dermatologist concerned about tanning beds, showed legislators the results of a survey

Contract lobbyists Lobbyists who work for different causes for different clients, in the same way that a lawyer represents more than one client.

POLICY IN PRACTICE
WHY SOME COMPANIES ARE BECOMING MORE PARTISAN

The retail giant Target has angered consumers on both sides of LGBT rights issues in recent years. In 2010, the company became the, well, target of a boycott after it donated $150,000 to a super PAC that supported a Minnesota gubernatorial candidate who opposed same-sex marriage. Six years later, social conservatives boycotted and picketed Target when a company blog post publicized its long-standing policy to allow transgender individuals to use bathrooms that conform with their gender identity.

While some big corporations make campaign contributions, they generally have shied away from otherwise engaging directly in partisan politics because of the risk of alienating a large share of their potential customer base. Doug Ducey was a cofounder of the Cold Stone Creamery chain before winning office as the governor of Arizona. He didn't discuss politics on the job. "We were selling ice cream to everyone," he told *National Review* in 2016. "You want every demographic."

Controversial corporate stances can lead to organized boycotts, with consumers refusing to support a company until it changes the offending practice or position. Boycotts have become more common because technology such as social media has made them cheaper and easier to organize. Between 1990 and 2007, only 213 boycotts were mentioned in the nation's six largest newspapers, according to data compiled by Timothy Werner, a business professor at the University of Texas. By comparison, the #GrabYourWallet campaign, which targeted companies that did business with President Donald Trump or members of his family, launched more than 50 boycotts of Trump-related products during the first 200 days of his presidency.

Werner says consumer boycotts can be effective, depending on how much media coverage they receive. About 25 percent of boycotts lead to concessions from targeted companies, he says, if the campaigns receive any sustained media attention. Often, however, boycotts are covered only when they are announced, if then.

But in a polarized era, pleasing consumers on one side of an issue might trigger a reaction from the other side. Following a mass shooting at a Florida high school in 2018, a number of major companies such as MetLife, Alamo, and National Car Rental ended the discount deals they offered to members of the National Rifle Association (NRA). All of them saw their favorability ratings go down, particularly among Republicans, according to a Morning Consult poll. One company in particular suffered a backlash to its bottom line. Georgia lawmakers ended a tax break on jet fuel that had been worth $38 million annually to Atlanta-based Delta Air Lines. "I will kill any tax legislation that benefits Delta unless the company changes its position and fully reinstates its relationship with NRA," tweeted Lieutenant Governor Casey Cagle. "Corporations cannot attack conservatives and expect us not to fight back."

It's become more difficult for brands to be all things to all people. Chief executives at a number of companies have taken stands on political issues that have nothing directly to do with their operations, such as racial tolerance and climate change. Researchers have found that young adults are more likely to buy products from a company such as Apple if they believe its values are in line with their own beliefs. Becoming associated with a cause can actually boost brand loyalty, whether among progressives or conservatives.

In today's polarized times, argue Aaron K. Chatterji and Michael W. Toffel, respectively professors at the Duke and Harvard business schools, it might be better to be intensely loved by some than to be seen as inoffensive by many. The "avalanche of companies abandoning the NRA is just the latest chapter in the gradual politicization of every square inch of the public sphere, which has compelled traditionally nonpartisan companies to take one partisan stand after another," Derek Thompson wrote in the *Atlantic* in 2018. "Many business leaders are getting political because they have determined that, in this environment, the noisiest position is often to remain silent in the face of national condemnation."

Source: Adapted from previous editions for the seventh edition by Alan Greenblatt.

she conducted, which found that of the 243 facilities responding, 65 percent allowed children as young as 10 to use tanning beds, with many of them providing misleading information about the risks.[82]

Legislators are always grappling with many issues at once: the state budget, education, the environment, and so on. It is up to lobbyists to keep legislators and their staffs apprised of who favors a particular bill and who would benefit from or be hurt by it. Lobbyists build up relationships with legislators over time, and legislators come to trust some of them for reliable information, even if they hold differing positions on particular issues. Often, members of trade associations and other groups will seek to inform legislators about their views without necessarily knowing whether the politicians they're meeting with agree with them or not; this is "lobbying as primarily engaged in providing information about constituency views, with groups pressing lawmakers to enact particular policies based on how constituents will respond," as one academic wrote after spending time working on Capitol Hill.[83] Of course, smart lobbyists don't pass up the chance to present their side of things.

Ben Jealous, a former president of the NAACP, won the Democratic nomination for governor of Maryland in 2018 over a county official with more support from party leaders. Like many Democrats that year, Jealous ran on an unapologetically progressive platform. He lost to popular GOP incumbent Larry Hogan.

Often they can hold tremendous sway over issues, particularly those that may be little studied by part-time legislators and little noticed by media outlets and the public.

In Louisiana, lobbyists love to get their clients tax breaks known as "tax exclusions." That means that lawmakers exclude specific types of business activities from being subject to the sales tax, such as rebates that manufacturers give to car buyers or school bus purchases by independent contractors. All told, these breaks are estimated to cost the state at least $320 million per year.[84] Lobbyists and the groups they represent are seeking the best deal they can possibly get from government. "There's almost no deception. It's almost completely transparent," North Dakota state representative Ben Hanson said of energy companies lobbying in his state. "They want you to pass these laws because it will make it easier for their companies to operate."[85]

Standing in contrast to the contract lobbyist is the **cause lobbyist**, someone who promotes a single-issue agenda, such as marijuana legalization or campaign finance reform. A cause lobbyist often plays an outsider's game, using the media to sway public opinion and pressure public officials. Groups that do not have an economic interest in legislative outcomes are able to get away with this tactic because their ideological position is clear for all to see. Major industries also occasionally play outside games as they seek to pressure politicians by stirring up interest through issue advertising.[86]

Contract lobbyists, by contrast, engage in **direct lobbying**, dealing directly with legislators in hopes of persuading them. Students trying to get public officials to divest from fossil-fuel companies earlier in this decade took part in **indirect lobbying**, building support for their cause through the media, rallies, and other ways of influencing public opinion, hoping that legislators would be swayed by the resulting buzz.

Using the media effectively can be trickier for private corporations and other entities directly affected by legislation. The media nearly always portray this third type of lobbyist in a negative light. If a politician sponsors a bill favoring a particular industry and individuals in that industry have made substantial donations to his or her campaign treasury, news stories are bound to be written about that money trail. Altria Group and Reynolds American, two big tobacco companies, gave $390,000 in campaign contributions between 2011 and 2016 to members of a California State Assembly committee that

Cause lobbyist A person who works for an organization that tracks and promotes an issue—for example, environmental issues for the Sierra Club or gun ownership rights for the National Rifle Association.

Direct lobbying A form of lobbying in which lobbyists deal directly with legislators to gain their support.

Indirect lobbying A form of lobbying in which lobbyists build support for their cause through the media, rallies, and other ways of influencing public opinion, with the ultimate goal of swaying legislators to support their cause.

In 2016, the **CALIFORNIA** Senate voted 24–8 to lift a two-year-old ban on fundraising during parts of the legislative season.

oversees tobacco, including $88,000 to Adam Gray, the committee's chair. "Money has no influence on what goes on with policy. It just doesn't," Gray said.[87] Maybe not, but his committee became a graveyard for tobacco control legislation, including an effort to regulate e-cigarettes. Gray's colleagues made an end run around the committee in a 2015 special session, passing the state's first significant tobacco control legislation in two decades.

Today, many interest groups try to combine the direct and indirect approaches, hitting up legislators for favors in private meetings while also running public relations campaigns through the media. Groups also are likely to join together in coalitions, hoping that a united front will not only present a more coherent and persuasive message but also prevent any individual group from looking as though it is acting out of narrow self-interest. Interest groups often look for surprising allies who will plead their case. For instance, groups wanting to increase funding for after-school programs will enlist law enforcement agencies to argue that the programs help cut crime by giving young people something constructive to do.

Interest groups tend to favor incumbents because the campaign contributions such groups make are generally based more on rewarding public officials for positions they already have taken than on trying to persuade them to take new positions altogether. In other words, if a legislator already has demonstrated support for gun owners' rights, the NRA will be inclined to support him or her. The group does not give donations to gun control advocates in the hope of changing their minds. The money follows the vote, in most cases, rather than the other way around. "Someone isn't going to vote one way or the other on gun control based on whether or not they received a contribution from the NRA," says John Weingart, associate director of the Eagleton Institute of Politics at Rutgers University. "But the example we always use here is that if there's a fight between ophthalmologists and opticians about what the regulations should be, a campaign contribution might make a difference because most people don't care."[88]

Numerous states, including Kentucky, Massachusetts, and Minnesota, have passed ethics laws in recent years that preclude lobbyists, who used to wine and dine legislators, from giving legislators anything of value, even a cup of coffee.[89] But the gift bans and other ethical restraints have not stopped the lobbying industry or deterred interest groups. Too much is at stake in too many state capitals for corporations, unions, or cause activists not to play an active role. At the beginning of the 20th century, one or two powerful home-state companies dominated many state political cultures. State capitals remained old boys' clubs, where just a few powerful interests typically held sway, until about World War II. Since then, states have come to rival Washington in terms of the buzz of activity among competing interests.

This points to a little-discussed reality about regulation. Business owners love to complain about the burden regulatory compliance imposes on them, but many regulations come about because business groups have asked for them. That is becoming especially clear with the advent of the so-called sharing economy. New firms that use the Internet to link service providers with customers, such as food trucks, Uber, and Airbnb, represent threats to traditional restaurants, taxi companies, and hotels. Those groups have been fighting it out in numerous states, with the newer firms arguing that they offer consumers a choice and the older businesses saying that such less regulated concerns have an unfair competitive advantage. "The first thing that comes out of regulators' mouths is, 'It's never consumers who ask us to regulate; it's always people in the industry,'" said Katelynn McBride, an attorney for the Institute for Justice, which advocates for less regulation. "New entrants are coming into the market, and they need to be shielded from competition."[90] Uber has given at least as good as it's gotten. By 2015, it employed 250 lobbyists around the country, which was a third more than Wal-Mart—a company with about 250 times as much revenue.[91]

Some regulations are needed to keep consumers from getting ripped off. It's good to know that there's someone to call if a housing contractor, for example, does dangerously shoddy work. But although states got into the professional licensing business in a big way to protect public health and safety, they are also pushed to enforce regulations by groups that want to set a bar high enough to discourage competition. Consider the case of Jestina Clayton, who moved at age 22 from a village in the West African nation of Sierra Leone to a town called Centerville in Utah. She started a business

MAP 6-3 ● State Corruption Report Card

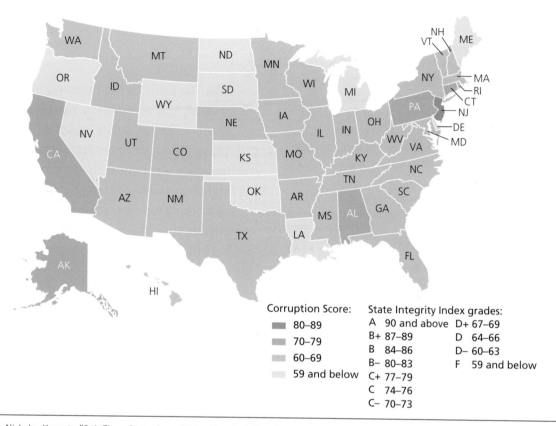

Corruption Score:
■ 80–89
■ 70–79
■ 60–69
□ 59 and below

State Integrity Index grades:
A 90 and above   D+ 67–69
B+ 87–89   D 64–66
B 84–86   D– 60–63
B– 80–83   F 59 and below
C+ 77–79
C 74–76
C– 70–73

Source: Nicholas Kusnetz, "Only Three States Score Higher Than D+ in State Integrity Investigation; 11 Flunk," Center for Public Integrity, November 9, 2015, updated November 23, 2015, https://www.publicintegrity.org/2015/11/09/18693/only-three-states-score-higher-d-state-integrity-investigation-11-flunk.

TABLE 6-1 ● Top Contributors to State Campaigns, by Sector, 2014

Sector	Contributions
Finance, insurance, and real estate	$399,175,515
Labor	$325,051,678
General business	$300,147,466
Health	$220,103,324
Lawyers and lobbyists	$158,680,488
Energy and natural resources	$144,654,869
Education and government agencies	$91,546,224
Agriculture	$81,202,278
Construction	$75,800,824
Communications and electronics	$75,502,333

Source: National Institute on Money in State Politics.

offering traditional African hair braiding, but soon enough she was warned that to practice her trade she needed a cosmetology license, which would require two years of schooling costing about $16,000 in tuition. She appealed to the state governing body—the Barbering, Cosmetology/Barbering, Esthetics, Electrology, and Nail Technology Licensing Board—for an exemption. The board, made up mainly of licensed barbers and cosmetologists, shot her down. Clayton then enlisted the help of a sympathetic state representative, but his bill to exempt hair braiding from the licensing law was blocked by full-force lobbying by the Professional Beauty Association, which favored regulation that would keep hair care the exclusive province of its professionals. "Only five states license shampooers," notes columnist Ramesh Ponnuru. "Presumably, that's not because shampooing is exceptionally dangerous in those states."[92]

Such scenarios are not uncommon, said Morris Kleiner, a University of Minnesota economist who coauthored a proposal at the federal level to abolish state licensing rules that do more harm than good. Approving such a proposal is good policy but "political suicide," Kleiner said. "When you talk about reductions in licensing, you have every occupation from the plumbers to the CPAs to the electricians lining up to argue why regulation should not be reduced."[93] Something other than safety is at play. At least 1,100 occupations are regulated by at least one state, but fewer than 60 are regulated in every state.[94] Only Louisiana regulates florists.

Even when it comes to issues such as health and safety, there's plenty of intramural competition between groups competing for business. Nurse practitioners have battled doctors to gain the right to see patients without a professional agreement in place with a physician. Orthopedic surgeons and podiatrists have faced off over who gets to treat ankle injuries, forcing legislators to debate whether the ankle is part of the foot. (The Colorado legislature decided it was, opening up the field to podiatrists.) Dog groomers fight veterinarians for the right to brush canine teeth.[95]

When an industry has relatively little credibility, it often will turn to allies to represent the public face of its cause. Tobacco companies favor hiring lobbyists who have earned the respect of state legislators as former colleagues or by working for other, less controversial clients. They also seek other groups to take the lead on a lot of their fights. When a state considers legislation that will regulate smoking in public places, for example, the most public opponents are more likely to be restaurant groups than representatives of the tobacco industry. "We're going to participate in a very upfront way," said a spokesman for the Philip Morris tobacco company. "But like any other industry, we're going to look to people who share that point of view on any given issue" to take a role as well.[96]

As in the case of tobacco companies fighting smoking bans, lobbyists spend the majority of their time playing defense, trying to kill bills they believe would harm their companies or clients. Still, interest groups and their desires stir up much of the activity in state capitals. "Frankly, the legislature in New Jersey exists for the lobbyist," said one lobbyist there.[97] What he was suggesting is that the governor may want five or six bills passed during a session, while individual legislators may want one or two of their own passed as

well. The remaining 99 percent of the thousands of bills introduced in a given year are a wish list reflecting the wants and needs of the lobbyists and the interests they represent.

When an industry has relatively little credibility, it often will turn to allies to represent the public face of its cause. Tobacco companies favor hiring lobbyists who have earned the respect of state legislators as former colleagues or by working for other, less controversial clients. They also seek other groups to take the lead on a lot of their fights.

That is why interest groups are an important part of the political landscape in every state. Certain groups play a disproportionate role in particular states—for example, the gambling industry in Nevada or the poultry industry in Arkansas[98]—but the full range of interest groups has crucial influence over the workings of every state. Clive S. Thomas and Ronald J. Hrebenar, two political scientists who have been studying interest group activity in the states for decades, rank the states according to which have policies that are most influenced by interest groups. In no state are interest groups subordinate to—that is, consistently outgunned by—other policy players, such as governors or political parties.

Those players are stronger in some states than in others. The relative weakness of political parties led Thomas and Hrebenar to argue that interest groups are most powerful in a few states in the South and West, such as Alabama, Nevada, and West Virginia.[99] Certain interest groups may hold greater sway at specific times. The importance of environmental issues, in particular, seems to ebb and flow. But Thomas and Hrebenar note that in the majority of states, the influence of interest groups as a whole remains fairly constant—and fairly strong.

The influence of interest groups is difficult to measure, but it is nonetheless quite apparent, part of the very air that policymakers breathe. Some groups may score a victory here and there: dentists looking for a regulatory change or animal rights activists looking to ban cockfighting. Other groups have become a permanent part of the landscape, such as business lobbies concerned with taxes, transportation, and education.

There are some interest groups that are powerful everywhere because their members are everywhere. Groups such as teachers' unions and associations of car dealers, restaurant owners, and real estate agents hold particular sway because they have members in every legislative district, and legislators are more likely to be persuaded by individuals or employers from their home districts. The political action committee of the National Association of Realtors raised more than $8 million for the 2016 election cycle, but the association also relies on its members to influence legislators, since Realtors tend to be well connected in their communities. The association makes it a point to encourage members of the real estate professional community to get to know the legislators from their districts and keep them up to date about issues of concern. Realtors, like members of other professions affected by government policy at the state level, also seek office themselves in part-time legislatures. During the 2005–2006 session, no fewer than 22 people who made their livings in real estate also served as members of the Utah legislature—including the president of the National Association of Realtors.[100] Self-dealing is not unusual in legislatures, as we will discuss in Chapter 7.

Taken together, interest groups are the means through which individual citizens and private companies, as well as governmental bodies, influence the policy decisions that affect their lives or ways of doing business. "I don't believe there are some states where interest groups are stronger and others where they're weaker," said Alan Rosenthal, a political scientist who was an expert on state politics at Rutgers University. "In every state, interest groups are important. That's the way interests are represented, through groups."[101]

Conclusion

In a partisan age, parties play an essential role by acting as organizing and fundraising sources for politicians.

Protests against a so-called bathroom bill were frequent in Raleigh in 2016, after North Carolina enacted a law weakening LGBT antidiscrimination protections. Among the issues was the question of whether transgender individuals should be able to use bathrooms that fit their gender identity.

CQ Roll Call via AP Images

Although other groups also recruit and fund candidates, it's the parties themselves that set the nominating rules and provide politicians the labels with which to identify themselves. The parties aggregate and articulate political interests and create and maintain majorities within the electorate and within government.

They are not the dominant organizing forces they once were, in part because voters and candidates—and nonparty fundraising organizations such as super PACs—have become more independent than they were decades ago. But for the past 150 years, two major parties—the Democrats and the Republicans—have dominated politics in the United States. Few candidates not belonging to either of these parties have won office at any level of government, and in most cases, the victories of those few have been based on personal appeal rather than on support for the third party they represented. The Republican and Democratic parties have been able to adapt to changing times and tastes in ways that have kept them in power, if not always in perfect favor.

With states regulating increasing numbers of industries, interest groups have proliferated so that there are now far more lobbyists than elected officials. Interest groups help push agendas subscribed to by individuals or corporations. Other interest groups push back. Their primary mission is to win as many political offices as possible, so the parties, with varying success, collate and mute the ideological agendas of their interest group allies. Parties cannot afford to have any one group's ideas play such a prominent role that other groups or voters are alienated. It is a difficult balancing act to try to appeal to the majority of voters at any given time while also standing for principles that are clear enough that most people are willing to support them.

THE LATEST RESEARCH

This chapter makes clear that political parties have critically important roles to play in democratic governance. How they go about fulfilling those roles has an enormous impact on politics and policy, in effect setting the boundaries of what will or can be done by the government. One aspect of how parties are executing those responsibilities has evolved into one of the dominant issues in contemporary American politics: the increasing polarization of the two major parties. Much of the evidence for and discussion of the increasing partisanship of Democrats and Republicans, however, is concentrated on the federal level, especially on Congress, where bipartisanship has faded with the near disappearance of moderates from both sides of the aisle. Yet scholars of state politics are also intensely interested in the development and direction of political parties and their associated interest groups, and by employing the comparative method, they have uncovered some fascinating insights about the polarized stances of political parties.

- **Ahler, Douglas J., and Gaurav Sood,** "The Parties in Our Heads: Misperceptions about Party Composition and Their Consequences," *Journal of Politics* 80 (July 2018): 964–981.

Perceptions matter when it comes to polarization. Ahler and Sood find that partisans have badly skewed ideas about the members of the other party. Through a survey of 1,000 Americans, they show that people considerably overestimate the share of stereotypical groups belonging to the other party. Republicans believe that the Democratic Party is made up of far more LGBT individuals, blacks, union members, and atheists than is the case in reality. Conversely, Democrats badly overestimate the number of Republicans who are old, southern, wealthy, and evangelical. Misperceptions are actually worse among people who pay more attention to political news. When provided information about the actual share of the various groups within the other party, "partisans come to see supporters of the out-party as less extreme and feel less socially distant from them," Ahler and Sood write. "Thus, people's skewed mental images of the parties appear to fuel contemporary pathologies of partisanship."

- **La Raja, Raymond J., and Jonathan Rauch,** "The State of State Parties—and How Strengthening Them Can Improve Our Politics," Center for Effective Public Management, Brookings Institution, March 2016, http://www.brookings.edu/~/media/research/files/papers/2016/03/08-state-parties-la-raja-rauch/states.pdf.

Relative to other players in the political system, such as super PACs, state parties are losing ground. While super PACs and social welfare organizations can raise and spend unlimited funds, state parties are regulated by their states and subject to federal campaign finance restrictions that limit their ability to influence elections or even do rudimentary tasks such as mobilizing voters to turn out. La Raja and Rauch note that eliminating restrictions on state parties' ability to coordinate with candidates and easing regulations on their fundraising would strengthen the parties. This, they argue, would be good for democracy, as parties have to appeal to a broader range of voters over longer periods of time than do the outside groups.

- **Masket, Seth E.,** *The Inevitable Party: Why Attempts to Kill the Party System Fail and How They Weaken Democracy* (New York: Oxford University Press, 2016).

Americans like to complain about political parties, but they are necessary to democracy, Masket writes—the best vehicles for lodging complaints about ruling regimes, proposing policy alternatives, and allowing for increased public involvement in the political process. Looking at states with political cultures shaped by the Progressive movement a century ago—California, Colorado, Minnesota, Nebraska, and Wisconsin—Masket shows that various attempts to "reform" parties, such as direct primary elections, changes in redistricting laws, and campaign finance overhauls, have by and large failed in their intended mission of weakening parties. The reason is that parties respond to altered circumstances. "Making some aspect of party behavior illegal doesn't remove or necessarily even weaken parties," Masket writes. "It just makes for a new business environment for the policy demanders."

- **Mason, Lilliana,** *Uncivil Agreement: How Politics Became Our Identity* (Chicago: University of Chicago Press, 2018).

Social scientists have long studied the effects of identities such as race and gender. Mason, a political scientist at the University of Maryland, argues that political scientists need to look at the "mega-identity" of partisanship. People's political identity has not only become polarized, but encompasses several types of group identity—race, gender, geographic preferences, and religious beliefs, among others. These collections of identities can have significantly different effects than any single identity looked at alone. "Any group member who feels connected to the group is powerfully motivated to evaluate other ingroup members more positively than nonmembers," she writes. "Partisans of the two parties are capable of coming to agreement on many issues, but today they will change their positions rather than agree with the other side."

- **Sides, John, Chris Tausanovitch, Lynn Vavreck, and Christopher Warshaw,** "On the Representativeness of Primary Electorates," *British Journal of Political Science,* March 13, 2018.

Earlier generations of political scientists found that primary voters were not more ideological or demographically dissimilar from the larger field of voters in general elections. In recent years, some political scientists have concluded that, at a time of partisan sorting, primary voters have become more ideological than the average voters in their party. It's become practically part of the conventional wisdom of contemporary politics that the small subset of more ideological voters who participate in the primaries is producing more extreme candidates and thus more polarization in Congress and legislatures. The authors take exception with such characterizations. Using large national surveys, they examine midterm and presidential elections from 2008 to 2014. They find that primary voters are not demographically distinct or ideologically extreme, compared to those who identify with the party or who voted for its presidential candidate in the general election. "These results suggest that the composition of primary electorates does not exert a polarizing effect above what might arise from voters in the party as a whole."

CHAPTER 6

for CQ Press

Want a better grade?

Get the tools you need to sharpen your study skills. SAGE edge offers a robust online environment featuring an impressive array of free tools and resources.

Access practice quizzes, eFlashcards, video, and multimedia at **edge.sagepub.com/ smithgreenblatt7e**

Top Ten Takeaways

1. The amount of influence parties have over American politics ebbs and flows over time.

2. For more than 150 years, American politics has been dominated by two main parties, the Republicans and the Democrats.

3. Candidates and voters have grown more independent of parties in recent decades, but parties remain important organizing forces and give shape to debates.

4. The two national parties are agglomerations of state parties, the effectiveness of which varies by state.

5. Parties are regulated by states, but for the most part not too strictly.

6. The ability of parties to ensure loyalty by doling out jobs through patronage has diminished greatly since the first half of the 20th century.

7. It is an exaggeration to argue that states can be divided neatly into Republican red or Democratic blue jurisdictions, but one party or the other now tends to have a major advantage in most states.

8. In recent years, the primacy of parties has been challenged by super PACs and other outside groups that are pumping large amounts of money into the political system.

9. Generally speaking, attempts to limit the influence of money in politics have ended in failure.

10. Interest groups such as corporations and unions, as well as individuals concerned with particular issues, make their political desires known not only through campaign contributions but also through efforts to lobby legislators and executive branch agencies.

Key Concepts

candidate-centered politics (p. 146)
cause lobbyist (p. 165)
closed primary (p. 153)
contract lobbyists (p. 163)
crossover voting (p. 153)
direct lobbying (p. 165)
factional splits or factions (p. 142)

general elections (p. 152)
independent expenditures (p. 158)
indirect lobbying (p. 165)
nonpartisan ballots (p. 151)
open primary (p. 153)
party conventions (p. 152)
polarization (p. 145)

political or party machines (p. 150)
political party (p. 141)
responsible party model (p. 147)
runoff primary (p. 153)
soft money (p. 158)
super PACs (p. 141)

Suggested Websites

- **ballotpedia.org.** Provides information on candidates and ballot measures in all the states.

- **www.dnc.org.** Website of the Democratic National Committee.

- **www.electproject.org.** Website offering statistics and research on elections, run by Michael McDonald of the University of Florida.

- **fivethirtyeight.com.** Statistician Nate Silver's blog, now hosted by ABC News, covering electoral polling and politics at the national and state levels.

- **www.followthemoney.org.** Website of the National Institute on Money in State Politics, which tracks political donations and lobbying in all 50 states.

- **www.gop.com.** Website of the Republican National Committee.

- **influenceexplorer.com.** Website run by the Sunlight Foundation; provides data on campaign finance and lobbying expenditures.

- **www.irs.gov/Charities-&-Non-Profits/ Political-Organizations/Political-Organization-Filing-and-Disclosure.** Website of the Internal Revenue Service providing information on political organizations' filings and disclosures.

- **www.ncsl.org.** Website of the National Conference of State Legislatures.

- **www.opensecrets.org.** Website of the Center for Responsive Politics, a nonpartisan organization that tracks money in politics.

- **www.politicalmoneyline.com.** CQ Roll Call's website that provides information on campaign finance, lobbying and lobbyists, and parties and candidates.

- **www.publicintegrity.org.** Website of the Center for Public Integrity, which produces, among other investigative journalism reports, pieces on campaign finance and lobbying activity in the states and Washington, D.C.

David Coleman/Alamy

Legislatures

The Art of Herding Cats

Every state capitol attracts school groups, protesters, lobbyists, and people only casually interested in getting a glimpse of their government in action.

Chapter Objectives

After reading this chapter, you will be able to

- Explain the role and activities of legislatures,

- Discuss how legislatures are organized and how they operate,

- Identify the characteristics of state legislators, and

- Describe the relationship between legislators and public opinion.

Republicans enjoyed supermajority control of both legislative chambers—the house and senate—in North Carolina for most of this decade, meaning they held two-thirds or more of the seats. When he was speaker of the house, Thom Tillis kept official documents from veto **overrides** (times when the legislature was able to override a governor's **veto** by voting again and passing legislation with supermajorities) under glass on his conference table as trophies and proof of the legislature's power. In recent years, majorities held by the Grand Old Party (GOP) have had virtually unimpeded control over state policy, setting a conservative course on budgets and on issues such as voting, abortion, and gay rights. Some of the laws they passed have been successfully challenged in court. Even after Democrat Roy Cooper was elected governor in 2016, however, Republican legislators were generally able to get their way. They had the votes to override his vetoes—even when it came to bills that stripped away authority from the governor himself.

In some ways, North Carolina presents an unusual case. In most states these days, the governor sets the agenda when it comes to major policy changes, or at least is able to act as a brake when a legislature tries to go too far, even when control over both branches resides within the same party. In some states, voters in recent years have elected governors from the less powerful party, seeming to want to put a curb on the dominant party, such as Republican governors elected in Democratic blue states such as Maryland. But, given overwhelming legislative majorities, a governor's veto becomes little more than an inconvenience. With one party or the other holding large majorities in most state legislative chambers, the other party sometimes hopes not to win back control, but simply to gain enough seats to have some chance of blocking legislation. All it takes is one-third of the vote, plus one, in either chamber to sustain a governor's veto. "We're not hoping actually to change the majority in the legislature—that's not likely," Anna Langthorn, chair of the Oklahoma Democratic Party, said in 2018, when the GOP went into the election boasting a 40–8 majority in the state senate and a 72–28 seat edge in the state house. "But we want to pick up enough seats to break the supermajority."[1] It has become more common than not for one party or the other to control all of a state's political branches of government—the governorship, house, and senate. But even within big party caucuses, the votes of individual legislators can make all the difference.

Legislatures are, in effect, the boards of directors of their states. They set policy that is then carried out by the governor and the rest of the executive branch. Getting legislators to agree on a budget or new law is a tricky business—that trickiness being central to the separation of powers that is a hallmark of American governance. The power of governors is constrained by what the legislature will or will not agree to. Within a legislature, the house and senate chambers often act as competing forces, each insisting on modifying proposals from the other. And within each chamber, individual legislators jealously guard their ability to tweak or defeat the bills that come before them.

Legislatures were not designed to be simple. The congressional system was designed to be difficult enough to

Override The process by which legislative chambers vote to challenge a gubernatorial veto; often requires a supermajority vote of two-thirds.

Veto A governor's rejection of legislation passed by the legislature.

prevent new laws that have not been properly thought through and debated from bothering everybody. "The injury which may possibly be done by defeating a few good laws will be amply compensated by the advantage of preventing a number of bad ones," wrote Alexander Hamilton in *Federalist* No. 73.[2] Most state legislatures share the basic structure of the U.S. Congress, with a house chamber and a senate chamber, each of which must approve a bill before it can go to the governor to be signed into law. That means that even if a bill makes its way through all the circuitous steps of getting passed by the house, including **committee** fights and winning a majority in the chamber, it can easily die if the senate refuses to sign off on an identical version. "If we passed the Lord's Prayer, we'd send it to the Senate and they'd amend it and send it back," said Bob Bergren in 2009, while he was speaker of the Montana House.[3] The road to a bill's passage into law is twisty and sometimes full of unexpected hurdles. In 2013, Massachusetts Republicans blocked all legislative activity in the house for weeks by objecting to a change in the rules that allowed all members to look into "the can," a small metal box that sits on the speaker's platform and contains copies of pending bills. John Dingell, D-Mich., the longest-serving member of the U.S. House of Representatives, perhaps best described the relationship between the actual substance of a bill and its prospects when he said in 1984, "If you let me write procedure and I let you write substance, I'll screw you every time."[4]

All these complicated dynamics are why legislative leadership has sometimes been compared to the job of herding cats. "You come into the Senate every day with a wheelbarrow of 33 cats," writes William Bulger, a former president of the Massachusetts Senate. "Your job is to get the wheelbarrow with 17 of those cats to the other side of the chamber."[5] William Howell, who served as speaker of the Virginia House, said the more apt comparison was to being a groundskeeper at a cemetery. Everyone is beneath you, but no one listens to you.

The circuitous legislative process not only leaves governors, lobbyists, and legislators themselves frustrated, but it also sometimes fuels the public

....

Committee A group of legislators who have the formal task of considering and writing bills in a particular issue area.

Majority rule The process in which the decision of a numerical majority is made binding on a group.

perception that politicians can't get anything done. In this chapter, you will gain a sense of how hard legislators work to address complex problems while sometimes coming up with results that fail to satisfy constituents. We will look at how legislatures have become more polarized, and we will examine what types of people become legislators and how they organize themselves within their institutions. As you read through this chapter, keep in mind the following questions:

- **Why do so many citizens think that legislatures accomplish so little—or accomplish the wrong things altogether?**

- **What constraints do legislatures face in making effective laws?**

- **Why are some legislators more powerful than others?**

The Job of Legislatures

It is the job of the legislature to set policy for the state, in consultation with the governor—or sometimes despite the governor's wishes, if there are sufficient votes to override his or her veto. If Republicans hold 60 seats in the Indiana House of Representatives and Democrats have only 40, the vast majority of the time the Republicans are going to get their way. This is called **majority rule**. In Missouri, Republicans hold supermajorities in both chambers—meaning they have more than two-thirds of the seats, which is enough to override a governor's veto.

You can't please everybody, and often legislators have to balance competing interests. They may have to choose between the desires of their party on one hand and the majority view of the state, as expressed in public opinion polls, on the other. They may have to choose which of two opposing interest groups they will offend, knowing that either choice is likely to put their political careers at risk. And they have to consult their consciences, too. In 2015, Nevada GOP governor Brian Sandoval asked legislators to approve a budget package that included a big tax hike to help pay for schools—$1.3 billion, which was the largest tax increase in the state's history. Republican legislators may have been inclined to support a governor of their own party on priority legislation, but some balked at raising taxes by such a substantial amount. The package passed and in 2016 Sandoval said he would endorse and campaign for only those legislators who voted for it, spurning those who voted no.

Keeping legislators together within party ranks has always been important, but in recent years, it's become the name of the game. Party caucuses in the state legislatures have grown further apart, with less agreement across party lines. For example, in Virginia in 2012, the legislature was weeks late completing its most basic job, writing a new state budget, because the Virginia Senate was evenly split between Democrats and Republicans—20 members on each side—and not a single member was willing to cross over and vote with the rival party.

Chris Neal/The Topeka Capital-Journal via AP

▲ Lobbyists and other interested parties pack legislative hearings that may get little attention from the press or the public, such as this hearing on Medicaid held by the Kansas House Health and Human Services Committee.

> It is the job of the legislature to set policy for the state, in consultation with the governor—or sometimes despite the governor's wishes, if there are sufficient votes to override his or her veto. Nevertheless, the decisions that legislators make are, by their nature, political. It's difficult to please everybody, and often legislators have to balance competing interests.

Bill sponsors seek to avoid such scenarios by engaging in **coalition building** or **logrolling**—finding ways to entice colleagues to support legislation by arguing that it would be in the best interest of their **districts**—or offering to swap their own votes on some future bill. Just as sponsors will try to build up the support they need for passage, an adamant opponent can stop a hated piece of legislation's progress through a chamber in many ways, including by mounting a **filibuster**, a kind of endless debate sometimes used in the U.S. Senate. But filibusters are not allowed in every

state. In 2017, Democrats in the Alabama House who were unhappy about a redistricting plan insisted that a machine read aloud all 539 pages of the bill. That took 16 hours, which delayed but didn't derail the bill, which passed 70–20. Another way to derail legislation is to attach unwanted amendments, or **riders**, to a bill.

As legislatures have grown more partisan, legislative leaders have been able to pass legislation without much **compromise**, counting on rank-and-file members to support party priorities. As political scientist Boris Shor notes, "About half of the states are even more polarized than Congress—which is saying a lot."[6] Polarization—the inability of members of the two major parties to

....

Coalition building The assembly of an alliance of groups to pursue a common goal or interest.

Logrolling A practice in which a legislator gives a colleague a vote on a particular bill in return for that colleague's vote on another bill.

Districts The geographical areas represented by members of a legislature.

Filibuster A debate that under U.S. Senate rules can drag on, blocking final action on the bill under consideration and preventing other bills from being debated.

Riders Amendments to a bill that are not central to the bill's intent.

Compromise The result when there is no consensus on a policy change or spending amount but legislators find a central point on which a majority can agree.

agree on much of anything—has stymied legislation in Congress in recent years, but it matters less now in states. When one party dominates a state, it is able to pass legislation pretty much to its heart's content.

Politics at the state level is becoming a zero-sum game, with one party prevailing and the other losing, and legislators sometimes display less interest in compromise than they used to. For decades, observers have talked about states as "laboratories of democracy," borrowing a phrase from Supreme Court justice Louis Brandeis, referring to experimentation with ideas that often blossom into national policy. Today, we have red labs and blue labs, with partisans pushing entirely different and opposite types of laws. Whether the topic is abortion, tax policy, voting rights, marijuana, or guns, Democratic (blue) states such as California and Oregon are bound to take a different tack than are Republican (red) states such as Georgia and Tennessee.

While Congress barely functions, state legislators are able to move through ambitious, if mostly partisan, legislative programs. At the state level, most bills are still passed with broad, bipartisan support. But on controversial matters, Republicans and Democrats are pursuing entirely divergent agendas, with little need to compromise. "In many state legislatures, the minority has fewer opportunities to obstruct than they do in Congress," said Peverill Squire, a political scientist at the University of Missouri. "It does give the majority in most states a greater opportunity to exercise its will."[7]

Whatever else you want to say about state politics these days, it is not sleepy. Although approval ratings for Congress are barely into the double digits, 62 percent of those surveyed by Gallup in 2016 had either a "great deal" or a "fair amount" of trust in how their state governments were handling issues.[8] Not surprisingly, approval of state government runs higher among Republicans in GOP-controlled states, and Democrats rate Democratic-led states more highly. Sizable minorities of voters in most states are likely to feel orphaned as their states pursue policies that aren't to their liking. This might be most apparent in "purple" states—those where voters are closely divided in terms of partisan loyalties. In North Carolina, Republican control of state government and the party's embrace of conservative legislation triggered years' worth of widely publicized "Moral Monday" protests organized by the National Association for the Advancement of Colored People (NAACP)—protests that accelerated in 2016 with the passage of a bill that limited rights for LGBT individuals.

Conversely, in Colorado, Democrats in 2013 pushed through environmental and gun control measures, leading to the recall of two state senators that year and the loss of Democratic control of the senate itself in 2014. Even John Hickenlooper, the state's Democratic governor, conceded that the totality of his party's agenda was too much, too fast. "You go back and look at everything that got passed, and we don't see things we would change," Hickenlooper said. "But I think there was a sense in the state that it was just a lot of change. I don't mean that we would do anything differently, but I think it made people uncomfortable. Doing so much so fast in one year was a big bite to take."[9]

If partisan majorities are guilty of overreach—pushing policies that go further than most of the public can accept—they may be punished at the polls. Colorado Democrats, for example, lost control of the state senate in 2014, and every statewide office but Hickenlooper's went to the Republicans. But in most states, partisan majorities are pretty well entrenched. Few legislative seats are up for grabs, due to the fact that more and more voters are living in like-minded communities—a natural trend that is exacerbated by redistricting methods that aim to maximize support for a single party within most districts. In 2018, the Supreme Court passed on cases from Wisconsin and other states that sought to set a standard for defining when mapmakers use methods that are so lopsided in favoring one party as to be unconstitutional.

There have always been differences between states that favor low-tax, limited-government policies, such as Texas, and those that want government to play a more activist role, such as California. But polarization within and between states is increasing. Legislatures today are not so much places where compromises are made and consensus is formed as they are places where legislative leaders drive a particular agenda and punish colleagues who break with their party on key votes.

What Legislatures Do

All state legislatures share four basic interrelated and often overlapping functions:

- *A lawmaking function:* They pass laws and create policy for their states.

- *A representative function:* They provide a means for various groups and individuals to have their interests represented in state policymaking.

- *A constituent service function:* They offer personalized constituent service to help residents sort out their problems with the state government.

- *An oversight function:* They oversee the activities of the governor and the executive branch and some private businesses through public hearings, budget reviews, and formal investigations.

Although state legislatures all address similar issues, including taxes, budgets, and a broad range of other matters (such as regulating office safety and updating environmental regulations), differences in timing, state history, and political culture may cause one state's laws on a topic to differ widely from those of other states. Occasionally, legislatures are pressured to pass uniform laws, as when the federal government, through the National Minimum Drinking Age Act of 1984, insisted that the states raise their legal drinking ages to 21 or lose highway funding. Louisiana resisted the longest, adopting a minimum drinking age of 21 in 1987. More often, legislators choose to adopt policies that have been tried in other states, such as particular restrictions on abortion. Often, states will collectively jump on a bandwagon when a new challenge presents itself. Between 2010 and 2016, for example, a total of 32 states enacted laws that made it easier to classify as illegal synthetic drugs such as fentanyl, which were becoming both more popular and more deadly.[10]

Often, laws are adapted to the local scene and are not easily molded to match other states' versions. Large insurance companies are regulated at the state level. They would love to have their agents qualified to sell in every state rather than having to take up to 50 different qualifying exams. "I'm still not sure what happens if Michigan says you can be an insurance agent if you can sign your name with your eyes shut, and New York says you've got to take a three-year course," said Alexander Grannis, a former chair of the insurance committee in the New York Assembly. "What happens if someone screws up—if we cancel a Michigan guy's license to practice here for malpractice, does that mean Michigan can retaliate and cancel a New Yorker's right to practice there?"[11]

Within a given state, the media and the public manage to register many failures of a legislature while sometimes failing to give the institution enough credit for its successes in balancing all the competing interests within the state. Ethics scandals generally receive greater coverage than do substantial debates; yet legislators debate and pass laws that cover everything from levels of Medicaid health insurance funding to clean-water protections to aid for local governments to workers' compensation payments to pensions for public employees. In most legislatures, easily 90 percent of the bills receive almost no media attention and are of interest only to those they directly affect. The news media—and the voting public—pay attention only when issues that affect the broadest range of people are considered, such as increases (or cuts) in property tax rates. Legislators do not have the luxury of tuning out when complex and boring but important issues crop up.

One of the arguments against term limits is that legislators have to cope with many complicated issues, getting quickly up to speed on such topics as water rights and regional transportation plans. If they can serve for only limited terms, there is the potential that legislatures will end up reopening fights that had been settled through painful negotiations years earlier, because no one is around who remembers what the earlier lawmakers went through. "You've got three groups of unelected people running government when you have term limits," said longtime Wisconsin state senator Fred Risser: legislative staff, agency officials, and lobbyists.[12]

State senators and representatives fight their biggest battles over budgets. Most of their power is derived from the fact that with the approval of the governor they can set fiscal policy, including spending levels and tax rates. Dealing with the question of how much money the state devotes to each of its programs is a way of revisiting all the problems that never go away. How much is enough to spend on education? How much of that education tab should the state pick up? Although public schools were once funded primarily by local property taxes, most states now pick up one-third of the bill or more. How much money should be spent on health care? How long should prison terms be for all manner of crimes, and what should be done to reintegrate offenders into society once they've served their time? How big an investment should the state make in roads or public transportation? How much can be spent overall before the state is taxing individuals and businesses too highly? Practically every state has a legal requirement to balance its budget every year, so legislators debate how to make spending match what the state takes in through taxes—or at least how to make the numbers look as though they match on paper. State legislatures annually address hundreds of such issues, large and small.

> State senators and representatives fight their biggest battles over budgets. Most of their power is derived from the fact that with the approval of the governor they can set fiscal policy, including spending levels and tax rates.

Lawmaking

Legislatures tend to be reactive institutions. After 2009, when media attention began to focus on the issue of concussion injuries among high school football players, every single state passed legislation to address the issue. Most of the new laws were designed largely to raise awareness of the problem, calling on schools to provide training and to remove players from the field who are suspected of having sustained concussions.

Most issues attract far less attention. The Texas state legislature grappled with more than 11,000 bills in 2015, while even much mellower Montana took up more than 1,000 that year.[13] Not everyone views passing more laws as a measure of success. "We passed the fewest laws in 20 years, proving that better government doesn't have to be more government," Texas governor Greg Abbott boasted at the state GOP convention in 2016.[14] Jerry Brown, the governor of California and the ideological opposite of Abbott, vetoed a number of bills during his years in office, such as a 2017 proposal to make it a crime to "willfully release" Mylar balloons, simply because there were already "too many laws" on the books. "Criminal penalties are not the solution to every problem," he wrote.[15]

Despite this amount of activity—or perhaps because of it—legislators generally do not go looking for issues to address. The typical bill is introduced for one of several reasons: it is a bill that has to be considered, such as the annual state budget; it is a bill dealing with a common problem modeled on another state's legislation; or it is something an individual or a group outside the legislature—such as constituents, the governor, or

lobbyists—wants considered. "It's very common practice that individuals, groups [and] third-party organizations have ideas and they may have representatives or senators that believe their viewpoints," said Texas representative Todd Hunter.[16]

It may not always seem like it, but constituents can have a lot of influence in government. In Massachusetts, for instance, legislators are obliged to consider petitions to introduce bills on any topic a state resident wants. In 2014, Chloe Stirling, a 12-year-old girl who had gotten busted for baking and selling cupcakes, helped convince the Illinois legislature to pass a law limiting the authority of local governments to regulate the sale of baked goods. She testified before a committee and presented the governor with a plateful of cupcakes. While she served in the Texas House, Sherri Greenberg received a letter from a constituent who was a paramedic. If emergency drivers got into an accident while on the job, it could affect their personal car insurance. She thought that public servants saving lives should get a break, so she wrote a bill decoupling their insurance rates from their official duties.[17]

Governors and the executive branch are also powerful players in the legislative process, promoting ideas they want legislators to work on. Some of these bills are designed to address immediate problems quickly. For example, in 2015, Wisconsin's legislature approved a bill promoted by Republican governor Scott Walker that put taxpayers on the hook for half of the $500 million construction cost of a new arena for the Milwaukee Bucks, in exchange for the NBA team's pledging to remain in the state's largest city.

Finally, lobbyists representing a client such as a beer company or auto manufacturer often will promote draft legislation in the hope that a member of the legislature or general assembly—as the legislatures are known in Colorado, Georgia, Pennsylvania, and several other states—will sponsor it as a bill. Uber and Lyft, the ride-sharing services, have made their presence known in numerous states with heavy lobbying campaigns seeking favorable legislation. Nebraska legislators spent the better part of a year working out a compromise that would allow the companies to operate legally in the state. Operators of traditional taxis are always opposed to the companies moving into their markets. Among other issues, legislators had to figure out ways to address insurance, since privately owned vehicles that are used for commercial purposes are typically not covered. State senator Heath Mello, who introduced the bill, called it "the most negotiated, time-consuming bill of my career."[18]

Although lobbyists promote bills, they also devote an enormous amount of energy to trying to kill bills. Part of the job of the legislature is to act as a sort of referee among a lot of competing interests. Any proposed change in state law that someone views as a positive step is likely to adversely affect—or at least frighten—someone else. Disputes between related industries or professions are common. "What's the demarcation between the foot (which podiatrists can treat) and the ankle (which they can't)? These are high-stakes disputes, and sometimes the licensing bodies have jurisdictional spats with each other, usually over 'scope of practice' issues," Texas Supreme Court justice Don Willett wrote in a 2015 opinion. "In 2010, this Court ended a nearly ten-year legal battle between, in one corner, the Texas Medical Association and Texas Orthopedic Association, and in the other, the Texas State Board of Podiatric Medical Examiners and Texas Podiatric Medical Association."[19]

Legislators react most strongly to bills in which they have a personal stake or that they know will affect their constituents directly. Let's say that environmentalists are concerned about a river's water quality and want to require new water filters at a paper mill. The mill's owners, concerned that the cost of the filters will be exorbitant, warn that they will have to lay off 300 employees if the bill goes through. A legislator from that area will have to worry about whether creating a healthier environment is worth being accused of costing people their jobs. Legislators who live clear across the state from the river and its mill, however, will hold the deciding votes. The people directly affected—the company, the workers, and the downstream residents worried about pollution—will all try to portray themselves as standing for the greater good. If no side is clearly right and favoring one side over the other can do political damage, the bill easily could die. Legislators could then be accused of doing nothing when in reality they are merely reflecting the lack of statewide consensus about how to solve the problem.[20]

AP Photo/Seth Perlman

▲

Pat Quinn, then the Illinois governor, is presented with cupcakes by Chloe Stirling, whose in-home cupcake business was shut down by the Madison County Health Department because she didn't have a license. The move garnered national attention and new state legislation to allow amateur bakers a limited number of sales without requiring a license.

Representation

The bulk of the work legislators do involves formulating the law and trying to keep an eye on the executive branch, but legislators' primary responsibility is to provide **representation** for their constituents. Basically, they ensure that the interests of those for whom they speak are properly considered as part of decision making at the state level. For example, in 2012, California state representative Roger Dickinson introduced a bill to create a Public Employees Bill of Rights in the state. The legislation set out a host of new rules to help government workers, such as mandating that they could not be required to work extra when their colleagues were fired unless they were paid extra for their time. Some critics mocked the concept. California has had some of the worst budget problems of any state. Why, the critics wondered, would the state offer new protections to government workers when it was already struggling to pay the salaries and benefits of its workforce and to maintain funding for basic services such as education and health care? "There is hardly a workplace in recession-battered America that

....

Representation Individual legislators acting as the voices of their constituencies within the house or senate.

LOCAL FOCUS

STATES DEBATE WHAT THEY OFFICIALLY HOLD MOST DEAR

Does your state have an official muffin? Five states do. State legislatures have adopted not just muffins but also other edibles as official state desserts, snacks, fruits, and vegetables. They've also designated official state plants, songs, and dog breeds.

Sometimes these designations reflect local pride. Boston cream pie is the official dessert of Massachusetts, for example, while key lime pie holds the honor in Florida. Usually, they are the handiwork of elementary or high school students, who propose an official state designation as a way of learning about civics. They persuade legislators to sponsor a bill and then watch it make its way through the process of becoming a law (or failing to do so). Yogurt became the official state snack of New York in 2014, thanks to the suggestion of fourth graders at Byron-Bergen Elementary School.

Almost inevitably, efforts to designate an official state cookie (snickerdoodles in Connecticut) or official state bat (Mexican free-tailed bat in both Oklahoma and Texas) are ridiculed by late-night comedians and newspaper columnists. Why waste time on such trivial matters when there's a budget that needs passing or some life-and-death issue is still awaiting compromise?

Often, legislators themselves raise objections. In 2015, a group of kids from Lincoln Akerman School in Hampton Falls, New Hampshire, proposed making the red-tailed hawk the state raptor. Not only did the proposal fail, but it also gave the kids an education in how acrimonious legislative debate can quickly become. One legislator said, in essence, that the kids were wasting her time. "I realize this may put me in hot water with fourth-grade teachers and students in our state," Representative Christy Bartlett said. "I understand and encourage engaging all residents in the governmental process, but would ask that consideration be given to more pressing matters on which we must debate, both in our committees and in the full House during our budget year."

Warren Groen, another state representative at the time, complained about the bird in fairly graphic terms, saying it "mostly likes field mice and small rodents. It grasps them with its talons and then uses its razor sharp beak to rip its victims to shreds and then basically tear it apart, limb from limb." He then likened the hawk to abortion providers. "I guess the shame about making this the state bird is it would make a much better mascot for Planned Parenthood." Groen was criticized for his remarks—not least by the school principal, who was dealing with kids asking him what Planned Parenthood is—but he said there is no better venue for the exercise of free speech than during legislative debate.

Legislators don't always wait for schoolchildren to make suggestions. State symbols are emblems of pride. In a polarized age, some state legislatures have adopted symbols that are more controversial than blueberry muffins. Since 2011, 11 states have designated official firearms. In 2016, Tennessee named the Barrett Model M82/M107, which is made in the state, as the official state rifle. "I love Goo Goo Clusters, I love Little Debbie cakes, and everything else—even Jack Daniel's whiskey—that have come from Tennessee," said then state senator Bill Ketron. "However, none of them have saved lives like this rifle has on the battle lines."

That same year, however, Tennessee legislators went too far, at least for the governor—they passed legislation naming the Bible as the official state book. GOP governor Bill Haslam vetoed the bill, warning that it not only violated the constitutional separation of church and state but also trivialized the Bible by treating it as something other than a sacred text. "If we believe that the Bible is the inspired word of God, then we shouldn't be recognizing it only as a book of historical and economic significance," Haslam wrote in his veto message.

Source: Written for the sixth edition by Alan Greenblatt.

has not been hit with layoffs," the *Modesto Bee* newspaper said in an editorial. "Private-sector workers regularly shoulder additional responsibilities along with pay cuts. It's how many deal with a drastically altered economic reality. Despite the valuable work that many of them do, government workers should not be shielded from such realities."[21] Dickinson, though, was just looking out for his constituents. His district is in Sacramento, California, where state agencies are headquartered. The city is home to more public workers than any other in the state.[22]

If a problem is real and persistent enough, a state's legislature will address it eventually. Sometimes there is a general recognition that a long-festering problem just needs to be fixed once and for all. That does not mean the fix is going to be easy. Some states, including Kansas, Ohio, and Pennsylvania, have had to tweak their school funding formulas continually in response to state supreme court decisions that found their education systems inadequate.

Legislatures often finish their work on an issue not because of outside pressure but because of internal changes. Prior to the 2012 elections, North Carolina Republicans hadn't controlled the political branches of state government—the legislature and governorship—since 1869. Once in power, as noted above, they passed a raft of conservative laws regarding voting rights, education spending, tax cuts, and crime. Similar turnovers have happened this decade in a number of southern states, with new GOP majorities pursuing similar agendas. In Tennessee, the new Republican majority quickly enacted an ambitious agenda that included many party priorities, such as phasing out the inheritance tax, weakening teacher tenure, enacting tort reform, and overhauling civil service rules.

Not surprisingly, states with stagnant leadership or long-term control by one party or the other may have a harder time making breakthroughs. Changes in partisan control bring in new leaders and, with them, new agendas that reflect new priorities and different constituencies. After all, before a bill can even get far enough to be debated, the idea for it must be developed. To get ideas for bills, legislators turn to each other, to staff, to colleagues in other states, and to outside sources such as companies with causes of their own or think tanks interested in pushing change. As the late Alan Rosenthal, who was a leading expert on state legislatures at Rutgers University, pointed out, "Legislation is becoming a national phenomenon."[23] National associations of legislators, such as the National Conference of State Legislatures and the American Legislative Exchange Council, promulgate ideas that quickly spread from state to state, as do bills pushed by national corporations and interest groups. And states may be addressing new issues that crop up on a similar time frame. In 2014, every state legislature that was in session that year (which was all but four of them) dealt with legislation meant to address the Common Core, a set of educational standards developed by states but promoted by the Barack Obama administration and private groups

such as the Bill and Melinda Gates Foundation. The Common Core was adopted quickly by most states but soon grew controversial. About 20 percent of the legislation introduced that year was designed to slow or stop its implementation. Sometimes private companies or other interest groups go "venue shopping," finding sympathetic legislators in a state who will pass a law that may become a model for other states. But most ideas are still homegrown.

Constituent Service

Aside from debating and passing laws, and ensuring that the interests of various groups are represented in decision making, legislators devote a good deal of time and energy to **constituent service**. They help clear up problems that citizens are having with public agencies or even private companies. They also act as liaisons between their constituents and unelected parts of the government in the executive branch, the bureaucracy that everyone knows and loves to hate. After a constituent asked Robin Vos, the Republican speaker of the Wisconsin Assembly, how he spends his day, Vos offered a description on his Facebook page: "I spent over an hour making calls back to constituents today. Hot topics I discussed with folks were problems with the 'GoWild' program run by the DNR [Department of Natural Resources] for our state's hunters, helping a woman who has become homeless access human services, Racine Unified Schools and the fear this gentleman had that the union would turn back progress in the district and a gentleman who would like us to consider changing state laws dealing with the allowed types of crossbows."[24]

Legislators and their staffs spend incredible amounts of their time dealing with constituent service requests, also known as **casework**.[25] Residents of a state may experience all manner of frustration coping with state laws or may merely want assistance in sorting through regulatory requirements. One of the advantages of being an **incumbent** is having the ability to dole out this kind of personalized help. At the state level, some legislators have staff members devoted solely to helping constituents. This is particularly true in their district offices—offices located back home in the area they

Constituent service The work done by legislators to help residents in their voting districts.

Casework The work undertaken by legislators and their staffs in response to requests for help from constituents.

Incumbent A person holding office.

TEXAS legislators approved a bill that would allow for random drug testing of thousands of high school athletes in an effort to stamp out steroid use.

represent, as opposed to their capitol offices. Typical issues include tracking down deadbeat dads for child support, figuring out how constituents can receive proper health coverage under Medicaid programs, and determining which federal agency to contact with questions about military matters.

The problem is that attempts to help individuals sometimes morph into policy decisions. That is, a legislator might not only write a letter to help a particular person but also write a bill that changes the way the state approaches a program, such as health insurance. Helping an individual may be all well and good, but changing the system based on the personal story of one constituent is not necessarily the best way to create policies that will affect thousands. In 2017, talk show host Jimmy Kimmel became an influential voice during a congressional debate over health

care. Lawmakers cited the care his newborn son got—he required multiple heart operations during his first year of life—as a standard. Kimmel then repeatedly took them to task for falling short. "We are in the midst of a serious public policy debate over the future of health care," wrote *Daily Beast* columnist Matt Lewis. "That debate should be decided using facts and logic—not on the anecdotal experience of one wealthy Hollywood comedian who endured a very difficult circumstance."[26]

Undoubtedly, it is important for legislators to hear about the real-world experiences of their constituents. Because they cannot meet with everybody, however, they need to rely on reports and studies to get a complete picture. They otherwise might be swayed too greatly by personal interactions. The danger of politicians' having to raise significant campaign finance treasuries is not so much that their votes can be bought but that they are much more likely to meet with the people or interest groups that give them the campaign contributions. Campaign donors often give money simply so they can have access to a legislator when they hand over the check. By contrast, people who do not or cannot give money may not get heard.

David Kidd/Governing

▲
Informal encounters are as important to the work of a legislature as committee hearings and floor debates. Here, Illinois state representative Sonya Harper confers with Paul Ferrero, an aide to the state attorney general.

....

Oversight The legislature's role in making sure that the governor and executive branch agencies are properly implementing the laws.

Oversight

Under the U.S. system of checks and balances, legislatures are charged with **oversight**, the task of making sure that the governor and the executive branch agencies are functioning properly. The executive branch is so called because it executes the laws written by the legislature. Legislators are only doing their job when they call governors and executive branch agencies to account through hearings, investigations, and audits for how they are carrying out those laws. Unfortunately, the most ubiquitous form of oversight is a legislator's intervening with administrative agencies on behalf of constituents or constituent groups in ways that are "episodic and punitive."[27]

For example, some years ago, the Arkansas Livestock and Poultry Commission filed suit against a livestock sales barn for failure to meet state regulations concerning an infectious livestock disease called brucellosis. The state senator from that district placed language to weaken those regulations in the bill to fund the commission, which prompted the commissioner to resign.[28] The commissioner had viewed the funding cut as a signal that his authority was being undermined, so he quit. That kind of scattershot approach—helping a particular constituent at the expense of the public good—is by its nature inequitable. The point of bureaucratic norms is to make sure that regulations and laws are applied fairly and evenly across the board.

Legislators may attack agencies for pursuing policies that hurt their constituents, but unfortunately, the legislative branch—despite its duty to keep an eye on executive branch functions—is not consistent about taking a hard look at whether ongoing programs are functioning as they should. Aside from unearthing an occasional scandal involving misspent funds, legislators reap little political reward for poking around in the business of the state. Staff aides regularly perform audits and evaluations, but legislatures make only sporadic use of the results in their follow-up decisions about funding. Most oversight comes in a less systematic way, through budget reviews and occasional committee hearings. In states that impose limits on the number of terms legislators can serve, there is even less opportunity to perform oversight. Members have less time to become expert in any particular area, and so they often rely heavily on expert testimony from the very executive branch they are meant to oversee.

And for each program, it seems, there are not only agency officials but also program beneficiaries and lobbyists who will question the motives of legislators or staffers who seek to audit the program's work. In other words, there's often not much reward for a legislator in taking the job of oversight seriously. The North Carolina legislature created the Program Evaluation Division, which was charged with compiling a scorecard to show how state agencies were performing, in much the same way information about the performance of private companies might be compiled for investors. John Turcotte, the division's founding director, said his goal was to "target programs for evaluation that are important to the General Assembly and also look at all state government programs collectively to avoid legislative oversight gaps."[29] Turcotte's first report looked at agricultural research stations. North Carolina had the most of any state in the country—21, compared with only 11 in the much larger state of California—and Turcotte's group concluded that there was no economic or strategic justification for the state to support so many. "That report was like setting off a nuclear weapon in the area of Raleigh," he said. "Any time you question the necessity of an institution or a major component of a program, you will create massive opposition."[30]

Organization and Operation of Legislatures

The U.S. system of representative democracy was designed to be messy. In their book *Republic on Trial*, Alan Rosenthal and his coauthors argue that the institutions of democracy should be more popular because they work pretty well, but they concede, "The American political system was not designed for people to understand."[31] Legislatures were created because, even in colonial days, this country was too large and its problems too complex to be addressed by its vast numbers of individual citizens. We elect legislatures in our republican form of government to argue out our problems at appointed times and in a single space, in sessions at the capitol. The ranks of the legislatures have become far more diverse over the past 30 years. Although the average state legislator is still a white male, there are nearly four times as many African Americans and about six times as many women serving in legislatures today as there were in 1970. Also over the past 40 years or so, legislatures have become better equipped to do their job by hiring more and better-trained staffers. None of these changes, however, have made state legislatures any more popular with the public.

Bicameralism

Every state has a constitution that describes a body that can pass state laws. In every state but Nebraska, which has a unicameral (one-house) legislature, the legislature is bicameral (divided into two houses), pretty much like the U.S. Congress. As mentioned earlier in this chapter, one chamber is normally called either the house of representatives or the assembly and the other is called the senate. The Tenth Amendment of the U.S. Constitution reserves to the states all powers not given to the federal government, and state legislatures can write any state law that does not interfere with federal laws.

The house, or assembly, is considered more of a "people's house," with its members representing fewer

FIGURE 7-1 ● How It Works

A One-Eyed Frog's View of the Legislative Process, or How a Bill Really Became a Law in Minnesota

The mechanisms by which a bill becomes a law at the state level are similar to the mechanisms at work at the federal level. And we've all seen the flowcharts that outline the ins and outs: A bill goes in one side, gets debated, marked up, and reported out, and then comes out the other side as a real-life law to be implemented, or it gets returned to the legislature for an override, or it gets "killed." You'd be forgiven for thinking that beneath that abstraction lies a more complex and interesting process.

You'd be right. Below is a different flowchart, this one fleshing out what actually happened when a group of Minnesota teens brought to light the fact that the frog population in their area was turning up with extra limbs and missing eyes. About eight months and $151,000 later, the frogs were in much better shape.

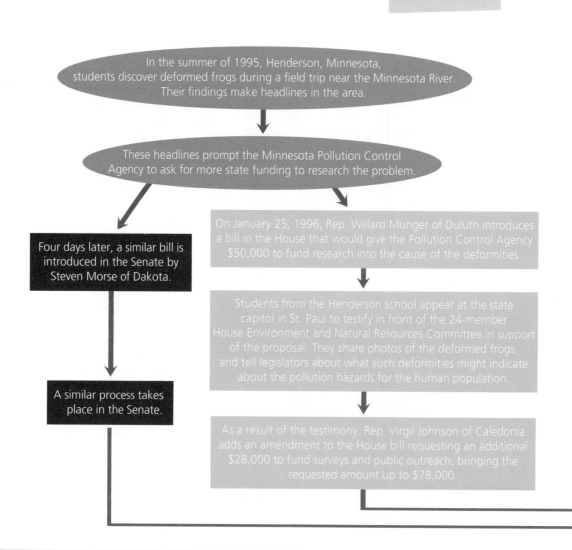

Source: Minnesota House of Representatives, Public Information Office, "Capitol Steps: How Six Bills Became Law."

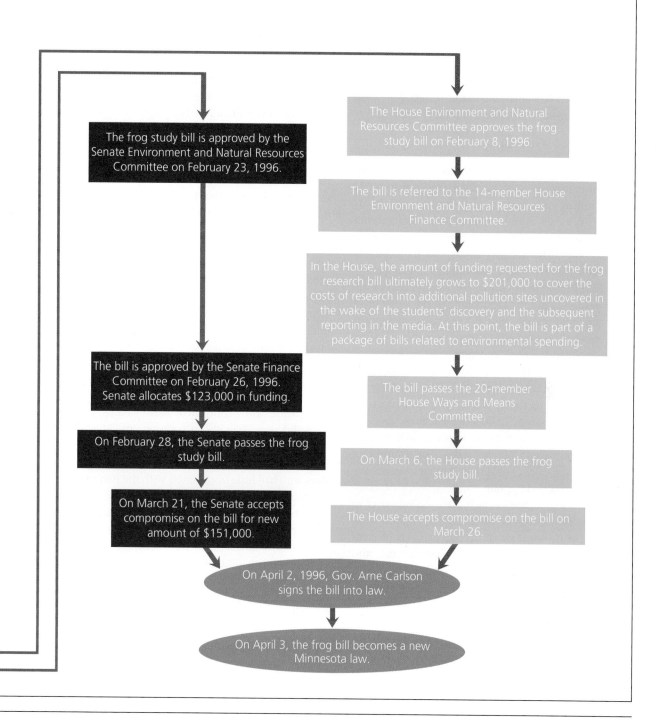

The frog study bill is approved by the Senate Environment and Natural Resources Committee on February 23, 1996.

The House Environment and Natural Resources Committee approves the frog study bill on February 8, 1996.

The bill is referred to the 14-member House Environment and Natural Resources Finance Committee.

In the House, the amount of funding requested for the frog research bill ultimately grows to $201,000 to cover the costs of research into additional pollution sites uncovered in the wake of the students' discovery and the subsequent reporting in the media. At this point, the bill is part of a package of bills related to environmental spending.

The bill is approved by the Senate Finance Committee on February 26, 1996. Senate allocates $123,000 in funding.

The bill passes the 20-member House Ways and Means Committee.

On February 28, the Senate passes the frog study bill.

On March 6, the House passes the frog study bill.

On March 21, the Senate accepts compromise on the bill for new amount of $151,000.

The House accepts compromise on the bill on March 26.

On April 2, 1996, Gov. Arne Carlson signs the bill into law.

On April 3, the frog bill becomes a new Minnesota law.

people for shorter terms than do their colleagues in the senate. The house always has more members, known as state representatives, than the senate does. There are 163 representatives in the Missouri General Assembly, for example, but only 34 senators. There are some exceptions, but generally senators serve four-year terms, whereas house members serve two-year terms. The two chambers operate independently, with separate leaders, committees, and agendas, although both chambers have to pass the same version of a bill before it can be sent to the governor to be signed into law or vetoed. Nebraska, with its unicameral legislature, is the one exception.

Legislative Leadership

Most state legislatures have essentially the same leadership structure, at least for their top positions. At the beginning of a session, each house votes in its speaker. This is generally someone picked beforehand by a **caucus**, the group of members belonging to the majority party. The majority leader and the minority leader rank just below the speaker of the house. *Majority* and *minority* here refer to the respective strengths of the major parties. Either the Democratic or the Republican Party may hold the majority of seats in a chamber. (In 2018, about three dozen legislators—out of more than 7,000 nationwide—were independents or members of third parties, with most of those serving either in Vermont or in Maine.) In the senate, the top leader is generally known as the president, president pro tempore, president pro tem, or majority leader.

Certain aspects of the leadership positions remain fairly constant across all the states. For example, a speaker will typically preside over daily sessions of the house or assembly, refer bills to the appropriate committees, and sign legislation as it makes its way over to the senate or the governor's desk. Leaders appoint committee chairs (in some states, all the members of committees), set or change committee jurisdictions, and offer staff or legislative help to rank-and-file members. They also often help with campaigns, including providing financial support.

The amount of power invested in the office of speaker or senate president does vary by state, however. In the Texas Senate, leadership powers are invested in the office of lieutenant governor. Lieutenant governors

normally do not possess much formal power, but in Texas, they appoint the members of committees and committee chairs in the 31-member body and decide which bills are considered and when. In some older legislatures, such as those in New Jersey and Massachusetts, the senate president performs all those functions, presides over debates, counts votes, and ensures member attendance. In California, those powers rest with the senate president pro tem. But regardless of how the formal duties are divided up, usually there is one individual who emerges as holding the most power and speaking for the chamber in negotiating with the other chamber and the governor.

With the exception of Nebraska, where parties are actually banned from the nonpartisan unicameral legislature, legislatures are divided along party lines (and even in Nebraska, the Democratic and Republican Parties endorse candidates for the legislature, so it's well known which lawmakers affiliate with which party). Not only does the majority party get to pick the top leader, but it gets to fill virtually all the important committee chairs as well. A party majority is worth much more than the comfort of knowing that your fellow Democrats or Republicans will help you outvote the opposition on most bills. Holding the leadership and chair positions means that the majority party gets to set the agenda—deciding which bills will be heard for a vote. From the 1950s into the early 1990s, Democrats held a 2–1 edge in the number of legislative seats held nationwide and controlled many more chambers than did their Republican counterparts. Much of the Democratic Party's dominance came from its strength in the South, where many Democrats were conservatives who had little in common with the national party. At the start of this century, Republicans pulled into parity in terms of both raw numbers of legislators and how many chambers they controlled. Heading into the 2010 elections, Democrats held the advantage in control of chambers, with 62 to the Republicans' 36. Following historic wins by the GOP in 2010 and 2014, those numbers basically reversed, with the GOP holding 68 of the 98 partisan chambers heading into the 2016 elections. Although Democrats hoped to gain ground in 2016, they failed to do so. The two parties each took control of three chambers, leading to no net change. Following the 2018 election, Republicans controlled both chambers in 31 states, and Democrats did so in 18. Only Minnesota was split—the first time there was only one divided legislature since 1914.

....

Caucus All the members of a party—Republican or Democrat—within a legislative chamber; also refers to meetings of members of a political party in a chamber.

TABLE 7-1 ● Total Number of State Legislators (House and Senate), 2018

State	Senate Members	House Members	Total Members	State	Senate Members	House Members	Total Members
Alabama	35	105	140	Nebraska	49	n/a	49
Alaska	20	40	60	Nevada	21	42	63
Arizona	30	60	90	New Hampshire	24	400	424
Arkansas	35	100	135	New Jersey	40	80	120
California	40	80	120	New Mexico	42	70	112
Colorado	35	65	100	New York	63	150	213
Connecticut	36	151	187	North Carolina	50	120	170
Delaware	21	41	62	North Dakota	47	94	141
Florida	40	120	160	Ohio	33	99	132
Georgia	56	180	236	Oklahoma	48	101	149
Hawaii	25	51	76	Oregon	30	60	90
Idaho	35	70	105	Pennsylvania	50	203	253
Illinois	59	118	177	Rhode Island	38	75	113
Indiana	50	100	150	South Carolina	46	124	170
Iowa	50	100	150	South Dakota	35	70	105
Kansas	40	125	165	Tennessee	33	99	132
Kentucky	38	100	138	Texas	31	150	181
Louisiana	39	105	144	Utah	29	75	104
Maine	35	151	186	Vermont	30	150	180
Maryland	47	141	188	Virginia	40	100	140
Massachusetts	40	160	200	Washington	49	98	147
Michigan	38	110	148	West Virginia	34	100	134
Minnesota	67	134	201	Wisconsin	33	99	132
Mississippi	52	122	174	Wyoming	30	60	90
Missouri	34	163	197	Total	1,972	5,411	7,383
Montana	50	100	150				

Source: National Conference of State Legislatures, "State Partisan Composition," April 9, 2018, http://www.ncsl.org/Portals/1/Documents/Elections/Legis_Control_041118_26973.pdf.

MAP 7-1 ● **Partisan Control of State Government, 1954**

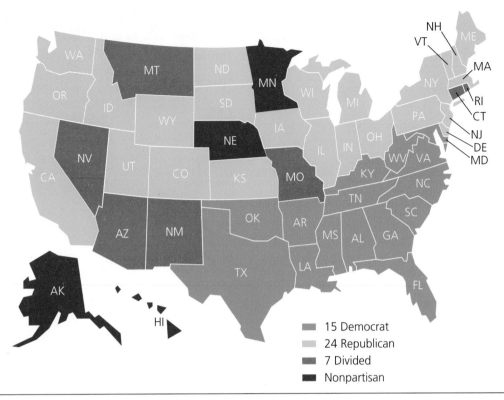

15 Democrat
24 Republican
7 Divided
Nonpartisan

Source: All data from Carl Klarner Dataverse, "State Partisan Balance Data, 1937–2011," https://thedata.harvard.edu/dvn/dv/cklarner.

Control over the political branches as a whole has ebbed and flowed over time. At the end of World War II, all but 7 of the 48 states had united governments, meaning one party controlled the governorship and both legislative chambers. By 1986, only 21 of 50 states had united governments.[32] The competitive nature of legislative politics has meant that every election cycle between 1984 and 2016 resulted in at least one tied chamber, but in most states, one party again has control of the entire government.[33] Today, most chambers have become lopsided, with one party dominating. When 2017 began, Republicans had control of both legislative branches and the governorship in 24 states, compared with just 5 for Democrats—the party's lowest number since the dawn of the Civil War, when there were 15 fewer states. Following the 2018 elections, Democrats had boosted their numbers to 14, but Republicans still had far more with 23 states.

Some leaders hold their positions for decades, although this is exceptional. Mike Madigan has been speaker of the Illinois House since 1983, with the exception of a two-year term during the 1990s when his party lost power. Mike Miller started his run as president of the Maryland Senate back in 1987 and was still going strong in 2018, although several of his top lieutenants lost their seats in primaries that year. Fred Risser is the nation's longest-serving state legislator; he was elected to the Wisconsin Assembly in 1956 and then to the Wisconsin Senate in 1962, and has served in a variety of legislative leadership positions over the past 50 years, including stints as majority leader, minority leader, and senate president.

Lots of legislative experience can be an advantage in getting leadership positions, but it is by no means required. Climbing the leadership ladder can take no time at all in states with term limits, such as California and Florida, where house members can serve only six and eight years, respectively, and speakers are sometimes chosen as freshmen. In contrast, Joe Hackney, who became speaker of the North Carolina House in 2007, had to serve more than a quarter-century before attaining that post. "When I came to the legislature,

MAP 7-2 ● Partisan Control of State Government, 2018

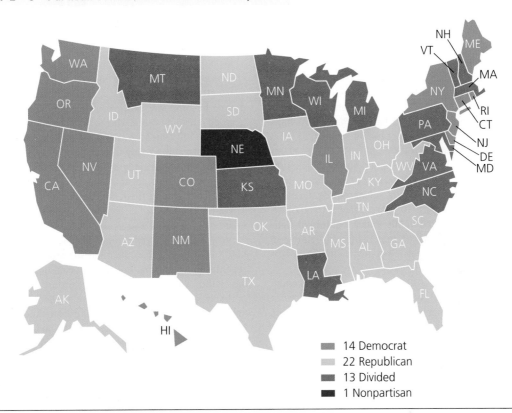

14 Democrat
22 Republican
13 Divided
1 Nonpartisan

Source: National Conference of State Legislatures, "Post Election 2018 State & Legislative Partisan Composition," November 21, 2018, http://www
.ncsl.org/Portals/1/Documents/Elections/Legis_Control_112118_26973.pdf.

I more or less regarded it as a long-term thing," he says. "It wasn't my plan to be there two or four or six years and quit. It was my plan to make a contribution, and I saw that those who make a contribution built up seniority and experience."[34] Hackney held the position of speaker for four years before Republican victories in 2010 forced him from power. His successor, Thom Tillis, by contrast, became speaker after serving just four years in the house.

Committees

Andy Gipson was one of the most influential legislators in Mississippi in 2014. As chair of the House Judiciary Committee, he was the main sponsor of the session's most complex bill, an act to overhaul the state's criminal justice system. He also shepherded two other high-profile bills regarding gay rights and abortion. Regardless of party control, after all, committees are where most

legislative work gets done. Legislators are divided into committees—usually about 15 or 20 per chamber—that grapple with particular issues, such as education, transportation, and taxes. Thousands of bills are introduced annually in each legislature. Most of these bills never reach the floor where the full house or senate meets. Basically, they never make it past the committee stage to be debated or voted on by the house or senate as a whole. Instead, they are sent to the appropriate committee, where they may be debated and amended but usually die without a hearing. Just as the senate president, house speaker, or other leader sets the agenda for floor action on bills, so the committee chair decides which bills are going to be heard and receive priority treatment at the committee level.

Legislators try to serve on the committees where they will have the most influence. The most prestigious committees are the budget committees, which set tax and spending levels. Other committees debate policies,

A DIFFERENCE THAT MAKES A DIFFERENCE
HOW MANY LEGISLATORS DOES A STATE NEED?

The California legislature may not be big enough. Each state senator represents about 930,000 people—far more than individual U.S. House members do. Those in the state assembly represent half as many, but that's still nearly a half-million constituents for each of them to keep track of and speak for.

As a result, the idea of expanding the legislature has been kicking around Sacramento for a long time. "I've been hearing the basic idea of increasing the number of seats for the past 10 years," said Eric McGhee, a research fellow at the Public Policy Institute of California. "There's no question that California, relative to the rest of the country, has legislative districts that are huge."

Leading into the 2018 elections, a businessman named John Cox, who became the GOP gubernatorial nominee that year, spent millions collecting signatures for an initiative to create what he called the "Neighborhood Legislature." State senators would represent 5,000 people, members of the assembly twice that many. Given California's size, that means there would be nearly 4,000 state senators and 8,000 assembly members. That's a lot of legislators. "I have a plan to make legislative districts small enough that anyone can run, and they won't need special interest money to do it," Cox said.

While there's an argument to be made that lawmakers representing a fraction as many people would be able to pay more attention to voters' specific concerns, it could also be argued that each individual member would have very little clout and would be hard pressed to pass any legislation at all. Similarly, when it comes to constituent services, the average person would have an easier time getting the attention of a legislator, but that politician, in turn, would have a harder time influencing state agencies.

Cox's initiative failed to make the ballot, as it had in his attempts in prior years. Even if it had been voted on and become law, however, it wouldn't actually have granted citizens more voices in Sacramento. There would be 100 times as many elected legislators, but there would still be only 40 senators and 80 members of the assembly actually meeting. That's because the new legislators would select senators and representatives from among their number to go to the capitol. There wouldn't be 12,000 legislators holding sessions at an arena.

Why adding a layer of elected officials to select an elite subgroup of 120 would make the process more representative is puzzling. And it is not clear just how many legislators are needed in a state to do the job. There probably is a "sweet spot"—a point at which legislators are representing the right number of constituents—said Nathan Monroe, a political scientist at the University of California, Merced. But what exactly is that? Most legislatures have somewhere between 150 and 200 legislators. That's more than California, which does have more people than any other state. But thousands—or even hundreds—might not be any better. State houses, Monroe noted, are larger than state senates, but not necessarily any better at representation.

The New Hampshire House is the nation's largest legislative chamber, with 400 members representing 1.3 million people. That doesn't mean legislators there do clearly superior work for their constituents than legislators elsewhere who represent several times as many people. "The theory is that it makes it so everybody knows who their state rep is," says Andrew Smith, a pollster at the University of New Hampshire. "The truth is, nobody knows who their state rep is. They're completely anonymous."

Source: Adapted from Alan Greenblatt, "How Many Lawmakers Does a Legislature Need?," *Governing*, January 2018, http://www.governing.com/topics/politics/gov-california-legislature-ballot-size.html.

but unless funding is provided to pay for those policies, they do not matter as much. If public officials ask themselves what they want to do, the second question should be how they can pay for it. Seats on a finance or appropriations committee are highly sought after, but members will also "request appointment to committees which will give them the most visibility and interest

in their districts."[35] Thus, a senator from a rural district may want to serve on an agriculture committee. A representative who previously served on a city council may want a seat on the local government committee.

While any member can introduce legislation on any topic, members of the education committee, for example, are more likely to introduce and influence bills that affect schools. When an education bill is being debated in the full house or senate, other members, who have other specialties, will turn to members of the education committee for guidance about what the bill would do and how they should vote. The same holds true for other issues, such as transportation and health care.

Rank-and-File Members

Not every legislator, of course, can be a leader. The majority of legislators—those who provide leaders with their votes—are known as **rank-and-file members** of the legislature. And no legislator—leader or rank-and-file member—can be fully versed in the details of all the dozens of bills that confront him or her every day during a session. Legislators are constantly being pulled in different directions by constituents, lobbyists, and colleagues demanding "just five minutes" of their time to be briefed or wooed on a subject. "You're just busy all the time," North Carolina state senator Cathy Dunn said during her freshman year in office. "I think the biggest factor is you're so busy, it feels like you can't get anything done."[36] Alan Becker, who chaired the board of Florida's economic development organization, complained that "their average attention span is 30 seconds."[37]

Legislators turn to many sources for information on how to vote. There is a classic notion, posited by the 18th-century political philosopher and statesman Edmund Burke, that divides legislators into **delegates**, who vote according to the wishes of their districts, and **trustees**, who vote according to their own consciences.[38] Given the proliferation of legislation, however, members never hear from a single constituent on perhaps 90 percent of the bills they must consider. Instead, they rely for guidance on staffers, other legislators, interest groups and lobbyists, executive branch officials, foundations, think tanks, and other sources.

That legislators cannot rely solely on their own judgment to vote is the source of many people's sense that legislators' votes can be bought—or at least rented. This is ironic, considering that political scientists note that most of the time most legislators are extremely attentive to their districts and vote according to their sense of their constituents' desires. Their primary goal, after all, is to win reelection. In addition, most states have made it tougher for lobbyists to get lawmakers' attention. It is difficult under the new ethics rules for a lobbyist to spring for a legislator's cup of coffee, much less treat him or her to lunch. In Kentucky, for example, there are far fewer of the receptions that once kept Frankfort well fed, and lobbyists are prohibited from making any personal contributions to candidates for the legislature. The goal is to avoid conflicts of interest, whether real or perceived. But some old-school legislators complain the clampdown makes it harder for them to socialize and get to know their colleagues the way they did at lobbyist-sponsored events in the past. "You can't even have a cup of coffee with a lobbyist, which is stupidity," complained Norma Anderson, a former Republican leader in the Colorado Senate. "We used to have parties where we would learn to know one another as people, rather than as politicians. That has been destroyed, so now, they're nothing but enemies."[39]

As with most things, times have changed. It used to be that rank-and-file members voted pretty much the way they were instructed to by their party leaders. In Connecticut, the legislature of the early 1960s was an assemblage of party hacks—members beholden to the party chair for patronage. This meant that most of the legislature's important decisions were made in small meetings to which the public—or even most rank-and-file members—were not invited. Today, leaders still call the shots, but they are careful not to go against the wishes of their caucuses too often, knowing that they can be ousted if enough members want to go in a different direction. Leaders help other legislators intervene with the governor or the rest of the executive branch and help green-light bills to build up political chits. "As long as it wasn't against the law, didn't require that I go to confession, or wouldn't break up my marriage, I did it," recalled Ralph Wright, onetime speaker of the Vermont House.[40]

Plenty of examples still exist of members caving in to party or leadership pressure—or being punished when they fail to do so. In 2017, Rudy Salas lost a committee chairmanship after being the sole Democrat in the California Assembly to vote against a gas-tax increase. Three years earlier, Missouri Democratic representative Keith English was stripped of his positions on four house committees after he joined with Republicans to override then governor Jay Nixon's veto of a tax-cut bill. English

....

Rank-and-file members Legislators who do not hold leadership positions or senior committee posts.

Delegates Legislators who primarily see their role as voting according to their constituents' beliefs as they understand them.

Trustees Legislators who believe they were elected to exercise their own judgment and to approach issues accordingly.

said he didn't take it personally. "Definitely, when you vote against the governor, or you vote against the Democratic position, there's retribution."[41] The combination of leadership pressure and possible targeting by outside groups means the incentive for most legislators, most of the time, is to go along with what their party wants.

The pendulum appears to have swung back toward greater power being held by legislative leaders, but they cannot simply bully their way through as they did a generation ago. There are two reasons for this. Leadership offices control fundraising efforts designed to build or maintain majorities, but these efforts are mainly directed toward the relatively few contests that will make or break a majority. Many rank-and-file members today can raise their own money and have access to expert advice for hire and separate sources of money, whether from political action committees run by industries or labor unions or elsewhere. We have already touched on the other factor—members do not have to rely on leaders as much as they once did for information about bills or for help in writing legislation. The proliferation of lobbyists and the **professionalization** of legislatures have meant that members in many states have their own resources.[42]

Apportionment

Another issue that profoundly affects all legislators is **apportionment**. Following the nationwide census that occurs every 10 years, each state draws new lines for its legislative districts. In states with more than one member of Congress, congressional districts are redrawn as well. The redistricting process is the most naked exercise of political power in the states. Within the legal limits that exist—Supreme Court rulings in the 1960s set the requirement that districts be roughly even in population, and there have been countless court decisions since—the incumbent party will do everything it can to preserve its hold on seats or, preferably, increase its numbers. Each party will seek to draw the maximum number of districts possible that are likely to elect members of its own party. The two major parties will fight each other as best they can to make certain that the

- -

Professionalization The process of providing legislators with the resources they need to make politics their main career, such as making their positions full-time or providing them with full-time staff.

Apportionment The allotting of districts according to population shifts. The number of congressional districts that a state has may be reapportioned every 10 years, following the national census.

MAP 7-3 ● The Upside-Down-Elephant District

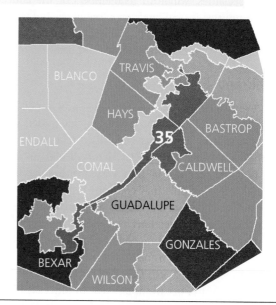

Texas's 35th Congressional District drew attention for its odd shape, the result of what many viewed as a partisan effort to redraw the district's lines.

Source: Texas Legislative Council.

other side does not gain the upper hand. "Just like there are no atheists in foxholes, there are no nonpartisans in redistricting," said Paul Green, the late director of the School of Policy Studies at Roosevelt University in Chicago. "You use whatever leverage you can."[43]

Travis County, Texas, where Austin is located, is one of the most Democratic jurisdictions in the state. President Obama won almost 64 percent of the vote in Travis County in 2008. In 2011, the Republican-controlled Texas legislature sliced and diced Travis County so that four of the five congressional districts that include parts of the county lean toward Republicans. They did that by packing Democrats into a single district that includes both parts of Austin and parts of San Antonio, three counties away—with the two halves connected only by a narrow strip of land. The district outline looked so strange on a map that the *Washington Post* held a contest to describe it; the winning entry was "Upside-down elephant (spraying water)."[44] Travis County's government, among other groups, challenged the redistricting in court, but judges allowed the five-way split to go into effect for the 2012 elections.[45]

Political district boundaries that link disparate communities or have odd shapes that resemble ear-muffs or moose antlers are known as **gerrymanders**, a term derived from the name of Elbridge Gerry, an early-19th-century governor of Massachusetts. **Malapportionment** occurs when districts violate the principle of equal representation. In the past, some state legislative districts could have many times the numbers of constituents in other districts. Votes in the smaller districts, in effect, counted for more. Relatively few people in, say, a sparsely populated rural district would have the same amount of representative clout in the legislature as many more people in a densely populated urban district.

As Texas's experience shows, the party in control of redistricting really does matter. Republicans took just 48.6 percent of the statewide, two-party vote for the Wisconsin Assembly in 2012, but won 60 of the chamber's 99 seats. In 2014, they won 63 seats with 52 percent of the statewide vote. This led to a lawsuit challenging the assembly map as a gerrymander that unconstitutionally favored the Republican Party. Plaintiffs used a political science measurement known as the "efficiency gap." According to this argument, all votes cast for a losing candidate and any votes for the winner beyond what was needed to win are considered "wasted." If too many districts have lopsided outcomes (where the party that drew the map "wasted" significantly fewer votes), the argument goes, that shows that the party drawing the map sought to game the system, creating districts that are totally safe for one party or the other and diluting its strength in neighboring districts. Democrats challenging the map showed that, as measured by the 2012 results, the Wisconsin Assembly was roughly three times more inefficient than the average legislature.

But, although lower courts had thrown out maps as unconstitutional partisan gerrymanders, the Supreme Court rejected the case in 2018 on technical grounds, while refusing to weigh in on cases from other states. The justices appear unlikely at this point to accept any standard for measuring when a gerrymander is so partisan as to be unconstitutional. Both parties press their partisan advantage when they have the chance. In 2011 in Illinois, Democrats drew a new congressional map that imperiled more than half the state's Republican incumbents. In 2018, the Supreme Court ruled Republicans had waited too long to challenge the congressional map Democrats had drawn in Maryland.

Legislatures define district boundaries in most states, but there are exceptions. Since the 1980s, Iowa's political maps have been created by the nonpartisan Legislative Services Agency. The agency uses software to draw 100 house districts and 50 senate districts according to rules that keep population as equal as possible from district to district, avoid splitting counties, and keep the districts compact. In contrast to maps drawn by legislators, those drawn by the agency do not take into account party registration, voting patterns, or the political territory of incumbents. Largely as a result, partisan control of the Iowa legislature has sometimes flipped in the election after the agency does its work.

While Iowa's system is unique, advocates elsewhere regularly try to find ways to prevent redistricting from flagrantly favoring one party over the other. Lately, they have won some important victories. In Florida in 2010, voters approved a constitutional amendment that mandated rules for redistricting, including forbidding the drawing of lines for the purpose of favoring incumbent officeholders or political parties. Leading up to the 2016 elections, both the congressional and state senate maps were redrawn following legal challenges that resulted in rulings that the state hadn't followed the amendment's requirement to draw competitive districts. California voters approved a pair of citizen initiatives in 2008 and 2010 that took redistricting out of the hands of state legislators and entrusted it to an independent commission. In 2018, voters in several states approved ballot measures to give redistricting duties to an independent commission if the legislature fails to draw maps that win broad bipartisan support. In 2015, deciding an Arizona case, the Supreme Court ruled that legislatures are not entitled to sole authority over redistricting and that the job can be done by organizations such as commissions created by ballot measures.

Partisanship is the primary concern of redistricting, but it is not the only one. Issues of representation also play a big part. African Americans are overwhelmingly Democrats, but some joined with Republicans following the 1980 and 1990 censuses to create majorityblack districts, especially in the South. For African Americans, this deal with the GOP offered the advantage of creating districts in which African American candidates were likely to be elected. It wasn't that they joined the Republican Party, of course. They simply allied

Gerrymanders Districts clearly drawn with the intent of pressing partisan advantage at the expense of other considerations.

Malapportionment A situation in which the principle of equal representation is violated.

themselves with the GOP to draw **majority–minority districts**, which guaranteed the election of more African Americans but also made the neighboring "bleached" districts more likely to elect Republicans. Following the Voting Rights Act of 1982, the federal Justice Department encouraged state legislators to create majority–minority districts whenever possible, until a series of U.S. Supreme Court decisions during the 1990s limited the practice. In a confusing and often contradictory series of rulings, the Court ruled that race could not be the "predominant" factor in redistricting.[46] In 2015, the Court ruled that Alabama had unconstitutionally relied on race in drawing legislative districts designed to have supermajority populations of African Americans. In 2018, the Court gave its blessing to a Texas map rejected by multiple lower courts, finding that the legislature had used race unconstitutionally as the dominant factor in drawing only one state house district.

Redistricting also changes representation in ways that go beyond race. With each new round of redistricting, power shifts to places that are growing quickly and away from those that are not. One of the major themes of the 2010 round of redistricting was a shift in power away from rural areas and to the suburbs and exurbs, which had experienced strong population growth in the previous 10 years.[47] Alaska legislators were so concerned about having fewer lawmakers representing rural areas—and about the remaining rural districts becoming even more massive—that they submitted a constitutional amendment to voters in 2010 to add more seats to the legislature. One of the lawmakers supporting the change was State senator Albert Kookesh, who represented the largest state legislative district in the country. From its southeastern corner, Kookesh's district extended 1,185 miles west—about the same distance as that from Jacksonville, Florida, to Minneapolis, Minnesota—and about 1,000 miles north—about the same as the distance from Phoenix, Arizona, to Portland, Oregon.[48] Getting around an area of that size cannot be done efficiently in a car; it's hard enough to do it by plane. "In order for me to get to one of my villages, Lime Village, I would have to go from Angoon to Juneau, Juneau to Anchorage, Anchorage to Fairbanks, Fairbanks to Aniak, and Aniak to Lime Village," Kookesh said.[49] Alaska voters rejected the plan to add legislative seats.

State Legislators

In 2014, the Pew Research Center conducted a survey of that small fraction of the population that ever runs for public office. It found that office seekers were disproportionately white, male, and college educated. Men were three times more likely to run for office than were women, and whites made up 82 percent of those who had ever run for office—easily a higher number than their share of the population.[50] If you were to make a composite drawing of the average state legislator, he—and it would be a he—would be white and in his mid- to late 40s. He would have at least some college education

A 2015 **OHIO** amendment requires that the state's apportionment commission include at least two members of each party.

Scott Keller/The Tampa Bay Times via AP

▲
In Florida, house freshmen generally pick a speaker-designate who will serve three terms hence, after all the more senior members have been term-limited out. Representative José Oliva, shown at right, was chosen to succeed Speaker Richard Corcoran, left, two years ahead of the start of the 2019 session.

. . . .

Majority–minority districts Districts in which members of a minority group, such as African Americans or Hispanics, make up a majority of the population or electorate.

and most likely more than one degree, describe himself as moderate or conservative, and have lived in the community he is representing for at least 10 years.[51] There are many, many exceptions to all the aspects of this composite. The type of person who runs for state legislative office has changed a good deal over the past 30 years—for example, far more women, Hispanics, and African Americans and fewer lawyers now run for office—but nonetheless, the type of middle- to upper-middle-class American male described here still predominates.

The nation's 7,383 state legislators come from all backgrounds, particularly in the states where the house and senate meet for only part of the year. In states with full-time legislatures, such as California and Pennsylvania, the legislators tend, not surprisingly, to be career politicians who have served in local or other elected offices or perhaps as members of legislative staffs. In states with part-time legislatures, such as Arkansas and Indiana, members come from many different walks of life, devoting perhaps one-third of their working hours to politics while earning their livings through some other means.

Professional Background

Some employers encourage the political hopes of their employees because they know legislative service can be good for business. This holds true especially for professions most directly affected by state lawmaking, such as big business. Buddy Dyer kept up his law practice while serving in the Florida Senate and in 2002 had to respond to complaints that the bills he proposed would have protected his industrial company clients from fines and lawsuits. His defense? "Probably not a bill that goes through the Legislature" that did not affect one of his firm's clients.[52]

Other groups enjoy considerable representation within legislative bodies. Often legislators will introduce bills that would help their industries or themselves, a practice known as self-dealing. In 2017, Kentucky state representative C. Wesley Morgan, who owns four liquor stores, filed a series of seven bills that would have forced his competitors to change some of their business practices. "It's no different than an attorney being for a law about tort reform or a doctor being for a law relating to medical practice," he said.[53] In 2015, Oregon state senator Chip Shields sponsored legislation to require contractors to use biodegradable lubricants in construction and maintenance projects that receive public funding. Guess what? Shields sells such products, and his

family owns a company that makes them. Back in 2006, Al Mansell stepped down from his leadership role as president of the Utah Senate to become president of the National Association of Realtors. He stayed in the senate, however, sponsoring legislation that helped members of his profession. He was one of 22 people who worked in real estate who were serving in the Utah legislature at that time. "I've got people who are on county commissions, mayors, state senators," said Chris Kyler, CEO of the Utah Association of Realtors. "Our lieutenant governor was president of our state association about 20 years ago. Our people are involved in the parties, too. We've got precinct chairs and vice chairs and county delegates throughout the state."[54] The online news site Texas Tribune noted in 2013, "At the Capitol, lawmakers rarely recuse themselves from legislation that has an impact on their livelihoods for one simple reason: They don't have to."[55] A count by the *Montana Standard* in 2016 found that, out of more than 900,000 legislative floor and committee votes over the previous four sessions, legislators abstained from voting due to a conflict of interest a grand total of three times, even though there were many instances where legislation would clearly have an impact on their day jobs.[56]

Consider public education. Teachers' unions are usually among the most active lobbying groups in any state, but schools do not necessarily have to rely on outsiders to influence the legislature. Teachers themselves are often members of legislatures, and employees of other institutions of higher learning also serve. In Maine, state law requires that teachers be granted leave from their jobs if they want to run for office. Maine's legislature meets for only six months every other year, but even that chunk of time is enough to play havoc with a person's work schedule, and there's a good deal of concern in the state that retirees are coming to dominate the legislative chamber.

The reality is that retired people account for only about 8 percent of state legislators nationwide.[57] About 15 percent of legislators are lawyers—a big decline from past decades. In 2015, Wisconsin's legislature had its lowest number of lawyers ever (15 out of 132), while Missouri had its fewest since 1891. In South Carolina, lawyers had become so scarce in the state senate that a textile executive chaired the Judiciary Committee—the first time that job had fallen to a nonlawyer.[58] Nowadays, the dominant group in legislatures nationwide comprises people with business backgrounds. They make up about 30 percent of today's legislators.

The remaining half or so come from education, health care, real estate, insurance, and agriculture.

Demographic Diversity

The numbers of women legislators have risen dramatically since the "second wave" feminist era of the late 1960s and early 1970s, but they still do not reflect the female share of the overall population. In 1970, women held just 4 percent of all state legislative seats.[59] Their numbers doubled quickly, to 8 percent of all legislators, by 1975, and they climbed to 18 percent by 1991. The ranks of women legislators held steady at just over 20 percent for about a dozen years before spiking to 23.5 percent after the 2006 elections. The figure ticked up to just above 24 percent following the 2008 campaigns, where it remained for a decade. Only in 2018 did their number pierce the 25 percent mark, rising to 28 percent. As late as 2018, only eight states—Arizona, Colorado, Illinois, Maine, Nevada, Oregon, Vermont, and Washington—could brag that a full third or more of their legislators were women, with only Arizona and Vermont having as many as 40 percent.[60] In 2009, the New Hampshire Senate became the first legislative chamber in the nation to have a majority of women members. Women served as its president and majority leader, and another woman served as speaker of the New Hampshire House.[61]

Back in the 1970s, when the first relatively large numbers of women legislators entered the capitols, they tended to be less politically ambitious than the men they served with, and thus less likely to enter the ranks of legislative leadership. They devoted more attention to constituent service matters and tended to serve on education, health, and welfare committees. They also tended to have less education than their male counterparts, and to come from jobs that were not as prestigious or well paying as those held by the men. During the 1980s, the average socioeconomic status of women legislators improved, and women served on a broader range of committees, but they mostly still focused on issues of women, family, and children. By the 1990s, women legislators held about 15 percent of all legislative leadership positions but were still unlikely to serve on tax committees.[62] Their backgrounds had become more varied, and they had also become more conservative, although they still were more liberal than men—and significantly more likely than their male colleagues to initiate legislation.[63] Women also became more likely than men to get their priority bills through the legislative process successfully.[64]

Women legislators, however, do not alter the fundamental political dynamics in legislatures, perhaps because they remain a fairly small minority in most states. For example, women legislators are more likely than their male counterparts to favor reproductive rights, but they do not have an especially powerful impact on a given state's policy regarding this issue. Whether a state devotes much funding toward abortion programs or places a number of restrictions on such programs, including requiring parental notification in the case of minors seeking abortions, depends more on whether the state's overall political culture is liberal or conservative than on whether women make up a large minority of legislative caucuses.[65] Still, gender composition of a state legislature is a difference that makes a difference: Women legislators do tend to bring up issues and concerns that would not be raised by an all-male legislature. One 2017 study, for example, found that states that were closer to gender parity in their legislatures had lower levels of infant mortality.[66] In Nevada in 2017, when 38 percent of the legislators were women, new laws included tax-free tampons, workplace accommodation for pregnant women, a new $500,000 family planning program, and a requirement that health insurers cover contraception and mammograms.

A similar dynamic also holds true when it comes to issues of concern to people of color. African Americans have made gains similar to those of women in legislatures over the past 40 years, growing from a microscopic minority to a larger minority, albeit one that still does not reflect their overall share of the population. The numbers of black legislators have nearly quadrupled, to about 625—less than 10 percent of all the legislators nationwide. Hispanics are even more poorly represented, as detailed below.

Although it can be both dangerous and wrong to generalize about any group, it has been observed that the interests of African Americans as a whole have long been fairly stable and predictable. "On questions of public policy, ideology, and candidate choice," writes Kerry L. Haynie in his 2001 book on black state legislators, "African Americans have been the most cohesive and consistent policy subgroup in United States politics."[67] The fact that there are more black legislators does not mean that voting trends have changed, however. Voting remains polarized along racial lines. Whites will support African American incumbents but are often reluctant to vote for black newcomers. The main reason for the growth in the number of black legislators, therefore, has been the creation of majority-black districts.[68]

Growth in the ranks of Hispanic legislators has been fairly rapid in recent elections, but it still does not nearly reflect the growing Hispanic share of the population as a whole. Hispanics accounted for 5 percent of state legislators nationwide in 2015—up from 3 percent in 2009—but that was still far short of their 17 percent share of the overall population. Hispanics' desires are no different from those of Anglos, suggested Alex Padilla, a former state senator who was elected in 2014 as California's first Latino secretary of state—"safe neighborhoods, clean air and water, good schools, equal opportunity, and sufficient income to raise a family."[69] No demographic group is a monolith, but each has its own priorities and concerns, which is why advocates push to have a more representative share of elected officials. Haynie found that a majority of African American legislators introduce bills that address issues of particular interest to blacks. White legislators seldom introduce such bills. The same holds true for other groups. After Ohio state representative Nickie Antonio, who is a lesbian, joined with colleagues in 2016 to introduce legislation that would classify intimidation or violence against LGBT individuals as hate crimes, the Victory Fund, which promotes LGBT candidates, tweeted, "This is what happens when you #ElectLGBT."[70] Alfonso Lopez, the only Hispanic state lawmaker in Virginia, has tried repeatedly to convince his colleagues to support in-state college tuition rates for students who have lived in the country illegally since childhood. "If we had a more diverse [legislature] and more Hispanics in the House of Delegates, I don't think it would be as difficult," he said.[71] But some legislators have sought to avoid being pigeonholed according to their ethnicity or gender identity. Danica Roem drew national attention in 2017 when she became one of the first transgender legislators elected in the nation by winning a seat in the Virginia House. Roem insisted that her focus would be on issues of universal concern, such as traffic—which, she noted, trans individuals are affected by, like everyone else.

Professional versus Citizen Legislators

As discussed above, legislatures, strictly white male playgrounds in the past, have become more inclusive of women and minorities and more attentive to their concerns. But even bigger changes in legislatures over the past 35 years have come in the very ways they do business. Whereas once legislatures were sleepy backwaters where not much got done—and even less got done ethically—now many chambers are highly professional operations. Most legislatures used to meet for short periods every other year. These days all but a handful meet every year and, in a few cases, nearly year-round. "No single factor has a greater effect on the legislative environment than the constitutional restriction on length of session," two leading legislative scholars wrote long ago.[72]

The most pronounced differences among the states are between "professional" legislatures that meet full-time, pay members high salaries, and employ large staffs and "amateur," or "citizen," legislatures that meet part-time, have members who usually hold other jobs, and have smaller staffs. To some extent, all legislatures have become more professional. Even "amateur" legislators devote a third of their time to legislative work. In the early 1940s, the legislatures of only four states—New Jersey, New York, Rhode Island, and South Carolina—met in annual sessions, but the number meeting yearly has climbed continuously.[73] Today, only four states do not meet in regular annual sessions. Expenditures per legislator have increased above the rate of inflation in nearly every state, and today the most professional legislatures have resources that rival those of the U.S. Congress.[74] Lately, however, that trend has slowed. The number of legislative staffers nationwide steadily dropped between 1996 and 2015 after decades of increases.[75] During tough budget times, legislators often feel they have to make cuts close to home first. In 2015, facing a serious budget shortfall due to declining oil revenues, Alaska's legislature cut its own research staff by 40 percent.[76]

There are many variations among states in the professionalism of their legislatures, and the level of professionalism has profound impacts on legislatures' effectiveness, how much institutional strength they have compared with governors, and how popular they are with the public. Some disagreement still exists about whether professional legislators really do a better job than their citizen-legislator cousins. Typically, however, the more professional a legislature, the more effective it is at the essential jobs of drafting and passing laws and overseeing the governor and the executive branch. With the exception of Texas, the more populous states have highly professional legislatures. Such legislatures are able to provide more resources to their chambers, which allows the chambers to keep up with the wider

STATES UNDER STRESS
#METOO MOVEMENT HELPED EXPOSE HARASSMENT IN LEGISLATURES

After the "me too" movement began to draw attention to problems of sexual abuse, assault, and misconduct among prominent media figures in fall 2017, a fair amount of attention turned to similar issues in state capitols. In 2017 and 2018, more than 40 legislators resigned or were forced from office amid misconduct allegations, including Jeff Hoover, the speaker of the Kentucky House.

"Each of us has endured, or witnessed or worked with women who have experienced some form of dehumanizing behavior by men with power in our workplaces," a group of 140 women who were involved in California politics wrote in 2017. "Men have groped and touched us without our consent, made inappropriate comments about our bodies and our abilities. Insults and sexual innuendo, frequently disguised as jokes, have undermined our professional positions and capabilities."

Sexual harassment scandals had already toppled many powerful lawmakers. In 2015, the Missouri House speaker lost his job after he was caught texting lewd messages to a 19-year-old intern. A year earlier, the assembly majority leader in Wisconsin went to jail for a groping incident. In 2013, one of the most prominent members of the New York Assembly stepped down before an expulsion vote, after an ethics commission found he harassed at least eight staffers. "I can say that as an elected official, as a state representative I have experienced this first-hand," Rhode Island state representative Teresa Tanzi told the *Providence Journal*. "I have been told sexual favors would allow my bills to go further."

Tennessee attorney general Herbert Slattery's office interviewed dozens of women in 2016 as it investigated sexual harassment complaints against then representative Jeremy Durham. Slattery's report not only implicated Durham, but it also cast a pall over the entire legislative culture in Nashville. "As legislative clerk Jane Doe #12 explained, when she told Rep. Durham that his requests for drinks with her in 2013 were inappropriate because he was married and she was engaged, she said his response was, 'Welcome to Capitol Hill,'" the report stated. The attorney general's office concluded that Durham had "inappropriate contact" with 22 women. The dossier included allegations that Durham sent inappropriate text messages, groped lobbyists, and had sex with a 20-year-old intern. In a rare move, the Tennessee House expelled Durham last September, by a 70–2 vote.

Even within the male-dominated political world, state legislatures can be especially fertile places for sexual harassment to thrive. A makeshift community of lawmakers, lobbyists, staff members, interns, and pages convenes for long hours, with many of them far from home. Socializing, often with the addition of alcohol, is par for the legislative course. And there are huge power disparities that make it difficult to police or punish sexual harassment. Legislatures don't have human resources, and legislators don't even have bosses women can complain to.

And it's not just legislators who harass women. It's lobbyists and staffers, too. "In this legislature, [sexual harassment] is more prevalent among the lobbyists than it is among the members," said Susan McKee, who served as a district director for Darrell Steinberg for 17 years, including his time as president of the California Senate. "The lobbyists have nothing to lose. They're not in the public eye. The members, even though they're not at home, they still have potential to be outed and named as harassers."

"One woman recalls being asked the color of her underwear while lobbying a lawmaker on a bill," the *Kansas City Star* reported. "Another talks of late-night texts from her boss asking if she would like to come to his apartment for a drink. A former intern says that when she finally got her boss to stop sending flirty text messages, he began treating her coldly and left her out of important projects."

"The culture of Jefferson City is very anything goes," said former state senator John Lamping, who left office in 2014. "We're in town three days a week, and we don't work particularly late very often. So the mentality is, 'Wow, this is so much fun. We're doing crazier stuff than we did in college. But now we have power, prestige, and money.'"

One of the big problems with changing the boys-club atmosphere in state capitols is that the culture is so ingrained, it's hard for anyone to change it, even if the number of women in the legislature increases. Most legislatures quickly changed their harassment policies and implemented new training regimens in the face of the "me too" movement. But it remains to be seen whether their cultures will change appreciably.

Source: Adapted from Daniel C. Vock, "As Outcry over Sexual Harassment Grows, Focus Shifts to State Legislatures," *Governing*, October 18, 2017, http://www.governing.com/topics/politics/gov-sexual-harassment-state-legislatures.html.

variety of issues that arise in densely populated states in comparison with most of their less populous neighbors. Legislatures in some states, such as Pennsylvania and California, meet essentially year-round; in contrast, Montana's part-time legislature meets for just 90 days in only odd-numbered years.

More populous states have the money to invest in the full-time legislatures that are necessary for their governments to keep on top of issues facing these states' more complicated and developed economies and diverse populations. The reason that Texas, with a population second only to California's, has a part-time legislature lies in the state's distrust of government in general. Texas is one of only nine states that do not impose an income tax, and a legislature that meets only part-time every other year is in keeping with this general low-tax, low-service point of view. Other states have traditions of embracing more expansive government. States with historic progressive traditions, such as Michigan and Wisconsin, have long used full-time, professional legislators with substantial staffs at their command.

As distrust of government has spread to more state capitols, there have been some moves to reverse the trend toward better-staffed, more expensive, more professionalized legislatures. Efforts to turn the Michigan legislature into a part-time body, although so far unsuccessful, have been launched repeatedly over the past dozen years. In Pennsylvania, efforts to scale back the legislature's spending on itself grew out of a double-digit pay increase legislators approved for themselves at 2:00 A.M. on July 7, 2005. Since then, one perennial idea promoted by some in the state has been to save money by having fewer legislators. No one could accuse Pennsylvania's house members of serving their own career interests when they voted in 2012 for a constitutional amendment that would have cut the house from 203 to 153 members.[77] The senate, which the amendment would have shrunk from 50 members to 38, did not act on the proposal. The house in 2014 tried again with a proposal that would have shrunk its own numbers by 50 but the number of senators by just 5. That didn't go any further, however. In 2016, Maine governor Paul LePage, a Republican who often feuded with his legislature, proposed shrinking the house from 151 to 100 members and the senate from 35 to 25 seats, in exchange for increasing legislative salaries by 25 percent—and more than doubling the governor's salary.[78]

The northeastern states have maintained their traditional interest in hands-on government, which grew out of their old practices of self-government, including town hall meetings. These states boast some of the largest legislatures. The New Hampshire House is the most extreme example, with 400 members—one for every 3,300 or so state residents. California's legislature is one of the best equipped and most professional in the country. It has to be, considering that each member of the assembly has more than 450,000 constituents.

Some states impose severe restrictions on the meeting times of their legislatures. In Colorado, the state constitution limits the house and the senate to no more than 120 days per year. Sometimes such limits are honored mostly in the breach. The governor may insist that the legislature meet in special session to address a budget crisis or other issue that cannot wait until the next regular session. Or the legislature may simply carve out a little more time for itself, as happened in 2002 in North Carolina. House rules require that the chamber be shut down by 9:00 P.M., so members stopped the clock one night at 8:50, essentially "freezing time," and then continued debate until 3:35 A.M. to finish a session that had run for months longer than expected.[79] Similarly, in Maryland, legislators in 2016 bought themselves some extra time at the end of what was scheduled to be a 90-day session. "For those keeping track at home, today is April 4th in the Senate and April 5th in the House," *Baltimore Sun* reporter Rachel Baye noted on April 11.[80]

Just like most of us, legislators feel intensely the pressure to get their work done on time. The fact that they have deadlines—for passing budgets or for adjournment—usually keeps them focused in much the same way that a final exam will make college students finally hit the books or do their serious Googling at term's end. Newspapers, however, routinely report on legislatures missing their budget deadlines and often publish commentary critical of the practice. The reality is that a legislature is pretty cheap to operate—in no state does it cost much more than 0.5 percent of the state budget—but elected officials know that their overtime does not play well with voters.[81]

TABLE 7-2 ● State House Demographic Diversity: Total Numbers and Percentages of Legislators Who Are Women, African American, and Hispanic, 2017

State	Total Number of Legislative Seats	Women State Legislators		African American State Legislators		Hispanic State Legislators	
		Total	Percentage of Total Seats	Total	Percentage of Total Seats	Total	Percentage of Total Seats
Alabama	140	20	14.3	34	24	0	0
Alaska	60	17	28.3	0	0	2	3.3
Arizona	90	32	35.6	1	1.1	19	21.1
Arkansas	135	27	20	15	11	0	0
California	120	31	25.8	11	9.2	23	19.2
Colorado	100	41	41	3	3	4	4
Connecticut	187	53	28.3	13	7	13	7
Delaware	62	15	24.2	4	6.5	2	3.2
Florida	160	40	25	25	16	21	13.1
Georgia	236	54	22.8	59	25	2	0.8
Hawaii	76	22	28.9	1	1.3	0	0
Idaho	105	29	27.6	1	1	0	0
Illinois	177	57	32.2	32	18.1	12	6.8
Indiana	150	32	21.3	12	8	2	1.3
Iowa	150	35	23.3	5	3.3	0	0
Kansas	165	41	24.8	8	4.8	5	3
Kentucky	138	24	17.4	7	5	1	0.7
Louisiana	144	17	11.8	32	22.2	1	0.7
Maine	186	54	29	2	1.1	0	0
Maryland	188	58	30.8	43	22.9	6	3.2
Massachusetts	200	52	26	6	3	6	3
Michigan	148	31	20.9	13	8.8	4	2.7
Minnesota	201	66	32.8	2	1	4	2
Mississippi	174	30	17.2	49	28.2	0	0
Missouri	197	49	24.8	18	9.1	2	1
Montana	150	47	31.3	0	0	2	1.3
Nebraska	49	10	20.4	2	4.1	0	0

State	Total Number of Legislative Seats	Women State Legislators		African American State Legislators		Hispanic State Legislators	
		Total	Percentage of Total Seats	Total	Percentage of Total Seats	Total	Percentage of Total Seats
Nevada	63	21	33.3	6	9.5	9	14.3
New Hampshire	424	123	29	4	0.94	0	0
New Jersey	120	36	30	17	14.2	11	9.2
New Mexico	112	30	26.8	1	0.9	41	36.6
New York	213	53	24.8	32	15	17	8
North Carolina	170	37	21.8	34	20	2	1.2
North Dakota	141	27	19.1	0	0	0	0
Ohio	132	33	25	15	11.4	3	2.3
Oklahoma	149	20	13.4	3	2	1	0.7
Oregon	90	28	31.1	2	2.2	3	3.3
Pennsylvania	253	45	17.8	20	8	3	1.2
Rhode Island	113	30	26.5	5	4.4	3	2.7
South Carolina	170	24	14.1	39	22.9	0	0
South Dakota	105	22	21	0	0	0	0
Tennessee	132	24	18.2	17	12.9	0	0
Texas	181	36	20	18	9.9	42	23.2
Utah	104	16	15.4	2	1.9	3	2.9
Vermont	180	73	40.6	2	1.1	2	1.1
Virginia	140	24	17.1	17	12	1	0.7
Washington	147	48	32.7	1	0.7	1	0.7
West Virginia	134	20	14.9	1	0.7	0	0
Wisconsin	132	33	25	7	5.3	3	2.3
Wyoming	90	12	13.3	1	1.1	2	2.2
Total	7,382	1,799	24.4	642	8.6	278	4.8

Source: National Conference of State Legislatures, "Legislator Demographics," 2016, http://www.ncsl.org/research/about-state-legislatures/who-we-elect-an-interactive-graphic.aspx.

Mississippi's largest newspaper, the *Clarion Ledger*, for instance, ran a typical editorial condemning legislators for wasting money in a special session in 2008, even though the extra time cost the state only $59,895 for the first day and $39,420 for each day after that. At that rate, the session would have had to drag on for weeks to add just 1 percent to the $90 million budget deficit the state faced the next year.[82] Such media coverage is one reason legislatures, even as they are becoming more professional and getting better at their jobs, remain unpopular with the public. Map 7-4 shows the breakdown of full-time, hybrid, and part-time legislatures among the states.

The Citizens' Whipping Boy: Legislators and Public Opinion

In the past, legislatures were, to put it bluntly, sexist, racist, secretive, boss ruled, malapportioned, and uninformed. Alabama's legislature was an extreme but representative case. In 1971, it ranked 50th out of the 50 state legislatures in independence, 50th in accountability, and 48th in overall performance in a Ford Foundation study. Yet, just three years earlier, 65 percent of the respondents in a statewide poll judged the institution favorably. By 1990, the legislature had freed

MAP 7-4 ● Full-Time, Hybrid, and Part-Time Legislatures

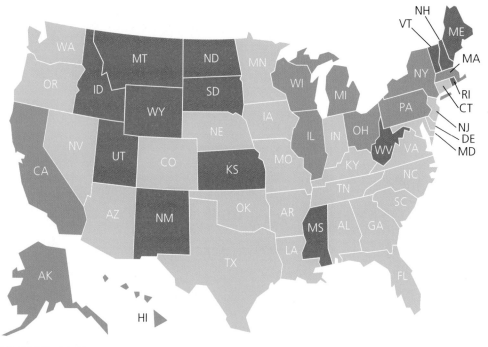

Category of Legislature	Average Time on the Job	Average Compensation	Average Staff per Legislature
Full-time	84%	$82,358	1,250
Hybrid	74%	$41,110	469
Part-time	57%	$18,449	160

- Full-time Legislatures
- Hybrid Legislatures
- Part-time Legislatures

Source: Data compiled from the National Conference of State Legislatures, "Full- and Part-Time Legislatures," June 14, 2017, http://www.ncsl.org/research/about-state-legislatures/full-and-part-time-legislatures.aspx.

itself of its institutional racism, secrecy, and malapportionment and was fully equipped to gather information and operate in a new state-of-the-art legislative facility. That year, it received an approval rating of 24 percent.[83] Remarkably, some legislatures have fallen even further than that in the public's opinion in recent years. During a leadership crisis in 2009, just 11 percent of New Yorkers said the state senate was doing an excellent or good job.[84] The California legislature's approval rating fell to 10 percent in fall 2010 and never exceeded 23 percent from September 2008 to February 2012.[85]

To a large extent, the general public does not view large staffs and good salaries as ways of ensuring that legislators do their jobs in a professional manner. Instead, these increases in legislative resources are seen as yet more proof that politicians want to exploit their offices for personal gain. Rather than reacting strongly to policy issues, the public is quick to anger over such ethical questions as legislative pay raises and other perks for elected officials. "The public does not want the same thing out of a legislature that you think they might want," says John Hibbing, a University of Nebraska political scientist who has written about the unpopularity of legislatures. "The public wants a legislature whose members are not in a position to feather their own nests."[86]

Legislators have done a poor job of selling the idea that what they do is important and necessary in a democracy. "It's our fault" that the legislature is viewed as "dysfunctional," "sheep," and "not independent," says Richard Brodsky, a member of the New York Assembly until 2010. "We have never gotten the message out in a coherent way of what we do well and right."[87]

For their part, the media are more concerned with dramatizing conflicts than with explaining what are sometimes awfully dry policy matters; therefore, they have not helped legislators to make their case. The media have made boo-boo coverage practically the mainstay of government reporting. This is not true in 100 percent of cases, of course, but the press's general attitude toward government was summed up well a few years ago by a reporter in Pennsylvania who told a public official, "Your job is to manage the public business and mine is to report when you do it wrong."[88] To be fair, a year doesn't go by without several legislators being charged with crimes. The *Sacramento Bee* couldn't resist pointing out that, with 3 out of the 40 California state senators arrested in 2014, the chamber had a higher arrest rate than any of the state's 25 largest cities.[89] The last time the New York legislature held a session in which no members resigned due to ethics or legal troubles was 2001–2002.[90]

Reporters may be cynical about what legislators are up to, but a bigger problem might be that there are so few reporters watching them. A primary job of the media in a democracy is to report on what the government is up to, but less and less media attention is devoted to legislatures. "The number of reporters covering the statehouse has dropped dramatically since I started here in 1980s," John Crangle, then head of Common Cause in South Carolina, said in 2017. "The *Greenville News* had three reporters, now it has one. The *Post and Courier* had four, now it has two. The *Spartanburg Herald* had three, now it has zero."[91] The story is similar in most states. According to the Pew Research Center, the number of reporters covering state capitols full-time dropped by 35 percent between 2003 and 2014. Less than a third of all newspapers and less than 15 percent of local television stations employed any statehouse reporters, with no full-time statehouse reporters from TV stations at all in 18 states. Students, who necessarily work part-time and have short tenures on the job, make up 14 percent of the total statehouse news corps.[92] "Every time you tweet about Justin Bieber, another state capital newspaper bureau shuts down," tweeted Brian Duggan, an editor with the *Reno Journal-Gazette*.[93]

Some of the slack has been taken up by new online-only publications, from blogs written by single activists and political junkies to nonprofit outlets with something closer to traditional newsrooms and staffs. Many of the nonprofits, such as MinnPost, the Texas Tribune, and CALmatters, have gone quickly from startups to leading sources of news for state government officials, lobbyists, and fellow reporters. They've broken big stories, such as California Watch's investigation of the earthquake risk of state schools. As newspapers can attest, however, good statehouse reporting does not guarantee a viable business model. And the total number of outlets and reporters paying attention to legislatures has declined. As a result of diminished coverage, says Gary Moncrief, a political scientist at Boise State University, "I'm not sure the American public is very attuned to the inner workings of legislatures and the fact that they probably do work better today than 30 or 40 years ago."[94]

While fewer reporters are covering statehouses, legislators have found ways to cut out the middleman. Through social media sites such as Facebook, YouTube,

Article III, Section 11, of the **SOUTH DAKOTA** Constitution gives legislators protections from arrest during sessions of the legislature and during their travel to and from sessions.

and Twitter, legislators are able to communicate directly with their constituents and the wider world more easily than ever before. In a typical example, New Jersey senator Jim Whelan held a town hall meeting in July 2012 during which he answered questions from a radio host on the Senate Democrats' Ustream channel while simultaneously accepting tweeted questions from the public via his own Twitter feed. Afterward, the chat was posted on the Democrats' Ustream channel, their YouTube page, and Whelan's own YouTube page.[95] "The media are very fractured right now," said Connecticut senator Bob Duff. "I have to find many ways to communicate with my constituents."[96]

The decline of general coverage and the rise of often partisan commentary and news sites on the Web are among the reasons that amateur legislatures are much more popular with their constituents than are more professional chambers. The urge to return legislatures to their more humble but lovable position as citizen institutions has been the main driver behind the term-limits movement. Limits on the number of terms an individual may serve in the house or senate have been approved in most of the states that allow ballot initiatives. There are 15 states with term limits, ranging from a low of 6 years of service per legislative chamber in Michigan to 12 years of service in states such as Nevada, Oklahoma, and Louisiana.

In 1990, California voters sent a strong message. When they limited terms, they also cut the legislature's budget and staffing levels by 40 percent—the third cut in six years. Legislators in California, as well as Arkansas, have since persuaded voters to increase the number of years a politician can serve in either the house or the senate, while keeping overall limits for service in the legislature intact.

Academic studies in term-limit states, including California, Colorado, and Maine, have found that legislators in those states make far fewer changes to governors' budgets than they used to, representing many billions of dollars in legislative discretion that is no longer exercised. "The crumbling of legislative power is clear across states," said Thad Kousser, a political scientist at the University of California, San Diego, and author of a book about term limits. "There's no more clear finding in the research than a shift in power where the legislature is becoming a less than equal branch of government."[97]

Conclusion

Legislatures have one of the toughest jobs in the political system. Imagine trying to get a hundred or more people—many of whom flat-out oppose your preferred choice—to sign off on something as controversial as, say, a welfare bill.

Senator Wendy Davis/Twitter

▲

Many state legislators attempt to keep their constituents informed about their doings through social media. On her Twitter feed, Texas Democratic state senator and 2014 candidate for governor Wendy Davis lets her supporters know where she'll be making appearances and what she thinks about events unfolding in the state.

Now imagine trying to do that over and over again—researching; negotiating; meeting; balancing partisan interests, special interests, and constituent interests; and, finally, hammering out an agreement that no one is fully satisfied with and everyone is willing to criticize. That gives you some idea of the reality of a legislator's job.

Historically speaking, legislators today do their jobs more effectively and more fairly than legislators at any previous time. For this achievement, they are mistrusted and disliked. Why? Ultimately, perhaps it is because a legislature can never give all the people everything they want. Democracy is simply not set up to do this, because people want very different things. Legislatures do not really create conflict; they simply reflect the disagreements that exist in the electorate. Or at least they do if the legislators are reasonably effective at representing the preferences of their constituencies. What democracy promises, and what state legislatures largely deliver, is not what everyone wants—on most issues, no such option exists. Rather, democracy is about reasonable compromises that most people can live with.

STATES UNDER STRESS
FIVE REASONS WHY STATE HOUSE SPEAKERS MAY BE PRONE TO CORRUPTION

The sight of legislative leaders being thrown in jail has become fairly common in recent years. Within a single month in 2016, former New York Assembly speaker Sheldon Silver and former New York Senate majority leader Dean Skelos were separately sentenced to years in prison on multiple federal corruption charges.

Both faced new trials in 2018 after their initial convictions were thrown out due to new guidance from the Supreme Court regarding public corruption cases. But when Silver was first charged in 2015, he became the fourth state house speaker in 10 months to enter into legal peril. The others were the speakers in Alabama, Rhode Island, and South Carolina. "It's not all 50 states, but four out of 50 is pretty bad," said Brendan Nyhan, an expert on political scandals at Dartmouth College. Ohio House speaker Cliff Rosenberger resigned in 2018 amid an FBI investigation into foreign trips he took that were sponsored by overseas interest and his occupancy of a condo owned by a major campaign donor.

Any politician might get into trouble, but this particular cluster of indictments opened up the question of whether there is something in the nature of the job of house speaker that makes corruption more likely to occur. There are some plausible reasons why a legislative leader could have extra chances to get into trouble.

1. Lots of Power . . .

Speakers are powerful figures, often able to control their chambers in a hierarchical way not available to many other political leaders. "The Speaker is at the top of that pyramid in a way that is rare even for the Senate," said Thom Little, research director for the State Legislative Leaders Foundation. "The power is greater pretty much than any other legislative office."

Speakers can kill bills quietly, Little noted, simply by assigning legislation to hostile committees. Governors may need to issue veto messages, but speakers can do much of their work secretly.

"Under Alabama's constitution, the speaker's position is by far the most powerful in the state," said journalist Bill Britt. "No legislation can move in the House without his approval."[a]

2. . . . but Not Much Scrutiny

Speakers may be powerful, but they receive comparatively little media attention. Most people can name their state's governor, but few people know who the speaker is. Do you know the name of the house speaker in your state? Did you know it before you signed up for this class?

"Legislative leaders have a great deal of power but face very little scrutiny," Nyhan said. "That's a combination that can certainly lead to corruption, especially in states where that tends to be more of a problem."

3. Limited Political Pressure

Speakers not only receive less media attention than governors, but they also answer to fewer voters than any comparably powerful politicians.

(Continued)

(Continued)

They might represent districts that account for one-hundredth of their state's population, or even a smaller fraction. "They're elected locally, but their impact is statewide," said Pam Wilmot, executive director of Common Cause in Massachusetts, where three of the last four speakers have resigned and pleaded guilty to criminal charges.

Not only are their districts small and generally safe, but often the majorities they lead are safe as well. In New York, Rhode Island, and South Carolina, it's been years since party control has changed in the house chambers. That's not the case in Alabama, but Republicans now control the whole of state government there, and scandals have involved politicians in other branches. Single-party control reduces the watchdog effect that an opposition party can have. "When you have one chamber controlled by the other party, they're looking at everything you do," Little said.

4. The Tendency to Play Let's Make a Deal

Speakers are able to direct huge sums of money. And, in an era when caucus leadership political action committees can dominate legislative campaign fundraising, they need huge sums of money. "Speakers have enormous power and the duty to raise large amounts of political money," said former North Carolina speaker Joe Hackney. Yet, he noted,

the job itself doesn't pay that much. "The confluence of those three things makes it really dangerous territory."

Hackney himself became speaker after his predecessor, Jim Black, became embroiled in a set of corruption scandals.

Not all speakers go looking for trouble. But the nature of the job is making deals, so politicians with that job have plenty of opportunities to cut themselves in. "There is a lot more deal-making in the legislative process than there is in the executive branch," said Wilmot, the Common Cause official.

5. Tempting Targets for Prosecutors

Making public corruption cases is always tough for prosecutors—there generally isn't tangible evidence like drugs waiting to be seized, quips Nyhan, the Dartmouth government professor—but elected officials, particularly those as prominent as state house speakers, still make tempting targets for ambitious prosecutors. Lots of New York legislators have gone to prison in recent years, but the power and prestige that Silver and Skelos held made them stand out.

"Prosecutors may choose to go after the big fish," said Nyhan. "They may choose to target the most powerful legislators in places where corruption is a problem, both as punishment and as a signal to others."

Source: Adapted from Alan Greenblatt, "5 Reasons State House Speakers May Be Prone to Corruption," *Governing*, January 26, 2015, http://www.governing.com/topics/politics/gov-speakers-indicted-new-york-rhode-island-south-carolina-alabama.html.

[a]Quoted in Joe Miller, "Is Mike Hubbard the Most Corrupt Politician in America?," *New Republic*, May 16, 2016, https://newrepublic.com/article/133504/mike-hubbard-corrupt-politician-america.

THE LATEST RESEARCH

This chapter has noted at various points the differences across legislatures that can make a difference. Term limits, partisanship and ideology, the sociodemographics of a legislature—all these can make a difference to legislative agendas, policy priorities, and whose political preferences are, or are not, represented. Given the importance

of these differences, it is not surprising that scholars are interested in their causes and consequences.

Below we summarize some of the latest research that employs the comparative method to explore how these legislative differences translate into power and policymaking.

- **Fouirnaies, Alexander, and Andrew B. Hall,** "How Do Electoral Incentives Affect Legislator Behavior?," paper in progress, http://www .andrewbenjaminhall.com/Fouirnaies_Hall_ Electoral_Incentives.pdf.

Some skeptics believe that it's hard for voters to hold politicians accountable simply because they don't have enough information or pay enough attention to how elected officials behave. To explore this question, the authors look at productivity among legislators, which they define as sponsoring bills, performing more committee service, and simply showing up for recorded votes. They have constructed a data set that covers more than 780,000 bills and more than 16 million votes cast over a 30-year period. They find that legislators are more productive when they face reelection and less productive when they are no longer allowed to seek reelection due to term limits. They find that this effect is especially strong in states with lifetime term limits (as opposed to those that allow legislators to return after a break) and in states where legislative salaries are higher and so "the desire to win reelection may be higher."

- **Jansa, Joshua M., Eric R. Hansen, and Virginia H. Gray,** "Copy and Paste Lawmaking: The Diffusion of Policy Language across American State Legislatures," *American Politics Research*, May 31, 2018.

Pressed for time and resources, state legislators often copy and paste prewritten text rather than writing policies from scratch; their sources for material include other states, interest groups, policy entrepreneurs, and intergovernmental agencies. Writing bills takes time, particularly the drafting of appropriate legal language. Politicians would rather spend their time raising money. They also may want to implement policies similar to those being adopted in other states. As a shortcut, they sometimes adopt language wholesale from other sources, especially if model legislation is being circulated from state to state by interest groups. Looking at 12 different policy proposals, Jansa and his colleagues find that copying is more common with those concerning economic matters than with those on social issues. They find no evidence that conservative bills are copied wholesale more often than liberal ones.

- **Makse, Todd,** "The Retention of Expertise and Productivity in State Legislative Committees," *State Politics and Policy Quarterly* 17, no. 4 (2017): 418–440.

Given the range and complexity of issues that state legislatures grapple with, specialization by legislators in various issue areas is crucial to their productivity. Most specialization occurs in committees, which are charged with generating and examining legislation in particular areas of jurisdiction, such as agriculture or finance. These committees, however, experience far more turnover than congressional committees. Over a 10-year period, "unforced" committee turnover (meaning changes in personnel not caused by departures of individual lawmakers) in the U.S. House was 15.8 percent, but in the 14 states examined by the author, the average was 24.5 percent. Comparing those states, he finds even small changes in committee membership retention have substantial effects on how much legislation is produced.

- **Richardson, Lilliard, and Jeffrey Milyo,** "Giving the People What They Want? Legislative Polarization and Public Approval of State Legislatures," *State and Local Government Review* 48, no. 4 (2016): 270–281.

Partisan polarization is a central issue in contemporary American politics. Elite observers frequently view it as a problem that contributes to governmental dysfunction. How do voters feel about it? The authors compare public approval of state legislatures with the polarization of those bodies. Not surprisingly, supporters of the parties out of power are unhappy, but they find that in general citizens do not hold negative views of legislatures that are more polarized or run by more extreme majority parties. Older and more educated individuals are significantly less likely to approve of their state legislature, while professionalized legislatures and those controlled by Democrats are also viewed more negatively. But "polarization by itself does not have a large negative effect on public approval. . . . Most citizens appear to prefer (or at least not mind) political polarization and major party extremism."

CHAPTER 7

for CQ Press

Want a better grade?

Get the tools you need to sharpen your study skills. SAGE edge offers a robust online environment featuring an impressive array of free tools and resources.

Access practice quizzes, eFlashcards, video, and multimedia at **edge.sagepub.com/ smithgreenblatt7e**

Top Ten Takeaways

1. Legislatures create and pass laws that set the policy direction for their states.

2. Legislators perform constituent service work, meaning they help residents of their districts navigate state agencies to get the services they need.

3. Legislators are responsible for government oversight, meaning they are supposed to monitor executive branch agencies.

4. Legislatures are heavily lobbied by interest groups promoting bills that favor their industries or causes. They face equal amounts of pleading from other groups seeking to kill bills they don't like.

5. The top leaders within each chamber hold enormous power in terms of determining which bills are given serious consideration and chance of passage.

6. Legislatures have become more diverse over the past generation, but they still do not reflect the demographics of the population as a whole.

7. Legislatures have become more professional over the past generation, but voters view them warily, skeptical of the need for support staff and put off by scandals.

8. With fewer traditional news outlets covering statehouses, voters have a harder time learning about what's happening in their capitals.

9. Term limits have served to weaken legislatures as institutions.

10. In a polarized era, there are huge variations among the states in the ways they approach contentious issues such as abortion, gay rights, gun control, and taxes.

Key Concepts

apportionment (p. 194)
casework (p. 183)
caucus (p. 188)
coalition building (p. 177)
committee (p. 176)
compromise (p. 177)
constituent service (p. 183)
delegates (p. 193)
districts (p. 177)

filibuster (p. 177)
gerrymanders (p. 195)
incumbent (p. 183)
logrolling (p. 177)
majority rule (p. 176)
majority–minority districts
   (p. 196)
malapportionment (p. 195)
override (p. 175)

oversight (p. 184)
professionalization (p. 194)
rank-and-file members
   (p. 193)
representation (p. 181)
riders (p. 177)
trustees (p. 193)
veto (p. 175)

Suggested Websites

- **www.alec.org.** Website for the American Legislative Exchange Council, an influential conservative organization that drafts model legislation. ALEC members include both legislators and private-sector interests.

- **americanlegislatures.com.** A website maintained by two political scientists that offers voting data for state legislative chambers dating back several decades.

- **www.csg.org.** Website for the Council of State Governments, which provides training and information to state government officials.

- **www.ncsl.org.** Website of the National Conference of State Legislatures; provides a wealth of information about legislative structures and procedures, as well as the major issues faced by legislators.

- **stateline.org.** A foundation-sponsored news service that provides daily news about state government.

David Kidd/Governing

Governors and Executives

There Is No Such Thing as Absolute Power

Gina Raimondo, the Democratic governor of Rhode Island, spent much of her first term touting jobs brought to the state by companies such as General Dynamics, Infosys, and Johnson & Johnson.

Chapter Objectives

After reading this chapter, you will be able to

- Describe the various roles of the governor,
- Identify the different types of power held by the governor,
- Discuss who becomes governor and how, and
- Identify other executive offices and their roles.

Scott Walker has done as much to reshape the political landscape of his state as any contemporary politician. Not long after taking office as governor of Wisconsin in 2011, the Republican convinced the legislature to pass a law stripping most public employees of collective bargaining rights, effectively eviscerating their unions. In 2015, he weakened unions in the private sector by signing a bill making Wisconsin a right-to-work state, meaning employees no longer had to pay union dues even at unionized companies. In 2016, Walker brought to an end the state's century-old civil service system, making it easier for the administration to fire employees and to give jobs to campaign contributors and other allies.

Along the way, Walker also promoted legislation restricting abortion rights and imposing voter identification requirements, slashed state support for higher education, cut taxes, and reduced environmental regulations. His agenda helped turn Wisconsin into arguably the most polarized state in the country, divided between conservatives who felt he had helped put a historically progressive state on a more sustainable course and liberals who believed he had weakened the state in order to aid corporate interests. "What's happened in Wisconsin is symptomatic of what's going on nationally," says James Conant, a political scientist at George Mason University who worked as an aide to a Democratic governor in Wisconsin. "They have a very clear philosophy and a clear approach to governing. They're going about systematically dismantling the public sector."[1]

Walker's agenda made him a conservative darling and a viable contender for the presidency—even an early frontrunner—although he ended his campaign for his party's presidential nomination just two months after he'd officially started it in 2015. He hoped that his narrative—that he had taken on unions and other

entrenched interests and won—would prove appealing on the national level. His candidacy faltered, but he returned to Wisconsin eager to continue his mission, becoming the only GOP (or Grand Old Party) governor out of many first elected in 2010 to seek a third term in 2018. (He lost.) Walker's career has demonstrated the extent to which one person—if he or she is a governor—can entirely change the terms of political debate within a state.

The governor, as head of the executive branch, is in charge of executing the laws passed by the legislature. "Ideology and politics stand in the way, but one way or another the roads must be fixed," Democratic governor Jerry Brown of California declared in 2016.[2]

But the governor also acts to shape the legislative agenda, generally setting the terms of debate when it comes to passage of budgets and often convincing legislators to pursue a particular policy course. Even a governor's friends in the legislature can feel big-footed by the executive. "In a world that is so driven by the executive branch, the legislative branch really should be more prominent than it is," says Robin Vos, the Republican speaker of the Wisconsin House. "My goal is that when I leave, the legislative branch is equally as important as the governor."[3]

Governors are like mini-presidents in their states. Like the president, the governor commands the lion's share of political attention in a state, is generally seen as setting the agenda for the legislative branch, and is basically the lead political actor—the figure most likely to appear on television on a regular basis. Also like the president, the governor tends to receive the blame or enjoy the credit for the performance of the economy. "We have a whole political system that judges our executives by the state of the economy, over which they have virtually no impact," Brown said in 2018. "So, you figure it out."[4]

The amount of power granted to governors varies by state. Even in states where the governors hold fewer cards, however, legislators hesitate to go up against them. "If you're a legislator and you look at the governor, he's calling the shots, whoever he is," Rutgers University political scientist Alan Rosenthal said—at the annual meeting of the National Conference of State Legislatures, no less.[5]

Governors are unique among state-level politicians in terms of the media attention they can attract. This helps them promote their causes. "The weakest governor has a built-in advantage over the strongest legislature," said Rosenthal, who wrote a book on governors titled *The Best Job in Politics*.

> **Governors are like mini-presidents in their states. Like the president, the governor commands the lion's share of political attention in a state, is generally seen as setting the agenda for the legislative branch, and is basically the lead political actor—the figure most likely to appear on television on a regular basis. Also like the president, the governor tends to receive the blame or enjoy the credit for the performance of the economy.**

Still, they must rely on other institutional players if they are going to accomplish more than making speeches. Like the president, the governor shares responsibility for running the government—implementing laws, issuing regulations, and doing the work of building the roads, maintaining the parks, and performing other public functions—with the help of a cabinet. Presidents appoint their cabinet officials to run the Departments of Defense and Agriculture and the like. Governors have help in running state-level departments of agriculture, finance, environmental protection, and so on. In most cases, the governor appoints officials to head these departments, but some other statewide officials, such as attorneys general and secretaries of state, often are elected on their own and may even represent another party. We explore the roles of these other executive branch officials later in this chapter. As you read, keep in mind the following questions:

- **How did governors get to be such powerful players, when for much of American history their offices were weak?**

- **Why do some states still give their governors more pomp than power?**

In this chapter, we look at how the office of governor has changed over the years. We examine the types of powers governors can command by virtue of the office and which powers they must create out of the force of personality. We also look at what sorts of people get elected governor and how they get elected. Finally, we survey some of the other important statewide offices, such as lieutenant governor and attorney general.

The Job of Governor

Recently, governors have become a lot better equipped to control the rest of the executive branch, and they are running states in fact as well as in theory. For more than 100 years after the founding of the American republic, governors were strong in title only, with little real power. Throughout the last decades of the 20th century, however, governors were given more and more formal control over the machinery of government at the same time the federal government was shifting greater control of many programs, including welfare, to the states. Governors have longer terms than they once did and enjoy greater authority to appoint the top officials in virtually all government agencies. (Only New Hampshire and Vermont still have two-year gubernatorial terms. The rest of the states have four-year terms. Only Virginia limits its chief executive to a single consecutive term—although two-term limits are common among the states.) These changes were the results of the enactment of laws in many states that were specifically designed to strengthen the office of governor in the hope of creating greater accountability and coherence in government. Governors are now, with few exceptions, not just the most famous politicians in their states but also the most powerful.

Following the American Revolution, governors had very little power for one simple reason—distrust. Colonial governors, appointed by the British, had imposed unpopular taxes and exploited their positions to make themselves rich. Americans did not want to invest too much power in individuals who might turn into mini-dictators. There was no national president, after all, under the original Articles of Confederation. In the states, most of the power was disbursed among many individuals holding office in legislatures and on state boards and commissions. Governors in all but three of the original states were limited to one-year terms. Some early state constitutions gave more power to legislatures than to governors, while some adopted a **plural-executive system**, in which the governor was but one elected administrator among many. Governors were not given control over state departments and agencies. Separately elected individuals, boards, or commissions ran these instead. After his state's constitutional convention, one North Carolina delegate said that the governor had been given just enough power "to sign the receipt for his salary."[6]

The number of agencies grew as government became more complex toward the end of the 19th century. Lack of central control over these agencies, however, meant that states had difficulty functioning coherently. Governors still lacked the authority to perform in ways the public expected of them, given their position at the top of the political pyramid. This problem persisted well into the 20th century.

Lynn Muchmore, a political scientist, sums up the sorts of frustrations governors had as late as the 1980s in terms of getting various parts of government to act as they wished. Muchmore lays out a theoretical case of a governor elected on a platform of promoting growth in the state's rural areas and documents the difficulties he had in making good on those promises. In this scenario, the new governor found that the highway department, which was run by a separate commission, had decided a decade ago to complete urban segments of the state's road system. This decision siphoned money away from plans to develop better roads in rural areas. The board that oversaw the public colleges and universities had a policy of phasing out satellite campuses in favor of investing in three urban campuses. The state's department of commerce would not work in any county that did not have a local economic development corporation. Many rural counties lacked such corporations because they did not have the population or tax base to support them. And the state legislature had passed restrictions that denied new businesses breaks on rural utility rates.[7] Despite his promises, the governor's battle to help rural areas was an uphill one.

Not every scenario is so extreme, but it is often the case that state agencies not headed by people appointed by the governor—and therefore not answering to him or her—have their own constituencies and concerns. They do not have in mind the big picture of how the different parts of state government can best work together to promote the general good. Only the governor sees the whole field in that way. Long after leaving office, former Maryland governor Marvin Mandel counted as his proudest accomplishment the consolidation of 248 independent agencies into 12 cabinet-level departments. "We reduced the government to a sizable figure of agencies where we could adequately work with them," he said. "You have no idea how difficult it was to get them to surrender their 'freedom,' as they called it."[8]

In recent decades, governors have been granted greater powers, including much more power over appointments than they once had. This means that they are able to put their own teams in place to carry out their policies. They have become important symbols of their states, not only at home but also in other states and abroad, as ambassadors who promote their states to businesses they hope to attract. YouTube is littered with clips of governors laying out their cases for why their states are the best. Rick Perry, a Republican who served as governor of Texas from 2000 to 2015, bragged that 7 million people had moved to the state during his tenure. "That's a lot of pickup trucks," he said.[9]

Terry Sanford, a former governor of North Carolina, sums up the job of the contemporary governor well:

> The governor by his very office embodies his state. He must . . . energize his administration, search out the experts, formulate the programs, mobilize the support, and carry new ideas into action. . . . Few major undertakings ever get off the ground without his support and leadership. The governor sets the agenda for public debate; frames the issues; decides on the timing; and can blanket the state with good ideas by using his access to the mass media. . . . The governor is the most potent political power in the state.[10]

Governors must be multitaskers. They propose legislation, which has to win approval from the legislature.

Plural-executive system A state government system in which the governor is not the dominant figure in the executive branch but, instead, is more of a first among equals, serving alongside numerous other officials who were elected to their offices rather than appointed by the governor.

They can implement regulations that help clear up how those laws actually are applied to individuals, businesses, and other groups. Increasingly in recent years, governors have become the strongest advocates and public relations people for their states, traveling to promote tourism and help close deals with out-of-state trading partners that might locate offices or operations in their states. Below, we explore all these roles in some detail.

Chief Legislator

Just as the president does not serve in Congress, governors do not sit as members of state legislatures. Like the president, however, they have enormous influence over the work legislatures do. Governors outline their broad proposals in inaugural and annual state of the state addresses. They and their staffs then work with individual legislators and committees to translate these proposals into bills.

Some governors are better than others at getting what they want from legislatures. Why? Part of it is personal charm, but a lot of it has to do with the powers granted to a governor in a given state. In Texas, for instance, much of the influence that the executive branch holds over legislation is given not to the governor but to the lieutenant governor, who presides over the state senate.

Emma McIntyre/Getty Images for Families Belong Together LA

▲
During his eight years as lieutenant governor of California, Democrat Gavin Newsom was practically invisible. After winning election as governor in 2018, he'll set the political agenda for the state.

....

Supermajority vote A legislative vote of much more than a simple majority—for instance, a vote by two-thirds of a legislative chamber to override a governor's veto.

Governors vary in terms of how much authority they have in blocking bills they do not like through use of the veto, or rejection, of the bills. Those variations in authority help determine how much clout a governor has in the legislature.

Governors never get everything they want from state legislatures, but they do have a great deal of impact on which bills become laws. There are a number of reasons for this. Bills almost never become law without the governor's signature, and governors have veto power. Legislators can get around a veto, but that often means that they have to pass the bill again by a **supermajority vote**, usually a vote of two-thirds or more. That means a governor needs the support of only one-third plus one vote in either chamber to sustain a veto. Because it is hard enough to get both legislative houses to agree on a bill in the first place, such a large vote against most governors rarely happens. If you can't pass a law without the governor's approval, it stands to reason that you will want to work with him or her to create a version of the bill that will win such approval.

Another factor that makes governors enormously influential in the legislative process is their command of state budgets. In nearly every state, the main responsibility for creating a state budget rests in the office of the governor. The governor proposes a budget that details the amounts of money that will go to every state agency, welfare program, highway department, and school district. There are often restrictions on how a state must spend much of its money from year to year, whether because of old laws or federal requirements. But the governor gets first crack at deciding how most of the state's money is going to be spent. Governors don't get everything on their wish lists, but they tend to set the general spending priorities for their states. "As far as legislators are concerned," one political scientist wrote, "the ability to create the budget is so powerful that it becomes *the* major tool for a governor in achieving his legislative programs."[11]

While the legislature might set the overall dollar amount that goes to the transportation department, the governor might get to decide, for instance, whether bridges are going to be built in particular districts. To get those bridges—or any other goodies they might want—legislators often have to give the governor what he or she wants in terms of passing major initiatives. "Any legislator who says he needs nothing from the governor's office is either lying or stupid," according to one observer of the Alabama political scene.[12]

Head of State Agencies

Governors at one time had very little control over who ran their states' departments. This meant that people with other agendas could set policy on taxes or health care or other issues. Only about half the governors chose their own cabinet officials in 1969, but nearly all of them do today.[13] "Reformers had long advocated strengthening the governor's office by lengthening the governor's term of office, allowing consecutive succession in office, broadening the veto power, increasing appointment and removal power, and increasing budgetary authority," noted a trio of political scientists in 2010. "States have generally responded by adopting many of the reformers' propositions, and by late in the twentieth century, most governors enjoyed significantly enhanced formal powers."[14]

The power to appoint people to run state departments offers obvious benefits for governors. They can pick their own people, who they know will pursue their policy preferences. "If you think you are in the governor's cabinet and can be a freelancer, you are mistaken," said Jim Aloisi, a former Massachusetts transportation secretary. "You have to adhere to the governor's philosophy."[15]

If a governor's appointees fail, they can be fired. Arguing for an expansion of the appointment power of New Hampshire governors, former legislator Marjorie Smith wrote in 2012:

> With the possible exception of Texas, New Hampshire's governor has power more limited than that of any other state's governor. We elect a governor with the expectation that she will shape the policy over the course of her term, but do not give her the power to name department heads who will carry out that policy.[16]

Just like any other boss, a governor may be disappointed in the performance of the people working for him or her. The ability to hire and fire people, however, as well as the ability to determine how much money the state's departments are going to get, means that the governor is truly the leader of the executive branch of government.

Chief Spokesperson for the State

Much of Texas stayed wet throughout spring 2016. The Houston area was pummeled by 17 inches of rain during a single 24-hour period in April, leading to more than a half-dozen deaths and the evacuation or rescue of hundreds of people. After the wettest May on record in the state, Governor Greg Abbott declared a state of emergency in 31 counties, freeing up state aid. "I want those who have been affected by these floods to know that Texas is here to help," Abbott said. "We are working with city and county officials who are working swiftly and effectively to do everything they can to protect you, your property, your lives, and to keep things as safe as possible as we weather the storm."[17]

It's always this way with disasters. People don't expect governors to lead rescue missions personally, but they do expect them to take charge and rise rhetorically to the occasion. "It's sort of like a leadership pop quiz," said Andrew Reeves, a political scientist at Washington University in St. Louis who has studied disaster relief politics.[18] When governors rise to the occasion, they're heroes. Responding to floods or severe storms is never the reason a politician seeks the office. But if governors aren't seen as responding swiftly and competently, it can imperil both their reelection chances and their broader agendas. "We've probably spent as much time on snow as we have on the budget," Massachusetts governor Charlie Baker said in 2015, not long after taking office.[19]

A governor acts as the chief spokesperson and public face of a state's government in good times as well as bad. Governors didn't always think it was part of their job description to attract jobs and industry to their states, but they do now. The template was set for them by Luther Hodges, who served as governor of North Carolina from 1954 to 1961, before becoming U.S. secretary of commerce. Hodges created a business development corporation in his state to supply capital to businesses, changed the state's corporate income tax rates, and employed the expertise of nearby University of North Carolina, North Carolina State University, and Duke University in the creation of the 5,000-acre Research Triangle industrial park, which in turn led to the development of the state's high-tech infrastructure. "My administration was considered by many to be 'industry hungry,'" Hodges once said. "It was!"[20]

Governors regularly send out press releases about their roles in helping land new jobs and companies through tax incentives, the creation of cooperative business ventures, and other economic development activities. Contemporary governors routinely take trips to China, Cuba, or wherever they think they can drum up trade or business for their state. Matt Bevin, the Republican governor of Kentucky, is fond of sending out tweets whenever a company expands within or relocates to his state, even if the number of jobs created can be counted on two hands. When Yum! Brands announced that several of its top executives would relocate from Louisville, Kentucky, to his state, Texas governor Abbott celebrated by eating at several of the company's restaurants—KFC, Pizza Hut, and Taco Bell—all on the same day.[21] When he was the governor of Florida, Republican Rick Scott was not shy about telling employers they should move to his state. In 2016, he publicly urged Yale University to move its 12,000 students and 4,000 faculty members to Florida, since the Connecticut legislature was considering a proposal to tax the university's endowment. "That would be fun, wouldn't it?" Scott said. "That would be a great day."[22]

Governors are also important lobbyists in Washington, seeking more federal money for their states. They are just about the only people lobbying in the nation's capital who can be sure that members of Congress and cabinet officials will meet with them directly rather than having them meet with staff.

Party Chief

Governors are the leading figures in their parties within their states. U.S. senators arguably might be more influential figures, but governors are more important politically at home. Governors command more foot soldiers. A governor may be able to call on thousands of state workers, whereas a senator's staff numbers in the dozens at most. Not all of a governor's workers are loyal members of the same party—in fact, changes in patronage laws and the creation of a civil service system mean that governors appoint far fewer state employees than they did some decades ago. Governors, however, have more people whose jobs depend on them than do any other elected officials.

Governors often pick state party chairs of their liking. They help recruit and raise money for candidates for other statewide offices and the legislature. They use the media attention they attract to campaign for those they support. They are still the titular heads of their parties in their states, and no modern politician (who isn't already rich) can avoid the duties of raising campaign contributions.

With the Democratic and Republican governors' associations having morphed into strictly campaign operations in recent years, governors are also taking a more partisan approach to politics outside their own state borders. Even 20 years ago, a governor who visited another state to campaign for his or her party's candidate would not speak ill of the incumbent. And that state's "host" governor would extend every courtesy, including offering the visiting governor the services of state troopers for protection. Today's governors are more willing to be openly critical of the other party and their peers. After North Carolina passed a law in 2016 curbing legal protections for gay and transgender individuals, Andrew Cuomo, New York's Democratic governor, signed an order barring state employees from taking "non-essential" trips to that state. Pat McCrory, then the Republican governor of North Carolina, called Cuomo's move "demagoguery at its worst."[23]

Commander in Chief of the National Guard

Even in this country's earliest days, when governors had few powers, each governor's military position was strong, "with all states designating him as commander-in-chief."[24] Southern governors perhaps most famously used their power to control the National Guard in resisting desegregation during the 1950s and 1960s. The National Guard in each state is a state agency, but the president has the power to federalize it, calling up units to perform federal service. That happened in the civil rights era, when the National Guard was ordered to work for the feds against governors who were resisting integration. Those serving in today's National Guard are more likely to fight alongside federal soldiers in hot spots such as Iraq and Afghanistan.

Governors do not use the National Guard as their private armies, however. Instead, they can call out units to respond to natural disasters or riots. Milton Shapp, governor of Pennsylvania during the 1970s, remembered his years in office in terms of emergency responses to floods, a pair of hurricanes, droughts, ice storms, fires, and a gypsy moth infestation, rather than in terms of lawmaking and policy agenda setting.[25] Still, the question of who controls the National Guard has become a politically potent one in recent years. The federal government pays for troop training and many of the National Guard's operations, and the Supreme Court has found that the feds—not governors—have the final say over where units are deployed.[26] In 2006, Congress passed a law that made it easier for the White House, rather than the statehouse, to take command of the National Guard during times of disaster. All 50 governors signed a letter protesting an earlier version of the law. In 2018, after President Donald Trump's "zero tolerance" policy, which called for arresting immigrants who were in the country illegally, led to the separation of children from their families, eight governors, including several Republicans, said they would withdraw guard troops or refuse to send them to the Mexican border.

The Powers of Governors

Anyone who follows sports understands that natural ability does not necessarily translate into success. Some players look great on paper—they're strong, they can run fast, they have whatever skills should help them dominate their sport. But, for whatever reason, these players sometimes squander their talents and are shown up by athletes who are weaker but who nevertheless have a greater understanding of the game, work harder, or simply find a way to win.

It is the same with governors. Some of them look incredibly strong on paper, and their states' constitutions give them powers that their neighbors can only envy. Nevertheless, states that have set up the governor's office to be strong sometimes end up with weak governors. Conversely, states in which the governor's **formal powers** are weak sometimes can have individuals in that office who completely dominate their states' politics. They are able to exploit the **informal powers** of their office—they manage to create personal powers, as opposed to relying on relatively weak institutional powers.

Below we outline the different types of powers governors actually do have—both the formal ones, those that come as part of the necessary equipment of the office, and the informal ones that individuals create for themselves by using the office as a platform.

Formal Powers

Most governors have a wide variety of formal powers granted to them by state constitutions or other laws. Among the most important of these are the power to appoint officials to run state agencies, the power to veto legislation, the power to craft budgets, the power to grant pardons, and the power to call legislatures into session. We examine each of these aspects of a governor's job description in this section.

Power to Appoint

The first governors lacked **appointment powers**. They could not pick their own people to run state agencies, which made those agencies more independent. Nowadays, governors can pick their own teams, giving them greater authority to set policy. When John Engler served as governor of Michigan during the 1990s, for example, he put in place a series of appointees with a strong ideological commitment to limited government. These appointees helped him carry out his desire to shrink the state's government. Engler's contemporary, Ann Richards of Texas, set out to change the face of state government by changing the faces of the people within it, appointing women, African Americans, and Hispanics to replace the white men who had always run things in Austin.

More than 2,100 National Guard troops were called on to support relief efforts in **NEW JERSEY** after Superstorm Sandy ravaged the state's coastline in 2012.

Having loyal foot soldiers on your team rather than free agents is important for governors who want things done their way. This is not the only benefit the power of appointment carries with it, however. Governors get to appoint dozens and sometimes thousands of people to full-time government jobs and to commissions and boards. For instance, if you are attending a public college, chances are that the governor appointed the board of governors of your school or university system. These are considered plum jobs, and giving them out is a way for a governor not only to influence policy but also to reward campaign contributors and other political allies.

Of course, there is a downside to the power of appointment, which is the risk of picking the wrong people. Earlier, we mentioned former Pennsylvania governor Milton Shapp, who remembered his administration

Formal powers The powers explicitly granted to a governor according to state law, such as being able to veto legislation and to appoint heads of state agencies.

Informal powers The things a governor is able to do, such as command media attention and persuade party members, based on personality or position, not on formal authority.

Appointment powers A governor's ability to pick individuals to run state government, such as cabinet secretaries.

A DIFFERENCE THAT MAKES A DIFFERENCE
CONTEMPORARY GOVERNORS ARE BECOMING MORE PARTISAN

When the National Governors Association (NGA) held its first meeting in Washington after President Donald Trump took office, various governors held news conferences to discuss health policy. The group's chairman and vice chairman—which is always a bipartisan pairing—held a joint news conference on Capitol Hill. But seven other governors, who were all Republicans, talked with reporters after a meeting at the White House to which Democrats were conspicuously not invited.

This kind of partisan divide would have been unusual even a decade ago. At least in Washington, governors from both parties generally tried to speak with one voice, while Democratic and Republican governors often worked together and learned from one another. Traditionally, governors have been among the least partisan figures in big-league American politics, more likely to borrow ideas from their peers of other parties than ever to campaign against them. Many were willing to buck fashions in their own parties to balance their budgets or try to improve high school graduation rates. Compromise was simply part of their job description.

These days, whether fueled by their own presidential ambitions or pressured by interest groups that figure they can get more action in states than from a gridlocked Congress, governors have become more polarizing figures. On taxes, gun control, abortion, voting rights, and a host of other issues, Democratic-controlled states are moving in entirely different directions than are their Republican-led neighbors. "There just seems to be more of a partisan edge," said former Democratic U.S. representative Jim Matheson, whose father was a popular governor of Utah. "They seem to be infected along with everyone else, there's no question about it."

Traditionally, once the campaign season was over, governors knew they had trains to run. The 50 governors saw themselves as belonging to a special breed—half the number of the U.S. Senate, the "world's most exclusive club," but with twice the accountability for solving problems. They collaborated with neighbors on border-crossing matters such as the environment while borrowing ideas from colleagues around the country on an ad hoc basis or through the NGA.

"Governors used to clearly learn from each other at NGA meetings and follow up on projects," said John Weingart, director of the Center on the American Governor at Rutgers University. "They'd send their staff to look at interesting things being done in other states, regardless of party."

Now, governors are more likely to openly criticize one another's approaches to pensions or tax policy. Twenty years ago, NGA was considered one of the most powerful lobbying forces in Washington, speaking with the full authority of the most important politicians out in the country. The landmark welfare overhaul law of 1996, for instance, was largely built on state-level experiments.

Today, with a more fractured group of governors, it's more difficult for NGA to present a united front. Instead, the separate Democratic and Republican governors' associations have become increasingly influential. The Republican Governors Association (RGA) raised $113 million for the 2018 campaign cycle by June of that year, a record haul, while the Democratic Governors Association (DGA) raised $67 million, a 24 percent increase over 2014, the previous major gubernatorial election cycle. Both groups receive big donations from corporations that are barred in many states from giving money directly to gubernatorial candidates, but can let the RGA and DGA know which candidates they're seeking to support. "The transition moved quickly when the Democratic and Republican governor groups started taking positions on controversial issues, and then sought to have the NGA reflect their views," says Dave Freudenthal, a former Democratic governor of Wyoming, citing matters such as climate change and health care.

Meanwhile, the internal politics of many states have grown more partisan, with one party or the other coming to dominate the legislature. "It used to be, you'd run from one side or the other, but you were forced to govern more from the middle," said Ray Scheppach, a former NGA executive director. "Now, they do worry about primary challenges more, so it keeps them aligned in that partisan approach."

There was a time when it was common for governors to please just about everyone, earning approval ratings in the 70s or 80s. Scott M. Matheson, for instance, was one of the most popular governors in the country in the 1980s, even as a Democrat in Utah, in part because he worked well with Republicans such as Norman Bangerter, who served under him as state house speaker and succeeded him as governor.

That sort of model has become more rare and doesn't bring with it national prominence. Instead, stars are born when governors take ownership of issues that excite the national party base—such as Republican governors taking on public employees' unions or talking about abolishing state income taxes, or Democrats banning assault-style weapons or expanding health coverage. "Certainly those that want a national profile, they may well need to be partisan, just because of the way the nominating process works," said Bill Pound, executive director of the National Conference of State Legislatures. "They've got to get out and appeal to whatever base it is, on either side."

"Being attractive to people in both parties used to be considered unambiguously a strength," said Weingart, the Rutgers professor. "Now, being seen as a moderate or someone who works well with the other party has not been a benefit in the last few cycles."

Source: Written for this edition by Alan Greenblatt.

---

mainly as a time of dealing with natural disasters. It is little wonder he preferred to remember his time in office that way, because many of his appointments turned into disasters of his own making. His secretary of property and supplies was sent to prison for contracting irregularities. The same fate befell a member of his turnpike authority. Other members of his administration came under ethical shadows as well. Even though Shapp himself was never touched by scandal, subsequent candidates—including the man who succeeded him as governor—ran campaigns against corruption. They won office by pledging to clean up Harrisburg.[27]

Power to Prepare State Budgets

The most powerful tool governors have may be their ability to shape their states' budgets, which gives them enormous influence in their dealings with the legislature. The same is true of their ability to maintain control over state agencies. In most states, agencies and departments submit their budget proposals to a central budget office that works as part of the governor's team. The governor's ability to deny them funds or shift money among departments helps make sure that agencies remain focused, at least to some extent, on the governor's priorities. "We have a structural imbalance in power, vis-à-vis the governor," says Shap Smith, the Democratic house speaker in Vermont.[28]

A governor can use the budget process to override old agency decisions, for example, to make sure that the transportation department fully funds bike trails that previously had been ignored. Even when an agency has some independence about how it spends its money, a governor can persuade officials to fund other priorities—such as a new law school at a state university—by threatening to withhold some percentage of their agency's overall budget. The governor's authority to set the terms of the budget varies by state. The governor of Texas can recommend a budget, but he or she has no

authority to make the legislature grapple with it seriously. Compare that to Maryland, where legislators can only accept or defeat the governor's spending proposals; they can make no fresh additions of their own.

Power to Veto

In talking about the governor as chief legislator, we touched on the governor's ability to veto legislation in every state. (North Carolina's governor was the last to win this power, in 1997.) Legislators can override vetoes, but that rarely happens, because of supermajority vote requirements. Members of the governor's own party usually are reluctant to vote to override a veto. That means that if the governor's party holds just one-third of the seats in a legislative chamber, plus one, a veto is likely to be sustained—meaning the governor wins.

Legislators, therefore, try to work with the governor or the governor's staff to craft a version of a bill that the governor will sign. There is little point in passing a bill if you know it is going to be rejected by the governor. Of course, a legislature will sometimes pass a bill just to get it vetoed, to make the governor's opposition official and public. That happened often when Gary Johnson was governor of New Mexico during the 1990s. "During his eight years as New Mexico's governor, Gary Johnson competed in the Ironman Triathlon World Championship, won the America's Challenge Gas Balloon Race, played guitar with Van Halen's Sammy Hagar, and helped save a house when massive wildfires struck Los Alamos," political scientists Thad Kousser and Justin H. Phillips write in their book *The Power of American Governors.*[29] Yet, they note, he never succeeded in persuading legislators to enact items on his legislative agenda.

That didn't mean Johnson was irrelevant. Johnson, who ran for president as the Libertarian Party candidate in 2012 and 2016, did not support any bill that increased the size of government, and so he ended up vetoing more than 700 bills. Legislators sent him bills that would increase funding for popular programs, such as education, in the hope that his vetoes would make him look bad. Whether that happened or not, Johnson almost always won the procedural battle. Not only was the legislature unable to override his vetoes except in one instance, but he also was reelected to a second term.

All but six governors—those in Indiana, Nevada, New Hampshire, North Carolina, Rhode Island, and Vermont—have a power known as the line-item veto; that is, they can reject just a portion of a bill. If there is a bill funding education, for example, the governor can accept all of it except for an increase in funding for a school in the district of a legislator who is a political enemy. Governors can use the line-item veto to try to cut spending, as when Florida governor Rick Scott eliminated $256.1 million in spending for several hundred items in the state budget in 2016. Scott even warned the legislature of his veto plan in advance, hoping it would encourage them to pony up the $250 million he wanted for an economic development fund. The governor's ability to cut legislators' pet projects out of the budget often forces them to support that governor's major initiatives. Congress tried to give the president line-item

veto authority, but the U.S. Supreme Court ruled the practice unconstitutional in 1998.

When Tommy Thompson was governor of Wisconsin during the 1990s, he used the line-item veto to an unusual degree. Some governors can strike not only projects from bills but individual words and letters as well. Thompson became notorious for vetoing just enough letters in a bill's wording to alter the meaning of the bill (see Chapter 3). The courts upheld his right to do so, but that power was soon curbed. Nevertheless, in 2005, Jim Doyle, the state's Democratic governor, was able to strike 752 words from a budget bill to cobble together a new 20-word sentence that shifted $427 million from transportation to education.[30] Prompted by Doyle's move—and by near-daily editorials in the *Wisconsin State Journal* newspaper and on the paper's website—the legislature in 2008 further restricted the governor's veto authority. The governor of Wisconsin can no longer stitch together words from different parts of a bill, but he or she can still delete words from individual sentences or change numbers—quickly converting $100 million to $10 million, for instance. "It seems like each governor gets more creative in their use of the partial veto, and this was clearly an abuse," said state senator Sheila Harsdorf, a sponsor of the successful veto referendum. "When people saw that veto, it was pretty hard to justify."[31]

Maryland GOP governor Larry Hogan twice successfully battled cancer while in office. His high approval ratings, though, came from cutting taxes and finding moderate policies that could appeal to his largely Democratic state.

David Kidd/Governing

Power to Grant Pardons

One clichéd motif of old movies and television dramas was the depiction of a prisoner about to be put to death only to be spared by a last-minute pardon from the governor. Governors, like the president, can forgive crimes or commute (change) sentences if they feel that particular persons have been convicted unfairly. They sometimes act on the recommendations of pardon boards, but the decision to pardon is theirs alone and not reversible.

A famous example of the use of pardon power happened in Illinois in 2003. During his last week in office, Republican governor George Ryan pardoned four prisoners condemned to death and commuted the sentences of the other 167 death-row prisoners to life in prison. Ryan had grown concerned that the number of capital cases that were being overturned because of new evidence, such as DNA lab work, indicated that the death penalty was being unfairly and inequitably applied. He appointed a commission to study the application of the death sentence and became convinced that the state could not impose the death penalty with such absolute certainty that innocent people would not be put to death. The move gained Ryan international celebrity among death penalty opponents but was criticized by prosecutors and others at home.

Not all governors use their pardon powers in such a high-minded way. In Tennessee in 1979, Lamar Alexander was sworn in as governor three days early to prevent outgoing governor Ray Blanton from commuting the sentences of any more prisoners. Blanton already had granted 52 last-minute pardons, and the Federal Bureau of Investigation (FBI) had arrested members of his staff for extorting money by selling pardons, paroles, and commutations. More recently, outgoing governor Haley Barbour of Mississippi drew national condemnation by pardoning some 200 people during his final days in office in 2012, including 5 who were still in prison and 5 others who had worked in the governor's mansion. Despite a challenge from Mississippi's attorney general, the state supreme court quickly ruled that Barbour's actions had been perfectly in keeping with his power. In part because they fear political backlash if pardoned criminals should reoffend, governors have greatly reduced their granting of pardons since the 1960s, and some governors currently in office have never pardoned anyone at all.[32]

Governors who do grant pardons are most likely to issue many of them just as they're leaving office, as happened in 2015, when outgoing Democrat Steve Beshear of Kentucky issued 201 pardons as his last official act in office.[33] Republican Eric Greitens of Missouri pardoned five people and commuted the sentences of four others less than two hours before leaving office amid scandal in 2018. Some, notably former GOP governor Robert Ehrlich of Maryland, have begun to push for expanded use of the authority, arguing that it can be an important corrective within the nation's system of justice. Some current governors, such as Republican Larry Hogan of Maryland, spoke during their campaigns about the importance of taking the pardon power seriously in office, which had rarely happened with earlier cohorts of governors.

Power to Call Special Sessions

Many legislatures meet only part-time and generally have fixed session schedules. When special sessions are necessary or desired, however, every governor has the power to call the legislature into session. Nearly half the nation's governors have the ability to set the agenda of a special session. This means that in such a session legislators can deal only with those issues that the governor wants addressed.

Special sessions can be useful for governors who want to deal with particular issues right away. In recent years, many governors have called special sessions when their states' revenues have fallen short so that the legislatures can help them cut spending. Sometimes a special session allows legislators to focus on a complex issue, such as changing medical malpractice liability laws. Such issues might get lost in the shuffle of a regular session, when most attention is devoted to passing a budget.

Although governors can call special sessions, they typically will not enjoy success unless they can work out deals on their pet bills in advance. "If a governor calls a special session without knowing what the outcome's going to be," said former Mississippi House speaker Tim Ford, "it's chaos for everybody."[34] Arkansas governor Mike Beebe waited to call a special session in 2014 until legislative leaders assured him that they'd reached consensus on bills that addressed prison funding, the state lottery, and changes to the state employee health insurance system. The legislature met and was able to pass the bills within 48 hours, and Beebe quickly signed them into law. Without a deal already in place, legislators who have been called into session will sit around reading newspapers and eating snacks while their leaders try to hammer out an agreement with the governor. They are likely to resent having to give up time from their regular jobs to sit idly in the capitol.

Informal Powers

The powers just outlined are spelled out in state constitutions and statutes. Governors either have line-item veto authority or do not. Much of the outcome of a governor's program, however, depends on the governor's individual ability to wield informal powers—the ability to leverage the power and prestige of the office into real influence in a way that may not be replicated by successors. Governors may be personally popular, have a special gift for working with legislators, or have some other skills that help them do their jobs well but that are not based on any authority granted by the state. They can "exert leadership," as onetime South Carolina governor Richard Riley put it, using informal powers "such as negotiations, public relations and strategizing."[35]

Popular Support

One thing that will always help a governor is popular support. A governor who comes into office with 51 percent of the vote has all the same formal powers as a governor who wins with 75 percent, but the more popular governor is clearly going to have an edge. Legislators and other officials will more readily accept the need to go along with a popular governor's program because they believe that program is what most voters in the state want. This is especially true if the governor had strong support for election in their districts. When Haley Barbour ran for governor of Mississippi in 2003, he rarely made a speech without mentioning tort reform. As governor, he was able to convert his political support into a successful push for a law to curb trial lawyers, overcoming the resistance of house Democratic leaders. Barbour then embarked on a "tort tour" to encourage other states to follow Mississippi's lead. "I think if a governor has strong popularity ratings, he's got a bigger **bully pulpit**," said former Ohio governor Bob Taft. "If a governor is strong and popular, whether or not he's going to use the electoral power that gives him, legislators still think that he might use that either for or against them in their reelection."[36]

It is a long time between gubernatorial elections—four years in most cases—so to maintain and build on their popularity, governors do all sorts of public relations work. They never fail to alert the press to all their good deeds, they travel their states constantly to appear in any number of forums—TV shows, groundbreakings, dedications, state fairs, church socials—where they can interact with the public, and they propose legislation that they believe will be popular. The fortunes of governors rise and fall with the health of the economies of their states, but individual governors can make themselves more or less popular depending on how well they appear to address the problems of the day.

....

Bully pulpit The platform from which a high-profile public official, such as governor or president, commands considerable public and media attention by virtue of holding office.

Party Support in the Legislature

Having members of their own party dominate the legislature certainly helps governors get their agendas passed. Governors can be successful if the other party controls the legislature, but it is a lot tougher. The reasons are fairly obvious. Republican legislators want to see a Republican governor succeed, and the same holds true, obviously, for Democratic legislators serving under a Democratic governor. Voters perceive politicians who belong to the same party as being part of the same team; therefore, the political fortunes of these politicians will be tied together during the next election. Members of the same party are likely to hold similar positions on such issues as taxes, levels of social service spending, and the environment.

Governors are more likely to grant favors to or raise money for legislators of their own party. This, in turn, makes those legislators more likely to support the governors' programs. Some governors curry favor with legislators because they used to be legislators themselves and still have friends in the house or senate. Onetime Tennessee governor Ned McWherter, for example, was a longtime legislator before taking the top office. As governor, he concentrated his attention on a few pet initiatives, such as a major overhaul of the state Medicaid system, and went along with whatever his pals in the legislature were thinking on most other matters.

More typically, "each party attempts to strengthen the institution it commands and to weaken the institution controlled by the opposition," notes one political scientist.[37] In other words, a Republican holding the governorship will try to make that office more powerful at the expense of a Democratic legislature and vice versa. When power is shared under divided government, however, the two parties cannot just attack each other's programs. If they share power, they also share responsibility in the eyes of the voters, and so they have to work together to forge compromises on central issues such as the budget.

Ability to Communicate

We have already touched on the advantage governors have over legislators in regard to media exposure. There is no law that says newspapers and TV stations have to pay more attention to pronouncements from the governor—but that is what happens anyway. Pretty much anything legislators say and do takes a back seat. The governor is a single, well-known individual who is important to every voter in the state. A legislator, by contrast, even a powerful one, is just an individual legislator among 120 or 150 legislators and represents a district that makes up only a fraction of the state. Whereas a governor speaks clearly with one voice, a legislature speaks with many—not just because it is made up of many individuals but also because there are differing points of view between the chambers and between the majority and minority parties.[38] "In any squabble, the governor had a distinct edge over what amounted to a gang of unknowns in the legislature," writes former Vermont House speaker Ralph Wright.[39]

Governors have to play both an inside game and an outside game. They have to appeal to capital insiders as well as to the public at large. A governor who makes every move based on the ability to turn it into a press release or who appeals to the public by bashing the "corruption" in the capital may score points with the media and the public but soon will have few friends in the legislature. In Illinois, Rod Blagojevich was elected governor thanks to his railing against the corruption of state government, and he did not change his theme song once he took office. He refused even to establish a permanent residence in the state capital of Springfield, instead commuting from his home in Chicago. "We're going to keep fighting to reform and change the system and give the people a government that stops spending their money like a bunch of drunken sailors," he said toward the end of his first year in office.[40] Needless to say, the legislators whom Blagojevich had likened to drunken sailors were not eager to cooperate with him any more than they had to—even though his own party had a majority in both chambers. They continued to feud with him throughout his tenure—one publicly called the governor "insane" in 2007[41]—and did not hesitate to impeach him in 2009 after federal investigators revealed tapes of phone conversations in which Blagojevich was caught trying to sell President Barack Obama's U.S. Senate seat, which the governor had the power to fill following Obama's ascension to the White House.

But governors often enjoy the upper hand in their relations with the legislature. Roy Barnes, who served one term as governor of Georgia from 1999 until 2003, said during his days in the state legislature, "When you are called down to the governor's office, it is a very impressive office, you're talking to the governor, and you know that he controls things that could be good or ill for your district. He controls grants, he controls roads, and other things."[42] In other words, the formal powers of the governor (the ability to control projects) merge with informal powers (the mystique of the office) to influence legislators and other supplicants.

Becoming Governor and Staying Governor

We have described governors as the most powerful and important political actors in their states. It should come as little surprise, then, given the history of politics in this country, that middle-aged white males have dominated the job. Women are being elected to governorships with greater frequency—only three women were elected governor during the nation's first two centuries—but plenty of states have yet to elect a woman for the top job.[43] In 2007, nine women served as governor, the highest number ever to serve at one time. (Their ranks have since been slightly depleted by retirements and presidential appointments; just five women governors were in office following the 2016 elections, and the number went back to nine following the 2018 election.) A record number of women received major-party nominations for governor in 2018—16 in all, including the first black, Native American, and transgender women ever nominated. In 1873, P. B. S. Pinchback, the black lieutenant governor of Louisiana, was elevated to the post of acting governor for 43 days, but only two African Americans have ever been elected governor of any state: Douglas Wilder of Virginia held the job during the first half of the 1990s, and Deval Patrick was elected to the office in Massachusetts in 2006.[44] David A. Paterson, who is African American and legally blind, became governor of New York following Eliot Spitzer's 2008 resignation due to a sex scandal. There have been a handful of Hispanic and Asian American governors, including Brian Sandoval of Nevada, Susana Martinez of New Mexico, and David Ige of Hawaii. In 2007, Bobby Jindal of Louisiana became the first Indian American to be elected governor; he was joined by Nikki Haley of South Carolina in 2010. In 2016, Democrat Kate Brown of Oregon became the first openly bisexual person elected as governor. In 2018, Jared Polis of Colorado became the first openly gay man elected governor.

Many nonpoliticians have been elected governor, including movie action hero Arnold Schwarzenegger of California, former wrestler Jesse Ventura of Minnesota, and business executives Pete Ricketts of Nebraska and Phil Murphy of New Jersey. Most governors, however,

TABLE 8-1 ● The Governors: Powers

State or Other Jurisdiction	Budget-Making Power		Item Veto Power					Authorization for Reorganization through Executive Order
	Full Responsibility	Shares Responsibility	Governor Has Item Veto Power on All Bills	Governor Has Item Veto Power on Appropriations Only	Governor Has No Item Veto Power	Item Veto—2/3 Legislators Present or 3/5 Elected to Override	Item Veto—Majority Legislators Elected to Override	
Alabama	*(a)	...	*	...	...	...	*	...
Alaska	*	...	...	*	...	*	...	*
Arizona	*(a)	...	...	*	...	*	(b)	...
Arkansas	...	*	...	*	...	...	*	*(c)
California	*(a)	...	...	*	...	...	...	*(c)
Colorado	...	*	...	*	...	*	...	*
Connecticut	...	*	*	...	...	*	...	...
Delaware	*(a)	...	*	...	...	...	...	*
Florida	...	*	...	*	...	*	...	*
Georgia	*	...	...	*	...	(b)	...	*
Hawaii	...	*	...	*	...	*	...	*
Idaho	..	*	*	...	...	*	...	*
Illinois	...	*	*	...	...	*	...	*
Indiana	*	...	...	...	*	...	...	*
Iowa	...	*	...	*	...	*	...	*
Kansas	*	...	...	*	...	*	...	*
Kentucky	*(a)	...	...	*	...	...	*	*
Louisiana	...	*	...	*	...	...	*(f)	*(g)
Maine	...	*	...	...	...	...	*	...
Maryland	*	...	*	...	...	*	...	*
Massachusetts	*	...	*	...	...	...	*(f)	*(c)
Michigan	*(h)	...	...	*(e)	...	...	*(f)	*
Minnesota	...	*	...	*	...	...	*(f)	*(i)
Mississippi	...	*(j)	...	*	...	...	...	*
Missouri	*(a)	...	...	*	...	*	...	*
Montana	*	...	...	*	...	*(f)	...	*(l)
Nebraska	...	*	...	*	...	*(m)	...	...
Nevada	*	...	...	...	*	...	...	*(t)
New Hampshire	*(a)	...	...	...	...	*	...	...
New Jersey	*(a)	...	...	*	...	...	*(f)	*(n)
New Mexico	*	...	...	*	...	*	...	...
New York	...	*	*	...	...	*	...	...
North Carolina	...	*	...	...	*	...	...	*(o)
North Dakota	*	...	...	*	...	*	...	*
Ohio	*	...	...	*	...	*	...	...
Oklahoma	...	*	...	*	...	...	*(f)	*(u)

State or Other Jurisdiction	Budget-Making Power		Item Veto Power					Authorization for Reorganization through Executive Order
	Full Responsibility	Shares Responsibility	Governor Has Item Veto Power on All Bills	Governor Has Item Veto Power on Appropriations Only	Governor Has No Item Veto Power	Item Veto—2/3 Legislators Present or 3/5 Elected to Override	Item Veto—Majority Legislators Elected to Override	
Oregon	...	*	...	*	...	*	...	*
Pennsylvania	*	...	...	*	...	*	...	...
Rhode Island	*	...	...	...	*	...	...	*
South Carolina	...	*	...	*	...	*	...	...
South Dakota	*	...	...	*	...	*(p)	...	*
Tennessee	...	*	...	*	...	...	*	*
Texas	...	*	...	*	...	*	...	*
Utah	...	*	...	*	...	...	...	*
Vermont	*	...	...	...	*	...	...	*
Virginia	*	...	...	*	...	*	...	*
Washington	*	...	*(q)	...	...	*	...	...
West Virginia	*	...	...	*	...	...	...	...
Wisconsin	*(a)	...	...	*(r)	...	*	...	...
Wyoming	...	*	...	*	...	*(p)	...	...
American Samoa	...	*	...	...	...	...	...	*
Guam	*	...	*	...	...	*	...	*
No. Mariana Islands	...	*	...	*	...	...	...	*
Puerto Rico	...	*	...	*	...	*	...	*(s)
U.S. Virgin Islands	*	...	...	*	...	*	...	*

Source: Council of State Governments, Book of the States 2016, June 6, 2016. Reproduced by permission of the Council of State Governments.

Key:

*—Yes; provision for.

. . .—No; not applicable.

(a) Full responsibility to propose; legislature adopts or revises and governor signs or vetoes.

(b) Two-thirds of members to which each house is entitled required to override veto.

(c) Authorization for reorganization provided for in state constitution.

(d) Legislature has full responsibility with regard to setting the state's budget.

(e) Governor may veto any distinct item or items appropriating money in any appropriations bill.

(f) Two-thirds of elected legislators of each house to override.

(g) Only for agencies and offices within the governor's office.

(h) Governor has sole authority to propose annual budget. No money may be paid out of state treasury except in pursuance of appropriations made by law.

(i) Statute provides for reorganization by the commissioner of administration with the approval of the governor.

(j) Governor has the responsibility of presenting a balanced budget. The budget is based on revenue estimated by the governor's office and the Legislative Budget Committee.

(k) If the legislature is not in session when the governor vetoes a bill, the secretary of state must poll the legislature as to the question of an override, but only if the bill had passed by a vote of two-thirds of the members present.

(l) The office of the governor shall continuously study and evaluate the organizational structure, management practices, and functions of the executive branch and each agency.

The governor shall, by executive order or other means within his authority, take action to improve the manageability of the executive branch. The governor may not, however, create an agency of state government by administrative action, except that the governor may establish advisory councils and must approve the internal organizational structures of departments.

(m) Three-fifths majority required to override line-item veto.

(n) Executive reorganization plans can be disapproved by majority vote in both houses of the legislature.

(o) Executive order must be approved by the legislature if changes affect existing law.

(p) Requires two-thirds of legislators elected to override.

(q) Governor has veto power of selections for nonappropriations and item veto in appropriations.

(r) In Wisconsin, governor has "partial" veto over appropriation bills. The partial veto is broader than item veto.

(s) Only if it is not prohibited by law.

(t) Only as to commissions, boards, and councils.

(u) The governor has the authority, through state statute, to enact executive orders that create agencies, boards, and commissions; and reassigns agencies, boards, and commissions to different cabinet secretaries. However, in order for the continued operation of any agency created by executive order, the state legislature must approve legislation that allows the agency to continue to operate; if not, the agency cannot continue operation beyond adjournment sine die of the legislature for the session.

have had a good deal of previous government experience. They have served in the U.S. Congress, the state legislature, or other statewide positions such as lieutenant governor, attorney general, or even state supreme court justice. Throughout the 20th century, in fact, only about 10 percent of governors had no prior elective experience.[45] Only a handful of independent or third-party candidates have been elected governor in recent years, including Lincoln Chafee of Rhode Island, who had served in the U.S. Senate as a Republican. In 2014, independent Bill Walker—a former Republican mayor of Valdez—won the Alaska gubernatorial election with the former Democratic nominee as his running mate.

One qualification for modern governors is quite clear—they must have the ability to raise money. Gubernatorial campaigns have become multimillion-dollar affairs, particularly in heavily populated states, where television ads are expensive to run because the media markets are competitive and costly. The amount raised by candidates themselves for the 36 governors' races in 2014 was $760.6 million—not counting millions more raised and spent by outside groups.[46]

Factors Driving Gubernatorial Elections

Like the Winter Olympics, gubernatorial elections in most states have been moved to the second year of the presidential term in what are called off-year elections. Thirty-four states now hold their gubernatorial elections in the off year. Another five states—Kentucky, Louisiana, Mississippi, New Jersey, and Virginia—hold their elections in odd-numbered years. Nine states—Delaware, Indiana, Missouri, Montana, New Hampshire, North Carolina, North Dakota, Utah, and Vermont—hold their elections at the same time as the presidential contest. In addition, New Hampshire and Vermont, the only states that have clung to the old tradition of two-year terms, hold elections for governor every even-numbered year.

The majority of governors are elected in even-numbered off years because states wanted to insulate the

J. B. Pritzker of **ILLINOIS** is the wealthiest governor in the United States, with a fortune estimated by *Forbes* at $3.4 billion. More than half a dozen governors have a net worth of more than $100 million.

contests from getting mixed up in national issues. Many states from the 1960s to the 1980s moved their gubernatorial elections to the presidential midterm because they hoped this would allow voters to concentrate on matters of importance to the states, without having their attention diverted to federal issues brought up in presidential campaigns. That may have been the intent, but the plan has not been too successful. In gubernatorial elections, the office of governor is often the biggest thing on the ballot, so voters frequently use these races as a way of expressing their opinions about who is *not* on the ballot. "There is simply no question that the primary motivation was to reduce presidential coattails on the election for governor and to increase the voters' attention on state rather than national issues," says Larry J. Sabato, director of the University of Virginia's Center for Politics. "What changed? Party polarization increased. It is easier to link the president and governor (and Congress and state legislatures) because almost all Democrats now are liberal and almost all Republicans are conservative, at least on critical social, tax, and spending issues."[47] Following the 2018 elections, Republicans held 27 governorships while Democrats had 23.

With American politics increasingly riven along partisan lines and media focus generally fixated on the presidency, governors are increasingly expected to weigh in on national issues. Overall, however, gubernatorial races are still less prone to following national trends than, say, elections for the U.S. Senate. The reason? Voters understand that the governor's position is important in and of itself. The dominant concern in most gubernatorial contests is the state economy. Even the most powerful politicians have only limited control over the economy at best, but voters tend to reward or punish the incumbent party based on the state's economic performance. If a state is faring poorly or doing considerably worse than its neighbors, the incumbent party is likely to struggle.

Voters more often use party as a guide in lower-profile contests, such as state legislative races, but are better informed about individual gubernatorial candidates. One reason is the greater news coverage of the races. Another important factor is the amount of money that candidates for governor spend to publicize themselves. Candidates create extensive organizations that promote their campaigns and use all the modern techniques of political consultants, polling, and media buys. Voters are far more likely, even in less populous states, to get to know the candidates through TV ads and brochures

(Text continues on page 236)

A DIFFERENCE THAT MAKES A DIFFERENCE
THE RISE OF THE RICH GOVERNOR

Donald Trump isn't the only rich guy to seek public office. In 2016, more than two dozen candidates funded their own campaigns for Congress, making contributions in excess of $250,000 apiece to promote their ambitions.

The trend is especially noticeable among governors. As of 2019, more than a half-dozen governors had personal fortunes in excess of $100 million. "The number of billionaires and mega-millionaires is absolutely unprecedented," says John Jackson, a Southern Illinois University political scientist.

It is not an entirely new phenomenon in a country where Rockefellers and Roosevelts have served as governors. But at a time of concern about the outsized influence of the überwealthy in politics, the idea of the rich running themselves leaves some wary. "This is your democracy," then Democratic representative Steve Israel of New York wrote in 2016. "But as the bidding grows higher, your voice gets lower. You're simply priced out of the marketplace of ideas. That is, unless you are one of the ultra wealthy."[a]

Republican Bruce Rauner of Illinois used his multi-million-dollar fortune to propel his successful run for governor in 2014. He subsequently became practically the sole source of support for the Illinois Republican Party. But Rauner was unseated in 2018 by J. B. Pritzker, a billionaire and part of the family that owns the Hyatt hotel chain.

Several other rich guys have started at the top. Republicans Matt Bevin of Kentucky, Doug Burgum of North Dakota, and Pete Ricketts of Nebraska, along with Democrats Phil Murphy of New Jersey and Tom Wolf of Pennsylvania, among others, all spent millions of their own dollars introducing themselves to voters during their gubernatorial runs. That obviously gave them an enormous boost. When Jared Polis, then the second-richest member of Congress, ran for governor of Colorado in 2018 and was spared having to raise money or the need to coordinate a message with outside groups, Jon Caldara of the Independence Institute wrote, "Unlike almost every major candidate for any office in Colorado, Polis has the very rare opportunity to run his own campaign, you know, like candidates used to do."[b]

If candidates can write their own checks—rather than present a drain on donors—parties are happy to have them run for any office. It's no secret why someone who is rich might want to run. For a person who is already enormously successful, politics offers the chance to become well known and influential, and presents plenty of new mountains to climb. "Many titans of industry have all the money and material goods they can enjoy in multiple lifetimes, so they crave success in other fields," says Larry J. Sabato, director of the University of Virginia Center for Politics. "What's a better match for loads of money than power?"

Being able to put millions into your own race is no guarantee of victory, as several rich-guy would-be governors have found out in recent years. But successful wealthy candidates have found a way to make being rich an advantage. Being rich, they say, means they can't be bought. That's been a persuasive argument for many voters, who like the idea that a politician won't have to trade favors for cash.

Many voters also have been impressed by candidates' achievements in other fields. "Voters have been choosing new ideas and new energy over the old formula of sheer time served in political office," Florida governor Rick Scott, whose estimated net worth is $150 million, wrote in *USA Today* as the presidential campaign got under way in 2016.[c]

Money is also a big help once in office. In theory, it shouldn't matter that the governor is worth 100 times as much as the state senate president. As a practical matter, however, the reality that a governor—and the governor's rich friends—can fund issue advocacy campaigns and candidates lends an already powerful figure that much more sway.

In a standoff between a rich governor and a house speaker of more modest means, money can become part of the conversation about who's going to give in first. "If your argument is, 'I earned my money and can't be bought by political contributors,'" says Thad Kousser, a University of California, San Diego, political scientist, "but then you turn around and try to buy others—that cuts against your claim that personal riches doesn't have undue influence."

Source: Adapted from Alan Greenblatt, "The Rise of the Rich Governor," *Governing*, June 2016, http://www.governing.com/topics/politics/gov-rich-governors-haslam.html.

[a]Steve Israel, "Confessions of a Congressman," *New York Times*, January 8, 2016, http://www.nytimes.com/2016/01/09/opinion/steve-israel-confessions-of-a-congressman.html.

[b]Jon Caldara, "Walker Stapleton Could Win," *Denver Post*, July 10, 2018, https://www.denverpost.com/2018/07/06/walker-stapleton-could-win/.

[c]Rick Scott, "Donald Trump Has America's Pulse," *USA Today*, January 7, 2016, http://www.usatoday.com/story/opinion/2016/01/06/trump-rubio-bush-florida-economy-rick-scott-column/78321590.

FIGURE 8-1 ● How It Works

Merging Formal and Informal Gubernatorial Powers: Florida's Governor Crist Takes on Category 5 Insurance Problems

As powerful as they are, there are some things governors may not be able to control. The weather is one. The insurance industry may be another. Florida's Republican governor Charlie Crist tackled both in his first term as he worked behind the scenes and in front of the cameras to pass legislation to stem rising insurance costs in the state.

Jeff Parker, Courtesy of Cagle Cartoons

THE PROBLEM. The disastrous 2004 and 2005 hurricane seasons left many of Florida's homeowners with more than just flattened roofs: it landed them with crushing insurance bills. The cost of insuring a home more than doubled in 2006, and many residents considered leaving the state altogether. Joining a chorus of voices advocating for a host of insurance reforms, Governor Crist urged Floridians to stay put and promised to work with lawmakers to help bring down insurance rates.

That's no small feat. Insuring property in a state that saw nearly $36 billion in storm damages in one year alone is an expensive business—and regulating that industry is the state's responsibility. Even the industry's harshest critics understand that the premiums homeowners pay on a regular basis to insure their homes must keep pace with the amounts that agencies anticipate will be paid out in future claims. That's basic math. But, critics say, insurers' profits have soared in recent years. Some agencies have adopted such misleading or unfair practices as creating differently named subsidiary companies that offer different rates than their parent agencies. Others offer restricted insurance plans to Floridians (for example, they offer auto but not homeowners' insurance). Still others refused to offer policies in that state, leaving many without coverage.

In their wake stands Citizens Property Insurance, a state-run agency created in 2002 by the Florida legislature as an insurance "safety net." Under its original rules, homeowners were allowed to switch to Citizens only if they had been denied coverage by a national company or if their premiums were quoted at more than 25 percent higher than Citizens' rates. By 2006, however, Citizens was set to become the insurer for more than half of all of Florida's homeowners—about 1.3 million policyholders—making it the state's largest insurance company rather than the agency of last resort.

With so many homeowners forced to pay exorbitant rates or cut loose from national policies altogether and Citizens stepping in to fill the gap, Governor Crist and Florida's lawmakers were made to reconsider the role that Citizens should (or could) play in wholesale insurance reform.

THE PROCESS. In January 2007, Crist called a weeklong special legislative session to try to hammer out a plan. Crist himself brought several aggressive measures to the table, including recommendations to lower threshold requirements for homeowners to get coverage through Citizens, to cap the agency's ability to raise rates, and to crack down on subsidiaries. He also asked for the power to appoint the company's director. But the hallmark of his plan was to make Citizens more competitive with private insurers. After the special session, the legislature continued the reform debate during its regular session.

Early predictions of Crist's likelihood of success were not good. The insurance lobby came on strong, as did a handful of legislators from his own party, who warned the public that increasing the role of the state-sponsored Citizens was tantamount to socialism and potentially could bankrupt the state. But having once been a state legislator himself, Crist knew how to work the ropes. His main advantage was his stratospheric popularity: he had plenty of political capital, and he wasn't shy about spending it.

To promote his plan, Crist put in rare appearances before several house and senate committees and stumped to persuade homeowners that the promised rate relief wasn't an illusion. He also traveled to Washington, D.C., to help Florida lawmakers appeal for a national disaster relief fund to help defray costs to that state's homeowners.

Crist and his staff continued to work behind the scenes, too, with the governor's staff "buttonholing" legislators. Then state senator J. D. Alexander reported that "there had been some political arm-twisting," adding, "You don't go against a governor with a 77-percent approval rating."[a]

Both the house and senate took up bills that included a number of Crist's original proposals; by the end of their regular session, they'd reached resolutions.

THE OUTCOMES. Crist got a lot of what he wanted. Legislators agreed to freeze Citizens' rates at 2006 levels through 2009. Policyholders will be allowed to choose coverage through Citizens if they receive quotes from national insurers that are more than 15 percent higher than Citizens' annual premiums. Other provisions also are in place to allow the agency to be more competitive with private insurers.

"You put the nail in the coffin this afternoon on the industry that was hurting our people. That's right and just fair and important, and you did it, and God bless you for fighting for the people of Florida," Crist told legislators. "I hear some groans from insurance lobbyists? Tough. That's right. We work for the people, not them."[b]

But Crist didn't get everything he asked for. Legislators killed an amendment giving him the power to appoint Citizens' director. Also rejected was a proposal that would have allowed the agency to write policies for auto, theft, and fire insurance that would have made it better able to amass greater financial reserves and offer lower premiums.

[a]Quoted in Paige St. John, "Crist Still Pushing for Property-Insurance Legislation," *Tallahassee Democrat*, May 3, 2007.

[b]Quoted in S. V. Date, "Session's End More like Recess Than Finale," *Palm Beach Post*, May 5, 2007.

TABLE 8-2 ● Governors' Institutional Powers, by State, 2015

State	Separately elected executive-branch officials (SEP)[a]	Tenure potential (TP)[b]	Appointment power (AP)[c]	Budget power (BP)[d]	Veto power (VP)[e]	Party control (PC)[f]	Total	GIPI[g]
Alaska	5	4	3.7	5	2	4	23.67	3.94
Kentucky	3	4	3	4	5	4	23	3.83
Maryland	4	4	2.8	5	5	2	22.83	3.81
Ohio	4	4	3.3	5	2.5	4	22.83	3.81
North Dakota	3	5	2.7	5	2.5	4.5	22.67	3.78
Massachusetts	4	5	3.3	5	4	1	22.33	3.72
Michigan	4	4	2.8	5	2.5	4	22.33	3.72
Connecticut	4	5	3.8	2	5	2	21.83	3.64
South Dakota	3	4	2.3	5	2.5	5	21.83	3.64
Kansas	3	4	2	5	2.5	5	21.5	3.58
Pennsylvania	4	4	3.8	5	2.5	2	21.33	3.56
New Mexico	3	4	3.8	5	2.5	3	21.3	3.55
New York	4	5	3.2	2	5	2	21.17	3.53
Wyoming	2	4	3.2	2	5	5	21.17	3.53
Tennessee	5	4	3.5	2	2	4.5	21	3.50
Utah	4	5	2.5	2	2.5	5	21	3.50
Washington	1	5	2.8	5	5	2	20.83	3.47
Delaware	2.5	4	3	4	5	2	20.5	3.42
New Jersey	5	4	3	4	2.5	2	20.5	3.42
Indiana	3	4	2.8	5	1	4.5	20.33	3.39
Nevada	2.5	4	3.3	5	1.5	4	20.33	3.39
Alabama	1.5	4	2.2	4	4	4.5	20.17	3.36
Hawaii	5	4	2.5	2	2.5	4	20	3.33
Missouri	2	4	2.5	4	2.5	5	20	3.33
Idaho	2	5	1.8	1	5	5	19.83	3.31
Illinois	3	5	2.8	2	5	2	19.83	3.31
Minnesota	4	5	3.8	2	2	3	19.83	3.31
Arizona	2.5	4	2.3	4	2.5	4	19.33	3.22
Maine	5	4	3.2	2	2	3	19.17	3.19
Montana	3	4	2.5	5	2.5	2	19	3.17
Iowa	3	5	3	2	2.5	3	18.5	3.08
Virginia	2.5	3	3	5	2.5	2	18	3.00
West Virginia	2.5	4	3	5	2.5	1	18	3.00
Florida	3	4	2.3	2	2.5	4	17.83	2.97
Nebraska	4	4	2.3	2	2.5	3	17.83	2.97
Georgia	1	4	1.2	5	2.5	4	17.67	2.94
Louisiana	2	4	3.2	2	2.5	4	17.67	2.94
Colorado	4	4	3	2	2.5	2	17.5	2.92

State	Separately elected executive-branch officials (SEP)[a]	Tenure potential (TP)[b]	Appointment power (AP)[c]	Budget power (BP)[d]	Veto power (VP)[e]	Party control (PC)[f]	Total	GIPI[g]
Wisconsin	3	2	2	4	2.5	4	17.5	2.92
Vermont	2	5	2.8	5	1.5	1	17.33	2.89
New Hampshire	5	2	2.7	4	1.5	2	17.17	2.86
Texas	2	5	1.7	2	2.5	4	17.17	2.86
Arkansas	2.5	4	2.2	2	2	4	16.67	2.78
California	1.5	4	2.5	4	2.5	2	16.5	2.75
Mississippi	1	4	2.3	2	2.5	4	15.83	2.64
Oklahoma	1.5	4	1.3	2	2.5	4.5	15.83	2.64
South Carolina	1	4	2.3	2	2.5	4	15.83	2.64
Rhode Island	2.5	4	3.5	2	1.5	2	15.5	2.58
North Carolina	1	4	2.8	2	1.5	4	15.33	2.56
Oregon	2	4	2.3	2	2.5	2	14.83	2.47
Fifty-state average	2.96	4.14	2.76	3.42	2.83	3.29	19.4	3.23

Source: Margaret Ferguson, "Governors and the Executive Branch," in *Politics in the American States*, 11th ed., ed. Virginia Gray, Russell L. Hanson, and Thad Kousser (Washington, DC: CQ Press, 2018).

Separately elected executive branch officials: 5 = only governor or governor/lieutenant governor team elected; 4.5 = governor or governor/lieutenant governor team, with one other elected official; 4 = governor/lieutenant governor team with some process officials (attorney general, secretary of state, treasurer, and auditor) elected; 3 = governor/lieutenant governor team with process officials and some major and minor policy officials elected; 2.5 = governor (no team) with six or fewer officials elected, but none are major policy officials; 2 = governor (no team) with six or fewer officials elected, but two are major policy officials; 1.5 = governor (no team) with six or fewer officials elected, but two are major officials; 1 = governor (no team) with seven or more process and several major policy officials elected.

Tenure potential: 5 = four-year term, no restraint on reelection; 4.5 = four-year term, only three terms allowed; 4 = four-year term, only two terms permitted; 3 = four-year term, no consecutive election permitted; 2 = two-year term, no restraint on reelection; 1 = two-year term, only two terms permitted.

Appointment powers: In six major functional areas: corrections, K–12 education, health, highway/transportation, public-utilities regulation, and welfare. The six individual offices scores are totaled and then averaged and rounded to the nearest 0.5 for the score. 5 = governor appoints, no other approval needed; 4 = governor appoints, and a board, council, or legislature approves; 3 = someone else appoints, and the governor approves or shares appointment; 2 = someone else appoints, and the governor and others approve; 1 = someone else appoints, and no approval or confirmation needed; 0 = separately elected statewide official.

Budgetary power: 5 = governor has full responsibility, legislature may not increase executive budget; 4 = governor has full responsibility, legislature can increase by special majority vote or subject to item veto; 3 = governor has full responsibility, legislature has unlimited power to change executive budget; 2 = governor shares responsibility, legislature has unlimited power to change executive budget; 1 = governor shares responsibility with another elected official, legislature has unlimited power to change executive budget.

Veto power: 5 = governor has item veto, and a special majority vote of the legislature is needed to override a veto (three-fifths of legislators elected or two-thirds of legislators present); 4 = governor has item veto, with a majority of legislators elected needed to override; 3 = governor has item veto, with only a majority of the legislators present needed to override; 2.5 = governor has item veto power on appropriations only, with a special majority vote needed to override; 2 = governor has item veto power on appropriations only, with a majority of legislators elected needed to override; 1.5 = governor has no item veto, with a special legislative majority needed to override; 1 = governor has no item veto, with only a simple legislative majority needed to override; 0 = governor has no veto power.

Party control: 5 = governor's party has a substantial majority (75 percent or more) in both houses of the legislature; 4.5 = governor's party has a substantial majority in one house and nearly a substantial majority in the other; 4 = governor's party has a simple majority in both houses (under 75 percent) or a substantial majority in one house and a simple majority in the other; 3.5 = governor's party has a simple majority in one house and split control in the other; 3 = split control in the legislature or a nonpartisan legislature; 2 = governor's party has a simple minority (25 percent or more) in both houses or a simple minority in one house and a substantial minority (under 25 percent) in the other; 1 = governor's party has a substantial minority in both houses.

Governor's institutional-powers index: To assess and compare how the 50 governors fared in their institutional powers, the scores of each indicator were combined into a single additive index. The six indicator scores for each state's governorship are averaged to remain within the framework of the five-point scale.

TABLE 8-3 ● Who's Who among U.S. Governors, 2019

State	Governor	Party	Education (highest degree obtained)	First Elected in	Previous Political Life
Alabama	Kay Ivey	Republican	Auburn University	—[a]	Lieutenant governor
Alaska	Mike Dunleavy	Republican	University of Alaska–Fairbanks (MA)	2018	State senator
Arizona	Doug Ducey	Republican	Arizona State University	2014	State treasurer
Arkansas	Asa Hutchinson	Republican	University of Arkansas (JD)	2014	Undersecretary of Homeland Security; member, U.S. House of Representatives
California	Gavin Newsom	Democrat	Santa Clara University	2018	Lieutenant governor
Colorado	Jared Polis	Democrat	Princeton University (BA)	2018	Member, U.S. House of Representatives
Connecticut	Ned Lamont	Democrat	Yale University (MBA)	2018	Selectman, Greenwich
Delaware	John Carney	Democrat	University of Delaware (MPA)	2016	Member, U.S. House of Representatives
Florida	Ron DeSantis	Republican	Harvard University (JD)	2018	Member, U.S. House of Representatives
Georgia	Brian Kemp	Republican	University of Georgia (BS)	2018	Georgia secretary of state
Hawaii	David Ige	Democrat	University of Hawaii (MBA)	2014	State senator
Idaho	Brad Little	Republican	University of Idaho	2018	Lieutenant governor
Illinois	J. B. Pritzker	Republican	Northwestern University (JD)	2018	Started at the top as governor; previously a businessman
Indiana	Eric Holcomb	Republican	Hanover College	2016	Lieutenant governor
Iowa	Kim Reynolds	Republican	Iowa State University	—	Lieutenant governor
Kansas	Laura Kelly	Democrat	Indiana University (MS)	2018	State senator
Kentucky	Matt Bevin	Republican	Washington and Lee University	2015	Started at the top as governor; previously a businessman
Louisiana	John Bel Edwards	Democrat	Louisiana State University (JD)	2015	State representative
Maine	Janet Mills	Democrat	University of Maine (JD)	2018	State attorney general
Maryland	Larry Hogan	Republican	Florida State University	2014	State secretary of appointments
Massachusetts	Charlie Baker	Republican	Northwestern University (MBA)	2014	State administration and finance secretary
Michigan	Gretchen Whitmer	Democrat	Michigan State University (JD)	2018	State senator
Minnesota	Tim Walz	Democrat	Minnesota State University, Mankato (MS)	2018	Member, U.S. House of Representatives
Mississippi	Phil Bryant	Republican	Mississippi College	2011	Lieutenant governor
Missouri	Mike Parson	Republican	University of Marylandb	—	Lieutenant governor
Montana	Steve Bullock	Democrat	Columbia University Law School (JD)	2012	Montana attorney general
Nebraska	Pete Ricketts	Republican	University of Chicago (MBA)	2014	Started at the top as governor; previously a businessman

State	Governor	Party	Education (highest degree obtained)	First Elected in	Previous Political Life
Nevada	Steve Sisolak	Democrat	University of Nevada, Las Vegas (MBA)	2018	Clark County commission
New Hampshire	Chris Sununu	Republican	Massachusetts Institute of Technology	2016	New Hampshire Executive Council
New Jersey	Phil Murphy	Democrat	University of Pennsylvania (MBA)	2017	U.S. ambassador to Germany
New Mexico	Michelle Lujan Grisham	Democrat	University of New Mexico (JD)	2018	Member, U.S. House of Representatives
New York	Andrew Cuomo	Democrat	Albany Law School (JD)	2010	New York attorney general
North Carolina	Roy Cooper	Democrat	University of North Carolina (JD)	2016	State attorney general
North Dakota	Doug Burgum	Republican	Stanford University (MBA)	2016	Started at the top as governor; previously a businessman
Ohio	Mike DeWine	Republican	Ohio Northern University (JD)	2018	State attorney general
Oklahoma	Kevin Stitt	Republican	Oklahoma State University (BS)	2018	Started at the top as governor; previously a businessman
Oregon	Kate Brown	Democrat	Lewis and Clark College (JD)	—	Secretary of state
Pennsylvania	Tom Wolf	Democrat	Massachusetts Institute of Technology (PhD)	2014	State secretary of revenue
Rhode Island	Gina Raimondo	Democrat	Yale University (JD)	2014	State treasurer
South Carolina	Henry McMaster	Republican	University of South Carolina	—	Lieutenant governor
South Dakota	Kristi Noem	Republican	South Dakota State University	2018	Member, U.S. House of Representatives
Tennessee	Bill Lee	Republican	Auburn University (BS)	2018	Started at the top as governor; previously a businessman
Texas	Greg Abbott	Republican	Vanderbilt University (JD)	2014	State attorney general
Utah	Gary Herbert	Republican	Brigham Young University[b]	—	Lieutenant governor
Vermont	Phil Scott	Republican	University of Vermont	2016	Lieutenant governor
Virginia	Ralph Northam	Democrat	Eastern Virginia Medical School (MD)	2017	Lieutenant governor
Washington	Jay Inslee	Democrat	Willamette University (JD)	2012	Member, U.S. House of Representatives
West Virginia	Jim Justice	Republican	Marshall University (MBA)	2016	Started at the top as governor; previously a businessman
Wisconsin	Tony Evers	Democrat	University of Wisconsin (PhD)	2018	State superintendent of public instruction
Wyoming	Mark Gordon	Republican	Middlebury College (BA)	2018	State treasurer

Source: National Governors Association, https://www.nga.org/governors/.

[a]Those individuals with no dates shown in this column (—) were not elected to the governorship when they first took that office; rather, each was elevated to the position after the elected governor left office for some reason.

[b]Did not graduate.

than through speeches or other personal appearances. As noted above, gubernatorial elections are now a billion-dollar business, with individual races sometimes costing in excess of $100 million. Candidates and outside groups spent more than $80 million in the unsuccessful recall election of Wisconsin Republican Scott Walker in 2012 (roughly $14 for every man, woman, and child in Wisconsin), more than doubling the previous gubernatorial record in that state.[48]

Keeping and Leaving Office

Governors are rarely booted out of office prematurely. In June 2004, Connecticut governor John Rowland resigned after being investigated by the legislature for accepting gifts from a contractor with business before the state. Faced with possible **impeachment** and a federal criminal investigation, Rowland, one of the nation's longest-serving governors at the time, chose to step down. Rod Blagojevich, the disgraced Illinois governor caught by the FBI on tape plotting to sell the appointment to President Obama's old U.S. Senate seat, continued to insist on his innocence even after he was impeached in 2009, but he was convicted in 2011 and sentenced to 14 years in prison. In 2003, Gray Davis of California was the first governor forced to leave office by a **recall election** since Lynn Frazier of North Dakota was booted out more than 80 years earlier on charges of corruption. Voters felt that Davis had dug the state into such a deep hole financially that it would take years to recover. His liberal views on such issues as gay marriage also had stirred up controversy. Arnold Schwarzenegger won the special election held on the same day as Davis's recall.

Wisconsin's Scott Walker in 2012 became the first governor to survive a recall election. He had angered labor unions and Democrats by pushing through

IOWA Republican Terry Branstad became the longest-serving governor in U.S. history in 2015, with 7,640 days in office.

legislation a year earlier that eliminated collective bargaining rights for most public-sector workers. The unions and their allies had no difficulty gathering more than a million signatures calling for his recall, which in Wisconsin amounts to a "do-over" election—Walker had to run for office again in midterm. He was able to beat back a repeat challenge by his 2010 opponent, Milwaukee mayor Tom Barrett, in part because he was able to amass enormous sums for the campaign and in part because even some Democrats felt it would be wrong to remove a governor in the middle of his term over a policy dispute, as opposed to a personal failing such as corruption or gross incompetence.

Arizona governor Evan Mecham was impeached and convicted in 1987 for impeding an investigation and lending state money to a car dealership that he owned. The most recent previous conviction dates back to 1929, when Henry Johnston of Oklahoma was removed for general incompetence by a legislature with possible political motives. A few governors, including Fife Symington of Arizona (1997), Jim Guy Tucker of Arkansas (1996), and Guy Hunt of Alabama (1993), have resigned following criminal convictions. More recently, several governors have resigned amid sex scandals: Robert Bentley of Alabama (2017), Eliot Spitzer of New York (2008), and Jim McGreevey of New Jersey (2004). John Kitzhaber of Oregon stepped down in 2015 amid complaints that his fiancée had advised him on clean energy issues while working as a paid private consultant on the issues. Eric Greitens of Missouri resigned in 2018 in the face of potential impeachment proceedings that sprang from complaints he'd skirted campaign finance laws and tried to blackmail his former lover. "Most top-ranking executive leaders survive political scandals while in office," concludes Brandon Rottinghaus, a University of Houston political scientist and author of the 2015 book *The Institutional Effects of Executive Scandals*. "That's especially true when the prospect of impeachment is low—usually because one party controls both the executive and legislative branches—and pre-scandal popularity was relatively high."[49]

A more common threat to gubernatorial staying power is term limits. Governors in 36 states are limited to either two terms or two consecutive terms in office. The only states that have two-year terms instead of four-year terms—Vermont and New Hampshire—place no limits on the number of terms a governor may serve. Howard Dean served five full terms as governor of Vermont before running for president in 2004.

Impeachment A process by which the legislature can remove executive branch officials, such as the governor, or judges from office for corruption or other reasons.

Recall election A special election allowing voters to remove an elected official from office before the end of his or her term.

TABLE 8-4 ● Recall Rules

State	Grounds for Recall	Specific Signature Requirement	Petition Circulation Time	Election for Successor
Alaska	Yes	25%	Not specified	Successor appointed
Arizona	No	25%	120 days	Simultaneous (5)
California	No	12%	160 days	Simultaneous (6)
Colorado	No	25%	60 days	Simultaneous (6)
Georgia	Yes	15% (1)	90 days	Separate special
Idaho	No	20% (1)	60 days	Successor appointed
Illinois	No	15%	150 days	Separate special
Kansas	Yes	40%	90 days	Successor appointed
Louisiana	No	33.3% (1)	180 days	Separate special
Michigan	Yes	25%	60 days	Separate special
Minnesota	Yes	25%	90 days	Separate special
Montana	Yes	10% (1)	3 months	Separate special
Nevada	No	25%	60 days	Simultaneous (5)
New Jersey	No	25% (2)	320 days (4)	Separate special
North Dakota	No	25%	Not specified	Simultaneous (5)
Oregon	No	15% (3)	90 days	Successor appointed
Rhode Island	Yes	15%	90 days	Separate special
Washington	Yes	25%	270 days	Successor appointed
Wisconsin	No	25%	60 days	Simultaneous (5)

Source: Adapted from the National Conference of State Legislatures, "Recall of State Officials," March 8, 2016, http://www.ncsl.org/research/elections-and-campaigns/recall-of-state-officials.aspx.

Note: Signature requirement is percentage of votes cast in last election for official being recalled. Exceptions: (1) percentage of eligible voters at time of last election; (2) percentage of registered voters in electoral district of official sought to be recalled; (3) percentage of total votes cast in officer's district for all candidates for governor in last election; (4) applies to governor or U.S. senator; all others 160 days; (5) recall ballot consists of a list of candidates for the office held by the person against whom the recall petition was filed; the name of the officer against whom the recall was filed may appear on the list; and (6) recall ballot consists of two parts: the first asks whether the officer against whom the recall petition was filed should be recalled, and the second lists candidates who have qualified for the election; the name of the officer against whom the recall was filed may not appear on this list.

So what do governors do once they leave office? Often, they run for higher offices, such as the presidency or a Senate seat. Four out of the five presidents who directly preceded Barack Obama, in fact, had been governors before winning the White House (see the "Difference That Makes a Difference" box "From State House to White House: Governors' Upward Mobility Blocked"). Governors also regularly run for the U.S. Senate. In 2016, 10 serving senators had previously been governors.

Entering the Senate or serving as a cabinet official generally is considered a step up the professional ladder from being a governor. Many politicians, however, find that being governor—able to make and implement

A DIFFERENCE THAT MAKES A DIFFERENCE
FROM STATE HOUSE TO WHITE HOUSE: GOVERNORS' UPWARD MOBILITY BLOCKED

In 2016, no fewer than 11 sitting or former governors ran for president. None of them got close to winning major-party nominations (although Gary Jacobson, a former Republican governor of New Mexico, was the Libertarian Party nominee). On the Democratic side, the governors could not match former senator and Secretary of State Hillary Clinton for experience. Among Republicans, none of the governors, even though they might not have worked in Washington, could top Donald Trump, the real estate mogul and reality TV star, in terms of projecting an "outsider" image.

Governors may live outside Washington, but they were viewed as part of government—and, therefore, part of the problem. "It's no longer about just being an outsider in principle," said Heather Stancil, cochair of the Madison County Republican Committee in Iowa. "People want somebody who is completely outside the system."[a]

Their poor showings came as something of a surprise. Prior to Barack Obama's elevation from the Senate to the White House in 2008, four of the five previous presidents had served as governor (Jimmy Carter, Ronald Reagan, Bill Clinton, and George W. Bush). Seventeen presidents in all had served earlier as governors. As the 2016 election season got under way, Gallup asked Americans who had the best résumé for becoming president. Their answer was clear: being governor offered the best preparation. After all, aside from foreign policy, the job description is largely the same. Like presidents, governors prepare budgets, oversee large agencies, and set a policy course. Of those surveyed by Gallup, 72 percent said being governor provided the right experience, compared with 51 percent who said the same about being a business executive.[b]

Governors have to run things. Members of Congress just vote. "Because the presidency is no place to begin to develop executive talents, the executive career clearly is preferable to the legislator," writes political scientist Larry J. Sabato. "If you live under a governor, you mainly care about his or her ability to govern."[c]

But the contemporary media landscape favors senators and other creatures of Washington. They stand ready and willing to pop off on cable talk shows or social media about whatever the cause or scandal of the moment might be. Governors might be closely associated with particular issues—such as cutting taxes or fighting crime—but they have no regular platform from which to spout off routinely. "We are into an age where it seems like your ability to get yourself on cable news and be a rock star in a reality-TV era matters more than what you've accomplished in a state like Texas or New Jersey or Florida," said Henry Barbour, who sits on the Republican National Committee. "It's tough, and it's not good, but it is reality."[d]

Running for president, though, often will not raise the standing of governors back home. Three of Trump's rivals in 2016—Chris Christie of New Jersey, Bobby Jindal of Louisiana, and Scott Walker of Wisconsin—saw their home-state approval ratings plummet into the 30s or even (in Jindal's case) into the 20s over the course of their presidential campaigns. Earlier governors saw their careers stall after failed national campaigns. Rick Perry had won three elections as governor of Texas but saw the handwriting on the wall after his presidential campaign imploded. He gave up the job of governor when his term ended, preparing another presidential run instead. "The collapse of Perry's 2012 presidential bid damaged his image in Texas as an invincible political juggernaut who had never lost a campaign in his political career," said Rice University political scientist Mark P. Jones. "While I believe Perry was already leaning towards not running for re-election in 2014, his failed 2012 presidential bid certainly emboldened potential challengers and likely influenced his decision to not stand for re-election."[e]

It's possible that governors are in for another long dry spell. Prior to the election of Carter in 1976, no one who had served as governor had been elected president since Franklin D. Roosevelt, back in 1932.

[a]Quoted in Glenn Thrush, "How Scott Walker Became an Asterisk," *Politico*, September 21, 2015, http://www.politico.com/story/2015/09/scott-walker-quits-2016-takeaways-213907#ixzz3mQla658Y.

[b]Jim Norman, "State Governor Best Experience for Presidency," Gallup, February 8, 2016, http://www.gallup.com/poll/189119/state-governor-best-experience-presidency.aspx.

[c]Larry J. Sabato, *Goodbye to Good-Time Charlie: The American Governorship Transformed*, 2nd ed. (Washington, DC: CQ Press, 1983), 33.

[d]Quoted in Alex Roarty, "Why Governors Are Struggling in the 2016 Race," *National Journal*, November 18, 2015, https://www.national-journal.com/s/98806/why-governors-are-struggling-2016-race.

[e]Quoted in Louis Jacobson, "Rocky Roads Ahead for Governors with Failed Presidential Bids," *Governing*, January 4, 2016, http://www.governing.com/topics/politics/gov-governors-post-presidential-careers.html.

decisions, with a large staff and all the machinery of state government at their disposal—is the best job they'll ever have. Dirk Kempthorne, who gave up a Senate seat to run for governor of Idaho in 1998, said that many of his colleagues regretted having to give up governorships to come to Washington and be just one more legislative voice among many. "They all said that being governor is the best job in the world," Kempthorne said on taking office. "I'm ready to find out."[50] Governor James Douglas took a post at Middlebury College rather than seeking federal office after he left the governorship in Vermont in 2011—one of a number of governors in recent years who have passed on the chance of continuing their careers in Washington. "Given the low repute in which Congress is now held, and its propensity to accomplish nothing or next to nothing, going to Washington is not a particularly appealing opportunity," he said.[51]

Many former governors in other positions complain that they never had it as good as back when they were running their states. "My worst day as governor was better than my best day as a United States senator," Thomas Carper, D-Del., said in 2009.[52] Wisconsin's Tommy Thompson openly lamented the second-guessing to which he was subjected as President George W. Bush's secretary of health and human services during a 2006 appearance before the National Governors Association, an organization he had once chaired. "When you're a governor, you can wake up in the morning and you can have an idea and you can have somebody working on it by 11 o'clock in the morning," Thompson said. "When you go to Washington . . . I get up, get the same idea, go in. Then you have to vet it with 67,000 people who all believe sincerely they're smarter than you."[53] He warned his successor, Scott Walker, not to accept a job in the Trump administration, telling him "a thousand times" that being governor was by far the better job.[54]

Other Executive Offices

Only the president is elected to the executive branch of the federal government. The vice president is the president's running mate and is elected as part of a package deal. The heads of all the cabinet departments—defense, transportation, energy, agriculture, and so on—are appointed by the president, subject to Senate approval. Voters do not get to say who gets in and who stays out.

Things work differently at the state level. The governor is the only statewide official elected in every state.

Most states, however, also have several other statewide officials elected in their own right. This is a holdover from earlier times when the governor was not invested with much power and authority was distributed among a number of officeholders. Texas still has two dozen officials who are elected statewide, whereas New Jersey for many years elected only the governor. (That changed in 2009, when Garden State voters elected a lieutenant governor for the first time.) In 2013, the Maine House voted down a proposal to allow voters to select the state's treasurer, secretary of state, and attorney general, who are all picked by the legislature. Most states have handfuls of officials elected statewide; we outline the responsibilities of a few of them below.

Lieutenant Governor

The office of lieutenant governor traditionally has been seen as something of a joke. Lieutenant governors, it's been said, have nothing to do but wait for their governors to resign or die so they can accrue some real power. That situation has changed in some places in recent years. Some states, such as Georgia and Virginia, responded to the budget shortfalls of recent years by slashing the budgets and limiting the powers of their lieutenant governors' offices. More states, however, have expanded the purview of the office, recognizing that there is plenty of work to go around and the skills of the second in command should be used more fully. Governors have turned to their lieutenants to set the course on issues such as economic development, homeland security, and opioid addiction. "We're seeing governors continue to tap lieutenant governors for really what are the top issues of the day," says Julia Hurst, executive director of the National Lieutenant Governors Association.[55]

In most cases, power is granted to the lieutenant governor because of the desire of the governor. The next person to hold the office may have very different responsibilities or nothing to do at all. Lots of contemporary lieutenant governors seem dissatisfied or have been unsuccessful. From 2012 to 2014, six lieutenant governors resigned, six saw their campaigns for governor or senator crumble, and three decided not to run alongside the governor for reelection. Republican lieutenant governor Peter Kinder of Missouri complained that during his first five years serving alongside Democratic governor Jay Nixon, "we've had one substantive discussion," and he wasn't even informed when the governor left the state.[56] Once, when similarly ignored lieutenant governor Gavin Newsom of California posed for a picture with a young boy who asked him what a lieutenant governor is, Newsom said, "I ask myself that every day."[57]

In some states, however, the lieutenant governor's responsibilities are laid out by law. In Indiana, for example, the lieutenant governor's portfolio includes the departments of commerce and agriculture. In half the states, the lieutenant governor presides over the state senate, having varying degrees of authority in that chamber from state to state. In Texas and Mississippi, lieutenant governors play much more than a ceremonial role. Not only do they preside over the senate, but they also set the agenda and appoint senators to committees. In both states, the lieutenant governor often is referred to as the most powerful figure in the state, with authority in both the executive and legislative branches. In 1999, Alabama Democrats in the state senate sought to strip control of their chamber, along with other powers, from Lieutenant Governor Steve Windom, a Republican. And they could have done it if only he had left the senate floor, but Windom refused. To stay present in and to keep control of the chamber for that day, and thus for the rest of his term, he did what was necessary, even urinating into a plastic jug in the chamber.[58]

In 25 states, the governor and lieutenant governor are elected as part of the same ticket. (New Jersey opted for this model after two recent governors left office prematurely. As noted above, the state elected its first lieutenant governor in 2009.) In 18 other states, the two are elected separately. The other 6 states—Arizona, Maine, New Hampshire, Oregon, Tennessee, and Wyoming—don't elect lieutenant governors, although in Tennessee the speaker of the senate is given the title. Electing the governor and lieutenant governor separately can be a source of mischief, especially if the people elected are not from the same party. After Mark Dayton, the Democratic governor of Minnesota, picked his lieutenant governor to take over a vacant U.S. Senate seat in 2017, her job in turn was filled by the president of the state senate, who was a Republican. "I'll do my best to stay healthy," Dayton quipped.[59]

The lieutenant governor often assumes the powers of the governor when the boss is out of the state. During the 1970s, Republican Mike Curb of California had a lot of fun appointing judges and issuing **executive orders** while Democratic governor Jerry Brown was busy out of the state doing, among other things, his own presidential campaigning. In 2014, when Brown was again serving as governor, his travels led the state to work its way through almost the entire line of succession. California had four acting governors in as many days when Brown went to Mexico on a trade mission, with the lieutenant governor, state senate president, and assembly speaker all doing the duty before all but one traveled out of state.

Attorney General

Perhaps the statewide office that has undergone the greatest transformation in recent years is that of attorney general. Always referred to as the top law enforcement officer in the state, the attorney general sometimes has had duties that have been quite minimal because most criminal prosecutions are taken care of at the county level. But attorneys general have become major political players, finding new power by banding together on a partisan basis to sue the federal government. It once was rare for more than one state attorney general to sue Washington in any given year. During the first year of the Trump presidency, however, Democratic attorneys general banded together to sue the feds no fewer than three dozen times.

Individual states such as California, Massachusetts, and Washington, in the meantime, sued to block Trump policies dozens of times, over issues including environmental policies, health funding, and a ban on travel from certain Muslim-majority countries. Democratic attorneys general said their actions are a necessary check on a president they described as out of control. "It is perhaps poetic justice that it's the son of immigrants who is wielding the legal slingshot against Donald Trump in protecting our constitutional and civil rights," said California attorney general Xavier Becerra, whose parents are from Mexico.[60]

Democratic attorneys general had borrowed a page from the Republican playbook. During the Obama presidency, Republican attorneys general got into the habit of suing the federal government at what was then an unprecedented pace. Among their number was Scott Pruitt, the attorney general of Oklahoma, who sued the Obama administration routinely, before serving as Trump's first Environmental Protection Agency administrator. During his 2014 campaign for governor, Texas

---

Executive orders Rules or regulations with the force of law that governors can create directly under the statutory authority given them.

attorney general Greg Abbott routinely boasted that his job consisted of going to the office, suing Obama (which he did more than two dozen times), and then heading home. "The AGs, who often attack the administration in packs, have done more than Republicans in Congress, statehouses, or anywhere else to block, cripple, undermine, or weaken Obama's initiatives," claimed the executive editor of the *Weekly Standard*.[61]

State attorneys general first flexed their collective muscles in multistate consumer protection cases against financial firms, toy manufacturers, and drug companies, among many other examples. In 2014, to cite one instance, California attorney general Kamala Harris announced that her state would receive $103 million as part of a $7 billion settlement reached with banking giant Citigroup to resolve claims that it misled investors about mortgage-backed bonds.

The granddaddy of all such cases was the series of lawsuits filed against the tobacco companies during the mid-1990s. The attorneys general argued that the cigarette makers had engaged in fraud and caused a great deal of sickness and health conditions that the states had ended up paying to treat through Medicaid and other programs. An initial agreement reached between the states and the industry was not ratified by Congress. Instead, in 1998, the attorneys general settled their lawsuits with the companies on their own. The tobacco companies agreed to pay the states an estimated $246 billion over 25 years.

The relatively few cases brought by more than one attorney general back in the 1980s typically involved fewer than five states. Today, there are far more cases involving far more actors. "Litigation involving over half of the nation's AGs, once an unusual event, represents over 40 percent of all the multistate cases conducted since 2000," Marquette University political scientist Paul Nolette writes in his book about contemporary attorneys general, *Federalism on Trial*.[62] In 2012, attorneys general in every state but one reached a $25 billion settlement with home mortgage servicers—the largest joint federal–state settlement in history. Beginning in 2007, Andrew Cuomo, then New York's attorney general, won $13 million in settlements from lenders and universities that had violated state laws with their student loan policies. One of the first things Cuomo did after taking office as governor in 2011 was to use the money to set up a national student loan center that would offer "unbiased" financial advice to students and their parents.

Not surprisingly, there has been a backlash against these newly powerful officials. In part, this has been based on the fact that for many attorneys general the job has been a successful launching pad toward the governorship. In 2014, half a dozen former attorneys general were serving as governors, with about as many seeking the office in elections that year. "It seems to be considered the second most prominent and important position to governor," said veteran Arkansas newspaper columnist John Brummett. "The other statewide offices are mostly clerical and pointless."[63] But the fight over control of the office of attorney general has largely been ideological. One of the great philosophical divides in U.S. politics is that between those with opposing views of how business should be regulated. On one side are those who believe that businesses have a right to conduct their affairs with a minimum of interference from state governments, which can only hinder their productivity and profits. On the other are those who believe just as strongly that conducting business in a state is a privilege that comes with a number of responsibilities that the state has the duty to enforce. The majority of state attorneys general over the past few years have acted as if they were members of the "privilege" camp, and that has fueled the rise of groups designed to combat what the business sector sees as excessive regulatory activism.

Attorneys general once were mainly Democrats, their campaigns funded by trial lawyers. Over the past couple of decades, the U.S. Chamber of Commerce and many other business groups have spent millions trying to defeat "activist" attorney general candidates. "Historically . . . attorney general races were off most business people's radar screens," said Bob LaBrant, a longtime leader of the Michigan Chamber of Commerce. Today, "there's greater incentive to get involved in an attorney general race because of the increased involvement of attorneys general across the country in litigation against the business community."[64] The Republican Attorneys General Association (RAGA) was founded in 1999 to elect candidates who believe that their colleagues have gone too far in the pursuit of business regulations and the revenues such cases can generate. Their strategy appears to have worked—the number of GOP attorneys general climbed from 12 in 1999 to 20 by 2003; as of 2019, 24 state attorneys general were Republicans, and 26 were Democrats. For years, the Republican and Democratic attorneys general associations had a handshake agreement that they wouldn't target seats held by incumbents from the other party. The Republican attorneys general voted to end that policy in

Andrew Cuomo followed both Eliot Spitzer, his predecessor as state attorney general, and his father, Mario Cuomo, into the New York governor's mansion. He won the 2010 election and has since presided over the closing of a $10 billion budget deficit and the legalization of same-sex marriage.

Aside from taking a more active role in elections, corporations that might be subject to investigation by state attorneys general have taken to courting them aggressively while they are in office, not just through campaign contributions but also through ongoing lobbying and personal appeals at lavish conferences—sometimes by former attorneys general who have been hired for the task. There are fewer disclosure requirements for attorneys general than for state legislators, and corporations with interests in banking, telecommunications, pharmaceuticals, and even energy drinks have spent millions to gain the ears of attorneys general and avoid exposure to costly litigation. "I don't fault for one second that corporate America is pushing back on what has happened," said John Suthers, a former Colorado attorney general, referring to multistate lawsuits brought against various industries. "Attorneys general can do more damage in a heartbeat than legislative bodies can. I think it is a matter of self-defense, and

2017, and the Democrats quickly followed suit. "RAGA has a clear mission to win races," says Zack Roday, the association's spokesman. "The decision was made: Where you have good candidates and can draw a clear difference, you don't leave those types of races on the table."[65]

TABLE 8-5 ● The Powers of State Offices

In Many States, Lieutenant Governors . . .	Secretaries of State . . .	Attorneys General . . .
Preside over the senate	File and/or archive state records and regulations, other corporate documents	Institute civil suits
Appoint committees	Administer uniform commercial code provisions	Represent state agencies and defend and/or challenge the constitutionality of legislative or administrative actions
Break roll-call ties	Publish state manual or directory, session laws, state constitution, statutes, and/or administrative rules and regulations	Enforce open meetings and records laws
Assign bills	Open legislative sessions	Revoke corporate charters
May be assigned special duties by governors	Enroll and/or retain copies of bills	Enforce antitrust prohibitions against monopolistic enterprises
Serve as cabinet members or members of advisory bodies	Register lobbyists	Enforce air pollution, water pollution, and hazardous waste laws in a majority of states
Serve as acting governors when the governors are out of state		Handle criminal appeals and serious statewide criminal prosecutions
		Intervene in public utility rate cases
		Enforce the provisions of charitable trusts

Sources: Compiled from Council of State Governments, ed., *The Book of the States 2003* (Lexington, KY: Author, 2003), 215, 221, and 224; the National Association of Attorneys General, http://www.naag.org; and the National Lieutenant Governors Association, http://www.nlga.us.

I understand it pretty well, although I have got to admit as an old-time prosecutor, it makes me a little queasy."[66]

Other Offices

Every state elects its governor, and most states elect a lieutenant governor and attorney general. In terms of which other offices are held by elected officials—as opposed to officials appointed by the governor or by boards and commissions—the states vary widely. The theory behind electing many officials directly is that it gives the public a greater voice in shaping a variety of state programs, instead of just selecting a governor and leaving it all up to him or her.

In 2003, New Mexico governor Bill Richardson convinced voters to approve a referendum that gave him the power to name the state's top education official directly. Richardson knew he would receive the credit or blame for running the schools anyway, so he wanted to have the power to shape policy in that office by being the boss of the person who ran it. In 2013, Republican governor Mike Pence of Indiana attempted to make an end run around the Democrat elected as the state superintendent of public instruction by creating a new state education agency to set policy. In 2016, the Wisconsin Supreme Court found unconstitutional a law passed five years earlier that stripped power from the state superintendent of education and gave it to the governor.

Only a few states, including Georgia, Montana, and Oregon, elect a state superintendent of education. In Nebraska, a state board of education is elected, and the board in turn selects a superintendent. Several states, mostly in the South, directly elect a secretary of agriculture. An increasing number of states allow citizens to vote for an insurance commissioner. Most states elect a secretary of state who, in turn, regulates elections in those states. Overall, many states structure their executive branches similarly—if there isn't an elected agriculture secretary, there is certain to be an appointed one.

Some believe, however, that electing separate department heads makes too much of government political. A state treasurer who has to worry about getting reelected might not make politically unpopular but fiscally necessary decisions to make sure that the state's books are balanced. The other trouble with electing officials is that the departments they head will squabble over money and power instead of working together as part of a team to promote the greater good.

Election officials themselves have become controversial in some cases. Secretaries of state often oversee elections, and some have been accused of partisan bias in this role. Colorado's former secretary of state Scott Gessler came to his job after a career as one of the GOP's top campaign lawyers in the state. He was accused by Democrats of retaining a partisan bias in office, notably in participating in a fundraiser to pay off a campaign fine levied by his office. He was sued no fewer than eight times during his first year in office.[67] Similarly, Democrats in other states complained that GOP secretaries of state favored their parties by making changes to early-voting rules and implementing voter identification laws that they claimed were meant to suppress voting by those likely to vote Democratic. The formerly low-profile office attracted millions of dollars in super PAC spending in 2014, as each party saw increasing value in electing the person who controls elections. Iowa was one of the few states that saw voter turnout increase in 2012. Brad Anderson was proud of the role he played in encouraging turnout there as state director of President Obama's campaign. In 2014, he ran for secretary of state, saying, "I have a plan to make Iowa No. 1 in voter turnout."[68] The fact that a former Obama operative wanted to run elections made some people nervous. But Anderson was part of a trend of overtly partisan figures running for a job designed to be neutral when it comes to election administration.

Secretaries of state are the top election officers in 37 states. They may have other duties, often including matters such as issuing business licenses. But as money and partisan interest in these races increase exponentially, there is a real danger that these offices will come to be viewed as little more than extensions of partisan movements, rather than as independent election watchdogs, their campaigns influenced by million-dollar support from super PACs. Once in office, secretaries of state now pursue separate agendas on a partisan basis. Democrats promote automatic voter registration to expand access to the ballot. Republicans, expressing concern about voter fraud, call for cuts to early-voting days and impose strict identification requirements.

Conclusion

How did governors become the most important political figures in their states? Over the years, their offices have become the centers of state power, with more and more authority given to them. The power of governors now matches, in most cases, the prestige they have always enjoyed. States have been involved in the difficult balancing act of trying to weigh the interests

POLICY IN PRACTICE
WHY ATTORNEYS GENERAL SOMETIMES DO NOT DEFEND THEIR OWN STATES

State laws get challenged all the time. Luckily, every state has a law firm on retainer—namely, the attorney general's office. But who defends the state when the attorney general is not willing to do it?

That question has come up repeatedly in recent years. Before the U.S. Supreme Court made same-sex marriage rights universal in 2015, several Democratic attorneys general (AGs) refused to defend their states' bans on the practice. In 2016, Roy Cooper, then North Carolina's attorney general, decided not to defend House Bill 2, which gutted antidiscrimination protections for gay and transgender people. Maine Republican governor Paul LePage sued Janet Mills, the state's Democratic attorney general, in 2017 for refusing to pursue legal actions he favored.

These conflicts emerge most often on high-profile issues where partisans hold strong and opposing positions, including governors and attorneys general from different parties. Defending state laws is one of the primary duties of attorneys general, something they should not refuse to do, argues Greg Zoeller, a former attorney general in Indiana. He had to defend all kinds of laws he didn't like, including the death penalty, which he opposes on religious grounds. It's one of the great clichés of the legal profession that lawyers take on cases and clients they don't believe in. Attorneys general who refuse to defend state laws typically say it is because those laws are unconstitutional, but Zoeller says that's not their call to make. "The courts are empowered to make the decision of whether a law is constitutional or not," he says. "To bring that question to the courts, there has to be a lawyer on both sides."

Zoeller points to the example of Proposition 8, the 2008 ballot measure that banned same-sex marriage in California. The attorney general there refused to defend the law, so the Supreme Court threw it out in 2013 on a question of standing, on the grounds that the ballot initiative's sponsors had no right to defend a state law if the state itself refused to do so. "It cost us two years of uncertainty," Zoeller says. "If the AG of California

defended the law, we would have had an answer [on same-sex marriage] two years earlier."

In practice, an attorney general's office expresses opinions about the constitutionality of laws all the time. On almost a daily basis, assistant attorneys general instruct legislators on how to craft bills so they stay within allowable bounds. One reason the attorney general gets to defend state laws is that constitutional expertise resides in that office.

Splitting authority within the executive branch was also a goal of most state constitutions. Few states follow the federal model, where the attorney general answers to the chief executive. There clearly could be dangers in making the attorney do whatever the governor wants. If governors can order attorneys general to sue, what would stop them from ordering the attorneys to step away from subjecting their campaign contributions to scrutiny? "State constitutions have a healthy fear of executive power," says Jim Tierney, who runs a program on attorneys general at Harvard University. "They don't want the governor to have legal power."

The desire to preserve a balance within the executive branch is one reason why the Kentucky House balked at a plan passed by the state senate in 2017 to strip Attorney General Andy Beshear of much of his authority. Beshear, a Democrat, repeatedly sued Republican governor Matt Bevin. Republican legislators may not like that, but they can still see the point of having an AG with independent watchdog authority.

When he was Maine's attorney general back in the 1990s, Tierney refused to defend a state law he felt was without merit. The state supreme court upheld his authority to exercise judgment about which state laws to defend and which ones to leave alone. It may seem problematic to have AGs decide on their own which state laws can stand up to scrutiny, but ultimately someone has to make the call. The American system of governance is all about splitting power. When it comes to legal questions, the attorney general is most often going to be the one who has the final word.

Source: Adapted from Alan Greenblatt, "What Happens When the Attorney General Refuses to Defend a Law?," *Governing*, August 2017, http://www.governing.com/topics/politics/gov-attorney-general-refusal-defend-state-laws.html.

of direct citizen selection of leaders against the need to have professional people appointed to pursue a coherent policy promulgated by a single accountable leader. In recent decades, the pendulum has mostly swung in favor of investing more power in the office of the governor.

Once weak, unable to set policy or budgets, governors have now become unquestioned leaders. They are able to select cabinets that run most of the state agencies according to the governors' priorities. Sometimes their staff picks prove to be embarrassments, but they are also able to fire such people in the hope of seeing their agendas pushed forward by more eager replacements. Many positions are designed with staggered terms so that governors cannot appoint their own people to every position. Strong governors, however, are able to combine their appointment powers with their ability to command attention from the mass media to set the terms of political issues and the direction these

issues take in their states. That clout extends to the judicial branch, with many governors able to appoint most state judges.

Their control of budgets and veto authority provide governors with enormous sway over the legislative branch as well. Although they never get everything they want from their legislatures, they almost always get more of what they want than do any individual legislators.

The unrivaled power of governors and their ability to command attention from the media and political donors make them the leading political actors at the state level. Their ability to put people to work in shaping policy and campaigns, as well as to raise money, makes them players in political races ranging from local and legislative contests all the way, in many instances, to the presidency.

Governors, in short, are the top dogs in the states. "As far as policy leadership goes," concludes Alan Rosenthal, "there may be big winners but there are no big losers among the nation's contemporary governors."[69]

THE LATEST RESEARCH

Understanding the evolving power and policy influence of governors through the comparative method has been a particular focus of political science for at least two decades. Much of this focus traces back to the late Thad Beyle, a professor at the University of North Carolina at Chapel Hill, who in the mid-1990s began developing and publishing quantitative measures of gubernatorial powers. Ever since, researchers have used these indices to examine how gubernatorial powers, and what types of powers, translate into political and policy influence.

Gubernatorial powers, however, are constantly shifting. Institutional reforms—such as increases in staff and expansion of appointment powers—may change formal power. Informal power, of course, shifts every time a new governor is elected and brings his or her own personal characteristics to the job. How do these changes shape the ability of chief executives to get their agendas enacted into law? Are these powers enough to give governors the tools they need to meet the increasingly heavy expectations voters place

on them? Are those expectations—especially of the economic variety—realistic given that even the most powerful governor leads a state that is open to economic forces beyond his or her control? Political scientists search for systematic answers through the comparative method, examining differences in power and expectations to see whether they predict differences in political influence and policy success. Below we summarize some of the most recent research on the powers and expectations of governors and other executive branch actors.

- **Barber, Michael, Alexander Bolton, and Sharece Thrower,** "Legislative Constraints on Executive Unilateralism in Separation of Powers Systems," working paper, April 5, 2018.

A central question in a political system based on separation of powers is when and whether executives are successfully constrained by legislatures. Political

(Continued)

(Continued)

science research at the federal level has consistently found evidence that seems counterintuitive—namely, that presidents issue fewer unilateral directives during periods of divided government. What explains this phenomenon in states? Governors are almost certain to veto bills that alter their unilateral directives or impose retaliatory costs on them. Such intended sanctions pose no threat to them, unless the legislative opposition controls a supermajority of seats that can override their vetoes. Some legislatures lack nonstatutory tools such as regulatory review. Thus, the authors state, executives are freer to act unilaterally when polarization is high and majorities are marginal, finding evidence for their conclusions by using a new data set of 24,232 executive orders issued between 1993 and 2013.

- **Nolette, Paul,** *Federalism on Trial: State Attorneys General and National Policymaking in Contemporary America* (Lawrence: University Press of Kansas, 2015).

Over the past two decades, state attorneys general have looked to litigation as a way not only to enforce the law but also to enable them to act as de facto national regulators. It was once rare for attorneys general to band together in legal actions, but in recent years it has become common practice. Attorneys general today are much more likely than their forebears not just to join hands with peers across state lines but also to act in concert with allied policy groups such as the Sierra Club or the U.S. Chamber of Commerce. A series of federal statutes offered them more resources and authority. Many social policies enacted since the Great Society of the 1960s carved out large enforcement roles for the judiciary, which in turn created openings for attorneys general. Attorneys general have collected billions of dollars in legal settlements for their states, but the main impetus for these actions has been their determination to convince entire industries, such as cigarette makers and home mortgage servicers, to change their ways. They have used the court system to push Washington to address a number of issues, such as climate change. "Rather than resisting the growth of a national regulatory state that threatens to expand federal power at the expense of states, AGs have more frequently used coordinated litigation to promote the expansion of national regulation," Nolette writes. Of course, attorneys general have also pushed back against the federal government, particularly during the Obama era. Republican attorneys general were "far more active" during that period than they were the last time a Democrat was president,

Nolette notes, seeking to block the administration in areas such as the Affordable Care Act and environmental regulations that were proposed, in fact, to answer complaints brought by earlier generations of attorneys general.

- **Rottinghaus, Brandon,** *The Institutional Effects of Executive Scandals* (New York: Cambridge University Press, 2015).

There has been no shortage of scandals involving governors in recent decades. What's rare is an executive willing to come clean. Examining scandals in which governors and other top political executives have been embroiled from 1972 to 2012, Rottinghaus found that almost half of them involved accusations of personal financial wrongdoing, such as taking bribes, failure to pay taxes, or embezzlement. Regardless of the scandal, though, governors try hard to change the subject, both by lying and by trying to turn attention toward issues such as education or tourism. The more serious the allegations, the less likely governors are to speak to them willingly. The stronger a governor's institutional powers, the more likely he or she is to stonewall. Most top-ranking executive leaders who face political scandals while in office survive them, especially when the prospect of impeachment is low because one party controls both the executive branch and the legislature.

- **Seifter, Miriam,** "Further from the People? The Puzzle of State Administration," University of Wisconsin Legal Studies Research Paper No. 1421 (2017).

One of the arguments often used in favor of federalism and sending power out from Washington to the states is that governments that are closer to the people can be checked more readily than the federal government. What if that argument is based on a false premise? Seifter notes that the scope and size of state administrative responsibilities have burgeoned in recent decades and now "do a lion's share of governance affecting people's day-to-day lives." Despite this, individuals, interest groups, and media outlets do a less thorough job monitoring, exposing, and impeding state governments than they do in Washington. State-level agencies are more opaque and increasingly politicized and have complex interactions with local governments, while public interest groups and media are either relatively weak or dwindling in the states.

CHAPTER 8

for CQ Press

Want a better grade?

Get the tools you need to sharpen your study skills. SAGE edge offers a robust online environment featuring an impressive array of free tools and resources.

Access practice quizzes, eFlashcards, video, and multimedia at **edge.sagepub.com/ smithgreenblatt7e**

Top Ten Takeaways

1. Governors are the leading political actors within their states, shaping the legislative agenda and getting the most attention from the media and the public.

2. The power of governors has increased over time. What were once almost figurehead positions have become repositories of real political power and influence.

3. There is still a great range across states in terms of the amount of formal authority that is invested within the governor's office.

4. But, as one political scientist has noted, "as far as policy leadership goes, there may be big winners but there are no big losers among the nation's contemporary governors."

5. Aside from helping to formulate laws and budgets, governors represent their states to outsiders, including businesses deciding where to locate and, sometimes, tourists.

6. Governors have become much more partisan in recent years. Rather than borrowing practical ideas from other governors regardless of party, governors today are much more likely to push agendas in line with fellow partisans.

7. Governors have become more diverse, but not as diverse as the holders of some other offices. Today, a governor is more likely to be a rich white man than a woman of any means or a member of an ethnic or minority group.

8. Governors are only rarely removed from office via recall or impeachment.

9. Being a governor isn't nearly as good a launching pad to the presidency these days as it was during the 1980s and 1990s.

10. Other state executive branch officials have gained power and stature in recent years, particularly state attorneys general.

Key Concepts

appointment powers (p. 219)
bully pulpit (p. 224)
executive orders (p. 240)
formal powers (p. 219)

impeachment (p. 236)
informal powers (p. 219)
plural-executive system
   (p. 215)

recall election (p. 236)
supermajority vote (p. 216)

Suggested Websites

- **www.csg.org**. Website of the Council of State Governments, a forum for state officials to swap information on issues of common concern, such as drugs, water, and other policy matters.

- **library.cqpress.com**. The CQ Press Library, which features an online voting and elections collection with a component for gubernatorial elections.

- **www.naag.org**. Website of the National Association of Attorneys General, which has become increasingly prominent as state attorneys general have banded together on a number of high-profile cases.

- **www.nga.org**. Website of the National Governors Association, which shares information among governors and also lobbies the federal government on their behalf.

- **www.stateside.com**. Website of Stateside Associates, a lobbying firm that keeps close tabs on policies and actions in the states.

9

Chris Neal/The Topeka Capital-Journal via AP File

Courts
Turning Law into Politics

Judges have increasingly found themselves in the midst of bitter partisan battles as they rule on cases related to important legislative issues such as voter identification. Some judicial decisions have raised accusations that "activist judges" are legislating from the bench. Judges often rule on cases concerning issues of great concern to legislators and the public, from gun rights and education to pipelines and death penalties, and their rulings will never please everyone.

Chapter Objectives

After reading this chapter, you will be able to

- Describe the role and structure of state courts,

- Explain how judges are selected,

- Identify the players and elements present in state-level criminal court cases, and

- Discuss the problems contributing to current changes in the courts.

At the dawn of the 20th century, the state of New York had a law on its books limiting the number of hours that bakers could work—no more than 10 hours per day, or 60 hours per week. A baker named Joseph Lochner was accused of letting an employee work more than 60 hours in a week. After he was fined, Lochner challenged the law. In 1905, in *Lochner v. New York*, the U.S. Supreme Court found that the state law violated the U.S. Constitution, by interfering with the right of employers and employees to enter into contracts pretty much as they saw fit. The case became the basis for a series of conservative judicial opinions invalidating economic regulation, including workplace protections.

During the New Deal period of the 1930s, however, the Court changed its approach. *Lochner* was never formally overturned, but the ideas underpinning the decision became judicial kryptonite. *The New Republic* ranked *Lochner* among the Court's worst decisions, arguing that a revival of the ideas in *Lochner* would undermine the government's ability to regulate workplace safety, employment discrimination, and minimum-wage rates.[1] That's not an uncommon reading among liberals. But even Robert Bork, the late conservative judicial icon, called *Lochner* "the symbol, indeed the quintessence, of judicial usurpation of power." U.S. Supreme Court chief justice John Roberts has cited *Lochner* numerous times, describing it as a "discredited decision." Since its repudiation, the courts have only rarely tossed out laws governing economic activity. "There's been this sense in constitutional law, at least for the last 70 to 80 years, that government has full power over regulation of economic matters," says Josh Blackman, a professor at the South Texas College of Law in Houston.[2]

In a 2015 opinion in a case known as *Patel*, Don Willett, a justice on the Texas Supreme Court, argued that the "Lochner bogeyman" had for too long stopped judges from doing their jobs, which include questioning the motivations and rationales of lawmakers when they impose new economic rules. "This case is fundamentally about the American dream and the unalienable right to pursue happiness without curtsying to government on bended knee," Willett wrote in a concurring opinion regarding occupational licensing requirements.[3] A few conservative legal scholars had previously promoted the idea that it was time to revive *Lochner* and get judges back in the game of challenging a broader range of economic regulation. The fact that Willett did so in a state supreme court opinion, joined by two of his colleagues, had far greater resonance. "Law professors, we can write whatever we want, and it serves no purpose," Blackman says. "When judges do it, it makes a big difference."

Willett was appointed to the U.S. Fifth Circuit Court of Appeals in 2017 and appeared on President Donald Trump's short list of possible Supreme Court picks. Willett has become a star in conservative legal circles for a number of reasons. The fact that some recent Supreme Court picks have danced around issues such as abortion and campaign finance on grounds of "judicial restraint" has left some conservatives looking to promote judges whose positions are more clear. Too many recent nominees, they complain, ended up drifting to the left after they reached the bench, in deference to progressive acts of Congress or state legislatures. In his opinion about *Lochner* and elsewhere, Willett offered abundant evidence that that wouldn't happen in his case. "This particular opinion wasn't just a break from the ordinary," says David Bernstein, a pro-*Lochner* professor at George Mason University law school. "To write a scholarly opinion taking a controversial stand shows that he's not a shrinking violet, that he'll stand up for what he believes."[4]

For years, conservatives have complained about **activist judges**, warning that liberal judges too often had created law themselves, rather than simply interpreting the laws as they are already written. At this point, it's pretty clear that one person's activist is another person's hero. Partisans on both sides cheer when judges interpret the law in the ways that they'd prefer. But conservative judges have at least paid lip service in recent years to the notion of restraint, for fear of being accused of legislating from the bench. Willett doesn't do that. In his *Patel* opinion, he wrote that he opposes judicial activism, but argued that "judicial passivism" is also "corrosive." He devotes a fair amount of space to describing how courts have been far more timid about calling out lawmakers when it comes to overreaching on economic issues than in other areas such as privacy or political speech. In his view, judges must intervene whenever the government tramples on an individual's right to pursue an economic path of his or her choice. "I believe that judicial passivity is incompatible with individual liberty and limited government," he wrote in *Patel*.

Willett also knows how to draw attention to his ideas. Texas Supreme Court justices have to run for reelection every six years. In an important but relatively obscure job, he found social media, in particular Twitter, to be an indispensable tool in getting his name in front of voters. Not many citizens can name the supreme court justices of their state, but in Texas, justices have to go after millions of votes. Willett understood an iron law of political life: "To do my job, I must keep my job," he says. His Twitter feed, which has largely gone silent since his ascension to the federal bench, was patriotic and Texas proud, but primarily nonpartisan, filled with puns, encomiums to bacon, and pictures of his kids. His jokes weren't hilarious, but in the often-scabrous context of Twitter, they came across as refreshing, perhaps especially coming from a prominent jurist. Willett built up a following of more than 100,000 on Twitter. By comparison, Nathan Hecht, the chief justice of the Texas Supreme Court, struggled to break the 2,000-follower mark. "There's not a very saturated market for judges who enjoy interacting with people and are good at it," says Chris Bonneau, a political scientist who studies courts at the University of Pittsburgh. "Willett rejects those old-school norms about how judges should only speak from the bench, and I think rightly so."[5]

During his 12 years on the Texas bench, Willett pushed libertarian ideas in language that was readily accessible to people who lack legal training. He appeared frequently at law schools and other public venues. Willett remained determined to write in his own voice, whether on Twitter or in formal opinions. Like Supreme Court justices Roberts and Elena Kagan, as well as the late Antonin Scalia, Willett tries to write so that laymen can follow his ideas. Most state supreme court opinions go unread; Willett's sometimes get shared on Twitter and Facebook. Coming up with a punchy phrase—and not shying away from occasional pop culture shout-outs—increases his chances to be quoted directly in news accounts, including public opinion and reaction to rulings. As with Scalia, it makes it more likely that Willett's opinions will be read and discussed by law students who are the future judges and legal activists. "Justice Willett has really typified the rejection of jargon and language that sounds like it came from Mt. Olympus rather than earth," says Evan Young, a former Scalia clerk who practices in Texas.[6]

Willett is only one judge, although a prominent one. But his career thus far typifies a number of trends in contemporary jurisprudence: the willingness to challenge old precepts and precedents; the belief that judges shouldn't cater or bend to the political branches of government; and a seemingly increasing willingness to use the courts to achieve political and policy goals. Americans want to view judges as neutral arbiters of justice, but the sense that the law is blind and impartial has become harder to sustain during a polarized era. During his last year in office as governor of Florida, Republican Rick Scott argued that he had the authority, including staving off a lawsuit, to replace three state supreme court justices who would be retiring due to age restrictions on the same day in 2019 when he was set to leave office, which would tip the partisan balance on the court. In 2016, both Arizona and Georgia expanded the number of seats on their state supreme courts, in order to allow Republican governors to appoint newcomers who would create conservative majorities. "The only reason why you would add justices to the court is to pack the court for political reasons," complained Steve Farley, a Democratic state senator in Arizona. "This is the executive making a power grab over the judiciary. If you don't like the decisions the Supreme Court is making, you don't pack the court."[7]

Supreme Court justices and often lower court judges appointed by Republican presidents can now

Activist judge A judge who is said to act as an independent policymaker by creatively interpreting a constitution or statute.

consistently be counted on to issue rulings that jibe with conservative beliefs. The opposite is true for justices and judges appointed by Democrats. This is a significant issue, because an impression of partisanship affects public confidence in the courts, which are institutions of tremendous importance. The authority of the courts comes, to a great extent, simply from people's willingness to bring their disputes to them and abide by the results.

This chapter provides an introduction to state court systems. First, we examine the types of courts and the different ways these courts are structured. Then the focus turns to the different ways state court judges are chosen and retained, and the controversies that these processes create. Many issues surround the various players in state justice systems, from prosecutors and defenders to victims and jurors; we explore these before turning to a discussion of some possible areas of reform. As you read through this chapter, keep in mind the following questions:

- **Why are some states' judges elected and some appointed?**

- **Why are some states' courts more likely than those in other states to impose the death penalty?**

- **What effects do state campaign finance rules have on judges and on the decisions they make?**

The Role and Structure of State Courts

Federal U.S. district courts hear several hundred thousand cases a year. By comparison, just over 100 million cases are filed in the lowest state courts every year. In 2014, Illinois alone saw more civil cases filed than were then active in the entire federal judiciary. State courts have the awesome responsibility of resolving the vast majority of the nation's disputes. If you crash your car or your landlord evicts you, if you get divorced and fight for child custody, if your neighbor's tree lands in your yard, or if your employer won't pay you, any legal remedy you seek will be decided in a state court. If you contest a traffic ticket, you will find yourself in a state court. State courts are also where virtually all criminal cases are tried, from drunk driving to murder, from misdemeanors to capital offenses.

There are two basic kinds of court cases: criminal and civil. **Criminal cases** involve violations of the law, with the government prosecuting the alleged perpetrators, or criminals. Those found guilty may go to jail. By contrast, **civil cases** involve disputes between two private parties, such as a dry cleaner and a customer with badly stained pants. In civil cases, individuals sue each other, usually for financial judgments. Both types of cases start out in **trial court**. If the parties in a case cannot reach agreement through a **settlement** or a **plea bargain**, they go to trial.

Every trial has a winner and a loser. The losing side, if unhappy with the trial's outcome, can file an **appeal**. Most states have two levels of courts that hear appeals from trial court judgments. The appeal first goes to an **intermediate appellate court**, which reviews the original trial's record to see if any errors were made. After the appellate court has ruled, a party who still is not satisfied can attempt to appeal to the highest state court of appeals, usually called the **state supreme court**. In most states, this court does not automatically have to take an appeal; rather, it can pick and choose among cases. Typically, a state supreme court will choose to hear only those cases whose resolutions will require novel interpretation of the state constitution or clarification of the law. Such resolutions could set **precedent** that will have consequences well beyond the specifics of the case being appealed.

The state supreme court is the highest legal body in the state court system. This gives it the ultimate power to interpret the state constitution, and its decisions are almost always final. Only the U.S. Supreme Court

....

Criminal cases Legal cases brought by the state intending to punish violations of the law.

Civil cases Legal cases that involve disputes between private parties.

Trial court The first level of the court system.

Settlement A mutual agreement between parties to end a civil case before going to trial.

Plea bargain An agreement in which the accused in a criminal case admits guilt, usually in exchange for a promise that a particular sentence will be imposed.

Appeal A request to have a lower court's decision in a case reviewed by a higher court.

Intermediate appellate court A court that reviews court cases to find possible errors in their proceedings.

State supreme court The highest level of appeals court in a state.

Precedent In law, the use of the past to determine current interpretation and decision making.

Mark Matson for the Texas Supreme Court

▲

At the apex of most state court systems is a supreme court. State supreme court justices, such as the Texas Supreme Court justices pictured here, typically have the final say on appeals from lower courts.

outranks the highest state courts. Even the nine justices in Washington, D.C., however, cannot review—that is, come up with a new decision for—a state supreme court judgment unless that judgment conflicts with the U.S. Constitution or federal law.

When such federal issues are involved, there is no question that state courts must follow the rulings of the federal courts. The chief justice of the Alabama Supreme Court, Roy S. Moore, should have learned this lesson in 2003 after he oversaw the installation of a 2.5-ton monument to the Ten Commandments in the rotunda of the state supreme court building. Federal judges ruled that such a display violated the First Amendment's separation of church and state, and they ordered Moore to have the monument removed. He refused and ultimately was expelled from office by a state ethics panel for having tried to place himself above the law. However, after being elected to the office again in 2012, he made headlines when he challenged the authority of the federal courts. After the U.S. Supreme Court recognized a constitutionally protected right to same-sex marriage in 2015, Moore responded by ordering all state probate judges not to issue marriage licenses to same-sex

couples. The federal district court ultimately had to issue orders stating that probate judges who obeyed Moore's order would be personally liable for failure to comply with the U.S. Supreme Court ruling, and Judge Moore was again suspended and then removed from the court on ethical charges. (Despite all his legal problems, Moore won the nomination of the Grand Old Party, or GOP, to fill a U.S. Senate seat in a special election in 2017. He narrowly lost amidst allegations of assault or questionable relations with underage girls.) The authority of the federal courts over state courts also played out in Kentucky, where a county clerk, Kim Davis, refused a federal order to issue same-sex marriage licenses, arguing that to do so would violate her religious faith. Federal judge David L. Bunning ruled that she was "free to disagree" with the Supreme Court, but "that does not excuse her from complying," and he sent her to jail for contempt.

Trial Courts

More than 84 million cases were filed in state courts in 2016, almost one case for every three citizens. The number of state court cases rose steadily from 2004 until the economic recession of 2008, and then steadily declined. More than half the cases in 2013 involved traffic offenses. Criminal cases outnumbered civil cases, 19.5 million to 16.9 million. Among them were 6.6 million domestic and juvenile cases, which, although comprising a relatively small percentage of the total, are generally the most resource-intensive cases.[8] The vast majority of these millions of cases were resolved through plea bargains or settlements. Only a small minority ever went to trial.

When parties do go to trial, they appear before a state court judge in what is often referred to as a **court of first instance**. In this court, nothing has been determined, and nothing is a "given." The trial is a blank canvas on which the parties can introduce documentary and physical evidence, such as fingerprints or DNA. Witnesses can testify as to what they saw or heard, and experts can try to help explain complex evidence.

....

Court of first instance   The court in which a case is introduced and nothing has been determined yet.

STATES UNDER STRESS

JUDGES FACE GROWING THREATS FROM UNHAPPY POLITICIANS

In 2018, the Pennsylvania Supreme Court threw out the state's Republican-drawn congressional map as an impermissible partisan gerrymander, which was a boon for Democrats hoping to flip control of the U.S. House. In response, a dozen Republican state legislators proposed impeaching four justices, elected as Democrats, who had signed on to the ruling. Cris Dush, the state representative who sponsored the impeachment resolution, said the judges had overstepped their bounds and violated the separation of powers between the branches. "This is basically junior high civics course material," he said.

Before the effort could get off the ground, two prominent Republicans came out against impeachment: Chief Justice Thomas G. Saylor and House Majority Leader Dave Reed. "Threats of impeachment directed against justices because of their decision in a particular case are an attack upon an independent judiciary, which is an essential component of our constitutional plan of government," Saylor said in a statement.

The impeachment effort in Pennsylvania joined other attempts by politicians to oust members of the judiciary due to policy disagreements. In 2018, the West Virginia House voted to impeach every sitting justice on the state supreme court. Partisans have become less politic about calling out judges they disagree with. In 2018, Dallas Woodhouse, the executive director of the North Carolina Republican Party, described former state supreme court justice Bob Orr as "detested" and "revolting." More formal attacks—including efforts to remove judges through impeachment or recall elections—have also become more common. "There was a point in time where these sorts of elections were relative one-offs," says William Raftery, a senior analyst with the National Center for State Courts. "Now we're starting to see one example somewhere in nearly every election cycle."

Retention elections are usually sleepy affairs where no opponent appears on the ballot and voters merely choose to either "retain" or "remove" the current judge. But on a few occasions in recent years, judges have found themselves facing aggressive and well-funded campaigns aimed at their removal. The most recent example of a successful ouster effort came in Iowa in 2010. The year before, the state supreme court had validated same-sex couples' right to marry. Critics of that decision organized a successful effort to defeat three justices who faced retention elections. "I think it will send a message across the country that the power resides with the people," Bob Vander Plaats, who led the campaign against the justices, told the *New York Times* after the results were in. "It's we the people, not we the courts." Still, talk of impeaching the remainder of the justices cooled, and the one justice who faced a retention election in 2012 was returned to the bench.

In 2010, conservative efforts to remove judges who faced retention elections failed in Alaska, Colorado, Kansas, Illinois, and Florida. "Most of these efforts fade out and don't succeed," Raftery says, adding that such attempts are "a shot across the bow" intended to remind judges that they're ultimately accountable to the people.

In Washington State in 2016, three justices targeted by pro-business interests, including the chief justice, managed to win reelection. The well-funded opposition cited rulings they considered anti-business, as well as a decision against school choice. That same year in Kansas, five state supreme court justices survived a concerted effort by conservatives to remove them in response to controversial decisions regarding school finance, as well as a murder case in which one of their rulings was eventually overturned by the U.S. Supreme Court. The ouster effort prompted upwards of $1 million in spending.

Douglas Keith, a counsel at the Brennan Center for Justice at the New York University School of Law, agrees that this don't-rock-the-boat pattern has prevailed nationally. The string of losing efforts to bounce judges, he says, "is likely due in large part to the condemnation they've been met with from across the political spectrum. The public gets that judges need to be independent and free from political pressure. There may be a handful of officials who think it is in their political interests to stir up impeachment talk, but, by and large, elected officials seem to know that voters aren't going to tolerate this kind of encroachment on basic separation of powers principles."

Source: Adapted from Louis Jacobson, "Judges Face Growing Threats from Unhappy Politicians," *Governing*, April 16, 2018, http://www.governing.com/topics/politics/gov-state-supreme-court-race-election-justice.html

The judge presides over the introduction of evidence; rules on objections, which occur when either of the parties thinks that the other party has said or done something improper, and issues of admissibility—that is, whether or not it is all right for specific evidence or facts to be included in the trial; and instructs the jury as to the relevant laws. The judge further instructs the jury members that they must apply the laws as stated to the facts as they find them. It is the jury, however, that must decide what the facts are. (In a **bench trial**, there is no jury, and fact-finding is done by the judge.) The jury (or the judge in a bench trial) must decide who and what to believe and what happened. Unless the jury's final decision is based on a legal mistake, such as improper evidence, hearsay testimony (testimony based on rumor), or a misleading statement of the relevant law, the result typically will be upheld on appeal. The business of the trial court is to examine the facts to resolve the dispute. Subsequent appellate courts review the trial court's application of the law to those facts.

A key distinction among state courts is between **general jurisdiction trial courts** and **limited or special jurisdiction trial courts**. A general jurisdiction trial court hears any case not sent to a special court, whether it is civil or criminal. The kinds of cases that can be tried in special jurisdiction courts are statutorily limited. Some are limited to cases of less seriousness, such as misdemeanors or civil cases that involve small amounts of money. Others are limited in regard to the types of parties involved, such as juvenile offenders or drug abusers.

Appeals Courts: Intermediate Appeals and Courts of Last Resort

When one of the parties in a trial is dissatisfied with the outcome, that party can challenge the result by filing an appeal. As a general rule, an appeal cannot be based on mere dissatisfaction with the trial's result. An appellant does not get a free second chance to try his or her whole case. Appellate courts do not decide issues of guilt or innocence or ensure that trials were conducted

perfectly. Instead, an appeal must be based on a claim that there were legal errors in the original trial. Further, it is not enough to show that an error occurred; the error had to have been **prejudicial**—that is, it had to have affected the outcome of the case. The appellant has to argue that there was a good chance the result would have been different if the error had not been made. This often is a very challenging argument to make.

To cite just one example, in 2006 the defense attorney representing the convicted murderer of an Indiana University freshman asked that the sentence be thrown out, arguing that the jurors may have been drinking during legal proceedings, given that some of the male jurors in the trial had painted their toenails and raced down a hotel hallway in a bailiff's backless high heels. "Two men with heels on, painting their toenails, it is not a normal activity unless they are intoxicated," the attorney said. The judge ruled against him, saying there was no indication of drunkenness in court or during the actual deliberations.[9]

There is no one way in which all the state appellate courts decide how to hear appeals from the trial courts. States have made different decisions about how many levels of review to grant an appeal, how the courts must choose which cases can be appealed, and how many judges will hear an appeal. These decisions combine to form the different appellate court structures.

For example, not all states have both an intermediate appellate court and a supreme court. Back in 1957, only 13 states had intermediate appellate courts. Today, only 11 states and the District of Columbia still resolve all their appeals with only one level of review. These states, which include Delaware, Montana, North Dakota, Rhode Island, South Dakota, Vermont, and Wyoming, have relatively small populations—seven have fewer than 1 million residents—and thus tend to have fewer cases to resolve than do more populous states. Smaller populations generally give rise to more manageable court caseloads. Until recently, the Nevada Supreme Court heard every appeal in that state, from murder cases to driver's license revocations. It had a caseload double that of any of the supreme courts in neighboring states, leading to lengthy delays and backlogs. Establishing an appellate court, however, required the voters to approve a constitutional amendment, which failed on the ballot three times before finally passing in 2014. Now all appeals are still filed with the Nevada Supreme Court, but then the court assigns roughly a third of its caseload to a new three-judge appellate court.

....

Bench trial A trial in which no jury is present and the judge decides the facts as well as the law.

General jurisdiction trial courts Courts that hear any civil or criminal cases that have not been assigned to a special court.

Limited or special jurisdiction trial courts Courts that hear cases that are statutorily limited by either the degree of seriousness or the types of parties involved.

Prejudicial error An error that affects the outcome of a case.

The majority of states recognize that the sheer volume of appeals makes it impossible for one appellate court to hear and resolve every appeal. To deal with burgeoning caseloads, almost all states have created another tier of review. In these states, appeals go first to an intermediate appellate court. Only after they have been reviewed at this level can they move on to the court of last resort, usually the state supreme court. The intermediate court makes it possible for the state judicial system to hear many more appeals and creates the possibility of a second level of appeal.

State appellate courts vary in whether they have **discretionary jurisdiction** or **mandatory jurisdiction**. In other words, in some states, the courts have a right to pick and choose which cases they hear. In other states, judges must consider every case, the principle being that everyone has the right to an appeal. It is widely accepted that a loser in a single-judge court ought to have the right to at least one appeal to a court with multiple judges. This one appeal, however, is generally considered sufficient to correct any prejudicial errors made in the trial courts. Even in states in which the court of last resort has discretionary jurisdiction, appeals may be mandatory in capital punishment cases.

One more variable in the state court system structure involves the number of judges at each level who hear a particular appeal. At the level of either the appellate court or the court of last resort, judges may hear an appeal **en banc**, or all together, or they may sit in smaller **panels**, typically of three judges. Sitting in panels may be more convenient, because appellate courts sit simultaneously in different locations. This allows more appeals to be heard and makes the courts more convenient to the parties. However, as with regional divisions, this may also lead to problems of unifying doctrine when various courts at the same level reach different decisions.

The most common pattern, adhered to by half the states, involves an intermediate appellate court, sitting in panels, which must consider all appeals. The decisions of these panels are then subject to review by a court of last resort, such as a supreme court, sitting en banc. Usually, this highest court hears just the cases it sees fit to hear. In states without intermediate courts of appeals, often the courts of last resort must hear all the cases that are sent to them. One such state, West Virginia, eliminated discretionary review for its supreme court in a historic change in 2010. In the next year, the number of appeals heard by the state's highest court more than tripled. In the District of Columbia, all appeals are heard by a court of appeals with nine justices, who often sit in panels of three and have mandatory jurisdiction over most cases.

In other words, no matter what state you are in, if you lose your case in court, you will have at least one chance—and sometimes more than one chance—to have your appeal heard. There is tremendous variation among states in courts and panels and rules; luckily, you need to know only the rules of the state where you file your case.

Selecting Judges

How judges are selected is a significant political decision. Historically, this decision has generated tremendous controversy, and the controversy continues today. The judiciary is one of the pillars of the U.S. political system, but at the same time, we want to believe that judges are above politics. We like to think that they are independent and will rule only as justice requires, based on the specific facts presented and the applicable law. But, of course, judges are only human. That's why we want them held accountable for their decisions. These competing values—independence and accountability—tug judicial selection procedures in different directions. If independence is seen as more important than accountability, it makes sense to appoint judges for lifetime tenures. This is done in the federal system. If accountability is seen as more important than independence, it makes sense to elect judges. Elections are a key element of judicial selection at the state level. Yet they are not the only component; states have formulated a variety of selection systems in an effort to balance the competing values of independence and accountability. These specifics matter. How a state structures its courts and chooses its judiciary may affect the types of decisions made by individual judges and the confidence citizens have in their courts to provide fair trials.

....

Discretionary jurisdiction The power of a court to decide whether or not to grant review of a case.

Mandatory jurisdiction The requirement that a court hear every case presented before it.

En banc Appeals court sessions in which all the judges hear a case together.

Panels Groups of (usually) three judges who sit to hear cases in a state court of appeals.

FIGURE 9-1 ●   How It Works

State Court Structure in Illinois and New York

It's easy to see why New York State's court system has been called Byzantine—just compare it with Illinois's (left). Although it encompasses 23 circuits with more than 850 justices, Illinois's trial court system looks like a model of clarity and simplicity compared with New York's 11 different trial courts. New York's 300-year-old town and village justice court system, in particular, has been subject to loud and persistent criticism for cronyism, corruption, fiscal mismanagement, and plain old inefficiency. Way back in 1927, the state's Crime Commission called the patchwork system of local justices "an obsolete and antiquated institution."

What can be done? In 2006, Judith S. Kaye, then New York's chief judge, recommended changes "across four broad areas: court operations and administration; auditing and financial control; education and training; and facility security and public protection."[a] But her main recommendation, that fewer courts be run by judges who were lawyers, went nowhere. "One of the difficulties is a legislature that seems to be very committed in keeping a system that they're very comfortable with," says Dennis Hawkins, executive director of the Fund for Modern Courts, which advocates for court restructuring.[b]

A commission on state court reform backed some of Kaye's ideas in 2008 with its suggestion that the state eliminate as many as 500 of the justice courts, but bills based on her ideas failed in the legislature. The idea of amending the state constitution to bar individuals who are not lawyers from serving as judges ran into opposition from the New York State Magistrates Association and failed as part of a larger push to hold a state constitutional convention in 2017. As late as 2018, Chief Administrative Judge Lawrence K. Marks complained that the court's structure, with its overlapping trial courts with differing levels of jurisdiction, was "confusing, cumbersome and complicated."[c] That year, Janet DiFiore, the state's new top judge, created a new task force to come up with recommendations for a judicial overhaul that might pass muster with legislators. But the combination of political entrenchment of the old system and the costs involved in creating a more professional system continue to prevent systemic reform from gaining traction.

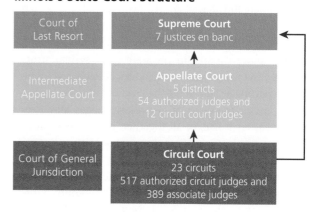

Illinois's State Court Structure

Court of Last Resort — **Supreme Court** 7 justices en banc

Intermediate Appellate Court — **Appellate Court** 5 districts, 54 authorized judges and 12 circuit court judges

Court of General Jurisdiction — **Circuit Court** 23 circuits, 517 authorized circuit judges and 389 associate judges

Almost no two states select judges in exactly the same way, although the states can be roughly divided into two camps of almost equal size. The first group includes states that choose judges through popular elections, either partisan or nonpartisan. In partisan elections, judicial candidates first run in party primaries, and then the winning candidates are listed on the general election ballot along with designations of their political parties. In nonpartisan elections, the names of candidates appear on the ballot without any party labels. The

New York State's Court Structure

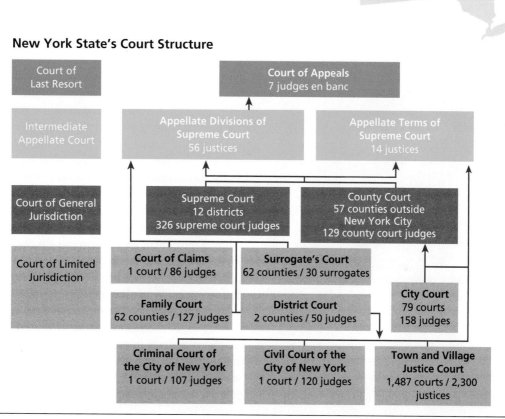

[a]Judith S. Kaye and Jonathan Lippman, *Action Plan for the Justice Courts* (Albany: State of New York Unified Court System, November 2006), https://www.nycourts.gov/publications/pdfs/ActionPlan-JusticeCourts.pdf.

[b]Phone interview with Dennis Hawkins, July 14, 2018.

[c]"New Coalition Pressing for Court Reform in New York State," *Proskauer for Good Blog*, May 8, 2018, https://www.proskauer.com/blog/new-coalition-pressing-for-court-reform-in-new-york-state.

second group consists of states that have appointed, rather than elected, judges. Under the appointment model, the governor or the legislature may appoint judges. In some states, only persons selected by a nominating committee are eligible for judicial appointments.

To make matters even more confusing, many states use different methods to choose judges at different levels of their judiciaries. A state might, for example, choose trial judges by popular election but appoint supreme court justices. What's more, regions within a given state often

The merit selection of judges, widely adopted by states across the country to fill some or all judicial vacancies, originated in Missouri from a power struggle between Governor Lloyd Stark, pictured here, and powerful political boss Tom Pendergast.

Courtesy of the Library of Congress, Prints and Photographs Division

NORTH CAROLINA passed a law in 2015 to require state supreme court justices to face retention elections, meaning voters would decide whether to keep justices on the court, but they wouldn't face opponents. The court itself struck down that law in 2016.

employ different methods. In Arizona, for example, trial courts in counties with populations greater than 250,000 choose judges through merit selection; less populous districts rely on nonpartisan elections. Indiana holds partisan elections in a portion of its judicial districts and nonpartisan elections in others. Finally, some states that generally elect their judges fill midterm judicial vacancies by appointment.

How states choose their judges has been historically volatile. Movements to change the methods for judicial selection rise up, gain popularity, and then, eventually, are supplanted by the next big reform movement. How a state originally chose its judges had much to do with which reform was in vogue at the time the state entered the Union and ratified its constitution. No single judicial reform has ever succeeded in completely replacing earlier methods, however, and so there is tremendous variation among the states in the way they select judges.

Under the U.S. Constitution, the president, with the advice and consent of the Senate, appoints all federal judges. Similarly, the original 13 states chose to appoint judges, giving the appointment power to one or both houses of the legislature or, less commonly, to the governor, either alone or with the consent of the legislature.[10]

Then, in the mid-1800s, during the presidency of Andrew Jackson—a period marked by distrust of government and a movement toward increased popular sovereignty—the appointive system came under attack. Every state that entered the Union between 1846 and 1912 provided for some form of judicial elections.[11] At the dawn of the 20th century, concern that judges were being selected and controlled by political machines led to a movement for nonpartisan elections. By 1927, 12 states employed this practice.[12]

During the second half of the 20th century, judicial reformers focused on persuading states to adopt a new method of choosing judges, referred to as **merit selection**. The variations of merit selection systems are discussed in detail in the following section on appointment. Basically, a merit system is a hybrid of appointment and election. It typically involves a bipartisan judicial nominating commission whose job is to create a list of highly qualified candidates for the bench. The governor appoints judges from this list, who must then face a **retention election**. The retention election for a newly appointed judge, which is usually set to coincide with the next general election, provides voters with a simple choice: to keep or not to keep the judge on the bench. If the vote is for retention, the judge stays on

Merit selection A hybrid of appointment and election that typically involves a bipartisan judicial nominating commission whose job is to create a list of highly qualified candidates for the bench from which the governor or legislature appoints judges. After serving a term, these judges are typically evaluated for retention either by the same commission or through uncontested popular elections.

Retention election An election in which a judge runs uncontested and voters are asked to vote yes or no on the question of whether they wish to retain the judge in office for another term.

the bench. If the vote is against retention (this is rare), the commission goes back to work to come up with another list of candidates for the post.

Under some merit systems, all judges (not just newly appointed ones) must face periodic retention elections, although the length of term and other specifics vary from state to state. Missouri became the first state to adopt such a judicial selection method in 1940, which is why judicial merit selection is sometimes referred to as "the Missouri Plan." The movement enjoyed considerable success from the 1960s to the 1980s. The number of states that embraced merit selection for choosing supreme court justices grew from 3 in 1960 (Alaska, Kansas, and Missouri) to 18 by 1980.[13] Recently, however, this approach appears to have lost momentum. About half the states still rely on merit selection to choose some or all of their judges, and no merit selection state has returned to selection through elections. However, since 1990, most states that have considered adopting merit selection, whether for trial courts or appellate-level courts, have rejected it. In Nevada, for example, the legislature sponsored a bipartisan ballot question in the 2010 election asking whether the Nevada Constitution should be amended to adopt the Missouri Plan. It was rejected by 58 percent of the voters.[14] In recent years, several states have debated doing away with merit selection altogether—including Missouri, where it began. In 2012, proposals to overhaul existing merit selection systems went before voters in Arizona, Florida, and Mississippi; they all lost.[15] In the sections that follow, we discuss at length each method for selecting judges and the issues it raises. (Map 9-1 shows the system of selection for each state.)

Popular Elections

Why do some states elect judges? Elections allow greater popular control over the judiciary and more public accountability for judges. Proponents argue that such elections are compatible with this country's democratic traditions and that voters can be trusted to make choices for judges that are as good as those that legislators or mayors would make. To these supporters, the appointment of judges smacks of elitism and raises worries about old-boy networks; that is, they fear that judges will get appointed because they are the cronies or political allies of elected officials.

Some argue that electing judges can increase the representation of women and minorities on the bench,

but studies have found negligible differences in judicial diversity between selection methods.[16] Regardless of system, state judiciaries have grown slightly more diverse over time, but the percentages of minority and women judges continue to trail these groups' proportions in the population at large. Nationwide, as of 2010, 43 (12 percent) state supreme court justices were members of minority groups, and 111 (33 percent) were women.[17]

There have been 14 states in which a majority of the supreme court justices were women. The most recent to join this list is **OHIO** with the appointment of Mary DeGenaro in 2018.

Those on the other side of the argument are critical of judicial elections in general, whether partisan or nonpartisan, asserting that such elections often become referendums on political issues rather than serving as forums that allow the public to evaluate the temperaments, backgrounds, and experience of the candidates. Opponents of judicial elections focus on what they see as the threat to the independence of the judiciary posed by the introduction of politics into the selection process and the danger that the need to solicit campaign contributions could make judges vulnerable to improper influence by donors. Further, opponents note that the tone of judicial elections has deteriorated substantially and in a manner that could damage the image of the judiciary and potentially undermine its perceived legitimacy. Given this, qualified candidates for office could choose not to run. "As the gatekeepers of justice, the court system should be considered impartial, above reproach, and operating with scrupulous decorum," the *Philadelphia Inquirer* editorialized in 2018. "The presence of money alone is not responsible for the judges who end up disgraced or behind bars, but its presence can taint even the best judges. The corrosive effects of money work over time until it is impossible for people to trust the court system. In Pennsylvania, the court system can be a circus peopled with clowns, grafters, scammers, and too often gives off the fetid whiff of elephant droppings."[18]

How a state chooses its judges has very real political impacts, with consequences for judicial impartiality, campaign fundraising, the role of interest groups,

MAP 9-1 ● Initial Judicial Selection, by Type of Court

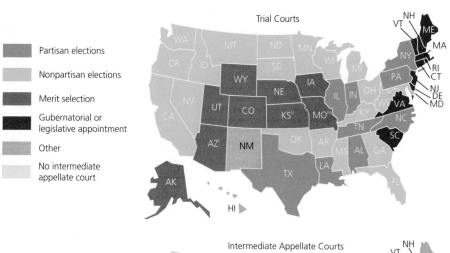

Trial Courts

Partisan elections

Nonpartisan elections

Merit selection

Gubernatorial or
legislative appointment

Other

No intermediate
appellate court

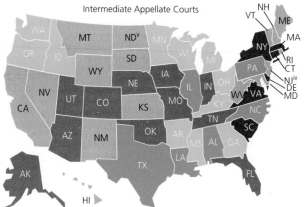

Intermediate Appellate Courts

Notes:
ⁱThe Arizona Constitution provides
for merit selection and retention
of judges in counties with populations of 250,000 or greater. Counties
whose populations are less than
250,000 may adopt merit selection
through ballot initiative.

ⁱⁱJudges are selected by merit
selection in 17 districts and by
partisan election in 14 districts.

ⁱⁱⁱJudges in Kansas City, Springfield,
and St. Louis are selected by merit
selection; all others are elected by
partisan election.

ⁱᵛThe chief justice of the supreme
court assigns superior court judges
to the appellate court division.

ᵛChosen from among active and
retired district judges, retired
supreme court justices, and
attorneys.

ᵛⁱCandidates who want to challenge
incumbent justices must be
nominated at party conventions.
Candidates appear without party
affiliation on the general election
ballot.

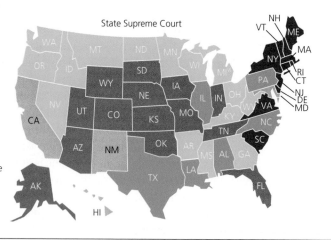

State Supreme Court

Source: Brennan Center for Justice, "Judicial Selection: An Interactive Map," http://judicialselectionmap.brennancenter.org/. Accessed August 13, 2018.

and the character of judicial campaigning. Some point to these impacts as reasons to move away from selecting judges through judicial elections and toward a merit selection system. Others argue that there is no need to abandon elections altogether; rather, any problems can be addressed through targeted changes. Die-hard supporters of judicial election see the increased politicization of the process as a positive thing; they assert that greater competitiveness translates into more meaningful choices for voters.

The legislative and executive branches are clearly political. Representatives of the people are chosen and held accountable through elections. Why shouldn't judges be elected in the same manner as other powerful players in the political system? Because, as Chief Justice Roberts wrote in a recent opinion, "judges are not politicians." The role of judges is designed to be different. Judges decide specific cases and controversies based on the evidence. They are supposed to rely only on statutes, case precedent, constitutional law, and the unique facts presented by each case. They are not supposed to rule based on the wishes of those who elect them or with the next election in mind. In 2015, comedian and political commentator John Oliver devoted a lengthy segment of his HBO program *Last Week Tonight with John Oliver* to highlighting the multiple problems inherent in choosing state judges through elections. "The problem with an elected judiciary is that sometimes the right decision is neither easy nor popular, and yet campaigns force judges to look over their shoulder on every ruling," Oliver said.[19] In 2018, Santa Clara County Superior Court judge Aaron Persky was recalled in response to the lenient sentence he'd given to Brock Turner, a former Stanford University swimmer convicted of sexually assaulting an unconscious woman. It was the first time since 1932 California voters had recalled a judge.[20]

A lot rides on the public's belief that judges are neutral and impartial. That belief underpins people's willingness to bring disputes to the courts and to abide by the results—the keys to both economic and political stability. Judges cannot, as political candidates do, make campaign promises about future decisions; to do so would be to undermine respect for the impartiality and independence of the judiciary. There are times when all judges, when doing their jobs properly, are compelled by the law to make unpopular judgments or to protect the rights of those without political power.

In 1999, U.S. Supreme Court justice Anthony Kennedy pointed out in an interview that there are times for every judge when the law requires the release of a criminal, whether the judge likes it or not. Characterizing the judge in such a case as "soft on crime" betrays a misunderstanding of the judicial process and the Constitution.[21] In the same television interview, Justice Stephen Breyer also expressed concerns about the way judicial elections require judges to court public opinion:

> Suppose I were on trial. Suppose somebody accused me. Would I want to be judged by whether I was popular? Wouldn't I want to be judged on what was true as opposed to what was popular? . . . We have a different system. And our system is based upon . . . neutrality and independence.[22]

Why are some courts more likely than others to impose the death penalty? Some research indicates that state supreme court justices facing reelection in states in which capital punishment is particularly popular are reluctant to cast dissenting votes in death penalty cases.

The effects of judicial selection ripple out beyond those cases that tackle politically volatile issues such as capital punishment and raise issues of improper influence of money on the judiciary. In 2006, the *New York Times* published the results of an examination of campaign financing over 12 years in regard to the Ohio Supreme Court. The investigators found that justices routinely sat on cases after receiving campaign contributions from the parties involved or from groups that filed supporting briefs and that justices, on average, voted in favor of contributors 70 percent of the time, with one particular justice voting for his contributor 91 percent of the time.[23] A 2012 report published by the Center for American Progress collects illustrations from six states with particularly expensive judicial elections: Alabama, Illinois, Michigan, Ohio, Pennsylvania, and Texas. The high courts in these states, the report notes, "are much more likely to rule in favor of big business and against individuals who have been injured, scammed or subjected to discrimination."[24] In one example, the Ohio legislature had passed three laws curtailing the right to sue an employer for on-the-job injuries. After the first two laws were held unconstitutional by the state supreme court, the insurance industry donated to judicial campaigns. The winning justices upheld the law on its third try.[25] It's not just corporations that seek to influence judicial elections. Lawyers and law firms involved in a case detailing sexual abuse and cover-ups in the Catholic Church gave seven Pennsylvania Supreme Court justices more than $180,000 in campaign donations leading up to the 2018 election. The justices had blocked the release of a grand jury report detailing abuse allegations.[26]

Describing judicial fundraising, Justice Paul E. Pfeifer, a Republican member of the Ohio Supreme Court, said, "I never felt so much like a hooker down by the bus station in any race I've ever been in as I did in a judicial race."[27] But the need to find dollars to run for a seat cannot supersede good judgment. In *Caperton v. Massey* (2009), the U.S. Supreme Court ruled that Justice Brent Benjamin of the West Virginia Supreme Court of Appeals should have recused himself from a case in which the chief executive officer (CEO) of the lead defendant, after losing a $50 million verdict in the trial court, raised $3 million to elect Benjamin to the court that was hearing the case's appeal. Benjamin was the deciding vote in favor of the defendants. Chastising Justice Benjamin for not sitting out this appeal, the U.S. Supreme Court stated, "Just as no man is allowed to be a judge in his own cause, similar fears of bias can arise when . . . a man chooses the judge in his own cause." In Benjamin's case, the $3 million from the CEO of A. T. Massey Coal Co. represented about 60 percent of his electoral war chest[28]—another piece of evidence that the funds required to run a campaign have been skyrocketing, particularly in state supreme court races. From 2000 to 2009, candidates for state supreme court seats raised more than $200 million, more than double the $83 million raised by such candidates in the previous decade.[29] Much of the money raised by judicial candidates comes from corporations, lawyers, litigants, and other groups with interests in the outcomes of litigation.

Then the Supreme Court's ruling in *Citizens United v. Federal Election Commission* (2010) invalidated laws placing limits on corporate campaign contributions and opened the door to spending by outside organizations and super PACs. The controversial decision did not specifically involve judicial elections, but concerns voiced by Justice John Paul Stevens in his dissent have proved prophetic:

> The consequences of today's holding will not be limited to the legislative or executive context. The majority of the States select their judges through popular elections. At a time when concerns about the conduct of judicial elections have reached a fever pitch . . . the Court today unleashes the floodgates of corporate and union general treasury spending in these races.[30]

In the wake of this opinion, spending in judicial elections has continued to increase. State supreme court races costing millions of dollars have become common. One Pennsylvania judicial contest in 2015 set a new record, with at least $15.8 million spent.[31] Ten states saw million-dollar judicial campaigns in 2015 and 2016, for a combined total of $30 million. Why do interest groups contribute so much money to judicial elections? As with any other political donation, there is at least some truth to the cynic's sense that campaign contributions are a good investment. The president of the Ohio State Bar Association concluded, "The people with money to spend who are affected by court decisions have reached the conclusion that it's a lot cheaper to buy a judge than a governor or an entire legislature, and he can probably do a lot more for you."[32] After all, from an interest group's standpoint, what is the point of getting laws passed if a judge will just declare them unconstitutional? When the judicial reform organization Justice at Stake surveyed 2,428 state court judges, one-quarter of them said that campaign contributions influenced their decisions.[33]

Prior to 2002, judges' campaigns generally were subject to codes of judicial conduct that placed tight restrictions on campaigning to prevent judges from discussing topics that might later come before them on the bench. In *Republican Party of Minnesota v. White* (2002), however, the U.S. Supreme Court struck down such restrictions as violations of judges' free speech rights. Since then, interest groups have asked judicial candidates to complete questionnaires, pressuring them to reveal their views on hot-button issues. The groups then target specific "bad" judges for removal. Some candidates themselves have run outspoken campaigns, stating their opinions on issues, such as school funding, that will clearly appear before the Court. However, the Supreme

Court's ruling in *Williams-Yulee v. Florida Bar* (2015) may signal, if not a reversal, a reluctance to extend the free speech argument further into judicial campaigning. In this narrowly divided case, Chief Justice Roberts, writing for the majority, held that Florida may forbid judicial candidates from personally soliciting campaign funds without running afoul of the First Amendment's free speech protections. "Judges, charged with exercising strict neutrality and independence," Roberts wrote, "cannot supplicate campaign donors without diminishing public confidence in judicial integrity." It is clear, though, that as long as judges need to run election campaigns, they will find ways to raise money.

In partisan elections, an additional danger is that the political parties may expect favors from the candidates they put forward. Thomas Phillips, onetime chief justice of the Texas Supreme Court, has asked:

> When judges are labeled as Democrats or Republicans, how can you convince the public that the law is a judge's only constituency? And when a winning litigant has contributed thousands of dollars to the judge's campaign, how do you ever persuade the losing party that only the facts of the case were considered?[34]

Appointment

The systems used by states in which judges are appointed rather than elected can be divided into two general categories: **pure appointive systems** and merit selection systems that rely on nominating committees. Federal judges have always been selected through a pure appointive system. The president appoints judges who, if they are confirmed by the Senate, "shall hold their Offices during good Behavior." No state, however, employs precisely this method of judicial selection.

In three states—California, Maine, and New Jersey—the governor appoints state court judges without a nominating commission; that is, these governors are not limited in their selections to lists of names provided by someone else.[35] Judges' nominations still require some kind of second opinion, however. In Maine, the governor appoints judges subject to confirmation by a legislative committee, the decision of which may be reviewed by the state senate. In New Jersey, the state senate must confirm the governor's appointees, who then serve an initial seven-year term, after which the governor may reappoint them. Senate confirmation is

not a mere formality, as Republican New Jersey governor Chris Christie learned when Democratic senate president Stephen Sweeney refused to give the governor's nominee a hearing—for six years. Finally, in 2016, Governor Christie withdrew his nomination and instead nominated a Democratic justice, who was confirmed. California's governor appoints judges after submitting names to a state bar committee for evaluation, but the governor is not bound by the committee's recommendation. New Hampshire used to be on this list, but in 2013, the governor created a judicial selection commission through executive order and now is limited to appointing judges nominated by this commission.[36] Virginia and South Carolina are the only two states that select judges through a vote of the legislature. Only Virginia, however, does so without a nominating committee. A majority vote of both houses of the Virginia General Assembly is required to appoint any judge.

Merit selection, initially endorsed by the American Bar Association in 1937, was conceived as a way to limit the intrusion of politics into judge selection and strike a balance between partisan election and lifetime appointment.[37] Under such a system, after an appointed judge serves an initial term, he or she must stand for a retention election. In this election, the judge runs unopposed. Voters may indicate only either yes or no on the question of whether the judge should be retained.

Most states that currently appoint judges rely on a method of merit selection through nominating committees. Twenty-four states and the District of Columbia rely on a merit selection plan for the initial selection of some or all judges. Another 10 states use such plans to fill midterm vacancies at some or all levels of the courts.[38]

What puts the *merit* into merit selection? It is misleading to describe merit selection as if it were a single method for selecting judges, because the details vary considerably from state to state. At its core, it requires that the state assemble a nonpartisan nominating committee. This committee forwards a list of names from which either the governor or the legislature chooses a judge. How a partisan, distrustful legislature solves the problem of creating a nonpartisan committee differs in almost every state. Some states require parity of political party affiliation or geographic diversity for

----

Pure appointive systems Judicial selection systems in which the governor alone appoints judges, without preselection of candidates by a nominating commission.

the commission members. In some states, the governor chooses all the members, and in others, the commission is chosen by some combination of the state bar, the governor, and legislative leaders. Some have adopted extremely complex methods to ensure the impartiality of nominating commissions.

While the details of how such commissions are chosen may seem innocuous and dry, they have significant impact on just how successful a merit selection plan can be in minimizing the politicization of the judiciary. In 2012, three merit selection states—Arizona, Florida, and Missouri—held referendums on the issue of increasing the power of governors and legislatures in the selection of judges. These efforts mostly focused on giving executives or legislatures more power to influence merit system selection committees. While retaining the basic framework of a merit system, giving partisan actors a greater role in selection committee appointments nudges a merit system toward giving greater weight to political concerns than to judicial qualifications. For example, Missouri has had several failed attempts in recent years to revoke merit selection entirely and replace it with partisan elections. Opponents eventually shifted tactics, focusing on an effort to give the governor the power to appoint a majority of the members of the judicial selection committee. The Missouri referendum did not pass, but such a move would have drastically increased the governor's power over who ends up sitting on the bench.

The ways judges are retained after they are appointed also vary by state. In most states, judges appointed through merit selection serve relatively short initial terms, usually one or two years. After that, they participate in retention elections. These special elections were conceived as a means to provide some public participation in the selection of judges while avoiding the intrusion of politics. In recent years, the national trend toward increased politicization of judicial retention elections has only accelerated. Some merit selection states have dispensed with elections altogether. For instance, in Connecticut and

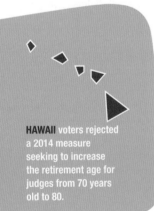

HAWAII voters rejected a 2014 measure seeking to increase the retirement age for judges from 70 years old to 80.

Delaware, once judges' initial terms are up, they are reappointed in exactly the same way they were initially appointed: the commission evaluates them, the governor appoints them, and the legislature approves. In Vermont, after an initial appointment through merit selection, a judge receives an additional term as long as the general assembly does not vote against it.[39]

Terms of Office

The length of a judge's tenure is another element in the balance between judicial independence and judicial accountability. In the federal court system, judges serve life terms "during good behavior"; that is, judges can be removed only through an impeachment process for cause. This life tenure is considered an important element, perhaps the most important element, in ensuring the independence of the federal judiciary.[40] There has never been a conviction of an impeached federal judge based solely on an unpopular judicial decision in the federal system.[41]

With only a few exceptions, state court judges serve fixed terms of office and must therefore seek reappointment or reelection. The rare exceptions are judges in Rhode Island, who serve life terms, and judges in Massachusetts and New Hampshire, who hold their positions until the age of 70. Judges in states with fixed terms typically serve for less than 10 years. New York trial court judges serve the longest terms among the states—14 years—and are required to retire at age 70. A 2013 attempt to raise the maximum age of judicial service to 80 failed at the ballot box.[42] The same happened in Hawaii the following year. But Pennsylvania voters in 2016 voted to raise the mandatory retirement age from 70 to 75, while Alabama voters agreed to the same change, albeit only for judges in a single county. "There is a growing belief that an age limit established long ago is too low by today's standards, and is arbitrarily depriving our courts of some experienced, thoughtful and highly capable judges," said Pennsylvania state senator Lisa Baker.[43] Laws placing an age limit on judges have been on the books a long time in most places, and are rooted in historical events in which jurists were incapacitated by dementia. But that shouldn't be as much of a problem anymore. Scott Makar, an appellate court judge in Florida who has studied the issue, notes that his state and others have commissions in place to remove judges who can't perform their duty. "All the evidence suggests that people are living longer, and

TABLE 9-1 ● Salaries and Rankings for Appellate and General Jurisdiction Judges, 2018 (dollars)

Courts of Last Resort		Intermediate Appellate Courts		Trial Courts	
Top Five		**Top Five**		**Top Five**	
California	244,179	California	228,918	DC	208,000
Illinois	229,345	Illinois	215,856	Hawaii	201,060
Hawaii	223,200	Hawaii	206,652	California	200,042
DC	220,600	New York	205,400	Illinois	198,075
New York	215,700	Pennsylvania	195,978	New York	194,000
Bottom Five		**Bottom Five**		**Bottom Five**	
West Virginia	136,000	Wisconsin	139,059	West Virginia	126,000
Kentucky	135,504	Oklahoma	138,235	Maine	125,632
South Dakota	135,270	Idaho	137,700	Kentucky	124,620
Maine	134,056	Kentucky	130,044	Kansas	123,038
New Mexico	131,174	New Mexico	124,616	New Mexico	118,384

Source: Data and rankings as of January 1, 2018, compiled from the National Center for State Courts, "Salaries and Rankings for Appellate and General-Jurisdiction Judges," *Survey of Judicial Salaries* 43, no. 1 (January 2018), https://www.ncsc.org/~/media/Microsites/Files/Judicial%20Salaries/2018-Judicial-Salaries.ash.

judging is the classic old-age profession," Makar says. "It takes what older people have, which is experience and judgment."[44]

Shorter tenures bring with them the increased danger that political interests and pressures will intrude on judicial decision making. Longer terms allow for judges to be evaluated on more complete records; any particular controversial decisions may have weaker effects when there are long periods between elections.

Impeachment

All states have provisions for the impeachment of state court judges. These typically mirror the language of the federal system and require a majority vote of the house of representatives and conviction by two-thirds of the senate. Many states have another provision similar to one in Michigan that allows the governor to remove a judge on a vote of two-thirds of the members of both houses of the legislature. Impeachable offenses are often limited by state constitutions to things like treason, bribery, and other high crimes and misdemeanors.

While impeachment has historically been extremely rare, in this era of intense political polarization, threats of impeachment have increasingly become a go-to tactic in the struggle between the judiciary and the other branches of government. According to the National Center for State Courts, judges faced more impeachment attempts in 2011 than in any previous year in history. In all but two instances, "the sole accusation was that the judges in question issued opinions that displeased members of the legislature."[45]

To date, no judge has been successfully impeached for an unpopular opinion. In Kansas, where state supreme court rulings on public education spending have drawn the fury of the governor and members of the legislature, the state senate narrowly passed a bill in 2016 that would have expanded the possible constitutional grounds for impeaching state judges to include "attempting to usurp power of the legislative or executive branches." The sponsor of the bill, Senator Dennis Pyle, explained the need for this change: "If you are going to make political rulings, then you should be politically accountable." An editorial in the *St. Louis*

Post-Dispatch, headlined "When Two Branches of Government Declare War on the Third," decried this move as a dangerous "politicizing of the judiciary."[46] The bill died in the house.

Prosecution and Defense of Cases in State Courts

A criminal case at the state court level most often involves a face-off between two state or county employees. The **prosecutor** pursues the case on behalf of the people and usually seeks the incarceration of the accused. Little difference exists among the states in the selection of the chief prosecutor; an elected county official almost always fills the position. The individual often is politically ambitious and views the job of chief prosecutor as a stepping-stone to higher elected office. For this reason, the policies of prosecutors tend to reflect the specific wishes of the county voters.

Private attorneys defend those individuals who can afford their services. In many cases, however, a **public defender**, an attorney also on the public payroll, represents the accused. Public defenders fulfill the state's constitutional requirement to provide indigent defense services—that is, defense services for those who are poor. There is much more variety in how states organize their systems of indigent defense than in their systems of prosecution. Some states employ statewide systems of public defenders. Others have established statewide commissions that set guidelines for local jurisdictions, sometimes distributing limited state funds to local programs that follow specific standards. Still others delegate the responsibility of deciding how to provide and fund indigent defense entirely to the counties.

The competing values of state oversight and local control play out differently depending on the cultural and political realities of each state, as well as any practical concerns involved. Even some states with statewide public defenders' offices exclude rural areas where the case volume would make supporting such offices impractical. In the current climate of runaway costs, government cutbacks, increased caseloads, and widespread litigation-challenging programs, the trend has been toward more state oversight.

....

Prosecutor A government official and lawyer who conducts criminal cases on behalf of the people.

Public defender A government lawyer who provides free legal services to persons accused of crimes who cannot afford to hire lawyers.

The Prosecutor

Commentators have gone so far as to say that the prosecutor has become the "most powerful office in the criminal justice system."[47] The prosecutor's office is run by an attorney referred to, depending on the state, as the chief prosecutor, district attorney, county attorney, commonwealth attorney, or state's attorney. Whatever the title, this lawyer represents the public in criminal and other cases. Most prosecutors are elected and typically serve four-year terms. It is a daunting job, particularly in major metropolitan districts, where the top prosecutor manages hundreds of lawyers and support staffers, deals with horrific crimes, and balances the need to serve justice with the "unavoidable scrutiny of won-lost statistics that become a factor in re-election campaigns."[48] This focus on statistics may, according to one commentator, undergird some prosecutors' resistance to the use of postconviction DNA testing to determine conclusively if the correct person was incarcerated for a crime.[49]

The authority to prosecute comes from the state, but prosecutors' offices are essentially local. A prosecutor's authority is over a specific jurisdiction, usually a county. County governments fund these offices, although close to half of them also receive some portion of their budgets from state funds.[50] Nationwide, there are more than 2,300 state court prosecutors' offices, employing about 78,000 attorneys, investigators, and support staffers.[51] They handle more than 2 million felonies and 7 million misdemeanors a year.

According to the most recent Department of Justice statistics, most chief prosecutors serve jurisdictions with fewer than 100,000 people and do so with an average total staff of 10 personnel, including 4 attorneys.[52] The top 5 percent of prosecutors' offices, however, serve districts with populations of 500,000 or more. They represent almost half the entire U.S. population.[53] In 2001, these large offices handled about 66 percent of the nation's serious crimes and had a median budget of more than $14 million.[54] The Los Angeles County District Attorney's Office has the largest staff, consisting of more than 2,200 people, including more than 1,000 attorneys, and a 2017–2018 budget of $174 million. The types of cases handled by these offices grow increasingly complex as prosecutors' offices encounter high-tech crimes, including identity theft and credit card fraud, and take on homeland security responsibilities.

A state's chief prosecutors have enormous discretion in the conduct of most of their responsibilities. The prosecutor makes all decisions as to whether or not

LOCAL FOCUS

A FRESH WAVE OF PROSECUTORS REDEFINES JUSTICE

In 2016, Kim Ogg was elected district attorney (DA) in Harris County, Texas, which includes Houston. For too long, she says, criminal justice in her county was run as a volume business, with Harris County not only leading the nation in executions, but also acting as one of the epicenters of mass incarceration. By targeting and prosecuting more and more people for "smaller and smaller crimes," she says, the county sacrificed quality for quantity. The jail is filled with people locked up on minor drug charges, while burglaries largely go uninvestigated. "Harris County has become in some sense a haven for robbers and burglars," Ogg said shortly after taking office, "because they know we're not doing a good job of catching them."

In order to prosecute crimes against people and property, Ogg wants her office, along with law enforcement in general, to pay less attention to minor drug offenses. A few weeks into the job, she announced she would no longer seek jail time in most cases for the crime of possessing up to four ounces of marijuana. Offenders are diverted toward treatment instead. "Two-thirds of the people in jail are minorities and nonviolent offenders, based on minor drug offenses," says Dwight Boykins, a member of the Houston City Council. "Kim's program touched me because I saw real change in the system, rather than just talk about it."

Ogg was part of a wave of reform-minded prosecutors elected nationwide in 2016 in major jurisdictions including Chicago, Cleveland, Denver, Orlando, Tampa, and Jacksonville. The trend has continued since, notably with the election of liberals Lawrence Krasner in Philadelphia in 2017 and Wesley Bell in St. Louis County and Satana Deberry in Durham County in 2018. Many, including Ogg, had significant financial backing from liberal donor George Soros. They didn't run on identical platforms, but each promised some form of change, whether it was skepticism about the death penalty and nonviolent drug cases, or greater scrutiny when police shoot unarmed suspects. Mark Gonzalez, who was elected in 2016 in Nueces County, Texas, which includes Corpus Christi, has the words *not guilty* tattooed across his chest. Even prosecutors, he says, should believe that suspects are innocent until proven guilty. "This idea that in the past

prosecutors have counted cases and wins like scalps on our belt is outdated, and it's just not supported by data that shows this isn't making people safer," Ogg says. "The new breed of prosecutors, especially from large urban areas, are looking at being more effective in reality at protecting people."

Prosecutors seeking to get elected followed the same formula for decades. Prosecutors typically run for office countywide and have long followed a set formula: talk tough and brag about how many rapists and murderers you've put away. "Prosecutors are responding to the incentives that our political system creates," says Vikrant Reddy, a senior fellow at the conservative Charles Koch Institute. "You're going to be rewarded electorally for locking up more and more people."

That meant prosecutors had been a missing piece of the criminal justice reform puzzle. Criminal justice is now one of a small number of issues on which conservatives and liberals have begun to adopt overlapping policy positions, if for different reasons. Conservatives worry about the expense of mass imprisonment; liberals talk about racial disparities and the social costs of hollowing out communities through incarceration. More than 30 states have approved laws that seek to reduce prison populations, while increasing funds for treatment or reentry programs that can cut down on recidivism. The results have been encouraging, with crime rates remaining low in most jurisdictions even as the number of prisoners drops.

But prosecutors have mostly lobbied against softer sentencing. They also can sometimes sabotage it if they don't like it. Prosecutors enjoy enormous authority and discretion. The way they frame charges determines whether an offender will face a long mandatory sentence or be diverted into treatment. "The prosecutors really are key because we make the decisions about who to prosecute and what to charge them with," says Beth McCann, the district attorney in Denver, who announced in 2017 that her office would no longer seek death penalty charges. "We really need to get prosecutors involved in this new way of thinking about the criminal justice system."

Prior to the "Soros sweep," there had been scattered examples of prosecutors taking a different tack.

(Continued)

(Continued)

After winning election as Dallas County DA in 2006, Craig Watkins created an in-house innocence project, using DNA to review old cases and exonerating some convicts. That approach seemed risky for a prosecutor at the time, but "conviction integrity" units have since become fairly common. In Seattle, King County prosecuting attorney Daniel Satterberg created a unit identifying prisoners who were rightfully convicted but may be ready for early release. "It's such a turnabout," says Marc Levin, policy director for Right on Crime, a conservative group promoting reform. "Normally, all the DA would do is intervene against people."

The first swell of the new reform wave may have hit shore in Brooklyn in 2013, when Kenneth Thompson unseated a longtime incumbent by campaigning against prosecutorial misconduct and racial discrimination by police. The prosecutors elected since then on reform platforms, including those in the class of 2016, represent a small fraction of their profession—about two dozen, out of more than 2,500 prosecutors nationwide. Still, many of them oversee significant jurisdictions. Harris County, with 4.4 million inhabitants, is more populous than half the states. The nation's 35 largest counties prosecute a third of all crimes nationwide. "It's a departure from what for many years everyone thought was the inevitable playbook in these elections," says David Sklansky, a Stanford law professor. "It's possible to win an election as DA, running against an incumbent, and not just arguing that you're going to be tougher but reform-oriented."

Source: Adapted from Alan Greenblatt, "Law and the New Order: A Fresh Wave of District Attorneys Is Redefining Justice," *Governing*, April 2017, http://www.governing.com/topics/public-justice-safety/gov-district-attorneys-houston-criminal-justice-reform.html.

to prosecute, whom to prosecute, and with what cause of action to prosecute. Discretion in charging is, in the words of one scholar, "virtually unchecked by formal constraints or regulatory mechanisms, making it one of the broadest discretionary powers in criminal administration."[55] Charging decisions are enormously important, particularly in states where statutory guidelines set minimum sentences or where the same act can be subject to a number of different charges. Prosecutors can pile on multiple charges to make it exceedingly dangerous for the accused to risk going to trial, regardless of guilt.

Several reasons exist for giving prosecutors such broad powers. One is the trend toward **legislative overcriminalization**, the tendency of legislatures to make crimes out of everything that people find objectionable.[56] By creating a large number of broadly defined crimes, legislatures have made it impossible for states to enforce all their criminal statutes, even as they have made it possible for

prosecutors to charge a single act under multiple, overlapping provisions.[57] This ability to charge the same act in multiple ways gives a prosecutor tremendous leverage over a defendant. It is a powerful tool to coerce a guilty plea to a lesser charge through the process of plea bargaining.

A second reason prosecutors are given broad discretion is the need to individualize justice. Each case involves a unique set of facts and issues, and requires careful weighing of the evidence. To determine how best to spend limited resources, a prosecutor must balance the severity of the crime against the probability of sustaining a conviction. Prosecutors have been reluctant to publish general guidelines regarding their charging decisions. A Florida prosecutor stated that his office declines to prosecute cases of cocaine possession when the amount of cocaine involved is deemed too small. But he refused to say just how much is too small. Understandably, he worried that drug smugglers would package their shipments in smaller batches than this arbitrary limit and thus escape prosecution.[58]

There are some limits to prosecutorial authority, for instance, in regard to the trial process itself. In many jurisdictions, before proceeding to trial, the government first must obtain an **indictment**, a formal criminal charge, from a **grand jury**. The U.S. Supreme

Legislative overcriminalization The tendency of government to make a crime out of anything the public does not like.

Indictment A formal criminal charge.

Grand jury A group of between 16 and 23 citizens who decide if a case should go to trial; if the grand jury decides that it should, an indictment is issued.

Court has noted that the grand jury historically has been regarded as the primary protection for the innocent. However, only prosecutors and their witnesses appear before a grand jury; no members of the defense are present. Prosecutors are able to offer their interpretation of the evidence and the law and have no obligation to inform the grand jury of evidence of a defendant's innocence. Grand juries hear only one side of any given case and thus almost always indict. For this reason, no discussion of grand juries is complete without mention of the immortal quip by former New York state judge Sol Wachtler that a grand jury could "indict a ham sandwich." It is also part of the reason that many states have abolished the grand jury and now rely instead on a preliminary hearing in which a judge decides if enough evidence exists to warrant a trial.

At trial, a criminal jury must determine guilt beyond a reasonable doubt. The possibility of **jury nullification** exists if the jury does not believe a case should have been brought to court. Trials, however, rarely come into play as a check on the discretion of prosecutors—nationwide, less than 3 percent of cases actually end up going to trial. Most are resolved through plea bargaining. Plea bargaining is another area in which prosecutors have broad discretion. Judges rarely question or second-guess plea bargains reached between prosecutors and defendants. Prosecutors ultimately have to answer to the voters, because chief prosecutors are elected everywhere other than Alaska, Connecticut, New Jersey, and Washington, D.C.[59]

There are positive and negative aspects to subjecting the prosecution of local crimes to the political process. On the positive side, the person deciding which laws to enforce and how to enforce them is answerable to the people of that district. More worrying is that political pressures—rather than the facts of a case—may guide the exercise of prosecutorial discretion. Prosecutors, for example, may choose not to charge politically connected friends. Some attributed the multibillion-dollar savings and loan scandal of the 1980s and 1990s to the reluctance of prosecutors to subject their friends and political allies to criminal indictment.[60] Discretion also can be misused when race enters the equation. A recent study of prosecutorial decision making in the New York County District Attorney's Office found more severe outcomes for minority defendants compared to similarly situated whites at every level of prosecution.[61] In another study, a national sample of outcomes in prosecutor elections revealed that a high percentage of races

are uncontested, and even when an incumbent faces a challenger, campaigns turn more on outcomes of a few high-profile cases than on overall larger patterns of outcomes.[62]

Defense Attorneys

Anyone with even a casual acquaintance with TV crime dramas knows that after the police make an arrest, they must inform the suspect of certain rights. One is that "you have the right to an attorney. If you cannot afford one, one will be appointed for you." This right derives from the Sixth Amendment to the U.S. Constitution: "In all criminal prosecutions, the accused shall enjoy the right . . . to have the assistance of counsel for his defense." In 1963, the U.S. Supreme Court found in *Gideon v. Wainwright* that this right to counsel is so fundamental and essential to a fair trial that the Constitution requires the state to provide a poor defendant with a lawyer at state expense. Nine years after *Gideon*, the Court extended this right to counsel to all criminal prosecutions, state or federal, **felony** or **misdemeanor**, that carry a possible sentence of imprisonment. The Court also has made it clear that the Sixth Amendment guarantees "the right to the *effective* assistance of counsel."[63] If an attorney is unprepared, drunk, or sleeping during a trial, that can be grounds for appeal.

No money came along with the constitutional mandate for counsel, and its scope is tremendous because most criminal defendants in the United States cannot afford to pay for legal services. In 1997, about three-quarters of state prison inmates reported that they had been represented by court-appointed lawyers.[64] The annual total cost of indigent defense nationwide was documented in a 2008 report as just over $5.3 billion,[65] although total spending can vary tremendously between states for a variety of reasons. For example, states with high numbers of individuals facing the death penalty have significantly higher indigent defense costs.

Not only did the mandate come with no funding, but it also lacked any specifications as to how indigent services must be provided. States and localities, as a

....

Jury nullification A jury's returning a verdict of "not guilty" even though jurists believe the defendant is guilty. By doing so, the jury cancels out the effect of a law that the jurors believe is immoral or was wrongly applied to the defendant.

Felony A serious crime, such as murder or arson.

Misdemeanor A less serious crime, such as shoplifting.

consequence, have devised differing systems, with the quality of service provided varying tremendously. Three primary models have emerged throughout the nation, with most states employing public defender programs, **assigned counsel**, **contract attorneys**, or some combination of these. The method chosen may vary from county to county within a state, or a state may rely primarily on one type and use either of the other types for casework overload or the inevitable cases involving conflict of interest. Among the nation's 100 most populous counties in 1999 (the latest figures available), 82 percent of indigent clients were handled by public defenders, 15 percent by assigned counsel attorneys, and 3 percent by contract attorneys.[66]

Public defenders' offices draw on salaried staffs of attorneys. They provide criminal legal defense services either as employees paid directly by the government or through public or private nonprofit organizations. Large public defenders' offices generally employ attorneys who are trained and supervised and who are supported by investigative, paralegal, and clerical staffers. In 2012, 950 public defenders' offices across the country received almost 6 million cases, at a cost of $2.3 billion.[67] In 22 states, public defenders' offices are funded almost exclusively by state sources; 11 states use a combination of state and county funds; and 16 use only county funds.[68] Louisiana is the only state that funds most of its public defender services with local traffic ticket revenue. It's not easy. In New Orleans, 60 public defenders manage roughly 20,000 cases a year.[69]

The American Bar Association (ABA) has observed, "When adequately funded and staffed, defender organizations employing full-time personnel are capable of providing excellent defense services."[70] The challenge is to fund and staff these offices adequately. "Public defenders in Kansas City, Missouri, staged a courtroom protest to decry their staggering caseloads—most handle 80 to 100 cases a week," *Stateline* reported in 2017. "And in the wake of proposed budget cuts, Amy Campanelli, the Cook County, Illinois, public defender, threatened to stop taking on new cases."[71] In California, the American Civil Liberties Union (ACLU) filed a lawsuit in 2016 alleging that the Fresno County Public Defender's Office was so underfunded that it was failing to provide constitutionally mandated adequate representation to criminal defendants. The ACLU subsequently filed additional lawsuits in Nevada and Missouri. The ABA and the National Advisory Commission on Criminal Justice Standards and Goals recommend caseload caps of 150 felony cases per attorney, but according to this lawsuit, Fresno's staff attorneys were carrying more than 600 such felonies at a time, leaving the attorneys "so little time with their clients that they often can't discuss the circumstances surrounding the person's arrest or whether evidence exists that could be used in their defense."[72] In Washington, the state supreme court entered this debate by setting explicit limits on acceptable public defender workloads. The court set these limits after overturning convictions in a number of cases because of inadequate defenses provided by overburdened public defenders. In one such case, a 12-year-old boy convicted of sexually molesting a neighbor child was represented by a public defender who handled about 500 cases a year. The defender failed to investigate the case and only spoke with the boy to urge him to plead guilty. After the high court granted the boy a new trial, he was completely exonerated.[73]

Another type of system uses assigned counsel; here private attorneys are chosen and appointed to handle particular cases, either on a systematic or an ad hoc basis, and are paid from public funds. Depending on the state, individual judges, assigned counsel program offices, or the court clerk's office may make the appointments. In the oldest type of assigned counsel program, judges make ad hoc assignments of counsel. Sometimes the only basis for these decisions is whoever is in the courtroom at the time. These arrangements frequently are criticized for fostering patronage (the granting of jobs to political allies), particularly in counties with small populations. Counsel appointed by the judges they appear before may also be less willing to take strong opposing positions that could be perceived as biting the hand that feeds them.

Most states using assigned counsel appoint lawyers from a roster of attorneys available for assigned cases. These rosters are compiled in various ways. Generally, defense attorneys need do no more than put their names on a list to be appointed to cases. No review of their experience, qualifications, or competence is conducted. Some states, particularly those with organized plans administered by independent managers, may require that attorneys receive specific training before they can be included on the roster. Assigned counsel are

---

Assigned counsel Private lawyers selected by the courts to handle particular cases and paid from public funds.

Contract attorneys Private attorneys who enter into agreements with states, counties, or judicial districts to work on a fixed-fee basis per case or for a specific length of time.

generally paid either a flat fee or an hourly rate, in some cases subject to an overall fee cap. Many are paid at very low rates, such that only recent law school graduates or those who have been unsuccessful in the business of law will agree to take assignments.[74]

Contract attorney programs are another way some states provide defense services. A state, county, or judicial district will enter into a contract for the provision of indigent representation. Such a contract may be awarded to a solo attorney, to a law firm that handles both indigent and private cases, to a nonprofit organization, or to a group of lawyers who have joined together to provide services under the contract. The contractor may agree to accept cases on a fixed-fee, per-case basis or to provide representation for a particular period of time for a fixed fee.

Regardless of the model used by a county or state, all indigent defense systems depend on adequate funding to successfully provide "effective assistance of counsel." Without such funding, the right to counsel becomes just another unfunded mandate, and justice for the rich becomes very different from justice for the poor. Inadequate funding leads to lawyers' carrying impossible caseloads. A 2013 documentary titled *Gideon's Army* shows young public defenders in Miami-Dade County, Florida, struggling to do right by their clients while carrying an average caseload of 500 felonies and 225 misdemeanors.[75] A 2012 study found that the average time spent by a public defender with a client at arraignment is often less than six minutes, and workloads are frequently multiples of the recommended 150 felony cases per year. The researcher concludes that, with these deficiencies, "it is impossible to represent individual clients while adhering to even minimal standards of professionalism."[76]

How secure would you feel if you were facing more than 20 years in jail for a felony you didn't commit, in Virginia, where your appointed lawyer could be paid a maximum of $1,235 to defend you?[77] If you didn't plead guilty quickly, your lawyer would lose money on your case. Recently, a wave of successful lawsuits against underfunded and overburdened public defender programs, assigned counsel programs, and contract attorneys by groups such as the ACLU has put pressure on legislators to enact reforms that "even the most skeptical observers admit have the potential to bring important changes to the process of criminal justice."[78]

Juries

If you vote, pay a utility bill, or have a driver's license, you may be called to serve jury duty at some point in your life. You may be asked to decide whether a defendant in a capital case lives or dies; whether someone spends the rest of his or her life in prison; whether a civil plaintiff, injured and unable to work, should be able to collect damages; or whether a civil defendant must be bankrupted by the large amount of damages ordered to be paid. Service on a jury may require spending days or weeks listening to intricate scientific evidence and expert testimony, some of it conflicting, and deciding who is credible and who is not to be believed. Or you may spend one day in a large room with other potential jurors, break for lunch, and go home at the end of that day without ever hearing a single case.

The right to a jury trial in state criminal proceedings is granted by the Sixth Amendment. Not all criminal prosecutions trigger the right to a jury trial. Minor offenses involving potential sentences of less than six months do not require juries. Neither do juvenile proceedings, probation revocation proceedings, or military trials.

The jury's role in a trial is that of fact finder. The judge has to ensure a fair and orderly trial, but the jurors must determine the facts of the case. In some instances, parties may agree to forgo a jury trial and, instead, choose a bench trial, in which the judge serves as both judge and jury. In a criminal bench trial, the judge alone decides guilt or innocence.

Stereotypes might lead you to think that juries are less capable than judges of separating emotion from reason or that juries decide cases more generously for injured plaintiffs or that grisly evidence in criminal cases may motivate juries to base their decisions on passion or prejudice. Not so.

Differences and similarities in how judges and juries rule have been the subject of much research and review. Stereotypes might lead you to think that juries are less capable than judges of separating emotion from reason or that juries decide cases more generously for injured plaintiffs or that grisly evidence in criminal cases may motivate juries to base their decisions on passion or prejudice. Not so. For instance, research shows that civil

A DIFFERENCE THAT MAKES A DIFFERENCE
AMERICA'S BAIL SYSTEM GOES ON TRIAL

One spring day, Houston police pulled over Maranda Lynn O'Donnell. The 22-year-old had driven through a toll plaza without paying. When officers ran the tags on her car, they found she was driving with a suspended license, didn't carry car insurance, and had already racked up $1,487.25 in unpaid tolls. The officers arrested her. During her intake at jail, a pretrial services agent interviewed her and recommended she be released on a "personal bond," which doesn't require any upfront payments. Nonetheless, the next day, a hearing officer set her bail at $2,500.

Some people have the resources to post bond on their own. But many do not. Instead, they turn to a bail agent who, for a fee—typically 10 percent of the total bond—puts up a promissory note for the total bail amount. In theory, the bonding agent will pay that amount if the person fails to appear. In 2017, a federal judge in Houston found that Harris County "has a consistent and systematic policy" of imposing cash bail on defendants in misdemeanor cases and that "these de facto detention orders effectively operate only against the indigent, who would be released if they could pay at least a bondsman's premium, but who cannot." Civil rights attorneys have brought, and in many cases won, similar cases in Alabama, Mississippi, and Tennessee. "It's long been a basic principle of constitutional law that no human being can be put in a cage because she can't make a payment," says Alec Karakatsanis of the nonprofit Civil Rights Corps, one of a group of organizations that sued Harris County over its bond practices. "Yet it's happening everywhere."

Every year, more than 10 million Americans are arrested and taken to jail. Most are released. However, on any given day, jails house some 700,000 people. A large majority of them are there because they can't afford to make bail. On a typical day in Harris County, 9,000 people are locked up in the county jail system. A significant number of them are low-risk offenders awaiting trial on misdemeanor charges who can't post bail.

Twenty years ago, 1 in 3 jail inmates in Texas were there awaiting trial. By 2017, that had escalated to 3 out of 4. Mostly, these were people who could not afford to make bail. Jail time cost people their jobs, their houses, even their families. It also cost Texas taxpayers: a billion dollars a year was spent on pretrial housing. The Texas Judicial Council duly recommended a series of fixes: expand the use of risk assessment tools to help judges better gauge flight risks and potential danger to the community; change the constitution to create a presumption of release on personal bond for low-risk defendants; and

allow judges to deny bail to any high-risk defendants. (As it was, judges could only deny bail in capital murder cases.)

But bail is a big business. Of the $14 billion in bonds that are issued across the country each year, some $2 billion is profit for bail bond companies themselves. Nationally, there are more than 25,000 such companies; Texas alone has hundreds, maybe thousands, of bail bondsmen. A proposed bill threatened the bail industry by encouraging courts to release more low-risk arrestees without requiring so-called surety bonds. Ironically, what elicited even greater opposition was that bail reform was too tough: letting judges deny bail to high-risk individuals was a blow to bail companies, since they earn higher fees on higher-risk defendants. The bill was defeated. "This is the classic case of a powerful special interest being able to block legislation that would change a system that they literally make millions of dollars off of every year," says John Whitmire, who chairs the Senate Criminal Justice Committee.

Bail is an ancient part of Anglo-American legal systems. In medieval England, courts released all but the most dangerous offenders before their trial. To guarantee that defendants appeared at trial, courts also required bail bonds. The amount of bond was pegged to the severity of the crime and the defendant's ability to pay.

Right now, America's cash bail system itself is on trial. According to the Laura and John Arnold Foundation, more than 40 states now have task forces or commissions considering changes to bail and pretrial detention. In 2017, Maryland's Court of Appeals issued rules that ban the practice of holding low-risk, misdemeanor offenders on money bonds. In other states, court systems are making changes proactively. In Arizona, a criminal justice task force convened by Chief Justice Scott Bales developed rule changes that have lowered the state's pretrial incarceration rate by encouraging judges to utilize nonjail alternatives and pay closer attention to defendants' financial circumstances when setting bail bonds. Courts in New Mexico began to operate under new rules that prohibit judges from requiring money bail for low-risk offenders who can't afford it.

The most sweeping changes, however, have taken place in New Jersey. In 2017, the state rolled out a new pretrial system. Three years in the making, it comprises statutory and constitutional changes, including ones that allow judges to detain high-risk arrestees. Previously, New Jersey, like Texas, could only deny bail to people arrested for capital murder. In addition, the New Jersey measure provides funding for a robust network of statewide pretrial services. The state has also adopted a risk assessment system (developed by the Arnold Foundation) that gives judges a better sense of the potential dangers posed by people being released from jail. One of the results of reform has been the virtual disappearance of commercial surety bonds from the criminal justice system in New Jersey.

The industry is fighting back in New Jersey and everywhere else. It has filed lawsuits challenging the reforms in New Jersey and New Mexico and is pushing Harris County to appeal the decision against it in court. It plans to urge the Maryland legislature to overturn the reform rules the state's court system put in place. These actions are part of a broader argument made by antireform factions: risk assessment is not a safe or effective substitute for cash bail.

In the 1960s, the Vera Institute of Justice began to explore an alternative: releasing people without a secured bail bond. The institute started with a question: what were the characteristics of people who showed up for trial without posting a secured bond? Certain features quickly surfaced, such as prior criminal record, employment history, and family connections to the community. The institute generated risk scores that could be used to make recommendations regarding pretrial release. After three years of trial, the project found that defendants released on nonfinancial conditions (based on risk scores) appeared for their day in court three times more frequently than similar defendants released on surety bail bonds.

Risk assessment was born. "Releases on recognizance" increased sharply in the 1970s and most of the 1980s, as judges made roughly equal use of surety bonds and personal recognizance. That began to change in the late 1980s. Congress passed legislation that allowed courts to factor into bail decisions not just the likelihood of a defendant appearing for trial but also the public safety risk he or she posed. Most states quickly passed similar directives. Judges responded to the increased concern about public safety by turning more frequently to cash bail. While most large jurisdictions still had pretrial services and made some use of risk assessment systems, they used them inconsistently and ineffectively, according to Cherise Fanno Burdeen, who heads the Pretrial Justice Institute. The result was a sharp rise in the use of cash bail.

Early in this century, Burdeen and others began to advocate for changes. Despite a decade of robust jail building and falling crime rates, jails were overcrowded. Reformers championed a new generation of risk assessment tools and expanded pretrial services. The Arnold Foundation developed one such risk assessment tool, which it piloted successfully in Kentucky

and encouraged other jurisdictions to adopt. The bail industry fought back politically, supporting legislation and ballot initiatives in Colorado, Florida, Georgia, and Virginia intended to expand the use of secured money bonds. During the Obama administration, however, the U.S. Justice Department hosted a symposium on bail to explore reform strategies, the first since 1968.

Investigators also looked into the operations of bail agents. In 2014, New Jersey's State Commission of Investigation published its results, which found that bail bond agencies were being operated by unlicensed individuals, some with criminal records. Bail bond agents often hired people in jail to drum up new clients. The commission also found that New Jersey's counties routinely failed to capture tens of millions of dollars in forfeited bail. Instead, penalties were often negotiated and settled for pennies on the dollar. The bail system as a whole, according to the commission, was "highly prone to subversion by unscrupulous and improper practices that make a mockery of the public trust." Soon thereafter, New Jersey began work on overhauling its system.

In states such as Colorado, Maryland, New Mexico, and Texas, the bail industry has mounted broad attacks on measures the states have put in place, raising questions of effectiveness, safety, and expense. One of the key arguments is that pretrial services and supervision—a key component of a risk assessment approach—will open sinkholes in state budgets. Pretrial services can indeed be expensive. Washington, D.C.'s pretrial services program is often held up as a model, but it costs $60 million a year. That's a figure that Tara Blair, who runs Kentucky's statewide pretrial services division, says "gives the cost of pretrial services a bad name." Her state manages to provide effective pretrial services to a population of 4.4 million for just under $14 million a year. Urban localities such as Toledo, Ohio; Allegheny County, Pennsylvania; and Denver, Colorado, have found ways to keep bail reform costs in check. Denver's Community Corrections Department, for instance, began to implement risk assessment in 2012 and enhanced its pretrial services program the following year.

Denver now releases without a secure bond 40 percent of people arrested on felonies. One cost of the program is the monitoring of those released on bond. Greg Mauro, who runs Denver's pretrial services department, says it's tempting to aggressively monitor lots of people after such systems are first put in place, but that most agencies find over time that it's not necessary. Although his corrections department uses GPS bracelets to monitor some arrestees, many are supervised using less-restrictive methods. One innovation that dramatically boosted court appearance rates: texting people reminders.

Source: Adapted from John Buntin, "The Fight to Fix America's Broken Bail System," *Governing*, October 2017, http://www.governing.com/topics/public-justice-safety/gov-bail-reform-texas-new-jersey.html.

plaintiffs in product **liability** and medical malpractice cases have more success before judges in bench trials.[79]

Historically, juries in the United States have been composed of 12 people who must come to a unanimous verdict. Since 1970, however, a series of U.S. Supreme Court decisions have allowed states to move away from this standard.[80] In state jury trials, whether unanimity is required depends on the size of the jury. A conviction by a 12-member jury may be less than unanimous, whereas a 6-member jury must have unanimity. A majority of states continue to require 12-member juries to make unanimous rulings in felony criminal cases, but seven states use 6-member or 8-member juries for noncapital felonies. The Florida jury that acquitted George Zimmerman in 2013 of murder charges stemming from the killing of Trayvon Martin had 6 people, in accord with state law. Oregon is the only state that does not require unanimous verdicts in such cases.[81] Louisiana voters did away with the practice of allowing 10–2 jury verdicts, which had been on the books since 1898, through a voter referendum in 2018. Most states provide for civil juries of 6 or 8 members. Those that still require 12 members typically allow the parties to civil cases to agree to smaller juries. Unanimity is not required in most civil trials; instead, most states provide for verdicts based on a supermajority of either five-sixths or two-thirds.

States develop and maintain master lists from which they identify potential jurors. Their sources include driver's licenses, motor vehicle registrations, telephone directories, tax rolls, utility customer lists, voter registration rolls, and lists of actual voters. It is very hard to avoid ever being called in for jury duty, and service is mandatory, like paying taxes. Failure to appear can result in civil or criminal penalties. Jurors must be residents of the county in which the court sits and must generally be at least 18 years old, although in Alabama and Nebraska the minimum age is 19 and in Mississippi and Missouri it is 21. States also usually have some sort of requirement regarding literacy and the ability to understand or communicate in English, or both. South Carolina requires that jurors have at least a sixth-grade education, and Tennessee explicitly excludes those of "unsound mind" and "habitual

drunkards." Most states also require that jurors not be convicted felons.

Sentencing

The total U.S. prison population has ballooned in the past 30 years, rising from fewer than 320,000 in 1980 to a high of 2.3 million in 2008.[82] The trend might be reversing, however; from 2008 to 2014, the total number of people incarcerated in local jails and prisons decreased by an average of 0.05 percent a year, marking the first period of decline in four decades.[83] During this period of declining rates of incarceration, crime rates also dropped. According to the Federal Bureau of Investigation, from 2009 to 2014, the rate of violent crime dropped from 432 to 366 per 100,000 persons. Property crimes similarly decreased.[84] There was no decrease, however, in state spending on corrections, which has been one of the fastest-growing items in state budgets. Although growth in spending on corrections slowed considerably after 2008 owing to widespread revenue shortfalls and limited state resources, it still totaled $55 billion in 2014, averaging 3.2 percent of total state spending and 6.9 percent of state general fund budgets.[85]

In most states, after a jury finds a defendant guilty, the judge holds a separate sentencing hearing. In capital cases, the U.S. Supreme Court has held that only a unanimous jury, and not the judge, can sentence a defendant to death.[86] In many states, capital juries are instructed that a sentence of life in prison without the possibility of parole is an option. In noncapital cases, by contrast, it is almost always the judge who sets the sentence. Only in Arkansas, Kentucky, Missouri, Oklahoma, Texas, and Virginia do juries choose the sentences of those they find guilty. In most of these states, the judge is free to reduce but not to increase the jury's sentence, except to comply with mandatory sentencing laws. Most of these states choose their judges through popular election, so having juries decide on sentences allows trial judges to evade political heat for sentencing.

The amount of discretion given to judges varies from state to state. Depending on the type of crime and where the defendant is charged, the sentence can be a matter of "do the crime, do the time" or whatever the judge or parole board thinks is best. Forty years ago, it was possible to talk of a predominant American approach to criminal sentencing. At all levels of the nation's criminal justice system, a concern for rehabilitation and deterrence led states to embrace **indeterminate sentencing**. Legislatures set very wide

....

Liability A legal obligation or responsibility.

Indeterminate sentencing The sentencing of an offender, by a judge, to a minimum and a maximum amount of time in prison, with a parole board deciding how long the offender actually remains in prison.

statutory sentencing margins within which judges had the discretion to impose sentences for imprisonment with little fear of appellate review. The sentencing was indeterminate because the parole board, not the judge, had ultimate control over the actual release date. Under this system, judges and parole boards had to apply their discretion to tailor punishments to the specific rehabilitative needs of individual defendants. This practice led to wide discrepancies in the sentences imposed on different persons convicted of the same crimes.

Indeterminate sentencing came under attack from several angles during the 1970s. The lack of guidance for judges led to the potential for discrimination in sentencing based on such factors as race, ethnic group, social status, and gender. There was also criticism of the ability of parole boards to determine successfully whether inmates had or had not been rehabilitated. Finally, rehabilitation lost favor as the country entered an era of tough-on-crime rhetoric and a "just deserts" theory of criminal sentencing.[87] Reformers sought to replace indeterminate sentencing with **determinate sentencing**. This led to the adoption of federal sentencing guidelines, a structured system of binding sentencing rules that greatly limited judicial discretion in sentencing in the federal courts.

By the year 2000, all states had adopted at least some features of determinate sentencing, although in greatly differing degrees. When it comes to sentencing reform, "the states have served as hothouses of experimentation during the last thirty years, with so much activity that the diversity of provisions among the states has become exceedingly complex."[88] Some of the major reforms adopted included sentencing guidelines (either presumptive, meaning the judge can deviate with a good reason, or purely voluntary), **mandatory minimum sentences** that are imposed for conviction of specified crimes, **habitual offender laws**, and **truth-in-sentencing laws**. With the implementation of these reforms, the time served in prison by those convicted started increasing as a percentage of the sentence imposed. In 1993, the average portion of a sentence that an offender spent in prison was 31.8 percent; that figure had increased to 46.7 percent by 2009.[89] The average length of an incarceration increased as well; offenders who were released from state prisons in 2009 served an average of almost three years behind bars, nine months longer than served by those released in 1990. According to a Pew study, those additional nine months cost states over $10 billion, and more than half of the inmates were nonviolent offenders.[90]

In the past few years, the pendulum appears to be swinging again on approaches to sentencing reform. A 2014 report by the Vera Institute of Justice shows that since 2000, at least 29 states have taken steps to roll back mandatory sentences, limit automatic sentence enhancements, and increase judicial discretion in sentencing.[91] This swing was necessitated in part by the considerable burden placed on the facilities and personnel of prison systems brought about by the reduction of judges' discretion and the increase in time spent by offenders in prison. In fact, most of these laws have been passed in the past five years alone, as states have increasingly recognized the consequences of the previous tough-on-crime sentencing policies. Indeed, states have been grappling with corrections costs that have roughly tripled in the past three decades and with dangerously overcrowded prisons.

In California, atrocious conditions caused by prison overcrowding have become such a problem that the U.S. Supreme Court held in *Brown v. Plata* (2011) that California prisons violate the Eighth Amendment ban on cruel and unusual punishment. The Court ordered the release over the next several years of tens of thousands of prisoners to reduce overcrowding to 137.5 percent of capacity. Voters, frustrated that the prisons were filled with low-level nonviolent criminals, passed Proposition 47 in 2014. Under this law, certain crimes such as drug possession and petty theft were dropped from felonies to misdemeanors, and those already serving time for such offenses could petition to be resentenced. In 2016, voters approved another measure making it easier for nonviolent offenders to win parole.

How Courts Are Changing

The organization of state courts is not static or carved in stone. States constantly evaluate the practices and procedures of their criminal justice systems as they attempt to adapt to changing demographic, economic,

Determinate sentencing The sentencing of an offender, by a judge, to a specific amount of time in prison depending on the crime.

Mandatory minimum sentences The shortest sentences offenders may receive upon conviction for certain offenses. The court has no authority to impose shorter sentences.

Habitual offender laws Statutes imposing harsher sentences on offenders who previously have been sentenced for crimes.

Truth-in-sentencing laws Laws that give parole boards less authority to shorten sentences for good behavior by specifying the proportion of a sentence an offender must serve before becoming eligible for parole.

and political conditions. This section discusses some reforms being adopted or at least being discussed in most states. Increasingly, states have transferred the financial responsibility for their criminal justice systems onto the defendants and offenders who interact with it, raising constitutional concerns. Specialized courts to handle drug offenses or family matters are currently in vogue as ways to accommodate increasing caseloads and lower costs, as are attempts to streamline and speed up court dockets.

The Problem of Increasing Caseloads and Crowded Courts

Nationwide, violent crime rates are down. State courts, nonetheless, have found themselves on the front lines dealing with the results of societal problems such as substance abuse and family violence since the 1980s. From 1984 to 1999, the U.S. population grew by only 12 percent, but the number of juvenile criminal cases grew by 68 percent, and the number of domestic relations cases grew by 74 percent. Criminal cases, mostly misdemeanors, grew by 47 percent.[92] While some of these caseload trends began to reverse after 2008, legal issues stemming from substance abuse and the "war on drugs" have continued to grow. According to The Sentencing Project, 19,000 people were in state prison on drug charges in 1980, but by 2016, that number had skyrocketed to more than 450,000.[93]

In reaction to such growth, many states have created "problem-solving courts." These include community courts, domestic violence courts, mental health courts, veterans' courts, and drug treatment courts. Their purpose is to deal decisively with low-level non-violent crimes while reducing congestion in the general jurisdiction courts. They work best for populations with recurring contact with the judicial system due to underlying problems such as addiction, homelessness, or, for returning combat veterans, post-traumatic stress disorder (PTSD). The solutions often involve closely monitored treatment plans meant to stop the revolving door of **recidivism**, or relapse into criminal behavior. Spokane, Washington, introduced a community court in 2014 that meets in a downtown library and provides free lunch. The court's jurisdiction is limited to the low-level crimes typical of the chronically homeless, and

its goal is to solve the underlying problems that lead to the commission of crimes. Typically, those charged meet with social service providers and get assistance with anything from getting a driver's license to getting health insurance coverage, substance abuse treatment, and mental health treatment. One indication of the program's success has been a drop in the levels of property crime in the downtown area.[94]

States also have been experimenting with integrated family courts. These courts, referred to as "one family/one judge" courts, adopt a holistic approach to all the issues that affect a single family in a single court system. Such integrated courts can address these issues more efficiently than can multiple courts, especially in cases where delays can leave children in foster care limbo. Many individuals who appear in such family courts traditionally would have been forced, instead, to face multiple proceedings in different courts: assault charges in county court, custody disputes in family court, and divorce issues in yet another court, with the potential for conflicting orders. The current trend is to put all of a family's problems before a single, informed judge to eliminate conflicting orders and multiple appearances. New York has estimated that its integrated domestic violence courts slashed the number of family court cases from more than 3,000 to fewer than 900 in the program's first two years, while reducing delay and duplication and increasing cost-effective case management.[95]

This increased focus on court administration and case management has not been confined to the criminal side of the court calendar. Until just a few years ago, crowded civil dockets and multiyear waiting periods were relatively common in many states. "Back in the 1980s, there was no incentive for an insurance company to settle a case for the first year," said Bill Sieben, who was then president of the Minnesota Trial Lawyers Association. "They knew the case wasn't even going to be nearing a trial for several years."[96] This is becoming less true as states focus on clearing their overcrowded and overly cumbersome civil dockets. Tom Phillips, former chief justice of the Texas Supreme Court, has attributed faster-clearing caseloads primarily to the rise of the managerial judge.[97] Most trial judges today may insist on strong case management systems, but a generation ago, when caseloads were smaller and more manageable, not many of them did.

In recent years, not content with merely handing down verdicts, forceful judges have seized control of their courts and made it clear that things will run

Recidivism Relapse into criminal behavior that generally refers to former inmates returning to jail or prison.

according to their schedules, not at the convenience of lawyers who never seem quite ready to go to trial. "A very strong component of civil cases is, just set a trial date and the case will go away," said Kevin Burke, formerly the chief judge of the Hennepin County Court in Minnesota. "Left to their own devices, lawyers aren't necessarily going to manage it to a speedy resolution."[98]

State initiatives to speed up dockets, or court case schedules, have included an increased reliance on **alternative dispute resolution (ADR)**, which incorporates a variety of methods, such as mediation and arbitration, to help parties resolve disputes without trial. In certain types of cases, ADR is now mandated, and lawyers are required to inform their clients about alternatives to standard court fights. These alternatives usually involve hashing things out in front of an independent third person, called a "neutral," who tries to help resolve or narrow the areas of conflict. Some courts have been creative in finding appropriately authoritative experts to serve as mediators. Hennepin County courts, for instance, refer disputes involving dry cleaning—complaints about stained pants, torn dresses, and busted buttons—to a retired owner of a dry cleaning business for speedy resolution. An accountant may serve as mediator in the resolution of a financial dispute. These innovations increase the efficiency of the court system and free up trial judges for more complex cases.

Several states have experimented with the **rocket docket**, patterned after an innovation in a Virginia federal court. In essence, this fast-tracked docket imposes tight, unbending deadlines on lawyers for the handling of pretrial motions and briefs. In the Vermont Supreme Court, the rocket docket applies to cases that present no novel issue likely to add to the body of case law. Rather than all five justices sitting en banc to hear these cases, each month they split and rotate through a smaller and less cumbersome panel of three that is able to reach consensus more quickly. The panel releases its decisions on 99 percent of rocket-docket cases within 24 hours.

Rocket dockets are not always a panacea, however. Florida implemented the approach as thousands of home foreclosures began clogging the courts in late 2006. The foreclosure courts could clear 250 cases a day, each in a matter of minutes. But, although it represented a success for the state, attorneys found fault with the system. The few homeowners who attended the hearings had little time to be heard, and one review of 180 cases in Sarasota found that only 1 in 4 had complete paperwork. By late 2009, one judge found a way to slow the rapid-fire process, at least a bit—he gave any homeowners who showed up at the courthouse an additional three months to work to save their homes or to move.[99]

Conclusion

State and local courts play a profound role in state governments. They resolve civil disputes and hand out justice in criminal cases. They are also one of three coequal branches of the state government and frequently find themselves in power struggles with the other branches. This conflict is perhaps inevitable, as one of the courts' most important roles is to protect the citizens of their states from unconstitutional behavior by the political branches of government. Despite the importance of this role, or perhaps because of it, judicial systems differ tremendously from state to state. There are organizational differences from initial trial to final appeal. Judges in some states are elected by voters and in others are appointed by the governor. Such differences reflect each state's unique orientation toward the values of politics, law, judicial independence, and accountability.

The focus in this chapter has been on the players involved as a case works its way through the judicial system. In a criminal case, the elected prosecutor has tremendous freedom to decide which charges to bring against an accused criminal. Anyone charged with a crime has the right to an attorney, and the state must provide attorneys to those unable to afford their own. Usually, the accused is represented by a public defender. If a plea bargain is not reached, the case goes to trial, and the fate of the accused rests in the hands of a panel of ordinary citizens who have been called to jury duty. Potential jurors are selected from a pool of individuals who may have done something as simple as paying a utility bill. This does not mean, however, that there is anything simple about a jury's task. Often, the members of a jury hold the future of another individual in their hands.

If an accused person is found guilty and sentenced to incarceration, the length of time the offender actually spends in jail depends a lot on how the values of rehabilitation, deterrence, and retribution have played out in that particular state's political system. Differences

....

Alternative dispute resolution (ADR) A way to end a disagreement by means other than litigation. It usually involves the appointment of a mediator to preside over a meeting between the parties.

Rocket docket Court schedule that fast-tracks cases that often have limited, specific deadlines for specific court procedures.

here can have enormous impacts. One state may try a nonviolent drug offender in a special drug court that focuses on treatment; another may try the same offense in a general trial court in which the judge has no choice under rigid minimum sentencing guidelines but to apply a sentence of lengthy incarceration.

None of the choices that states make in structuring their courts is fixed and unchanging. States are always responding to altered societal, economic, or political realities; experimenting with what works; and adapting to political movements. Some of the areas of reform and change examined in this chapter were triggered by the political rise of victims' rights movements; by the realities of changing caseloads, overcrowded prisons, and stressed state budgets; or by a perception that the selection of judges has become increasingly political.

THE LATEST RESEARCH

State courts, like state constitutions, are one of the aspects of government that remain relatively understudied by political scientists. Although there is a long record of court studies, especially by law scholars, truly systematic research using the comparative method dates back only a few decades and is considerably less common than research examining state legislatures and executives. This is unfortunate because, as this chapter has explained in detail, state courts shoulder enormous responsibility for the administration of criminal and civil justice, and their decisions have far-reaching policy implications.

As this chapter makes clear, one of the perennial controversies in this branch revolves around how states can best select judges. Above we have given a flavor of the increasing politicization of the bench. Some champion this development as increasing democratic accountability, whereas others lament it as reducing the independence of the courts. Ultimately, which of these values is best to emphasize in selecting judges? Below we summarize some of the latest research on state courts and prosecutors. Most of these studies focus on the impact of elections, which are at the center of controversies regarding judicial selection.

- **Baum, Lawrence, David Klein, and Matthew J. Streb,** *The Battle for the Court: Interest Groups, Judicial Elections, and Public Policy* (Charlottesville: University of Virginia Press, 2017).

Judicial elections that see big money pouring in often have a similar set of characters. Business groups representing industries such as health and insurance seek to elect judges who will cast a wary eye on big payoffs in personal injury cases and related matters. Trial lawyers and labor unions often counter them. Despite the interests in both sides in tort cases, the advertising campaigns they underwrite focus on crime, offering often lurid and misleading versions of cases that may have been decided by judicial candidates. The authors offer a history of judicial elections and examine how they have evolved due to increasing participation from moneyed interest groups, using Ohio as their predominant case study.

- **Bonica, Adam, and Maya Sen,** "Judicial Reform as a Tug of War: How Ideological Differences between Politicians and the Bar Explain Attempts at Judicial Reform," *Vanderbilt Law Review* 70 (2017): 1781–1811, https://s3.amazonaws.com/vu-wp0/wp-content/uploads/sites/89/2017/11/28132124/Judicial-Reform-as-a-Tug-of-War.pdf.

Where does judicial reform come from? The authors examine the political tug of war caused by polarization between the plaintiffs' attorney bar and political players, looking at the overlay with judicial selection procedures. "How states choose their judges is a product of deep political forces and tensions, and political actors may have strong reasons to favor one kind of selection mechanism over another." The more liberal the bar and the more conservative the political actors, or vice versa, the more likely politicians are to introduce ideology into the judicial selection process. For example, under most ideological configurations, conservatives will, depending on how liberal they perceive the bar to be, push reform efforts toward partisan elections and executive appointments, while liberals will work to maintain merit-oriented commissions. The authors, political scientists at Harvard, examine how these dynamics play out in real life by offering three case studies: Florida in 2001, Kansas in the 2010s, and North Carolina in 2016.

- **Christiansen, Jeremy M.,** "Originalism: The Primary Canon of State Constitutional Interpretation," *Georgetown Journal of Law & Public Policy* 15 (2017): 341–408, https://ssrn.com/abstract=2827872.

Legal scholars devote a lot of attention to questions surrounding originalism, such as whether it's partisan or harmful or where it came from. Almost all their focus, however, is on federal cases and the U.S. Constitution. Most state courts of last resort have been invoking originalism for a long time—as early as 1804—and identify originalism as their primary canon of state constitutional interpretation. Although they don't always cite or follow original meanings in their rulings, state courts have been invoking originalism for longer and more consistently than their federal brethren. Christiansen offers a history of the ways in which state courts have considered originalism over time, as well as a discussion of the different schools of legal thought that have evolved under this particular umbrella.

- **Sklansky, David Alan,** "The Changing Political Landscape for Elected Prosecutors," *Ohio State Journal of Criminal Law* 14 (2017): 647, https://ssrn.com/abstract=2828803.

Since most prosecutors are elected, they have to be politicians. For years, that meant they had to appear tough, unforgiving, and "staunchly pro-police." All a prosecutor had to do to be reelected, it seemed, was to pledge to convict bad guys. Just in the last few years, however, a surprising number of district attorneys have been elected on a platform of reducing the charges they'd seek for certain offenses, being more vigilant about protecting against wrongful convictions, and promising greater scrutiny of police practices. This shows not only that prosecutors can win with a new message, at least in large metropolitan areas, but that elections for prosecutors are not automatic slam dunks and can provide some accountability. Having said that, Sklansky, a law professor at Stanford, warns that as prosecutorial elections become more contested, they run the risk of becoming "inappropriately politicized," with victory or defeat perhaps turning on the handling of particular high-profile cases.

CHAPTER 9

for CQ Press

Want a better grade?

Get the tools you need to sharpen your study skills. SAGE edge offers a robust online environment featuring an impressive array of free tools and resources.

Access practice quizzes, eFlashcards, video, and multimedia at **edge.sagepub.com/smithgreenblatt7e**

Top Ten Takeaways

1. State courts are the primary engines of justice in the United States, resolving 98 percent of the nation's legal disputes and criminal cases.

2. A state supreme court is the final interpreter of the state's constitution. Only if a state court's ruling directly conflicts with the U.S. Supreme Court's interpretation of the

(Continued)

(Continued)

federal constitution can the highest court in a state be overturned.

3. A state's court system makes up one of the three branches of government in the state system, and it can find itself in a power struggle with the political branches, which may control court system budgets, have a role in choosing new judges, and sometimes threaten impeachment of judges.

4. The power of the judiciary comes from the confidence the public has in the integrity of the judicial system.

5. There is a great deal of variety in how states organize their court systems, but cases usually start out in trial courts. The losing side in a trial court, if unhappy with the result, can appeal that decision at least once.

6. How a state selects its judges involves balancing the competing values of independence and accountability. Roughly half the states select their judges primarily through either partisan or nonpartisan elections; in the other half, judges are appointed, either by some combination of the governor and the legislature or through merit selection.

7. Merit selection of judges was originally conceived as a compromise between appointment and election. Judges are still appointed, usually by the governor, but the governor's choices are limited to a list of names provided by a bipartisan judicial nominating commission.

8. In the last decade, the amount of money involved in judicial elections has increased dramatically. The elections have become not only more expensive but increasingly nasty and partisan as well.

9. State prosecutors are generally elected and have total discretion to decide whom to charge with a criminal offense, what charges to bring, and whether to accept a plea bargain before trial.

10. How long someone spends in prison for an offense depends on how a state balances the competing values of rehabilitation, deterrence, and retribution.

Key Concepts

activist judge (p. 252)
alternative dispute resolution (ADR) (p. 279)
appeal (p. 253)
assigned counsel (p. 272)
bench trial (p. 256)
civil cases (p. 253)
contract attorneys (p. 272)
court of first instance (p. 254)
criminal cases (p. 253)
determinate sentencing (p. 277)

discretionary jurisdiction (p. 257)
en banc (p. 257)
felony (p. 271)
general jurisdiction trial courts (p. 256)
grand jury (p. 270)
habitual offender laws (p. 277)
indeterminate sentencing (p. 276)
indictment (p. 270)

intermediate appellate court (p. 253)
jury nullification (p. 271)
legislative overcriminalization (p. 270)
liability (p. 276)
limited or special jurisdiction trial courts (p. 256)
mandatory jurisdiction (p. 257)
mandatory minimum sentences (p. 277)

merit selection (p. 260)

misdemeanor (p. 271)

panels (p. 257)

plea bargain (p. 253)

precedent (p. 253)

prejudicial error (p. 256)

prosecutor (p. 268)

public defender (p. 268)

pure appointive systems
(p. 265)

recidivism (p. 278)

retention election
(p. 260)

rocket docket (p. 279)

settlement (p. 253)

state supreme court
(p. 253)

trial court (p. 253)

truth-in-sentencing laws
(p. 277)

Suggested Websites

- **www.americanbar.org.** Website of the American Bar Association, the largest voluntary professional association in the world, with a membership of more than 400,000.

- **www.americanjudicaturesociety.org.** Website of the American Judicature Society, a nonpartisan organization with a national membership that works to maintain the independence and integrity of the courts and increase public understanding of the justice system.

- **www.bjs.gov.** Website of the Bureau of Justice Statistics, which provides statistics and other information on a variety of justice system–related areas, including courts, sentencing, crimes, and victims.

- **www.brennancenter.org.** Website of the Brennan Center for Justice, a nonpartisan center at New York University that conducts research and advocates on a range of judicial topics, including state court reform and campaign financing.

- **www.ncsc.org.** Website of the National Center for State Courts, an independent nonprofit organization that assists court officials to better serve the public.

Dougal Brownlie/The Gazette via AP

Bureaucracy

What Nobody Wants but Everybody Needs

Haircuts are not what usually springs to mind when you think of government bureaucracy. In order to practice their trade legally, however, barbers and beauticians have to be licensed to do so by state government.

Chapter Objectives

After reading this chapter, you will be able to

- Identify the five organizational characteristics of a bureaucracy,

- Explain how bureaucracy makes and implements policy,

- Describe why rural states with smaller populations often have more bureaucracy than urban states with larger populations,

- Relate the advantages and disadvantages of using a traditional bureaucracy to deliver public services,

- Explain how the key organizational characteristics of bureaucracy help ensure neutral competence,

- Compare the spoils system with the merit system,

- Discuss how public labor unions and affirmative action have changed the merit system, and

- Summarize new public management and identify attempts to incorporate private-sector management practices into the public sector.

In early 2017, Juan Carlos Montes de Oca helped organize Haircuts for the Homeless, a charitable event in Tucson, Arizona, that offered manicures and barber services to the needy. Who could object to that? Well, the Arizona State Board of Cosmetology, that's who. Montes de Oca was a cosmetology student, but not yet professionally licensed. Lacking the state's official blessing to snip locks and trim nails meant those free hairdos were a legal hair-don't. Montes de Oca was formally investigated by the board and feared losing his cosmetology career before he'd even really started it.[1]

It appeared this was just one more example, as if we needed it, of everything that's wrong with government bureaucracy. Here's some big-hearted guy trying to help out the needy, and what does he get for his trouble? Big Brother shows up, shuts him down, and threatens to prevent him from getting the occupational license he needs to make a living. Just goes to show what an overbearing, overreaching, interfering, and needless complication in citizens' lives government bureaucracy really is, right? Wrong. States require cosmetologists and barbers to be licensed for good reasons.

Think about it. Would you want an untrained person putting potentially toxic chemical substances—and that's what a lot of hair treatments are—on your head? Using a cutthroat razor on you? Not understanding what practices avoid or encourage the transmission of diseases of the hair, skin, and nails? Neither does the state of Arizona, which is why it requires people to pass a stringent set of professional qualifications before being allowed to spend their working days wielding very sharp tools in close proximity to people's noggins. It sounds kind of silly, but unlicensed cosmetology is no joke. There are thousands of reports every year of unlicensed barbers and cosmetologists leaving their customers with chemical burns, nicks, and cuts, not to mention unflattering haircuts. One unlicensed New York cosmetologist even accidentally killed a customer by, of all things, injecting silicone into her buttocks.[2]

Besides, it's not like the barber police just showed up and shut Montes de Oca down. Someone filed a complaint with the state's cosmetology board saying he was practicing without a license. Once that sort of a complaint is filed, the board is obligated to follow up. No one suggested that Montes de Oca had anything but the best of intent or was trying to do anything other than a good deed. But a central job of government bureaucracy is to make sure everyone plays by the same rules; it does not get to pick and choose when and to whom those rules apply. That would be playing favorites, and one of the reasons we have the bureaucracy we do is to help ensure government doesn't play favorites.

The villainous red tape that shuts down free haircuts for the homeless highlights not bureaucracy's inherent silliness or uselessness but its paradoxical nature. On one hand, bureaucracy inevitably does mean rules and regulations that can be inconvenient at best and may defy common sense at worst. Yet bureaucracy does not produce or enforce these rules just for fun. Like it or not, there are good reasons for the rules and good reasons for bureaucracy to enforce them. Bureaucracy represents what is perhaps the political system's greatest contradiction. We do not particularly like it, yet we seem unable to live without it. Like a trip to the dentist, bureaucracy often is inconvenient, involves too much paperwork, and can result in a certain amount of pain. Ultimately, however, it turns out to be good for us.

This chapter explores this workhorse of the U.S. political system—the state and local bureaucracies that implement and manage most public programs and services. We discuss what bureaucracy is and why it plays such an important role. Most important, we use the comparative method to arrive at some explanations for why the American political system has so much bureaucracy when many citizens seem to value it so little. As you read through this chapter, keep in mind the following questions:

- **Why do we have so much bureaucracy?**

- **How good—or bad—a job does bureaucracy actually do?**

- **How should we decide who gets to work for a public bureaucracy, and how much pay and power should they get?**

What Is Bureaucracy?

For our purposes, **bureaucracy** consists of the public agencies and the public programs and services that these agencies implement and manage. Thus, **bureaucrats** are simply the employees of the public agencies. Most of these agencies—generically known as government bureaucracies—are located in the executive branches of state and local governments. Although these agencies vary greatly in terms of the programs and services they manage and deliver, the vast majority of them are organizationally similar. A specific set of organizational characteristics is associated with bureaucracy:

- *Division of labor.* Labor is divided according to task and function. Most large bureaucracies, for

example, have separate technical, personnel, and financial specialists.

- *Hierarchy.* There is a clear vertical chain of command. Authority is concentrated at the top and flows down from superiors to subordinates.

- *Formal rules.* Bureaucracies are impartial rather than impulsive. They operate on the basis of rationally formulated guidelines and standardized operating procedures.

- *Maintenance of files and records.* Bureaucracies record their actions.

- *Professionalization.* Employees of bureaucratic agencies earn their jobs based on qualifications and merit.[3]

Virtually all large, complex organizations have these characteristics, not just government agencies. Wal-Mart and Amazon have these characteristics and can thus be considered bureaucratic organizations, even though they are private companies. What separates a public bureaucracy such as the state department of motor vehicles or the local school district from a private bureaucracy such as IBM is a difference in goals. In the end, what separates public bureaucracies from private bureaucracies is not what they are but what they do.

What Does Bureaucracy Do?

Public bureaucracies play two fundamental roles in state and local political systems. First, they are the key administrators in the democratic process. They are charged with carrying out the decisions and instructions of elected public officials. This is the central focus of the academic discipline of public administration. Their second role is more controversial. It involves trying to figure out exactly what those decisions and instructions are. Interpreting the will of elected officials can be a tricky business; state laws and city ordinances can be complex and vague. The job of bureaucracy is to be specific and take action. Extracting specifics means that bureaucracies not only carry out the decisions of the democratic process but also have a fairly important say in what those decisions are.

Bureaucracy as Policy Implementer

The first job of bureaucracy is to be the active manifestation of the will of the state. This is just a fancy way

---

Bureaucracy Public agencies and the programs and services they implement and manage.

Bureaucrats Employees of public agencies.

of saying that bureaucracy does what the government wants or needs done.[4] The whole process is known as **policy implementation**. Agencies implement policy by issuing grants and contracts, by enforcing laws and regulations, and by undertaking and managing programs directly. For example, when elected officials decide to build a new road, they do not adjourn the legislature to go survey land, drive bulldozers, and lay asphalt. A public agency negotiates to buy and survey the land. The agency either issues the contracts to build the road or takes on the job of construction using its own employees and equipment. This is what makes private and public bureaucracy different: Amazon and Wal-Mart exist to make money, whereas public agencies exist to serve the public interest by turning the decisions of elected officials into concrete reality.

The job of the bureaucracy is staggering in its scope and complexity. Citizens ask government for a lot: roads, education, health benefits, safe drinking water, parks, reliable power grids—the list is virtually endless. Governments respond by passing laws that create programs or policies, which then must be put into action and then managed or enforced. Governments respond, in other words, with bureaucracy. State and local bureaucracies manage not only state and local programs but federal programs as well. The federal government relies on state and local agencies to implement the vast majority of its welfare, education, and highway programs.[5]

> Citizens ask government for a lot: roads, education, health benefits, safe drinking water, parks, reliable power grids—the list is virtually endless. Governments respond by passing laws that create programs or policies, which then must be put into action and then managed or enforced.

In their roles as implementers, managers, and enforcers, state and local government bureaucracies shape the day-to-day lives of citizens more than does any other part of government.[6] The single largest form of bureaucracy in the United States is a fundamental part of virtually every community: public schools. Employing about 3.2 million teachers, public schools serve about 51 million students and have a combined budget of $623.5 billion.[7]

Other public agencies regulate and set the licensing requirements for professions ranging from lawyer to bartender. Think of the need to ensure that professionals are qualified to deliver the services they sell. Look around at all the public libraries, swimming pools, and parks that offer recreational and educational opportunities at little or no cost. Think of programs for garbage removal, law enforcement, and fire protection. From the barber who is licensed to cut our hair to the street sweeper who is hired to clean the paths we walk, bureaucracy literally covers us from our heads to our toes.

Inside Erie County, **NEW YORK**, there are 3 cities, 25 towns, 15 villages, and almost 1,000 special fire, sewer, and lighting districts.

Bureaucracy as Policymaker

The second fundamental role of the bureaucracy is more controversial than its job as the government's agent of implementation. Public bureaucracies not only help translate the will of a government into action but in many instances also actually determine the will of the government. Put bluntly, bureaucracies do not just implement policy; they also make it.[8] They do this in at least three ways.

The first way is through what has been called the power of the **street-level bureaucrat**. Street-level bureaucrats are the lower-level public employees who actually take the actions that represent government law or policy. In many cases, street-level bureaucrats have the discretion, or ability, to make choices about what actions they do or do not take. In making these choices, they are essentially making policy. For example, the street-level bureaucrat associated with speed limits is the traffic cop. This public employee is actually on the highway with a radar gun making certain that motorists abide by the speed limits specified by state or local law. The legislature may have passed a law setting a maximum highway speed of 65 miles per hour, but if the

....

Policy implementation The process of translating the express wishes of government into action.

Street-level bureaucrat A lower-level public agency employee who actually takes the actions outlined in law or policy.

Even if it drives you to drink, you can't escape government bureaucracy: some states mandate minimum training requirements for bartenders.

iStock.com/Click_and_Photo

traffic cop decides to go after only those motorists doing 75 miles per hour or faster, what really is the speed limit that motorists must obey? And who has set that limit? Arguably, it is not the legislature but, rather, the street-level bureaucrat.[9]

This is not to suggest that street-level bureaucrats are power-hungry tyrants. In many cases, they have no choice but to make choices. On a road where speeding is common, it may be impossible to stop every lead foot putting pedal to the metal. Doesn't it make more sense to concentrate on the most flagrant offenders who pose the most risks to safety? Street-level bureaucrats have to balance the goals, laws, and regulations relevant to their agencies with the practical demands of the day-to-day situations they deal with. That often means making, not just implementing, policy.

The second way bureaucracies make policy is through rulemaking. **Rulemaking** is the process by which laws or mandates approved by legislatures are turned into detailed written instructions on what public agencies will or will not do.[10] Rules are necessary because most laws passed by legislatures express intention, but they do not specify the details of how to make that intention

a reality. For example, the Nebraska state legislature created the Nebraska Game and Parks Commission to enforce a number of laws related to hunting, fishing, wildlife preservation, and boating. The details of enforcing those laws—such as setting permit fees, determining bag limits for particular types of fish, and designating no-wake zones on lakes—are rules established by the commission rather than by laws passed by the legislature. This makes sense. The legislature would quickly become bogged down if it had to delve into the myriad details that must be addressed to put a public program into action. These details are left to individual agencies.

Once a rule is approved, it typically becomes part of the state's administrative code, which is the bureaucratic equivalent of state statutes. These rules have the force of law—violate them, and you could face fines. Just ask anyone who has ever been caught fishing without a license. Given this, rules are not left to the discretion of the street-level bureaucrat. Most state agencies have to follow a well-defined process for making rules. This process includes seeking input from agency experts, holding public hearings, and, perhaps, listening to special interests. The Nebraska Game and Parks Commission is required to give public notice of any intention to create a rule and must hold a public hearing to allow interested parties to have their say. If this sounds a lot like the process of making laws in a legislature, that's because it is. Rulemaking is probably the most important political activity of bureaucracy. In effect, it is a large lawmaking operation that most citizens do not even know exists.

Finally, bureaucracies also contribute to policymaking directly by pursuing political agendas. Street-level discretion and rulemaking are *passive* policymaking in the sense that they involve bureaucrats responding or not responding to something such as a speeding car or a newly signed bill. Yet bureaucracies and bureaucrats also take *active* roles in politics. They do so in a number of ways. At the state and local levels, the heads of many public agencies are elected. Such positions include everything from county sheriff to state attorney general. As elected officials, these agency heads often

Rulemaking The process of translating laws into written instructions on what public agencies will or will not do.

make campaign promises, and, once in office, they try to get their agencies to deliver on those promises.

Because of the visibility and importance of their positions, these elected state and local agency heads have long been recognized as critical and influential players in the process of policy formulation, not just policy implementation.[11] Therefore, some agencies become the tools used to deliver on political agendas. It is also true that other bureaucrats, not just elected agency heads, try to influence policy. As we will see later in this chapter, unions are powerful political actors in many states, lobbying for better pay and benefits and getting actively involved in election campaigns.

The implementation and political roles of bureaucracy make it a particular target for citizen concern and, at times, scorn. It is easy to see that we need some bureaucracy. Somebody has to manage all those programs and services we want from government. Yet government bureaucracy has a terrible reputation for inefficiency, incompetence, and mismanagement.[12] Many question whether we have too much bureaucracy, and still others are concerned about the powerful political role played by individuals who are mostly unelected officials. Why do we have so much bureaucracy? How good a job does it really do? Could we get by with less of it? Is there a better way to run public programs and services? Is there too much bureaucracy and too little democracy in state and local government? These are reasonable questions that the comparative method can help answer.

What Is "Enough" Bureaucracy?

Most people believe that, whatever the merits of bureaucracy, there is too much bureaucracy in government and in our lives. Undeniably, state and local governments have a lot of bureaucracy. How much? Some insight into the size and scope of state and local agencies can be gleaned from Table 10-1, which lists the numbers of employees on state and local government payrolls and breaks down the totals by selected function. Combined, state and local governments have more than 14.5 million full-time employees (they also employ roughly 5 million part-timers). Most of these—nearly 11 million—are employees of local rather than state governments.[13] Whether at the local or state level, the vast majority of these individuals work in what we would recognize as a bureaucracy.

The numbers displayed in Table 10-1 confirm that there are a lot of state and local bureaucrats, but numbers alone give little insight into whether there is too much or too little bureaucracy. In reality, the size of the bureaucracy and the extent of its role in the day-to-day life of any given individual vary from state to state and locality to locality for two main reasons. First, across localities, citizens make different kinds of demands on state and local government agencies. Some localities need more of one particular resource, whereas others need less. In Eden Prairie, Minnesota, the public demands more cross-country ski trails, and in Yuma, Arizona, the citizens want more public swimming pools. As a result, the size and role of the public sector can vary significantly from place to place—more demand equals more bureaucracy.

Second, there is no universally agreed-on yardstick for measuring what constitutes a "reasonably" sized bureaucracy. Where one person sees a bloated public sector overregulating citizens' lives, a second sees the same set of agencies providing important public goods and services. At the very least, to compare the size of bureaucracy across states and localities, we need to explore not just the total number of public employees but also the size of a specific public sector relative to the size of the public it serves. Table 10-2 shows one way to do this. It lists the states with the five largest and the five smallest bureaucracies as measured by the number of government employees for every 10,000 citizens.

By this measure, it looks as though more urban and populous states such as California, Pennsylvania, and Michigan have smaller bureaucracies than do more rural, less populous states such as Alaska, Kansas, and Wyoming. How can this be? Why on earth would Wyoming have more bureaucracy than Pennsylvania? The answer is actually pretty simple. Fewer people do not necessarily mean less demand on the government. Even the most rural state still needs an education system, roads, and police and fire protection, as well as social welfare agencies to help administer programs such as Medicaid. These are all labor-intensive propositions. Indeed, they may be even more labor-intensive in rural states. To understand why, consider education. All states are required to support and maintain public elementary and secondary education systems, but in a rural state with a widely dispersed population, an education system has to either build lots of small schools or figure out a way to transport lots of students over considerable distances to a smaller number of large schools. In contrast, more urban, densely populated states can take advantage of the economies of scale that come with centralized locations. Basically, less bureaucracy is needed where the citizens being served are close by.

TABLE 10-1 ● State and Local Government Full-Time Employment by Selected Function, 2016

Function	Total Individuals (in thousands)	State Government (in thousands)	Local Government (in thousands)
Elementary and secondary education	5,237	42	5,195
Higher education	1,557	1,317	240
Hospitals	867	348	519
Police protection	883	100	783
Corrections	690	436	254
Streets and highways	471	205	266
Public welfare	489	235	254
Other government administration	405	166	239
Electric power and gas supply	89	5	84
Judicial and legal	398	171	227
Financial administration	380	164	216
Fire protection	331	0	331
Parks and recreation	184	29	155
Social insurance	69.5	69	0.5
Libraries	87.5	0.5	87
All functions (including those not listed above)	14,528	3,763	10,764

Source: U.S. Census Bureau, "2016 Government Employment and Payroll Tables," 2017, https://www.census.gov/data/tables/2016/econ/apes/annual-apes.html.

Note: Total column may not equal state and local columns due to rounding.

The same tale is told when we use expenditures—in this case, total state expenditures—to measure the size of bureaucracy. Alaska and Wyoming are among the five states with the largest bureaucracies as measured by both number of employees and per capita expenditure. (See Table 10-3.)

Expenditures and employees tell us something about the size of the bureaucracy, but they do not tell us much about its influence or power over the daily lives of citizens. An undermanned bureaucracy with a small budget still can have considerable impact on the interests of an individual. If you have ever spent time in a university financial aid office, you probably already understand the point here—when people complain about bureaucracy being too big, they often mean the red tape and rules that come with it, not its budget or payroll. For the number of forms you fill out at the financial aid office, you may feel that the bureaucracy owes you a free meal, but there is only so much money in the pot. It is very easy to recognize this sort of thing as a central part of bureaucracy; it is very hard

TABLE 10-2 ● States with the Most and the Least Bureaucracy by Number of Employees, 2016

State	State and Local Employees (per 10,000 citizens)
Top Five	
Wyoming	750
Alaska	650
Kansas	610
Mississippi	596
New Mexico	554
Bottom Five	
California	388
Pennsylvania	385
Michigan	363
Arizona	354
Nevada	332

Source: Calculated by the authors using data from the U.S. Census Bureau.

TABLE 10-3 ● States with the Most and the Least Bureaucracy by Expenditures, Fiscal Year 2015

State	State and Local Expenditures (dollars per capita)
Top Five	
Alaska	19,965
Wyoming	14,322
New York	13,033
North Dakota	11,976
Vermont	11,065
Bottom Five	
Nevada	6,407
Tennessee	6,671
Georgia	6,637
Arizona	6,600
Idaho	6,407

Source: Calculated by the authors using data from the U.S. Census Bureau.

to measure it objectively. The lack of good measures of "red tape" or "rules" makes drawing comparisons difficult. If there are no comparative measures, it is harder to use the comparative method to examine why some bureaucracies have more influence than others.

Despite this, there is little doubt that public bureaucracies play a more powerful role in the day-to-day lives of citizens in large urban areas than they do in less populous rural areas. Why? It is not because bureaucracy is more power hungry in cities but, rather, because populations that are more concentrated require more rules. Building codes are more critical in urban areas because of the associated fire-safety and health risks—a problem with one building can pose risks for those working or living in the surrounding buildings. Building regulations thus tend to be more detailed, and the enforcement of these rules tends to be a higher priority, in urban than in rural areas. In this sense, urban areas do have more bureaucracy than rural areas.

Measuring Bureaucratic Effectiveness: It Does a Better Job Than You Think

So far, our application of the comparative method has given us a sense of how big bureaucracy is and why it is so big—because characteristics such as urbanization and geography result in different demands being placed on government. These different demands translate into public agencies of different sizes and with varying levels of involvement in our day-to-day lives. What the comparative method has not told us is how good (or bad) a job public agencies do. The widespread belief is that such agencies are, at best, mediocre managers of public programs and services.[14] Although this negative stereotype is held by many, for the most part it is wrong. Public agencies, as it turns out, are very good at what they do.

How good? Well, in many cases, they are at least as good as, if not better than, their private-sector counterparts. The assumption is that the private sector is more efficient and more effective than the public sector, but numerous studies have found that this assumption is based more on stereotypes than on facts.[15] For example, **contracting out** is a term used to describe having private or nonprofit organizations rather than government agencies deliver public services. The basic idea is that rather than using an expensive and inefficient bureaucracy to provide a public good or service, the job is awarded to an outside organization through a competitive bidding process. The bidder that can do the best job with the least charge to the taxpayer gets the business, and government reaps the efficiency benefits of the market. At least, that's the theory. The record of contracting out in practice is much more mixed. While it certainly works well in some circumstances, it is far from being a magic bullet.[16]

For example, faced with rising health care costs and a reluctance to increase student fees on top of rising tuition bills, over the past couple of decades a number of colleges and universities have experimented with contracting out student health care services. These attempts to privatize such services have met with very mixed success. The University of Northern Colorado outsourced the operation of its student health center in 2003, but the large health care provider that took over asked to be released from its contract a few years later when it found it couldn't make a profit. Auburn University outsourced its student health center's operations in 1999, but one of the private companies that won the contract went bust in 2001. These teething problems were overcome, however, and Auburn's health center privatization is now generally recognized as a success. The same cannot be said for the University of Denver's student health center, where an experiment with privatization was largely a failure. The health care company that took over student health care services seemed to focus too much on its bottom line and too little on the outreach services central to the original health center's mission. The university brought its health center back in-house and funded it with student fees.[17]

Some of the problems often associated with contracting out include a loss of accountability and transparency, difficulty in specifying contracts to cover all possible contingencies (e.g., who bears the costs if bad weather delays road construction), and a clash of public service versus make-a-profit value systems. All this can create conflict between private contractors and governments, conflict that can be messy, litigious, and expensive. After experimenting with contracting out, some governments end up deciding that it causes more headaches than it's worth. This is a pretty common experience; local governments that contract out services frequently bring those services back in-house after a year or two.[18] One review of the by now extensive pile of research studies on contracting out finds pretty mixed results: contracting out might cut costs in some circumstances, but it also creates new management and oversight problems for governments and creates clashes between private- and public-sector values.[19] The bottom line seems to be that a traditional public bureaucracy might seem old-fashioned, but it generally can be counted on not just to get the job done but also to be responsive to its elected bosses rather than to its profit–loss statement.

Although popularly viewed as inferior to their private-sector counterparts, public agencies actually come out equal to or better than the private sector on a wide range of employee characteristics used to identify effective organizations. Public- and private-sector employees are roughly equal in terms of their job motivation, their work habits, and their overall competence. Compared with private-sector employees, however, public-sector employees tend to have higher levels of education, express a greater commitment to civic duty and public service, abide by more stringent codes of ethical behavior, and are more committed to helping other people.[20] Various studies have shown that over the past 30 years state and local agencies have become more productive and more professional, and they have done so during an era when they have shouldered an increasing share of the burden for delivering programs and services from the federal government.[21]

There *is* wide variation between and within the states when it comes to how well public bureaucracies are managed. Good management has an enormous impact on the capacities and effectiveness of programs and agencies. States that engage in prudent, long-range fiscal planning are better positioned to deal with economic downturns, and they generally can deliver programs more efficiently. States that do a better job of attracting qualified employees with a strong commitment to public service almost certainly are going

....

Contracting out Government hiring of private or nonprofit organizations to deliver public goods or services.

to be rewarded with more effective public agencies. States that make training their employees a priority are likely to enjoy similar benefits. The bottom line is that well-managed public agencies lower costs and improve results, whereas the reverse is true for badly managed agencies.[22]

So how can we tell if agencies are being well managed or not? This is not exactly clear. During the past decade or two, various states and localities have tried to come up with some at least semi-objective performance evaluation measures for public-sector bureaucracies. These efforts, however, have rarely been comprehensive and comparative; in other words, they have tended to focus on agencies in one city or one state. Despite the enormous effort and energy expended in attempts to create performance evaluation metrics, it is not at all clear that much has been accomplished. Performance measures generally indicate that public bureaucracies are doing reasonably good jobs. More worrying is the increasing evidence that performance measures don't seem to change much, even when they do highlight problems. A big claim of the performance measurement movement has been that these metrics can help create a virtuous circle; they clarify agency objectives and measure performance on those objectives, and the resulting data can be used to improve management practices to improve performance, thus resulting in more effective and efficient goal achievement. One recent study on performance evaluations at the municipal level gloomily concluded that, despite all the associated effort and expense, we know little about the impact, if any, of all the efforts to "grade" public agencies, and "we may need to ask ourselves how much it matters and how much effort should continue to be placed in promoting it."[23]

This lesson may be reflected in what was probably the biggest and most truly comprehensive evaluation effort for state-level public agencies. The idea behind the Government Performance Project (GPP) was to hold state governments publicly accountable for the quality of management within their jurisdictions and prod them into making improvements.[24] Starting in 1999, the GPP did this by researching management practices and performance in four areas (money, people, infrastructure, and information) and issuing states grades for performance in each area. The GPP was not around long enough to have any lasting impact. The last grades were issued in 2008—just before the Great Recession hit and shook up the budgets, objectives, and management practices of public agencies in ways the GPP never did.

Is There a Better Way to Run Public Programs and Services?

Looking at bureaucracy comparatively, we learn how big it really is, we see why it is so big, and we might even get some insight into how well it performs. But is a traditional bureaucracy really the best way to run public programs and services? Do we really need less democracy and more bureaucracy? Do we really need millions on the state and local government payrolls? The short answer is no. As we have already discussed, public services and programs could be contracted out through a competitive bidding process and delivered by the private sector. Public agencies could be staffed and run by political party loyalists or special-interest supporters. Things could be done differently. Before we abandon the traditional public bureaucracy, however, it is worth considering why public agencies are so, well, bureaucratic.

Remember the key characteristics of bureaucratic organizations listed earlier? (Here's a reminder: division of labor, hierarchy, formal rules, record keeping, and professionalization.) These turn out to be important advantages when it comes to running public programs and services. For one thing, bureaucracies tend to be impartial because they operate using formal rules, not partisan preferences, bribes, or arbitrary judgments. If you need some form of license or permit, if your shop is subject to some form of environmental or business regulation, or if you are trying to receive benefits from a public program, it does not matter to the bureaucracy if you are rich or poor, liberal or conservative, an influential high roller or an average citizen; it does not matter if you are more interested in doing good deeds than making money. What matters to the bureaucracy are the rules that define the application process, eligibility, and delivery of the necessary service or program. Following bureaucratic rules can be maddening, but these rules do help ensure that public agencies are more or less impartial.

The bureaucratic characteristics of hierarchy and record keeping help hold public agencies accountable. Public agencies are expected to be accountable for their actions. They have to justify to legislatures, executives, the courts, and citizens why they do what they do.[25] An action at a lower level of bureaucracy almost always can be appealed to a higher level. Students at most colleges and universities, for example, can appeal their grades. In such an appeal, the bureaucrat responsible for issuing the grade—the instructor—is expected to justify to the appeals board and the dean why the grade represents a fair and reasonable application of the rules of the class and the grading policies of the university. Setting rules, requiring records, and setting up a clear chain of authority all help ensure that bureaucrats and bureaucracies do not exceed their authority or act unfairly. If they do, these same factors provide a means for holding the bureaucrat or bureaucracy accountable.

Professionalization is another bureaucratic characteristic that is desirable in public agencies because it promotes competence and expertise. To get a job in most state and local bureaucracies, what you know is more important than who you know. Getting a job as a professor at a state university requires a specific set of professional qualifications. The same is true for an elementary school teacher, an accountant at the Department of Revenue, or a subway operator. Of course, setting and enforcing such qualifications as the basis for employment and promotion means another set of rules and regulations. These qualifications also help ensure that merit—rather than partisan loyalty, family connections, or political influence—is the basis for an individual's gaining public-sector employment.

The great irony of public bureaucracy is that the very characteristics that help ensure neutrality, fairness, and accountability also produce the things people dislike about bureaucracy: red tape and inefficiency. Formal rules help guarantee equity and fairness, but—as anyone who has spent time filling out forms and waiting in line can attest—they can be a pain. Enforcing rules, or "going by the book," may mean bureaucracy is fair, but it is not particularly flexible. Treating everyone the same is an advantage from an equity standpoint, but the fact is that not everyone *is* the same. Surely there are ways to make bureaucracy more responsive to the individual. Well, yes, there are. But the history of bureaucratic reform in the United States suggests that the cures are often worse than the problem. Although going through this history is not a particularly comparative exercise, it is a necessary step toward understanding why bureaucracy is the way it is.

Professionalization The rewarding of jobs in a bureaucratic agency based on applicants' specific qualifications and merit.

Spoils system A system under which an electoral winner has the right to decide who works for public agencies.

Patronage The process of giving government jobs to partisan loyalists.

State Bureaucracy: From Patronage to Professionalism

Public agencies have undergone a remarkably radical transformation during the past century. They have become more professionalized, more organized, and more able to shoulder a large share of the political system's responsibilities.

For much of the early history of the United States, there was little in the way of state and local bureaucracy. State and local government functions that we now take for granted, such as public schools, libraries, and fire protection, were left largely to the private sector. In most cases, this meant they did not exist at all or were available only to those who could afford them. Public education is the single largest public program undertaken by state and local governments. Yet public education in the contemporary sense did not exist until the last half of the 19th century, roughly 100 years after the nation's founding. As the nation grew, however, so did the demands on government. The country needed to build roads, regulate commerce, clean the streets, and curtail crime. And taxes had to be collected to make all this happen. There was no centralized plan to expand public bureaucracy—it evolved in fits and starts as governments took on the jobs citizens wanted done.

At the federal level, staffing the bureaucracy was initially a job for which only the educated elite were considered qualified. This example often was followed at the state and local levels. Public service was seen as an obligation of the aristocratic class of a community or state. This "gentlemen's" system of administration was swept away following the election of Andrew Jackson to the presidency in 1828.

Jackson believed in the **spoils system**—that is, the right of an electoral winner to control who worked for the government. The intent was to democratize government and make it more accountable by having regular citizens who supported the electoral winners run the government agencies. This process of giving government jobs to partisan loyalists is called **patronage**.

Instead of producing a more democratic bureaucracy, the spoils system and patronage invited corruption. Following Jackson's example, electoral winners used positions in the administrative arms of many state and local governments as ways to pay off political favors or to reward partisan loyalty. Perhaps the most famous examples are the big-city political machines that flourished well into the 20th century and produced some of the most colorful characters ever to wield power in state and local politics. As discussed in Chapter 6, political or party machines were organizations headed by party committees or party bosses. A committee or boss led a subset of ward or precinct leaders whose job it was to make sure voters in their districts supported the machine-endorsed candidates. Supporters of the machine were, in turn, rewarded with government jobs and contracts. They also were often expected to contribute a set percentage of their salaries to the machine.[26] This created a well-regulated cycle, or machine—votes in one end, power and patronage out the other.

Political machines dominated politics in many urban areas and even whole states in the 19th and early 20th centuries. They produced some of the most fascinating characters in U.S. political history: Boss Tweed of New York, Tom Pendergast of Kansas City, and Gene Talmadge of Georgia, to name just a few. These men wielded enormous power, aided in no small part by their ability to dole out government jobs and contracts. Some machines survived well into the 20th century. Mayor Richard Daley of Chicago ran what many recognize as a political machine well into the 1960s.

Courtesy of the Library of Congress, Prints and Photographs Division

▲ Political machines were powerful organizations that dominated many state and local governments for parts of the 19th and 20th centuries. Their power was based on their ability to control government jobs, awarding these positions to supporters or, as this cartoon suggests, to the highest bidder.

While the machines made for lively politics and brought almost unlimited power to their leaders, they were often corrupt. Machine politics meant that getting a government job was based on whom you knew rather than on what you knew. Job security lasted only as long as you stayed in your political patron's good graces or until the next election. Understandably, then, there was a tremendous incentive to make the most of a government position. Kickbacks and bribery inevitably made their way into many state and local agencies.

The founders of the modern conception of government bureaucracy were the progressive reformers of the late 19th and early 20th centuries. They wanted a lasting solution to the gross dishonesty and inefficiency they saw in public administration. Toward this end, these reformers created a new philosophy. At its center was the idea that the administrative side of government

needed to be more insulated from the political arena.[27] Reformers promoted **neutral competence**, the idea that public agencies should be the impartial implementers of democratic decisions, not partisan extensions of whoever happened to win the election.

To achieve these ends, progressive reformers began to push for public agencies to adopt the formal characteristics of bureaucratic organizations. This was accomplished in no small part through lobbying for the merit system as an alternative to the spoils system. In a **merit system**, jobs and promotions are awarded on the basis of technical qualifications and demonstrated ability instead of given out as rewards for political loyalty. A merit system also makes it harder for public employees to be dismissed without due cause. But this does not mean a guaranteed

....

Neutral competence The idea that public agencies should be the impartial implementers of democratic decisions.

Merit system A system used in public agencies in which employment and promotions are based on qualifications and demonstrated ability; such a system blends very well with the organizational characteristics of bureaucracy.

job. The idea is to create a system within which public employees can be fired only for failing to do their jobs and not because they missed a payment to a political boss. The overall goal was to make government bureaucracies less political and more professional.

The federal government shifted from the spoils system to the merit system in 1883 with the passage of the Pendleton Civil Service Reform Act. The main features of this merit system were (1) competitive examination requirements for federal jobs, (2) security from political dismissals (i.e., people could not be fired simply because they belonged to the "wrong" party or supported the "wrong" candidate), and (3) protection from being coerced into political activities (so workers were no longer expected or required to contribute a portion of their salaries to a political party or candidate). The basic principles of merit systems have since been expanded to include equal pay for equal work; recruitment, hiring, and promotion without regard to race, creed, national origin, religion, marital status, age, or disability; and protection from reprisals for lawful disclosure of lawbreaking, mismanagement, abuse of authority, or practices that endanger public health—called whistleblower laws.

States and localities once again followed the example of the federal government and began shifting from spoils systems to merit systems. New York State was the first to do so, adopting a merit system in the same year that the Pendleton Act became law. In 1935, the federal Social Security Act made merit systems a requirement for related state agencies if they wished to receive federal grants. This stimulated another wave of merit-based reforms of state and local bureaucracies. By 1949, nearly half the states had created merit-based civil service systems. Fifty years later, virtually all states and many municipalities had adopted merit systems. All this helped professionalize state and local bureaucracies, and turned what had been sinkholes of patronage and corruption or marginally competent old-boy networks into effective instruments of democratic policymaking.

Politics and the Merit System

Although using merit as the basis for public bureaucracy has effectively created agencies that are competent and professional, it has its drawbacks. Remember the two key roles of the bureaucracy, policy implementation and policymaking? Merit systems have positive and negative implications for both.

In some ways, merit-based bureaucracy is a victim of its own success. The whole idea of shifting to a merit system was to insulate public agencies and their employees from undue political influence. We want bureaucrats to work for the public interest, not for the interests of party bosses. We want bureaucrats to apply rules neutrally, not to interpret them through the lens of partisan prejudices. To a remarkable extent, merit systems have had exactly that effect. Rules are rules, and bureaucracies more or less competently and impartially enforce them, regardless of which party controls the legislature or who sits in the governor's mansion. The merit system has undoubtedly been an enormous positive for the policy implementation role of bureaucracy.

The impact of merit systems on the policymaking role of bureaucracy is more open for debate. Merit systems did not eliminate the political role of the bureaucracy; they merely changed it. Under the spoils system, bureaucracy was an agent of a particular boss, party, or political agenda, and it favored the supporters of electoral winners. The merit system cut the connection between the ballot box and the bureaucracy. Distancing bureaucracy from elections, however, can make it less accountable to the democratic process—a big concern if bureaucracy is policymaker as well as policy implementer.

Once distanced from the ballot box, public agencies and public employees discovered their own political interests and began to pursue them with vigor. Organized interests outside the bureaucracy also began to realize that being able to influence lawmaking and, especially, rulemaking offered enormous political opportunities. All you have to do is get your favored policy written into the rules, and bureaucracy will enforce it well beyond the next election. These sorts of developments raise serious questions about the drawbacks of the merit system. As examples of how these concerns play out in state and local agencies, let us consider two issues: public labor unions and affirmative action.

Public Labor Unions

Historically speaking, public-sector labor unions are a relatively new political force. Unions were almost exclusively a private-sector phenomenon until the 1960s. That changed in 1962 when President John F. Kennedy issued an executive order that recognized the right of federal employees to join unions and required federal agencies to recognize those unions. The 1960s and 1970s saw a considerable expansion in the numbers of state and local employees joining unions. Today, roughly five times as many public-sector as private-sector workers belong to unions. In 2017, 6.5 percent of private-sector workers belonged to a labor union, while approximately 34 percent of public employees belonged to a union.[28]

The reasons for the expansion in public-sector union membership are not hard to fathom. For much of their history, public employees received lower wages than did their private-sector counterparts. Public employees also had limited input with regard to personnel decisions. Despite the merit system, many still saw favoritism and old-boy networks as having too much influence in pay and promotion decisions. Public-sector labor unions pushed for the right to engage in **collective bargaining**, a process in which representatives of labor and management meet to negotiate pay and benefits, job responsibilities, and working conditions. The vast majority of states allow at least some public unions to bargain collectively.

What should not be missed here is that the outcomes of collective bargaining are important policy decisions. They are decisions in which the voter—and sometimes the legislator—has little say. Negotiations about pay and benefits for public employees are, in a very real sense, negotiations about taxes. A raise won by a public employee represents a claim on the taxpayer's pocketbook. And it is a claim that is worked out not in an open democratic process but often in closed-door negotiations.

And it is not just money. Collective bargaining agreements can result in fairly complex rules about what public employees are and are not expected to do. Such rules reduce both the flexibility of agency managers, who are constrained from redirecting personnel from their assigned jobs, and the responsiveness of bureaucracy to legislatures and elected executives.

Labor unions have given public employees more than just collective bargaining muscle; they also have started to do some heavy lifting in electoral politics. Unions that are able to deliver their members' votes can have a powerful say in who holds office. Understandably, people seeking public office pay attention to the policy preferences of public-sector unions. By raising money, mobilizing voters, and even running independent campaigns, unions exercise considerable political clout that has, at least historically, given them the power to shape how the merit system actually works. For

example, a basic principle of the merit system is that competence is supposed to be rewarded. Expertise and job performance are supposed to be the bases of promotion and pay increases. In contrast, unions tend to advocate **seniority**—the length of time spent in a position—as the basis for promotions and pay increases.

NEW YORK is home to the highest concentration of union workers of any state, at 23.6 percent.

Public employees with more experience may—and often do—deserve such rewards, but it is not always the most senior employee who is the most productive or who contributes the most to an agency's success. Even in the absence of unions, seniority plays a considerable role in the pay and benefits of public employees. This is much to the chagrin of critics who view civil service protections as failing the public interest. For example, some critics view tenure at colleges and universities as a system that rewards laziness and allows "deadwood"—unproductive faculty members—to collect healthy paychecks.[29]

In many states, the success of unions in securing things like strong collective bargaining rights and seniority protections has generated powerful political opposition. Those conflicts have increasingly mirrored and amplified the polarized partisan divide that so frequently characterizes contemporary politics. As a group, public unions tend to

Unions represented 9.4 percent of WISCONSIN's workforce in 2016, down from 12.5 percent in 2014 and 15.1 percent in 2010.

offer more political support to sympathetic, left-leaning Democrats than to conservative Republicans, who are not only more likely to be on the receiving end of well-funded and organized union political activity but also

....

Collective bargaining A process in which representatives of labor and management meet to negotiate pay and benefits, job responsibilities, and working conditions.

Seniority The length of time a worker has spent in a position.

POLICY IN PRACTICE
WILL KILLING AGENCY FEES KILL PUBLIC UNIONS?

Mark Janus is not the sort of guy central casting would pick as a union killer. He's not a conservative politician or a crusading free marketer. He's an Eagle Scout. He makes his living as a child support specialist for the Illinois Department of Healthcare and Family Services, where a big part of the job involves helping out kids dealing with the stress of their parents divorcing.

Clearly he's someone who takes public service seriously. You certainly do not become a social worker working for a public bureaucracy to make money, let alone to radically reshape the entire public-sector labor market. You do it because you want to help people and make a difference. Yet, at least according to a study done by the Illinois Economic Policy Institute, Janus could reduce membership in public-sector unions by 726,000, cost state and local government employees nearly $2,000 a year in salary and benefits, and shave at least $12 billion off the nation's gross domestic product. In other words, he really could be a public union killer.

How the heck could Janus do all that? Simple. He took legal action because he did not like being forced to give a portion of his paycheck to the American Federation of State, County and Municipal Employees (AFSCME), a trade union for public employees. AFSCME was the union chosen as the collective bargaining agent for state employees in Illinois. Janus did not belong to the union, and no one ever asked him if he wanted to be represented by AFSCME. Under state law, however, Janus is required to pay so-called agency fees to the union, money used to support the union and its collective bargaining efforts.

Union supporters say such fees are important and critical to ensure unions can continue to function as effective negotiators on behalf of state workers. Without such fees, the argument goes, people will not join unions at all. If you get the benefits they negotiate whether you contribute or not, why bother giving them anything? That worries some people because if people do not join, or at least financially support,

unions, then union power collapses, and the government gets to keep wages and benefits low, cut vacation days, and generally force a worse deal for public agency employees.

Janus doesn't buy that argument. It's no secret that Illinois is in a budgetary mess, and Janus believes the unions have a big hand in that. To put it mildly, Janus does not like AFSCME's politics, saying the union "has backed legislation that has bankrupted the state . . . bankrolls politicians for whom I didn't vote . . . the union is wrangling taxpayers for higher wages and pension benefits for state workers—benefits that Illinoisans cannot afford."

His disagreement with the union was so strong he sued to overturn the law requiring him to involuntarily support the union financially. His argument is simple—those agency fees essentially mean he is being coerced into supporting a political agenda he does not support, and he wants out.

Public union supporters say it's not that simple. If state employees do not contribute to the collective bargaining agent—in other words, the union—all the benefits won at the negotiating table are at risk. These benefits—which are very real—could dissipate, leaving not just social workers but police officers, teachers, and lots of other public agency employees with a lower quality of life. It means fewer of the best and brightest will be attracted to public service careers, harder times and lower morale for those already working in the public sector, and knock-on effects that hurt not just government workers but the economy more generally.

The Supreme Court didn't buy that argument, and in 2018 ruled in favor of Janus. That decision meant no more agency fees, which in turn meant a big financial blow for all public unions in the 22 states where such fees were being collected. Will the *Janus* decision really kill off public unions? At this point, who knows. But even if Janus's actions do not kill public unions, they will certainly leave them weaker.

Sources: Mark Janus, "I'm Forced to Pay Union Fees as a Government Employee and I Want Out," *USA Today*, February 26, 2018, https://www.usatoday.com/story/opinion/2018/02/26/unions-dont-represent-me-shouldnt-pay-their-fees-mark-janus-supreme-court-column/352460002/; Frank Manzo IV and Robert Bruno, "After *Janus*: The Impending Effects on Public Sector Workers from a Decision against Fair Share," Illinois Economic Policy Institute (2018), https://illinoisepi.files.wordpress.com/2018/05/ilepi-pmcr-after-janus-final.pdf.

much more likely to disagree with unions philosophically on issues such as collective bargaining rights and seniority protections.

In recent years, Republican gubernatorial administrations in several states have made concentrated efforts to curtail the power of public unions, especially their rights to collective bargaining. Wisconsin governor Scott Walker, for example, successfully championed reforms to severely restrict the collective bargaining rights of public unions in his state. The most significant and potentially most far-reaching of these efforts was a legal case backed by Illinois governor Bruce Rauner that focused on a state employee who argued that being forced to pay so-called agency fees amounted to being coerced to support a political agenda. Agency fees are mandatory contributions collected from nonunion members to help cover the costs of collective bargaining. So, for example, police officers or teachers who decide not to join a union may still be required to pay an agency fee to the union that conducts the collective bargaining negotiations on their behalf. The basic logic here is to prevent free-riding. Even if they do not belong to the union, those police officers or teachers will get the same benefits the union negotiates with the city or school district. As they get the same salary increases, health benefits, vacation days, and so on won by the union in collective bargaining negotiations, the argument is that they should help cover some of the costs of union operations. The argument against agency fees is that it is not always clear that the money collected is used for those communal benefits. Unions, as already discussed, engage in political and electoral activities, and nonunion members may disagree strongly with the political stands supported by the union. Should they be compelled to contribute financially to an organization with political views they disagree with? In 2018, the U.S. Supreme Court considered exactly this question in *Janus v. American Federation of State, County, and Municipal Employees*. The court, in a narrow 5–4 decision, ruled that employees cannot be forced to make financial contributions to unions. While it will take some years to fully understand the impact of this ruling, it almost certainly will weaken the membership and power of public labor unions (see Policy in Practice box "Will Killing Agency Fees Kill Public Unions?").

Underneath the titanic political and legal struggles pitting unions against conservative-leaning elected officials, there is the broader conundrum about the future of merit systems as the basis of staffing public bureaucracies.

For example, at the heart of state merit systems are civil service rules, which spell out how employees of public agencies are to be hired, fired, and promoted. Pretty much everyone agrees with the general intent behind these rules—that is, to ensure that public agencies are staffed with people who are qualified and good at their jobs, and to protect them from arbitrary discrimination or retribution. In many cases, however, these rules have become incredibly complex and convoluted.

For example, consider civil service exams. Such exams are used to determine hiring and promotion opportunities and are designed to identify the people best suited for these opportunities. So far, so good. This sounds like the merit system in action; if you want to be a firefighter or social worker (or whatever), then part and parcel of the application or promotion process is a test designed to figure out which applicants are the most knowledgeable firefighters or social workers. The problem is that scores on these tests have become increasingly subject to legal "adjustments." In Massachusetts, for example, civil service test scores can be readjusted on the basis of more than a dozen "preferences." In other words, your test grade is effectively curved if you meet one of those preferred characteristics. Affirmative action, or giving priority based on minority group membership, is probably the best known and most controversial of these (see discussion below). In Massachusetts, though, preferred groups also include veterans, children of police officers or firefighters injured in the line of duty, and widows of veterans killed in the line of duty. Recalculate test scores by applying a long list of such preferences, and the results of those civil service exams can seem pretty distorted. At one point, the city of Boston was hiring 25 firefighters, and no one who scored 100 percent on the civil service exam even made it onto the list of the top 200 candidates because of "adjustments." One individual who scored 100 percent was ranked number 1,837.[30] In other states, personnel systems have simply become antiquated and too rigid to deal with the 21st-century labor market. Tennessee, for example, recently enacted a massive civil service reform with the primary objective of allowing agency managers to hire the best people for the job.[31] The fact that a top-to-bottom reform of the personnel management system was deemed necessary to achieve that objective shows just how far state officials at all levels believed the civil service had drifted from the core philosophy of the merit system over the years.

Affirmative Action

Public unions show how a political role for bureaucracy can be generated internally—public employees get organized and pursue their interests in the political arena. Yet bureaucracies can be politicized from the outside as well. Consider **affirmative action**, the set of policies used to get government to make a special effort to recruit and retain certain categories of workers who historically have been underrepresented, to achieve better and fairer representation. It is illegal for government agencies to have employment, evaluation, or promotion practices that discriminate on the basis of race, age, color, creed, gender, physical disability, or other characteristics not related to the job or job performance. Although such discrimination has been banned outright, public bureaucracies are not particularly diverse in a number of these factors, especially race and gender.

Consider K–12 teachers, who make up the largest single group employed by state and local governments. There are huge gender and race imbalances in this group: Roughly 77 percent are female, and more than 80 percent are white. That suggests males and nonwhites are massively underrepresented among grade school teachers.[32] The lack of diversity among teachers is unusual only in that women are overrepresented. Among all state and local government employees, more than half are male and roughly two-thirds white, and that gender and racial imbalance tends to be more pronounced in management and leadership positions.[33] Consider the New York Police Department (NYPD), which in 2015 had 35,160 uniformed officers. Of that total about 51 percent were white, 15 percent were black, and 27 percent were Hispanic. In contrast, the city they served was roughly 33 percent white, 22 percent black, and nearly 30 percent Hispanic.[34]

The demographic disproportionality in the ranks of the NYPD is probably not the result of the outright racism of individuals. A bigger problem is that the nondiscriminatory hiring practices that form the foundation of the merit system are passive; they ensure access to hiring opportunities but make no guarantees about jobs or promotions. In choosing who should be hired or promoted, the merit system is predicated on looking at factors such as experience, qualifications, and performance on civil service exams. This strict approach, though, does not account for gender, race, or ethnicity, and this is potentially a problem because minorities historically have had fewer educational opportunities. Less education means fewer qualifications. This translates into a tougher time gaining access to jobs. The end result is that, even if race is not an explicit factor in hiring and promoting, whites tend to have more education and better connections in bureaucratic hierarchies.[35] This strikes many as unfair.

One of the remedies offered to address this unfairness is affirmative action, a set of policies that, in essence, constitute proactive attempts to increase diversity. Such policies are highly controversial—are they necessary to remove institutionalized racism from the merit system, or are they simply a way for certain groups to profit from a double standard that makes a mockery of the merit system? Defenders argue that such

Policies to help organizations recruit and promote historically underrepresented groups such as women and African Americans, broadly known as affirmative action, create more diversity in public agencies. Such policies can be controversial, with critics arguing that they undercut the principle of technical competence at the heart of the merit system.

iStock.com/Roberto Galan

....

Affirmative action A set of policies designed to help organizations recruit and promote employees who are members of disadvantaged groups.

policies are necessary because of the political role of the bureaucracy.

The desire for multiracial balance is only a part of this argument. A fairly long-standing theory in the field of public administration suggests that more diverse bureaucracies actually may be more effective. According to the theory of **representative bureaucracy**, public agencies that reflect the diversity of the communities they serve are more likely to account for the interests of all groups when managing programs and delivering services.[36] To serve a diverse and democratic society well, a bureaucracy should include affirmative action as an important part of its hiring and promoting practices. Remember our street-level bureaucrat, the traffic cop deciding which speeders to stop? What if all the traffic cops were white and most of the speeders stopped were black—or vice versa? Regardless of who was going how fast, this sort of situation would likely create friction. Some may view the agency as unfair, which could make the bureaucracy's job harder. If traffic cops are ethnically diverse, the bureaucracy will be less likely to be seen as playing favorites and will be better able to focus on its job.

Opponents of affirmative action reject such arguments. Males and whites often resent establishing preferential recruitment and promotion policies for women and for racial and ethnic minorities. Some see the policies as little more than reverse discrimination. From this perspective, affirmative action represents the success of special interests in getting their favored agendas written into the law and the rules that run bureaucracies. In a merit system, technical qualifications and job performance—not race or gender—are supposed to drive personnel decisions in the ideal bureaucracy. Opponents of affirmative action argue that it produces quotas and favoritism for certain groups. In effect, affirmative action has bureaucracy wage politics on behalf of the favored groups. Speeders should be stopped, and the race or gender of the driver and of whoever issues the ticket should be irrelevant.

Which of these viewpoints is correct is a matter of fierce debate. Whatever the underlying pros and cons, the fight comes down to what is the best way to recruit and promote public employees, and who—if anyone—should be given preferential treatment. This is ultimately a political fight about who gets government jobs. In *Ricci v. DeStefano* (2009), the U.S. Supreme Court ruled that public agencies cannot simply ignore well-established merit system procedures to achieve greater racial diversity. At the heart of this case were 19 white and Hispanic firefighters from the city of New Haven, Connecticut. They sued after the city threw out their scores on an exam that would have qualified them for promotions, fearing a lawsuit from minority employees. The Supreme Court sided with the firefighters and ruled New Haven's actions impermissible, but the ruling was relatively narrow and did not resolve the larger question of whether bending merit system rules to promote racial diversity is necessarily a violation of the constitutional right to equal protection. In short, the ruling left this area of employment law as gray as ever, ensuring that the fight will go on.[37]

If Not Merit . . . Then What?

At least in theory, traditional bureaucracy and the merit system have some clear advantages: equity, competence, and something approaching neutrality. They also have disadvantages: a measure of red tape and inefficiency, a lack of flexibility and accountability, and a political role that makes many uncomfortable. No clear answer exists on whether the pros outweigh the cons, or vice versa, but this has not stopped the nearly constant search for a better way to do things. Bureaucratic reform is a perennial issue in American politics.

Many of the reform efforts are variations on a single theme that reflects a popular belief that government would be better if it were run more like a business. In practice, this means introducing competition into the delivery of public programs and services, making the organizations that deliver these goods and services less hierarchical, and making greater use of the private sector to deliver public services.[38] The idea is to introduce the benefits of the market into the public sector, which in theory could lead to more efficiency through lower costs while increasing responsiveness, because competition means paying attention to your customers or going out of business. The great difficulty facing reformers is how to get these benefits without leaving behind the advantages of the traditional, tried-and-true, merit-based bureaucracy.

Over the past two decades, reformers have made a sustained effort to try to change the entire philosophy of delivering public programs and services from the use of a traditional bureaucracy to the use of a more

Representative bureaucracy The idea that public agencies that reflect the diversity of the communities they serve will be more effective.

business-based model. Although these reforms come in many different packages, collectively they often are described as new public management. New public management has six core characteristics that have been widely pursued and adopted by state and local governments:

> **The basic problem with trying to run government more like a business is simply that government is not a business.**

1. A focus on productivity that emphasizes "doing more with less"—that is, providing public services with fewer resources

2. A market orientation that looks increasingly to the private sector to deliver public services, typically done through a process of competitive bidding, during which private companies vie to gain a government contract to run a public program

3. A drive to improve customer satisfaction with public services

4. A decentralization of decision-making power, an effort to push policymaking choices as close as possible to the people who are going to be affected by them

5. A movement to improve the government's capacity to make, implement, and manage public policy and public programs

6. An effort to maintain accountability—that is, to make the government deliver on its service promises[39]

These characteristics all sound fairly positive when presented as a simple list. In practice, however, they have proved to be a mixed bag. The basic problem with trying to run government more like a business is simply that government is not a business. For the most part, we as citizens do not like rules and red tape—until there is a problem or a scandal. Then we want to know what went wrong and who is to blame. We want government agencies to act more like businesses until bureaucracy takes a calculated risk—as businesses do routinely—and loses taxpayer money. We want bureaucrats to be given the freedom to be flexible and make choices—until those choices result in favoritism or program failure. We like the idea of competition and the profit motive; we like it until a private company contracted to provide public services puts profit above the public interest.

Although most efforts to make government bureaucracy more market-like have produced very mixed results, they have done little to reduce the widespread belief that government is best run as a business. This belief has spawned a veritable alphabet soup of business-oriented reform movements. Reinventing government (REGO) stresses making public agencies entrepreneurial. Total quality management (TQM) emphasizes having public programs and services designed and shaped by the clients who actually consume those services, and focuses on preventing problems rather than reacting to them. Management by objectives (MBO) and performance-based management (PBM) are approaches that focus on setting goals and achieving them, and Six Sigma is an approach predicated on improving outputs by systematically focusing on the processes that produce those outputs. There are many other such movements. All originated in private-sector management trends that do not fully account for the unique problems of the public sector. Support and enthusiasm for making government more like a business tend to fade when these systems are put into practice and it becomes apparent that there are good reasons government is not run like the typical 9-to-5 corporation.

As the problems with these proffered replacements for traditional bureaucracy become clear, public agencies gravitate back to their tried-and-true bureaucratic ways of doing things, at least until they get swept up in the next big reform movement. Some of these movements are counterproductive from the beginning because they spread more confusion than efficiency and leave public managers with vague or complicated sets of guidelines that are both difficult to implement and based on concepts that are hard to understand.

Another big drawback to trying to replace the traditional merit-based bureaucracy is that the advantages of such a bureaucracy get overlooked until they are no longer there. Many of the attempts to radically reform the bureaucracy by either making agencies more like businesses or eliminating the merit system end up doing little more than returning public programs and services to the spoils system.[40]

FIGURE 10-1 ● **Changes in State and Local Government Employment, 2014–2017**

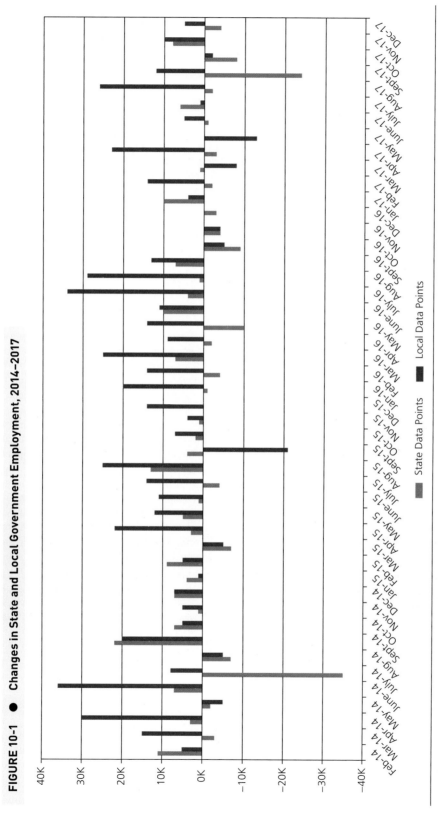

■ State Data Points   ■ Local Data Points

Source: "State and Local Government Employment: Monthly Data," *Governing,* last updated January 11, 2018, http://www.governing.com/gov-data/public-workforce-salaries/monthly-government-employment-changes-totals.html.

LOCAL FOCUS

POACHING PERSONNEL

States and localities are facing an increasing problem with government workers: there's not enough of them to go around. Baby boomers are retiring, creating lots of vacancies in everything from teaching to law enforcement. The problem is, fewer people seem to want a government job.

There are good reasons for this. Salaries in the public sector have been shrinking for a decade, and other traditional perks that might have once tempted people into working for a public agency have also taken a hit. Government jobs are not as secure as they used to be, the pensions are less generous, and other benefits—everything from health care to vacation days—are being cut. About the only thing that hasn't changed is the public's general disdain for government bureaucracies and the people who work for them. As you might imagine, low pay, poor benefits, and the ire of a disgruntled public are not exactly calculated to lure in job seekers who have a lot of private-sector choices in an era of low unemployment.

This has ramped up the pressure on the people trying to recruit people to work for public bureaucracies. Traditionally, local governments have hired locally, but there's an emerging national labor market for public-sector jobs because agencies are being increasingly aggressive about recruiting out of state. In that competition, some public agencies have quickly figured out where they may have a recruiting advantage. Cities in California and Florida, for example, can not only tempt people away from positions in Midwestern states with comparatively higher pay; they can also promise something cities in Indiana and Wisconsin cannot: year-round sunshine.

Brian Mahone, a recruiting supervisor for the Indianapolis Police Department, has seen police departments from sunnier climates thousands of miles away show up to job fairs in his state. "They come here in the wintertime," he says, "and they try to draw people from our applicant pool." That's either sneaky or sound recruiting strategy, depending on your perspective.

All's fair, though, in love and poaching personnel. The Los Angeles Police Department, for example, has a lot of jobs to fill and about 20 employees whose full-time job is trying to get them filled. To do that, they are increasingly targeting well-qualified people in midsize cities where wages are lower and there's no Southern Cali beaches or weather.

It's not just police departments. Everything from water agencies to schools districts are aggressively recruiting out of state. To recruit good people—and to prevent good employees from being picked off by other agencies—public bureaucracies are starting to experiment with new ways to keep people happy. If pay and pensions are being squeezed, what else can they do to make public-sector jobs attractive?

Well, the Arizona Department of Health Services lets parents bring their babies to work. The city of Memphis, Tennessee, offers departmental appreciation nights at basketball games and movies. The city of Atlanta, Georgia, gives its employees free access to nap pods and a juice bar at a new wellness center.

In an era when public-sector jobs do not pay well and it's tough to fill open slots, public agencies are figuring out often creative ways to prevent their people from being poached by other public agencies.

Sources: Adapted from Katherine Barrett and Richard Greene, "Sunshine and Pay Raises: How Governments Poach Employees from Other Governments," *Governing*, August 2017; Katherine Barrett and Richard Greene, "Can New Perks Make Up for Smaller Pensions," *Governing*, September 2017. Supplementary source: Andrew G. Biggs and Jason Richwine, *Overpaid or Underpaid? A State-by-State Ranking of Public-Employee Compensation*, AEI Economic Policy Working Paper 2014-14 (Washington, DC: American Enterprise Institute for Public Policy Research, April 2014), http://www.aei.org/wp-content/uploads/2014/04/-biggs-overpaid-or-underpaid-a-statebystate-ranking-of-public-employee-compensation_112536583046.pdf.

This is not to say that it is impossible to implement long-lasting changes in public bureaucracies. Indeed, the Great Recession brought about some of the biggest and potentially longest-lasting changes to public agencies in at least a generation. One of the most obvious of these changes is that, personnel-wise, public agencies shrank. Cash-strapped state and local governments started shedding jobs shortly after the financial crunch hit in 2008, and their staffing levels have never fully recovered. In December 2007, there were approximately 14.5 million people on local government payrolls and 5.13 million on state government payrolls.

In December 2017, a decade later, there were roughly 30,000 fewer local government employees and more than 100,000 fewer state employees.[41] In short, we're living an era where the population is growing and with it the demand for public services, while at the same time the state and local bureaucracies tasked with providing those services are shrinking (see Figure 10-1).

Conclusion

Although bureaucracy is often despised and disparaged, it is clear that the effectiveness of government bureaucracy is underestimated, and bureaucratic agencies do not get the credit they actually deserve. A wide range of state and local agencies support and deliver the programs and services that make up social and economic life as we know it. The comparative method shows us that bureaucracy is big—but only as big as we want it to be. If we want less bureaucracy, we can choose to make fewer demands on government. For the most part, bureaucracies do their jobs remarkably well. In contrast to the popular stereotype, most public agencies tackle difficult jobs that are unlikely to be done better by any other alternative. Perhaps the most astonishing thing about bureaucracy is how much we take it for granted. Public schools, safe drinking water, working utility grids, and roads are simply there. We rarely contemplate what astounding administrative and logistical feats are required to make these aspects of everyday life appear so mundane.

Indeed, perhaps the one thing that makes us pay attention to the upside of bureaucracy is when that bureaucracy is not there. There are fewer bureaucrats on state and local government payrolls today than there were a decade ago. Some may think that is a good thing in the abstract—who could argue against having fewer expensive government bureaucrats to support with our tax dollars? In reality, though, what this means is fewer police, fewer teachers, fewer librarians, and big difficulties in maintaining pre-recession levels of public goods and services. The high cost of those services has prompted an ongoing debate about what government should do, and it may result in a shift of more of what was traditionally considered public administration toward the private sector.

Bureaucratic reform movements should be viewed, at least in some ways, with skepticism. Criticizing the bureaucracy is a traditional sport in American politics, and a lot of reforms turn out to be little more than fads that quickly fade when the pleasing rhetoric meets the real-life challenge of delivering the goods. Some reforms are almost certainly overdue for state civil service systems that have evolved away from ensuring neutral competence and toward favoring seniority and similar preferences. How to do that without making public employees vulnerable to retribution or discrimination, though, remains a tricky and controversial proposition. Regardless of how such reforms play out, however, one thing will almost certainly remain constant: whatever the government is and whatever it does, it will rely on bureaucracy to get it done.

THE LATEST RESEARCH

As discussed above, among the political tensions surrounding bureaucracy are the sometimes conflicting social goals of neutral competence and ensuring that bureaucracies reflect the diverse nature of the citizens they serve. Neutral competence, as embedded in merit systems, has been a bedrock of state and local civil service systems for a century or more. The basic idea is that you should get a job in a public agency because you are the most qualified, not because you advance or reflect some political interest. While that sounds great in the abstract, there are persuasive arguments that traditionally underrepresented minorities are systematically disadvantaged by traditional personnel systems. Affirmative action programs can help address those imbalances, but they are controversial because many suspect they move bureaucracy away from a focus on neutral competence and toward the fulfillment of broader political goals. Scholars grappling with the difficult questions raised by these issues have long been attracted to the notion of representative bureaucracy (also discussed above), which suggests that agencies that reflect the clients they serve also objectively do a better job of running public programs and policies. Research on the pros and cons of representative bureaucracy is growing rapidly, and the studies

(Continued)

(Continued)

reviewed below provide an introduction to the current state of the field.

- **Gooden, Susan T.**, "*PAR's* Social Equity Footprint," *Public Administration Review* 75, no. 3 (2015): 372–381.

The *Public Administration Review* (*PAR*) is the flagship journal of the field of public administration. It is where scholars and practitioners (that is, bureaucrats) exchange research and insights on a broad range of bureaucracy-related topics, everything from effective implementation to personnel and budgets. This study examines how much attention the journal, and by implication the entire field, pays to social equity. Just how focused are scholars and bureaucrats on social equity in the bureaucracy? Gooden finds mixed results. There is little doubt that the *PAR* has provided a valuable platform for addressing and improving understanding of gender and racial inequities in bureaucracy at all levels of government. Yet women and racial minorities are far from the only groups who may be treated inequitably by or within public agencies (see the discussion on New Haven firefighters above). This article examines seven decades of *PAR* publications and finds that nearly 70 percent of the articles addressing social equity issues focus on gender and race/ethnicity. The pages of the *PAR* reflect much less concern about social inequity as it relates to sexual orientation (less than 1 percent of all social equity articles since the 1940s), disability (less than 4 percent), and age (less than 3 percent). Gooden argues that it is critically important for scholars and bureaucrats to recognize that the programs and policies managed by public bureaucracies must reflect a basic social fairness if they are to be trusted and successful. That also means expanding the traditional notion of what social fairness encompasses.

- **Riccucci, Norma, Gregg Van Ryzin, and Huafang Li**, "Representative Bureaucracy and the Willingness to Coproduce: An Experimental Study," *Public Administration Review* 76, no. 1 (2016): 121–130.

One of the central ideas behind representative bureaucracy is the notion that if citizens can relate to bureaucrats, they are more likely to cooperate with the goals of that agency. So, for example, if you interact with a police officer, a teacher, a librarian, or even a representative of the state's cosmetology board, you are more likely to positively respond to whatever policy aim he or she is pursuing if you share key sociodemographic traits with him or her. This research study puts this hypothesis to the test. To do this, these researchers conducted an experiment looking at willingness to engage in recycling efforts, a social behavior local governments are trying to encourage for a range of environmental and financial reasons. They conducted a survey where respondents were asked to listen to an announcement about a recycling program and then asked about their willingness to do things like separate out plastic and compostable items from their garbage for recycling. The announcement contained the names of four public officials heading up the recycling program. Some people were randomly assigned a version of the announcement where all those listed had stereotypically male names, others heard four stereotypically female names, and the rest had a mix of male and female names. What the researchers found is that people generally, but especially females, were more likely to indicate a willingness to recycle when they got the announcement where all the public officials were women. The researchers argue this provides evidence supporting a key element of the representative bureaucracy theory.

- **Nicholson-Crotty, Sean, Jason A. Grissom, Jill Nicholson-Crotty, and Christopher Redding**, "Disentangling the Causal Mechanisms of Representative Bureaucracy: Evidence from Assignment of Students to Gifted Programs," *Journal of Public Administration Research and Theory* 26, no. 4 (2016): 745–757, doi:10.1093/jopart/muw024.

Research into the theory of representative bureaucracy has mostly focused on organizations rather than on individuals. In contrast, this study uses the individual as the unit of analysis, and its findings show why the individual-level focus may be important. The primary purpose in this research is to examine whether black students are more likely to be tracked into gifted programs if they have black teachers and/or if they are in a school with a higher proportion of black teachers irrespective of whether their own classroom teachers are black. The results show that having a black teacher increases the probability that a black student will be classified as gifted, but having more black teachers in the school generally does not. This suggests that it is the diversity of the street-level bureaucrats that people interact with, not necessarily the proportional representation of minorities on a bureaucracy's staff, that makes the difference in representing and advancing minority interests.

CHAPTER 10

Want a better grade?

Get the tools you need to sharpen your study skills. SAGE edge offers a robust online environment featuring an impressive array of free tools and resources.

Access practice quizzes, eFlashcards, video, and multimedia at **edge.sagepub.com/ smithgreenblatt7e**

Top Ten Takeaways

1. Public bureaucracies, though among the least loved branches of government, generally do a much better job than they get credit for.

2. A bureaucracy can be defined as a type of organization that has five particular characteristics: division of labor, hierarchy, formal rules, record keeping, and professionalism.

3. Government bureaucracy consists of all the public agencies—the vast majority of them having the classic characteristics of bureaucratic organizations—that manage and implement public programs and policies.

4. Bureaucracies do not just implement and manage public programs; they also influence and even make public policy. Examples run from the traffic cop who sets the speed limit to agency heads who lobby legislatures.

5. Formally, bureaucracies make policy through a process of rulemaking. Rules specify the actions an agency will (or will not) take in order to translate laws into action. Effectively, they have the power of law.

6. Staffing sizes, per capita costs, and activities of public bureaucracies range widely from state to state. As measures of efficiency do not always agree, it is hard to say which, if any, states have "too much" bureaucracy.

7. At a minimum, the private businesses to which some public programs and services have been contracted out have not consistently done a better job than public agencies.

8. The staffing of bureaucracies has evolved from a system of patronage to merit systems that seek to institutionalize neutral competence.

9. Merit systems face political pressure on a number of fronts, ranging from unions that favor seniority over merit as a basis for career advancement to affirmative action programs that seek to advance diversity in addition to merit.

10. Public bureaucracies have been under intense political pressure over the past decade. State governments have cut jobs, sought to rein in the power of public-sector labor unions, and put downward pressure on wages.

Key Concepts

affirmative action (p. 300)
bureaucracy (p. 286)
bureaucrats (p. 286)
collective bargaining (p. 297)
contracting out (p. 292)
merit system (p. 295)
neutral competence (p. 295)

patronage (p. 294)
policy implementation
    (p. 287)
professionalization (p. 294)
representative bureaucracy
    (p. 301)
rulemaking (p. 288)

seniority (p. 297)
spoils system (p. 294)
street-level bureaucrat
    (p. 287)

Suggested Websites

- **www.aspanet.org.** Website of the American Society for Public Administration, the largest professional association for those who work for or study public agencies.

- **www.governing.com.** Web version of *Governing* magazine, which is dedicated to covering state and local issues; includes numerous stories and other resources on agency leaders and performance, e-government, and more.

- **www.pewtrusts.org/en/topics/ us-state-policy.** State and consumer initiatives section of the website of the Pew Charitable Trusts, home to a number of analyses of government effectiveness and efficiency, including the Government Performance Project.

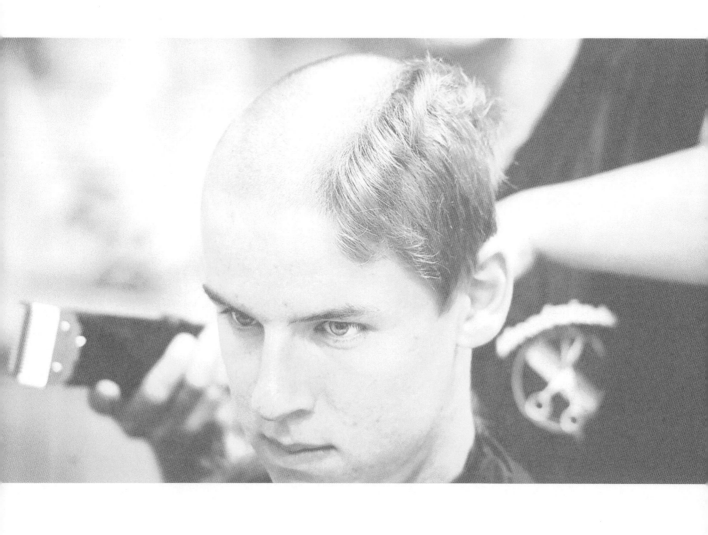

11

iStock.com/DnHolm

Local Government
Function Follows Form

The ancient Greeks pledged allegiance to their cities, not to any nation-state. There are still plenty of people who make formal commitments to serve local government, including police officers and firefighters.

Chapter Objectives

After reading this chapter, you will be able to

- Identify the three main types of local government and how they are different,

- Describe the three basic forms of county government,

- Explain the four basic governance systems used by municipalities,

- Summarize Dillon's Rule and how it shapes the relationship between state and local governments, and

- Discuss how politics and political participation are different at the local level compared with the state and federal levels of government.

Section 25.082 of the Texas Education Code requires all students in public schools to recite the Pledge of Allegiance at least once a day. They've got lots of company. Every school day, millions of students repeat the same oath of commitment and loyalty to the United States of America. Similar promises of fealty to a political community can be found throughout history, though the community in question does not have to be a nation. Wind back a couple of thousand years, and one well-known group was regularly pledging allegiance to a city rather than a country.

The Athenian Oath, recited by the citizens of ancient Athens, is still cited as a model code for civic duty and responsibility. Citizens who took this oath pledged: "We will never bring disgrace on this our City by an act of dishonesty or cowardice. . . . We will revere and obey the City's laws, and will do our best to incite a like reverence and respect in those above us who are prone to annul them or set them at naught."[1] Clearly, the ancient Greeks were seriously committed to the political jurisdiction of their city.

In contrast, Americans rarely center their patriotic attachments at the municipal level. As the Pledge of Allegiance demonstrates, such loyalties are directed toward the nation, or perhaps the state. Americans tend to think of themselves as, well, Americans. They might also think of themselves as Texans, Hoosiers, or Huskers. In other words, their sense of identity with a political jurisdiction is firmly tied to the nation or to their state, but only rarely to a locality. Even New Yorkers and Angelenos bursting with municipal pride rarely focus their political interests—let alone their political identity—at the city level. Which is kind of odd. Why? Well, think about it.

How do you feel about the U.S. government? If you're like most Americans, you are not happy with it. Less than a fifth of Americans trust the federal government to do the right thing.[2] What about state government? Much better. About 60 percent of Americans say they trust state government. It's local government, though, that Americans really seem to believe and have confidence in. More than 70 percent say they trust local government.[3]

What accounts for these big differences in confidence and trust? Why do Americans put so much stock in local government, which, at least technically speaking, is relatively powerless compared to other levels of government? Clearly, part of the answer to these questions is the perceived poor performance of the federal government in dealing with important issues. Some of that negative image is now shared by state governments, which like their federal counterpart have become increasingly polarized and partisan. Maybe more important is the general notion that local governments do a good job and are less profligate spenders of the taxpayers' money. In bang-for-buck assessments, local governments are seen as doing more with less in comparison with state and federal governments, which suggests that Americans, as a general rule, prefer, value, and trust government down at the grassroots level.[4] Given those attitudes, it is somewhat paradoxical that local government is, technically speaking, the weakest level of government. The federal government and state governments are sovereign powers, equal partners in the federal system that draw their powers from their citizens. Pull a state out of the federal system and view it independently, however, and what you find is not a federal system but a unitary system. (See Figure 11-1.) Hierarchically speaking, as discussed in

FIGURE 11-1 ● **Substate "Unitary" System**

At the state level, state government grants power to local governments.

some depth in this chapter, states are superior to local governments. Local governments are not sovereign; they can exercise only the powers granted to them from the central authority of the states.

An individual state, however, is a strange sort of unitary system. Whereas a state government is clearly the seat of power, below the state are an astonishing number and variety of political jurisdictions, many of them piled on top of one another and related to one another in no clear organizational fashion. Many of them operate independent of one another even when they occupy the same geographical space and provide services to the same citizens. For example, a city and a school district may overlap entirely but have different governance structures, different leaders, and different purposes. One of these governments is not the boss of the other; the city cannot tell the school district what its tax rate should be any more than the school district can tell the city to build another library.

It is down here in the crazy quilt of local governments that much of the grunt work of the political system takes place. Local governments provide law enforcement, roads, health services, parks, libraries, and schools; they are mostly responsible for regulating (or even providing) utilities, such as sewer and water; they run airports, public transportation systems, mosquito control programs, and community recreation centers. The list goes on—and on. Collectively, these are the public services we encounter most in our daily lives, generally take for granted, and almost certainly could not get along without. No wonder citizens tend to think that local governments give them good value for their money (well, at least compared with what they get from state and federal governments). They may not pledge allegiance to any of these governments, and the sight of the city seal or the water district's logo may not trigger the same

sense of pride that a state flag does, but people depend on these governments for critical programs and services, and for the most part these governments deliver.

Local governments, however, go well beyond just providing services. They must make political and philosophical decisions that affect their residents' quality of life and reinforce community values. In short, local governments are worth getting to know. This chapter examines the powers, responsibilities, and specific forms of local government; how and why these forms evolved; how they differ by state and region; and how the political process works within the astonishing number and variety of substate governments. As you read through this chapter, keep in mind the following questions:

● **Why do local governments vary so much within and between states?**

● **How and why have local governments changed over the years?**

● **What are the positive and negative aspects of Dillon's Rule?**

● **Should state governments be able to override policies put in place by local governments?**

The Many Faces of Local Government

The importance of local governments to the American political system is evident, on one level, from their sheer numbers. According to the U.S. Census Bureau, at last count roughly 90,000 local governments were operating in the United States. (See Table 11-1.) That works out to about one local government for every 3,630 people.[5]

TABLE 11-1 ● **Numbers of Government Units, Ranked by State and Type**

State	All Government	Counties	Municipalities	Towns or Townships	School Districts	All Special Districts
Alabama	1,208	67	461	—	132	680
Alaska	177	14	148	—	—	15
Arizona	674	15	91	—	242	568
Arkansas	1,556	75	502	—	239	979
California	4,425	57	482	—	1,025	3,886
Colorado	2,905	62	271	—	180	2,572
Connecticut	643	—	30	149	17	464
Delaware	339	3	57	—	19	279
Florida	1,650	66	410	—	95	1,174
Georgia	1,378	153	535	—	180	690
Hawaii	21	3	1	—	—	17
Idaho	1,168	44	200	—	118	924
Illinois	6,963	102	1,298	1,431	905	4,132
Indiana	2,709	91	569	1,006	291	1,043
Iowa	1,947	99	947	—	366	901
Kansas	3,826	103	626	1,268	306	1,829
Kentucky	1,338	118	418	—	174	802
Louisiana	529	60	304	—	69	165
Maine	840	16	22	466	99	336
Maryland	347	23	157	—	—	167
Massachusetts	857	5	53	298	84	501
Michigan	2,875	83	533	1,240	576	1,019
Minnesota	3,672	87	853	1,784	338	948
Mississippi	983	82	298	—	164	603
Missouri	3,768	114	954	312	534	2,388
Montana	1,265	54	129	—	319	1,082
Nebraska	2,581	93	530	417	272	1,541
Nevada	191	16	19	—	17	156
New Hampshire	541	10	13	221	166	297

(Continued)

TABLE 11-1 ● (Continued)

State	All Government	Counties	Municipalities	Towns or Townships	School Districts	All Special Districts
New Jersey	1,344	21	324	242	523	757
New Mexico	863	33	103	—	96	727
New York	3,453	57	614	929	679	1,853
North Carolina	973	100	553	—	—	320
North Dakota	2,685	53	357	1,313	183	962
Ohio	3,842	88	937	1,308	668	1,509
Oklahoma	1,852	77	590	—	550	1,185
Oregon	1,542	36	241	—	230	1,265
Pennsylvania	4,897	66	1,015	1,546	514	2,270
Rhode Island	133	—	8	31	4	94
South Carolina	678	46	270	—	83	362
South Dakota	1,983	66	311	907	152	699
Tennessee	916	92	345	—	14	479
Texas	5,147	254	1,214	—	1,079	3,679
Utah	622	29	245	—	41	348
Vermont	738	14	43	237	291	444
Virginia	518	95	229	—	133	194
Washington	1,900	39	281	—	295	1,580
West Virginia	659	55	232	—	55	372
Wisconsin	3,128	72	596	1,255	440	1,205
Wyoming	805	23	99	—	55	683

Source: U.S. Census Bureau, "2012 Census of Governments," https://www.census.gov/programs-surveys/cog.html.

The forms these local governments take, the responsibilities and powers they exercise, and the numbers of particular kinds of governments that exist in given geographical or demographic areas vary wildly from state to state. The number of local governments within a state's boundaries, for example, depends on the state's history, culture, and administrative approach to service delivery. New England states have a tradition of active civic participation and social spending that accommodates a large number of local governing units. By contrast, states in the South have much less of a tradition of civic engagement in local government, and even today a relatively small number of powerful county leaders dominate such services as school governance.

In terms of differences, local governments make state governments look as though they were all stamped from the same cookie cutter. Take the average of 3,630 people for each local government. That number can be misleading because local governments are not evenly spread out demographically. Hawaii has relatively few local governments. Think of a munici-pality such as a city as a type of cor-poration, specifically an organization incorporated under state law to pro-vide government services to a com-munity. Think of a county as just a geographic subdivision of state gov-ernment. By those definitions, Hawaii has no incorporated **municipalities**, just 4 **counties**, and the consolidated city–county government of Honolulu. Georgia, on the other hand, has 153 counties, and all of them are vested with municipal-like powers. The same types of local governments can serve wildly different sorts and sizes of populations. The city of New York, for example, has a resident population of roughly 8.6 million. The village of Monowi, Nebraska, has a population of 1. No, that's not a typo. Monowi is, at least as of the last census, the small-est incorporated municipality in the United States. Monowi's only resident is Elsie Eiler, who serves as the town's mayor, librarian, and local bartender. If you want to know what a town with only one resident looks like, just type "Monowi" into YouTube's search engine—you'll find a number of short documentaries on the place.

Local governments are not evenly spread out geo-graphically, either. They range from villages covering less than a square mile to counties that cover nearly 125,000 square miles. Within or adjacent to their bor-ders may be mountains, deserts, beaches, urban centers, or vast stretches of nothingness. These differences help explain why some local governments are interested in maintaining subways and others worry about maintain-ing clean beaches.

Political and cultural traditions also vary at the local level. For instance, the degree of loyalty that citizens display toward a local governing entity often depends on whether they personally identify with the area or whether they ignore their membership and regard the area as an artificial construct. Put another way, a Manhattanite probably feels more community pride than, say, a user of the Buncombe County, North Carolina, Metropolitan Sewerage District.

Despite all these differences, however, there are only three general forms of local government in the United

Tim Mosenfelder/WireImage

▲
Strong attachments to localities are not unusual. New Orleans has faced its fair share of troubles since the dawn of the century, dealing with everything from a devastating hurricane to political unrest. Its distinct culture, however, gives all of its residents a strong sense of identity. Part of that is reflected by and anchored in the city's music scene.

States: counties, munici-palities, and special districts. Counties tra-ditionally are viewed as geographical and administrative subdivi-sions of states. The exact definition of a munici-pality varies from state to state, but municipali-ties generally are political units that are distinguished geographically from coun-ties by being more compact and distinguished legally by being independent cor-porations rather than "branch offices" of the state government. Special districts cover a huge range of local governments. Typically, special dis-tricts are single-purpose governments. Unlike counties

ILLINOIS has 6,963 local governments, the most of any state. **HAWAII** has 21 local governments, the fewest of any state.

....

Municipalities Political jurisdictions, such as cities, villages, or towns, incorporated under state law to provide governance to defined geographi-cal areas; more compact and more densely populated than counties.

Counties Geographical subdivisions of state government.

and cities, which are general-purpose governments, special districts usually are created to provide specific public services rather than a range of services. School districts are a good example. These are geographically defined local units of government created to provide educational services. Other special districts include water management and sewage treatment districts.

The Organization and Responsibilities of Local Governments

Even within each of the three basic categories of local government, there is considerable variation in organizational structure, autonomy, and responsibilities. These categories are distinct enough, however, to wrangle those roughly 90,000 local governments in the United States into a general understanding of what local governments are and why they take on the forms they do.

Between the County Lines

To learn what county government is all about, you might find it instructive to take a trip to your local county courthouse. There you are likely to find signs pointing you toward a variety of self-explanatory government offices: district attorney, coroner, sheriff, treasurer, and the like. You also may find signs for offices whose purposes are not quite so self-evident. President Harry Truman once walked into the courthouse in Allegheny, Pennsylvania, and was taken aback by one of the signs he saw. "What the hell is a prothonotary?" he famously asked. Well, a prothonotary, Mr. President, is the chief record keeper of a civil court. Truman's bewilderment over this obscure county office encapsulates some of the confusion over what county government is and what it does. People might be asked to vote on a prothonotary come election time, but chances are very few of them know what the heck a prothonotary is or why the position is necessary.[6]

In your particular courthouse, the prothonotary might travel under a less mysterious title, such as clerk of the civil court. Regardless, however, the office of prothonotary illustrates what county government is often about: the unglamorous, but undoubtedly necessary, administration of state government functions. Civil courts and criminal courts for the most part function under the framework of state rather than county authority. Yet at the county courthouse, the court's record keeper,

prosecutor, and judge are typically county-level elective offices. It is the county government that represents the local face of the state government.

The unglamorous utilitarian governing unit known as the county grew out of a 1,000-year-old tradition brought over from England, where it was known as the shire. (Many English county names still carry this suffix; one of the authors of this book was born in the county of Oxfordshire.) In the United States, counties "are nothing more than certain portions of the territory into which the state is divided for the more convenient exercise of the powers of government," wrote U.S. Supreme Court chief justice Roger B. Taney in *Maryland ex. rel. Washington County v. Baltimore & Ohio Railroad Co.* (1845).[7] Centralizing day-to-day governance for an entire state in the state capital was, and largely still is, simply impractical. Thus, states divided themselves into smaller geographical units—counties—and created a governance structure within each to provide a local "branch office" of the state government.

Called parishes in Louisiana and boroughs in Alaska, more than 3,000 counties are drawn on the maps of the remaining 48 states. How many county governments reside within a state varies wildly. Rhode Island and Connecticut are the only states that have no county governments (they actually have counties; they just don't have county governments—as geographically compact states, they have no need for such administrative subunits of state government). Some states have just a handful. Delaware, for example, has only 3 counties. Supporting the claim that everything is bigger in Texas, that state has 254 counties—the most in the nation.

Geographically speaking, counties are typically the largest local governments, although, like their numbers, their sizes can vary enormously. Arlington County, Virginia, covers 42 square miles, which is on the smallish side. North Slope Borough, Alaska, encompasses 142,224 (mostly uninhabited) square miles. Measured by population, counties range from more than 10 million people in Los Angeles County, California, to fewer than 90 people in Kalawao County, Hawaii. (See Tables 11-2 and 11-3.)

Because among substate governments counties generally cover the largest amounts of geographical territory, they bear much of the burden of providing services widely, if not lavishly. The majority of the million citizens in California's Sacramento County, for example, live in unincorporated territory. This means that their property is not part of any city, town, or township that can provide municipal services. Hence, the burden falls

TABLE 11-2 ● Twenty-Five Largest U.S. Counties by Population, 2016

Rank	County, State	Population (estimate)
1	Los Angeles County, California	10,137,915
2	Cook County, Illinois	5,203,499
3	Harris County, Texas	4,589,928
4	Maricopa County, Arizona	4,242,997
5	San Diego County, California	3,317,749
6	Orange County, California	3,172,532
7	Miami-Dade County, Florida	2,712,945
8	Kings County, New York	2,629,150
9	Dallas County, Texas	2,574,984
10	Riverside County, California	2,387,741
11	Queens County, New York	2,333,054
12	Clark County, Nevada	2,155,664
13	King County, Washington	2,149,970
14	San Bernardino County, California	2,140,096
15	Tarrant County, Texas	2,016,872
16	Bexar County, Texas	1,928,680
17	Santa Clara County, California	1,919,402
18	Broward County, Florida	1,909,632
19	Wayne County, Michigan	1,749,366
20	Alameda County, California	1,647,704
21	New York County, New York	1,643,734
22	Middlesex County, Massachusetts	1,589,774
23	Philadelphia County, Pennsylvania	1,567,872
24	Sacramento County, California	1,514,460
25	Suffolk County, New York	1,492,583

Source: U.S. Census Bureau, "Annual Estimates of the Resident Population: April 1, 2010 to July 1, 2016," https://factfinder.census.gov/faces/tableservices/jsf/pages/productview.xhtml?src=bkmk.

TABLE 11-3 ● Twenty-Five Smallest U.S. Counties by Population, 2016

Rank	County, State	Population
1	Kalawao County, Hawaii	88
2	Loving County, Texas	113
3	King County, Texas	289
4	Kenedy County, Texas	404
5	Arthur County, Nebraska	469
6	Blaine County, Nebraska	484
7	Petroleum County, Montana	489
8	McPherson County, Nebraska	493
9	Loup County, Nebraska	591
10	Yakutat City and Borough, Alaska	601
11	Borden County, Texas	633
12	Grant County, Nebraska	641
13	Harding County, New Mexico	665
14	Treasure County, Montana	692
15	San Juan County, Colorado	694
16	Hooker County, Nebraska	708
17	Thomas County, Nebraska	716
18	Mineral County, Colorado	732
19	Slope County, North Dakota	763
20	Kent County, Texas	769
21	Logan County, Nebraska	772
22	Wheeler County, Nebraska	776
23	Hinsdale County, Colorado	788
24	Esmeralda County, Nevada	790
25	Keya Paha County, Nebraska	791

Source: U.S. Census Bureau, "Annual Estimates of the Resident Population: April 1, 2010 to July 1, 2016," *Population Estimates 2016*, https://factfinder.census.gov/faces/tableservices/jsf/pages/productview.xhtml?src=bkmk.

on the county to provide these residents with such services as law enforcement, parks and recreation, and stormwater management.

The autonomy and authority of county governments also vary considerably from state to state. There are some regional patterns to such differences. For example, in the Northeast, local government traditionally is centered in towns and villages. These are the units of government that attract the most participation, make the most high-profile decisions, and are the focus of the most attention. County governments in this region are historically viewed as just the local offices of state government, representing a form of government and governance more remote than the village board.

In the South, counties are also technically creatures of state government in that they were formed and granted their authority by state legislatures, yet county governments in other regions are much more likely to be a central focus of local government than are counties in the South. County government tends to be the form of local government that wields the most political power and policy influence, and thus it tends to be the focus of local political elites. The reason for these differences has to do primarily with the more urban nature of the Northeast compared with the historically more rural South. Rural areas by definition lack substantial urban centers, which means they lack large and powerful city or village governments. County governments thus occupy the center of local government, and the county seat—the place where county government is physically located—becomes the locus of local politics.

Counties are distinct from municipalities (which are discussed in depth later), although the distinctions have become blurred. County governments are historically rural governments that help conduct state government business. The quintessential county government is a keeper of public records (such as property deeds, birth and death certificates, and mortgages) and an administrator of property taxes, local road maintenance, election results certification, criminal courts, and jails run by county sheriffs. The typical U.S. municipality, on the other hand, performs such day-to-day functions as police and fire protection, sewage disposal, sanitation, and the maintenance of public parks and other infrastructure facilities, including stadiums, airports, and convention centers.

In the messy real world, however, such clear distinctions often disappear. Many modern county governments—particularly urban ones—have their official fingers in these classic city functions as well. In many regions, there is substantial overlap between county and city functions, and county and city governments operate cheek by jowl. For example, in Lincoln, Nebraska, city hall and the Lancaster County government offices share the same building.

As a general rule, however, counties tend to be kept on a tighter leash by state governments than are municipalities (especially large urban cities). In New Hampshire, state legislators still approve county budgets. In Texas,

state government mandates that each county appoint a county judge-at-large and four commissioners, regardless of whether the county's population numbers in the hundreds or the millions. Loving County, Texas, for example, had barely 100 full-time residents in 2016, but still had not only four county commissioners but also a sheriff, a county clerk, a tax assessor, an auditor, and a constable. It was in theory and practice a full-service subunit of state government—all for a population that could squeeze into a Starbucks in Los Angeles.

County governments, like all other subnational governments, have independent sources of revenue. The primary funding source controlled by county governments is the property tax, which historically accounts for about 30 percent of county government income. As with everything else about local government, however, there is considerable variation in where county governments get their money and what they spend it on. In 2018, real estate taxes accounted for about 65 percent of Fairfax County, Virginia's $4.1 billion in revenues, and personal property taxes accounted for another 15 percent. In Orange County, California, in contrast, only about 15 percent of revenue came from sales and property taxes combined; the county's biggest source of income was intergovernmental transfers—that is, money from the state and federal governments.[8]

Just as there are huge variations among counties in terms of revenue, there are similar variations in spending priorities. Where county governments focus their spending depends on geography, politics, and relations with neighboring jurisdictions. A significant chunk of the roughly half a trillion dollars that county governments spend every year is invested in basic social services, including public welfare, hospitals, and other health care programs. Counties also own and maintain more than 40 percent of the nation's roads and bridges, operate airports, maintain water and sewage plants, and run more than 3,000 sheriffs' and police departments.[9]

The Structure of County Government

There are three basic forms of county government: commission, council–executive, and commission–administrator. What differentiates the three forms is the degree of separation between legislative and executive powers and who is responsible for the day-to-day administration of the executive side of government.

The most common form is the **county commission system**, which concentrates legislative and

County commission system A form of county governance in which executive, legislative, and administrative powers are vested in elected commissioners.

executive functions and powers into an elected board of commissioners. For example, the commission exercises legislative powers by passing county ordinances and approving the budget. Further, it wields executive powers, as it is responsible for a broad range of hiring and firing decisions and exercises considerable control over many administrative offices.

Depending on the state and the county, members of these county-level legislatures may be called county commissioners, supervisors, selectmen, county board members, or judges. In Louisiana, these locally elected legislators are called parish jurors. In New Jersey, the county legislatures are called boards of chosen freeholders. Whatever their official titles, commissioners are typically members of small groups elected to serve staggered two- or four-year terms.

The most significant reform of county government since its inception has been the separation of executive and legislative powers through the creation of an independent county-level executive office. A county government using a **council–executive system** typically has an independently elected officer who serves as the county-level equivalent of a governor. County executives frequently have the power to veto ordinances passed by the board of commissioners and the authority to appoint key department heads. Thus, the main difference between the commission and council–executive forms of county government is the approach to separation of powers. (See Figure 11-2.)

The **commission–administrator system** of county government stands somewhere between the commission and council–executive forms. In this form of government, an elected commission retains most legislative and executive powers but appoints a professional administrator to actually run the government. County administrators usually serve at the pleasure of the commissioners—that is, they can be hired and fired as the county commissioners see fit. In practice, commissioners typically delegate considerable powers to administrators, including the powers to hire and fire department heads and to prepare a budget for the commission's approval.

Commission–administrator and, to an even greater extent, council–executive structures have been popular reforms to the traditional commission form of county government. Diffuse and ineffective decision making and outright corruption were the primary reasons for the shift away from commissions in the 20th century. Reformers were concerned that under the commission approach, power was so diffuse that county governments tended to drift in the absence of clear leadership; also, commissioners too often appointed their friends to important positions. As a result, an increasing number of counties, as many as 15 percent, now are run by elected county executives who exert firm leadership on policy and hiring. This reduces the role of the commissioners to something closer to an advisory level. Another 12 percent of counties are led by appointed administrators. State policymakers have contributed to this trend—Arkansas, Kentucky, and Tennessee now mandate that their counties be headed by elected executives.

Although such reforms have reduced entrenched corruption, even in the modern era there are examples of county governments going very badly astray. In such cases, states can step in and take over county government, or even put them out of business altogether. Though such cases are very rare, they do happen. For example, in 1997, the Massachusetts House of Representatives voted to abolish the government of Middlesex County, which it believed had become a corrupt, debt-ridden, and expensive administrative burden. The state retained a handful of county-based positions (e.g., the sheriff, district attorney, and register of deeds) as independently elected offices, but it simply absorbed much of the rest of the county government. Still today, the most populous county in the state of Massachusetts (roughly 1.6 million residents) does not have a county government.

Most counties, however, continue to have representative forms of government that include elected heads of a broad range of administrative and executive offices. These typically include a district attorney, a sheriff, a treasurer, a clerk of records, and, yes, sometimes even a prothonotary.

Municipalities

A municipality is a political jurisdiction formed by an association of citizens to provide self-governance within a clearly defined geographical area. Municipalities

....

Council–executive system A form of county governance in which legislative powers are vested in a county commission and executive powers are vested in an independently elected executive.

Commission–administrator system A form of county governance in which executive and legislative powers reside with an elected commission, which hires a professional executive to manage the day-to-day operations of government.

FIGURE 11-2 ● How It Works

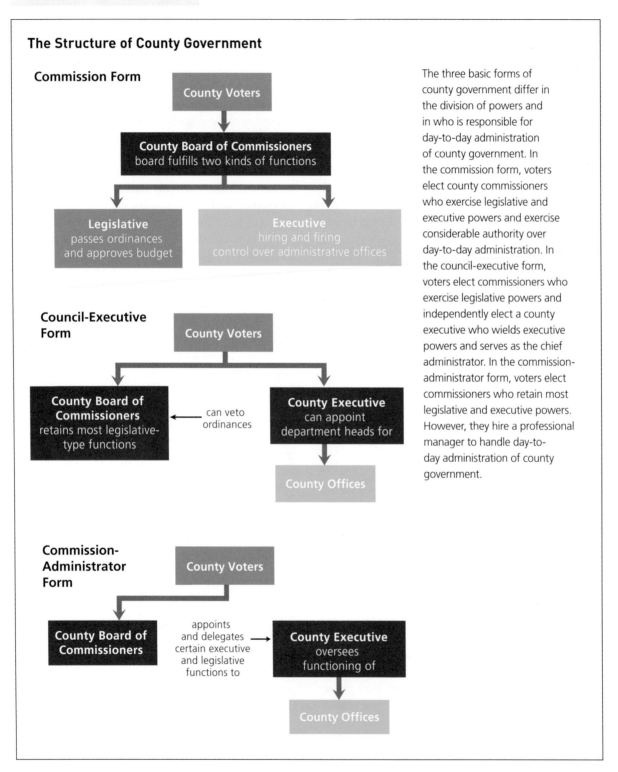

The Structure of County Government

The three basic forms of county government differ in the division of powers and in who is responsible for day-to-day administration of county government. In the commission form, voters elect county commissioners who exercise legislative and executive powers and exercise considerable authority over day-to-day administration. In the council-executive form, voters elect commissioners who exercise legislative powers and independently elect a county executive who wields executive powers and serves as the chief administrator. In the commission-administrator form, voters elect commissioners who retain most legislative and executive powers. However, they hire a professional manager to handle day-to-day administration of county government.

encompass two basic forms of government: townships and cities. **Cities** are corporations. In other words, they are legal entities incorporated under state law for the purpose of self-government at the local level. This is a central difference between counties and cities. Counties were created by the state from the top down; states mandated these political jurisdictions and delegated to them certain powers and functions. Cities are bottom-up creations. A local community seeks the authority of self-governance by incorporating itself as a legal entity with certain powers and responsibilities under state law. Such corporate municipal governments also may be called villages, towns, or boroughs (although, somewhat confusingly, in some states the terms *town* and *borough* can also refer to nonincorporated governments).

Townships (or towns) constitute an interesting category of local government that all but defies general description. In some states, townships are little more than geographical subdivisions of counties vested with little in the way of responsibility or power. In others, townships are vested with a considerable range of responsibilities and essentially function as mini–county governments. They typically are run by boards of commissioners or township supervisors—a county commission form of government in miniature. These more active townships typically are responsible for such functions as snowplowing rural roads.

In still other states, townships exercise as much power as cities do, if not more. This is particularly true in the New England states, where the township is the traditional form of local governance. These kinds of townships function as municipalities. Like cities, they are bottom-up institutions, political entities formed by groups of local citizens for the purpose of self-governance. Many are incorporated, like cities, and some of them have been working units of government longer than the United States has been in existence. The Maine town of Dover-Foxcroft, for example, was incorporated in 1769, seven years before the Declaration of Independence was approved.[10] Townships, in other words, can be viewed as being like counties, like cities, or like large geographical spaces with little in the way of governance structure within them. Which of these descriptions is accurate depends on state law and the traditions of local governance.

What distinguishes cities and city-like townships from counties and county-like townships is that they are formed by associations of citizens rather than brought to life as designated subunits of states. Municipalities are general-purpose governments that provide a range of public services and address a variety of political issues at the local level. They are brought into existence because groups of citizens, usually those concentrated in compact urban areas, want to exercise a degree of political self-determination over their community. Accordingly, they incorporate, bringing to life a legal entity—a municipality—that grants them the right to a broad degree of self-governance.

Governance arrangements vary even more at the municipal level than at the county level. In municipalities, there is variation in the powers of the executive, or **mayor**, and the legislature, typically a **city council**. A strong role often is played by an appointed administrator, or **city manager**, who is given the day-to-day responsibility for running municipal operations. Municipal governance systems can be divided into four basic types: the mayor–council system, the city manager system, the commission system, and the town meeting system.

Mayor–Council Systems

One of the most common forms of municipal governance is the **mayor–council system**. It is distinguished by a separation of executive and legislative powers. According to the National League of Cities, more than half of U.S. cities use this system.[11] Executive power is vested in a separately elected mayor, although the powers a mayor is actually allowed to exercise vary considerably.

· ·

Cities Incorporated political jurisdictions formed to provide self-governance to particular localities.

Townships Local governments whose powers, governance structure, and legal status vary considerably from state to state. In some states, townships function as general-purpose municipalities; in others, they are geographical subdivisions of counties with few responsibilities and little power.

Mayor The elected chief executive of a municipality.

City council A municipality's legislature.

City manager An official appointed to be the chief administrator of a municipality.

Mayor–council system A form of municipal governance in which there is an elected executive and an elected legislature.

Mayor–council systems can be broken down into **strong mayor** and **weak mayor systems**. (See Figures 11-3 and 11-4.) In discussions of city governance, these terms have less to do with a politician's personality than with the powers that a given mayor enjoys when stacked up against the powers of the city council and the bureaucracy. Under the strong mayor system, the executive is roughly the municipal-level equivalent of a governor. Strong mayors exercise a great deal of power, and typically they have the authority to make appointments to key city offices, to veto council decisions, to prepare budgets, and to run the day-to-day operations of municipal government in general. The mayor of New York City, for example, has the power to hire and fire the heads of more than 40 city agencies, including the police commissioner and the school chancellor; appoints judges to the Criminal Court of the City of New York; and is responsible for proposing the city's budget, which in 2018 topped $88 billion.

A weak mayor system retains the elected executive, but this is more of a ceremonial than a real policymaking office. In a weak mayor system, the council wields both executive and legislative power. Executives in weak mayor systems still can exercise considerable influence, but they have to do this by using their powers of persuasion rather than the authority vested in their office. In many cities where mayors have limited powers, individuals with strong personalities are nevertheless able to exert huge influence. They do this by fostering cooperative relationships with their powerful city managers. Examples are Pete Wilson, the mayor of San Diego in the 1970s, and Henry Cisneros, the mayor of San Antonio in the 1980s.

Strong mayor system A municipal government in which the mayor has the power to perform the executive functions of government.

Weak mayor system A municipal government in which the mayor lacks true executive powers, such as the ability to veto council decisions or appoint department heads.

FIGURE 11-3 ● Strong Mayor–Council Form of Government

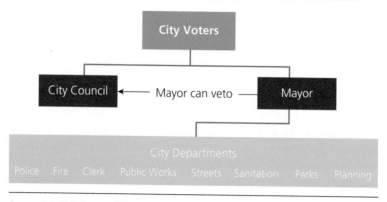

Source: John P. Pelissero, "The Political Environment of Cities in the Twenty-First Century," in *Cities, Politics, and Policy: A Comparative Analysis*, ed. John P. Pelissero (Washington, DC: CQ Press, 2003), 15.

FIGURE 11-4 ● Weak Mayor–Council Form of Government

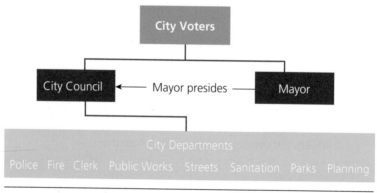

Source: John P. Pelissero, "The Political Environment of Cities in the Twenty-First Century," in *Cities, Politics, and Policy: A Comparative Analysis*, ed. John P. Pelissero (Washington, DC: CQ Press, 2003), 15.

In both strong and weak mayor systems, the council serves as the municipal-level legislature and can wield extensive policymaking power. No major policy or program can get far in a city without massaging from the city council. Councils average 6 members, but in many large jurisdictions, 12 to 14 members are elected. Los Angeles, for example, has 15. Chicago has a whopping 50 council members, and New York City has 51. The number of people a city council member represents also varies wildly. A city of 60,000 with a 6-member council means a local legislator is representing roughly 10,000 constituents. In contrast, a member of the Los Angeles City Council represents more than 265,000. Regardless of how many of them serve on the council or how many constituents they represent, these individuals exert a major influence over a city's livability. They steer policies on such vital issues as zoning and urban renewal, as well as the provision of a wide range of public services—everything from law enforcement and fire protection to libraries and parks.

> **Like legislatures at the state and federal levels, however, councils are subject to conflict, gridlock, and disagreement with the executive branch. While some councils are exemplars of good democratic governance, others are notorious for their levels of self-interest and corruption.**

Like legislatures at the state and federal levels, however, councils are subject to conflict, gridlock, and disagreement with the executive branch. While some councils are exemplars of good democratic governance, others are notorious for their levels of self-interest and corruption. Illinois politics has long had a reputation for high levels of corruption—four of the last eight Illinois governors ended up serving prison terms for various forms of malfeasance—and the Chicago City Council has played its part in that reputation. The council consists of 50 aldermen, each elected from a neighborhood **ward**. Between the late 1970s and 2013, more than 30 Chicago aldermen were convicted of or pled guilty to bribery, extortion, or similar crimes.[12] In 2013, roughly half of Chicago's aldermen were accused of taking illegal campaign contributions.[13] Pledges for cleaner government followed, though they didn't last long. In 2016, Alderman Willie B. Cochran—a former Chicago police officer—was hit with a 15-count federal indictment, charged with stealing charitable contributions meant for his own impoverished constituents.[14] While few other councils can rival that level of questionable activity, council members in many cities report that they are frustrated with the more typical legislative issues of gridlock and conflict, which are exacerbated by interest group pressures and media coverage.[15] In some cases, all it takes is just one or two individuals to hold up their hands or raise objections in council chambers, and entire city operations can grind to a halt.

Council–Manager Systems

Rather than separating executive and legislative functions, the **council–manager system** is based on the principle of separating the political and administrative functions of government. In such a system, a council makes policy decisions but places the implementation of those decisions in the hands of a professional administrator, usually called a city manager, hired by the council. (See Figure 11-5.)

In 2015, Alan Baker served as mayor of Nenana, **ALASKA**, for just 17 days. He took office on October 12 and submitted his resignation letter on October 29, saying that the city's government was a mess.

The origins of this system are in the Progressive reform movement that swept through government at all levels beginning at the end of the 19th century. As discussed elsewhere in the context of state-level party politics, a century ago political machines ran the typical large city in the United States. Places such as Boston, Chicago, and New York were governed by charismatic politicians who took advantage of their ties to ethnic minorities, such as the Irish or the Italians. Patronage jobs were given out to their personal friends, whose chief qualification was that they were campaign supporters. Elections were fraught with partisanship, which produced high incumbent reelection rates. Many machine insiders got themselves elected as city commissioners and were given authority to run individual departments, including police, fire, and sanitation services. This resulted in politically powerful, but often corrupt and incompetent, municipal governments.

During the first half of the 20th century, reform groups began pressuring city governments to become more professionalized and less politicized. The National Municipal League (now the National League of Cities), which focused on small to medium-size cities, was one such group. The U.S. Conference of Mayors, whose members head larger cities, and the International City/County Management Association (ICMA) were

....

Ward A division of a municipality, usually representing an electoral district of the city council.

Council–manager system A form of municipal governance in which the day-to-day administration of government is carried out by a professional administrator.

FIGURE 11-5 ● Council–Manager Form of Government

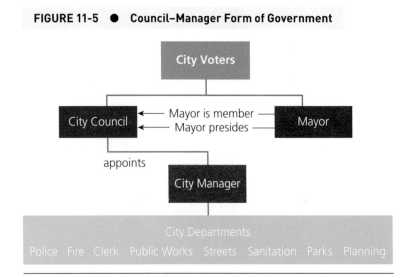

Source: John P. Pelissero, "The Political Environment of Cities in the Twenty-First Century," in *Cities, Politics, and Policy: A Comparative Analysis*, ed. John P. Pelissero (Washington, DC: CQ Press, 2003), 16.

two others. In the belief that the top vote-getters in a given city may not be the best managers, the National Municipal League drafted a model charter that laid out the powers of mayors, city councils, and administrators.

In 1913, Dayton, Ohio, became the first major U.S. city to create a position for a strong manager, largely in response to suburbanization (the establishment of residential communities on the outskirts of the city) and the rise of an educated middle class. The idea was that a government run by a professional city manager would be less prone to corruption and partisan favoritism than one led by the classic big-city mayor. Such managers are generally more interested in implementing organizational systems than they are in glad-handing voters and trolling for campaign cash.

This reform movement by no means eliminated the urban political machines or the power wielded by strong executives. For example, Richard J. Daley, mayor of Chicago from 1955 to 1976, continued to run the city with unequaled influence, even though Chicago had a supposedly independent city council. He swayed his city council members, the national Democratic Party, and the Chicago-area delegation to the U.S. Congress. Even today there are a handful of mayors with political influence that extends far beyond municipal borders. For example, Rahm Emanuel, Daley's modern-day successor, continues the tradition of high-profile, powerful, and often controversial Chicago mayors. Prior to being

elected mayor in 2011 (and reelected in 2015), Emanuel was President Barack Obama's chief of staff, and before that he was a member of the House of Representatives and chair of the Democratic Caucus in that chamber. While Emanuel does not have Daley's political machine, his political résumé and national-level political network, and the clout that these imply, make him a formidable mayor.

Worries about mayors or city councils wielding political power for their own interests rather than the public interest were at least part of the motivation behind the notion of a city manager. This is an individual who is appointed, not elected, and who, at least in theory, can counter the powers of commissioners or city council members with nonpartisan technical administrative expertise. In some cities, this manager is paired with a mayor. In such cases, the mayor acts as more of a ceremonial figurehead and seldom blocks anything that the manager or the council members want. Supported by a legislative body that is elected by popular vote and meets about every two weeks to deal with policy issues, the manager is empowered to hire and fire all city employees, set pay scales, prepare an annual budget that is approved by elected officials and implemented by staff, and make policy recommendations.

Today, the council–manager system of city government is used by roughly half of municipalities with populations of more than 2,500. It is most popular in medium-size cities, primarily in the South and the West. The reason council–manager systems tend to be concentrated in cities of medium size is that smaller cities cannot afford to pay a full-time manager's salary and big cities tend to want a more partisan mayor. However, there are exceptions to this rule. Large cities that use a council–manager system include Dallas, Texas, and San Diego and San Jose, California.[16]

And the trend toward professionalization continues. ICMA estimates that a majority of city managers have advanced degrees. A recent study of city managers in North Carolina found them to be a highly educated and fairly mobile group. Most do not work their way up the administrative ranks from within a city, but rather are appointed from the outside. Success on the job seems to be dependent on training, experience, and the ability to make sound administrative decisions, in addition to the ability to maintain good relationships with city council members.[17]

Commission Systems

Similar to its county-level counterpart, the **city commission system** concentrates executive and legislative powers into a single elected body. This body makes key policy decisions in the same way a legislature does. Yet each commissioner is also the head of an executive department. Commissioners run for office not as representatives in a legislative body but as the heads of particular city departments: commissioner for public safety, commissioner for public works, and so on. Most commission systems also have a mayor. The position usually is held by a commissioner chosen to preside over commission meetings; it is not an independent executive office but more of a ceremonial position.

As a form of municipal (as opposed to county) governance, the commission system originated in Galveston, Texas, in the early 1900s. Galveston had suffered a devastating hurricane that killed thousands and left the city in ruins. The existing city government proved ineffective in dealing with the aftermath of this disaster. In response, the Texas legislature approved a completely new form of municipal government—the commission system—to try to deal with the huge task of rebuilding the city. It proved successful; Galveston was rebuilt and put back on the civic track.

This success led other municipalities to follow Galveston's lead and adopt the commission form of governance. The commission system's success has been limited, however, and only a relative handful of cities currently operate under it. This type of system has two main drawbacks. First, the merging of elected and administrative positions leads to commissioners becoming the entrenched advocates of their departments. Second, winning an election and administering a large bureaucracy are very different skills. Good politicians, in other words, do not always make good department heads.

Less than 1 percent of municipalities use the commission form of government.[18] The drawbacks of commission governments are much the same as the drawbacks of commission systems at the county level—executive authority is so diffuse it tends to produce a government with no real direction. Because commissioners serve as the heads of their own departments, with no real central authority above their positions, commission systems

at the municipal level function as legislatures consisting of elected executives. This can make coordinating departments difficult and providing a strong sense of direction for the government overall even harder.

Town Meetings

The **town meeting form of government** is largely unique to the United States and is mostly found in towns in New England states (in New England, towns are basically municipalities, although they may also have some of the functions traditionally associated with county government in other states). Although not a particularly widespread form of local governance, it is probably the oldest, and it is certainly the most democratic. Its origins are rooted in the religious communities that made up early colonial settlements in New England. A high premium was put on consensus in these communities, and the town meeting evolved as a means to reach such widespread agreement. Town meetings allowed citizens to have a direct role in deciding which laws they would pass and who would be responsible for implementing and enforcing those laws. In many cases, the politics were worked out before the actual meetings took place, with neighbors talking to neighbors across their fences and in taverns. The grassroots agreements hashed out in these informal discussions then were expressed as community consensus in the town meeting.[19]

What all this boils down to is that the legislative functions are concentrated in the citizens themselves. A town meeting is convened through a warrant, or an announcement of the date, time, and place of the meeting and the items to be discussed. It is open to all community citizens, and all have an equal vote in matters of town policy. Such legislative power often is exercised directly; for example, budgets are approved by town meetings. Some authority, however, may be delegated to a representative board, whose members are called selectmen. The board of selectmen exercises whatever authority is granted to it and is responsible for seeing that policies enacted in the town meeting are carried out.

Towns also have incorporated some elements of the council–manager system by voting to hire professional managers to handle the administrative side of government.

City commission system A form of municipal governance in which executive, legislative, and administrative powers are vested in elected city commissioners.

Town meeting form of government A form of governance in which legislative powers are held by the local citizens.

▲

The town meeting form of government is largely unique to the United States and even in the United States is mostly confined to the Northeast. In this form of local governance, legislative powers are vested in citizens, who exercise those powers during town meetings of local residents. Here, residents in Burke Hollow, Vermont, are meeting to discuss local issues.

The manager system seems to work well with this type of government; for example, roughly 30 percent of the towns in Maine—most of them small communities with fewer than 2,500 residents—have managers but hold town meetings as well.[20]

Pelham, MASSACHUSETTS, has the oldest town hall in continuous use for town meetings, built in 1743.

The town meeting is probably the most idealized form of government that has ever existed in the United States. Thomas Jefferson, for example, saw this grassroots democratic approach to self-governance as "the wisest invention ever devised by man."[21] Alexis de Tocqueville, the 19th-century French aristocrat who wrote one of the most celebrated analyses of the American political system, referred to towns as the "fertile germ" of democracy.[22] For even modestly large communities, however, this approach simply isn't practical. A gathering of citizens that runs

into the thousands would be too unwieldy, and the likelihood of getting broad agreement from such a large group on any number of policy issues is pretty low. Such considerations go a long way toward explaining why this approach is largely confined to smaller communities in New England.

Special Districts

Special districts, for the most part, are fundamentally different from the other forms of local government already discussed. Counties and municipalities are general-purpose governments that provide a broad range of public services within their given jurisdictions. Special districts, on the other hand, are mostly single-purpose governments. They are created to provide specific services that are not being provided by a general-purpose government.

With few exceptions, special districts exist outside the consciousness of the average citizen. More than 50,000 special districts have been created across the country—and often across borders of other units of government—to administer single programs or services. Still, most people know very little about these governments. The single biggest exception to this general rule of special district anonymity is the school district; there are roughly 14,000 independent school districts in the United States. Public schools are often one of the best-known and most widely used local public institutions. Few might know a lot about a school district's politics, but a lot of people will know teachers, students, and administrators; how the school sports teams are doing; and which schools have good or poor reputations for academic performance. That level of knowledge and intimacy drops off quickly for other types of special districts. Among the most numerous forms of special districts are sewer and water system districts, which account for about one-third of special districts nationwide. Few people know much at all about these sorts of districts—many may be completely unaware of their existence.

Other types of special districts administer firefighting and housing services, public transportation, soil conservation, mosquito control, and even libraries.

....

Special districts Local governmental units created for a single purpose, such as water distribution.

Commuters may not know it, but hundreds of thousands of them use some pretty well-known special districts every day. The Port Authority of New York and New Jersey, Boston's Massachusetts Bay Transportation Authority, and the Washington Metropolitan Area Transportation Authority of the District of Columbia collectively cover hundreds of square miles and cross dozens of government borders.

Why use special districts to provide single programs or services? Why not just have the county or municipality add those services to its governing portfolio? Well, in certain situations, single-purpose governments can seem like attractive solutions to political and practical problems. For example, special districts sometimes are implemented as a way of heading off threats of political annexation of one local government by another. They also are used as tools for community and business improvement. Freed of local tax authority, administrators of special districts often can get infrastructure items built and services provided without dipping into any one locality's funds. For example, farmers in special water districts, particularly in the West, are eligible for discounted federal loans to help them with irrigation. In addition, special districts can use private-sector business techniques in management, such as paying market rates instead of government rates to contractors.

While there are clear advantages to special districts, their comparative lack of visibility often leads to low levels of accountability. This is potentially a problem, as special districts frequently have taxing authority, and while that adds to the tax burden of citizens—mostly in higher property taxes—these governments are rarely targeted by voters upset about tax levies. It doesn't help that many special districts are not particularly transparent— their budgets can be hard to find online, and most of them do not bother publishing annual reports. The difficulty in finding information on what are already low-visibility governments make it difficult for the average voter to have even a vague notion of whether special districts are doing a responsible job for taxpayers (see the box "Local Focus: What Are Special Districts Doing with Your Taxes?").

Working within Limits: The Powers and Constraints of Local Government

Local governments, regardless of their particular form, differ from state and federal governments in a fundamentally

important way—they are not sovereign. This means that local governments draw their power not from the citizens they serve but from the government immediately above them—the state government (this is why states considered in isolation are referred to as unitary governments in the introduction to this chapter).

This is not to say that local governments are powerless. Far from it. Local governments are charged with the primary responsibility for delivering a broad range of public services (such as education, law enforcement, roads, and utilities), and they have broad authority to levy taxes and pass regulations and ordinances (an ordinance is a law passed by a nonsovereign government). Local governments can also exercise the power of eminent domain. Yet, despite all their responsibilities and powers (not to mention their sheer numbers), not all forms of local governments are, at least technically, equal partners in government. They are subordinate to the state governments that grant their power.

Why is this the case? The short answer is the Tenth Amendment to the U.S. Constitution. Local governments are not mentioned anywhere in the U.S. Constitution, which divides power between the federal and state governments. Despite the long-standing cultural practice of having strong local governments, legally these governments fall under the purview of the Tenth Amendment's guarantee of state sovereignty. This means the power to determine the scope of authority of local governments is among the powers "reserved to the States respectively, or to the people." In other words, states get to say what localities can and cannot do. They set the limits and define the terms.

Dillon's Rule

The legal doctrine that defines the division of power between state and local governments is known as

OKLAHOMA was one of five territories to gain statehood in the 20th century. At one point, American Indians initiated efforts to create a state from land in the Indian and Oklahoma Territories. Today, the state is home to more members of recognized tribes than any other state in the country, and, like other native groups in the United States, many of these tribes have their own government and judicial systems.

LOCAL FOCUS

WHAT ARE SPECIAL DISTRICTS DOING WITH YOUR TAXES?

Ever turn on a faucet? Visit a library? Fly out of an airport? Use a bathroom? If so, chances are you've used services provided by special district governments. Special districts often run water and sewer services, airports, and libraries, not to mention public schools, cemeteries, and programs ranging from flood control to mosquito abatement. While you might use these services, though, it's a good bet you know little about the government entity that actually provides them. It's a rare voter who can name the board of directors of his or her local water district, let alone know any details about that board's taxing and spending decisions.

Special districts spend a lot of taxpayer money—roughly $200 billion annually according to one estimate. In Massachusetts, for example, total expenditures by special districts are roughly equal to a third of the entire state government's budget. All that taxing and spending, though, gets much less scrutiny than state budgets. What exactly are special districts doing with all that money, and are they making wise decisions with it?

The slightly alarming answer is that no one is really sure. In 2017, U.S. PIRG (a public interest research group) published what is almost certainly the first national survey of transparency practices by special districts. What the researchers found is that most special districts fail to meet even basic transparency standards about financial information. Not even half published their budgets online, and less than a third published comprehensive financial reports. Some districts didn't report anything at all, at least not in the sense of making information readily accessible online.

The difference in reporting expectations between special districts and city and county governments, let alone state governments, is stark. Budgets for those governments get a lot of scrutiny from a lot of stakeholders, and they expect—and generally get—easy access to financial information. "We really didn't see the same level of transparency that we'd come to expect from general purpose governments," said Michelle Surka, who coauthored the report. "The difference is really striking."

Other studies of special district financial reporting have come to similar conclusions. For example,

a review of special districts in Kentucky found that 40 percent of them didn't even bother to submit a budget. Obviously, it is hard to hold government accountable at the ballot box if you can't even find out how much money it is spending and what it is spending on.

Ironically, part of the problem here is the higher financial transparency and accountability expectations of general-purpose governments. As state governments and local governments have come under increasing pressure to keep taxes low, they have reduced a swath of public programs and services. However, that does not mean demand for those services were also reduced. As higher levels of government cut programs to save costs, special districts sprang up in response to public demand for those same services. In Colorado, for example, the vast majority of local governments—nearly 90 percent—are now special districts, many of them formed to pick up the slack in public services caused by a constitutional amendment limiting the state government's ability to raise taxes.

While lawmakers and special interest groups pore over easily accessible state government balance sheets and battle over limiting taxes and expenditures, few voters seem to have noticed that as a result government spending is shifting rather than shrinking. It's simply being pushed out to special districts where financial information is often harder to come by.

What can be done to improve financial transparency and accountability in special districts? Stringent accounting and reporting requirements by state governments would certainly help, as would enforcement of such standards where they do exist. The lack of transparency, however, is not simply due to lazy bookkeeping or a desire to keep taxpayers in the dark. Some special districts are run by volunteer boards, and many of them are organizations that lack the qualified staff to keep up-to-date financial information accessible online. The only way they could become more transparent and accountable is to expend more resources—in other words, by spending more of the taxpayers' money to demonstrate they are not wasting the taxpayers' money.

Sources: Mike Maciag, "Most Special Districts Lag in the Transparency Department," *Governing*, April, 2017; Frank Shafroth, "The Secret Tax Explosion," *Governing*, September 2013; Frank Shafroth, "Redefining 'Special Districts' Could Have Big Taxing Consequences," *Governing*, May 2016.

Dillon's Rule, named for Iowa Supreme Court justice John F. Dillon. In addition to having a fine legal mind, Dillon was a highly respected and well-read scholar of local government. An argument he formulated in 1868 has served ever since as the basis for understanding and justifying the power—or, more accurately, the lack of power—of local government. Dillon's Rule is built on the legal principle of *ultra vires*, which means "outside one's powers." In a nutshell, it states that local governments are limited to the powers expressly granted to them by their state and to those powers indispensable to the stated objectives and purposes of each local government.

> " Dillon's Rule is built on the legal principle of *ultra vires*, which means "outside one's powers." In a nutshell, it states that local governments are limited to the powers expressly granted to them by their state and to those powers indispensable to the stated objectives and purposes of each local government.

What Dillon essentially did was build a legal argument that the Tenth Amendment secures power for the states but not for local governments. As Dillon himself put it in his famous 1868 ruling in *City of Clinton v. Cedar Rapids and Missouri Railroad*, local governments are "mere tenants at the will of their respective state legislatures." The rule has structured legal thinking on the power of local governments ever since, although it has always had its critics. It was challenged as early as the 1870s, when Missouri legislators rewrote the state constitution specifically to allow municipalities a degree of independence from the constraints of state government.[23]

For the most part, however, Dillon's Rule holds: state power trumps local government power, which means that state legislatures invariably win when they engage in power struggles with local governments. In Virginia, for example, antitax lawmakers continually prevent localities from restructuring their tax systems to raise revenue. It should come as no surprise that ambitious state legislators hoard power over their county and city counterparts. States have the authority to limit even traditionally exercised local government powers, such as eminent domain, or the right to take private property for public use without the owner's consent.

Yet, although Dillon's Rule says state governments can grant powers to local governments and retract those powers as they see fit, Dillon himself felt that it would be a bad idea for state governments to take full advantage of this legal authority. The bottom line is that the division of labor between local and state governments, broadly speaking, works. It makes sense, Dillon argued, for states to respect local government autonomy because of cultural tradition and sheer practicality. Accordingly, the independence and powers that state governments grant to localities vary considerably. Some state governments are more willing than others to let local governments make their own decisions. Many of these differences can be explained by state culture and degree of citizen participation. Idaho and West Virginia reserve the most local powers to the state; Oregon and Maine give localities the most freedom.[24]

The powers granted to substate political jurisdictions, in other words, reflect the cultural traditions, politics, and practicalities of governance unique to each state. This variation is a difference that can make a difference. For example, it can make a difference in taxes. What local governments can or cannot tax, and by how much, is structured by state law. For example, Virginia allows cities with populations greater than 5,000 to operate independently from the counties of which they are a part. It also gives these communities the right to impose sales taxes on meals, lodging, and cigarettes. On the other hand, counties in Virginia rely heavily on a single revenue source—property taxes—to pay their bills.[25] This can pose a serious dilemma for county leaders. When the housing market is booming, many homeowners watch their property assessments, and hence their annual taxes, rise relentlessly. In many cases, the property taxes rise faster than their incomes. These homeowners, subsequently, take out their annoyance with the tax increases on county leaders come election time.

And taxes are not the only issue. State governments can, and sometimes do, place regulatory limits on local government in areas ranging from taxes to titles, from personnel to pensions. For example, the city of Buffalo, New York, is prevented from controlling the salaries

....

Dillon's Rule The legal principle that says local governments can exercise only the powers granted to them by state government.

and pensions of its uniformed workers because of New York State labor laws. In 2015, the state of Missouri passed a law preventing St. Louis from setting a city-wide minimum-wage law and banning single-use plastic grocery bags. In 2016, the North Carolina legislature met in special session with the specific aim of preventing cities from passing protections for LGBT people. In 2017, Texas passed a law outlawing so-called sanctuary cities within the state (essentially municipalities where local law enforcement agencies do not cooperate with federal immigration officials—see the box "Local Focus: What Is a Sanctuary City?"). These and other examples of state governments stepping in and squelching city-level policy agendas are at least partially attributable to a growing ideological and partisan divide between densely populated cities and state governments. Even though governments in most cities are technically non-partisan, there is little doubt that big urban areas tend to lean liberal and Democratic; in 2018, only 4 of the nation's 25 largest cities had Republican mayors, and two of those (Fort Worth and El Paso) were in the single state of Texas. State governments, on the other hand, have shifted heavily toward conservative Republican control following the 2010 "Red Tide" election. In 2018, 32 states had Republican-controlled legislatures, and 33 had Republican governors. The end result of this trend is a growing divide between the policy preferences of left-leaning cities and the policy preferences of right-leaning legislatures.[26]

This political friction reflects a bottom-up version of the often contentious battles between state governments opposed to what they perceive as federal overreach and the federal government as it tries to implement coherent and uniform national policies and programs. Yet state governments often care less for local government control than the federal government does for state control. There is a certain irony in this; many of the same governors and state legislatures who staunchly resist the imposition of federal policy preferences in the name of local control have little compunction about

forcefully imposing state preferences on cities. The big difference in these battles, of course, is that the states are sovereign, so they have a strong legal weapon to resist the power of the federal government. Local governments do not have that same legal power. Dillon's Rule essentially means that in a clash of policy preferences between local and state governments, the state will inevitably win.

Home Rule

Dillon's Rule establishes a clear legal hierarchy between state and local governments. Local governments are unquestionably subordinate to state governments; yet states, if they so choose, can grant considerable autonomy to local governments. Many states make such grants of autonomy formal by giving local governments **home rule**, or the freedom to make local decisions without interference from state government. Home rule typically is enshrined in a **charter**, which spells out the powers and purposes of the local government. In effect, a charter is the municipal equivalent of a constitution.

The movement for such charters started in the 19th century and peaked in the early 1970s. A charter can be adopted only after voters approve a council-approved or citizen-written petition. Of the 48 states that use a county form of government, 36 allow charters or some form of home rule, according to the National Association of Counties. This can free these communities from both state and county obligations. Even under home rule, however, the state may place some strict limits on local governmental autonomy. And even those who might be thought of as natural advocates of home rule support keeping a measure of state control. For instance, city or county employees may prefer state protections to giving the local mayor or city manager too much authority. Antitax groups often fear that independent cities free of state regulation will raise new taxes.

Home rule can be granted in two basic forms. Legislatures may approve home rule in **general act charters**, which apply to all cities, or in **special act charters**, each of which affects only one community. Either type can be initiated by state legislators, local councils, or citizens' groups. In cases of citizen initiatives, advocates gather the requisite number of signatures on petitions, which are then converted into legislation or language for a ballot referendum that is put before voters. States being states, of course, there are a number of variations on these general rules.

Home rule The right of a locality to self-government, usually granted through a charter.

Charter A document that outlines the powers, organization, and responsibilities of a local government.

General act charters Charters that grant powers, such as home rule, to all municipal governments within a state.

Special act charters Charters that grant powers, such as home rule, to a single municipal government.

For example, in California, state law allows but does not require cities to adopt their own charters. The basic difference between charter cities and so-called general law cities is that the former have more autonomy in conducting municipal affairs. What counts as a "municipal affair" is not comprehensively defined, but it certainly can include more flexibility to do things like regulate local elections, parks, and libraries; set parking regulations; negotiate salaries for municipal employees; and generally have more leeway in how cities tax and spend. While that autonomy certainly sounds attractive, it also has its downsides. In the past decade, several charter cities in California—the list includes San Bernardino, Stockton, and Vallejo—have been forced into bankruptcy. Critics argue it's no coincidence that charter cities are more vulnerable to such shocks—the price of having more autonomy is more freedom to make bad decisions.[27] This may be one reason why only about a quarter of California's cities have voted to adopt charters.

Although voters generally support the notion of local government autonomy and generally oppose the idea of state or federal government making decisions on behalf of local communities, there clearly are benefits to state and federal oversight. What is lost in local control can be offset by the deeper pockets of the larger, sovereign governments. Much of what local leaders wish to accomplish requires infusions of funds from Washington and state capitals. Those intergovernmental sources of revenue are especially critical during hard economic times, when the traditional local government sources of funding, such as property and sales taxes, tend to take a hit. With oversight, at least local governments also get some cold, hard cash. The superior capacity of state governments and the federal government to raise revenues is another limit on the powers of localities.

The important point here is that there are trade-offs that go along with greater local government autonomy. County officials, for example, are responsible for the building and maintenance of extensive road systems, as well as for enforcing traffic and safety laws on those roads. That's an expensive proposition, and counties generally welcome state and federal money to support these critical public services. Yet the Golden Rule—he who has the gold makes the rules—means that those funds inevitably come with strings. The obligations that come with the money, in the form of state or federal mandates, are not nearly as popular as the cash. This sets up a love–hate relationship between local authorities and the state and federal governments above them. In addition, state and federal governments cause frustration by restricting the decision-making freedom of local authorities. Restrictions and conditions, however, are often the price of the intergovernmental grants that underwrite important local government functions.

Participation in Local Government

Local governments are distinguished from state and federal governments not only by their power (or lack thereof) but also by their politics. Comparatively speaking, state and federal politics are dominated by political parties, which contest elections, mobilize voters, and organize government. Things are different down at the local level, where more than two-thirds of governments are nonpartisan. Since the decline of the big-city political machines of the early 20th century, candidates for county boards and city councils run on their personal competence, for the most part, rather than on ideology or past affiliation. Only about a quarter of city councils hold partisan elections, according to ICMA.[28] Yet in some cities, party labels that have been abolished officially continue to play a role unofficially. This has occurred in Chicago, where city government has been officially nonpartisan since the 1930s, but Democrats continue to dominate the heavily African American city.

Council members usually run in **ward or district elections**. The advantage of organizing such elections on the basis of defined geographical areas is that this system assures each neighborhood of having a local on the city council who knows the streets and residents by name. This is especially important for minorities, who may be grouped together by housing patterns. Very large cities, however, have to balance the desire to have districts small enough that council members really know the neighborhood concerns with the practical matter of having a municipal legislature that has a reasonable number of members. In some places, the populations of council districts are themselves the equivalent of midsize cities. Los Angeles, for example, is split into 15 city council districts. Given the city's population of roughly 3.9 million, that means each district has something like a quarter-million constituents.

....

Ward or district elections Elections in which voters in municipal wards vote for candidates to represent them on councils or commissions.

▲
Although their ranks in high office are far below the roughly 50 percent of the population they represent, women hold some of the most important leadership positions in local government. Pictured is Keisha Lance Bottoms, mayor of Atlanta.

Other jurisdictions permit candidates to run in **at-large elections**. This means that they can hail from any part of the jurisdiction. The advantage of having candidates run at-large, and the reason most cities opt for this system, is that it makes room for the largest possible pool of highly qualified and talented people who, presumably, look at the interests of the city as a whole rather than just the parochial interests of their own wards or neighborhoods. Some city charters require a combination of ward representatives and at-large members. But the use of at-large elections can be controversial. In 1991 in Dallas, court-ordered redistricting required a switch from an at-large system to one in which 14 city council members were chosen by districts. The result was that more Hispanics and African Americans won seats.

....

At-large elections Elections in which city or county voters vote for council or commission members from any part of the jurisdiction.

There is perhaps no better example of the unique nature of local politics than the town meetings that define local governance in New England. Usually held twice a year when the elected council or clerk issues a warrant, or agenda, these gatherings epitomize direct democracy in action. Citizens can do everything from passing a budget to opposing a developer's plan for a new golf course. There simply is no equivalent to this comprehensive citizen legislature at the state or federal level, nor, as a practical matter, could there be.

One of the paradoxes of local government is that, although it is the level of government that citizens support the most, it is also the level of government in which they participate the least. The voter turnout in local elections is routinely only half, or even less, of the national turnout average of 55 percent in a presidential election.[29] This reflects a general indifference among many citizens toward the prosaic affairs of local government. That indifference can even extend to local election officials. In 2016, Philadelphia city commissioner Anthony Clark was reelected to chair the board that oversees city elections, a position that paid $138,612 a year. The irony was that Clark had not voted in any election for a four-year span and had been widely criticized for his general inactivity and inattention to the job.[30] Yet voters voted for the nonvoting election commissioner, and he went on overseeing elections that most voters didn't vote in. There's more votes and voters in that last sentence than in some municipal wards. The general absence of popular fervor over local issues does not mean that local offices are not important. Indeed, politics at this level can have implications for state and even national politics. For example, local government offices often serve as proving grounds for up-and-coming politicians who go on to higher office at the state or national level. New immigrants, particularly Asians and Latinos, increasingly are working their way into public office on this level. By the end of the 20th century, one-third of all cities with more than 200,000 residents had elected either a Hispanic or an African American mayor.[31] In 2017, there were almost 6,600 elected Hispanic or Latino officials at all levels of government in the United States. The vast majority of these, roughly 6,200, were holding local offices.[32] The increase in the numbers of black local officials during the final third of the 20th century was similarly dramatic. According to the Washington-based Joint Center for Political and Economic Studies, from 1970 to 2001, the number of black mayors rose from 48 to 454, the number of black city council members rose from

552 to 3,538, and the number of black county commissioners rose from 64 to 820.

Women also have made great gains in local government, although they remain far from matching their proportion as half the total population. According to the Center for American Women and Politics in Washington, D.C., in 2018, 59 cities with populations greater than 100,000 had female mayors. Roughly 1 in 5 of the nation's largest 100 cities had female mayors, including Fort Worth, Texas; Baltimore, Maryland; and Las Vegas, Nevada.[33]

Where partisan affiliations are allowed at the local level, there have been some historically important divisions among voters. For example, Democratic candidates have tended to draw votes from minority groups, Catholics, and the liberal intelligentsia. Republicans have tended to draw votes from WASPs (white Anglo-Saxon Protestants), big business, and law-and-order enthusiasts.

The payoff for winning local office is more likely to come in the form of visibility and personal satisfaction than in cold, hard cash. Mayors, many of whom work part-time, earn an average of less than $10,000 per year. Former New York City mayor Michael Bloomberg shelled out more than $100 million to win a third term in 2009, but he declined to take a salary; he worked for a token $1 per year. Typically, mayors of big cities get considerably more than that. In 2018, Los Angeles mayor Eric Garcetti was at the top end of the scale with an annual salary of $232,000. Most mayors, though, are nowhere near these two extremes. According to payscale.com (a website devoted to compensation analysis), the median salary for a mayor is approximately $56,000, with roughly 25 percent making more than $100,000 and 25 percent making less than $48,000. On the other hand, the job of professional city or county manager tends to be a fairly well-compensated, white-collar position. According to payscale.com, the median annual salary for city managers in 2018 was nearly $87,000.

City council members generally earn less than mayors and managers. Especially in small and medium-size cities, being a member of the city council is more of a public service than a part-time job. And just because the pay is low doesn't mean the workload is light. The weekly average time that council members spend on the job in small, medium, and large cities is 20, 25, and 42 hours, respectively. Less than 10 percent of council members in cities of fewer than 200,000 receive more than $20,000 in annual salary, and many of them receive nothing. The pay is a bit higher for council members in large

cities, with three-quarters of council members in cities with populations over 200,000 receiving at least $20,000 in annual pay.[34] Given the low pay and relatively high workloads, it is not surprising that 66 percent of city council members surveyed by the National League of Cities said they wanted a raise. Many citizens oppose large salaries for their local officials, particularly at the school board level, because they feel that the nominal fees the officials receive are not an hourly wage but, rather, a stipend that honors public spiritedness.

> **Many citizens oppose large salaries for their local officials, particularly at the school board level, because they feel that the nominal fees the officials receive are not an hourly wage but, rather, a stipend that honors public spiritedness.**

Conclusion

Alexis de Tocqueville viewed local governments in the United States as sort of mini-republics. He saw them as civic entities in which citizens were closest to government and in which government reflected accurately what citizens desired. In many ways, that perspective is still valid. Local governments wield actual power, and they are responsible for important programs and services. They come in a bewildering variety of types, many of which reflect state or regional history, culture, and preferences. Taken as a whole, all these differences can seem confusing. Yet in any single place—your hometown or local county—the government and what it does or does not do probably seem perfectly reasonable and natural.

Local government certainly remains the most common form of government in the United States, and it is still the form of government the average citizen is most likely to come into contact with on a day-to-day basis. Counties, municipalities, and special districts build and maintain roads, police those roads, run schools, manage libraries, and provide other programs and services too numerous to list. And they do all this while employing very different approaches to government. Some are run by powerful executives, others are run by more egalitarian councils or commissions, and still others are mostly run by professional managers.

LOCAL FOCUS

WHAT IS A SANCTUARY CITY?

The federal government wanted the politicians running them hauled into court. Texas passed a sweeping law designed to shut them down. So did Tennessee. Mississippi banned them even though it didn't have any. Between 2017 and 2018, roughly 80 bills were floating around state legislatures seeking to outlaw them. They were sanctuary cities.

By one count, more than 200 local jurisdictions around the United States—counties as well as cities—have been labeled as sanctuary cities, and clearly they are up to something that the federal government and a lot of state governments are not happy with. But what is that something, exactly? What is a sanctuary city? While definitions vary, a sanctuary city is typically a political jurisdiction where local law enforcement limits its cooperation with U.S. Immigration and Customs Enforcement (ICE). This typically takes the form of not asking suspects, detainees, or witnesses about their immigration status; not complying with requests from ICE to detain people suspected of being illegal immigrants; and/or refusing to share information about immigration status with ICE.

Some people, especially ICE officials and anti-immigration conservatives, find this beyond frustrating. From their perspective, these local governments are at a minimum turning a blind eye to scofflaws and at worst aiding and abetting fugitives. Entering the United States without permission of an immigration officer, after all, is a federal crime. Shouldn't law enforcement be interested in upholding the law?

Officials in sanctuary cities often have a very different perspective. Illegal immigration might be a federal crime, but it has little to do with state or local laws. Sheriff's deputies and city cops have enough on their plates without asking every speeder to demonstrate legal residency and, if no proof is forthcoming, haul them off to the local jail until ICE shows up. That eats up scarce time and resources needed to deal with the state and local laws they are charged with enforcing, let alone the federal ones they are not.

It's more than that, though. Especially in large urban areas with sizable populations of illegal immigrants, cooperating with ICE can make it harder for local law enforcement officers to actually do the job they have. If the members of that community are reluctant to cooperate with local law enforcement because they fear the risk of deportation, it makes it harder to investigate crimes or, if people are reluctant to report violations, even know when one has been committed.

At least part of the furor over sanctuary cities is thus anchored in a differing set of political and policy priorities that divide cities and counties on the one hand from states and the federal government on the other. At the local level, law enforcement officers need the cooperation of the community to do their job. And elected officials in large, urban areas often have the political support of diverse communities to go the sanctuary city route. Federal and many state governments want illegal immigrants identified and detained for ICE to deal with.

When this federal/state rock meets the municipal hard place, it invariably is going to be local governments that lose. That's because the state holds the whip hand when it comes to the laws localities must abide by and enforce. Most laws aimed at nixing sanctuary cities are, in one form or another, mandates requiring local officials to ask people about their immigration status and share that information with ICE. In other words, states have the power to make immigration matters part of the job of local law enforcement. This is just another example of Dillon's Rule in action.

Sources: Natalie Delgadillo, "Can Politicians Be Jailed for Supporting Immigrant Sanctuary Policies?", *Governing*, January 8, 2018, http://www.governing.com/topics/public-justice-safety/gov-sanctuary-cities-thomas-homan-officials-crime-jailed.html; Mike Ward and Lindsay Ellis, "Texas Governor Signs 'Sanctuary Cites' Ban into Law," *Governing*, May 8, 2017, http://www.governing.com/topics/politics/TNS-Texas-sanctuary-cities-ban.html.

Yet local government is far from ideal. These mini-republics are constrained by Dillon's Rule. They tend to have relatively low voter turnout for elections. The idiosyncrasies of local government structure can mean that someone with no real administrative experience may be elected to run a complicated bureaucracy with a multimillion-dollar budget.

Local governments today face significant challenges. Politically, some local governments, especially large cities, face frustration as their policy agendas are reined in by state governments that do not agree with their policy choices. Local governments increasingly find themselves entangled in policy areas such as immigration, which are beyond their traditional jurisdictions. In short, partisan and ideological polarization that has defined Congress and has seeped into state legislatures and governors' mansions seems to be trickling down to the local level. Yet, despite such challenges, local government will undoubtedly endure.

THE LATEST RESEARCH

Despite their numbers and importance to the day-to-day lives of citizens, local governments are surprisingly understudied by political scientists. Certainly, systematic comparative studies on local governance are few and far between in the discipline's major journals. Part of the reason for this may be the astonishing variety of local governments and their sometimes bewildering numbers of responsibilities. It is hard to say something generalizable about local governments because, unlike state governments, they are not necessarily comparable units. This does not rule out comparative research, however. Similar cities can be compared, similar forms of government can be compared, and similar policy problems can be compared. The research summarized below offers a slice of the issues that can be addressed by employing the comparative method. By comparing different jurisdictions, researchers can investigate a wide array of questions that reflect the multilayered and complex environment of local government. What makes a better mayor? What are urban politics about: policy differences or racial differences? Is the council–manager form of government really more effective? These are the sort of questions that the difference-makes-a-difference comparative approach can help answer at the local level.

- **Ferreira, Fernando, and Joseph Gyourko**, "Does Gender Matter for Political Leadership? The Case of U.S. Mayors," *Journal of Public Economics* 112 (2014): 24–29.

As discussed in the text, while women remain proportionally underrepresented among the elected ranks of local government, their numbers have been growing. Females now hold the top elected office in roughly a fifth of the nation's largest cities. This study examines whether the emergence of powerful female mayors carries with it any substantive policy impacts. It looks at mayoral elections over more than a half-century—from 1950 to 2005—to see whether shifting from a male to a female mayor leads to any changes in things such as expenditure patterns, crime rates, and the size of local government. The authors find pretty much no evidence of a gender effect. Policy-wise, cities led by female mayors look pretty much like the same as cities with male mayors. The big noticeable difference seems more intangible—voters like female mayors, or

at least female mayoral incumbents, more than their male counterparts. Females running for reelection tend to have a five-point incumbency advantage over comparable males. This suggests that even if there are no policy differences, the political skill sets of female mayors give them greater standing with votes.

- **Hajnal, Zoltan, and Jessica Trounstine**, "What Underlies Urban Politics? Race, Class, Ideology, Partisanship, and the Urban Vote," *Urban Affairs Review* 50, no. 1 (2014): 63–99.

One of the questions that fascinates scholars of local governments concerns the character and nature of local politics. What is local politics all about? Is it primarily about local issues and concerns? Is it simply an extension of the ideological and partisan conflicts that characterize state and national politics? Hajnal and Trounstine consider all of these possibilities and more. What they find, however, is that the dominant factor driving local elections is something else: race. Analyzing data from exit polls taken from 63 elections for local offices in five cities, they find that race is a consistent trait dividing vote choice. While other factors—including ideology, partisanship, and class—certainly play a role, race consistently seems to be the key underlying factor driving local politics. At least in the cities these researchers studied, members of racial and ethnic groups—especially African Americans—tend to vote as a bloc, and these racial divisions tend to overshadow any other divisions among voters.

- **McGuire, Michael, and Jered Carr**, "What Have We Learned about the Performance of Council–Manager Government? A Review and Synthesis of the Research," *Public Administration Review* 75 (2015): 673–689.

This article reviews and assesses the research on the council–manager form of municipal government. McGuire and Carr's primary aim in conducting their review was to try to come to some evidence-based conclusions about whether the council–manager form of municipal government outperforms the more traditional mayor–council approach. They conclude that, despite a fairly extensive set of studies, there really is no

(Continued)

(Continued)

clear evidence pointing toward one form of government as better than the other. Indeed, they note that there seems to have been a curious reluctance among scholars to engage in serious heads-up comparisons investigating whether the council–manager approach leads to better-administered local government (as its advocates propose) or whether the mayor–council approach is more representative of citizens' preferences (as its supporters assert). Given the stakes—figuring out which form of local government is the most efficient, representative, and accountable—this gaping hole in local government research is more than a little surprising.

CHAPTER 11

for CQ Press

Want a better grade?

Get the tools you need to sharpen your study skills. SAGE edge offers a robust online environment featuring an impressive array of free tools and resources.

Access practice quizzes, eFlashcards, video, and multimedia at **edge.sagepub.com/ smithgreenblatt7e**

Top Ten Takeaways

1. There are more than 90,000 local governments in the United States, and they have enormously varied responsibilities, organization, and visibility.

2. County governments are multipurpose governments that were essentially created as geographic subdivisions—"branch offices"—of state government. Their responsibilities generally include law enforcement, courts, record keeping, road maintenance, and election oversight.

3. Most county governments have a commissioner form of government, though some have council–executive or commission–administrator systems.

4. Municipalities are multipurpose governments formed by associations of citizens. Cities are corporations, legal entities created under state law to provide governance and public services at the local level.

5. Cities use a variety of governance systems. The most common is the mayor–council system, but many cities use the council–manager system, and a smaller number employ a commission system.

6. Special districts are single-purpose governments. They are created to deliver particular services not provided by general-purpose governments. School districts, created to provide K–12 educational services, are the most common form of special district.

7. Unlike state governments, local governments are not sovereign. Dillon's Rule defines the relationship between state and local governments, stating that local governments can exercise only the powers granted to them by state government.

8. Home rule is a form of legal autonomy that many states grant at least some local governments. Home rule essentially means

that the state gives the local government the freedom to make decisions with minimal state interference.

9. Although local governments provide critically important programs and services, they tend to be low profile. Voter turnout tends to be much lower in local elections than in state or federal elections.

10. As state governments have become increasingly conservative and Republican, and large cities have become more liberal and Democratic, state governments have become more willing to step in and overturn local policies on issues such as the minimum wage, recycling, protections for LGBT people, and cooperation with federal officials on immigration.

Key Concepts

at-large elections (p. 332)
charter (p. 330)
cities (p. 321)
city commission system (p. 325)
city council (p. 321)
city manager (p. 321)
commission–administrator system (p. 319)
council–executive system (p. 319)

council–manager system (p. 323)
counties (p. 315)
county commission system (p. 318)
Dillon's Rule (p. 329)
general act charters (p. 330)
home rule (p. 330)
mayor (p. 321)
mayor–council system (p. 321)

municipalities (p. 315)
special act charters (p. 330)
special districts (p. 326)
strong mayor system (p. 322)
town meeting form of government (p. 325)
townships (p. 321)
ward (p. 323)
ward or district elections (p. 331)
weak mayor system (p. 322)

Suggested Websites

- **www.brookings.edu**. Website of the Brookings Institution, one of the oldest think tanks in Washington, D.C.; pursues independent, nonpartisan research in such areas as metropolitan policy and governance.

- **www.naco.org**. Website of the National Association of Counties, the only national organization that represents county governments in the United States.

- **www.natat.org**. Website of the National Association of Towns and Townships, which seeks to strengthen the effectiveness of town

and township governments by exploring flexible and alternative approaches to federal policies to ensure that smaller communities can meet federal requirements.

- **www.nlc.org**. Website of the National League of Cities, the oldest and largest national organization representing municipal governments in the United States.

- **www.usmayors.org**. Website of the U.S. Conference of Mayors, which is the official nonpartisan organization of the 1,183 U.S. cities with populations of 30,000 or more.

Metropolitics

The Hole Problem of Government

Critics of urban governance argue that there is a hole in local government. Not a hole quite as literal as this one but, rather, the general absence of meaningful regional government. While many issues—such as transportation and highway maintenance—are essentially regional in nature, there is a notable lack of regional political jurisdictions.

Chapter Objectives

After reading this chapter, you will be able to

- Describe the "missing level of government" and the difficulties its absence creates for local governance,

- Identify the key characteristics of sprawl and how they shape urban development patterns,

- Summarize the negative impacts of sprawl and metropolitan growth,

- Discuss current approaches to creating regional governance,

- Contrast the Tiebout model with efforts to reform metropolitan governance by creating regional governments, and

- Describe the big challenges of "rural metropolitics" and how they differ from the big challenges of metropolitics in more urban areas.

Illinois's official state slogan is "Land of Lincoln." Its unofficial slogan might as well be "Land of Lots of Government." It has more of them than any other state by a considerable margin, nearly 7,000 in all. No matter where you live in Illinois, you are, on average, living within at least six local government jurisdictions that can levy taxes on your property: a municipality, a township, a county, two school districts (primary and secondary), plus a community college district.[1] There are plenty of people who live within more than that. An analyst for the Illinois Policy Institute once totaled up the number of local taxing bodies making a claim on his pocketbook and found that it was an astonishing 18. There were the standard three general-purpose governments (Village of Buffalo Grove, Lake County, Vernon Township), school and community college districts, plus a slew of special districts responsible for everything from the local library to maintaining roads and bridges.[2] Most people, though, have never done this exercise. They have no clue how many local jurisdictions they belong to. Even the state government in Illinois seems only dimly aware of what all those jurisdictions are up to. Given the sheer numbers, maybe that's not too surprising. To help out, the Illinois Commission on Intergovernmental Cooperation once printed a list of local governments to help legislators keep track of them. It ran for 123 pages.[3]

If that sounds kind of overwhelming, it is. Nobody keeps systematic track of what all those 7,000 governments are doing. Many of them, including those that occupy the same piece of real estate, often have only a vague notion of what adjacent local governments are doing. If you think that's a recipe for redundancy, hit-and-miss planning, and big problems for accountability and rational cooperation, you're right. It is. Having several layers of general-purpose governments piled on top of each other, and scattered through each a set of independent special districts handling sanitation, parks, libraries, mosquito abatement, museums, street lights, hospitals, schools, and lots of other things, makes rational coordination and policy planning difficult and comprehensive efficiency nearly impossible.

Illinois is far from the only place suffering from this sort of problem. Allegheny County in Pennsylvania, for example, includes 130 municipalities, 40-plus school districts, and more than 100 special districts. In that single county, in other words, there's something like 300 local governments, everything from the city of Pittsburgh to the West Mifflin Sanitary Sewer Municipal Authority. It averages out to one government for every 2.7 square miles in the county.[4] Of course, they don't all come in nice distinct geographic packets; a lot of them are just piled on top of each other. What coordinates all these governments to ensure they are not working at cross-purposes, doing the same thing twice, or doing something that could be handled more effectively and cheaply by one of the other governments? The short answer is, well, pretty much nothing. They all just chug along doing their own thing the way they always have.

For some who study local government, that's a problem. There's a lot of differences down at the local level, and they certainly make a difference. Identically valued houses within blocks of each other may lie in very different local jurisdictions, a difference that can mean not just different tax bills, but differences in the quality of public services, or even what public services are available. On the other hand, there are those who are less worried by all these governments and say, "Vive la différence." Allegheny County, like many big metropolitan areas, can be a pretty terrific place to work, live, attend school, and raise a family. So what if there are a lot of local governments? The positive side to having a lot of different local governments, with their different tax rates and levels of public services, is choice, and lots of it. Choice is a good thing, isn't it?

There's certainly something to that argument, and it's one we'll return to later in this chapter. There's no doubt, though, that the economic and social problems that local governments must address are increasingly regional rather than local in nature. Think traffic, economic development, crime, and the environment. Yet the United States has no tradition, and few examples, of governments designed to address such problems at the regional level. Instead, it has a lot of local governments with limited abilities and limited incentives to cooperate and act regionally. How to fashion coherent responses to regional problems while lacking any true form of regional government is the central challenge of governance in urban areas.

It is not just densely populated urban areas that are struggling with the problem of too many governments and too little coordination. Rural areas are being forced to grapple with regional-level coordination issues because shrinking populations cannot provide the tax base needed to support general-purpose governments in small communities. Thus, local governments in rural areas, like local governments in urban areas, are trying to figure out how to collectively and cooperatively address problems that are not confined to the borders of any single jurisdiction. So, urban or rural, the biggest challenge for everyone is dealing with a world in which the problems are regional but the governments are local. This chapter delves into the often confusing issues involved in how local governments handle—or in many cases fail to handle—problems that are regional rather than purely local in nature. As you read through the chapter, keep in mind the following questions:

- **What is the "hole" in government?**

- **Why do the decisions of one local government affect the decisions of other local governments?**

- **Why do patterns of growth create pressure for new forms of local government?**

The Missing Level of Government

You might not have noticed, but, according to some scholars, there is a hole in the organizational structure of the federal system. The basic organization of the federal government and the powers and responsibilities of state and federal governments are covered by the U.S. Constitution. The organization of the state governments and the powers and responsibilities of state and local governments are covered by individual state constitutions. The hole is at the regional level. There is nothing in the U.S. Constitution and virtually nothing in state constitutions that addresses even the notion of regional government, let alone its organization or powers and responsibilities.

In some ways, this is understandable. The federal arrangement set up by the Constitution is the bedrock of the U.S. political system and is deeply woven into the fabric of society. No one seriously proposes to fundamentally alter this arrangement. Even though local governments stand on less legal authority—remember, they are not sovereign—there is a strong tradition of local government. People tend to be oriented toward their local communities and tend to place more faith in city hall than in the state or national capitol. In contrast, there are no strong legal foundations for regional governments and no strong tradition of regional government either. Regional government is the poor relation of the U.S. political system: little thought of and, outside the community of urban scholars and a handful of officials, not much loved.

Yet the majority of local governments in the United States are, like the hundreds of governments in Allegheny County, embedded in larger metropolitan regions. These regions have similar policy challenges and problems that have common sources and call for common solutions. This absence of some sort of regional umbrella government has been called a "fundamental flaw in America's governance structure." This is due to the fact that "metropolitan regions have become the most important functional units of economic and social life in almost all modern societies."[5] Labor and jobs, for example, rarely are concentrated in a single local political jurisdiction. The bottom line is that localities are intertwined economically and socially but are governed as if such matters can be isolated within the preexisting geographical boundaries of political jurisdictions.

MAP 12-1 ● Pittsburgh Metropolitan Statistical Area (MSA) and Surrounding MSAs

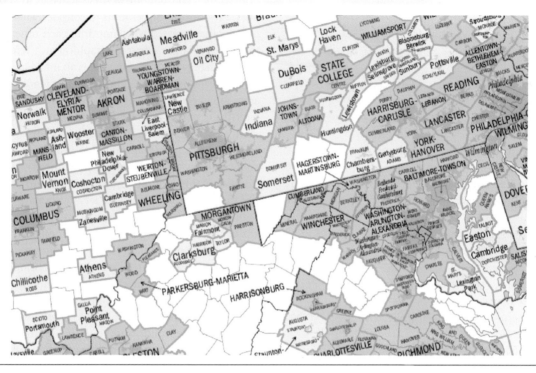

Source: U.S. Census Bureau, Population Division.

The basic problem, then, is that political geography no longer lines up with economic and social geography. The center of economic and social life in the United States is increasingly less a city or a county and more a larger metropolitan area. The U.S. Office of Management and Budget defines a **metropolitan area** as a region with "a large population nucleus, together with adjacent communities having a high degree of social and economic integration with that core." It is important to note that this definition goes on to specify that a metropolitan area comprises "one or more entire counties."[6]

For data-gathering and reporting purposes, the federal government formally defines metropolitan areas using the concept of the **metropolitan statistical area (MSA)**, an area made up of a city of 50,000 or more people, together with adjacent urban communities that have strong ties to the central city. As of 2017, there were 382 MSAs in the United States (and 7 more in Puerto Rico), and roughly 279 million people—about 85 percent of the entire population—lived in such metropolitan areas.[7] These metros are where some of the most important policy challenges of the 21st century are not just concentrated but also irretrievably interconnected.

Consider traffic congestion. According to metro scholar Bruce Katz, roughly 60 percent of all the vehicular miles logged in the United States occur in the top 100 metropolitan areas. This reflects not just the population concentration of those areas or just the challenges of traffic congestion and maintaining transportation infrastructure but also the effects of such concentration on global warming (that much traffic produces a lot of greenhouse gases) as well as on global trade, shipping, and freight.[8]

Local governments in these metros, like it or not, simply cannot confine their problems or their ambitions within their own borders, any more than they can independently control global trade or air pollution. In metros, the cities, their suburbs, and the counties in which they are geographically located all blend together into a dense urban concentration. The vast majority of Americans live, work, and play in such urban areas,

....

Metropolitan area A populous region typically comprising a city and surrounding communities that have a high degree of social and economic integration.

Metropolitan statistical area (MSA) An area with a city of 50,000 or more people, together with adjacent urban communities that have strong ties to the central city.

TABLE 12-1 ● Metropolitan Statistical Areas at a Glance, 2016

10 Largest MSAs by Population	Rank
New York–Newark–Jersey City, NY–NJ–PA, Metro Area	1
New York–Jersey City–White Plains, NY–NJ, Metro Division	2
Los Angeles–Long Beach–Anaheim, CA, Metro Area	3
Los Angeles–Long Beach–Glendale, CA, Metro Division	4
Chicago–Naperville–Elgin, IL–IN–WI, Metro Area	5
Chicago–Naperville–Arlington Heights, IL, Metro Division	6
Dallas–Fort Worth–Arlington, TX, Metro Area	7
Houston–The Woodlands–Sugar Land, TX, Metro Area	8
Washington–Arlington–Alexandria, DC–VA–MD–WV, Metro Area	9
Philadelphia–Camden–Wilmington, PA–NJ–DE–MD, Metro Area	10

10 Smallest MSAs by Population	Rank
Vernon, TX, Micro Area	389
Craig, CO, Micro Area	388
Lamesa, TX, Micro Area	387
Ketchikan, AK, Micro Area	386
Vermillion, SD, Micro Area	385
Zapata, TX, Micro Area	384
Pecos, TX, Micro Area	383
Jayuya, PR, Micro Area	382
Sweetwater, TX, Micro Area	381
Spencer, IA, Micro Area	380

Top 10 MSAs by Percentage Change, 2010–2016	Rank
Farmington, NM, Metro Area	1
Pine Bluff, AR, Metro Area	2
Johnstown, PA, Metro Area	3
Danville, IL, Metro Area	4
Sierra Vista–Douglas, AZ, Metro Area	5
Weirton–Steubenville, WV–OH, Metro Area	6
Flint, MI, Metro Area	7
Charleston, WV, Metro Area	8
Saginaw, MI, Metro Area	9
Decatur, IL, Metro Area	10

Source: U.S. Census Bureau, "Metropolitan and Micropolitan Statistical Areas Totals: 2010–2016," https://www.census.gov/programs-surveys/metro-micro/data/tables.2016.html.

more often than not crossing local government jurisdictions as they go from one of these activities to another. But there are even bigger units to consider. These dense metropolitan areas often bump into each other, forming an even larger urban geographical area referred to as a **megaregion**. A megaregion is an urban area made up of several large cities and their surrounding urban areas—in effect, a string of MSAs. Megaregions represent a relatively new type of urban geography, a merging of metropolitan areas into a massive interlocking economic and social system. Megaregions may spill across multiple counties or even multiple states, but there is typically no overarching institution at this level with anything like the powers of a municipal, let alone a state, government. Instead, within megaregions are dozens and dozens of governments trying to balance local and regional interests, with mixed success. All these different governments share a set of interests because a decision by any one jurisdiction in a megaregion has implications for the other jurisdictions. This interdependence fuels an increasing recognition of the need for local governments to coordinate with one another in policy and decision making on everything from transportation infrastructure to economic development to public housing.

Achieving that sort of coordination is highly problematic because of the relative lack of regional government in the United States. Because these metropolitan areas span not just county but also state and even national borders, exercising any form of centralized planning over their growth and operation is incredibly difficult. For example, in the Northeast, there is a densely populated urban corridor that is anchored in the south by Washington, D.C., then extends to the north to encompass Baltimore, Maryland; Philadelphia, Pennsylvania; New York, New York; and Boston, Massachusetts. Within that massive megaregion, hundreds of local governments across several different states are making thousands of decisions, often with little coordination or thought to their regional effects. Not only does this fragmentation of political authority make it hard to address regional problems, but it is also arguably the cause of some of those problems.

Take, for example, the rise of so-called **edgeless cities**. These are sprawling, unplanned office and retail complexes that are not pedestrian-friendly and often become ghost towns at night. They do have obvious

Megaregion An urban area made up of several large cities and their surrounding urban areas that creates an interlocking economic and social system.

Edgeless cities Office and retail complexes without clear boundaries.

economic attractions—they mean jobs, sales taxes (people who work in them buy stuff, even if it is just gas and incidentals at a convenience store), and property taxes (office complexes are valuable properties). Yet, whatever local benefits they produce, they also export a set of costs to the larger region. Most of the people who work in edgeless cities commute home to greener residential areas. This means that such developments segregate and put considerable geographical distance between where people live and where they work. The end results—traffic congestion and smog—affect all communities in the region, but individually, there is not much any local government can do about such problems.

Sprawl: How Metropolitan Regions Grow

The fragmented nature of governance in metropolitan areas creates an interconnected set of problems that are difficult to address in a systematic and coordinated fashion. To understand the causes and consequences of these problems, as well as the challenges involved in addressing them effectively, it helps to have a little historical background on the roots of metropolitan growth.

Metropolitan areas (and certainly megaregions) are a relatively new concept. As recently as the 1920s, scholars recognized that the growth of suburbs, rapid and easily accessible transportation, and new forms of communication were transforming urban areas into a new social and economic phenomenon. They also recognized that existing forms of local government were ill equipped to deal with this new urban reality, and some even went so far as to call for a new form of metropolitan government to address the gap between state and local political jurisdictions.[9]

It was not until after World War II, however, that the country really saw the explosive growth of metropolitan areas and the broad-scale governance problems that accompanied it. In some ways, this growth was inevitable. A population boom created enormous pressure for new development, and that development typically took place on the peripheries of large cities or urban areas in the form of low-density suburban housing and commercial developments. This created an interrelated set of problems that can be traced to the catchall phenomenon of **sprawl**. Although the term *sprawl* is often used generically to refer to the rapid growth of any metropolitan area, most urban scholars consider it to be a particular type of growth. There is no universal definition of sprawl, but this type of growth does have a set of specific characteristics:

single-use zoning, low-density development, leapfrog development, car-dependent living, and fragmentation of land-use powers.[10] We discuss each in turn below.

Single-Use Zoning

One of the central political powers of local government is control over land use. This power is typically exercised through **zoning laws**, which can allow land to be used for a mix of commercial, recreational, and residential development or for single uses, when land is used for single-purpose developments. Local governments in metropolitan areas have tended to favor the latter approach. The end result has been the geographical separation of the places where people work, live, and play.

Low-Density Development

The growth of metropolitan areas has been defined not only by single-use development but also by **low-density development**. In effect, local governments have exercised their powers over land use to dictate that the growth in metropolitan areas will be out rather than up. Rather than multifamily developments such as high-rise condominiums and apartments, suburbs and other urban municipalities have favored single-family developments. These developments make for lower population densities, but obviously, they also require more land. For example, the population of the Milwaukee, Wisconsin, metropolitan area increased roughly 3 percent between 1970 and 1990, but geographically, the metro area increased by 38 percent. Los Angeles is a classic case of how low-density development can consume vast stretches of land. Population-wise, Los Angeles grew about 45 percent between 1970 and 1990; land-wise, it grew by 300 percent.[11]

Leapfrog Development

In **leapfrog development** practices, developments jump—or leapfrog—over established developments, leaving undeveloped or underdeveloped land between developed areas. This puts a particular strain on infrastructure—not just roads but also water and sewer

---

Sprawl The rapid growth of a metropolitan area, typically as a result of specific types of zoning and development.

Zoning laws Regulations that control how land can be used.

Low-density development Development practices that spread (rather than concentrate) populations across the land.

Leapfrog development Development practices in which new developments jump—or leapfrog—over established developments, leaving undeveloped or underdeveloped land between developed areas.

facilities. When new development bypasses undeveloped land, utilities have to be stretched out farther to serve the newly developed areas.

Leapfrog development is partially driven by the economic incentives of developers. Most established municipalities like to create uniform requirements for developments within their own jurisdictions—for example, by enforcing specific building codes. They may even impose what are sometimes called **impact fees**. Municipalities charge builders of new housing or commercial developments impact fees to help offset the costs of extending services such as parks, schools, law enforcement, and fire protection to these developments. A new housing development, for instance, may require the building of a new fire station, and impact fees can help offset that cost. It is not hard to see, then, why developers often favor building in unincorporated areas, typically on land with geographical separation from municipal borders that is still close enough to make for an easy commute to the urban center. The land in unincorporated areas tends to be cheaper, and there are fewer regulations to deal with.

One of the consequences of urban development patterns is traffic congestion. Because people tend to live in one place and work in another, commuting by car is a daily ritual for millions of Americans.

Impact fees Fees that municipalities charge builders of new housing or commercial developments to help offset the costs of extending services.

Car-dependent living A situation in which owning a car for transportation is a necessity; an outcome of low-density development.

Car-Dependent Living

Developing metropolitan areas through single-use, low-density developments means that citizens have to be highly mobile. Getting from a suburban home to a job in a commercial office development and from home to the kids' soccer game on the weekend pretty much requires an automobile. In low-density housing developments, it is often impossible—or at least impractical—to do something such as "run to the corner store." Getting a six-pack to watch the game or a bag of sugar to bake cookies, even arranging a play date for the kids, requires transportation. Because public transportation systems are, for the most part, not set up for convenient and efficient transportation across large, multijurisdictional geographical areas, having a car becomes a necessity for anyone living in a metropolitan area.

The rise of the automobile-centric society was largely a post–World War II phenomenon. Between 1950 and 1990, the population of the United States increased by about 40 percent, but the number of miles traveled in cars increased 140 percent. The imbalance between population growth and the growth in automobile use is a direct consequence of how land has been developed in metropolitan areas. The rise of **car-dependent living** exacts an environmental toll. Governments have done a reasonably good job of controlling "point" sources of pollution (concentrated sources of pollutants that tend to be limited in number, such as factories and power plants) over the past three decades or so. However, nonpoint sources of pollution are harder to identify and control because they consist of many sources, each putting out a relatively small amount of pollutants but collectively having a large-scale impact on the environment. Cars are a classic example of a nonpoint source of pollution and are a major cause of air-quality problems in metropolitan areas.[12]

Fragmentation of Land-Use Powers

A key characteristic of sprawl is the division of powers among local political jurisdictions, in particular the power over land use. Local governments frequently have strong incentives to use these powers in ways that provide benefits for those within their particular local jurisdictions but create costs for neighboring communities.

The basic characteristics described above have defined the growth and development of many major metropolitan areas in the United States during the past half-century or so. The result has been largely unplanned growth (growth with no systematic coordination to balance local benefits with regional costs) spread out across ever-larger geographical regions, gobbling up previously rural areas and replacing them with low-density, single-use developments.

The Cons of Metropolitan Growth

By now it should be fairly obvious that the characteristic sprawl-like growth of metropolitan areas over the past 50 or 60 years has contributed to, and in some cases is a primary cause of, problems such as traffic congestion and smog. According to many academics who study urban politics and growth, these same development patterns produce a wide range of other problems as well. These problems include the concentration of poverty and crime in certain neighborhoods, segregation by race and class, and inequality in public services, fiscal resources, and political power.

As new low-density housing developments began popping up around core cities after World War II, the middle and upper classes began moving from the cities to the suburbs. There were "push" and "pull" reasons for the migration of the better-off classes to the suburbs. One reason was the lure of the lifestyle—the home with the white picket fence on a leafy suburban lane—that "pulled" people out of the city. Another was the racial desegregation of public schools in the 1960s and 1970s; increasing numbers of less well-off nonwhites began to make up an even greater proportion of urban schools, acting as an incentive for whites to move, "pushing" them out to the suburbs.

The racial—and perhaps racist—undertones of this demographic shift have been noted repeatedly by academics.[13] Because the middle and upper classes were largely white, this demographic phenomenon became known as **white flight**. As whites left the dense, multiuse neighborhoods of cities for the lure of single-family homes on large lots in suburbia, minorities became concentrated in the core urban areas. Because racial minorities also were much more likely to be less socioeconomically well-off than whites, this meant that inner-city neighborhoods became poorer.

As the city neighborhoods became poorer, the remaining middle-class residents felt more pressure to move to the suburbs, and a self-reinforcing trend set in; the poor and ethnic minorities became increasingly concentrated in core city neighborhoods. In the past couple of decades, this trend has started to occur in the suburbs themselves. Minorities who managed to get far enough up the socioeconomic ladder to move to an inner-ring suburb have triggered another round of white flight; as these comparatively less white, less well-off people move into the inner-ring suburbs, the better-off move farther out. The end result is the increasingly racial and socioeconomic homogeneity of particular political jurisdictions.

One result is that certain local jurisdictions are well-off and have property values that support high-quality public services. Middle- and upper-class suburbs, for example, tend to have high-quality public schools. So do **exurbs**, or municipalities in more rural settings that serve as bedroom communities, with residents commuting to jobs in the cities or suburbs during the day and returning to their homes after work. This tends to be in stark contrast to some inner-city neighborhoods and inner-ring suburbs in which poverty is concentrated. Property values are low in such neighborhoods, which means that they cannot support high-quality public services.

It is important to note that the end result is economic *and* racial segregation based on housing patterns. This trend is made apparent by school districts. In some urban areas, for example, African Americans make up less than 3 percent of the total population but constitute 70 percent of the enrollment in school districts.[14] These are invariably schools that serve poor communities, where crime and other social problems place enormous strains not just on public education but also on social and economic opportunities in general. While people can, and do, experience challenge and struggle out in the suburbs, suburban communities are much more likely to have the fiscal capacity to support such public services as good school systems. And because good schools play an important role in determining where the middle class wants to live, again this becomes a self-reinforcing trend.

In other words, here is a difference that makes a big difference to the quality of life of millions of people.

....

White flight A demographic trend in which the middle and upper classes leave central cities for predominantly white suburbs.

Exurbs Municipalities in rural areas that ring suburbs. They typically serve as bedroom communities for the prosperous, providing rural homes with easy access to urban areas.

LOCAL FOCUS

DEALING WITH HIGH-TECH SPRAWL

In 2017, Apple opened its new headquarters in Cupertino, California. It was the most expensive office building in history—it cost about $5 billion to build—and it was also one of the biggest. It had nearly 3 million square feet of office space and a parking lot that could hold 3,000 cars. As you'd expect from one of the premier technology companies on the planet, it looked like something out of the future and came with all the latest gizmos and gadgets. It was nicknamed "the spaceship."

The spaceship is, without a doubt, a building fit to serve a corporate titan of the modern era. Visionary. Cutting-edge. Pioneering. It also is emblematic of the very old-fashioned problem of urban sprawl. Plop a massive corporate campus down in a suburb like Cupertino, and you create a series of predictable knock-on effects that add up to sprawl. Start with the required commute. There's no train station near that campus; employees have to drive. That means every day thousands of cars head into the community on their way to that massive parking lot.

Lots of people, of course, will try to cut down the driving by living closer to work. The problem is that suburbs tend to have zoning laws that discourage high-density housing developments. People go to the 'burbs, after all, for space and the white picket fence, not to replicate the cheek-by-jowl living arrangements of city centers. In other words, there's a limited pool of housing to go around for all those high-tech employees. Obeying the law of supply and demand, housing prices near the corporate campus start heading north.

That's a problem not just for those looking to cut their commute time. For example, people on the lower end of the wage scale working retail and service industries in those communities now have a hard time affording rent, let alone getting on the property ladder. So they move to where the housing is more affordable and commute back to their jobs. More cars on the road. More congestion. More strip malls and gas stations to serve all those commuters. In other words, more sprawl.

It's not just Apple. Other Silicon Valley giants like Google and Facebook have followed the same development patterns that have had similar sprawl-inducing ripple effects. Ironically, all these cutting-edge, high-tech firms are following development patterns that are at least a half-century old. Back in the 1950s and 1960s, there were a lot of open spaces and inexpensive land, and mobility by car was cheap and easy. Yet, even back in the day, that was a recipe for sprawl, and today, spaces are not so wide open, land is expensive, and getting around by car in urban areas can be a nightmare.

What, if anything, can be done to stop this cycle? Well, the San Francisco Bay Area Planning and Urban Research Association (SPUR), thinks a relatively simple solution would be to encourage corporate relocations to focus more on situating themselves closer to transit hubs. Less than a third of Bay Area offices that opened between 2011 and 2015, for example, were close to rail stations. In other words, there was not much choice about commuting by car to those places. In contrast, some companies—General Electric and Red Hat are examples—are moving their headquarters from the suburbs to downtown locations within walking distance of rail stations.

That doesn't completely solve the problem of sprawl, but it sure helps. It encourages people to live in higher-density urban areas where there's less need for a car to work, shop, or just get out and enjoy yourself. And those who do live out in the 'burbs can have an easier commute into work via rail without worrying about putting upward pressure on housing costs in outlying communities.

Sources: Adapted from Daniel C. Vock, "A New Idea to Fight Silicon Valley Sprawl," *Governing*, April 2017.

Place matters because wealth is segregated by communities across metropolitan regions, communities that are themselves concentrated in different political jurisdictions. As one well-known study of metropolitan politics and policy concludes, where you live in a given metropolitan area both affects your quality of life and shapes your social and economic opportunities. Place affects access to jobs, public services, level of personal security (crime tends to be higher in some socioeconomically stressed neighborhoods), availability of medical services, and even the quality of the air we breathe (the people commuting in from the exurbs contribute to urban smog but escape to the cleaner rural air after the workday is done).[15]

> Place matters because wealth is segregated by communities across metropolitan regions, communities that are themselves concentrated in different political jurisdictions. As one well-known study of metropolitan politics and policy concludes, where you live in a given metropolitan area both affects your quality of life and shapes your social and economic opportunities.

Critics of the consequences of sprawl argue that the end result will be metropolitan areas that continue to promote and reinforce economic and racial segregation and create disparities in tax bases that lead to huge differences in the quality of public services among local political jurisdictions. On top of that, from a regional perspective, the patterns of metropolitan growth are economically inefficient (jobs and the labor market are disconnected) and environmentally dangerous (all those cars pump out a lot of toxic emissions).[16] Others, however, wonder if these concerns are exaggerated. Current development patterns are taking account of sprawl, and people are rediscovering the advantages of living in higher-density areas. Traditional development patterns that trigger sprawl, however, continue to be fairly mainstream (see the box "Local Focus: Dealing with High-Tech Sprawl"). But urban revitalization is not necessarily a cure for the inequalities that have long accompanied development patterns. As businesses and wealthier families move into urban neighborhoods, they drive up property values and the general cost of living, which may squeeze out not only some poorer residents but also whole lower-class communities. Ironically, the latter may end up relocating to the suburbs, which are seeing poverty rates skyrocket as the middle class moves back into the cities.[17]

Government Reform in Metropolitan Areas

Racial and economic segregation, inequities in tax bases and public services, and, above all, political

fragmentation that creates difficulty in coordinating rational and effective responses to regional challenges—the problems of governance in metropolitan areas are well known. But what can be done about them?

There is no single answer to this question. One option is complete regional centralization—in other words, sweeping away a patchwork of local governments and replacing them with a single consolidated regional government. Another approach is to keep all the existing governments as they are and simply promote more effective collaboration and cooperation among them. In between are a wide range of possibilities, from creating special districts to handle specific region-wide issues (such as transportation) to creating what amount to regional confederal governments out of local general-purpose governments.[18] Advocates of greater centralization favor the **reform perspective**, which assumes that the key problems and challenges of governance in metropolitan areas are regional in nature and, as such, should be addressed regionally. Proponents also tend to argue that many of the problems have been created by political fragmentation in the first place, in that there are lots of smaller governments making decisions that may produce local benefits but export the costs to other jurisdictions. If the root cause of these problems is political fragmentation, government consolidation is the obvious solution. In other words, new regional governing structures should be created to fill the hole in the federal system; such governments would be better positioned to respond effectively to the interconnected problems of large metropolitan areas.[19] In contrast, advocates of decentralization view having lots of local governments as the regional governance solution rather than the problem. Having many competing local governments can, at least in theory, create a market for public services, and those competitive market forces offer the most effective and efficient way to deal with governance problems.

Clearly, there is no universal response to dealing with the big challenge of regional governance. Instead, there are a number of different strategies that range from creating new pan-regional governments to eliminating long-standing local jurisdictions to keeping all those local jurisdictions and encouraging them to collaborate or compete with each other.

....

Reform perspective An approach to filling gaps in service and reducing redundancies in local governments that calls for regional-level solutions.

Regional Governments

Adherents of the reform perspective are strong advocates of creating regional authorities to address regional problems. This can be done in a couple of ways. First, new government structures can be created to sit above existing political jurisdictions and be given the authority to oversee regional issues such as land-use planning. A couple of well-known examples of such regional planning authorities are frequently cited by advocates as examples of the benefits of taking a top-down approach to land-use regulation. One of these is the metropolitan service district in Portland, Oregon, known simply as Metro. Metro is a true regional government that covers Clackamas, Multnomah, and Washington Counties and the 25 municipalities in the Portland metropolitan area; all told, its jurisdiction extends across about 1.5 million people, or about 40 percent of Oregon residents. It is governed by an elected legislature (a six-member council) and an elected executive (the council president).[20] Metro exercises real regulatory authority in areas such as land-use planning, regional transportation, recycling and garbage disposal, and a host of other policy areas that are regional rather than local in nature.

A number of academic observers have concluded that Metro's top-down approach to regional planning has reaped considerable benefits not seen in metropolitan areas that have no comparable regional governance. For example, white flight has been markedly lower in Portland than in other cities. In contrast to the pattern seen in many other major cities, in Portland, members of the middle class—especially young, highly educated individuals—tend to settle in the central city rather than in the suburbs or nonmetropolitan areas.[21]

One of the notable characteristics of Portland's Metro is the presence of an **urban growth boundary (UGB)**. A UGB controls the density and type of development by establishing a boundary around a given urban area. Land inside the UGB is slated for high-density development; land outside the UGB is slated for lower-density, rural sorts of development. In effect, this type of planning regulation forces cities to grow vertically rather than horizontally and, thus, sets limits on sprawl and the problems it generates.

....

Urban growth boundary (UGB) A border established around an urban area that is intended to control the density and type of development.

Regional council A planning and advisory organization whose members include multiple local governments; often used to administer state and federal programs that target regions.

Critics of UGBs argue that they have a significant downside. By limiting the land available for development, UGBs drive up prices for land in particular and real estate in general. The end results are high property values and limited supplies of affordable housing. Evidence for the negative impact of UGBs is mixed, with studies showing that even when UGBs do restrain development, the impact is pretty negligible.[22] For example, property values in Portland are generally considered reasonable compared with the rest of the West Coast, and reformers have pointed to that success to promote the adoption of similar policies in other urban areas. Three states—Oregon, Tennessee, and Washington—now mandate cities to establish UGBs.

Regional Councils

Metro is a very rare example of a true regional government—the vast majority of metropolitan areas in the United States lack anything with comparable authority and policymaking power. There are, however, a large number of regional planning authorities that provide at least a rudimentary form of coordination among the local governments packed into their metropolitan areas.

Probably the most common method of attempting to rationalize local policymaking across multijurisdictional metropolitan areas involves the formation of regional councils. A **regional council** is "a multiservice entity with state- and locally-defined boundaries that delivers a variety of federal, state, and local programs while carrying out its function as a planning organization, technical assistance provider, and 'visionary' to its member local governments."[23]

Regional councils are made up of member governments, such as municipalities and school districts, although other nonprofit, civic, private, or academic organizations also may be included. They originated in the 1960s and 1970s as vehicles for delivering state and federal programs to regional areas. Since then, they have grown to become an important means of making and coordinating region-wide policy and planning in such areas as land use, transportation, economic development, housing, and social services. Regional councils are a way to recognize that decisions made in one community can trigger domino effects in neighboring communities and that it therefore makes sense to address some problems regionally rather than locally. There are more than 500 such bodies in the United States, and of the roughly 39,000 general-purpose local governments in the country (which include counties, cities, municipalities, villages, boroughs, towns, and townships), about 35,000 are served by regional councils.[24]

A related form of regional authority is the **metropolitan planning organization (MPO)**. MPOs are regional organizations that decide how federal transportation funds are allocated within their regions. MPOs are interesting because they represent a specific recognition by federal law that regions—as opposed to localities—are central functional policy units. The Intermodal Surface Transportation Efficiency Act of 1991 mandated that every metropolitan region had to identify an institution (an MPO) to serve as the central coordinating authority for federal transportation funds in that area. These MPOs have the responsibility of developing transportation plans and programs for their metropolitan regions. Every transportation project involving federal money—which is to say virtually every major transportation project—has to be approved by an MPO. Some MPOs administer billions of dollars in federal transportation grants, and control over such large amounts of money, coupled with the MPOs' authority over critical transportation programs, translates into major political clout.[25] There have been some efforts to coordinate the decision making of MPOs within megaregions, which would extend their influence on transportation infrastructure policy across even wider geographic areas.

Regional councils and MPOs, however, should not be confused or equated with Portland's Metro. They are more vehicles for intergovernmental cooperation than actual forms of government with executive and legislative authority independent of local government interests. Formal organizations of local governments in metropolitan areas have existed in some form or another for decades; regional councils and MPOs are just the more common and better-known examples. Hashing out roles and responsibilities, not to mention making decisions, involves a complicated—and often contentious—give-and-take among the local governments that constitute the membership of these regional bodies.

Intergovernmental institutions such as regional councils are, at best, confederal sorts of regional governments that are creatures of the often conflicting interests of their members. This complicates decision making and makes it harder for these bodies to exert firm regulatory authority over critical areas such as land use. Still, in most parts of the country, they come the closest to filling the hole in the organizational structure of the federal

system. A move in this direction has been the growing support for regional planning efforts that promote **smart growth**, development practices that emphasize more efficient infrastructure and less dependence on automobiles. Smart growth is reflected in regional, or even single-jurisdiction, policies that promote mixed-use developments that are pedestrian- and bicyclist- friendly, emphasize building community rather than just structures of bricks and mortar, and consciously account for development's impact on the environment.

WASHINGTON, D.C., and neighboring Arlington County, VIRGINIA, announced in 2016 that they would spend $70,000 to study the feasibility of installing an aerial gondola system to ferry commuters across the Potomac River.

The bottom line on regional councils and MPOs is that, for the most part, there is a considerable mismatch between their governance capacities and the need for effective and coordinated responses to regional issues. As one study of regional councils concludes, "Despite the efforts of progressive reformers to push strategies encouraging . . . strong, centralized regional government institutions, most regional institutions find it difficult to address issues affecting the quality of life in a metropolitan area."[26] Despite their obvious limitations, these councils are currently the only politically viable regional governance mechanisms that "most local jurisdictions can use to address multiple and cross-cutting issues."[27]

Many local governments also engage in looser, informal cooperative arrangements rather than creating formal institutions such as regional councils or MPOs. This sort of arrangement, known as an **interjurisdictional agreement (IJA)**, is becoming increasingly common. An IJA may take the form of a binding agreement. For example, a town may contract with the county for law

Metropolitan planning organization (MPO) A regional organization that decides how federal transportation funds are allocated within that regional area.

Smart growth Environmentally friendly development practices, particularly those that emphasize more efficient infrastructure and less dependence on automobiles.

Interjurisdictional agreement (IJA) A formal or informal agreement between two or more local governments to cooperate on a program or policy.

enforcement services or for dispatch services. Other IJAs may be much more informal and rest on nothing more than good-faith agreements between two or more local governments to provide a service jointly or to work together on planning or management issues. No one really knows how many IJAs there are or how effective they are in promoting successful integrated responses to regional problems. Given the shortcomings of more formal institutions such as regional councils and MPOs, however, IJAs often represent one of the few viable alternatives for multijurisdictional governance.[28]

Government Consolidation

One way to regularize or rationalize governance in a metropolitan region is to create a pan-regional institution. As already discussed, such an institution can take the form of a new level of government, such as Portland's Metro, or a formal institution of intergovernmental cooperation, such as a regional council. A second approach is to reduce the number of governments through merger or consolidation. This is typically done through the merging of a city with a county.

On the face of it, this makes a good deal of sense. Cities and urban counties share the same geographical space and provide similar services. A classic example is law enforcement services. Think of an urban county sitting on top of a large city. The county will have a sheriff's office; the city will have a police department. Each can have its own jails, dispatch centers, training facilities, and purchasing departments. It strikes many that there is a lot of redundancy and inefficiency in duplicating these services in such close quarters. Why not consolidate at least some of these functions? That is exactly what the city of Des Moines and Polk County, Iowa, did with their city and county jails. The county and city jails sat on opposite sides of the Des Moines River—directly across from each other—and consolidating facilities and operations just seemed to make sense.

If consolidating operations can reduce redundancy and improve efficiency, why not go whole hog and merge municipal and county governments into a single government? Cities and counties often duplicate bureaucracies and paperwork, so there seems to be an obvious logic to **city–county consolidation**. With as many as 75 percent of all major urban areas in the United States contained within single counties, it would

seem to make sense that such mergers would be common and easy. But they aren't, and it doesn't.

According to the National Association of Counties, of the nation's more than 3,000 counties, only about 40 (roughly 1 percent) have consolidated with cities. Between 2000 and 2010, there were more than 20 formal proposals to consolidate city and county governments, less than half of which actually passed.[29] Unsuccessful efforts include the attempts to merge the city of Gainesville with Alachua County in Florida and the city of Spokane with Spokane County in Washington.

Despite the glacial pace of city–county consolidation, it is an idea that has been around for a long time. The earliest consolidation dates back to 1805, when the city of New Orleans was consolidated with New Orleans Parish (remember, in Louisiana, counties are called parishes). The practice even enjoyed an era of popularity in the 1960s and 1970s. Proposals for consolidation often come in response to state initiatives or regional challenges. For example, the citizens of Jacksonville, Florida, in Duval County, were experiencing industrial waste in their river, underachieving high schools, and clashes between city and county officials during the 1960s. Local business leaders lobbied the state legislature for help. The legislature created a commission that proposed a consolidation plan. The plan was approved in 1967 by the legislature and, subsequently, by the voters in a referendum.

For the most part, this merger has worked for the two governments involved. But even after the merger, there were municipalities in Duval County (Atlantic Beach, Baldwin, Jacksonville Beach, and Neptune Beach) but outside Jacksonville city limits that continued as independent local governments. These communities periodically have considered splitting off from Jacksonville/Duval and forming a new county (Ocean County) as a means to recover a county government less tied to the city of Jacksonville. Thus far, however, these efforts have not progressed beyond the discussion stage, and all these municipalities remain a part of Duval County. The bottom line is that there's only been a few dozen successful mergers in 200 years, and a lot of cities and counties are left sitting right on top of each other, duplicating services. Why haven't city–county consolidations happened more often? The answer lies, in part, in who supports and who opposes the mergers when they are proposed.

Consolidation typically is advocated by business groups and others who favor efficiency in government

City–county consolidation The merger of separate local governments in an effort to reduce bureaucratic redundancy and service inefficiencies.

spending and regulation over local control of government. These groups and individuals seek a reorganization of government to reduce bureaucratic redundancy and to allow communities to speak "with one voice." The politics of consolidations, however, are tricky. Middle-class suburbanites may be concerned that mergers will benefit mostly downtown residents while raising taxes in the suburbs; inner-city minorities may fear their voting power will be diluted. Elected officials reflect these concerns and perhaps add some of their own. Consolidated governments mean fewer elected politicians and, most likely, fewer public employees. This creates internal pressure to resist merger movements.

There is also plain, old-fashioned community loyalty. The point has been made before about the strong tradition of local government in the United States. People identify with their local governments and tend to trust them (at least compared with state and federal governments). There is no tradition of regional government, and citizens and public officials treat these new and unknown entities with a degree of mistrust.

All this combines to make city–county consolidations a tough political undertaking, even when most objective observers agree they make a good deal of sense. The difference between successful and unsuccessful consolidation attempts seems to boil down to several key factors. One is the proposed new government structure and its jurisdiction and responsibilities. For example, consider a municipal utility that has taken on debt—that sounds pretty technical, but it can create a huge barrier to consolidation if county taxpayers not served by the utility see consolidation as a vehicle to get them to pay off that debt. Another factor is the nature of the area's demographics. Successful consolidations tend to involve cities and counties that have populations that are roughly similar in demographic terms, with no clear "town versus country" divide. The legal context also plays a big role. Put simply, state legislatures can either encourage or discourage consolidation, and which way they lean makes a big difference.[30]

The political hurdles that make successful consolidation proposals so rare frustrate reform perspective advocates, who see consolidation as a reasonable path to addressing key problems of regional governance. St. Louis County, Missouri, for example contains 90 municipalities, not including the city of St. Louis, which holds a distinct legal status as an "independent city." On top of all the usual issues surrounding policy coordination, the municipalities in St. Louis County are notable

for their stark differences in class, race, tax burdens, and level of public services. One of those municipalities is Ferguson, which gained national attention in August 2014 when weeks of civil unrest were triggered by the shooting of Michael Brown, an unarmed black man, by a white police officer. The attention highlighted differences between Ferguson and other cities in the county, in everything from tax burden to quality of public services. One proposed solution to such inequities that emerged in the wake of the events in Ferguson was the establishment of "big box" government—that is, some sort of consolidated government—in St. Louis County, even if it did not include all 90 municipalities. The idea was that this would help smooth out some of the inequities driving the unrest in places like Ferguson. Once more, however, the theoretical benefits of consolidation failed to convince many of the political players whose support was needed to make it a reality, and St. Louis County remains home to lots of independently operated local governments.[31] Some view consolidation in places like St. Louis County as a long-term possibility because of the benefits they believe consolidation can bring (see the box "Policy in Practice: Fighting the Urge to Merge").

History suggests that those hopes are not likely to be realized. If any city–county pairing is in a position to reap the benefits of consolidation, it is Pittsburgh and Allegheny County, Pennsylvania. Consolidation between these two governments has been seriously discussed in academic circles at least since the 1920s.[32] In the first decade of the 21st century, a series of blue-ribbon panels, committees, and commissions studied the pros and cons of an Allegheny–Pittsburgh consolidation, mostly concluded that the pros outweighed the cons, and recommended consolidation: "There's no question you could save money and provide much better service," stated David O'Laughlin, who served on one such panel.[33] As recently as 2017 and 2018, there was another spate of calls for an Allegheny–Pittsburgh consolidation and for many of the municipalities in Allegheny County to disincorporate (essentially putting themselves out of business) to reduce service redundancies and tax burdens.[34] Yet despite continued recommendations to merge, and despite some baby steps toward government integration (e.g., centralization of 911 call centers), full-scale consolidation remains a long way off. The bottom line is that local governments as a general rule do not want to share customers, and they definitely do not want to put themselves out of business. Like a good marriage, the consolidation of a

TABLE 12-2 ● Consolidated City–County Governments

Cities–Counties Operating Primarily as Cities		Metropolitan Governments Operating Primarily as Cities		Areas with County-Like Offices in Other Governments (city, township, special district, state)	
Alaska	City and borough of Anchorage	Tennessee	Hartsville and Trousdale County	Florida	County of Duval (city of Jacksonville)
	City and borough of Juneau		Lynchburg and Moore County	Georgia	County of Clarke (city of Athens)
					County of Chattahoochee (city of Cusseta)
					County of Echols (city of Statenville)
	City and borough of Sitka		Nashville and Davidson County		County of Muscogee (city of Columbus)
	City and borough of Yakutat				County of Richmond (city of Augusta)
					County of Quitman (city of Georgetown)
					County of Webster (city of Preston)
California	City and county of San Francisco			Hawaii	County of Kalawao (state of Hawaii)
Colorado	City and county of Broomfield			Indiana	County of Marion (city of Indianapolis)
	City and county of Denver			Kansas	County of Greeley (city of Tribune)
				Kentucky	Lexington-Fayette Urban County
Hawaii	City and county of Honolulu			Louisiana	Parish of East Baton Rouge (city of Baton Rouge)
Kansas	Unified government of Wyandotte County and city of Kansas City				Parish of Lafayette (city of Lafayette)
Montana	Anaconda–Deer Lodge County				Parish of Orleans (city of New Orleans)
	Butte–Silver Bow County				Terrebonne Parish Consolidated Government
				Massachusetts	County of Nantucket (town of Nantucket)
					County of Suffolk (city of Boston)
				New York	Counties of Bronx, Kings, New York, Queens, and Richmond (all part of the city of New York)
				Pennsylvania	County of Philadelphia (city of Philadelphia)

Source: National League of Cities, "List of Consolidated City–County Governments," https://www.nlc.org/list-of-consolidated-city-county-governments.

POLICY IN PRACTICE
FIGHTING THE URGE TO MERGE

St. Louis County, Missouri, contains roughly 90 municipalities. The largest of these will almost certainly sound familiar: the city of St. Louis, with a population somewhere north of 300,000. Chances are you've never heard of the smallest. That would be the village of Champ, population 13. No, we didn't forget a digit. Champ was incorporated in 1959 by Bill Bangert, a former boxer and pro football player who had dreams of fostering municipal glory as a mayor. He was duly elected to serve in that office by the village's constituents (otherwise known as his family). The dreams never quite took off, and he eventually moved off to California, but the village of Champ remains, a small municipality in a large county.

Champ has lots of company. Population-wise, about half of the incorporated local governments in St. Louis County range somewhere between tiddler (a few hundred) and Census Bureau rounding error (five to six thousand). All of those general-purpose governments are sitting right next to each other and within another general-purpose government (i.e., the county).

Local civic leaders in St. Louis have been bemoaning this governmental fragmentation and the redundancies, petty rivalries, and socioeconomic segregation they foster at least since the city of St. Louis split from the county in 1876. The problems that concern them are real. For example, local governments in the county compete with each other, offering sweetheart tax deals to lure employees from one jurisdiction to another, which might only be a mile or two distant geographically. There's a reason this sort of competition can be so intense. The tax base of many of these municipalities is so small that they are financially dependent on court fees and fines. Ferguson was one such city, and its practice of financing itself using court fees disproportionately levied on its African American residents became enormously controversial in 2014 when a white police officer shot and killed Michael Brown.

By one estimate, having all these governments carpeting the county like mushrooms leads to at least a billion dollars in wasteful spending every year. This helps explain why in 2017 both St. Louis mayor Lyda Krewson and county executive Steve Stenger came out in support of a study calling for consolidating many of these local governments. The basic idea is that government could be cheaper and more effective if there was less of it and what remained was more regionally oriented than focused on one small patch of the county.

Champ and its many neighbors, however, are unlikely to disappear anytime soon. Everyone is against too much government until you try to take it away. There was an immediate pushback to the calls for consolidation, with opponents arguing any cost savings likely to be brought by consolidation are exaggerated and, regardless, people like things the way they are. Several municipalities started circulating resolutions opposing a city–county merger, and a political scientist estimated local residents were willing to pay 10 to 15 percent more in taxes to keep the status quo.

The bottom line is that no matter how logical municipal mergers seem to be in places like St. Louis County, chances are they are not going to happen. Politically, they are going nowhere.

Source: Adapted from Alan Greenblatt, "Consolidation Makes Sense, Yet Few Cities Have the Urge to Merge," *Governing*, October 2017.

---

city and a county depends critically on partners that trust each other and can make equal contributions to the merger. For example, Phoenix, Arizona, has won awards for its state-of-the-art management innovations. Surrounding Maricopa County, in contrast, has a reputation for management inefficiency. Good luck getting those two governments down the aisle.[35]

Annexation

Rather than forming new governments like Portland's Metro or merging old ones, another option for dealing with the problems of sprawl, traffic congestion, and uneven economic development is to make the existing political jurisdictions bigger. **Annexation** is the legal incorporation of one jurisdiction or territory into another. Usually, the jurisdiction that does the annexing is the more politically powerful, whereas the "annexee" is weaker and may not be enthusiastic about becoming the latest addition to a larger municipal neighbor. This approach is relatively common in the South and

....

Annexation The legal incorporation of one jurisdiction or territory into another.

West, regions where there are large tracts of unincorporated land adjacent to major cities. Cities such as El Paso, Houston, and Phoenix have annexed hundreds of square miles and, in doing so, have turned themselves into regional governments by sheer geographical size. Oklahoma City, for example, has more than 620 square miles within its city limits, with much of that added over the years through annexations.[36]

Annexation is a tool used principally by municipalities that want to control development along their peripheries and engage in planned expansions of their tax bases. Remember that cities like to place uniform requirements on area developers, leading developers to favor unincorporated areas where land is cheaper and there are fewer regulations. One way cities can put a stop to developers' avoiding regulation and impose a more coherent and orderly plan on metropolitan growth is simply by annexing that unincorporated land.

A city government that wishes to annex a tract of land must organize the citizens of the unincorporated area to sign a petition. Some communities seek to expand by annexing prospectively, working to incorporate still-undeveloped parcels of land farther out from suburban parcels already being transformed from woods or farmland into subdivisions. This, in turn, may alienate rural landowners, including farmers, who value their traditional identity as separate from that of the city.[37] Annexation, in short, can create a lot of conflict, with some residents of unincorporated areas seeing it as a land grab that threatens to develop their rural communities out of existence.

Given this sort of conflict, it should not be too surprising to find that states make it tough for cities to annex new land. For example, in 1963, the California legislature created 58 local agency formation commissions as boundary watchdogs to discourage annexation. Among other things, these commissions are supposed to discourage urban sprawl. However, because urban sprawl pretty much describes metropolitan growth in the past four decades in large parts of the state, many Californians believe that these commissions are too weak to deal with rapid suburbanization.

Annexation can make sense from a big-picture perspective in that it can help impose the orderly expansion of urban municipalities, but there is no getting around the fact that it creates losers as well as winners. And the losers often are not interested in losing at all. Townships, for example, may be less than pleased at the prospect of their rural character being changed when municipalities decide to gobble up unincorporated land in the name of development.[38]

Annexation does have natural limits—there has to be land available to annex. Although municipalities tend to have the upper hand over sparsely populated, unincorporated territories, if they bump up against other cities, it's a different story. Unlike cities in the South and West, many cities in the North and East are ringed by incorporated suburbs; in effect, core cities are fenced in by other cities, with no real option to expand. Pittsburgh covers about 58 square miles—a fraction of Oklahoma City's 600-plus square miles—and is surrounded by suburbs that are municipalities in their own right. Outside of a merger with Allegheny County, it is unlikely that Pittsburgh is going to grow geographically to anywhere near the size of Oklahoma City.

The Case against Reform: Public Choice and the Tiebout Model

Although metropolitan areas undoubtedly have problems, not everyone agrees that these problems require stronger regional governments. Indeed, some argue that at least a few of the underlying problems have been exaggerated, or at least not balanced adequately against the benefits of metropolitan growth.

Backing this argument is the fact that cities are, for the most part, pretty decent places to live. Core cities have not been swirling down into a uniform death spiral of relentless flight to the suburbs, leaving poverty, racial segregation, and crime. In many MSAs, the core cities remain the economic and social hubs of their regions. Scholars and musicians, business leaders and actors—people in a wide range of fields are still more likely to be attracted to the city to pursue their opportunities and dreams than to an exurb or single-use housing tract. Core cities remain exciting places—centers of innovation and culture, shopping and business activity.

So, despite the undeniable downsides to longtime growth patterns in metropolitan areas, there are also some positives, at least for some people. First and foremost are the quality-of-life benefits. That house in the suburbs can be a pretty darn nice house, in a pretty darn nice neighborhood. Good-quality schools are not hard to find in the suburbs, and neither are relatively crime-free developments with nice parks and maybe even a golf course nearby. This can look very attractive to those who have the means to take advantage of such opportunities. The same developments that often are castigated by academic critics of urban planning (or the lack thereof) can be job-generating machines.

For example, many consider Levittown in Nassau County, New York, to be the original "cookie-cutter" modern suburban housing development. Eventually totaling more than 17,000 homes, Levittown was built in an unincorporated area in the late 1940s and early 1950s. It was, literally, a community built from the ground up. First came the housing development; then public services (schools and parks) followed. Levittown served as a model for suburban growth across the United States, and what is notable about it for present purposes is that it was designed as an affordable housing development. The houses were nothing fancy—brand new, they cost less than $8,000, which even by the standards of the early 1950s was a good price for a single-family home. What they offered was not economic segregation for the moneyed class but, instead, the American Dream of homeownership for a generation of World War II veterans.[39]

And the middle and upper classes have not abandoned every neighborhood in every city. Indeed, some decaying urban areas have undergone a renaissance, with old warehouses being turned into upscale condos and downtown neighborhoods becoming the focus of thriving cultural scenes. This process of physical rehabilitation of urban areas, which attracts investment from developers and drives up property values, is known as **gentrification**. Gentrified neighborhoods do present something of a double-edged sword, however. Although gentrification clearly can resuscitate decaying areas, the rise in property values means that poorer people (the original residents) can no longer afford to live there. In essence, gentrification creates pockets of middle-class wealth within cities.

In short, there is a glass-half-full perspective that sees innovation and vitality, high standards of living, and social and economic opportunities in the cities; this contrasts with a glass-half-empty perspective that focuses on segregation, smog, and economic inequality. There are also strong theoretical arguments against any large-scale movement to replace multiple local jurisdictions with larger regional governance structures.

▲ Gentrification, the physical rehabilitation of urban areas, is a double-edged sword. It can improve property values and attract new investment, but it can also disrupt long-standing local communities and cultures. Those communities may politically resist outsiders seeking to change their neighborhood.

Erik Mc Gregor/Pacific Press/LightRocket via Getty Images

In Portland, **OREGON** 58.1 percent of eligible tracts gentrified from 2009 to 2013—more than in any other U.S. city.

In short, there is a glass-half-full perspective that sees innovation and vitality, high standards of living, and social and economic opportunities in the cities; this contrasts with a glass-half-empty perspective that focuses on segregation, smog, and economic inequality.

Gentrification The physical rehabilitation of urban areas, which attracts investment from developers and drives up property values.

The **public choice model** of politics views governments and public services in market terms. In this model, governments are seen as producers of public services, and citizens are seen as consumers. As in most markets, competition among producers is seen as a good thing. With lots of local jurisdictions, citizens can choose their favored "producers" by moving to the cities or towns that have the mixes of taxes and public services that suit them best. If local governments fail to satisfy individual citizen consumers—in other words, if their taxes go too high or their public services drop too low—the citizens can vote with their feet and move to other jurisdictions with more attractive tax–public service packages.

Multiple jurisdictions mean multiple producers, a set of competing "products" in the form of different mixes of taxes and public services. That competition keeps governments responsive to their constituents and puts pressure on the governments to be efficient and to keep the quality of public services as high as possible and taxes as low as possible. If local governments are inefficient—that is, their taxes are high and their public services are poor—they risk having their constituents move to other jurisdictions that offer better deals. From a public choice perspective, then, concentrating local governments into regional governments, through either formal or informal mechanisms, risks a considerable downside. Government consolidation basically represents the creation of monopoly service providers and brings with it all the problems of monopolies that are well understood from private markets: lack of response to consumers, high costs, and indifferent quality.

This perspective on local government was most famously articulated by Charles Tiebout in the 1950s. The **Tiebout model** of local government calls for a metro area made up of a series of micropolitical jurisdictions. If each jurisdiction can control its tax-service package, fully mobile citizens will respond to the available packages by gravitating to the one that suits them best. Or, as Tiebout put it, the mobility of citizens will provide "the local public goods counterpart to the private market's shopping trip."[40]

In addition to highly mobile citizens, the Tiebout model requires informed citizens. If people do not know what different governments are offering in the way of alternative tax-service packages, they are not going to be very good local government "shoppers," and local governments may be able to take advantage of that ignorance by becoming lazy and inefficient producers of public goods and services.

If the mobility and information requirements are met, the Tiebout model makes a strong theoretical case for political fragmentation in metropolitan areas, obviously arguing against the reform perspective of pushing for government consolidation. From the Tiebout model perspective, a regional government or a merged city and county government represents a big monopoly, which is likely to produce a large, inefficient bureaucracy that is unresponsive to citizens and has little incentive to keep quality high and costs low.

The "if" on the mobility and information requirements, however, is a big one. A number of scholars have argued that citizens are neither fully mobile nor fully informed. The constraints on mobility are fairly obvious: Where you can live is determined by how much money you can earn. This means the well-off, if they so choose, can be fairly mobile. The less well-off, on the other hand, are more likely to find their mobility limited by their pocketbooks. They simply cannot afford to move to better neighborhoods, even if they want to, because property prices are too high. There are some important implications here. The Tiebout model, remember, makes a good case that local governments will be responsive to people who have a real exit option—in other words, people who can pack up and move if they do not like what the local government is doing. If those people are defined by wealth, it means governments in metropolitan areas are likely to be more responsive to the concerns of the well-off than to those of the poor.

The requirement that citizens be informed also turns out to be a fairly restrictive burden on using the Tiebout model as a practical template for metropolitan governance. Studies show that citizens are not particularly mobile and are pretty uninformed about local services. Indeed, if anything, citizens know more about local services when they live in an area with a single centralized local government compared with areas where there are lots of local governments.[41] These findings raise questions about whether the Tiebout model can serve as a practical guide to governance in metropolitan areas.

....

Public choice model A model of politics that views governments and public services in market terms; governments are seen as producers of public services, and citizens are seen as consumers.

Tiebout model A model of local government based on market principles wherein a metro area is made up of a series of micropolitical jurisdictions that, on the basis of their services and costs, attract or repel certain citizens.

Regardless, the Tiebout model demonstrates that there is at least a theoretical case to be made for political fragmentation in metropolitan areas. Coupled with high suburban standards of living and gentrification in the core cities, there is a reasonable counterargument to the calls for more centralized government in metropolitan areas.

Rural Metropolitics

Rural governments frequently face a different set of challenges from those that confront the urban areas discussed thus far. For example, some rural counties are dealing with shrinking and aging populations, as younger people move from rural agricultural areas to more metropolitan areas in search of educational, social, and economic opportunities.

Consider that nationwide there are roughly 300 counties with fewer than 25,000 people that lost at least 10 percent of their population between 2000 and 2010.[42] At least in part, this reflects a population exodus that tracks a massive consolidation in agriculture as family farms give way to vast corporate operations. Fewer farms means fewer agricultural jobs, which means that younger people move to the cities, where the jobs are, leaving smaller rural communities with fewer shoppers, fewer schools, and fewer businesses. That is a recipe for decline that can be hard to reverse. By one estimate, half of the U.S. population lives in just 146 highly urbanized counties. In contrast, less than 20 percent of Americans live in rural areas.[43] What that means is a small fraction of the total population is spread out across thousands of counties accounting for the vast majority of the nation's geography. Loving County, Texas, for instance, is a big place—it covers roughly 670 square miles—with few people. The Census Bureau estimates that in 2016 the population of the entire county was 113, a population density of roughly 1 person for every 6 square miles. Indeed, there's a decent chance that the county's biggest and only city, Mentone, is smaller than your college class on state politics—it has a population of just 19.

Loving County is just a rather extreme example of a common problem rural governments are struggling to deal with. Rather than white flight, rural states with agriculture-based economies, such as Iowa, Kansas, and Nebraska, face **rural flight**, the movement of the young and the middle class to more urban areas. Although the underlying cause is different, the end result can be pressure for a solution that sounds familiar to any veteran of the political battles over urban growth—regional government. Iowa, for example, is a mostly rural state. It has a population of roughly 3.1 million and more than 1,000 general-purpose governments. If special districts (schools and the like) are included, Iowa has something like one government for every 1,600 residents. Most counties in Iowa do not have a lot of people; what they have is a lot of government. Adams is the least populated county in Iowa, with roughly 3,700 residents in 2017. In addition to the county government, in Adams there are five general-purpose municipalities and two school districts. If we stop counting right there, Adams County has about one government for every 460 residents. And Adams County is losing people—its population shrank by about 8.5 percent between 2010 and 2015. (See Map 12-2 for county-by-county population changes in Iowa.)

The bottom line is that declining populations in rural areas can leave redundant layers of government sitting on stagnant tax bases. That puts upward pressure on property taxes, and it also creates incentives to make government more efficient. Consolidating governments is one way to do this, and it is an option that increasingly is being considered in rural states. Schools are typically among the first sets of merger candidates. As student populations decrease in a rural community, it is harder to fund a comprehensive K–12 school system. If there is another community within busing distance, it can make a good deal of financial sense for the two communities to split educational services—for example, to have elementary schools in both communities, the junior high in one town, and the high school in the other.

These sorts of pressures have made for a steady stream of school district consolidations in rural states. For example, in 2000, Nebraska had nearly 600 public school districts. As of 2017, it had 245. So, in less than two decades,

Chicago, **ILLINOIS**, became the only large U.S. city to have a declining population after losing 2,890 residents in 2015.

Rural flight The movement of youth and the middle class from rural areas to more urban areas.

MAP 12-2 ● Population Changes by County, Iowa, 2010–2017

County	Value
Lyon	1.8
Osceola	−6.5
Dickinson	3.2
Emmet	−8.4
Winnebago	−2.6
Worth	−0.7
Mitchell	−1.3
Howard	−1.6
Winneshiek	−4.1
Allamakee	−3.1
Sioux	3.4
O'Brien	−4.1
Clay	−3.0
Palo Alto	−3.5
Kossuth	−3.5
Hancock	−5.0
Cerro Gordo	−2.6
Floyd	−3.4
Chickasaw	−3.5
Plymouth	1.0
Cherokee	−6.3
Buena Vista	−0.7
Pocahontas	−6.3
Humboldt	−2.5
Wright	−3.4
Franklin	−4.8
Butler	−1.8
Bremer	2.6
Fayette	−5.2
Clayton	−3.0
Woodbury	0.2
Ida	−3.2
Sac	−5.1
Calhoun	−4.2
Webster	−3.7
Hamilton	−3.6
Hardin	−2.8
Grundy	−1.0
Black Hawk	1.2
Buchanan	1.2
Delaware	−3.4
Dubuque	3.6
Monona	−5.4
Crawford	−0.2
Carroll	−2.4
Greene	−3.8
Boone	0.7
Story	8.9
Marshall	−0.9
Tama	−4.0
Benton	−1.7
Linn	6.1
Jones	−0.5
Jackson	−2.4
Harrison	−5.4
Shelby	−1.9
Audobon	−8.8
Guthrie	−2.6
Dallas	31.9
Polk	11.9
Jasper	0.3
Poweshiek	−3.2
Iowa	−1.5
Johnson	14.0
Cedar	0.3
Clinton	−4.3
Scott	4.4
Muscatine	0.3
Pottawattamie	0.3
Cass	−5.8
Adair	−8.2
Madison	2.1
Warren	8.5
Marion	−0.6
Mahaska	−0.7
Keokuk	−3.4
Washington	2.7
Louisa	−1.8
Mills	0.1
Montgomery	−5.6
Adams	−8.5
Union	−0.7
Clarke	0.9
Lucas	−4.1
Monroe	−1.6
Wapello	−1.6
Jefferson	9.4
Henry	−1.4
Des Moines	−2.3
Fremont	−6.6
Page	−4.5
Taylor	−2.2
Ringgold	−1.9
Decatur	−6.0
Wayne	1.1
Appanoose	−4.2
Davis	2.4
Van Buren	−5.5
Lee	−4.4

Legend: Decline | 0 to 1.4 percent | More than 1.4 percent

Source: Calculated by the authors using data from Iowa State University, "Annual Estimates of the Total Population for Counties," http://www.icip .iastate.edu/tables/population/counties-estimates.

more than half of the public school districts in the entire state consolidated or went out of business.[44] It is not hard to fathom the economics behind this massive contraction of governments. School consolidations make financial sense from the standpoint of the statewide taxpayer: larger districts can take advantage of economies of scale, rationalize class sizes, and lower per-pupil spending. From a community perspective, however, school consolidations are less about dollars and cents and more about identity, or even survival. A rural community that loses its school loses a central social and cultural institution, and the loss of teachers also means the loss of a significant chunk of a town's middle class. Many see the loss of a school, especially a high school, as a devastating blow to a rural community.

When economics come up against strong loyalties to local governments, the local loyalties often win, but those victories mean higher property taxes and fewer public services. Back in 2005, Iowa governor Tom Vilsack tried to do something about his state's surplus of government, arguing that Iowans simply could not support that level of public infrastructure. Vilsack proposed a truly radical solution—replacing the grab bag of hundreds of local governments with about 15 regional governments. These regional governments, Vilsack reasoned, would be not only cheaper but also better positioned to drive economic development in rural areas. His plan landed with a thud; it got little support at the local level and a chilly reception in the legislature.[45] Iowans preferred higher taxes and/or lower levels of service to losing their traditional local governments, a preference that is almost certainly still prevalent in most rural states.

Rural flight is a demographic phenomenon whose causes and consequences tend to attract less scholarly and media attention than do white flight and the problems it causes for core cities and urban areas. The governance and political issues raised by rural flight, however, clearly have distinct parallels with the broader story of metropolitics told in larger urban areas.

Conclusion

The central issue of metropolitics—and its rural equivalent—boils down to the gap that exists between local and state governments. Local governments were founded and organized in a horse-and-buggy era, and those organizational structures do not always make for a rational fit with 21st-century realities. Dense urban concentrations, or metros, are where most economic activity in the United States is located, and such activity is integrated and interconnected across a region rather than confined within a single local government's borders. In rural areas, dispersed and shrinking populations squeeze local tax bases and can make providing even basic public services a struggle for small, independent jurisdictions. These urban and rural realities create a set of policy challenges that are clearly regional in nature, yet there is no real level of government capable of taking a truly regional perspective on those issues.

In short, the broad array of region-wide social and economic challenges exposes a hole in government organization. The politics of metropolitan areas—and,

in many cases, rural areas—boils down to differences about what, if anything, should fill that hole. A true regional government, with the authority to develop and effectively enforce policy solutions to problems of transportation, land use, and the like, means that established local governments must cede their power to this new government. In the case of consolidation, they have to, in effect, put themselves out of business. The politics involved can be contentious. The end result is resistance to changing the status quo. And so, in most places in the United States, there simply are no strong central or general-purpose governments at the regional level.

Despite the difficulties, however, the realities on the ground are pushing local governments toward regional perspectives through cooperative agreements and joint action. The social and economic challenges that are regional in nature demand that the hole in government be filled. The unanswered question is how.

THE LATEST RESEARCH

Local government in the United States is organized for a 19th-century social and economic environment, not for its 21st-century equivalent. As this chapter has made crystal clear, we have many local governments, often crammed into the same metropolitan area, all making decisions that affect one another and the broader region, with varying levels of cooperation and coordination. While there is more or less universal agreement on these points, there is less agreement on what a 21st-century model of local governance should look like. Should it involve more city–county consolidation and a move to true regional governments, like Portland's Metro? Or do we want less centralization and more fragmentation, a concentrated effort to create a flexible and efficient market for public services along the lines of the Tiebout model? In a political system with no real level of regional government, is it even possible to rein in development patterns that result in sprawl? As the studies described below suggest, the latest research on these questions gives conflicting answers.

- **Landis, John D.**, "The End of Sprawl? Not So Fast," *Housing Policy Debate* 25, no. 5 (2017): 659–697.

Gentrification and the increasing attractiveness of city living have led a number of observers to wonder whether we are in an era that may see the end of sprawl. If people are flocking to high-density urban areas and are less interested in being car dependent to get to work or play, shouldn't that act as a natural brake on the growth of sprawl? This study looks at the current state of sprawl in 178 of the largest cities in America to try and address this question. It comes up with mixed answers. On the one hand, average population densities are declining, which suggests sprawl is at least slowing if not coming to a complete halt. It also finds some anti-sprawl regulations can work, though the impact is hit-and-miss. The tentative conclusion here is that sprawl is slowing, but whether this is a pause or a permanent decline in these sorts of development patterns is still an open question.

(Continued)

(Continued)

- **Uden, Amy B.,** "A Checklist for Alternatives in City–County Consolidation Decisions: From Separation to Unification," *State and Local Government Review* 48, no. 1 (2016): 49–62.

As discussed above, city–county consolidations are often considered but very rarely adopted. Why? In this study, Uden examines some of the assumptions underlying consolidation efforts and tries to identify the characteristics of successful and (more likely) unsuccessful consolidation efforts. What is unique about this study, however, is not the list of traits associated with more versus less successful consolidation efforts, but Uden's attempt to translate that knowledge into a practical guide to figuring out the best—or at least the most realistic—path to shared regional governance. She develops a straightforward checklist for navigating consolidation options that includes everything from assessing the outcomes of greater unification that are most valued by localities (increased taxation equity? public-sector efficiency?) to legal and demographic contexts. This checklist is sort of like a regional governance personality test—its results are designed to shed light on what unified governance options are politically realistic. Those options can range from full unification (i.e., the creation of a true metropolitan government) to the retention of completely separate local governments. In between these two extremes are options that include networked government that stresses cooperation and a shared services system that creates regional public programs or services (e.g., law enforcement) while retaining independent local governments. What is notable about this approach is that it systematically clarifies the range of regional governance options within any given local context. This contrasts with the arguments made by committed advocates of the reform perspective or the Tiebout model, which tend to present regional governance options as an either/or choice between centralization and decentralization.

- **Taylor, Charles, Dagney Faulk, and Pamela Schaal**, "What Are the Cost Savings in City–County Consolidation?," *Journal of Urban Affairs* 39, no. 2 (2017), 185–204, doi.org/10.1111/juaf.12308.

One of the primary arguments made in favor of consolidating city and county governments is efficiency. The basic argument is that it is cheaper to run one law enforcement agency or one roads department rather than two. But does that actually happen? This study

takes a look at expenditure patterns in four city–county jurisdictions for roughly a decade before and after they decided to consolidate. It does find differences in expenditures pre- and post-consolidation, but not necessarily the differences predicted by supporters or opponents of consolidation. There clearly are some cost savings, but these are uneven across jurisdictions, are far from automatic, and sometimes dissipate over time. Generally speaking, administrative expenditures do decrease after consolidation, validating the argument that having multiple layers of general-purpose government exacts a literal cost on the taxpayer. Those savings, though, tend to be short term. Expenditure patterns over the long term often head back to what they were pre-consolidation.

- **Savitch, H. V., and Sarin Adhikari**, "Fragmented Regionalism: Why Metropolitan America Continues to Splinter," *Urban Affairs Review* 53, no. 2 (2017), doi:10.1177/1078087416630626.

As this study points out, the average metropolitan statistical area contains about 635,000 residents and 104 local governments. A number of powerful incentives push those governments away from each other. For example, they all have a strong incentive to attract businesses, even at the expense of other local governments, because they need the tax bases to pay for the services they provide. Yet there are also opposing forces pushing local governments together. For example, they all have a big stake in regional transportation infrastructure and in combatting common problems like air pollution. This study is an in-depth look at these contradictory push–pull forces and their consequences. Local governments jealously guard their own turf, but they are also acutely conscious of the need to address regional challenges collectively. Savitch and Adhikari argue that this paradox is at least partially dealt with through the creation of "public authorities," which are corporations created by one or more governments to provide regional services. An example is the Los Angeles County Metropolitan Transportation Authority, which has a board of directors with members representing Los Angeles County, the city of Los Angeles, and 87 other municipalities in Los Angeles County. Savitch and Adhikari assert that such authorities play an underappreciated role in keeping regional government decentralized. Essentially, these public authorities provide just enough in the way of collective action to address regional issues, and, in doing so, they also help head off any greater movement toward centralization.

CHAPTER 12

for CQ Press

Want a better grade?

Get the tools you need to sharpen your study skills. SAGE edge offers a robust online environment featuring an impressive array of free tools and resources.

Access practice quizzes, eFlashcards, video, and multimedia at **edge.sagepub.com/ smithgreenblatt7e**

Top Ten Takeaways

1. In the United States, most economic and social activity is focused in urban regions that include many independent local governments.

2. Many of the central challenges of governance are regional in nature, but the United States has very few truly regional governments.

3. Sprawl has contributed to the extreme fragmentation of local government in metropolitan regions. Growth patterns characterized by single-use zoning, low-density development, leapfrog development, car-dependent living, and fragmented land-use powers have created huge urban areas where people work in one place, live in another, and seek entertainment and recreation in others.

4. Fragmented government and sprawl have contributed to segregated housing patterns, service and tax inequities between neighboring communities, and difficulties in addressing issues such as transportation infrastructure and environmental concerns.

5. Critics of fragmentation argue that it also creates redundancy and inefficiencies in the provision of public goods and services.

6. To address inefficiency, redundancy, and inequities, champions of the reform perspective advocate a move toward creating more centralized regional governments.

7. Reforms that require big structural changes, such as city–county consolidation, are difficult to achieve. They are not popular with voters and are resisted by local governments reluctant to give up their powers. The result is that true regional governments are very rare in the United States.

8. There are also champions of decentralization who oppose centralizing reforms. The public choice and Tiebout models of government argue that having lots of local governments competing to attract citizen "consumers" is the most effective and efficient way to provide public goods and services.

(Continued)

(Continued)

9. Because of falling populations leading to stagnant tax bases, many rural areas are facing increasing pressure to replace multiple local governments with fewer regional governments.

10. Local government in the United States is essentially built on a 19th-century understanding of economic, social, and political activity. Although there clearly are increasing pressures to create regional governments to deal with 21st-century challenges, it seems unlikely that any widespread adoption of true regional governments will take place soon.

Key Concepts

annexation (p. 353)
car-dependent living
  (p. 344)
city–county consolidation
  (p. 350)
edgeless cities (p. 342)
exurbs (p. 345)
gentrification (p. 355)
impact fees (p. 344)
interjurisdictional agreement
  (IJA) (p. 349)

leapfrog development
  (p. 343)
low-density development
  (p. 343)
megaregion (p. 342)
metropolitan area (p. 341)
metropolitan planning
  organization (MPO)
  (p. 349)
metropolitan statistical area
  (MSA) (p. 341)

public choice model (p. 356)
reform perspective (p. 347)
regional council (p. 348)
rural flight (p. 357)
smart growth (p. 349)
sprawl (p. 343)
Tiebout model (p. 356)
urban growth boundary
  (UGB) (p. 348)
white flight (p. 345)
zoning laws (p. 343)

Suggested Websites

- **www.ampo.org.** Website of the Association of Metropolitan Planning Organizations (AMPO), the national organization for MPOs. AMPO is mainly oriented toward transportation issues, but the site includes downloadable studies and publications on a range of issues facing metropolitan areas.

- **www.narc.org.** Website of the National Association of Regional Councils, an organization of MPOs that seeks to promote cooperation between governments; covers urban, suburban, and rural governments.

- **www.oregonmetro.gov.** Website of Portland, Oregon's Metro, a rare example of a true regional government in the United States; includes the history of Metro's formation and information on a range of its activities.

Bill Pugliano/Getty Images

Education

Reading, Writing, and Regulation

Education is one of the single biggest categories of expenditure for state and local governments. Even so, teachers' wages have lagged for years in many states, and educators have been pressuring state governments to increase spending on public schools.

Chapter Objectives

After reading this chapter, you will be able to

- Describe key education policymakers and how they help shape and implement education policy,

- Explain why per-pupil spending varies so much,

- Summarize how educational performance is measured and what those measures say about public school performance,

- Describe the aims and objectives of the Common Core State Standards and other major education reform movements,

- Discuss key alternatives to public schools, and

- Identify key interest groups seeking to influence education policy.

"Learning is earning" isn't just a rah-rah cliché trotted out by high school counselors and parents discouraging teenagers from blowing off course work. It is also, quite literally, true. In 2016, the median weekly earnings for a high school dropout were roughly 500 bucks. For those who got the diploma, that number jumped to almost $700, which works out to be a 40 percent wage premium for finishing high school. For those who went on to college and finished a bachelor's degree, the typical weekly wage climbed to about $1,155—nearly three times that of the typical dropout. Learning really *is* earning.[1]

And that's true not just for individuals, but also for states. States with stronger public education systems and better-educated populations tend to be better off economically.[2] And education does more than improve everyone's bottom line. Better-educated people are not just wealthier, but also healthier.[3] They are more likely to vote and less likely to divorce.[4] Public education has long been seen as critical to supporting democratic government and as a handy cure-all that can address pretty much any social ill. Thomas Jefferson said, "An educated citizenry is a vital requisite for our survival as a free people." President Lyndon B. Johnson called education "the answer to all our national problems."[5] Talk about a difference that makes a difference.

The bottom line is that it is hard to underestimate the importance of education to our individual and collective well-being. That puts a lot of responsibility on state governments. That's because the vast majority of schooling that occurs within the United States takes place within public education systems, and those systems are almost without exception legally mandated, financially supported, and regulated by the states. While a good deal of administrative control and financial independence is often delegated down to other forms of government—think school districts and public universities—ultimately it is the states that are responsible for public education systems. And there are systems, plural. Even with recent efforts to bring more uniformity to public education (more on that in a bit), there is enormous variation in how states approach education. Some take more central financial and regulatory roles; others let local districts fend more for themselves. Requirements for teacher certification and graduation vary, as do everything from textbooks to teacher salaries to tuition rates. All those differences, don't forget, mean differences in economic success, civic engagement, family stability, and health, so education is clearly a very big deal. Public education is a big part of every state's budget for a good reason: it is inarguably one of the most important functional areas of subnational government.

The basis of all state public education systems is the **common school**, which is simply a school funded at taxpayer expense to provide primary or secondary educational services to all residents of school age. These are typically organized into school districts, a form of special district that often has its own taxing authority and some degree of freedom in making budgetary and curricular

....

Common school In a democratic society, a school in which children of all income levels attend at taxpayer expense.

decisions. Most states also have a **state board of education**, which is made up of gubernatorial appointees (in some states, they are independently elected) and exercises primary policymaking power over K–12 education.

A perennial obsession of parents, education reformers, and lawmakers at state and federal levels is that these common schools, and public education in general, could and should be doing better. Over the past few decades, there has been a series of more or less continuous reform efforts in pursuit of that goal. These have focused on everything from **back to basics**, to new curriculum **standards**, to **high-stakes standardized testing**, to experiments with nontraditional organizational arrangements like charter schools. In this chapter, we take an in-depth look at education policy, the politics that surround it, and some of the reform efforts those politics have driven. As you read through this chapter, keep in mind the following questions:

- **Why are some school systems so much stronger than others?**
- **Why do curricula vary so much from state to state?**
- **Why are there so many different brands of school reform?**
- **What is the appropriate role for the federal government in education, which is traditionally a function of local and state governments?**

Organization and Leadership: Schools Have Many Bosses

The United States is one of the few industrialized countries with no national ministry of education. The federal government does have a cabinet-level education agency—the U.S. Department of Education—but its regulatory and funding authority is limited. The agency

State board of education Top policymaking body for education in each of the 50 states, usually consisting of appointees selected by the governor.

Back to basics A movement against modern education "fads," advocating a return to an emphasis on traditional core subjects such as reading, writing, and arithmetic.

Standards In education, fixed criteria for learning that students are expected to reach in specific subjects by specific grade years.

High-stakes standardized testing Testing of elementary and secondary students in which poor results can mean either that students fail to be promoted or that the school loses its accreditation.

was created in 1978 as the fulfillment of a campaign promise by President Jimmy Carter, and its existence has been controversial ever since. Many critics, especially conservatives and Republicans, argue that education is not the federal government's policy concern and that Washington has no business sticking its large bureaucratic nose into a primary concern of the states. In 1980, Ronald Reagan campaigned on an explicit promise to abolish the Department of Education, and during his 2016 campaign for president, Donald Trump promised to shrink the agency drastically if not kill it outright. The department has proved to be remarkably resistant to such plans, yet its survival and expansion over the past three decades have not come close to centralizing governance over education at the federal level. The primary authority for running schools remains with the 50 states. The reason education is controlled by states rather than the federal government is the Tenth Amendment, which dictates that the powers not delegated by the Constitution to the federal government are reserved for the states. In effect, that means regulatory authority over education ultimately rests with the states. The big exception to this is the District of Columbia, which technically is a federal city and not a state; its board of education derives its funds from the city's appropriation from Congress.

In contrast to the Johnny-come-lately federal government, states have been taking on the task of schooling their citizens for a very long time. For example, in 1857, Minnesota's constitution proclaimed that because the "stability of a Republican form of government depends upon the intelligence of the people, it is the duty of the legislature to establish a general and uniform system of public schools."[6] In other words, the consensus was that creating a well-educated population not only helps individual citizens prosper but also helps entrench the democratic process. Indeed, most state constitutions justify their provisions for taxpayer-supported education systems and compulsory school attendance laws not by citing economic reasons but by arguing that democracy needs an educated citizenry to function.[7]

Fifty varying traditions make for a lot of bosses in a democratic approach to education. A system that permits local innovations and variations is a far cry from the systems in use in other countries. Legend has it that a national education chief in Europe can look at a clock on any given weekday and know precisely which lesson is being taught in classrooms across the country at that moment. This is not the case in the United States, where education systems can be very different from state to state.

Generally speaking, state legislatures working with state **departments of education** are the major players dealing with state education policy questions and large-scale resource issues. A state legislature can raise teacher salaries statewide, equalize funding among districts, and set up health benefits and retirement plans for the state's pool of teachers. It can borrow money by floating state bonds to provide schools with construction funds, which commits taxpayers to long-term debts. The states are also the main players in determining **teacher licensure procedures**. For example, they determine whether or not teacher candidates must take standardized tests and how schools are awarded **accreditation**. States also set curricular standards and graduation requirements.

The more complex state decisions are proposed and implemented by an experienced educator who is the chief state school officer. Such an official may be appointed by the governor, as in Iowa, Maine, and New Jersey, or by a state board of education, as in Louisiana, Utah, and Vermont. In some states, the top school official is elected, whether on a partisan ballot, as in North Carolina and Oklahoma, or on a nonpartisan ballot, as in North Dakota and Oregon. This official works closely with the state board of education, the members of which are also appointed or elected, depending on the state. The members of a state's board usually represent all the regions of the state.

While regulatory authority over education is concentrated at the state level, the actual administration of schools is widely decentralized. Most public schools are run not directly by the state but by **local education agencies (LEAs)**, which have been formed in roughly 14,000 **school districts** scattered over cities, counties, and townships. School districts are staffed with full-time professionals, but they carry out policies set by **school boards** or other locally elected officials.

The extent of policymaking authority enjoyed by each LEA or district is determined by the state's legislature, and this is a difference that can make a difference. In New England, for example, there is a long tradition

MARK RALSTON/AFP/Getty Images

In response to a series of mass shootings, tens of thousands of students across the country staged a walkout in 2018 to bring attention to the issue of gun violence on school campuses.

of strong local control. In contrast, legislatures in the Deep South have retained a more centralized state role. Even within states, there are huge differences in economies, traditions, and demographics that seep into differences in education. Think of rural, mountainous Northern California versus densely populated, arid Southern California. Northern Virginia, an affluent suburban area of Washington, D.C., tends to favor active government and is very different from Virginia's rural areas, in which folks tend to favor limited government.

Departments of education State-level agencies responsible for overseeing public education.

Teacher licensure procedures The processes states use to qualify teacher candidates to work in school districts; requirements for licensing typically include attainment of certain academic degrees, work experience, and adequate performance on adult standardized tests.

Accreditation A certification process in which outside experts visit a school or college to evaluate whether it is meeting minimum quality standards.

Local education agencies (LEAs) School districts, which may encompass cities, counties, or subsets thereof.

School districts Local administrative jurisdictions that hire staff and report to school boards on the management of area public schools.

School boards Elected or appointed bodies that determine major policies and budgets for school districts.

The degree of flexibility in education that states can give to localities depends greatly on scale. It also depends on how passionate local citizens are about participating in school governance. The nation's school districts are a patchwork quilt, the parts of which evolved as individually as the states themselves. Texas, for example, contains more than 1,000 school districts. These vary widely, from the liberal college town of Austin to the conservative business center of Dallas. Enrollment-wise, they range from the Adrian Independent School District, which in 2016 had a total enrollment of 120 students, to the Houston Independent School District, which had roughly 214,000.[8] In contrast, Hawaii has one school district covering the whole state, which in 2017 had about 168,000 students plus another 11,000 in independent charter schools.[9]

School boards are quintessentially U.S. democratic institutions that got their start in the Progressive Era at the end of the 19th century. These citizen boards were envisioned as a way to end the spoils system. Individuals would no longer be able to show partisan and political favor by awarding school jobs to their followers. This would make way for the shared pursuit of effective public education.

Looking back now, that promise seems quaint; various groups have long targeted school board elections to further special interests rather than the public interest. In Virginia, school board elections were actually abolished in the early 1950s because southern white traditionalists feared that too many candidates were sympathetic to the then-growing school desegregation movement. It was not until 1992 that elected members once again replaced appointed members. Political activists of various stripes have targeted school board elections as battlegrounds on issues ranging from school prayer, LGBT rights, and "intelligent design" to tax rates and curricular requirements.

Some critics say school boards actually produce fewer school improvements than they do campaign bumper stickers. That is one reason they were curbed by city governments during the 1990s in Boston, Chicago, Cleveland, and Detroit, and a little later in New York.[10] Faced with stagnating test scores and an exodus of families to private or parochial schools, urban leaders argued that emergency action to arrest the decline of the schools was more important than the democracy of a thousand voices.

The idea is that a centralized authority figure, such as a mayor or school chief, is more visible and thus

> Legend has it that a national education chief in Europe can look at a clock on any given weekday and know precisely which lesson is being taught in classrooms across the country at that moment.

more accountable than are low-profile school board members, who are often more worried about getting reelected than they are about making difficult decisions. Members appointed by an elected mayor are more likely to take decisive action and worry less about glad-handing, returning campaign favors, and seeking reelection. The jury is still out on such propositions, and proposals to abolish elected school boards tend to appear only in districts that are in dire straits.

To be fair, most school boards are genuinely focused on their responsibilities, but they often face formidable challenges. Keep in mind that by law a public school must accept all students who live within its jurisdiction. This makes planning tricky, because different student populations can have wildly differing needs, including accommodations for pupils who speak little English or have disabilities. Many school boards do not have taxing authority, but most prepare budgets for approval by the county board or city council, which must balance education spending against spending on police and fire protection and transportation. The board hires the superintendent, who hires the principals, who in turn hire the teachers.

Money Matters

Public education is funded almost exclusively by state and local governments; indeed, public education is by far the largest single category of spending for these governments. In 2015 (the latest data available), state and local governments spent roughly $650 billion on K–12 education.[11] State governments spend another $200 billion on higher education.[12] In contrast, the federal government kicks in roughly $100 billion at all education levels, roughly 10 percent of the total. All told, spending at all levels of government on all levels of education is somewhere in the region of a trillion dollars (that's a one followed by 12 zeros).

Public schools are funded from a variety of different revenue sources. Many states and localities raise school funds from income taxes and sales taxes. Twenty-seven states also earmark lottery funds for education, although the budgetary impact of this often controversial revenue source is debatable. While lotteries no doubt can provide funds to support public schools, those moneys tend to be a modest fraction of overall education budgets. Even when they do add significant dollars to public education budgets, they do not necessarily result in an equally significant increase in education spending. This is because state legislatures often view the "extra" money from lotteries as an opportunity to reallocate funds that otherwise would have been dedicated to education. In other words, the lottery funds often do not boost overall education budgets; they simply displace tax dollars that are sent elsewhere.[13]

While education is funded by a diverse revenue stream, there is no doubt that the biggest and often most controversial local source of school funds is local property taxes. These taxes are paid by homeowners and businesses based on the assessed value of their homes and businesses, usually a percentage of each $100 in assessed value.

There is logic to using property values as a basis for education funding. All taxpayers in a given community are believed to benefit from a high-quality school system—it helps maintain attractive real estate values and contributes to an educated workforce. And property taxes are progressive, meaning that homeowners whose property is worth more pay more in nominal amounts, although all pay the same percentage. Most mortgage companies inconspicuously collect these tax funds for homeowners. The money is then kept in the homeowners' personal escrow accounts until the taxes are due.

The downside of property taxes is that as property gains in value, the assessment and corresponding property taxes also rise—irrespective of whether the homeowner's income is rising along with the property value. This vicious circle is what fueled passage of California's famous Proposition 13 in 1978. As discussed in Chapter 3, this statewide ballot measure capped property taxes and ignited a tax revolt in other states.

An even deeper problem with funding schools through property taxes is that wealthier jurisdictions are able to keep such taxes at an attractively low percentage rate and still produce enough revenue dollars to support good schools. For example, in affluent Beverly Hills, California, property was—and still is—very expensive. Yet the tax rate cited in *Serrano v. Priest* (1971), a famous school-funding equity case, was only $2.38 per $100 in assessed

value. Place this up against the $5.48 per $100 in the low-income Baldwin Park area. There the schools were demonstrably inferior, and the community was able to spend only half the amount spent in Beverly Hills. The California Supreme Court agreed that families in Baldwin Park were being denied a "fundamental right" to good-quality schools.[14] The court ordered the legislature to find a way to make school funding more equitable.

VERMONT has the fewest enrolled public school students (76,102 in fall 2015). **CALIFORNIA** has the most (6,230,003).

A slightly different principle was spelled out by the U.S. Supreme Court in the 1973 ruling in *San Antonio Independent School District v. Rodriguez*. In this case, attorneys for a largely Mexican American population found that their clients were paying a tax rate 25 percent higher than that paid by people in nearby affluent school districts. These less affluent districts, however, were able or willing to fund schools with only 60 percent of the amount enjoyed by wealthy San Antonio neighborhoods. Here the Supreme Court acknowledged the disparities but ruled that equal school funding is not a federal constitutional right: "The Equal Protection Clause does not require absolute equality or precisely equal advantages," the justices wrote. Despite this ruling, the precedent was set. State courts began to see themselves as protectors of poor and rural students, and the movement for school funding equity at the state level gathered more steam.

These two cases launched a decades-long period of constitutional litigation on school funding that has spread to nearly every state and is still ongoing. It pits the principle of local control against pressures to close the gap between wealthy and poor districts. Jurists, educators, parents, and tax activists continue to fight about the key to school equity. Understandably, citizens in affluent districts like to see their tax dollars spent in their own communities, and they will lobby and push to keep their schools the best. Many middle-class and upper-class taxpayers say they paid extra for their homes so their children could attend schools that do not lack for essentials. Citizens in poor districts, by contrast, argue that dilapidated school buildings, meager resources, and teachers at the low end of the profession's already low pay scale are the chief reasons for the achievement gap between their children and those in wealthier districts. (See Map 13-1.) They assert that resources should be distributed among all districts in a way that ensures all students receive an essentially equitable level of education. Should individuals from less affluent areas be denied access to a good education? Must funneling more resources into disadvantaged communities require "penalizing" affluent communities? These questions have taken on even sharper political overtones in recent years as squeezed state budgets have pushed more of the education funding burden onto local school districts (see the box "States under Stress: How Much Should We Spend on Public Schools?").

The Pressure to Perform

Except in the minds of some nostalgists, it is doubtful there ever was a halcyon era of consensus among education's disparate stakeholders. For example, traditionalists who hark back to the classic education students received in the early 20th century seem to forget that in 1900, only 6 percent of children in the United States finished high school. Back then, the best that most could count on was a solid job in, say, manufacturing. For many, college wasn't an option.[15] The bottom line is that there are far too many views about the nation's public schools for all parties ever to agree that public education achieved some satisfactory level of quality at *any* point in time. Today's charge that schools are going to the proverbial hell in a handbasket has been a rallying call for education reformers going back to at least the 1940s and 1950s.

MAP 13-1 ● Spending per Student, Fiscal Year 2015

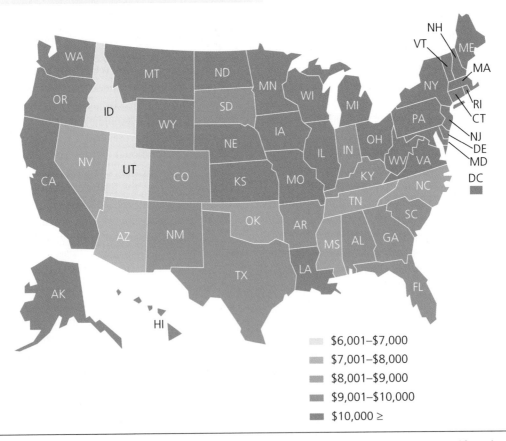

Legend:
- $6,001–$7,000
- $7,001–$8,000
- $8,001–$9,000
- $9,001–$10,000
- $10,000 ≥

Source: National Center for Education Statistics, "Current Expenditure per Pupil in Fall Enrollment in Public Elementary and Secondary Schools," Table 236.65, https://nces.ed.gov/programs/digest/d17/tables/dt17_236.65.asp?current=yes.

STATES UNDER STRESS

HOW MUCH SHOULD WE SPEND ON PUBLIC SCHOOLS?

What's the right amount to spend on public schools? There is, of course, no easy or universal answer to that question. There is an increasing consensus, however, that whatever the right number is, it has more zeros in it than the current one.

In many states, the real fight isn't even over spending more. It's about not spending less. Consider that, as of 2017, roughly half of the states were spending less per student in inflation-adjusted terms than they were in 2008. In other words, pretty much an entire school generation went through the K–12 experience with less—in some cases way less—access to resources than the previous generation.

There's no doubt the Great Recession of 2008–2009 was an economic catastrophe that hit public schools hard. There really was no avoiding it. Public education is the biggest chunk of most state budgets, and given the fiscal realities, public education took an unavoidable hit. The recession ended years ago, though, and the economy has recovered. But, in many states, education budgets did not. Why?

There's a number of answers. Economic recovery was simply slower in some states than others. In other states, though, the underfunding of education has been at least partially a deliberate policy choice rather than a lingering effect of a long-ago economic downturn. For example, following the end of the recession, some states like Oklahoma and Kansas cut taxes rather than spend more on schools. The hope was that this would act as an economic stimulus, and economic growth would eventually help school finances. That didn't happen. Government revenues simply shrank and put downward pressure on educational expenditures for a decade. That led to larger classes, cutting Advanced Placement (AP) and honors courses, and eliminating art programs. In Oklahoma, four-day school weeks were instituted as a cost-saving measure, and teachers did not receive a state-funded pay raise for a decade.

In 2018, teachers who had seen their incomes shrunk by inflation, their benefits cut, and their class sizes increased had finally had enough. Teachers in West Virginia went on strike, and walkouts in Oklahoma and Arizona followed. In response, state governments grudgingly started to loosen the purse strings, agreeing to increase teacher salaries and find a few more bucks for public schools. Even states where increasing taxes is traditionally a tough sell started to recognize the negative long-term consequences of underfunding education. In 2018, for example, Oklahoma passed a $450 million tax increase to boost education spending. That's a big deal—it's hardly the sort of tax-and-spend package typical for a conservative-leaning legislature where any tax increase needs a three-quarters majority to pass.

While those sorts of spending increases certainly help, it's far from clear that they can make up for a decade of nickel-grubbing parsimony. By kicking the can down the road for so long, governments simply made the underfunding problem bigger and bigger. Filling that hole is going to take a truckload of cash. For example, committing to spending that extra $450 million annually will certainly be enough to give teachers in Oklahoma a substantial pay increase. They'll likely still be earning less on average than their colleagues next door in Texas, though. And it's not like teachers in Texas are exactly rolling in dough—starting salaries there can be below $30,000 and average about $50,000.

And that's just salaries. Reducing class sizes and bringing back those AP and honors courses would mean hiring more teachers at those newly increased wage rates. Old textbooks need to be replaced, deferred maintenance caught up on, new technology purchased. That also costs money. Lots of it. There's a broad consensus that states will have to find more money to do this sort of stuff. But how much more? And who is going to foot the bill in the form of higher taxes? Those are tough questions that some states will likely be grappling with for the next ten years.

Source: Adapted from Liz Farmer, "Nation's Least-Funded Schools Get What They Pay For," *Governing*, June 2017.

These days, the most frequently cited evidence for public school underperformance consists of comparisons of standardized test scores. The claim is that test scores within the United States are falling, or at least not increasing, and/or that American students come out poorly in international comparisons of test performance. These charges are nothing new. In 1983, Reagan administration education secretary Dr. Terrel Bell published a high-profile and highly controversial report titled *A Nation at Risk*. It is worth pointing out that *A Nation at Risk* was a research

MAP 13-2 ● Student Enrollment in Public Schools by State, 2018

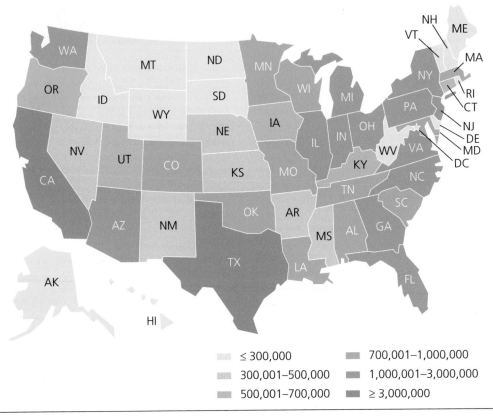

≤ 300,000	700,001–1,000,000
300,001–500,000	1,000,001–3,000,000
500,001–700,000	≥ 3,000,000

Source: National Center for Education Statistics, *Digest of Education Statistics* (Washington, DC: U.S. Department of Education), Table 203.20, "Enrollment in Public Elementary and Secondary Schools, by Region, State, and Jurisdiction: Selected Years, Fall 1990 through Fall 2027," https://nces.ed.gov/programs/digest/d17/tables/dt17_203.20.asp.

NEW YORK leads the states in total spending per pupil for elementary/secondary education, at $20,000 in 2016. **UTAH** spends about one-third as much.

report that employed the comparative method. It compared states on a wide variety of performance metrics in four broad areas (curriculum content, learning expectations, teaching, and time) and found that not many states fared well in these comparisons. When states were compared with other nations, they looked even worse. The publication of this comparative research report sparked an education reform movement that is still ongoing. In spite of all the resources and energy consumed by

this movement, the worry that public schools are not up to standard has not changed much at all. In 2008, the U.S. Department of Education published a 25-year follow-up to *A Nation at Risk*. Its big conclusion was this: "If we were 'at risk' in 1983, we are at even greater risk now."[16]

Traditionalists who hark back to the classic education students received in the early 20th century seem to forget that in 1900, only 6 percent of children in the United States finished high school. Back then, the best that most could count on was a solid job in, say, manufacturing. For many, college wasn't an option.

There are certainly some empirical reasons for the seemingly constant worry that the nation's public schools are failing. It is true that school test scores have been relatively stagnant for many years. It is hard to argue that a yawning achievement gap has not persisted between the preponderance of African American and Hispanic students at the lower end of the achievement scale and the frequently more affluent whites and Asian Americans near the top. Yet test scores are not locked into a downward spiral. There is a glass-half-full perspective to public education in America. Look at the nation's ever-replenishing supply of successful entrepreneurs. Look at the country's proliferation of Nobel Prize winners. Look at how American corporations continue to compete and succeed in the world economy. If public education plays a foundational role in supporting the economy and promoting new knowledge, America's schools must be doing something right. Americans seem to recognize this. In 2017, polls showed that half of Americans would give their local schools a letter grade of A or B, and more than 70 percent of parents give the schools their children attend an A or B. Yet only 24 percent of Americans gave schools nationally an A or B. In other words, when people look at the education institutions they are most familiar with—local schools—they clearly see them doing a pretty good job. Given all the bad news they hear about education, though, they also seem to think everyone else's schools must be in serious trouble.[17]

Measuring School Performance

How do you know if schools or teachers are doing a good job? How do you know if they are getting better? Come to that, what is it, exactly, that we want students to get out of schools? Basic numeracy and literacy? Broader skills and traits associated with being good citizens and involved community members? High levels of academic achievement? Vocational skills? What about athletics and the arts—should they figure in there somewhere too? If schools are expected to do all these things, how can you capture all of that in some sort of performance measure? Is a good school one that produces a lot of students who go to college, go on to get good jobs, earn a lot of money, and become community leaders, or students who become good moms, dads, and citizens? Or maybe schools are supposed to do all of that? Whatever schools are supposed to be doing, should we judge them not just on how well they do it but also on how equitably they impart those skills and traits

across different gender, racial, and economic groups? We seem to want schools to do everything from providing a decent meal to putting up a decent showing at the Friday-night football game, from teaching economically valuable skills to training well-rounded citizens. American society places a crushing set of expectations on schools. How do we measure whether they are doing an adequate job of accomplishing any or all of that?

There is no obvious answer to that question. Standardized test scores are, by far, the most common way school performance is measured. Yet it is not at all clear what standardized test scores tell us. There are huge controversies about whether test scores capture student and family traits rather than school or teacher performance. Some critics argue that standardized tests are biased against certain ethnic or cultural groups. Entire books have been written in an effort to parse what standardized tests do or do not say about schools and teachers.[18] If there is any scholarly consensus about what test scores tell us, it is that they probably tell us something about school performance, although what—and how much—is considerably narrower and smaller than policymakers frequently assume. Critics are increasingly bemoaning the trend of "teaching to the test," which skews classroom time toward the subjects covered on these tests—often at the expense of classes such as art and music. Public opinion polls suggest that less than half of Americans believe test scores say much about school quality.[19]

Despite this skepticism, public school students take a lot of standardized tests. Indeed, the sheer number and variety of standardized testing regimes can be mind-boggling. There are the broadly familiar exams like the Comprehensive Test of Basic Skills, the Iowa Assessments (formerly the Iowa Test of Basic Skills), the Stanford Achievement Test Series, and the most common college admission tests, the SAT and the ACT (originally the Scholastic Aptitude Test and the American College Test; controversies over what these tests measure led to a series of name changes that eventually left them being called just by their three-letter acronyms). States have also developed their own independent tests to assess whether students are meeting state curriculum standards. In the past few years, most states have adopted new standardized testing programs as part of the Common Core initiative (discussed in the next section). If anything, this stew of different testing regimes makes it harder to judge school and state educational performance. Not all states and schools use the same tests, so performance measures are not necessarily comparable, and even when the same tests are widely employed—the SAT and ACT are prime examples—they are not representative (this is because not all students take these tests, and those who do may not accurately reflect the academic performance of all students in their schools, districts, or states).

In an effort to provide some uniformity and continuity in testing, the federal government has administered its own test since 1969—the **National Assessment of Educational Progress (NAEP)**. Nicknamed "the nation's report card," it is administered in volunteer sample districts to students in Grades 4, 8, and 12. Over the years, NAEP scores have remained essentially flat, with subgroups' scores rising and falling. For example, between 1990 and 2015, scores on mathematics increased for 4th and 8th graders, but 12th graders showed no improvement. In reading, scores improved slightly for 4th and 8th graders between 1992 and 2015, but scores for 12th graders actually declined.[20]

Another key performance indicator coordinated by the U.S. Department of Education is the **Trends in International Mathematics and Science Study (TIMSS)**. Designed to compare the academic achievement of students in dozens of countries, the 2015 TIMSS (the latest for which data are available) found, for example, that the scores for U.S. 4th and 8th graders exceeded the TIMSS averages for both math and science. That's the good news. The bad news is that the United States just barely cracked the top 10 in these rankings.[21]

All this testing has provided reform advocates with plenty of ammunition—falling on the lower end of district, state, or national test comparisons is frequently presented as evidence of public education failure and justification for policy changes. Yet even if we assume that test scores are good measures of school performance—an assumption that is highly debatable—it is not clear what all this testing is telling us. For example, using TIMSS results to compare the performance of public schools in the United States to schools in other countries

is in a very real sense not a good use of the comparative method. Why? Well, other countries have national public education systems. The United States does not—it has 50 separate systems. In international comparisons, some states come off looking pretty good, while others lag behind. If we stick to comparing states to states, NAEP scores might give us a sense of which states are doing better than others, but those state averages cover up some huge variations. In the worst-performing states, there are still some schools with excellent test scores, and in the highest-performing states, there are test score laggards.

Test scores clearly have problems as educational performance measures. Are there any other options? Sure. High school graduation rates are also widely used as a performance measure. Graduation rates, however, have some inherent drawbacks as a comparative measure. Historically, the states have applied a patchwork of methods for determining these rates, and experts have long pointed out the temptation for districts and schools to calculate rates by simply subtracting the number of dropouts from the number of students collecting diplomas. That approach can result in misleading figures, because some dropouts transfer to other schools in a **general equivalency diploma (GED) program**, get their GEDs on their own, or are incarcerated.

It is often difficult to account for these missing students because they can be hard to track down. Furthermore, states and districts have little incentive to invest scarce resources to rectify such gaps in their accounting, because the poor performance of these students can contribute to the perception of "failure" on the part of the school or district. Unsurprisingly, few states spend the money required to perform longitudinal studies of the fates of such students. Some districts have even deliberately ignored these students in an effort to make their graduation rates look higher than they really are. Most famously, in 2003, city high schools in Houston, Texas, were found to be spectacularly underreporting dropout rates to appear to be performing better under the state's accountability plan. The officially reported citywide dropout rate was 1.5 percent, when in reality the rate was somewhere between 25 and 50 percent.[22]

For these reasons and others, graduation rates have historically not been comparable from state to state (or even year to year) and not fully reliable. The U.S. Department of Education has in recent years tried to provide some uniformity by adopting the Average Cohort Graduation Rate (ACGR) as the preferred measure. The

ACGR is the percentage of all first-time 9th graders (the "cohort") within a state in a given year who graduate four years later, with the numbers in the cohort adjusted to reflect students who transferred out or in. The ACGR for 2015–2016 (the latest data available) was 84 percent, which indicates that more than four out of five students who started high school four years earlier got a diploma. That average, though, reflects a lot of variation. The ACGR for New Mexico was 71 percent, 20 points behind Iowa, which had an ACGR of 91 percent. There are also huge differences in ACGR between racial groups. The ACGR for Asian students was 91 percent, closely followed by whites at 88 percent. The comparable figures for Hispanic students (79 percent) and black students (76 percent) were considerably lower.[23]

Even if all the measurement issues are cleared up, though, it is not at all clear graduation rates are any better than standardized test scores for measuring school performance. Graduation requirements and expectations can vary considerably from state to state, and even from school to school. Is a state or school with higher graduation standards and a lower graduation rate really doing a worse job than another state or school with lower standards and a higher graduation rate? There is no easy, obvious answer to that question. While lots of people agree that standardized testing is a far from perfect way to measure school performance, test scores continue to be the main yardstick used because alternatives like graduation rates are, at best, no better and arguably even worse.

Many Brands on the School Reform Shelf

Whatever the level of school performance, policymakers, teachers, parents, and students broadly believe that it could, and probably should, be better. Yet it is one thing to theorize about how to improve schools and quite another to implement real-world programs that get results. Decades of promising techniques—and sometimes utopian promises—have rotated through solutions that span **site-based management**, early-reading programs, and smaller class sizes, to name just a few. No consensus has materialized, only more debate. Still, the main schools of thought on school reform can be boiled down to those addressed in the sections below.

Standards and Accountability

The **standards movement** first drew attention at a 1989 education summit in Charlottesville, Virginia.

Attended by President George H. W. Bush and state governors, including future president Bill Clinton, the summit created a national panel to set and monitor education targets that would become Goals 2000, or the Educate America Act. That same year, the Kentucky Supreme Court struck down that state's entire education system, which prompted the enactment of the Kentucky Education Reform Act the following year.

CALIFORNIA had the largest number of public high school graduates in the 2014–2015 school year (452,530), while WYOMING had the fewest graduates (5,429).

This paved the way for the standards movement nationwide and opened the door for the strong—some might say excessive—focus on standardized testing discussed in the preceding section.

The premise of the standards movement was simple: define what students should be able to do at each grade in each subject, align tests to that content, and then evaluate students on those standards. Professional associations, starting with the National Council of Teachers of Mathematics, began producing grade-appropriate standards. As momentum built in the early 1990s, the Clinton administration worked to give the movement a national framework in its reauthorization of the **Elementary and Secondary Education Act (ESEA)**, originally passed in 1965. In 2002, the federal government passed the No Child Left Behind Act, which was largely a standards-based revision of ESEA. **No Child Left Behind (NCLB)** significantly ramped up federal involvement in public schools. It held schools

Site-based management A movement to increase freedom for building administrators such as school principals to determine how district funds are spent at individual schools.

Standards movement An effort to create benchmarks of adequate learning in each subject for each grade level so that students and teachers can be evaluated on the mastery of this predetermined material.

Elementary and Secondary Education Act (ESEA) Federal law passed in 1965 as part of President Johnson's Great Society initiative; steered federal funds to improve local schools, particularly those attended primarily by low-income and minority students.

No Child Left Behind Act (NCLB) Federal law enacted in January 2002 that introduced new accountability measures for elementary and secondary schools in all states receiving federal education aid.

accountable for academic progress, required standardized testing to measure that progress, and required states to set benchmarks on achievement. From its inception, the NCLB was controversial. It proved expensive to implement and tricky to administer. Critics charged the law with setting unrealistic standards and representing an unwarranted intrusion in Tenth Amendment territory by the federal government. Bipartisan opposition to NCLB became so strong that in 2015 Congress passed the Every Student Succeeds Act. This effectively killed the NCLB initiative, backing the federal government away from regulating public schools and clearing the way for states to take the lead on education reform.

Standards-based reform efforts at the state level were percolating at the state level for a number of years prior to the Every Student Succeeds Act. As early as summer 2002, 47 states not only had formulated standards criteria but also were issuing "report cards" on student achievement. Not quite half were breaking the data down by racial subgroups, level of income, and/or English-language proficiency. Among teachers, according to an *Education Week* survey, 8 in 10 reported that their curricula were now more demanding; 6 out of 10 said their students were writing more.

The state-level standards movement reached something of a threshold in 2009 with the beginning of a coordinated effort by states to formulate a uniform, national set of academic standards. This effort, known as the **Common Core State Standards (CCSS)**, was backed by the National Governors Association and the Council of Chief State School Officers. The basic objective was to develop a consistent, rigorous set of standards aligned with the academic skill sets students need to get good jobs or pursue higher-education opportunities.[24] The hope was that the CCSS would provide a consistent and uniform framework that would replace the often-idiosyncratic academic standards and testing programs states were then using. As of 2018, 41 states and the District of Columbia had voluntarily adopted and implemented the CCSS, which at least in theory set a common set of achievement expectations in English and mathematics across most of the nation. It's important to note that the Common Core does not set a standard curriculum; it is designed to establish basic benchmarks for what students are expected to learn regardless of what curricular patterns and specifics their schools or states require.[25]

As with the other standards initiatives like NCLB, the Common Core has encountered a strong political backlash. Critics argue that there is little evidence of what the CCSS can or cannot do to improve education and that such a massive reform of curricula in schools should not be undertaken in the absence of proof that it will actually work. Others do not like the one-size-fits-all approach embraced by the CCSS—they want states to remain free to do whatever they decide is best. Some

AP Photo/David Zalubowski

School reform efforts have brought a new focus on test scores as proof of student improvement and achievement. Standardized tests have become common nationwide, and students increasingly must pass exams to advance in grade or to graduate.

....

Common Core State Standards (CCSS) An education initiative that has created a uniform set of learning expectations in English and math for students at the end of each grade. Although participation is voluntary, most states have joined this initiative.

parents have been alarmed to discover that some students who were earning good grades did poorly on the new standardized tests. Others have been suspicious of some of the new approaches to old subjects that came with the CCSS or have been worried about the retooling teachers had to go through to teach the new curricula. Some have been concerned about the growing clout of the companies that produce the tests and about the administrative bungling in the implementation of the CCSS (e.g., many states adopted the new standards without updating high school graduation requirements that did not comply with them). Some state governments, even those initially supportive, have cooled on the CCSS. Some suspect the federal government might use the Common Core as a stalking horse, stepping in at some future point to nationalize the initiative and exert greater centralized control over public education. A number of states, including Arizona, Florida, and New Jersey, repealed participation in the CCSS, and other states that have adopted the Common Core have made significant revisions in how they implement it. Minnesota, for example, adopted the English standards part of the CCSS, but rejected the math standards.

Recruiting Good Teachers

Research has demonstrated that the single most important factor in student learning—more important than curriculum, family income, student health, or parental involvement—is good teaching.[26] Economists have even quantified the effect, estimating that the best teachers give their students an extra year's worth of learning and perhaps increase their standardized test scores by 50 points.[27] Such gains are seen particularly with minority students, many of whom enter school with social or economic disadvantages.

While the importance of teachers is recognized, finding qualified teachers and holding on to them can be a problem for schools. This problem is particularly pronounced in high-poverty schools, which tend to suffer from heavy staff turnover. More generally, there are notable shortages of teachers in certain subject areas, including special education, mathematics, science, bilingual education, and technology, and in some states these shortages can be acute. For example, in the 2017–2018 school year, Oklahoma had teacher shortages in 17 subject areas, ranging from computer science and math to art and music.[28] In 2018, teacher shortages were so acute in some areas that states were lowering licensure requirements and issuing hundreds, or even thousands,

of emergency teaching credentials just to get instructors into the classroom.[29] According to a U.S. Department of Education study, more than a quarter of middle school English, mathematics, and science classes are taught by instructors with either college majors or certification in the subject areas they are teaching.[30]

There are at least two reasons for this shortage of teachers. First, fewer people are choosing to go into primary and secondary education as a career. These days, less than 5 percent of college freshmen say they intend to major in education. That's less than half the typical proportion of incoming college students saying they are headed toward becoming grade school teachers over the past 45 years.[31] The second reason is that even those who do go into teaching often leave. All told, roughly 13 percent of teachers leave the profession every year, a loss of expertise and human capital that costs states and schools districts an estimated $2.2 billion a year.[32] With low pay and increasingly challenging working conditions, teaching is simply a less attractive career option than it used to be.

Choosing Wisely: Alternatives to Public Schools

For several decades, reformers have been pushing for alternatives to traditional public schools. The proposed alternatives include everything from charter schools to voucher programs to the abandonment of the public education system entirely for homeschooling. Collectively known as school choice, these alternatives account for a relatively small fraction of students. For example, less than 4 percent of students are homeschooled, and about 5 percent attend charter schools. That still adds up to a lot of students—4 or 5 million.[33] In 2017, advocates of the school choice movement got a considerable boost from the administration of President Donald Trump. Trump appointed Betsy DeVos, a longtime champion of school choice, to head the U.S. Department of Education. DeVos's nomination was controversial. She had no hands-on experience in educational administration, had difficulty answering some basic policy questions at her Senate confirmation hearing, and attracted a good deal of bipartisan opposition. Her confirmation vote was 50–50 in the Senate, requiring Vice President Mike Pence to cast a tiebreaking vote, putting her in charge of the federal education agency by the narrowest of margins. Despite this opposition, it meant for the first

POLICY IN PRACTICE
THE RISING COST OF SCHOOL SHOOTINGS

School shootings are one of the most high-profile and alarming issues facing education officials. In the spring semester of 2018, school shootings were occurring at the rate of about one per week. Notably, 17 students and staff members were gunned down in Parkland, Florida, and another 10 lost their lives in Santa Fe, Texas. The problem extends far beyond the multi-fatality incidents that make national news. According to one estimate, in the past two decades, more than 200,000 students at more than 200 schools have experienced gun violence in some form within the United States. Disturbingly, the number of school shootings seems to have ticked upward in the past half-decade or so. These events inflict lasting pain on a community. They also can create significant financial burdens for schools and state governments.

Connecticut spent $50 million rebuilding Sandy Hook Elementary School after a shooting spree that left 26 dead in 2012. The total cost of the 1999 Columbine High School shooting in Littleton, Colorado, has been estimated at a similar amount. Parkland plans on tearing down and rebuilding the part of the school where the shootings occurred, and the Florida state government helped pay for funeral costs. Litigation, victim compensation, funeral expenses, trauma counseling, new security measures—these costs can be enough to overwhelm a government. And this doesn't touch the psychological and reputational costs to the communities where these shootings occur.

This helps explain why more school districts are considering shelling out for insurance policies that will help cover the financial burdens of dealing with a school shooting. While there are no firm numbers, some insurance companies report that inquiries about these sorts of policies jumped dramatically during 2018. Those policies don't come cheap, and many school districts are already strapped for extra cash.

Those policies, however, can be a financial lifesaver if the unthinkable happens. They help cover medical expenses, liability costs associated with lawsuits, and even extra security. This is why after every mass shooting insurance brokers are fielding more calls from schools and government agencies. As Paul Marshall, a broker for a large insurance underwriting firm, put it, "People just feel vulnerable . . . that's when we get phone calls, because it feels inevitable and very difficult to handle."

Source: Adapted from Natalie Delgadillo, "With Active Shootings on the Rise, Schools Turn to 'Active Shooter' Insurance," *Governing*, June 2018, http://www.governing.com/topics/education/gov-cost-of-active-shooters-insurance.html.

---

time an avowed champion of school choice—her critics would claim a firm opponent of public schools—was in charge of the national government's education policy.

Charter Schools

Entrepreneurs who want to launch their own schools with public money have been applying to run **charter schools** since the early 1990s. These schools reflect less an educational philosophy than a variation on school governance. Charter schools range in theme from Montessori to the fact-based niche curriculum called Core Knowledge to ranching to online (distance) learning. Sponsors have included former public and private school principals, parent groups, universities, social service agencies, and nonprofits such as the YMCA. In 2017, there were an estimated 6,700 charter schools in the United States, with more than 3 million students enrolled.[34]

In principle, students who attend charter schools are given the same per-pupil expenditure as are students in mainstream schools, although the founders often must scrounge to find facilities. The willingness of a state to encourage the establishment of charter schools depends on the condition of its public schools and the energies of would-be charter school founders. Some states set up special chartering boards, whereas others allow local school boards to approve the applications.

State charter laws vary widely. Arizona's loose regulations allow any public body, private organization, or private person to open a charter school, and guarantee base-level funding from the state, plus a range of

Charter schools Public schools, often with unique themes, managed by teachers, principals, social workers, or nonprofit groups. The charter school movement was launched in the early 1990s.

results-based financial incentives. Other states only allow nonprofits, institutions of higher education, or groups that include some combination of parents and licensed teachers to open charter schools. They may also put tighter restrictions on how charters are funded. In Kansas, for example, it is up to the local school district to decide how charter schools are funded.[35]

Backers see charter schools as laboratories of innovation that bypass staid bureaucracies and satisfy the parental desire for choice. Evidence of the academic achievement of charter schools is mixed. Some schools have been forced to close because of corruption, such as embezzlement by administrators, or because they have failed to attract enough students or to maintain physical facilities. In one high-profile case, California's largest charter school operator announced in August 2004 that it would be closing at least 60 campuses amid an investigation into its academic and financial practices, leaving 10,000 students stranded just weeks before the start of the school year.[36] In addition, critics worry that charter schools will balkanize public education and that states may exploit them as a way to avoid dealing with unionized teachers. Some observers fear that these schools may present administrative headaches to those school superintendents charged with monitoring them to prevent abuses of funds. Critics of charter schools also worry that they have the potential to drain funding from traditional schools—every student who walks out the door of a traditional public school to a charter school takes taxpayer dollars with him or her.

To determine whether particular charter school models should be scaled up and duplicated throughout the country, researchers do not just want to know whether a charter's own students' test scores improve; they want to know if the schools these children's families chose to leave are using the departures as an incentive to do better.[37] To that end, numerous studies have been carried out. The results generally suggest charters have achieved mixed results, sometimes doing a bit better on various performance and outcome measures

than traditional schools, and sometimes a bit worse.[38] In short, while some charter schools have done well, as a whole they have not provided the clear and comprehensive improvement over the public school status quo their advocates hoped for.

Vouchers

School vouchers are a more radical reform than charter schools. The idea of the **school voucher movement**, which has existed in one form or another since the 1950s, is simple: rather than give money to schools, governments give families public grants (vouchers) that they can use to enroll their children at any accredited schools—not just public schools but also private and parochial (religious) schools. Supporters argue that voucher programs create real markets for educational services, providing parents with real choices and breaking up the "monopoly" of public education bureaucracy. The goal is that the competitive market forces

Mark Wilson/Getty Images

▲
A range of alternatives to traditional public school arrangements have been proposed, including school vouchers and charter schools. U.S. secretary of education Betsy DeVos has been a strong supporter of these alternatives.

....

School voucher movement A movement, dating back to the 1950s, to allow taxpayer dollars to be given to families for use at whatever public, private, or parochial schools they choose.

will force schools to innovate and respond to consumer demand or face going out of business. In recent years, many have also advanced the argument that vouchers serve a civil rights function, in that they can rescue low-income black families from failing schools in low-income neighborhoods.

Opponents worry that vouchers spell the beginning of the end of society-wide efforts to maintain and improve universal public education. They note that private schools can be selective about which students they accept. In addition, the proposed amounts for vouchers are often less than half the actual tuition charges at many schools. In some communities, the number of available slots at area private schools is insufficient for the number of interested applicants. Voucher proponents aren't without counterarguments, however. They assert that the programs create competition that forces public schools to improve, and that they give lower-income students opportunities they might not otherwise have.[39]

Critics also object to the widespread participation of religious schools in voucher programs. Many are uncomfortable with the idea that, through vouchers, taxpayer funds go to institutions that support the inculcation of particular sets of religious beliefs. Despite these concerns, in June 2002, the U.S. Supreme Court ruled that vouchers can go to a religious school as long as the school's chief purpose is education—in other words, a school that offers a comprehensive secular curriculum, albeit with religious rituals and instructors, as opposed to a Sunday school or Bible study school.

Generally speaking, vouchers tend to have less political support than charters. For example, many states have voted on voucher-related ballot initiatives, and the majority of these have been defeated by considerable margins. Despite mixed political support, some voucher programs have been in place for decades. Probably the two best known are programs that, at least initially, were aimed at long-troubled and racially isolated schools in Cleveland, Ohio, and Milwaukee, Wisconsin. Cleveland's voucher program was folded into Ohio EdChoice, a statewide voucher program, in 2006. EdChoice offers up to 60,000 renewable scholarships to students attending schools considered in "academic emergency" or on "academic watch," the state's two lowest rankings for school performance.[40]

Milwaukee's program offers vouchers to low-income families (family income may not exceed 300 percent of the federal poverty level). These vouchers can be used to enroll students in more than 100 private schools that participate in the program. The program included only secular schools when it started, but in 1995, it expanded to include parochial schools, a measure protected by the 2002 Supreme Court ruling. Currently, more than two-thirds of the schools in the program are religiously affiliated. In 2017–2018, there were roughly 28,700 students participating in this program, and the average value of the voucher received by each student was $7,503.[41] Whether students who use vouchers experience achievement gains is a matter of fairly intense debate. Dozens—likely hundreds—of studies have produced mixed evidence. Studies backed by advocacy groups, unsurprisingly, have found significant gains for voucher students.[42] More academic studies have a much more mixed record, with some showing significant gains and others showing no impact. A 2012 study of the Milwaukee school choice program, for example, found that voucher students have slightly higher reading test scores than do comparable nonvoucher students but found no differences in math test scores between these groups.[43] Generally speaking, the weight of evidence from the nearly three-decade experiment in Milwaukee shows that in terms of academic achievement, voucher programs produce little improvement over traditional public schools.[44]

Homeschooling

A major school reform movement gaining popularity is **homeschooling**. In 1999, according to a survey by the U.S. Department of Education, an estimated 850,000 students were being taught at home. By 2012, that number had jumped to more than 1.7 million.[45]

As the movement has grown, homeschooling parents have organized sports leagues, field trips, proms, and graduation ceremonies. Supporters of homeschooling have even organized a legal defense network and a sophisticated lobbying effort. And there are plenty of homeschooling success stories, including Harvard acceptances and solid scores on standardized tests.

Homeschooling advocates are a diverse group, but the two main strands are fundamentalist Christians and "free school" advocates who favor more student choice of subject matter. Parents who can make the time to homeschool like the security and the personal imprint they can leave on their youngsters. A study by

Homeschooling The education of children in the home; a movement to grant waivers from state truancy laws to permit parents to teach their own children.

the National Center for Education Statistics found that 30 percent of homeschooling parents surveyed wanted the flexibility to teach their children moral or religious lessons. Another 31 percent cited concerns about the environment of traditional schools.[46]

Of course, throughout the history of this country, there always have been those who have chosen to teach their children at home. The modern homeschooling movement, however, really started taking off in the 1980s. State governments have accommodated home-schoolers to varying degrees. Some require a parent to have a bachelor's degree to homeschool. Others require parents to submit their curricula for approval, and still others give parents the choice of having their children take standardized tests selected by the school district or hiring their own qualified evaluators.[47]

Critics fear that homeschooled students miss important opportunities for social development and that many parents are not qualified to teach. They also worry that some homeschooling parents isolate their children and instill in them religious prejudice. Some state and local officials consider homeschooling an inconvenience because it forces them to come up with policies on home visits, gauge assessments that may be out of sync with conventional report-card grades, and wrestle with dilemmas such as whether a homeschooled student can play in the public high school band.

Can't Tell the Players without a Program: Groups That Influence Public Education

Public education is consistently at the top of state government policy agendas. Budgetary commitments alone are enough to keep education on policymakers' radar, but the incessant scrutiny of education by state and local governments is driven by a lot more than budgets. Everyone has a stake in public education, not just parents and students. Public schools provide the basic educational foundation for future ditch diggers as well as future doctors, and how well public schools do this job plays a massive role in the social, economic, and political health of communities, states, and the nation. It is little wonder that education attracts so much attention.

Similarly, it is not surprising that a range of interest groups have a stake in defending the education status quo or advocating radical change. Here is a roster of the most familiar players in the education dramas that unfold across the country.

Teachers' Unions

For decades, the major **teachers' unions** have been the National Education Association (NEA), which boasts 3 million members, and the American Federation of Teachers (AFT), with about 1.7 million members.[48] These groups organize teachers from the preschool level through K–12 to the university level, forming state and local affiliates. They engage in collective bargaining, lobby for resources, and seek to upgrade teacher professionalism through training and publications.

For years, these two unions, both headquartered in Washington, D.C., have flirted with a merger, but style differences always intervene. The AFT was quicker than the NEA to join the school reform parade, for example, by participating in the creation of standards and charter schools. By the late 1990s, however, both organizations had soured on the school choice movement, which they consider a threat to public education and their members' livelihoods. Both were also critical of NCLB, with the NEA leading the charge in lawsuits challenging the federal government's administration of the law. Teachers' unions have provided mixed support for the Common Core initiative. Both the AFT and the NEA were initially supportive of the intent of the CCSS, but this enthusiasm has cooled somewhat as implementation and political challenges have surfaced. Regardless of their specific policy stands, both unions align themselves with the Democratic Party—one reason most Republicans blame them for obstructing school reform.

Parent Groups

The **National PTA**, with millions of members, bills itself as "a powerful voice for all children . . . and a strong advocate for public education."[49] For decades, this umbrella group for local parent–teacher associations and organizations was stereotyped as a klatch of moms putting on bake sales. Today, however, the PTA has school-based state and national organizations that combine to form a sophisticated lobbying and policy force. For the most part, the organization works to boost parent involvement and to encourage parent–teacher cooperation.

....

Teachers' unions Public-sector unions that organize employees at all educational levels to form state and local affiliates. In the United States, the two major teachers' unions are the National Education Association and the American Federation of Teachers, both headquartered in Washington, D.C.

National PTA An umbrella organization founded in 1897 consisting of state-based and school-based parent–teacher associations of volunteers who work to improve and support schools.

The National PTA has strict rules about remaining nonpartisan. Despite this, local PTAs' occasional endorsements of state legislative candidates based on school funding commitments have gotten some in hot water. Other parent groups have emerged over the years to focus on narrower school-related issues, such as the school desegregation efforts of the Mississippi-based Parents for Public Schools.

National Political Parties

For much of the latter part of the 20th century, education was Democratic Party turf, at least on the national level. This was because Democrats traditionally wanted to expand government spending to close the gap between affluent and low-income schools. Republicans, on the other hand, emphasized local control and social issues, such as efforts to overturn the ban on school prayer. During the Reagan administration, Republicans vowed to abolish the federal Department of Education set up by President Carter. Many of them opposed proposals made during the mid-1990s to introduce a national standardized test. They based their protests on the need to preserve local control of schools.

President George W. Bush moved the Republicans dramatically to the center of the education debate with NCLB. NCLB was modeled in part on the system used since the early 1990s in Texas, borrowed its name from the liberal Children's Defense Fund, and received critical support from key Democratic lawmakers. The bipartisanship and general optimism over Bush's signature domestic achievement, however, dissolved because of inter- and intraparty disappointments regarding how NCLB was implemented (see the discussion above). While support for NCLB was collapsing across the partisan spectrum, bipartisan enthusiasm reappeared for the Every Student Succeeds Act, the legislation that pulled the federal government away from the trajectory it had been on and toward tighter regulation of public schools (the bill passed in the House on a vote of 359–64, and the vote in the Senate was 85–12). Mostly what this did, however, was move partisan battles from Washington, D.C., to the states, where battles over the Common Core have sometimes been fought along party lines, with conservative Republicans generally leading the fight against the CCSS and more liberal Democrats supporting the initiative.

While education is one of the few policy areas where Republicans and Democrats have, at least sometimes, worked in bipartisan accord over the past decade or so, there are still clear differences between the parties in their approaches to education. For example, the Grand Old Party (GOP) tends to be much more supportive of school vouchers than are Democrats, due to the strong support that Democrats depend on from anti-voucher teachers' unions and the Democrats' general skepticism about market-based alternatives to government programs.

Business Groups

Corporations and small businesses have been among the most vocal organizations pushing for school reform. They cite what they perceive as a decline in the writing and math skills of young job applicants as industry has become more complex technologically. The Gates Foundation, Microsoft founder Bill Gates's philanthropic organization, played a key role in funding and spearheading development of the Common Core initiative, and business-affiliated groups such as the U.S. Chamber of Commerce have also been strong supporters. Businesses view themselves as having a critical stake in public schools, which are responsible for ensuring that students master certain basic skills that businesses need their current and future employees to have.

Professional and Advocacy Groups

Within the education "establishment," each of the managerial groups—administrators, principals at the elementary and secondary levels, and school boards—has its own association. The official decision makers in these groups usually win their jobs through prerequisite sets of academic credentials, years of experience in the classroom, and dues paid on the front lines of management.

Also influencing public education are research groups such as the Education Trust, which is based in Washington, D.C., and performs research to encourage those in higher education to help with elementary and secondary school reforms. And then there are the advocacy groups, such as the Center for Education Reform, which promotes school choice, and the Network for Public Education, which seeks to preserve and promote traditional public schools.

Conclusion

Be it NCLB, CCSS, or whatever acronym describes the next big initiative, there is little doubt that efforts to reform public education will remain a central part of both state and federal policy agendas. There is also little doubt that controversy will swirl around the federal role in public education whenever it bumps into the centuries-old tradition of state and local control. Advocates of increased funding targeting the poor will still lock horns with those who stress reforms in pedagogy and new incentives. The ongoing battles over the Common Core initiative are just the latest chapter in a very long story of reform.

That story seems unlikely to conclude with a happily-ever-after ending anytime soon. The governance of the U.S. public education system is rooted in local control and wide variations in state and community traditions. This guarantees that it always will be characterized by diverse approaches and active political maneuvering. The quest for the ideal school continues to be more art than science. The results? They are as glorious—and as messy—as democracy itself.

THE LATEST RESEARCH

Education is such a sprawling, perennially high-profile topic that it should come as no surprise that a very large research industry is devoted to examining its every dimension and nuance. Many political scientists, economists, and sociologists study education issues, as do many more researchers from exclusively education-based disciplines, such as educational psychology—not to mention the large number of scholars in university teaching colleges and departments who not only train educators but also conduct studies on everything from curricular development to best practices in educational administration. Entire academic journals are devoted to research in education (e.g., *American Journal of Education*, *American Educational Research Journal*). Given this, it is all but impossible for us to summarize here anything but a narrow slice of the latest education research.

That said, one of the more interesting developments in the latest research is an ongoing examination of the effectiveness of many of the key reform initiatives discussed in this chapter, especially the standards and accountability movement and the expansion of school choice. For decades, dueling studies have claimed to provide evidence to support or contradict assertions of the efficacy of such reforms. While a lot of that continues, over the past half-decade or so, scholars have been increasingly paying attention to what the mixed messages of all this research mean. Do the inconsistent reports on the efficacy, or lack thereof, of these reforms mean that the evidence on the impacts is not clear, even though some of the reforms have been in place for decades? Does it mean that the studies are, consciously or unconsciously, being conducted to serve political agendas rather than to get at objective assessments of what works and what does not? Are the

studies' results simply being cherry-picked by key players in the reform debate who ignore contradicting evidence and the often careful caveats that study authors place on the interpretation of their findings? Given the high stakes involved for state governments, which have often invested heavily in these reforms, these are important questions. Below we discuss some representative research looking hard for answers, especially in trying to understand the actual payoffs of charter schools, which have been touted in many states and on both sides of the aisle in the federal government as effective alternatives to traditional public schools.

- **Berends, Mark**, "Sociology and School Choice: What We Know after Two Decades of Charter Schools," *Annual Review of Sociology* 41 (2015): 159–180.

This is a review of two decades' worth of academic studies on school choice and charter schools in particular. It explains what charter schools are and why various scholars and reform advocates expect them to do different things than traditional public schools. In terms of academic performance and educational attainment, the results are clearly mixed. Charter schools have scored some performance successes, notably in urban areas where achievement levels have been low and education reforms have historically been ineffective. Other research, however, raises questions about any positive impact of charters on achievement. A reasonable conclusion is there may be some overall positive gains, but these are almost certainly pretty small. Though the evidence is again mixed, the key area where charter schools do seem to have an edge on comparable traditional schools is in improving graduation rates.

(Continued)

(Continued)

- **Shober, Arnold F.**, *In Common No More: The Politics of the Common Core State Standards* (Santa Barbara, CA: Praeger, 2016).

Shober is a political scientist who studies the politics of education. In this book, he traces the political history of the CCSS. As he details, in some ways the trajectory of the whole Common Core initiative has been a case of history repeating itself. The initiative's aims are broadly supported across the political spectrum, and it initially gathered enthusiastic bipartisan support, with backing from business groups as well as teachers. And then it ran into the political fault lines that have long bedeviled education reform—the role of the federal government in education policy, the desire of states to protect their prerogative to go their own way, the inevitable disagreements that happen when good theory meets the vexing problems of implementation. These are the sorts of political questions that have ensnared the CCSS: Will it lead to a loss of local control? Constrain the ability of teachers to do what they think best for their students? Denigrate training in arts, humanities, and citizenship and evolve into a taxpayer-supported appendage of business interests? Tear down the status quo at great financial and political cost for little gain in school performance? That these sorts of questions would create troubles for the initiative was in many ways predictable. They are, in one form or another, the same questions that have created controversy for most other education reforms of the past half-century.

- **Clark, Melissa A., Philip M. Gleason, Christina Clark Tuttle, and Marsha K. Silverberg**, "Do Charter Schools Improve Student Achievement?," *Educational Evaluation and Policy Analysis* 37, no. 4 (2015): 419–436.

This article seeks to provide just the sort of reliable, empirical-based analysis that many education policy experts are calling for. This team of researchers examines the impact of 33 charter schools in 13 states. A key aspect of this research is that admission to the middle school charters included in the study was based on a lottery, so students were randomly selected to attend, or not to attend, a charter school. This created a naturally occurring experiment that allowed any achievement differences between students attributable to charter schools to be statistically isolated. The results were, at best, mixed. Some charter schools were associated with more positive achievement outcomes than more traditional schools, while other charters were associated with more negative outcomes. Overall, the average effect of charter schools on achievement was negative, though not statistically significant. In other words, no real overall achievement differences could be found between charter schools and their more traditional counterparts.

CHAPTER 13

for CQ Press

Want a better grade?

Get the tools you need to sharpen your study skills. SAGE edge offers a robust online environment featuring an impressive array of free tools and resources.

Access practice quizzes, eFlashcards, video, and multimedia at **edge.sagepub.com/ smithgreenblatt7e**

Top Ten Takeaways

1. Education is broadly viewed as critically important to the economic and social success of individuals, communities, states, and the nation. As such, there is a broad consensus in the United States that education reform is an effective way to address a wide range of social and economic problems.

2. Education has traditionally been within the policy jurisdiction of states and localities. A series of federal initiatives over the past half-century, however, have increased the federal government's role in regulating education.

3. Greater federal government involvement in education has created a good deal of political conflict, as states and localities have pushed back against attempts by Congress to increase the federal role in education.

4. Despite greater federal government policy activity, control over public education remains primarily in the hands of states and localities. Education is the single largest functional expenditure of state budgets, and states and localities provide roughly 90 percent of the funding for public K–12 schools.

5. Equity in funding across school districts is a subject of long-running political controversy. Locally, schools are funded mainly by property taxes, meaning wealthier communities can afford to spend more on education. State funding seeks to even out these inequities, but big differences in per-pupil spending can occur even between neighboring school districts.

6. There is widespread agreement that public schools could be doing better, and education reform efforts are constantly trying to improve schools' performance.

    Yet it is not clear how to measure performance. School performance is gauged primarily through comparisons of standardized test scores, but different tests are not comparable, and they may say more about the traits of students than about the job schools are doing.

7. One of the dominant education reform initiatives of recent years is the Common Core State Standards. The implementation of the CCSS was supported by the federal government, but it is primarily a project of state governments working cooperatively together. The basic idea of the CCSS is to create a set of rigorous, uniform standards for achievement in areas such as English and math that will be common across all states.

8. There is a nationwide problem with recruiting and retaining teachers. While there is a good deal of variation in the extent of this problem across states and school districts, low pay and challenging working conditions are among the reasons that more than 10 percent of teachers leave the profession every year.

9. There is a well-established movement to create alternatives to traditional public schools. Broadly known as school choice, these alternatives include charter schools, voucher programs, and homeschooling. Research on the effectiveness of these alternatives has produced mixed findings, with traditional public schools generally doing at least as well on test score–based measures of achievement and performance.

10. Given the high social, political, and economic stakes, a wide range of organized interest groups participate in education reform politics. These include groups representing parents and teachers, as well as business and professional groups.

Key Concepts

accreditation (p. 367)
back to basics (p. 366)
charter schools (p. 378)
Common Core State
    Standards (CCSS)
    (p. 376)
common school (p. 365)
departments of education
    (p. 367)
Elementary and Secondary
    Education Act (ESEA)
    (p. 375)
general equivalency diploma
    (GED) program (p. 374)

high-stakes standardized
    testing (p. 366)
homeschooling
    (p. 380)
local education agencies
    (LEAs) (p. 367)
National Assessment of
    Educational Progress
    (NAEP) (p. 374)
National PTA (p. 381)
No Child Left Behind Act
    (NCLB) (p. 375)
school boards (p. 367)
school districts (p. 367)

school voucher movement
    (p. 379)
site-based management
    (p. 375)
standards (p. 366)
standards movement (p. 375)
state board of education
    (p. 366)
teacher licensure procedures
    (p. 367)
teachers' unions (p. 381)
Trends in International
    Mathematics and Science
    Study (TIMSS) (p. 374)

Suggested Websites

- **www.aasa.org.** Website of AASA, The School Superintendents Association. Founded in 1865, AASA has more than 13,000 members worldwide. Its mission is to support and develop individuals dedicated to the highest-quality public education for all children.

- **www.aft.org.** Website of the American Federation of Teachers, which represents the economic, social, and professional interests of classroom teachers. The AFT has more than 3,000 local affiliates nationwide, 43 state affiliates, and more than 1.3 million members.

- **www.cep-dc.org.** Website of the Center on Education Policy, a national independent advocate for more effective public schools.

- **www.ed.gov.** Website of the U.S. Department of Education, which oversees the federal government's contributions to public education.

- **www.edexcellence.net.** Website of the Thomas B. Fordham Institute, whose mission is to advance the understanding and acceptance of effective reform strategies in primary and secondary education.

- **www.edreform.com.** Website of the Center for Education Reform, a national organization dedicated to the promotion of more choices in education and more rigorous education programs.

- **www.edweek.org.** Website of *Education Week*, a weekly publication devoted to primary and secondary education and funded by Editorial Projects in Education. *Education Week* publishes *Quality Counts*, an annual evaluation of K–12 education in all 50 states.

- **www.nationsreportcard.gov.** Website of the National Assessment of Educational Progress, the program that administers standardized tests to students in Grades 4, 8, and 12 across the United States.

- **www.nea.org.** Website of the National Education Association, which is dedicated to advancing public education. The organization has 2.8 million members across every level of education, from preschool to university graduate programs, and affiliates in every state, as well as in more than 13,000 local communities across the United States.

- **www.nsba.org.** Website of the National School Boards Association, a not-for-profit federation of state associations of school boards across the United States.

Michael Nigro/Pacific Press/LightRocket via Getty Images

Crime and Punishment

In March 2016, thousands of protesters took to the streets of Cleveland, following the decision by a grand jury not to indict two police officers who had shot and killed 12-year-old Tamir Rice, less than two seconds after arriving at the park where Rice was playing with a toy gun. Protests against police sometimes turn violent and are met with massive demonstrations of force from law enforcement.

Chapter Objectives

After reading this chapter, you will be able to

- Outline the basic operations of the criminal justice system,

- Describe the origins and legacies of the American penal and policing systems,

- Assess critiques of the criminal justice system made by both conservatives and liberals, and

- Discuss contemporary issues and debates on crime and punishment.

The election of Donald Trump looked like it would end momentum toward an approach known as criminal justice reform.

Criminal justice reform is a complicated subject, but it's based on some simple ideas. The vast majority of incarcerated individuals will be released from prison before their natural lives are over. Too many of them get sent back to prison, with recidivism rates, meaning the number of people who commit new offenses and get sent back to prison within three years of release, nearing 70 percent. Simply by cutting down on their numbers, the governments that house prisoners (which is all levels of government) can save huge amounts of money.

Since the ultimate goal of drug treatment and employment programs and the like is to help prevent individuals from committing fresh crimes, public safety is enhanced, as well. "Certainly prisoners should be punished for their crimes, but if you reduce recidivism rates, you reduce incarceration rates and ultimately make communities safer," says Ronald J. Lampard, director of the criminal justice task force for the American Legislative Exchange Council (ALEC), a conservative group that brings state legislators together with businesses to craft policy.[1]

This philosophy is a rebuke, in short, to the "tough on crime" policies that dominated discussion during the 1980s and 1990s. Back then, when murder rates were rising fast and the crack cocaine epidemic was rotting cities from within, politicians shied far from the idea that it was worth trying to rehabilitate prisoners. In 1974, a sociologist named Robert Martinson wrote a highly influential study examining prison rehabilitation programs called "What Works?" His conclusion? Nothing works. At least, that was the takeaway for policymakers. The "nothing works" doctrine dominated discussion

through the 1980s and 1990s. It was impossible to rehabilitate criminals, so you just have to lock people up.

In response to the crime wave, states passed changes to sentencing laws, including determinant sentencing guidelines (which gave judges less discretion toward leniency), mandatory minimum sentences for crimes such as drug trafficking, and "three strikes" laws, which sent repeat offenders to prison without possibility of parole. Inevitably, such policies meant more convicts went to prison, often to serve longer sentences. Over the course of about 30 years starting in the mid-1970s, the prison population nationwide more than quadrupled, making corrections the fastest-growing cost in many state budgets, in some places surpassing spending on higher education.

Over the past dozen years, a majority of states have rethought their approach, pursuing the criminal justice reform agenda briefly outlined above. We'll discuss this approach in more detail later in the chapter. Here, it's worth noting that Trump ran and won in 2016 using "tough on crime" rhetoric of the sort that had been dominant in earlier decades.

Trump clearly came out of the earlier, more punitive tradition. As his first attorney general, he appointed Jeff Sessions, who as an Alabama senator had helped kill a criminal justice reform bill toward the end of Barack Obama's presidency. But it turns out that Trump himself was open to a more complicated argument about how to combat crime.

Alongside progressives concerned with mass incarceration and racial disparities in sentencing, several conservative groups had been preaching the criminal justice reform gospel for years, including Heritage Action, the American Conservative Union Foundation, FreedomWorks, Right on Crime, and R Street Institute. Once in office, Trump talked with lobbyists from those groups, who offered him a ready-made policy platform that was more nuanced than his anti-crime campaign slogans. They'd spent years building a coalition of support within the Republican Party, winning over many hard-line conservatives in Congress and elsewhere. "The last 10 years of policies and politics have been about building a reform movement," says Vikrant Reddy, a senior fellow at the conservative Charles Koch Institute. "The opposing agenda didn't really exist, outside of his attorney general."[2]

These groups' efforts were immeasurably aided by Jared Kushner, the president's son-in-law and senior advisor. Charles Kushner, Jared's father, served two years in federal prison on charges of witness tampering, tax evasion, and illegal campaign donations. By all accounts, his father's experience taught Jared Kushner to think about prisoners and their treatment in a new way. Kushner has worked closely not just with conservative groups but with Democrats who were otherwise ideological enemies. Kushner organized a prison reform summit at the White House in 2018, offering the most flattering platform possible for advocates of the "smart on crime" approach. "Prison reform is an issue that unites people from across the political spectrum," Trump said at the event. "It's an amazing thing. Our whole nation benefits if former inmates are able to reenter society as productive, law-abiding citizens." He promised, in his characteristically humble way, that America's criminal justice system would emerge as "the best of its kind anywhere in the world."[3]

It represented a remarkable change in positions, not just for Trump but for the Republican Party as a whole. Four days after the summit, the House overwhelmingly approved, 360–59, a prison reform bill. Among other things, the bill would authorize $50 million annually over the next five years for the FBI to spend on education, job training, and drug treatment programs. The bill would also allow prisoners to earn "good time credits" toward early release by participating in educational or job training programs.

A grand total of two Republicans voted against the bill in the House. Most of the no votes came from progressive Democrats who complained the bill was not ambitious enough in scope and did nothing to address problems with sentencing. Similar complaints came up in the Senate, including from senators who had become convinced of the approach.

The increasing appeal of criminal justice reform at the federal level, however, demonstrates two things. For one, it's an example of federalism at work, with ideas being tried out at the state level and then gaining currency in Washington. "We were seeing a lot of success in my home state of Georgia," says representative Doug Collins, the lead Republican sponsor of the House bill. "We were saving money and also seeing less recidivism."[4] The other thing it shows is that it's possible for policymakers to change course on a central issue of concern. The congressional vote represented the most ambitious effort in a quarter-century to move away from the "tough on crime" tactics that had been at the root of the last major federal crime law, which was enacted in 1994.

The growing bipartisan consensus about ways to rethink crime and punishment is one of the most impressive developments of the current era in crime policy. We'll talk about it at greater length in this chapter, while also exploring the American penal and policing system's origins and how the crime explosion that began in the early 1960s led to a crackdown whose effects we are still dealing with today. We'll discuss the rise of the Black Lives Matter movement and explore the critiques of the criminal justice system that have been put forward in recent years. Along the way, we'll examine how the court system operates differently for different segments of society, even as the flow of money into judicial elections remakes the system as a whole.

Today, the criminal justice system is at a pivotal moment. At the end of this chapter, you'll understand how the system works today, what a smarter system in the future would look like, and what forces could propel or derail much-needed reforms. As you read through this chapter, keep in mind the following questions:

- **What factors contribute to the strained relationship between police and minority communities?**

- **Why does the United States incarcerate a higher proportion of its population than any other developed country?**

- **What options are state and local governments considering to reduce both imprisonment and crime?**

Private Wrongs, Public Justice

One of the most striking features of the U.S. criminal justice system is that the state initiates and dispenses punishment for such crimes as homicide, assault, robbery, and burglary. To Americans, this seems entirely natural. Crime is thought of as an offense not just against an individual but also against society itself. As a result, the state initiates the punishment—and the punishment can be severe. It can take the form of imprisonment or **probation**. Punishment deemed to be cruel and unusual, such as torture, is not allowed under the U.S. Constitution, but for homicide, the death penalty is still an option.

A look at the historical record reveals something interesting: The distinctions that Americans see as natural are, in fact, not at all universal. For most of human history, from ancient Greece to monarchical Europe, private prosecution was the norm.[5] In medieval Britain, the attorney general initiated cases only for the king. Justices of the peace began prosecutions only when there was no private individual to initiate punishment.

Until relatively recently, the governments of most nations simply set the rules for how offended parties should pursue justice. Their role was essentially that of umpire. Governments had to fight long and hard to establish that they had the *exclusive* right to punish wrongdoers.[6] A key figure in this transference of the right of retaliation from the wronged party to the state was the public prosecutor. For reasons that historians still do not fully understand, public prosecutors first appeared in North America—in Great Britain's Atlantic colonies.

On the whole, the state's successful monopoly on punishment has brought enormous benefit to the United States. Conflicts such as the famous one between the Hatfields and McCoys notwithstanding, the nation is essentially free of ongoing feuds or vendettas.

Principle versus Practice in Common Law

Americans are governed by a mixture of formal (statutory) law and case (or common) law. Statutes are laws enacted by the sovereign. The most famous example is the Napoleonic Code, drafted by the French emperor Napoleon Bonaparte in the early 19th century. Most countries today have statutes and justice systems in which disputes are adjudicated by a magistrate. The United States has statutes, too, of course, at both the state and federal levels of government. But the U.S. justice system is also rooted in the English **common law**.

> **The common law is made up of legal opinions written by judges that recognize commonly accepted community practices, and it evolves gradually over time as a community's ideas change. Forty-nine states operate within this common-law tradition.**

The common law is made up of legal opinions written by judges that recognize commonly accepted community practices, and it evolves gradually over time as a community's ideas change. Forty-nine states operate within this common-law tradition. (The exception is Louisiana. As a former French colony, the state instead operates under the Napoleonic Code.) Common law makes the U.S. system quite unlike the legal systems of most other countries. In most of the world, law is enacted by a single sovereign power: a legislature, a monarch, or some combination. The United States has both statutes and a body law.

Many of the other institutions that characterize the U.S. criminal justice system have their roots in the English system as well. County sheriffs are the most notable example. At more than 1,000 years old, the office of sheriff is the oldest law enforcement office within the common-law system. The king of England appointed a representative called a reeve to act on behalf of the king in each shire or county. *Shire reeve*, or king's representative, became *sheriff* as the English language changed. In 2018, Sessions, then the U.S. attorney general, was criticized in some quarters for saying, during an address to the National Sheriffs' Association, that "the office of sheriff is a critical part of the Anglo-American heritage of law enforcement." Some heard a racial dog whistle in that phrase, but there's no question that Sessions's sense of history was correct.

Sheriffs in Anglo-Saxon England sometimes apprehended criminals, but their main job was in-person tax collection, threatening or doling out violence until they received a satisfactory sum—much of which they kept

Probation Supervised punishment in the community.

Common law Law composed of judges' legal opinions that reflects community practices and evolves over time.

LOCAL FOCUS

SHERIFFS SELDOM DISCIPLINED WHEN THEY ABUSE THEIR POWER

Tapping into the food fund has become a tradition for sheriffs in Morgan County, which hugs the Tennessee River in northern Alabama. Back in 2001, a judge ruled that the food served to prisoners was "inadequate in amount and unsanitary in presentation," and required that nutritionally adequate meals be served. But that court order was violated several years later by the next sheriff, who bought a truckload of corn dogs at a discount, served them up twice daily for three months, and pocketed $212,000 from the food fund over a period of three years. So the court order was expanded to state specifically that the food money was to be spent solely on food. Nonetheless, the next sheriff, Ana Franklin, took $160,000 out of the food budget and invested most of it in a used car lot.

She was forced to repay the money and was slapped with a $1,000 fine. Still, the case illustrates a fact of life among sheriffs. They control pots of money with little oversight and a good deal of potential for abuse. Because most are independently elected, there isn't much that other officials at the local level can do to control them. A police chief may be fired by a mayor or town council for malfeasance or simply on a whim, but short of impeachment, there is usually no way to remove a sheriff, no matter the offense. "In many states, if the sheriff does something wrong, it's not clear who's supposed to do something about it, which means no one is going to do anything about it," says Mirya Holman, a political scientist at Tulane University who studies sheriffs. "A combination of large budgets and little information provides an environment where corruption is certainly possible, if not probable."

Like many peers, the sheriff in Morgan County oversees more than a dozen discretionary funds. The money that passes through a typical sheriff's hands ranges from pistol permit fees and garnishment of prisoners' wages to cash from the seizure of cars or other assets used in the commission of a crime—or sometimes when no crime has been charged.

In most states, the powers of the sheriff are spelled out in the constitution, so there's little hope of rewriting their list of duties when they abuse their power.

And, with more than 3,000 sheriffs elected nationwide, there are always at least a few who do.

The duties of sheriffs vary tremendously by state. In the Northeast, they may do nothing more than provide security in the courthouse. But in most other states, they're responsible for highway patrols, and in many, they handle general policing and corrections. The job can be incredibly complex, involving the oversight of law enforcement across multiple jurisdictions; managing jails, which often makes them the largest provider of mental health services in the county; performing evictions; sometimes running the coroner's office; and, if they're near water or mountains, running search and rescue functions.

Sheriffs' duties may vary, but the demographics of the officeholders are strikingly consistent. A survey of sheriffs by Holman and Emily Farris of Texas Christian University found that 95 percent of them are male and 99 percent are white. Accusations of racial profiling and excessive force are common, and there are always a few lawsuits pending around the country for wrongful deaths.

A few cases of sheriff misconduct have drawn attention from prosecutors, or at least plaintiffs' attorneys. But most sheriffs are never called to account for their misdeeds. Individuals who have confronted sheriffs—whether they are deputies, prosecutors, or members of the public—recall campaigns of harassment and intimidation. In some states, governors have the power to remove a sheriff, but they are slow to do so, generally considering it a local matter. State legislatures have reduced some of the powers of sheriffs in recent years, placing limits on civil asset forfeiture and requiring state approval for some large contracts. But sheriffs are often able to block bills they see as a threat. They are a powerful lobbying force, well connected in every part of a state.

In theory, sheriffs should be highly accountable, since they have to answer directly to voters. But in practice, while a police chief may be lucky to serve three years, it's not unusual for a sheriff to be around for 20. There's often meager interest in challenging a sheriff politically.

Source: Adapted from Alan Greenblatt, "Why There Are So Many Bad Sheriffs," Governing, April 2018, http://www.governing.com/topics/public-justice-safety/gov-bad-sherriffs.html.

for themselves. That's one reason England has eliminated all but their ceremonial duties. "They had a direct financial incentive in raising money because that's how they were paid," said Seth Stoughton, a former police officer who teaches at the University of South Carolina law school. "That incentive problem is why the sheriff of Nottingham was a bad guy."[7]

Sheriffs can award contracts to campaign contributors, with ex-sheriffs often funding lucrative retirements by winning no-bid contracts on equipment or services from their successors. But the most troubling source of money swirling around sheriffs is civil asset forfeiture. Sheriffs can seize almost any property used in the commission of a crime. They argue it's a necessary tool in the fight against drugs. That may be so, but abuses of the process have been well documented, from sheriffs shaking down travelers for the exact amount of cash they happen to have on their person, to sheriffs ordering deputies to work traffic on just one side of the highway—the side being used to bring back cash, not the side on which the drugs initially come in.

The United Kingdom also gave us the model for today's police. European cities had night watchmen since the Middle Ages, but it was not until British home secretary Sir Robert Peel established the Metropolitan Police Service in 1829 that a recognizably modern police force with uniforms, a regular chain of command, and a philosophy of interacting with the citizenry that prefigures community policing came into being. (British police officers are called "Bobbies" in Peel's honor.) U.S. cities such as Philadelphia, Boston, and New York quickly followed suit. These police departments were only the most visible part of American law enforcement. County sheriffs make up the vast bulk of the law enforcement capacity in the United States, and states operate law enforcement agencies, too, from state highway patrol departments to more specialized bureaus of investigation that operate much like the Federal Bureau of Investigation.

The existence of multiple agencies with jurisdictional overlap can lead to confusion. Congress and the state legislatures each make laws, as do county and city governments, though these typically operate under the jurisdiction of the states. Citizens must obey these laws or risk punishment. Yet sometimes states enact laws that contradict federal laws.

Take the issue of marijuana, for example. In 2012, Washington and Colorado legalized the recreational use of marijuana for adults. Other states have followed, while cities such as Philadelphia have decriminalized the possession of small amounts of marijuana. Possession, which had once been a misdemeanor offense, is now punishable with a $25 civil fine. It's like a cheap parking ticket. Yet the possession of marijuana remains a federal offense. Colorado is collecting taxes on marijuana growers (who must submit to a whole range of regulations), but the federal Drug Enforcement Administration could still arrest them.[8]

Perhaps our most important inheritance from the common-law tradition is the institution of the jury. Serving on a jury is *the* defining act of citizenship. It is just about the only thing every citizen must do if called upon. (Men between the ages of 18 and 25 must also register with the Selective Service System in the event that the government needs to reinstitute a military draft.) In most states, ignoring a jury summons is a crime. Failing to appear for jury duty without being properly exempted constitutes contempt of court and may present a somewhat less appealing opportunity to experience the criminal justice system, such as fines or even imprisonment. Unless you commit a crime or have the misfortune of being one of the roughly 5 million people who fall victim to a crime every year, serving on a jury probably will be your primary interaction with the criminal justice system.[9]

As discussed in Chapter 9, there are two types of juries. In most states east of the Mississippi River, a grand jury determines whether there is sufficient evidence for the state to prosecute someone for a crime. In states west of the Mississippi, the district attorney usually has the authority to indict someone and take that person to trial. Presented with a less clear instance of wrongdoing, a prosecutor also may impanel an investigative grand jury to study the evidence and determine exactly who should be targeted for prosecution. Once a grand jury or the district attorney has indicted an individual, another trial begins, and another jury is formed to hear the case.

So what is the role of a juror? Most jurors are given clear instructions by the presiding judge. The word **verdict** comes from the Latin phrase *vera dicere*, "to speak the truth." Jurors usually are told that their role is to determine exactly what the truth of a case is. They are to apply the law, regardless of whether they personally agree with it or not. As a result, the role of the juror often is that of a cog—albeit a very important one—in the criminal justice machine. But, in fact, the jury system is at the heart of America's criminal justice process.

....

Verdict A jury's finding in a trial.

The history of the jury system underscores the importance of the checks that Americans, as inheritors of the English common-law tradition, have historically placed on the state, as well as the awesome powers and responsibilities that our system of justice gives to a group of citizens duly impaneled and sworn to uphold the law. But it is also clear that for a significant portion of the U.S. population, the system has gone terribly wrong.

Prison Nation

The most striking aspect of the U.S. system is how many people we incarcerate. At the end of 2016, some 6.6 million Americans were under the supervision of adult correctional systems. Even though prison populations had dropped for nine straight years, some 2.16 million of those people were in state or federal prisons. Another 740,000 were in local jails. How does that compare to the rest of the world? By one estimate, a quarter of the world's prisoners are housed in the United States, a country with under 5 percent of the world's population. Another 4.5 million Americans were on probation (3.7 million) or parole (874,800).[10]

The United States incarcerates more individuals than any other country. Only China, Iraq, Iran, and Saudi Arabia execute more people than does the United States. These are not typically countries that Americans like to be grouped with. The United States also holds some 9,000 inmates in **solitary confinement**, a practice in which a prisoner is confined to a cell (typically the size of a small bathroom or walk-in closet) 23 hours a day, 7 days a week. In the United States, solitary confinement is used to punish disciplinary infractions as well as to separate gang members and other dangerous prisoners from the general population. Yet psychologists say that isolating individuals in this way can cause or exacerbate mental illness. A disproportionate number of prisoners with mental illnesses also end up in solitary. No other developed country uses this practice on a large scale.[11]

An additional 80,000-odd inmates are held in restrictive segregation units. Most states and the federal government also operate stand-alone **supermax prisons**.[12] Then there is the regular system. Some 41,000 inmates in this country are serving life sentences without parole;

in England, that number is just 41. Not surprisingly, all this prison use is expensive. In 2010, the United States spent $80 billion on jails and prisons—about $280 per person.[13]

The second standout characteristic of the U.S. justice system is how much more punishment minorities experience. On average, black men receive sentences that are 20 percent longer than the sentences whites and Latinos receive for similar offenses. According to an estimate by the Bureau of Justice Statistics, at current rates of imprisonment, 1 in 3 black men will serve time in prison in their lifetimes. University of Washington professor Becky Pettit found that on any given day in 2008, 1 in 9 black men were incarcerated and a full 37 percent of young, black, male high school dropouts were behind bars.[14]

But incarceration is only the most visible part of the problem. Governments don't just punish offenders; they profit from them. Consider Orange County, California, which outsourced its "supervised electronic confinement program" to a private company that monitors movements, oversees case management, and tests participants for drug and alcohol use—all for free. The catch is that the company then charges probationers $35 to $100 a month, a sum that can be challenging for many to pay. Some observers see this system as smart and fair. Others, such as journalist Thomas Edsall, have described it as "poverty capitalism." "In this unique sector of the economy," writes Edsall, "costs of essential government services are shifted to the poor."[15]

For young men with criminal records in high-crime areas, it's even worse. Sociologist Alice Goffman studied the lives of a group of young men and women, as well as their extended families and romantic partners, in inner-city Philadelphia over the course of four years. In her book *On the Run: Fugitive Life in an American City*, she describes "hidden systems of policing and supervision" that "are transforming poor black neighborhoods into communities of suspects and fugitives," where "a climate of fear and suspicion pervades everyday life, and many residents live with the daily concern that the authorities will seize them and take them away."[16]

The Crime Explosion
and the War on Drugs

Many of the get-tough crime policies started in response to rising murder and crime rates. The story begins in the 1960s. In 1962, the United States experienced

Solitary confinement The practice of keeping a prisoner isolated in a cell without human contact.

Supermax prisons High-security prisons designed to house violent criminals.

LOCAL FOCUS

POLICE MISCONDUCT CREATES MORE LEGAL LIABILITY THAN SOME CITIES CAN BEAR

Cities have to pay out settlements due to police misconduct all the time. That's a matter of concern not only because of the allegations of abuse or wrongful death that are involved, but also to the civic bottom line.

For big cities, the costs can be alarming. In the first eight weeks of 2018 alone, Chicago paid out $20 million to settle police misconduct lawsuits, well exceeding the city's average of $47 million a year over the previous six years. Chicago still pays less than New York, which in 2017 doled out a record $302 million.

For small cities, the financial impact can be even bigger, at least as a percentage of their overall budgets. Most small governments have liability insurance to help them with lawsuits, but legal costs for police misconduct can still place huge strains on budgets. In some cases, it can lead to law enforcement agencies being disbanded entirely.

In Lakewood, Washington, a jury returned a $15 million verdict for the death of Leonard Thomas, who was unarmed when a police sniper shot him. Lakewood's insurance is expected to cover a portion of that payout, but the city still had to spend $6.5 million on punitive damages. That amount is equivalent to 18 percent of the city's total annual spending.

When misconduct lawsuits start mounting, insurance companies can withdraw coverage. Without insurance, a single claim against a local police department has the potential to bankrupt a small municipality. As a result, cities in California, Illinois, Louisiana, Ohio, Pennsylvania, and Tennessee have opted to disband their police departments after losing coverage.

Police misconduct lawsuits are an overlooked area of taxpayer spending and management, says David Eichenthal, executive director of the PFM Group's Center for Safety & Justice Finance. "The ability to limit your future liability by taking preventive steps upfront isn't just good policing policy, but important financial policy," he says.

Ron Serpas, New Orleans's former police chief and a consultant with PFM, agrees. He says training and active monitoring of new hires can make a big difference. "You see numerous times that a poor decision in hiring or succession planning results in multimillion-dollar lawsuits in cities," Serpas says.

In Sorrento, Louisiana, for example, a newly hired cop in 2013 slammed into a car on a highway during a high-speed chase in pursuit of another driver who was speeding. The driver who was hit sued. It was later revealed that the officer was already one of the town's most zealous issuers of speeding tickets, hundreds of which were later thrown out in court. That incident, combined with other lawsuits against the police department that served the small town of 1,500 people, prompted the city's insurer to drop its coverage. The town disbanded its police department shortly thereafter.

Some small towns have been able to make a turnaround before losing insurance. In 2017, University of Chicago law professor John Rappaport detailed examples of such efforts, which ranged from firing a police chief in Tennessee to adopting new training and supervision of SWAT teams in Wisconsin following some botched raids.

Eichenthal says local governments shouldn't wait until the threat of bankruptcy or the cancellation of insurance forces them to start dealing with misconduct. "I used to have a boss who'd say it's cheaper to build a guardrail at the top of a cliff than station an ambulance at the bottom," he says. "It's really about building those guardrails in the right places."

Source: Adapted from Liz Farmer, "Police Misconduct Is Increasingly a Financial Issue," *Governing*, June 20, 2018, http://www.governing.com/topics/finance/gov-police-misconduct-growing-financial-issue.html.

4.2 murders per 100,000 residents. By 1964, the homicide rate had climbed to 6.4; by 1972, it had risen to 9.4. And that was just the homicide rate. Another category of violent crime, robberies, had risen far more sharply. In 1959, the rate was 51.2 for every 100,000 residents; by 1968, the rate had nearly tripled. Crime, the political scientist James Q. Wilson concluded, "had assumed epidemic proportions." (See Figure 14-1.)

Wilson looked primarily to cultural changes to explain this explosion in criminality. However, he and University of Chicago economist Gary Becker posited another cause as well: Crime was rising because the

FIGURE 14-1 ● **The Rise and Fall of Crime Rates: Aggravated Assault, Robbery, and Homicide Rates per 100,000 Residents, 1960–2016**

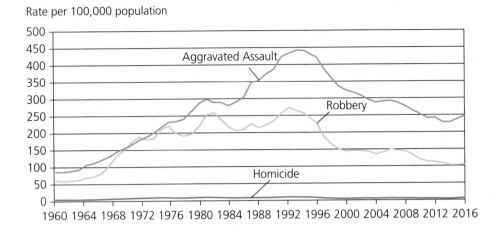

Rate per 100,000 population

Source: "Estimated Number and Rate (per 100,000 Inhabitants) of Offenses Known to Police, by Offense, United States, 1960–2012," in *Sourcebook of Criminal Justice Statistics*, School of Criminal Justice, University at Albany, 2013, http://www.albany.edu/sourcebook/pdf/t31062012.pdf. Data for 1997 through 2016 are from https://ucr.fbi.gov/crime-in-the.u.s/2016/crime-in-the-u.s.-2016/tables/table-1.

risk of punishment was falling. Crime was up, but the number of prison beds was down. By 1974, the "average" punishment per committed burglary was 4 days of incarceration. The average punishment per committed aggravated assault was 8 days; for robbery, 28. In short, crime increasingly "paid." That gave rise to a straightforward solution: incarcerate more people for longer periods of time.

It was an idea that resonated with voters. From 1968 to 1990, "crime" consistently polled as American voters' top domestic concern. As a result, states went on a prison-building spree. States also increased punishment in other ways. Between 1975 and 2002, all 50 states adopted mandatory sentencing laws that curbed judicial discretion by mandating minimum sentences. Many also enacted "three strikes" laws, which led to lengthy convictions for repeat offenders, even if their third crime was comparatively minor. By 1996, the United States had regained the level of punitiveness (calculated by dividing crimes committed by punishment given out) of 1962, the year before the crime spike of the 1960s began. By 1996, crime rates were beginning to fall.[17] Incarceration rates had held remarkably steady throughout most of the 20th century. From the 1920s, when national prison statistics were first captured, and into the 1970s, roughly 110 individuals for

every 100,000 residents were in jail or prison. But what criminologists call "stability of punishment" was suddenly disrupted during the 1970s. Prison rates rose and then continued to climb without cessation until the first reductions in incarceration came on the heels of criminal justice reform laws at the state level.

Between 1985 and 2008, state prison populations nearly tripled. According to the Vera Institute of Justice, corrections spending rose even faster, by more than 600 percent. It now makes up 7 percent of state general fund spending. By 2008, some 2.3 million Americans were in prison or jail—that's 1 percent of the adult population. Another 5 million were under court supervision on probation or parole. Some 40 percent of the inmates were black. What had happened?[18]

Part of the answer has to do with the war on drugs. In 1971, President Richard Nixon declared war on illegal drugs. "If we cannot destroy the drug menace in America, then it will surely in time destroy us," Nixon told a joint session of Congress. "I am not prepared to accept this alternative."[19]

The war did not go well. By 1978, one-third of all kids ages 12 to 17 admitted to having tried an illegal drug.[20] Faced with a seemingly unstoppable rise in violence, more and more states responded by increasing the penalties for dealing and possessing drugs. Nelson

Rockefeller, the liberal Republican governor of New York State, led the way. In 1973, Rockefeller and the state legislature agreed to impose new drug laws that were among the toughest in the nation. Anyone found in possession of 4 ounces or more of a narcotic such as heroin or cocaine faced the likelihood of a mandatory 15-year prison sentence. Selling as little as 2 ounces of the same narcotic could result in a similar penalty. The hope was that such harsh penalties would drive up drug prices and deter potential users. New York's strategy was an application of **deterrence theory**, the idea that if the punishment is severe enough, it will keep people from committing the crime. Other states and many cities quickly followed suit. State legislatures upped the penalties for the possession of illegal narcotics, and local and county law enforcement officers focused their resources on catching dealers.[21]

It didn't work. The tough new penalties directed against drug users had a minor effect at best on drug use. What they did succeed in doing was putting a lot more people in jail. In 1973, New York State incarcerated about 10,000 people. By 1980, that number had reached 20,000. To many, it seemed that things could hardly get worse—but by the mid-1980s, they did.

In the early 1980s, intrepid drug dealers discovered that they could add baking soda and water to high-quality powder cocaine and bake the resulting solution to create small rocks. These rocks could be smoked in homemade pipes. Nicknamed "crack," for the crackling sound the rocks make when broken, the drug could be bagged in small portions that could be sold for as little as $5 each. Before, cocaine had been a yuppie drug, available only to those with the right connections and the right amount of cash. Now a teenager could buy it for less than a week's allowance.

Crack delivered a potent high at a bargain price. As a result, it quickly found users—with devastating results. Highly concentrated, it created a craving in most users that was so intense they would do shocking things to get more. Some crack addicts abandoned their children. Some began engaging in prostitution to get money to support their habits. Crack addicts broke into condemned buildings and stripped them of their contents, even the plumbing pipes, just to make more money to buy crack.

To keep up with the demand, open-air drug markets sprang up on street corners across urban America. In drug-infested neighborhoods, teenagers often occupied the perfect dealing niche. Many were juveniles and thus were hard to arrest or at least to prosecute. Because the profits were so large, dealing drugs on a street corner was often a violent business. Street-level dealers became popular robbery targets, so they started carrying handguns. Neighborhood fistfights and gang brawls turned into running gun battles. Homicide rates, which had been rising slowly for years, skyrocketed. More than half the males arrested in nine major cities in 1988 tested positive for cocaine. In Washington, D.C., the figure was 59 percent, up from 14 percent in 1984. In Manhattan, the figure was more than 80 percent. A 1987 survey found that police classified more than a third of murders and two-thirds of robberies and burglaries as drug related.[22]

Policing's Race Problem

Policing is also a profession at the crossroads. Despite nearly two decades of falling crime, police relations with minority communities are strained. Central to the perception that law enforcement operates unfairly is the practice of stopping, questioning, and frisking residents in high-crime neighborhoods. It's a common tactic with a troubled history. Prior to the 1960s, police departments employed tactics that would outrage most citizens today. Police routinely (and sometimes arbitrarily) arrested people for "vagrancy." To apprehend criminals, big-city police departments would blockade entire neighborhoods, stopping and searching all cars and pedestrians entering or leaving the area. In 1968, however, the Supreme Court established a new method of conduct in *Terry v. Ohio*. The case concerned a Cleveland detective, Martin McFadden, who observed two men who seemed to be casing a store in the neighborhood. Detective McFadden confronted the men, identified himself as a police officer, and asked the men for their names. Their response was unclear, so McFadden spun one of the men around and patted down his outside clothing. He felt a revolver. The officer ordered the men to line up against the wall. There he patted down another man, finding another gun. All three were taken to the local police station. There, two were arrested for illegally carrying concealed weapons. At trial, the defense argued that Detective McFadden's actions amounted to an unconstitutional search and seizure.

....

Deterrence theory A theory advanced by criminologists that harsh penalties will deter people from committing crimes.

FIGURE 14-2 ● U.S. Incarceration Rate, 1920–2016

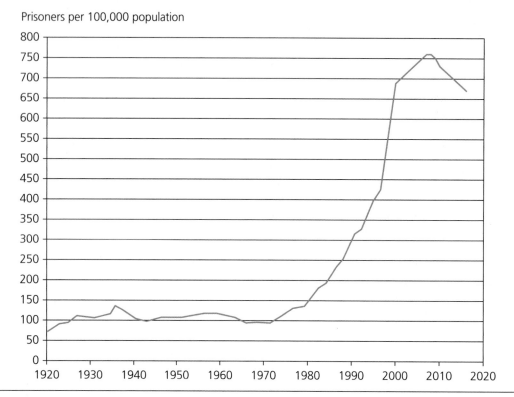

Prisoners per 100,000 population

Sources: Margaret Werner Cahalan, *Historical Corrections Statistics in the United States, 1850–1984*, Bureau of Justice Statistics Report NCJ 102529 (Washington, DC: U.S. Department of Justice, 1986); E. Ann Carson and Daniela Golinelli, *Prisoners in 2012: Trends in Admissions and Releases, 1991–2012*, Bureau of Justice Statistics Bulletin NCJ 243920 (Washington, DC: U.S. Department of Justice, December 2013, revised September 2, 2014), Table 18, http://www.bjs.gov/content/pub/pdf/p12tar9112.pdf; E. Ann Carson and William J. Sabol, *Prisoners in 2011*, Bureau of Justice Statistics Bulletin NCJ 239808 (Washington, DC: U.S. Department of Justice, December 2012), http://www.bjs.gov/content/pub/pdf/p11.pdf; William J. Sabol, Heather C. West, and Matthew Cooper, *Prisoners in 2008*, Bureau of Justice Statistics Bulletin NCJ 228417 (Washington, DC: U.S. Department of Justice, December 2009, revised June 30, 2010), http://www.bjs.gov/content/pub/pdf/p08.pdf; Danielle Kaeble and Mary Cowhig, *Correctional Populations in the United States, 2016*, Bureau of Justice Statistics Bulletin NCJ 251211 (Washington, DC: U.S. Department of Justice, April 2018), https://www.bjs.gov/content/pub/pdf/cpus16.pdf.

The Supreme Court disagreed. "Where a reasonably prudent officer is warranted in the circumstances of a given case in believing that his safety or that of others is endangered, he may make a reasonable search for weapons of the person believed by him to be armed and dangerous," wrote Chief Justice Earl Warren in his decision. A new type of police interaction with the citizenry—**stop and frisk**—was born.[23]

Stop and frisk soon became a familiar—and often resented—ritual in many high-crime, minority communities. Nowhere was it embraced with more enthusiasm

than in New York City. There the tactic of stopping and frisking large numbers of people was bound up with a concept known as "broken windows" policing. The idea, as elaborated by the political scientist James Q. Wilson and criminologist George Kelling in the early 1980s, was that minor kinds of disorder, such as shoplifting and vandalism, often give rise to much more serious types of disorder and crime, such as robbery and arson. The two social scientists went on to make a larger point about policing. Those police officers whom researchers in the 1950s observed walking around and resolving disputes actually might have been doing something important. By their very presence, they had been maintaining order. It was time, Wilson and Kelling wrote, to go back to the past.[24]

Stop and frisk A police tactic that allows police officers to stop, question, and search citizens under a set of narrowly defined circumstances.

Wilson and Kelling argued for a dramatic break from the **professional model of policing**. This approach to fighting crime emphasizes squad cars and quick response times; police departments across the country embraced it during the 1970s. The reason for this was an important new innovation—the 911 emergency number. Cops who had once walked the beat and played the role of friendly neighborhood supervisor now were put into squad cars. Response time—how quickly the police responded to a call for assistance—became the criterion by which departments were judged as successes or failures. It was an all-or-nothing situation because there simply were not enough police officers available to monitor neighborhoods *and* answer emergency calls.

Wilson and Kelling's article caused a sensation among policymakers and the public; however, the criminologists weren't interested in exploring the "broken windows" theory, which held that enforcement of minor violations would help make a community feel more secure and better policed. In 1983, the National Institute of Justice prepared to fund an experimental assessment of the proposition that reducing disorder could reduce crime, but at the last minute, the project was rejected. Not until 1990 was the idea tested on a large scale. That's when Boston police chief Bill Bratton took command of the New York City transit department (the nation's seventh-largest police force).

Bratton thought of his job as a police chief as akin to that of a doctor treating a sick patient. In his previous jobs, many of which had involved turnarounds of troubled agencies, he had begun to develop what he thought of as a doctor's kit for damaged police departments. For example, he thought that morale was important, so when he arrived in New York, he improved both the uniforms (adding commando-style sweaters) and the weapons (issuing modern Glocks, a distinct improvement on the old revolvers) of the transit police. Bratton also upgraded the department's radio system so the transit cops could communicate underground.

But the most celebrated aspect of Bratton's tenure as transit chief was his embrace of **"broken windows"**

Police in Chicago frisk a woman and search her car. Critics of the practice of stop and frisk allege that police departments often hassle minorities in high-crime neighborhoods without probable cause, a practice they say constitutes unconstitutional racial profiling. Some police departments nevertheless defend it, saying the ability to stop, question, and frisk people in situations where officers have reason to be concerned about their safety is constitutional and appropriate.

policing. Along with Kelling, who was working as a consultant for the transit police, he emphasized catching fare beaters. The transit cops who, following his orders, started arresting turnstile jumpers made a surprising discovery: 1 in 7 were wanted on an outstanding warrant, and 1 in 21 were carrying a weapon. In short, enforcing the law was also an excellent way to arrest felons and fugitives, which in turn drove down crime rates and public fear. Bratton's subway successes vindicated broken windows as a policing strategy and put Bratton on track to become Rudy Giuliani's commissioner of the New York Police Department (NYPD) in 1994.[25]

Bratton's immediate predecessors at the NYPD had promoted **community policing**, an approach to policing that emphasized police officers forming

....

Professional model of policing An approach to policing that emphasizes professional relations with citizens, police independence, police in cars, and rapid responses to calls for service.

"Broken windows" policing Policing that emphasizes maintaining public order, based on the theory that unattended disorder breeds crime.

Community policing An approach that emphasizes police officers forming relationships with neighborhood residents and engaging with them in collaborative problem solving.

relationships with neighborhood residents and engaging with them in collaborative problem solving. But exactly what community policing entailed had always been somewhat vague. Bratton disagreed with the idea that young cops who'd grown up in places such as Staten Island or Long Island could go into New York's most challenging neighborhoods and problem solve. Instead, he expected the captains of New York City's 77 precincts to take responsibility for reducing crime.

Bratton's book about his time in New York, *Turnaround*, provides a comprehensive account of the many changes he made to the NYPD and its operations.[26] The key innovation, however, was a new computerized crime-mapping system known as CompStat. This system allowed the police to map crime in virtual real time, identify patterns or problems, and then shift resources and devise solutions accordingly. Before the creation of CompStat, the NYPD compiled crime statistics every quarter. CompStat provided fresh numbers every week and allowed police commanders to look for crime patterns and "hot spots." It also encouraged officers to try new tactics and introduced an element of accountability into policing.[27]

The New Criminal Frontier

Bratton left the NYPD after only two years as commissioner. By the time he left, crime was down 40 percent. Not surprisingly, police departments around the country rushed to adopt his tactics. Yet exactly what New York had done was somewhat unclear. In his book *The City That Became Safe*, Franklin Zimring reports that broken windows was a tactic that was only occasionally used by the NYPD during Bratton's tenure.[28] Yet many outsiders seemed to view an extreme version of broken windows as its essence. They called it "zero tolerance": the idea was that the police should enforce every law, no matter how minor. Kelling saw this approach as a disaster waiting to happen. "Broken windows has always been a negotiated sense of order in a community, in which you negotiate with residents about what is appropriate behavior in an area," said Kelling. "If you tell your cops, 'We are going to go in and practice zero tolerance for all minor crimes,' you are inviting a mess of trouble."[29]

Yet to some extent that is what the NYPD itself did. Misdemeanor arrests rose by roughly 70 percent over the course of the 1990s and continued to climb in the years that followed. Mayor Michael Bloomberg and his police commissioner, Ray Kelly, justified the tactics as a form of deterrence: If there was a high probability of interacting with a police officer, youth would not carry guns. Without ready access to firearms, the seemingly petty disputes that ignited so many conflicts in high-crime neighborhoods would be less likely to turn violent. Intent on driving crime down, the NYPD steadily increased its use of stop and frisk. In 2002, the NYPD made 97,296 stops. By 2011, the number of stops had risen to 685,724, with 90 percent of them involving blacks and Latinos. Only 2 percent resulted in arrests. Critics alleged that this constituted racial profiling; the police responded that they were simply going where the crime was.[30]

In 2008, a class action lawsuit was filed against the department, and in August 2013, federal judge Shira A. Scheindlin ruled that the police department had resorted to a "policy of indirect racial profiling" as it increased the number of stops in minority communities. That had led to officers routinely stopping "blacks and Hispanics who would not have been stopped if they were white." Scheindlin appointed a monitor to reform the department's stop-and-frisk practices. But just two months later, an appeals court stayed her order and removed her from the case, saying that Judge Scheindlin "ran afoul" of the judiciary's code of conduct by compromising the "appearance of impartiality surrounding this litigation" by actively seeking to hear the 2008 case in her courtroom.[31]

In January 2014, newly elected mayor Bill de Blasio announced that the NYPD would voluntarily adopt Judge Scheindlin's remedies. The department had already scaled back police contacts with citizens—with no adverse effects on the city's homicide rates. De Blasio also appointed a new police commissioner, Bill Bratton. During his time away from New York, Bratton had served as chief of the Los Angeles Police Department (LAPD) for seven years. There he oversaw a remarkable improvement in the LAPD's relationship with Los Angeles's black community. By the time he left in 2009, surveys showed that 83 percent of Angelenos believed that the LAPD was doing a good or excellent job, up from 71 percent two years earlier. The percentage of residents

The first police car went on patrol in Akron, **OHIO**, in 1899. It was electric powered and could reach a speed of 16 miles per hour.

saying that the police in their communities treated members of all racial and ethnic groups fairly "almost all the time" or "most of the time" rose from 44 percent in 2005 to 51 percent in 2009. When asked to assess personal experiences, a majority of every racial and ethnic group in Los Angeles reported that most LAPD officers treated them, their friends, and their family with respect. Bratton accomplished this while driving crime down dramatically—especially violent crime. The crime rate during his final year in Los Angeles was 54 percent lower than it had been during his predecessor's final year.

Getting Tough on Crime through Sentencing

State and local government officials responded to violence and crime during the 1960s through the 1980s by making fundamental changes to their sentencing practices. For most of the post–World War II era, courts across the United States had enjoyed considerable leeway in determining the severity of the punishments they delivered. In academic-speak, this was known as indeterminate sentencing (see Chapter 9).

Stories of judges releasing hardened criminals with little more than a slap on the wrist resulted in a growing number of states moving toward determinate sentencing. "Truth in sentencing" laws were passed. These restricted judges' ability to set penalties and curtailed parole boards' freedom to release prisoners early. All 50 states passed mandatory sentencing laws. Many states went even further. Fourteen states abolished discretionary parole and parole boards altogether. In 1994, California voters approved a "three strikes" law, under which individuals arrested and convicted of three felony crimes were to be imprisoned for a minimum of 25 years, if not for the rest of their lives. In 2004, the U.S. Supreme Court further constrained judges' sentencing flexibility, but also set the stage for potentially shorter sentences, when it ruled that only juries, not judges, can increase sentences beyond the maximums suggested by sentencing laws.

AP Photo/Jeff Roberson, File

▲

Police wearing riot gear point weapons at a man before arresting him on August 11, 2014. He was among the many protesters who gathered in Ferguson, Missouri, following the shooting death of Michael Brown by a local police officer. Protests continued for months and spread around the country after grand juries decided not to indict that officer or another police officer in New York who killed Eric Garner using a forbidden chokehold.

Crackdowns on crack cocaine and other drugs, the broadening of offenses classified as felonies, the introduction of mandatory sentencing, and a tendency toward longer sentences in general soon led to a surge in the numbers of prisoners. States expanded their prison systems accordingly. Between 1983 and 1990, California added 21,000 prison beds at a cost of $3.2 billion. During that same period, New York added 17,780 cells. And the prison building was only getting started. The increased reliance on incarceration had a big effect on state budgets. In 1978, state governments spent about $5 billion on maintaining prisons and jails. By 2007, prison spending had risen to $44 billion, or 10 percent of state expenditures. More than 1 in every 100 U.S. adults were under lock and key.[32] Spending has since ticked down a bit, but states still spend an average of 7 percent of total general revenue funds—$1 out of every $14—on prisons.[33]

Problems of a Prison Nation

In 1994, California voters enacted a "three strikes" law in response to the horrific murder of 12-year-old Polly

Klaas by a convicted felon with a long criminal record. The law imposed a sentence of 25 years to life for almost every crime, no matter how minor, if the defendant had two prior convictions for crimes defined as serious or violent by the California Penal Code. Serious crimes included drug possession and burglary. The result was a surge in prisoners (including a man in Torrance who was given a 25-year sentence for stealing a slice of pizza)—and more prison beds, of course. The state auditor would estimate that in the 12 years before its emendation in 2012, "three strikes" cost the state $19 billion. Some 45 percent of the people affected were African American.

By 1990, California's prisons were severely over-crowded, a condition that in time led to two lawsuits alleging that overcrowding and inadequate health care in the prisons amounted to a violation of the U.S. Constitution's ban on cruel and unusual punishment. By the early 21st century, the state was spending about $8 billion a year to incarcerate some 173,000 prison-ers. Forget the image of cell blocks: state facilities were so overcrowded that triple-height bunk beds spilled out into hallways and filled gymnasiums. A significant number of the inmates were mentally ill. Some of these prisoners were held in telephone booth–sized cages pending sentencing. An outside investigation found that an average of one inmate a week was dying of mal-treatment or neglect.

In 2006, a federal judge in San Francisco appointed someone to oversee California's prison health system. The overseer found that it would cost the state $8 bil-lion to meet constitutional requirements, money the state legislature failed to provide. In August 2009, a panel of federal judges ruled that overcrowding in California's prisons was so severe that it endangered the health and safety of inmates and prison staff in a way that violated the U.S. Constitution's prohibition on cruel and unusual punishment. The court ruled that California must reduce its prison population by 137.5 percent in two years' time. In concrete terms, that meant that the state had to cut its inmate population by some 33,000 prisoners to bring the overall number down to 110,000.[34]

The state appealed the decision to the U.S. Supreme Court, but two years later, the Court upheld the rul-ing. Citing conditions whereby suicidal inmates were held in "telephone-booth-sized cages without toilets," Justice Anthony Kennedy, writing for a 5–4 majority, declared that a "prison that deprives prisoners of basic sustenance, including adequate medical care, is incom-patible with the concept of human dignity and has no place in civilized society."

In response, the state decided to move responsibil-ity for supervising parolees to California's 58 counties. It also began moving low-level offenders from state-run prisons to county jails. This process was known as "realignment."[35] By mid-2013, the state had moved 100,000 felons from state prisons or parole to county jail or probation. Experts have described California's prison reform process as the nation's most ambitious attempt to remake a correctional system. To date, reac-tions have been mixed. Probation officers and public defenders have generally welcomed the greater public control. Prosecutors have been critical; sheriffs' reac-tions have varied depending on the capacity of local jails. Levels of violent crime did not increase during this period; however, rates of property crime did.

Despite these mixed results, California voters have demonstrated a commitment to changing crime policy. In 2014, Golden State voters approved a ballot measure that reduced sentences for many nonviolent crimes, including drug possession. The result was a sharp drop in the prison population. Between November 2014 and August 2015, the prison population fell by almost 7,800. The state system achieved the court-ordered reduction level in January 2015 and has remained below the cap ever since.[36] In 2016, voters approved a proposition that allowed nonviolent offenders to earn credit toward early release by taking educational courses or avoiding disciplinary complaints while in prison. "For gover-nor Jerry Brown, Proposition 57 is an effort to, in part, undo what he helped create almost four decades ago: a system where prison sentences became less flexible and helped fuel the largest inmate population in the nation," according to the *Los Angeles Times*.[37] California voters are expected in 2020 to vote on a measure that would partially roll back some of these changes they've recently approved. California took action to reduce its prison population only after being ordered to do so by the U.S. Supreme Court. However, a growing number of states have acted to reduce the growth of their cor-rectional systems on their own. This is a change that started in an unlikely place—Texas, a state famous for its "tough on crime" culture. While all 50 states saw incarceration rates rise dramatically, beginning in the 1970s, Texas outdid them all (with the possible excep-tion of Louisiana). The Lone Star State incarcerates roughly 1,000 out of every 100,000 people. (In contrast, the state with the lowest level of incarceration, Maine, locks up 300 people per 100,000.) Its prison system, second in size only to California's, holds more people than do the prison systems of Germany, France, Belgium, and the Netherlands—combined. And that's not counting the roughly 700,000 people the state supervises who are on probation or parole. It also executes more prisoners than any other state. Indeed, since 1976, when the U.S. Supreme Court reinstated the death penalty, Texas alone has carried out roughly a third of the country's executions.[38]

Mass Arrests and Incarceration

Racial disparities are an issue throughout the criminal justice system. Bruce Western, a sociologist at Harvard University, has calculated that black men born between 1975 and 1979 who do not earn a high school degree have a 68 percent chance of ending up in prison. "This means that for certain men—black men without a high school degree—imprisonment is *modal* in statistical terms," notes Yale Law School professor Tracey Meares. "In everyday language, it is *normal*. For these men, going to prison is an ordinary life experience along one's life course trajectory, just like graduation, marriage, a first job, or having children is for everybody else."[39]

In recent years, the legitimacy of the criminal justice system has come under some withering criticism. In her best-selling book *The New Jim Crow: Mass Incarceration in the Age of Colorblindness*, Ohio State University law school professor Michelle Alexander examines how minorities have fared under the U.S. criminal justice system.[40] By 2006, 5 percent of all black males in the United States were serving time either in a state prison or in a city or county jail. That stood in sharp contrast to the 1 percent of white males jailed during the same period. Nearly one-third of all black males ages 20 to 29 were either in prison or under some form of supervision, such as probation or **parole**. One study estimated that in 1997 black males had a 32 percent chance of going to prison at some point in their lives. In contrast, Hispanic males had a 17 percent chance of being imprisoned, and white males had a 5.9 percent chance.[41]

The primary cause of this difference in treatment is the **war on drugs**—specifically, the war on crack cocaine. "Drug offenses alone account for two-thirds of the rise in the federal inmate population and more than half of the rise in state prisoners between 1985 and 2000," notes Alexander. About 500,000 of the nearly 2.5 million people incarcerated today are serving time for drug offenses—versus fewer than 50,000 people in 1980. "Nothing," Alexander concludes, "has contributed more to the systematic **mass incarceration** of people of color in the United States than the War on Drugs."[42]

But in Alexander's view, the war on drugs wasn't the real issue; the real issue was racism. "The War on Drugs, cloaked in race-neutral language, offered whites opposed to racial reform a unique opportunity to express their hostility toward blacks and black progress, without being exposed to the charge of racism," she writes. Had the war on drugs really been about drugs, she continues, then "the drug war could have been waged primarily in overwhelmingly white suburbs or on college campuses. SWAT teams could have rappelled from helicopters in gated suburban communities and raided the homes of high school lacrosse players known for hosting coke and ecstasy parties after their games. . . . All of this could have happened as a matter of routine in white communities, but it did not." The so-called crack epidemic was, in Alexander's opinion, a sensationalized media phenomenon that was created by the far right.[43]

That goes too far for many of the people who saw crack's impact firsthand. Indeed, David Kennedy, a professor at the John Jay College of Criminal Justice, disagrees. In his book *Don't Shoot: One Man, a Street Fellowship, and the End of Violence in Inner-City America*, Kennedy responds to the claim that "crack sparked a 'moral panic': that it was never really that bad, that the public and political and law enforcement response was just a fevered overreaction," with a single, italicized

The feud between the Hatfields of **WEST VIRGINIA** and the McCoys of **KENTUCKY** came to involve the U.S. Supreme Court and the National Guard before the families agreed to end the conflict in 1891.

Parole Supervised early release from prison.

War on drugs An effort by the federal government to treat drug abuse as a law enforcement issue rather than a public health problem.

Mass incarceration The phrase used to describe the United States' strikingly high rate of imprisonment.

▲
Demonstrators in Ferguson, Missouri, raise their arms and chant "hands up, don't shoot" in protest of the shooting death of Michael Brown in 2014. The police officer who pulled the trigger was not charged with any wrongdoing, but the killing of the unarmed teen led to weeks of protest and national debate about use of force by police.

Joe Raedle/Getty Images

Americans have suffered from . . . a lack of effective criminal justice, and this, more than anything, is the reason for the nation's long-standing plague of black homicides," she writes. Leovy notes that in Los Angeles County blacks are killed at 2 to 4 times the rate of Latinos (even Latinos residing in the same high-crime neighborhoods as African Americans) and at 12 times the rate of whites. Yet black homicides rarely receive top priority.[45] Leovy contributes a valuable perspective. The more common argument, however, is that in minority communities law enforcement operates with excessive, indiscriminate zeal. Central to the perception that law enforcement operates unfairly is the practice of stopping, questioning, and frisking residents in high-crime neighborhoods.

Columbia professor Jeffrey Fagan and his colleagues found that 18- and 19-year-old African Americans residing in New York City had a 78 to 80 percent chance of being stopped in 2006. Latino teenagers of the same age had a 35 to 40 percent chance of being stopped. For white teenagers, the numbers were between 1 and 13 percent. In Los Angeles, the black stop rate is 3,400 stops higher than the white stop rate. It's hardly surprising that many African Americans see this as **racial profiling**.

Other parts of the criminal justice system also work in ways that are often discriminatory and destructive. The rise of cell phone cameras has helped fuel national awareness about lethal encounters with police. One example in 2014 triggered nationwide protests, the killing of Michael Brown, an unarmed black teen, by a police officer named Darren Wilson in Ferguson, Missouri. One month earlier, Eric Garner died after being arrested for selling "loosies" (single cigarettes) without a license on Staten Island and being put into a chokehold by one of the NYPD officers. After being cuffed and shoved to the ground, Garner complained that he could not breathe. He died before reaching the hospital. Four months later in Cleveland, 12-year-old Tamir Rice was gunned down after police responded to a call about "a black male sitting on a swing and pointing a gun at

epithet—"*Bullshit.*" Kennedy got a firsthand look at the crack epidemic 25 years ago, at Nickerson Gardens, a thousand-unit housing project in Los Angeles. "I've never been so scared before or since," writes Kennedy of the day he spent walking through the housing development with two LAPD patrol officers. (In fact, Kennedy's LAPD companions would later tell him that the dealers had been scared of *him*; they had seen a white guy in a suit in the projects and thought, "Fed.") But while Kennedy rejects Alexander's belief that the criminal justice system is a tool of racist oppression, he shares her view that something has gone terribly wrong with the way this country polices its inner-city communities. "We are destroying the village in order to save it," he writes.[44]

The war on drugs is just part of the problem; the other part is how law enforcement operates. Some critics have argued that police operate with insufficient zeal in high-crime neighborhoods. In her book *Ghettoside*, Jill Leovy, founder of the *Los Angeles Times* murder blog The Homicide Report, explores the long history of official indifference to black-on-black crime. "African

Racial profiling The alleged police practice of targeting minorities when enforcing the law.

people" in a park. The gun turned out to be a toy. Police described the shooting as a tragic mistake and claimed that Rice had been given multiple warnings. Video from a nearby surveillance camera, however, showed officers arriving and immediately shooting Rice. In April 2015, a police officer in North Charleston, South Carolina, shot a fleeing motorist, Walter Scott, in the back.

How common are officer-involved killings? Until recently, this question was unanswerable. The United States has 18,000 federal, state, and local government law enforcement agencies, yet no government agency keeps track of the number of police killings. So two newspapers, the *Washington Post* and U.K. paper the *Guardian*, set out to gather the data. The *Post* identified 990 people who had been fatally shot by police in the United States in 2015. Compared with other developed countries, that's quite a high number. In 2015, the number of police shootings in Great Britain (a country whose population is a fifth that of the United States) was 3. Police shootings are so common in high-crime U.S. neighborhoods that there's even a name for it— "death by cop."[46]

The killings in Ferguson, Staten Island, Chicago, and South Carolina ushered in a new protest movement led by digital activists organized around the hashtag #blacklivesmatter.[47] Attitudes toward the police polarized along racial lines. A 2014 Pew Research Center study found that just 10 percent of African Americans believed that police did an "excellent" or "good" job of treating blacks and whites equally, compared with 38 percent of whites.[48] In 2017, using a different measure, Pew found that just 30 percent of black Americans express warm attitudes toward police, compared with 74 percent of whites.[49]

Although nationwide crime rates remain flat, violent crime has begun to increase in some of America's largest cities. Conservative writers such as the Manhattan Institute's Heather Mac Donald blame this on the so-called Ferguson effect, which Mac Donald describes as "the phenomenon of officers backing off of proactive policing and thereby emboldening criminals."[50] Many criminologists have rejected this claim, arguing that the crime increase in St. Louis began before events in Ferguson in 2014 and that crime rates nationwide remain low. But as crime rates in the nation's largest cities started to rise (according to *Vox,* the country's 50 largest cities saw homicide rates rise by 17 percent between 2014 and 2015), the concern that police have pulled back became more widespread.[51] But violent crime in large cities ticked back down after that temporary spike and several academic studies have rejected the notion of a "Ferguson effect" on policing.

The Bipartisan Search for Solutions

Between 1985 and 2005, Texas built prisons with gusto, increasing its inmate population from roughly 64,000 in 1993 to 154,000 in 2007. That year, the Texas Department of Criminal Justice approached the state legislature with a request for $523 million in additional funding for three new prisons, which would allow the prison population to grow to more than 168,000 by 2012. The department had good reason to expect a positive response. The chairman of the Senate Criminal Justice Committee, John Whitmire, was a conservative Democrat from Houston and the author of Texas's famously tough penal code. His counterpart in the Texas House, Jerry Madden, was a conservative Republican from Plano. Governor Rick Perry and Lieutenant Governor David Dewhurst were on board.

But instead of okaying the request, Whitmire and Madden did something unexpected. They teamed up to convince the legislature, governor, and lieutenant governor to spend $241 million on treatment, mental health, and rehabilitation instead. These programs are designed to help ex-felons stay out of prison following release by providing them with help such as drug treatment and job training. Some 95 percent of prisoners, after all, will return to their home communities at some point after their incarceration ends. Madden recalls that when Texas House speaker Tom Craddick appointed him as chair of the corrections committee, he offered simple instructions: "Don't build new prisons, they cost too much."[52]

By all accounts, this approach worked. In the three years that followed the adoption of the legislature's reform package, Texas's prison population declined by some 15,000 prisoners. (It had been expected to rise.) Probation recidivism fell by nearly a quarter, probation

In 2016, the average bail set in **PENNSYLVANIA** for 15- to 17-year-olds charged as adults was $248,000. As a result, almost all juvenile suspects are locked up for months or years without being convicted of a crime.

A DIFFERENCE THAT MAKES A DIFFERENCE
THE SLOW DEATH OF CAPITAL PUNISHMENT

In 1972, the U.S. Supreme Court found that the application of the death penalty in many states had been cruel, arbitrary, and unconstitutional. A moratorium, or indefinite delay, was placed on all executions. Four years later, the Court lifted the moratorium. By then, the states had passed sentencing guidelines that addressed the Court's concern that the death penalty was being applied in an arbitrary fashion. Today, the statutes of 31 states allow prosecutors to request the death penalty. (The federal death penalty, of course, can apply anywhere in the country. However, in practice, it is rarely used. There have been just three federal executions in the past half-century.) More than 1,300 prisoners have been executed since capital punishment was reinstated, and another 2,943 people were on death row as of January 1, 2016, according to the Death Penalty Information Center.

The fact that most states sanction capital punishment does not mean that they use it in similar ways. Some counties and states are much more enthusiastic in its use than are others. For example, suburban counties tend to apply the death penalty with more zeal than do urban counties. In 2009, San Mateo County, a suburb of San Francisco, had 17 people on California's death row; by contrast, San Francisco itself, a larger city with twice as many murders, had sentenced only 4 people to death.

During the 1990s, the scientific breakthrough of DNA testing shook up the capital punishment systems. In state after state, lawyers and public interest groups convinced courts and prosecutors to reexamine forensic evidence. They found that many people had been convicted of crimes they had not committed. Since 1973, more than 150 people have been released from death row after evidence of their innocence emerged. That works out to three to five releases over the course of a typical year. The impact of this new research has been felt. In January 2000, Illinois governor George Ryan, a Republican and previously an avowed supporter of capital punishment, became the first governor in the nation to halt executions in his state.

Other states began examining the most widely used method of execution—lethal injection—after the U.S. Supreme Court ruled in June 2006 that lower courts must consider the possibility that the process can be cruel and painful, a finding that would make the procedure unconstitutional. Several states proposed adding an anesthesiologist to monitor executions and confirm that the three-drug process, intended to sedate, paralyze, and finally kill the prisoner, was working properly. There was just one problem—anesthesiologists balked at presiding over executions because that would go against their Hippocratic Oath to "do no harm." States also began to lose access to the drugs most typically used to induce unconsciousness, stop breathing, and stop the heart. In 2014, a series of botched executions in which inmates retained or appeared to retain consciousness or feel pain while dying raised pointed questions about whether death by lethal injection is an efficient standard after all. In light of these challenges, some experts are calling for a return to other execution methods, including the electric chair and the firing squad. "We've known for a long time that there are better methods, but states don't want to look bad and horrifying," says Deborah Denno, a law professor at Fordham University who has written about the death penalty.

Instead, states have slowed down. In 2016, 20 prisoners were executed, with 23 more put to death in 2017. Those totals were down sharply from the peak execution year of 1999, when 98 people were executed. Moreover, capital punishment has become a distinctly southern punishment. Just six states—Texas, Georgia, Missouri, Oklahoma, Florida, and Virginia—accounted for all 28 executions in 2015. But even there, attitudes are changing. As David J. Burge, a leader of the Georgia Republican Party, put it, "Capital punishment runs counter to core conservative principles of life, fiscal responsibility and limited government. The reality is that capital punishment is nothing more than an expensive, wasteful and risky government program."

Sources: Nathan Koppel and Chris Herring, "Lethal Injection Draws Scrutiny in Some States," *Wall Street Journal*, October 15, 2009, A13; "The Slow Death of the Death Penalty," *Economist*, April 26, 2014; Death Penalty Information Center, "Facts about the Death Penalty," updated August 30, 2016, http://deathpenaltyinfo.org/documents/FactSheet.pdf; David von Drehle, "The Death of the Death Penalty," *Time*, June 8, 2015.

violations plummeted, and overall crime rates declined. Instead of adding thousands of prison beds, the state was able to close three adult and six juvenile prisons. "This is not a Republican or Democratic issue," said Madden. "It's about what's smart for Texas."[53]

It turned out there were some promising new approaches. Cognitive-behavioral therapy helped prisoners come up with practical strategies for identifying the people and places that might trigger their criminal or addictive behavior. States also found it made sense to handle different offenders differently. They began setting up specialized courts to handle cases involving, for instance, drug abuse or mental issues. The aim was to address the underlying causes of criminal behavior, as opposed to simply locking people away. Among prisoners, it made sense to get them into drug treatment programs before they went before the parole board, rather than waiting until they were ready for parole to prepare them to leave. "If you have a druggie that comes to prison and you don't treat them, that's called stupid," Madden says. "They're a captive audience." If they're not treated, he says, "they'll be in prison and come out and commit crimes caused by the need for drugs."

The bill included a fail-safe: if the new program wasn't working, the governor was authorized to build new prisons. That never happened. Over the next two years, the state added just 529 new prisoners—one-tenth the amount that had been projected. After peaking in 2010, the prison population started to come down, despite the state's rapid growth in population overall, demonstrating the effectiveness of the alternative treatments and punishments.

Whitmire and Madden's pioneering work in Texas did something remarkable: it made corrections reform a bipartisan issue. Since 2007, legislatures in more than 30 states have passed corrections reform packages. Some of the most ambitious packages have been enacted in the most conservative states, including Arkansas, Georgia, Kentucky, Mississippi, Missouri, Ohio, Oklahoma, and

Robert Daemmrich Photography Inc/Corbis via Getty Images

▲
Texas state senator John Whitmire, a leader of the criminal justice reform movement, visits prison inmates at the maximum-security Darrington Unit outside of Houston. The inmates are students in a program to become Christian ministers through the Southwestern Baptist Theological Seminary.

South Carolina. An analysis by the nonprofit group GiveWell suggests that these reforms will reduce state prison populations by 11 percent in 5 years' time and save states billions of dollars. Prominent conservatives such as former House speaker Newt Gingrich and Tea Party stalwart Mike Lee, a Republican senator from Utah, teamed up to form the conservative group Right on Crime to promote smart penal policies. In the process, corrections reform has become the rare issue on which policymakers from both parties can find common ground. The approach has demonstrated some striking results. In 2018, the Pew Charitable Trusts released a study looking at 23 states that found they'd experienced a 23 percent drop in recidivism rates between 2005 and 2012.[54] No one planned it, but the credibility of Texas on law-and-order issues helped sway legislators in other states. Cost savings and statistics that might on paper have been just as impressive out of California or Vermont would not have swayed so many red-state legislators. "It was a tremendous stroke of luck for the country that Texas was the first to step out of the gate," says Adam Gelb, who directs the Pew Charitable Trusts'

In 2015, **CALIFORNIA** requested a total of 1,761,079 federal firearm background checks. Total federal firearm background checks climbed to a record high of 23.1 million in 2015.

Public Safety Performance Project, which provides technical assistance to states on criminal justice policies. "Texas is the very symbol of law and order in this country," he continues. "Nobody thinks that Texas is going to do something that's soft on crime. What they did resonated loudly in capitals across the country."[55]

Corrections isn't the only part of the criminal justice system that has seen stirrings of reform. The past couple of decades have seen a tremendous growth in **drug courts**, special tribunals that offer nonviolent drug offenders a chance at reduced or dismissed charges in exchange for their undergoing treatment or other rehabilitation, an initiative that got under way during the Bill Clinton administration. As of May 2018, more than 3,100 drug courts were operating across all 50 states. National Institute of Justice researchers found evidence that the programs are successful in both reducing recidivism and lowering long-term costs. They report that enrolling a participant in a drug court program saves more than $12,000 in criminal justice and victimization costs.[56]

Drug courts are closely connected to the **community, or restorative, justice movement**. This movement's basic goal is to give neighborhoods a voice in determining which kinds of criminals prosecutors should pursue. Sometimes restorative justice involves sentences that are tailored to fit both the crime and the perpetrator. A woman convicted of stealing from a nursing home

Drug courts Special tribunals that offer nonviolent drug offenders a chance at reduced or dismissed charges in exchange for their undergoing treatment or other rehabilitation; an alternative forum for sentencing nonviolent drug offenders.

Community, or restorative, justice movement A movement that emphasizes nontraditional punishment, such as community service.

MAP 14-1 ● Incarceration Rates per 100,000 Population, 2018

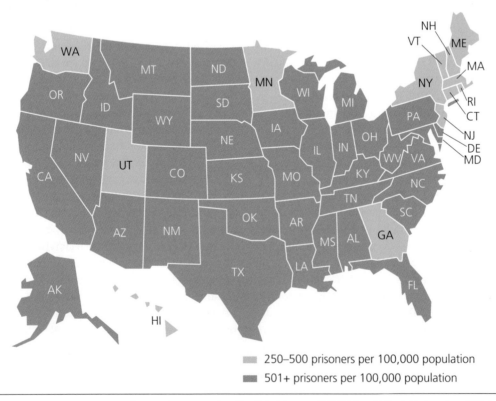

■ 250–500 prisoners per 100,000 population
■ 501+ prisoners per 100,000 population

Source: Peter Wagner and Wendy Sawyer, "States of Incarceration: The Global Context 2018," Prison Policy Initiative, June 2018, https://www.prisonpolicy.org/global/2018.html.

POLICY IN PRACTICE

HOW FAR TO TAKE GUN CONTROL?

Would tougher gun control laws save lives? For some people, the answer is obvious. In 2016, the United States suffered 11,000 gun-related homicides, according to the FBI. Countries with strict gun control laws, such as Great Britain and Japan, had well under 50 apiece. Frequent, highly publicized mass shootings—49 people killed at an Orlando nightclub in 2016; 58 killed and 851 injured at a Las Vegas concert in 2017; 17 killed and 17 others injured at a high school in Parkland, Florida, in 2018—have led to widespread calls for gun control. "We are going to be the kids you read about in textbooks," said Emma González, a survivor of the Parkland shooting. "Not because we're going to be another statistic about mass shooting in America, but because . . . we are going to be the last mass shooting."

The Parkland shooting helped spark a mass movement, with millions participating in protests calling for stricter gun control. But, as with every major shooting, advocates of gun owners' rights called for different solutions. After Parkland, President Donald Trump revived an idea that had been promoted by the National Rifle Association (NRA) after the Sandy Hook school shooting in 2012, which left 20 first-grade students and six adults dead—namely, that teachers or other school personnel should be armed.

Some have argued that allowing citizens to carry concealed weapons would improve overall public safety. They claim that the country would be safer if more Americans carried guns. The massacre of 32 people at Virginia Tech in 2007 led some states to make it easier to carry concealed weapons on college campuses.

For millions of Americans, the very suggestion of outlawing handguns is outrageous. Many gun owners view individual firearms ownership as a basic constitutional right—a point of view the Supreme Court has upheld twice in the past few years. The Second Amendment proclaims, "A well-regulated militia being necessary for the security of a free state, the right to keep and bear arms shall not be infringed."

Still, the extent of your right to bear arms varies depending on where you live. All states allow law-abiding citizens to carry concealed weapons with a permit; six states require no permit. Ten states give law enforcement agencies the discretion to issue or deny concealed weapons licenses based on a variety of factors. In general, though, the trend has been in the other direction: 42 states have passed laws preventing cities in their states from enacting gun control laws.

Both sides of the gun debate believe that they argue for actions that will increase public safety. The advocates of gun ownership point out that localities with strict gun control laws often have very high crime rates, and all that bans on handguns do is ensure that only criminals have guns. The advocates of gun control acknowledge that problem but counter that the real problem is that borders are porous and other surrounding jurisdictions often have very weak gun control laws. In fact, according to criminologist Garen Wintemute at the University of California, Davis, a dispassionate look at the evidence seems to support the key claims of both sides. Studies have shown that certain types of gun restrictions—waiting periods, background checks, and some level of screening for gun buyers—work. In Wintemute's words, "They reduce rates of criminal activity involving guns and violence among people who are screened out and denied purchase of a gun—about 25 percent to 30 percent of those who are screened."[a] Other types of restrictions, such as gun buybacks, do not. Buybacks often encourage people to turn in only old, sometimes inoperable guns.

The argument for thinking about gun violence in different terms—as a public health problem—is stronger. Gun wounds, most of which are accidental, are among the leading causes of death in the United States.[b] Academics believe that regulations focusing on consumer safety (such as trigger locks) could significantly reduce accidental deaths. It's hard to say with any certainty, though. For years, the NRA has blocked most efforts at serious gun research.[c]

---

[a]Quoted in Jeremy Travis and Michelle Waul, *Reflections on the Crime Decline: Lessons for the Future? Proceedings from the Urban Institute Crime Decline Forum* (Washington, DC: Urban Institute Justice Policy Center, August 2002), 16, http://www.urban.org/uploaded-pdf/410546_crimedecline.pdf.

[b]For a discussion of the public health approach to gun violence, see David Hemenway, *Private Guns, Public Health* (Ann Arbor: University of Michigan Press, 2004). For statistics related to injuries and fatalities by year, see the Centers for Disease Control and Prevention's National Center for Injury Prevention and Control, http://www.cdc.gov/injury/index.html.

[c]Gary Gutting, "The N.R.A.'s Blockade on Science," *New York Times*, December 20, 2102, http://opinionator.blogs.nytimes.com/2012/12/20/the-blockade-on-science-on-gun-violence; Kevin Qualy and Margot Sanger Katz, "Compare These Gun Death Rates: The U.S. Is in a Different World," *New York Times*, June 14, 2016; J. B. Wogan, "Would Other States' Gun Laws Have Prevented Orlando?," *Governing*, June 14, 2016.

patient may have to fill vases with potpourri for a senior center, for instance, or an artist convicted of drunk driving may have to paint a picture for the organization whose lawn she drove over. Although such sentences are sometimes belittled as not just soft but mushy on crime, some communities have found that they are more effective than traditional probation in leading perpetrators to commit fewer offenses in the future. In practice, community justice initiatives range from the modest (placing prosecutors in local police stations, where they can see the neighborhood needs firsthand) to the ambitious (alternative courts that may require juvenile offenders to apologize to the people they have harmed and perform community service in an attempt to rectify the harm done by the crime committed).

The Shifting War on Drugs

The war on drugs began with the decision to criminalize the use of illicit drugs and to punish not just the production and distribution of drugs but also possession and use with severe criminal penalties. Today, some authorities are turning away from criminal sanctions. Instead, many states are embracing a public health approach. This can be seen with the greatest drug scourge of our time, opioids. Abuse of both illegal substances such as heroin and prescription painkillers have led to frequent overdoses—an estimated 64,000 Americans died from opioids in 2017—and other major societal problems and costs. For every three fatal overdoses, a local government's public safety costs can increase by an average of 1 percent, or $150,000, according to research from the data platform OpenGov.[57] Once deaths start spiking, government costs tend to steadily increase at that rate for about three years until they begin to plateau. President Trump declared in 2017 that opioid abuse was a national public health emergency.

We'll cover the opioid epidemic in some detail in Chapter 15. Within the context of crime, it's worth noting that the drugs that authorities are targeting are also changing—and subsiding to some degree as a concern. Cocaine use has fallen sharply since 2002. So have alcohol use and nicotine use. During this same period, illicit prescription drug use and heroin use have risen sharply.

Marijuana use has risen since 2007, and so has public support for decriminalization, if not legalization. In 1990, less than 20 percent of Americans supported the legalization of marijuana use. Today, about 60 percent do. Not surprisingly, since 2007, marijuana-related

arrests have fallen sharply—by nearly 40 percent, according to an analysis of crime data by Keith Humphreys, a Stanford University psychiatrist and former senior drug policy advisor to the Obama administration. At the same time, the number of people smoking marijuana has increased by 20 percent.[58]

The more meaningful metric, though, is total pot consumption. (See Figure 14-3 for Colorado's consumption.) Survey results suggest that a small number of people consume the vast majority of marijuana; in fact, people who use marijuana more than 21 times a month account for 89 percent of total marijuana consumption. Not coincidentally, these heavy if not daily users tend to be less educated and poorer; many also have mental health issues. From a public health viewpoint, this has clear policy implications. People who occasionally use marijuana are not a major public health concern. Daily users are. A strong case can be made that the number of heavy users should be minimized through high taxes that discourage heavy consumption, caps on THC content (to reduce marijuana dependency), and limits on advertising and points of sale in vulnerable communities.

More than half the states allow marijuana use for medical purposes. The trend toward legalization for

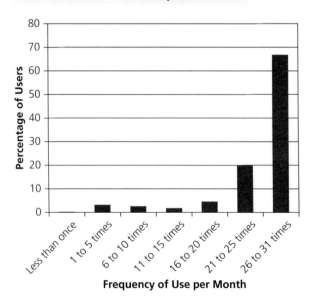

FIGURE 14-3 ● Colorado's Marijuana Consumption

Source: Miles K. Light, Adam Orens, Brian Lewandowski, and Todd Pickton, "Market Size and Demand for Marijuana in Colorado," Table 8, prepared for the Colorado Department of Revenue, Marijuana Policy Group, 2014.

recreational purposes is strong. The number of states that legalized marijuana doubled in 2016, to eight. As they do, state legislatures will ultimately have to decide what kind of regulatory structure will prevail. In doing so, states will have to weigh their desire for revenues from marijuana taxes—a stream of revenue that would benefit from increases in consumption—against public health needs.[59]

Conclusion

Today, America's prison system is in flux. A 2009 study by the human rights group Amnesty International found that more than 20,000 prisoners continued to be held in conditions of extreme isolation in supermax prisons. According to a Justice Department survey of former inmates released in 2012, nearly 10 percent of prisoners suffer sexual abuse while incarcerated in state prisons, local jails, or postrelease treatment centers. Nearly 4 percent said they were forced to have nonconsensual sex with another prisoner, while more than 5 percent reported incidents involving facility staff. For many of these prisoners, rape may be just the beginning. Male prisoners who are passive or effeminate may end up as slaves, forced to do menial jobs and sometimes "rented out" to other inmates to be used sexually.[60] The prison bill passed by the U.S. House in 2018 sought to address the issue of sex crimes and safety in prison.

The United States also leads the world in the execution of people with mental impairments. An estimated 56 percent of state prisoners and 64 percent of local jail inmates suffer from mental health disorders, including serious conditions such as schizophrenia, bipolar disorder, and depression. That's more than a million mentally ill prisoners and inmates—far more than the number of patients in mental hospitals.[61]

But there are promising changes in the nation's criminal justice reform. A growing number of states are embracing corrections reform and showing that there are smarter ways to reduce crime and punishment than mere severity in the process. That example has prompted a reevaluation of policies at the federal level, including the White House. And the criminal justice system as a whole has wakened to its problems with race, even if the search for solutions is just beginning.

THE LATEST RESEARCH

After a long period of decline, violent crime has reemerged as an issue of concern to policymakers and the public. Protests over police shootings have become common. At the same time, while crime remains historically low, recent increases in the murder rates in a few cities have sparked debate about whether the right deterrence policies are in place. The studies reviewed below look at the factors that contribute to racial disparities, incarceration, and gun violence, as well as questions concerning the effects of criminal justice reform on recidivism.

● **Baumgartner, Frank R., Derek A. Epp, and Kelsey Shoub,** *Suspect Citizens: What 20 Million Traffic Stops Tell Us about Policing and Race* (New York: Cambridge University Press, 2018).

To determine whether police racially profiled individuals, North Carolina became the first state to mandate collection of data about traffic stops. Since 2002, the state has collected data from virtually every policy agency in the state, as well as the state highway patrol. It hasn't done much with it, though. The state department of justice is supposed to report periodic findings to the legislature, but has yet to do so. But the data are publicly available, allowing this comprehensive look by academic researchers. They found that black and Hispanic drivers are more likely to be pulled over. Blacks make up 22 percent of North Carolina's population, but make up 32 percent of the traffic stops, even though studies show whites drive more. Once they're stopped, black drivers are much more likely to be searched. After the stop, 2.35 percent of white drivers are searched, compared with 5.05 percent of black drivers and 4.74 percent of Hispanics. "This means that blacks are subjected to about twice the odds of being pulled over, and then after that more than twice the odds of being searched: A double-whammy that means they are four times as likely to be searched."

● **Carr, Jillian, and Jennifer Doleac,** "The Geography, Incidence, and Underreporting of

(Continued)

(Continued)

Gun Violence: New Evidence Using ShotSpotter Data," working paper, April 26, 2016.

According to the FBI, the United States experiences more than 8,000 gun deaths a year—the equivalent of about 27 people shot dead every day of the year. That's nearly 15 times the gunshot homicide rate of European countries such as Germany, the Netherlands, and Austria. However, Carr and Doleac suggest that the U.S. gunshot homicide rate actually understates the rate of gun violence. Drawing on data from Washington, D.C., and Oakland, California, from ShotSpotter, a tool that records sounds of gunfire, Carr and Doleac calculate that only 12 percent of gunfire incidents result in 911 calls to report gunshots. Only 2 to 7 percent of incidents result in a reported assault with a dangerous weapon. These extremely low reporting rates suggest that gun violence may be even more widespread than researchers previously believed.

- **Pelletier, Elizabeth, Bryce Peterson, and Ryan King**, "Assessing the Impact of South Carolina's Parole and Probation Reforms," Urban Institute, April 2017, https://www.urban.org/sites/default/files/publication/89871/south_carolina_jri_policy_assessment_final_1.pdf.

In 2009, there were 24,612 people serving time in South Carolina's prisons, a population expected to grow by 13 percent over the next five years, at a cost of $458 million. In response, the legislature passed a comprehensive criminal justice reform bill that restructured sentences for some crimes, allowed prisoners to earn more "good time" in prison, and broadened eligibility for parole. This paper focused on the effect of administrative responses to parole and probation violations. The average number of responses received per person per year increased nearly 42 percent between 2010 and 2015, in essence meaning there was more supervision. Recidivism among people on supervision has declined every year since. Almost 10 percent of people who began supervision in 2010 were incarcerated or reincarcerated within a year. That share was cut in half by 2014.

- **Phelps, Michelle S., and Devah Pager**, "Inequality and Punishment: A Turning Point for Mass Incarceration?," *The ANNALS of the American Academy of Political and Social Science* 663 (January 2016): 185–203.

Mass incarceration has been much studied, with the total U.S. prison population growing more than fivefold between the 1970s and 2000s. But now incarceration rates are declining. What explains the drop? Examining prison population rates across states between 1980 and 2013, Phelps and Pager found that the story isn't the same in every state. Not surprisingly, states with high rates of violent crime didn't see their prison populations drop on a comparative basis. Those that felt the greatest budget pressures during and after the recession of 2007–2009 were the most likely to reduce prison populations after 2010, suggesting that financial pressure was an important contributor to downward trends. States dominated by Republican legislators and governors continue to be associated with higher incarceration rates, with racial demographics and economic inequality also remaining key factors.

CHAPTER 14

for CQ Press

Want a better grade?

Get the tools you need to sharpen your study skills. SAGE edge offers a robust online environment featuring an impressive array of free tools and resources.

Access practice quizzes, eFlashcards, video, and multimedia at **edge.sagepub.com/smithgreenblatt7e**

Top Ten Takeaways

1. Much of the American system of justice is rooted in British traditions.

2. The United States incarcerates a much larger proportion of its population than do other rich nations.

3. There is considerable evidence that people of color are targeted, arrested, and incarcerated in disproportionate numbers.

4. Official and unofficial videos of police encounters with the public have raised new questions about police use of excessive force.

5. Some police forces have been accused of using arrests as a means of collecting revenues rather than improving public safety.

6. Some conservatives worry that law enforcement officers are hamstringing themselves because of the so-called Ferguson effect.

7. After a long decline, homicide rates have risen in some cities, such as Chicago.

8. Drug addiction and violent crimes led to an enormous prison-building boom in recent decades.

9. Now, many states are looking to change their criminal justice systems in order to help cut down on recidivism.

10. Application of the death penalty has declined sharply in recent years.

Key Concepts

"broken windows" policing (p. 399)
common law (p. 391)
community policing (p. 399)
community, or restorative, justice movement (p. 408)
deterrence theory (p. 397)
drug courts (p. 408)
mass incarceration (p. 403)
parole (p. 403)
probation (p. 391)
professional model of policing (p. 399)
racial profiling (p. 404)
solitary confinement (p. 394)
stop and frisk (p. 398)
supermax prisons (p. 394)
verdict (p. 393)
war on drugs (p. 403)

Suggested Websites

- **www.bjs.gov**. Website of the Bureau of Justice Statistics; pulls together a wide variety of information on the criminal justice system.

- **www.fbi.gov**. Website of the Federal Bureau of Investigation; offers information on national and international criminal activities as well as crime prevention tips.

(Continued)

414 Governing States and Localities

(Continued)

The FBI's Uniform Crime Report is the best source of information on felony and violent crime nationwide.

- **www.manhattan-institute.org**. Website of the Manhattan Institute; includes archived articles from the institute's *City Journal*, which addresses such issues as the effectiveness of various policing strategies.

- **www.themarshallproject.org**. Website of a new nonpartisan, nonprofit news organization, The Marshall Project, that focuses on the work of the criminal justice system.

- **www.ncjrs.gov**. Website of the National Criminal Justice Reference Service; provides statistics on a variety of topics involving crime.

- **www.nij.gov**. Website of the National Institute of Justice, the research, development, and evaluation agency of the U.S. Department of Justice; the agency researches crime control and justice issues, particularly at the state and local levels.

- **www.pewtrusts.org/en/projects/public-safety-performance-project**. Website of the Pew Charitable Trusts' Public Safety Performance Project; offers up-to-date information on corrections reform and on the crime–prison connection.

- **www.sentencingproject.org**. Website of The Sentencing Project; offers data and information about racial disparities in the U.S. criminal justice system.

- **www.urban.org/research-area/crime-and-justice**. Website of the nonpartisan Washington, D.C.–based Urban Institute; offers an excellent collection of criminal justice research.

- **www.vera.org**. Website of the Vera Institute of Justice, a nonprofit organization that conducts research, demonstration projects, and technical assistance to improve the justice system.

Joe Raedle/Getty Images

Health and Welfare

State, Heal Thyself!

Undeniably, the patients aren't the only ones who are sick in the U.S. health care system. The system itself needs more than an aspirin and an apple a day to heal itself, and it remains to be seen whether the federal health care reform package will provide that solution. Meanwhile, states and localities continue to pick up the slack. Here, Dr. Gwen Wurm, a pediatrician with the University of Miami Health System, checks 5-year-old Christina Brownlee's ears.

Chapter Objectives

After reading this chapter, you will be able to

● Discuss variations in public health programs and how political culture influences how states define public health,

● Explain how federal and state governments became involved in health care,

● Describe health care reform efforts from the 1980s to the 2010s,

● Relate how the rise of managed care resulted in greater state involvement in health care,

● Identify current issues in U.S. health care, and

● Compare how different states and the federal government have sought to define good health.

Opioids have become a trillion-dollar problem, the result of lost earnings, decreased productivity, and, of course, health care costs. In Kentucky, 1,565 people died from drug overdoses in 2017, which represented a 40 percent increase from 2012 and an 11.5 percent jump from just the year before. Kentucky is one of the states hit hardest by opioids, but it's far from alone. Just across the Tug Fork River, two pharmacies dispensed 20.8 million prescription painkillers over the course of a decade in Williamson, West Virginia, a town with just 3,191 residents. Towns that average hundreds or even thousands of pills for every man, woman, and child are not uncommon. "These numbers will shake even the most cynical observer," said Don Perdue, a former West Virginia delegate and a retired pharmacist. "Distributors have fed their greed on human frailties and to criminal effect. There is no excuse and should be no forgiveness."[1]

Drug overdoses killed 63,362 Americans in 2016, according to the federal Centers for Disease Control and Prevention (CDC). More than 40,000 involved an illicit or prescription opioid, a group that includes prescription painkillers such as oxycodone, hydrocodone, codeine, morphine, and fentanyl, as well as heroin. The death toll from opioids could exceed 500,000 over the next decade, according to public health forecasters.[2] Already, opioids are blamed for drops in life expectancy in both 2015 and 2016—the first time life expectancy dropped in two consecutive years since the 1960s. Things may get worse before they get better. More than 2 million Americans are struggling with opioid abuse

or addiction, according to the U.S. Surgeon General's office. Most addicts started out taking prescribed painkillers. "The nation has weathered drug epidemics before, but this crisis is different," federal Food and Drug Administration commissioner Scott Gottlieb said in 2018. "It's more insidious, more pervasive and more devastating."[3]

In response, a number of states have filed lawsuits against drug manufacturers. All but four states agreed to a compact outlined by Massachusetts governor Charlie Baker to take steps such as establishing more public awareness campaigns; pursuing Good Samaritan laws, which protect individuals from arrest if they help at an overdose scene; and changing prescription guidelines. A number of cities now equip police officers with the antidote drug naloxone to reverse opioid overdoses in emergency situations. Every state except Missouri now has a prescription drug database intended to stop potential users from doctor-shopping to obtain more drugs. Many states have tried to limit supply by restricting the number of pain-relief pills doctors can prescribe. They might limit patients, for instance, to a three-day supply.

After growing for years, the national prescription rate peaked in 2012 at more than 255 million, or 81.3 prescriptions for every 100 persons. By 2017, the prescribing rate declined to its lowest level in a decade, at 58.7 per 100 persons, with 191 million opioid prescriptions in total.[4] That's still a lot of pills. Lawmakers are grappling with the fact that any policies they put in place will take years to make a difference. "Most of the things we do, we realize are not going to take that immediate effect," said Van Ingram, executive director of the Kentucky Office of Drug Control Policy.[5]

Part of the challenge for public officials is that the opioid epidemic is really a fight on two distinct fronts: the increased use of heroin in young adults in urban and suburban areas, and older adults abusing prescription drugs like Oxycontin in more rural areas. "You can cut the state of Virginia in half," Virginia governor Terry McAuliffe said in 2017. "On the East Coast, around Virginia Beach, it's all heroin and now the more potent fentanyl. Then I can drive eight hours to Abingdon in the southwest corner of the state, and I can tell you there are no heroin problems there. It's all prescription drugs."[6]

That makes the current crisis different from previous drug epidemics involving methamphetamines or crack cocaine. Even if officials in the United States were to pursue every available solution, the approaches can seem frustratingly piecemeal, like plugging a hole in a dike only to see two leaks spring up elsewhere. Naloxone can reverse overdoses in an emergency, but it doesn't reduce addiction rates. Prescription databases prevent people from doctor-shopping for more pills, but those users often just start buying their drugs illegally. Limiting the supply of prescription opioids like Oxycontin has led to a surge in fentanyl, an opioid that's 50 times stronger than heroin and 100 times more potent than morphine. Fentanyl is so powerful that an Ohio police officer accidentally overdosed on the substance while searching the car of a suspected drug dealer. He passed out after brushing some of the powder off his shirt; other officers had to administer four doses of naloxone to revive him. Another emerging opioid, carfentanil, is an elephant tranquilizer that's 10,000 times stronger than morphine and has been blamed for hundreds of recent overdoses. These increasingly potent substances continue to make the epidemic a moving target.

The scale and challenge of the opioid epidemic, as well as the enormous costs involved, help illustrate why all levels of government have health care as a central part of their missions (and budgets). There's certainly disagreement about the extent to which government should be involved. President Donald Trump and other Republicans have sought to scale back the effort and expenditures at the state and federal levels. Many

Democrats now argue that health care is "a human right," with progressives calling for some form of universal health care that would be largely or wholly underwritten by the government.

Health care is an issue where governmental policies now split notably along partisan lines. As of August 2018, 17 states, mostly in the South and Midwest and all with Republican leadership, had rejected the Medicaid expansion that was a central part of the Affordable Care Act (ACA), a 2010 federal law that sought to cover most individuals who didn't have health insurance through their employers. Voters in states such as Idaho, Maine, and Utah have sought to implement the expansion through ballot measures. Abolishing the Affordable Care Act has been a priority for President Trump, something he has been unable as yet to achieve, but he has undone some of its key components. The uneven implementation of the law has led to some striking disparities between states in terms of their uninsured populations, their overall health costs, and the balance sheets of many health care providers, notably hospitals in rural areas that rely on Medicaid reimbursements to pay for care. Blue states are considering insurance requirements that would mimic those currently being weakened or ended by the Trump administration. Red states are looking for ways to allow insurers to offer plans that are cheaper but provide less complete coverage than mandated by the federal law. "Without question I think we're going to see a natural experiment in the states and a growing divergence in outcomes," said Sabrina Corlette, a research professor at Georgetown University's Health Policy Institute.[7]

The argument surrounding the Affordable Care Act isn't all about dollars and cents; partly, it reflects differences in ideology. One of the ongoing arguments in American politics is over how much—and how best—to help the poor. Giving people handouts, such as through welfare—the cash assistance program also known as **Temporary Assistance for Needy Families (TANF)**—only enables them to remain mired in poverty, argue many conservative politicians and others. While he was governor of Kansas, Republican Sam Brownback refused to implement the Medicaid expansion and also cut his state's TANF caseload by about a third through changes in eligibility benefits. Rather than giving poor people a "pittance," he said, government policies should prod them into finding work. "Our country has spent billions of dollars and decades supporting a welfare system that has shown no improvement getting people out of poverty," Brownback says.

Temporary Assistance for Needy Families (TANF) The next-generation welfare program (passed in 1996) that provides federal assistance in the form of block grants to states, which have great flexibility in designing their programs.

"Instead of focusing on spending more money on a system that creates dependency, we need to reform our welfare system to provide the opportunity for people to learn the skills to be self-sufficient, which is what we are doing here in Kansas."[8] Perhaps the strongest current trend in health and human services on the Republican side is to impose work requirements on individuals benefiting from government assistance programs.

Many states—and not just ones run by Republicans—cut social service programs during recent years of recession. Government cannot cure all social ills, but over the years, Americans have come to count on the various levels of government to provide many benefit programs. Chief among these is health care. The Affordable Care Act relies primarily on employers and private insurance companies to expand coverage, stopping short of the type of government-funded health coverage that progressives favor and that is common in other rich nations. But the act represents the latest and one of the most important expansions of the government's role in regulating and underwriting health care.

In this chapter, we will discuss the ways in which states differ in terms of their generosity in paying for health care and social welfare programs for their residents. In addition to differing in regard to the resources they're willing to expend caring for individuals, states differ in how they address public health—that is, the health of the population as a whole and how it might be affected by threats such as epidemics. We will also look at the long history of how governments got into the business of paying for health care in the first place. As you read through this chapter, keep in mind the following questions:

- **Why does access to health care vary so widely across the country?**
- **How has federal health care reform affected states, cities, and counties?**
- **What roles do state and local governments play in maintaining public health?**

Government's Role in Health

Seeking Universal Health

When it comes to health policy, it always boils down to money. Back during the 1980s, President Ronald Reagan's administration floated the idea of having the federal government pay the entire cost of Medicaid in exchange for states' fully funding welfare, which is also a joint federal–state responsibility. The proposal went nowhere, in part because governors and other state officials balked. In a sense, that argument is being replayed today, with some state leaders happy to take money from Washington while others suspect that doing so would result in hidden costs for them down the road.

Even states that have shown little interest in taking on new responsibilities have found that health care is an unavoidable issue. This is due largely to **Medicaid**, the joint state–federal health insurance program for low-income individuals and children, the elderly, and people with disabilities. When Congress created it in 1965, it was supposed to be a modest program that served only a small number of extremely poor people. But it didn't work out that way.

As soon as it was created, Medicaid expenditures started rising quickly—and never stopped. Medicaid now provides health insurance and services to more than 67 million Americans. The federal government pays a majority of the program's costs, but Medicaid has still grown as a share of total state spending from 20.5 percent in 2008 to 29.0 percent in 2017.[9] Medicaid spending reached a new high in 18 states in 2016, with the program taking up a larger share of each state-generated dollar than in 2000 (ranging from a one-cent increase in Hawaii and New York to an increase of nearly 14 cents in Louisiana).[10] Such expenses are one reason Republicans have mostly opposed the Affordable Care Act, sometimes called Obamacare after President Barack Obama, and its expansion of Medicaid.

Congressional Republicans held dozens of votes to repeal Obamacare, but those were meaningless so long as Obama held the veto pen. In 2016, Trump campaigned on the idea of getting rid of Obamacare, or at least most of its provisions. In May 2017, the House passed a bill to repeal parts of the Affordable Care Act, including the individual mandate, which required people to have health insurance or pay a fine. Trump hosted a celebration in the Rose Garden. But it turned out the bill didn't have enough support to make it through the Senate, where it died in a dramatic vote in July 2017. The House-passed bill would have increased the number of Americans without health insurance by 14 million in 2018 and by 23 million by 2026.

Medicaid A joint state and federal health insurance program that serves low-income individuals, the elderly, and people with disabilities.

Since its passage, the Affordable Care Act had always been controversial, with more people saying they disapproved of the law in polls than saying they approved of it. Once the law was under real threat, however, public opinion started to shift. In February 2018, a poll conducted by the Kaiser Family Foundation found that 54 percent of people viewed the law favorably, which was its high-water mark since its initial passage.[11] Governors whose residents had benefited from expanded coverage, including Republicans, helped block the repeal, persuading home-state senators of its value. Medicaid expansion had been "a winner for people of our state," said Nevada governor Brian Sandoval, a Republican. "I have to be comfortable that those 210,000 lives are going to continue to enjoy the quality of life and health care that they have right now."[12]

The failure of the congressional repeal has not stopped Trump from ending what he calls the "Obamacare nightmare." As part of a tax-cut package passed at the end of 2017, Congress eliminated the Affordable Care Act's individual mandate, meaning people without health coverage will no longer be hit with a tax penalty beginning in 2019. In February 2018, Republican attorneys general from 20 states, led by Texas, filed a lawsuit claiming that the Affordable Care Act was unconstitutional. The Supreme Court had upheld the law in 2012 because the individual mandate was constitutional under Congress's taxing authority. The attorneys general argued that the elimination of the individual mandate also made other parts of the law unstable, since insurers could not count on healthy young people to buy insurance and in effect subsidize others with preexisting conditions. In June 2018, the Trump administration informed a court that it would not defend the Affordable Care Act against the states' challenge. In 2018, some Republican candidates pledged they would preserve requirements for coverage of preexisting conditions, even as they participated in the suit to eliminate them under the Affordable Care Act.

That same month, Trump announced that a new Labor Department regulation would make it easier for small businesses to band together to pay for health insurance plans that would be exempt from some mandates under the Affordable Care Act, meaning they would not have to provide "essential health benefits" such as mental health, emergency services, maternity and newborn care, and prescription drugs. In other words, the allowable plans would be cheaper but offer fewer benefits. "You're going to save massive amounts of money and

have much better health care," Trump told the National Federation of Independent Business, a small-business association. "It's going to cost you much less."[13]

The idea of creating a universal health coverage plan had been a dream of Democrats for decades. In 2010, Obama came close. Enjoying large Democratic majorities during his first two years in office, Obama pushed through the Affordable Care Act, which used various methods to expand coverage with federal subsidies. Most people remained covered through plans subsidized by their employers, but people with limited incomes and no insurance through their jobs would receive support when buying insurance from private companies. The poor would rely on a major expansion of the Medicaid program, which had been created in 1965.

The Medicaid expansion was a good deal for states—the federal government would pick up 100 percent of the cost for the first three years, from 2014 to 2016, and no less than 90 percent after that—but many Republican officials decided that they couldn't afford it anyway. Already, Medicaid eats up a sizable percentage of state budgets (states pay, on average, 43 percent of traditional Medicaid costs, and total spending on the program nationwide was $553 billion in 2016).[14] Rather than making Medicaid bigger, a number of Republican governors and legislators argued, the goal should be to make the program more efficient. And some were skeptical that the federal government would pay its promised share. It wouldn't be the first time Washington started a program and then left states to make up the difference when funding dropped. "We believe in the end the track record of the federal government has been to pull away from their commitments to the states," said governor Scott Walker of Wisconsin. "We believe confidently going forward this federal government is likely to renege from its promises on Medicaid to the states. And we won't be exposed to that."[15]

Not taking the money was costing Wisconsin money, however. Rather than having the federal government pick up 100 percent of the costs for some Medicaid patients, Wisconsin was paying about 40 percent of the costs for those covered under traditional Medicaid rules—which amounted to about $100 million a year for the state. And lots of other Wisconsin residents who might have been able to receive coverage found themselves ineligible. Various studies have shown that the Medicaid expansion saves states money, because it makes the federal government absorb the health care costs for people who were receiving treatment through other programs. "One reason new enrollees do not substantially burden states' Medicaid budgets is that expansion absorbs some of the costs states were already bearing prior to expansion," says Mark Hall, director of the Health Law and Policy Program at Wake Forest University's School of Law. "Various categories of previously covered Medicaid recipients (such as 'presumptive' enrollees) can now enroll under the ACA's expansion program."[16]

Those who remain unenrolled have caused problems for hospitals, which are required to provide emergency medical care regardless of ability to pay. One study found that in the first four months of the Medicaid expansion, uncompensated care of patients without insurance dropped by 30 percent at 465 hospitals in 30 states that had embraced the new program. In states that hadn't expanded Medicaid, the amount of uncompensated care was essentially unchanged.[17] The big price tag of uncompensated care is one reason hospitals have been pressing states to accept the Medicaid expansion.

Some of the Affordable Care Act's provisions are popular, and may yet be preserved by Congress, such as the requirement that insurers allow parents to keep their children on their plans until age 26. (Formerly, young people could be dropped at 18.) A study by the Department of Health and Human Services in 2016 found that 6.1 million Americans between the ages of 19 and 25 were enrolled on a parent's plan and that most of them wouldn't have been able to have that coverage prior to passage of the law.[18] As a result, the number of young adults without health insurance had declined from 3 million to 1 million.[19]

As noted earlier, some Republican governors and legislators have become convinced that no matter how much they may disdain Obamacare, it makes sense in terms of their revenues. After all, their residents pay federal taxes—and thus underwrite the Medicaid expansion—even if their states don't participate. Not surprisingly, overall Medicaid costs are expanding fastest in states that have accepted the expansion, but costs rose at a rate 50 percent lower for those states themselves in 2014 and 2015 than for the states that blocked expansion. State representative Steve Clouse, the Republican who chairs the Alabama Ways and Means General Fund Committee, said he favors repealing the Affordable Care Act but argues that as long as it's the law, it would make sense for his state to bring in the Medicaid dollars. The net gain for his state if it accepted the expansion would be $935 million by 2022, according to an Urban Institute study. It's "the hand we've been dealt by the feds," Clouse said.[20]

Retaining State Authority

States continue to play a central role in setting policy even under the federal health care regime. As part of its 2012 ruling, the Supreme Court placed the decision of whether to expand Medicaid in the states' hands. The law as written left the states some important powers. The Obama administration announced in 2011 that states would have broad discretion to make a key decision under the law: the level of coverage a health insurance plan must meet, at a minimum, to count as health insurance.[21] The Affordable Care Act has attempted to expand health insurance by creating state health insurance exchanges, online marketplaces where consumers can choose among different health insurance plans. The exchanges represent an alternative to employer-provided insurance. For low-income and middle-income people, the cost of insurance purchased through the exchanges is subsidized by federal tax credits. In following the exchange model, the Affordable Care Act borrowed from ideas that had already been tried at the state level. Massachusetts established a health insurance exchange in a law enacted under Governor Mitt Romney in 2006 to expand access to health insurance.

Under the federal law, states themselves can run the exchanges if they choose. States that administer their own exchanges get to make important choices, such as whether to allow every health insurance plan that meets basic criteria into the exchange or to provide more structure to consumers' options.[22] But most states opted not to set up their own exchanges, as part of their campaign of resistance against the Affordable Care Act. Most people who sign up through the exchanges receive subsidies for insurance based on their incomes. The law states that subsidies are available to people who purchase insurance through "an exchange established by the state." That led to a legal fight over whether people signing up through the federal exchange—not the ones established by states—were eligible to receive financial assistance. In 2015, the Supreme Court ruled that they were eligible, since it was clear that Congress intended for subsidies to flow through exchanges operated by governments, not just "states." Justice Antonin Scalia, writing in dissent, derided this as "interpretive jiggery-pokery."[23]

The Affordable Care Act largely forbids states to reduce the number of people who are eligible for

Medicaid, but it doesn't stop them from scaling back coverage in certain ways. In 2012, for example, Florida cut the number of days most Medicaid patients could spend in hospitals from 45 to 23, and Maine eliminated coverage for podiatry, optometry, and dental care.[24] In 2011, California tried to end a well-regarded adult day-care program for Medicaid patients that had succeeded in keeping seniors and people with disabilities out of nursing homes. Lawmakers were tempted by the possibility of saving $145 million immediately, even though having more people in nursing homes would likely have cost the state more money in the long term.[25] After opponents of the cuts sued, the state agreed to maintain a more modest program.

Under the Affordable Care Act, the federal government paid the full cost of the expansion through 2016. Now it's tapering back its share to 90 percent by 2020. Taking the deal doesn't just mean more people will have health coverage; it also means billions of dollars will be pumped into states' economies via their health care systems. In certain ways, states are saving money: if fewer people are uninsured, fewer will seek treatment in hospital emergency rooms and stick the state with the bills. On the other hand, the Medicaid expansion is so large that even the remaining 10 percent will mean millions of dollars a year in fresh costs for many states. Given the precarious condition of many states' budgets, adding any new costs is a difficult sell.[26]

Beyond Medicaid

Although Medicaid is the states' biggest immediate health care expense, it is hardly their only one. States provide health insurance to their own employees and, in many cases, to their former employees after they retire. As with employee pension costs, paying for retired state employees' health care costs has emerged over the past decade as one of the states' leading long-term budget challenges. Traditionally, states have paid for the retiree health care bill that shows up each year, rather than setting aside money in advance. The looming bills for the coming decades are so large, though—as of 2016, states had promised $587 billion more in retiree health care than they had assets set aside—that many states are starting to rethink that strategy.[27] In 2012, West Virginia, which has a long-term bill of $10 billion, became the first state to dedicate a specific amount of tax money for retiree health care, committing $30 million per year. West Virginia also did what many other states

have done: it made retiree health care benefits less generous for future retirees. State and local employees have gone along with the changes reluctantly. "Does it give me heartburn?" asked Josh Sword, political director of the American Federation of Teachers–West Virginia. "Sure. But at the end of the day, the state cannot continue to afford this level of benefit."[28]

States are also responsible for providing health care for inmates in state prisons. No state has struggled more with inmate health care than California, where state prisons have long been massively overcrowded. In 2006, a federal judge said that one inmate a week was dying unnecessarily because of the low quality of care, a violation of the U.S. Constitution's prohibition of cruel and unusual punishment. The judge took control of the prisoner health care system away from the state and placed it in the hands of an independent receiver. Since then, the state has made some gradual improvements—improvements that have come at a cost. The state spends well above $10,000 per prisoner each year for medical care, far more than most other states.[29]

County and city governments spend significant amounts on health care as well. In many parts of the country, hospitals and clinics funded by counties and cities continue to function as a critical social safety net for people without health insurance. These are people who earn too much to qualify for Medicaid but too little to be able to pay for private health insurance.

In states that haven't expanded Medicaid under the Affordable Care Act, many hospitals are struggling to pay for care for the uninsured. Assuming that states would expand insurance coverage through Medicaid, the health care law reduced payments to hospitals for the uninsured. That has hurt hospitals' bottom lines in states that have refused the Medicaid expansion. Between 2010 and 2018, 83 rural hospitals closed nationwide, representing about 4 percent of the total, predominantly in states that hadn't expanded Medicaid.[30] "And now, beginning in 2010, we've had another series of cuts that are all combining to create another expansion of closures just like we saw in the '90s," said Brock Slabach, senior vice president of the National Rural Health Association (NRHA). "We don't want to wake up with another disaster."[31]

This can be traced back in large measure to the Affordable Care Act, which upended the overall health care system by encouraging a move away from a traditional fee-for-service model. As that happens, critical-access hospitals—hospitals in rural areas that have no more than 25 inpatient beds but provide emergency care—are entirely reliant on fee-for-service. With the new law also came new regulations and mandates. Hospitals have to adopt electronic systems for keeping health records and new forms of reporting or face penalty fees for not complying with new initiatives. These regulations have tightened finances for many hospitals, but rural ones have been especially affected because they operate with much smaller and less flexible financial bases.

But despite the law's costs, the rural hospitals that have suffered the most have been those in states that have not taken up the Affordable Care Act's offer to expand Medicaid coverage at the federal government's cost. In Kansas, for instance, the state hospital association has told lawmakers that the state's failure to expand Medicaid is having dire consequences, costing individual hospitals millions in unreimbursed care. While no particular rural area of the country is safe from hospital closures, Alan Morgan, chief executive of the NRHA, notes that "if you pull up a map of where conditions like diabetes, hypertension, [and] obesity are most prevalent, those are the areas that have seen the most rural hospitals close." In effect, he's referring to the southeastern corner of the country, where those chronic conditions are dishearteningly common. Hospitals in states with high rates of diabetes, obesity, and other conditions are also suffering. Georgia has been especially hard hit. More than half of its rural hospitals are classified as at-risk, and five of them closed between 2011 and 2016. Medicaid expansion still isn't on the table in Georgia.

That's why Adam O'Neal decided to take a long walk. He is the mayor of Belhaven, North Carolina, and soon after the hospital in his town shut down in 2014, O'Neal started off on a 273-mile walk to Washington, D.C., where he hoped to draw attention to the plight of rural hospitals. The closure of Pungo District Hospital in his eastern North Carolina town meant that townspeople had to travel 75 miles to the nearest emergency room. O'Neal shared the story of a woman who had died four days after the hospital closed, just as a medevac helicopter arrived an hour after it was called to airlift her for treatment. "Before, she would have been given nitroglycerin, put in the back of an ambulance and been to a hospital in about 25 minutes," O'Neal said. "In that hour that she lived, she would have received 35 minutes of emergency room care and she very well could have survived."[32]

How Government Got into the Health Care Biz

Any serious discussion of health care soon arrives at a basic question: who should pay for what? It wasn't always so complicated. For most of the nation's history, elected officials believed that the government should serve as the health and welfare provider of last resort for society's poorest and sickest members. The level of government that officials had in mind, however, was not the federal government and not even state governments. It was local government.

The role of local governments in health and welfare goes back to the very beginning of U.S. history. In colonial America, local communities maintained almshouses to feed and clothe people who could not care for themselves and who had no families to care for them. "They frequently griped about the cost of these expenditures," writes Gabriel Loiacono, a historian at the University of Wisconsin, Oshkosh, "but for about three centuries from the beginning of British North America, almost no one thought government-provided health care for the poor should go away."[33] Back then, few distinctions were made among the sick, the mentally ill, and people without means of support. As sociologist Paul Starr has noted, almshouses "received dependent persons of all kinds, mixing together promiscuously the aged, the orphaned, the insane, the ill, the debilitated."[34] Those with infectious diseases, such as typhoid fever and cholera, were sent into quarantine in pesthouses to survive as best they could.

That began to change in the 19th century. By the middle of the century, elected officials, social reformers, and physicians—who were just beginning to establish medicine as a respectable profession—came to believe that mixing juveniles, beggars, the mentally ill, widows, and others in almshouses was no longer the best course of action. In effect, physicians and public officials began to distinguish between the sick and the destitute. A new institution was needed—the hospital.

From the early to mid-1800s, cities such as Philadelphia and New York transformed some of their almshouses into hospitals.[35] Privately organized charitable hospitals, many run by religious groups, appeared in many cities too. Even state governments made modest forays into health care. By 1860, most states had established mental hospitals and homes for the blind and the deaf.

STATES UNDER STRESS
STATE STRATEGIES FOR ADDRESSING RISING MEDICAID COSTS

States are concerned about the rising costs associated with Medicaid. During the first couple years of Medicaid expansion under the Affordable Care Act, the federal government paid 100 percent of the additional coverage costs. That funding started winding down in 2016 and will drop to 90 percent in 2020. "It can't be avoided, and every state will be looking at this," says Stacey Mazer, a policy analyst for the National Association of State Budget Officers.

Most of the states that chose to expand Medicaid will use their general fund budget to make up the difference. Thirteen states, however, are either tapping into tax revenues for it, making hospitals help, or cutting other Medicaid costs to make room in the budget. Faced with losing Medicaid benefits, Oregon voters in 2018 approved a ballot measure to raise taxes on hospitals and health insurance plans to pay for expansion. California voters similarly approved two ballot initiatives in 2016 that will fund the state's share. One makes a hospital fee permanent, and another raises cigarette taxes. In 2018, New Hampshire Republican governor Chris Sununu signed a proposal that earmarks 5 percent of liquor sales tax revenue for Medicaid expansion. "I knew this was going to be the most important challenge the state was going to face from day one," Sununu said.

New Hampshire is also one of several states seeking to use work requirements to cut Medicaid costs and free up money for expansion. Requiring people to meet employment criteria will limit the number of people eligible for Medicaid in general. Arkansas, Kentucky, and Indiana have also gotten the green light from the federal government to add work requirements to Medicaid, with Arkansas's taking effect this month. Kentucky's, however, are tied up in the courts after a federal judge ruled that they were unconstitutional. Work requirements in New Hampshire and Indiana are being phased in, starting in 2019. The decision to require Medicaid beneficiaries to work or volunteer is a controversial one, but "it is likely these requirements will save states money," says Ben Sommers, a health care economist at Harvard University. But it's not yet clear the requirements are legal. A similarly controversial policy—charging a premium for Medicaid—is also being used by Kentucky to plug holes.

In some states, the conversation about expansion costs is just starting. Rhode Island Democratic governor Gina Raimondo, for instance, proposed putting the funding burden on Medicaid beneficiaries and adding a copay requirement for emergency room visits and generic drugs. The legislature balked at that proposal.

Although states have to prepare to pay a bigger share of the Medicaid tab, health policy experts say the cost of expansion will be relatively small compared to other Medicaid costs such as prescription drugs. "The population that is covered by Medicaid expansion tends to be less expensive than others," Sommers says. "It is a real cost, but if you hear a politician say that Medicaid expansion alone is going to bust the budget, then that's just a political argument."

Source: Adapted from Mattie Quinn, "As Federal Medicaid Money Fades, How Are States Funding Expansion?," *Governing*, July 23, 2018, http://www.governing.com/topics/health-human-services/gov-medicaid-expansion-funding-states.html.

Like almshouses, the first hospitals were institutions for unfortunates without money or family. For people with family or money, a house call from the doctor was the preferred form of medical care. According to Starr, "Almost no one who had a choice sought hospital care."[36] Hospitals were regarded with dread, and rightly so. They were dangerous places, in part because of the medical and hygienic practices of the time. Sick people were safer at home. The few who became hospital patients did so because of special circumstances. They might be seamen in strange ports, travelers, the homeless, or the solitary aged, individuals who, whether traveling or destitute, were unlucky enough to fall sick without family, friends, or servants to care for them.[37]

Hospitals and physicians made a spirited effort to improve their image. Hospitals moved their sickest residents—as well as patients who were dissolute or morally objectionable—to other institutions. In 1847, for instance, Bellevue Hospital in New York decided to move the penitentiary and almshouse off its grounds and concentrate on medical care.[38] The hospital was beginning to emerge as a distinct institution.

A DIFFERENCE THAT MAKES A DIFFERENCE
WORK REQUIREMENTS FOR MEDICAID RECIPIENTS WON'T COME CHEAP OR EASY

Just hours before work requirements for Medicaid recipients in Kentucky were set to go into effect in July 2018, a federal judge struck them down, ruling that they were "arbitrary and capricious." It would have been the first time in the United States that some people applying for the federal–state health care program had to meet a certain number of hours working or job training.

The ruling left at least 10 states that had asked the Donald Trump administration for permission to impose work requirements in limbo, as they awaited the response from the federal Centers for Medicare and Medicaid Services (CMS). "We are conferring with the Department of Justice to chart a path forward," said CMS administrator Seema Verma.

Republican governors have been promoting the work requirements as a way to put impoverished individuals on a more productive path, while also providing a source of labor to employers. The state plans largely exempted pregnant women, new mothers, and children. "It is imperative to provide expectations for all of our citizens who are able to work," Oklahoma governor Mary Fallin said when she signed her state's law. "Medicaid recipients who are able-bodied will be able to take advantage of job-training programs and work opportunities that lead to a stable job, self-sufficiency and success."

Critics of the work requirements focus on the people who could lose health insurance in the process and believe health care is key to getting and keeping jobs. Ideological differences aside, health policy experts warn that changing decades-old rules and systems won't come cheap. "I don't know if states realize how fundamentally they'll have to change their eligibility systems," says Jennifer Wagner, a senior policy analyst at the Center on Budget and Policy Priorities, a progressive think tank. She estimates that states could be looking at "tens of millions of dollars to the eligibility system alone."

There are two big costs that come with implementing these kinds of changes. There's the technology side: updating systems that house beneficiary data, or in some cases creating entirely new ones. Then there's the personnel side: hiring more staff to track compliance and appeals, while training current staff on the new requirements.

Medicaid is not the first government program to add work requirements. In 1996, federal law called for work requirements under welfare (formally known as Temporary Assistance for Needy Families, or TANF). When Tennessee implemented TANF work requirements, the state spent more than $70 million, according to the Sycamore Institute, a nonpartisan policy institute. In New York City, the cost of just implementing job training programs for welfare recipients was about $17 million. In 2018, Virginia governor Ralph Northam estimated that the commonwealth would be on the hook for $100 million for the first two years if it added a work requirement to Medicaid.

In most cases, states can get Washington to pick up part of the tab through a federal match for new administrative costs. Most of the time, that would be 50 percent, but Matt Salo, executive director of the National Association of Medicaid Directors, says states can sometimes get up to a 90 percent match for information–technology systems development. The Trump administration has warned state Medicaid directors that it will not help pay for "job training or other employment services, child care assistance, transportation, or other work supports to help beneficiaries prepare for work or increase their earnings."

Source: Adapted from Mattie Quinn, "Implementing States' Medicaid Wishes Won't Be Cheap," *Governing*, February 19, 2018, http://www.governing.com/topics/health-human-services/gov-medicaid-work-requirements-states-cost-implement.html.

The Idea of a Social Safety Net

The arrangement described above continued in the United States until well into the 20th century. The duty of providing health care and welfare remained firmly in the hands of local governments. States assisted those with mental illnesses and people with disabilities. The federal government ran a compulsory health insurance system for the merchant marine, so that sick sailors could get care in any port, and provided pensions and health care to military veterans.

By the end of the 19th century, a new idea was percolating in progressive circles. Many social reformers came to believe that the federal government should take a much larger role in securing health care and pensions for the working class.

The idea first arose in Germany. In 1883, the conservative government of German chancellor Otto von Bismarck created the world's first compulsory sickness and unemployment insurance fund, which required employees and employers to set aside money to cover the costs of medical treatment for workers. Bismarck later created a compulsory retirement program, the cost of which was divided among employees, employers, and the national government, in much the same way that the Social Security system operates in the United States today. These innovations were momentous in the development of the state. Before Bismarck, most talk of health care, unemployment insurance, and pensions had come from socialists and communists. He showed that conservative capitalist countries could enact such programs too. Indeed, they could take the lead in developing a generous social safety net. Over the course of the next 30 years, other European countries followed Germany's lead.

The United States, however, did not. During the heyday of the Progressive movement in the early 20th century, discussions about national health insurance were widespread. Eventually, opposition from physicians and from the country's largest labor union, the American Federation of Labor (the forerunner of today's AFL-CIO), fearful of government control of the health care system, effectively derailed the idea. During the 1920s, many states took the first small steps toward creating a social safety net by setting up workers' compensation funds for injured workers. However, amid the affluence of the times, there was little support for a more ambitious social safety net.[39] That changed with the start of the Great Depression.

On Thursday, October 24, 1929, the stock market in New York City collapsed in what the *New York Times* called "the most disastrous trading day in the stock market's history."[40] By spring 1933, it was clear that the United States had entered an unprecedented economic slump—the Great Depression.

In response to this economic disaster, the federal government for the first time took on some of the social safety net functions that European governments had pioneered decades earlier.[41] In 1935, President Franklin Delano Roosevelt and Congress teamed up to pass the Social Security Act. This act established two social safety net programs. The first was a joint federal–state program of unemployment compensation. The second was a federally run program of retirement benefits for senior citizens, which soon would be known simply as Social Security.

The federal government also created **Aid to Families with Dependent Children (AFDC)**, the purpose of which was to provide monetary assistance to widowed women with children, women who had been abandoned by their husbands, and women who were in some way incapacitated. Funded by the federal government, the program was administered by the states.

The Roosevelt administration briefly considered adding a compulsory health insurance program to the Social Security Act. However, given the medical industry's continued vehement opposition to such a program due to fear of too much government control, the proposal was eventually dropped as too controversial. Instead, the Social Security Act provided federal grants to help states pay for programs for the disabled and the aged and to provide child welfare services, public health services, and vocational rehabilitation.[42] As a result, responsibility for providing a health care safety net remained in the hands of state and local governments.

A Multibillion-Dollar Afterthought

State governments became major participants in the U.S. safety net system almost by accident. After the assassination of President John F. Kennedy in 1963, Lyndon B. Johnson ascended to the Oval Office. Johnson and congressional Democrats were determined to pass legislation that would cover hospital costs for senior citizens. Congressional Republicans, however, had a different proposal in mind. They supported a voluntary health insurance program that would cover the cost of physician visits for seniors. In 1965, the two parties decided to compromise in classic Washington fashion—by doing both. The result was **Medicare**, the federal health insurance program for the elderly.

But Congress didn't stop there. While it was on a roll, it also created Medicaid. Despite their similar names, Medicare and Medicaid are very different programs. Medicare is run and paid for entirely by the federal government. As with Social Security, every senior who worked for 10 years and paid taxes—or whose spouse worked for 10 years and paid taxes—is eligible to

Aid to Families with Dependent Children (AFDC) The original federal assistance program for women and their children, started under Roosevelt's New Deal.

Medicare The federal health insurance program for elderly citizens.

participate, as are people with certain types of disabilities. The program is financed in part by a payroll tax. Most retirees, however, take far more out of Medicare than they contributed during their working years.[43] Understandably, Medicare almost immediately became a popular program.

Medicaid, on the other hand, is a joint state–federal program that is paid for in part by the general revenue funds of state and local governments. The federal government does pick up most of the cost, however. On average, it covers nearly 60 percent of Medicaid expenditures; for poorer areas, the percentage is higher. Arkansas, Idaho, Kentucky, Mississippi, South Carolina, and West Virginia all receive at least 70 percent of their Medicaid expenditures from the federal government.[44] Wealthier states split the cost 50–50. The federal government's share is larger for states that have taken the Medicaid expansion under the Affordable Care Act. States do not have to participate in Medicaid; however, since 1982—when Arizona finally signed on—all states do.

Therefore, Medicaid is not an unfunded mandate; the federal government does not force states to participate in it. (The Supreme Court, in its 2012 decision on the Affordable Care Act, ruled that the federal government could not force states to participate in the expansion of Medicaid, which the law required them to do or risk their traditional Medicaid funding.) Medicaid is, however, an **entitlement program**; that is, it does create legally enforceable rights. In fact, it is a double entitlement program. First, states have a right to a certain amount of federal money for Medicaid every year; second, individuals who meet eligibility thresholds are entitled to Medicaid services, regardless of the cost. States are required to provide coverage to certain populations, including children in families with income below the **poverty line or poverty threshold** and parents who qualify for TANF.[45]

Beyond these basics, the states enjoy considerable leeway when setting eligibility standards. (See Table 15-1.) They have created health care safety nets with very different levels of generosity. As of April 2018, Alabama was the least generous state in the country. It allowed only those adults earning less than 13 percent of the federal poverty level—the threshold set by the U.S. Census Bureau to measure poverty—to receive Medicaid. That means that a working parent with two children who earned more than $218 a month—slightly more than $2,610 a year—earned too much to qualify. Few states want to be stingy when it comes to health coverage,

but they need to balance their budgets, and paring back eligibility levels is one way to make the numbers work, especially when Medicaid expenditures increase by double-digit percentages every year.

The most generous states, such as Connecticut, Massachusetts, and Minnesota, allowed families earning up to 133 percent of the federal poverty level to receive Medicaid benefits. (Washington, D.C., allowed families to earn up to 216 percent.)[46] The United States may have one safety net for seniors, but for everyone else, it is a country with many different safety nets. One of the goals of the Affordable Care Act was to set the same baseline of at least 133 percent of the poverty level for Medicaid eligibility, but with many states not participating in the program expansion, that is not the case.

In 2014, Medicaid expenditures accounted for 8 percent of **WYOMING'S** total budget but 35.8 percent of **OHIO'S**.

Oops! The Unexpected Cost of Health Insurance

Medicare and Medicaid were structured very differently, but the two programs soon revealed a common trait. They both quickly proved to be fantastically expensive. From 1965 to 1970, the annual rate of increase in state and federal health expenditures was 20.8 percent.[47] By 2016, the federal government and state governments spent just over $550 billion annually on Medicaid alone.

As Medicaid spending soared, another disturbing trend was becoming evident. The number of women with children receiving financial assistance under AFDC was soaring, too. After two decades of slow growth, the number of AFDC beneficiaries took off in the late 1960s, rising from slightly more than 2 million recipients in 1960 to more than 10 million recipients by 1972.

The composition of AFDC recipients also was changing. The widows of the 1940s were being replaced by

....

Entitlement program A government-run program that guarantees unlimited assistance to those who meet its eligibility requirements, no matter how high the cost.

Poverty line or poverty threshold An annual income level, set by the federal government, below which families cannot afford basic necessities.

TABLE 15-1 ● State Medicaid and Children's Health Insurance Program (CHIP) Income Eligibility Standards, April 2018

	Children				Pregnant Women		Adults (Medicaid)	
	Medicaid Ages 0–1[a] (%)	Medicaid Ages 1–5[a] (%)	Medicaid Ages 6–18[a] (%)	Separate CHIP[b] (%)	Medicaid (%)	CHIP[c] (%)	Parent/ Caretaker[d] (%)	Expansion to Adults (%)
Alabama	141	141	141	312	141	N/A	13	No
Alaska[e]	203	203	203	N/A	200	N/A	139 ($)	133
Arizona	147	141	133	200	156	N/A	106	133
Arkansas	142	142	142	211	209	N/A	17 ($)	133
California	261	261	261	f	208	N/A	109	133
Colorado	142	142	142	260	195	260	68	133
Connecticut	196	196	196	318	258	N/A	133	133
Delaware	212	142	133	212 (1–19)	212	N/A	87	133
District of Columbia	319	319	319	N/A	319	N/A	216	210[g]
Florida	206	140	133	210 (1–19)	191	N/A	29 ($)	No[h]
Georgia	205	149	133	247	220	N/A	34 ($)	No
Hawaii[e]	308	308	308	N/A	191	N/A	105	133
Idaho	142	142	133	185	133	N/A	23 ($)	No
Illinois	142	142	142	313	208	N/A	133	133
Indiana	208	158	158	250	208	N/A	19 ($)	133
Iowa	375	167	167	302 (1–19)	375	N/A	53 ($)	133
Kansas	166	149	133	235	166	N/A	33	No
Kentucky	195	159	159	213	195	N/A	24 ($)	133
Louisiana	212	212	212	250	133	N/A	19	133
Maine	191	157	157	208	209	N/A	100	No[h]
Maryland	317	317	317	N/A	259	N/A	123	133
Massachusetts	200	150	150	300	200	N/A	133	133[g]
Michigan	212	212	212	N/A	195	N/A	54	133
Minnesota	283[j]	275	275	N/A	278	N/A	133	200[k]
Mississippi	194	143	133	209	194	N/A	23 ($)	No
Missouri	196	150	150	300	196	300	18[i] ($)	No[i]
Montana	143	143	143	261	157	N/A	24	133
Nebraska	213	213	213	N/A	194	N/A[c]	58	No
Nevada	160	160	133	200	160	N/A	32 ($)	133
New Hampshire	318	318	318	N/A	196	N/A	67 ($)	133
New Jersey	194	142	142	350	194	200	31 ($)	133
New Mexico	300	300	240	N/A	250	N/A	45 ($)	133
New York	218	149	149	400	218	N/A	133	200[k]
North Carolina	210	210	133	211 (6–19)	196	N/A	43 ($)	No[h]
North Dakota	147	147	133	170	147	N/A	52 ($)	133

	Children				Pregnant Women		Adults (Medicaid)	
	Medicaid Ages 0–1ᵃ (%)	Medicaid Ages 1–5ᵃ (%)	Medicaid Ages 6–18ᵃ (%)	Separate CHIPᵇ (%)	Medicaid (%)	CHIPᶜ (%)	Parent/ Caretakerᵈ (%)	Expansion to Adults (%)
Ohio	206	206	206	N/A	200	N/A	90	133
Oklahoma	205	205	205	N/A	133	N/A	41ⁱ ($)	Noⁱ
Oregon	185	133	133	300	185	N/A	40 ($)	133
Pennsylvania	215	157	133	314	215	N/A	33	133
Rhode Island	261	261	261	N/A	190	253	116	133
South Carolina	208	208	208	N/A	194	N/A	62	No
South Dakota	182	182	182	204	133	N/A	56 ($)	No
Tennessee	195	142	133	250	195	N/A	101 ($)	No
Texas	198	144	133	201	198	N/A	15 ($)	No
Utah	139	139	133	200	139	N/A	55ⁱ ($)	Noⁱ
Vermont	312	312	312	N/A	208	N/A	52 ($)	133
Virginia	143	143	143	200	143	200	48 ($)	No
Washington	210	210	210	312	193	N/A	40 ($)	133
West Virginia	158	141	133	300	158	N/A	19 ($)	133
Wisconsin	301	186	151	301 (1–19)	301	N/A	95ⁱ	No/95
Wyoming	154	154	133	200	154	N/A	54 ($)	No

Source: "Medicaid, CHIP, and BHP Eligibility Levels," Centers for Medicare and Medicaid Services, April 1, 2018, https://www.medicaid.gov/medicaid/program-information/medicaid-and-chip-eligibility-levels/index.html.

Note: This table reflects the principal but not all modified adjusted gross income (MAGI) coverage groups. All income standards are expressed as a percentage of the federal poverty level (FPL). As of 2018, FPL for the 48 contiguous states and the District of Columbia was $12,140 for one person, with $4,320 for each additional person in the household. For the eligibility groups reflected in the table, an individual's income, computed using the MAGI-based income rules described in the Code of Federal Regulations, is compared to the income standards identified in this table to determine if the individual is income eligible for Medicaid or CHIP. The MAGI-based rules generally include adjusting an individual's income by an amount equivalent to 5 percent FPL disregard. Other eligibility criteria also apply, for example, with respect to citizenship, immigration status, and residency.

ᵃThese eligibility standards include CHIP-funded Medicaid expansions.

ᵇCHIP covers birth through age 19 unless otherwise noted in parentheses.

ᶜStates have the option to cover pregnant women under CHIP. This table shows coverage of pregnant women only.

ᵈReflects Medicaid state plan coverage of the eligibility group for parents and other caretaker relatives. Parents and caretaker relatives with income over the income standard for coverage under this group may be eligible for coverage in the adult group in states that have expanded to cover the adult group. In states that use dollar amounts based on household size, rather than percentages of the FPL, to determine eligibility for parents, we converted those amounts to a percentage of the FPL and selected the highest percentage to reflect the eligibility level for the group. States that actually use dollar amounts in making determinations are indicated by ($).

ᵉThe dollar values that represent the FPLs in Alaska and Hawaii are higher than in the contiguous 48 states. For example, as of 2018, 100 percent of the FPL for a family of four was equal to $31,380 in Alaska and $28,870 in Hawaii, compared to $25,100 in the other 48 states and the District of Columbia.

ᶠThe separate CHIP in California covers certain children up to age 2 with incomes up to 317% of the FPL statewide. It covers children up to age 19, also up to 317% of the FPL, in three counties only.

ᵍIn addition to covering the adult group up to 133% of the FPL, the state covers ages 19 and 20 up to the following levels: D.C., 216 percent; Massachusetts, 150%.

ʰThe state covers some 19- and 20-year-olds—Florida, 29 percent; Maine, 156 percent; North Carolina, 44 percent.

ⁱThe state has a section 1115 demonstration that provides Medicaid coverage to some additional low-income adults. The demonstration includes limitations on eligibility and/or benefits, is not offered to all residents of the state, and/or includes an enrollment cap.

ʲMinnesota covers children up to age 2 with income up to 283 percent of the FPL.

ᵏAdults with incomes between 133 percent and 200 percent of the FPL are covered through the Basic Health Program.

divorced and separated women with children as well as single mothers who had never been married. By 1979, single mothers made up nearly 80 percent of all AFDC recipients.[48]

As the group benefiting from welfare changed, the program became increasingly unpopular with the public. During the late 1970s and early 1980s, Reagan and other conservative politicians railed against what they saw as the excesses of the welfare state. They evoked racially charged images of "welfare queens" who drove Cadillacs and paid for steak dinners with fat rolls of food stamps.[49] Reagan's welfare queen proved to be more myth than reality, but it was arguably true that the United States had created a set of permanent dependents of the sort that Roosevelt had warned against when he called government relief "a narcotic, a subtle destroyer of the human spirit."[50]

The Devolution Revolution

The supporters of Reagan weren't the only people who were fed up. State and local officials were, too. Many were frustrated by the high-handed way the federal government administered welfare and Medicaid. Medicaid was theoretically a joint state–federal program, but the federal government always held the whip hand over state governments. The Centers for Medicare and Medicaid Services (CMS) is the federal agency responsible for administering both Medicare and Medicaid. Formerly called the Health Care Financing Administration, this agency monitors state governments in much the same way that a reform-school principal might monitor juvenile offenders.

Of course, the federal government sometimes had reason to be suspicious. Many states, most notably Louisiana, have long sought to shift as many Medicaid expenses to the federal side of the ledger as possible. Despite sometimes questionable actions on the part of states, even federal officials began to come around during the 1980s to the idea that perhaps the states should be given greater freedom to experiment with their welfare and Medicaid programs. In the late 1980s, the U.S. Department of Health and Human Services, the parent organization of CMS, began to grant states demonstration waivers that allowed them to experiment with how they provided welfare and health care. By 2006, every state had received at least one waiver for a portion of its Medicaid program. States were able to extend or augment health insurance for more than 7 million individuals who otherwise would not have been eligible to receive it.[51] Recently, with the Affordable Care Act, the federal government has taken the lead role in offering health insurance to more people. States, however, are at the forefront of a different type of innovation. They have experimented with new ways to coordinate care in the hope of improving patients' health outcomes and saving money simultaneously.

Welfare Reform

One of the first states to take advantage of federal flexibility was Wisconsin. In 1987, Tommy Thompson entered the governor's office, and one of his first acts was to bring together about a dozen people for lunch at the state executive mansion to discuss one of the most contentious topics in American politics—welfare reform. Thompson's first lunch underscored that he was eager to think outside the box and achieve real reform. Unlike most governors, Thompson didn't invite policy wonks or advocates, either pro or con. Instead, he invited welfare mothers so he could hear firsthand about the obstacles that made it difficult for them to get and keep jobs.[52]

Thompson took the answers he got that day and, during his subsequent yearly lunches, set out to radically reorient welfare in Wisconsin. In doing so, he managed to avoid the dead ends that previous reformers had encountered. In the past, most states had attempted to move welfare recipients into the job market by providing training and education opportunities. All these programs were expensive, and only some were successful. Thompson decided to focus on getting welfare recipients jobs—any jobs. Virtually all welfare recipients were required to work. If a recipient was unable to find a job, then a subsidized position or one in community service was made available. In addition, if a welfare recipient needed child care during the workday or transportation to get to work, the state provided it.

Essentially, Thompson subverted one of the major arguments for ending welfare—namely, that welfare recipients were free-riding on the taxpaying public. In doing so, he actually increased funding for child care, health care, and transportation. Once recipients were working, they were provided with one-on-one job counseling, education, training, and other support services.[53] The program also sought to use dollars to promote better behavior. Funds were cut off to the parents of truant children. Also, marriage incentives were created for teenage parents.

By forcing welfare recipients to get jobs *in addition to* offering them the support they realistically needed to enter the job market, Thompson disarmed both conservative and liberal critics and pointed the way to workable reforms to the system. Other states soon followed suit. Work requirements were strengthened, and time limits on benefits were imposed. New assistance with child care and transportation was offered. By summer 1996, more than 40 states had received statewide waivers that allowed them to vary the work requirements for AFDC recipients.[54]

Thompson's reforms, coercive or otherwise, were remarkably effective. Providing services such as child care and transportation increased per capita welfare costs in the short run, but in the long run, it paid off. State welfare costs fell by about 65 percent over the course of the decade. The state saved more than $1 billion. Such successes later earned Thompson the position of secretary of health and human services under President George W. Bush.

In 1996, Congress and President Bill Clinton formally embraced the reforms that the states had initiated and abolished the existing AFDC, or welfare, program and replaced it with a system of block grants to the states called Temporary Assistance for Needy Families, or TANF. As part of this new program, the Personal Responsibility and Work Opportunity Reconciliation Act put a five-year cap on federal payments to welfare recipients. It also required states to put a large portion of welfare recipients to work.

Federal block grants gave state governments the leeway to design their own personalized, work-oriented, time-limited welfare programs. The new legislation was most notable, however, for what it did not require. Gone were most of the requirements that the federal government sign off on the state plans. TANF gave states the freedom to set benefit levels, eligibility requirements, and financial incentives and penalties as they saw fit. The result has been a profusion of sometimes very

MAP 15-1 ● TANF Income Eligibility Thresholds, 2013

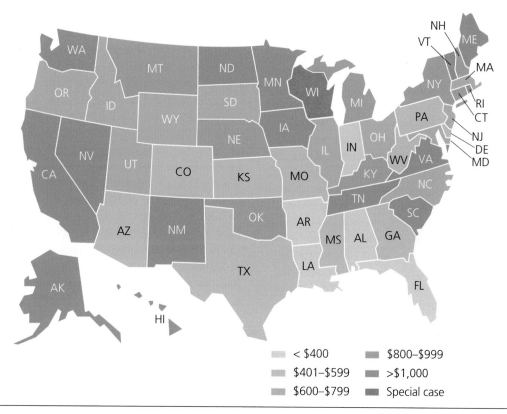

Legend:
- < $400
- $401–$599
- $600–$799
- $800–$999
- >$1,000
- Special case

Source: Urban Institute, Welfare Rules Database, "TANF Policy Tables," Table I.E.3, "Standards for Estimating Eligibility, July 2013," https://wrd.urban.org/wrd/Query/query.cfm.

different welfare-to-work programs. In the past, people who met eligibility guidelines had been legally entitled to welfare, no matter the cost. Now, the federal government provides only a finite amount of money to the states. At first, the federal payout was quite generous. The intent was to give states plenty of funds to devise and implement the support programs of their choice. Over time, however, the federal contribution grew smaller and smaller.

The number of welfare recipients declined sharply, from about 6 million in 1996 to fewer than 4 million by 2008 and fewer than 2 million by 2013. Poverty rates for single-parent households also fell. By and large, the alarming outcomes predicted by opponents of the welfare reform bill failed to materialize. Still, even as the economy weakened with the recession that ended in 2009, fewer people were receiving TANF benefits than in 2005. That stands in contrast to entitlement programs such as food stamps, which grew rapidly during the recession and its aftermath.[55]

The Feds Falter

When Bill Clinton took office in 1993, he and his administration were prepared to let states take the lead on welfare reform. After all, the president's previous job had been governor of Arkansas. However, the president and his wife, Hillary Clinton, did see the problem of the number of Americans without health insurance as primarily a federal one. In early 1994, Clinton introduced the Health Security Act, legislation that would have provided universal health insurance to all Americans.

Senate Republicans initially countered with a proposal that would have extended health insurance coverage dramatically but would still have fallen short of universal health insurance. Clinton rejected this counterproposal, vowing to veto any measure that failed to provide 100 percent coverage.[56] The two major parties were unable to find common ground. Nine months later, the Clinton health insurance proposal was defeated.[57]

Fast-forward more than 15 years. In 2010, the year Congress approved the Affordable Care Act, 50 million Americans lacked health insurance—fully 16 percent of the population.[58] (See Map 15-2 for more recent uninsured rates by state.) The Kaiser Commission on Medicaid and the Uninsured has estimated that some 20 percent of

uninsured residents are noncitizens, who often work in low-wage jobs that do not include health coverage.[59]

The Rise of the Health Care State

The collapse of health care reform efforts in the 1990s at the federal level left states in a tricky position. They were being squeezed between the pincers of the rising costs of state Medicaid programs and the rising demands for assistance from citizens struggling with prescription drug costs and a lack of health insurance. Finally, in the mid-1990s, states found what looked like a good way both to contain costs and to expand coverage—**managed care**.

Proponents of managed care originally saw health maintenance organizations (HMOs) as a way to improve the quality of care patients received. Most medical care that patients receive in the United States is poorly coordinated. Different doctors often cannot easily share a patient's medical records. In addition, physicians have little incentive to offer preventive services because they get paid for dealing with sickness. Paul Ellwood, the physician who coined the phrase *health maintenance organization* in the early 1970s, believed that HMOs would rationalize and coordinate the medical care that patients received. This would improve the quality of health care for members of an HMO; moreover, HMOs would reduce costs by emphasizing preventive health care.

Under managed care, instead of paying doctors a fee for each service provided, states typically paid an HMO a flat fee for each Medicaid patient enrolled in a plan. The fees that states offered HMOs were designed to be lower than the expenses the states would have incurred if patients had remained in a traditional fee-for-service Medicaid program. HMOs agreed to these lower rates because they believed that, even with lower reimbursement rates, they would still be able to squeeze inefficiencies out of the system and turn a profit.

Medicaid recipients benefited, too. They were able to join health plans that gave them access to physicians and services that often had been unavailable under the old program. Traditional fee-for-service Medicaid reimbursement rates were so low that many physicians simply refused to see Medicaid beneficiaries. Ultimately, the states saved money, at least theoretically.

A Promising Beginning

For a while, the HMO approach seemed to work. By 1998, about half of all Medicaid recipients nationwide were

---

Managed care An arrangement for the provision of health care whereby an agency acts as an intermediary between consumers and health care providers.

MAP 15-2   ●   Rates of Uninsurance among Nonelderly, 2016

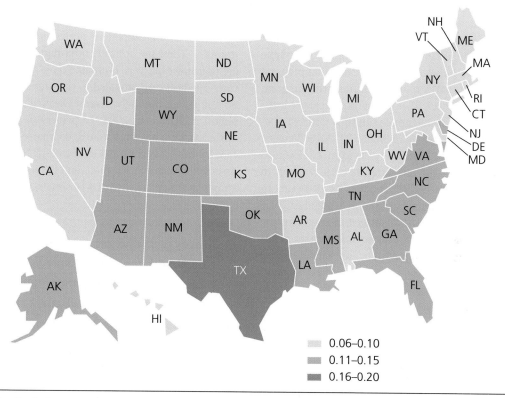

0.06–0.10
0.11–0.15
0.16–0.20

Source: Kaiser Family Foundation, "Uninsured Rates for the Nonelderly by Race/Ethnicity," 2016, https://www.kff.org/uninsured/state-indicator/rate-by-raceethnicity.

in managed-care programs.[60] As enrollment increased, health costs slowed. From 1995 to 1999, Medicaid expenditures grew at the relatively modest rate of 4.3 percent annually. This was dramatically lower than the unprecedented 27 percent growth of the early 1990s.[61] In addition, as the economic expansion that began in the early 1990s gained momentum and swelled state coffers, a growing number of state officials and health care advocates began to think about addressing other problems of the uninsured. Advocates set their sights on a new state–federal partnership. The first goal: to extend health insurance to uninsured children in families that earned too much to qualify for Medicaid but too little to pay for health care on their own.

In August 1997, Congress created the **Children's Health Insurance Program (CHIP)** at the behest of President Clinton. CHIP was designed to provide health insurance to roughly 6.5 million children in low-income families without health insurance.[62] As with Medicaid, CHIP would be designed and administered by the states

and paid for primarily by the federal government. The federal government would spring for about 80 percent of total costs.

The states were given considerable flexibility in designing their child health programs. They were free to fold CHIP into their Medicaid programs or create stand-alone CHIP programs. As with Medicaid, they determined the eligibility levels. They also could cap CHIP enrollments and force recipients to pay some of the costs for the health insurance they received.[63]

Not surprisingly, states have taken advantage of this flexibility. Fourteen states allow children living in families earning up to 300 percent of the federal poverty level to qualify for CHIP. (The federal contribution for CHIP is higher than that for Medicaid, with the federal government picking up 70 percent of the cost.) New York

. . . .

Children's Health Insurance Program (CHIP) A joint federal–state program designed to expand health care coverage to children whose parents earn income above the poverty line but still are too poor to afford insurance.

allows the highest amount at 400 percent—or roughly $80,000 a year for a family with one adult and two children. Just two states, Idaho and North Dakota, cap coverage at less than 200 percent of the poverty level.

Congress reauthorized the program in 2009 with an additional $33 billion in federal funds, and the Affordable Care Act further bolstered CHIP by extending program funding through 2015 and establishing the program itself until at least 2019. There's just one catch: the legislation mandates that states maintain their CHIP eligibility standards as they existed on March 23, 2010. Between 1999 and 2013, CHIP coverage grew from 2 million to 8.1 million, cutting the uninsured rate for children in half. Congress renewed CHIP funding for two years in 2015. Federal CHIP funding expired in September 2017. States made up for the lack of federal money by using reserves and received a short-term injection of funds from Congress in December 2017, but several states came close to running out of money, leading them to make contingency plans to reduce coverage. In January 2018, Congress passed a six-year extension of the program.

The Safety Net Widens

What effects do these different policies have on the residents of the states? Researchers have found a strong correlation between having health insurance and access to and use of health care services.[64] In addition, giving more people more access to public health care is one direct way to increase their health care use. Some research shows that expanding Medicaid results in lower death rates and that Medicaid participants report being in better health.[65] Thanks to the Affordable Care Act, the number of uninsured Americans is expected to drop by half, from about 45 million in 2012 to 23 million by 2023, according to CMS.

Not having health insurance does not necessarily translate into having no health care. Government-supported community health centers provide health care to more than 20 million uninsured Americans in thousands of communities across the country every year. These clinics treat people regardless of their ability or inability to pay.[66] In addition, hospitals are required to provide treatment to people who come into their emergency rooms whether these people can pay or not. As noted at the beginning of this chapter, that is why many hospitals support expanding Medicaid and other provisions of the Affordable Care Act.

Along with community health centers, public hospitals have long assumed a particularly important role in providing services to the uninsured. For many low-income individuals, the emergency room of a public hospital is their first and only way to access medical care. Many public hospitals border high-crime neighborhoods and provide essential advanced emergency and trauma services, as well as outpatient clinics for these same communities. These are critically important functions. They are not, however, very profitable ones. Uncompensated care—medical care provided to the uninsured that they do not pay for themselves—cost the medical system $85 billion in 2013.[67] In 2008, 16 percent of public hospitals' costs were uncompensated, compared with 5.8 percent for hospitals nationwide, according to the National Association of Public Hospitals and Health Systems (now known as America's Essential Hospitals).[68]

> **Many public hospitals border high-crime neighborhoods and provide essential advanced emergency and trauma services, as well as outpatient clinics for these same communities. These are critically important functions. They are not, however, very profitable ones.**

The result is that public hospitals have a tough time staying open. Between 1996 and 2002, the number of public hospitals in the nation's 100 largest cities fell from 730 to 645.[69] The recent recession crunched them even further; public hospital systems across the country cut back on programs, including mental health services, pharmacies, and oncology clinics. New York cut 400 positions from its public hospitals in 2009.[70]

Although the Affordable Care Act has helped address the problem of uncompensated care, particularly in those states participating in the Medicaid expansion, it has exacerbated other problems. As cost-control measures under the law started to expire, insurance premiums began to climb, often by double-digit percentages. In California, for instance, insurers offering policies through the state insurance exchange, known as Covered California, raised premiums for 2017 by an average of 13 percent—more than triple the average increases of the previous two years.[71]

The law also contributed to another problem—lack of physicians. "The Affordable Care Act will add hundreds of thousands of people to the rolls of the insured. That's good," said Dr. G. Richard Olds, the founding dean of the medical school at the University of California, Riverside. "But where are the primary care physicians going to come from to serve that population?"[72]

A majority of the counties even in a well-served state such as California do not have enough primary care doctors, according to guidelines set by the American Medical Association. The Association of American Medical Colleges warns that the nation will be short 95,000 doctors by 2025. Admittedly, this association has a vested interest in promoting the training of more doctors. In many states, the gap in care is being made up partially by expanded use of nurse practitioners and other health professionals who are not physicians. But, remember from our discussion of interest groups in Chapter 7 that doctors do not necessarily care for other clinicians providing care on their turf.

Lack of access to care is certainly not an issue limited to cities and suburbs. Rural areas long have been plagued by fragmented health care systems and shortages of doctors and nurses, as well as the closure of hospitals that we noted earlier. Even worse, rural residents tend to be older and poorer than their urban and suburban counterparts, factors that often translate into a greater need for health care services.[73] It's not a formula for a healthy population.

Missouri tried a novel approach to addressing this problem in 2014, passing a law to allow graduates fresh out of medical school to practice primary care in underserved areas under the supervision of a "collaborating physician." Every state had required physicians to complete a year's residency in a teaching hospital before practicing primary care. The Missouri State Medical Association promoted the bill, but the American Medical Association formally opposed special licensing pathways for physicians who aren't enrolled in an accredited postgraduate program or who don't have at least a year of additional education in the United States under their belt. The reason is simple, said Atul Grover, the chief public policy officer at the Association of American Medical Colleges: Their education is often grounded in theoretical and academic work, with the assumption that a future doctor will spend time in a residency afterward. "That education is designed to pair them up with residency," he said. "It's not designed to pair them up with immediate independent practice."[74]

Beyond Managed Care

The use of managed care in Medicaid programs is alive and well. As of 2016, 81 percent of Medicaid patients were enrolled in managed-care plans.[75] The trend has been for states to shift ever more patients into managed care, with Florida, Illinois, and South Carolina all deciding in 2011 to virtually end traditional fee-for-service Medicaid. Yet, more and more, states are deciding that managed care on its own isn't enough.

The accountable care organization (ACO) has emerged as a possible successor to the HMO. ACOs are partnerships of health care providers—including primary care doctors, specialists, and sometimes hospitals—that agree to a set budget for serving all the health and long-term-care needs of a defined group of patients. In other words, ACOs are a lot like HMOs, except that health care providers themselves, rather than third-party entities, manage the care they provide. Under the ACO model, the health care providers have a financial incentive to work together to keep patients healthy, to treat those who are sick efficiently, and to help patients who have chronic illnesses control the effects of their diseases. If costs fall below a set budget, the ACO shares in the profits. If costs exceed the budget, some ACOs share in the losses. Budgets are set based on the overall health of the population to be served, and payments are tied to quality measurements.[76]

At a basic level, an ACO gives doctors, hospitals, and clinics the responsibility to provide care for a group of patients within a specified budget. If health care providers better coordinate care to provide good quality for less money, they can share in the savings. ACOs started out as mostly a private-sector phenomenon. As recently as 2010, only 41 such practices existed. By 2015, that number had exploded to at least 744. ACOs have already started to take root in Medicare; now they're making their way into Medicaid.

Borrowing heavily from the ACO model, in 2011, Oregon approved a law to move close to a million people—including Medicaid enrollees, but also teachers and other government employees—into coordinated care organizations.[77] "We have the opportunity to do something that no other state has done, and something that has eluded our nation for decades," Oregon governor John Kitzhaber said at the time. "That is creating a system that actually improves the health of the population at a cost we can afford."[78]

Minnesota is one of the other leaders behind the accountable care movement. It launched an initiative in 2013 to test ACOs in Medicaid. For the first year, the setup was pretty straightforward: The state let provider groups set risk terms they were comfortable with. Any savings realized were shared with those ACOs that came in under budget—that is, those that provided care for less than the targeted amount. By 2014, some larger health systems had to pay the state back if they went over budget. Managing that risk is much easier for larger providers, with several revenue streams and control over every segment of care. The larger systems that took on downside risk in the second year were building toward a 15 percent goal—meaning they would split savings or overages with the state up to 15 percent above or below their spending goal. "They wanted to ease us into it so they could increase the trust level that would allow us to take risk in the following year," said Greg Klugherz, the chief financial officer at St. Cloud Hospital, a facility 60 miles northwest of Minneapolis. He viewed the risk-sharing change as strengthening the system's focus on long-term priorities, such as reducing hospital-acquired infections.[79]

Time for Reform

The defeat of federal health care reform in the 1990s left the states in charge of efforts to expand health insurance coverage. Maine and Massachusetts unveiled universal (or near-universal) health care plans that served as precursors to the federal health care reform bill passed in 2010.

When Dirigo Health, Maine's plan, began in 2004, 14 percent of the state's residents lacked health insurance, and 80 percent of the uninsured worked for small businesses that could not afford to provide coverage. Private insurers agreed to provide coverage, which the state would administer and, for the first year, subsidize. In the first phase of enrollment, geared toward small businesses and self-employed workers, 250 businesses and 1,000 individuals signed up.[80] By late 2006, however, researchers found that, even though the program had enrolled more than 16,000 Mainers, it had reduced the state's uninsured population by less than 10 percent. They also reported that the state had raised insufficient funds to support Dirigo.[81] The plan ultimately ran into financial problems and capped enrollment well below its original goal.[82] "The time has passed for states to go it alone; DirigoChoice helps prove that," wrote Maine representative Sharon Anglin Treat, chair of the state's Joint Standing Committee on Insurance and Financial Services, in a letter to the editor of the *Wall Street Journal* in 2009.[83]

Maine's experience did not stop Massachusetts from launching an even more ambitious plan of its own. The plan required every resident of the state to have health insurance by July 2007 or face tax penalties. Under the law, every resident below the federal poverty line can receive insurance fully subsidized by the state; subsidies are extended on a sliding scale to those earning between 100 and 300 percent of the established federal poverty line. Businesses that do not provide health insurance are required to pay the state $295 per employee per year; this money is used to fund the coverage subsidies. However, calling the Massachusetts plan "universal health care" isn't exactly accurate. State officials estimated that the law would extend health insurance coverage to as much as 95 percent of the state's population. They expected that the remaining residents would accept the tax penalties rather than pay for insurance that may still be too expensive, despite the government subsidies.[84]

By 2008, just 6.1 percent of the state's population was uninsured, the lowest rate in the nation. But Massachusetts was beginning to suffer under the strains of the initiative's expense. The Massachusetts Taxpayers Foundation estimated that the program added more than $700 million per year in annual costs, which the state split 50–50 with the federal government. The state cut its payments to hospitals for uncompensated care and raised its cigarette tax by $1 a pack, but, coupled with declining revenues, its efforts weren't sufficient to close the gap.[85] In response, Massachusetts adopted an ambitious, multifaceted new plan in 2012 designed to limit the state's expenses. Among other things, the plan now limits by law how fast the state's health care costs are allowed to rise and redirects more patients into managed care, ACOs, and other arrangements that are designed to spend less by improving coordination.[86]

Shortly after taking office, President Obama declared that the federal government would, once again, take on health care reform. Members of Congress invoked the Massachusetts program often during their debates; those in favor of reform pointed to its success in reducing the uninsured population, while those opposed singled out its costs. Ultimately, after nearly a year of hearings and speeches, President Obama signed the Affordable Care Act into law on March 23, 2010. Major federal health care changes had finally been accomplished, but, as we have seen, the debate was far from over.

Issues to Watch

Passing federal health care reform legislation was just the first step. States will continue to grapple with the

A DIFFERENCE THAT MAKES A DIFFERENCE
STATES TRY NEW APPROACHES TO LIMIT OR UPHOLD ABORTION RIGHTS

In July 2018, Massachusetts legalized abortion. Of course, abortion was already legal in the state, as it was in every state, thanks to the Supreme Court's ruling in the 1973 case *Roe v. Wade*, which found that access to the procedure was a constitutional right. But suddenly, with President Donald Trump's second Supreme Court pick making it look like there would be five justices prepared to overturn *Roe*, states recognized that the question could soon return to them to decide.

Massachusetts overturned a 173-year-old state law that prohibited "procuring a miscarriage." It was one of 10 states with abortion bans that predated *Roe* still on the books. The others are Alabama, Arizona, Arkansas, Michigan, Mississippi, New Mexico, Oklahoma, West Virginia, and Wisconsin. "How quickly those states would enforce those laws [if *Roe* is overturned] is really going to vary," says Andrea Miller, president of the National Institute for Reproductive Health.

Alabama and Arkansas, for example, have passed extensive restrictions on abortion in recent years, so it's likely that they would enforce a pre-*Roe* abortion ban. But, Miller adds, "Rhode Island and New Mexico might be less inclined." Lawmakers in those two states have committed to repealing their laws when the legislature meets again in 2019.

A bill to repeal New Mexico's abortion law was introduced in 2017. It failed to make it to the governor's desk, but the bill's sponsor, Democratic state representative Joanne Ferrary, plans to make it a priority. "I will be introducing this bill again in 2019 with the new governor—hopefully Michelle Lujan Grisham, who is also committed to protecting safe and legal abortions," she told the *New Mexico Political Report* in 2018.

Conversely, four states—Louisiana, Mississippi, North Dakota, and South Dakota—have "trigger laws" that would automatically ban abortion if *Roe* is overturned. North Dakota passed legislation to ban abortions after 6 weeks of pregnancy, while Arkansas imposed a ban after 12 weeks. Both laws were quickly overturned in 2014, but those state legislatures had made their preferences known.

In Texas, the number of abortion clinics was cut in half by a 2013 law that required physicians to have hospital admitting privileges and clinics to meet safety standards required for surgical procedures.

In 2016, the Supreme Court ruled that these requirements placed an unconstitutional "undue burden" on women seeking to exercise their constitutional right to access to abortion. But with the makeup of the court looking a lot different, states on either end of the political spectrum are expected to take up more abortion bills, widening the chasm in access between blue and red states.

Source: Adapted from Mattie Quinn, "Not Just Massachusetts: 10 Other States Have Abortion Bans Still on the Books," *Governing*, July 26, 2018, http://www.governing.com/topics/health-human-services/gov-abortion-massachusetts-nasty.html.

law's effects inside their borders, and they must continue to address a number of other burgeoning challenges, including those discussed below.

Long-Term Care

Unlike private-sector health insurance plans, state Medicaid programs have an additional responsibility. Medicaid provides long-term care to the elderly and other services to people with disabilities. These services can range from providing nursing home care for low-income Medicaid recipients to developing rehabilitation plans for people with disabilities. All these services are extremely expensive. Although the elderly and disabled make up only about 25 percent of the people enrolled in Medicaid, they account for nearly two-thirds of total Medicaid spending.[87] Nearly 10 million Americans now use some form of long-term care.[88]

Moreover, the cost of long-term care is growing fast. According to the Congressional Budget Office, caring for elderly and disabled Medicaid beneficiaries accounted for more than 72 percent of the program's cost increases between 1975 and 2002. States' long-term-care bills hit $147 billion in 2009; although that figure has since ticked down, it may reach as much as $346 billion by 2040.[89]

Demographics are largely driving those cost increases. According to the U.S. Census Bureau, the number of

There have always been complaints from practitioners that Medicaid doesn't pay them well or promptly enough. Back in 1968, three years after the program was created, a pharmacist in New York put a sign in his window warning Medicaid patients that he would no longer fill their prescriptions.

people 85 years of age and older will grow by 40 percent by 2020. By 2040, that population is expected to grow by more than 300 percent, to 18 million people.[90] As it does, the number of people with serious disabilities will almost certainly increase. Many of these people will be unable—or unwilling—to pay for long-term care on their own.

Some states, such as Oregon, have kept costs down by shifting the elderly away from expensive care in nursing homes and toward less expensive at-home care and assisted living centers. Seniors overwhelmingly prefer such alternatives to nursing homes. The federal government has encouraged states' efforts in this direction

....

Public health The area of medicine that deals with the protection and improvement of citizen health and hygiene through government agencies.

despite opposition from the strong nursing home lobby. The percentage of Medicaid long-term-care spending that went to noninstitutional care more than tripled between 1995 and 2010, rising to 45 percent.[91] The Affordable Care Act uses financial incentives to move states more aggressively toward the provision of home-based services.

Despite the expense to states, the long-term-care coverage provided under Medicaid comes with a big drawback. To qualify, a patient must have almost nothing in assets. Examples abound of long-term-care patients' spending down hundreds of thousands of dollars in life savings before they qualify for Medicaid.[92] The Affordable Care Act attempted to find a new model. It created the first national long-term-care insurance plan, a voluntary program to be financed through payroll deductions.[93] During the debate over the law, however, Republicans who were concerned about the potential cost of the program succeeded in convincing Congress to include a provision requiring the federal government to design the program in such a way that it would pay for itself over the course of 75 years. In October 2011, the Obama administration conceded that making the program financially solvent wasn't possible and abandoned it.

Public Health

One of the most important functions of government is protecting **public health**. Public health is the area of medicine that deals with the protection and improvement of citizen health and hygiene through government agencies. After public health systems at all levels of government were bulked up following the terrorist attacks of 2001, funding for these programs has steadily eroded in recent years. Public health officials like to say that a town wouldn't wait until fire broke out to build a firehouse, and it wouldn't shut the firehouse down if there weren't any fires. Yet something like that happens with public health. The United States has no single public health system. The federal CDC is a highly regarded agency, but states and localities carry out much of the work of educating the public on health issues and combating epidemics. The picture varies so much from state to state—and so much within states—that a coherent or consistent response to health threats isn't always possible, suggests Celine Gounder, an infectious disease specialist. "We can't just keep running from one fire to the next, whether the current most pressing threat is Zika, Ebola, Legionnaire's disease or lead in the water supply," Gounder wrote in 2016. "Yet historically, there's little long-term political will to sustain public health funding."[94]

State and local governments also have taken the lead in responding to public health crises. In practice, this includes responses as simple as making sure an ambulance or fire truck is dispatched to a 911 call and as complex as managing an epidemic. A century ago, the latter might have involved yellow fever, cholera, or influenza. In 1918, it involved a flu **pandemic** that killed an estimated 600,000 Americans and 100 million people worldwide.[95] Such diseases pose continued threats.

During the initial response to the Ebola outbreak in 2014, hospitals, cities, and state governments seemed to struggle, unclear on proper protocols for treating patients as well as on the question of whether health providers who had potentially been exposed to the disease should be quarantined. Rules and strategies regarding protective gear, use of isolation wards, and handling of blood changed rapidly as new cases emerged. Responding to novel health threats is always a challenge. States and cities seem at first to fall back on a generic playbook, whether a crisis is caused by measles or a dirty bomb. "To think the first patients would go flawlessly [is] an overestimation of our systems," said Dr. Craig Smith, medical director for infectious disease at University Hospital in Augusta, Georgia, in response to Dallas's handling of the first case of Ebola diagnosed in the United States. "I would expect there would be a few stumbles."[96]

A 2016 study by the Trust for America's Health, a nonprofit advocacy group, found that public health spending remained lower than it had been prior to the recession of 2007–2009. The nation ramped up public health funding in response to the terrorist attacks of 2001, but funding for the CDC and for the federal program that provides grants to states and localities for responding to public health emergencies was down from the peak levels set more than a decade earlier. Many states had cut their own funding in recent years as well.

Public health officials who complained that politicians too often forced them to lurch from crisis to crisis worried that the nation was no longer even able to lurch effectively. "Congress has shown me that even in a major crisis they're unable to respond in a timely way," said Georges Benjamin, executive director of the American Public Health Association. "Preparedness money has been cut, so the core capacity of the public health system has diminished to the lowest I've seen in many, many years." Just how active state and local governments should be on chronic issues that affect the public health is often a source of heated debate. According to the CDC, smoking tobacco causes more than 480,000 deaths a year in the United States.[97] In addition, a growing percentage of Americans are overweight

In 2017, **WEST VIRGINIA** had the highest obesity rate in America at 37.7 percent.

or suffer from **obesity**. Some state and local officials have made combating obesity a major priority. They have pushed for educational programs for parents and, for children, have restored physical education classes and removed soft drink machines from schools. Others resist the idea that obesity is a problem that should be addressed through government policy.

The scope of public health programs varies from state to state. Some state health departments have just a handful of employees, while others have hundreds. Some states are generous providers of assistance to their low-income citizens to cover the expenses associated with illness and hospitalization. Other states are much more restrictive.

How state governments define public health has a lot to do with the distinctive political cultures of their regions. All public health officials would agree that certain issues, such as HIV/AIDS or the potential for biological attacks perpetrated by terrorists, are important public health issues. No one would argue that a flu epidemic or the contamination of a major watershed would not also qualify. In recent years, with drug overdoses becoming more common and resulting in a spiking number of deaths, states have crafted new regulations to crack down on excessive prescribing of pain medications known as opioids and, in some cases, have stepped up their substance abuse treatment efforts.

Other topics are not so easily categorized. Is gun violence a public health issue? Researchers at the CDC think so. They point out that gun-related deaths, most of which are accidental, are the country's second leading

---

Pandemic An outbreak of a disease that spreads across a large geographical area and affects a high proportion of the population.

Obesity The medical condition of being excessively overweight; defined as having a body mass index of more than 25.

▲ A group of ninth graders participate in a Teen Talk High School class at Carlmont High School in Belmont, California. Sex education in some American high schools is evolving beyond pregnancy and disease prevention to include lessons aimed at curbing sexual assaults.

AP Photo/Jeff Chiu

research to identify patterns of risk, illuminate productive targets for intervention, and assess the effectiveness of interventions. Unfortunately, the United States lacks a comprehensive public health approach to gun violence, due in large part to the absence of federal funding for research on gun violence for more than 2 decades."[98]

On other health fronts, some cities have attempted to reduce the transmission of dangerous blood-borne illnesses, such as HIV and hepatitis C, by providing drug addicts with clean needles. Others have rejected these needle exchange programs, charging that they give rise to disorder and crime and send the message that intravenous drug use is acceptable.

Then there is the always controversial question of sexual health and education. Should parents, educators, and other adult role models emphasize **abstinence** with teenagers or teach them to use condoms? Or is instruction in a variety of options that include both abstinence and birth control the answer? What role should government play in providing access to contraception?

As we have seen before, often different policies reflect very different political cultures. Oregon has granted terminally ill patients the right to physician-assisted suicide. A number of states have debated bills to require random drug testing of people receiving welfare or unemployment benefits. States such as Massachusetts and Maine sought to expand health care coverage to nearly every resident in advance of the passage of federal health care reform in 2010, whereas other states have shown no great enthusiasm for providing health care to low-income citizens.

cause of death. The American Medical Association now advises doctors to talk with patients about the proper handling and storage of any guns they may own. Many gun owners, however, vehemently reject the idea that guns are in any way a public health issue. In 2016, Republicans in Congress rejected an attempt by Democrats to allow the CDC to study gun-related injuries and deaths as a health issue, something it had mostly been blocked from doing for the preceding 17 years. "Effective public health strategies have reduced such threats as motor vehicle injury, tobacco use, accidental poisonings, and drownings," Victor J. Dzau and Alan I. Leshner, respectively the president of the National Academy of Medicine and the CEO emeritus of the American Association for the Advancement of Science, wrote in 2018. "Effective strategies are built on

In **FLORIDA** in 2014, conducting drug tests on welfare recipients as a condition of their benefits was ruled unconstitutional.

Abstinence Refraining from sexual activity, usually intercourse.

As noted above, the topic of sexual health and education remains controversial in many communities. One in nine girls between the ages of 16 and 19 become pregnant outside of marriage, yet a considerable number of parents remain opposed to their children learning about sexuality in the classroom. These parents helped resurrect abstinence-only sex education programs, which have received $1 billion in federal funding since 1998, when only 2 percent of schools offered such programs. By 2002, the proportion of schools teaching abstinence as the only way to avoid sexually transmitted diseases and pregnancy had risen to 23 percent.[99] Congressional Democrats allowed the funding to expire in June 2009, but it was partially revived as part of a federal health care compromise. The bill provided $250 million over five years for abstinence education—if states could provide 75 percent matching funds. It also allocated $375 million for comprehensive sex education.[100] In 2016, as part of his last budget proposal, President Obama called for the end of federal support for abstinence-only programs.

Evaluations of abstinence-only programs report conflicting findings that are often used by both proponents and opponents to advance their positions. One study conducted by a Pennsylvania State University researcher found that, compared with counterparts who had taken comprehensive sex education classes, fewer middle school students who were enrolled in an abstinence-only education program engaged in sexual activity within two years. Further, more students in both groups remained sexually inactive in comparison with students who had no sex education at all.[101] Regardless of the teaching method, the statistics seem headed in the right direction: in 2010, the rate of births to teenage mothers fell to the lowest level since the 1940s.[102]

The states are also battlegrounds in the debate over access to contraception. At least 29 states have passed laws that require insurers that cover prescription drugs to include coverage of contraceptives. Of these states, however, 21 allow exemptions for employers who oppose such coverage for religious reasons.[103] In this way, the states foreshadowed a debate that would take place in early 2012 at the federal level. The Affordable Care Act requires health insurance to cover contraceptives. Initially, the Obama administration said that even religious groups with objections to contraception coverage would be required to provide it to their employees. But, facing a backlash even from some of its allies, the administration decided on a compromise instead. Religious organizations themselves wouldn't be required to provide contraception, but employees of the religious groups would still be offered the coverage

Ted Soqui/Corbis via Getty Images

▲ California hosts an informational Covered California event to mark the opening of the state's health insurance exchange in 2013. Federal and state health care exchanges throughout the 50 states are a result of President Obama's health care reform law known as the Affordable Care Act, but they may be killed under the Trump administration.

directly from their health insurance companies. This deal borrowed directly from the states: it was called the "Hawaii rule" because it mimicked a policy in that state.[104] Many religious conservatives weren't satisfied with the deal, however, including some in state capitols. Arizona approved a law in May 2012 to permit religious employers not to cover contraception and, in so doing, directly challenged the federal mandate.[105] In 2014, the Supreme Court ruled that closely held private companies (those with five or fewer owners) could not be required to provide contraceptive coverage. In 2016, with the number of justices down to eight and thus unable to reach a majority, the Court kicked another contraception case down to the lower courts, asking them to find a compromise.

What Is Good Health Anyway?

As if these issues were not enough, local health officials are increasingly wrestling with another question we have not yet touched on in this chapter: what exactly constitutes a health issue anyway?

Consider obesity. Nearly 40 percent of all adult Americans are considered obese. Media attention has turned to this issue as an ever-growing list of health studies proclaims just how out of shape Americans are. The films *Super Size Me* (2004) and *Fast Food Nation* (2006) addressed people's obsession with fast food. (See Map 15-3.) Kids are getting heavier, too. In the past two decades, the number of overweight and obese children has nearly tripled. Today, according to the CDC, roughly 18 percent of children between the ages of 6 and 11 are overweight—up from just 4 percent in the early 1970s. The number is 18 percent for adolescents between the ages of 12 and 19, too; that is also a significant change from the early 1970s, when just 6 percent of teens weighed too much.[106]

Obesity contributes to a variety of ailments, among them heart disease, certain types of cancer, diabetes, stroke, arthritis, breathing problems, and psychological disorders such as depression. Overweight individuals suffer from these and other related conditions at much higher rates than do people who are not overweight.

Indeed, in the United States alone, researchers attribute about 112,000 deaths each year to obesity.[107] In 2008, obesity in the United States cost an estimated $147 billion in medical spending.[108] Researchers at Emory University have estimated that if the United States could curb the rate of increase of obesity, the nation could save $821 per adult by 2018.[109]

In 2006, New York City reignited the debate over government's role in promoting healthy eating habits when it banned the use of trans fats (some of the most dangerous fats) in city restaurants. Soon after, other cities and states began to consider similar legislation. Parent groups and health organizations demanded better, healthier fast-food options, and the fast-food restaurants quickly took notice. McDonald's, the world's largest fast-food chain, received such a negative rap for its unhealthy products that it was under strong pressure to take immediate action. It began expanding its "healthy" meal options with great fanfare, shooting

MAP 15-3 ● Obesity Rates among U.S. Adults, 2018

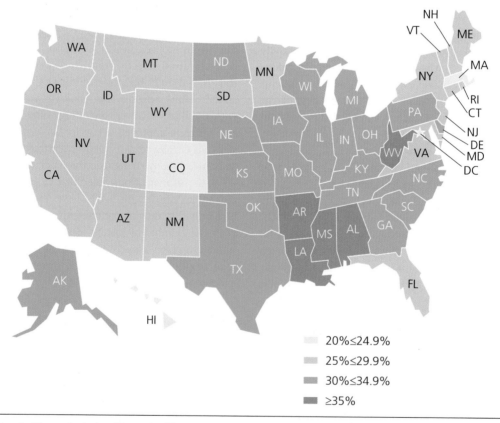

20%≤24.9%
25%≤29.9%
30%≤34.9%
≥35%

Source: Centers for Disease Control and Prevention, "Overweight and Obesity: Adult Obesity Prevalence Maps," September 2018, http://www.cdc.gov/obesity/data/prevalence-maps.html.

STATES UNDER STRESS
THE NATION'S MOST HARMFUL DRUG IS LEGAL

The national conversation around addiction has been dominated in recent years by opioids. But the fact is that alcohol kills roughly 88,000 Americans each year, more than double the number of opioid deaths. Almost half of alcohol fatalities come from chronic health problems attributed to excessive alcohol consumption, such as liver cirrhosis, breast cancer, and heart disease. Those alcohol-induced deaths are on the rise. Excluding certain acute causes, such as homicides and traffic fatalities, the rate of alcohol-induced deaths increased by about 47 percent between 1999 and 2015.

Most Americans have a general sense that drunken driving isn't as bad a problem as it was a generation ago. Few realize how much those numbers changed in a relatively short period of time. When the federal government started counting alcohol-impaired traffic deaths in 1982, there were more than 21,000 a year. By 2011, the death toll was down 53 percent. States had raised the legal drinking age to 21 and adopted a common rule that a blood alcohol concentration (BAC) of .08 meant "too drunk to drive."

Many states also mandated the installation of interlock devices to prevent those with a history of drunken driving from turning on their ignition unless they were sober. Those laws, coupled with education and prevention campaigns, helped reduce drunk driving deaths to fewer than 10,000 in 2011.

But the total number of alcohol-impaired traffic fatalities actually rose in both 2015 and 2016. "Drunk driving has been around since the automobile was invented and it's still the biggest killer on the highway," says J. T. Griffin, the chief government affairs officer for Mothers Against Drunk Driving (MADD). Indeed, alcohol causes more traffic deaths per year than either speeding or driving without a seat belt. In 2018, the National Academies of Sciences, Engineering, and Medicine issued a report about the problem. "Yes, we made progress. No, we didn't get rid of it," says David Jernigan, a Boston University public health researcher who helped write the report. "Ten thousand deaths are too many."

The report provided a package of policy recommendations, one of which was for every state to lower the legal BAC limit from .08 to .05. In practical terms, that would mean most women couldn't drive after two glasses of wine in an hour; most men couldn't drive after three. The report is only the latest to call for a more stringent BAC limit: The National Transportation Safety Board has also called for a lower level. Up to now, no state had imposed a limit of .05 until Utah at the end of 2018. Delaware, Hawaii, New York, and Washington State have also considered legislation to lower the limit. "It will change the conversation from, 'If you have been drinking too much, you shouldn't drive,' to, 'If you've been drinking, you shouldn't drive,'" says Utah state representative Norm Thurston, who sponsored the .05 limit. The new message—that driving shouldn't occur after even moderate drinking—"is probably what it should have been all along," he says.

American alcohol policy is in a curious state of flux. While public officials are united in the fight against opioids, they are struggling to adjust their strategy toward a substance that is legal, widely available, and increasingly popular among American consumers.

On one hand, states and localities continue to tax alcoholic beverages not only to raise revenue but also to educate the public about the risks associated with drinking. On the other hand, states are passing laws that make alcohol easier to purchase by permitting sales on Sundays, in movie theaters, and at grocery outlets. In 2017, Congress cut federal alcohol excise taxes to the tune of $4.2 billion over two years. The reduction is expected to bring down prices and increase consumption.

Public health specialists say it's time for a broader national dialogue about substance misuse, one that includes alcohol. "There continues to be a [reluctance to accept that] alcohol is an addictive substance because it's legal, because it's widely used, because people believe that unless it's a drunk driving accident you don't really die from it," says Phyllis Randall, chair of the Loudoun County, Virginia, Board of Supervisors and a former mental health therapist who worked for 15 years treating offenders with substance abuse problems in an adult detention center.

When it comes to alcohol abuse, one troubling development is that women are closing the gender gap. Over the last decade, the percentage of women who drink, the number of days they drink per month, and the percentage who engage in binge drinking have all increased. Women are also visiting emergency rooms more often for alcohol-related reasons.

Ira Chasnoff, a pediatrician at the University of Illinois College of Medicine in Chicago, is working with a handful of states, including Arizona, Illinois, and Iowa, to improve the way hospitals screen for prenatal

(Continued)

(Continued)

alcohol exposure and provide treatment to families. Over the last decade, Congress has updated federal law to require that physicians ask expectant mothers about alcohol use. In the past, doctors were only supposed to ask about illicit drugs. But even today, most physicians still don't ask about or report alcohol use by pregnant mothers. Some research suggests many of them don't know Congress changed the requirement. The upshot is that hospitals identify only a small fraction of the more than 400,000 children born each year with prenatal exposure to alcohol or illicit drugs.

Historically, the federal government hasn't prioritized alcohol in the way it has illicit drugs or, in today's opioid crisis, prescription painkillers. "The federal government reacts to and bounces [from crisis to crisis]," says Chasnoff. "A few years ago, it was the methamphetamine crisis, and before that it was cocaine. The list goes on and on."

Source: Adapted from J. B. Wogan, "The Deadliest Drug," *Governing*, July 2018, http://www.governing.com/topics/health-human-services/gov-alcohol-abuse.html.

commercials showing Ronald McDonald rollerblading and exercising with children instead of sitting in the restaurant eating, and posting fact sheets on its website announcing how much healthy food it had sold worldwide. Wendy's, KFC, Chili's, and other restaurant chains began using oils free of trans fats for frying.

One of New York City's next public health initiatives required chain restaurants to post calorie counts on their menus, based on the theory that if diners eating fast food knew how many calories were in their meals, they would eat less. Some research showed that the calorie labels didn't succeed in encouraging consumers to eat less, at least initially.[110] Nonetheless, the Affordable Care Act nationalized the concept, requiring all chain restaurants with at least 20 locations to post calorie counts. Even before the rule went into effect, McDonald's announced that it was updating its menus at its 14,000 locations nationwide to include calorie labels.

> One of New York City's public health initiatives required chain restaurants to post calorie counts on their menus, based on the theory that if diners eating fast food knew how many calories were in their meals, they would eat less. The Affordable Care Act nationalized the concept, requiring all chain restaurants with at least 20 locations to post calorie counts.

Not all efforts by states and localities to discourage the consumption of fast food and junk food have gone so smoothly. In 2010, several states, including California, Kansas, New York, Rhode Island, and Washington, engaged in spirited debates about new taxes on soft drinks. Every state has a cigarette tax, and research shows that these taxes have succeeded in helping discourage young people from starting smoking. (States are also explicitly prohibiting young people from smoking, with Hawaii and California both deciding in 2016 to raise the legal age for buying cigarettes to 21.)

The idea behind the proposed soda taxes was that they would have the same effect—reducing consumption of unhealthy sugary beverages while raising money for states. Yet most of the states didn't end up enacting soda taxes. Washington did approve such a tax, only to have voters repeal it in November 2010. The soda industry fought back against attempts to tax its products by portraying the efforts as examples of overly intrusive government. "It's government digging into the grocery cart of people," said Chris Gindlesperger, director of communications at the American Beverage Association.[111] Once again, New York City wasn't willing to let the issue rest. In September 2012, the city's board of health banned the sale of many sugary beverages by restaurants, movie theaters, and other vendors in containers larger than 16 ounces. Soon after, the beverage industry sued to block the rule. In 2014, voters in Berkeley, California, approved the nation's first local tax on sugary drinks. One early study there found that soda consumption quickly dropped by as much as 20 percent in some neighborhoods.[112] Two years later, Philadelphia became the first major city to impose a soda tax, quickly followed by San Francisco; Cook County, Illinois; and several other jurisdictions. In 2018, California legislators reluctantly passed a ban on local soda taxes. The beverage industry had collected signatures for a ballot initiative that would have made it difficult for local governments to raise any taxes unless state lawmakers agreed to a ban on soda taxes.

Conclusion

State and local governments have played an important role in providing health care and assistance to the poorest members of society for a long time. They also have the responsibility to protect and promote public health. Things changed in the 1960s, however, when Congress passed legislation that created the Medicare program for the elderly and the Medicaid program for low-income Americans. This set into motion a process that continues to this day. In recent decades, Medicaid has emerged as one of the most expensive and most important functions of state government.

States have been forced to look for ways to save money on one hand and extend health insurance coverage on the other. Despite the difficulty in reconciling these tasks, some state governments

In 2016, Philadelphia, **PENNSYLVANIA**, implemented a tax on soft drinks of 1.5 cents per ounce. The soda tax is the first in any big U.S. city and is expected to raise more than $90 million a year for education and parks.

THE LATEST RESEARCH

As we have seen in this chapter, the federal Affordable Care Act is an attempt to provide health insurance to tens of millions of Americans—an attempt in which, willingly or unwillingly, states are intimately involved. It became clear almost as soon as its major provisions took effect in 2014 that the law's goal of expanding insurance coverage had significant effects. Supporters of the law also cheered initial reports that overall health spending increased by relatively low amounts. But it was not clear whether enduring savings would be possible as more people sought care.

And not every state was seeing the same results. Following the Supreme Court's ruling in 2012, states get to decide whether or not to expand their Medicaid programs under the law. The Medicaid expansion is one of the central ways the act attempts to expand health insurance coverage to nearly every American, but Republican officials at the state level remained resistant. Direct repeal of the Affordable Care Act looks unlikely for now, but the president will continue to press for changes to a law he describes as "disastrous."

Much of the focus on health remains concerned with major entitlement programs and their costs, but policymakers are also grappling with the opioid epidemic and other public health challenges, while gearing up for a renewed season of argument over abortion.

• **Hacker, Jacob S., and Paul Pierson**, "The Dog That Almost Barked: What the ACA Repeal Fight Says about the Resilience of the American Welfare State," *Journal of Health Politics, Policy and Law* 43 (2018): 551–577.

It is difficult, as political science research has demonstrated, to dismantle large-scale social programs. Forces in favor of the status quo, both individuals and organized groups, fight hard to protect the benefits they already enjoy. How was it that Republicans came close to dismantling the Affordable Care Act and making deep cuts in Medicaid in 2017? They lacked popular support. The ACA never enjoyed the popularity of more entrenched programs such as Social Security and Medicare, but polling support rose for the law once it was under threat and fewer than one in six Americans supported the House-passed repeal legislation. Support was uneven, however. Republicans had succeeded in blocking much of its implementation in a significant number of states, preventing millions from enjoying its benefits. The party's own supporters remained more opposed to the law than the country as a whole, and Republican politicians, the authors posit, felt insulated anyway from a possible backlash due to negative partisanship. "Voters haven't just become increasingly loyal to their party," Hacker and Pierson write. "Their

(Continued)

(Continued)

political preferences are increasingly driven by hatred or fear of the other party." The repeal legislation fell thanks in part to opposition from almost every major organization with a stake in health care. Despite the lack of popular or interest group support, the Republican plan fell just short in the Senate, a victim of the party's narrow majority. President Trump continues to tack the law piecemeal through legislation and administrative rulemaking. "It is now possible to see activities that would have been unthinkable a generation ago—like a direct assault on a major part of the welfare state," the authors write. "The political 'tree line' for extreme policies has shifted, so that today even slim majorities can translate into radical legislative drives."

- **Jerman, Jenna, Lori Frohwirth, Megan L. Kavanaugh, and Nakeisha Blades**, "Barriers to Abortion Care and Their Consequences for Patients Traveling for Services: Qualitative Findings from Two States," *Perspectives on Sexual and Reproductive Health* 49 (2017): 95–102

Access to abortion is not equal everywhere. In 2014, 90 percent of the nation's counties lacked abortion clinics, while five states had only one. Seven percent of women who obtained an abortion traveled to another state to do so, often traveling significant distances. The authors interviewed 29 women in Michigan and New Mexico who had traveled either across state lines or more than 100 miles within their states. They experienced a number of barriers, including travel-related issues, limited clinic options, financial considerations, and state or clinic restrictions such as waiting periods. "The experience of barriers complicated the process of obtaining an abortion," they write. "The experience of multiple barriers appeared to have a compounding effect, resulting in negative consequences for women traveling for abortion."

- **Nadelmann, Ethan, and Lindsay LaSalle**, "Two Steps Forward, One Step Back: Current Harm Reduction Policy and Politics in the United States," *Harm Reduction Journal* 14 (2017): 37.

The United States is in the midst of the "worst drug overdose epidemic in history," according to the Centers for Disease Control and Prevention. What are policymakers doing about it? Surveying practices at the federal and state levels, the authors contend that the nation is still low in adopting effective strategies to combat addiction. They applaud the United States as "the global pioneer" in legalizing and regulating cannabis, but when it comes to other illicit drugs, the country lags well behind much of Western Europe. Too much emphasis remains on punitive, supply-reduction strategies such as prescription drug monitoring and crackdowns on physicians and users. "There is little evidence that these approaches have reduced opioid misuse or overdose," they write. But they note that ideological resistance to harm reduction is slowly fading. Conservative jurisdictions are beginning to accept syringe exchange programs and the value of opioid agonist therapy. "Abstinence-only treatment programs still dominate but harm reduction precepts and practices are proliferating as a new generation of treatment professionals assert their influence. The opioid epidemic in the US is forcing much of this new openness, especially in more conservative parts of the country, as mostly Republican-elected officials struggle to respond to cries for help by desperate, disproportionately white, constituents," the authors write. Nearly every state has improved access to naloxone, while 36 states have passed Good Samaritan laws to shield those who respond to overdoses from legal liability. Local law enforcement officials now say they would rather administer naloxone than "handcuff a corpse."

- **Sommers, Benjamin D., Bethany Maylone, Kevin H. Nguyen, Robert J. Blendon, and Arnold M. Epstein**, "The Impact of State Policies on ACA Applications and Enrollment among Low-Income Adults in Arkansas, Kentucky, and Texas," *Health Affairs* 34 (2016): 1010–1018.

Although the Affordable Care Act is a national law, state policy choices have had major impacts on the enrollment experiences of low-income adults and on their overall perceptions of the law. A survey of 3,000 low-income adults in late 2014 found that less than half had heard some or a lot about the law. The survey covered three different states with three different approaches to implementation. Kentucky expanded Medicaid and operated a successful health insurance exchange. Arkansas used Medicaid dollars to subsidize private insurance, and its residents used the federal exchange. Texas did not expand Medicaid and put restrictions on "navigators" who are trained to help individuals and companies find coverage through the federal exchange. The percentage of people who applied for Medicaid or exchange coverage was a bit higher in Kentucky than in Arkansas, but it was far higher in both states than in Texas. The same was true in terms of receiving help from navigators or social workers. Twice as many respondents felt the Affordable Care Act had helped them as reported that it had hurt them.

have achieved notable successes. Medicaid and the Children's Health Insurance Program, known as CHIP, have made health insurance available to most American children, and in some cases, experimental programs have brought coverage to their parents as well. Even after the passage of federal health care reform legislation in 2010, states continue to be at the center of health care expansion in the United States. Thanks to a 2012 ruling by the U.S. Supreme Court, states get to decide whether or not to expand Medicaid under the law. Congress failed to repeal the Affordable Care Act, but President Trump is ending provisions he finds too expensive or onerous. At stake in those choices are many billions of dollars and health insurance for millions of Americans.

At the same time, state and local governments are grappling with new public health challenges. Illnesses such as influenza show that local governments still have a role to play in guarding public health. The threat of biological and chemical terrorism, as well as the emergence of new or newly threatening diseases such as Zika and Ebola, also presents local public health officials with a grave responsibility. In addition, governments' expenses continue to mount for treating diseases caused by obesity and smoking. All this means that health care will almost certainly continue to be a major concern of state and local governments for the foreseeable future.

CHAPTER 15

for CQ Press

Want a better grade?

Get the tools you need to sharpen your study skills. SAGE edge offers a robust online environment featuring an impressive array of free tools and resources.

Access practice quizzes, eFlashcards, video, and multimedia at **edge.sagepub.com/ smithgreenblatt7e**

Top Ten Takeaways

1. The Affordable Care Act has had profound effects on the nation's health care system. It remains politically controversial, and parts of it are bound to be repealed under the Trump administration.

2. Although the Affordable Care Act is mostly funded by the federal government, states retain considerable authority in terms of expanding Medicaid coverage and running health insurance exchanges through which private subsidies flow.

3. Prior to the 20th century, providing for health and welfare was largely left to local governments.

4. States now spend a sizable portion of their budgets on health care, not just through Medicaid but also in providing health care for prisoners and government employees.

5. During the 1990s, Congress changed the old welfare law, letting states design programs that required recipients to

(Continued)

(Continued)

work. Caseloads subsequently dropped dramatically.

6. Also during the 1990s, a presidential push toward universal health coverage failed abysmally, but Congress did create a new program known as CHIP to insure children.

7. States have enacted hundreds of restrictions on abortion during this decade, but federal courts have struck down many of the most significant ones.

8. States also differ on other issues where social mores intersect with health, such as guns and sex education.

9. As the nation's population ages, costs for long-term care are increasing rapidly.

10. State and local governments have traditionally played a role in protecting and promoting public health, seeking to stop the spread of epidemics. In recent years, the definition of public health has been broadened beyond infectious disease to address matters such as obesity, even as public health funding has been shrinking.

Key Concepts

abstinence (p. 440)
Aid to Families with
    Dependent Children
    (AFDC) (p. 426)
Children's Health Insurance
    Program (CHIP) (p. 433)

entitlement program (p. 427)
managed care (p. 432)
Medicaid (p. 419)
Medicare (p. 426)
obesity (p. 439)
pandemic (p. 439)

poverty line or poverty
    threshold (p. 427)
public health (p. 438)
Temporary Assistance for
    Needy Families (TANF)
    (p. 418)

Suggested Websites

- **www.americashealthrankings.org.** Website of America's Health Rankings, a 25-year project tracking health indicators at the state level.

- **www.astho.org.** Website of the Association of State and Territorial Health Officials.

- **familiesusa.org.** Website of Families USA, a liberal advocacy group that promotes a more activist government policy.

- **www.tfah.org.** Website of Trust for America's Health, a nonprofit organization dedicated to protecting public health.

- **kff.org.** Website of the Henry J. Kaiser Family Foundation; offers a wealth of detail on state health care initiatives in general and Medicaid in particular. See, especially, kff.org/statedata for detailed information on states.

- **khn.org.** Website of Kaiser Health News, a nonprofit news organization covering state and federal health care issues, funded by the Kaiser Family Foundation.

- **www.naccho.org.** Website of the National Association of County and City Health Officials.

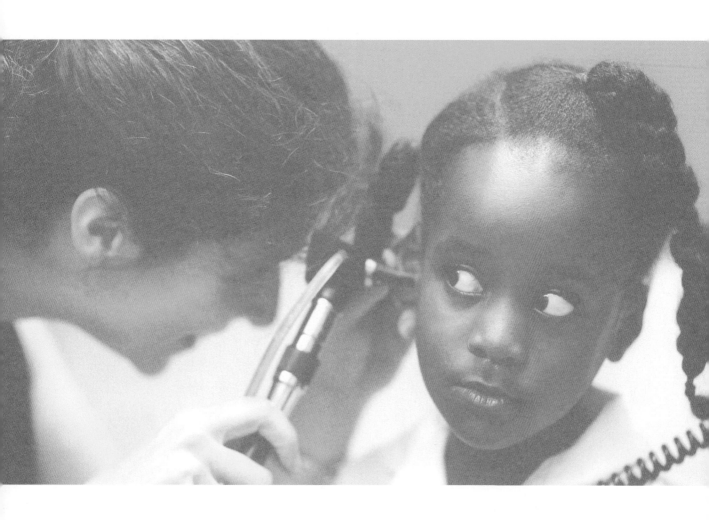

REUTERS/Jonathan Bachman

Environment and Climate Change
Thinking Globally, Acting Locally

Hurricane Harvey turned a never-ending line of Houston residents into temporary climate refugees in 2017. The massive storm was fueled by record warm seawater, further proof to scientists that while no single event can be blamed on climate change, global warming is affecting the intensity of storms.

Chapter Objectives

After reading this chapter, you will be able to

* Discuss the various measures states and cities have taken to protect the environment,

* Describe the role of adaptation in dealing with climate change, and

* Identify contemporary issues, debates, and agreements on the environment.

Jared Polis wants Colorado to get 100 percent of its energy from renewable sources such as wind, solar, and hydropower by 2040. The Democrat made this ambitious target central to his candidacy for governor in 2018. "For our climate, for our national security, for our health, and for our economic growth, we need a bold goal of 100 percent renewable energy," he said during the campaign.

Bold, indeed. Oregon, the state that gets the largest share of its energy from renewables, still gets more than half its energy from fossil fuels. In Colorado, the share of renewables was less than a third. The state not only consumes considerable amounts of fossil fuels, but also relies on its $30 billion oil and gas industry as an important source of jobs and economic activity. "His proposals and others like them would have multibillion-dollar negative impacts on the state of Colorado," said Jeff Hays, who chairs the state Republican Party.[1] Hays called Polis's proposal "heartless," saying that even if Colorado cut out its fossil-fuel production and use entirely, it would have a meager impact on greenhouse gas production worldwide. In the meantime, tens of thousands of jobs in the state would be lost. "If he succeeds with renewable energy, it's going to be difficult to sell a house in Weld County," the state's top energy-producing area, Hays said.

Would that be such a terrible thing? Lori Vienneau, a Weld County resident and Polis supporter, didn't think so. She says that her community is overrun with drilling rigs. "You can't turn around without running into another oil and gas drill," she said. "I'm very concerned about the health risks of the drilling that's going on next to our houses and our day care centers."[2]

These opposing points of view reflect the partisan schism in environmental politics. Republicans celebrate the fact that increased drilling in the United States has made the country more energy independent. "Gone are the days of America's crippling dependence on foreign energy sources," Rick Perry, the federal energy secretary and a former Texas governor, wrote in 2018. "True energy independence is finally within our grasp and we are exporting more of our energy to our allies. Nowhere is this stunning turnaround more dramatic than with natural gas."[3]

Shortly after Donald Trump's election, President Barack Obama met with Xi Jinping, the president of China and Obama's partner on some climate deals. Xi said that China would continue—along with the rest of the world—to treat climate as a serious issue, even if Trump pulled out of the Paris Agreement (which he soon did). "That's very wise of you," Obama said. "I think you'll continue to see an investment in Paris in the United States, at least from states, cities and the private sector."[4]

After all, states and cities banding together to address climate change is nothing new. During the presidency of George W. Bush, there was little to no action on climate issues at the federal level. Instead, leadership was taken up by states such as California. With Washington under Trump actively hostile to climate efforts, state and local leaders again are trying to push changes such as the renewable energy drive in Colorado or Washington State Democratic governor Jay Inslee's so far unsuccessful efforts to impose a carbon tax. There are limits to what any state or group of states can do, but the participants in the U.S. Climate Alliance represent 40 percent of the nation's population. Separately, hundreds of mayors around the country are taking steps to reduce emissions through purchases of renewable energy and green vehicles and requirements for more efficient buildings.

Climate change is a generational challenge that moves in fits and starts. States and cities have not been able to find a reliable partner in the federal government, but many continue to devote time and serious money to reducing fuel consumption, while also working on ways to adapt to the climate changes that are already happening. But, given the partisan divide on the issue, not all lawmakers in states or cities are convinced of the need. "We have to get other states and other nations on a similar path forward," said Jerry Brown, the Democratic governor of California, in 2014. "That is enormously difficult, because it requires different political jurisdictions, different political values, to unite around this one challenge of making a sustainable future."[5]

In this chapter, we will explore this dynamic, looking at how federalism and partisanship combine to make climate an especially complicated problem to solve. We will look at how some states and cities have sought to regulate emissions and promote renewable energy, while others have stepped up their extraction of fossil fuels—or bemoaned recent declines in fields such as coal extraction. As you read through the chapter, keep in mind the following questions:

- **How did states become important voices on a global problem?**

- **Why has climate change become a partisan issue?**

Environmental Conflict between Washington and the States

One April day in 2018, the Trump administration attacked California's environmental policies on two fronts. The Environmental Protection Agency (EPA) announced it would revoke penalties for automakers that do not meet strict Obama-era emission standards, which were based in part on a California law. The agency also said it would challenge California's ability under the Clean Air Act to set fuel standards that are more stringent than required nationally. "Cooperative federalism doesn't mean that one state can dictate standards for the rest of the country," said Scott Pruitt, then the EPA administrator. "It is in America's best interest to have a national standard."[6]

California and other states have sued the Trump administration repeatedly over a variety of issues (as Republican attorneys general sued Obama when he was in office, including Pruitt, then the attorney general of Oklahoma). One of their major areas of conflict

has been environmental regulation, where Democratic state officials want to pursue an entirely different course than Trump. After Trump announced he would start the process of abolishing the Obama administration's Clean Power Plan, which sought to cut carbon pollution from power generators by 32 percent below 2005 levels, a group of 28 states moved to block him. They were unsuccessful, with a federal judge in 2017 granting the administration's request to suspend the lawsuits.[7]

Also in 2017, Trump announced he would remove the United States from the Paris accord, an agreement negotiated in 2015 that every other country in the world is a party to. The goal of the accord is to keep the global average temperature from rising as much as 2 degrees Celsius above preindustrial levels. Complying with the accord could cost the United States 2.7 million jobs by 2025, Trump said. "The Paris Climate Accord is simply the latest example of Washington entering into an agreement that disadvantages the United States to the exclusive benefit of other countries," he said, "leaving American workers—who I love—and taxpayers to absorb the cost in terms of lost jobs, lower wages, shuttered factories, and vastly diminished economic production."[8]

The United States' withdrawal was a global disaster, celebrated physicist Stephen Hawking told the BBC a few months before he died. "We are close to the tipping point where global warming becomes irreversible," he said. "Trump's action could push the Earth over the brink, to become like Venus, with a temperature of two hundred and fifty degrees, and raining sulphuric acid."[9] In 2018, the Intergovernmental Panel on Climate Change, a group of scientists convened by the United Nations, warned that the planet faces severe risk of catastrophic effects from climate change as early as 2040 unless carbon emissions are reduced dramatically.[10]

As noted above, state lawmakers continue to pursue numerous policies to address the issue, absent federal action. States are pursuing taxes on carbon, pushing for more use of renewable energy, encouraging use of electric and other clean-energy vehicles, and promoting cap-and-trade programs of their own to regulate and limit industrial use of carbon. Not all of these efforts have been successful by any means, even in states dominated by Democrats. And the policies that have been put in place don't have the same impact a uniform federal standard might.

Not only is Trump a climate skeptic, but he has stocked his administration with officials who promote

A DIFFERENCE THAT MAKES A DIFFERENCE
DEMOCRATIC STATES TRY BUT FAIL TO TAX CARBON

In 2018, Washington looked like it might become the first state in the nation to pass a tax on carbon pollution. Democratic governor Jay Inslee had made it one of his top priorities, and his party had taken full control of the legislature, thanks to a special state senate election in 2017. "The public really is understanding the critical nature of this existential threat," Inslee said. "What used to be a graph on a chart are now our forests burning down and hurricanes and massive precipitation events, so this is something people are now experiencing in their own lives and their own retinas, and they understand we have to act."

But Inslee was ultimately forced to concede that he didn't have the "one or two votes" needed for passage. This wasn't Washington's first pass at a carbon tax, which could be used to reduce carbon pollution by placing a tax or fee on either fossil fuels or emissions. Voters soundly rejected a ballot measure in 2016 after the state's major environmental, labor, and liberal groups came out against it, largely because of disagreements over how the tax revenue would be spent.

But the ballot measure's failure didn't deter Inslee from trying again. "Doing so will allow us to reinvest in all the things that drive down emissions," he said in his 2018 state of the state address. "We can build more solar panels. We can put more electric cars on the road. We can help more Washingtonians purchase energy-saving insulation for their homes and businesses."

Although Inslee hasn't yet made the sale in Washington, the state is far from alone in pursuing a carbon tax. Nine other states introduced some two-dozen bills in 2018 that propose studying or using financial penalties to deter the use of fossil fuels and to encourage the growth of alternative fuel sources, according to Ryan Maness, a senior policy analyst and tax counsel at the consulting firm MultiState Associates, Inc. The states are Hawaii, Maryland, Massachusetts, New Hampshire, New Mexico, New York, Oregon, Rhode Island, and Vermont.

The proliferation of bills comes on the heels of President Donald Trump's decision to withdraw the United States from the Paris climate agreement. Following the president's announcement, many states and municipalities independently pledged to adhere to the agreement's goals. "The current administration has no interest in advancing carbon policy," says Jordan Stutt, a policy analyst at Acadia Center, a clean-energy advocacy group. "State legislators are realizing they have the opportunity to craft carbon policy."

But enacting a carbon tax is a complex task, Maness notes. Legislators first need to work out what will and won't be taxed, at what rate fuel sources or emissions will be taxed, and what the tax revenue will be used for. The bill in Washington, for example, would have imposed a new tax of $12 per metric ton of carbon emissions on the sale or use of fossil fuels such as gasoline and natural gas. It would eventually have increased each year until the tax hit $30 a ton, raising roughly $1 billion for the state. Half of the money raised would have gone toward energy projects that reduce greenhouse gas emissions.

Twenty percent would have addressed climate resilience through forest health, wildfire prevention, and other natural resources projects. The rest would have provided assistance for low-income families and workers in the fossil-fuel industry. Inslee acknowledged that Washington consumers would have paid more in fuel and energy costs if the carbon tax had been enacted, hurting low-income residents. It was this increase in prices that ultimately doomed the bill.

British Columbia and California already price carbon, but Washington would have been the first to impose a direct tax on carbon emissions. The carbon tax defeat was "a setback," says Maness, "but it wasn't the kind of rousing defeat that I think will keep lawmakers from thinking about it in the future. It will definitely be back," he says, at least in Democratic states. "It's a very 'coming soon to a theater near you' type of thing."

Source: Adapted from Elizabeth Daigneau, "After Carbon Tax Fails in Washington, Focus Turns to 9 Other States," *Governing*, March 20, 2018, http://www.governing.com/topics/transportation-infrastructure/gov-carbon-tax-states-washington-inslee.html.

---

energy use and cast doubt on climate change. Pruitt, who was ousted as EPA administrator in July 2018 amid various ethical scandals, argued that technology and the marketplace, not government mandates, were the correct way to reduce the nation's carbon footprint. Senior officials at agencies including the U.S. Department of Agriculture, the Department of Homeland Security, and the Department of Housing and Urban Development have expressed doubts about climate projections made by the government's own researchers. The White House has deleted mention of climate change from government websites and booted scientists from advisory boards. In 2018, the National Park Service deleted all references to human contributions to climate change in a draft of a report on sea-level rise and storm surges.

The administration has excluded rising temperatures from the list of threats in its official national security strategy, reversing a position taken under both the Obama and George W. Bush administrations. In 2017, weeks before Hurricane Harvey pounded Houston, the administration rescinded Obama's executive order that projects built with federal dollars take into account the potential effects of warming temperatures. "Inefficiencies in current infrastructure project decisions, including management of environmental reviews and permit decisions or authorizations, have delayed infrastructure investments, increased project costs and blocked the American people from enjoying improved infrastructure that would benefit our economy, society and environment," Trump wrote in an executive order of his own.[11]

States are seeking to step into the void on climate regulation left by the administration's actions. The U.S. Climate Alliance, which includes 16 states and Puerto Rico, is collaborating on various initiatives to cut greenhouse gas emissions, including finding new ways to finance clean-energy projects, updating their electric grids in hopes of using and storing wind and solar power, and improving construction standards. States are also working on improving resilience, so that populations and structures are better able to withstand the effects of climate change, including sea-level rise. States are also working individually or on a regional basis, including the cap-and-trade programs in place in California and the Northeast. "Donald Trump cannot stop my state from fighting climate change," Inslee said in 2018. "He cannot stop us from adopting a renewable portfolio standard. He cannot stop us from developing a carbon tax."[12]

Some amount of sea-level rise is already locked in. The Earth is already warming, polar ice is already melting, and nothing currently stands in the way of those trends continuing. The wild card is how much more will occur, and when. "What we do from now on can determine what's going to happen in the second half of the century," said Astrid Caldas, senior climate scientist with the Union of Concerned Scientists. "The thing is, we don't know the trajectory."[13]

But making serious inroads against climate change requires real sacrifices—less energy usage, less consumption in general, allowing developers to build smaller, denser housing units. That's why proposals to reduce emissions run into serious opposition even in the bluest states, where most voters say something must be done to address the issue. One study published in the *Journal of Environmental Psychology* in 2018 found that people who were the most "highly concerned" about climate were supportive of government efforts to address the problem, but were the least likely to change their individual behaviors. Those who were rated as "skeptical" opposed governmental policy actions but were the most likely to change their own environmental behaviors.[14]

The Partisan Divide on Climate

In 2018, Gallup found that 91 percent of Democrats worry about **climate change** a great deal or a fair amount. Eighty-two percent of them believe that the effects of **global warming** are already starting to take place. The same poll found that Republicans were far less worried. Only a third of them were worried about climate change or thought it's starting to take effect. Sixty-nine percent of them said that the seriousness of global warming has been exaggerated.[15] This chasm in partisan beliefs about climate is borne out by other surveys. "While clear majorities of Democrats have long said the Earth's temperature is rising, the current share (92 percent) is as high as it has ever been in surveys since 2006," Pew reported in 2017. "About half of Republicans and Republican-leaning independents (52 percent) say there is solid evidence of rising global temperatures, up from 39 percent in 2014. Still, while the share of Republicans who say there is solid evidence of global warming has increased in recent years, it remains lower than a decade ago."[16]

As the Pew comment suggests, Republicans and Democrats weren't always so divided on climate. In the early 2000s, many of the voices calling loudest for a policy response were Republicans. Senator John McCain, R-Ariz., the Republican presidential nominee in 2008, had sponsored cap-and-trade legislation. Some of the most prominent governors cheerleading for action on the issue were Republicans, including Arnold Schwarzenegger of California, George E. Pataki of

Climate change A shift in global temperatures.

Global warming Rising average temperatures worldwide.

New York, Charlie Crist of Florida (who later switched to the Democratic Party), Jon Huntsman Jr. of Utah, and Tim Pawlenty of Minnesota. It was still easier to muster support for climate change legislation among Democrats than among Republicans at all levels of government, but the issue was far less partisan in nature than, say, health care or taxes.

By the 2010 midterm election season, however, it was hard to find a Republican who was raising climate change as an issue—unless it was to denounce it. Some Republicans who had advocated tough environmental measures have left the scene, such as Schwarzenegger, who signed a landmark California law capping carbon emissions in 2006 but was term-limited out of office as governor in 2010. Others had switched their position, now advocating more of a market response and shying away from strict governmental controls. That's especially true among Republicans reaching for higher office—including the presidency. Insisting on caps on energy use has become something of a nonstarter for candidates in the Grand Old Party, or GOP.

A number of individual politicians have switched their positions on the issue. In 2008, Republican governor Pawlenty of Minnesota appeared with Janet Napolitano, then the Democratic governor of Arizona, in a nationwide radio advertisement criticizing Congress for not addressing climate change. But appearing on NBC's *Meet the Press* in February 2010, Pawlenty, who was briefly a candidate for the presidential nomination in 2012, said, "Cap and trade . . . would be a disaster." "With Tim Pawlenty, I guess he sees that there's a need to talk about climate change in a more skeptical frame to make himself more appealing in a Republican primary," said Jim DiPeso, vice president for policy and communications at Republicans for Environmental Protection.[17] Sarah Palin had always expressed skepticism that climate change was human-made, but when she was governor of Alaska, she thought her state should prepare for its effects. In late 2010, however, she tweeted that climate science was "bogus."[18] Marco Rubio, as speaker of the Florida House, declared in 2007 that "this nation—and ultimately the world—is headed toward emission caps."[19] He backed the idea of creating a state cap-and-trade program the following year. In his 2010 campaign for the U.S. Senate, however, Rubio blasted Crist, his primary opponent, for having pushed the cap-and-trade idea. Rubio said that he doesn't believe the scientific evidence for human-influenced climate change.

In 2016, the GOP's platform rejected the Paris accord to cut carbon emissions. It also called for less spending on renewable energy and on international programs meant to help communities adapt to the changes wrought by global warming. "In four pages devoted to energy and climate, the platform tosses aside an environmental regulatory structure built on congressional legislation and judicial rulings over more than four decades, dating to the creation of the Environmental Protection Agency under President Richard M. Nixon," the *Washington Post* reported.[20] By contrast, the Democratic Party's 2016 platform referred to climate change as "a defining challenge of our time" and called for "using every tool available to reduce emissions now."

The changes in opinion among Republican leaders and rank-and-file voters lead straight to a chicken-and-egg question: Are elected officials growing more skeptical about climate change legislation because of concerns raised by their political base? Or are GOP voters following a shift among top officials and the conservative media? "Many ordinary citizens take their cues on complex political issues from leaders of the political party that they identify with," said DiPeso.[21] But Daniel J. Weiss, senior vice president of the League of Conservation Voters, thinks it is public opinion that is leading the leaders in this case. He cited the frequent attacks against global warming legislation efforts launched by Rush Limbaugh and commentators on Fox News Channel. "That has really riled up their highly conservative base," Weiss said.[22]

He also noted that elected officials are well aware of the opposition to congressional climate change legislation led by energy companies and the U.S. Chamber of Commerce. In 2012, fossil-fuel companies devoted more than $150 million to advertising focused on energy issues. "If you're a Republican," Weiss asked, "would you really stand up to them and risk getting on their wrong side when they have so much money to spend?"[23] From 2014 to 2016, Republican attorneys general, who led the fight against Obama's Clean Power Plan, and their association received nearly $5 million in donations from energy companies.[24]

Billionaire investor Tom Steyer sought to level the playing field in 2014, spending millions to promote candidates who took climate change seriously and to defeat those who didn't. He spent upwards of $70 million during the 2014 campaign season, including more than $10 million supporting Charlie Crist in his effort to get reelected as Florida's governor, this time running as a Democrat. He spent even more in 2016, devoting somewhere in the neighborhood of $100 million through his NextGen America political action committee to supporting candidates and convincing voters that the time had come to take a stand and demand action on the issue. But climate was barely mentioned during the presidential campaign, save for Trump's pledges to withdraw from the Paris Agreement and undo Obama's Clean Power Plan. *Investor's Business Daily* dubbed Steyer "the biggest loser of the 2016 election."[25] In 2016, a group of construction unions threatened to back out of a plan to launch a $50 million super PAC to get out the vote for Democrats unless Steyer was dropped from the group, due to his opposition to projects the unions thought could create jobs, such as the Keystone XL oil pipeline extension. By 2018, Steyer had turned much of his attention to promoting the idea of impeaching Trump.

States Get Serious about the Environment

Unlike education, crime, taxes, and budgets, the environment is a relatively recent policy concern for state

Western fires are becoming more common and more intense. Since the 1980s, the number of fires has increased more than 400 percent, and on average, they are lasting five times as long.

U.S. Environmental Protection Agency (EPA) The federal agency charged with protecting the environment.

Kyoto Protocol A 1997 international treaty that sought to reduce emissions of greenhouse gases.

and local governments. Indeed, it is a relatively recent policy concern for the federal government. The modern environmental movement got its start in the 1960s and led to a concerted federal response in the early 1970s. This included the passage of landmark laws regarding air and water quality, as well as the creation of the **U.S. Environmental Protection Agency (EPA)**. Enforcing and expanding environmental policy has since become one of the central responsibilities of the federal and, increasingly, state and local governments. "Today, after nearly four decades, environmental protection is the most heavily funded regulatory responsibility in the United States," writes Marc Allen Eisner, a political scientist at Wesleyan University.[26]

At the heart of contemporary environmental debates is climate change, which has become a hot issue not just among national (and international) policymakers but also for state and local officials. It's worth remembering, however, that policymakers at all levels have taken this issue seriously for a relatively short time. "We're still very much at the embryonic stage of dealing with climate change in this country," said John Cahill, who worked on environmental legislation as a gubernatorial aide in New York.[27]

The federal government has, to put it mildly, a mixed record in dealing with the climate change challenge. Environmentalists derided President George W. Bush for not seriously addressing global warming, but his predecessor's record was not notably stronger. Congress rejected President Bill Clinton's 1993 proposal to impose a tax on energy, and the Senate passed a unanimous resolution in 1997 that it would reject U.S. participation in the **Kyoto Protocol** if it harmed the U.S. economy.

At least initially, states followed the skeptical approach of the federal government. It soon became clear, however, that many states were eager to address the problem of global warming, particularly after Bush's formal rejection of the Kyoto Protocol in 2001. "Ironically . . . American states may be emerging as international leaders at the very time the national government continues to be portrayed as an international laggard on global climate change," Barry G. Rabe, a public policy professor at the University of Michigan, wrote in 2004.[28]

Most of the initial state-level efforts were largely symbolic, lacking specific mandates or resources. Unlike the federal government, however, some states actually put teeth into their efforts. As early as 1989, New Jersey governor Thomas Kean, a Republican, signed an executive order instructing all state agencies to take the lead in reducing **greenhouse gases**. In 2001, Massachusetts governor Jane Swift, also a Republican, issued a rule limiting a variety of pollutants from six major power plants; the rule included the nation's first **carbon dioxide** standards. "The new, tough standards will help ensure older power plants in Massachusetts do not contribute to regional air pollution, acid rain and global warming," Swift said.[29] Her action was soon copied in New Hampshire.

Indeed, it was actually a state government—California's—rather than the federal government that emerged as the leader in addressing climate change–related policies. California stepped into this policy arena not simply because of its green-leaning political constituencies or its large economy or its role as a national cultural trendsetter, although all these factors certainly played their roles. "California will become a petri dish for international efforts to slow global warming . . . forcing one of the world's largest economies to squeeze into a dramatically smaller carbon footprint," the *Los Angeles Times* reported after passage in 2016 of another iteration of the state's ambitious climate policy.[30]

As the only state allowed to set air pollution controls stricter than those mandated by federal law, thanks to a provision in the **Clean Air Act**, California occupies a unique policymaking niche in the federal system. That law—written at a time during the early 1970s when Southern California was notorious for its **smog**—gives California the authority to regulate any such pollutant as long as the state can get a waiver from the EPA. Other states are then allowed to follow California's rules. Following the 1998 elections, there was strong pressure from environmentalist forces within California to move on the issue of greenhouse gases, with both the legislature and the governor's mansion in Democratic hands for the first time in two decades. Thus, on a series of important environmental issues, California began to act. Other states, following California's lead, began experimenting with innovative environmental policies. One of the biggest obstacles the states faced in these efforts was the federal government.

Regulating Vehicles

In 2002, California lawmakers enacted a measure to regulate **tailpipe emissions**, or greenhouse gases released by vehicles, which in 1999 accounted for 37 percent of carbon dioxide emissions in the state.[31] The idea came from Bluewater Network, a San Francisco environmental group that has since become part of Friends of the Earth, a global organization. The group found its sponsor in Fran Pavley, a Democratic freshman state representative willing to take on the fight when more prominent legislators were avoiding it. "We were happy at that point to find any progressive author, because we knew it would be a difficult bill," said Bluewater executive director Russell Long.[32]

The legislation survived a committee challenge and was ready to reach the floor by the middle of 2001, but Pavley held off on a vote until 2002 so she could broaden her backing. Carmakers and oil companies spent an estimated $5 million attempting to sink it, and she was ardently attacked by talk-radio hosts for impinging on the freedom of Californians to drive SUVs and other large vehicles.

Pavley responded with polls demonstrating overwhelming popular support for the bill, even among SUV owners. She also got help from water-quality districts, religious leaders, technology executives from Silicon Valley, and celebrities such as Tom Hanks and former president Clinton, who made calls to wavering lawmakers.

Her bill's progress was also helped immeasurably by legislative leaders who showed the former civics teacher some parliamentary tricks to ensure its passage. One was to put language into the bill all in capital letters highlighting the fact that the California Air Resources Board would not have the power to ban SUVs or other specific types of vehicles, as bill opponents were warning would be the case in their advertisements. One of Pavley's colleagues called these the "We Really Mean It" amendments. The substance of the bill was not

Greenhouse gases Emissions—primarily carbon dioxide but also other gases such as methane—that are believed to contribute to global warming.

Carbon dioxide A naturally occurring gas, the prevalence of which is increased by the burning of fossil fuels.

Clean Air Act The law, initially enacted in 1970, that provides authority for federal regulation of air pollution.

Smog A type of air pollution; the word comes from the combination of *smoke* and *fog*.

Tailpipe emissions Greenhouse gases released by cars and other vehicles.

changed, but the amendments were "put in to clarify it for the public," Pavley said. "Admittedly, in all the years I taught 'how a bill becomes law,' we didn't talk about that possibility."[33]

But her law did require the Air Resources Board to adopt "cost-effective" and "reasonable" restrictions on carbon dioxide emissions from cars and light trucks by 2005, with automakers having until 2009 to comply. Not surprisingly, carmakers fought the law through numerous court challenges.

More than a dozen other states enacted laws saying they would abide by California's rules once they were approved, and several others pledged to do so, but the Bush administration refused to grant California the necessary waiver. "All we asked for was permission to enforce, because the rules were all in place," California Air Resources Board spokesman Stanley Young said in a 2008 interview. "We've been ready for 2 years on Pavley. The rules were fully fleshed out. They were formally adopted back in 2005, and we're ready to move on them as soon as we get the green light."[34]

Challenging the Environmental Protection Agency

In the face of federal reluctance to regulate greenhouse gas emissions, several environmentalist groups as early as 1999 had petitioned the EPA to use its authority under the Clean Air Act to regulate the gases. The agency denied it had such authority and also argued that the link between greenhouse gases and climate change was not firmly established.

Massachusetts and 11 other states appealed the EPA's denial. In April 2007, the Supreme Court ruled 5–4 in the states' favor, noting that they had standing to bring such a case due to the "risk of catastrophic harm" they faced as sovereign entities. Justice John Paul Stevens wrote that the EPA had provided "no reasonable explanation for its refusal to decide whether greenhouse gases cause or contribute to climate change." In his dissent, Chief Justice John Roberts argued that it was an issue better decided by Congress and the executive branch.[35] But the Court's majority had determined that carbon dioxide was indeed an air pollutant under the federal Clean Air Act.

The 2007 Supreme Court decision set the political stage for Congress to enforce a new mileage standard for cars and light trucks. In December 2007, President Bush signed into law requirements that a car manufacturer's entire fleet average 35 miles per gallon by 2020.

Just hours after that bill was signed, however, EPA administrator Stephen L. Johnson dashed hopes that the *Massachusetts v. EPA* decision would lead the agency to approve California's waiver application for enforcement of the Pavley bill. "The Bush administration is moving forward with a clear national solution, not a confusing patchwork of state rules, to reduce America's climate footprint from vehicles," Johnson said in a statement.[36]

California had been granted more than 50 waivers under the Clean Air Act, which allowed it to develop such innovations as the catalytic converter, which reduces tailpipe emissions; tighter fuel caps to reduce gasoline evaporation; and computerized detectors to warn when a car's smog controls are not working. California's standards have often been adopted by other states and, thus, by carmakers. "If not for California's leadership, I think it's fair to say that cars wouldn't be as clean as they are today," said Ron Burke, Midwest climate change director for the Union of Concerned Scientists. "We would have suffered through more bad air days over the last 30 years."[37]

As noted earlier, the waiver had to wait until President Obama granted it—representing the federal government's first step toward regulating greenhouse gases. (Trump now wants to roll it back.) Under rules finalized in April 2010 by the EPA and the Department of Transportation, emission and mileage standards for new vehicles would require an average performance of 35.5 miles per gallon by 2016. "The rules are expected to cut emissions of carbon dioxide and other heat-trapping gases about 30 percent from 2012 to 2016," the *New York Times* reported.[38] The Obama administration estimated that the new standards would add $985 to the price of a car but would save the consumer $4,000 in fuel costs over the life of the vehicle.

Canada adopted identical standards the same day. The federal rules were largely based on the California law, but they also reflected an agreement hammered out with carmakers. Two years later, the Obama administration finalized rules calling for cars and light-duty trucks to average 54.5 miles per gallon by 2025. But in 2018, the Trump administration announced plans to freeze the Obama-era anti-pollution and fuel efficiency requirements.

Cap and Trade

Cars are not the only source of greenhouse gas emissions. In 2006, Pavley and other California lawmakers worked successfully for the passage of a piece of legislation, known as AB 32, that sought to address the stationary sources of pollution, such as power plants, oil refineries, and cement plants. The law aims to reduce industrial carbon dioxide emissions by 25 percent by 2020. AB 32 represents the first imposition of statewide enforceable limits on greenhouse gas emissions that includes penalties for noncompliance. The legislation was the first in the nation to require a cap-and-trade system to address greenhouse gases.

Cap and trade puts an overall limit—or cap—on the emission of a pollutant, such as carbon dioxide. Once the limit is set, polluters are given or sold some number of emissions allowances—in essence, permits to pollute. The amount of pollution they can release—say, 1,000 tons of carbon dioxide at a power plant—is slowly reduced over time. If they come in below their limits, they can sell or trade their excess permits; if not, they have to pay fines or buy extra permits from other polluters. That's the trade part. Late in 2012, California held its first auction of 23.1 million carbon emission permits, which sold for $10.09 apiece. When the law took effect at the beginning of 2013, California became the world's second-largest carbon market, after the European Union.[39]

Cap-and-trade systems have been used by the federal government and by other states to address environmental concerns. Congress created such a system to address acid rain in the 1990 Clean Air Act. (Acid rain is rain that contains a high concentration of sulfur dioxide; it was blamed for polluting lakes and streams.)

Ten states in the Northeast and Mid-Atlantic—Connecticut, Delaware, Maine, Maryland, Massachusetts, New Hampshire, New Jersey, New York, Rhode Island, and Vermont—signed on to a cooperative effort known as the Regional Greenhouse Gas Initiative (RGGI), which uses cap and trade. (New Jersey dropped out in 2011 under Republican governor Chris Christie but rejoined in 2018 under newly elected Democrat Phil Murphy.) These states have capped carbon dioxide emissions from large power plants, requiring gradual reductions that will bring emissions down 50 percent by 2020.

Governors from seven states began RGGI negotiations in 2003, reached a formal agreement in 2006 (with the last three states, Maryland, Massachusetts, and Rhode Island, signing on the following year), and began auctioning pollution permits to power companies in 2009. The history of RGGI includes many touch-and-go moments when states dropped out of or rejoined the program. RGGI stayed afloat based on the hope that, once carbon emissions carried a price, utilities would burn less coal, oil, and natural gas because it would be in their economic interest to do so, which would then make carbon-free alternatives comparatively more attractive.

The early auctions were considered a success, but not everyone is convinced that the most optimistic scenarios about reducing emissions will play out as intended. The region-by-region approach has left open plenty of opportunities for undermining the system.

The other regional initiatives have not been as productive as RGGI. The midwestern regional initiative outlined a cap-and-trade system, with an advisory group releasing its final recommendations and model rules in May 2010, but the states involved then failed to follow through on their greenhouse gas reduction goals through the accord. The Western Climate Initiative, originally comprising seven states and four Canadian provinces, appeared bolder in its approach than did RGGI, targeting not just carbon dioxide but other greenhouse gases as well, but every U.S. member state, save California, had dropped out of the initiative by 2012. The three regional initiatives joined forces in 2012 with the creation of America 2050: A Partnership for Progress, a group of 16 states and four Canadian provinces designed to share ideas and techniques for moving toward a low-carbon economy. California has since signed climate deals with China and Mexico, but those agreements only lay the groundwork for increased cooperation, as opposed to setting any binding targets for new reductions in greenhouse gas emissions. In 2018, the California Air Resources Board announced that the state's total carbon emissions fell by 12 million tons in 2016, meeting the state's goal of reducing emissions back to 1990 levels four years before its target date of 2020.

California's own cap-and-trade system caps the total amount of greenhouse gases that can be released and requires companies to buy permits, each of which allows 1 metric ton of emissions. During an auction in 2016, only 11 percent of the permits on offer were purchased. Proceeds are meant to pay for other projects to cut greenhouse gases, but the auction brought in only $2.5 million out of the $150 million expected for a high-speed rail

Cap and trade A system for limiting pollution by assigning allowances to polluters, who can sell their excess permits if they succeed in reducing their emissions.

MAP 16-1 ● Renewable and Alternative Energy Portfolio Standards, 2018

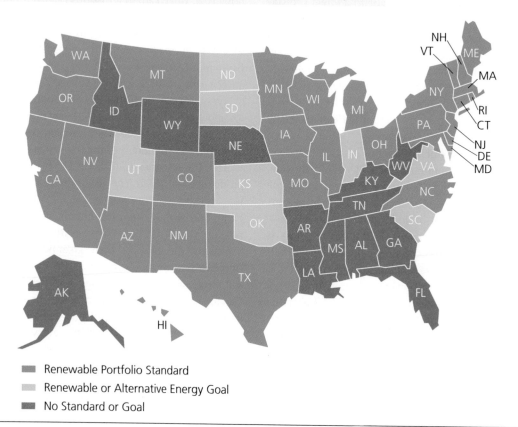

■ Renewable Portfolio Standard
■ Renewable or Alternative Energy Goal
■ No Standard or Goal

Source: National Conference of State Legislatures, "State Renewable Portfolio Standards and Goals," July 20, 2018, http://www.ncsl.org/research/energy/renewable-portfolio-standards.aspx.

project.[40] In 2017, the legislature voted to extend the cap-and-trade program for 10 additional years.

A cap-and-trade proposal was central to the approach taken by the 2009 bill passed by the U.S. House, but the concept itself became highly charged over the course of congressional debate. Critics derided the idea, calling it "cap and tax" and claiming that it would add billions to the nation's energy costs.

As White House counsel under President George H. W. Bush, C. Boyden Gray was an architect of the 1990 Clean Air Act cap-and-trade program designed to address acid rain. Nevertheless, he added his voice to the chorus of complaints about the cap-and-trade model proposed by federal climate change legislation. "The proponents always say they're copying the highly successful cap-and-trade program of the Clean Air Act and they're most decidedly not, because they've thrown in this auction function," Gray said. "It's purely

a revenue function, and that becomes a tax. You pull 2 or 3 trillion dollars out of the economy and that's what people are objecting to."[41] In 2014, the U.S. Conference of Mayors—a group that has long supported efforts to address climate change—dropped its call for Congress to pass a cap-and-trade bill because of differences of opinion within the group's own ranks. "Rather than split mayors up over partisan disagreements, we wanted to focus on actually doing something," said Democratic mayor Bill Finch of Bridgeport, Connecticut, cochair of the group's climate task force.[42]

Clean Power Plan

States have long taken different approaches to environmental protection. Coastal states such as California and Maine traditionally put a higher premium on clean air and clean water than do the industrial states of the

Midwest and coal-producing states such as West Virginia and Kentucky. Over the past decade, however, when questions about climate change have at times been a top-priority concern, the differences between states have seemed to become more pronounced. In addition to regional differences in priorities and willingness to spend large sums of money, climate questions have become—like so many other issues—a matter of partisan debate.

When the Obama administration unveiled the Clean Power Plan in 2014, calling on states to reduce their carbon emissions from power plants by 30 percent from 2005 levels by the year 2030, it was applauded in some of the Democratic-led states that had already made major efforts to increase energy efficiency, and perhaps even seen as insufficiently bold to address the challenge at hand. The northeastern states participating in RGGI had already slashed their combined carbon dioxide emissions by more than 30 percent from 2005 levels and were upping their target to 45 percent. "The announcement is a little bit of a non-event here in New England," said Dan Dolan, president of the New England Power Generators Association.[43]

In more conservative states, however, officials saw the announcement as one more regulatory intrusion from the federal EPA that would cost jobs. Two months after the plan was announced, a coalition of attorneys general from a dozen coal-reliant states sued to block it, arguing that the EPA was overstepping its authority under the Clean Air Act. The agency's proposed rule would have "devastating effects on West Virginia jobs and its economy" by forcing some coal-fired plants to close, argued Patrick Morrisey, that state's attorney general.[44] States including Kansas, Kentucky, and West Virginia moved swiftly to pass laws directing their environmental agencies to develop carbon emission plans that would consider the "unreasonable costs" of compliance for power plants.

Ultimately, half the states sued to block the Clean Power Plan. They succeeded in convincing the Supreme Court in 2016 to put the plan on hold while legal challenges were pending. As noted earlier, Trump made good his campaign pledge to end the Clean Power Plan, with a lawsuit from states—this time involving Democratic attorneys general—blocked by the courts.

Republicans continue to stress the importance of taking care not to make changes in pursuit of addressing climate change that could cost big money and jobs. "I do think it's sensible for a Republican candidate to express skepticism about this headlong rush . . . a lot of Democrats seem to be having to kill the coal industry," said Dick Wadhams, a former chair of the Colorado Republican Party.[45] But some Republicans do not dismiss climate change out of hand, even if they differ with Democrats about the right approaches or even the question of whether human activity is at fault. The same polls that show a partisan divide on the issue find that younger Republicans are much less skeptical about climate than older voters. Millennial Republicans are much more likely to favor government action than are members of the baby boom generation or Generation X.

That may be in part because the scientific consensus about climate change and its effects becomes firmer every year—and more dire. The proof may also be all around us. "Extreme weather" conditions, such as severe droughts in California, Texas, and the Midwest, along with a proliferation of powerful storms, have politicians talking about climate change in more urgent tones. In 2017, damage from a record season of wildfires and large-scale disasters such as Hurricane Harvey cost the United States a record $306 billion, easily shattering the previous single-year record by nearly $90 billion, according to the National Oceanic and Atmospheric Administration (NOAA).[46] "We now have very strong evidence that global warming has already put a thumb on the scales, upping the odds of extremes like severe heat and heavy rainfall," Stanford University climate scientist Noah Diffenbaugh said. "We find that global warming has increased the odds of record-setting hot events over more than 80 percent of the planet, and has increased the odds of record-setting wet events at around half of the planet."[47]

The state of Louisiana has already lost its distinctive boot shape as more and more of its shoreline has been swallowed by the Gulf of Mexico. One town, Isle de Jean Charles, which was settled in the early 1800s, has been sinking. It was the subject of a documentary in 2014 and the inspiration for the feature film *Beasts of the Southern Wild*. It became known as "the Louisiana town devoured by climate change." Early in 2016, the federal Department of Housing and Urban Development devoted $48 million to help the entire community move off the island, making its inhabitants the first American "climate refugees."[48] "In 2011, the federal government retired 35 place names for islands and bays and passes and ponds that had simply ceased to exist," the *New York Times* reported in 2018. "State planners believe another 2,000 square miles, or even

STATES UNDER STRESS
DURING DISASTERS, STATES LEARN TO RELY ON EACH OTHER

A mutual aid pact among U.S. states and territories is changing the way governments plan for major disasters. The Emergency Management Assistance Compact (EMAC) allows states to reach out to each other—instead of the federal government—to get the resources they need.

Massachusetts and other states sent more than 4,700 responders on 120 missions to Puerto Rico in 2017 to help with disaster relief efforts following Hurricane Maria. That came on top of nearly 5,300 who had been sent to Texas after Hurricane Harvey, and nearly 4,000 who were dispatched to Florida after Hurricane Irma. The EMAC volunteers also helped Nevada coroners after the Las Vegas mass shooting, battled forest fires and winter storms in California, and provided law enforcement to North Dakota during the Standing Rock pipeline protests. In total, for missions that began in 2017, states sent out 17,818 people, by far their busiest year for mutual aid since Hurricanes Katrina and Rita hit the Gulf Coast in 2005.

"Every state can't have every resource, especially with the pattern of severe weather events we've been having in the last couple of years," says Mike Sprayberry, North Carolina's emergency management director and the president of the National Emergency Management Association, which runs EMAC. "Every state can't have urban search and rescue teams with structural collapse capabilities, swift water rescue teams, helicopter rescue teams and all of the different things you need. So you have EMAC, which allows us to very quickly get resources out the door from other states, so they can rally at the site of the disaster. You can't overestimate the value of it."

The value of the arrangement has grown, as states have started to offer—and request—a broader array of services through EMAC. The responders now go far beyond police and National Guard units. States have called on mental health experts, agricultural specialists, veterinarians, and electric line workers. Meanwhile, the back-office services that support the mutual aid missions have improved as well. That means it's now easier to show disaster-stricken states what resources are available, track responders and their equipment, and allow for easy reimbursements.

The growing capabilities of EMAC, along with the anxiety among members of Congress and federal officials about the rising costs of disaster relief, make it likely that state-based mutual aid will play an even bigger role in future disaster responses, says EMAC program director Angela Copple. "We expect the use of the EMAC system to go up and [for there to be] less reliance on federal response elements."

State-to-state disaster aid got its start in the early 1990s, at a time when federal disaster relief programs were failing badly. Governors and local officials chastised the Federal Emergency Management Agency (FEMA) for tardy and disorganized responses to Hurricanes Hugo and Andrew, which hit the southeastern United States in 1989 and 1992, respectively. The federal agency at the time was notoriously bureaucratic. When the Puerto Rican governor mailed a request for disaster aid as Hugo approached the island, FEMA sent it back through the mail because he forgot to check one section. That delayed federal relief for days.

A month after Andrew hit, Florida governor Lawton Chiles proposed a mutual aid system among nearby states. A year later, 19 states in the region joined an emergency management compact, and by 1995, they decided to allow any state to join. Congress ratified EMAC the following year. Under the agreement, the governor of the affected state must declare an emergency or a disaster before requesting help. The state asking for help is responsible for reimbursing states that send aid. For severe disasters, FEMA will, in turn, reimburse the affected state. By 2000, 36 states were part of the network.

It was the hurricanes in 2004 and 2005 that brought about a major change in the way the interstate agreement worked. "Prior to the 2004 hurricane season, it was primarily fire resources, emergency management resources and the National Guard," says Copple of EMAC. "In 2004, that really shifted to any resource a state would have that they could share with another state."

During the 2004 season, when Florida was hit by four hurricanes, the state brought in 715 emergency responders from 35 states. The next year, by comparison, Florida alone dispatched 7,000 people to help Louisiana and Mississippi. All told, the hurricane-stricken states brought in 67,048 responders from all over the country to cope with the aftermath of Katrina and Rita. Of all the out-of-state personnel responding to Hurricane Katrina on September 10, 2005 (two weeks after the storm hit), 52 percent had been called up through EMAC. FEMA personnel made up just 11 percent.

But the massive influx of responders also brought new complications. At the time, many of the contracts between states were handwritten. They had to be signed, faxed, signed by the other state's official, and faxed back again. Sometimes the paperwork couldn't keep up with the demand. Florida sent search and rescue teams, law enforcement personnel, and even water and ice to Mississippi without contracts in place. Mississippi welcomed the help. "Will police up paperwork later—you have my guarantee," Mississippi's emergency management director e-mailed his Florida counterpart. Those ad hoc arrangements made it difficult for Louisiana and Mississippi to reimburse states that had helped them. Many states didn't even have written policies for reimbursements. Even in those that did, responders often didn't understand or know about them.

In the years following Katrina, emergency managers tried to simplify things and speed up response times by using preplanned mission packages. The response teams would figure out ahead of time what they would

need to do their work in another state for two weeks, and how much that would cost. That way, when a disaster strikes, all the team has to do is figure out its travel expenses and give the affected state a cost estimate.

Today, emergency managers can use the web-based system to alert other states that they need help, see what teams are available, track reimbursements, and keep better tabs on responders. If communications break down, another state can run the EMAC system remotely for the affected state. Such features make it possible for states to take disaster planning to a level they've never been able to reach before.

"States that have disasters like Louisiana, where we're prone to hurricanes and flooding, have learned the hard way," says Victoria Carpenter, Louisiana's EMAC coordinator. "We know we need assistance from other states. We know we can't handle the number of resources needed in a catastrophic event."

Source: Adapted from Daniel C. Vock, "The Pact Changing How Governments Respond to Disaster," *Governing*, March 2018, http://www.governing.com/topics/transportation-infrastructure/gov-emergency-management-local-federal-fema-states.html.

double that, could be overtaken in 50 years as the land sinks, canals widen and sea levels rise because of climate change."[49] In August 2016, more than 26 inches of rain fell on Louisiana in a week, causing at least 13 deaths and nearly $9 billion in property damage—the worst natural disaster in the United States since Superstorm Sandy in 2012. The following month, NOAA said that the likelihood of such heavy downpours had been more than doubled by human-made climate change.[50] In 2014, the Pentagon released a report concluding that climate change poses immediate national security threats, leading to increased risks from terrorism, infectious disease, poverty, food shortages, and extreme weather. The report described ways the military would have to adapt to increased droughts, storms, and rising sea levels.[51] A draft United Nations report that same year said that global warming had already cut grain production by several percentage points' worth and warned that sea levels could rise, periods of high heat would increase, and other climate issues would worsen unless greenhouse gas emissions were brought under control. Scientists and even the Obama White House were careful to assert that no single episode of extreme weather—no storm, no flood, no record-breaking heat wave, and no drought—could be attributed specifically to global climate change. But weather everywhere seemed to be

affected by the continuing buildup of greenhouse gases. "The new reality in New York is we are getting hit by 100-year storms every couple of years," said Andrew Cuomo, the state's Democratic governor.[52] In 2014, he signed a law known as the Community Risk and Resiliency Act that amended a number of statutes to require consideration of the impact of climate change for many projects and permits. The state's public service commission ordered Consolidated Edison, the utility company serving New York City and some of its suburbs, to spend $1 billion on upgrading its equipment and physical plants to prevent future damage from flooding and other weather events.

How to address the effects of climate change—if not climate change itself—has become a top challenge for states and localities. It's true that roughly half the states have taken little to no action related to climate change, either because they are concerned that the price of addressing the issue, through limiting energy use, is simply too high or because their leaders and political cultures remain skeptical that global warming is anthropogenic (i.e., caused largely by human activity). In general, states have lately come to concentrate less on limiting energy consumption than on promoting the development of energy resources. Numerous states were undergoing booms in oil and natural gas production prior to the recent decline in energy prices. Many states, however, have put in place new measures meant to limit reliance on fossil fuels. More than half the states have adopted renewable energy portfolio standards requiring utilities to rely on renewable sources such as wind and solar energy to generate a significant share of their electricity (25 percent in most states) in future years. "They're committed to moving forward on various measures that they've already started in the absence of federal action," said Jessica Shipley, a fellow at the Center for Climate and Energy Solutions. "Definitely, states are still working hard on climate, in conjunction with federal action."[53]

This represents an important role for states, which traditionally have taken a back seat to federal efforts when it comes to environmental issues. The major environmental laws of the early 1970s, such as the Clean Air Act and the Clean Water Act, set out strict federal guidelines that states had to follow. In contrast to this "command and control" model, in which the federal government called all the shots, in the area of climate change the American states are leading, influencing not only federal policy under Obama but also efforts in many other countries through state partnerships with regions and provinces in other nations.

Approaches to climate change, then, have become a particularly interesting exercise in federalism. States have sought to fill the vacuum left by the absence of federal leadership on an issue that state leaders themselves realize calls for a national—indeed, international—set of solutions. "States have been tripping all over themselves to show national leadership on this issue," says public policy professor Barry Rabe. "California, I would argue, has made as heavy an investment in time and treasury into climate change as any government on Earth, including the European Union."[54]

In 2018, California enacted a law requiring the state to generate 60 percent of its energy from renewable sources by 2030, up from the previous target of a 50 percent reduction sought by a 2015 law. That law, known as SB 100, also set a target for 100 percent of the state's electricity supply to come from carbon-free sources by 2015.

The 2015 law also required building owners to double the energy efficiency of their structures by 2030. The bill was stripped of a provision that would have cut petroleum use by 50 percent, due to opposition from the oil industry. Oil companies spent $10.7 million in three months on a lobbying and media campaign against the requirement.[55] The following year,

California extended its landmark 2006 climate change law, which had been set to expire in 2020, until 2030. It also increased the ambition of the law's goals. Rather than reducing greenhouse gas emissions to 1990 levels by 2020, the state is now aiming to reduce emissions to 40 percent below 1990 levels by 2030. The *Los Angeles Times* ran a column about the bill's passage headlined "With New Climate Legislation, Gov. Brown Gets Even with the Oil Industry."[56] In short, inaction by the federal government and differences across states and localities have resulted in significant obstacles to a coordinated response to environmental problems, especially problems associated with global warming. Climate change is certain to remain an important issue among states and localities, but whether a subset of the subnational governmental units of the United States can make a significant impact on greenhouse gas emissions in the absence of further action at the national and international levels remains very much in question.

International Agreements

Just a couple of weeks after he was elected president in November 2008, Barack Obama offered a videotaped address to state leaders gathered at a climate change policy summit in California. "When I am president, any governor who's willing to promote clean energy will have a partner in the White House," he said.[57] When he came into office, he made it clear that climate change was among his highest priorities.

Obama's promise of support was welcome news to those assembled at the summit, an audience of policymakers who had felt frustrated by the lack of attention that global warming had received under President George W. Bush. Some were openly emotional, believing the president-elect's remarks signaled a new day. Many state and local leaders had gotten involved in climate change policy only because of the lack of federal action—a state of affairs they felt certain was at its end.

But by the time of Obama's election, it was clear that many states and localities were already too invested in the issue simply to cede the ground to Washington. They became highly vocal lobbyists during deliberations in Congress, as well as in international forums. In contrast to the general run of environmental issues, where policies have largely been set by the federal government even though responsibilities are carried out by the states, climate change had become an issue in which states and localities had already claimed their ground. In large part because its effects are felt differently in different locales, many states and cities had become convinced of the need to formulate their own strategies and plans, even if the logjam in Washington looked as though it was ready to be broken.

As it turned out, state leaders who believed greenhouse gas emissions needed to be lowered were still acting on their own. Obama and other world leaders failed to reach any serious agreement at a summit in Copenhagen in December 2009, the purpose of which had been to revamp and update the international treaty on greenhouse gases that had been written in Kyoto a dozen years earlier. A two-week UN meeting in Doha at the end of 2012 led to little agreement beyond the idea of extending the old Kyoto Protocol. The United States and China did announce a climate agreement in November 2014, and renewed UN talks on climate took place in Paris at the end of 2015. Knowing he was unlikely to get approval of any treaty through the Senate, Obama floated the idea well ahead of those negotiations of a "name and shame" strategy that would taunt countries into cutting their emissions.

At the Paris summit, representatives from 195 nations agreed to commit to limiting greenhouse gas emissions. The agreement was hailed as a historic breakthrough, the first calling on all nations to reduce greenhouse gas emissions. Under the agreement, countries are required to reconvene every five years to update their plans to limit emissions. They are also required to report publicly on how much they are actually cutting emissions. Every country in the world has agreed to the accord, with the exception of the United States, which has withdrawn. Other rich countries may not hold up their ends of the deal. For instance, poor nations had hoped that a pledge of $100 billion a year to help them mitigate and adapt to climate change would be legally binding, but it is not. And scientists have noted that even if the agreement holds up in total, it will cut greenhouse gas emissions by about half as much as necessary to prevent an increase in atmospheric temperatures of 3.6 degrees Fahrenheit above preindustrial averages, which is the point at which rising sea levels, storms, droughts, and flooding are expected to become catastrophic.

Projections about the consequences of climate change, meanwhile, keep getting worse. A study from the University of Massachusetts in 2016 estimated that by 2100 sea levels could rise by twice the level previously expected—6 feet rather than 3 feet—if current rates of greenhouse gas emissions held steady.[58]

Another study released that year found that sea levels are rising at the fastest rate in the past 28 centuries.[59] In 2015, Pope Francis released a lengthy encyclical calling on global leaders and citizens to devote themselves to combating climate change. "We may well be leaving to coming generations debris, desolation and filth," the pope wrote. "The pace of consumption, waste and environmental change has so stretched the planet's capacity that our contemporary lifestyle, unsustainable as it is, can only precipitate catastrophes, such as those which even now periodically occur in different areas of the world. The effects of the present imbalance can only be reduced by our decisive action, here and now."[60]

Issues to Watch

Promoting Renewable Energy

Meanwhile, all but a dozen states are pushing forward on another front intended to reduce greenhouse gas emissions and lower U.S. dependence on fossil fuels. Most states outside the South and the Great Plains region now require utilities to rely on **renewable energy** sources, such as wind, solar, biofuels, and geothermal power, to generate a significant share of electricity—usually up to 25 percent in future years. That's nearly three times as many states as had renewable portfolio standards in place in 2004. Burlington, Vermont, reached an important milestone when it purchased a hydroelectric project in 2014, allowing it to generate 100 percent of its electricity from wind, water, or biomass sources and helping the state on its way toward the goal of meeting 90 percent of its electricity needs with renewable sources by 2050. The following year, San Diego, California, became the first major city to set a legally binding target of using 100 percent renewable energy by 2035. More than 50 other cities have since followed suit. Pursuing renewable energy sources is "an important step in the process of weaning ourselves from foreign oil," said then Rhode Island state senator David E. Bates, who helped push through legislation in 2004 that requires a 20 percent renewable energy portfolio in his state by 2020. "We provided incentives for companies to produce renewable energy. We also took great pains to make it a workable formula. You can't tell a national grid to produce green energy in twenty years

Renewable energy Power generated using natural sources that can be replenished, such as wind and solar energy, as opposed to nonrenewable fossil fuels.

LOCAL FOCUS

COAL INDUSTRY'S TROUBLES ARE FAR FROM OVER

One of the worst gaffes of Hillary Clinton's 2016 presidential campaign concerned coal. Speaking on CNN, Clinton said, "We're going to put a lot of coal miners and coal companies out of business, right?" In context, it was clear that she was calling for economic development help for coal-dependent regions, which were seeing the industry shrink. She called for $30 billion in aid for those regions. But Republicans used the quote as proof of a Democratic "war on coal." The remark hurt Clinton in Appalachia in both the primaries and the general election.

Clinton's diagnosis was correct: Even as the use of coal continues to grow around the world, the U.S. coal industry is in decline. Hundreds of coal-fired power plants have closed since 2010, with domestic coal production falling 40 percent between 2008 and 2016. Most of the major American coal companies have filed for bankruptcy. "At the time [the Obama] administration took office, there were hundreds of functional coal mines in West Virginia that were producing," John O'Neal, a West Virginia state representative, said in 2016. "Only 30 some are actually producing coal right now."[a]

The center of the American coal industry has actually shifted from Appalachia to Wyoming, which now produces 40 percent of the nation's coal. But all of coal mining is shedding jobs: employment dropped by 19 percent from 2014 to 2015.

The industry blamed federal regulation. That played a part, but market forces are also undermining coal. Wind and solar power are on the rise, but the biggest change has been the rise of natural gas. Natural gas prices have been falling rapidly over the past decade, as energy companies flood the market with gas extracted through hydraulic fracking. In 2016, for the first time, more of the nation's electricity was generated with natural gas than with coal.

As far as environmentalists are concerned, the decline of coal is good news. Fossil-fuel-fired power plants, most of which use coal, are the nation's leading source of greenhouse gas emissions, accounting for 37 percent of the total. Former New York mayor Michael Bloomberg has devoted $80 million to the Sierra Club's Beyond Coal Campaign, which seeks to eliminate coal-fueled electricity. "You'd think the politicians would at least care about the air they breathe themselves," Bloomberg said.[b]

Donald Trump pledged in 2016 to put coal miners back to work, but even industry officials, while welcoming his anti-regulatory stance, were skeptical that many jobs would be restored. "I would not expect to see a lot of growth because of the Trump presidency," Nick Carter, the head of the Kentucky Coal Association, said after the election.[c] A year after Trump's inauguration, the number of coal jobs was still near historic low levels, with a third as many workers as during the mid-1980s, according to the Bureau of Labor Statistics. "The fact is, putting coal miners back to work is no more possible from a business standpoint than putting telegraph operators back to work taking Morse code or putting Eastman Kodak employees back to work manufacturing film rolls," Bloomberg wrote in 2017.[d]

---

[a]Quoted in Chuck Holton, "Obama's War on Coal Decimating 'America's Powerhouse,'" CBN News, May 9, 2016, http://www1.cbn.com/cbnnews/us/2016/may/obamas-war-on-coal-decimating-americas-powerhouse.

[b]Quoted in Michael Grunwald, "Inside the War on Coal," Politico, May 26, 2015, http://www.politico.com/agenda/story/2015/05/inside-war-on-coal-000002.

[c]Quoted in Daniel Desrochers, "McConnell: It's 'Hard to Tell' If Ending 'War on Coal' Will Bring Back Jobs," Lexington Herald-Leader, November 14, 2016, https://www.kentucky.com/news/politics-government/article114197923.html.

[d]Michael Bloomberg, "Trump's Promise to Bring Back Coal Jobs Is Worse Than a Con," Washington Post, May 2, 2017, https://www.washingtonpost.com/opinions/trumps-promise-to-bring-back-coal-jobs-is-worse-than-a-con/2017/05/02/8aecd0b4-2e91-11e7-8674-437ddb6e813e_story.html.

without making sure the energy is available."[61] A decade after Bates's bill passed, Rhode Island passed a law aiming to reduce greenhouse gas emissions by 45 percent below 1990 levels by 2035 and by 80 percent by 2050.

Meeting the required targets remains quite a challenge, however, especially in coal-dependent regions such as the South and the Midwest. Coal is used to generate about half the nation's electricity. As governor of West Virginia, Joe Manchin touted wind energy but noted in 2008 that his state's coal production is the key source of electrical power for the entire Eastern Seaboard. "Economists and scientists . . . will tell you that coal is going to be the primary factor that's going to power this nation and most of the world for the next thirty to fifty years."[62]

According to the American Wind Energy Association, U.S. wind energy capacity has been growing rapidly, with wind turbines installed by 2017 capable of generating 85,000 megawatts of additional electricity. That's up from 17,000 megawatts of capacity as recently as 2007. Investment in geothermal energy has also grown steadily. Solar power generation grew 40 percent between 2016 and 2017 alone, providing 1.9 percent of the nation's electricity—roughly doubling its share in just two years. Four states—California, Hawaii, Nevada, and Vermont—drew more than 10 percent of their energy from solar.[63] The costs of production are coming down for all renewable sources.

Cutting Back on Coal

At the same time that states are promoting the generation of energy from renewable sources, some are also simply clamping down on coal. Nowadays, wherever a coal-fired plant is proposed, the Sierra Club or an allied group steps forward with a lawsuit to block it.[64] Environmentalists believe that delays, and their concomitant costs, can only serve to move power generation away from coal. "Each time you step back and reassess the politics and economics of coal," said Bob Eye, a Sierra Club attorney and former counsel to the Kansas Department of Health and Environment (KDHE), "things are more difficult for the coal plant proponents."[65]

In 2007, Rod Bremby, then the KDHE secretary, blocked a pair of massive coal-fired power plants. Citing that year's *Massachusetts v. EPA* Supreme Court decision (which sought to force the EPA to regulate greenhouse gases), Bremby overruled his own staff and rejected Sunflower Electric Power Corporation's application to build a $3.6 billion power plant project outside Holcomb. Bremby was the first regulator to block a power plant strictly out of concern for climate change and without getting specific statutory cover from the legislature. "To approve the permit didn't seem a reasonable option, given that carbon dioxide is a pollutant and we're talking about 11 million tons of carbon," he said.[66] Since Bremby's original decision, more than 120 power plants have been retired or new projects have seen their permits denied, delayed, or withdrawn for reasons similar to the ones he cited.

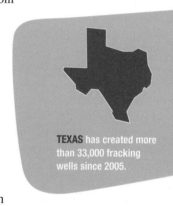

In 2016, **OREGON** became the first state in the nation to pass legislation to completely eliminate coal from its resource mix.

A lot of this had to do with environmentalists' complaints and regulation, but another factor was at work as well. Thanks to a boom in **fracking**, natural gas prices dropped in 2012 below $3 per million British thermal units (BTUs), down from about $8 in 2008, and some gas-fueled plants were able to generate electricity for about 2 cents per kilowatt, or less than half what it costs to run many coal-fired operations.

TEXAS has created more than 33,000 fracking wells since 2005.

That year, "natural gas pulled even with coal as a fuel source for power plants," according to the *Washington Post*, with coal usage down 17 percent and natural gas up 27 percent.[67]

Fracking itself remains controversial. New technologies have made it possible to extract oil from rock as thick as concrete through horizontal drilling and fracking, which involves pumping a mixture of water, sand, and chemicals into the ground to extract natural gas and oil. As a result, states such as North Dakota have experienced an energy boom. The high price tag of those

Fracking A process in which water, sand, and chemicals are pumped into the ground to enable the extraction of natural gas and oil.

extraction techniques means they're economically feasible when the price of a barrel of crude oil at times hovers around $100. Oil companies are rushing to tap the ground before the cheap pre-boom leases they signed with mineral rights owners expire, and North Dakota is reaping the benefits. By the end of 2010, the state had more than 6,000 wells capable of producing oil and gas, and an additional 20,000 wells could be drilled within the next 10 or 20 years, followed by more than 30 years of pumping oil.

In summer 2014, the unemployment rate in North Dakota was less than 3 percent—the lowest in the nation and less than half the national rate. For the past hundred years, the number of people in North Dakota has remained virtually stagnant. It's the only state in the country that had more residents in 1930 than it does today. Fracking brought about a population boom in the western part of the state; the state added 50,000 residents from 2010 to 2013, boosting its total population by 8 percent. "This boom is just wild and crazy," said Ward Koeser, mayor of Williston, the largest city in the center of the oil activity. "It's more than you can fathom."[68]

Fracking has been around in one form or another since 1947, but the vast increase in its use in recent years has made it perhaps the top environmental concern facing states, and they differ in how they balance the risks and rewards. The benefits of fracking are readily apparent. According to the Heritage Foundation, the process has been used to retrieve more than 7 billion barrels of oil and more than 600 trillion cubic feet of natural gas. One trillion cubic feet of natural gas is enough to heat 15 million homes for one year. Fracking has made it possible to tap the Marcellus Shale in the Mid-Atlantic region, one of the richest natural gas deposits in the world. This rock formation lies more than a mile beneath the earth's surface, and until fracking came along, there was no economical way to extract the gas. Ohio Republican governor John Kasich has referred to the formation as "a gift from heaven." All this exploration has helped lower energy prices and create jobs. Natural gas production

NEW JERSEY has 114 Superfund sites, uncontrolled or abandoned places where hazardous waste is located. That's the most of any state.

in the United States rose by 30 percent from 2008 to 2015, thanks to fracking, and overall U.S. gas output hit a new record in 2016 for the sixth year in a row. The steep decline in energy prices in 2015 and 2016, however, cooled the fracking industry's growth.

Along with its benefits, fracking presents many potential environmental hazards. Industry officials insist that their processes are safe, but environmentalists are worried that the chemicals released in fracking pollute both air and groundwater. A federal Department of Energy study released in 2014 found no evidence that chemicals or brine water contaminated drinking water at a site in western Pennsylvania. After 18 months of monitoring—the first time an energy company allowed independent researchers to study a drilling site—the scientists found that chemical-laced fluids used to free gas stayed almost a mile below drinking water supplies. A separate study in 2014 found that faulty well construction, not fracking itself, caused water pollution near some drilling sites.

The sheer amount of water that fracking requires has also raised concerns. Each well can use up to 5 million gallons of water per year—in some parts of the country, even more. In Carroll County, Ohio, alone, the state has issued permits to drill 161 wells.

In addition to concerns about water consumption and pollution, activists who say "no fracking way" point to the increase in seismic activity in states such as Colorado and Texas where fracking has been employed. The problem seems to be related to the wastewater—the water that has been used in fracking and then retrieved and injected into waste wells. The waste wells can be thousands of feet deep, under high pressure that can build up for months or years, eventually causing earthquakes. A study released in 2014 said that the 2,500 small earthquakes over the previous five years in Jones, Oklahoma, were likely triggered by oil and gas extraction. The largest earthquake in the state's history, a magnitude 5.7 quake in 2011 that damaged about 200 buildings, was "likely caused by fluid injection," according to scientists from the University of Oklahoma, Columbia University, and the U.S. Geological Survey. In 2016, the U.S. Geological Survey said that Oklahoma and parts of Kansas had become as prone to earthquakes as California. (Oil production is causing more earthquakes in Kern County, California, as well.)

Scientists say that the earthquake risk caused by fracking could be reduced by regulations demanding more careful placement and construction of wells. Following a series of earthquakes in 2011, Ohio instituted a moratorium on new wastewater injection permits. It resumed issuing the permits the following year, after putting more safeguards in place. In 2016, after a cluster of at least a dozen earthquakes struck north of Oklahoma City in less than a week, the Oklahoma Corporation Commission ordered injection well operators to reduce the volume of wastewater they were disposing.

In general, the fracking boom has been so rapid that it has seen comparatively little regulation. A study released in 2012 by OMB Watch, a research and advocacy group, found that only 13 of the 30 states engaged in natural gas drilling had passed legislation related to fracking. Hundreds of other bills were under consideration in other states.

Some government officials, however, have demanded further study

Erik McGregor/Pacific Press/LightRocket via Getty Images

▲ The Spectra Algonquin Incremental Market Project began transporting natural gas across New York State in 2016. Environmentalists tried to stop the project because it passes near suburban neighborhoods and at one point lies within 105 feet of a nuclear power plant.

before allowing fracking to proceed. Even as neighboring states such as Pennsylvania were going full steam ahead with fracking, then Maryland governor Martin O'Malley, a Democrat, placed a de facto moratorium on the practice in 2011, pending completion in 2014 of a $1.5 million study by the state Department of the Environment. The report warned that fracking would cause air pollution and create jobs that were dangerous for workers.

Another Democrat, New York governor Andrew Cuomo, had appeared to be ready to give fracking the green light, but after seven years of study, he decided to put off lifting the state's moratorium, pending still more review. Antifracking protesters had been stalking Cuomo for months—not just at speaking engagements but at his home and office—while celebrities such as Lady Gaga lined up to express their disapproval of fracking. "I literally see them everywhere I go," Cuomo said of the hydraulic fracturing opponents in 2014. "One of my daughters joked, we were pulling up to an event and she said, 'We must be in the wrong place. There's no fracking protesters.'"[69]

Limiting Land Use

In addition to addressing the consumption of energy directly, states are looking at ways to cut back on individuals' use of fuel. Many environmentalists blame sprawl—the growth of suburban and exurban communities far from central cities and existing transit and transportation infrastructure—for contributing to the greater consumption of natural resources.

Tom Adams, a former president of the California League of Conservation Voters, argues that his state must cut down on sprawl to meet its long-term environmental goals. In 2008, the state took a big step in the direction that Adams favored by enacting a major new land-use law.

Typically, land-use policies are decided at the local level, with cities or counties passing zoning laws, or ordinances, that, for instance, keep industrial sites separate from residential areas or require that no more than one house be built on each quarter acre of land. Some areas impose only loose zoning restrictions—or none at all, as in Houston. But state governments often do influence land-use policy, if only through their transportation programs. Numerous states, led by Maryland, have enacted policies in recent years aimed at cutting down on sprawl—saying that the state will not build infrastructure outside approved development areas, for instance. Most such laws have proved to be largely toothless.

California's 2008 law known as SB 375 goes further than most. SB 375 directs the California Air Resources

Board to come up with targets for reducing emissions from cars and trucks. Regional planning boards must then revise their master growth plans in ways that seek to meet those targets—for instance, by planning more housing near existing mass-transit lines. The regions that come closest to the goals are rewarded with extra federal and state transportation dollars.

It's no surprise that SB 375 was backed by environmentalists, but it also had the support of California's home builders, who liked the prospect of greater predictability in the zoning process. One of the main goals of the bill is to induce localities to coordinate their major planning tasks: transportation, land use, and housing. Few had been doing that. In addition, SB 375 provides relief from certain air-quality standards that had, perversely, discouraged developers from undertaking infill projects. "Builders thrive on certainty, knowing what the rules are," said Tim Coyle of the California Building Industry Association.[70] Local governments also supported the law; it provides incentives and creates a policymaking framework, but it doesn't create specific mandates for any individual region. "It's really a very important piece of legislation," said Peter Kasabach of New Jersey Future, a smart-growth group. "How we

develop our land is going to impact our greenhouse gas targets. A lot of folks think that if we drive hybrids or change our lightbulbs, we'll be okay. But a significant amount of our greenhouse gas targets will be met by how we get around and reduce vehicle miles traveled."[71]

But various regions of California have struggled to meet requirements under the law. For instance, a judge ruled in 2012 that a transportation plan put forward by the San Diego Association of Governments relied too much on temporary measures such as telecommuting to meet specific emission reduction targets, with the pace of reductions to be achieved slipping over time (from 14 percent per capita in 2020 to 9 percent by 2050). In addition, Tea Party activists and other conservatives have come to oppose such zoning restrictions, seeing them as a challenge to private-property rights. One particular document that has drawn their ire is Agenda 21, a sustainability program adopted by the United Nations back in 1992. Police have been called out to quell protests against the plan even in such pro-zoning jurisdictions as California and Maryland. In 2012, the Republican Party made opposition to Agenda 21 part of its official platform.

In 2018, California state senator Scott Wiener became something of a national celebrity among urbanists by introducing SB 827, which would have overruled local zoning restrictions to allow for much higher building heights and a higher density of new projects within a half-mile radius of any transit stop. Wiener amended SB 827 to bring more groups on board—the automatic height allowance was dropped to four- and five-story buildings, rather than permitting eight stories—and Wiener clarified that only the immediate areas around rail, subway, and ferry stops would be subject to the full height allowances. (The bill still permitted somewhat higher density—that is, multifamily housing—around bus stops.) Those changes helped bring around groups such as the Non-Profit Housing Association of Northern California and the Natural Resources Defense Council. But by then, the damage had already been done, and the bill failed in its first test at the committee level. Still, the notion that sprawl is bad both

AP Photo/Rich Pedroncelli

▲
State senator Scott Wiener (D–San Francisco) is convinced California has to be more aggressive about promoting density to address its housing failures, over the objections of local governments.

for the environment and for the health of communities has become fashionable over the past decade—perhaps nowhere more so than in Miami. That's surprising because, when it comes to building and construction, Miami has always been a wide-open town, home to endless rows of towering condo buildings. In late 2009, the city council approved a new zoning code that is likely to have a profound effect on development. Ardently promoted by Miami mayor Manny Diaz but drafted in large part by architect Elizabeth Plater-Zyberk, the code embraces the **New Urbanism** principles that made Plater-Zyberk and Andrés Duany (her husband and professional partner) famous.

The new code, known as Miami 21, seeks to encourage street-level pedestrian activity and reduce automobile dependence. The hope is that neighborhoods will fit within a comfortable scale, with plenty of shops out front and buildings that conform to fixed height limits, with upper-story setbacks from the street. At the same time, the goal is to create corridors with enough density that public transit will be viable. But the most important idea may be the decision to focus on entire neighborhoods rather than on individual projects.

Codes influenced by the principles of New Urbanism have been adopted in various places around the country for new projects in previously unbuilt areas (greenfields) and for specific areas undergoing redevelopment, such as riverfronts. But Miami became the first city of any size to attempt to apply these principles throughout its borders.

Advocates of the approach are making grand claims about its potential to transform much of the landscape and have explicitly promised that it will make Miami far more environmentally friendly as well. "A whole city is changing its strategy consistent with this idea of preventing climate change," says Armando Carbonell, chair of the Department of Planning and Urban Form at the Lincoln Institute of Land Policy.[72] Developers, looking for a hedge against the next downturn, over the past couple of years have taken advantage of Miami 21's mixed-use provisions to help convert all-condo buildings into combined live–work spaces; this approach has succeeded in increasing residency in areas such as the city's downtown and Wynwood Arts District.

Adaptation

In 2006, the U.S. Army Corps of Engineers proposed a plan to help protect Long Beach, home to 33,000 people on a barrier island just off of Long Island, New York. The plan involved the erection of sand dunes and the elevation of beaches along more than 6 miles of coast to protect the island. But the project would have cost $98 million, and the city would have had to chip in a $7 million share. And people just didn't like the idea of having their ocean views obscured and giving up their nice, wide, flat beaches. So the city council voted unanimously to block the project.

It was a decision Long Beach came to regret. In 2012, the storm known as Sandy did some $200 million worth of property damage to the town. Neighboring communities on the barrier island had approved construction of 15-foot-high dunes and were able to avoid suffering catastrophic losses in the storm.[73]

The effects of Superstorm Sandy in 2012 and other high-impact weather events turned the attention of some policymakers away from the question of how to prevent climate change and toward planning for coping with its effects. If climate change is already having real impacts—and will continue to do so, even if efforts to reduce greenhouse gas emissions succeed—state and local governments have little choice but to deal with these effects. So how should state and local governments begin to adapt to the resulting problems, such as flooding, coastal erosion, and species loss? Should they, for example, build higher seawalls to offset rising sea levels? Many officials in areas affected by Sandy became believers, but facing price tags potentially reaching into the hundreds of billions of dollars, some remained skeptical. "I don't think there's any practical way to build barriers in the oceans," then New York City mayor Michael Bloomberg said in 2012. "Even if you spent a fortune, it's not clear to me that you would get much value for it."[74]

Up until 2007 or so, most environmentalists dismissed talk about **adaptation** to climate change. Their concern seemed to be that shifting the policy debate away from efforts to prevent climate change by cutting down on carbon emissions amounted to conceding to conservatives' denials that human activity causes global warming. They also felt that planning for the effects brought about by climate change was defeatist. "It was seen as a potential smokescreen behind which

New Urbanism A design movement that seeks to promote walkable communities through transit-oriented, mixed-use development.

Adaptation Taking steps to prepare for and deal with the effects of climate change.

LOCAL FOCUS

CLIMATE ADAPTATION TAKING PLACE FAR FROM COASTS

In recent decades, Tulsa, Oklahoma, has become an unlikely model for strong flood control efforts. Back in the 1970s, so-called 100-year floods occurred nearly every year, with creek beds overflowing and damaging property. Following a particularly devastating storm in 1984, which killed 14 people and damaged more than 6,000 homes, the city decided it was time to take a new approach. Since then, it has put in place a series of detention ponds—excavated basins designed to hold water following severe storms—and uses flood maps more demanding than those required by the Federal Emergency Management Agency (FEMA). It's also pursued an ambitious plan to move or tear down homes that have been subject to repeated flood damage. All told, the city has paid to transport or destroy roughly 1,000 houses, an effort that's ongoing.

Tulsa has done more to address its exposure to a serious natural threat than just about any other city in the country. Not that long ago, Tulsa had the highest flood insurance rates in the nation. Now, its rates are just about the lowest. Other Oklahoma cities continue to suffer extensive damage when sudden storms known as "toad stranglers" pass through. But Tulsa hasn't flooded on those occasions, even during recent months that have been among the wettest on record. "In 2015, there was flooding in the suburbs, but we didn't have any," says Bill Robison, the city's floodplain manager.

As a conservative oil town sitting 500 miles north of Houston and the Gulf of Mexico, Tulsa is a surprising setting for one of the nation's most extensive climate adaptation efforts. Its example, though, shows that local leadership and investment can do a lot to prevent damage from the predictable threats that are likely to worsen with climate change. Communities like Tulsa, far from any coast, still face increased risks from a variety of disasters, including fires and tornadoes. Coping with these problems may take decades of investment and political fighting. It can be a tough sell for local governments that want to create a safer and more secure future. It seems to be human nature to believe that disaster will not strike one's own home. Even when the worst does happen, people have a hard time accepting that it could easily happen again. "A natural disaster is not enough, in and of itself, to push cities to make real policy change," says Rachel Krause, a political scientist at the University of Kansas who studies responses to climate change. "Frankly, it takes deaths."

What's more, progress won't always happen under the words "climate change." In Tulsa, environmentalists have learned that in a town founded and fueled by the oil economy, the term is a surefire way to shut down discussion. They talk instead about "extreme weather," emphasizing the need to plan for reoccurring storms. The same is true in many places. Progressive coastal cities such as Boston and Seattle now formally worry about sea-level rise and other effects from climate change as part of their policymaking process. But in many areas of the country, the idea that the climate is changing in permanent and unpredictable ways is not an accepted fact. That doesn't mean, however, that no thought is given to recurrent problems such as flooding, hurricanes, and wildfires. Every city has some plan in place for dealing with natural disasters and emergencies. Thinking about climate could simply mean taking possible effects into account as part of broader planning and response efforts. "We don't freak out, to use a highly technical term, if for political reasons, folks don't want to say 'climate change,' as long as they are taking steps to address climate change," says Otis Rolley of the Rockefeller Foundation's 100 Resilient Cities effort, which has provided funding to Tulsa.

By its very nature, climate change will have unpredictable effects. But many of its main effects are entirely predictable. Places that are prone to natural disasters will likely see more of them. If a region experiences hurricanes, for example, it will have more intense hurricanes. If it is routinely hit by floods, there will be more flooding. And regardless of whether climate change is an accepted fact, it's clear that the gears of nature's disaster-making machinery are speeding up. During the 1980s, the nation endured, on average, fewer than three natural disasters per year that caused $1 billion in damage, in constant dollars. Now, the annual count is higher than 10. "Raising additional money is harder without the impetus of a catastrophe," says Janet Bly, general manager of the Miami Conservancy District in Dayton, Ohio, a flood control agency created a century ago. The lack of problems since then in her area have made it hard to keep people focused on the potential for devastation, she says.

"We're almost the victim of our success when it comes to that."

What the story of Tulsa shows is that protecting against climate effects is an effort that has to be more or less permanent, stretching across generations. It is certainly not easy, either from an engineering stand-point or from a political one. The only places that will make the attempt are the ones where people realize that, practically speaking, there's no better choice. The alternative is continuing destruction and death. "We're never, ever going to be able to say we're done with disasters," says Tim Lovell, executive director of the Disaster Resilience Network, a nonprofit group in Tulsa. "Disasters are going to continue. The question is whether you can design your community so that they don't have the impact they might have."

Source: Adapted from Alan Greenblatt, "The City Preparing for Climate Change without Ever Saying the Words," *Governing*, November 2017, http://www.governing.com/topics/transportation-infrastructure/gov-tulsa-climate-change-resilience-adaptation-flooding.html.

high-emission countries could hide so they wouldn't have to make binding agreements to reduce," said Nathan Hultman, a professor of science, technology, and international affairs at Georgetown University.[75]

Some advocates still argue that discussion about how to adapt to climate shifts amounts to a distraction from the larger project of reducing emissions. "There are people out there working on adaptation, but I have to say the overwhelming effort is to try to reduce our emissions," said Tom Adams, the former California League of Conservation Voters president. "At this point, some fairly significant climate impacts are inevitable, but a lot of us feel that this is a genuine planetary emergency, and it's imperative that we cut emissions."[76] But the notion that talking about adaptation is just a smoke-screen to conceal the lack of effort to reduce greenhouse gases seems to have faded away.

As a practical matter, policymakers are increasingly concerned about how to plan for the climate-related changes their communities are facing. In 2017, Moody's, a credit rating agency, warned local governments they could face a downgrade if they didn't prepare for climate effects. **Resilience** has become a big buzzword for civic leaders who are looking for ways their communities can cope with and bounce back from environmental changes that are already widely evident—not just shocks such as fires and floods but ongoing differences across areas such as the availability of fresh water. The Rockefeller Foundation is running a program to offer assistance to 100 cities around the world that are finding ways to become more resilient. While noting the importance of British Columbia's first-on-the-continent carbon tax, Vancouver mayor Gregor Robertson said his city is not only striving to reduce greenhouse gases through greener building codes and the like but also preparing to deal with the damage that existing emissions are already causing. "The successful cities of the future will be those making the investments and changes necessary to adapt to the impacts of climate change," he wrote. "Climate change poses a serious risk to global economic and social stability, and resilient cities will prove to be attractive draws for people and capital."[77]

According to an online clearinghouse of state efforts compiled by the Georgetown Climate Center, fewer than half the states in 2014 were attempting to pro-tect themselves from the effects of climate change.[78] Not surprisingly, the issue has drawn the most atten-tion in areas along coastlines, such as in Maryland and Oregon. In 2011, the city of Boston released a cli-mate action plan to prepare for a rise in sea level of 2 to 6 feet by the end of the century, depending on the rate of polar ice melt. When a hurricane storm surge is added, some models show parts of Boston under 10 feet of water. Researchers have warned city officials that by midcentury, such storms could happen every two to three years. The University of Massachusetts released a report in 2018 that found that neighborhood projects in Boston could cost $2.4 billion, with an even bigger bill to protect Boston's downtown from storm surges and flooding. "We're not very vulnerable to the impacts

Resilience Like *adaptation*, a term borrowed from biology to describe efforts to prepare for effects of climate change.

LOCAL FOCUS

SCHOOL DISTRICTS ARE FINALLY TESTING THEIR WATER FOR LEAD

The crisis caused by lead in the water in Flint, Michigan, drew national attention in 2016 and increased public awareness of the problem of lead contamination nationwide. Despite the fact that the ingestion of lead poses a potential danger to children, neither the federal government nor state governments had required schools to test their water regularly for the toxic metal.

That has started to change. In 2016, New York became the first state to require lead tests for water in schools. "Lead is such a lethal contaminant and threat to human health, especially to youngsters, that we must make every effort to ensure that the water our school-children drink is lead free," said assembly speaker Carl Heastie, a Democrat who backed the measure.

About a tenth of the nation's schools operate their own water systems, which means they're already subject to regular testing. In the past three years, 278 school systems showed lead levels above the minimum set by the Environmental Protection Agency. (Health officials stress that there is no safe level of lead in water.) Most schools, though, are connected to municipal or other water utilities. The water in those systems is also tested, but the results may not capture high lead levels in the school buildings themselves. There typically isn't a problem with the quality of the water as it leaves a treatment plant. Instead, what's important is what happens once the water leaves the water main under the street and flows toward a building and through its plumbing. In schools, that plumbing could be several decades old.

Congress banned lead in plumbing in 1986, but many schools still have lead pipes that were installed earlier. Schools sometimes have especially long service lines because they're often set far back from the street. The longer lead pipes increase the chances of contamination because the water must travel further through them.

In 1988, Congress required states to come up with a plan for eliminating lead in schools and day-care centers. But a federal appeals court struck down that law in 1996, ruling that it violated the Tenth Amendment. Despite the decision, the federal government and many states have still worked to try to reduce the lead levels in schools' drinking water. But none required regular testing until New York passed its law.

When the water in schools has been tested, many big problems have come to light. In Oregon, Portland's longtime school superintendent stepped down in 2016 after it was revealed that the district kept secret for several months test results that showed two schools had water with high levels of lead. The district shut off all of its schools' water fountains over the summer until they could be retested.

Newark, New Jersey, also shut down water fountains in 30 schools in 2016, ordering blood tests for 17,000 students after high levels of lead were found in more than half the district's schools. Officials later released information showing that the lead problems went back at least six years, but the public had not been notified.

The New York legislation came as schools in Ithaca and Binghamton had to shut off taps because of high lead levels. New York City retested many of its own schools in light of the scrutiny, and those tests also revealed several schools with lead levels that exceeded the federal maximum. The district created a website that allows parents and the public to find basic information about lead testing in individual schools.

New York State representative Catherine Nolan, who chairs her chamber's education committee, said that even though New York might be the first state in the nation with a testing law, it came too late. "This testing requirement should have been in place years ago," she said.

Source: Adapted from Daniel C. Vock, "Why Water in Schools Is So Susceptible to Lead Poisoning," *Governing*, July 26, 2016, http://www.governing.com/topics/transportation-infrastructure/gov-new-york-schools-lead-testing.html.

of climate change and we've experienced it pretty intensely in recent months with flooding," said Sheila Dillon, Boston's housing director.[79]

In 2014, Massachusetts officials announced a $50 million resilience plan that included projects to rebuild

seawalls, repair dams, and help coastal communities rebuild natural defenses against storm surges. That same year, Washington governor Jay Inslee signed an executive order updating the state's emission limits and creating a cap-and-trade program modeled on California's, stressing the need for the state to reduce energy use and also adapt to the effects of climate change. "This is not a hypothetical thing for governors on the West Coast—this is fire alarms and floods," he said. "It's not a next-century issue. This is a next half-hour issue."[80]

But because climate change will manifest itself differently in different locales, adaptation questions are drawing attention all over. For instance, government officials in Vermont have been working with the state university to begin crafting plans to help the forestry and farming industries cope with the local effects of climate change.

In California's Sierra Nevada, snowpack was 43 percent below normal levels in 2018. That could seem like a good year in the future. By the end of the century, snowpack will be down 64 percent from its average at the end of the 20th century, according to a University of California, Los Angeles, study.[81] In parts of the Cascade Range in Washington State, snowpack has already declined by as much as 60 percent. In response, nearby King County, which includes Seattle, has begun planning backward from 2050, formulating plans to adapt to the climate change effects that are seen as likely to occur even if carbon emissions are cut significantly between now and then. For example, officials expect coastal erosion problems associated with rising sea levels, health effects such as new infectious diseases and heat stroke, increasing numbers of forest fires, and ecological issues affecting salmon. In 2007, the county council agreed to a tax inspired by such looming dangers, part of then county executive Ron Sims's $335 million plan to bolster river levees and reduce flood risks. The county is now building climate change risks into all its long-term planning and policy development.

Like most environmentalists, Ron Burke, who is now executive director of the Active Transportation Alliance, says that both responses to climate change—reduction of carbon emissions, or **mitigation**, and adaptation—are important. Still, he says, "If you had to argue one

versus the other, which I don't think is really helpful, I think mitigation is a higher priority given the urgency with which we need to create these reductions. You see that reflected in how most cities and states are going about their planning. They're definitely doing the mitigation piece first and then moving onto adaptation."[82]

In 2016, voters in **CALIFORNIA**'s San Francisco Bay Area approved property tax increases to pay for wetlands restoration to defend against sea-level rise.

Gilles Mingasson/Getty Images

Environmentalists hope that the conversion to cleaner energy technologies such as wind power will not only curb carbon emissions but also provide a new source of jobs. Here, Cerro Coso Community College instructor Mike Cervantes explains safety procedures to students about to make their first climb on a wind turbine in Tehachapi, California. His students enrolled in the technical course after being laid off from auto or construction work.

One of the world's biggest adaptation efforts is taking place in the Netherlands. The Dutch are spending billions to create "floating communities" that can rise with floodwaters and to otherwise reengineer their long

Mitigation Reduction of emissions of greenhouse gases and other steps taken to curb the forces that cause climate change.

> **States and local governments face a practical challenge when it comes to crafting adaptation plans: Much of the science in this area has been, not surprisingly, global in scope. Thus, in planning for climate change's local impacts, experts need to downscale the large-scale data to make them applicable to and useful for communities.**

coastline. They expect to spend $100 per year per person on climate-proofing over the next century, according to the *Washington Post*. Although some may view their efforts as excessive, U.S. officials have consulted with the Dutch about how to protect New Orleans and other low-lying coastal areas.[83]

Relatively few jurisdictions in the United States have turned their full attention to adaptation and planning questions. Even normally proactive California has barely paid attention to adaptation issues and is unprepared for the flooding, coastal erosion, and loss of wildlife habitat predicted to occur in coming decades as the results of higher temperatures.[84] In 2012, the San Francisco Bay Conservation and Development Commission amended its San Francisco Bay Plan to make sure projected sea-level rise is accounted for by new projects, such as a planned $1.5 billion development on Treasure Island, which rests in the bay midway between San Francisco and Oakland. In 2016, voters in nine Bay Area counties approved an increase in property taxes to pay for wetlands restoration to defend against sea-level rise.

States and local governments face a practical challenge when it comes to crafting adaptation plans: Much of the science in this area has been, not surprisingly, global in scope. Thus, in planning for climate change's local impacts, experts need to downscale the large-scale data to make them applicable to and useful for communities. According to Sims, it is imperative

for states, cities, and counties to accept the need to make decisions based on scientific modeling rather than historical experience. "With all the discussion we've had on global warming, I am stunned that people haven't realized that it's actually going to occur," he said in 2007. "The ice caps are melting now. They're not going to refreeze next year because we reduce our emissions. We're going to live in that world. So plan for it."[85]

Conclusion

Climate change has seen considerable policy debate and innovation at the state and local levels over the past decade. In some ways, this is surprising. Global warming, by its name and nature, is an issue that calls for solutions on an international level as opposed to a subnational one. And states historically have left policy on most environmental issues up to Washington.

But the opposition of federal policymakers to serious curbs on energy use at a time when global warming concerns were at their height led many state and local leaders to chart their own courses. Not all states are convinced that promoting renewable energy sources or curbing carbon emissions is the right or even a necessary course. And there are plenty of critics who charge that most of the policies pursued at the state and local levels have been largely symbolic. It's easy to set targets that won't take effect for several years. An increasingly loud chorus of voices maintains that even effective measures will not be worth the high cost that they might impose on the economy. Climate change is an issue that now tends to break fairly neatly along partisan lines.

Many states and cities, however, have taken real action to curb their own energy use and to promote conservation and renewable energy sources throughout their economies. They have done this in spite of years of the current opposition at the national level and in spite of the difficulties in coordinating policy responses that are inherent in the federal system. Despite the challenges, having gotten into this game, many state and local governments clearly intend to stay. Without a partner in Washington, they want to be able to pursue policies and programs that by now are pretty well entrenched.

THE LATEST RESEARCH

This chapter has illustrated the ways many states have emerged as policy leaders on climate issues. For decades, the federal government was the driver on environmental policy, but lack of anything like consensus in Washington in recent years has allowed states to take various approaches (including none at all) to addressing climate change. Policy innovations among individual states and regional consortia have provided frameworks not just for the erstwhile efforts of the Obama administration but for efforts at the provincial level in other countries as well.

States have sought ways of addressing climate change only over the past couple of decades, with many important laws passed only in the past few years. Perhaps for that reason, scholarship in this field has emerged relatively slowly, certainly in comparison with other long-standing state and local government concerns, such as budgets, political parties, and crime. This has proved to be a robust field of inquiry nonetheless, as academics can grapple not only with policy innovations and their efficacy but also with a number of questions regarding federalism and intergovernmental relations, since climate is a topic that is inherently cross-jurisdictional in scope.

- **Hall, Michael P., Neil A. Lewis Jr., and Phoebe C. Ellsworth**, "Believing in Climate Change, but Not Behaving Sustainably: Evidence from a One-Year Longitudinal Study," *Journal of Environmental Psychology* 56 (2018): 55–62.

Nearly all scientists believe in climate change, but significant numbers of Americans do not. The researchers conducted a longitudinal study of 600 Americans, measuring their climate change beliefs and their pro-environmental behaviors every eight weeks over the course of a year. They divided participants into three groups: those who were "highly concerned" about climate change, those who were "cautiously worried," and others who were "skeptical." What they found was that the highly concerned individuals were the most supportive of government action to address climate, but also the least likely to maintain environmentally friendly habits, such as riding public transportation or using reusable shopping bags. Climate change skeptics, conversely, were more likely to report that they had engaged in such habits in their personal lives, even as they opposed federal climate policies.

- **Meyer, Andrew**, "Political Parties and Climate Change Skepticism: Evidence from Close Gubernatorial Elections," February 13, 2018; available at SSRN: https://papers.ssrn.com/sol3/papers.cfm?abstract_id=3123547.

Public opinion surveys consistently show that self-identified Republicans are much more likely to be skeptical about climate change than Democrats. Why is that? The author compares data from national surveys on energy and environment with gubernatorial election results from all 50 states and finds a causal link between the stances of a political leader and climate change beliefs of constituents. When confronted with a complex issue such as climate change, individuals tend to look for cues from the political elite of their party when forming their opinion. When Republicans win gubernatorial contests, it significantly decreases the probability of a Republican voter believing in global warming, by approximately 11 to 16 percentage points. Republican wins have no significant effects on Democratic voters. "It will likely remain difficult to convert climate change skeptics so long as their political leaders publicly exhibit skeptical positions," Meyer writes.

- **Rabe, Barry G.**, *Can We Price Carbon?* (Cambridge, MA: MIT Press, 2018).

Economists have long argued that carbon taxing would offer an effective way to cut down on carbon emissions. That may be so, but it overlooks the political difficulties involved in creating such regimens. An idea that makes good policy sense has often run into fierce opposition. The book examines carbon-pricing schemes around the world that have managed to survive for at least half a decade, comparing them with comparable cap-and-trade systems. Rabe examines what sort of political foundations of support are necessary to sustain carbon pricing, primarily looking at American examples but also some from Canada and other countries.

- **Rosenbloom, Jonathan D.**, "Fifty Shades of Gray Infrastructure: Land Use and the Failure to Create Resilient Cities," *Washington Law Review* 93 (2018): 317–384.

Local communities around the country collectively have massive amounts of mostly unseen infrastructure,

(Continued)

(Continued)

including a million miles of drinking-water pipes and almost 15,000 wastewater treatment facilities. This often-deteriorating infrastructure is not prepared for climate change. Still, only a portion of the nation's infrastructure is built and maintained by the public sector. Much is paid for by the private sector and is necessary for critical services, including potable water and energy distribution. Privately maintained pipes, culverts, detention basins, and other "gray infrastructure" is typically designed to maintain a fixed level of performance established at a single point in time. Cities including Los Angeles and Dubuque, Iowa, have set up systems to track the performance of gray infrastructure over time, developing standards and methods that allow for flexibility of performance in response to changing circumstances.

CHAPTER 16

Want a better grade?

Get the tools you need to sharpen your study skills. SAGE edge offers a robust online environment featuring an impressive array of free tools and resources.

Access practice quizzes, eFlashcards, video, and multimedia at **edge.sagepub.com/ smithgreenblatt7e**

Top Ten Takeaways

1. Climate change and environmental issues in general have become highly polarized, with Republicans tending to dismiss the concerns expressed by many Democrats.

2. Although there are political arguments about climate change, the scientific consensus is clear.

3. Major entities such as the Pentagon and states and cities are trying to come up with ways to cope with the effects of climate change.

4. States have sought various ways to limit greenhouses gases, from seeking stricter fuel standards for cars to limiting emissions from power plants.

5. Many states and some cities have passed laws requiring utilities to obtain a percentage of their power from renewable sources. However, in some states, conservatives are pushing back against the requirements.

6. The coal industry is hurting, with environmentalists fighting to block the opening of power plants fueled by coal and to close existing ones. The rise of natural gas production is also contributing to coal industry losses.

7. Even with the decline in the price of oil, states such as North Dakota, Ohio, and Pennsylvania have enjoyed a boom from fracking.

8. Many state and local governments have adopted policies that seek to limit sprawl and create more density, in part to cut down on fuel usage.

9. Scientists continue to find alarming evidence of the effects of climate change, including sea-level rise.

10. Although often described as one of the greatest long-term challenges facing the nation and the world, climate change does not elicit nearly as much concern among the public as do other issues, such as the economy.

Key Concepts

adaptation (p. 471)
cap and trade (p. 459)
carbon dioxide (p. 457)
Clean Air Act (p. 457)
climate change (p. 454)
fracking (p. 467)

global warming (p. 454)
greenhouse gases (p. 457)
Kyoto Protocol (p. 456)
mitigation (p. 457)
New Urbanism (p. 471)
renewable energy (p. 465)

resilience (p. 473)
smog (p. 457)
tailpipe emissions (p. 457)
U.S. Environmental Protection Agency (EPA) (p. 456)

Suggested Websites

- **www.aspanet.org**. Website of the American Society for Public Administration, the largest professional association for those who work for or study public agencies.

- **www.c2es.org**. Website of the Center for Climate and Energy Solutions, a think tank devoted to finding ways to address climate change.

- **www.governing.com**. Web version of *Governing* magazine, which is dedicated to covering state and local issues. Includes numerous stories and other resources on agency leaders and performance, e-government, and more.

- **www.iclei.org**. Website of ICLEI, an international network of local governments working to combat climate change and promote sustainable economies and infrastructure.

- **www2.ucar.edu**. Website of the University Corporation for Atmospheric Research, a nonprofit consortium of more than 100 North American colleges and universities focused on research and training in atmospheric and earth sciences.

• Notes •

Chapter 1

1. Eun Kyung Kim, "'I Don't Want It to Be about My Age,' Says 18-Year-Old Saira Blair, Nation's Youngest State Lawmaker," *Today*, November 7, 2014.

2. Kevin Eagan, Ellen Bara Stolzenberg, Hilary B. Zimmerman, Melissa C. Aragon, Hannah Whang Sayson, and Cecilia Rios-Aguilar, *The American Freshman: National Norms Fall 2016* (Los Angeles: Higher Education Research Institute, UCLA, 2015), https://www.heri.ucla.edu/monographs/TheAmericanFreshman2016.pdf.

3. National Center for Education Statistics, *Digest of Education Statistics* (Washington, DC: U.S. Department of Education, December 2016), Table 303.10, "Total Fall Enrollment in Degree-Granting Postsecondary Institutions, by Control and Level of Institution: 1947 through 2026," https://nces.ed.gov/programs/digest/d16/tables/dt16_303.10.asp.

4. Michael Mitchell, Michael Leachman, and Kathleen Masterson, "A Lost Decade in Higher Education Funding," Center on Budget and Policy Priorities, August 23, 2017, https://www.cbpp.org/research/state-budget-and-tax/a-lost-decade-in-higher-education-funding.

5. "Who Pays for Public Higher Education," *Chronicle of Higher Education*, March 2, 2014, http://chronicle.com/article/Who-Pays-More/145063.

6. National Center for Education Statistics, "Fast Facts: Tuition Costs of Colleges and Universities," 2015, https://nces.ed.gov/fastfacts/display.asp?id=76.

7. Mitchell et al. 2017.

8. National Center for Education Statistics, "Fast Facts: Financial Aid," 2014, http://nces.ed.gov/fastfacts/display.asp?id=31.

9. National Center for Education Statistics, *Digest of Education Statistics* (Washington, DC: U.S. Department of Education, December 2016), Table 105.20, "Enrollment in Elementary, Secondary, and Degree-Granting Postsecondary Institutions, by Level and Control of Institution, Enrollment Level, and Attendance Status and Sex of Student: Selected Years, Fall 1990 through Fall 2026," https://nces.ed.gov/programs/digest/d16/tables/dt16_105.20.asp?current=yes.

10. Kenneth J. Meier, *Politics and the Bureaucracy* (Pacific Grove, CA: Brooks/Cole, 1993), 2.

11. Christopher Z. Mooney, "Why Do They Tax Dogs in West Virginia? Teaching Political Science through Comparative State Politics," *PS: Political Science & Politics* 31 (June 1998): 199–203.

12. J. F. Chriqui, S. S. Eidson, and F. J. Chaloupka, "Fact Sheet: State Sales Tax on Regular Soda (as of January 2014)," Bridging the Gap Program, Health Policy Center, Institute for Health Research and Policy, University of Illinois at Chicago, April 2014, http://www.bridgingthegapresearch.org/_asset/s2b5pb/BTG_soda_tax_fact_sheet_April2014.pdf.

13. Estimates based on a standard ordinary least squares regression analysis conducted by the authors using the data from Figure 1-1, with mean tuition and fees as the dependent variable and per-student appropriation as the independent variable.

14. U.S. Census Bureau, "QuickFacts: United States," https://www.census.gov/quickfacts/fact/table/US/PST045217.

15. Richard Morrill, "The Urban US: Growth and Decline," *NewGeography*, April 11, 2012, http://www.newgeography.com/content/002769-the-urban-us-growth-and-decline.

16. U.S. Census Bureau, "QuickFacts."

17. Daniel J. Elazar, *American Federalism: A View from the States* (New York: Crowell, 1966). This book has gone through three editions, the most recent of which was published in 1984.

18. Quoted in Robert D. Putnam, *Bowling Alone: The Collapse and Revival of American Community* (New York: Simon & Schuster, 2000), 293.

19. Laura McKenna, "Why Do Different States Have Such Wildly Different Ideas about Government?," *Pacific Standard*, February 7, 2014, http://www.psmag.com/politics-and-law/different-states-government-ideas-political-culture-73037.

20. Jesse R. Harrington and Michele J. Gelfand, "Tightness-Looseness across the 50 United States," *Proceedings of the National Academy of Sciences* 111, no. 22 (2014): 7990–7995.

21. Russell Hanson, "Political Culture Variations in State Economic Development Policy," *Publius: The Journal of Federalism* 21, no. 2 (1991): 63–81; Kevin B. Smith, *The Ideology of Education: The Commonwealth, the Market, and America's Schools* (Albany: State University of New York Press, 2003).

22. Bureau of Economic Analysis, "Per Capita Real GDP by State," 2014, http://www.bea.gov/iTable/iTable.cfm?re qid=70&step=1&isuri=1&acrdn=2#reqid=70&step=1& isuri=1.

23. Phillip W. Roeder, *Public Opinion and Policy Leadership in the American States* (Tuscaloosa: University of Alabama Press, 1994); J. Wolak and C. K. Palus, "The Dynamics of Public Confidence in U.S. State and Local Government," *State Politics & Policy Quarterly* 10 (2010): 421–445; Justin McCarthy, "Americans Still More Trusting in Local over State Government," *Gallup News*, September 19, 2016, http://news.gallup .com/poll/195656/americans-trusting-local-state-gov ernment.aspx.

24. Bruce Wallin, "State and Local Governments Are American Too," *Political Science Teacher* 1 (1988): 1–3.

25. National Center for Education Statistics, "Fast Facts: Teacher Trends," https://nces.ed.gov/fastfacts/display .asp?id=28.

26. U.S. Census Bureau, "State & Local Government Finances by Level of Government and by State: 2015," October 19, 2017, https://factfinder.census.gov/faces/ tableservices/jsf/pages/productview.xhtml?pid=SLF_20 15_00A1&prodType=table.

27. Evan J. Ringquist and James C. Garand, "Policy Change in the American States," in *State and Local Politics*, ed. Ronald E. Weber and Paul Brace (New York: Chatham House, 1999).

28. David Osborne and Ted Gaebler, *Reinventing Government: How the Entrepreneurial Spirit Is Transforming the Public Sector* (New York: Plume, 1993).

Chapter 2

1. Sean Williams, "Ka-Ching! Here's How Much Marijuana Colorado Sold Last Year," *The Motley Fool*, January 28, 2018, https://www.fool.com/investing/2018/01/28/ ka-ching-heres-how-much-marijuana-colorado-sold-la .aspx.

2. James Collier and Christopher Collier, *Decision in Philadelphia* (New York: Random House, 1986).

3. Quoted in ibid., 3.

4. Ellen Perlman, "The Preemption Beast: The Gorilla That Swallows State Laws," *Governing*, August 1994, 46–51.

5. Quoted in Harry N. Scheiber, "The Condition of American Federalism: An Historian's View," in *American Intergovernmental Relations*, ed. Laurence J. O'Toole Jr. (Washington, DC: CQ Press, 2000), 71.

6. Ibid.

7. Kala Ladenheim, "History of U.S. Federalism," March 16, 1999, http://libertyparkusafd.org/Madison/Federalism/ History%20of%20U.%20S.%20Federalism.htm.

8. Scheiber, "Condition of American Federalism."

9. Ellis Katz, "American Federalism, Past, Present and Future," *Issues of Democracy* 2, no. 2 (1997).

10. Paul L. Posner, *The Politics of Unfunded Mandates: Whither Federalism?* (Washington, DC: Georgetown University Press, 1998), 13.

11. National Conference of State Legislatures, "Mandate Monitor," http://www.ncsl.org/state-federal-commit tees/scbudg/mandate-monitor-overview.aspx.

12. Timothy Conlan, "Federalism and Competing Values in the Reagan Administration," *Publius: The Journal of Federalism* 16, no. 4 (1986): 29–47.

13. Thomas J. Anton, "New Federalism and Inter-governmental Fiscal Relationships: The Implications for Health Policy," *Journal of Health Politics, Policy and Law* 22, no. 3 (1997): 691–720.

14. Richard L. Cole and John Kincaid, "Public Opinion and American Federalism: Perspectives on Taxes, Spending, and Trust," *Spectrum: The Journal of State Government* 74, no. 3 (2000): 14–18.

15. "Same-Sex Marriage: Federal and State Authority," *Congressional Digest* 75 (November 1996): 263.

16. Peter Harkness, "Potomac Chronicle: Obama and the States," *Governing*, January 1, 2009, 18.

17. Barton Aronson, "The Rising Tide of Federalism," CNN. com, February 1, 2001, http://www.cnn.com/2001/ LAW/02/columns/fl.aronson.federalism.02.01.

18. Timothy Conlan, "The Changing Politics of American Federalism," *State and Local Government Review* 49, no. 3 (2017): 1–14.

19. Greg Goelzhauser and Shanna Rose, "The State of American Federalism 2016–2017: Policy Reversals and Partisan Perspectives on Intergovernmental Relations," *Publius: The Journal of Federalism*, 47, no. 3 (2017): 285–313.

20. Michael S. Greve, *Real Federalism: Why It Matters, How It Could Happen* (Washington, DC: AEI Press, 1999), 17.

21. Jeffrey G. Homrig, "*Alden v. Maine*: A New Genre of Federalism Shifts the Balance of Power," *California Law Review* 89, no. 1 (2001): 183–205.

22. David G. Savage, "Justices Rule U.S. Can Ban Medical Pot," *Los Angeles Times*, June 7, 2005.

23. John Dinan, "The State of American Federalism 2007–2008: Resurgent State Influence in the National Policy Process and Continued State Policy Innovation," *Publius: The Journal of Federalism* 38, no. 3 (2008): 381–415.

24. Brady Baybeck and William Lowry, "Federalism Outcomes and Ideological Preferences: The U.S. Supreme Court and Preemption Cases," *Publius: The Journal of Federalism* 30, no. 1 (2000): 73–96.

Chapter 3

1. Section 26, Alabama state constitution.

2. Donald Kettl, "Governor Rehnquist," *Governing*, July 1999.

3. Alan Tarr, *Understanding State Constitutions* (Princeton, NJ: Princeton University Press, 1998), 6–8.

4. Christopher W. Hammons, "Was James Madison Wrong? Rethinking the American Preference for Short, Framework-Oriented Constitutions," *American Political Science Review* 93, no. 4 (1999): 837.

5. "State & Local Government," https://www.whitehouse .gov/about-the-white-house/state-local-government/.

6. Ibid. See also John G. Kester, "Amendment Time," *Washingtonian*, March 1995.

7. Adam Clayton, "Why Are Some Institutions Replaced While Others Persist? Evidence from State Constitutions," *State Politics & Policy Quarterly* 16, no. 3 (2016): 267–289.

8. Janice C. May, "Trends in State Constitutional Amendment and Revision," in *The Book of the States 2003*, ed. Council of State Governments (Lexington, KY: Council of State Governments, 2003), 8.

9. Robert J. Taylor, ed., *Massachusetts, Colony to Commonwealth* (New York: Norton, 1961).

10. Quoted in Willi Paul Adams, *The First American Constitutions: Republican Ideology and the Making of the State Constitutions in the Revolutionary Era* (Chapel Hill: University of North Carolina Press, 1980), 53.

11. Quoted in ibid., 61.

12. Quoted in ibid., 207.

13. Tarr, *Understanding State Constitutions*, 121.

14. W. B. Stouffer, Cynthia Opheim, and Susan Bland Day, eds., *State and Local Politics: The Individual and the Governments* (New York: HarperCollins, 1996).

15. Bruce Sundlun, "R.I.'s Martyr for Democracy," *Providence Journal-Bulletin*, August 11, 2002.

16. Delaware is the only state that does not refer constitutional amendments to the electorate as a whole. The legislature may enact constitutional amendments on its own if a measure receives support in two consecutive legislative sessions.

17. Council of State Governments, ed., *The Book of the States 2001* (Lexington, KY: Council of State Governments, 2001), 5. In South Carolina, a majority of both houses of the legislature must vote to approve a constitutional amendment a second time, after it has passed a popular referendum, before it can go into effect.

18. Initiative and Referendum Institute, http://www .iandrinstitute.org. The institute's website includes detailed timelines of initiative and referendum activity in each state.

19. Juan B. Elizondo Jr., "Ratliff: Time to Rewrite Constitution; Lawmaker Joined by Watchdog," *Austin American-Statesman*, October 28, 1999.

20. Alan Greenblatt, "New York Voters Reject Chance to Rewrite State Constitution," *Governing*, November 7, 2017, http://www.governing.com/topics/politics/gov-new-york-constitutional-convention.html.

21. Council of State Governments, ed., *The Book of the States 2003* (Lexington, KY: Council of State Governments, 2003), 3–4.

22. Isaiah J. Ashe, "Alabama Constitutional Revision Commission Finishes Work with Disappointing Results in Key Areas," *AL.com*, October 14, 2013, http://www .al.com/opinion/index.ssf/2013/10/alabama_constitu tional_revisio.html.

23. Hammons, "Was James Madison Wrong?," 839.

24. Joni James, "Voters Hold Key to Big Shake-Up in State Cabinet: The Revision Would Eliminate Three Posts, Give the Governor More Power, and Shift Control of Education Policy," *Orlando Sentinel*, October 20, 1998, D1.

25. Stuart MacCorkle and Dick Smith, *Texas Government* (New York: McGraw-Hill, 1960).

26. Daniel J. Elazar, *American Federalism: A View from the States*, 3rd ed. (New York: Harper & Row, 1984), 115.

27. Hammons, "Was James Madison Wrong?," 846.

28. See ibid. for a more complete argument along these lines.

29. Melinda Gann Hall, "State Judicial Politics: Rules, Structures, and the Political Game," in *American State and Local Politics*, ed. Ronald Weber and Paul Brace (New York: Chatham House, 1999), 136.

30. National Conference of State Legislatures, "Gubernatorial Veto Authority with Respect to Major Budget Bill(s)," December 2008, http://www.ncsl.org/Issues Research/BudgetTax/GubernatorialVetoAuthority withRespecttoMajor/tabid/12640/Default.aspx.

31. Andrew Taylor, "Line Item Budget Barely Trims Spending at State Level," *Denver Rocky Mountain News*, January 15, 1995.

32. Scott Milfred, "Some Want to Clip Gubernatorial Wings: A Resolution in the Legislature Would Curtail Wisconsin Governor's Exceptionally Broad Veto Power," *Wisconsin State Journal*, September 23, 2001, A1.

33. Quoted in Virginia Gray, Herbert Jacob, and Kenneth N. Vines, eds., *Politics in the American States: A Comparative Analysis* (Boston: Little, Brown, 1983).

34. In 2003, the U.S. Supreme Court invalidated laws prohibiting sodomy. Until that time, Alabama, Florida, Idaho, Louisiana, Massachusetts, Mississippi, North Carolina, South Carolina, Utah, and Virginia had laws that explicitly prohibited sodomy. Kansas, Oklahoma, and Texas prohibited same-sex sodomy only. LAMBDA Legal Defense and Education Fund website, http:// www.lambda.org.

35. James Madison, *Federalist* No. 10, in Alexander Hamilton, James Madison, and John Jay, *The Federalist Papers*, ed. Charles Kesler and Clinton Rossiter (New York: Penguin Putnam, 1961), 76.

36. Ibid. Hamilton, Madison, and Jay envisioned other safeguards as well. One was the well-known principle of the separation of powers among the three branches of

government. The other was the large size of the republic itself. Previous theorists of democracy had worried about republics that became too large to govern. In *Federalist* No. 10, Madison makes the novel claim that a more extensive republic would be less likely to succumb to factionalism than were the smaller republics of old.

37. Quoted in David Broder, *Democracy Derailed: Initiative Campaigns and the Power of Money* (New York: Harcourt, 2000), 27.
38. Ibid.
39. Initiative and Referendum Institute, "The History of Initiative and Referendum in the United States," http://www.iandrinstitute.org.
40. Richard Ellis, *Democratic Delusions: The Initiative Process in America* (Lawrence: University Press of Kansas, 2002).
41. Broder, *Democracy Derailed.*
42. Ballotpedia, "2016 Ballot Measures," https://ballotpedia.org/2016_ballot_measures#By_state.
43. Keon S. Chi, "Emerging Trends Shaping State Governments: 2005 and Beyond," in *The Book of the States 2005*, ed. Council of State Governments (Lexington, KY: Council of State Governments, 2005).
44. Christine Mai-Duc, "Get Signatures, Make Money: How Some Gatherers Are Making Top Dollar in This Year's Flood of Ballot Initiatives," *Los Angeles Times*, August 10, 2016, http://www.latimes.com/politics/la-pol-ca-signature-gatherers-ballot-initiatives-california-20160627-snap-htmlstory.html.
45. Broder, *Democracy Derailed*, 1.
46. Lawrence F. Keller, "Municipal Charters," *National Civic Review* 91, no. 1 (2002): 155–161.

Chapter 4

1. National Association of State Budget Officers, *State Expenditure Report: Examining Fiscal 2015–2017 State Spending* (Washington, DC: Author, December 2017), https://higherlogicdownload.s3.amazonaws.com/NASBO/9d2d2db1-c943-4f1b-b750-0fca152d64c2/UploadedImages/SER%20Archive/State_Expenditure_Report__Fiscal_2015-2017_-S.pdf.
2. National Center for Education Statistics, "Fast Facts: Teacher Trends," https://nces.ed.gov/fastfacts/display.asp?id=28.
3. PayScale, "Hourly Rate for All K–12 Teachers," https://www.payscale.com/research/US/All_K-12_Teachers/Hourly_Rate.
4. Alexia Fernandez Campbell, "Oklahoma Teachers Say They're Going on Strike Next Week," *Vox*, March 29, 2018, https://www.vox.com/2018/3/29/17164284/oklahoma-teachers-strike.
5. Mireya Garcia, "Consumer Watch: Living on Teacher Pay," *Fox 25 News*, September 27, 2016, http://okcfox.com/news/consumer-watch/consumer-watch-living-on-teacher-pay.
6. U.S. Census Bureau, "State and Local Government Finances by Level of Government and by State: 2015," https://factfinder.census.gov/faces/tableservices/jsf/pages/productview.xhtml?pid=SLF_2015_00A1&prodType=table.
7. Ibid.
8. Federation of Tax Administrators, "State Excise Tax Rates on Cigarettes," January 1, 2018, http://www.taxadmin.org/assets/docs/Research/Rates/cigarette.pdf.
9. William F. Fox. "History and Economic Impact," March 13, 2002, http://cber.bus.utk.edu/staff/mnmecon338/foxipt.pdf.
10. Scott Drenkard and Jared Walczak, "State and Local Sales Tax Rates in 2015," Tax Foundation, April 8, 2015, http://taxfoundation.org/article/state-and-local-sales-tax-rates-2015#_ftn23.
11. Donald Bruce, William F. Fox, and LeAnn Luna, "E-tailer Sales Tax Nexus and State Tax Policies," *National Tax Journal* 68 (2015): 735–766.
12. Liz Farmer, "The Week in Public Finance: States Dare Online Retailers to Sue, a Local Government Shutdown Threat and More," *Governing*, February 26, 2016, http://www.governing.com/topics/finance/gov-week-finance-online-tax-paterson.html.
13. Elaine S. Povich, "Beyond Amazon: States Prepare to Pounce on Online Sales Taxes," *Governing*, March 14, 2018, http://www.governing.com/topics/finance/sl-online-sales-taxes-supreme-court-states.html.
14. U.S. Census Bureau, "State and Local Government Finances by Level of Government and by State: 2015."
15. Tax Foundation, *Facts and Figures 2015: How Does Your State Compare?* (Washington, DC: Author, 2015), Table 31, http://taxfoundation.org/sites/taxfoundation.org/files/docs/Fact%26Figures_15_web_9_2.pdf.
16. U.S. Census Bureau, "2013 State and Local Summary Table,"https://www.census.gov/data/tables/2013/econ/gov-finances/summary-tables.html.
17. Emma Brown, "In 23 States, Richer School Districts Get More Local Funding Than Poorer Districts," *Washington Post*, March 12, 2015, https://www.washingtonpost.com/news/local/wp/2015/03/12/in-23-states-richer-school-districts-get-more-local-funding-than-poorer-districts.
18. Alan Greenblatt, "The Loathsome Local Levy," *Governing*, October 2001.
19. U.S. Census Bureau, "State and Local Government Finances by Level of Government and by State: 2015."
20. Fifteen states allow certain localities to impose income taxes as well, but for the most part, income tax receipts are a minor source of funds for cities and counties.

21. Alaska Department of Revenue, *Revenue Sources Book: Spring 2017*, April 24, 2017, Table 1-1, http://www .tax.alaska.gov/programs/documentviewer/viewer .aspx?1331r.

22. Tax Foundation, *Facts and Figures 2018: How Does Your State Compare?* (Washington, DC: Author, 2018), Table 13, https://files.taxfoundation.org/20180411102900/ Facts-Figures-2018-How-Does-Your-State-Compare.pdf.

23. Alaska Department of Revenue, *Revenue Sources Book*.

24. U.S. Census Bureau, "State and Local Government Finances by Level of Government and by State: 2015."

25. Ibid.

26. Kaiser Family Foundation, "Federal and State Share of Medicaid Spending," https://www.kff.org/medicaid/ state-indicator/federalstate-share-of-spending/?data View=1&currentTimeframe=0&sortModel=%7B%22c olId%22:%22Location%22,%22sort%22:%22asc%22 %7D.

27. Alan Greenblatt, "Enemies of the State," *Governing*, June 2002.

28. Tax Foundation, *Facts and Figures 2018*, Table 13.

29. Tax Foundation, *Facts and Figures 2015*, Tables 19 and 31.

30. Tax Foundation, "Income per Capita by State, Fiscal Year 2010," February 16, 2012, http://taxfoundation .org/article/income-capita-state-fiscal-year-2010.

31. Tax Foundation, *Facts and Figures 2018*, Table 2.

32. See the Mayflower Compact for further insights into the mind-set of the founders of the Massachusetts Bay Colony, http://www.pilgrimhallmuseum.org/ap_may-flower_compact.htm.

33. Elizabeth Campbell, "Illinois Cut Near Junk by Moody's and S&P, Lowest Ever for a U.S. State," *Chicago Tribune*, June 2, 2017, http://www.chicagotribune.com/busi ness/ct-illinois-bond-rating-20170601-story.html.

34. For a detailed discussion of the state budget process, see National Association of State Budget Officers, *Budget Processes in the States* (Washington, DC: Author, 2008).

35. These states are Connecticut, Hawaii, Indiana, Kentucky, Maine, Minnesota, Montana, Nebraska, Nevada, New Hampshire, North Carolina, North Dakota, Ohio, Oregon, Texas, Virginia, Washington, Wisconsin, and Wyoming. Ron Snell, "State Experiences with Annual and Biennial Budgeting," National Conference of State Legislatures, April 2011, http://www.ncsl.org/issues-research/budget/state-experiences-with-annual-and-biennial-budgeti.aspx.

36. Pew Charitable Trusts, "Rainy Day Funds and State Credit Ratings," May 2017, http://www.pewtrusts .org/~/media/assets/2017/05/statesfiscalhealth_credi tratingsreport.pdf.

37. U.S. Census Bureau, "State and Local Government Finances by Level of Government and by State: 2015."

38. "State and Local Government Employment: Monthly Data," *Governing*, 2017, http://www.governing.com/ gov-data/public-workforce-salaries/monthly-govern ment-employment-changes-totals.html.

39. U.S. Census Bureau, "State and Local Government Finances by Level of Government and by State: 2015."

40. Ibid.

41. "Table 1: State Fiscal Support for Higher Education, by State, Fiscal Years 2012–13, 2015–16, 2016–17, and 2017–18," in *Grapevine* (Normal: College of Education, Illinois State University, 2018), http://education.illi noisstate.edu/grapevine/tables.

42. National Association of State Budget Officers, *State Expenditure Report*, 46.

43. Ibid.

44. Kaiser Family Foundation, "Status of State Action on the Expansion Decision," April 5, 2018, https:// www.kff.org/health-reform/state-indicator/state-activity-around-expanding-medicaid-under-the-affordable-care-act/?currentTimeframe=0&sortM odel=%7B%22colId%22:%22Location%22,%22s ort%22:%22asc%22%7D.

45. Kaiser Family Foundation, "Where Are States Today? Medicaid and CHIP Eligibility Levels for Children, Pregnant Women, and Adults," March 28, 2018, https://www.kff.org/medicaid/fact-sheet/where-are-states-today-medicaid-and-chip/.

46. Pamela J. Loprest, "How Has the TANF Caseload Changed over Time?," Urban Institute, Brief #8, March 2012, https://www.acf.hhs.gov/sites/default/files/opre/ change_time_1.pdf.

47. U.S. Department of Health and Human Services, "A.1: Federal TANF and State MOE Expenditures Summary by ACF-196 Spending Category, FY 2014," http://www .acf.hhs.gov/sites/default/files/ofa/tanf_financial_ data_fy_2014.pdf.

48. U.S. Census Bureau, "State and Local Government Finances by Level of Government and by State: 2015."

49. "Law Enforcement Officers per Capita for Cities, Local Departments," *Governing*, http://www.governing.com/ gov-data/safety-justice/law-enforcement-police-department-employee-totals-for-cities.html.

50. National Association of State Budget Officers, *State Expenditure Report*, 57.

51. U.S. Census Bureau, "State and Local Government Finances by Level of Government and by State: 2015."

52. Joseph Henchman, "Gasoline Taxes and User Fees Pay for Only Half of State and Local Road Spending," Tax Foundation, January 3, 2014, http://taxfoundation .org/article/gasoline-taxes-and-user-fees-pay-only-half-state-local-road-spending.

53. National Association of State Budget Officers, *State Expenditure Report*, 67.

54. Pew Charitable Trusts, "The State Pension Funding Gap: 2015," April 20, 2017, http://www.pewtrusts.org/en/research-and-analysis/issue-briefs/2017/04/the-state-pension-funding-gap-2015.

55. Jeff Hurley, "At What Cost? NSCL President Testifies on Unfunded Mandates," National Conference of State Legislatures, March 1, 2016, http://www.ncsl.org/blog/2016/03/01/at-what-cost-ncsl-president-testifies-on-unfunded-mandates.aspx.

56. Greenblatt, "Enemies of the State."

57. Bill Piper, *A Brief Analysis of Voter Behavior Regarding Tax Initiatives: From 1978 to March 2000* (Washington, DC: Citizen Lawmaker Press, n.d.).

58. This section is adapted from the February 2003 *Governing* special issue on state tax systems; see Katherine Barrett, Richard Greene, Michele Mariani, and Anya Sostek, "The Way We Tax: A 50-State Report," *Governing*, February 2003.

59. Soledad Artiz Prillaman and Kenneth J. Meier, "Taxes, Incentives and Economic Growth: Assess the Impact of Pro-business Taxes on U.S. State Economies," *The Journal of Politics* 76 (2014): 364–379.

Chapter 5

1. Richard L. Hasen, "Scalia's Goal of Unwinding Voter Protections Is Becoming a Reality," *Talking Points Memo*, April 2, 2018, https://talkingpointsmemo.com/cafe/scalias-goal-of-unwinding-voter-protections-is-becoming-a-reality.

2. Earl Black and Merle Black, *Divided America: The Ferocious Power Struggle in American Politics* (New York: Simon & Schuster, 2007), 10.

3. David S. Bernstein, "Donald Trump Needs 7 of 10 White Guys," *Politico*, March 4, 2016, http://www.politico.com/magazine/story/2016/03/donald-trump-needs-7-of-10-white-guys-213699.

4. Tom Hamburger, "Cruz Campaign Credits Psychological Data and Analytics for Its Rising Success," *Washington Post*, December 13, 2015, https://www.washingtonpost.com/politics/cruz-campaign-credits-psychological-data-and-analytics-for-its-rising-success/2015/12/13/4cb0baf8-9dc5-11e5-bce4-708fe33e3288_story.html.

5. Chris Evans, "It's the Autonomy, Stupid: Political Data-Mining and Voter Privacy in the Information Age," *Minnesota Journal of Law, Science & Technology* 13 (2012): 868.

6. Sasha Issenberg, "The Best-Laid Free Media Plan of Marco Rubio," *Bloomberg Politics*, March 3, 2016, http://www.bloomberg.com/politics/articles/2016-03-03/the-best-laid-free-media-plan-of-marco-rubio.

7. Quoted in W. Gardner Selby, "Light a Match to Greg Abbott's Ridiculous Claim about 'Rampant Voter Fraud,'" *PolitiFact*, March 17, 2016, http://www.politifact.com/texas/statements/2016/mar/17/greg-abbott/light-match-greg-abbotts-claim-about-rampant-voter.

8. Randy Ludlow, "Husted Refers Franklin County Fraud Cases for Prosecution," *Columbus Dispatch*, June 25, 2015, http://www.dispatch.com/content/stories/local/2015/06/25/voting_fraud.html.

9. Justin Levitt, "A Comprehensive Investigation of Voter Impersonation Finds 31 Credible Incidents Out of One Billion Ballots Cast," *Washington Post*, April 30, 2014, http://www.washingtonpost.com/blogs/wonkblog/wp/2014/08/06/a-comprehensive-investigation-of-voter-impersonation-finds-31-credible-incidents-out-of-one-billion-ballots-cast.

10. Michael McDonald, Twitter post, August 6, 2014, https://twitter.com/ElectProject/status/497034025081798656.

11. Quoted in Max Bayer, "Univ. of Wisconsin Students Protest New Voter Registration Law," *USA Today College*, February 18, 2016, http://college.usatoday.com/2016/02/18/univ-of-wisconsin-students-protest-new-voter-registration-law.

12. Aaron Blake, "Republicans Keep Admitting That Voter ID Helps Them Win, for Some Reason," *Washington Post*, April 7, 2016, https://www.washingtonpost.com/news/the-fix/wp/2016/04/07/republicans-should-really-stop-admitting-that-voter-id-helps-them-win.

13. Michael Wines, "Some Republicans Acknowledge Leveraging Voter ID Laws for Political Gain," *New York Times*, September 16, 2016, http://www.nytimes.com/2016/09/17/us/some-republicans-acknowledge-leveraging-voter-id-laws-for-political-gain.html.

14. Todd Allbaugh, Facebook post, April 5, 2016, https://www.facebook.com/permalink.php?story_fbid=221323231557115&id=100010383187417.

15. Quoted in Patrick Marley, "Attorney General Brad Schimel Suggests Donald Trump Won Wisconsin Because of the State's Voter ID Law," *Milwaukee Journal Sentinel*, April 13, 2018, https://www.jsonline.com/story/news/politics/2018/04/13/attorney-general-brad-schimel-suggests-donald-trump-won-wisconsin-because-states-voter-id-law/514628002/.

16. Patrick Marley and Jason Stein, "Wisconsin Voter ID Law Deterred Nearly 17,000 from Voting, UW Study Says," *Milwaukee Journal Sentinel*, September 25, 2017, https://www.jsonline.com/story/news/politics/2017/09/26/wisconsin-voter-id-law-deterred-nearly-17-000-voting-uw-study-says/702026001/.

17. Josh Voorhees, "Did a Voter ID Law Really Cost Clinton a Victory in Wisconsin?," *Slate*, May 10, 2017, http://www.slate.com/blogs/the_slatest/2017/05/10/

the_problem_with_the_civis_study_blaming_
clinton_s_wisconsin_loss_on_a_voter.html.

18. Mary Lou Miller, "Photo ID Not That Easy to Obtain," *San Antonio Express-News*, June 12, 2015, http://www.mysanantonio.com/opinion/commentary/article/Photo-ID-not-that-easy-to-obtain-6324060.php.

19. U.S. Government Accountability Office, *Elections: Issues Related to State Voter Identification Laws*, report to congressional requesters (Washington, DC: Author, September 2014), http://www.gao.gov/assets/670/665966.pdf.

20. Zoltan Hajnal, Nazita Lajevardi, and Lindsay Nielson, "Voter Identification Laws and the Suppression of Minority Votes," University of California, San Diego, 2016, http://pages.ucsd.edu/~zhajnal/page5/documents/voterIDhajnaletal.pdf.

21. Adam Liptak and Michael Wines, "Strict North Carolina Voter ID Law Thwarted after Supreme Court Rejects Case," *New York Times*, May 15, 2017, https://www.nytimes.com/2017/05/15/us/politics/voter-id-laws-supreme-court-north-carolina.html.

22. Jack Citrin, Donald P. Green, and Morris Levy, "The Effects of Voter ID Notification on Voter Turnout: Results from a Large-Scale Field Experiment," *Election Law Journal* 13, no. 2 (2014): 228–242.

23. Nicholas Valentino and Fabian Guy Neuner, "The Participatory Consequences of Voter ID Laws: Demobilization and Counter-mobilization," *Political Psychology*, forthcoming.

24. Quoted in Lisa Mascaro, "GOP-Backed Limits on Voting Lead to Spirited Backlash from Democrats," *Los Angeles Times*, October 9, 2014, http://www.latimes.com/nation/la-na-voting-backlash-20141010-story.html.

25. Thom File, *The Diversifying Electorate—Voting Rates by Race and Hispanic Origin in 2012 (and Other Recent Elections)*, Current Population Survey P20-568 (Washington, DC: U.S. Census Bureau, May 2013), https://www.census.gov/prod/2013pubs/p20-568.pdf.

26. Jan Leighley and Jonathan Nagler, "Oregon's New Voter Registration Law Will Make Voting Easier—but Higher Turnout Will Depend on Parties and Candidates," London School of Economics, American Politics and Policy Blog, April 3, 2015, http://eprints.lse.ac.uk/61963/1/blogs.lse.ac.uk-Oregons%20new%20voter%20registration%20law%20will%20make%20voting%20easierbut%20higher%20turnout%20will%20depend%20on%20parties%0a.pdf.

27. Sean McElwee, "Oregon's AVR Increased Diversity in 2016 Electoral Participation across All Age Groups," Demos, August 28, 2017, http://www.demos.org/blog/8/28/17/oregons-avr-increased-diversity-2016-electoral-participation-across-all-age-groups.

28. Rob Griffin, Paul Gronke, Tova Wang, and Liz Kennedy, "Who Votes with Automatic Voter Registration?," Center for American Progress, June 7, 2017, https://www.americanprogress.org/issues/democracy/reports/2017/06/07/433677/votes-automatic-voter-registration/.

29. Simon Jackman and Bradley Spahn, "Unlisted in America," Stanford University, August 20, 2015, 1, http://gbytes.gsood.com/wp-content/uploads/2015/08/jackman_unlisted.pdf.

30. Steven Hill, *Fixing Elections: The Failure of America's Winner Take All Politics* (New York: Routledge, 2002), 119.

31. Steven Conn, "It's the Geography, Stupid; or Why the Democratic Party Should Stop with Its Appeals to the White Working Class," *Belt Magazine*, January 30, 2018, http://beltmag.com/its-the-geography-stupid/.

32. Interview with Rhodes Cook, December 11, 2006.

33. Jeffrey M. Jones, "Americans' Identification as Independents Back Up in 2017," Gallup, January 8, 2018, https://news.gallup.com/poll/225056/americans-identification-independents-back-2017.aspx.

34. Kevin J. Coleman, Thomas H. Neale, and Joseph E. Cantor, "The Election Process in the United States," Congressional Research Service, Washington, DC, July 6, 1995, 69.

35. National Conference of State Legislatures, "Straight-Ticket Voting States," September 10, 2018, http://www.ncsl.org/research/elections-and-campaigns/straight-ticket-voting.aspx.

36. Election Data Services, *The Election Data Book: A Statistical Portrait of Voting in America* (Lanham, MD: Bernan Press, 1992), appendix.

37. Vauhini Vara, "'Instant Runoff' Faces Test," *Wall Street Journal*, October 21, 2011, http://online.wsj.com/article/SB10001424052970204776045766312122294462 84.html.

38. Kay Lawson, "How State Laws Undermine Parties," in *Elections American Style*, ed. A. James Reichley (Washington, DC: Brookings Institution, 1987), 241.

39. Cited in William C. Binning, Larry E. Esterly, and Paul A. Sracic, *Encyclopedia of American Parties, Campaigns, and Elections* (Westport, CT: Greenwood Press, 1999), 95.

40. Quoted in Reid Wilson, "Runoff Elections a Relic of the Democratic South," *Washington Post*, June 4, 2012, http://www.washingtonpost.com/blogs/govbeat/wp/2014/06/04/runoff-elections-a-relic-of-the-democratic-south.

41. E-mail correspondence with Richard Winger, July 24, 2012.

42. Quoted in Robert Draper, "The Future of Battleground Texas," *Texas Monthly*, February 16, 2015, http://www.texasmonthly.com/story/future-battleground-texas.

43. Quoted in Paul Singer, "For Third-Party Candidates, Playing Field Is Uneven by State," *USA Today*, July 10, 2012, http://usatoday30.usatoday.com/news/politics/

story/2012-07-08/third-party-ballot-access/5609 8480/1.

44. Lawson, "How State Laws Undermine Parties," 246.
45. E-mail correspondence with Richard Winger, April 16, 2016.
46. Quoted in Jesse McKinley, "California Puts Vote Overhaul on the Ballot," *New York Times*, May 27, 2010, A1.
47. Larry Sabato, Twitter post, December 24, 2011, https://twitter.com/BuzzFeedBen/statuses/150620246800220162.
48. Binning et al., *Encyclopedia of American Parties*, 95.
49. Quoted in Zachary Roth, "Why Does New York Make It So Hard to Vote?," MSNBC, April 15, 2016, http://www.msnbc.com/msnbc/why-does-new-york-make-it-so-hard-vote.
50. Commission on Federal Election Reform, "Building Confidence in U.S. Elections," September 2005, https://www.eac.gov/assets/1/6/Exhibit%20M.PDF.
51. Melissa Santos, "Facebook: Source of Baby Pictures, Memes and . . . Record Number of Washington Voter Registrations," *Olympian*, April 4, 2016, http://www.theolympian.com/news/politics-government/article69938612.html.
52. Quoted in Megan Riesz, "Register to Vote through Facebook? Washington Reveals New App," *Christian Science Monitor*, July 18, 2012, http://www.csmonitor.com/Innovation/2012/0718/Register-to-vote-through-Facebook-Washington-reveals-new-app.
53. Alan Greenblatt, "Meet the High School Student Who Took Down a State Legislator," NPR, May 15, 2014, http://www.npr.org/blogs/itsallpolitics/2014/05/15/312494574/meet-the-high-school-student-who-beat-a-state-lawmaker.
54. Phone interview with Curtis Gans, September 4, 2003.
55. Phone interview with Steven Hill, September 11, 2003.
56. Jens Manuel Krogstad and Mark Hugo Lopez, "Black Voter Turnout Fell in 2016, Even as a Record Number of Americans Cast Ballots," Pew Research Center, Hispanic Trends, May 12, 2017, http://www.pewresearch.org/fact-tank/2017/05/12/black-voter-turnout-fell-in-2016-even-as-a-record-number-of-americans-cast-ballots/.
57. Kate Linthicum, "Low Turnout Weakens Power of Latino Vote," *Los Angeles Times*, September 11, 2015, http://www.latimes.com/nation/politics/la-na-latino-voters-20150910-story.html.
58. Interview with Ruy Teixeira, April 2006.
59. Philip Bump, "The Remarkable California Turnout Curve," *Washington Post*, January 17, 2015, https://www.washingtonpost.com/news/the-fix/wp/2015/01/17/the-remarkable-california-turnout-curve.
60. Steve Kraske, "Young People Don't Vote, and It's Costing Them," *Kansas City Star*, December 12, 2014, http://www.kansascity.com/news/local/news-columns-blogs/local-columnists/article4453144.html.
61. Initiative and Referendum Institute, University of Southern California, http://www.iandrinstitute.org.
62. John F. Camobreco, "Preferences, Fiscal Policy, and the Initiative Process," *Journal of Politics* 60, no. 3 (August 1998): 822.
63. Reid Wilson and Niraj Chokshi, "Ballot Initiatives Become Pricey Playgrounds of Parties and Corporations," *Washington Post*, August 27, 2014, http://www.washingtonpost.com/blogs/govbeat/wp/2014/08/27/ballot-initiatives-become-pricey-playgrounds-for-corporations-and-political-parties.
64. National Conference of State Legislatures, "Recall of State Officials," March 8, 2016, http://www.ncsl.org/research/elections-and-campaigns/recall-of-state-officials.aspx.
65. Seth Masket, "The Recall Is the New Normal," *Pacific Standard*, September 17, 2013, http://www.psmag.com/navigation/politics-and-law/recall-election-now-thing-permanent-campaign-election-66344.
66. Alan Greenblatt, "Total Recall," *Governing*, September 2003, 27.
67. "Political Recall Efforts, 2017," Ballotpedia, https://ballotpedia.org/Political_recall_efforts,_2017.
68. Phone interview with Randall Gnant, August 7, 2003.
69. Barney Frank, *Frank: A Life in Politics from the Great Society to Same-Sex Marriage* (New York: Farrar, Straus and Giroux, 2015), 156.
70. V. O. Key, *Public Opinion and American Democracy* (New York: Knopf, 1964), 7.
71. Interview with Doug Duncan, November 15, 2006.
72. Interview with Mike Haridopolos, August 8, 2012.
73. Quoted in Ryan Lizza, "A House Divided," *New Yorker*, December 14, 2015, http://www.newyorker.com/magazine/2015/12/14/a-house-divided.
74. Ron Littlefield, "4 Important Lessons from 40 Years of Civic Engagement," *Governing*, City Accelerator blog, July 7, 2015, http://www.governing.com/cityaccelerator/blog/4-important-lessons-from-40-years-of-civic-engagement.html.
75. Sam Sturgis, "Should Cities Give Hackathons Another Look to Improve Digital Infrastructure?," *CityLab*, December 18, 2014, http://www.citylab.com/tech/2014/12/should-cities-give-hackathons-another-look-to-improve-digital-infrastructure/383848.
76. Rob Gurwitt, "The Demise of the Public Hearing," *Governing*, October 2013, http://www.governing.com/topics/mgmt/gov-demise-of-public-hearing.html.
77. See, especially, Robert S. Erikson, Gerald C. Wright, and John D. McIver, *Statehouse Democracy: Public Opinion and Policy in the American States* (New York: Cambridge University Press, 1993).
78. Paul Brace, Kellie Sims-Butler, Kevin Arceneaux, and Martin Johnson, "Public Opinion in the American

States: New Perspectives Using National Survey Data," *American Journal of Political Science* 46, no. 1 (January 2002): 173–189.

79. Susan Herbst, "How State-Level Policy Managers 'Read' Public Opinion," in *Navigating Public Opinion: Polls, Policy, and the Future of American Democracy*, ed. Jeff Manza, Fay Lomax Cook, and Benjamin I. Page (New York: Oxford University Press, 2002), 176.

80. Logan Dancey and Paul Goren, "Party Identification, Issue Attitudes, and the Dynamics of Political Debate," *American Journal of Political Science* 54 (July 2010): 686–699.

81. Phone interview with Greg Shaw, September 3, 2003.

82. Phone interview with Paul Brace, September 10, 2003.

Chapter 6

1. "Clinton, Trump Supporters Have Starkly Different Views of a Changing Nation," Pew Research Center, August 18, 2016, http://assets.pewresearch.org/wp-content/uploads/sites/5/2016/08/08-18-2016-August-political-release.pdf.

2. Art Swift, "Americans Split on Whether NAFTA Is Good or Bad for U.S.," Gallup, February 24, 2017, https://news.gallup.com/poll/204269/americans-split-whether-nafta-good-bad.aspx.

3. Steven Shepard, "Poll: Few Voters Think Tariffs Will Help U.S. Economy," *Politico*, June 6, 2018, https://www.politico.com/story/2018/06/06/poll-tariffs-us-economy-trump-628586.

4. Atif Mian, Amir Sufi, and Nasim Khoshkhou, "Partisan Bias, Economic Expectations, and Household Spending," Chicago Booth Research Paper, July 2017, http://faculty.chicagobooth.edu/amir.sufi/research/papers/miansufikhoshkhou_partisanbias.pdf.

5. "Positive Views of Economy Surge, Driven by Major Shifts among Republicans," Pew Research Center, March 22, 2018, http://www.people-press.org/2018/03/22/positive-views-of-economy-surge-driven-by-major-shifts-among-republicans/.

6. Douglas J. Ahler and Gaurav Sood, "The Parties in Our Heads: Misperceptions about Party Composition and Their Consequences," *Journal of Politics* 80 (July 2018): 964–981.

7. Perry Bacon Jr., "Democrats Are Wrong about Republicans. Republicans Are Wrong about Democrats," *FiveThirtyEight*, June 26, 2018, https://fivethirtyeight.com/features/democrats-are-wrong-about-republicans-republicans-are-wrong-about-democrats/.

8. Lilliana Mason, *Uncivil Agreement: How Politics Became Our Identity* (Chicago: University of Chicago Press, 2018), 19.

9. Scott Jennings, "Chasing Mitch McConnell: You Aren't Hurting Him, You Are Helping Him," *LEO Weekly*, July 18, 2018, https://www.leoweekly.com/2018/07/chasing-mitch-mcconnell/.

10. Shanto Iyengar and Sean J. Westwood, "Fear and Loathing across Party Lines: New Evidence on Group Polarization," *American Journal of Political Science* 59 (2015): 690–707.

11. Liam Stack, "Denounced by His Party as a Nazi, Arthur Jones Wins Illinois G.O.P. Congressional Primary," *New York Times*, March 20, 2018, https://www.nytimes.com/2018/03/20/us/politics/arthur-jones-illinois.html.

12. Twitter feed of Alex Seitz-Wald, May 31, 2018, https://twitter.com/aseitzwald/status/1002334472602378241.

13. Quoted in Dan Balz, "The GOP Has Two Weeks to Take Down Donald Trump," *Washington Post*, March 1, 2016, https://www.washingtonpost.com/politics/2016/03/01/d2774da4-dfb1-11e5-846c-10191d1fc4ec_story.html.

14. Quoted in Peter Overby, "Outside Group Mirrors Successful Strategies of Political Parties," NPR, August 22, 2014, http://www.npr.org/sections/itsallpolitics/2014/08/22/342354175/outside-group-mirrors-successful-strategies-of-political-parties.

15. Quoted in Karen Tumulty, "Super PACs' Spending Isn't Always Welcomed by Candidates They Support," *Washington Post*, August 5, 2014, http://www.washingtonpost.com/politics/super-pacs-spending-isnt-always-welcomed-by-candidates-they-support/2014/08/04/ecc36ed6-18ed-11e4-9349-84d4a85be981_story.html.

16. Julia Azari, "Weak Parties and Strong Partisanship Are a Bad Combination," *Vox*, November 3, 2016, https://www.vox.com/mischiefs-of-faction/2016/11/3/13512362/weak-parties-strong-partisanship-bad-combination.

17. Seth Masket, "Are the Parties Devolving?," *Mischiefs of Faction*, March 3, 2014, http://www.mischiefsoffaction.com/2014/03/are-parties-devolving.html.

18. Ronald Brownstein, "There Are Absolutely Two Americas. Sometimes in the Same State," CNN, July 20, 2018, https://www.cnn.com/2018/07/20/politics/2018-midterms-brownstein-two-americas-in-virginia/index.html.

19. David A. Graham, "Really, Would You Let Your Daughter Marry a Democrat?," *Atlantic*, September 27, 2012, http://www.theatlantic.com/politics/archive/2012/09/really-would-you-let-your-daughter-marry-a-democrat/262959.

20. Stephen P. Nicholson, Chelsea M. Coe, Jason Emory, and Anna V. Song, "The Politics of Beauty: The Effects of Partisan Bias on Physical Attractiveness," *Political Behavior* (April 5, 2016), doi:10.1007/s11109-016-9339-7.

21. Ed Kilgore, "Diagnosing Dems," *Blueprint*, May 17, 2006.

22. Quoted in Mark Leibovich, "The Tea-Party Primary," *New York Times Magazine*, January 10, 2010, 29.

23. Republican National Committee, "Growth and Opportunity Project," March 18, 2013, https://www.documentcloud.org/documents/624581-rnc-autopsy.html.

24. Theda Skocpol, "Who Owns the GOP?," *Dissent*, February 3, 2016, https://www.dissentmagazine.org/online_articles/jane-mayer-dark-money-review-koch-brothers-gop.

25. John Celock, "Steve Morris, Kansas Senate President, Blames Moderates' Defeat on Conservative Attack Ads," *Huffington Post*, August 8, 2012, http://www.huffingtonpost.com/2012/08/08/steve-morris-kansas-senate-koch-brothers_n_1757928.html.

26. Quoted in Jeff Greenfield, "Hayes's Ride," *Washington Monthly*, March 2003.

27. Alvin Kess, *Politics in New York State* (Syracuse, NY: Syracuse University Press, 1965), 29.

28. David R. Mayhew, *Placing Parties in American Politics: Organization, Electoral Settings, and Government Activity in the Twentieth Century* (Princeton, NJ: Princeton University Press, 1986), esp. 24.

29. Quoted in Bertil L. Hanson, "County Commissioners of Oklahoma," *Midwest Journal of Political Science* 9 (1965): 396.

30. Joel H. Sibley, "The Rise and Fall of American Political Parties, 1790–1990," in *The Parties Respond: Changes in the American Party System*, ed. L. Sandy Maisel (Boulder, CO: Westview Press, 1990), 9.

31. Daniel C. Vock, "Both Illinois Candidates for Governor Avoid the State's Most Pressing Issue," *Governing*, March 21, 2018, http://www.governing.com/topics/politics/gov-illinois-governor-primary-state-budget-rauner-pritzker.html.

32. Quoted in Simon van Zuylen-Wood, "Marty Walsh Is Not Tom Menino," *Boston Magazine*, April 2016, http://www.bostonmagazine.com/news/article/2016/04/03/marty-walsh-profile.

33. Mayhew, *Placing Parties in American Politics*, 185.

34. John F. Bibby and Thomas M. Holbrook, "Parties and Elections," in *Politics in the American States: A Comparative Analysis*, 7th ed., ed. Virginia Gray, Russell L. Hanson, and Herbert Jacobs (Washington, DC: CQ Press, 1999), 71.

35. Leon D. Epstein, *Political Parties in the American Mold* (Madison: University of Wisconsin Press, 1986), 155.

36. Malcolm E. Jewell and Sarah M. Morehouse, *Political Parties and Elections in American States*, 4th ed. (Washington, DC: CQ Press, 2001), 76.

37. John F. Bibby, "State and Local Parties in a Candidate-Centered Age," in *American State and Local Politics: Directions for the 21st Century*, ed. Ronald E. Weber and Paul Brace (New York: Chatham House, 1999), 198.

38. Bibby and Holbrook, "Parties and Elections," 70.

39. Ibid., 71.

40. Bibby, "State and Local Parties," 198.

41. Rhodes Cook, "Republican Brawls through the Century Helped Define Party for Years to Come," *Congressional Quarterly Weekly Report*, April 6, 1996, 942.

42. John R. Schmidt and Wayne W. Whalen, "Credentials Contests at the 1968—and 1972—Democratic National Conventions," *Harvard Law Review* 82 (May 1969): 1456.

43. Alan Greenblatt, "History: Winds of War Blew through Chicago," *Congressional Quarterly Weekly Report*, August 17, 1996, 23.

44. Quoted in Joe Wagner, "Former Mayor John Coyne of Brooklyn, 97, Remembered as Influential Politician," *Plain Dealer*, July 21, 2014, http://www.cleveland.com/metro/index.ssf/2014/07/post_239.html.

45. Quoted in Alan Greenblatt, "Wired to Win," *Governing*, October 2006, 26.

46. Bibby, "State and Local Parties," 199.

47. "Politics by Numbers," *Economist*, March 26, 2016, http://www.economist.com/news/special-report/21695190-voters-america-and-increasingly-elsewhere-too-are-being-ever-more-precisely.

48. Jewell and Morehouse, *Political Parties and Elections*, 22–23.

49. William H. Frey and Ruy Teixeira, "America's New Swing Region: The Political Demography and Geography of the Mountain West," in *America's New Swing Region: Changing Politics and Demographics in the Mountain West*, ed. Ruy Teixeira (Washington, DC: Brookings Institution Press, 2012), 43.

50. Quoted in Alan Greenblatt, "How California Is Turning the Rest of the West Blue," NPR, August 29, 2013, http://www.npr.org/blogs/itsallpolitics/2013/08/29/216150644/how-california-is-turning-the-rest-of-the-west-blue.

51. Emily Hoban Kirby and Kei Kawashima-Ginsberg, "The Youth Vote in 2008," Center for Information and Research on Civic Learning and Engagement, August 17, 2009, http://www.civicyouth.org/PopUps/FactSheets/FS_youth_Voting_2008_updated_6.22.pdf.

52. William A. Galston and Clara Hendrickson, "How Millennials Voted This Election," Brookings Institution, November 21, 2016, https://www.brookings.edu/blog/fixgov/2016/11/21/how-millennials-voted/.

53. Shane Goldmacher, "This Man Is the Future of Super PACs," *National Journal*, May 5, 2014, http://www.nationaljournal.com/magazine/this-man-is-the-future-of-super-pacs-20140505.

54. Quoted in Dave Davies, "Coming to a Mayor's Race Near You: SuperPACs Moving into Cities," NPR, October 26, 2015, http://www.npr.org/sections/itsallpolitics/2015/10/26/451946805/coming-to-a-mayoral-race-near-you-superpacs-moving-into-cities.

55. Nicholas Confessore, Sarah Cohen, and Karen Yourish, "Small Pool of Rich Donors Dominates Election Giving," *New York Times*, August 1, 2015, http://www.nytimes.com/2015/08/02/us/small-pool-of-rich-donors-dominates-election-giving.html.

56. Martin Gilens and Benjamin I. Page, "Testing Theories of American Politics: Elites, Interest Groups, and Average Citizens," *Perspectives on Politics* 12, no. 3 (2014): 575.

57. Thomas B. Edsall, "Would Stronger Parties Mean Less Polarization?," *New York Times*, October 21, 2014, http://www.nytimes.com/2014/10/22/opinion/would-stronger-parties-mean-less-polarization.html.

58. Alan Greenblatt, "Soft Money: The Root of All Evil or a Party-Building Necessity?," *Congressional Quarterly Weekly Report*, September 26, 1997, 2064.

59. Quoted in Ruth Marcus, "Party Spending Unleashed; Justices Say Independence from Candidate Is Key," *Washington Post*, June 27, 1996, A1.

60. Don Van Natta Jr. and Richard A. Oppel Jr., "Parties Set Up Groups to Elude Soft Money Ban," *New York Times*, November 2, 2002, A1.

61. OpenSecrets.org, "Outside Spending," https://www.opensecrets.org/outsidespending/summ.php?disp=O.

62. Interview with Larry J. Sabato, May 2002.

63. "Party Affiliation," Gallup, https://news.gallup.com/poll/15370/party-affiliation.aspx.

64. Pew Research Center, "Trends in Party Identification, 1939–2014," April 7, 2015, http://www.people-press.org/interactives/party-id-trend.

65. James K. Glassman, "Save the Republican Party: Vote for Clinton," *New York Times*, Sept. 6, 2016, http://www.nytimes.com/2016/09/06/opinion/save-the-republican-party-vote-for-clinton.html.

66. Quoted in Joel Siegel, "Party's Over for Liberals," *Daily News*, February 24, 2003, 20.

67. Quoted in Alan Greenblatt, "Politics and Marketing Merge in Parties' Bid for Relevance," *Congressional Quarterly Weekly Report*, August 16, 1997, 1967.

68. Dana R. Fisher, "Here's Who Actually Attended the March for Our Lives. (No, It Wasn't Mostly Young People.)," *Washington Post*, March 28, 2018, https://www.washingtonpost.com/news/monkey-cage/wp/2018/03/28/heres-who-actually-attended-the-march-for-our-lives-no-it-wasnt-mostly-young-people/.

69. Twitter feed of Lawrence Mower, March 3, 2018, https://twitter.com/lmower3/status/96994885196414976/photo/1.

70. Quoted in James Surowiecki, "Taking on the N.R.A.," *New Yorker*, October 19, 2015, https://www.newyorker.com/magazine/2015/10/19/taking-on-the-n-r-a.

71. Brad Bumstead and Mike Wereschagin, "Investigation Puts Scrutiny on Lobbyists, Political Ties," *Pittsburgh Tribune-Review*, May 28, 2016, http://triblive.com/news/allegheny/10490790-74/lobbying-nyquist-state.

72. Quoted in Reid Wilson, "Amid Gridlock in D.C., Influence Industry Expands Rapidly in the States," *Washington Post*, May 11, 2015, https://www.washingtonpost.com/blogs/govbeat/wp/2015/05/11/amid-gridlock-in-d-c-influence-industry-expands-rapidly-in-the-states.

73. Dante Chinni, "With Gridlock in Washington, Lobbyists Turn to Statehouses," *Wall Street Journal*, January 14, 2016, http://www.wsj.com/articles/with-gridlock-in-washington-lobbyists-turn-to-state-houses-1452825384.

74. Frank J. Sorauf, *Political Parties in the American System* (Boston: Little, Brown, 1964), 13.

75. Clive S. Thomas and Ronald J. Hrebenar, "Interest Groups in the States," in *Politics in the American States: A Comparative Analysis*, 8th ed., ed. Virginia Gray and Russell L. Hanson (Washington, DC: CQ Press, 2004), 114–115.

76. Leah Rush, "Hired Guns," Center for Public Integrity, December 20, 2007, updated August 19, 2011, http://www.publicintegrity.org/2007/12/20/5895/influence-booming-business.

77. John Myers, "Nearly $300 Million Spent on Calif. State Lobbying in 2013," KXTV, February 3, 2014, https://www.abc10.com/article/news/politics/john-myers/nearly-300-million-spent-on-calif-state-lobbying-in-2013/103-277668517.

78. Liz Essley Whyte and Ben Wieder, "Amid Federal Gridlock, Lobbying Rises in the States," Center for Public Integrity, February 11, 2016, https://www.publicintegrity.org/2016/02/11/19279/amid-federal-gridlock-lobbying-rises-states.

79. Joseph O'Sullivan, "Many of the State's Powerful Lobbyists Work from One Olympia Neighborhood," *Seattle Times*, April 15, 2018, https://www.seattletimes.com/seattle-news/politics/where-the-lobbyists-are-many-of-the-states-most-powerful-influencers-work-from-this-olympia-neighborhood/.

80. Virginia Gray and David Lowery, "Interest Representation in the States," in *American State and Local Politics: Directions for the 21st Century*, ed. Ronald E. Weber and Paul Brace, *American State and Local Politics* (New York: Chatham House, 1999), 267.

81. Quoted in Alan Rosenthal, *The Third House: Lobbyists and Lobbying in the States*, 2nd ed. (Washington, DC: CQ Press, 2001), 17.

82. Alex Stuckey, "St. Louis Doctor's Crusade Finally Ends with Tanning Bed Bill," *St. Louis Post-Dispatch*, May 20, 2014, http://www.stltoday.com/news/local/govt-and-politics/st-louis-doctor-s-crusade-finally-ends-with-tanning-bed/article_7ea484ae-9a3b-54f4-9559-3cd85a66552b.html.

83. Lee Drutman, "The Complexities of Lobbying: Toward a Deeper Understanding of the Profession," *PS: Political Science & Politics* 43, no. 4 (October 2010): 835.

84. Tyler Bridges, "Inside Look at 'Tax Exclusions,'" *Advocate*, April 26, 2016, http://www.theadvocate.com/baton_rouge/news/politics/legislature/article_24a041ff-8001-5fd4-9bc7-69f1f2025cec.html.

85. Quoted in Whyte and Wieder, "Amid Federal Gridlock."

86. Richard L. Hall and Molly E. Reynolds, "Targeted Issue Advertising and Legislative Strategy: The Inside Ends of Outside Lobbying," *Journal of Politics* 74, no. 3 (July 2012): 888–902.

87. Quoted in Nicholas Kusnetz, "How Big Tobacco Lobbies to Safeguard E-Cigarettes," Center for Public Integrity, March 25, 2016, https://www.publicintegrity.org/2016/03/25/19468/how-big-tobacco-lobbies-safeguard-e-cigarettes.

88. Phone interview with John Weingart, August 18, 2010.

89. Christopher Swope, "Winning without Steaks and Cigars," *Governing*, November 2000. See also Rob Gurwitt, "Cookie-Jar Clampdown," *Governing*, April 2007.

90. Quoted in Alan Greenblatt, "Illinois Declares Truce in Cupcake War," NPR, June 6, 2014, http://www.npr.org/2014/06/06/319413152/illinois-declares-truce-in-cupcake-war.

91. Karen Weise, "This Is How Uber Takes Over a City," *Bloomberg*, June 23, 2015, http://www.bloomberg.com/news/features/2015-06-23/this-is-how-uber-takes-over-a-city.

92. Ramesh Ponnuru, "Is Your Fortune Teller Licensed?," *Bloomberg View*, March 28, 2014, http://www.bloombergview.com/articles/2014-03-28/is-your-fortune-teller-licensed.

93. Quoted in Jacob Goldstein, "So You Think You Can Be a Hair Braider?," *New York Times*, June 12, 2012, http://www.nytimes.com/2012/06/17/magazine/so-you-think-you-can-be-a-hair-braider.html.

94. U.S. Department of the Treasury Office of Economic Policy, Council of Economic Advisers, and U.S. Department of Labor, *Occupational Licensing: A Framework for Policymakers* (Washington, DC: White House, July 2015), https://obamawhitehouse.archives.gov/sites/default/files/docs/licensing_report_final_nonembargo.pdf.

95. Rosenthal, *Third House*, 78.

96. Quoted in Alan Greenblatt, "Secondhand Spokesmen," *Governing*, April 2002, http://www.governing.com/topics/health-human-services/Secondhand-Spokesmen.html.

97. Quoted in Rosenthal, *Third House*, 61.

98. Clive S. Thomas and Ronald J. Hrebenar, "Lobby Clout," *State Legislatures*, April 1999.

99. Thomas and Hrebenar, "Interest Groups in the States," 121–122.

100. Alan Greenblatt, "Real Power," *Governing*, June 2006, 46.

101. Phone interview with Alan Rosenthal, February 6, 2007.

Chapter 7

1. Phone interview with Anna Langthorn, June 27, 2018.

2. Alexander Hamilton, *Federalist* No. 73, https://www.congress.gov/resources/display/content/The+Federalist+Papers.

3. Bob Bergren, presentation at the Council of State Governments western regional meeting, October 7, 2009.

4. Quoted in Philip D. Duncan and Christine C. Lawrence, *Congressional Quarterly's Politics in America 1998* (Washington, DC: CQ Press, 1997), 755.

5. William M. Bulger, *While the Music Lasts: My Life in Politics* (Boston: Houghton Mifflin, 1996), 71.

6. Boris Shor, "How States Are Polarized and Getting More Polarized," *Washington Post*, January 14, 2014, http://www.washingtonpost.com/blogs/monkey-cage/wp/2014/01/14/how-u-s-state-legislatures-are-polarized-and-getting-more-polarized-in-2-graphs.

7. Quoted in Rex Santus, "With Congress Deadlocked, NCSL Says Eyes Are on State Legislatures," *Denver Post*, August 8, 2014, http://www.denverpost.com/politics/ci_26295129/congress-deadlocked-ncsl-says-eyes-are-state-legislatures.

8. Justin McCarthy, "Americans Still More Trusting in Local over State Government," Gallup, September 19, 2016, https://news.gallup.com/poll/195656/americans-trusting-local-state-government.aspx.

9. Quoted in Zach Patton, "John Hickenlooper: The Man in the Middle," *Governing*, August 2014, http://www.governing.com/topics/politics/gov-colorado-hickenlooper.html.

10. Sarah Breitenbach, "Synthetic Drugs Send States Scrambling," *Stateline*, April 29, 2016, http://www.pewtrusts.org/en/research-and-analysis/blogs/stateline/2016/04/29/synthetic-drugs-send-states-scrambling.

11. Quoted in Rob Gurwitt, "The Riskiest Business," *Governing*, March 2001, 21.

12. Phone interview with Fred Risser, May 12, 2015.

13. Texas Legislature, "General Reports," https://capitol.texas.gov/Reports/General.aspx; e-mail correspondence with Montana Legislative Services Division, May 20, 2016.

14. Quoted in Texas for Abbott, Twitter post, May 12, 2016, https://twitter.com/AbbottCampaign/status/730786194145959936.

15. John Myers, "Gov. Jerry Brown Vetoes a Bill That Would Make It a Crime to 'Willfully Release' Helium Balloons," *Los Angeles Times*, July 31, 2017, http://www.latimes.com/politics/essential-politics/la-pol-ca-essential-politics-updates-gov-jerry-brown-vetoes-a-crackdown-on-1501538095-htmlstory.html.

16. Rachel Osier Lindsey, "Who Actually Writes the Bills Your Texas Legislators Sponsor?," KERA, April 24,

2017, http://keranews.org/post/who-actually-writes-bills-your-texas-legislators-sponsor.

17. Ibid.

18. Quoted in Paul Hammel, "Measure to Let Uber, Lyft Operate in Nebraska Advances," *Omaha World-Herald*, April 21, 2015, http://www.omaha.com/money/measure-to-let-uber-lyft-operate-in-nebraska-advances-mello/article_d57b7923-c401-5628-9f6a-e6b6ad4ddcf9.html.

19. Don Willett, "Patel v. Texas Department of Licensing and Regulation," Texas Supreme Court, June 26, 2015, http://www.txcourts.gov/media/1008502/120657c1.pdf.

20. Judith C. Meredith, *Lobbying on a Shoestring*, 2nd ed. (Dover, MA: Auburn House, 1989), 4.

21. "Government Workers Don't Need Even More Protections," *Modesto Bee*, February 17, 2012.

22. Melissa Maynard, "A Bill of Rights for State Workers?," *Stateline*, April 3, 2012, http://www.pewstates.org/projects/stateline/headlines/a-bill-of-rights-for-state-workers-85899380541.

23. Alan Rosenthal, *Engines of Democracy: Politics and Policymaking in State Legislatures* (Washington, DC: CQ Press, 2009), 310.

24. Robin Vos, Facebook post, May 10, 2016.

25. See Gary F. Moncrief, Joel A. Thompson, and Karl T. Kurtz, "Old Statehouse Ain't What It Used to Be," *Legislative Studies Quarterly* 21, no. 1 (February 1996): 57–72.

26. Matt Lewis, "What Jimmy Kimmel's Monologue about His Son Didn't Mention," *Daily Beast*, May 3, 2017, https://www.thedailybeast.com/what-jimmy-kimmels-monologue-about-his-son-didnt-mention.

27. Alan Rosenthal, *Governors and Legislatures: Contending Powers* (Washington, DC: CQ Press, 1990), 187.

28. Diane D. Blair, *Arkansas Politics and Government* (Lincoln: University of Nebraska Press, 1988), 182, cited in Rosenthal, *Governors and Legislatures*.

29. Katherine Barrett and Richard Greene, "B&G Interview: Questions for John Turcotte," *Governing*, February 1, 2008, http://www.governing.com/column/bg-interview-questions-john-turcotte.

30. John Turcotte, presentation at the annual meeting of the National Conference of State Legislatures, July 21, 2009.

31. Alan Rosenthal, Burdett Loomis, John Hibbing, and Karl Kurtz, *Republic on Trial: The Case for Representative Democracy* (Washington, DC: CQ Press, 2003), 26.

32. Wes Clarke, "The Divided Government and Budget Conflict in the U.S. States," *Legislative Studies Quarterly* 23, no. 1 (February 1998): 5.

33. National Conference of State Legislatures, "In Case of a Tie ... ," November 8, 2017, http://www.ncsl.org/legislatures-elections/legislatures/incaseofatie.aspx.

34. Quoted in Alan Greenblatt, "Reformer in Power," *Governing*, January 2009, 20.

35. Meredith, *Lobbying on a Shoestring*, 34.

36. Quoted in Mat Batts, "Life in the Legislature: Two Freshmen Lawmakers Settle in While Watford Gains a Level of Comfort," *Dispatch*, March 4, 2017, http://www.the-dispatch.com/news/20170304/life-in-legislature-two-freshmen-lawmakers-settle-in-while-watford-gains-level-of-comfort.

37. Quoted in Steve Bousquet, Twitter post, August 20, 2015, https://twitter.com/stevebousquet/status/634364558757494786.

38. Edmund Burke, "The English Constitutional System," in *Representation*, ed. Hannah Pitkin (New York: Atherton Press, 1969).

39. Phone interview with Norma Anderson, July 5, 2018.

40. Quoted in Rosenthal, *Engines of Democracy*, 237.

41. Quoted in Bill Reker, "Rep. English Stripped of Committee Positions after Tax Cut Vote," KMOX, May 8, 2014.

42. Richard A. Clucas, "Principal-Agent Theory and the Power of State House Speakers," *Legislative Studies Quarterly* 26, no. 2 (May 2001): 319–338.

43. Quoted in Alan Greenblatt, "The Mapmaking Mess," *Governing*, January 2001, 23.

44. Aaron Blake, "Name That District Winner: 'Upside-Down Elephant,'" *Washington Post*, The Fix blog, August 12, 2011, http://www.washingtonpost.com/blogs/the-fix/post/name-that-district-winner-upside-down-elephant/2011/08/11/gIQABOTABJ_blog.html#pagebreak.

45. Nolan Hicks, "New Congressional Redistricting Maps Very Close to Greg Abbott's Plan," *Houston Chronicle*, Texas on the Potomac blog, February 28, 2012, http://blog.chron.com/txpotomac/2012/02/new-congressional-redistricting-maps-very-close-to-greg-abbotts-plan.

46. Greenblatt, "The Mapmaking Mess," 22.

47. Josh Goodman, "The Future of Redistricting and Rural America," *Governing*, November 2010, http://www.governing.com/topics/politics/future-redistricting-rural-america.html.

48. Josh Goodman, "Introducing America's Largest State Legislative District," *Governing*, Politics blog, February 11, 2010.

49. Quoted in Sean Cockerham, "Lawmakers Spar over Adding Seats to Legislature," *Alaska Dispatch News*, February 2, 2010.

50. Seth Motel, "Who Runs for Office? A Profile of the 2%," Pew Research Center, Fact Tank, September 3, 2014, http://www.pewresearch.org/fact-tank/2014/09/03/who-runs-for-office-a-profile-of-the-2.

51. National Conference of State Legislatures, "Legislator Demographics," 2016, http://www.ncsl.org/research/

about-state-legislatures/who-we-elect-an-interactive-graphic.aspx#.

52. Quoted in Howard Troxler, "Choice for Attorney General Not So Easy," *St. Petersburg Times*, October 18, 2002, 1B.

53. Quoted in Tom Loftus, "7th Liquor Bill Filed by State Lawmaker Who Owns Liquor Stores," *Louisville Courier-Journal*, February 14, 2017, https://www.courier-journal.com/story/news/politics/ky-legislature/2017/02/14/7th-liquor-bill-filed-state-lawmaker-who-owns-liquor-stores/97889378/.

54. Quoted in Alan Greenblatt, "Real Power," *Governing*, June 2006, 46.

55. Jay Root, "For John Carona, Conflicts and Interests," *Texas Tribune*, May 20, 2013, https://www.texastribune.org/2013/05/20/conflicts-and-interests-sen-john-carona/.

56. James DeHaven, "Investigation Shows Montana Lawmakers Rarely Refrain from Voting on Personal Interests," *Montana Standard*, March 27, 2016, http://mtstandard.com/politics/montana/investigation-shows-montana-lawmakers-rarely-refrain-from-voting-on-personal/article_fa9dd22f-e2b2-58eb-9ae9-4398ab0e83e4.html.

57. Karl Kurtz, "Who We Elect: The Demographics of State Legislatures," *State Legislatures*, December 2015, http://www.ncsl.org/research/about-state-legislatures/who-we-elect.aspx.

58. Alan Ehrenhalt, "Why It's Important to Know Legislators' Day Jobs," *Governing*, October 2015, http://www.governing.com/columns/assessments/gov-state-legislator-professions.html.

59. Kathleen Dolan and Lynne E. Ford, "Change and Continuity among Women Legislators: Evidence from Three Decades," *Political Research Quarterly* 50 (March 1997): 137–152.

60. Center for American Women and Politics, "Women in State Legislatures 2018," n.d., http://www.cawp.rutgers.edu/women-state-legislature-2018.

61. Renee Loth, "The Matriarchy Up North," *Boston Globe*, April 30, 2009, 15.

62. Thomas H. Little, Dana Dunn, and Rebecca E. Deen, "A View from the Top: Gender Differences in Legislative Priorities among State Legislative Leaders," *Women and Politics* 22, no. 4 (2001): 29–50.

63. Donald E. Whistler and Mark C. Ellickson, "The Incorporation of Women in State Legislatures: A Description," *Women and Politics* 20, no. 2 (1999): 84.

64. Ibid.

65. Michael B. Berkman and Robert E. O'Connor, "Do Women Legislators Matter? Female Legislators and State Abortion Policy," *American Politics Quarterly* 21, no. 1 (January 1993): 105.

66. Patricia Homan, "Political Gender Inequality and Infant Mortality in the United States, 1990–2012," *Social Science and Medicine* 182 (June 2017): 127–135.

67. Kerry L. Haynie, *African American Legislators in the American States* (New York: Columbia University Press, 2001), 19.

68. Bernard Grofman and Lisa Handley, "Impact of the Voting Rights Act on Black Representation in Southern State Legislatures," *Legislative Studies Quarterly* 16 (1991): 111–128.

69. Quoted in Louis Jacobson, "The Hispanic Dynamic," *State Legislatures*, June 2015, http://www.ncsl.org/bookstore/state-legislatures-magazine/the-hispanic-dynamic.aspx.

70. Victory Fund, Twitter post, May 20, 2016, https://twitter.com/VictoryFund/status/733655676304646144.

71. Quoted in David Lieb, "Divided America: Minorities Missing in Many Legislatures," Associated Press, June 16, 2016, http://lasvegassun.com/news/2016/jun/16/divided-america-minorities-missing-in-many-legisla.

72. Malcolm E. Jewell and Samuel C. Patterson, *The Legislative Process in the States* (New York: Random House, 1966), 138.

73. William Pound, "State Legislative Careers: Twenty-Five Years of Reform," in *Changing Patterns in State Legislative Careers*, ed. Gary F. Moncrief and Joel A. Thompson (Ann Arbor: University of Michigan Press, 1992).

74. James D. King, "Changes in Professionalism in U.S. State Legislatures," *Legislative Studies Quarterly* 25, no. 3 (May 2000): 327–343.

75. National Conference of State Legislatures, "Size of State Legislative Staff," October 2, 2018, http://www.ncsl.org/legislatures-elections/legisdata/staff-change-chart-1979-1988-1996-2003-2009.aspx.

76. Pat Forgey, "In Cutting Their Own Budget, Alaska Lawmakers Drop Ax on Research Staff," *Alaska Dispatch News*, September 7, 2015, http://www.adn.com/politics/article/legislatures-own-budget-cuts-focus-research-staff/2015/09/08.

77. Josh Goodman, "Pennsylvania Takes Step toward Smaller Legislature," *Stateline*, April 11, 2012, http://www.pewstates.org/projects/stateline/headlines/pennsylvania-takes-step-toward-smaller-legislature-85899381094.

78. Steve Mistler, "LePage Bills Would More Than Double Next Governor's Salary, Slash Size of Legislature," *Portland Press-Herald*, March 29, 2016, http://www.pressherald.com/2016/03/29/lepage-submits-bill-to-increase-next-governors-salary-slash-size-of-legislature.

79. Wade Rawlins, "Lawmakers Adjourn," *News & Observer* (Raleigh), October 4, 2002.

80. Rachel Baye, Twitter post, April 11, 2016, https://twitter.com/.

81. Ellen Perlman, "The 'Gold-Plated' Legislature," *Governing*, February 1998, 37.

82. Editorial, *Clarion Ledger*, April 21, 2008, 6A.

83. Alan Ehrenhalt, "An Embattled Institution," *Governing*, January 1992, 30.

84. Marist Poll, "6/30: NY State Senate Unrest Irks Voters," June 30, 2009, http://maristpoll.marist.edu/630-ny-state-senate-unrest-does-not-sit-well-with-voters.

85. Field Poll, "Brown's Job Rating Remains Favorable. Very Poor Appraisal of the Legislature. Yet, Voters Oppose Having Lawmakers Work Part-Time," February 25, 2012, 6.

86. Interview with John Hibbing, October 15, 2002.

87. Quoted in Nicholas Confessore, "Perception of Being Slighted Stoked Revolt by Lawmakers," *New York Times*, February 9, 2007, B7.

88. Jonathan Walters, "How to Tame the Press," *Governing*, January 1994, 30.

89. Phillip Reese, "Arrest Rate in California Senate Higher Than State's Largest Cities," *CaliforniaCityNews.org*, August 28, 2014, https://www.californiacitynews.org/2014/08/arrest-rate-california-senate-higher-state%E2%80%99s-largest-cities.html.

90. Citizens Union of New York, "Albany Corruption Tracker," 2016, http://www.citizensunion.org/albany_corruption_tracker.

91. Phone interview with John Crangle, January 6, 2017.

92. Katerina Eva Matsa and Jan Lauren Boyles, *America's Shifting Statehouse Press* (Washington, DC: Pew Research Journalism Project, July 10, 2014), http://www.journalism.org/2014/07/10/americas-shifting-statehouse-press.

93. Brian Duggan, Twitter post, January 29, 2014, https://twitter.com/brianduggan/status/428669730329612288.

94. Interview with Gary Moncrief, October 2, 2002.

95. New Jersey Senate Democrats, "Media Advisory—Senator Whelan to Hold 'Twitter Town Hall' Live on Monday," July 6, 2012.

96. Quoted in Jon Kuhl, "Tools of the Trade: Social Media Rules!," *State Legislatures*, June 2013, http://www.ncsl.org/bookstore/state-legislatures-magazine/tools-of-the-trade_june-2013.aspx.

97. Quoted in Alan Greenblatt, "The Truth about Term Limits," *Governing*, January 2006, 24.

Chapter 8

1. Phone interview with James Conant, July 11, 2015.

2. Quoted in Cathleen Decker, "He's an Angry Young Man No Longer," *Los Angeles Times*, January 22, 2016, http://www.latimes.com/politics/la-pol-ca-jerry-brown-analysis-20160121-story.html.

3. Robin Vos, remarks made at *Governing*'s conference Outlook 2016, Washington, DC, February 3, 2016.

4. Quoted in Jose A. Del Real, "Jerry Brown Warns of Recession and Reveals His Final Budget," *New York Times*, January 11, 2018, https://www.nytimes.com/2018/01/11/us/california-today-jerry-brown-warns-of-recession-and-reveals-his-final-budget.html.

5. Quoted in Alan Greenblatt, "When Governors Don't Play Nice," *Governing*, November 2012, 9.

6. Quoted in Larry J. Sabato, *Goodbye to Good-Time Charlie: The American Governorship Transformed*, 2nd ed. (Washington, DC: CQ Press, 1983), 4.

7. Lynn R. Muchmore, "The Governor as Manager," in *Being Governor: The View from the Office*, ed. Thad Beyle and Lynn R. Muchmore (Durham, NC: Duke University Press, 1983), 83.

8. Quoted in Adam Clymer, "Marvin Mandel, Progressive Maryland Governor Convicted of Fraud, Dies at 95," *New York Times*, August 30, 2015, http://www.nytimes.com/2015/08/31/us/marvin-mandel-former-maryland-governor-dies-at-95.html.

9. Quoted in Bryan Lowry, "In KC visit, Rick Perry Touts Texas and Says Governments Shouldn't Be 'Big Brother,'" *Kansas City Star*, May 17, 2017, https://www.kansascity.com/news/politics-government/article151046767.html.

10. Terry Sanford, *Storm over the States* (New York: McGraw-Hill, 1967), 185–188, quoted in Eric B. Herzik and Brent W. Brown, "Symposium on Governors and Public Policy," *Policy Studies Journal* 17 (1989): 761.

11. E. Lee Bernick, "Gubernatorial Tools: Formal vs. Informal," *Journal of Politics* 42 (1979): 661.

12. Quoted in Alan Rosenthal, *Governors and Legislatures: Contending Powers* (Washington, DC: CQ Press, 1990), 14.

13. Muchmore, "Governor as Manager," 13.

14. Ann O'M. Bowman, Neal D. Woods, and Milton R. Stark II, "Governors Turn Pro: Separation of Powers and the Institutionalization of the American Governorship," *Political Research Quarterly* 63, no. 2 (June 2010): 307.

15. Quoted in Daniel C. Vock, "Massachusetts' Unlikely Transit Team," *Governing*, April 2016, http://www.governing.com/topics/transportation-infrastructure/gov-massachusetts-transit-stephanie-pollack.html.

16. Marjorie Smith, "NH's Executive Branch Needs Reform," *Manchester Union-Leader*, August 1, 2012, 7.

17. Quoted in Office of the Governor, Texas, "Governor Abbott Takes Aerial Tour, Receives Briefing and Holds Press Conference on Texas' Response to Ongoing Severe Weather," press release, June 3, 2016, http://gov.texas.gov/news/press-release/22365.

18. Quoted in Alan Greenblatt, "In Emergencies, Politicians Are Expected to Master Disaster,"

NPR, September 17, 2013, http://www.npr.org/blogs/itsallpolitics/2013/09/17/223389847/in-emergencies-politicians-are-expected-to-master-disaster.

19. Quoted in Eric Levenson, "Baker 'Frustrated, Disappointed' in MBTA," *Boston Globe*, February 9, 2015, http://www.boston.com/news/local-news/2015/02/09/baker-frustrated-disappointed-in-mbta-suggests-changes-coming.

20. Quoted in Jon C. Teaford, "Governors and Economic Development," in *Legacy of Innovation: Governors and Public Policy*, ed. Ethan G. Sribnick (Philadelphia: University of Pennsylvania Press, 2008), 113.

21. Greg Abbott, Twitter post, February 25, 2016, https://twitter.com/GregAbbott_TX/status/702942445143728130.

22. Quoted in Gary Fineout, "Rick Scott Says Yale Should Move to Florida," Associated Press, March 30, 2016, https://www.bostonglobe.com/news/nation/2016/03/29/rick-scott-says-yale-should-move-florida/chNSGV1jl6S918mEeBOTOM/story.html.

23. Quoted in Chris Johnson, "McCrory to Cuomo: Boycott Your Own State for Not Having Trans Law," *Washington Blade*, March 31, 2016, http://www.washingtonblade.com/2016/03/31/mccrory-to-cuomo-might-need-to-boycott-his-own-state.

24. Sabato, *Goodbye to Good-Time Charlie*, 4.

25. See Muchmore, "Governor as Manager."

26. Alan Greenblatt, "Tug of War," *Governing*, August 2004, 32.

27. Rob Gurwitt, "The Governor's People," *Governing*, March 1991, 28.

28. Shap Smith, remarks made at *Governing*'s conference Outlook 2016, Washington, DC, February 3, 2016.

29. Thad Kousser and Justin H. Phillips, *The Power of American Governors* (New York: Cambridge University Press, 2012), 26.

30. Daniel C. Vock, "Govs Enjoy Quirky Veto Power," *Stateline*, April 24, 2007.

31. Quoted in Alan Greenblatt, "Killing Frankenstein," *Governing*, June 2008, 17.

32. Maggie Clark, "Governors Balance Pardons with Politics," *Stateline*, February 8, 2013.

33. Jack Brammer, "Steve Beshear Issues 201 Pardons in Final Act as Governor," *Lexington Herald-Leader*, December 7, 2015, http://www.kentucky.com/news/politics-government/article48539005.html.

34. Quoted in Alan Greenblatt, "Why Are We Meeting Like This?" *Governing*, August 2002, 40.

35. Quoted in Alan Rosenthal, *The Best Job in Politics: Exploring How Governors Succeed as Policy Leaders* (Washington, DC: CQ Press, 2013), 28.

36. Quoted in Kousser and Phillips, *Power of American Governors*, 40.

37. Laura A. Van Assendelft, *Governors, Agenda Setting, and Divided Government* (Lanham, MD: University Press of America, 1997), 1.

38. Rosenthal, *Best Job in Politics*, 29.

39. Ralph Wright, *Inside the Statehouse: Lessons from the Speaker* (Washington, DC: CQ Press, 2005), 88.

40. Quoted in Alan Greenblatt, "States of Frustration," *Governing*, January 2004, 26.

41. Quoted in Alan Greenblatt, "Rod Reeling," *Governing*, September 2007, 18.

42. Quoted in Van Assendelft, *Governors, Agenda Setting, and Divided Government*, 71.

43. Jan Reid, "The Case of Ann Richards: Women in Gubernatorial Office," in *A Legacy of Leadership: Governors and American History*, ed. Clayton McClure Brooks (Philadelphia: University of Pennsylvania Press, 2008), 185.

44. Raphael J. Sonenshein, "Can Black Candidates Win Statewide Elections?," *Political Science Quarterly* 105 (1990): 219.

45. Rosenthal, *Best Job in Politics*, 58.

46. Audrey Wall, "Gubernatorial Elections, Campaign Costs and Winning Governors of 2014," Knowledge Center, Council of State Governments, September 1, 2015, http://knowledgecenter.csg.org/kc/content/gubernatorial-elections-campaign-costs-and-winning-governors-2014.

47. Quoted in Alan Greenblatt, "All Politics Is National," *Governing*, October 2012, 28.

48. Wisconsin Democracy Campaign, "Recall Race for Governor Cost $81 Million," July 25, 2012, updated January 31, 2013, http://www.wisdc.org/pr072512.php.

49. Brandon Rottinghaus, "Here Are Six Key Lessons from 40 Years of Political Scandals," *Washington Post*, May 26, 2016, https://www.washingtonpost.com/news/monkey-cage/wp/2016/05/26/heres-what-happens-when-your-governor-gets-tangled-in-a-scandal.

50. Quoted in Thomas Clouse, "Kempthorne at the Helm," *Idaho Statesman*, January 5, 1999, 1A.

51. Lou Jacobson, "Where Have All the Governors Gone?," *Governing*, March 4, 2013, http://www.governing.com/Where-Have-All-the-Governors-Gone.html.

52. Quoted in Brian Friel, "For Governors in Congress, No More King of the Hill," *National Journal*, June 27, 2009.

53. Quoted in Clayton McClure Brooks, "Afterword: Governing the Twenty-First Century," in *A Legacy of Leadership: Governors and American History*, ed. Clayton McClure Brooks (Philadelphia: University of Pennsylvania Press, 2008), 219.

54. Twitter feed of Theo Keith, February 6, 2017, https://twitter.com/TheoKeith/status/828680070487240704/photo/1.

55. Phone interview with Julia Hurst, January 11, 2016.

56. Quoted in Jo Mannies, "Kinder Says He's Tired of Being Ignored by Governor," *St. Louis Public Radio*, January 22, 2014, http://news.stlpublicradio.org/post/kinder-says-hes-tired-being-ignored-governor.

57. Quoted in Michael J. Mishak, "Gavin Newsom a Rising Star Who's in Eclipse as Lt. Governor," *Los Angeles Times*, July 15, 2013, http://www.latimes.com/local/la-me-gavin-newsom-20130715-dto-htmlstory.html.

58. Associated Press, "The Decatur Daily on Windom Candidacy," October 4, 2001.

59. Quoted in Erin Golden, "Fischbach Said She'll Juggle Two Jobs; DFLers May Contest That," *Minneapolis Star Tribune*, December 13, 2017, http://www.startribune.com/republican-senator-to-become-minnesota-s-lieutenant-governor/463950133/.

60. Michael Krasny, "California Attorney General Xavier Becerra Talks DACA, Taking on Trump," KQED, January 15, 2018, https://www.kqed.org/forum/2010101863403.

61. Fred Barnes, "The Last Redoubt," *Weekly Standard*, July 22, 2013, https://www.weeklystandard.com/fred-barnes/the-last-redoubt.

62. Paul Nolette, *Federalism on Trial: State Attorneys General and National Policymaking in Contemporary America* (Lawrence: University Press of Kansas, 2015), 22.

63. Quoted in Josh Goodman, "The Second Best Job in the State," *Governing*, April 2009, 34.

64. Quoted in Alan Greenblatt, "Where Campaign Money Flows," *Governing*, November 2002, 44.

65. Quoted in Alan Greenblatt, "State AGs Used to Play Nice in Elections. Not Anymore," *Governing*, November 15, 2017, http://www.governing.com/topics/politics/gov-state-attorneys-general-elections-2017-2018-raga-daga.html.

66. Quoted in Eric Lipton, "Lobbyists, Bearing Gifts, Pursue Attorneys General," *New York Times*, October 28, 2014, http://www.nytimes.com/2014/10/29/us/lobbyists-bearing-gifts-pursue-attorneys-general.html.

67. Megan Verlee, "Secretaries of State at Center of Election Battles," NPR, January 18, 2012, http://www.npr.org/2012/01/18/145351397/secretaries-of-state-at-center-of-election-battles.

68. Quoted in Alan Greenblatt, "Once Obscure State Job Is Now Attracting Millions of Campaign Dollars," NPR, February 21, 2014, http://www.npr.org/blogs/itsallpolitics/2014/02/19/279659009/once-obscure-state-job-is-now-attracting-millions-of-campaign-dollars.

69. Rosenthal, *Best Job in Politics*, 199.

Chapter 9

1. Brian Beutler, "The Rehabilitationists," *New Republic*, August 30, 2015, https://newrepublic.com/article/122645/rehabilitationists-libertarian-movement-undo-new-deal.

2. Phone interview with Josh Blackman, June 7, 2017.

3. Don Willett, *Patel vs. Texas Department of Licensing and Regulation*, Texas Supreme Court, June 26, 2015, http://www.txcourts.gov/media/1008502/120657c1.pdf.

4. Phone interview with David Bernstein, June 6, 2017.

5. Phone interview with Chris Bonneau, May 30, 2017.

6. Alan Greenblatt, "Don Willett's Lone Star Legal Show," *Governing*, August 2017, http://www.governing.com/topics/public-justice-safety/gov-don-willett-conservative-justice.html.

7. Quoted in Howard Fischer, "Senate OKs Expanding AZ Supreme Court by Two," *Arizona Daily Star*, May 2, 2016, https://tucson.com/news/local/govt-and-politics/senate-oks-expanding-az-supreme-court-by-two/article_2d229e71-009f-54ed-ae73-3f401fe46ed8.html.

8. Robert C. LaFountain, Shauna M. Strickland, Richard Y. Schauffler, Kathryn A. Holt, and Kathryn J. Lewis, *Examining the Work of State Courts: An Overview of 2013 State Court Caseloads* (Williamsburg, VA: National Center for State Courts 2015), http://www.courtstatistics.org/~/media/Microsites/Files/CSP/EWSC_CSP_2015.ashx.

9. Diana Penner, "Judge: Jurors Antics Harmless," *Indianapolis Star*, November 30, 2006, 1.

10. Sari S. Escovitz, *Judicial Selection and Tenure 4* (Chicago: American Judicature Society, 1975).

11. Caleb Nelson, "A Re-evaluation of Scholarly Explanations for the Rise of the Elected Judiciary in Antebellum America," *American Journal of Legal History* 37 (April 1993): 190–224.

12. Larry C. Berkson, "Judicial Selection in the United States: A Special Report," *Judicature* 64, no. 4 (1980): 176–193, updated 1999 by Seth Andersen.

13. G. Alan Tarr, "Rethinking the Selection of State Supreme Court Justices," *Willamette Law Review* 39, no. 4 (2003): 1445.

14. Doug McMurdo, "Voters Reject Changing Judge Selection," *Las Vegas Review-Journal*, November 3, 2010.

15. William Raftery, "Judicial Selection in the States," Trends in State Courts, National Center for State Courts, December 2013, http://www.ncsc.org/sitecore/content/microsites/future-trends-2013/home/Monthly-Trends-Articles/Judicial-Selection-in-the-States.aspx.

16. Ciara Torres-Spelliscy, Monique Chase, and Emma Greenman, *Improving Judicial Diversity*, 2nd ed. (New York: Brennan Center for Justice, New York University School of Law, 2010), https://www.brennancenter.org/sites/default/files/legacy/Improving_Judicial_Diversity_2010.pdf.

17. American Judicature Society, "Judicial Selection in the States: Diversity of the Bench," 2010, http://www.judicialselection.us/judicial_selection/bench_diversity/index.cfm?state.

18. "Close Down the Circus: Replace Judicial Elections with Merit Selection," *Philadelphia Inquirer*, July 13, 2018, http://www.philly.com/philly/opinion/editorials/judicial-election-merit-selection-pennsylvania-election-reform-20180713.html.

19. John Oliver, "Elected Judges," *Last Week Tonight with John Oliver*, February 23, 2015, https://www.youtube.com/watch?v=poL7l-Uk3I8 (the segment includes some funny and some horrifying ads run by judicial candidates).

20. Augie Martin, Holly Yan, and Dan Merica, "Voters Oust Judge Who Gave Brock Turner 6 Months for Sex Assault," CNN, June 6, 2018, https://www.cnn.com/2018/06/06/us/judge-aaron-persky-recall-results-brock-turner/index.html.

21. "Justice for Sale: Interview, Justices Stephen Breyer and Anthony Kennedy," *Frontline*, PBS, http://www.pbs.org/wgbh/pages/frontline/shows/justice/interviews/supremo.html.

22. Ibid.

23. Adam Liptak and Janet Roberts, "Campaign Cash Mirrors a High Court's Rulings," *New York Times*, October 1, 2006.

24. Billy Corriher, *Big Business Taking Over State Supreme Courts: How Campaign Contributions to Judges Tip the Scales against Individuals* (Washington, DC: Center for American Progress, August 2012), 2.

25. Ibid., 14.

26. Liz Navratil and Angela Couloumbis, "Pa. Supreme Court Justices Got More Than $180K in Donations from Law Firms in Clergy Abuse Case, Records Show," *Philadelphia Inquirer*, July 11, 2018, http://www.philly.com/philly/news/pa-supreme-court-justices-received-campaign-cash-from-lawyers-in-catholic-clergy-abuse-case-20180711.html.

27. Quoted in Liptak and Roberts, "Campaign Cash," sec. 1, 1.

28. *Caperton v. Massey*, Brennan Center for Justice, New York University School of Law, June 8, 2009, https://www.brennancenter.org/legal-work/caperton-v-massey.

29. Justice at Stake, "Money and Elections," 2014, http://www.justiceatstake.org/issues/state_court_issues/money_elections.cfm.

30. *Citizens United v. Federal Election Commission*, 558 U.S. 310 (2010) (Stevens, dissenting).

31. Tyler Bishop, "The Most Expensive Judicial Election in U.S. History," *Atlantic*, November 10, 2015, http://www.theatlantic.com/politics/archive/2015/11/the-most-expensive-judicial-election-in-us-history/415140.

32. Quoted in Sheila Kaplan, "Justice for Sale," *Common Cause Magazine*, May–June 1987, 29–30.

33. Justice at Stake, "State Judges Frequency Questionnaire," November 5, 2001–January 2, 2002, https://www.brennancenter.org/sites/default/files/2001%20National%20Bipartisan%20Survey%20of%20Almost%202%2C500%20Judges.pdf.

34. Quoted in Mark A. Behrens and Cary Silverman, "The Case for Adopting Appointive Judicial Selection Systems for State Court Judges," *Cornell Journal of Law and Public Policy* 11, no. 2 (Spring 2002): 282.

35. Raferty, "Judicial Selection in the States."

36. Maggie Hassan, Governor, State of New Hampshire, Executive Order 2013-06, April 23, 2013, http://sos.nh.gov/ExecOrdersHassan.aspx.

37. Berkson, "Judicial Selection in the United States."

38. "Assisted Appointment (Judicial Selection)," Ballotpedia, 2016, https://ballotpedia.org/Assisted_appointment_(judicial_selection).

39. National Center for State Courts, "Methods of Judicial Selection: Selection of Judges," 2016, http://www.judicialselection.us.

40. Luke Bierman, "Beyond Merit Selection," *Fordham Urban Law Journal* 29 (2002): 851, 864–865.

41. Charles Gardner Geyh, "Why Courts and Congress Collide, and Why Their Conflicts Subside," *Insights on Law & Society* 7, no. 1 (Fall 2006): 9.

42. "New York Mandatory Judicial Retirement Age Amendment, Proposal 6 (2013)," Ballotpedia, 2016, https://ballotpedia.org/New_York_Mandatory_Judicial_Retirement_Age_Amendment,_Proposal_6_(2013).

43. Quoted in Alan Greenblatt, "How Old Is Too Old to Be a Judge? Voters in 4 States Got to Decide," *Governing*, November 9, 2016, http://www.governing.com/topics/elections/gov-judicial-retirement-2016-state-ballot-measures.html.

44. Ibid.

45. Bill Raftery, "2011 Year in Review: Record Number of Impeachment Attempts against Judges for Their Decisions," *Gavel to Gavel*, December 27, 2011, http://gaveltogavel.us/site/2011/12/27/2011-year-in-review-record-number-of-impeachment-attempts-against-judges-for-their-decisions.

46. "When Two Branches of Government Declare War on the Third" (editorial), *St. Louis Post-Dispatch*, April 14, 2016.

47. Robert L. Misner, "Recasting Prosecutorial Discretion," *Journal of Criminal Law and Criminology* 86 (1996): 741.

48. Steve Weinberg, "Inside an Office: An Elected Prosecutor Explains," Center for Public Integrity, June 26, 2003, http://www.publicintegrity.org/2003/06/26/5521/inside-office.

49. Daniel S. Medwed, "The Zeal Deal: Prosecutorial Resistance to Post-conviction Claims of Innocence," *Boston University Law Review* 84 (2004): 125–183.

50. Steven W. Perry, *Prosecutors in State Courts 2005*, Bureau of Justice Statistics Bulletin NCJ 213799 (Washington, DC: U.S. Department of Justice, July 2006).

51. Steven W. Perry and Duren Banks, *Prosecutors in State Courts, 2007—Statistical Tables,* Bureau of Justice Statistics, Statistical Tables NCJ 234211 (Washington, DC: U.S. Department of Justice, December 2011).

52. Ibid.

53. Carol J. DeFrances, *State Court Prosecutors in Large Districts 2001,* Bureau of Justice Statistics Special Report NCJ 191206 (Washington, DC: U.S. Department of Justice, December 2001).

54. Ibid. "About two-thirds of Part I Uniform Crime Report (UCR) offenses reported to the police in 1998 occurred in the prosecutorial district served by these offices" (2).

55. Shelby A. Dickerson Moore, "Questioning the Autonomy of Prosecutorial Charging Decisions: Recognizing the Need to Exercise Discretion—Knowing There Will Be Consequences for Crossing the Line," *Louisiana Law Review* 60 (Winter 2000): 374.

56. Wayne R. LaFave, "The Prosecutor's Discretion in the United States," *American Journal of Comparative Law* 18 (1970): 532, 533.

57. Misner, "Recasting Prosecutorial Discretion."

58. Telephone interview with Kenneth Noto, deputy chief of the narcotics section at the U.S. Attorney's Office for the Southern District of Florida, cited in William T. Pizzi, "Understanding Prosecutorial Discretion in the United States: The Limits of Comparative Criminal Procedure as an Instrument of Reform," *Ohio State Law Journal* 54 (1993): 1325n88.

59. Perry, *Prosecutors in State Courts 2005.*

60. Moore, "Questioning the Autonomy."

61. Besiki Luka Kutateladze and Nancy R. Andiloro, "Prosecution and Racial Justice in New York County," report submitted to the National Institute of Justice, January 31, 2014, http://archive.vera.org/sites/default/files/resources/downloads/race-and-prosecution-manhattan-technical.pdf.

62. Ronald F. Wright, "How Prosecutor Elections Fail Us," *Ohio State Journal of Criminal Law* 6 (2009): 581–610.

63. *McMann v. Richardson,* 397 U.S. 759, 771 n.14 (1970). ("The right to counsel is the right to the effective assistance of counsel.")

64. Caroline Wolf Harlow, *Defense Counsel in Criminal Cases,* Bureau of Justice Statistics Special Report NCJ 179023 (Washington, DC: U.S. Department of Justice, November 2000), Table 16, http://www.bjs.gov/content/pub/pdf/dccc.pdf.

65. Holly R. Stevens, Colleen E. Sheppard, Robert Spangenberg, Aimee Wickman, and Jon B. Gould, "State, County and Local Expenditures for Indigent Defense Services Fiscal Year 2008," report prepared for the American Bar Association Standing Committee on Legal Aid and Indigent Defendants Bar Information Program, November 2010.

66. Carol J. DeFrances and Marika F. X. Litras, *Indigent Defense Services in Large Counties 1999,* Bureau of Justice Statistics Bulletin NCJ 184932 (Washington, DC: U.S. Department of Justice, November 2000), http://www.bjs.gov/content/pub/pdf/idslc99.pdf.

67. Erinn Herberman and Tracey Kyckelhahn, *State Government Indigent Defense Expenditures, FY 2008–2012—Updated,* Bureau of Justice Statistics Special Report NCJ 246684 (Washington, DC: U.S. Department of Justice, July 2014, revised April 21, 2015), http://www.bjs.gov/content/pub/pdf/sgide0812.pdf.

68. Lynn Langton and Donald J. Farole Jr., *Public Defender Offices, 2007—Statistical Tables,* Bureau of Justice Statistics Selected Findings NCJ 228538 (Washington, DC: U.S. Department of Justice, November 2009, revised June 17, 2010), http://www.bjs.gov/content/pub/pdf/pdo07st.pdf.

69. Teresa Wiltz, "Public Defenders Fight Back against Budget Cuts, Growing Caseloads," *Stateline,* November 21, 2017, http://www.pewtrusts.org/en/research-and-analysis/blogs/stateline/2017/11/21/public-defenders-fight-back-against-budget-cuts-growing-caseloads.

70. Criminal Justice Standards Committee, American Bar Association, *Standards for Criminal Justice: Providing Defense Services,* 3rd ed. (Chicago: American Bar Association, 1992).

71. Wiltz, "Public Defenders Fight Back."

72. "The ACLU Foundation of Northern California Sues over Failing Public Defense System," ACLU of Northern California, April 13, 2016, https://www.aclunc.org/our-work/legal-docket/phillips-v-state-california-fresno-public-defense.

73. Gene Johnson, "State High Court Limits Public Defender Caseloads," *Seattle Times,* June 15, 2012.

74. Adele Bernhard, "Take Courage: What the Courts Can Do to Improve the Delivery of Criminal Defense Services," *University of Pittsburgh Law Review* 63 (2002): 305.

75. *Gideon's Army,* documentary, directed by Dawn Porter (Montclair, NJ: Trilogy Films, 2013), http://gideon-sarmythefilm.com.

76. Thomas Giovanni, *Community-Oriented Defense: Start Now* (New York: Brennan Center for Justice, 2012), 2, http://www.brennancenter.org/sites/default/files/legacy/publications/COD_WEB.pdf.

77. State of Virginia, Chart of Allowances, July 1, 2018, http://www.courts.state.va.us/courtadmin/aoc/fiscal/chart.pdf. Virginia recently created a fund from which attorneys could petition to exceed the cap, but the fund rarely lasts for the whole year.

78. Andrew Rachlin, "Rights of Defense," *Governing,* January 2007.

79. Kevin Clermont and Theodore Eisenberg, "Trial by Jury or Judge: Transcending Empiricism," *Cornell Law Review* 77 (1992): 1124.

80. See *Williams v. Florida*, 399 U.S. 78 (1970), approving 6-member juries; and *Apodaca v. Oregon*, 406 U.S. 404 (1972), allowing nonunanimous verdicts.

81. David Rottman and Shauna M. Strickland, *State Court Organization, 2004* (Washington, DC: Bureau of Justice Statistics, 2004), http://www.bjs.gov/content/pub/pdf/sco04.pdf.

82. Pew Center on the States, *One in 31: The Long Reach of American Corrections* (Washington, DC: Pew Charitable Trusts, March 2009), http://www.pewtrusts.org/~/media/assets/2009/03/02/pspp_1in31_report_final_web_32609.pdf.

83. Danielle Kaeble, Lauren Glaze, Anastasios Tsoutis, and Todd Minton, *Correctional Populations in the United States, 2014*, Bureau of Justice Statistics Bulletin NCJ 249513 (Washington, DC: U.S. Department of Justice, December 2015, revised January 21, 2016), http://www.bjs.gov/content/pub/pdf/cpus14.pdf.

84. Federal Bureau of Investigation, "Crime in the United States 2014," September 2015, https://ucr.fbi.gov/crime-in-the.u.s/2014/crime-in-the-u.s.-2014.

85. National Association of State Budget Officers, *2014 State Expenditure Report: Examining Fiscal 2013–2015 State Spending* (Washington, DC: Author, 2015), 54–56.

86. In *Ring v. Arizona*, 536 U.S. 584 (2002), the Supreme Court invalidated Arizona's capital sentencing procedures, holding that the jury, not the judge, must find the aggravating factors necessary to impose the death penalty. Similar procedures in Colorado, Idaho, Montana, and Nebraska also were ruled unconstitutional.

87. Robert Mosteller, "New Dimensions in Sentencing Reform in the Twenty-First Century," *Oregon Law Review* 92 (2003): 16–17.

88. Marguerite A. Driessen and W. Cole Durham Jr., "Sentencing Dissonances in the United States: The Shrinking Distance between Punishment Proposed and Sanction Served," *American Journal of Comparative Law* 50 (2002): 635.

89. Thomas P. Bonczar, "National Corrections Reporting Program: Sentence Length of State Prisoners, by Offense, Admission Type, Sex, and Race," Bureau of Justice Statistics, 2009, Table 9, https://www.bjs.gov/index.cfm?ty=pbdetail&iid=2056.

90. Pew Center on the States, *Time Served: The High Cost, Low Return of Longer Prison Terms* (Washington, DC: Pew Charitable Trusts, June 6, 2012), https://www.pewtrusts.org/~/media/legacy/uploadedfiles/wwwpewtrustsorg/reports/sentencing_and_corrections/prisontimeservedpdf.pdf.

91. Ram Subramanian and Ruth Delaney, *Playbook for Change? States Reconsider Mandatory Sentences* (New York: Vera Institute of Justice, 2014), http://archive.vera.org/sites/default/files/resources/downloads/mandatory-sentences-policy-report-v3.pdf.

92. Brian Ostrom, Neal Kauder, and Robert LaFountain, *Examining the Work of the State Courts, 1999–2000: A National Perspective from the Court Statistics Project* (Williamsburg, VA: National Center for State Courts, 2000).

93. The Sentencing Project, "Fact Sheet: Trends in U.S. Corrections," June 2018, "Number of People in Prisons and Jails for Drug Offenses, 1980 and 2016" (graph), 3, http://sentencingproject.org/wp-content/uploads/2016/01/Trends-in-US-Corrections.pdf.

94. Rachel Alexander, "Spokane's Community Court an Experiment That's Paying Off," *Spokesman-Review*, March 7, 2016, http://www.spokesman.com/stories/2016/mar/07/spokanes-community-court-an-experiment-thats-payin.

95. Judith S. Kaye, "The State of the Judiciary, 2003: Confronting Today's Challenge," annual address, Albany, NY, January 13, 2003, 4.

96. Quoted in Alan Greenblatt, "Docket Science," *Governing*, June 2001, 40.

97. Ibid.

98. Quoted in ibid. For discussion of the reforms to the Hennepin County courts, see the profile of Kevin Burke in "Court Reform," *Governing*, November 2004.

99. Todd Ruger, "'Rocket Docket' Can Be Slowed," *Sarasota Herald-Tribune*, September 27, 2009, BN1; Todd Ruger, "Two Minutes, and Home Goes Away," *Sarasota Herald-Tribune*, May 14, 2009, A1.

Chapter 10

1. "Tucson Cosmetology Student under Investigation for Giving Free Haircuts," *Tucson News Now*, February 9, 2017, http://www.tucsonnewsnow.com/story/34472284/tucson-cosmetology-student-under-investigation-for-giving-free-haircuts.

2. "The Perils of Unlicensed Hair Stylists," *CBS News*, July 29, 2010, https://www.cbsnews.com/news/the-perils-of-unlicensed-hair-stylists/. Fox News, "Jury Finds Unlicensed Cosmetologist Guilty in Silicone Buttocks Injection Death," November 11, 2011, http://www.foxnews.com/health/2011/11/11/jury-finds-unlicensed-cosmetologist-guilty-in-silicone-buttocks-injection-death.html.

3. Max Weber, *From Max Weber: Essays in Sociology*, ed. H. H. Gerth and C. Wright Mills (New York: Oxford University Press, 1946).

4. Ronald C. Moe and Robert S. Gilmour, "Rediscovering Principles of Public Administration: The Neglected Foundation of Public Law," *Public Administration Review* 55, no. 2 (March–April 1995): 135–146.

5. John J. Gargan, "Introduction and Overview of State Government Administration," in *Handbook of State Government Administration*, ed. John J. Gargan (New York: Marcel-Dekker, 2000).

6. Jerrell D. Coggburn and Saundra K. Schneider, "The Quality of Management and Government Performance: An Empirical Analysis of the American States," *Public Administration Review* 63, no. 2 (March–April 2003): 206–213.

7. National Center for Education Statistics, "Fast Facts: Back to School Statistics," 2018, http://nces.ed.gov/fastfacts/display.asp?id=372.

8. Charles Barrilleaux, "Statehouse Bureaucracy: Institutional Consistency in a Changing Environment," in *American State and Local Politics*, ed. Ronald E. Weber and Paul Brace (New York: Chatham House, 1999).

9. Michael Lipsky, *Street-Level Bureaucracy* (New York: Russell Sage Foundation, 1980).

10. Cornelius Kerwin, *Rulemaking: How Government Agencies Write Law and Make Policy*, 3rd ed. (Washington, DC: CQ Press, 2003).

11. Deil S. Wright, Chung-Lae Cho, and Yoo-Sun Choi, "Top-Level State Administrators: Changing Characteristics and Qualities," in *The Book of the States 2002*, ed. Council of State Governments (Lexington, KY: Council of State Governments, 2002).

12. Charles T. Goodsell, *The Case for Bureaucracy: A Public Administration Polemic*, 4th ed. (Washington, DC: CQ Press, 2003).

13. U.S. Census Bureau, "2016 Government Employment and Payroll Tables," 2017, https://www.census.gov/data/tables/2016/econ/apes/annual-apes.html.

14. Goodsell, *Case for Bureaucracy*.

15. George W. Downs and Patrick D. Larkey, *The Search for Government Efficiency* (Philadelphia: Temple University Press, 1986).

16. Amanda M. Girth, Amir Hefetz, Jocelyn M. Johnston, and Mildred E. Warner, "Outsourcing Public Service Delivery: Management Responses in Noncompetitive Markets," *Public Administration Review* 72, no. 6 (November–December 2012): 887–900.

17. Kevin Abourezk, "University Health Privatization a 'Mixed Bag,'" *Lincoln Journal-Star*, September 27, 2012, http://journalstar.com/news/local/education/university-health-privatization-a-mixed-bag/article_bd064c84-4524-5581-8f07-37512ebf7ee1.html.

18. Scott Lamothe and Meeyoung Lamothe, "The Dynamics of Local Service Delivery Arrangements and the Role of Nonprofits," *International Journal of Public Administration* 29 (2006): 769–797.

19. H. George Frederickson, Kevin B. Smith, Christopher W. Larimer, and Michael J. Licari, *The Public Administration Theory Primer* (Boulder, CO: Westview Press, 2016), 119–123.

20. J. Norman Baldwin, "Public Versus Private Employees: Debunking Stereotypes," *Review of Public Personnel Administration* 12 (Winter 1991): 1–27.

21. Barrilleaux, "Statehouse Bureaucracy," 106–107.

22. John J. Dilulio Jr., Gerald Garvey, and Donald F. Kettl, *Improving Government: An Owner's Manual* (Washington, DC: Brookings Institution, 1993).

23. Mary Bryna Sanger, "Does Measuring Performance Lead to Better Performance?," *Journal of Policy Analysis and Management* 32, no. 1 (2013): 200.

24. Pew Center on the States, "The Government Performance Project," 2010, http://www.pewstates.org/projects/government-performance-project-328600.

25. Barbara Romzek and Melvin Dubnick, "Accountability in the Public Sector: Lessons from the Challenger Tragedy," *Public Administration Review* 47, no. 3 (May–June 1987): 227–238.

26. Alfred Steinberg, *The Bosses* (New York: Macmillan, 1972).

27. Dwight Waldo, *The Administrative State* (New York: Holmes and Meier, 1948).

28. U.S. Department of Labor, "Union Members Summary," Bureau of Labor Statistics, January 19, 2018, https://www.bls.gov/news.release/union2.nr0.htm.

29. Charles J. Sykes, *Profscam: Professors and the Demise of Higher Education* (New York: St. Martin's Press, 1989).

30. Charles Chieppo, "The Civil Service Systems Governments Need for the Modern Era," *Governing*, September 2013.

31. Katherine Barrett and Richard Greene, "How Tennessee Transformed the Way It Hires and Fires People," *Governing*, November 2015.

32. National Center for Education Statistics, *Digest of Education Statistics* (Washington, DC: U.S. Department of Education, October 2013), Table 209.10, "Number and Percentage Distribution of Teachers in Public and Private Elementary and Secondary Schools, by Selected Teacher Characteristics: Selected Years, 1987–88 through 2015–16," https://nces.ed.gov/programs/digest/d17/tables/dt17_209.10.asp?current=yes.

33. U.S. Equal Opportunity Commission, "State and Local Government Information (EEO-4), 2015: National Employment Summary," https://www.eeoc.gov/eeoc/statistics/employment/jobpat-eeo4/2015/table1/table1.html.

34. William Bratton, *Crime and Enforcement Activity in New York City (Jan 1–Dec 31, 2015)* (New York: NYPD, 2016), Appendixes C and B, http://www.nyc.gov/html/nypd/downloads/pdf/analysis_and_planning/year_end_2015_enforcement_report.pdf.

35. C. J. Chivers, "For Black Officers, Diversity Has Its Limits," *New York Times*, April 2, 2001.

36. Sally Selden, *The Promise of Representative Bureaucracy: Diversity and Responsiveness in a Government Agency* (Armonk, NY: M. E. Sharpe, 1997).

37. Steven Greenhouse, "Supreme Court Ruling Offers Little Guidance on Hiring," *New York Times*, June 29, 2009; Adam Liptak, "Supreme Court Finds Bias against White Firefighters," *New York Times*, June 29, 2009.

38. Donald F. Kettl, *The Global Public Management Revolution: A Report on the Transformation of Governance* (Washington, DC: Brookings Institution Press, 2000).

39. H. George Frederickson, Kevin B. Smith, Christopher W. Larimer, and Michael J. Licari, *The Public Administration Theory Primer*, 2nd ed. (Boulder, CO: Westview Press, 2012), 227.

40. James S. Bowman and Jonathan P. West, "Ending Civil Service Protections in Florida Government: Experiences in State Agencies," in *American Public Service: Radical Reform and the Merit System*, ed. James S. Bowman and Jonathan P. West (Boca Raton, FL: CRC Press, 2007).

41. "State and Local Government Employment: Monthly Data," *Governing*, last updated December 1, 2017, http://www.governing.com/gov-data/public-work-force-salaries/monthly-government-employment-changes-totals.html.

Chapter 11

1. This translation of the oath is available on the National League of Cities website, http://www.nlc.org/build-skills-and-networks/resources/cities-101/city-factoids/the-athenian-oath.

2. Pew Research Center, "Public Trust in Government: 1958–2017," December 14, 2017, http://www.people-press.org/2017/12/14/public-trust-in-government-1958-2017/.

3. Justin McCarthy, "Americans Still More Trusting in Local over State Government," Gallup, September 19, 2016, http://news.gallup.com/poll/195656/americans-trusting-local-state-government.aspx.

4. Richard Cole and John Kincaid, "Public Opinion on U.S. Federal and Intergovernmental Issues in 2006," *Publius: The Journal of Federalism* 36, no. 3 (2006): 443–459.

5. This figure is based on an estimated total population of 300 million.

6. David Y. Miller, *The Regional Governing of Metropolitan America* (Boulder, CO: Westview Press, 2002).

7. Quoted in Jonathan Walters, "Cry, the Beleaguered County," *Governing*, August 1996.

8. Fairfax County, Virginia, "FY 2018 Adopted Budget Summary," https://www.fairfaxcounty.gov/budget/sites/budget/files/assets/documents/fy2018/adopted/overview/15_general_fund_revenue_overview.pdf; County Executive Office, Orange County, California, "FY 2017–18 Annual Budget," http://bos.ocgov.com/finance/2018FN/charts_frm.asp.

9. National Association of Counties, *Counties Matter* (brochure) (Washington, DC: National Association of Counties, February 2016), http://www.naco.org/sites/default/files/attachments/Counties_Matter_brochure.pdf.

10. Miller, *Regional Governing of Metropolitan America*, 26.

11. National League of Cities, "Forms of Municipal Government," https://www.nlc.org/forms-of-municipal-government.

12. "Chicago Aldermen and Corruption Cases: Hall of Shame," *Chicago Tribune*, December 14, 2016, http://www.chicagotribune.com/news/local/breaking/ct-chicago-convicted-aldermen-htmlstory.html.

13. Austin Berg, "FBI Seizes Files as Chicago Aldermen Oust Oversight," Illinois Policy Institute, November 17, 2015, https://www.illinoispolicy.org/fbi-seizes-files-as-chicago-aldermen-oust-oversight.

14. Jason Meisner, Jeremy Gorner, and Hal Dardick, "Al. Willie Cochran Indicted on Thefts from Ward Charity," *Chicago Tribune*, December 14, 2016, http://www.chicagotribune.com/news/local/breaking/ct-alderman-willie-cochran-indicted-20161214-story.html.

15. National League of Cities, "Serving on City Councils," Research Brief on America's Cities, no. 2003-5, Washington, DC, September 2003.

16. Roger L. Kemp, ed., *Model Government Charters: A City, County, Regional, State, and Federal Handbook* (Jefferson, NC: McFarland, 2003), 10.

17. Bonnie G. Mani, "Determinants of a City Manager's Tenure in Office: The Person, Job, Municipality, and Election System," *SAGE Open* (January–March 2014): 1–16, doi:10.1177/2158244014522069.

18. National League of Cities, "Forms of Municipal Government."

19. Michael Zuckerman, *Peaceable Kingdoms: The New England Towns of the 18th Century* (New York: Knopf, 1970).

20. Miller, *Regional Governing of Metropolitan America*, 41.

21. Quoted in Anwar Syed, *The Political Theory of the American Local Government* (New York: Random House, 1966), 40.

22. Alexis de Tocqueville, *Democracy in America: A New Translation*, trans. George Lawrence, ed. J. P. Mayer (New York: HarperCollins, 2000), 33.

23. Penelope Lemov, "Infrastructure Conference Report: Building It Smarter, Managing It Better," *Governing*, October 1996, 40.

24. Ann O'M. Bowman, "Urban Government," in *Handbook of Research on Urban Politics and Policy in the United States*, ed. Ronald K. Vogel (Westport, CT: Greenwood Press, 1997), 133.

25. Kemp, *Model Government Charters*, 59.

26. National Conference of State Legislatures, "State Partisan Composition," http://www.ncsl.org/research/about-state-legislatures/partisan-composition.aspx.

27. Jeremy Rozansky, "The Problem and Promise of Charter Cities," *City Journal*, August 17, 2012, https://

www.city-journal.org/html/problem-and-promise-charter-cities-11070.html.

28. National League of Cities, "Partisan vs. Nonpartisan Elections," http://www.nlc.org/build-skills-and-networks/resources/cities-101/city-officials/partisan-vs-nonpartisan-elections.

29. Makie Maciag, "Voter Turnout Plummeting in Local Elections," *Governing*, October 2014, http://www.governing.com/topics/politics/gov-voter-turnout-municipal-elections.html.

30. Claudia Vargas, "Philadelphia Re-elects Elections Chief Who Hasn't Voted in Years," *Governing*, January 7, 2016, http://www.governing.com/topics/elections/tns-philadelphia-elections-anthony-clark.html.

31. Lana Stein, "Mayoral Politics," in Pelissero, *Cities, Politics, and Policy: A Comparative Analysis*, ed. John P. Pelissero (Washington, DC: CQ Press, 2003), 162.

32. National Association of Latino Elected and Appointed Officials, "Latino Elected Officials in America," 2017, http://www.naleo.org/at_a_glance.

33. Center for American Women and Politics, "Women in Elective Office 2018," http://www.cawp.rutgers.edu/women-elective-office-2018.

34. National League of Cities, "City Councils," https://www.nlc.org/city-councils.

Chapter 12

1. Brian Costin, "Too Much Government: Illinois' Thousands of Local Governments," Illinois Policy Institute, https://files.illinoispolicy.org/wp-content/uploads/2013/11/Too_much_gov-1.pdf.

2. Brian Costin, "Illinois Ranks First in Number of Local Taxing Bodies," Illinois Policy Institute, https://www.illinoispolicy.org/illinois-ranks-first-in-the-nation-in-number-of-local-taxing-bodies/.

3. Illinois Commission on Intergovernmental Cooperation, "Legislator's Guide to Local Governments in Illinois," http://ilga.gov/commission/lru/SpecialDistricts.pdf.

4. Rae Archibald and Sally Sleeper, *Government Consolidation and Economic Development in Allegheny County and the City of Pittsburgh* (Santa Monica, CA: RAND Corporation, 2008); Christopher Briem, "A Primer on Local Government Fragmentation and Regionalism in the Pittsburgh Region."

5. Anthony Downs, "The Devolution Revolution: Why Congress Is Shifting a Lot of Power to the Wrong Levels," Policy Brief no. 3, Brookings Institution, July 1996, http://www.brookings.edu/research/papers/1996/07/governance-downs.

6. Office of Management and Budget, "2010 Standards for Delineating Metropolitan and Micropolitan Statistical Areas," *Federal Register* 75, no. 123 (June 28, 2010), https://www.federalregister.gov/documents/2010/06/28/2010-15605/2010-standards-for-delineating-metropolitan-and-micropolitan-statistical-areas.

7. U.S. Census Bureau, "Estimates of Resident Population Change and Rankings: July 1, 2016 to July 1, 2017—United States—Metropolitan Statistical Area; and for Puerto Rico," https://factfinder.census.gov/faces/tableservices/jsf/pages/productview.xhtml?src=bkmk.

8. Bruce Katz, "A Nation in Transition: What the Urban Age Means for the United States," speech presented at the Urban Age Conference, New York, May 4, 2007.

9. David Y. Miller, *The Regional Governing of Metropolitan America* (Boulder, CO: Westview Press, 2002), 1.

10. Shima Hamidi, Reid Ewing, Illana Preuss, and Alex Dodds, "Measuring Sprawl and Its Impacts: An Update," *Journal of Planning Education and Research* 35 (2015): 35–50.

11. David Cieslewits, "The Environmental Impacts of Sprawl," in *Urban Sprawl: Causes, Consequences, and Policy Responses*, ed. Gregory D. Squires (Washington, DC: Urban Institute Press, 2002).

12. Ibid.

13. See, for example, Myron Orfield, *American Metropolitics: The New Suburban Reality* (Washington, DC: Brookings Institution Press, 2002).

14. Ibid., 41.

15. Peter Dreier, John Mollenkopf, and Todd Swanstrom, *Place Matters: Metropolitics for the Twenty-First Century* (Lawrence: University Press of Kansas, 2001).

16. Orfield, *American Metropolitics*, 10.

17. Daniel C. Vock, "Suburbs Struggle to Aid the Sprawling Poor," *Governing*, February 2015, http://www.governing.com/topics/health-human-services/gov-suburban-poverty-gentrification-series.html.

18. David K. Hamilton, *Measuring the Effectiveness of Regional Governing Systems: A Comparative Study of City Regions in North America* (New York: Springer, 2013), 4–6.

19. G. Ross Stephens and Nelson Wikstrom, *Metropolitan Government and Governance: Theoretical Perspectives, Empirical Analysis, and the Future* (New York: Oxford University Press, 1999).

20. Metro, "What Is Metro?," http://www.oregonmetro.gov/regional-leadership/what-metro.

21. Heike Mayor and John Provo, "The Portland Edge in Context," in *The Portland Edge: Challenges and Successes in Growing Communities*, ed. Connie P. Ozawa (Washington, DC: Island Press, 2004).

22. Judith Dempsey and Andrew Plantiga, "How Well Do Urban Growth Boundaries Contain Development? Results for Oregon Using a Difference-in-Difference Estimator," *Regional Science and Urban Economics* 43 (2013): 996–1007.

23. National Association of Regional Councils, "What Is a Regional Council or Council of Governments?," 2013, http://narc.org/about-narc/cogs-mpos.

24. National Association of Regional Councils, "Regional Councils, COGs and MPOs," 2016, http://narc.org/about-narc/cogs-mpos.

25. Miller, *Regional Governing of Metropolitan America*, 103.

26. James F. Wolf and Tara Kolar Bryan, "Identifying the Capacities of Regional Councils of Government," *State and Local Government Review* 41 (2010): 61.

27. Ibid., 67.

28. Simon Andrew, "Recent Development in the Study of Interjurisdictional Agreements: An Overview and Assessment," *State and Local Government Review* 41 (2010): 133–142.

29. National Association of Counties, "City–County Consolidation Proposals, 1921–Present," 2010, http://www.naco.org/sites/default/files/documents/City%20County%20Consolidations.01.01.2011.pdf.

30. Amy B. Uden, "A Checklist for Alternatives in City–County Consolidation Decisions: From Separation to Unification," *State and Local Government Review* 48, no. 1 (2016): 49–62.

31. Aaron Renn, "The Myths of Municipal Mergers," *Governing*, January 2015, http://www.governing.com/columns/eco-engines/gov-ferguson-and-splintered-governance.html.

32. Rowland Egger, "City–County Consolidation in Allegheny County, Pennsylvania," *American Political Science Review* 23 (1929): 121–123.

33. Quoted in Jeffrey Cohan, "Reports Outline Options in Merging Pittsburgh–Allegheny County Services," *Pittsburgh Post-Gazette*, April 2, 2004.

34. Molly Born, "Officials to Propose Plan for Disbanding Municipalities," *Pittsburgh Post-Gazette*, May 10, 2017, http://www.post-gazette.com/local/city/2017/05/11/disincorporation-plan-allegheny-county-disbanding-financially-distressed-municipalities/stories/201705110053.

35. National League of Cities, "Serving on City Councils," Research Brief on America's Cities, no. 2003-5, Washington, DC, September 2003.

36. World Population Review, "Oklahoma City, Oklahoma Population 2018," http://worldpopulationreview.com/us-cities/oklahoma-city-population/.

37. Ann O'M. Bowman, "Urban Government," in *Handbook of Research on Urban Politics and Policy in the United States*, ed. Ronald K. Vogel (Westport, CT: Greenwood Press, 1997), 139.

38. Rob Gurwitt, "Annexation: Not So Smart Growth," *Governing*, October 2000.

39. Barbara Kelly, *Expanding the American Dream: Building and Rebuilding Levittown* (Albany: State University of New York Press, 1993).

40. Charles Tiebout, "A Pure Theory of Local Expenditures," *Journal of Political Economy* 64, no. 5 (October 1956): 422.

41. William Lyons, David Lowery, and Ruth Hoogland DeHoog, *The Politics of Dissatisfaction: Citizens, Services, and Urban Institutions* (Armonk, NY: M. E. Sharpe, 1992).

42. Dante Chinni, "Rural Counties Are Losing Population and Aging, but Are They Really 'Dying'?," PBS, *NewsHour*, March 4, 2011, https://www.pbs.org/newshour/economy/as-the-2010-census.

43. U.S. Census Bureau, "Measuring America: Our Changing Landscape," December 8, 2016, https://www.census.gov/library/visualizations/2016/comm/acs-rural-urban.html.

44. Nebraska Department of Education, "Data and Information Archives," https://www.education.ne.gov/dataservices/data-reports/data-and-information-archives/.

45. Alan Greenblatt, "Little Mergers on the Prairie," *Governing*, July 2006, 49–50.

Chapter 13

1. U.S. Bureau of Labor Statistics, "Weekly Earning by Educational Attainment in First Quarter 2016," *TED: The Economics Daily*, May 11, 2016, https://www.bls.gov/opub/ted/2016/weekly-earnings-by-educational-attainment-in-first-quarter-2016.htm.

2. Norman Baldwin and Stephen Borrelli, "Education and Economic Growth in the United States: Cross-national Applications for an Intra-national Path Analysis," *Policy Sciences* 14, no. 3 (2008): 183–204.

3. Catherine Ross and Chia-Ling Wu, "The Links between Education and Health," *American Sociological Review* 60, no. 5 (1995): 719–745.

4. Wendy Wang, "The Link between a College Education and a Lasting Marriage," Pew Research Center, December 4, 2015, http://www.pewresearch.org/fact-tank/2015/12/04/education-and-marriage/.

5. Quoted in David Tyack and Larry Cuban, *Tinkering toward Utopia: A Century of Public School Reform* (Cambridge, MA: Harvard University Press, 1995), 2.

6. Quoted in Michael A. Rebell, "Fiscal Equity Litigation and the Democratic Imperative," *Journal of Education Finance* 24, no. 1 (1998): 23–50.

7. Ibid.

8. Texas Education Agency, "Student Enrollment Reports," April 4, 2018, https://rptsvr1.tea.texas.gov/adhocrpt/adste.html.

9. Hawaii State Department of Education, "Department Announces 2017–18 Enrollment Figures for Public and Charter Schools," press release, September 8, 2017, http://www.hawaiipublicschools.org/ConnectWithUs/

MediaRoom/PressReleases/Pages/2017-18-enrollment.aspx.

10. Charles Mahtesian, "Too Much Democracy," *Governing*, January 24, 2000.

11. Stephen Cornman, Lei Zhou, Mali Howell, and Jumaane Young, *Revenues and Expenditures for Public Elementary and Secondary Education: School Year 2014–15 (Fiscal Year 2015)*, NCES 2018-301 (Washington, DC: National Center for Education Statistics, 2018), Table 1, https://nces.ed.gov/pubs2018/2018301.pdf.

12. National Association of State Budget Officers, *State Expenditure Report: Examining Fiscal 2015–2017 State Spending*, https://higherlogicdownload.s3.amazonaws.com/NASBO/9d2d2db1-c943-4f1b-b750-0fca152d64c2/UploadedImages/SER%20Archive/State_Expenditure_Report__Fiscal_2015-2017_-S.pdf.

13. Elizabeth Chuck, "Powerball Windfall? Schools Don't Always Benefit from Lottery Sales," *NBC News*, January 13, 2016, http://www.nbcnews.com/news/us-news/powerball-windfall-schools-don-t-always-benefit-lottery-sales-n494746.

14. Rebell, "Fiscal Equity Litigation."

15. "Quality Counts 2003: If I Can't Learn from You . . .," *Education Week*, January 9, 2003, 22, http://www.edweek.org/media/ew/qc/archives/QC03full.pdf.

16. U.S. Department of Education, *A Nation Accountable: Twenty-Five Years after "A Nation at Risk"* (Washington, DC: U.S. Department of Education, April 2008), 1, http://www2.ed.gov/rschstat/research/pubs/accountable/accountable.pdf.

17. "The 49th Annual PDK/Gallup Poll of the Public's Attitudes toward the Public Schools," *Phi Delta Kappan*, supplement, September 2017, http://pdkpoll.org/assets/downloads/PDKnational_poll_2017.pdf.

18. Good examples are Alfie Kohn, *The Case against Standardized Testing* (Portsmouth, NH: Heinemann, 2000); Peter Sacks, *Standardized Minds* (New York: Perseus, 2001).

19. "49th Annual PDK/Gallup Poll."

20. National Center for Education Statistics, "The Nation's Report Card," http://www.nationsreportcard.gov.

21. National Center for Education Statistics, "Trends in International Mathematics and Science Study: Selected Findings from TIMSS 2015," https://nces.ed.gov/timss/timss2015/findings.asp.

22. Rebecca Leung, "The 'Texas Miracle,'" *CBS News*, January 6, 2004, http://www.cbsnews.com/stories/2004/01/06/60II/main591676.shtml.

23. National Center for Education Statistics, "Public High School Graduation Rates," https://nces.ed.gov/programs/coe/indicator_coi.asp.

24. Common Core State Standards Initiative, http://www.corestandards.org.

25. Common Core State Standards Initiative, "Standards in Your State," http://www.corestandards.org/standards-in-your-state/.

26. Kati Haycock, "Good Teaching Matters: How Well-Qualified Teachers Can Close the Gap," *Thinking K–16* 3, no. 2 (1998).

27. Economists Steven G. Givkin and Eric A. Hanushek, cited (along with researcher William Sanders) in "Quality Counts 2003," 10.

28. U.S. Department of Education, "Teaching Shortage Areas Nationwide Listing 1990–1991 through 2017–2018," May 2017, https://www2.ed.gov/about/offices/list/ope/pol/tsa.html?exp=0#list.

29. Sophie Qunton, "As Teacher Shortages Plague Every State, Some Take Action," *Governing*, December 28, 2017, http://www.governing.com/topics/education/sl-teacher-shortage.html.

30. Stéphane Baldi, Catharine Warner-Griffin, Chrystine Tadler, and Chelsea Owens, *Education and Certification Qualifications of Public Middle Grades Teachers of Selected Subjects: Evidence from the 2011–12 Schools and Staffing Survey*, NCES 2015-815 (Washington, DC: U.S. Department of Education, 2015), http://nces.ed.gov/pubs2015/2015815.pdf.

31. Mary Ellen Flannery, "Survey: Number of Future Teachers Reaches All-Time Low," *NEA Today*, March 14, 2016, http://neatoday.org/2016/03/15/future-teachers-at-all-time-low/.

32. Alliance for Excellent Education, *On the Path to Equity: Improving the Effectiveness of Beginning Teachers* (Washington, DC: Author, July 2014), http://all4ed.org/wp-content/uploads/2014/07/PathToEquity.pdf.

33. National Center for Education Statistics, *Digest of Education Statistics* (Washington, DC: U.S. Department of Education, October 2016), Tables 206.10 and 216.30, https://nces.ed.gov/programs/digest/d16/.

34. National Alliance for Public Charter Schools, "Estimated Number of Public Charter Schools and Students, 2016–17," February 2017, https://www.publiccharters.org/sites/default/files/migrated/wp-content/uploads/2017/01/EER_Report_V5.pdf.

35. Education Commission of the States, "50-State Comparison: Charter School Policies," https://www.ecs.org/charter-school-policies/.

36. Erika Hayasaki, "Charter Academy Shuts 60 Schools," *Los Angeles Times*, August 16, 2004, http://articles.latimes.com/2004/aug/16/local/me-charter16.

37. Charles S. Clark, "Charter Schools," *CQ Researcher*, December 20, 2002; Brian P. Gill, P. Michael Timpane, Karen E. Ross, and Dominic J. Brewer, *Rhetoric Versus Reality: What We Know and What We Need to Know about Vouchers and Charter Schools* (Santa Monica, CA: RAND Corporation, 2001), xviii.

38. Mark Berends, "Sociology and School Choice: What We Know after Two Decades of Charter Schools," *Annual Review of Sociology* 41 (2015): 159–180.

39. Kenneth Jost, "School Vouchers Showdown," *CQ Researcher*, February 15, 2002.

40. Ohio Department of Education, "2018–2019 EdChoice Scholarship Program Fact Sheet," http://education .ohio.gov/getattachment/Topics/Other-Resources/ Scholarships/EdChoice-Scholarship-Program/EC-Fact-Sheet-1.pdf.aspx?lang=en-US.

41. EdChoice, "Wisconsin—Milwaukee Parental Choice Program," https://www.edchoice.org/school-choice/ programs/wisconsin-milwaukee-parental-choice-program/.

42. John Robert Warren, "Graduation Rates for Choice and Public School Students in Milwaukee, 2003–2008," School Choice Wisconsin, February 2010.

43. John F. Witte, Deven Carlson, Joshua M. Cowen, David J. Fleming, and Patrick J. Wolf, *MPCP Longitudinal Educational Growth Study: Fifth Year Report*, Report of the School Choice Demonstration Project (Fayetteville: University of Arkansas, Department of Education Reform, 2012).

44. National Education Policy Center, "Reports, Reviews Offer Little to Commend Milwaukee Voucher Schools," April 19, 2012, http://nepc.colorado.edu/newslet-ter/2012/04/review-Milwaukee-Choice-Year-5; U.S. General Accounting Office, *School Vouchers: Publicly Funded Programs in Cleveland and Milwaukee*, GAO 01-914 (Washington, DC: U.S. General Accounting Office, 2001), 4; Zachary M. Seward, "Long-Delayed Education Study Casts Doubt on Value of Vouchers," *Wall Street Journal*, July 15–16, 2006.

45. National Center for Education Statistics, "Number and Percentage of All Students Ages 5–17 Who Were Homeschooled and Homeschooling Rate, by Selected Characteristics, 2011–2012."

46. National Center for Education Statistics, *The Condition of Education* (Washington, DC: U.S. Department of Education, 2005).

47. Home School Legal Defense Association, "Homeschool Laws in Your State," http://www.hslda.org/content/ laws/.

48. See the NEA and AFT websites, http://www.nea.org and http://www.aft.org/about.

49. National PTA, "About PTA," http://www.pta.org/ about/?navItemNumber=503.

Chapter 14

1. Phone interview with Ronald J. Lampard, May 1, 2018.

2. Phone interview with Vikrant Reddy, July 20, 2018.

3. "Remarks by President Trump at White House Prison Reform Summit," White House, May 18, 2018, https:// www.whitehouse.gov/briefings-statements/remarks-president-trump-white-house-prison-reform-summit/.

4. Phone interview with Doug Collins, July 18, 2018.

5. Danielle S. Allen, *The World of Prometheus: The Politics of Punishing in Democratic Athens* (Princeton, NJ: Princeton University Press, 1999), 3.

6. For a discussion of how this transformation came to pass, see Sir Frederick Pollock and F. W. Maitland, *History of English Law before the Time of Edward I* (Cambridge: Cambridge University Press, 1969).

7. Quoted in Alan Greenblatt, "Why There Are So Many Bad Sheriffs," *Governing*, April 2018, http://www.gov erning.com/topics/public-justice-safety/gov-bad-sher riffs.html.

8. For a comprehensive statement of the Obama administration's position on marijuana, see Drug Enforcement Administration, *The DEA Position on Marijuana* (Washington, DC: U.S. Department of Justice, April 2013).

9. Marc Mauer, "The Crisis of the Young African American Male and the Criminal Justice System," presentation to the U.S. Commission on Civil Rights, Washington, DC, April 15–16, 1999, 6.

10. "U.S. Correctional Population Declined for the Ninth Consecutive Year," Bureau of Justice Statistics, April 26, 2018, https://www.bjs.gov/content/pub/press/cpus 16pr.cfm.

11. Erica Goode, "Solitary Confinement: Punished for Life," *New York Times*, August 3, 2015; Peter Baker and Erica Good, "Critics of Solitary Confinement Are Buoyed as Obama Embraces Their Cause," *New York Times*, July 21, 2015. For more on solitary confinement and its many permutations, see Solitary Watch, www.solitarywatch.org.

12. The degree to which states put inmates in isolation units varies widely. As of 1999, Arizona, Colorado, Maine, Nebraska, New York, Nevada, Rhode Island, and Virginia all kept between 5 and 8 percent of their prison population in isolation. In contrast, Indiana had 85 supermax beds; Georgia had only 10. See Atul Gawande, "Hellhole: The United States Holds Tens of Thousands of Inmates in Long-Term Solitary Confinement. Is This Torture?," *New Yorker*, March 30, 2009. See also Angela Browne, Alissa Cambier, and Suzanne Agha, "Prisons within Prisons: The Use of Segregation in the United States," *Federal Sentencing Reporter* 24, no. 1 (October 2011): 46–49, https://www .vera.org/publications/prisons-within-prisons-the-use-of-segregation-in-the-united-states.

13. Eduardo Porter, "In the U.S., Punishment Comes before the Crimes," *New York Times*, April 29, 2014; "The Slow Death of Capital Punishment," *Economist*, April 26, 2014.

14. Becky Pettit, "Black Progress? Not When You Include the Incarcerated," *Washington Post*, November 13, 2012, http://www.washingtonpost.com/blogs/therootdc/post/black-progress-not-when-you-include-the-incarcerated/2012/11/13/1412b6b2-2da0-11e2-9ac2-1c61452669c3_blog.html.

15. Thomas Edsall, "The Expanding World of Poverty Capitalism," *New York Times*, August 26, 2014, http://www.nytimes.com/2014/08/27/opinion/thomas-edsall-the-expanding-world-of-poverty-capitalism.html?_r=0.

16. Alice Goffman, *On the Run: Fugitive Life in an American City* (Chicago: University of Chicago Press, 2014), xiv, 8.

17. The rise in incarceration levels almost certainly had something to do with the crime decrease. Estimates of what percentage of the crime reduction it accounts for range from 10 to 40 percent. See Steven Levitt, "Understanding Why Crime Fell in the 1990s: Four Factors That Explain the Decline and Six That Do Not," *Journal of Economic Perspectives* 18, no. 1 (2004): 163–190.

18. Lauren E. Glaze and Thomas P. Bonczar, *Probation and Parole in the United States, 2008*, Bureau of Justice Statistics Bulletin NCJ 228230 (Washington, DC: U.S. Department of Justice, December 2009), http://www.bjs.gov/content/pub/pdf/ppus08.pdf.

19. Quoted in German Lopez, "Everything You Need to Know about the War on Drugs," *Vox*, October 6, 2014, http://www.vox.com/cards/war-on-drugs-marijuana-cocaine-heroin-meth/war-on-drugs-goals.

20. This figure—from the Office of National Drug Control Policy—does not include alcohol, which is, of course, the most popular drug of all.

21. See Robert MacCoun and Peter Reuter, *Drug War Heresies: Learning from Other Vices, Times, and Places* (New York: Cambridge University Press, 2001), 26, 29.

22. "Crack; A Disaster of Historic Dimension, Still Growing," *New York Times*, May 28, 1989.

23. *Terry v. Ohio*, 392 U.S. 1 (1968).

24. James Q. Wilson and George L. Kelling, "Broken Windows: The Police and Neighborhood Safety," *Atlantic Monthly*, March 1982.

25. John Buntin, "The LAPD Remade: How William Bratton's Police Force Drove Crime Down—and Won Over Los Angeles's Minorities," *City Journal*, Winter 2013.

26. William Bratton, *Turnaround: How America's Top Cop Reversed the Crime Epidemic* (New York: Random House, 1998).

27. For an account of how CompStat was created and how it is used, see John Buntin, *Assertive Policing, Plummeting Crime: The NYPD Takes on Crime in New York City*, Kennedy School of Government Case Study (Cambridge, MA: Harvard University, August 1999).

28. Franklin Zimring, *The City That Became Safe: New York's Lessons for Urban Crime and Its Control* (New York: Oxford University Press, 2011).

29. Quoted in Buntin, "LAPD Remade."

30. New York Civil Liberties Union, "Stop and Frisk Facts," https://www.nyclu.org/en/stop-and-frisk-facts.

31. Joseph Goldstein, "Judge Rejects New York's Stop-and-Frisk Policy," *New York Times*, August 12, 2013; Joseph Goldstein, "Court Blocks Stop-and-Frisk Changes for New York Police," *New York Times*, October 31, 2013.

32. Pew Center on the States, "One in 100: Behind Bars in America 2008," February 28, 2008, https://www.pewtrusts.org/~/media/legacy/uploadedfiles/pcs_assets/2008/one20in20100pdf.pdf.

33. "Crack; A Disaster of Historic Dimension"; National Association of State Budget Officers, *State Expenditure Report, 2008* (Washington, DC: 2009), 58.

34. Mike Nizza, "California's $8 Billion Surprise," *New York Times*, August 13, 2008; Jennifer Steinhauer, "Prisons Push California to Seek New Approach," *New York Times*, December 11, 2006.

35. Keith Humphreys, "California's Strange, Tragic Embrace of Prisons," *Reality-Based Community*, August 13, 2014, http://www.samefacts.com/2014/08/drug-policy/californias-strange-enduring-embrace-of-prisons.

36. Joan Petersilia, "California Prison Downsizing and Its Impact on Local Criminal Justice Systems," *Harvard Law & Policy Review* 8 (2014): 327–357; Magnus Lofstrom and Brandon Martin, "Public Safety Realignment: Impacts So Far," Public Policy Institute of California, September 2015, http://www.ppic.org/main/publication_quick.asp?i=1164.

37. John Myers, "What You Need to Know about the 17 Propositions on November's Statewide Ballot," *Los Angeles Times*, July 3, 2016, http://www.latimes.com/politics/la-pol-ca-november-ballot-propositions-guide-20160630-snap-htmlstory.html.

38. Marie Gottschalk, "American Hell," *New Republic*, June 28, 2010.

39. Tracey Meares, "The Legitimacy of Police among Young African-American Men," *Marquette Law Review* 92, no. 4 (2009): 655, http://digitalcommons.law.yale.edu/cgi/viewcontent.cgi?article=1527& context=fss_papers.

40. Michelle Alexander, *The New Jim Crow: Mass Incarceration in the Age of Colorblindness* (New York: New Press, 2010).

41. Thomas P. Bonczar and Allen J. Beck, *Lifetime Likelihood of Going to State or Federal Prison*, Bureau of Justice Statistics Special Report, NCJ 160092 (Washington, DC: U.S. Department of Justice, March 1997), http://bjs.gov/content/pub/pdf/Llgsfp.pdf.

42. Alexander, *New Jim Crow*, 60.

43. Ibid., 54, 124.

44. David M. Kennedy, *Don't Shoot: One Man, a Street Fellowship, and the End of Violence in Inner-City America* (New York: Bloomsbury, 2011), 18.

45. Jill Leovy, *Ghettoside: A True Story of Murder in America* (New York: Spiegel & Grau, 2015), 8.

46. "Overkill," *Economist*, August 23, 2014; Michael Wine, "Race and Police Shootings: Are Blacks Targeted More?," *New York Times*, August 30, 2014.

47. Jay Caspian Kang, "Our Demand Is Simple: Stop Killing Us," *New York Times Magazine*, May 4, 2015, http://www.nytimes.com/2015/05/10/magazine/our-demand-is-simple-stop-killing-us.html?_r=0.

48. Pew Research Center, "Few Say Police Forces Nationally Do Well in Treating Races Equally," August 25, 2014, http://www.people-press.org/2014/08/25/few-say-police-forces-nationally-do-well-in-treating-races-equally.

49. Hannah Fingerhut, "Deep Racial, Partisan Divisions in Americans' Views of Police Officers," Pew Research Center, September 15, 2017, http://www.pewresearch.org/fact-tank/2017/09/15/deep-racial-partisan-divisions-in-americans-views-of-police-officers/.

50. Heather Mac Donald, "In Denial about Crime," *City Journal*, Winter 2016, http://www.city-journal.org/html/denial-about-crime-14118.html.

51. Dara Lind, "The 'Ferguson Effect,' a Theory That's Warping the American Crime Debate, Explained," *Vox*, May 18, 2016, http://www.vox.com/2016/5/18/11683594/ferguson-effect-crime-police.

52. Phone interview with Jerry Madden, May 3, 2018.

53. John Buntin, "The Correctionists," *Governing*, 2010, http://www.governing.com/poy/jerry-madden-john-whitmire.html; Betsy Woodruff, "Bipartisan Prison Reform: Many Conservatives and Liberals Agree: We're Putting Too Many People in Jail," *National Review Online*, January 20, 2014, http://www.nationalreview.com/article/368877/bipartisan-prison-reform-betsy-woodruff.

54. Adam Gelb and Tracy Velázquez, "The Changing State of Recidivism: Fewer People Going Back to Prison," Pew Charitable Trusts, August 1, 2018, http://www.pewtrusts.org/en/research-and-analysis/articles/2018/08/01/the-changing-state-of-recidivism-fewer-people-going-back-to-prison.

55. Phone interview with Adam Gelb, May 16, 2018.

56. National Institute of Justice, "Do Drug Courts Work? Findings from Drug Court Research," U.S. Department of Justice, Office of Justice Programs, May 1, 2018, https://www.nij.gov/topics/courts/drug-courts/pages/work.aspx.

57. Liz Farmer, "How to Calculate What Opioid Overdoses Cost Government," *Governing*, June 4, 2018, http://www.governing.com/topics/finance/gov-opengov-opioid-overdose-deaths-cost-governments.html.

58. William A. Galston and E. J. Dionne Jr., "The New Politics of Marijuana Legalization: Why Opinion Is Changing," *Governance Studies at Brookings*, May 2013, https://www.brookings.edu/wp-content/uploads/2016/06/Dionne-Galston_NewPoliticsofMJLeg_Final.pdf; Marc Fisher, "Even as Marijuana Gains Ground, Some Tightly Enforce Laws," *Washington Post*, June 21, 2014.

59. Keith Humphreys, "Three Ways of Looking at Marijuana Consumption Data," Reality-Based Community, July 21, 2014, http://www.samefacts.com/2014/07/drug-policy/three-ways-of-looking-at-marijuana-consumption-data.

60. Robert Weisberg and David Mills, "Violence Silence: Why No One Really Cares about Prison Rape," *Slate*, October 1, 2003, http://www.slate.com/id/2089095. See also Human Rights Watch, *No Escape: Male Rape in U.S. Prisons* (New York: Human Rights Watch, 2001), http://www.hrw.org/reports/2001/prison/report.html.

61. Doris J. James and Lauren E. Glaze, *Mental Health Problems of Prison and Jail Inmates,* Bureau of Justice Statistics Special Report NCJ 213600 (Washington, DC: U.S. Department of Justice, September 2006), http://www.bjs.gov/content/pub/pdf/mhppji.pdf.

Chapter 15

1. Gabe Gutierrez, Adam Reiss, and Corky Siemaszko, "Welcome to Williamson, W.Va., Where There Are 6,500 Opioid Pills per Person," *NBC News*, February 1, 2018, https://www.nbcnews.com/news/us-news/welcome-williamson-w-va-where-there-are-6-500-opioid-n843821.

2. Max Blau, "STAT Forecast: Opioids Could Kill Nearly 500,000 Americans in the Next Decade," *STAT News*, June 27, 2017, https://www.statnews.com/2017/06/27/opioid-deaths-forecast/.

3. Scott Gottlieb, "In Search of More Rational Prescribing," U.S. Food and Drug Administration, April 4, 2018, https://www.fda.gov/NewsEvents/Speeches/ucm603651.htm.

4. "U.S. Opioid Prescribing Rate Maps," Centers for Disease Control and Prevention, October 3, 2018, https://www.cdc.gov/drugoverdose/maps/rxrate-maps.html.

5. Quoted in Adam Beam, "Kentucky Drug Overdose Deaths Jump 11.5 Percent in 2017," Associated Press, July 25, 2018, https://abc6onyourside.com/news/local/kentucky-drug-overdose-deaths-jump-115-percent-in-2017-07-26-2018-102610870.

6. Mattie Quinn, "Is America Talking about Opioids the Wrong Way?," *Governing*, July 2017, http://www.governing.com/topics/health-human-services/gov-opioid-epidemic-conversation-countries.html.

7. Quoted in Margot Sanger-Katz, "A Big Divergence Is Coming in Health Care among States," *New York*

Times, February 28, 2018, https://www.nytimes.com/ 2018/02/28/upshot/health-care-obamacare-states-divergence.html.

8. Quoted in Alan Greenblatt, "Can Tough Love Help Reduce Poverty?," *Governing*, November 2013, http:// www.governing.com/topics/health-human-services/ gov-can-tough-love-help-reduce-poverty.html.

9. "State Expenditure Report," National Association of State Budget Officers, November 16, 2017, https://higherlogicdownload.s3.amazonaws.com/ NASBO/9d2d2db1-c943-4f1b-b750-0fca152d64c2/ UploadedImages/SER%20Archive/State_Expenditure_ Report__Fiscal_2015-2017_-S.pdf.

10. Matt McKillop and Jessica Carges, "More Than 17 Cents of Each State Revenue Dollar Goes to Medicaid," Pew Charitable Trusts, June 20, 2018, http://www.pewtrusts .org/research-and-analysis/articles/2018/06/20/more-than-17-cents-of-each-state-revenue-dollar-goes-to-medicaid.

11. Ashley Kirzinger, Bryan Wu, and Mollyann Brodie, "Kaiser Health Tracking Poll—February 2018: Health Care and the 2018 Midterms, Attitudes towards Proposed Changes to Medicaid," Kaiser Family Foundation, March 1, 2018, https://www.kff.org/ health-reform/poll-finding/kaiser-health-tracking-poll-february-2018-health-care-2018-midterms-proposed-changes-to-medicaid/.

12. Quoted in Jonathan Martin and Alexander Burns, "Governors from Both Parties Denounce Senate Obamacare Repeal Bill," *New York Times*, July 14, 2017, https://www.nytimes.com/2017/07/14/us/politics/ governors-oppose-senate-affordable-care-act-repeal .html.

13. Quoted in Robert Pear, "New Trump Rule Rolls Back Protections of the Affordable Care Act," *New York Times*, June 19, 2018, https://www.nytimes.com/2018/06/19/ us/politics/trump-affordable-care-act-health-insur ance.html.

14. Centers for Medicare and Medicaid Services, "NHE Fact Sheet," July 15, 2016, https://www.cms.gov/research-statistics-data-and-systems/statistics-trends-and-reports/nationalhealthexpenddata/nhe-fact-sheet.html.

15. Quoted in Patrick Marley, "Wisconsin Loses $206 Million by Not Fully Expanding BadgerCare," *Milwaukee Journal Sentinel*, August 17, 2014, http:// www.jsonline.com/news/statepolitics/wisconsin-loses-206-million-by-not-fully-expanding-badgercare-b99331674z1-271552321.html.

16. Mark Hall, "Do States Regret Expanding Medicaid?," Brookings Institution, March 26, 2018, https:// www.brookings.edu/blog/usc-brookings-schaeffer-on-health-policy/2018/03/26/do-states-regret-expanding-medicaid/.

17. Chris Kardish, "Uncompensated Care Dropping Fast in Medicaid Expansion States," *Governing*, June 17, 2014, http://www.governing.com/topics/health-human-ser vices/gov-uncompensated-care-dropping-fast.html.

18. U.S. Department of Health and Human Services, "Health Insurance Coverage and the Affordable Care Act, 2010–2016," March 3, 2016, https://aspe.hhs.gov/ pdf-report/health-insurance-coverage-and-affordable-care-act-2010-2016.

19. David Blumenthal and Sara R. Collins, "Health Care Coverage under the Affordable Care Act—A Progress Report," *New England Journal of Medicine* 371 (2014): 275–281.

20. Quoted in Tony Pugh, "States That Decline to Expand Medicaid Give Up Billions in Aid," *McClatchyDC*, September 2, 2014, https://www.mcclatchydc.com/ news/nation-world/national/article24772552.html.

21. Robert Pear, "Health Care Law Will Let States Tailor Benefits," *New York Times*, December 16, 2011, http:// www.nytimes.com/2011/12/17/health/policy/health-care-law-to-allow-states-to-pick-benefits.html?_r=2&.

22. Kaiser Family Foundation, "Establishing Health Insurance Exchanges: An Overview of State Efforts," May 2, 2013, http://kff.org/health-reform/issue-brief/ establishing-health-insurance-exchanges-an-overview-of.

23. Quoted in Adam Liptak, "Supreme Court Allows Nationwide Health Care Subsidies," *New York Times*, June 25, 2015, http://www.nytimes.com/2015/06/26/ us/obamacare-supreme-court.html.

24. Christine Vestal, "States Push to Contain Health Costs," *Stateline*, June 15, 2012, https://www.pewtrusts.org/ en/research-and-analysis/blogs/stateline/2012/06/15/ states-push-to-contain-health-costs.

25. Christine Vestal, "In California, Adult Day Care Program Is Threatened with Extinction," *Stateline*, June 10, 2011, http://www.pewstates.org/projects/stateline/ headlines/in-california-adult-day-care-program-is-threatened-with-extinction-85899376889.

26. Christine Vestal, "For Some States, Medicaid Expansion May Be a Tough Fiscal Call," *Stateline*, July 11, 2012, http://www.pewstates.org/projects/stateline/head-lines/for-some-states-medicaid-expansion-may-be-a-tough-fiscal-call-85899404110.

27. Kil Huh and Sarah Babbage, "Long-Term Obligations Vary as a Share of State Resources," Pew Charitable Trusts, May 17, 2016, http://www.pewtrusts.org/en/ research-and-analysis/analysis/2016/05/17/long-term-obligations-vary-as-a-share-of-state-resources.

28. Quoted in Stephen C. Fehr, "West Virginia Tackles Retiree Health Costs," *Stateline*, March 13, 2012, https://www.pewtrusts.org/en/research-and-analysis/ blogs/stateline/2012/03/13/west-virginia-tackles-retiree-health-costs.

29. Mac Taylor, "Providing Constitutional and Cost-Effective Inmate Medical Care," California Legislative Analyst's Office, April 19, 2012, http://www.lao.ca.gov/reports/2012/crim/inmate-medical-care/inmate-medical-care-041912.pdf.

30. Ayla Ellison, "State-by-State Breakdown of 83 Rural Hospital Closures," Becker's Hospital CEO Report, January 26, 2018, https://www.beckershospitalreview.com/finance/state-by-state-breakdown-of-83-rural-hospital-closures.html.

31. Quoted in Guy Gugliotta, "Rural Hospitals, Beset by Financial Problems, Struggle to Survive," *Washington Post*, March 15, 2015, https://www.washingtonpost.com/national/health-science/rural-hospitals-beset-by-financial-problems-struggle-to-survive/2015/03/15/d81af3ac-c9b2-11e4-b2a1-bed1aaea2816_story.html.

32. Quoted in Tony Pugh, "An N.C. Mayor Treks 273 Miles to Help Rural Hospitals," *McClatchyDC*, July 28, 2014, https://www.mcclatchydc.com/news/nation-world/national/article24771118.html.

33. Gabriel Loiacono, "Government Paid for Poor Citizens' Health Care Some 300 Years before Obamacare," *Atlantic*, April 2, 2017, https://www.theatlantic.com/politics/archive/2017/04/history-health-care-america-obamacare-aca/521541/.

34. Paul Starr, *The Social Transformation of American Medicine* (New York: Basic Books, 1992), 149.

35. Ibid., 72.

36. Ibid.

37. Ibid.

38. NYU Langone Medical Center, "Bellevue Hospital," https://med.nyu.edu/emergency/patient-care/bellevue-hospital.

39. Samuel Gompers, the head of the AFL, viewed compulsory health insurance as "paternalistic" and worried that it might weaken the labor movement by causing workers to look to employers instead of to unions for benefits. Starr, *Social Transformation of American Medicine*, 254–255.

40. "Stocks Collapse in 16,410,030-Share Day, but Rally at Close Cheers Brokers," *New York Times*, October 30, 1929.

41. Scholars such as Theda Skocpol have argued that the federal government's first major foray into safety net programs actually came much earlier, in the form of lavish pensions for Union veterans of the Civil War. Theda Skocpol, "America's First Social Security System: The Expansion of Benefits for Civil War Veterans," *Political Science Quarterly* 108 (Spring 1993): 85–86.

42. "Social Security," in *Columbia Encyclopedia*, 6th ed. (New York: Columbia University Press, 2001).

43. Jay Bhattacharya and Darius Lakdawalla, "Does Medicare Benefit the Poor? New Answers to an Old Question," Working Paper 9280, National Bureau of Economic Research, Cambridge, MA, October 2002.

44. Kaiser Family Foundation, "Federal and State Share of Medicaid Spending," 2014, http://kff.org/medicaid/state-indicator/federalstate-share-of-spending.

45. Center for Budget and Policy Priorities, "Policy Basics: Introduction to Medicaid," updated May 8, 2013, http://www.cbpp.org/cms/index.cfm?fa=view&id=2223.

46. All Medicaid eligibility figures are from Centers for Medicare and Medicaid Services, "Medicaid and CHIP Eligibility Levels," April 1, 2018, https://www.medicaid.gov/medicaid/program-information/medicaid-and-chip-eligibility-levels/index.html.

47. John Klemm, "Medicaid Spending: A Brief History," *Health Care Financing Review* 22, no. 1 (2000). For more recent data, see the Kaiser Family Foundation's State Health Facts website, http://www.statehealthfacts.org.

48. By 1983, the number of single mothers had fallen back to about 50 percent of AFDC recipients. By 1992, that number had crept back up to 55 percent. National Research Council, *Evaluating Welfare Reform in an Era of Transition*, ed. Robert A. Moffitt and Michele Ver Ploeg (Washington, DC: National Press, 2001), 17.

49. Steven Roberts, "Food Stamps Program: How It Grew and How Reagan Wants to Cut It Back," *New York Times*, April 4, 1981.

50. Quoted in Lou Cannon, *Governor Reagan: His Rise to Power* (New York: Public Affairs, 2003), 349. Of course, Roosevelt made this statement to argue for government-funded work programs—a measure that Reagan never supported as president.

51. Andy Schneider, *Medicaid Resource Book* (Washington, DC: Kaiser Commission on Medicaid and the Uninsured, July 2002), 97–98.

52. "Public Officials of the Year: Leading in Good Times and in Bad," *Governing*, December 1997.

53. Charles Mahtesian, "Captains of Conservatism," *Governing*, February 1995.

54. National Research Council, *Evaluating Welfare Reform*, 19.

55. Pamela M. Prah, "Why Are Welfare Rolls Flat, While the Food Stamp Program Grows Rapidly?," *Stateline*, July 2, 2012, http://www.pewtrusts.org/en/research-and-analysis/blogs/stateline/2012/07/02/why-are-welfare-rolls-flat-while-the-food-stamp-program-grows-rapidly.

56. For a comprehensive account of this health care debate, see Haynes Johnson and David Broder, *The System: The Way of American Politics at the Breaking Point* (Boston: Little, Brown, 1996).

57. Ibid.

58. U.S. Census Bureau, "Income, Poverty and Health Insurance Coverage in the United States: 2011," September 12, 2012, http://www.census.gov/newsroom/releases/archives/income_wealth/cb12-172.html.

59. Kaiser Commission on Medicaid and the Uninsured, "The Uninsured: A Primer—Key Facts about Health Insurance on the Eve of Coverage Expansions," October 23, 2013, https://kaiserfamilyfoundation.files .wordpress.com/2013/10/7451-09-the-uninsured-a-primer-key-facts-about-health-insurance.pdf.

60. Christopher Swope, "The Medicaid Windfall: Enjoy It While It Lasts," *Governing*, September 1998.

61. Medicaid expenditures grew at an annual rate of 27.1 percent from 1990 to 1992. Kaiser Commission on Medicaid and the Uninsured/Alliance for Health Care Reform, "Medicaid 101 Briefing Charts," February 28, 2003.

62. Kaiser Commission on Medicaid and the Uninsured, "Enrolling Uninsured Low-Income Children in Medicaid and SCHIP," May 2002.

63. National Conference of State Legislatures, "NCSL Resources—SCHIP General Information," 2009.

64. John Holahan and Brenda Spillman, *Health Care Access for Uninsured Adults: A Strong Safety Net Is Not the Same as Insurance*, Policy Brief No. B-42 (Washington, DC: Urban Institute, January 2002), http://www.urban.org/ sites/default/files/alfresco/publication-pdfs/310414-Health-Care-Access-for-Uninsured-Adults.PDF.

65. Benjamin D. Sommers, Katherine Baicker, and Arnold M. Epstein, "Mortality and Access to Care among Adults after State Medicaid Expansions," *New England Journal of Medicine* 367 (2012): 1025–1034. Also see Amy Finkelstein, Sarah Taubman, Bill Wright, Mira Bernstein, Jonathan Gruber, Joseph P. Newhouse, Heidi Allen, and Katherine Baicker, "The Oregon Health Insurance Experiment: Evidence from the First Year," National Bureau of Economic Research, Working Paper 17190, July 2011, http://www.nber.org/papers/ w17190.pdf.

66. National Association of Community Health Centers, "Health Centers at a Glance: Research Snapshots and Infographics," 2013.

67. Teresa A. Coughlin, John Holahan, Kyle Caswell, and Megan McGrath, "Uncompensated Care for the Uninsured in 2013: A Detailed Examination," Kaiser Family Foundation, May 30, 2014, http://kff.org/unin sured/report/uncompensated-care-for-the-uninsured-in-2013-a-detailed-examination.

68. Obaid S. Zaman, Linda C. Cummings, and Sari Siegel Spieler, *America's Public Hospitals and Health Systems, 2008* (Washington, DC: National Public Health and Hospital Institute, 2010).

69. Katherine Vogt, "Public Hospitals Seen Slipping Away, Changing into Other Entities," *American Medical News*, September 12, 2005.

70. Kevin Sack, "Immigrants Cling to Fragile Lifeline at Safety-Net Hospital," *New York Times*, September 24, 2009, A16.

71. Melody Peterson and Noam N. Levey, "California Obamacare Rates to Rise 13% in 2017, More Than Three Times the Increase of Last Two Years," *Los Angeles Times*, July 19, 2016, http://www.latimes.com/business/la-fi-covered-california-rates-20160718-snap-story.html.

72. Quoted in David Westphal, Emily Bazar, John Gonzales, Richard Kipling, Deborah Schoch, and Lauren M. Whaley, "California Faces Headwinds in Easing Doctor Shortages," Center for Health Reporting, California Healthcare Foundation, June 29, 2012, http://centerforhealthreporting.org/article/ california-faces-headwinds-easing-doctor-shortages.

73. Agency for Healthcare Research and Quality, "Challenges Facing Rural Health Care," U.S. Department of Health and Human Services, November 7, 2012, https://innovations.ahrq.gov/perspectives/ challenges-facing-rural-health-care?id=3752.

74. Quoted in Chris Kardish, "Missouri's Unprecedented Push to Ease the Doctor Shortage," *Governing*, July 22, 2014, http://www.governing.com/topics/health-human-services/gov-missouri-medical-residency-law.html.

75. Kaiser Family Foundation, "Total Medicaid Managed Care Enrollment," https://www.kff.org/medicaid/ state-indicator/total-medicaid-mc-enrollment/?curren tTimeframe=0&sortModel=%7B%22colId%22:%22Loc ation%22,%22sort%22:%22asc%22%7D.

76. Christine Vestal, "Accountable Care Explained: An Experiment in State Health Policy," *Stateline*, October 11, 2012, http://www.pewstates.org/projects/stateline/ headlines/accountable-care-explained-an-experiment-in-state-health-policy-85899422676.

77. Quoted in John Buntin, "Coordinating More Care in Oregon," *Governing*, August 23, 2011, http://www .governing.com/topics/health-human-services/ coordinating-more-care-oregon.html.

78. Quoted in John Buntin, "What Experts Think of Five Medicaid-Savings Strategies," *Governing*, August 31, 2011, http://www.governing.com/topics/health-human-services/what-experts-think-five-medicaid-sav ings-strategies.html.

79. Quoted in Chris Kardish, "How Can States Fix Their Medicaid Programs?," *Governing*, September 2014, http://www.governing.com/topics/health-human-ser vices/gov-states-fix-medicaid.html.

80. Katherine Barrett, Richard Greene, and Michele Mariani, "Insurance Coverage: Access Denied," *Governing*, February 2004; "Dirigo Agency Reaches Deal with Anthem to Extend DirigoChoice," Associated Press, September 22, 2006; Penelope Lemov, "Maine's Medical Gamble," *Governing*, November 2004.

81. Debra J. Lipson, James M. Verdier, and Lynn Quincy, "Leading the Way? Maine's Initial Experience in Expanding Coverage through Dirigo Health Reforms,"

Mathematica Policy Research, December 2007, http://www.mathematica-mpr.com/~/media/publications/PDFs/dirigooverview.pdf.

82. "No Maine Miracle Cure," *Wall Street Journal*, August 20, 2009, http://online.wsj.com/article/SB10001424052970204619004574322401816501182.html.

83. Sharon Anglin Treat, "Competing Lessons from Maine's Health Insurance Plan," *Wall Street Journal*, August 25, 2009, A14.

84. Anna C. Spencer, "Massachusetts Going for Full Coverage," *State Health Notes*, April 17, 2006.

85. Richard Wolf, "Mass. Has Lessons for Health Care Debate," *USA Today*, July 23, 2009.

86. Christine Vestal, "Massachusetts Tackles Health Costs," *Stateline*, August 16, 2012, http://www.pewstates.org/projects/stateline/headlines/massachusetts-tackles-health-costs-85899411644.

87. Kaiser Family Foundation, "Distribution of Medicaid Enrollees by Enrollment Group, FY2014," http://kff.org/medicaid/state-indicator/distribution-by-enrollment-group; Kaiser Family Foundation, "Distribution of Medicaid Payments by Enrollment Group, FY2011," http://kff.org/medicaid/state-indicator/payments-by-enrollment-group.

88. Lauren Harris-Kojetin et al., "Long-Term Care Providers and Services Users in the United States: Data from the National Study of Long-Term Care Providers, 2013–2014," National Center for Health Statistics, *Vital and Health Statistics* series 3, no. 38 (February 2016), http://www.cdc.gov/nchs/data/series/sr_03/sr03_038.pdf.

89. Christine Vestal, "Hope for the Long Term," *Stateline*, April 15, 2010, http://www.pewtrusts.org/en/research-and-analysis/blogs/stateline/2010/04/15/hope-for-the-long-term.

90. Jennifer M. Ortman, Victoria A. Velkoff, and Howard Hogan, *An Aging Nation: The Older Population in the United States*, Current Population Reports P25-1140 (Washington, DC: U.S. Census Bureau, May 2014), https://www.census.gov/prod/2014pubs/p25-1140.pdf.

91. Kaiser Commission on Medicaid and the Uninsured, "Medicaid and Long-Term Care Services and Supports," June 2012, https://kaiserfamilyfoundation.files.wordpress.com/2013/01/2186-09.pdf.

92. See, for example, William Galston, "Live Long and Pay for It: America's Real Long-Term Cost Crisis," *Atlantic*, September 12, 2012, http://www.theatlantic.com/business/archive/2012/09/live-long-and-pay-for-it-americas-real-long-term-cost-crisis/262247.

93. Vestal, "Hope for the Long Term."

94. Celine Gounder, "Zika Is a Warning to the US Public Health System to Stop Rushing from Fire to Fire," *Quartz*, April 18, 2016, http://qz.com/664283/zika-is-a-warning-to-the-us-public-health-system-to-stop-rushing-from-fire-to-fire.

95. John Barry, *The Great Influenza: The Epic Story of the Deadliest Plague in History* (New York: Viking Penguin, 2004).

96. Quoted in Sharon Begley and Yasmeen Abutaleb, "Cities, States Scramble after Dallas's Ebola Missteps Expose Planning Gaps," Reuters, October 11, 2014, http://www.reuters.com/article/2014/10/11/us-health-ebola-planning-idUSKCN0I00CT20141011.

97. Centers for Disease Control and Prevention, "Tobacco-Related Mortality," last updated August 18, 2015, http://www.cdc.gov/tobacco/data_statistics/fact_sheets/health_effects/tobacco_related_mortality.

98. Victor J. Dzau and Alan I. Leshner, "Public Health Research on Gun Violence: Long Overdue," *Annals of Internal Medicine*, June 19, 2018, http://annals.org/aim/fullarticle/2675740/public-health-research-gun-violence-long-overdue.

99. Jane Brody, "Abstinence-Only: Does It Work?," *New York Times*, June 1, 2004; Nicholas Kristof, "Shaming Young Mothers," *New York Times*, August 23, 2002.

100. Erik W. Robelen, "Program Promoting Sexual Abstinence Gets Resurrected; Instructional Approach Winds Up in Health-Care Law," *Education Week*, April 7, 2010, 6.

101. Faye Flam, "Study Offers Nuanced View of Abstinence Education: Penn's Sex-Education Study," *McClatchy-Tribune Business News*, February 16, 2010.

102. Brady E. Hamilton and Stephanie J. Ventura, "Birth Rates for U.S. Teenagers Reach Historic Lows for All Age and Ethnic Groups," Centers for Disease Control and Prevention, NCHS Data Brief No. 89, April 2012, http://www.cdc.gov/nchs/data/databriefs/db89.pdf.

103. "Insurance Coverage of Contraceptives," Guttmacher Institute, October 1, 2018, https://www.guttmacher.org/state-policy/explore/insurance-coverage-contraceptives.

104. Helene Cooper and Laurie Goodstein, "Rule Shift on Birth Control Is Concession to Obama Allies," *New York Times*, February 10, 2012, http://www.nytimes.com/2012/02/11/health/policy/obama-to-offer-accommodation-on-birth-control-rule-officials-say.html?_r=2&pagewanted=all&.

105. Jessica Arons and Elizabeth Rich, "State Efforts to Reject Contraceptive Coverage Laws on Religious Grounds," Center for American Progress, July 30, 2012, http://www.americanprogress.org/wp-content/uploads/issues/2012/07/pdf/state_contraception.pdf.

106. Cynthia Ogden and Margaret Carroll, "Prevalence of Obesity among Children and Adolescents: United States, Trends 1963–1965 through 2007–2008," Centers for Disease Control and Prevention, June 2010, http://www.cdc.gov/nchs/data/hestat/obesity_child_07_08/obesity_child_07_08.pdf.

107. Todd Zwillich, "CDC: Obesity Is Still an Epidemic," WebMD, June 2, 2005, http://www.webmd.com/diet/news/20050602/cdc-obesity-is-still-epidemic.

108. Centers for Disease Control and Prevention, "Adult Obesity Causes & Consequences," last updated March 5, 2018, https://www.cdc.gov/obesity/adult/causes.html.

109. United Health Foundation, American Public Health Association, and Partnership for Prevention, "The Future Costs of Obesity: National and State Estimates of the Impact of Obesity on Direct Health Care Expenses," November 2009, http://www.nccor.org/downloads/CostofObesityReport-FINAL.pdf.

110. Anemona Hartocoolis, "Calorie Postings Don't Change Habits, Study Finds," New York Times, October 6, 2009, http://www.nytimes.com/2009/10/06/nyregion/06calories.html?_r=1&.

111. Quoted in Josh Goodman, "Spread of Soda Taxes Fizzles," Stateline, February 14, 2012, https://www.pewtrusts.org/research-and-analysis/blogs/stateline/2012/02/14/spread-of-soda-taxes-fizzles.

112. Dan Charles, "Berkeley's Soda Tax Appears to Cut Consumption of Sugary Drinks," NPR, August 23, 2016, http://www.npr.org/sections/thesalt/2016/08/23/491104093/berkeleys-soda-tax-appears-to-cut-consumption-of-sugary-drinks.

Chapter 16

1. Interview with Jeff Hays, July 9, 2018.

2. Interview with Lori Vienneau, July 11, 2018.

3. Rick Perry, "Energy Secretary Rick Perry: 'True Energy Independence Is Finally within Our Grasp,'" CNBC, July 29, 2018, https://www.cnbc.com/2018/07/29/energy-secretary-perry-true-energy-independence-is-finally-within-ou.html.

4. Quoted in Ben Rhodes, The World as It Is: A Memoir of the Obama White House (New York: Random House, 2018), xv.

5. Quoted in Jennifer Medina, "Climate Issues Moved to Fore in California by Governor," New York Times, May 20, 2014, A12.

6. "EPA Administrator Pruitt: GHG Emissions Standards for Cars and Light Trucks Should Be Revised," Environmental Protection Agency, April 2, 2018, https://www.epa.gov/newsreleases/epa-administrator-pruitt-ghg-emissions-standards-cars-and-light-trucks-should-be.

7. Juliet Eilperin and Brady Dennis, "Court Freezes Clean Power Plan Lawsuit, Signaling Likely End to Obama's Signature Climate Policy," Washington Post, April 28, 2017, https://www.washingtonpost.com/news/energy-environment/wp/2017/04/28/court-freezes-clean-power-plan-lawsuit-signaling-likely-end-to-obamas-signature-climate-policy/?utm_term=.16a1c354d066.

8. "Statement by President Trump on the Paris Climate Accord," White House, June 1, 2017, https://www.whitehouse.gov/briefings-statements/statement-president-trump-paris-climate-accord/.

9. Quoted in Pallab Ghosh, "Hawking Says Trump's Climate Stance Could Damage Earth," BBC News, July 2, 2017, https://www.bbc.co.uk/news/science-environment-40461726.

10. "Global Warming of 1.5 C," Intergovernmental Panel on Climate Change, October 8, 2018, http://www.ipcc.ch/report/sr15/.

11. "Presidential Executive Order on Establishing Discipline and Accountability in the Environmental Review and Permitting Process for Infrastructure," White House, August 15, 2017, https://www.whitehouse.gov/presidential-actions/presidential-executive-order-establishing-discipline-accountability-environmental-review-permitting-process-infrastructure/.

12. "Washington Gov. Jay Inslee Pushes Nation's First Carbon Tax," Here and Now, January 29, 2018, http://www.wbur.org/hereandnow/2018/01/29/washington-jay-inslee-carbon-tax.

13. Quoted in Christopher Swope, "Rising Seas," CQ Researcher, February 16, 2018.

14. Michael P. Hall, Neil A. Lewis Jr., and Phoebe C. Ellsworth, "Believing in Climate Change, but Not Behaving Sustainably: Evidence from a One-Year Longitudinal Study," Journal of Environmental Psychology 56 (2018): 55–62.

15. Megan Brenan and Lydia Saad, "Global Warming Concern Steady Despite Some Partisan Shifts," Gallup, March 28, 2018, https://news.gallup.com/poll/231530/global-warming-concern-steady-despite-partisan-shifts.aspx.

16. "The Partisan Divide on Political Values Grows Even Wider," Pew Research Center, October 5, 2017, http://www.people-press.org/2017/10/05/the-partisan-divide-on-political-values-grows-even-wider/.

17. Phone interview with Jim DiPeso, March 23, 2010.

18. Quoted in Alan Greenblatt, "How Republicans Learned to Reject Climate Change," NPR, March 25, 2010, http://www.npr.org/templates/story/story.php?storyId=125075282.

19. Quoted in William March, "Rubio Questions Climate Change," Tampa Tribune, February 13, 2010, 7.

20. Steven Mufson, "GOP Platform, Which Calls Coal 'Clean,' Would Reverse Decades of U.S. Energy and Climate Policy," Washington Post, July 19, 2016, https://www.washingtonpost.com/news/energy-environment/wp/2016/07/19/gop-platform-which-calls-coal-clean-would-utterly-reverse-decades-of-u-s-energy-and-climate-policy.

21. Phone interview with DiPeso.

22. Phone interview with Daniel J. Weiss, March 19, 2010.

23. Ibid.

24. Steven Koff, "Group Raises Questions about Ohio Attorney General Mike DeWine's Connection to Polluting Industries," *Plain Dealer*, June 2, 2016, http://www.cleveland.com/open/index.ssf/2016/06/liberal_group_says_mike_dewine.html.

25. Craig Richardson, "The Biggest Loser in the 2016 Election? Tom Steyer," *Investor's Business Daily*, November 14, 2016, https://www.investors.com/politics/commentary/the-biggest-loser-in-the-2016-election-tom-steyer/.

26. Marc Allen Eisner, *Governing the Environment: The Transformation of Environmental Regulation* (Boulder, CO: Lynne Rienner, 2007), 1.

27. Phone interview with John Cahill, December 5, 2008.

28. Barry G. Rabe, *Statehouse and Greenhouse: The Emerging Politics of American Climate Change Policy* (Washington, DC: Brookings Institution Press, 2004), xiv.

29. Quoted in ibid., 77.

30. Chris Megerian and Liam Dillon, "Gov. Brown Signs Sweeping Legislation to Combat Climate Change," *Los Angeles Times*, September 8, 2016, http://www.latimes.com/politics/la-pol-ca-jerry-brown-signs-climate-laws-20160908-snap-story.html.

31. Alan Greenblatt, "Fran Pavley: Legislative Prodigy," *Governing*, September 2002, 80.

32. Quoted in ibid.

33. Phone interview with Fran Pavley, September 3, 2002.

34. Phone interview with Stanley Young, November 21, 2008.

35. Quoted in Linda Greenhouse, "Justices Say EPA Has Power to Act on Harmful Gases," *New York Times*, April 8, 2007, A1.

36. Quoted in John M. Broder and Felicity Barringer, "EPA Says 17 States Can't Set Greenhouse Gas Rules for Cars," *New York Times*, December 20, 2007, A1.

37. Phone interview with Ron Burke, November 20, 2008.

38. John M. Broder, "Limits Set on Pollution from Autos," *New York Times*, April 2, 2010, B1.

39. "California Greening," *The Economist*, November 24, 2012, 36.

40. Chris Megerian and Ralph Vartabedian, "California's Cap-and-Trade Program Faces Daunting Hurdles to Avoid Collapse," *Los Angeles Times*, June 14, 2016, http://www.latimes.com/politics/la-pol-sac-climate-change-challenges-20160614-snap-story.html.

41. Phone interview with C. Boyden Gray, April 5, 2010.

42. Quoted in J. B. Wogan, "Mayors Group Scraps Cap-and-Trade Support," *Governing*, July 8, 2014, http://www.governing.com/topics/transportation-infrastructure/gov-mayors-group-scraps-cap-and-trade-in-new-climate-plan.html.

43. Quoted in Brian Dowling, "New England Leading the Way in Capping Carbon Emissions," *Hartford Courant*, June 3, 2014, A1.

44. Quoted in Neela Banerjee, "12 States Sue the EPA over Proposed Power Plant Regulations," *Los Angeles Times*, August 4, 2014, http://www.latimes.com/business/la-fi-epa-lawsuit-20140805-story.html.

45. Quoted in Alex Roarty, "Republicans Are Talking Differently about Climate Change," *National Journal*, June 18, 2014, http://www.nationaljournal.com/politics/republicans-are-talking-differently-about-climate-change-20140618.

46. "Assessing the U.S. Climate in 2017," National Oceanic and Atmospheric Administration, January 5, 2018, https://www.ncei.noaa.gov/news/national-climate-201712.

47. Quoted in "Extreme Heat and Wildfires Made Worse by Climate Change, Say Scientists," Associated Press, July 28, 2018, https://www.nbcnews.com/news/weather/extreme-heat-wildfires-worsened-climate-change-say-scientists-n895496.

48. Coral Davenport and Campbell Robertson, "Resettling the First American 'Climate Refugees,'" *New York Times*, May 3, 2016, http://www.nytimes.com/2016/05/03/us/resettling-the-first-american-climate-refugees.html.

49. Kevin Sack and John Schwartz, "Left to Louisiana's Tides, a Village Fights for Time," *New York Times*, February 24, 2018, https://www.nytimes.com/interactive/2018/02/24/us/jean-lafitte-floodwaters.html.

50. Seth Borenstein, "NOAA: Global Warming Increased Odds for Louisiana Downpour," Associated Press, September 7, 2016, https://www.usnews.com/news/news/articles/2016-09-07/noaa-global-warming-increased-odds-for-louisiana-downpour.

51. Office of the Deputy Under Secretary of Defense for Installations and Environment, *2014 Climate Change Adaptation Roadmap* (Alexandria, VA: U.S. Department of Defense, June 2014), https://www.acq.osd.mil/eie/downloads/CCARprint_wForward_e.pdf.

52. Quoted in Dan Vock, "A Climate of Change," *Governing*, September 2014, 28.

53. Phone interview with Jessica Shipley, November 18, 2009.

54. Phone interview with Barry Rabe, December 8, 2008.

55. Jeremy B. White, "Oil Industry's Spending Surged as It Fought California Climate Bill," *Sacramento Bee*, November 2, 2015, http://www.sacbee.com/news/politics-government/capitol-alert/article42348678.html.

56. George Skelton, "With New Climate Legislation, Gov. Brown Gets Even with the Oil Industry," *Los Angeles Times*, August 25, 2016, http://www.latimes.com/politics/la-pol-sac-skelton-california-climate-change-legislation-20160825-snap-story.html.

57. Quoted in Samantha Young, "Schwarzenegger Opens Climate Summit with Obama," Associated Press, November 19, 2008.

58. Robert M. DeConto and David Pollard, "Contribution of Antarctica to Past and Future Sea-Level Rise," *Nature* 531 (March 31, 2016): 591–597.

59. Justin Gillis, "Seas Are Rising at Fastest Rate in Last 28 Centuries," *New York Times*, February 22, 2016, http://www.nytimes.com/2016/02/23/science/sea-level-rise-global-warming-climate-change.html.

60. Pope Francis, "Encyclical Letter of the Holy Father Francis on Care for Our Common Home," Vatican, May 24, 2015, http://w2.vatican.va/content/francesco/en/encyclicals/documents/papa-francesco_20150524_enciclica-laudato-si.html.

61. Quoted in Chelsea Waugaman, "Voltage Charge," *Governing*, November 2005, 76.

62. Quoted in Mannix Porterfield, "Manchin Wants Aggressive Renewable Energy Policy," (Beckley, WV) *Register-Herald*, October 20, 2008.

63. "Electric Power Monthly," U.S. Energy Information Administration, July 2018, https://www.eia.gov/electricity/monthly/current_month/epm.pdf.

64. Judy Pasternak, "Coal at Heart of Climate Battle," *Los Angeles Times*, April 14, 2008, A1.

65. Phone interview with Bob Eye, May 15, 2008.

66. Quoted in Alan Greenblatt, "Guarding the Greenhouse," *Governing*, July 2008, 21.

67. Steven Mufson, "The Coal Killer," *Washington Post*, November 25, 2012, G1.

68. Quoted in Ryan Holeywell, "North Dakota's Oil Boom Is a Blessing and a Curse," *Governing*, August 2011, http://www.governing.com/north-dakotas-oil-boom-blessing-curse.html.

69. Quoted in Jon Campbell, "Cuomo: Fracking Protesters Are 'Everywhere,'" *PressConnects*, September 10, 2014, http://www.pressconnects.com/story/news/local/new-york/2014/09/09/new-york-fracking-cuomo-protest/15351419.

70. Quoted in Alan Greenblatt, "Confronting Carbon," *Governing*, December 2008, 14.

71. Quoted in ibid.

72. Quoted in Alan Greenblatt, "Miami's Vision," *Governing*, November 2009, 15.

73. Mireya Navarro and Rachel Nuwer, "Resisted for Blocking the View, Dunes Prove They Blunt Storms," *New York Times*, December 4, 2012, A1.

74. Quoted in Alan Feuer, "Protecting the City, Before Next Time," *New York Times*, November 4, 2012, MB1.

75. Quoted in Alan Zarembo and Thomas H. Maugh II, "U.N. Says It's Time to Adapt to Warming," *Los Angeles Times*, November 17, 2007, A1.

76. Phone interview with Tom Adams, November 18, 2008.

77. Gregor Robertson, "Cities Can Lead on Climate Change to Build a More Resilient Future," World Bank, *Development in a Changing Climate* blog, September 15, 2014, http://blogs.worldbank.org/climatechange/cities-can-lead-climate-change-build-more-resilient-future.

78. Georgetown Climate Center, "State and Local Adaptation Plans," Georgetown Law, 2014, http://www.georgetownclimate.org/adaptation/state-and-local-plans.

79. Sheila Dillon, remarks at the Lincoln Institute of Land Policy, April 13, 2018.

80. Quoted in Medina, "Climate Issues Moved to Fore," A12.

81. "Climate Change in the Sierra Nevada: California's Water Future," UCLA Center for Climate Science, April 2018, https://www.ioes.ucla.edu/wp-content/uploads/UCLA-CCS-Climate-Change-Sierra-Nevada.pdf.

82. Quoted in Alan Greenblatt, "Confronting Warming," *CQ Researcher*, January 9, 2009, 10.

83. Anthony Faiola and Juliet Eilperin, "Dutch Defense against Climate Change: Adapt," *Washington Post*, December 6, 2009, A1.

84. Louise Bedsworth and Ellen Hanak, *Preparing California for a Changing Climate* (San Francisco: Public Policy Institute of California, November 2008), http://www.ppic.org/content/pubs/report/R_1108LBR.pdf.

85. Quoted in Christopher Swope, "Local Warming," *Governing*, December 2007, 25.

• Glossary •

Abstinence: Refraining from sexual activity, usually intercourse.

Accreditation: A certification process in which outside experts visit a school or college to evaluate whether it is meeting minimum quality standards.

Activist judge: A judge who is said to act as an independent policymaker by creatively interpreting a constitution or statute.

Adaptation: Taking steps to prepare for and deal with the effects of climate change.

Ad hoc federalism: The process of choosing a state-centered or nation-centered view of federalism on the basis of political or partisan convenience.

Affirmative action: A set of policies designed to help organizations recruit and promote employees who are members of disadvantaged groups.

Aid to Families with Dependent Children (AFDC): The original federal assistance program for women and their children, started under Roosevelt's New Deal.

Alternative dispute resolution (ADR): A way to end a disagreement by means other than litigation. It usually involves the appointment of a mediator to preside over a meeting between the parties.

Annexation: The legal incorporation of one jurisdiction or territory into another.

Appeal: A request to have a lower court's decision in a case reviewed by a higher court.

Appointment powers: A governor's ability to pick individuals to run state government, such as cabinet secretaries.

Apportionment: The allotting of districts according to population shifts. The number of congressional districts that a state has may be reapportioned every 10 years, following the national census.

Appropriations bills: Laws passed by legislatures authorizing the transfer of money to the executive branch.

Assigned counsel: Private lawyers selected by the courts to handle particular cases and paid from public funds.

At-large elections: Elections in which city or county voters vote for council or commission members from any part of the jurisdiction.

Back to basics: A movement against modern education "fads," advocating a return to an emphasis on traditional core subjects such as reading, writing, and arithmetic.

Balanced budget: A budget in which current expenditures are equal to or less than income.

Ballot initiatives: Processes through which voters directly convey instructions to the legislature, approve a law, or amend the constitution.

Bench trial: A trial in which no jury is present and the judge decides the facts as well as the law.

Bicameral legislatures: Legislatures made up of two chambers, typically a house of representatives, or assembly, and a senate.

Bill of Rights: The first 10 amendments to the U.S. Constitution, which set limits on the power of the federal government and set out the rights of individuals and the states.

Block grants: Federal grants-in-aid given for general policy areas that leave states and localities with wide discretion over how to spend the money within the designated policy area.

Bonds: Certificates that are evidence of debts on which the issuer promises to pay the holders a specified amount of interest for a specified length of time and to repay the loans on their maturity.

"Broken windows" policing: Policing that emphasizes maintaining public order, based on the theory that unattended disorder breeds crime.

Budget deficits or shortfalls: Cash shortages that result when the amount of money coming into the government falls below the amount being spent.

Budget process: The procedure by which state and local governments assess revenues and set budgets.

Bully pulpit: The platform from which a high-profile public official, such as governor or president, commands considerable public and media attention by virtue of holding office.

Bureaucracy: Public agencies and the programs and services they implement and manage.

Bureaucrats: Employees of public agencies.

Candidate-centered politics: Politics in which candidates promote themselves and their own campaigns rather than relying on party organizations.

Cap and trade: A system for limiting pollution by assigning allowances to polluters, who can sell their excess permits if they succeed in reducing their emissions.

Capital investments: Investments in infrastructure, such as roads.

Carbon dioxide: A naturally occurring gas, the prevalence of which is increased by the burning of fossil fuels.

Car-dependent living: A situation in which owning a car for transportation is a necessity; an outcome of low-density development.

Casework: The work undertaken by legislators and their staffs in response to requests for help from constituents.

Categorical grants: Federal grants-in-aid given for specific programs that leave states and localities with little discretion over how to spend the money.

Caucus: All the members of a party—Republican or Democrat—within a legislative chamber; also refers to meetings of members of a political party in a chamber.

Cause lobbyist: A person who works for an organization that tracks and promotes an issue—for example, environmental issues for the Sierra Club or gun ownership rights for the National Rifle Association.

Centralized federalism: The notion that the federal government should take the leading role in setting national policy, with state and local governments helping implement the policies.

Charter: A document that outlines the powers, organization, and responsibilities of a local government.

Charter schools: Public schools, often with unique themes, managed by teachers, principals, social workers, or nonprofit groups. The charter school movement was launched in the early 1990s.

Children's Health Insurance Program (CHIP): A joint federal–state program designed to expand health care coverage to children whose parents earn income above the poverty line but still are too poor to afford insurance.

Cities: Incorporated political jurisdictions formed to provide self-governance to particular localities.

City commission system: A form of municipal governance in which executive, legislative, and administrative powers are vested in elected city commissioners.

City council: A municipality's legislature.

City–county consolidation: The merger of separate local governments in an effort to reduce bureaucratic redundancy and service inefficiencies.

City manager: An official appointed to be the chief administrator of a municipality.

Civil cases: Legal cases that involve disputes between private parties.

Clean Air Act: The law, initially enacted in 1970, that provides authority for federal regulation of air pollution.

Climate change: A shift in global temperatures.

Closed primary: A nominating election in which only voters belonging to that party may participate. Only registered Democrats can vote in a closed Democratic primary, for example.

Coalition building: The assembly of an alliance of groups to pursue a common goal or interest.

Collective bargaining: A process in which representatives of labor and management meet to negotiate pay and benefits, job responsibilities, and working conditions.

Colonial charters: Legal documents drawn up by the British Crown that spelled out how the colonies were to be governed.

Commission–administrator system: A form of county governance in which executive and legislative powers reside with an elected commission, which hires a professional executive to manage the day-to-day operations of government.

Committee: A group of legislators who have the formal task of considering and writing bills in a particular issue area.

Common Core State Standards (CCSS): An education initiative that has created a uniform set of learning expectations in English and math for students at the end of each grade. Although participation is voluntary, most states have joined this initiative.

Common law: Law composed of judges' legal opinions that reflects community practices and evolves over time.

Common school: In a democratic society, a school in which children of all income levels attend at taxpayer expense.

Community, or restorative, justice movement: A movement that emphasizes nontraditional punishment, such as community service.

Community policing: An approach that emphasizes police officers forming relationships with neighborhood residents and engaging with them in collaborative problem solving.

Compact theory: The idea that the Constitution represents an agreement among sovereign states to form a common government.

Comparative method: A learning approach based on studying the differences and similarities among similar units of analysis (such as states).

Compromise: The result when there is no consensus on a policy change or spending amount but legislators find a central point on which a majority can agree.

Concurrent powers: Powers that both federal and state governments can exercise.

Confederacy: A voluntary association of independent, sovereign states or governments.

Constituent service: The work done by legislators to help residents in their voting districts.

Constitutional amendments: Proposals to change a constitution, typically enacted by a supermajority of the legislature or through a statewide referendum.

Constitutional convention: An assembly convened for the express purpose of amending or replacing a constitution.

Constitutional revision commissions: Expert committees formed to assess constitutions and suggest changes.

Contract attorneys: Private attorneys who enter into agreements with states, counties, or judicial districts to work on a fixed-fee basis per case or for a specific length of time.

Contracting out: Government hiring of private or nonprofit organizations to deliver public goods or services.

Contract lobbyists: Lobbyists who work for different causes for different clients, in the same way that a lawyer represents more than one client.

Cooperative federalism: The notion that it is impossible for state and national governments to have separate and distinct jurisdictions and that both levels of government must work together.

Council–executive system: A form of county governance in which legislative powers are vested in a county commission and executive powers are vested in an independently elected executive.

Council–manager system: A form of municipal governance in which the day-to-day administration of government is carried out by a professional administrator.

Counties: Geographical subdivisions of state government.

County commission system: A form of county governance in which executive, legislative, and administrative powers are vested in elected commissioners.

Court of first instance: The court in which a case is introduced and nothing has been determined yet.

Criminal cases: Legal cases brought by the state intending to punish violations of the law.

Crosscutting requirements: Constraints that apply to all federal grants.

Crossover sanctions: Federal requirements mandating that grant recipients pass and enforce certain laws or regulations as a condition of receiving funds.

Crossover voting: Voting by a member of one party in another party's primary. This practice is not allowed in all states.

Delegates: Legislators who primarily see their role as voting according to their constituents' beliefs as they understand them.

Departments of education: State-level agencies responsible for overseeing public education.

Determinate sentencing: The sentencing of an offender, by a judge, to a specific amount of time in prison depending on the crime.

Deterrence theory: A theory advanced by criminologists that harsh penalties will deter people from committing crimes.

Devolution: The process of taking power and responsibility away from the federal government and giving it to state and local governments.

Dillon's Rule: The legal principle that says local governments can exercise only the powers granted to them by state government.

Direct democracy: A system in which citizens make laws themselves rather than relying on elected representatives.

Direct lobbying: A form of lobbying in which lobbyists deal directly with legislators to gain their support.

Discretionary jurisdiction: The power of a court to decide whether or not to grant review of a case.

Discretionary spending: Spending controlled in annual appropriations acts.

Districts: The geographical areas represented by members of a legislature.

Dividend: A payment made to stockholders (or, in Alaska's case, residents) from the interest generated by an investment.

Drug courts: Special tribunals that offer nonviolent drug offenders a chance at reduced or dismissed charges in exchange for their undergoing treatment or other rehabilitation; an alternative forum for sentencing nonviolent drug offenders.

Dual constitutionalism: A system of government in which people live under two sovereign powers. In the United States, these are the government of their state of residence and the federal government.

Dual federalism: The idea that state and federal governments have separate and distinct jurisdictions and responsibilities.

Edgeless cities: Office and retail complexes without clear boundaries.

Electorate: The population of individuals who can vote.

Elementary and Secondary Education Act (ESEA): Federal law passed in 1965 as part of President Johnson's Great Society initiative; steered federal funds to improve local schools, particularly those attended primarily by low-income and minority students.

En banc: Appeals court sessions in which all the judges hear a case together.

Entitlement: A service that government must provide, regardless of the cost.

Entitlement program: A government-run program that guarantees unlimited assistance to those who meet its eligibility requirements, no matter how high the cost.

Enumerated powers: Grants of authority explicitly given by the Constitution.

Estate taxes: Taxes levied on a person's estate or total holdings after that person's death.

Excise or sin taxes: Taxes on alcohol, tobacco, and other similar products that are designed to raise revenues and reduce use.

Exclusive powers: Powers given by the Constitution solely to the federal government.

Executive orders: Rules or regulations with the force of law that governors can create directly under the statutory authority given them.

Expenditures: Money spent by government.

Exurbs: Municipalities in rural areas that ring suburbs. They typically serve as bedroom communities for the prosperous, providing rural homes with easy access to urban areas.

Factional splits or factions: Groups that struggle to control the message within a party; for example, a party may be split into competing regional factions.

Federalism: A political system in which national and regional governments share powers and are considered independent equals.

Felony: A serious crime, such as murder or arson.

Filibuster: A debate that under U.S. Senate rules can drag on, blocking final action on the bill under consideration and preventing other bills from being debated.

Fiscal federalism: The system by which federal grants are used to fund programs and services provided by state and local governments.

Fiscal year: The annual accounting period used by a government.

Focused consumption taxes: Taxes that do not alter spending habits or behavior patterns and therefore do not distort the distribution of resources.

Formal powers: The powers explicitly granted to a governor according to state law, such as being able to veto legislation and to appoint heads of state agencies.

Fourteenth Amendment: Constitutional amendment that prohibits states from depriving individuals of the rights and privileges of citizenship and requires states to provide due process and equal protection guarantees.

Fracking: A process in which water, sand, and chemicals are pumped into the ground to enable the extraction of natural gas and oil.

Franchise: The right to vote.

Full faith and credit clause: Constitutional clause that requires states to recognize each other's public records and acts as valid.

General act charters: Charters that grant powers, such as home rule, to all municipal governments within a state.

General elections: Decisive elections in which all registered voters cast ballots for their preferred candidates for a political office.

General equivalency diploma (GED) program: A program offering a series of tests that an individual can take to qualify for a high school equivalency certificate or diploma.

General jurisdiction trial courts: Courts that hear any civil or criminal cases that have not been assigned to a special court.

General obligation bonds: Investments secured by the taxing power of the jurisdiction that issues them.

General revenue sharing grants: Federal grants-in-aid given with few constraints, leaving states and localities almost complete discretion over how to spend the money.

General welfare clause: Constitutional clause that gives Congress an implied power through the authority to provide for the "general welfare."

Gentrification: The physical rehabilitation of urban areas, which attracts investment from developers and drives up property values.

Gerrymanders: Districts clearly drawn with the intent of pressing partisan advantage at the expense of other considerations.

Gift taxes: Taxes imposed on money transfers made during an individual's lifetime.

Global warming: Rising average temperatures worldwide.

Grand jury: A group of between 16 and 23 citizens who decide if a case should go to trial; if the grand jury decides that it should, an indictment is issued.

Grants-in-aid: Cash appropriations given by the federal government to the states.

Greenhouse gases: Emissions—primarily carbon dioxide but also other gases such as methane—that are believed to contribute to global warming.

Habitual offender laws: Statutes imposing harsher sentences on offenders who previously have been sentenced for crimes.

High-stakes standardized testing: Testing of elementary and secondary students in which poor results can mean either that students fail to be promoted or that the school loses its accreditation.

Home rule: The right of a locality to self-government, usually granted through a charter.

Homeschooling: The education of children in the home; a movement to grant waivers from state truancy laws to permit parents to teach their own children.

Impact fees: Fees that municipalities charge builders of new housing or commercial developments to help offset the costs of extending services.

Impeachment: A process by which the legislature can remove executive branch officials, such as the governor, or judges from office for corruption or other reasons.

Implied powers: Broad, but undefined, powers given to the federal government by the Constitution.

Income taxes: Taxes on wages and interest earned.

Incumbent: A person holding office.

Independent expenditures: Funds spent on ad campaigns or other political activities that are run by a party or an outside group without the direct knowledge or approval of a particular candidate for office.

Indeterminate sentencing: The sentencing of an offender, by a judge, to a minimum and a maximum amount of time in prison, with a parole board deciding how long the offender actually remains in prison.

Indictment: A formal criminal charge.

Indirect lobbying: A form of lobbying in which lobbyists build support for their cause through the media, rallies, and other ways of influencing public opinion, with the ultimate goal of swaying legislators to support their cause.

Individualistic culture: A political culture that views politics and government as just another way to achieve individual goals.

Informal powers: The things a governor is able to do, such as command media attention and persuade party members, based on personality or position, not on formal authority.

Insurance trust funds: Money collected from contributions, assessments, insurance premiums, and payroll taxes.

Intergovernmental transfers: Funds provided by the federal government to state governments and by state governments to local governments.

Interjurisdictional agreement (IJA): A formal or informal agreement between two or more local governments to cooperate on a program or policy.

Intermediate appellate court: A court that reviews court cases to find possible errors in their proceedings.

Interstate commerce clause: Constitutional clause that gives Congress the right to regulate interstate commerce. This clause has been broadly interpreted to give Congress a number of implied powers.

Jim Crow laws: Legislative measures passed in the last decade of the 19th century that sought to systematically separate blacks and whites.

Judicial federalism: The idea that the courts determine the boundaries of state–federal relations.

Judicial review: The power of courts to assess whether a law is in compliance with the constitution.

Jury nullification: A jury's returning a verdict of "not guilty" even though jurists believe the defendant is guilty. By doing so, the jury cancels out the effect of a law that the jurors believe is immoral or was wrongly applied to the defendant.

Kyoto Protocol: A 1997 international treaty that sought to reduce emissions of greenhouse gases.

Laboratories of democracy: A metaphor that emphasizes the states' ability to engage in different policy experiments without interference from the federal government.

Leapfrog development: Development practices in which new developments jump—or leapfrog—over established developments, leaving undeveloped or underdeveloped land between developed areas.

Legislative overcriminalization: The tendency of government to make a crime out of anything the public does not like.

Liability: A legal obligation or responsibility.

Limited or special jurisdiction trial courts: Courts that hear cases that are statutorily limited by either the degree of seriousness or the types of parties involved.

Line-item veto: The power to reject a portion of a bill while leaving the rest intact.

Local education agencies (LEAs): School districts, which may encompass cities, counties, or subsets thereof.

Logrolling: A practice in which a legislator gives a colleague a vote on a particular bill in return for that colleague's vote on another bill.

Low-density development: Development practices that spread (rather than concentrate) populations across the land.

Majority–minority districts: Districts in which members of a minority group, such as African Americans or Hispanics, make up a majority of the population or electorate.

Majority rule: The process in which the decision of a numerical majority is made binding on a group.

Malapportionment: A situation in which the principle of equal representation is violated.

Managed care: An arrangement for the provision of health care whereby an agency acts as an intermediary between consumers and health care providers.

Mandatory jurisdiction: The requirement that a court hear every case presented before it.

Mandatory minimum sentences: The shortest sentences offenders may receive upon conviction for certain offenses. The court has no authority to impose shorter sentences.

Mass incarceration: The phrase used to describe the United States' strikingly high rate of imprisonment.

Mayor: The elected chief executive of a municipality.

Mayor–council system: A form of municipal governance in which there is an elected executive and an elected legislature.

Medicaid: A joint state and federal health insurance program that serves low-income individuals and children, the elderly, and people with disabilities.

Medicare: The federal health insurance program for elderly citizens.

Megaregion: An urban area made up of several large cities and their surrounding urban areas that creates an interlocking economic and social system.

Merit selection: A hybrid of appointment and election that typically involves a bipartisan judicial nominating commission whose job is to create a list of highly qualified candidates for the bench from which the governor or legislature appoints judges. After serving a term, these judges are typically evaluated for retention either by the same commission or through uncontested popular elections.

Merit system: A system used in public agencies in which employment and promotions are based on qualifications and demonstrated ability; such a system blends very well with the organizational characteristics of bureaucracy.

Metropolitan area: A populous region typically comprising a city and surrounding communities that have a high degree of social and economic integration.

Metropolitan planning organization (MPO): A regional organization that decides how federal transportation funds are allocated within that regional area.

Metropolitan statistical area (MSA): An area with a city of 50,000 or more people, together with adjacent urban communities that have strong ties to the central city.

Misdemeanor: A less serious crime, such as shoplifting.

Mitigation: Reduction of emissions of greenhouse gases and other steps taken to curb the forces that cause climate change.

Model constitution: An expert-approved generic or "ideal" constitution that states sometimes use as a yardstick against which to measure their existing constitutions.

Moralistic culture: A political culture that views politics and government as the means to achieve the collective good.

Municipal bonds: Bonds issued by states, counties, cities, and towns to fund large projects as well as operating budgets. Income from such bonds is exempt from federal taxes and from state and local taxes for the investors who live in the state where they are issued.

Municipal charter: A document that establishes operating procedures for a local government.

Municipalities: Political jurisdictions, such as cities, villages, or towns, incorporated under state law to provide governance to defined geographical areas; more compact and more densely populated than counties.

National Assessment of Educational Progress (NAEP): A regularly conducted, independent survey of what a nationally representative sample of students in Grades 4, 8, and

12 know and can do in various subjects; known as "the nation's report card."

National PTA: An umbrella organization founded in 1897 consisting of state-based and school-based parent–teacher associations of volunteers who work to improve and support schools.

National supremacy clause: Constitutional clause that states that federal law takes precedence over all other.

Nation-centered federalism: The belief that the nation is the basis of the federal system and that the federal government should take precedence over state governments.

Natural law or higher law: A set of moral and political rules based on divine law and binding on all people.

Necessary and proper clause: Constitutional clause that gives Congress an implied power through the right to pass all laws considered "necessary and proper" to carry out the federal government's responsibilities as defined by the Constitution.

Neutral competence: The idea that public agencies should be the impartial implementers of democratic decisions.

New Federalism: The belief that states should receive more power and authority and less money from the federal government.

New Urbanism: A design movement that seeks to promote walkable communities through transit-oriented, mixed-use development.

No Child Left Behind Act (NCLB): Federal law enacted in January 2002 that introduced new accountability measures for elementary and secondary schools in all states receiving federal education aid.

Nonpartisan ballots: Ballots that do not list candidates by political party; still often used in local elections.

Nonpartisan election: An election in which the candidates do not have to declare party affiliation or receive a party's nomination; local offices and elections are often nonpartisan.

Nullification: The process of a state's rejecting a federal law and making it invalid within state borders.

Obesity: The medical condition of being excessively overweight; defined as having a body mass index of more than 25.

Office group (Massachusetts) ballot: A ballot in which candidates are listed by name under the title of the office they are seeking.

Open primary: A nominating election that is open to all registered voters regardless of their party affiliations.

Override: The process by which legislative chambers vote to challenge a gubernatorial veto; often requires a supermajority vote of two-thirds.

Oversight: The legislature's role in making sure that the governor and executive branch agencies are properly implementing the laws.

Pandemic: An outbreak of a disease that spreads across a large geographical area and affects a high proportion of the population.

Panels: Groups of (usually) three judges who sit to hear cases in a state court of appeals.

Parole: Supervised early release from prison.

Party column (Indiana) ballot: A ballot in which the names of candidates are divided into columns arranged according to political party.

Party conventions: Meetings of party delegates called to nominate candidates for office and establish party agendas.

Patronage: The process of giving government jobs to partisan loyalists.

Plea bargain: An agreement in which the accused in a criminal case admits guilt, usually in exchange for a promise that a particular sentence will be imposed.

Plenary power: Power that is not limited or constrained.

Plural-executive system: A state government system in which the governor is not the dominant figure in the executive branch but, instead, is more of a first among equals, serving alongside numerous other officials who were elected to their offices rather than appointed by the governor.

Plurality: The highest number of votes garnered by any of the candidates for a particular office but short of an outright majority.

Polarization: A split among elected officials or an electorate along strictly partisan lines.

Policy implementation: The process of translating the express wishes of government into action.

Political culture: The attitudes and beliefs broadly shared in a polity about the role and responsibility of government.

Political or party machines: Political organizations controlled by small numbers of people and run for partisan ends. In the 19th and 20th centuries, these organizations controlled party nominations for public office and rewarded supporters with government jobs and contracts.

Political party: An organization that nominates and supports candidates for elected offices.

Poverty line or poverty threshold: An annual income level, set by the federal government, below which families cannot afford basic necessities.

Precedent: In law, the use of the past to determine current interpretation and decision making.

Preemption: The process of the federal government's overriding areas regulated by state law.

Prejudicial error: An error that affects the outcome of a case.

Privileges and immunities clause: Constitutional clause that prohibits states from discriminating against citizens of other states.

Probation: Supervised punishment in the community.

Professionalization: The process of providing legislators with the resources they need to make politics their main career, such as making their positions full-time or providing them with full-time staff (Chapter 7). The rewarding of jobs in a bureaucratic agency based on applicants' specific qualifications and merit (Chapter 10).

Professional model of policing: An approach to policing that emphasizes professional relations with citizens, police independence, police in cars, and rapid responses to calls for service.

Progressive tax system: A system of taxation in which the rate paid reflects ability to pay.

Prosecutor: A government official and lawyer who conducts criminal cases on behalf of the people.

Public choice model: A model of politics that views governments and public services in market terms; governments are seen as producers of public services, and citizens are seen as consumers.

Public defender: A government lawyer who provides free legal services to persons accused of crimes who cannot afford to hire lawyers.

Public health: The area of medicine that deals with the protection and improvement of citizen health and hygiene through government agencies.

Pure appointive systems: Judicial selection systems in which the governor alone appoints judges, without preselection of candidates by a nominating commission.

Racial profiling: The alleged police practice of targeting minorities when enforcing the law.

Rank-and-file members: Legislators who do not hold leadership positions or senior committee posts.

Ratification: A vote of the entire electorate to approve a constitutional change, referendum, or ballot initiative.

Recall: A way for voters to oust an incumbent politician prior to the next regularly scheduled election; they collect signatures to qualify the recall proposal for the ballot and then vote on the ouster of the politician.

Recall election: A special election allowing voters to remove an elected official from office before the end of his or her term.

Recidivism: Relapse into criminal behavior that generally refers to former inmates returning to jail or prison.

Reconstruction: The period following the Civil War when the southern states were governed under the direction of the Union army.

Redistricting: The drawing of new boundaries for congressional and state legislative districts, usually following a decennial census.

Referendums: Procedures that allow the electorate to accept or reject a law passed by the legislature.

Reform perspective: An approach to filling gaps in service and reducing redundancies in local governments that calls for regional-level solutions.

Regional council: A planning and advisory organization whose members include multiple local governments; often used to administer state and federal programs that target regions.

Regressive taxes: Taxes levied on all taxpayers regardless of income or ability to pay, placing proportionately more of a burden on those with lower incomes.

Renewable energy: Power generated using natural sources that can be replenished, such as wind and solar energy, as opposed to nonrenewable fossil fuels.

Representation: Individual legislators acting as the voices of their constituencies within the house or senate.

Representative bureaucracy: The idea that public agencies that reflect the diversity of the communities they serve will be more effective.

Representative government: A form of government in which citizens exercise power indirectly by choosing representatives to legislate on their behalf.

Resilience: Like *adaptation*, a term borrowed from biology to describe efforts to prepare for effects of climate change.

Responsible party model: The theory that political parties offer clear policy choices to voters, try to deliver on those policies when they take office, and are held accountable by voters for the success or failure of those policies.

Retention election: An election in which a judge runs uncontested and voters are asked to vote yes or no on the question of whether they wish to retain the judge in office for another term.

Revenue bonds: Investments secured by the revenue generated by a state or municipal project.

Revenues: The money governments bring in, mainly from taxes.

Riders: Amendments to a bill that are not central to the bill's intent.

Rocket docket: Court schedule that fast-tracks cases that often have limited, specific deadlines for specific court procedures.

Rulemaking: The process of translating laws into written instructions on what public agencies will or will not do.

Runoff primary: An election held if no candidate receives a majority of the vote during the regular primary. The top two finishers face off again in a runoff to determine the nominee for the general election. Such elections are held only in some states, primarily in the South.

Rural flight: The movement of youth and the middle class from rural areas to more urban areas.

Sales taxes: Taxes levied by state and local governments on purchases.

School boards: Elected or appointed bodies that determine major policies and budgets for school districts.

School districts: Local administrative jurisdictions that hire staff and report to school boards on the management of area public schools.

School voucher movement: A movement, dating back to the 1950s, to allow taxpayer dollars to be given to families for use at whatever public, private, or parochial schools they choose.

Secession: The process of a government's or political jurisdiction's withdrawal from a political system or alliance.

Secret (Australian) ballot: A ballot printed by a state that allows voters to pick and choose among different candidates and party preferences in private.

Seniority: The length of time a worker has spent in a position.

Separation of powers: The principle that government should be divided into separate legislative, executive, and judicial branches, each with its own powers and responsibilities.

Settlement: A mutual agreement between parties to end a civil case before going to trial.

Severance taxes: Taxes on natural resources that are removed from a state.

Site-based management: A movement to increase freedom for building administrators such as school principals to determine how district funds are spent at individual schools.

Smart growth: Environmentally friendly development practices, particularly those that emphasize more efficient infrastructure and less dependence on automobiles.

Smog: A type of air pollution; the word comes from the combination of *smoke* and *fog*.

Sociodemographics: The characteristics of a population, including size, age, and ethnicity.

Soft money: Money not subject to federal regulation that can be raised and spent by state political parties. A 2002 law banned the use of soft money in federal elections.

Solitary confinement: The practice of keeping a prisoner isolated in a cell without human contact.

Sovereign immunity: The right of a government not to be sued without its consent.

Special act charters: Charters that grant powers, such as home rule, to a single municipal government.

Special districts: Local governmental units created for a single purpose, such as water distribution.

Spoils system: A system under which an electoral winner has the right to decide who works for public agencies.

Sprawl: The rapid growth of a metropolitan area, typically as a result of specific types of zoning and development.

Standards: In education, fixed criteria for learning that students are expected to reach in specific subjects by specific grade years.

Standards movement: An effort to create benchmarks of adequate learning in each subject for each grade level so that students and teachers can be evaluated on the mastery of this predetermined material.

State board of education: Top policymaking body for education in each of the 50 states, usually consisting of appointees selected by the governor.

State-centered federalism: The belief that states are the basis of the federal system and that state governments should take precedence over the federal government.

States' rights: The belief that states should be free to make their own decisions with little interference from the federal government.

State supreme court: The highest level of appeals court in a state.

Stop and frisk: A police tactic that allows police officers to stop, question, and search citizens under a set of narrowly defined circumstances.

Straight ticket: Originally, a type of ballot that allowed voters to pick all of one party's candidates at once; today, voting a straight ticket refers to voting for all of one party's candidates for various offices—for instance, voting for all Democrats or all Republicans.

Street-level bureaucrat: A lower-level public agency employee who actually takes the actions outlined in law or policy.

Strong mayor system: A municipal government in which the mayor has the power to perform the executive functions of government.

Supermajority vote: A legislative vote of much more than a simple majority—for instance, a vote by two-thirds of a legislative chamber to override a governor's veto.

Supermax prisons: High-security prisons designed to house violent criminals.

Super PACs: Political action committees that can spend unlimited funds on behalf of political candidates but cannot directly coordinate their plans with those candidates.

Tailpipe emissions: Greenhouse gases released by cars and other vehicles.

Tax burden: A measurement of taxes paid as a proportion of income.

Tax capacity: A measure of the ability to pay taxes.

Tax effort: A measure of taxes paid relative to the ability to pay taxes.

Teacher licensure procedures: The processes states use to qualify teacher candidates to work in school districts; requirements for licensing typically include attainment of certain academic degrees, work experience, and adequate performance on adult standardized tests.

Teachers' unions: Public-sector unions that organize employees at all educational levels to form state and local affiliates. In the United States, the two major teachers' unions are the National Education Association and the American Federation of Teachers, both headquartered in Washington, D.C.

Temporary Assistance for Needy Families (TANF): The next-generation welfare program (passed in 1996) that provides federal assistance in the form of block grants to states, which have great flexibility in designing their programs.

Tenth Amendment: Constitutional amendment guaranteeing that a broad, but undefined, set of powers be reserved for the states and the people.

Tiebout model: A model of local government based on market principles wherein a metro area is made up of a series of micropolitical jurisdictions that, on the basis of their services and costs, attract or repel certain citizens.

Town meeting form of government: A form of governance in which legislative powers are held by the local citizens.

Townships: Local governments whose powers, governance structure, and legal status vary considerably from state to state. In some states, townships function as general-purpose municipalities; in others, they are geographical subdivisions of counties with few responsibilities and little power.

Traditionalistic culture: A political culture that views politics and government as the means of maintaining the existing social order.

Trends in International Mathematics and Science Study (TIMSS): A regularly updated study launched by the United States in 1995 that compares the performance in science and mathematics of students in 46 countries.

Trial court: The first level of the court system.

Trustees: Legislators who believe they were elected to exercise their own judgment and to approach issues accordingly.

Truth-in-sentencing laws: Laws that give parole boards less authority to shorten sentences for good behavior by specifying the proportion of a sentence an offender must serve before becoming eligible for parole.

Unfunded mandates: Federal laws that direct state action but provide no financial support for that action.

Unicameral legislatures: Legislatures that have only one chamber. Nebraska is currently the only U.S. state with a unicameral legislature.

Unitary systems: Nations in which legal authority is held exclusively by a central government.

Urban growth boundary (UGB): A border established around an urban area that is intended to control the density and type of development.

U.S. Environmental Protection Agency (EPA): The federal agency charged with protecting the environment.

User fees: Charges levied by governments in exchange for services. Such fees constitute a type of hidden tax.

Variance: The difference between units of analysis on a particular measure.

Verdict: A jury's finding in a trial.

Veto: A governor's rejection of legislation passed by the legislature.

Voter turnout: The percentage of voting-eligible citizens who register to vote and do vote.

Ward: A division of a municipality, usually representing an electoral district of the city council.

Ward or district elections: Elections in which voters in municipal wards vote for candidates to represent them on councils or commissions.

War on drugs: An effort by the federal government to treat drug abuse as a law enforcement issue rather than a public health problem.

Weak mayor system: A municipal government in which the mayor lacks true executive powers, such as the ability to veto council decisions or appoint department heads.

White flight: A demographic trend in which the middle and upper classes leave central cities for predominantly white suburbs.

Zoning laws: Regulations that control how land can be used.

• Index •

Note: Figures, maps, tables and notes are indicated by *f, m, t,* or *n* following the page number.